Ordeal of the Union

VOLUME 2

The Emergence of Lincoln:

DOUGLAS, BUCHANAN, AND PARTY CHAOS
1857–1859

PROLOGUE TO CIVIL WAR
1857–1861

by ALLAN NEVINS

With a new Introduction by
James M. McPherson

Collier Books
MACMILLAN PUBLISHING COMPANY
NEW YORK

MAXWELL MACMILLAN CANADA
TORONTO

MAXWELL MACMILLAN INTERNATIONAL
NEW YORK   OXFORD   SINGAPORE   SYDNEY

Collier Books
Macmillan Publishing Company
866 Third Avenue
New York, NY 10022

Maxwell Macmillan Canada, Inc.
1200 Eglinton Avenue East
Suite 200
Don Mills, Ontario M3C 3N1

Macmillan Publishing Company is part of the Maxwell Communication Group of Companies.

Library of Congress Cataloging-in-Publication Data
Nevins, Allan, 1890–1971.
    Ordeal of the union / by Allan Nevins; with a new introduction by James M. McPherson.—1st Collier Books ed.
        p.   cm.
    Vol. 1 originally published: Ordeal of the Union. New York: Scribner, 1947; v. 2 originally published: The emergence of Lincoln. New York: Scribner, c1978; v. 3–4 originally published: The war for the Union. New York: Scribner, 1959–1971.
    Includes bibliographical references and indexes.
    ISBN 0-02-035441-X (v. 1).—ISBN 0-02-035442-8 (v. 2).—ISBN 0-02-035443-6 (v. 3).—ISBN 0-02-035445-2 (v. 4)
    1. United States—History.   I. Title.
E468.N428   1992   92–3522   CIP
973—dc20

Macmillan books are available at special discounts for bulk purchases for sales promotions, premiums, fund-raising, or educational use. For details contact:

            Special Sales Director
            Macmillan Publishing Company
            866 Third Avenue
            New York, NY 10022

First Collier Books Edition 1992

10   9   8   7   6   5   4   3   2   1

Printed in the United States of America

This Chronicle of Lincoln and Douglas
Is Inscribed by the Author
A Son of Their Prairie State
To His Alma Mater
The University of Illinois

GENERAL INTRODUCTION

ALLAN NEVINS's life illustrated the American dream of upward mobility that he wrote about in many of his books. Born on an Illinois farm, Nevins became America's foremost historian and the recipient of the top honors of his profession, including two Pulitzer prizes, a National Book award, and the presidency of both the American Historical Association and the American Academy of Arts and Letters. In an active career that spanned sixty years, he wrote at least fifty books, edited seventy-five others, and authored uncounted hundreds of articles and reviews. At the time of his death in 1971, fourteen different publishers had books written by Nevins in print.

This prodigious output was achieved not only by inspiration but also by the ninety-nine percent perspiration that Thomas A. Edison defined as genius. Nevins did not have armies of research assistants and collaborators to do his work. The twelve-to-fourteen-hour days he had put in on the farm as a youth trained him for even longer hours as a journalist and historian. Stories abound of missed appointments, skipped lunches, and disappearances into his study during dinner parties at his home where bemused guests would soon hear his typewriter clacking away. Nevins learned how to write under the pressure of deadlines during nearly two decades as a journalist before he joined the faculty of Columbia University as DeWitt Clinton Professor of American History in 1931. But it would be far from accurate to characterize his historical writings as "journalism." The prose flows lucidly and pulses with energy—and, admittedly, with an occasional tinge of purple. But Nevins's books were the product of exhaustive research, thorough mastery of sources, and a professional command of the historiography of his subject.

The subject was most often biography, of the life-and-times genre, which won him Pulitzer prizes in 1932 and 1937 for biographies of Grover Cleveland and Hamilton Fish. But Nevins's crowning achievement was his eight-volume series on the era of the Civil War, published from 1947 to 1971. The final two volumes won Nevins a posthumous National Book award in 1972. The title originally intended for the whole series, *Ordeal of the Union*, became the title for the first two volumes, covering the period from the Mexican War to the Inauguration of James Buchanan in 1857. The next two, with the title *The Emergence of Lincoln*, carry the story down to Lincoln's Inauguration in 1861. The final four volumes, one for each year of the Civil War, bear the general title of *The War for the Union*. The grandeur and sweep of these eight volumes—four thousand pages, one million, seven hundred thousand words—are worthy of the great theme they treat, the drama and trauma of internecine conflict, the *ordeal* of American nationality in which the United States was preserved and purged of its great anomaly, slavery, in a war that cost nearly as many American lives as all the rest of the nation's wars combined. The Civil War was America's *Iliad* and Allan Nevins was its Homer. Befitting Nevins's skill at biography as well as the Homeric model, the narrative and interpretation are carried forward by the story of the dominant individuals of the age, chiefly Abraham Lincoln who makes brief appearances in the first two volumes and "emerges" in the next two, becoming in the final four the Agamemnon of this American *Iliad*.

Each of the two pairs of volumes in the original series has been combined into one volume for this edition, and the whole given the main title originally intended, *Ordeal of the Union*.

INTRODUCTION TO THIS VOLUME

The subtitle of the present volume, *The Emergence of Lincoln*, expresses its principal theme. As a leader of the "anti-Nebraska" coalition in Illinois pledged to stop the expansion of slavery into any more territories, the Kansas–Nebraska Act had propelled Abraham Lincoln into political activism. By 1856 this coalition had emerged nationally as the Republican party, which came close to winning the presidency in its first try in 1856 on a platform of excluding slavery from the territories.

When the narrative in this volume begins with the Inauguration of James Buchanan as president in 1857, Lincoln is still an Illinois lawyer and a peripheral leader of the opposition party. But as the pace of political events ominously quickens toward the sectional rupture of 1860, Lincoln emerges as the party's most articulate spokesman of the moderate antislavery position—moderate but firmly principled and uncompromising on the territorial issue, a stance that earns Lincoln the Republican presidential nomination in 1860. The election of this "Black Republican" (so-called because Democrats, to win the votes of fearful whites in both South and North, branded the Republicans as advocates of racial equality) as president precipitated the secession of the lower South. The volume closes with Lincoln's inaugural address as the nation teeters on the brink of war.

The sense of impending crisis that ebbed and flowed in Volume I builds steadily and rapidly toward a climax in these pages. The focus becomes increasingly political. Only five of thirty-one chapters deal with social, economic, and cultural developments compared with eleven of thirty-one in Volume I. Nevins's prose style, which magically blends a magisterial stateliness with a throbbing energy, captures the accelerating pace of political confrontations that threatened the unity, indeed the very survival of the United States. Although the events of these crucial four years have attracted the attention of many outstanding historians, none has treated them in such comprehensive, lucid fashion as Nevins, who makes clear their interrelationships: the Dred Scott Case; the Lecompton constitution in Kansas; the Lincoln–Douglas debates; the southern demand for a territorial slave code; the sectional schism in the Democratic party; the nomination of Lincoln; the four-party election of 1860 which aroused more passion and brought out the highest percentage of eligible voters than any in American history; the secession of seven states; the failure of compromise; and Lincoln's Inauguration as what many feared would be the last President of the United States.

Underlying all of these events was the institution of slavery. In the long-running debate about the causes of secession, Nevins leaves no uncertainty about where he stands. He dismisses with impatience the alternative explanations advanced over the years, mostly by southern-born historians embarrassed that their ancestors left the Union and brought on a disastrous war in defense of human bondage. Yes, of course, writes Nevins, there were significant differences between the culture and values of the agrarian South and the industrializing North, and sectional differences over economic issues such as the tariff and internal improvements. There were radicals and extremists on both sides who exacerbated sectional tensions for self-serving purposes. There were differences of opinion over the constitutional balance between federal power and state's rights. But none of these alone, not even all of them together, were enough to provoke the divisive bitterness that led to separation. And in any case, suffusing them all was the slavery issue; it caused most of the sectional differences and sharpened the remainder to the point of deadly conflict. "The issue of slavery remained fundamental," Nevins writes. "Could the problems of the labor system and racial adjustment in the South have been solved, all other discords might have proved transient."

Lincoln had it right: " 'A house divided against itself cannot stand.' I believe this government cannot endure, permanently half *slave* and half *free*." As a candidate for the Senate in 1858, Lincoln made it clear that "the *opponents* of slavery," including himself, intended "to arrest the further spread of it, and place it where the public mind shall rest in the belief that it is in the course of ultimate extinction."

This was precisely what the southern ruling class feared. Their primary commitment was not to state's rights as opposed to national power, but to slavery. They were quite content to wield national power in defense of slavery, as they did with the Fugitive Slave Law of 1850 or with their demand for a federal slave code enforced in the territories, which split the Democatic party in 1860. It was their loss of this national power by Lincoln's election that precipitated them out of the Union. They apprehended that Lincoln's accession to power was the first step in that "ultimate extinction" which spelled the end of their way of life if they remained in the Union.

Thus Nevins would agree with his illustrious predecessor James Ford Rhodes, whose seven-volume history of the Civil War era stood as the monumental work until superseded by Nevins's *magnum opus*. "Of the American Civil War," Rhodes had written in 1913, "it may be safely asserted that there was a single cause, slavery." But Nevins carries this assertion an important step further: "The main root of the conflict . . . was the problem of slavery *with its complementary problem of race-adjustment.*" It was their fears of the racial consequences of emancipation that wedded non-slaveholding southern whites to slavery, that caused many northern whites of conservative or racist bent to deplore any talk of abolition, that inhibited even such liberals as Thomas Jefferson from taking any practical steps to end slavery—in short, that paralyzed Americans in both sections and across the social spectrum from facing up squarely to the slavery issue.

This important insight of Nevins, spelled out explicitly in the concluding pages of this volume, runs like a black thread through the two thousand pages of his treatment of the coming of the Civil War. It is a somber theme; it is also Nevins's most important interpretive contribution to our understanding of this era. The America of 1860 was not able to resolve these issues of slavery and race-adjustment peacefully. The war that ensued cut the Gordian Knot of slavery but left the complementary problem as a legacy for future generations.

JAMES M. MCPHERSON

CONTENTS

ILLUSTRATIONS

THESE TWO VOLUMES are complete in themselves. They are, however, also a sequel to the author's two previous volumes entitled *Ordeal of the Union* —the four covering the history of the United States 1846–1861.

Such a work must necessarily rest upon the firm foundation laid by many previous writers. Although I have worked from the sources, I owe a great debt to the historians who have done so much to lay open the field. No period of the American past has received more careful attention than this era just preceding the Civil War. Two men who lived through it as expert observers of events wrote general histories which no student can neglect: Horace Greeley in *The American Conflict* (appropriately dedicated to John Bright), and Henry Wilson in *The Rise and Fall of the Slave Power*. Antagonistic to these in point of view, George Lunt's *The Origin of the Late War* furnishes at some points a useful corrective. Rather a history of the period than a biography, John G. Nicolay's and John Hay's ten-volume *Abraham Lincoln: A History* is an indispensable compendium of details. Among other treatments of Lincoln, I have specially profited from those of Carl Sandburg, James G. Randall, and Albert J. Beveridge. The lives of Stephen A. Douglas by George Fort Milton (*The Eve of Conflict*) and Allen Johnson, each admirable in its own way, have yielded me much that I could not easily have found elsewhere. Four other biographical studies, Ulrich B. Phillips's *Robert Toombs*, the full-packed *Life of Alexander H. Stephens* by Richard M. Johnston and William H. Browne, the two-volume *Seward* by my oldtime friend and mentor Frederic Bancroft, and the *John Brown: A Biography Fifty Years After* by another mentor, Oswald Garrison Villard, require special mention.

No writer on the period can fail to pay tribute to the general works by four great figures in historical literature: James Ford Rhodes, whose breadth of view, keen sense of what was practically significant, and skill in portraiture give his books enduring merit; James Schouler, who accurately minuted many facts; John Bach McMaster, who wrote on social ferment and Western growth with special felicity; and Edward Channing, who brought a finished scholarship to bear upon a succession of issues and aspects. I have frequently disagreed with their conclusions, but never without hesitation. If I have also frequently disagreed with parts of Avery Craven's *The Coming of the Civil War*, it is with respect for his scholarship, courage, and acuteness, and a concurrence in his belief that we must look behind propagandist distortions to find the realities of the time. As a compactly expert survey of the era, the first ten chapters of James G. Randall's *The Civil War and Reconstruction* are invaluable. I regret that in the large cooperative history of the South now under way, only the able volumes by E. M. Coulter and Charles S. Sydnor (in the later period) were available for my use.

Without the numerous expert monographic studies of the last quarter century, such a work as this could have had little value. Beyond specific debts acknowledged in the footnotes, I owe a great general obligation to scores of writers. It is perhaps not invidious to mention U. B. Phillips, Charles S. Sydnor, Ralph B. Flanders, J. W. Coleman, Charles S. Davis, and W. E. B. DuBois on various aspects of slavery; William S. Jenkins, Robert S. Cotterill, Jesse Carpenter, Clement Eaton, and W. J. Cash on the Southern mind; Arthur C. Cole on the social history of the period; Dwight L. Dumond, Gilbert H. Barnes, Wilbur H. Siebert, and Henrietta Buckmaster on antislavery movements; Carter G. Woodson, John Hope Franklin, and W. E. B. DuBois on the Negro; the books of W. L. Mathieson and Frederic Bancroft on the foreign and domestic slave trade; the studies of Frank L. Owsley, Everett Dick, and Lewis E. Atherton in ante-bellum Southern society; and the writings of Cardinal Goodwin, W. J. Ghent, Robert G. Cleland, and J. W. Caughey on the development of the West. I have leaned heavily on the studies of Roy F. Nichols in Democratic Party history, and especially upon his *The Disruption of American Democracy*. The standard writings of Thomas A. Bailey and Samuel Flagg Bemis upon diplomatic affairs; the investigations of James C. Malin into Kansas history; Philip Foner's treatment of New York businessmen and slavery; the thorough work of Paul M. Angle, David Donald, Jay M. Monaghan, Benjamin P. Thomas, Harry E. Pratt, and Roy P. Basler upon various aspects of Lincoln's career; the admirable volumes by William E. Baringer on *Lincoln's Rise to Power* and *A House Dividing*; the analyses of the campaign of 1860 by E. D. Fite, Reinhard H. Luthin, and Ollinger P. Crenshaw; the work of Dwight L. Dumond on *The Secession Movement, 1860–1861;* and David M. Potter's treatment of Lincoln in the crisis of 1860–1861—all these have been indispensable.

Such a short list omits many writers whom I would like to name. I should add that in my opinion no understanding of the period is possible without much reading in the best literature of the time; in Emerson, Hawthorne, Lowell, Melville, Simms, Longfellow, Whittier, Timrod, Bryant, and Whitman.

The author must give special thanks to three friends who have patiently read all of this work, and who have given him indispensable aid in improving it: Mr. Frank E. Hill, Professor David Donald, and Professor Michael Kraus. He thanks also the men and women who have dealt with special parts of it and offered incisive criticism: Professors Henry Steele Commager, Frank Tannenbaum, Louis M. Hacker, and Joseph H. Dorfman; Mr. Boyd B. Stutler, who not only read the sections on John Brown but opened his rich Brown collection; Mr. Henry Seidel Canby, who read the chapter on literature; Mrs. Laura Roper, who fruitfully criticized the pages on Olmsted; Professors Roy F. Nichols, Charles S. Sydnor, Arthur C. Cole, Herbert O. Brayer, and James C. Malin;

Mr. Kirke Mechem of the Kansas State Historical Society and his associates; Mr. Jay Monaghan of the Illinois State Historical Library; and Mr. Roy P. Basler and Benjamin P. Thomas of the Abraham Lincoln Association. From a circle of friends—George Fort Milton, Merle Curti, Dr. Reinhard Luthin, Holman Hamilton, and Ralph Newman—he derived counsel and encouragement. For help in the early stages of the work he must thank Miss Margaret Clapp, now president of Wellesley College, Professor Basil Rauch of Barnard College, and Dr. W. J. Niven. Mr. Foreman M. Lebold generously admitted the author to his rich private manuscript collection. For aid in dealing with constitutional questions he is indebted to Mr. Charles Warren, Professor E. S. Corwin, Rev. Vincent Hopkins, S.J., and Mr. Frederic R. Coudert.

It would be impossible for the author to thank by name all the librarians and archivists who have assisted him. But he is especially grateful to Carl White, Librarian of Columbia University; to Robert W. Hill of the New York Public Library, and R. W. G. Vail, Director of the New York Historical Society; to Miss Ellen FitzSimons, long the expert and courteous head of the Charleston Society Library; to Robert L. Meriwether and J. G. De Roulhac Hamilton, who have made the collections at the Universities of South Carolina and North Carolina so valuable; to Stanley Pargellis, head of the Newberry Library, and Paul Angle, head of the Chicago Historical Society; to Kirke Mechem of the Kansas State Historical Library; to W. J. Van Schreeven of the Virginia State Archives; and to St. George L. Sioussat and Solon J. Buck of the Library of Congress.

New York, May 15, 1950.

ALLAN NEVINS

PART I

The Emergence of Lincoln

DOUGLAS, BUCHANAN, AND PARTY CHAOS
1857–1859

1

Moods, Attitudes, and Leaders

WHEN AN explorer on an unknown river finds the current quickening under his boat, hears a faint but increasing roar, and sees above the farthest treetops a mist of spray, he knows that he is nearing a cataract. Yet if he is bold, if his craft is strong, and if on a prosperous voyage he has already shot other foaming rapids with success, he may push blithely into the unknown, confident that he can override all dangers.

A bold temperament, a blithe outlook—these we can better understand if we glance at the exuberant American nation in the mid-century.

Few decades in our history are more easily misinterpreted than that between the Compromise of 1850 and the election of Lincoln. An excessive emphasis on politics has led most observers to regard the period too exclusively as one of turmoil and uncertainty. It is true that the mounting antislavery agitation and the problems left by the Mexican War had brought the republic into white waters of political peril. Yet, in any broad view, the period stands conspicuous for a peaceful growth and prosperity greater than any that Americans had previously seen. All the territorial gains of the past decade were being consolidated. The dazzled nation, when the fifties began, was just beginning to realize that it held a permanent frontage on the Pacific and was neighbor to the Orient. By 1860, California had become one of the wealthiest of the States; Oregon had fixed her star in the flag; a frenzied horde of miners (with sober settlers on their heels) had made the name of Colorado familiar. From Montana glaciers to New Mexican deserts, sharp-eyed prospectors were scattering into a thousand mountain pockets. Minnesota, her wheatfields waving red, had pushed into the Union; while the farmers of Kansas were knocking at the door. The industrial revolution was gaining momentum in the North. The South exulted in the apparently insatiable demand of the world for its staples.

This was a more restless period than any before known. The energy of the fast-growing population channeled itself into countless outlets—business, trade, politics, reform, religion, letters, art. But the thrust was strongest toward materialistic objects. Already lusty and opulent, the nation instinctively reached for

3

greater strength and greater riches. Walt Whitman was soon to define in *Democratic Vistas* the two grand preparation stages of America, and to emphasize the fact that the country was in the midst of the second. The first had been "the planning and putting on record the political foundation rights of immense masses of people;" the second (in which these masses were now healthfully immersed) was the creation of "material prosperity, wealth, produce, labor-saving machines, iron, cotton, local, State, and continental railways, intercommunication and trade with all lands, steamships, mining, general employment, organization of great cities, cheap appliances for comfort, numberless technical schools, books, newspapers. . . ."

Critics complained that the land was much too materialistic, too intent on selfish aggrandizement. "We speculate how to get rich; we build railroads and ships, to increase our stores; we spy out the neighboring lands which promise us luxurious harvests hereafter"—so exclaimed a writer in *Putnam's Magazine* in the fall of 1855.[1] Once men had dreamed of a high destiny for the young land, fresh and unpolluted from the hand of its Creator; now, he wrote, the spirit of Timour-Mammon was in the ascendent. But such reflections, however natural to a cultivated New Yorker, did not occur to citizens of St. Paul and Sacramento, which had not existed when the Mexican War ended and were thriving towns in 1860; they did not occur to hustlers who lifted Michigan during the decade to third place in iron ore production; they did not occur to the speculators and toilers who created a new industry in Pennsylvania petroleum. These men were too busy to worry about Timour-Mammon. No such reflections occurred to the Southerners who knew the arguments of David Christy's *Cotton Is King* without reading the book, and who agreed that the $200,000,000 cotton crop of 1858–59 was an indispensable pillar of world economy. "Take from New York, or Boston, or Philadelphia, for one month, Southern exports and Southern trade, and widespread ruin and disaster would follow."[2]

The sunshine of economic prosperity bathed the country throughout the decade, as indeed it bathed the whole Western World. If one brief panic occurred, it was little more than the reaction against too reckless an advance. Great Britain, with her middle classes established in full power, her technological revolution almost completed, and the Peel-Russell system of free trade benefiting manufacturers, merchants, and consumers alike, was enjoying one of the golden ages of her history. Her wealth and prestige had never been greater. Louis Napoleon, proclaiming at Bordeaux in 1852, "L'Empire, c'est la paix," was developing railways, canals, and harbors, half-rebuilding Paris and other cities, encouraging iron mills and textile factories, and by other ostentatious activities assuring

1 *Putnam's Magazine*, "The Kansas Question," October, 1855.
2 New Orleans *Picayune*, September 10, 1859.

employment to artisans and shopkeepers. Prussia and Bavaria, which witnessed an astonishing multiplication of business corporations in this decade, were beginning the creation of industrial Germany. Gold from California and Australia helped force the draught of economic activity. Even the brief wars in which Napoleon, Cavour, and Victor Emmanuel so blithely embarked did something to stimulate production and trade in America.

Vast numbers of people in the Western nations were acquiring wealth; and, in Europe and the United States alike, prosperity bred self-confidence, and egotism engendered an aggressive temper. It was not difficult to measure the arrogance of the British ruling classes which, under the leadership of Palmerston, supported war in the Crimea, applauded Lord Elgin's capture of Peking, and avenged the Sepoy Mutiny, while the arrogance of the French bourgeoisie and the gilt-and-tinsel nobility of the Second Empire was written large in Napoleon's exploits at Magenta and Solferino. Plenty of arrogance was always latent in Prussia. Nor was there any lack of self-assurance and arrogance in the United States. Many Northern businessmen, politicians, and lawyers—the Caleb Cushings, Ben Wades, and Zack Chandlers—after pushing to success in highly competitive fields, deemed themselves capable of solving any problem whatsoever. Their bumptiousness impressed foreign travelers; they were ready to teach the world.[3] Slaveholding planters and politicians meanwhile assured their section that it possessed a superior culture and gentility. Such men as John Slidell, Howell Cobb, and Robert Toombs believed the South the main support of the world's economy. Southerners took pride in Senator James H. Hammond's "Cotton is King" speech—a speech summarized in his boast in 1859 that they were "at this moment unquestionably the most prosperous people on earth, realizing ten to twenty per cent on their capital with every prospect of doing as well for a long time to come;" [4] and their consciousness of material success made them stubbornly insistent on having their own way.

In a period of expansion and explosion, this hardening of temper, this strutting egotism of the self-made and newly rich, carried distinct dangers. Both North and South, large bodies of pushing, successful men were more ready to bluff their way, spurn compromises, and trust to luck than if times had been sterner and failure more frequent. The principal reason why a different outlook was needed lay in the dangerous divisions of the land.

3 Hear D. W. Mitchell on the Northerner: "His mind is always at work, engaged seriously on something useful or profitable; and he wears himself out with unceasing anxious thought about gaining and saving. . . . The most serious faults in his character are too much thought of his own personal independence and dignity, too much jealousy of any superiority, and an unduly excited pride and ambition." *Ten Years in the United States* (1862), pp. 194, 195.

4 James Hammond to W. G. Simms, April 22, 1859, Hammond Papers, LC.

[I]

Silently and irresistibly, the ferments released by the materialistic forces of the time were emphasizing the differences among the three great American sections, the East, Northwest, and South. The industrial revolution was well advanced in the East. From the Penobscot to the Potomac, railroads were scarring the fields, factories banking the streams, streets of offices replacing village lanes. A proletariat, largely immigrant, was being created. The sensational cheap press, the ward boss, the rooming houses and parochial schools, the saloon, the labor union, the baseball nine, the slum, all furnished tokens of a novel culture. Radical leaders, especially after the panic of 1857, were lifting demands for new economic rights, the freedoms earlier preached by William Leggett, George Henry Evans, and Elizur Wright. In New England and the North Atlantic States, the great middle class of yeomen farmers, village artisans and storekeepers, and small professional men was still solidly in control of affairs; but this body was increasingly conscious of the growing number of unpropertied, unrooted, and restless wage earners.

While Atlantic coastal communities were yielding to urbanization and the mill whistle, the sway of the frontier in other parts of the half-empty continent was being extended. The great West, a beckoning terrain in which freemen might plant their farms and shops, was in many essential traits precisely what the West had been since colonial days. It was a region of plentiful opportunity and general prosperity, with unrestrained individual energy, much speculative optimism, faith in the common man (and woman), stubborn insistence on political and social equality, and strong national loyalties. Yet the West was changing. It developed primary and even secondary industries with astonishing rapidity, so that by 1860 many communities from Milwaukee to Cincinnati, from Quincy to Ashtabula, were becoming fairly homogeneous with the factory cities of Pennsylvania and Massachusetts. The second or third generation farmer in the West was much more conscious than his father of the importance of foreign markets. Farming for profit, not subsistence, he was more of a businessman and more alert to see his margin of profit defended. Railways, speedy mails, cheap periodicals, and lyceums placed the Hoosier township in the heart of progressive nineteenth century culture.

The egalitarian radicalism of the frontier had always possessed a strong kinship with the radicalism of the town-bred worker. A highly democratic temper marked the farm and village population of the upper Mississippi Valley in these years. This body of Americans was not at all revolutionary-minded; rather it was distinctly moderate on economic and political issues. Yet it felt itself in the forefront of an advancing western civilization, it disliked aristocratic stratifications, and it was impatient with outworn and obsolescent ideas. The *Prairie Farmer* of John S. Wright well expressed the temper of the Northwest. It carried on incessant campaigns against land speculation, dishonest produce grading, and poor roads. It demanded crop diversification, soil analysis, and better farm implements. It proclaimed its belief in a democratic population of small landholders busy making the most creative use possible of their acres. Farmers of the Middle West might indict slavery mildly as Wright did, or attack it sternly as his fellow leader Jonathan B. Turner did; but all were instinctively hostile to the great planters of the South.[5]

Though the South was by no means static in any absolute sense, it seemed so by comparison with the North and West. The basic elements of its economic life were merely soil, climate, and low-skilled labor. While large bodies of farmers in the border regions and uplands closely resembled their Northwestern brethren, in plantation areas the way of life was hostile to variegation and progress. The ruling class of Southerners (and it was a *class*) clung to the aristocratic and conservative ideals which the North and West instinctively disliked. As Northern capital, technology, and labor-saving machinery forced the pace of industry, the gulf between the sections grew deeper. Those who crossed the Potomac felt they were entering a foreign land. According to his predilections, the traveler might pronounce one side or the other superior; he might agree or disagree with De Tocqueville, who had found the Kentucky bank of the Ohio River ill-populated and half-tilled, while the Northern shore was marked by abundant harvests, elegant dwellings, and the confused hum of industry;[6] he might discover more taste and charm among the slaveholders; but the essential fact was the difference. It grew from year to year. Like the differences between the industrial and rural areas of England depicted in Mrs. Gaskell's *North and South*, it created two sharply divergent populations; the people (when the novelists came to discover them) of Thomas Nelson Page and George W. Cable on one side, and of Howells and Hamlin Garland on the other.

Numerous exceptions to the rule of sectional contrast, and many crosscurrents in the broad flow of tendencies, could of course be noted.

Democratic change was by no means wholly victorious in the North, where

5 "I know, and you know, that a revolution has begun. Twenty Senators and a hundred Representatives proclaim in Congress today, sentiments and opinions, and principles of freedom, which hardly so many men, even in this free State, dared to utter in their homes twenty years ago. While the Government of the United States has been all that time surrendering one plain and castle after another to slavery, the people of the United States have been no less steadily and perseveringly gathering together all the forces with which to recover back again all the fields, and all the castles, which have been lost." Seward's Rochester speech, 1858 (*Works*, II, 352).

6 De Tocqueville, *Democracy*, Part 1, Ch. 18.

powerful conservative and aristocratic elements could be found. A landed gentry flourished in the valleys of the Hudson, Genesee, and Susquehanna. In Boston, New York, and Philadelphia the merchant groups were inveterately cautious. From these, and from the new founders of industrial dynasties, millionaires were emerging. Already proud mansions were numerous in the Northern cities. Meanwhile, moderate public men of the type of Edward Everett, Rufus Choate, Hamilton Fish, and John A. Dix strove to prevent the new wine from splitting the old bottles. The North had important elements which preferred the good old ways and the aristocratic approach, which tacitly disliked egalitarianism and the consent-of-the-governed theory, and which took a chilly attitude toward talk of reforms and rights.

Again, in parts of the South, frontier radicalism was as strong as on the borders of Iowa and Wisconsin. Albert Gallatin Brown championed the small farmers of southern and eastern Mississippi against the planting interest of the river country. Reform had its intrepid champions like Daniel R. Goodloe of North Carolina, Cassius M. Clay of Kentucky, and "Parson" Brownlow of Tennessee, while the non-slaveholding whites found numerous voices for their discontent—Hinton Rowan Helper's was only the loudest.

The political and social psychology of the city masses in the North, and especially the Irish and Germans who fell naturally into the Democratic Party, offered an interesting field for study. The followers of Fernando Wood in New York, for example, tenement dwellers without culture or capital, toilers given a reckless temper by their harsh struggle for bread, immigrants resentful of the airs and ease of the richer classes, tended to align themselves against the conservative forces of the North. Yet, just because they hated many features of their environment, they were ready to join hands with aristocratic Southern leaders. Rejecting one form of privilege, they accepted alliance with another.

While confusion, conflict, and incongruity were to be found in every section, and while it would be a fatal error to personify North, South, and West with any idea that they represented unified and unchanging entities, the gulf between free-labor and slave-labor societies was real and deep. What Turner has said of the frontier West was true of the South; it was "a form of society rather than an area." Its special psychology, traditions, and principles ran far back into history. The doctrines of the Virginia school on State Rights and strict construction, crystallized by Madison and Jefferson in the Resolutions of 1798–99, continued to find a wide acceptance. The Richmond *South* affirmed in 1857 that these tenets were still as popular in theory as when first expounded, though in practice they commanded less observance; and the hostile *National Intelligencer* agreed that this was so. Many Southerners felt a deep-seated injury in the "centralizing" tendencies of the national government, and in a long succession of measures enacted since Hamilton had prepared his *Report on Manufactures*.[7] Calhoun's literary executor, R. K. Crallé, and ex-Governor Hammond in 1857 stirred up the Southern Rights Associations of the various slaveholding States to lay before Congress a detailed list of the acts which had operated injuriously on the interests and security of the section; and it was with Hamilton that they began.[8] Aggrieved elements in the South, conscious of their peculiar character and interests, had considered radical action in 1798, more radical action in 1832, and still more radical action in 1850. A belief that consolidated power spelt danger had become deeply ingrained.

North and South had always, from early colonial days, found difficulty in understanding each other. William Byrd of Virginia and John Winthrop of Massachusetts Bay had approached life from totally different points of view. By 1830 the divergent psychologies of the two sections presented the most serious obstacles to mutual comprehension. What an Alabamian meant by "liberty" and "democracy" was something very different from what a New Yorker meant by those terms. The Southerner's liberty was more restricted, and his democracy had to be reconciled with a more patrician leadership. "Self-government" had connotations in the Illinois of Lincoln and Douglas quite unlike those it carried in the South Carolina of Calhoun and Pickens.

Perhaps the word "Union," which a European might have supposed could have but one meaning, best illustrated the differences in state of mind. The Yankee and the Westerner thought of the Union with the high emotional fervor which they had learned from Daniel Webster. They thrilled to the term with an intense spirit of nationality, a passionate attachment to the republic as a whole, a conviction that the people must stand as a unit in defense of national honor and freedom. If Union died, liberty died with it. Jackson, Webster, Benton, and Clay had inculcated an ideal of the Union which imparted a grand devotion to the uprising of the North in 1861. The dominant elements of the Lower South held quite a different conception. Their Union had to be yoked with State Rights; it was, next to their sectional liberties, most dear. As a Southern publicist put it, they clung to Calhoun's definition of the Union: "a peculiar association in which sovereign States were held by high considerations of good faith; by the exchanges of equity and comity; by the noble attractions of social order; by the enthused sympathies of a common destiny of power, honor, and renown." [9]

Naturally, the South thought of itself more and more as a separate nation. By 1857 it *was* in many ways a separate nation. Had secession been crowned with success, historians would have said what John Adams wrote of American

7 Richmond *South*, quoted in *National Intelligencer*, April 30, 1857.
8 R. K. Crallé, Columbia, S. C., to Hammond, December 4, 1857; Hammond Papers, LC.
9 Edward A. Pollard, *The Lost Cause*, 52, 53.

withdrawal from the Empire, that separation was a fact before fighting began. Many Northerners wished to recognize the separation. "So perish all compromises with tyranny!" exclaimed Garrison as at Framingham on July 4, 1854, he burned a copy of the Constitution; and he ceaselessly proclaimed in the *Liberator* that but one honest course was open—"The Union must be dissolved!" Southern radicals talked of the South as if it were another Holland under the Spaniards, another Lombardy under the Austrians. "Ireland *would* be free and independent, if she *could*," wrote one of Senator Hammond's Charleston friends; "the South *could* be, if she *would*. It is because of this opinion, that I would urge the straight and open policy of Disunion, and on its general merits. I only want a pretext to announce and enter upon it—such would be the election of an Abolitionist or protectionist." [10]

The extent to which the South cherished the ideal of separate nationality was demonstrated in the resolutions of the Southern Commercial Convention which met at Savannah in the month following Buchanan's election. Not merely did this body call for direct trade with Europe in place of the "triangular trade" which had enriched New York, and for the construction by the Southern States and Territories of a railroad from the Mississippi by way of El Paso to the Pacific; not merely did it urge the Kentucky legislature to build the final Louisville-Cumberland Gap link in the railroads connecting the Potomac and Mississippi: the Convention went far beyond such measures. It wanted Southern ships built in Southern yards, and Southern seamen trained in large numbers by Southern States. It created a committee of Southern scholars, including William Holmes McGuffey, Augustus Baldwin Longstreet, the historian Gayarré, and the scientist Joseph LeConte, to prepare a series of distinctively Southern texts in every department of study, which Southern legislatures might then order used in the schools. It asked for the encouragement of Southern periodicals, books, and institutions of learning. It exhorted the States to see to the establishment of foundries for casting artillery and arsenals for the manufacture of arms—for the South was to be armed as a separate nation. In the same spirit, it directed Southern Representatives in Congress to inquire whether their States had received due quotas of arms, and to see to it that Southern ports were amply equipped for defense.[11]

Gradually, upon many Southern eyes, had dawned the splendid vision of a republic stretching from Cape Hatteras to the Gulf of California, a nation with a future boundless as the hopes of its people. The South that had produced Washington, Jefferson, and Marshall, whose sons had generally held the Presidency, the chief justiceship, and the control of the Senate, would surely con-

10 John Cuningham to Hammond, Charleston, April 18, 1859; Hammond Papers, LC.
11 *Proceedings*, December, 1856; pamphlet, 48 pp.

tinue to exhibit a rich political genius. This new republic would have a historical tradition, a culture, and an economy all its own. Under the bright sun of independence its dormant gifts would quicken into life. Its harbors would nourish a vigorous commerce, its capital would make laws suiting its peculiar conditions, and its wealth would go to developing its own resources. Architects greater than Latrobe, sculptors more talented than Clark Mills, authors more original than Poe and Simms, orators transcending Henry and Calhoun would arise to express its spiritual greatness. Let the latent energies of the South find outlets under the spur of nationalism—let it show what a defiant people could accomplish. A record equalling that of Greece under Pericles and England under Elizabeth might be written by the free and happy people whose domain embraced the plantations of Virginia and South Carolina, the pine-shaded savannahs of Georgia, the bluegrass farms of Kentucky, the mountains and waterfalls of Tennessee, the iron and coal mines of Alabama, the sugar-cane fields of Louisiana, and the cattle-dotted plains of Texas. Their past role in the political and military annals of America was ample guarantee for accomplishment in the future.

While the South had the dream, the North and West had realities. They had the steady growth of industrial power, which meant wealth and higher living standards; more immigration, and a faster increase in population; the wider areas suited to their free-labor system. The spirit of the modern world was reinforcing their demand for the containment of slavery, which was sure to be followed by demands for its regulation or gradual elimination. For the nation as a whole, irresistible economic pressures were strengthening free society. Resist it as the South might, the movement for tariffs, free homesteads, agricultural education, internal improvements, and a better banking system could not long be withstood; halt the thrust one year, and the next it had enhanced force. By 1860 it was plain that if the country held together, every forward step would strengthen the free society as against the slave society.

[II]

Among the manifold causes of division or divergence of interest—tariffs, public lands, ship subsidies, internal improvements, immigration, the Pacific railroad, Federal powers—the issue of slavery remained fundamental. Could the problems of the labor system and racial adjustment in the South have been solved, all other discords might have proved transient. Year by year the slavery question intensified the conflict, increased the misunderstanding, and heightened the prejudice. By the eighteen-fifties the aura of emotion which surrounded it was so dense that no one could view it without distortion. The emotion was compounded of many elements—suspicion, contempt, anger, but above all fear. In many quarters both North and South it had generated a mass hysteria. No comprehension of the later fifties is possible unless we realize that this emotional tension, this hysteria, magnified every incident to portentous size.

Each side, according to its convictions, was right. The South thought slavery a positive good—and in one sense it *was* a positive good. The Negro was better off on a well-managed Southern holding than anywhere else on earth; better off than in Africa, the West Indies, Brazil, or (arguably) some free-Negro settlements of the North. "Oh, dey ain't no place in de worl' like Ole Virginny for niggers, massa," an intelligent sailor-slave told Olmsted.[12] The North thought slavery a positive evil—and except as a transitional status, it *was* a positive evil. The essence of the dispute between the two sections may be found in Robert Toombs's statement of 1856 in Tremont Temple, Boston. "The white is the superior race," said Toombs, "and the black the inferior; and subordination, with or without law, will be the status of the African in this mixed society; and, therefore, it is in the interests of both, and especially of the black race, and of the whole society, that this status should be fixed, controlled, and protected by law."[13] Most Southerners regarded this as unanswerable logic. Most Northerners would have declared that the moment the major premise, the assumption of racial inferiority, was disproved, the argument collapsed; and even accepting the premise, the question was, *what* status? A fixed status, or an evolutionary status? The latter alone was tolerable.

Logic counted for little, however, in the prevalent hysteria. A deep sense of crisis now pervaded the air. Emotion not merely magnified every collision; it made recurrent collisions inevitable. The Brooks-Sumner assault, the Lecompton battle, the John Brown raid were essentially symptoms, not detached realities. To fasten attention primarily upon them would be as erroneous as to fancy that the rocks in the bed of the Niagara rapids, throwing spray into the air, are the primary force rather than the weight of water pouring torrentially down the gorge. Fundamental loyalties are always a matter of emotion; and these were now so challenged as to create in both North and South a sharp sense of fear— fear among Northerners that slavery would be made universal, fear among Southerners that four million slaves would be suddenly freed amid such scenes of violence and rapine as Haiti had witnessed.

The slaveholding States, a Southern woman resident in Philadelphia wrote in 1851, were slumbering upon a volcano. "It is a truth; every day's information, every paper you take up, teems with the same news—the constant warfare

---

12 F. L. Olmsted, *A Journey through the Seaboard Slave States,* 107.
13 W. W. Brewton, *The Son of Thunder,* gives the entire lecture of Toombs on slavery, 218–249.

against us from North, East, West; and all the haters, too, they are sending their inflamed missiles against us; all, all about slavery and the slave bill. What are we to do if the South goes on sleeping?" Five years later, even though Buchanan had just been elected, Governor James H. Adams of South Carolina anticipated Seward by declaring the conflict irrepressible:

Slavery and Freesoilism can never be reconciled. Our enemies have been defeated—not vanquished. A majority of the free States have declared war against the South, upon a purely sectional issue, and in the remainder of them, formidable minorities fiercely contended for victory under the same banner. The triumph of this geographical party must dissolve the confederacy, unless we are prepared to sink down into a state of acknowledged inferiority. We will act wisely to employ the interval of repose afforded by the late election, in earnest preparation for the inevitable conflict. The Southern States have never demanded more than equality and security. They cannot submit to less, and remain in the Union, without dishonor and ultimate ruin.[14]

The violence of 1856 in Washington and in Kansas propagated a feeling that violence might soon become general. That common-sense Yankee, Henry Wilson, telling a friend early the next year of the constant threats offered him, said he never left his lodging to go to his Senate seat without wondering whether his papers were arranged as he should wish if he were never to return alive.[15] Wendell Phillips had thought just after the passage of the Kansas-Nebraska Act that the aggressive Slave Power was now in full control of the government. It would seize Cuba within a year or two, annex Mexico within five, and attempt to reopen the slave trade. Indeed, the future unfolded a vast slave empire united with Brazil and darkening the whole Western Hemisphere. Only one remedy existed—disunion: "it is now with nine-tenths only a question of time." [16] Theodore Parker was soon to tell Bostonians that the time had gone by when the great American question of the nineteenth century could be settled without bloodshed, while Thomas Wentworth Higginson was to ask concerning slavery: "Is it destined, as it began in blood, so to end? Seriously and solemnly I say, it seems as if it were." [17] The continuous intensification of fear and hatred came out horrifyingly in the letters exchanged by Lydia Maria Child and Governor Henry A. Wise just after John Brown's raid in 1859. Mrs. Child wrote scathingly of the "slave oligarchy" and its "continual success in aggression," while Wise assured her that he would not let Virginians insult even a woman "who whetted knives of butchery for our mothers, sisters, daughters, and babes." [18]

14 James H. Adams, *Governor's Message*, November 24, 1856.
15 *Letters of Lydia Maria Child*, 88, 89.
16 F. J. and W. P. Garrison, *Wm. Lloyd Garrison*, III, 410–412.
17 *Ibid.*, 472; T. W. Higginson, May 11, 1858; Theodore Parker, May 26, 1858.
18 *Letters of Lydia Maria Child*, 103–116.

The Slave Power, the Freesoil Power—each feared the other, and each mistook defensive postures for aggression. The question of the ultimate source of political power was obviously involved, and it presented a fundamental issue. Edmund Ruffin spoke for a multitude of apprehensive slaveholders when in the spring of 1857 he predicted that Kansas would soon come in free, that other Territories would hold the same complexion, and that, probably within twenty years, three-fourths of the States would be freesoil. Slavery would then be extinguished either directly or indirectly. The North had no such apprehension that increasing population and wealth would make its enemies irresistible. Its fear was that the South, already holding undisputed possession of the official strongholds of government, directing the Executive, managing the Legislative, and keeping in reserve the Judicial department, would continue to rule by intimidation and manipulation—and would use its power in reckless territorial expansion. Charles Francis Adams, a man as moderate as he was shrewd, told the South in 1855 just why his section was deeply worried:

This slave power consists, in fact, of about three hundred and fifty thousand active men, spreading over a large territorial surface, commanding the political resources of fifteen States directly, and, through their connections, materially affecting those of five or six more. These persons, and all their numerous friends and dependents, in and out of the slaveholding region, are held together in interest by a common bond, in the sum of two thousand million dollars worth of what they consider property. For the sake of protecting this against the prevailing tendencies of the age, and the effect of public sentiment created by a large body of their own countrymen, it is impossible that they should escape adopting a system of policy aggressive upon the rights of the freemen. They become, in their action, to all intents and purposes, men of one idea. This idea necessarily includes the extension of their own power, whether they are sensible of its influence in that direction or not. They throw into the public councils their allotted portion of representatives, all equally pledged to be faithful to it, whatever they may think upon other subjects. The unity of policy thus secured for all the time spreads its influence far beyond the limits of its own circle. It is always at hand to wield an umpirage in its own favor, between the contending factions and the rival aspirations of prominent statesmen of the free states. It never relaxes in its vigilance over public events. It never is turned aside by the temptation of an incidental pursuit. The sense of danger overrides every other consideration. Around it have been arrayed, for its protection, alike the conservative and the destructive elements of society in the free States—the richest and the poorest class, the best citizens and the worst: the former from an instinctive dread of anything that looks like an attack upon prescriptive rights to property; the latter from an adhesion to the superiority of caste, the more tenacious by reason of the sense of self-degradation in every other particular.

In addition to all this, it must be admitted that the best abilities of the people in the slaveholding region are enlisted in the defence of their rights. There is no path to distinction but that of public life, and that path leads but one way.

Literature, science, and mechanical invention lag far behind, relatively to the progress they make elsewhere. Commerce and navigation are managed by the citizens of the free States; agriculture, by the slaves. With slaveholders, the mind must either lie fallow in sensuality and indolence, or it must seek its exercise in politics directed to one end—the support of slavery. As a consequence, the representation of the slave power in the federal councils becomes one of more than average capacity, of trained experience, of substantial harmony in the adaptation of means to ends, and last, but not least, of quite flexible public morality.[19]

That Adams's arguments possessed force was admitted by some Southerners. A Louisiana planter who contributed to *De Bow's Review* in 1856 an article deprecating the "artificial" Southern passion of fear and excitement, denied, in correspondence with De Bow, that all the aggression was on the other side. "Well—admit the two millions interested in slavery—shall they give the law to the other twenty-odd millions? Are not the rights of majorities as sacred as those of minorities?" [20] This planter represented the capitalist and conservative groups which, in both sections, were ready to resist terroristic movements and confess that the great issue had two sides. But as the years slipped by, the issue of ultimate political authority grew more burning. In the final paroxysm of 1860–61, large bodies of Southerners were filled with frenzy at the idea that a hostile Freesoil Power, already seizing control of Presidency and House, might soon gain the Senate, the Judiciary, and a sufficient number of States to pass constitutional amendments. Large bodies of Northerners were grimly implacable in resisting the idea that a compact Slave Power could continue to nullify their numerical majority, and could retain the opportunity of expanding their institutions over wide Caribbean domains. Fear was largely the product of ignorance, and ignorance—or misinformation—largely the product of propaganda.

Two stereotypes were created. Readers of even moderate Northern newspapers found them full of articles on Southern aggressions in Kansas, Southern filibustering enterprises against Cuba and Nicaragua, Southern domination in Washington, and Southern cruelties to slaves. Readers of even moderate journals in the South found them full of items about Northern slums and poverty, Northern exploitations of immigrant labor, Northern incitations to slave revolts, Northern aggressions in Washington and Kansas, and Northern desire to reduce the South to a fiefdom. Little thinking of the time was a process of reasoning from fact-buttressed premises to logical conclusions. Anybody who measures the political conduct of the fifties from such a premise is bound to be as confused as if he were a believer in Ptolemaic astronomy making careful observations of the Copernican heavens. The thinking was largely irrational, governed

19 C. F. Adams, "What Makes Slavery a Matter of National Concern?" Lecture in New York, January 30, 1855, pamphlet.
20 R. B. Brashear, February 8, 1856; De Bow Papers, Duke University.

by subconscious memories, frustrated desires, and the distortions of politicians and editors.

When L. W. Spratt reported to the Southern Commercial Convention at Montgomery in 1858 in favor of reopening the slave trade, he argued that the North already had one more State than the South; that it had six million more people; that not only was its native increase far larger, but it gained hundreds of thousands of immigrants each year; and that without some drastic preventive, it would soon control the fortunes of the South. Northern commentators promptly raised their own cries of fear. The South, they said, having won the right by the Nebraska Act and Dred Scott decision to carry Negroes into the Territories, now wished the slave trade so that she might fill the West with Africans and gain a permanent national ascendancy. Each section saw the other as a wanton attacker, itself as an heroic defender.[21]

"Take an extreme case," wrote the editor of the Nashville *Union and American* in 1859. "Take a South Carolina fire-eater who declares himself ready for disunion and the establishing of a Southern Confederacy rather than submit to the unconstitutional wrongs and aggressions of the North, and what is his offence compared with that of the filthy, fanatical abolitionist, who, regardless of all right and justice, is seeking to *usurp* the control of the government, destroy the equality of the States, and trample in the dust the sacred guarantees of the Constitution? The extremist of the South errs upon policy in resisting oppression. The abolitionist in the North violates a principle of right, justice, and the Constitution." With equal sincerity, the editor of the Warsaw (Illinois) *Bulletin* was accusing the South of grasping at Kansas, seeking to seize Cuba, and smuggling in thousands of slaves. "The South is not satisfied with what she is fairly entitled to under the Constitution. She wants more. She aspires to nothing short of absolute supremacy. . . . On behalf of the interests of freedom, the Republicans in self-defense have been compelled to resist; and thus the contest will go on, until one or the other shall have achieved an undisputed supremacy."[22]

These stereotypes were steadily reinforced. Leaders on each side made frantic efforts to propagandize their own people. During the first five months of the Congressional session of 1857–58, with its critical battle over the Kansas constitution, Senators of the free States franked out six hundred and eight thousand speeches, Senators of the slaveholding States one hundred and thirty thousand. And each side paid inadequate attention to the views of the other section. In the North, few men ever saw *Russell's*, *De Bow's*, and other Southern maga-

---

21 Spratt's report is in *De Bow's Review*, June, 1858. On the danger of exaggerating the rational element in human affairs, see Graham Wallas's *Human Nature in Politics* (3rd ed., 1921).

22 *Union and American*, July 31, 1859; *Bulletin*, July 28, 1859.

zines; still fewer had the liberality of outlook which Lincoln showed in sub-scribing for the Charleston *Mercury* and Richmond *Inquirer* to learn their opinions. As for the South, it lay under two great tabus, criticism of slavery and displays of religious heterodoxy being equally debarred.

A considerable freedom of thought existed in the North, where many Demo-crats expounded Southern political ideas and Bishop John H. Hopkins and Charles O'Conor freely defended slavery. Opinion was much more restricted in the South. Illiteracy, political agitation, and the "black terror" or alleged danger of servile insurrection were deterrents to freedom of discussion. In South Carolina, wrote B. F. Perry, Calhoun had "thought for the State and crushed out all independence of thought in those below him." A Southern bishop, H. B. Whipple, declared that illiteracy rendered the masses the "dupes" of designing politicians, the ignorant being obviously more fanatical than the well-read. Most Southern States had laws which made it a penal offense to cir-culate any newspaper, pamphlet, or handbill having a tendency to excite discon-tent among the slaves. Under such a law, even in Maryland a colored minister was sentenced to ten years in prison in 1857 for possessing a copy of *Uncle Tom's Cabin*. Humboldt complained that, while his *Political Essays on the Island of Cuba* was freely read in Madrid, it could not be purchased in the United States except with the deletion of all passages condemnatory of slavery.[23]

No iron curtain separated the two sections. Travel was free. Southerners by tens of thousands read Harriet Beecher Stowe, while Northerners discussed the Southern polemics. But a gauze curtain did exist, more opaque on the Southern side than the Northern, distorting the vision of all who tried to peer through.

Basically, the struggle lay between two radically different assumptions. The Northern freesoilers assumed that slavery was morally, socially, and econom-ically wrong, and must therefore be presently circumscribed and ultimately dis-solved. The Southern majority assumed that slavery was morally right, eco-nomically profitable, and socially indispensable, and must therefore be protected and allowed to expand. Each side defended its assumption with full conviction of right. To many Northerners it seemed monstrous that a great people could believe slaveholding ethical. To many Southerners it seemed equally monstrous that a great people could forget how recently the North had held slaves, over-look the immense benefits the Negro had received on American soil, and ignore the terrible problem of racial readjustment if black men were hastily freed. This last consideration cut very deep, for many Southerners would readily have admitted that slavery was unfortunate if they had known what racial controls

23 Clement Eaton, *Freedom of Thought in the Old South, passim;* N. Y. *Weekly Tribune,* May 22, 1858, for franking of Congressional speeches; *ibid.,* June 5, 1850, for Humboldt's letter. The Maryland statute under which the minister was sentenced is in *Md. Laws of 1835,* Ch. 325.

to put in its place. The South in 1860 had a slave population of 3,949,557. The States of Georgia, Alabama, and Mississippi each had between 435,000 and 465,000 slaves. What helpful steps did the North propose to take in assisting the South to release this ignorant, penniless, and perhaps unruly horde? Massachusetts had a white population about twice as great as Georgia's; for how many liberated Negroes would the Bay State offer homes, employment, and cultural facilities? The answer is that no help whatever was either asked or offered.

In this sectional conflict, as Lincoln said, a crisis had to be reached and passed. The danger point of the crisis would be at hand when one side realized that it must break up the Union, or admit that its basic assumption was no longer tenable. By the late eighteen-fifties, all the forces of the time indicated that the South would have to make this fateful choice. The election of a Republican President, sure to come sooner or later, was the crisis that would have to be reached and passed. If the South reconciled itself to the idea of a Republican Administration, it tacitly accepted the idea that slavery must be contained within the existing limits, and methods studied for its gradual supersedence. The ruling system of the South in 1857 was in the position of the ruling system of France in 1785, or Russia in 1910; it had time for a few more decisions, but it had to think fast and think courageously. A failure to make a decision would be as fatal as an error in deciding.

Yet when the situation demanded the utmost seriousness of thought both North and South, the quarrel over slavery, State Rights, and ultimate power was rendered doubly dangerous by an irresponsible levity among politicians and people. Posturing and finessing were never more recklessly used by leaders than in this period. Senator Hammond, looking about Washington in 1859, found few men who thought for a moment of the good of the country, the maintenance of the Constitution, or even of justice. Shams, filibustering, and crass maneuvering for advantage, he wrote, were the order of the day. "We are not rushing so fast to disunion, as we are to utter anarchy—*at once*." Many a lover of national concord echoed this observation. The genial essayist Donald Grant Mitchell, writing from Connecticut to his Virginia friend, A. Dudley Mann, declared that he would tenfold rather see the country become two distinct nations than continue listening to the mad abuse. "Has it not come to this, that with you a man must villify the North to gain applause and place; and with us, it is equally essential that a politician must depreciate and calumniate the South?" Rufus Choate, Edward Everett, and Hamilton Fish in one section, William Cabell Rives, W. A. Graham, and John Bell in the other, found that a man who undertook to defend conservative positions lost most of his influence. Rives wrote Washington Hunt of New York in 1859 that too many politicians were inflaming public opinion by taking extreme stands on slavery, that the issue was being used to divert attention from flagrant corruptions, and that if this demagogy were not stopped, disaster would ensue. But what could he do? [24]

Levity was equally evident in the popular attitude toward the price of disunion. Americans had never fought a really bloody war. The only conflict which most men recalled, that against Mexico, had furnished drama, heroism, and solid national gains at an absurdly cheap price. As the crisis deepened, both sections indulged the delusion that peace could always be preserved, while if by bad luck it were broken, the struggle would be brief. Northern men thought that slaveholders who talked secession were raising the old cry of Wolf! Wolf! and that the sight of a bayonet would quiet this bluffing. Southern men thought with the editor, J. D. B. De Bow, that the North could not make war for three good reasons: it lived by Southern trade, and would submit to anything rather than lose these profits; it had no means to make war except what it got by preying on the South; and its people were too divided, half of them taking the Southern side. Others believed that the Yankees were cowardly. They accepted Franklin Pierce's private assurances to Jefferson Davis that a Yankee army marching to attack the South would first have to fight a bloody battle with Northern Democrats. Disbelieving in the possibility of war, the two sections drifted into a position that made war unavoidable. But then war itself held no connotations grimmer than those of New Orleans or Palo Alto; a little gallant fighting, and the other side would give in.

In all periods of prolonged peace, the longing of hot-blooded elements for action, adventure, and power is translated into a readiness to spring to war. Not a little jingoism, to use a later term, might have been discerned in America of the fifties. For one evident reason, more of the lust for martial excitement was abroad in the slaveholding area than in the North. The industrial revolution drained off much of the restless demand of Yankee lads for risk and desperate effort. Young men like Rockefeller, Carnegie, Jay Cooke, and Collis P. Huntington had no need to think of the thunder of cannon and shock of charging cavalry. When war came, they were so busy harnessing the industrial forces of the land that it seemed an interruption of larger enterprises. The young blades growing up on Southern plantations and farms, however, found that politics and pioneering by no means occupied all their energies. Having a romantic bent, they romanticized war! Hence it was that Charles Francis Adams, Jr., living with his father in Washington in 1859–61, thought that a good many proud "Southrons"—Keitt, Porcher Miles, and Roger B. Pryor—were

24 Hammond to W. G. Simms, January 21, 1858, Hammond Papers, LC; D. G. Mitchell to Mann, August 15, 1858, Miscellaneous Files, Duke Univ.; Rives to Hunt, May 19, 1859, Rives Papers.

"spoiling for a fight." [25] As he says, they got their bellyful of it—and so did their opponents.

Basically, what light-hearted Northerners and Southerners lacked in regarding the grim face of Janus was imagination. If by some prevision the chief political leaders could have seen the four years of carnage, the million graves, and the devastation of broad States, they would have drawn back in horror. Could they have glimpsed for one minute the reeking field of Chancellorsville or Gettysburg, they would have acted far more responsibly. Hugh McCulloch writes that a Senator who visited the Wilderness at the close of the battle told him: "If that scene had been presented to me before the war commenced, anxious as I was for the preservation of the Union, I should have said, 'The cost is too great; erring sisters, go in peace.'" Secession had to be resisted; but it would never have occurred had Americans realized what a great war meant.

[III]

The divisions of the country bring us to the question of leadership. The sentiment of the American majority had never lain with the extremists. They had proved that fact in 1850 and 1852. They had proved it again in 1856, when all the Presidential candidates professed moderate principles, and Buchanan, Frémont, and Fillmore so divided the vote that the first-named fell far short of a majority. Where could the nation find the moderate and constructive leaders whom it wished to follow?

In the debate on Pierce's provocative final message in December, 1856, two radicals, Wade of Ohio and Mason of Virginia, hurled defiance at each other. The North was determined, said Wade, to confine slavery to the States where it existed, letting it into no Territory whatever. The South, averred Mason, would tolerate no interference with slavery in the Territories any more than in the States; and for that reason it had been ready, if Frémont had won the election, to break up the Union. [26] This exchange defined the immediate ground of difference. What path could possibly be found between these two opposed views, each powerful if not dominant in its section? The answer lay in mollification, reassurance, and delay. Time, however, was running short. "In the next four years is, I think, locked up the fate of the Union," wrote Jefferson Davis on April 9, 1857. "If the issues are boldly and properly met my hope is that the Constitution will prevail; if the attempt is made to postpone them the next Presidential election will probably bring us to the alternative of resistance to oppressive usurpation or the tame surrender of our birthright." [27]

25 C. F. Adams, Jr., *An Autobiography*, 44, 45; R. G. Osterweis, *Romanticism and Nationalism in the Old South*, 90–94.
26 *Cong. Globe*, 34th Cong., 3rd Sess., 16, 26, 27.
27 To E. De Leon, De Leon Papers, LC.

The hope of peaceful adjustment (for, despite fatalistic interpretations of history, in 1857 such a possibility existed) rested on the chance that statesman-like leaders would suppress immediate rancors, plead for patience, lay bare the immense difficulties of race adjustment which underlay the slavery issue, show that time was needed for dissolving them, and bring into the foreground those economic issues which were genuinely pressing. The enveloping national prosperity, the materialistic preoccupations of the people, and the rush of energy into continental development, would assist such leaders. Race adjustment, even though some bold initial steps were vital, was a task for generations. The Pacific railroad, the best use of public lands, a fair compromise between Hamiltonian and Jeffersonian schools on the tariff, and the promotion of scientific agriculture, were subjects of immediate urgency. Could the statesmanship be found which would trace a patient way between exigent and distant problems, teaching the electorate to take long views?

All government is a process of experimentation, full of errors and blind gropings; and the use of government to help evolve a new social and economic order, first in the border States and then in the Lower South, would have been a peculiarly delicate and dangerous matter. Still, it was conceivably not beyond the power of a nation which had produced the Revolutionary Fathers. The eminent Americans of the fifties offered a great variety of character and talent; to what men, if any, could the country look for a leadership paralleling that of its formative period?

On careful examination it becomes clear that the old-fashioned effort to put the leaders in this crisis into radical, moderate, and conservative groups is misleading. To be sure, in 1857 any astute observer would have said that Charles Sumner, Ben Wade, John P. Hale, and Zack Chandler, in the North, and Slidell, Toombs, Henry A. Wise, and R. B. Rhett, in the South, were radicals. He would have said that Seward, F. P. Blair, Sr., Lyman Trumbull, and Douglas, in the North, with Jefferson Davis, Judah P. Benjamin, R. M. T. Hunter, and Alexander H. Stephens, in the South, were moderates. He might fairly have termed J. J. Crittenden, Hamilton Fish, Lewis Cass, and Edward Bates conservatives. But such categories, subject to constant revision, are unenlightening. The essential questions with respect to any leader were three: Did he have a firm grasp on principles—on fundamental realities? Did he possess both tact and courage in supporting principles? Above all (and this was the supreme test before which nearly all failed) was he able to appeal to the nation's imagination, its idealism, its sense of a great historic mission?

Seward, short, rusty-looking, his face and head insignificant, his dress antiquated and badly cut, his only outward title to distinction his quickness of perception and heady flow of talk, possessed talents of a high order. Many thought him the first statesman of the land. He was beloved by all who knew him well;

those who saw his affectionate and unselfish deportment in his family circle, his genuine, hearty fellowship with his Auburn neighbors, who gathered about him as freely as the Marshfield farmers had collogued with Webster, were much impressed. His grasp of mind was unquestioned. Carl Schurz thought that he gave an impression of abilities never fully used, of possessing "hidden, occult powers which he could bring into play if he would." His courage had sometimes been conspicuous. Modeling his public career on John Quincy Adams, whose life he had written, he could take large views of public affairs, a trait he had shown as a young governor in promoting public education and legal reform, and would show when an old Secretary of State in buying Alaska. He was an astute politician, quick to measure men at their true worth and subtle in using them. A man of magnanimous heart, he never exaggerated party differences, never sulked under failure (even when he lost the Presidential nomination in 1860), and never showed pettiness. When his constant opponent Jefferson Davis was ill, he was an assiduous and affectionate visitor. "Benjamin," Seward said, as the Louisiana Senator finished some vituperative remarks, "give me a cigar, and when your speech is printed send me a copy." [28] He was always full of talk, badinage, and kindly offices to others.[29] E. L. Godkin thought him in 1859 the best constitutional lawyer in the country, the least of a demagogue among public men, and the clearest-headed statesman.[30]

But Seward lacked the cardinal requisite of steady judgment. For one thing, he was deficient in tact, in sense of timing, and in verbal discretion, so that most people thought this wary politician rash, and many believed this moderate leader (who had been slow to leave the Whig Party) an extremist. In the debate on Pierce's final message, Senator Mason reminded him that he had told a crowd in 1848 that slavery "can and must be abolished, and you and I must do it." So he had, and though the occasion, a speech in favor of the slaveholder Zachary Taylor, and the context, which was mild, had to be considered, the sentence was indiscreet. His "higher law" speech in 1850 was not only poor politics but bad statesmanship, and the "irrepressible conflict" address of 1858 was still more unfortunate. While rash in the use of words, Seward was also occasionally too complicated, devious, and crafty in action; at one time the high-minded statesman, he was at others the partner of the sly Thurlow Weed, who made politics pay in crass ways. His best biographer describes him as a Jekyll and Hyde personality.[31] Save in devotion to the Union, he seemed to lack constancy. He was capable of taking a bold position one day and retracting three-quarters of it the

28 Schurz, *Reminiscences*, II, 34; H. B. Stanton, *Random Recollections,* 204
29 W. R. Thayer, *John Hay*, I, 253-255.
30 Rollo Ogden, *Life and Letters of E. L. Godkin*, I, 258.
31 Frederic Bancroft, *Seward*, I, 200, 201; II, 88.

next, and he frankly told Mrs. Jefferson Davis that he often spoke without conviction.[32]

In short, Seward was erratic. Perhaps an excess of imagination contributed to some of his worst blunders, as when in 1861 he suggested provoking a European war in order to bring back the South; perhaps his emotions sometimes overruled his head. His abundant letters and diary notes show an appealing streak of artistry. Whatever the cause of his instability, this brilliant little Welsh wizard was most valuable when he could lean upon a more massive strength, like Lincoln's.

Jefferson Davis, a man of elegant accomplishments and—despite his humble origin—a gentleman to the core, possessed the dignity of manner and the distinction that Seward lacked. This West Pointer, the son of a Revolutionary veteran, had some of the best traits of a soldier, for he was reserved, self-controlled, and punctiliously courteous, yet plainly not to be trifled with. He was a scholar, who had used his plantation leisure to read widely in military history and the British classics. He was a practical politician, steeped in precedents and instances. Not an orator, he spoke with a finish, lucidity, and force which produced an impression of great logical power—and with a haughty, defiant mien, as one who would not brook contradictions.[33] As Secretary of War under Pierce he showed himself a resourceful administrator, enlarging the army, pushing forward the construction of the Capitol, and experimenting with camels in the Southwest. He was brooding in these years over a plan for saving both the South and the Union; a plan for something like dominion status for the fifteen slave States, making their domestic institutions untouchable.[34]

Those who studied him closely, however, discerned a burning intellectual vanity beneath his impassive exterior, and saw that it was the wellspring of two fatal qualities—selfishness and obstinacy. His future wife, Varina Howell, noted at their first meeting his grim, moody temper, and his way of assuming that when he expressed an opinion, everyone would agree to it. She found him "the kind of person I should expect to rescue one from a mad dog at any risk, but to insist upon a stoical indifference to the fright afterwards."[35] In the Senate, he could never bear contradiction or opposition. When Douglas half-humorously told his Southern opponents on what terms he would admit them to the Democratic Party if ever he gained control of that body, Davis leaped to his feet with blazing passion: " I scorn your quarter!"

Men saw, too, that despite his brilliant public record, his attainments were rather of the study than of practical affairs. Aristocratic, fastidious, self-

32 Gamaliel Bradford, *Union Portraits*, 200–209.
33 E. A. Pollard, *Jefferson Davis*, 33.
34 N. W. Stephenson, *Typical Americans and Their Problems*, 51.
35 Allen Tate, *Jefferson Davis*, 74, 75.

preoccupied, he was Byronically aloof. He disliked meeting men in offhand give and take; he lacked the strong common sense, the practical sagacity, of tamer spirits like Polk or Sam Houston; and his constraint sealed the book of human nature to him. Hence when he attained power, he made grotesque errors in estimating lieutenants, overrating Bragg and underrating Joseph E. Johnston. Having none of the homely, earthy quality which the best democratic leader must possess, he was never willing to place his faith, like Jefferson, Jackson, and Lincoln, in the aggregate wisdom of the people. Moreover, on Southern rights his touchiness led him to hold it "a true maxim to meet danger on the frontier in politics as in war." His stiff sectional feeling estopped him from taking truly national views, and hence long views.

As a parliamentary combatant, the most impressive figure in the country was Stephen A. Douglas. A dozen years younger than Seward, five years junior to Davis, he was still in his early forties when Buchanan was inaugurated; yet he was a political veteran, for he had been elected State's attorney in Illinois at twenty-one, and had been in Congress in Tyler's time. No man excelled him in riding the storm. He had been in the thick of the struggle for the Compromise of 1850, had labored ambitiously for the Presidential nomination in 1852 and 1856, and had given the country the most controversial measure of the decade in his Nebraska Bill. Indeed, ever since the day when, an ill-educated stripling of twenty with hardly enough law to write a simple instrument, he had hung up his shingle in the Morgan County courthouse, he had been ceaselessly fighting his way forward. He had two elementary articles of faith: he believed in the growth of the country—believed that, as it had pushed across the Mississippi, the plains, and the Rockies to the Pacific, it must continue to expand, either north or south; and he believed in popular self-government. When he flung himself into battle it was with tigerish ferocity. In an early run for Congress he had so enraged his opponent, the stalwart John T. Stuart, that this Whig candidate tucked Douglas's head under his arm and dragged him around the Springfield square. John Quincy Adams had stared in amazement when the five-foot Illinoisan, roaring out one of his first speeches in the House, had stripped off his cravat, unbuttoned his waistcoat, and with convulsed face and frantic gesticulation had "lashed himself into such a heat that if his body had been made of combustible matter, it would have burnt out." Schurz had watched him send his sentences like cannon balls, crashing and rending, into his opponents' ranks. Few were the Senators who dared stand against him.[36]

Yet Douglas's limitations were as striking as his gifts. His conduct was sometimes deplorably lax. Charles Francis Adams has left a graphic vignette of

36 Allen Johnson, *Stephen A. Douglas*, 43; Adams, *Memoirs*, XI, 510; Schurz, *Reminiscences*, II, 30–35.

the man invading a sleeping car in 1860, whiskey bottle in hand and half drunk, to try to drag Seward out to address a Toledo crowd. One day Douglas might be leading his party in the Senate, the next be found with his arm about the neck of a crony in a Washington saloon.[37] Deeply versed in political history, he was ill-informed in almost all other fields of knowledge. He had read little but lawbooks, debates, and government manuals, and had seldom found time for that deeper type of reflection which produces statesmen. A marvellously effective floor debater, he had no real power of abstract thought, and no ability to present such general ideas as are associated with Hamilton and Jefferson, Calhoun and Webster. He had never produced a genuine state paper. While he grappled friends to him with hooks of steel, he taught them to act on practical expediency rather than far-reaching principle.

Above all, he was an improviser. His whole genius, backed by irresistible personal force, was for meeting practical situations with some rapidly devised measure, taking little thought of ultimate consequences, and trusting to the country's growth for remedying all defects. He had improvised as State's attorney and judge when he knew little law and no jurisprudence. He had improvised as a young Congressman supporting Polk and the Mexican War. He had improvised policies and bills; above all the reckless measure, the worst Pandora's box in our history, for organizing Kansas Territory. As he improvised he battled implacably, for he loved nothing more than political combat. The great weakness of the born improviser is that he oversimplifies the problem he faces and forgets that remote results are often far more important than the immediate effect. The great penalty paid by the born fighter is that he gradually accumulates a phalanx of enemies. Douglas by 1857 was a doughty champion, famous for his power to give and take blows, but he had still to reckon his final bill of profit and loss.

The best trait of Douglas was his faith in the expansive energies of the American people. Europe, he had said, is one vast graveyard. "Here everything is fresh, blooming, expanding, and advancing. We wish a wise, practical policy adapted to our condition and position."[38] He must be credited, too, with a fervent belief in the masses—in democracy. But he had a number of less happy traits. One was his chauvinism, for he constantly inveighed against the "tyranny" and "aggressions" of European nations, and showed no appreciation of our cultural debt to older lands. Another was his readiness in debate to twist logic, darken counsel, and even misstate facts. Still another was his constant exaltation of material considerations and depreciation of moral factors: the slavery question, he said on the eve of the Civil War, is exclusively "one of climate, of

37 C. F. Adams, *Autobiography*, 65, 66; cf. Milton, *Eve of Conflict*, 258, 259.
38 *Cong. Globe*, 32nd Cong., Sp. Sess., 273.

political economy, of self-interest." [39] Finally, he often suffered from his head-long impetuosity.

In 1857 the brightest pages of his brilliant career lay before him. His successful fight against a proslavery constitution for Kansas was to be one of the most gallant episodes of the time; and in 1860 he was to play a more farsighted and heroic role than any other Presidential candidate. But he lacked the capacity to plan, the patient wisdom, and the conciliatory gifts of a great national chieftain.

So we might run down the beadroll of leaders of the time, some of them exhibiting great gifts. How fine in various ways was Charles Sumner, with his broad cosmopolitan culture, his Alpine elevation, his friendship with Brougham, Grote, Macaulay, Longfellow, Prescott, and Tocqueville; yet how petty he could be, too! When he returned to the Senate in 1860, after four years of illness and partial exile, he had an opportunity to deliver a speech full of magnanimity, generosity, and Olympian wisdom. Instead, he poured forth a diatribe on "The Barbarism of Slavery," full of erudite venom and personal abuse. Like Douglas, he was incapable of appealing to the highest instincts of the people whom he apostrophized. How able was Salmon P. Chase, who had taken a leading place at the Ohio bar, written for the *North American Review*, helped pioneer the antislavery movement in Ohio, and served with distinction as Senator and governor! Of majestic stature, fine head, and keen eye, he looked like the statesman he was. Unfortunately, he had a touchy self-importance, he let political ambition warp his outlook, he never learned to make friends of national leaders, partly because he could never subordinate himself to others, and he almost totally lacked the arts of popular appeal.[40] He thirsted for the Presidency, yet could never command a large following. How brilliantly capable was Alexander H. Stephens, and how truly national in outlook! High-minded, devoted to principle, well-read and thoughtful, he was the strongest of the Southern moderates. Yet as one of his admirers admits, he was too quick-tempered, too unwilling to yield on details, too eager to score victories for personal prestige or party credit, to carry through any great purpose; while his invalidism made him a bundle of nerves.[41]

[IV]

Where, then, were leaders equal to the crisis to be found—leaders who united intellectual power, moderation of temper, moral earnestness, and the power of lifting the popular heart? All the men named, and others like Lyman Trumbull, J. J. Crittenden, Robert Toombs, and R. M. T. Hunter, seemed

39 *Cong. Globe*, 36th Cong., 1st Sess., 552–559.
40 A. B. Hart, *Salmon P. Chase*, 415–425.
41 Ulrich B. Phillips in *Dictionary of American Biography*.

statesmen *manqués*. And could a fit leader be found in time? For the hysteria, the mounting hatreds and fears made time all too short.

Here and there a new voice of promise was raised. Nobody in the East and few in the West paid any attention to one which was heard at a Republican banquet in Chicago on December 10, 1856. A lanky attorney from Springfield, known only as a man who had served one term in Congress, who had narrowly missed the nomination for Senator that Trumbull got, and who had received some votes for the latest Vice-Presidential nomination, spoke on Pierce's message. He mentioned contemptuously the President's vaunt that the recent election had vindicated "State equality." Then he went on to appeal to the imagination of his hearers and to their high sense of national destiny:

All of us who did not vote for Mr. Buchanan, taken together, are a majority of four hundred thousand. But in the late contest we were divided between Frémont and Fillmore. Can we not come together in the future? Let everyone who really believes, and is resolved, that free society is not and shall not be a failure, and who can conscientiously declare that in the past contest he has only done what he thought best, let every such one have charity to believe that every other one can say as much. Thus let bygones be bygones; let past differences as nothing be; and with steady eye on the real issue, let us reinaugurate the good old "central idea" of the republic. We can do it. The human heart is with us; God is with us. We shall again be able not to declare that "all States as States are equal," nor yet that "all citizens as citizens are equal," but to renew the broader, better declaration, including both of these and much more, that "all men are created equal." [42]

If the Union could yet be saved, if the Ship of State was not to go over the cataract whose thunders ahead shook the air, it would be by some leaders, somewhere, who thus reminded Americans that their republic must be kept the last, best hope of mankind. Lincoln appealed to the older faith in America as "a bulwark for the cause of men." That a deep reservoir of idealistic feeling existed in the nation, and that beneath turbid surface eddies the old moral forces still flowed with pomp of waters, unwithstood, was demonstrated, as we shall now see, by the best literary voices of the young republic.

42 *Complete Works* (Nicolay and Hay ed.), I, 225-226.

2

"Not from a Vain or Shallow Thought"

THE MAIN impression given by American life in the fifties was of health, strength, and constructive force. Slavery was the most dangerous problem of the nation—the more dangerous because of popular self-confidence, the tendency toward regional division, and the mediocre character of most political leadership. But after all, this was only one element in the complex of national affairs. The history of civilization was, as it must always be, more important than the history of politics; when Aristotle wrote of man as a political animal he meant gregarious or social animal, and the busy States cannot be understood if we do not scrutinize many aspects of their life. Some of these aspects were making strong competitive demands upon the country's stock of brains, vision, and character. No part of American civilization in this decade was more arresting than what might be termed the culturally creative element.

We must include among the creative achievements of the time the continued development of government; for the Jeffersonian and Jacksonian impulses were still strong, the bold use of universal manhood suffrage was proving successful, and the world's largest experiment in federalism served as effectively for three million square miles as for two. We must include impulses foreshadowing the distinctively American contributions of the next generations in technology and mass production. America could point to the light suspension bridges of Roebling, the swift slender steamships designed by Jacob Bell and others, the Yankee clippers of Donald McKay, the ingenious balloon-frame house, and the locomotives of basketlike flexibility made by Baldwin or Eastwick. It could point to such feats of invention as the telegraph, sewing machine, and reaper. It could tell of progress in mass production on the interchangeable-part principle, introduced by Eli Whitney and carried forward in Colt's arms works, the Waltham watch factory, and McCormick's reaper works. It could point to a new kind of integrated manufacturing procedure illustrated by the assembly line of meat-packing plants and the planning of elaborate flour mills.

In a different field, Americans could take pride in the high development some States had given to general public education, and in Horace Mann's contributions to teacher-training. They could assert that the lyceum had been a useful path in adult education. In not a few philanthropies and reforms— children's aid, training of the deaf and dumb, prison management—American effort led the world. The nation could claim credit in medicine for one of the great advances of history, the discovery of surgical anaesthesia by W. T. G. Morton, Crawford Long, and others. American theology as represented by Andrews Norton and Horace Bushnell, and American jurisprudence as expounded by Story and Taney, were on a high level; while Henry Wheaton's pre-eminence in international law was widely recognized. In science the United States still lacked names of the highest distinction; but it had bred its own Joseph Henry, naturalized Agassiz, and given oceanography the "pathfinder of the seas," M. F. Maury.

In a variety of endeavors Americans of the fifties made a mark of signal talent or heroic devotion. Now it was the explorer Elisha Kent Kane, scurvy-ridden, driving his *Advance* into yet more perilous Arctic wastes. Now it was the impoverished inventor Charles Goodyear, borrowing money to place his rubber devices in the London and Paris exhibitions of 1851 and 1855. Now it was the critic W. J. Stillman making the *Crayon* one of the best art magazines on the globe.[1] Now it was the topographer Frémont leading his doomed band into the icy fastnesses of the Sangre de Cristo Mountains to prove their mid-winter passage feasible. Now it was John Carter Brown of Providence and James Lenox of New York making the first impressive collections of rare books and literary manuscripts. It was Elizabeth Cady Stanton and Susan B. Anthony keeping the flag of women's rights defiantly flying. It was Charles Loring Brace toiling sixteen hours daily on a thousand dollars a year to make his Children's Aid Society effective. It was Francis James Child beginning his lifework of scholarship on the British ballads, and the Le Conte family winning scientific laurels for the South. It was Cyrus W. Field, undaunted by bankruptcy, debt, the burning of his business quarters, and four successive failures, raising funds for the fifth attempt to lay an Atlantic cable. It was the devoted endeavor of John R. Thompson and William Gilmore Simms to give the South magazines for its writers.

In the realms of art and literature, transcendent achievement had proved slow, for it depended upon social and cultural elements which were the growth of time. Something more than large cultivated groups, a clash of minds, and

1 Charles Eliot Norton wrote to William Porcher Miles of the *Crayon*: "It is very different from most of our American journals and magazines. There is no claptrap about it, no writing down to the low level of popular taste. It addresses the small audience of true artists and lovers of art. Besides very well written, clearly thought, and high bred essays upon subjects connected with art, it contains much pleasant information upon matters of art both at home and abroad." June 26, 1855; Miles Papers.

accumulations of artistic and literary materials had to be provided. In the soul of a nation, spiritual strength comes from maturity and travail. Americans were for the most part a new people—many had arrived at Castle Garden only yesterday; and most of their travail and social turmoil lay ahead. The best thought and artistry came from old, long-ripened communities, and from areas where layer on layer of troubled history had been laid down. It came, that is, from Boston and its old colonial suburbs, from cosmopolitan New York, from Philadelphia, once the second city in the British Empire, from Tidewater Virginia, and from the basin of the Cooper and Ashley. Yet at last it was coming—particularly in literature. For the first time, men and women throughout the country were recognizing that great writers were among them, and that great writing was being done.

American art, though not attaining the distinction that letters reached, was groping toward it. Here the social basis for achievement was being created: the schools of design, the sales galleries, the fellowship of eager practitioners, the stir of public interest. Italy remained full of American sculptors. Let us call New York the City of Studios, said *Putnam's* in May, 1857, for no fewer than three hundred palettes are set up in Manhattan every morning by as many artists. What was needed was not merely high talent, but a modernized technique and a more spiritual vision. Of the competent, sincere, and commonplace the country had enough in sculptors like Crawford and Story, portrait painters like Chester Harding, and landscape painters like William Hart and Thomas Doughty. It had artists who loved nature as deeply as J. F. Kensett, whose paintings of the Hudson Valley were full of sincere feeling. It had painters of imagination, or at least of a certain grandiosity of outlook, such as F. E. Church of the erupting "Cotopaxi." But as yet, for all its virtues of self-respect, conscientiousness, and skilled craftsmanship, American art had produced no sculptor or painter who united a modern technique with rich distinction of mind and personality.

Art, we say, was groping toward the light. One of the prolific portrait painters, Charles Loring Elliott, several times struck out a work of genius, as in his portrait of Ericsson (1845), called the best American work in the field since Stuart, and that of Fletcher Harper, admired at home and in France. A greater figure, George Inness, with the soul of a mystic and poet, came back from Paris in the middle fifties afire with the lessons taught him by Corot and Rousseau. He began to put into the meticulously detailed canvases characteristic of the Hudson River school a passion which his associates had never admitted. His "Juniata River near Harrisburg" (1856) was full of dryly precise detail. "But," writes Royal Cortissoz, "what a queer thing is genius! This picture cannot die. A mysterious life is stirring in it, the energizing touch of an artist who could not be merely photographic though he tried. . . . All the time that Inness was

just taking pains with his subject there was at the back of his mind the general-
izing instinct that goes to the making of great works of art." [2] Inness was to do
better work—work completely American, as typical of his country as a Vermont hillside in autumn or an upper New York snowscape, executed with the
best European expertness. Something of the same freakish touch of genius
gave strength to Henry K. Brown's equestrian statue of Washington (1856),
making it stand out from the insipid neo-classic sculpture of the period.

As yet it was only dawn in art, but there were signs of sunrise; the sunrise
of Winslow Homer, La Farge, Whistler, and Eakins in painting, of Saint-
Gaudens and Daniel Chester French in sculpture. In literature, however, the
country was well beyond the dawn represented by Irving and Cooper. Letters
by the middle fifties were the most noteworthy aspect of the American scene
from any cosmopolitan point of view.

[I]

At the beginning of the century the country had possessed little more than
the hope of a literature. The work of Franklin, Jefferson, Paine, and Freneau
had been special or incidental. But by 1844, when Rufus W. Griswold brought
out a large volume on *The Poets and Poetry of America*, it was evident that
the country had writers of high and enduring distinction. To be sure, at first
there was the usual difficulty in separating genius from talent. Griswold gave
inordinate space to such minor authors as Brainard, Dawes, Pike, Ware, Wilde,
Peabody, and Sands; while E. P. Whipple, reviewing Griswold in *Essays and
Reviews* (1850), devoted as much attention to Sprague, Dana, and Percival as
to Holmes, Longfellow, and Whittier. Time, however, quickly separated gold
from brummagem metal. Even Griswold pronounced Emerson the country's
greatest poet, and by 1855 readers were well aware that Longfellow, Whittier,
Emerson, Bryant, and Poe stood far above the Percivals and Spragues. Not a little
heart burning accompanied this sieving process. New Yorkers were jealous of
New England, while Southerners complained that the work of M. B. Lamar,
Philip Cooke, and Simms was unjustly neglected; but the verdict had to stand. [3]

One after another the memorable works appeared. While Taylor and Scott

2 *American Artists*, p. 113.
3 The Raleigh *Register*, replying to an article in *Putnam's*, listed the living Southern
writers of renown: "Such names as Simms, Kennedy, Hawks, Grayson, Louisa McCord,
Calvert, M. F. Maury, John Esten Cooke, Anna Estelle Lewis, P. H. Hayne, Longstreet,
Brantz Mayer, Webber, Benton, Badger, Hammond, Bledsoe, Marion Harland, Gayarré, and
twenty others." It recalled Poe's statement that Simms's genius had been neglected because he
was Southern. Quoted in Charleston *Courier*, March 10, 1857. Actually most Northern
reviewers were quite fair to Southern books; the *Atlantic* was conspicuously generous.
Simms complained of Southern rather than Northern neglect. Southern and Northern
authors maintained cordial relations to the last. Jared Sparks, for example, sent Caleb Cushing
a copy of W. H. Trescot's new book on the diplomacy of the Revolution with high praise.
July 29, 1852; Cushing Papers.

were defeating the Mexicans, Lowell published his *Biglow Papers*, Hawthorne his *Mosses from an Old Manse*, Longfellow his *Evangeline*, Prescott his *Conquest of Peru*, and Melville his *Typee* and *Omoo*. The year 1848 found Thoreau printing his *Ktaadn* in magazine form, and Lowell his *Fable for Critics*, while the next year saw Thoreau bring out his *Week on the Concord and Merrimac*. In the twelve months of Clay's last great compromise appeared Emerson's *Representative Men*, Longfellow's *The Seaside and the Fireside*, Melville's *White Jacket*, and Hawthorne's *Scarlet Letter*—books to make any year notable. Whittier, too, was busy; that year he published *Songs of Labor* and *Old Portraits and Modern Sketches*. Yet 1851 was of almost equal importance, illuminated as it was by Melville's *Moby Dick*, Longfellow's *The Golden Legend*, and Hawthorne's *The House of the Seven Gables*. The stream was now flowing full, and we can mention but a few of the outstanding and perdurable titles. In 1854 appeared *Walden*. Another *annus mirabilis* in 1855 gave the country Whitman's *Leaves of Grass*, Longfellow's *Hiawatha*, and the first two volumes of Prescott's *Philip II*. Motley's *Rise of the Dutch Republic* emerged to its resounding success in 1856, the year too of Emerson's *English Traits*. In 1858 Holmes's *Autocrat of the Breakfast Table* divided attention with Longfellow's *Courtship of Miles Standish*.

The political incandescences of the time had no effect upon the great writers save to fire their pens and stimulate their production. Bryant alone, giving his energies to the *Evening Post*, perhaps spent some of his genius unwisely.[4] Irving was still busy, issuing his life of Washington, 1855–59. The stream of Holmes's wit ran on into *The Professor at the Breakfast Table* (1859) and *Elsie Venner* (1861). The year of Lincoln's election Emerson produced what Carlyle thought his best book, *The Conduct of Life*, and Hawthorne one of his greatest romances, *The Marble Faun*, while Whitman reissued his *Leaves of Grass* with additional poems. Where in the history of American letters is another dozen years equal to 1848–60?

[II]

It was of no small moment that these imaginative achievements heightened American pride, proving that the new republic, for all its materialistic pre-

---

4 Bryant brought out his collection *A Forest Hymn* in 1860, the year also of Whittier's *Home Ballads and Other Poems*. But the hot sun of political controversy tended to dry up his fancy. Emerson had written in his Notebooks on March 20, 1842, that the "Humanity and Reform men trample on letters and poetry." Writers of the South suffered from the necessity, as they saw it, of giving half their energies to controversy. The *Southern Literary Messenger* of October, 1856, carried a long article on "The Duty of Southern Authors," urging them to take up their pens against the North and to write a vindicatory history of slavery.

occupations, could touch the finer chords of the spirit. The same Sydney Smith who had asked in 1820 who read an American book, later predicted that when Prescott visited England he would find a Caspian Sea of soup awaiting him. In London in the summer of 1848, young Charles Eliot Norton glowed with pride to see the historian lionized, and to hear people say, even while reading *In Memoriam*, that England had no poet to compare with Longfellow. In the *Athenaeum* he could have found a reviewer who ranked *The Scarlet Letter* among the most powerful, if also the most painful, of all recent books; a work strangely compounded of passion and Puritan reserve, of the allegorical and the real, and shot through with imaginative fire. In *Blackwood's*, long so savage in treating things American, he could have found a discussion of Herman Melville which, highly appreciative of the exotic color of *Typee* and *Omoo*, and of the frank, manly style of *Redburn*, credited the Yankee with introducing a new genre in literature—a combination of Swift, Defoe, the *Arabian Nights*, nautical terminology, and American yarning.[5]

Such praise had real value, for if Americans were anywhere lacking in exuberant self-confidence, it was in cultural endeavors; but after all, large and appreciative native audiences were infinitely more important than the comment of foreign critics. Moreover, much British commendation was coupled with unreasonable demands. Most British critics asked that the rising writers of the West be wildly, shaggily North American, that they bear the stamp of an untamed New World. Why should Longfellow go to Europe for *The Golden Legend* when so much history and folklore lay at home? Why should Bayard Taylor's *Rhymes of Travel* dip into Old World streams when the most magnificent forms of nature awaited description in his own land? Why should Thoreau in his *Week on the Concord and Merrimac* echo Carlyle when a dozen passages made it clear that if he trusted to his genius he might become a prophet

5 The *Athenaeum*, a real power, was conspicuously friendly toward American authors, praising all the great writers of the period—though it gave an adverse judgment upon *Moby Dick*, which it called an ill-compounded mixture of romance and matter of fact (October 25, 1851). In reviewing *Hiawatha* it declared that for many years it had preached "the poetical doctrine of America for the Americans," and it praised that long poem warmly, saying that the tale was beautiful, fanciful, and new, and that the author had given variety even to a metre chosen for its sad and tender monotone (November 10, 1855). Hawthorne was regarded by the *Athenaeum* with marked admiration. *The Scarlet Letter* received praise for its high originality, its delicacy and restraint, its imaginative power, and its touch of the fantastic (June 15, 1850). *The House of the Seven Gables* was greeted as placing Hawthorne "amongst the most original and complete novelists that have appeared in modern times" (May 24, 1851). Of the *Blithedale Romance* the weekly said that it put the seal on the author's reputation as "the highest, deepest, and finest imaginative writer whom America has yet produced" (July 10, 1852). *The Marble Faun* again received warm praise. Melville was done better justice by the reviewer of *White Jacket*, who declared him incomparable in rendering "the poetry of the ship," and placed him high above Marryat. He was credited with "more vivacity, fancy, color, and energy than ninety-nine out of a hundred" of those who understood to poetize monsters of sea or land (February 2, 1850).

of rank in his own right? Let Americans be *national*, insisted Chorley's *Athenaeum* and other periodicals in reviewing books; let them find home themes and develop home ideas. In their great continent they had a wealth of untouched material for song, story, and essay almost as great as that of weary old Europe.

Within limits this was good advice, for it was time that Americans ceased to be imitative. When pushed too far, however, the demand was false and misleading. One reason for its falsity lay in the fact that Americans were not a new stock; they were Euro-Americans and their culture was mainly Anglo-American. Though *The Courtship of Miles Standish* dealt with English folk newly landed on a colonial shore, it was more authentically American, less alien and outlandish, than *Hiawatha*. In every important sense Hawthorne's *Our Old Home* (published a little later, in 1863) was as penetratingly American as Parkman's *California and Oregon Trail*. Parkman's book had high significance in its vivid description of the hunter's and fur-trader's frontier, of the pioneer and the Indian. Who can forget his picture of the dog feast at Fort Laramie, of Jim Beckwourth teaching the Crows how to fight, of the cluttered, smelly Oglalla Sioux village, of the prairies black with buffalo? But Hawthorne's book described some of the enduring roots of Anglo-American civilization. Americans today can name particulars in which they were influenced by Stratford, Epworth, and Cambridge as vitally as they were influenced by the Oregon Trail. It was not for Americans to face West alone or East alone; they naturally faced in both directions.

The larger reason for the falsity of any demand for a *forced* Americanism (and such demands were heard at home as well as in Europe) was that as literature enters the higher realms of feeling, thought, and art it knows less and less of national peculiarities and limitations. Hawthorne, delving into problems of personality, did better with Miriam and Donatello under Italian skies than with Zenobia in a Yankee setting. Emerson's "Saadi" holds a larger measure of American truth, as part of world truth, than his prosaic poem "The Adirondacs." Thoreau's *Walden* dealt with a very American experience, but its value lay in the distinction with which he discussed universal topics. His chapter on "Reading" in that book was not an exhortation to be provincial and national by going through the native works published by Harper's and Little, Brown. On the contrary, he recommended Homer, Aeschylus, Vergil, Dante, and Shakespeare. The important object was not that Americans should strike a cisatlantic note, but simply that they should trust themselves, and look within their hearts and write.

Once they did so, it was inevitable that decade by decade they *would* become more American. As the subsoil of American ideas, folklore, and history grew thicker, as American culture became more satisfying, with better colleges,

THE
ATLANTIC MONTHLY.

PHILLIPS, SAMPSON & COMPANY'S
NEW MAGAZINE,
Devoted to Literature, Art, and Politics.

ITS AIM WILL BE

FIRST: In Literature, to leave no province unrepresented, so that while each number will contain articles of an abstract and permanent value, it will also be found that the healthy appetite of the mind for entertainment in its various forms of Narrative, Wit, and Humor, will not go uncared for. The publishers wish to say, also, that while native writers will receive the most solid encouragement, and will be mainly relied on to fill the pages of the ATLANTIC, they will not hesitate to draw from the foreign sources at their command, as occasion may require, relying rather on the competency of an author to treat a particular subject, than on any other claim whatever. In this way they hope to make their Periodical welcome wherever the English tongue is spoken or read.

SECOND: In the term ART they intend to include the whole domain of æsthetics, and hope gradually to make this critical department a true and fearless representative of Art, in all its various branches, without any regard to prejudice, whether personal or national, or to private considerations of what kind soever.

THIRD: In Politics, the ATLANTIC will be the organ of no party or clique, but will honestly endeavor to be the exponent of what its conductors believe to be the American idea. It will deal frankly with persons and with parties, endeavoring always to keep in view that moral element which transcends all persons and parties, and which alone makes the basis of a true and lasting national prosperity. It will not rank itself with any sect of *antics*, but with that body of men which is in favor of Freedom, National Progress, and Honor, whether public or private.

As an earnest of the material at their command, they subjoin the following list of literary persons interested in their enterprise; wishing it, however, to be distinctly understood, that they shall hope for support from every kind of ability which desires the avenue of their columns, and in the remuneration of which they shall be guided purely by their sense of intrinsic merit:—

WILLIAM H. PRESCOTT,
RALPH WALDO EMERSON,
WM. C. BRYANT,
HENRY W. LONGFELLOW,
REV. F. H. HEDGE, D. D.,
NATHANIEL HAWTHORNE,
JOHN G. WHITTIER,
OLIVER WENDELL HOLMES,
JAMES R. LOWELL,
J. LOTHROP MOTLEY,
GEORGE WM. CURTIS,
HERMAN MELVILLE,
PROF. C. C. FELTON,
PROF. F. J. CHILD,
E. P. WHIPPLE,
EDMUND QUINCY,
    Author of "Wensley,"
THOMAS W. PARSONS,
J. T. TROWBRIDGE,
    Author of "Neighbor Jackwood," &c.

MRS. H. BEECHER STOWE,
MRS. GASKELL,
    Author of "Ruth," "Mary Barton," &c.
MRS. L. MARIA CHILD,
MRS. C. M. KIRKLAND,
MRS. PIKE,
    Author of "Ida May," "Caste," &c,
MISS ROSE TERRY,
WILKIE COLLINS,
    Author of "The Dead Secret," &c.
G. RUFFINI,
    Author of "Doctor Antonio," &c.
SHIRLEY BROOKS,
    Author of "Aspen Court," &c.
E. M. WHITTY,
    Author of "Political Portraits," &c.
JAMES HANNAY,
    Author of "Singleton Fontenoy,"
O. W. PHILLEO,
    Author of "Twice Married."

The Publishers will aim to have each number of the magazine ready in time for distribution and sale, in the more remote parts of the country, on or before the first day of the month for which it is intended.

TERMS.—The ATLANTIC MONTHLY can be had of Booksellers, Periodical Agents, or from the Publishers, at Three Dollars a year, or Twenty-five Cents a Number.

Subscribers remitting three dollars, in advance, to the publishers, will receive the work for one year, *post paid*, in any part of the United States within 3000 miles.

A liberal discount made to wholesale dealers, and to postmasters and others who act as agents, to whom specimen numbers will be furnished without charge.

The Publishers will not be responsible for contracts made by agents. All persons ordering through that medium must look to them for their supply.

All communications for the Atlantic must be addressed to the Publishers.

35

libraries, newspapers, art collections, and highly literate groups, as American themes supplied a bolder impulse to the imagination, writers would look less to the Old World. Naturally—not in the dogged spirit of Emerson's *American Scholar*—our authors by 1850 were writing more as Americans than ever before.

By that date the eminent authors could be divided into several main groups. Some used foreign themes almost exclusively. That could be said, for example, of Prescott with Spain and Spanish America as his field, and of Motley, devoting his pen to the struggles of Protestant Europe for liberty. Another group chose European or American subjects almost impartially, for education, background, and temperament gave them a cosmopolitan outlook. This was true of Longfellow, whose muse was equally at home in old Norway, Germany, or Massachusetts; true of Lowell, writing his "Legend of Brittany" and lays of Italy with as much gusto as his "Pictures of Appledore"; and even true of Emerson (thorough Yankee though he was), ranging the whole globe and all history for ideas and inspiration. Still another group were so much interested in the American scene and spirit that they seldom forsook the topics of their own land. These writers, Whitman, Thoreau, Whittier, Mrs. Stowe, William Gilmore Simms, Parkman, and others, were instinctively possessed by home subjects. All of Whitman's strength sprang from native ground; Whittier's home ballads and songs of labor were bounded by Monadnock and Cape Ann; Thoreau as a philosopher might belong to the world, but as a naturalist he was all Concord's; Simms had Cooper's own feeling for local scene-painting and indigenous types of humanity; Parkman, haunted from boyhood by images of the wilderness, devoted his life to the history of the struggle for North America. As Lowell grew older, he kept more closely within his national orbit.

Then, too, the question of idiom enters. Some authors, like Longfellow and Hawthorne, wrote with a European tone and accent. Save for its frequent Biblical phrasing, Whittier's language differs little from Tennyson's—even the chant of the fishermen's wives denouncing Floyd Ireson might be by an English poet. But some authors broke frequently into an American vernacular. Lowell did so in the "Biglow Papers" and "The Courtin'," Emerson in many a line of verse ("Drain sweet maple-juice in vats") and many *Journal* entries ("Dumb and unhappy like an Indian in church"), and Mrs. Stowe in the delicious Yankee dialogue of *The Minister's Wooing*. In two writers, Thoreau and Whitman, the American accent is pervasive, lending a homely strength throughout. Nobody could ever believe that Emerson's essays were written by anyone but a firmly planted American using his native idiom.

But the essential fact was that the nation in the fifties could be proud of its authors. If they were not the peers of Dickens and Thackeray, Tennyson and Browning, Hugo and De Musset, Balzac and Heine, they were nevertheless touched with fire by a New World muse. Such authors could be left to follow their own bent.

[III]

The chief values which the country derived from its best creative works in this era were two. They enriched the national scene, transforming its bare landscapes by a multicolored investiture; and still more important, they deepened and invigorated the national spirit. It may be added that although their impact was only beginning to be felt by the late fifties, they also quickened the flow of American ideas. But this was a less noteworthy function. For ideas, readers went not to the imaginative creations, but to books of a tougher, tamer quality. They sought their political ideas in Calhoun, St. George Tucker, and Francis Lieber, and their economic ideas in the Careys, Hezekiah Niles, and Francis Bowen. They found European ideas transmitted by a hundred ready pens—Charles A. Dana, for example, reporting the revolutions of 1848 on the instant. To be sure, Emerson's essays, Thoreau in "Civil Disobedience" and other polemic papers, and Whitman and Lowell as well, were full of ideas. But their best coin was not such silver; it was gold minted with an imaginative and moral stamp.

It is imagination that furnishes and tapestries the national house. As men had looked on the Hudson with brightened eye after "Rip Van Winkle," so they looked with a novel delight on the Plymouth shore after *Miles Standish*, on Louisiana bayous after *Evangeline*, and on the South Carolina uplands after Simms's *The Yemassee*. Most people never fully see their own land until the poet and novelist fit glasses to their eyes. Old New York had been the first to profit largely in this fashion. Readers of Philip Freneau's poems dreamed of the British prison ships firing their evening gun over the black tide of the East River, of Benedict Arnold gloomily sailing for England from the Battery, and of shopkeepers crowding the gallery of Congress Hall. Readers of Drake and Halleck found the "Croaker Papers" mirroring the Park Theatre, the snug bar of Niblo's Hotel, and the busy newspaper offices. Long Island Sound and Montauk Point had been made romantic ground by *Miles Wallingford* and Cooper's other sea tales. As for Otsego Lake, who could see it without thinking of Hutter's "castle," and the rendezvous between Deerslayer and Chingachgook on Otsego Rock? Cooper had done as much for the Lake George country in *The Last of the Mohicans*, and still more for the blood-stained border country of Westchester in *The Spy*. White Plains, Four Corners, and the dales that Harvey Birch, the pretended peddler, fearlessly traversed while the Neutral Ground was being ravaged by miscreants who preyed on both patriot and loyalist, were now seen with an inward as well as outward vision; they had a double existence.

Without these writers, the Empire City and State would have been all foreground, bathed in the hard hot sunlight of the present alone. Irving had done most of all to give them a long cool background. His historian Diedrich Knickerbocker, relating how in the golden reign of Wouter Van Twiller the town of New Amsterdam rose out of the mud to become marvellously polite, how William the Testy carried on the Oyster War, and how Peter Stuyvesant, after leading an army, brimful of wrath and cabbage, to wrest Fort Christina from the Swedes, had to surrender to a legion of British beef-fed warriors, succeeded all too well in lifting the old Dutch regime from the level of realism. As a historian, Irving now had time to repent his grotesque sallies of the imagination. A greater author, Whitman, not only chanted of "Crossing Brooklyn Ferry," but turned his face occasionally to the past, and did his part to give romance to old Long Island, and even to a bloody defeat on Brooklyn ground as recalled by a Revolutionary veteran:

> The years recede, pavements and stately houses disappear;
> Rude forts appear again, the old hoop'd guns are mounted;
> I see the lines of rais'd earth stretching from river to bay. . . .
> As I talk I remember all—I remember the Declaration;
> It was read here—the whole army paraded—it was read to us here.
> *   *   *   *   *   *   *
> It sickens me yet, that slaughter!
> I saw the moisture gather in drops on the face of the General. . . .

It was New England, however, which by 1861 had fared best in this imaginative transformation. Minor writers were assisting the process; Jones Very of Salem, for example, in verse and essay, and Sylvester Judd in *Margaret*, his fine bucolic study of Massachusetts life just after the Revolution. Yet the great romancers and poets needed no aid. How clearly had Americans seen the Yankee sailor until R. H. Dana, Jr., pictured him in *Two Years Before the Mast*, or the Yankee ports until Longfellow sang of the black wharves and slips, the sea tides tossing free, and the beauty and mystery of the vessels? How well had they known the coastal villagers until Whittier struck out "Skipper Ireson's Ride" and Hawthorne presented the all-too-ordinary facts of tragedy in "The Wives of the Dead?" How vivid had a Northern snowstorm really been to Americans until Whittier told how it came on, the sun rising cheerless and darkly circled over hills of gray to give a noonday light sadder than waning moon; until Emerson described its frolic architecture, with white bastions round every fence stake, Parian wreaths hung on coop and kennel, and swan-like forms investing the hidden thorn—the housemates meanwhile, as the tempest lasted, sitting about the radiant fireplace enclosed in a tumultuous privacy of storm; until Hawthorne touched the very poetry of the new-fallen drifts in his tale of the little snow-sister made by playing children? The Yankee yarn-teller had never been properly identified until Hawthorne's pen caught him—whenafter his counterpart was noted in every grocery and groggery in the land:

One of Uncle Parker's eyes had been blown out with gunpowder, and the other did but glimmer in its socket. Turning it upward as he spoke, it was his delight to tell of cruises against the French, and battles with his own shipmates, when he and an antagonist used to be seated astride of a sailor's chest, each fastened down by a spike nail through the trousers, and there to fight it out. Sometimes he expatiated on the delicious flavor of the hagden, a greasy and gooselike fowl, which the sailors catch with hook and line on the Grand Banks. He dwelt with rapture on an interminable winter at the Isle of Sables, where he had gladdened himself, amid polar snows, with the rum and sugar saved from the wreck of a West India schooner. And wrathfully did he shake his fist, as he related how a party of Cape Cod men had robbed him of that lawful spoil, and sailed away with every keg of old Jamaica, leaving him not a drop to drown his sorrow.

Something much above historical, reportorial, or descriptive talent is needed to people an empty land with living people, and paint pictures of fancy on brown hillsides. The typical Shaker village of the time was lifted out of its evanescent reality into enduring ideality in Hawthorne's story of "The Canterbury Pilgrims." It became as difficult for cultivated Americans to visit the White Mountains without thinking of "The Great Stone Face" as to voyage up the Hudson to Albany without thinking of Irving's "Dolph Heyliger." Not until 1856 was the manuscript of Governor Bradford's great history, miraculously discovered in the Lambeth Palace Library, completely published; good secondary accounts did not exist; and the story of the Pilgrims had never been properly written.[6] All the more marvellous was Longfellow's feat in bringing to bright-hued immediacy the wintry sea, the springtime woods, the village street, the Pilgrim settlers, the little human triangle of Priscilla, John Alden, and Miles Standish. He anticipated history and almost made it unnecessary; no prose writer could overthrow his image of Standish any more than a historian could overthrow Shakespeare's Richard III, for both entered into the heart of the people. The magic of Herman Melville's eye and hand was not so quickly recognized. Yet even in the fifties, if few understood the philosophical overtones of *Moby Dick*, many found in Captain Peleg, who was the very type of

6 The best-known sourcebook until Bradford's history was published was Alexander Young's dry compilation of 1841, *Chronicles of the Pilgrim Fathers of the Colony of Plymouth, 1602–1605*, which contained Nathaniel Morton's *New England's Memorial* and Edward Winslow's *Relation*.

Nantucket Quaker mariner, in Stubb and Starbuck, quintessential whaling men, and in that strangest figure of all, Captain Ahab, with the sea adventures in which they figured, material for understanding the maritime frontier of the United States as they had never understood it before.

Leaf from Ticknor, Reed and Fields catalogue, spring, 1851.

The South, which had produced an immortal in Poe, had its lesser Irving in John P. Kennedy, its lesser Cooper in Simms, and its other minor romancers like John Esten Cooke. That under happier circumstances, with more leisure, better home criticism, and greater freedom from political preoccupation, Simms might almost have equalled Cooper is evident to all readers of his Revolutionary series: *The Partisan, Mellichampe, Katharine Walton, The Scout, Eutaw,* and *Woodcraft.* He could be as interesting a storyteller, and if he totally failed in that work of character creation which made Long Tom Coffin, Hawkeye or Leatherstocking, and Harvey Birch really distinct and memorable personages, he excelled Cooper in his use of historical elements. The six novels named, all delightful if read in the same fashion in which they were written—at headlong, careless pace—give a fuller, more graphic, and more affectionate picture of oldtime Charleston and of the Carolina countryside, checkered by Marion's rangers and Tarleton's cavalry, than Cooper gives of any eastern area. The author write of *Katharine Walton*, in which his historical matter is richest, that it was the product of many different studies pursued for years under the guidance of the best authorities, that the portraits were mostly of real persons, that the descriptions of manners and social life were drawn from unquestionable sources, and that the very anecdotes and repartees were often taken from tradition. His presentation in *Woodcraft* of the prosperous post-Revolution plantation Glen-Eberley, with its hospitable owner, its loyal, industrious slaves, and its books, dogs, horses, and boats, and hunting rifles, is a faithful piece of genre painting, almost comparable to Scott's best work.

On a lower plane, the South had been a fertile field for a broad journalistic type of humor, which became important in a few literary productions, and still more important in its influence upon future writers like Bret Harte and Mark Twain. The *Georgia Scenes* of Augustus Baldwin Longstreet, published as the 1840's opened, cast its genial rays afar, finding ultimate reflection even in a few pages of Thomas Hardy's *The Trumpet-Major*. The courtship of Major Jones, and the adventures of Captain Simon Suggs, as celebrated by William T. Thompson and J. J. Hooper respectively, were in crude fashion an anticipation of the local colorists who were to become so abundant in another generation or two. The best of all these works, Joseph Glover Baldwin's *The Flush Times of Alabama and Mississippi*, which appeared in 1853, has a special appeal to students of history. The unsettled, rough, cheerful life of the nearer Southwestern frontier was sketched as graphically in its pages, and with nearly as much literary art, as that of the Indiana and Illinois frontier was soon to be drawn in Edward Eggleston's books. The time was the halcyon period 1835–37, when, as Baldwin put it, shinplasters were the sole currency, bank bills drifted as thick as autumn leaves in Vallambrosa, and credit could be had for the asking. The crash came, with personal tragedies aplenty. Both literary and historical values of no mean sort can be found in the section of the book which describes the ups and downs of the Virginia migrants to the Southwest, relating how these sanguine, spendthrift, genial sons of the Old Dominion were ruined, and how they then turned to tavern-keeping, school-teaching, or even overseerships for the wealthy planters.

The enrichment of the national scene by the romancer's imagination and the poet's vision was perhaps the greatest single gain in American wealth during this period. Scotland before Burns and Sir Walter Scott was one of the poorest of lands; Scotland after "Tam O' Shanter," "The Cotter's Saturday Night," and the Waverley novels was one of the richest. By 1860 Americans could feel what they did not in 1840—that they, too, had a picturesque, varicolored social life, a brilliant landscape, a heroic historical background; for the great writers had shown it all to them and to the world. Year by year the tapestry was widened. When Harriet Beecher Stowe in 1858 began *The Minister's Wooing* in the *Atlantic*, Lowell read it with enthusiasm and pronounced it her best work, because it presented with such simple beauty the New England life which she probably knew more intimately than any other author. As yet the realist had not thrown down the gauntlet to the romancer. Tokens of an emerging realism appeared, however, as in the powerful Pennsylvania story which Rebecca Harding Davis published in 1861—"Life in the Iron Mills." In romance and poem, in Whittier's ballads, Hawthorne's allegories, Simms's adventure tales, Whitman's chants, Bayard Taylor's travel studies, and in experimental work by younger hands, America was finding its landscape irradiated and its feeling for social experience vitalized.[7]

[IV]

Americans were learning also that their spiritual life was debtor to the deep underlying seriousness of their best literature. To instruct, to reform, and to elevate were purposes from which the greatest authors were never beguiled by hedonism, paganism, or any cult of art for art's sake. With only one notable exception, Irving, these authors were crusaders. All the eminent New Englanders save Hawthorne enlisted in the antislavery legions; the noble-hearted Simms believed ardently in the cause of Southern nationalism; and Whitman battled for his faith in democracy, brotherhood, and national feeling. The historians, who then had a wider following than at any other period in our national life, felt no desire to be coolly objective. Prescott and Motley dealt with the desperate European struggles in which political and religious liberalism had achieved a partial victory over bigotry and tyranny; Bancroft described with panegyric enthusiasm the growth of democracy in America; and Richard Hildreth, most philosophic-minded and politically conservative of them all, defended the principles of Federalism as exemplified by Washington, John Adams, and Hamilton.

The New Englanders in particular struck two dominant notes: they were unwearying foes of mediocrity and falsity, and they were imbued with a deeply felt moral passion. Emerson, who though he left the church never left off preaching, was the precentor of the group. Always insisting upon excellence—the best

7 Probably never have newspapers reprinted more good poetry than in this period. Indexes to the Burlington (Vermont) *Free Press* show that in 1856–61 it published nine poems of Longfellow, including "Paul Revere's Ride" and long excerpts from *Hiawatha;* twenty of Whittier's; six of Lowell's; seven of Bryant's; and half a dozen of O. W. Holmes's.

that a man, a community, or a nation could do—and always defending the right, he drenched his books in ethical didacticism. This homiletic trait was already recognized by some as his chief title to greatness. As a poet he was uneven, rough-tongued, and short of flight. As a philosopher he made no pretensions to profundity. As a reformer he was too retiring and scholarly to be effective; he had been noticeably tardy in joining the abolitionist movement. As a man of letters he lacked the higher creative gifts. As an ethical teacher, however, he found no equal in his time in America, and no superior anywhere except that more religious, intense, and prophetic genius, Carlyle. He tried always to reach the intellect rather than the emotions, believing that the duty of the preacher "is to convert life into truth." His gospel made a natural appeal to American opti- mism and individualism, for he minimized evil, urged men to trust in themselves, and extolled the grand intuitive forces in human nature. At the same time, he ex- horted his hearers to explore the universe under the direction of thought. His ideal of America was a land intellectually alert and morally earnest; a country impatient of the second-best and ardent in pursuit of the superlative.

Emerson had come home from England in 1848 animated with a warmer love of his native land than ever. Almost as much as Whitman, he took joy in the expansive energy, the variety, and the driving power of the people—their march to the West, their ability to raise cities overnight, their capacity for digesting masses of immigrants. Attending the Concord town meetings, he renewed his faith in democracy as he saw Yankee farmers and tradesmen manage their public affairs with integrity and foresight. He was soon writing passages that Jefferson would have applauded. "Try the rough water as well as the smooth," ran one. "Rough water can teach lessons worth knowing. When the state is unquiet, per- sonal qualities are more than ever decisive. Fear not a revolution which will constrain you to live five years in one. Don't be so tender about making an enemy now and then." The American idea, even in this stormy decade, seemed to him superior to any Old World idea. "I wish," he wrote in his *Journal*, "to cast out the passion for Europe by the passion for America." [8]

Yet the defects of American society did not escape him. The people lacked maturity; they were unripened, like peaches and grapes needing a fortnight more of sun. They were overpractical: "The providing means of living now absorbs them, to the exclusion of the ends. Nothing but the brandy of politics will wake them from brute life." Being ill-educated, they thought too much of machines, of railroads, telegraphs, balloons, and newspapers. Slavery, a reproach in itself,

---

8 "We have our culture, like Allston, from Europe, and are Europeans. Perhaps we must be content with this, and thank God for Europe for a while yet, and there shall be no great Yankee, until, in the unfolding of our population and power, England kicks the beam, and English authors write to America; which must happen ere long." *Journals*, VI, 264, 265 (1842). See also his essay "Culture" in *Conduct of Life*.

was still more shameful in the way it made cowards among Massachusetts and other Northern men. "Oh for a Roman breath and the courage that advances and dictates!" he exclaimed in the year of Buchanan's inauguration.

It was not until the Compromise of 1850, with Webster's Seventh of March speech and the Fugitive Slave Act, that Emerson had enlisted in the abolitionist crusade. Then he awoke in earnest. He felt infamy in the air; he carried about all day a painful sensation which, when traced home, was "the odious remembrance of that ignominy which has fallen on Massachusetts, which robs the landscape of beauty, and takes the sunshine out of every hour." [9] The Kansas-Nebraska Act confirmed his belief in Southern aggression, so that he later wrote of the crisis as "the years when Southern slavery broke over its old banks, made new and vast pretensions, and wrung from the weakness or treachery of the Northern people fatal concessions." [10] His was a purely moral view of slavery; if it was good, then theft, arson, and homicide were all good. He rejected the doctrine of racial inferiority, quoting Montesquieu's remark that the slaves might be better men than the slaveholders. To determine a nice question of right or wrong, he declared, he would not go to Louis Napoleon, a political hack, or a slavedriver. He did not expect a quick solution of the problem. "Liberty is never cheap. It is made difficult, because freedom is the accomplishment and perfectness of man." Yet he was certain that slavery would be overthrown. "Slowly, slowly, the Avenger comes, but comes surely. The proverbs of the nations affirm these delays, but affirm the arrival. They say, 'God may consent, but not forever.' " And Emerson quoted a verse anticipating the Second Inaugural: [11]

> For evil word shall evil word be said,
> For murder-stroke a murder-stroke be paid,
> Who smites must smart.

Never really at home in politics, Emerson was at his best when he left controversial issues alone and lifted his audiences to a higher plane of thought. He taught self-trust and self-communion as emphatically as Whittier, with his simple Quaker religiosity, taught self-distrust and self-questioning. Emerson's definition of transcendentalism as idealism was derived from Kant; for while Locke had declared that nothing could be found in the intellect which was not previously in the experience of the senses, Kant (and Emerson) held that the mind possessed an important body of intuitive ideas, which did not come by experience, but through which experience was acquired. Emerson's self-communion also owed

---

9 See repeated entries in the *Journals* for May and June, 1850. "This filthy enactment," he wrote in July, "was made in the nineteenth century, by people who could read and write. I will not obey it, by God."
10 See essay on Theodore Parker in *Miscellanies*, Concord ed., 290.
11 For Emerson's opinion of slavery see *Miscellanies*, Concord ed., 179–244.

much to the individualism of the Yankee come-outers. He believed that every man had in his own breast a deity which, intensely personal, yet embraced the world. He distilled this creed into his "Brahma" and still more lucidly into "The Problem," with its assertion that the wisdom of all bibles came from the hearts of peoples, that the litanies of nations rose from a volcanic core below, and that Michelangelo, in rounding Peter's dome, builded better than he knew because he built on the inspiration of an inner power, not on mere knowledge. Countless young Americans found stimulus in Emerson's exhortation to live in the spirit, to seek beauty, to be self-reliant, and to trust to their purer spontaneities.

Countless Americans, too, found a wholesome invigoration in Emerson's optimism. It was characteristic of the Concord seer that he never liked Shelley, whose themes of pantheism, melancholia, and rebellion against the universe repelled him; characteristic also that he disliked *The Scarlet Letter*, pronouncing it ghastly in its gloom and morbidity.[12] To Emerson, one cardinal duty of the poet was to cheer and encourage the soul. He recognized the dualism of nature, all experience finding a double form—good and evil, light and darkness, knowledge and ignorance. But his was what a later critic called a vanishing dualism, for he thought that each man could find in himself the "soul of the whole; the wise silence; the universal beauty; the eternal One." That the ultimate tendency of his ideas was to generate an excessively facile kind of optimism might be argued; that they made spiritual salvation seem too cheap and easy has often been asserted; but that their immediate effect was to brighten the outlook and strengthen the courage of men was unquestionable.[13]

Great as a preacher, he was also great as a teacher of that knowledge which he ranked so much below the inner afflatus. Nearly all his best prose work was cast in the form of the teacher's short discourse, his vocation of lecturer molding his essays. Each paper represented the quintessence of long and wide reading in the master minds of the past and of much ripe thinking, squeezed first into his journals and then refined into his essay. He holds a place with other tremendous readers and quoters—with Montaigne, Bacon, Sir Thomas Browne, Burton, Pascal, and Hazlitt—and his own reflections are as good as the thoughts he borrows from classic lore. Year by year those who heard and read him got the benefit of an encyclopedic explorer of human wisdom from Plato to Comte and Spencer. Oliver Wendell Holmes computed that the essays contained nearly 3,400 quotations from 868 writers; W. C. Brownell has written that the very titles of his discourses are a liberal education. The breadth, the spaciousness, the gem-encrusted wealth of his writings reminded Americans that they were the heirs of all the ages and that they could never afford to lose the culture of past centuries.

12 E. P. Whipple, *Reminiscences of Eminent Men*, 147, 149.
13 Cf. Paul Elmer More's estimate of Emerson, *Shelburne Essays*, First Series.

They spurred ardent minds to further reading, as they spurred ardent spirits to high endeavor.

Yet however much a cosmopolite, a citizen of all ages and all countries, Emerson was not lacking in a deep vein of pure Americanism. The national past was still so new that the question of how to regard it had an urgent importance. The radical instinct was to turn one's back on the past and seek new truth alone. The scholarly instinct was to record the facts, to preserve the more picturesque traditions and legends, and to explain the best ideas of bygone generations. The artistic instinct was to transform old lore and legend by making them more finely decorative and more deeply symbolic. Radical though he was, Emerson had his share of the preservative instinct. He felt the same affection for his national past that Plutarch, Bacon, and Montaigne had shown for theirs. While an illustration from Hindu scriptures or Byzantine story occurred to him as readily as an incident from Washington's career, he was always eager to commemorate the Yankee lares and penates.[14] When the town of Concord began its third century in 1835, he had pronounced his noble Historical Discourse, a summary of the contributions made by one provincial village to the cause of human liberty. He kept a strong sense of the merits of the old Puritanism whose formal creed he had forsaken. Two lines, certain to endure as long as anything he wrote,

> Tis man's perdition to be safe
> When for the truth he ought to die

were transmuted by him from an old Puritan divine writing in the iron year, 1642. His "Historic Notes on Life and Letters in New England" (not composed until 1867) are full of salty appreciation of the past of his section, from William Bradford's day to John A. Andrew's. His study of his witty aunt, Mary Moody Emerson, his sketch of the old Roman-spirited jurist and commissioner to South Carolina, Samuel Hoar, and his essay on Thoreau, all show a fine preservative instinct. His poems "Monadnock" and "Boston" have apt commemorative touches, while the shots of Concord battlefield were made to echo immortally around the world in his stanzas.

[V]

Second only to Emerson in his power as a moral teacher for this era stood Hawthorne. (Not until a later generation was Walt Whitman to come into his own.) Hawthorne had emerged but slowly into general recognition. At first glance this fact might seem difficult to explain. His early sheaves, *Twice Told Tales*, *The Snow Image and Other Tales*, and *Mosses from an Old Manse*, pos-

14 "A good scholar," wrote Emerson in his *Journals* for April, 1847, "will find Aristophanes and Hafiz and Rabelais full of American history."

sessed many qualities to commend them to general readers. Their themes, drawn from the old chronicles and traditions of Massachusetts, were fairly familiar: "The Gentle Boy" echoed the persecution of the Quakers, "The Gray Champion" told of the regicide judges, and the stories of the Province House dealt with important historical episodes. To these materials he gave a beautiful transforming touch. His style, pure, sweet, and graceful, with haunting poetic strains, was as simple and lucid as that of the Bible itself. Yet the moral intensity of the writer made him difficult to accept on his own terms. His pages reflected a lonely, gloomy outlook on life; they had a faint but pervasive subacidity, not quite bitter but at times decidedly misanthropic; they seemed the work of a man who had often probed the sources of spiritual unhappiness but seldom touched the fountains of spiritual joy. Readers who plunged into his tales found themselves shivering in a darker, sadder world. Even his humor had the brightness of Lapland moonlight or December sunshine, for it irradiated without warming.

Then, too, the stories and even the later novels seemed out of touch with active everyday life. As a writer in the *Atlantic* put it in 1860, the fictions suggested a shy recluse, alternately diffident in conduct and bold in thought, whose original and varied gifts "seemed to have developed themselves in the shade, without sufficient energy of will or desire to force them, except fitfully, into the sunlight." [15] He himself often spoke of his creations as unsubstantial or phantom-like, as when he wrote that Hepzibah Pyncheon appeared like someone walking in a dream. His early plaint to Longfellow explains much in his career. Writing from one of the busiest corners of the energetic New World, with a teeming, variegated, hustling life all about him, this self-bound recluse explained that he lived in an owl's nest, never going abroad till dark. He sympathized when Mrs. Longfellow died. "But," he wrote Longfellow, "I assure you that trouble is the next best thing to enjoyment, and that there is no fate in the world so horrible as to have no share in either its joys or its sorrows." Little known, little applauded, he held his pen with numbed fingers. "I have another great difficulty, in the lack of materials; for I have seen so little of the world that I have nothing but thin air to concoct my stories of; and it is not easy to give a lifelike semblance to such shadowy stuff. Sometimes, through a peephole, I have caught a glimpse of the real world; and the two or three articles in which I have portrayed such glimpses, please me better than the others." [16] Though he knew more of the

15 Unsigned article, May, 1860.
16 Samuel Longfellow, *Longfellow*, I, 264, 265. But he had another feeling about his long imprisonment in his lonely Salem chamber. It had benefited him in that "if I had sooner made my escape into the world, I should have grown hard and rough, and been covered with earthly dust, and my heart would have become calloused by rude encounters. . . ." Newton Arvin, *Hawthorne*, 91. For another view see Randall Stewart, *Hawthorne*.

world, and played a larger part in its activities, than this plaint would suggest, his early experience was too limited for a full-bodied fiction.

But if his absorption with a shadowy sphere of the imagination, and with the darker aspects of psychology, deprived his work of throbbing vitality, it deepened his moral vision. Hawthorne has been treated by one critic as an author reacting against Transcendentalism.[17] While the view has some justice, he is more accurately to be seen as a latter-day New Englander preoccupied with and reacting against Puritanism, which had an overmastering fascination for him. Indeed, he anticipated a struggle between Puritanism and a freer attitude, to reach its climax early in the twentieth century. When in 1850 he brought out *The Scarlet Letter*, readers saw that he had imparted a deeper feeling than ever before to his work; that putting real passion into it, he had for the first time achieved a true act of creation. His genius shone forth with such power that the book immediately became famous in both Britain and America. Yet its harshness and gloom repelled readers who declared that while it took everybody captive, it captivated nobody. Brooding over the primitive era in New England, in an effort to delineate its spiritual features, Hawthorne seized upon the sternest side of the Puritan ideal of discipline. He presented Hester Prynne and Arthur Dimmesdale as figures sealed into an icy glacier of social condemnation and hostility. They suffered under the concepts of law and justice which Increase and Cotton Mather had stated with such fierce inflexibility; they experienced none of that forgiveness and loving-kindness with which John Winthrop or Samuel Sewall would actually have treated them. The Puritans had their dogmas of grace and love no less than of punishment. New Englanders complained, with justice, that Hawthorne had brought out the iron relentlessness of their forebears in their bleakest moods, but had failed to portray their relieving interludes of humanity, compassion, and gaiety.[18]

Yet it was well for Americans to be reminded of those truths which Puritanism had at times inflexibly enforced. It was well that, in the greatest work of art produced down to that memorable year 1850 on New World soil, they should learn again the power of sin to brand an individual heart with a far more burning stigma than the letter "A" embroidered on Hester's breast. The moral symbolism which gave the book its chill, crepuscular power lifted it to the classic plane.

In *The House of the Seven Gables*, the most variegated, delightful, and lively

17 John Erskine, in *Cambridge Hist. Am. Lit.*, II, Ch. XI.
18 Indeed, Hawthorne delivers himself of iron moralizing: "And be the stern and sad truth spoken, that the breach which guilt has once made into the human soul is never, in this mortal state, repaired. It may be watched and guarded. But there is still the ruined wall, and near it the stealthy tread of the foe that would win over again his unforgotten triumph."

of the American stories, a book which (says Henry James) has a vague indefinable charm, like the sweetness of a piece of music or the softness of a September day, the drama is similarly enacted not so much for its own interest as for its symbolic value.[19] The novel possesses a sunniness unknown elsewhere in Hawthorne. It contains more social observation than the other novels, just as *The Scarlet Letter* contains more history. Several of the characters exhibit a picturesque quality, heightened by idiosyncrasy, which suggests that the author had taken some hints from Dickens. Miss Hepzibah Pyncheon, mistress of the penny shop, a stiff, antique gentlewoman of decayed fortune, spurred on by necessity yet restrained by dignity as she sells gingerbread and toys; her brother Clifford, fresh from prison, dishonored, enervated, collapsing in mind and body; the cheerful, affectionate, efficient country cousin, Phoebe Pyncheon, who comes to succor this forlorn pair, a girl as fresh, sweet, and heart-warming as she is sensible and practical; Judge Pyncheon, that imposing, bland, benevolent-seeming, hard-natured pillar of society, outwardly strong and inwardly rotting—these are the finely imagined members of a sinking family. With lighter touch Hawthorne has sketched the garrulous old wood-sawer, Uncle Venner, and the ethereal little Pearl. But for all its approach to a study of contemporaneous American life, and for all its varied charm, the novel is fundamentally stern and forbidding. Hawthorne has carried out with much fancy, but also with unsparing force, the moral purpose which he frankly avowed: to show how "the wrongdoing of one generation lives into the successive ones, and, divesting itself of every temporary advantage, becomes a pure and uncontrolled mischief."

What power is possessed by the *Blithedale Romance*, a breezy, lively book of less finish and depth, is likewise largely derived from its ethical seriousness. Zenobia dominates the story. In some respects she was unquestionably sketched from Margaret Fuller, a woman imperious, high-spirited, and eloquent; in other respects this beautiful and richly temperamental woman was a creation of Hawthorne's imagination. Almost equally robust is the portrait of Hollingsworth, a typical New England theorist. The novel shows how the flaws inherent in the characters of these two, and of their associates Miles Coverdale and Westervelt, drive them on to an inevitable catastrophe. If the moral conception of the book is narrow, it is nevertheless important.

At the end of the fifties, and near the end of Hawthorne's life, came the grandest though not the greatest of his books, a work of exquisite originality. *The Marble Faun* lacks the four-square strength, the simplicity, the poignant characters of *The Scarlet Letter*. Yet it has a richness all its own. Never has a book depended less upon its plot. It was aptly said at the time that the story began in a mystery and ended in a mist. No small part of its appeal rested upon

19 Henry James, *Nathaniel Hawthorne*, 121.

its ripe appreciation and subtle description of Italian scenery, customs, and social life generally, its acute criticism of ancient and modern art, its illuminating comments upon the architecture, history, politics, and culture of Rome.[20] At the same time, its chief personages, Hilda, Miriam, and Donatello, though types or symbols rather than warm flesh and blood, were the most imaginative and

THE MARBLE FAUN:

OR, THE

ROMANCE OF MONTE BENI.

BY
NATHANIEL HAWTHORNE,
AUTHOR OF "THE SCARLET LETTER," ETC., ETC.

IN TWO VOLUMES.
VOL. I.

BOSTON:
TICKNOR AND FIELDS.
M DCCC LX.

Title page of the original edition of *The Marble Faun.*

romantic of all Hawthorne's creations. Once more, as in *The Scarlet Letter* and *The House of the Seven Gables*, the story is overshadowed by a past sin or crime in which one of the characters, Miriam, has some implication. Once more the power of sin to stigmatize and transform a life is studied. The faunlike,

20   As George Edward Woodberry remarks, he looked beyond the Italy of flowers, ruins, music: "The assumption of the myth of the world before sin, the Rousseau-like state of nature, the prehuman, fawn-and-nymph world, is easily made in that land of classical fragments and visible joy; and Hawthorne describes it with his New England pen of light fantasy and wild nature." *Hawthorne,* 185.

innocent Donatello commits an impulsive murder; the dark act matures his character and converts him into a moral being; while the equally innocent Hilda, his companion, finds that her very knowledge of the crime throws a burden upon her conscience, impairs her joy in art and nature, and awakens in her a deeper thirst for rectitude and truth. The once-happy Donatello, who had been able to call furry and feathered creatures to him, is miserable on finding that they avoid his presence. "They shun me!" he cries. "All nature shrinks from me, and shudders at me! I live in the midst of a curse, that hems me round with a circle of fire! No innocent thing can come near me!" The cloudy ending of the story lessens its force as a moral apologue, but apologue it is, and one of wild, haunting beauty.

In all the New England writers this ethical vein was prominent. Whittier was a true son of the Quaker faith in his religious piety, his belief in toleration, his reformative impulses, his abhorrence of violence (which made him condemn John Brown's raid), and his emphasis upon the humbling of self. In many controversial essays, of which "Democracy and Slavery" is the most important, he pressed home his ethical attitude toward public issues. His antislavery poems, beginning with his apostrophes to William Lloyd Garrison and Toussaint l'Ouverture in 1832–33, were destined to rise to a fine climax in such pieces as "The Battle Autumn of 1862" and "Barbara Frietchie." All his poetry was strongly moralized; when he told a tale or pictured a scene, he never let the reader make application for himself. The same could be said of that transplanted New Englander, William Cullen Bryant. His favorite themes were death, to which he wrote more than one hymn, the inexorable march of years, the circle of eternal change in nature, the duty of man to his native land, and the still greater duty of communion with God. Even June reminded him of mortality—it was a happy month in which to be buried, when through the long summer hours the golden light might slant across his grave; even the fringed gentian, fixing its blue eye upon the autumn heavens, inspired a wish that in his fatal hour hope might blossom in his breast. He wrote of American virtues in "O Mother of a Mighty Race," and urged fortitude in "The Battlefield:"

> Truth, crushed to earth, shall rise again,
> Th' eternal years of God are hers;
> But Error, wounded, writhes in pain,
> And dies among his worshippers.

Holmes, touching in the *Autocrat* papers on a multitude of subjects, was affluent in wit, humor, and sagacious insights. His lightness of touch and hints at heterodoxy in religion led many to suspect him of levity. Actually his essays are full of didacticism, and he sometimes preaches as if his ministerial father Abiel were furnishing him a sermon. Jolly as is "The Wonderful One-Hoss

Shay," it cannot be fully understood except in connection with Holmes's essay on Jonathan Edwards; the issue of the *Atlantic* (September, 1858) that carried it also contained his lively piece of moralizing, "The Chambered Nautilus."

Lowell may also be given high rank among the humorists. He had displayed his rare spirits, ebullient humor, and satiric gift in the *Fable for Critics* and the *Biglow Papers*, while he was one of the few genuine epigrammatists that the country has produced. His approach to life was cultivated, genial, and intensely literary; despite his social activity, his journalistic work, and his gay versatility, it was even bookish. He seemed to have read everything of importance in Spanish, Italian, and French, as well as in English literature: he was equally at home in Cervantes, Dante, Molière, and Shakespeare. With the highest standards of classic expression he was thoroughly familiar, and with them in mind he wrote in 1857 an effective condemnation of didactic poetry: "Put all your beauty in your rhymes, your morals in your living." Yet he frequently touched the moral chord—and with resounding force, as his "Sir Launfal" of 1848 had proved.[21]

Heartiest teacher of them all was Walt Whitman, poet of the masses (though they read him but little) and voice of the democratic ideal—a man who sang "the greatness of Love and Democracy" and the song of Companionship; a believer in individualism and "the beauty of all adventurous and daring persons." In Whitman we touch a force far broader, more humane, and more electric than is found in any of his New England contemporaries. He had drawn much from his Quaker forebears, much from Emerson, much from various pagan influences, and most of all from his contacts with the plain people. Out of his experience and reading he painted pictures of the wide national scene and the multitudinous varieties of social action; and he infused his sketches with a sense of American energy, joviality, confidence in the future, and democratic ease. He wrote of Yankee clippers, cutting the sparkle and scud, of clam diggers gathering around the chowder kettle, of the fur-clad trapper marrying a lithe Indian girl in a glade beneath the Tetons, of the foot-bruised runaway slave sinking exhausted at a Northern door, of Texas Rangers massacred by the Mexicans, of an old-fashioned sea fight of the days of 1812. He wrote, above all, of his own appetites, emotions, and aspirations. His *Leaves of Grass* had a surging vitality; it was suffused with a semi-religious feeling for democracy as the very essence of the republic's life.[22]

21 Herman Melville, too, a man of deep moral insights, brought them out in *Mardi* and *Billy Budd*; while he had his direct reform objects as well. *Redburn* was aimed at the reformation of bad conditions in the merchant marine, *White Jacket* in the naval service.
22 Emerson writes in his *Journals* that George Bancroft and Bryant were historical democrats interested in dead or organized liberty, not in the work of organizing liberty. This was unjust; for though Whitman was much more concerned with organizing liberty than Bancroft, Bryant's great work for that cause on the *Evening Post* is unforgettable. On Whitman, see Cleveland Rodgers and John Black, eds., *The Gathering of the Forces*.

Whitman's verse was often of a nebulous kind, at its worst harsh and monotonous, and even at its best sometimes seeming to need an alchemic change to precipitate it in true poetic form. His gospel of self-reliance, comradeship, national loyalty, and democracy was sometimes nebulous too, or disjointed and inarticulate—but it was infinitely suggestive; if at times it left the reader baffled and irritated, it usually left him heartened and buoyant. Whitman's faults lay all on the surface, while some of his merits were not fully grasped for half a century. Yet even in 1855 there were many who saw that he was achieving a new and stirring form of verse melody. He conceived it his business to "take hold of muscular democratic virilities without wincing and put them into verse;" and if he frequently fell into prose and even bathos, he also frequently touched felicity. Prophet, mystic, and poet in one, he was willing to speak himself even if he startled others:

> Do you take it I would astonish?
> Does the daylight astonish? Does the early redstart twittering through
>   the wood?

And in speaking his broad sympathies ("Whoever walks a furlong without sympathy walks to his own funeral drest in his shroud") he could occasionally convey his feeling with the happiest diction and rhythm. The music of his familiar hymn to earth and night—"Press close, magnetic nourishing night!"—was matched by his pictorial vividness in passage after passage:

> Where the quail is whistling betwixt the woods and the wheat-lot,
> Where the bat flies in the Seventh-month eve, where the great gold-bug
>   drops through the dark,
> Where the brook puts out of the roots of the old tree and flows to the
>   meadow,
> Where cattle stand and shake away flies with the tremulous shuddering
>   of their hides. . . .
> Where band-necked partridges roost in a ring on the ground with their
>   heads out,
> Where burial coaches enter the arch'd gates of a cemetery,
> Where winter wolves bark amid wastes of snow and icicled trees,
> Where the yellow-crowned heron comes to the edge of the marsh at
>   night and feeds upon small crabs,
> Where the splash of swimmers and divers cools the warm noon.

His gospel of self-reliance, self-release, emotional honesty, and democratic individualism peculiarly fitted the mood of mid-century America. A superbly liberating gospel, it had a foundation of long meditation and self-searching, and it was destined to blow like a fresh wind through the world poetry of succeeding generations. Now he spoke the ideals of the masses—"the dense-packed cities all and the teeming wharves and ways." Now he spoke of the self-realization of the individual soul, as in his description ("Out of the Cradle Endlessly Rocking"; 1860) of the boy listening to a bird-song by the seashore:

> Demon or bird! said the boy's soul,
> Is it indeed toward your mate you sing? or is it mostly to me?
> For I, that was a child, my tongue's use sleeping,
> Now I have heard you,
> Now in a moment I know what I am for—I awake,
> And already a thousand singers—a thousand songs, clearer,
>   louder, and more sorrowful than yours,
> A thousand warbling echoes have started to life within me,
> Never to die.

Whitman was broadening the language of verse by marrying the American idiom to literature; no other poet in 1855 would have dared to say, "We have had ducking and deprecation enough." But his greater object was to broaden the spirit of the nation by a challenge to inert conventionality: by persuading men to be like himself, one who had "hated tyrants, argued not concerning God, had patience and indulgence toward the people, taken off my hat to nothing known or unknown, gone freely with powerful uneducated persons and with the young, and with the mothers of families."

[VI]

The creation of this resplendent if uneven body of literature had been impossible until various social foundations had been laid. One prerequisite was a broad measure of freedom of individual expression. The goal stated by Mill in his *Essay on Liberty*, a goal difficult of attainment under modern conditions, was within reach of countless citizens in this era. No restrictions checked the spontaneous growth of individuality; no tyrannic forces ground men down to an average norm. The humanities of the people had full opportunity to develop. Almost everywhere except in the Deep South a broad freedom of thought and expression existed. In that area the two before-noted tabus, slavery and religious heterodoxy, laid a stern restraint upon public utterance. As the tensions of the decade increased, it is true that intolerance on the slavery issue rose. Even Massachusetts punished Commissioner Loring for merely doing his sworn duty under the Fugitive Slave Act. But all sections had their courageously independent editors and politicians. The South could point to the brilliant John H. Pleasants, the tenacious Benjamin F. Perry, the belligerent Cassius M. Clay and John Minor Botts, speaking unpopular views; South Carolina admired the arch-Unionist Petigru. And nowhere, North or South, were the religious dogmas of the time important as restraints upon literature.[23]

23 Clement Eaton, *Freedom of Thought in the Old South,* 162–195.

Northerners enjoyed Hawthorne without repining because he sneered at abolitionism in his life of Franklin Pierce. They delighted in the *Autocrat* without worrying much over Holmes's trenchant rationalism and anti-Calvinism, and in Whitman without resenting his dislike of creeds. The defensive attitude of the South did fetter its writers. But the *Southern Quarterly Review*, praising Longfellow for his gifts of fancy, grace, and taste, merely remarked in passing that he had penned sundry ignorant verses on slavery in a moment of fanaticism, and went on to extol him as one of the most charming of poets in English.[24]

As important as freedom of expression was a wide, appreciative, and growing body of readers. The demand for books in this decade was such as to delight an author's heart. Technical improvements, such as the invention of electrotyping about 1850, had greatly reduced the costs of publishing; book production rose by one-half during the first decade of the fifties; and one publisher estimated that in 1856 Americans bought sixteen million dollars' worth of books published at home, and another million dollars' worth imported from abroad. Harper & Brothers were issuing three million books a year.[25] Anthony Trollope was soon to remark that while an English publisher contented himself with thousands of copies, his Yankee counterpart would deal with ten thousands.[26] Just how many bookstores the country contained it is difficult to say. According to the census of 1860, fewer than nineteen hundred persons reported their occupation as booksellers and stationers; but many shops sold books among their other wares. New York State in 1859 had 422 booksellers, or at least book outlets, in 157 cities and towns; Pennsylvania had 329 in 78 towns; and Maryland had 54 in 13 towns. The *American Publishers Circular and Literary Gazette*, which collected these figures, found that Massachusetts had 237 booksellers, and Connecticut 81. The South, if we may accept the carefully gathered statistics of this journal, did surprisingly well. In 1860 Virginia had 73 booksellers, North Carolina 66, South Carolina 35, Georgia 67, Alabama 80, and Mississippi 70.[27] These figures, North and South, may include general stores which carried a few religious books. But then many books were sold by mail, while book peddlers took orders for standard sets.

The magazines which printed genuinely able reviews, awarding praise and blame with discrimination, were now numerous. The critical pages of *Graham's*, *Russell's*, and the *Southern Literary Messenger* were of fair quality, *Putnam's* was good if uneven, and the *Atlantic*, with Lowell's hand prominent, was excellent, lifting American criticism to a higher plane from the date of its establish-

24 September, 1850.
25 See Eighth Census, Manufactures, cxxxiii; Harper, *House of Harper*, 90, 117, 118.
26 *North America*, 271.
27 *Publishers' Circular*, August 6, September 10, 1859, March 24, 1860.

ment.[28] Newspapers of the time played a greater part in popularizing literature, and especially poetry, than later. They gutted travels and histories, and reprinted verse from all the standard magazines. Lowell's "The Courtin'," Holmes's "Chambered Nautilus," and Bryant's "The Constitution" were thus scattered from the Atlantic to the Pacific. Whittier, however, was the poet most quoted at the North. The newspapers also published admiring articles on the chief literary personages. The *National Intelligencer*, for example, carried in 1856 an essay by a travelling Washingtonian upon "the Athens of America" (Concord), assuming the familiarity of all readers with *Mosses from an Old Manse*, treating Thoreau, Ellery Channing, and Margaret Fuller appreciatively, and lauding Emerson to the skies. "If Emerson has ever written an unimportant word," the writer exclaimed, "I should like to treasure it up . . . as a certificate that Jove sometimes nods." [29]

The professional man of letters could now begin to live by his pen. Prescott and Motley greatly augmented their fortunes by their histories; Hawthorne was lifted out of poverty by his major books; and even so minor a poet as Fitz-Greene Halleck, with three editions of his works published 1848–58, reaped a considerable return.[30] On the day *Hiawatha* was published Longfellow wrote that four thousand out of the first five thousand copies had been sold, and another three thousand ordered. *The Courtship of Miles Standish* was an even greater success. By noon of the day of publication five thousand copies had been sold in Boston alone; two editions of ten thousand copies each were printed or printing. A week later Longfellow wrote that the book had marched steadily on. "Another five thousand are in press; in all, an army of twenty-five thousand— in one week." [31]

The West and South alone failed to offer their writers an appreciative public, the West because it was too new, the South because social conditions were unfavorable. The slave States in the forty years before the war could be said to have two professional writers, and only two. One was Poe, who took refuge in the North and almost starved even there! The other was Simms, who fared nearly as badly.

Early in 1860, poor, in debt, with a dilapidated plantation, torn by care and anxiety, Simms wrote William Porcher Miles a pathetic letter upon the failure

28 Emerson had written in his *Journals* on October 2, 1841, that the country needed severe literary criticism. "I cannot help seeing that Dr. Channing would have been a much greater writer had he found a strict tribunal. . . . It is very easy to reach the degree of culture that prevails round us; very hard to pass it, and Dr. Channing, had he found Wordsworth, Southey, Coleridge, and Lamb around him, would as easily have been severe with himself and risen a degree higher as he has stood where he is."
29 *National Intelligencer*, August 16, 1856.
30 J. G. Wilson, *Halleck*, 478 ff.
31 Samuel Longfellow, *Longfellow*, II, 364, 365.

of his latest volume. "I have been overworked; I have been unsuccessful all my life; my books fail to pay me; I am myself a failure! . . . The labor is wasted upon a people who have seemingly decided that, so far as my labor is to depend upon their favor, I shall die. I shall appear again on no stage. I have heart for nothing, I am resigned to obscurity, and can struggle no more, except to pay off creditors and feed and clothe my poor little children." [32] Three distinguished Southern writers, A. B. Longstreet, John P. Kennedy, and Beverley Tucker (whose *George Balcombe* was called by Poe the best American novel of its time) depended on law, politics, or education for a living. The shy young poet Henry Timrod was a plantation tutor.

Simms prophesied that no Southern literature worthy of the name would ever exist under a slaveholding aristocracy. His views were echoed by Paul Hamilton Hayne, who edited *Russell's Magazine* for two years without pay, and who in 1859 complained that he had sold fewer than two hundred copies of a small book of poems issued two years earlier largely at his own expense. "There's encouragement for you!" he exclaimed. Thanking Lowell for a friendly review in the *Atlantic*, he deplored the unliterary character of the Southern people. To a young literary aspirant, it was hard to learn "that his *very profession* is looked upon with contempt, or at best a sort of half-pitying patronage by those he would fain delight and satisfy." [33] The sparse population of the section, the paucity of large, well-stocked bookshops and public libraries, the preoccupation with politics, and the belief that literature was best regarded either as a proslavery weapon or a proof of elegant leisure, were unpropitious to Southern authorship.

Still another prerequisite for literary achievement was a large and varied body of craftsmen, vying with one another for distinction. By mid-century, America had its swarm of writers. A series of important new types appeared. In the serious field James Parton, with his *Greeley*, *Burr*, and other biographies, represented the hitherto unknown school of journalist-historian; a group which also produced Richard Hildreth. Friedrich Kapp and Francis Lieber led in the column of transplanted European writers of erudition and talent. Artemus Ward and George H. Derby rose to notice in the fifties as newspaper humorists of a fresh kind. Bayard Taylor, George W. Curtis, and others made the light volume of travels more popular than ever before. The painstaking Benson J. Lossing, whose *Pictorial Field Book of the Revolution* was published in 1850–52, showed how interesting the labors of the antiquarian might become. Henry S. Randall set a new standard for scholarly biography in his *Jefferson*, issued in three solid volumes in 1858. On every hand, in fact, authors were hewing out new channels.

32 January 13, 1860; Miles Papers, U. of North Carolina.
33 December 28, 1859; D. M. McKeithan. *A Collection of Hayne Letters.*

Charles Eliot Norton and William Wetmore Story were giving currency to the first really original and incisive art criticism in America, framed in studies of Italian life.[34] It may be said that such figures bear no relation to the masterpieces of Hawthorne, Melville, and Whitman. But if a country does not have a large body of small writers, it is not likely to have a small body of great ones.

The growing swarm of litterateurs made possible the rise of coteries, like the Saturday Club in Boston, the circles that met in Pfaff's restaurant and the Century Club in New York, the friends of the bibliophile Henry D. Gilpin in Philadelphia,[35] and the group that sat in Russell's Bookshop in Charleston. Here, wits were sharpened and spiritual stimuli interchanged. No one can read the letters of Lowell or the journals of Longfellow and Emerson without feeling how immeasurably they profited by the frequent meetings of the whole Concord-Boston group—in the Old Corner Bookshop, at Felton's dinner table or in Harriet Hosmer's drawing room, on the Common, or at the Club; meetings where Prescott was sunny and jovial, where James T. Fields reported on Hawthorne's new book, where Sumner told historical anecdotes, or where Holmes shot out his latest pun; contacts which kept learning and ideas in circulation.[36] No one can read W. D. Howells's account of his meeting with Walt Whitman at Pfaff's on an August night in 1860 without realizing how much a single handclasp from a figure of eminence might mean to a neophyte.[37] And no one can go through the papers of an isolated writer like John Esten Cooke without a poignant understanding of his hopeless craving for literary companionship. Cooke hailed a letter from Simms with joy. "Simms is a hearty, cordial, openhearted man—a capital companion, and as true as steel. It is refreshing now and then to see such a 'high-pressure steamboat,' as he is—it stirs my languid pulse, and wakes me from my indolence." He wrote Thomas Dunn English asking how his New York friends were doing, and what that nice gentleman Aldrich of the *Home Journal* was up to. Alas, the few Southern men of letters had little contact with their Northern fellows or with each other.[38]

We might speak of still other factors in this literary efflorescence. At its roots, no doubt, lay social forces of an indefinable kind. As T. S. Eliot has said, a true culture is not the creation of a special class or set of institutions; it must spring from a way of life, from an ethos that pervades a whole society and embraces all its activities and interests.[39] No complete explanation is possible and none is necessary. The important fact was simply that America did have the

34 As in Norton's *Travel and Study in Italy* (1859).
35 See *Memorial of Henry D. Gilpin* (Philadelphia, 1860).
36 See Edward Emerson, *The Early Years of the Saturday Club.*
37 *Literary Friends and Acquaintance*, 74-76.
38 See letter May 13, 1858, to Edward St. George Cooke, and other letters in the small collection of Cooke Papers in Duke University.
39 *Notes Toward the Definition of Culture.*

vigorous budding of a great literature. This burgeoning of letters was of the first importance to the national mind and spirit. As we have said, it gave the country confidence in its power to contribute to the world's stock of aesthetic treasures; it transformed and enriched the national scene, brightening it with the light never seen on land or sea; and above all, by its high import and moral elevation it fortified the heart of the republic. The soul of a country is best realized in pure literature; here, at last, the American soul was finding expression. Next to its partial demonstration of the value of democratic self-government, America could point to this literature as its proudest achievement.

3

Buchanan Prepares for His Task

THE FIRST DAYS of 1857 found Americans opening the initial number of a bright sixteen-page illustrated magazine: *Harper's Weekly, a Journal of Civilization*. Its leading feature was a first-page, four-column editorial on the recent Presidential election. The result, declared the editor, had proved the strength of the "great conservative element." It was a mandate for preserving the vast national interests by "harmony and concession."

This opinion was generally held, and was borne out by impartial analyses of the returns. The combined vote for Buchanan and Fillmore, an impressive majority of the total, might well be regarded as a conservative vote. In the critical States of Pennsylvania and Indiana, in particular, the electorate had been profoundly moved by apprehensions of civil strife. Union was the controlling desire of the nation, and the Democratic Party had been maintained in power because it was the one chief bond of union. All this seemed reassuring. Did any ground for anxiety still exist? If so, it was not primarily because Mississippi and Georgia were laying down a new "ultimatum," while Greeley's *Tribune* was insisting that the Republicans would never compromise on freedom for the Territories. It was because the main bond of union, the Democratic Party, was itself increasingly disunited.

For the campaign and its results, as viewed by optimists of the day, scarcely reflected the real state of the country. The first issue of *Harper's Weekly* suggested certain sombre aspects of the national scene in touching on polygamy in Utah and a suspected slave insurrection in Tennessee. In the latter State an accused Negro had been whipped, to die after receiving 750 lashes. That episode stood as an unhappy symbol of the tensions between North and South; of rifts that had destroyed the Whig organization, had given birth to the Republican Party, and were now putting a heavy strain on the Democracy. Campaign excitements had thrown a concealing web across the chasm dividing Douglas's popular sovereignty wing from the Southern State Rights wing. While Douglas insisted that the settlers in a Territory might exclude slavery practically from the outset, Jefferson Davis and his associates maintained that the settlers must admit slavery until in forming a new State they gained power to exclude or perpetuate it. The country expected Buchanan to uphold national unity. But the initial question was whether he could restore the unity of his own party. What was his equipment for that task?

[I]

James Buchanan had been so long in public life that neither his character nor his views should have been mysterious. It was forty-three years since he had entered the Pennsylvania legislature, thirty-seven since he had first gone to Congress. Yet he was less understood than many a younger but more salient figure. No great law, no dramatic event, no revealing speech, was associated with his name. The country knew him as a man of dignified bearing, balanced judgment, and conciliatory ways. It knew that, holding many offices—Senator, Secretary of State, minister to Russia and Britain—he had risen in the political firmament by industry, ability, and adroitness. Toiling early and late, he had always mastered his duties thoroughly; he had always spoken clearly and temperately; he was versed in the law, and a learned expositor of the Constitution. But no dramatic act, no gallant episode, had ever revealed the man's soul. His character was unsullied, but it seemed a limited character.

What would latter-day psychiatrists have made out of this stiff, capable, unadventurous man? A toilsome childhood as son of a Mercersburg farmer and merchant; highly ambitious college years at Dickinson, where he would have led his class but for some rule-breaking; an apprenticeship at law, studying hard all day and practicing extempore speeches at night—this is a commonplace story. Within three years of entry to the bar his annual income exceeded $11,000, proof of brains and address. The most striking event of his early life was the sudden death of his fiancée, following a lovers' quarrel between them. The circumstances are not fully known (in his instructions to executors he ordered the pertinent papers destroyed), but he was barred from the funeral, and the tragedy left a scar that forbade all thought of marriage. Though he made warm friends, his life thereafter was lonely. The key to his character, however, is to be found in a quality not easily explained: in a deep irresolution. His deficiency in humor, his meagre imagination, his secretive vein, his tortuous ways, were all connected with this trait. So, too, was his tendency to lean on others; for while in small matters he was reticent, in large affairs he did not trust himself.

To contemporaries, his character seemed strangely at variance with his personal and political antecedents. Of the same Scotch-Irish stock as Jackson, Calhoun, and Polk, he showed hardly a rusty fleck of the iron in these notable men. The typical Ulster Scot was stern, emphatic, and daring, ready for a word and a blow, the blow first. Buchanan had invariably been cautious, peaceloving, and soft-spoken. To be sure, he possessed a few salient traits of his ancestry; he was religious, a man of prayer; he was self-denying and stubbornly tenacious. As Martin Van Buren saltily remarked, he was "amply endowed with those clear perceptions of self-interest and of duties connected with it that are almost inseparable from the Scottish character."[1] He had accumulated a modest fortune, perhaps $300,000, from which he gave generously to charity. But he was totally devoid of stern fighting qualities. It was also plain that, although a Jacksonian, he had little trace of Jackson's unbending devotion to the Union and impatience of sectionalism. Quite ignorant of the trans-Allegheny region, he knew nothing of the Western spirit of nationalism; but he might have displayed as much attachment to national unity as his fellow-Jacksonians of the East, Bancroft and Bryant. On the contrary, he explicitly said that a continuance of the abolitionist agitation would justify the South in seceding. Another contradiction lay in his attitude toward slavery. He had been reared at Mercersburg, educated at Carlisle, and admitted to practice at Lancaster, all in Pennsylvania; he represented a free State; yet he was more partial to slavery than many Virginians.

All these contradictions arose from his irresolution—from the combination of timidity, pliability, and self-seeking in his character. He was too timid to be a fighter; too pliable to stand firmly for the Union; too self-seeking to say a word against slavery when he knew that his political future rested upon slave-State favor. He had thus far tactfully wormed his way through obstacles that had foiled the direct attack of Benton and Webster. His success had sometimes been marvellous. As Jackson's star rose, he had hitched his chariot to it. In 1827, Jackson, insisting on his charges of bargain and corruption in the late election, asserted that Buchanan had been an agent for Clay in the latter's efforts to gain high office for giving up the Presidency. This was untrue, for Buchanan had never been an intermediary in any attempted bargain. He had to deny Jackson's statement. Yet he did it so adroitly that he managed to keep Jackson's favor. During the controversy in Congress over the right of petition, similarly, he somehow managed to take the sound constitutional ground that it must not be abridged, and yet to retain Southern liking by insisting that the petitions be laid on the table without debate. As Polk's Secretary of State, again, Buchanan with one hand made firm demands on Mexico, and with the other offered conciliatory blandishments, leaving it to the President to take the steps which ended in war. He had thus pleased the South without estranging the North. But in managing and leading politicians (as distinguished from placating them), he had practically no experience whatever.

1 Martin Van Buren, *Autobiography*, 406.

Endowed with industry, capacity, and tact, Buchanan was admirably qualified for judicial or diplomatic positions. It was a cruel fate which kept him from
the Supreme Court in 1844 (when Tyler offered him a seat) to raise him to the
White House thirteen years later.[2] As a diplomat, despite the stain left on his
name by the Ostend Manifesto, he had served with high ability. In negotiating
with Russia and Britain, he always showed a firm Americanism, and by his persistence, thorough mastery of facts, and cautious preparation, he usually achieved
success. In his overseas career he again showed his adroitness. Although Martin
Van Buren, spending a month or so with him in London, found that his pertina-
cious Yankee aims had become a subject of general remark, he enjoyed a distinct
social success in England. Oxford had given him a D.C.L. But for an executive
post, especially in a time of grim pressures, he was unsuited. His wariness, his
legalistic temper, his meekness whenever faced by a belligerent associate, and
his taste for shifty maneuvers were heavy disqualifications. Where iron nerve,
decisive action, and a power of bending men to his will were needed, he was
helpless to supply them. Moreover, he totally lacked imagination or inspiration.
No electric spark, no glow of genius, ever lighted up his mind. He had
never coined an epigram or written an eloquent passage; he could not even
quote aptly, for he had no interest in literature. "I do not think he ever
uttered a genuine witticism in his life," states his intimate friend Henry S.
Foote.[3]

President Polk's shrewd eye had perceived the irresolute character of
Buchanan. "It is one of his weaknesses," wrote Polk, "that he takes on and mag-
nifies small matters into great and undeserved importance." William H. Trescot,
who served under him in the London legation, termed him cold, calculating, and
heartless, so devious that he was sometimes false and so circumspect that he was
often crafty; an excessively harsh judgment, but with much truth. His great
admirer, Jeremiah S. Black, speaks of an excess of craftiness. "Even among close
friends," writes Senator Foote, "he very rarely expressed his opinions at all
upon disputed questions, except in language especially marked with a cautious
circumspection almost amounting to timidity." Like other weak men, he could
be a vengeful fighter when attacked; and again like other weak men, he never
confessed himself wrong. Needing the aid of more robust natures, he delighted
in a small circle of cronies, but as Foote remarks, he did not like men of high
intellectual attainments about him. Never very resourceful, he became more stiff
and inflexible with increasing years, as his book *The Administration on the Eve
of the Rebellion* shows. In the final crisis of his term he grew panicky (the word

2 Charles Warren, *Hist. Supreme Court*, II (1926 ed.) 116; cf. *Atlantic*, LII, 708.
3 Foote, *Casket of Reminiscences*, 112.

is endorsed by Jefferson Davis on the basis of their conversations) for both the nation and his personal safety.[4]

In his defense it can be said that he was passionately attached to peace and convinced that appeasement was the one way to stay the South from rash courses. But in iron times our verdict on appeasers must be severe. In a line of mediocre Presidents, not one of whom would be esteemed fit today to head a large corporation, bank, or university, he had more ability than Taylor or Fillmore, more steadiness than Pierce, and more civil experience than the three combined. Yet he was as ill-equipped for a supreme test as they. By half-measures, evasions, and stealthy approaches, by all the arts of weakness, he had gained the Presidency at just the moment when a man of all but superhuman vision and strength was needed.

Since it was natural for him to cling to some strength greater than his own, throughout his career he had shown a strict allegiance to party. He had accepted all the Jacksonian doctrines, good or bad; he had hewn to the Democratic line under Polk. While often statesmanlike in his speeches and papers, he had also often been cheaply partisan. This party constancy, however, was less remarkable than his equally unswerving alignment with the Southern proslavery wing of his party.

The campaign documents of 1856, in appealing to Southern voters, had described this side of his record in detail. During the middle thirties, he had spoken against the abolition of slavery in the Federal District, had declared for tabling the abolitionist petitions in silence, and had pressed for the admission of Arkansas as a slave State. He had espoused a measure making it unlawful for postmasters to distribute printed material touching upon slavery if this was forbidden by State enactment. He had supported all of Calhoun's resolutions of December 27, 1837—the famous resolutions asserting the compact-theory of the Union, assailing the abolitionists, declaring it the duty of the national government to give increased stability to slavery in any State possessing it, and denouncing any Northern attempt to interfere with the acquisition of new lands simply because such annexation would expand the domain of slaveholders. Ten years later, Buchanan had advocated a division of California and New Mexico between slavery and freedom by the extension of the Missouri Compromise line to the Pacific. In the autumn of 1850 he had assured the people of Philadelphia that this Compromise line had "passed away." He had remonstrated against an

4 Polk, *Diary*, September 1, 1846; Foote, *op. cit.*, 112. Buchanan's papers contain some striking instances of his timidity when faced by belligerent men. For example, John M. Clayton, his successor in the State Department, wrote him a nasty letter April 6, 1849. Some dispute had arisen over a petty appointment. Clayton wrote that his first inclination had been "to tell you to go to the devil," and called one of Buchanan's statements untrue. Buchanan replied in conciliatory and honeyed terms. Buchanan Papers.

act of the Pennsylvania legislature obstructing the recovery of fugitive slaves. He had supported proposals for the purchase of Cuba at a cost of a hundred millions or more, and had been a ready participant in the Ostend Manifesto upon acquisition of the island.[5]

Each one of these acts was from his standpoint arguably correct. It was nevertheless remarkable that this son of Franklin's State, this fellow townsman of Thaddeus Stevens, had never once deviated from a line congenial to advanced proslavery men.

Buchanan's closest personal friends in Congressional days had been Southerners like John Slidell and William R. King. He had asserted in 1850 that the Compromise was a hard bargain for the South. He wrote in 1851 that he had been fighting the battle of the South on the slavery issue for fifteen years. He had declared in 1856 that a Republican victory would be a decree of outlawry against fifteen slave States, and that disruption of the Union would immediately and inevitably ensue. Taking the view that the North alone was aggressive, he held that the central requirement of the hour was simply that the slave area be left alone. While he never expressed any moral repugnance to slavery (though he had spoken regretfully of its existence), he had uttered some bizarre ideas on its practical aspects. Thus he had assured the Senate in 1844 that the annexation of Texas would be the means of limiting, not enlarging, the slavery domain. "In the government of the world," he remarked, "Providence generally produces great changes by gradual means. There is nothing rash in the councils of the Almighty." (In fact, the Almighty was cautious, evasive, and timid, like James Buchanan.) The acquisition of Texas, he argued, would operate to draw slaves farther south, into a clime more congenial to their nature; and they would probably thus "pass off into Mexico, and there mingle with a race where no prejudice exists against their color." He shared this strange opinion with Robert J. Walker, his Cabinet associate, who likewise believed that Texas would serve as a funnel for draining slavery away, "by diffusion," into the boundless regions of Mexico, Central America, and beyond.[6]

As sectional feeling rose, the dread of secession had become an obsessive idea with the weak-nerved Buchanan. During the recent campaign he had felt that nothing mattered but "the grand and appalling issue of union or disunion."

5 Von Holst, *Calhoun*, Ch. VII; George Ticknor Curtis, *Buchanan*, I, 215–543 *passim*. See the Democratic pamphlet of 1856, "The Agitation of Slavery. Who Commenced and Who Can End It? Buchanan and Fillmore Compared."

6 *Cong. Globe*, June 8, 1844. One caller in these years says he heard Buchanan state again and again that if the two sections separated on the slavery question, it was doubtful with which Pennsylvania would take her stand. W. M. Corry in Cincinnati *Daily Commercial*, quoted in N. Y. *Weekly Tribune*, December 3, 1859. Buchanan requested Sir William Gore Ouseley never to express "abolitionist" opinions in his presence. Ouseley to Buchanan, August 19, 1858; Buchanan Papers.

Republican defeat had stayed the danger, but would it not recur? Another obsession, derived from his Southern friends, was the danger of a servile insurrection. As early as 1826 he had dwelt upon the possibility of Haitian horrors in the cotton States. "There are portions of the Union in which, if you emancipate your slaves, they will become your masters. There can be no middle course. Is there any man in this Union who would for a moment indulge the horrible idea of abolishing slavery by the massacre of the chivalrous race of men in the South? . . . For my own part I would, without hesitation, buckle on my knapsack." He was thus persuaded that slavery represented not a mere political issue, but a question of life or death for the Southern people. "What agony of mind the abolitionist publications are causing!" he exclaimed in 1836. "Many a mother clasps her infant to her bosom when she retires to rest, under dreadful apprehensions that she may be roused from her slumbers by the savage yells of the slaves by whom she is surrounded." As President, he repeatedly touched the same chord. Secession by the South would be justified, he believed, if the antislavery agitation continued; and he held that it would have been justified had Frémont been elected, for the Republican Party was largely made up of abolitionists.[7]

Leaning toward the Southern view of all public issues, sharing the mental processes of his many Southern friends, well aware that but twenty-five miles from his own town of Lancaster lay the slaveholding Marylanders, Buchanan took the Southern position on the great difference in doctrine which divided the Democratic Party. Could the people of a Territory decide against slavery before they formed a State Constitution? He thought not. In his speech to his Wheatland neighbors just after the October elections, he had said that the residents of a Territory should make their decision when about to enter the Union as a State.[8] For various reasons, Buchanan was certain to take an impatient attitude toward Douglas and his popular sovereignty tenets. He had long disliked the "Young America" spirit and its denunciation of old fogies; he disliked Douglas personally, thinking him bumptious, ill-mannered, and aggressive; he thought Douglas's Kansas-Nebraska Act regrettable; he well remembered that if Douglas could have held the whole of the New York delegation at the Cincinnati convention instead of only half, no other man could have been nominated; and he consorted with men who, like Slidell, were enemies of Douglas. Always conservative in his interpretation of the Constitution, he accepted the argument that all citizens had an equal right to carry their property into the Territories. He awaited only the proper hour to trample squatter sovereignty, and with it the Illinois Senator, underfoot.

For if cautious and conciliatory on grim national questions, Buchanan was

7 Curtis, *Buchanan*, I, 317; II, 68.
8 *Ibid.*, II, 176.

harshly unyielding on party discipline. He detested Democratic "guerrillas" and "disorganizers" only less than he detested Republicans. He deemed it the first duty of an Administration to suppress factions. Jackson's imperious attack upon Calhoun, his rough ousting of three Calhounite members, Ingham, Branch, and Berrien, from the Cabinet, his stringent measures to break William J. Duane when that Secretary opposed his Bank policy, and his other acts to marshal his followers into a firm party front, had deeply impressed Buchanan. President Polk's firmness in carrying through his program without regard for the dissent of Benton or any other Democratic chieftain seemed to him equally admirable. Buchanan would not be a fighting President, but he would be an implacable defender of Democratic regularity.[9]

[II]

The making of the Cabinet was a matter of supreme importance, for the Cabinet rather than the President was to determine Administration policies. Throughout the next four years the country was to be governed by a Directory. Not merely was Buchanan cautious, impressionable, ill-trained in executive posts, and readily moved by stronger natures; he believed in the principle of action by a united Cabinet. In his opinion, a President should choose aides who represented like groups, who thought alike, and who would act alike. The Chief Magistrate who tried to conciliate opposing elements by placing determined agents of each in his official family would find that he had simply strengthened discord, and had deepened party divisions. Unity was essential; in Polk's day, he recalled, the Cabinet council scarcely ever failed, after free consultation and discussion, to agree at last—and it was its undivided action "which rendered Mr. Polk's administration so successful." [10] Following this principle, Buchanan often submitted questions to Cabinet vote. But unlike Polk, he was ready to let his own judgment be overruled. In 1859, for example, he and his Postmaster-General were in favor of calling a special session to vote the post office appropriation which the recently adjourned Congress had omitted; the other six members of the Cabinet outvoted these two; and to the disgust of the New York *Times* and the *National Intelligencer*, he yielded.[11]

In short, Buchanan failed to comprehend the vital difference between a unified Cabinet which is managed by the President, and a unified Cabinet which manages the President.

His chief advisers in choosing his official family were the familiar circle of personal friends; Slidell, W. W. Corcoran, Henry A. Wise of Virginia, Jesse

9 Letter to Pierce, December 11, 1852; Curtis, *op. cit.*, II, 69–74.
10 *Idem.*
11 *National Intelligencer*, March 26, 1859.

D. Bright of Indiana, Governor William Bigler of Pennsylvania, and Representative J. Glancy Jones of the same State. They were by no means ideal counsellors. Slidell and Wise were radical slavery men.[12] It was absurd to think of Bright as a spokesman for the Northwest; he was the owner of a slave-stocked plantation in Kentucky, an associate of the slavery circle in Washington, and an enemy of all freesoilers. Corcoran, a genial, philanthropic, and conservative banker whose social relationships were chiefly with Southerners, was deeply concerned lest the nation be disrupted. Bigler, a cautious, phlegmatic man, could furnish nothing but the advice of a machine politician, while Glancy Jones, another political heeler, was useful merely for reporting currents of Washington opinion. Not a single statesman could be found in Buchanan's entourage.

Buchanan moved deliberately, for he believed in the rule (he said it was Washington's) not to decide weighty questions until the final moment for doing so had nearly approached. He believed too that he ought to visit the capital for conferences. The result was that he soon found himself subjected to every variety of pressure, intrigue, cajolery, and wire-pulling. His once-peaceful retreat at Wheatland was overrun with callers, who rapped at the door as he got out of bed at seven and implored his attention as the clock struck midnight. By letters, telegrams, personal visits, and the use of intermediaries, a thousand party manipulators and office hunters beleaguered him. The drain on his larder and wine cellar threatened him with bankruptcy. Buchanan had never possessed a personal secretary; but now he summoned his nephew, James Buchanan Henry, a young man just beginning law practice, and, with many warnings against the temptations he would meet, installed him at a desk. For a confidential assistant he turned to John Appleton of Maine, an experienced man of ready pen—journalist, lawyer, and politician—who had worked with Buchanan before, having been secretary of legation in London. Appleton, a friend of the historian Bancroft, possessed cultivation, wit, and integrity.

Still endlessly harassed, early in January, 1857, Buchanan made a stealthy visit to Philadelphia. His mind was as yet apparently quite open with respect to the Cabinet and other high offices, and politicians flocked to his hotel like bees to an oozing comb. Then on January 27 he dropped quietly into Washington, his arrival unexpected by the most knowing observers.

This Washington trip was a characteristic exhibition of caution. Four years earlier, Buchanan had written President-elect Pierce that he ought not to make his final decisions on his Cabinet without visiting the capital, the best place to

---

12 Wise had been one of the leaders in threatening secession and military action if Frémont were elected; Nevins, *Frémont*, 451. He and John B. Floyd led one of the two main factions of the Virginia Democracy, R. M. T. Hunter the other.

consult disinterested Democratic leaders. He knew that he could see a wide range of men in Washington, especially Southerners. The sojourn was more eventful than he had expected. Arriving the day of Preston Brooks's sudden death, he attended the funeral ceremonies in the House, and watched Republican members, when Representative Savage of Tennessee declared that the world had applauded the justice of Brooks's chastisement of Sumner, leave the chamber in abrupt dudgeon. At the National Hotel he contracted the mysterious "disease" connected with that place, apparently amoebic dysentery, attributed by many to its bad plumbing. But above all, he carried out his main purpose; he made certain that the conservative appointments upon which he was fixing would find favor among the Southern groups whom he so deeply respected.[13]

The cardinal question was whether Robert J. Walker or Lewis Cass should be Secretary of State. Both were old-time friends; both were staunch Jacksonian Democrats; both had agreed with Buchanan in publicly supporting but privately disapproving the Kansas-Nebraska Act; both were strong Unionists and sternly conservative on the slavery question. Both were expansionists. It was at Walker's house in Washington that Buchanan had been staying when he was appointed minister to Great Britain. The President-elect had been intimate with both men in the Senate, and he remembered pleasantly his association with Walker in Polk's councils. On personal grounds he could readily have accepted either, and on grounds of fitness there was little to choose; the question therefore must be left to party pressures.

Such active groups pressed Walker's claims that for a time it seemed almost certain that he would become Buchanan's chief lieutenant—and probably his controlling guide. Some radical Southern expansionists, like C. C. Clay of Alabama and Alfred Iverson of Georgia, who believed that he would take steps to annex Cuba and other Gulf areas, threw their weight behind him. Jefferson Davis was said to regard him favorably. The familiar agents of "Young America," including George N. Sanders and Daniel Sickles, deemed him their best hope. Senator Douglas, though very friendly to Cass, seemed to incline toward him. Every possible plea for Walker was presented by Buchanan's young newspaper friend, the ebullient, mercurial John W. Forney, whose activities had been vital the previous fall in carrying Pennsylvania. As the author of the tariff of 1846, Walker was naturally a favorite of the anti-protectionists.

Yet as the weeks passed, antagonism toward the baldish little Mississippian gained ground. This bustling, courageous, highly ambitious politician had cheerfully made many enemies in his long climb to eminence. An excitable man with a taste for the melodramatic, he had for years written hard-hitting newspaper

13 N. Y. *Herald,* February 8–17, 1857.

articles on a wide variety of issues. Essentially independent, he was no enthusiast about slavery, and some Southerners recalled how heartily Calhoun had condemned his lukewarm attitude toward its expansion. His ventures into land speculation and railroad promotion had convinced many that he was a reckless, perhaps even an unscrupulous, business plunger. In the New York *Herald,* James Gordon Bennett raked him with a withering fire, blasting his connection with Pacific Railroad schemes and his intimacy with greedy New York politicians who might use the new Administration to fatten their pocketbooks. Even Slidell shared this view. "While I have great respect for Walker and high appreciation of his talents," he wrote Buchanan, "I do not like the men by whom he is surrounded and to a great degree controlled. . . . I fear that from his extreme facility of temper he may be led to say and do things that his own judgment would disapprove." [14] Obviously, many Northern conservatives would be aghast at the choice for Secretary of State of a Manifest Destiny man, who in 1846 had wished to annex all Mexico, and who had since been an open abettor of filibustering; and Europe would take alarm.

Various other considerations helped incline Buchanan to Cass. It seemed important to place Howell Cobb in the Treasury. Not only did he have energy and brains, but he combined political boldness with a talent for administrative system. The proud Georgian made it clear, however, that he would play second fiddle to no man of his own station or years; he would take a lower Cabinet appointment than the venerable Cass or Marcy, but he would not sit below Robert J. Walker.[15] The North, too, must be given some places, and the appointment of Cass would help to supply a sectional balance.

If we may believe various newspapers and G. P. R. James (the acute British consul in Richmond), the Russian and French legations, well aware of Cass's Anglophobic views, did their utmost to rally the press behind him. The *Herald* spoke of their sleepless "intrigues." A correspondent of the Albany *Argus* declared that the Russian envoy was spending large sums to fill Southern and Western newspapers with laudatory articles and items, even corrupting many small country weeklies. "I have every reason to conclude," James wrote the Foreign Office early in the year, "that one-half the newspaper paragraphs, stating General Cass's appointment and acceptance to be certain, proceed from Russian sources; the object being to work up a popular feeling in favor of his appointment, and thereby influence, if not control, the President-elect." He thought Russia very adroit. "She used the newspaper press of America with great skill and success during the late [Crimean] war; and if she can now raise a general expectation that Mr. Cass is to be Secretary of State, it might puzzle Mr. Buchanan to avoid making him so." James knew many American politicians,

14 He thought Sanders the chief operator; February 14, 1857, Buchanan Papers.
15 William Bigler, December 29, 1856, to Buchanan; Buchanan Papers.

heard much political gossip, and believed that he had a correct estimate of Cass; the man was incompetent from age, full of vanity, and swayed by foolish antipathies.[16]

The result of all the arguments and pressures was that Buchanan, on his return to Wheatland, determined to appoint Cass to the State Department— under certain rigid conditions. He would not take the corpulent, constitutionally indolent, ailing old Michigan leader, now in his seventy-fifth year, unless Cass accepted an efficient aide: John Appleton, with his experience as chief clerk in the State Department, chargé in Bolivia, and secretary of the London legation, must be made Assistant Secretary. Obviously, he would be expected to guide Cass's hand. Moreover, Cass must explicitly renounce his anti-British views. These stipulations, embodied in a formal letter, were unhesitatingly accepted by Cass. The State Department was counted the post of highest dignity and greatest ease in the Cabinet; he could enjoy its honors without being crushed by its burdens, and it would save him from a humiliating retirement to Detroit. Michigan was now a Republican state, and Zachariah Chandler was about to take Cass's seat in the Senate. The way was thus opened for the appointment of Howell Cobb to the Treasury. He too accepted with alacrity—for his would clearly be the post of chief authority.[17]

The lesser Cabinet places were filled without great difficulty, although the Attorney-General and the head of the Navy were not selected until after Buchanan went to Washington for his inauguration. It would be tedious to rehearse all the factional squabbling and personal intriguing which attended the bestowal of the various places, and we may content ourselves with a statement of results. A proffer of Cabinet seats to Wise, Bright, and Slidell was politely rejected. Wise desired to serve out his four-year term as Governor of Virginia; Bright and Slidell preferred to continue in the Senate. "There is no respectable office in the United States that I would not rather take than a Cabinet place," wrote Bright, who told friends the apocryphal story that he might have been Secretary of State had he chosen. He thought of himself as a Senatorial viceroy for the Northwest, dispensing Administration patronage in that quarter, and he had dreams of the White House.[18] When Wise, who also had dreams, declined a place, his Virginia friends rallied about John B. Floyd,

16 N. Y. *Herald*, January 14, 1857; F. O. 5/677, G. P. R. James to Lord Clarendon, January 9, February 28, 1857. The *Herald* remarked that if the hardheaded Lord Elgin came over as minister, "we suspect that the intrigues of the Russian and French embassies would be very rapidly brought to a close, and that the course of opinion in Washington would not be, as it has been lately, persistently hostile to England."
17 Nichols, *Disruption of the American Democracy*, 66; A. C. McLaughlin, *Lewis Cass*, 377.
18 Bright, April 16, 1857, to Wm. H. English; English Papers. N. Y. *Weekly Tribune*, February 27, 1857. Bright liked to go to his Kentucky farm, living "in my log Cabbin (very much such a one) as Genl Harrison was described as living in in 1840," and companioned only by "Niggers and Dogs." May 5, 1857, to Corcoran; Corcoran Papers.

a former governor who was best remembered by most Americans as the man who had advocated laying a tax on the products of those Northern States which would not return fugitive slaves to Virginia. He was formally designated by a meeting of Virginia members of the electoral college, and Buchanan gave him the War portfolio.

Since in Howell Cobb the Cabinet would have a leader who had supported the Compromise of 1850, the timid Buchanan thought it advisable to include some Southerner who had opposed it. Jacob Thompson of Mississippi, a Southern Rights man who had served in Congress from 1839 to 1851, was less objectionable to the nation at large than Pickens, Quitman, and Soulé, simply because he had done less to lift his radical views into notice. He was given the Interior Department; a logical place, for he had once been head of the House committee on public lands and Indian affairs.

The Post Office Department went to A. V. Brown of Tennessee, a former law partner of Polk and an able governor of his State in Mexican War days. He was a stump orator of rough hard-hitting qualities, and a proslavery expansionist who had been a delegate to the Nashville Convention. Now an elderly man of infirm health, he was destined to die in office. As the Post Office and Interior controlled a great part of the appointments and contracts of the government, and as the latter department did much to regulate the pace at which the Western areas were converted into free States, the South was pleased to have both in its hands.

Because New England had to be recognized, the Navy Department was assigned to an elderly political hack of Hartford, Isaac Toucey. He might earlier have gone into the Supreme Court, but he too, almost incredibly, had dreams of the Presidency! [19] At the last minute Buchanan bestowed the Attorney-Generalship upon his faithful friend, Jeremiah Black.

[III]

It was not a brilliant Cabinet, as Pierce's had been. Indeed, it was distinctly mediocre. Cass compared ill with the sagacious Marcy, Floyd with the energetic, far-sighted Jefferson Davis; Cobb was less of a practical financier than Guthrie, and Black less learned in the law than Caleb Cushing. Still, in routine ability it would do well enough.

19 Senator Dixon, December 2, 1858 to Welles; Gideon Welles Papers. Welles's opinion of Toucey was scorching. "Cold and selfish by nature and by calculation, Toucey was never known to make a sacrifice for his friends, his party, or the state, but would readily sacrifice either or all to promote his own aggrandizement. . . . In past conflicts the Southern States . . . had usually been successful; he therefore made it a point to identify himself with that section, without considering that it involved a reversal of principles." Papers Relating to Gideon Welles, LC.

The strongest criticism of the Cabinet naturally came from Republicans, who regarded it, in Greeley's words, as proslavery to the hub. Of the seven places, the South took four. And how much could be said of the aged Cass and the meek, time-serving Toucey as Northern representatives? The Michigan Polonius meant well, but he had long been inert, and was now subject to attacks of vertigo and incapable of prolonged concentration. Only a month before inauguration he had fallen on the Interior Department steps, and been picked up insensible and bleeding.[20] His appointment gave him a new lease of life, and for a time he showed heightened briskness and industry. Donning a new brown wig, shaving more closely than before, dressing with greater care, and taking a daily constitutional, he performed ordinary duties with promptness, and entertained with seeming pleasure.[21] However, a lover of ease and a man of conciliatory temperament, hesitant in taking any stand, he was certain to avoid home controversies. It was significant that although chosen a member of the Senate committee on the Brooks-Sumner assault he had failed to say a word against that outrage.

As for Toucey, he had long shown himself aware that his political bread was buttered on the Southern side. Every Northern freesoiler knew that he had urged a stern enforcement of the Fugitive Slave Act, had attacked the constitutionality of the Missouri Compromise, and had espoused the Nebraska Bill. He was destined to play an equivocal part in the early drama of secession. In fact, his role was to be such that Montgomery Blair called it treason, that E. M. Stanton secretly urged his arrest, and that the Connecticut legislature indignantly removed his portrait from the gallery devoted to ex-governors. Cass and Toucey could make no stand against such strong-willed Southerners as Cobb, A. V. Brown, and Jacob Thompson. It was a Cabinet controlled by slavedrivers, scornfully commented the New York *Tribune*.[22]

Of course Buchanan cared nothing for Republican censure. He cared little that conservative Whigs complained bitterly of their exclusion; that members of the Pierce Administration resented his failure to consult with them in Washington; and that New York Democrats felt left out in the cold. Much more important to the nation's future was the offense taken by the popular sovereignty Democrats of the North.

Buchanan's chief error in dispensing offices was his needless estrangement of the most powerful leader of the Northwest, the very man whose timely withdrawal at Cincinnati had made his nomination possible—Stephen A. Douglas. In these early weeks of the Administration we find the germ of a quarrel pregnant

20 *National Intelligencer*, February 9, 1857.
21 MS Journal of Samuel Ryan Curtis (Ill. State Hist. Lib.), January 1, 1860; *National Intelligencer*, March 31, 1859.
22 N. Y. *Tribune*, February 18, 1857.

with the direst consequences to party and nation. Douglas had believed that the Northwest was entitled to two places in the Cabinet. He was anxious that William A. Richardson of Quincy, Illinois, defeated for Congress the previous autumn, should get one seat, and willing that Cass should get the other. He had hoped that his friend Judge Samuel Treat of St. Louis might represent the border States. But it was soon plain that neither Treat nor Richardson stood a chance. Buchanan, determined to apply his principle that faction must be crushed, was going to form an Administration that would stand as a unit behind the Southern antipathy to squatter sovereignty. When the President-elect made his unexpected descent on Washington, Douglas visited him, got a frosty reception, learned that his enemies would drive the Administration chariot, and departed glowering with anger. He wrote Judge Treat:

Under all the circumstances the inference is irresistible that the patronage of the North West was disposed of before the nomination. Bright is the man who is to control it if they dare to carry out their designs. Slidell, Bright, and Corcoran (the banker) assume the right to dispose of all the patronage. If this purpose is carried out and I am the object of attack I shall fight all my enemies and neither ask nor give quarter. I do not decline to urge friends, provided the opportunity is presented to do so under any prospect of success. At present, I am an outsider. My advice is not invited nor will my wishes probably be regarded. I want nothing but fair play. I want only a fair show for my friends. I desire the brave true men who fought the battle to be sustained. If this can be done I am content. If on the contrary, the power of the Administration is to be used for plunder or ambition I shall return every blow they may give.[23]

Never was resentment more justifiable. Douglas was the ablest man in the party, its most formidable speaker in the Senate, the author of its most important legislation during the past decade, a leader who had borne the heat and danger of conflict while Buchanan was safe in a foreign haven. He should have been the nominee in 1856, for his Nebraska Act was the chief plank in the party platform. Had New York's Soft Delegation been seated and had Tennessee stayed in line, he might well have been chosen.[24] He was the champion of a host of Northern Democrats whose aid would be indispensable to future victory. Now he was not merely ignored; his enemy Bright, the Indiana slaveholder, the man whom Wise called a "money pimp of Corcoran's" and "a land-whore in the Northwest," the Midwestern tool of Southern leaders, was preferred over him.[25] It is no wonder that Douglas exploded in open hatred of Bright, that he showed Slidell, when they met, a front of suspicion and dislike, and that this alarmed gentleman reported that the Illinoisan was ready to run amok like a

23 February 5, 1857; Treat Papers. On the hostility of Buchanan and Slidell to Douglas, see P. G. Auchampaugh, *James Buchanan and his Cabinet*, 36, 37.
24 Milton, *Eve of Conflict*, 226–230.
25 Wise to Buchanan, January 5, 1857, Buchanan Papers.

maddened Malay.[26] He was not a man to sit tamely inert while he and his section were being wronged.

The three most vigorous figures of the Cabinet, Howell Cobb, Jacob Thompson, and Jeremiah S. Black, were the men who with Senator Slidell would control Buchanan at critical moments. Of these, the ambitious and active Cobb, still in his early forties, was the most attractive figure. He knew how to season his labors with jollity and wit. Sunny-tempered and generous-spirited as well as able, he was a delightful conversationalist, with just a dash of Falstaffian coarseness. It is not strange that Buchanan grew fond of him, and that whenever Mrs. Cobb's domestic responsibilities (she was a Lamar, sprung from one of the wealthiest and most aristocratic families of Georgia) kept her at home in Athens, he became an inmate of the White House. He had a high reputation for personal honor. When his father, plunging into land speculation, went bankrupt in 1837, the son, as an endorser of his notes, scrupulously paid every penny, although the act cost him a large estate and embarrassed him for years. He also had a reputation for hard, painstaking work. At the bar he had neglected no point in preparing his cases; in office he was careful, methodical, and a firm disciplinarian. With his Assistant Secretary Clayton and his law officer, Junius Hillyer, he placed the Treasury on a high level of efficiency. It could be said that he was first and always a politician, and, with patronage and contracts absorbing much of his time, took party rather than national views; but it could never be said that he neglected his duties.[27]

As a great planter-lawyer, with more than a thousand slaves calling him master, Cobb naturally held the opinions of the ruling class in the Lower South. He was a conservative by taste and habit, but his conservatism was all for the welfare of his own section. In 1850 he had been for the Compromise because it meant Southern peace and safety; he was presently to be for secession because he thought that it alone could give the South security. For good or ill, this imperious Georgia grandee was now to be Buchanan's chief personal guide.

Jacob Thompson had a prosaic name, and with his clean-shaven, rugged, rather homely face and stocky figure looked as prosaic as a butcher; but his career, with its alternations of wealth and ultimate ruin, honor and final exile, was to prove romantic enough for any novel. Compared with the aristocratic Cobb, he belonged to the newly rich of the South. A poor graduate of the University of North Carolina, he had gone west to practice law and had rapidly coined wealth out of raw Mississippi land. Now he held, besides minor tracts, a "home place" of 550 acres at Oxford with a fine mansion, another plantation

26 February 14, 1857, Buchanan Papers.
27 Samuel Boykin, *Howell Cobb, passim.* Boykin says that he knew from personal contact that Secretary Cobb enjoyed the unbounded confidence of Buchanan, and was really prime minister of the Administration.

in the same county of 2,720 acres, and a third on the Mississippi River of 1,783 acres. As a chairman of the trustees of the State University, he had lent its strongest men, Augustus B. Longstreet and Frederick A. P. Barnard, a shoulder in their progressive policies, aiding them also in trying to reclaim nearly a million of State-guaranteed funds which had been lost in bank crashes. Living at the university seat, Oxford, he profited from his intimacy with the professors, who temporarily included Longstreet's brilliant son-in-law, L. Q. C. Lamar.[28]

One singularly romantic episode had lighted up Thompson's early life. He had fallen in love with a poor girl of fourteen; had married her in 1840; and without consummating the marriage, had hurried her off to Paris for four years of schooling. Mrs. Thompson, a gay, beautiful woman in her early thirties, was now to shine as one of the social ornaments of Washington.

Another striking episode of Thompson's early life, destined to have important national consequences, was his quarrel with Robert J. Walker. It happened that Thompson and James K. Polk, both educated at Chapel Hill, were long-time friends. The spring of 1845 found Polk making up his Cabinet, and Thompson, a Representative from Mississippi, urging him—successfully—to make Walker head of the Treasury, instead of Attorney-General as first planned. Walker thereupon perpetrated an act of bad faith. When he resigned his seat in the Senate, the governor appointed Thompson to fill out Walker's term. He sent the commission to Walker for delivery to Thompson, so that the latter might remain on hand for special session after March 4, 1845. Walker received it. But he wished to be succeeded by his friend William M. Gwin, and though he saw Thompson several times, he never handed him the commission! The result was that Thompson returned to Oxford and accepted a renomination for the House before he learned of his appointment, which then went to a man named Chalmers. Walker never came back to the State, while Gwin migrated to California. For years Thompson loathed both men; and, though he was ultimately reconciled to Gwin, his detestation of Walker persisted. He thought Walker an unprincipled fellow, of flighty weathercock views, likely to be controlled by any man of strong will. Before the year 1857 expired, this opinion was to have its bearing on grave Cabinet decisions.[29]

Thompson himself, a ruthless, ambitious leader, ready for anything—during

28 The memoir of Thompson in the first volume of Claiborne's *Mississippi as Province, Territory, and State,* was dictated by himself to his niece.

29 See Dorothy Z. Oldham, MS Life of Thompson, Univ. of Mississippi Library. Jefferson Davis was a close personal friend of Thompson's. As head of the House Public Lands Committee, Thompson had learned much about the deficiencies of the Interior Department. Its important bureaus (public lands, Indian affairs, patents, census, pensions, and public buildings and grounds) worked independently of each other. Thompson resolved to unify the department and make himself the controlling head; and against not a little opposition, he did so.

the Civil War he supported a scheme for burning Northern cities—was not excessively troubled by principle. He meant to manage his department efficiently while looking out for the main chance. More than a year earlier, while standing for the Senate before the Mississippi legislature, he had tried to bribe the editor of the Washington *Sentinel*, a journal of some Southern influence, to support him; so, at least, that editor assured Jefferson Davis. He had offered "pecuniary favors to any reasonable amount." [30] On the slavery issue he was frankly radical. "You Illinoisans," he told one Congressman, "ought to concede that slaves are property, and treat them as such." "That," replied the Representative with asperity, "is the very point at issue." [31]

A third member of the ruling Directory, Jeremiah S. Black, stood out in craggy relief from the other appointees. Grim, intense, prejudiced, narrow, he could throw his powerful but unimaginative mind behind the most exasperatingly partisan doctrines. He scolded, fought, and jested like John Knox. And like that greater Calvinist, he was rigidly honest according to his lights, while he never tired of battle. A product of the Pennsylvania frontier, he had managed to attend an academy and had broadened his education by diligent reading. Steeped in the English classics and religious literature, he spoke with thunderous precision, and wrote with signal effectiveness. His was a fine mind, but a very legalistic mind. As a lawyer, he showed a passion for reducing the complexities of codes and statute books to first principles, which he expounded with learning. He displayed an unalterable devotion to justice, and an unchallengeable integrity. As member and head of the Supreme Court of Pennsylvania, he had handed down decisions of marked power, especially on points of corporation law. His oration on the character of Andrew Jackson and his speech of 1856 in defense of religious liberty were fine examples of his championship of the fundamentals of democracy.

This keen-witted, argumentative Scotch-Irishman, able to quote Shakespeare, St. Paul, and John Marshall with equal appositeness, always biased and sometimes excessively emotional, loving a saturnine jest, could be more voluble than discreet. Eccentric in appearance—tall, loose-jointed, and subject to spasmodic jerks—he was highly temperamental in spirit, giving rein to exaggerated loves and hates. His friends worried over his notorious forgetfulness of engagements, his carelessness of details, and his tactlessness. But his intellectual power and stubborn will made him refreshingly independent. For a time he was curiously subservient to Buchanan, whose experience and rank awed him; then, as if suddenly recognizing the President's weakness, he brusquely asserted himself. While Cass dozed, and Toucey yielded, Black was

30 H. J. Harris, August 16, 1856; Davis Papers, Duke University.
31 Samuel Ryan Curtis, MS Journal, Dec. 26, 1859.

not the man to let the Southern leaders hoodwink or intimidate him. In the ultimate crisis he stood up courageously for the Union, and when Buchanan showed his lack of backbone Black was ready to supply plenty of it.[32]

These men, together with Slidell, would help the President sway the rod of government. And Slidell, though outside the Cabinet, was a power. Now sixty-four, he had behind him lucrative years at the New Orleans bar, service in Congress, the use of fraud in Plaquemines parish to carry Louisiana for Polk, and an abortive mission to Mexico; he was the ruling boss of Louisiana, and one of the Senate leaders. Firm and unscrupulous, a shrewd wire-puller who had contributed much to Buchanan's nomination and election, he could count on the President's gratitude. For all his New York birth, Slidell was a Southern nationalist, anxious to acquire Cuba, and full of zeal for all the Gulf State demands.

Little need be said of Cass, who, after giving public assurance that he would drop his Anglophobe tendencies, contributed no ideas and no vision to the Administration. Buchanan blocked out the main foreign policies. Most of Cass's dispatches were written or rewritten for him by Appleton, Black, or the President.[33] He made a firm stand against British claims to the right of visitation and search on the high seas, and he cooperated with Buchanan in an aggressive policy in the Western Hemisphere.

Secretary Floyd proved equally clumsy and hapless. Scion of an old Virginia family, elected governor because his father had been one, he was an amiable cipher. Shrewd men soon saw that his dullness and laziness made him easy to victimize, and an odor of corruption rose from the War Office.

As for Toucey, a stiff, dignified gentleman, he exercised more vigilance. Naval officers and bureaucrats generally ran his department for him, but he prevented thefts. Postmaster-General Brown was interested in distributing offices and in securing his wealthy second wife a high social position. He took an elegant mansion, and an entertainment there, with his consort presiding in rose-colored brocade and his stepdaughter showing her white arms at the harp, was an occasion to delight the social reporters.[34]

It took time for the great defects of the Cabinet to show themselves. The general view was that it would serve well enough, and the South, with Virginia, Georgia, Tennessee, and Mississippi all represented (Kentucky might be added for Bright) purred with complacency. To be sure, the Cabinet represented the

---

32 See W. N. Brigance, *Jeremiah S. Black*; biographical sketch in C. F. Black, *Essays and Speeches of Jeremiah S. Black.*
33 "The real Secretary during the four years preceding the Civil War was President James Buchanan, who directed the foreign affairs of the United States with great ability." Lewis Einstein, in S. F. Bemis, ed., *American Secretaries of State*, VI, 297.
34 Mary J. Windle, *Life in Washington*, 249, 250.

moderate rather than the radical South. Duff Green, the fearless old Jacksonian editor, now engaged in railway promotion, thought Buchanan should be warned that the fire-eaters were dissatisfied and hostile; warned, too, that Calhoun in his grave was no less potent than in his senatorial chair.[35] The Calhounites hoped to convert or cow the Southern members. Some Northern freesoilers also waited hopefully for disaster. Lincoln's partner Herndon assured Lyman Trumbull that this group of moderate slavery men, ground between two extremes, could never withstand the pressure of the revolutionary times. A soft, fat, good-natured parcel of men, it would soon split. "Buchanan and his Cabinet must go north or go south, or perish." [36] The majority of Americans, however, were (as always) optimistic.

Howell Cobb and Jacob Thompson were less good-natured than they looked, and Slidell, the Senate whip, was not good-natured at all. Buchanan was justified in choosing a predominantly Southern Cabinet—if he used it. The South was losing ground; all the great social and economic forces were against it; it must adjust itself to painful concessions. A President could better reconcile it to the inevitable surrenders, as in Kansas, if upheld by a Southern Cabinet. But he must dominate his Cabinet and employ it to persuade the South. The grand error of Buchanan was that, having chosen a Southern Cabinet, he did not use it; he let it use him.

[IV]

On the eve of taking office, Buchanan sustained a serious blow in his own State. His editorial friend Forney, thwarted by party enemies in his desire to gain control of the Washington *Union*, eagerly coveted a place in the Senate. The President-elect was duly grateful for the man's twenty years of devotion. He therefore intervened openly, expressing a hope that the legislature would give Forney the seat about to be vacated by the mediocre Richard Brodhead. In doing so he took distinct risks. Many Pennsylvania Democrats disliked Forney, and some men in Washington and Harrisburg thought that Brodhead was entitled to a reelection. Jefferson Davis, related by marriage to the Brodhead family, was reported "mad as fury." For a time the situation looked so hopeful that veteran politicians predicted the victory of Forney, who was jubilant. Then as a little group of Democrats in Western Pennsylvania showed a rebellious temper, the astute Simon Cameron saw his chance.

If there was a man on earth whom Buchanan hated, it was this devious intriguer, once a Democrat but now a Republican. "Cameron, after having be-

35 To G. M. Dallas, September 1, 1857; Duff Green Papers, LC.
36 March 4, 1857; Trumbull Papers.

trayed me at the Baltimore convention, has since been moving heaven and earth to destroy me," Buchanan had written in 1851. "His election to the Senate would be a disgrace to the State, and would inflict a most serious blow on the Democratic party." [37] After Cameron's change of party and his warm espousal of Frémont, Buchanan's enmity toward him intensified. Yet the aggressive Harrisburg politician stepped into the confused hurly-burly of the legislature with the ease of a gallant in a ballroom, deftly blocked his rival, and bore off the prize. He was chosen Senator for six years—six years in which he would take charge of the Republican organization in Pennsylvania and make eager preparations for his party's victory in 1860!

How did Cameron do it? The chagrined Democrats, counting the vote (67 for Cameron, 58 for Forney, 8 scattered), hardly knew. They talked of bribery, and forty-four members of the House petitioned Congress for an investigation, alleging corrupt and unlawful acts. In Schuylkill County the Democrats held a public meeting to condemn the "atrocious" conduct of two Representatives who had inexplicably violated their solemn party pledges. Everybody knew that Cameron was not above the purchase of votes. But in this instance it may not have been necessary. He still had some warm personal friends among the Democrats. His papers show that for years he had been in the habit of lending legislators small sums on their notes, with the understanding that these would never be presented for payment if the beneficiaries furnished some *quid pro quo*. He was president of the Lebanon Valley Railroad, with offices at Reading, and prominent in other business enterprises—coal, banking, insurance —which offered possibilities in the way of pressure or reward. In short, he could wave his hand with fair confidence that a number of Harrisburg Democrats would instantly fall into line.[38]

The essential fact was that Buchanan had received a sharp rebuff in his own State, and that the Republicans had gained a dexterous new political leader in the Senate. Greeley, Thurlow Weed, and the allied Republican editors rent the air with their huzzas. Slidell and other Democrats in Washington were dumfounded. And the President-elect, smarting from the blow, was worried to find Forney behaving with childish petulance. The editor began drinking heavily, demanded impossible offices, inspired his wife to ask for the Post Office

37 January, 1851; American Autograph Shop, Merion Station, Pa.
38 Pennsylvania House-Senate Journal, January 9, 1857. The Cameron Papers contain much matter on this election. They also contain other curious data. For example, one C— writes from Carlisle, July 13, 1857, that Cameron contributed $200 toward his election to the State Senate, that he gave a note which he understood to be a receipt, never to be presented for payment, and that he also agreed to "do a certain thing." Another correspondent wrote on August 4 that he had been given a "loan" of $300 by Cameron in return for supporting the sale of the main line of the Pennsylvania public works. Both were indignant when Cameron's son tried to collect on the notes.

on his behalf, and indulged in wild fits of scolding. He was momentarily a case for a neurologist if not an alienist. For a time Buchanan put up patiently with his querulous rages and his officious advice on appointments. Then, in the presence of a tittering company at Wheatland, he uttered a rebuke that the editor never forgot;[39] and thereafter he simply brushed Forney aside. The mercurial journalist felt crushed. "I go to Washington at the Inauguration to sell my furniture and to retire to a country newspaper," he wrote.[40]

Some other changes in the Senate were of national interest. It is not often that a prosperous middle-aged dry-goods merchant can be converted into a political chieftain of force, but Zach Chandler, the former mayor of Detroit who had organized the overthrow of Cass, was an exception. A rough-spoken, imperious man, who expected to rule Michigan as an honest, iron-fisted boss, he was quite fearless. He would face the Southern fire-eaters with anger as quick and a roar as dogmatic as their own. He had been the dominant figure in the Buffalo convention of 1854 to concert plans for promoting the freesoil migration to Kansas. The recent Presidential canvass had revealed him as one of the most effective of stump speakers.[41]

Another businessman, the yarn manufacturer James F. Simmons, came forward from the Rhode Island Republicans to replace a Democrat; he was a devotee of tariff reform and a man of some expertness in finance. Wisconsin sent a brilliant attorney, James R. Doolittle, to Washington. He had proved his independent stamp when in 1848, a rising young politician of western New York, he had cast aside his Democratic allegiance to become a Free Soiler. His powerful frame, Hobart College education, and trenchant personality had quickly brought him to the front in the Northwest. Still another former Democrat turned Republican, the sagacious Preston King, appeared from the northern border of New York to occupy Hamilton Fish's old seat. These men added much to Republican power. They showed how rapidly the new party was gaining in talent as in numbers. Missouri did little to offset them when she put one of the bitterest anti-Bentonian Democrats, James S. Green, into the Senate.[42]

But just before Buchanan took office, a sharp trick in Indiana gave the Administration one Senator to whom it was not entitled. The story behind this maneuver illustrates the low political morals of the State. In 1854 the Republicans, carrying Indiana by about 12,000, had won a decisive majority on joint ballot of the two houses. They were entitled to elect a Senator for the term expiring March 4, 1855. The Democrats, however, kept a majority of two in the upper chamber, refused to go into joint session, and thus caused a vacancy.

39 Forney, *Anecdotes of Public Men*, II, 421.
40 February 18, 1857; *Toombs, Stephens, Cobb Corr.*, 397.
41 George Frisbie Hoar, *Autobiography*, II, 75, 76.
42 N. Y. *Weekly Tribune*, January 17, 24, 1857,

When the election of 1856 came, the Democrats carried the lower chamber but fell short of success in the upper. It was now the turn of the Republicans to play an obstructionist game. They stubbornly refused to go into joint session, demanding one of the two senatorships. Jesse Bright's term expired March 4, 1857, and the possibility loomed up that he might lose his place—that Indiana would have two vacancies until the election of 1858. Some chicanery was necessary. The Democratic minority in the Senate therefore joined the House majority in an irregular session. Though they had less than a quorum of either body, they reelected Bright; and they chose as his colleague Dr. G. N. Fitch, a Logansport physician. This was on February 4, 1857, and the two at once claimed their seats in Washington.

The irregular election of both men, under the rule just laid down by the Senate in debarring James Harlan of Iowa, a Republican chosen by a rump legislature, should have been voided. But an investigation would take some time. Indiana Democrats counted on having the inquiry prolonged until after March 10, 1857, when the State legislature was constitutionally required to adjourn, not to meet for two years. This plan was duly carried out. When the two doughfaces took their places under the unfinished Capitol dome, Lyman Trumbull urged immediate action to debar Fitch. But Toombs, arguing that his credentials were in proper form, asked for a leisurely inquiry by a select committee. Fitch was sworn in, and Bright shortly entered on his new term. The Indiana legislature had adjourned, and the two men were temporarily safe. From Republican newspapers arose a chorus of wails and denunciations. In equity, Bright should have been reelected, but the Republicans should have been given the other seat.[43]

[V]

The debates of the expiring Congress on Pierce's last message, with its denunciation of Republicans, exhibited the feverish rancors of section and party. Republican leaders, denying that they had fomented disunion, carried the attack into the enemy trenches. It was Pierce's party, they said, which by introducing the Nebraska bill had blown flame into dying sectional embers. The recent election had not endorsed this Democratic action; it had repudiated it. The Democrats had nominated Buchanan because he was unconnected with the Kansas-Nebraska iniquity. They had carried Pennsylvania, Indiana, and the election on the slogan, "Buchanan, Breckinridge, and Free Kansas." Even so, they had barely won; and Pierce, thrust into outer darkness by the North,

43 N. Y. *Weekly Tribune*, February 7, 14, 21, 1857; review by "Amicus" in *National Intelligencer*, December 2, 1858; *Cong. Globe*, 34th Cong., 3d. Sess., 774–776.

was but venting his spiteful bile. "I hope he may live to a hale old age," snapped John Sherman, "and have time to reflect that in politics, as in morals, honesty is the best policy." [44]

The Republicans scored heavily when they pointed out how utterly the Northwestern and Southern Democrats differed on the interpretation of their own platform. The Douglas wing believed that settlers could exclude slavery from a Territory almost from the beginning. The Slidell-Toombs men held that slavery could not be excluded until the Territory was adopting its constitution for statehood. "Behold," said Humphrey Marshall of Kentucky, "the crack behind the smooth Democratic facade!" Their spokesmen had been boastfully speechifying, he said—and then some cruel outsider asked whether they believed in popular sovereignty. The question was devastating. "It told upon that portion of the House as though a 24-pound shot had fallen into a battalion. You could *see* its effects." [45]

Quite visibly, Congress had two Democratic parties. While the Cass-Douglas Democrats reiterated that a territorial legislature might interdict slavery, most Southern members vehemently asserted that neither Congress nor a legislature could touch slavery in any Territory. Some men hoped for a judicial determination of the issue. "Well, sir," complacently remarked Keitt of South Carolina, "if the Supreme Court decides that this power is not conferred upon the territorial legislature, then the Northern portion of the Democratic Party do not claim the power, but are satisfied with the decision." [46] Preston Brooks echoed him, saying that the Supreme Court would hew a channel through "the shoal which is threatening us with wreck." With this view English of Indiana agreed. John Sherman asked him whether Southerners might carry their slaves into a Territory, even if the settlers objected. That, said English, is purely a question of constitutional law; it would probably soon be decided by the Supreme Court; and he would acquiesce in the decision.

Would all Northerners, however, be as ready as English to accept an adverse ruling? Already some leaders were stating the view later elaborated by Douglas in his famous Freeport Doctrine. Ex-Speaker Orr of South Carolina declared, in effect, that no court decision would have much practical significance. The people alone would establish the character of popular sovereignty. Personally, he did not accept the theory of squatter sovereignty, but it was of little consequence what anybody in Washington thought:

In every slaveholding community of this Union, we have local legislation and local police regulations appertaining to that institution, without which the

44 *Cong. Globe,* 34th Cong., 3rd Sess., 53 ff.
45 *Ibid.,* 100.
46 "The Democratic Party," added Keitt, "makes this a judicial question." *Ibid.,* 100.

institution would not only be valueless, but a curse to the community. Without them the slave-holder could not enforce his rights when invaded by others; but if you had no local legislation for the purpose of giving protection, the institution would be of no value. I can appeal to every gentleman on this floor who represents a slaveholding constituency to attest the truth of what I have stated upon that point.

Now, the legislative authority of a Territory is invested with a discretion to vote for or against laws. We think they ought to pass laws in every Territory, when the Territory is open to settlement, and slaveholders go there, to protect slave property. But if they decline to pass such laws, what is the remedy? None, sir. If the *majority* of the people are opposed to the institution, and if they do not desire it engrafted upon their Territory, all they have to do is simply to decline to pass laws in the Territorial legislature for its protection, and then it is as well excluded as if the power was invested in the Territorial legislature, and exercised by them, to prohibit it.[47]

As the statements of Keitt, English, and Orr indicated, the case of Dred Scott was now exciting close attention. This humble Negro had been born a slave in Virginia about 1795. Taken by his master to St. Louis, he was sold to an army surgeon, Dr. John Emerson. As a household servant he accompanied Emerson to Rock Island in Illinois and to Fort Snelling in Wisconsin Territory, thus dwelling on free soil during most of the years 1834–38. Carried back to St. Louis, he was transferred on Emerson's death to the widow and her brother, John F. A. Sanford, as part of a trust estate. Mrs. Emerson tried to make some use of Dred, hiring him to various families, but he was infirm and inefficient, and became increasingly dependent on his owners and those who befriended him. In 1850 Mrs. Emerson married a Massachusetts physician, Calvin G. Chaffee, who had political ambitions and in due course was elected to two terms in Congress as a Know-Nothing; the ownership of Dred thus becoming a greater embarrassment than ever. Since neither Mrs. Chaffee nor Sanford wanted him, and he was a drain on the charity of the sons of his original owner —one of whom, the able businessman Henry Taylor Blow, was a strong supporter of the freesoil cause and was later, in 1860, to become a supporter of Missouri Republicanism—it is not remarkable that the idea of giving him freedom gained currency. As early as 1846 Dred and his wife brought suit, perhaps at the instance of some lawyer who hoped to share in the collection of fourteen years' wages, perhaps on the prompting of some humane friend, for their liberation. The Blow family then lent their assistance.[48]

47 *Ibid.*, 103, 104.
48 See John D. Lawson, *American State Trials*, XIII, 220 ff.; Helen T. Catterall, "Some Antecedents of the Dred Scott Case," *Am. Hist. Rev.*, XXX, 56–71; and the pamphlet "Case of Dred Scott in the Supreme Court of the United States." H. T. Blow's letters in the E. D. Morgan Papers throw light on his freesoil fervor. His papers are in the Missouri Hist. Soc. Vincent Hopkins, in "The Dred Scott Decision," a doctoral dissertation completed at Columbia University in 1940. shows that under Missouri law Mrs. Chaffee, after her re-

The decisions in the State courts had been contradictory. First a circuit court, following the general line of Missouri decisions, held that Dred's long residence on free soil had made him a free man. An appeal was prosecuted, however, and the Missouri supreme court in 1852 reversed the lower tribunal.[49] In doing so it made a curious acknowledgment of influences not pertinent to law or equity. The times, it said, "are not as they were when the former decisions on this subject were made. Since then not only individuals, but States, have been possessed by a dark and fell spirit in relation to slavery, whose gratification is sought in the pursuit of measures whose inevitable consequences must be the overthrow and destruction of our government. Under such circumstances, it does not behoove the State of Missouri to show the least countenance to any measures which might gratify this spirit."

The suit was then remanded to the circuit court of St. Louis County, where it was continued. It was shortly decided, however, that the case, still continued, should be taken to the Federal district court. Full control over Dred, since Mrs. Chaffee's new marriage, now rested in Sanford, who at this time was a citizen of New York. Dred, averring himself to be a citizen of Missouri, brought a totally new action in the Federal district court; and thence an appeal was entered on the docket of the Supreme Court in Washington in the closing days of 1854. Delays ensued. Finally an initial argument of the case early in 1856 was followed by an order for a reargument.

This reargument opened in December, 1856—and at once the crucial importance of the litigation became evident. It involved the very point which Northern Democrats and Southern Democrats were so sternly debating in Congress; the question whether either Congress or a local legislature had power to exclude slavery from territorial confines. The eminence of the counsel engaged showed that the case was meant to settle issues immeasurably greater than the ownership of a Negro whom nobody wanted to own. On Dred's side appeared Montgomery Blair of St. Louis, scion of the most powerful border family, and George Ticknor Curtis, one of the leaders of the American bar. On the owner's side appeared a former Attorney-General of the United States, Reverdy Johnson of Maryland, and Senator Henry S. Geyer, the oldest and most distinguished attorney of St. Louis. Such giants did not plead in minor cases. They were on their mettle, too. The argument of Reverdy Johnson, delivered before a crowded courtroom, had defects of style and temper but

---

marriage, could not act in any capacity with respect to Emerson's estate, which had been left in trust to a daughter, Henrietta Emerson. Her brother and his St. Louis agent looked after matters. Dr. Hopkins also shows that the usual statement that Blow instigated the suit of 1846 is erroneous. But after the inception of the suit, some member of the Blow family appeared in it at every stage.

49 Scott . . .vs. Emerson, 15 Missouri, 577–592.

exhibited him at the height of his powers, while that of Curtis was pronounced by one associate justice of long tenure, Catron, the best plea on a question of constitutional law that he had ever heard.[50]

Before Christmas arrived, Washington was full of speculation and discussion on the case. Interest was particularly keen, as James S. Pike told readers of the *Tribune,* among those who realized the transcendent importance of the coming decision. To be sure, the bench might evade a broad pronouncement. "Yet the urgency of the Slave Power is so great—the temper of the slaveholders within the bar and without the bar, to say nothing of the bench, is roused to crush the rebellious spirit of the North, and a decision of the Supreme Court is eagerly desired which shall promote this end." The depth of feeling among the contestants was disclosed when Reverdy Johnson made two astonishing statements to the court. In one he said that slavery promised to exist through all time; in the other that the expansion of slavery might prove the only means of preserving the constitutional freedom of the nation.[51] While Southerners applauded such doctrine, freesoilers held up their hands in horror.

Various newspapers, including the New York *Commercial Advertiser,* urged the judges to hand down a broad decision, not failing to rule on the constitutionality of the Missouri Compromise.[52] Senator Lyman Trumbull asked a friend if it was really possible that the Court would decide that slavery followed the flag everywhere outside the free States. Indeed it is, replied his correspondent; it may yet go further, plant its heel on the neck of the North, and claim for slavery a place within the States themselves.[53] Gossip was soon busy with reports upon the positions taken by the nine justices. One rumor had it that Curtis of Massachusetts, Nelson of New York, and McLean of Ohio were for upholding the constitutionality of laws excluding slavery from a Territory; that Campbell of Alabama, Wayne of Georgia, and Daniel of Virginia wished to deny the constitutionality of any restriction; and that Taney of Maryland, Grier of Pennsylvania, and Catron of Tennessee were undecided. "Thus it will be seen that the division is geographical and sectional," wrote James S. Pike; "of the three judges who hold the balance of power, two live well up to the Ohio River, and Mason and Dixon's Line." [54] He added that Grier was well known to be proslavery in sentiment. Such gossip was worthless except as an

50 Warren, *History of the Supreme Court,* II (1926 ed.), 287.

51 N. Y. *Tribune,* December 23, 1856. George Ticknor Curtis said on the occasion of Johnson's death: "It was the forcible presentation of the Southern view of our Constitution in respect to the relation of slavery to the Territories and of the Territories to the nation, that contributed more than anything else to bring about the decision that was made in this case." B. C. Steiner, *Reverdy Johnson,* 38.

52 *Commercial Advertiser,* January 17, 1857.

53 D. L. Phillips to Trumbull, January 18, 1857; Trumbull Papers.

54 N. Y. *Tribune,* December 24, 1856.

indication that Washington was eagerly forecasting a decision, that the judges seemed inclined to give it a sweeping character, and that most people expected the panel to divide along lines of sectional sympathy.

By mid-January, reports were thickening that the Supreme Court would soon deny the power of Congress to exclude slavery from a Territory. This, said indignant Republicans, was a naked scheme to use the judicial power in a political maneuver. "If the Supreme Court were today to decide that Congress had no power over slavery in the Territories," wrote Pike, "the decision would be simply a majority decision, carrying no moral power with it in the North, and if a speedy change were possible in one or two individuals composing the court, such a decision would be unceremoniously reversed at the very next session." [55] Many Southerners were obviously thirsting to have the question resolved in their favor by the Court; so were many freesoil Northerners, who wanted to keep up the sectional agitation. Sooner or later, thought Greeley's Washington correspondent, the Court would give slavery men what they wanted. He hoped they would do it at once, while the Northern mind was still excited, and when Congress, Court, and President could be identified by the people as fellow conspirators in the work of extending the slavery domain.[56]

[VI]

Meanwhile, the nation was exuberantly prosperous. Its interests were many and diverse. Sectional animosities seemed to dwindle as the debate on Pierce's message wore itself out. The country was reading about war in China, Richard Burton's expedition in East Africa, and the desperate troubles of William Walker in Nicaragua as overwhelming forces hemmed in his little army. General Scott and Jefferson Davis were conducting a newspaper quarrel with such ferocious epithets as "falsehood" and "hypocrisy." A report that the Empress Eugénie had appeared without hoops aroused vast feminine excitement.

From such topics the nation turned at the beginning of March to Buchanan's inaugural ceremonies. Pomp and glitter attended the great day. The President-elect came down from Lancaster in a special car. A huge concourse poured into the capital, the Baltimore & Ohio alone bringing more than thirty thousand from the north.[57] Attired in a well-advertised suit of homespun, and escorted by a colorful parade of regulars, marines, and militia from various States, Buchanan rode to the Capitol with Pierce, and received the oath from Chief Justice Taney —a reception at the White House following.[58]

55 *Idem.*
56 N. Y. *Weekly Tribune*, January 10, 1857.
57 N. Y. *Express*, March 6, Washington *Union, National Intelligencer*, March 5, 1857.
58 MS Recollections of Mrs. C. C. Clay, Duke University.

That night, in a large building erected on Judiciary Square, a ball offered the grandest spectacle of the kind yet seen in Washington. From outside, the impromptu structure looked like a huge railroad-constructor's shanty; but the interior, lined with glazed cambric and handsomely beflagged, with chandeliers lighting its ceiling of white cloth and golden stars, was attractive. Buchanan, his niece Miss Lane, and Breckinridge made a brief appearance. Members of Congress attended, Slidell and Douglas being prominent. It was recorded that Gautier, the caterer, provided 500 gallons of oysters, 800 chickens, huge quantities of venison, beef, turkey, pheasants, ham, and lobster, and 100 gallons of ice cream. Ladies predominated, for they entered free while men paid ten dollars. As guests drove home through the clear moonlight, they agreed that the ball promised a brilliant social future for the Administration.[59]

But if the ceremonies were imposing, the inaugural address was uninspired. No eloquence of phrase or glint of original thought lighted up its turgidity. Buchanan reiterated his determination to serve only one term. This was an error, for his political authority would have been far greater had he concealed his intent. The one striking passage of his discourse dealt with the Supreme Court and might better have been omitted. It was now widely believed that the judges would soon present a decision annulling the Missouri Compromise. The Chicago *Times*, for example, on February 26, 1857, had accurately predicted that the Court would declare the Compromise restriction unconstitutional, with only Justices Curtis and McLean dissenting. The new President should prudently have avoided the subject. Instead, after pointing out that men differed as to the time when the people of a Territory should decide for slavery or freedom, he went on:

This is happily a matter of but little practical importance, and besides, it is a judicial question, which legitimately belongs to the Supreme Court of the United States, before whom it is now pending, and will, it is understood, be speedily and finally settled. To their decision, in common with all good citizens, I shall cheerfully submit, whatever this may be, though it has ever been my individual opinion that, under the Kansas-Nebraska Act, the appropriate period will be when the number of actual residents in the Territory shall justify the formation of a constitution with a view to its admission as a State into the Union.

For the rest Buchanan expatiated upon the importance of maintaining the Constitution and the Union; proposed to use the Treasury surplus in extinguishing the national debt, increasing the navy, and strengthening the coast defenses; declared against squandering the public lands; and recommended a military road to the Pacific. Though he spoke of expanding the American realm, he stipulated that new territory should be acquired only by honorable means. All this was

59 N. Y. *Times*, March 6, 7, 1857.

commonplace. The central defect of the American governmental system at the moment was that it had no policy-making agency other than the President. In Britain, the Cabinet did consider long-range policy, and did sometimes lead Parliament effectively in implementing it; in America, the Cabinet merely dealt *ad hoc* with exigent issues, while Congress had no planning machinery. The problem which now required planning was slavery—and Buchanan showed that he did not understand its nature.

For the most significant part of the address was his denunciation of the long slavery agitation and his expression of a fatuous hope that it would soon cease. During the whole previous twenty years, he remarked, the agitation had done no positive good to any human being, but had been a prolific source of evils to the master, the slave, and the nation. This was partially true. It was equally true that no fever resulting from an inner malady, no riot provoked by a social mal-adjustment, and no depression caused by economic blunders ever produces much positive good. They are not, however, to be regarded as detached phenomena. If weighed in connection with their causes, it becomes plain that only a removal of the source will eliminate their "great evils." Buchanan remarked that by let-ting slavery severely alone in the States, and remitting it in the Territories to the principle of popular sovereignty, the matter might easily be settled. Since no other question would then remain for adjustment, the protracted controversy might speedily become extinct.

When the new President said this, he knew that the Supreme Court was about to decide that slavery should range freely through any Territory until the moment came for its admission to the Union. His statement thus amounted to a cool proposal that the Republican Party, built on a demand for the exclu-sion of slavery from all Territories, should disband; it amounted to an equally cool proposal that the Douglas, or squatter sovereignty, wing of the Democracy, built on a demand for early territorial autonomy, should give up its basic tenet. Nor was Buchanan's statement a mere rhetorical flight. The amazing fact is that he really believed that his proposal might be realized.

4

The Dred Scott Decision

FORTUNATELY for the country, few administrations open with a thunder-clap. Usually the new President and Cabinet find a few quiet months in which to settle routine affairs, and to take their bearings, before they have to deal with controversial problems. Buchanan was unfortunate when his long courtship of political quiet ended only two days after his inauguration, and the Dred Scott decision broke upon the nation with a confusing crash. His friends assured the country that the Supreme Court bolt had scattered his enemies and cleared his path for a successful term of office. It was quickly evident, however, that the thunder had brought not victory and peace, but a furious political storm.

The full implications of Dred Scott can be grasped only if we remember to what a savage pitch Pierce's recent castigation of Republican doctrines had raised the dispute upon the constitutional position of slavery in the Territories, and with what fierceness the defenders of the three main views had sprung to arms. During December and January, Congress had quivered with the debate. Senator Cass expounded his and Douglas's view that the settlers of a Territory alone had definitive power over slavery. Lyman Trumbull and John P. Hale argued that Congress possessed full power to regulate it, like other domestic institutions, throughout the public domain. Alexander H. Stephens and Senator Mason of Virginia declared that neither Congress nor the territorial legislatures had any authority to limit slavery, and that the late election had sustained the principle that the institution could not be prohibited in lands belonging to the whole nation. Perhaps the ablest speech was by Collamer of Vermont, reviewing the many historical instances in which Congress *had* acted to interdict or restrict slavery in certain Territories; but it made no Southern converts.

Everybody knew that this issue of the Negro in the Territories was the central question before the country; and the Congressional debates, running concurrently with the courtroom arguments on Dred Scott, were caught up by the press. Justice McLean's essay, arguing that Congress certainly had no power to institute slavery in a Territory where it did not exist, had lately been reprinted. Many people remembered Attorney-General Cushing's extended opinion of

90

November, 1855, on the subject, written at Pierce's request. He had held that the United States never possessed any "municipal sovereignty" in the common territory, and that the Missouri Compromise of 1820 must have been declared by any court to be null and void because it gave certain new States a position unequal with the old States; that is, it deprived the States north of 36° 30′ of the right to decide on slavery for themselves. Editors now worried the topic as dogs chew a juiceless bone.[1] Yet for all the debate, the Court decision, far more sweeping than had been anticipated, took the country aback.

[I]

March 6, 1857: Another bright, clear day. The sunlight filtered through even into the cool, dim apartment of the Capitol basement which, beneath the throbbing discussions of Senate and House, was reserved for the Supreme Court. At eleven exactly, the procession of black-garbed judges moved from their robing room to the chamber, the younger members, as they kicked up the long gowns with their heels, adjusting their gait to that of the tremulous chief, Roger B. Taney. They found the tiny courtroom jammed. Indeed, it had been packed the previous day in expectation of the great decision, which was deferred. By this time the crowd of distinguished public men, the reporters with pad and pencil, were not disappointed. The judges bowed to the lawyers, the lawyers bowed to the judges; the crier opened the session with the immemorial "Oyez! Oyez!" that had echoed through English-speaking courts since Plantagenet days; and the Chief Justice, gathering his papers before him, began reading in a high, thin voice. He continued, with signs of ebbing strength, until half-past one, though his words became almost inaudible long before he had finished.[2]

The general tenor of the decision was no surprise, for word of it had confidentially passed around Washington. The correspondent of the New York *Commercial Advertiser* had explicitly stated on March 5 that the Court would give judgment seven to two against the Missouri Compromise. James S. Pike had simultaneously written the *Tribune* that the judges would declare slavery coextensive with the nation outside of the free States, and would rule that its expansion must keep pace with every gain of territory. As Taney pronounced the Compromise restriction on slavery invalid, disappointment gathered on the face of John J. Crittenden of Kentucky, Clay's disciple, and indignation on the brow of Henry Wilson of Massachusetts, Webster's successor. Reporters caught a gleam of exultation on Caleb Cushing's visage, and watched anger deepen in Lewis Cass's eyes. As Justices Nelson and Catron followed Taney, the audience

1 Claude Fuess, *Caleb Cushing*, II, 153, 154.
2 Full texts of the decisions are in 19 *Howard*, 393–633.

melted away. By midafternoon the wires were humming with the news which fell upon Northern readers next morning like a bludgeon-stroke: "Slavery Alone National—The Missouri Compromise Unconstitutional—Negroes Cannot Be Citizens—The Triumph of Slavery Complete."

The questions caught up in Dred Scott's suit for freedom were now familiar to all well-informed citizens. One issue in the case was whether any man of Dred's color, descent, and status could be a citizen of a State and hence entitled to sue in the Federal courts. Another issue was whether Dred's residence at Rock Island and Fort Snelling, on free soil, had given him a title to liberty which continued to hold good when he returned to Missouri. Bound up with this, obviously, was the third issue: the question whether the Missouri Compromise restriction, which made slavery illegal in the Territory embracing Fort Snelling, was constitutional. To everyone but Dred the third issue overshadowed all the other considerations. With some bitterness, freesoilers pointed out that the Supreme Court had once included two justices who, when members of Congress, had voted for the Compromise: Philip P. Barbour of Virginia, and Henry Baldwin of Pennsylvania. What would these men have said of the constitutionality of the law they had helped to pass?

On the question whether Dred, or any other Negro of slave ancestry, could be a citizen (the question of jurisdiction), only three judges pronounced a broad and explicit negative. They were Judges Taney, Wayne, and Daniel, who found grounds for stating that citizenship was impossible to any such person. Not one of the three cited any apposite precedent, for, while Taney mentioned that the issue of citizenship had been raised in the famous Prudence Crandall case in Connecticut, he noted that no final opinion had then been handed down upon it. Indeed, no precedent was to be found in any work of reference known in 1857, though one has since been discovered: in 1793 the Federal circuit court in Connecticut had decided that a free Negro of Massachusetts possessed the right to sue.[3] Of the other judges, John McLean and Benjamin R. Curtis firmly asserted that a free Negro *was* a citizen, while the four others avoided the broad abstract question. Justice John A. Campbell, for example, held that Dred was a slave and hence not a citizen; but he skirted what seemed to him the academic issue whether the man, had he been a freeman, would have possessed citizenship.[4] It was an important fact that only three judges found that no Negro, even when free, could be a citizen—that is, that the Federal courts were closed to all such persons. If five or more judges had so held, the case would have been halted then and there. As matters stood, it had to be pushed one step further.

This step was to determine whether Dred Scott's residence at Rock Island

3 *Columbian Centinel*, May 15, 1793; information supplied by Charles Warren.
4 H. G. Connor. *John A. Campbell*, 63.

and Fort Snelling had freed him from bondage. In most of the Missouri cases bearing on this point the removal of the slave to free soil had been with a view to *permanent* domicile, something quite different from Dred's temporary sojourn. A majority of judges, led by Taney, held that the status of the Negro with respect to freedom or slavery was fixed, not by the law of areas in which he held transitory residence, but by that of the State in which he lived when the question was raised. As Judge Campbell put it: "The claim of the plaintiff to freedom depends upon the effect to be given to his absence from Missouri, in company with his master, in Illinois and Minnesota, and this effect is to be ascertained by reference to the laws of Missouri." The action of the Missouri Supreme Court was therefore upheld.

One justice, Daniel of Virginia, stated his opinion as to the controlling influence of Missouri law with vituperative emphasis. He pointed out that various slaveholding States had passed acts which limited the power of masters to set their slaves free. The arguments in behalf of Dred, he remarked, would permit any owner to emancipate his slave without reference to those legal restrictions; he need only take the slave to free soil and then bring him back: "At assumptions anomalous as these, so fraught with mischief and ruin, the mind at once is revolted." Judge McLean, on the other hand, held that the rule of interstate comity required Missouri to give due effect to the constitution and laws of Illinois. He noted that, as lately as 1851, the South Carolina Court of Appeals (following precedents in other Southern States) had recognized the principle that a slave when taken to reside in a free State lost his condition of bondage.[5]

Since, of the nine judges, a majority concurred in holding that the Missouri law did control Dred's status, that he remained a slave, and that he therefore had no right as citizen to maintain a suit in a Federal court, the case might have been halted at this stage. Why go on to explore the constitutionality of the Congressional enactments making the Territory of Wisconsin and the other Territories free?

This, however, is precisely what the Court did. Only one justice, Nelson of New York, stopped short with the judgment that Dred had no right to come before the tribunal. Concurring with the verdict that the plaintiff was a slave, and that the Federal circuit court therefore had no jurisdiction, he halted at that point. Chief Justice Taney and the other seven associate justices went further. They dealt with the whole field of Congressional power. Six, including the Chief Justice, held that Congress had no right to exclude slavery from any Territory,

5 In *Commonwealth* vs. *Pleasants*, 10 Leigh Reports 697. Chief Justice Gamble of the Missouri Court, in his dissenting opinion, had written: "In this state it has been recognized, from the beginning of the government, as a correct position in law, that the master who takes his slave to reside in a state or territory where slavery is prohibited, thereby emancipates his slave." J. D. Lawson, *American State Trials*, Vol. XIII. But one question was whether Dred had really been taken to "reside."

and that the Missouri Compromise was therefore unconstitutional. (Of these six, Taney, Wayne, and Daniel held that a Negro like Dred could not be a citizen; Grier, Catron, and Campbell left the issue of citizenship untouched.) Two judges, Curtis and McLean, dissented from the decision *cum ira;* they argued that Congress had ample power under the Constitution to debar slavery from any Territory. The vagueness and ambiguity of the instrument gave full room for an honest difference of interpretation.[6]

Taney's judgment on this constitutional issue was read by Americans with emotions varying from white-hot indignation in parts of the North to jubilant rejoicing in most of the South. Whenever new areas were acquired outside the limits of the United States, he reasoned, they were held for the common benefit of the people of the whole nation. The general government must act simply as trustee for the people, administering the areas for them until made part of the Union. It was undoubtedly necessary for Congress to establish some local government over the Territories, but it must not be on a discretionary or discriminatory basis as regards persons and property. The Georgian with his slave must have equality in the Territory alongside the Vermonter with his horse. He argued that what authority Congress did possess was derived, not from the clause empowering it to make necessary rules and regulations for the Territories (this being a mere emergency provision for the lands ceded to the Confederation), but from the power to create new States and to acquire land by treaty. It was therefore a power to acquire territory and prepare it for statehood; it was not a broad internal police authority. His language was emphatic: "No word can be found in the Constitution which gives Congress a greater power over slave property, or which entitles property of that kind to less protection, than property of any other description." Congress could not exclude slavery, for as Taney broadly construed it, this would violate the "due process of law" clause of the Fifth Amendment. It had "only the power coupled with the duty of . . . protecting the owner in his rights." [7]

The five judges who concurred with Taney in holding the Missouri Compromise unconstitutional were Wayne, Daniel, Grier, Campbell, and Catron—

6 The power of Congress over Territories had been exhaustively discussed by George Ticknor Curtis in his *History of the Constitution* (1854), II, 351–358. For the hasty way in which the Constitutional Convention, near the end of its work, wrote the territorial clause, see Charles Warren, *The Making of the Constitution,* 598–600.

7 Taney's reasoning is analyzed by E. S. Corwin in "The Dred Scott Decision in the Light of Contemporary Legal Doctrines," *Amer. Hist. Review,* XVII (1911), 52–69. The stands taken by the various judges (a tangled and in part obscure set of opinions) are lucidly summarized in G. T. Curtis's *Constitutional History of the United States* (prepared at the end of his long career and published in two volumes in 1896), I, 266–278. The "due process" clause had hitherto been generally held to limit governmental procedure, but not substantive legislation. Taney's dictum stands with the New York decision in *Wynehamer* vs. *New York* (13 N.Y. 378) as the first notable attempt to apply it to legislative acts.

Southerners, all but one. The position of James Catron of Tennessee was somewhat peculiar. While in his brief, crudely expressed opinion he joined the majority in pronouncing the Missouri Compromise restriction invalid, he declared that Congress was invested with a broad authority to make needful regulations concerning the Territories. Having hanged men under the power of Congress to pass laws for the western domain, he was anxious to insist that Congress and he had acted properly. He held, in short, that the national government had large powers—but not quite large enough to permit the interdiction of slavery. Justice Daniel once more used improper language. Some groups, he wrote, in attempting to exclude slavery from Territories, had "asserted a power in Congress, whether from incentives of interest, ignorance, faction, partiality, or prejudice, to bestow upon a portion of the citizens of this nation that which is the common property and privilege of all—the power, in fine, of confiscation." This, likes his use of the terms "iniquity" and "absurdity," was undignified name-calling.

To sum up, three Southern judges declared that no Negro of slave ancestry could be entitled to citizenship; five Southern judges, with Nelson of New York, decided that Dred's status depended upon the laws of Missouri; five Southern judges, with Grier of Pennsylvania, maintained that any law excluding slavery from a Territory was unconstitutional; and two Northern judges, McLean and Curtis, held that Dred was a citizen, that Missouri law did not control his status, and that Congress had a constitutional right to pass laws debarring slavery from any Territory.[8]

The majority having made its decision, all territorial restrictions on slavery were dead; wherever the flag advanced into new regions, it carried slavery with it. The doctrine of squatter sovereignty seemed equally dead. So long as any area held the status of a Territory, its people were theoretically as helpless as Congress to bar out the slaveholders with their slaves. But what would be the actual force of the decision? Would all good citizens, as Buchanan had predicted in his inaugural, cheerfully submit to it, or would the Northern people, legislators, and courts, as several freesoil members of Congress had threatened in advance, disregard it? The answer was not left in doubt for a single day. The greater part of the North instantly rejected the judgment on the ground that, handed down by a bench overwhelmingly biased in favor of one section, one party, and one slaveholding interest, it had no moral validity, and would retain legal validity only until a truly national bench overruled it.

8 The five men who joined Taney in holding the compromise restriction unconstitutional had various approaches. Writes Corwin, *op. cit.,* 52–69: "When the student finds six judges arriving at precisely the same result by three distinct processes of reasoning, he is naturally disposed to surmise that the result may have induced the processes rather than that the processes compelled the reasoning."

[II]

The storm of anger which instantly swept the North emphasized first and foremost the moral argument. Freesoilers believed that the fathers of the republic, anticipating a sentiment of the civilized world which by 1857 had become well-nigh irresistible, had regarded slavery as an evil which must eventually wither and die. It was therefore important to circumscribe and weaken it.[9] The Constitution ought to be interpreted in the light of this basic principle; instead, it had been interpreted in such wise as to diffuse and strengthen slavery. Greeley called for the creation of an enlightened public opinion to place all departments of the government in "the hands of men who love the Constitution and the Union much, but Liberty, Eternal Justice, and the Inalienable Rights of Man, still more." [10] A number of editors raised the cry that if the Constitution recognized no difference between slave property and other property, then a State legislature was as powerless as Congress or a territorial legislature to deprive any slave owner of the full use of his property. The Lemmon case, an appeal from the New York appellate court involving the status of a slave carried into that State, was pending. The Supreme Court, said these alarmists, had now indicated what would be its decision. Let its doctrine be established by law, and Toombs's reputed boast that he would yet call the roll of his slaves under Bunker Hill Monument might be realized. Meanwhile, William Cullen Bryant was denouncing Taney's decision as morally intolerable:

Hereafter, if this decision shall stand for law, slavery, instead of being what the people of the slave States have hitherto called it, their peculiar institution, is a Federal institution, the common patrimony and shame of all the States, those which flaunt the title of free, as well as those which accept the stigma of being the Land of Bondage; hereafter, wherever our jurisdiction extends, it carries with it the chain and the scourge—wherever our flag floats, it is the flag of slavery. If so, that flag should have the light of the stars and the streaks of morning red erased from it; it should be dyed black, and its device should be the whip and the fetter.

Are we to accept, without question, these new readings of the Constitution —to sit down contentedly under this disgrace—to admit that the Constitution was never before rightly understood, even by those who framed it—to consent that hereafter it shall be the slaveholders' instead of the freemen's Constitution? Never! Never! [11]

9 George Mason had said in the Constitutional Convention: "He held it essential, in every point of view, that the general government should have power to prevent the increase of slavery." Elbridge Gerry had said: "He thought we had nothing to do with the conduct of the states as to slaves, but ought to be careful not to give any sanction to it." Madison Papers, Rives ed., 1391, 1394.
10 N. Y. *Tribune*, March 18, 1857.
11 Nevins, *New York Evening Post*, 254, 255.

The Northern revulsion against Taney's judgment was deepened by several passages which suggested a certain harshness of outlook. In building a historical foundation for his doctrine that Negroes were ineligible to citizenship and hence could not sue, he, like Daniel, exaggerated the public antipathy to Negroes in colonial days. History, he wrote, showed that for more than a century prior to the adoption of the Constitution they had been regarded as "beings of an inferior order, and altogether unfit to associate with the white race, either socially or politically; and so far inferior that they had no rights which the white man was bound to respect." The black man might be reduced to slavery, bought and sold, and treated as an ordinary article of merchandise. "This opinion at that time was fixed and universal in the civilized portion of the white race." A substantial inferiority had indeed existed. Charles R. Ingersoll had said in the Connecticut legislature in 1787 that Negroes in that State were "universally regarded as a servile, subject, exceptional class, in no sense fitted for . . . American citizenship." Yet Taney painted the situation too blackly. All the chief British colonies contained free Negroes who held property, made contracts, sued and were sued. Many Negroes served valiantly in the Revolution, Taney's own Maryland gladly accepting their services. Many were highly respected. As for the opinion of the "civilized portion" of mankind, everyone knew that in 1773 Lord Mansfield had forever established the rule that no Negro could be held to slavery within the realm of England; and that Jefferson's first draft of the Declaration of Independence had contained a reprobation of slavery which was omitted only in deference to Georgia and South Carolina.

In another unhappy passage, Taney asserted that the decision to abolish slavery in the Northern States had not resulted from any changed opinion upon the Negro, but from the fact that the North had found slave labor unsuited to its climate and productions. This was an untenable simplification of a complex process, its emphasis on materialistic elements doing injustice to salient moral considerations. A truer statement would be that moral opposition to slavery, increasingly strong in both sections during the Revolutionary period, was promoted in the North but checked in the South by economic factors. The contribution of reformative idealism to Northern emancipation was decisive; the labors of John Woolman, Anthony Benezet, and Franklin in America and of Granville Sharp, Wilberforce, and Clarkson in Britain had nothing to do with dollars or pounds. Numerous followers of these reformers were actuated by justice and philanthropy to the detriment of their pockets. Taney also remarked that Northern unregeneracy was illustrated by the continued activity of slave-traders plying from Northern ports, their traffic being "openly carried on and fortunes accumulated by it, without reproach from the people of the States where they resided." It was well known that the few Northerners who engaged

in the slave trade after 1800 were held in bad repute, and their business had sul-
lied the name of their descendants.

Next to the moral argument, indignant Northerners emphasized a belief that
the decision constituted a flagrantly improper intrusion into the political domain.
Men declared that while the supreme bench must sometimes touch political
issues, a body of judges so predominantly Southern and sympathetic with slaveholding culture had no right to present a decision so manifestly sectional and
partisan. Had they vindicated their impartiality by a decision adverse to their
personal predilections, a different view might have been taken of their course.
But in a great national crisis, said freesoilers, they had stooped, with political
motives, to an act which all too obviously favored their own half of the country.
Bryant's *Evening Post* on March 7, and James Watson Webb's *Courier* on
March 13, set up the cry of "political conspiracy"; it spread throughout half the
Northern Press; and its wide acceptance is indicated by the fact that Abraham
Lincoln soon took it up. A political motive was believed even where the idea
of a conspiracy was rejected.

Throughout the North and West, the dissenting opinions of Curtis and
McLean (particularly Curtis's, which contained much the greater panoply of historical and legal facts) exercised a profound influence. They had weaknesses of
evidence and logic. But taken together, they offered a large body of evidence to
rebut Taney's findings on Negro citizenship and on Congressional power.

Nothing could be more erroneous, urged Curtis, than this denial of the
Negro's historic status. The Constitution spoke of "citizens of the United States
at the time of adoption" of the instrument. It was therefore clear that citizens of
the several States under the Confederation were citizens of the United States
under the Constitution; and it was a fact that in 1787 free native-born Negroes
of five States (New Hampshire, Massachusetts, New York, New Jersey, North
Carolina) were not merely citizens, but held suffrage rights on equal terms with
white men. Curtis cited the opinion of Judge William Gaston of North Carolina
that free Negroes had voted in his State for years until a constitutional amendment deprived them of the ballot.[12] Both McLean and Curtis pointed out that
under the Treaty of Guadelupe Hidalgo the United States had given citizenship
to persons of color in the lands annexed from Mexico. It had done the same,

12 At a later date, free Negroes were allowed to vote in Tennessee until the Constitutional
Convention of 1834 deprived them of the right. P. M. Hamer, *Tennessee: a History*, I, 468.
When James Monroe was minister to Great Britain, he gave a passport to Essex White, a
slave of John Randolph of Roanoke, describing him as a "citizen of the United States."
Passports were given to free Negroes of the United States, as citizens, until Franklin Pierce's
Administration in 1856 issued instructions to legations abroad stopping the practice (Amer.
Antislavery Soc., *Report, 1860*, 220, 221). But Curtis and Taney did not meet squarely.
Curtis argued that citizenship, for persons born in the republic, came through the States.
Taney held that "a citizen of the United States" gained his status through some form of
Federal intervention; and he regarded Curtis's historical instances as irrelevant.

they argued, in treaties covering Louisiana, Florida, and the Cherokee and Choc-taw domains. Nor was it true, asserted Curtis, that the Constitution was made exclusively for white people. Its preamble declared that it was to secure to the people of the United States the blessings of liberty, and "people" certainly in-cluded the free Negroes voting in five States.[13]

As for Congressional power over slavery in the Territories, McLean and Curtis offered arguments based both on theory and on precedent. In theory, McLean contended that the power to acquire carries the power to govern; that Congress had always exercised this authority; and that if it deemed slavery in-jurious to any Territory, it had a right to prohibit it. In this argument he was able to cite Chief Justice Marshall, who had described the right of governing as "the inevitable consequence of the right to acquire." It necessarily followed, he believed, that when the United States gained a new area by conquest or pur-chase, Congress might govern it in any manner and for any length of time it saw fit, so long as it remained a dependency external to the Union. Curtis laid down the same doctrine still more emphatically. Chief Justice Taney's contracted interpretation of the powers of the general government was inconsistent, he held, with the nature and purposes of the Constitution. That instrument gave Con-gress authority "to dispose of and make all needful Rules and Regulations re-specting the Territory or other property" of the nation; it could deal *both* with jurisdiction and soil; and so long as the laws were "needful" (that is, not arbi-trary, capricious, or unnecessary), their scope could be left to Congressional discretion.[14]

In citing precedents, Curtis found that Congress had passed two classes of acts. In eight distinct instances, beginning with the first Congress and coming down to 1848, it had excluded slavery from various Territories. In six distinct instances, beginning with the first Congress and coming down to 1822, it had recognized slavery in a Territory and contained it therein. These laws had been signed by seven Presidents, including all who were in public life when the Con-stitution was adopted. This fact, he believed, should have much weight in inter-preting the Constitution, while it was difficult to resist the force of the acts themselves. (When the Missouri Compromise became law, all the Southern Senators, a large majority of Southern Representatives, and the whole executive branch deemed it constitutional. President Monroe, as J. Q. Adams's diary shows, propounded to the Cabinet—Adams, Calhoun, Crawford, McLean, and

13 *1 Peters*, 543.
14 Curtis cited Marshall's famous opinion in *American Insurance Co. vs. Canter* (1828) as showing that Congressional power did come from the rules-and-regulations clause as well as from the power to acquire land. Edward S. Corwin concludes that on the question of citizenship Taney's argument was the stronger; "The Dred Scott Decision in the Light of Contemporary Legal Doctrines," *Amer. Hist. Review*, XVII, 52–69.

Wirt—the question of power and they unanimously concurred with him as to its existence.) Indeed, for a half-century the Congressional power was hardly challenged.

If it could be shown by the Constitution itself that when it gave Congress authority to make all needful rules and regulations slavery was excepted, then, said Curtis, he would give due weight to that fact; but no such demonstration was possible. He must find something more than Taney's theoretical reasoning to make him believe that the Constitution did not mean *all* when it said all; especially as the Court had repeatedly balked efforts to introduce exceptions not found in the Constitution. Under the power to regulate commerce, Congress had embargoed all ships, thus prohibiting the use of a special kind of property belonging mainly to citizens of the Northeastern States; yet the Court had held this constitutional. If the power to govern commerce extended to an indefinite prohibition of the use of vessels, did not the power to make all needful rules respecting the territory of the United States extend to a prohibition of slavery?

[III]

Would the prestige of the Court, which for sixty years had been gathering dignity and influence, override all opposition? "Mr. President," Senator Cass had exclaimed in the Senate two years earlier, "it is an impressive spectacle, almost a sublime one, to see nine men . . . establishing great principles essential to public and private prosperity and to the government; whose influence is felt throughout the whole Union, and whose decrees are implicitly obeyed. It is the triumph of moral force." [15] Yet Cass knew that the interpretation of the Constitution was a human process, and that the conclusions of the nine judges must in the last analysis harmonize with the will of the people, or they would be swept aside; he acknowledged this fact when he said that the Court "lives and breathes upon public confidence," and that "it cannot carry into effect a single decree without calling upon the other departments of government to aid it." For two main reasons all Republicans and many freesoil Democrats were quite unwilling to acknowledge the finality of the decision; one being the biased composition of the Court, the other the widespread suspicion of some political maneuvering or even conspiracy behind its decision.

Northern spokesmen had for years repeatedly declared that public confidence in the Supreme Court was impaired by the lack of balance in its membership. Of the nine judges who heard the Dred Scott case, five, including the Chief Justice, were Southerners, and four Northerners. Of these four, Grier of Penn-

15 *Cong. Globe,* February 8, 1855; see *Ordeal of the Union,* I, 171.

sylvania was as pronouncedly Southern in his sympathies as Buchanan.[16] So far as sectional inclination went, the Court stood six to three. As for party affiliation, seven of the nine were Democrats, McLean was a Republican, and Curtis still called himself a Whig. The Court plainly had an excessive party and sectional bias. Representative Stanton of Ohio, early in 1857, had introduced a resolution calling on the House Judiciary Committee to inquire into an equalization of the population and business of the judicial circuits. As critics pointed out, the seventh circuit (Ohio, Indiana, Illinois, Michigan), with four and a half million people, had more white inhabitants than three Southern circuits combined.

The bias would have been excessive even had the times been perfectly calm. But the Court had been called upon to decide the constitutionality of the Missouri Compromise restriction just when President Pierce, Attorney-General Cushing, and Secretary Jefferson Davis were condemning that law as a monumental error, and just when President-elect Buchanan and the Southern leaders were hailing the late election as a sweeping verdict against any restrictions.

The character of the judges, whose attainments ranged, as always, from consummate ability to mediocrity, offered no guarantee that party and sectional pressure would be withstood. Of the intellectual power and profound learning of the Chief Justice no question could exist. Strength of mind and elevation of spirit were stamped upon Taney's face. Tall, thin, bent with his eighty years, his skin a parchment yellow, his features deeply furrowed, his hair drooping over his high forehead, his plain black garb ill-brushed, his long arms and bony fingers giving him a spidery look as he took nervous notes, he was not an attractive figure.[17] Yet fire dwelt in his eyes, and intensity marked his movements. From the time in 1836 when Henry Clay had violently denounced his appointment, political opponents had spoken of him harshly. Counsel familiar with the Court, however, paid tribute to his spotless character, his sagacity, his vast legal erudition, his serene dignity as presiding officer, and his painful conscientiousness in holding the scales of justice even between litigants.[18] Deploring slavery, he had long since freed all his bondsmen. A devout Catholic, he made it a daily custom to implore heaven for guidance. Even hostile editors admitted that in the sincerity of his convictions and his intellectual authority, he was no unworthy suc-

16 There may or may not be significance in the fact that Grier was a distant relative of the mother of Alexander H. Stephens, and that his daughter married a Kentuckian who became a Confederate officer. J. Z. Rabun, "Alexander H. Stephens, 1812–1861," MS Dissertation, Univ. of Chicago; N. Y. *Tribune*, September 27, 1870.

17 Born the year of the battle of Saratoga; March 17, 1777.

18 Caleb Cushing in due course penned a glowing tribute to Taney. He spoke of the Chief Justice's erudition, masterly style in written opinions, and kind deportment toward members of the bar. "He was one of those men who possess such tenacity of vitality as half to suggest that the human body may sometimes endure to extreme old age by the mere force of a great mind within it, as the will may have power to withstand physical decay, and repel the attacks of death." Undated MS; Cushing Papers.

cessor of John Marshall; while "affectionate reverence" was the term used by Judah P. Benjamin for the feeling which he inspired among friends.[19] To his trenchant power as a political thinker, later generations would do full justice.

It could nevertheless be said that, penetration and not breadth being his chief mental attribute, he sometimes displayed a narrow stubbornness; that he was strongly molded by his early Calvert County environment, the tobacco-planting, slaveholding tidewater strip of Maryland, and was deeply sympathetic with Southern ways and manners; and that his conduct as a judge had not been untinged by partisanship. As a member of Jackson's Cabinet, helping make war upon the Bank of the United States, he had developed an anti-monopolist feeling which expressed itself on the bench in a desire to restrain mercantile and financial concentrations. The tendency of his decisions was to a strict construction of national powers conferred in the Constitution, and to a protection of the States in a full and unfettered use of their retained authority.[20] His judgment in the Charles River case was one of several which almost caused Justice Story to resign, and inspired James Kent's indignant protest.[21] Even sympathetic biographers admit that his opinion in one case involving the Bank and his own previous action as Attorney-General went to the verge of impropriety.[22]

It might be noted that, in the famous Prigg case, he and Justice Daniel had stood together in holding that States could pass laws for the surrender of escaped slaves, but not laws which impaired the master's right to recover them. A champion of human rights in the economic field, he had an agrarian instinct, a feeling for the rural South as against the wealthy, partially industrialized North, which was bound insensibly to color his judicial thought. He felt that the South, and with it the Union, were in imminent danger.

Of the four other judges from slaveholding States, John A. Campbell, only forty-six this year, was easily the ablest, and had gained national reputation as an attorney before Pierce lifted him to the Supreme Court. The son of an eminent Georgia lawyer, he grew up in the same aristocratic town as Toombs —Washington—and graduated from the University of Georgia. Removing to Montgomery, Alabama, he distinguished himself by studious tastes, a remarkable memory, and undeviating regard for principle. His charge to the grand jury in New Orleans in 1854, denouncing William Walker and other filibusters, was a long-remembered exemplification of his courage. Genial, gentle, and philosophical, a close and accurate reasoner, he was never strongly partisan. He labored

19 *Cong. Globe,* 35th Congress, 1st Sess., 1065–1072.
20 G. W. Biddle in T. M. Cooley et al., *Constitutional History,* 195 ff.
21 *Appleton's Cyc. Amer. Biography,* VI, 29.
22 *Bank of Augusta vs. Earle;* C. B. Swisher, *Roger Brooke Taney,* 380–386.

nearly to the last against secession, although he believed it a right.[28] Unhappily, his three Southern associates had a less rigid impartiality.

James M. Wayne of Georgia, an intelligent, hard-working, and in no way brilliant man, who bore his sixty-seven years sturdily and who had been a member of the Court since Jackson's Presidency, was deeply attached to the Union; a fact proved in 1861 when, unlike Justice Campbell, he stuck to it. But he was also sternly positive in defense of Southern institutions. His specialty was admiralty law. Another judge of Jacksonian antecedents, John Catron of Tennessee, was a big, forthright, awkward frontier lawyer who spoke his common-sense (and commonplace) mind in a booming and unmelodious voice. A shrewd politician, he had won his place on the bench by helping Jackson in his Bank contest, and a politician he remained. There was much that was likeable in a rough western way about Catron; he had shouldered a rifle at New Orleans and had resented insults to his honor with duelling pistols. The stamp of Nashville, not as the Athens of the South but as the capital of slaveholding Tennessee, with her old interest in western expansion, was upon him.

Equally picturesque was Peter B. Daniel, a tall, thin, sharp-visaged, fidgety Virginian of aristocratic family, who had studied law under Washington's Attorney-General, Edmund Randolph, and married his daughter. While he had a fine library, read widely, and cultivated music, he made few pretensions to legal learning. He was simply an old-school gentleman of taste and logical intellect. His weakness lay in his fanatical temper, for if Wayne was an extremist in defending slavery, Daniel was a bigot. He told his grandnephew, Moncure D. Conway, that the antislavery men were "monsters," and his language in the Dred Scott case was so intemperate that his friend W. W. Seaton gravely rebuked him in the *National Intelligencer*. The portrait of Daniel reveals a wild gleam in his eye, an intolerant set about his mouth.[24]

These five members from the slaveholding region constituted a majority of the Court. Of the two judges from the Middle States, Samuel Nelson of New York was the more easily appraised. He was a conservative up-State Democrat who, while chief justice of the State Supreme Court, had been raised to the national tribunal by Tyler. Plodding, blunt, honest, and hard-working, he was perfectly trustworthy. His interest was in technical questions of maritime, patent, and international law rather than in broad constitutional issues. While his views might be limited, he stuck to them without regard for politics, personalities, or public opinion.[25] The other, Robert C. Grier of Pennsylvania, one of

23 E. I. McCormac, "Justice Campbell and the Dred Scott Decision," *Miss. Valley Hist. Review*, XIX (1933), 565–571, shows that Campbell wrote Calhoun in a long and careful letter, March 1, 1848, that Congress had a full right to exclude slavery from the Territories. He suggests that this was Campbell's real view, changed in 1857 for political reasons.
24 Conway, *Autobiography*, I, 223; *National Intelligencer*, June 18, 1857.
25 *The Green Bag*, June, 1907.

Polk's appointees, had of late been ceaselessly attacked in his own section as a fickle tool of slavery. Like Taney (class of 1795) and Buchanan (class of 1809), he was a graduate of Dickinson College (class of 1812) at Carlisle. During recent years his zeal in upholding the Fugitive Slave Law had evoked Southern praise and freesoil wrath.[26] "He succumbs to touch and returns to shape upon its removal," wrote James S. Pike of this rotund, cheerful jurist. "He is ardent and impressible." A neighbor and friend of Buchanan, he was eager for the success of the Administration and the party. It was to Grier that the President-elect had written just after his triumph the previous fall that he meant to destroy the dangerous slavery agitation, strengthen the Democratic Party, and thus restore peace to the distracted nation.[27]

Grier's pliability was coupled with an inadequate instinct for propriety and dignity. The Buchanan Papers contain some curious letters showing that at this very time Grier's family affairs were embarrassed; indeed, he was always heavily burdened, for he had toiled hard to support his mother and help educate ten younger brothers. To mend his circumstances, he was anxious to install a relative as clerk of the circuit court in Philadelphia, a position held by an efficient party lieutenant, George Plitt. The justice first asked Buchanan to give Plitt another office, which the President coldly refused to do. Grier then brought pressure upon Plitt to resign. The clerk declined. "You and I and the public too," he wrote Grier, "if aware of all the facts, would know that by resigning I should make myself party to an apparent traffic in official trusts, which . . . the President, when it was hinted to him, promptly rebuked." Yet Grier persisted, and in the face of a memorial signed by numerous members of the Philadelphia bar brought about Plitt's removal.[28] This improper act was much resented. Grier, to be sure, had certain good qualities; a former head of Northumberland College, he was broadly cultivated, while his Civil War record was to prove creditable. But he was a weak man.[29]

Altogether, it is not strange that countless Northerners regarded the Dred Scott decision as the political stroke of a sectional, proslavery majority of judges. Many press reports were highly colored. Describing the panel on March 6, some Northern journalists pictured them as guilt-haggard conspirators. The general air of the majority, wrote Pike of the *Tribune*, was one of "nervous exultation over their attempt to garrote the free States." [30] He presented a series of caustic vignettes of the Southern members. Daniel, he wrote, was a palsied, fretful old gentleman in glasses, with the politics of a Virginia slaveholder and abstraction-

26 Castner Hanway, correspondence, *National Intelligencer*, November 10, 1853.
27 November 14, 1856; Buchanan Papers.
28 Letters, January-February, 1858, Buchanan Papers.
29 See obituaries, N. Y. *Tribune*, N. Y. *World*, September 27, 1870.
30 J. S. Pike in N. Y. *Tribune*, March 8, 1857.

ist who still swore by the resolutions of 1798. Catron's errors would more often spring from obtuseness than from original sin. Campbell was more Southern than the extreme South from which he hailed. Wayne, who had shown his ill temper by uttering loud comments while Curtis read his judgment, would dispute the right of any Northern man to an opinion on slavery or its relations. But Pike's sharpest barbs were reserved for Taney. Not content with saying that the inverted step, narrow forehead, sunken eyes, and "sinister expression" of the Chief Justice made him look like a man of malign disposition, he impugned his honor. Reverdy Johnson, he declared, had overcome the opposition in the Senate when Jackson appointed Taney head of the Court, and Taney was duly grateful. Hence the eagerness of the slavery men to hire Reverdy Johnson to argue the Dred Scott case! [31]

While such calumny was deplorable, Northern insistence that the one-sided decision would shortly be rectified by a truly national court was perfectly defensible. Freesoil men held that the decree was valid insofar as it affected Dred Scott, but not in its more sweeping pronouncements, and that as soon as a freesoil President could change the list of judges, the Court would restore the old reading of the Constitution. Every Republican editor caught up the cry. "The remedy," stated the Chicago *Tribune*, "is union and action; the ballot box. Let free States be a unit in Congress on the side of freedom. Let the next President be Republican, and 1860 will mark an era kindred with that of 1776." [32] The Springfield *Republican*, Albany *Journal*, and other sheets pointed out that the judgments of the Court were always reversible. If the Court had affirmed the constitutionality of the Alien and Sedition Acts, the people would nevertheless have annulled them and paid back the penalties exacted under them. The Court had pronounced the Bank of the United States constitutional, but the people had made a contrary decision. The tribunal of final jurisdiction was the American nation massed at the polls.

Declaring that six million whites of the South had more weight in the Supreme Court than sixteen million people in the free areas, the New York *Tribune* called for a reapportionment; "Make the judicial districts equal, let judges be fairly selected therefrom, and the Dred Scott decision will soon be overthrown and effaced." [33]

The conviction of Republicans upon the bias of the Court was enhanced by their belief that more "national" nominations to the bench had been defeated

31 N. Y. *Weekly Tribune*, March 21, 1857; for the close friendship between Taney and Reverdy Johnson, begun when they were young lawyers together in 1815, see B. C. Steiner, *Reverdy Johnson*, 10, 11, 31. Ex-Senator J. W. Bradbury of Maine told Rhodes that Northern Democrats in 1857 had said that Johnson prevailed on Taney to give his decision; Rhodes, *United States*, II, 269, 270. No evidence exists for this piece of gossip.
32 Chicago *Tribune*, March 19, 1857.
33 N. Y. *Tribune*, March 18, 1857.

mainly by Southern votes. President Tyler had nominated John C. Spencer and Chancellor Reuben Walworth, both New Yorkers of high standing and both Whigs, but the Senate had refused confirmation. When Polk had nominated George W. Woodward of Pennsylvania, he had been rejected because of his alleged nativist views, because of the dislike of Simon Cameron, then a Democrat, and because some Senators feared Woodward would be hostile to slavery. Fillmore had nominated George E. Badger of North Carolina, a Whig, twice a Cabinet member, and a distinguished Senator. The Democratic press had deluged him with abuse, one editor terming him worse than an abolitionist because he believed the Wilmot Proviso constitutional, and the Senate blocked him. Had these four men gone into the Supreme Court, its character in 1857 would have been very different.[34]

[IV]

While charges against the Court's impartiality were serious, those against its probity were far graver. The theory that the majority decisions had originated in a conspiracy between Buchanan and Taney was bitterly asserted by several newspapers, and caught up by Republican politicians. Eminent leaders soon adopted it. In a resounding speech of March 3, 1858, Seward declared that before entering office Buchanan had approached or been approached by the Supreme Court; that his reference to the decision in the inaugural was proof of a coalition between Court and President "to undermine the national legislature and the liberties of the people;" and that the plot culminated in dishonorable "whisperings" between Buchanan and Taney just before the new President took his oath.

Taney was revolted by this charge. He long afterward told his first biographer that if the scoundrel Seward had been chosen President in 1860, he would have declined to administer the oath of office to him. That Seward wronged the Chief Justice, in bringing so harsh an accusation, there can be no doubt. While there had been a most improper exchange of views between the President-elect and two associate justices, there had certainly been no collusion between Taney and Buchanan.[35] But, setting aside the misstated charge of conspiracy, we must

34 A House Committee of the Vermont legislature brought in a report early in 1858 which sternly indicted the Court: "The judges, without check or control except by the President, combine with him and with the Government to legalize oppression and wrong. Instead of judges they become tyrants . . ." Report of the Select Committee on Slavery and the Dred Scott decision (pamphlet).

35 Buchanan left among the papers used by his official biographer an uncandid document. He spoke of "the infamous and unfounded assertion of Mr. Seward that in a conversation with Chief Justice Taney, he [the Chief Justice] had informed him what the opinion would be." Curtis, *Buchanan*, II, 306, 307. Virtuous indignation! But Seward's statement was erroneous merely in detail. Buchanan's information came in writing from Grier and Catron, not orally from Taney.

still ask why the Court entered so unnecessarily upon the dangerous question of Congressional power in the Territories. When it was decided that Missouri law controlled Dred's status, it was beside the point to explore the validity of the Missouri Compromise. Did the Southern members of the Court wantonly intrude upon this political terrain, or did the fault lie elsewhere? Conflicting evidence requires the closest possible analysis.

Let us review what had happened. From the moment Congress met in December, 1856, and found the Court ready to hear argument, Southern and Democratic pressure was brought upon the judges to make a clear-cut decision on the Compromise. Alexander H. Stephens, a close friend of his fellow-Georgian Wayne, vigorously urged a broad judgment on this controverted issue. He wrote his brother Linton in mid-December that he was active and hopeful.[36] The Washington correspondent of the New York *Express*, a Know-Nothing organ which prided itself on the best capital intelligence in the country, stated that a comprehensive decision was expected by those who knew the situation. "The Democracy is especially anxious that the bench should relieve them from the territorial issues of the slavery question, and it is understood are bringing whatever influence they may to bear upon the court." [37] On New Year's Day, another of its correspondents added that some of the judges had made up their mind on the territorial issue. "Their opinion has found partial expression in the Dred Scott case, and you will find that, before six months shall have expired, the unconstitutionality of territorial legislation upon the question will be regarded as settled, both by the North and the South." [38] The Washington *Union*, precentor of the Administration press, simultaneously prophesied that the Court would find the Compromise restriction unconstitutional by a vote of seven to two, McLean and Curtis dissenting.[39] It and other Democratic sheets were patently anxious for a sweeping decision.

When reargument began in mid-December, the Chief Justice had carefully framed the two main questions to be treated *de novo:* (1) Whether a Negro of Dred's position and lineage could be a citizen of the United States and entitled to sue, and (2) Whether Congress had constitutional authority to exclude slavery from the Territories. It was noteworthy that counsel dealt with the whole range of issues. Reverdy Johnson, with much undignified gibing at "Sambo" and "Cuffee" combined with sarcasm, partisan prejudice, and appeals to South-

36 The day set for the second argument of the case was December 15, 1856. That very day Alexander H. Stephens wrote his brother: "I have been urging all the influence I could bring to bear upon the Sup. Ct. to get them no longer to postpone the case on the Mo. Restriction before them, but to decide it. They take it up today. If they decide as I have reason to believe they will that the restriction was unconstitutional . . . then the . . judicial question as I think will be ended. . . ." Stephens Papers, Manhattanville College. Taney and Stephens had been members of the same Congressional mess, 1844–46.
37 Washington correspondence N. Y. *Express*, December 19, 1856.
38 N. Y. *Express*, January 3, 1857.
39 Quoted in N. Y. *Express*, January 5, 1857.

ern emotion, covered the widest possible ground. He held that slavery, as a beneficent institution, should be perpetual and should be given the right to expand.[40] On Dred's side, Montgomery Blair argued the right of the Negro to citizenship, and George Ticknor Curtis the right of Congress to prohibit slavery in the Territories. Indeed, Curtis, the first of whose two learned volumes on *The History of the Origin, Formation, and Adoption of the Constitution of the United States* had appeared three years earlier, furnished a searching examination of the use Congress had made of its authority to devise "all needful rules and regulations" for the Territories. Geyer also argued the constitutionality of the Missouri Compromise.[41] Press reports and editorial comment covered the whole subject, and with Democratic papers confident and Republican journals apprehensive, the public gained the impression that a broad decision impended.[42]

Alexander H. Stephens, who was in touch with Justice Wayne, thought that such a decision was about to be rendered. On New Year's Day he wrote a friend that he felt a deep solicitude over the judgment. "From what *I hear sub rosa* it will be according to my own opinions upon every point as abstract political questions. The restriction of 1820 will be held to be unconstitutional. The Judges are all writing out their opinions I believe *seriatim*. The Chief Justice will give an elaborate one." [43] Montgomery Blair, who was on the alert to pick up every grain of news, also expected a sweeping decision. He informed ex-President Van Buren on February 5 that it seemed to be the impression that the Court would decide against Dred, and also against the power of Congress over the Territories.[44]

At this point an extraordinary correspondence began between the President-elect and Judge Catron. Buchanan, aware that he would be expected to say something about popular sovereignty in his inaugural, and that any explicit statement would anger either the Cass-Douglas or the Southern wing of the party, wished with characteristic caution to fall back on the Supreme Court. He wrote his old Jacksonian friend on February 3, asking whether he might say that the Court would soon decide the question. Catron immediately replied (February 6) that it rested with Chief Justice Taney to move in the matter, and that so far he had said nothing to him about it. A conference might have been held earlier, he thought, but for the prostration of Judge Daniel by the tragic death of his beautiful young wife, whose clothing had accidentally caught fire. This delay was really unnecessary, for Daniel "will surely deliver his own opinion in the case, *at length*." Probably Catron knew how profoundly Daniel's feelings were stirred.

40 N. Y. *Weekly Tribune*, March 21, 1857.
41 Correspondence, N. Y. *Times, Herald, Tribune*, December 16, 17, 18, 1856. Curtis's second volume appeared in 1858.
42 Curtis, *Const. Hist. U. S.*, I, 266–278.
43 January 1, 1857; Stephens Papers, Manhattanville College.
44 Warren, *Supreme Court* (1926 ed.), II, 293.

He promised to keep Buchanan informed. Four days later, February 10, he wrote again:

The Dred Scott case will be decided next Saturday [that is, would be discussed in conference on Saturday, February 14] but it is not at all probable that you will be helped by the decision in preparing your Inaugural. Some of the judges will not touch the question of [Congressional] power, others may, but that it will settle *nothing*, is my present opinion.

No opinions can be expected to be announced before the end of this month.[45]

Catron went on to make it plain that he himself believed the Missouri Compromise unconstitutional, simply because the Louisiana Purchase had guaranteed slavery in that region. His letters must have provoked Buchanan. They made it evident that Daniel would surely express his fanatical opinions at length, that other judges might touch the Compromise issue, and that Catron himself had fixed views on the subject—but that he doubted whether the decision would settle the matter. On February 14, however, Glancy Jones, who operated his own listening post in the capital, sent Buchanan a different view. "The Supreme Court will give their decision soon and the reasoning of the opinion will cover Squatter Sovereignty. To anxious inquirers on this subject in your inaugural I have answered I believe you would rest on the decision of the Supreme Court." [46]

What, meanwhile, was the Court actually doing? Rules of secrecy and judicial reticence envelop the subject in a murky haze through which we can peer but dimly, and dogmatic assertions on the critical point are impossible. It appears that when conferences began on or about the fourteenth,[47] the majority wished to stop short with the decision that after Dred's return the Missouri law determined his status as slave, and he had no right to sue in a Federal court. Judge Nelson was deputed to prepare the majority opinion on the subject, and did so; the question of Congressional power would lie untouched. It also appears that various members contested this majority action, and a series of stormy debates began. What members? Catron had mentioned Judge Daniel's wish to express himself *at length;* evidence exists that Judge Wayne, pressed by Stephens, had already begun to write a broad opinion. Indeed, Judge Campbell later stated that several opinions had been begun before the first conference, and that Wayne shortly urged Chief Justice Taney to write a full decision instead of letting Nelson pen a brief judgment.

"The instruction of the majority, in reference to the preparation of this opinion," writes Campbell,[48] "was to limit the opinion to the particular circum-

45 Catron, February 6, 10, 1857; Buchanan Papers.
46 Glancy Jones, February 14, 1857; Buchanan Papers.
47 Warren says the fifteenth, but that day was Sunday.
48 In Samuel Tyler, *R. B. Taney*, 384; Campbell's letter is dated November 24, 1870.

stances of Dred Scott; and Mr. Justice Nelson prepared his opinion, on file, under this instruction, to be read as the opinion of the Court. Subsequently, and before it was read, upon a motion of Mr. Justice Wayne, who stated that the case had created public interest and expectation, that it had been twice argued, and that an impression existed that the questions argued would be considered in the opinion of the Court, he proposed that the Chief Justice should write an opinion on all of the questions as the opinion of the Court. This was assented to; some reserving to themselves to qualify their assent as the opinion might require." [49]

If we accept this statement, Wayne apparently convinced Taney, Catron, and Campbell that a broad verdict was needed—Daniel already taking that view. But Judge Grier, as a Northerner who had been under heavy fire for "subservience," was reluctant to act. If he held to his position, the Compromise restriction would be declared unconstitutional by five slave State judges. This, from the Southern point of view, was undesirable; at least one Northern judge should join the others. Something must be done!

For the Southern majority, Catron took action. Resuming his correspondence with Buchanan, he asked him to bring pressure upon his close friend Grier. Writing February 19, he stated that the omens were better, that the case had been before the judges several times since Saturday the fourteenth, and that Buchanan could safely pass responsibility to the Court. "You may say in your inaugural that the constitutionality of the Compromise is now before the tribunal," he wrote, "and you may add, 'It is due to its high and independent character to suppose that it will settle and decide a controversy which has so long and uselessly agitated the country, and which *must* ultimately be decided by the Supreme Court.' " But would the President-elect please lend a hand? "A majority of my brethren will be forced up to this point by two dissentients. Will you drop Grier a line, saying how necessary it is, and how good the opportunity is, to settle the question by an affirmative decision of the Supreme Court, the one way or the other? He ought not to occupy so doubtful a ground as the outside issue—that admitting the constitutionality of the Missouri Compromise law of 1820, still, as no domicile was acquired by the Negro at Fort Snelling, and he returned to Missouri, he was not free. He has no doubt about the question on the main contest, but has been persuaded to take the smooth handle for the sake of repose." [50] Catron knew that Grier readily yielded to manipulation.

Buchanan was quite ready to act. In fact, he had a special reason for doing so; for if Catron stuck to what was apparently his original position, that the

49 Wayne in conversation corroborated this; Curtis, *Benjamin R. Curtis,* I, 234, 235.
50 Buchanan, *Works,* X, 106.

Missouri Compromise was void merely because of the Louisiana Purchase treaty, then only a minority of four judges (Taney, Wayne, Daniel, Campbell) would declare that Congress had no power over slavery in the Territories in general. The President-elect sent Grier a letter, since lost, which urged him to join in quashing the slavery agitation. Grier replied on February 23 with all the expected complaisance. He had at once shown Buchanan's letter to Taney and Wayne, he wrote. "We fully appreciate and concur in your views as to the desirableness at the time of having an expression of the opinion of the Court on this troublesome question."

Indeed, he explained, they had already reached this conclusion. At first, Nelson had been commissioned to write an opinion leaving the difficult issues of citizenship and Congressional power untouched. "But it appeared that our brothers who dissented from the majority, especially Justice McLean, were determined to come out with a long and labored dissent, including their opinions and arguments on both the troublesome points, although not necessary to a decision of the case. In our opinion both the points are *in* the case and may be legitimately considered. Those who hold a different opinion from Messrs. McLean and Curtis on the power of Congress and the validity of the Compromise Act feel compelled to express their opinions on the subject." [51]

Grier was anxious, he continued, that no line of latitude should seem to have determined the Court's decision; anxious, too, that the majority opinion should have a general unity of view. Conversing with Taney, he had agreed to concur with him, while he had also agreed to labor with Wayne to get Daniel, Campbell, and Catron to do the same. He feared that some Southern members might throw out extreme views. But at any rate, six judges would declare the Missouri Compromise unconstitutional. "We will not let any of our brethren know the *cause of our anxiety* to produce this result." [52] This missive greatly relieved Buchanan and Catron. But they continued under some anxiety. As late as February 21, eleven days before the inauguration, Buchanan was writing Catron again to urge prompt action, and two days later Catron was replying that he had hoped to have the opinion delivered before the third of March, that most of his colleagues were ready, and that "I want Grier speeded." [53]

What does all this come to? On the letters of Grier and Catron many writers have founded a dogmatic statement that the dissenters, McLean and Curtis,

---

51   *Ibid.*, 106–108; C. B. Swisher, *Taney*, 499.
52   What was "the cause of our anxiety"? Obviously, Buchanan and Grier were anxious to annul the compromise restriction so as to cripple the Republicans and to destroy Douglas's doctrine, thus (as they hoped) unifying the Democratic Party. They were also anxious that at least one Northerner join in the annulment. Grier may have referred to either anxiety, or both. In any event, he was assuring Buchanan that he and Wayne would work upon their fellow judges, from a secret motive, for a political end.
53   Catron to Buchanan, February 23, 1857; Buchanan Papers.

forced a broad decision; [54] but hastily written letters usually give but a partial view of the truth. One curious contradiction in these epistles is evident at a glance. Catron asked Buchanan to induce Grier to support a sweeping judgment; Grier wrote Buchanan that he would try to get Catron to agree to one! The two men did not clearly understand each other. For half a dozen reasons, which are discussed in the first appendix of this work, we may doubt their accuracy in placing the main responsibility for the broad decision upon McLean and Curtis; for this oversimplifies a very complex transaction.

[V]

Rosy hopes of benefit and prestige from the decision danced before the Administration eyes. The truculent Douglas would have to "cave in"; Republicans would find themselves battling the Constitution and the Union. "There was but one thing needful to give to the result in the presidential contest the force of an absolute and final settlement of the sectional issue," exulted the Washington *Union*. "That thing was the judgment of the Supreme Court in confirmation of the Democratic doctrines which had received the popular endorsement. . . . The people have decided that sectional agitation must cease, and the highest judicial authority has declared that the people have decided in accordance with the Constitution." The attacks of Republicans on the decision it stigmatized as "the last dying fit of fanatical sectionalism." [55]

In the minds of Buchanan, Taney, Wayne, and wishful-thinking leaders of the Southern Democracy, a certain confusion existed. The Supreme Court "settled" great national questions. When it handed down its decision in *Marbury* vs. *Madison*, the right of judicial interpretation was "settled"; men ceased to contest it. When it spoke in *Gibbons* vs. *Ogden*, the jurisdiction of the national government over navigation was "settled"; thereafter none denied it. When it decided the Dartmouth College case, the sanctity of certain contracts was "settled"; acceptance was general. It was natural to believe that when the Court gave explicit judgment on the position of slavery in the Territories, that too would be settled. Good citizens would cease to hold an adverse view. Multitudes of Republicans would say, resignedly: "Well, I had thought we possessed some ground for believing slavery could be excluded from the Territories. I see now that it cannot. We shall have to pull our party over to the tariff, or some other new dogma."

The fact that a deep and insuperable difference existed between a demand that individuals should abandon a legal theory, and a demand that a great party

54 For example, F. H. Hodder in "Some Phases of the Dred Scott Decision," *Miss. Valley Hist. Review*, XI (1929), 3–22.
55 Washington *Union*, March 11, 1857.

should abandon a basic conviction, escaped these observers. Men could be persuaded by the logic of the Court to give up an interpretation which touched only property interests or the mechanics of government. They could not be persuaded to give up a party doctrine upon which they believed the whole destiny of the republic—nay, its very position as the hope of mankind—depended. Points of law could be determined by a decision from the Capitol basement; main lines of national development could not. Even had the Court in 1857 been a body of Olympian majesty, its purity unquestioned, millions of Republicans would have said: "Some issues can be decided only at the polls—only by the masses."

Thomas Hart Benton, now dying of cancer, expressed this conviction with characteristic vigor. Filled with indignation, he was determined to give his last energies to a long and minute exposé of the errors of the Court. He objected to its decision, he wrote, not so much because it was mistaken as because it violated a great principle. Recalling the failure of two efforts in Congress in 1848–49 to pass a bill carrying the Constitution (and slavery) into the Territories, he exclaimed: "And this is what the Supreme Court has decided—the judicial power deciding a political question!—and in a way which the political power had twice repulsed!" [56]

The wave of denunciation that swept across the North and West was long in subsiding. Lincoln dealt with the decision in a widely reported speech in Springfield on June 12, 1857, notable for its appeal to first principles. The position of the slave, he declared, had grown worse. Masters had largely been prevented from emancipating them. Provisions had been written into State constitutions to prevent legislatures from abolishing slavery. The Supreme Court now decided that Congress could not keep slavery out of the Territories. Once the Declaration of Independence had been held sacred, but now it was assailed, construed, and hawked at until its framers would not recognize it—and all to make the bondage of the Negro universal and eternal. "All the powers of earth seem rapidly combining against him. Mammon is after him, ambition follows, philosophy follows, and the theology of the day is fast joining the cry. They have him in his prison-house; they have searched his person and left no prying instrument with him. One after another they have closed the heavy iron doors upon him; and now they have him, as it were, bolted in with a lock of a hundred keys, which can never be unlocked without the concurrence of every key—the keys in the hands of a hundred different men, and they scattered to a hundred different and distant places; and they stand musing as to what invention, in all the dominions of mind and matter, can be produced to make the impossibility of his escape more difficult than it is." He appealed to the rightful meaning of the

56 T. H. Benton, *Hist. and Legal Examination of Dred Scott Case*, 120.

Declaration. Its authors intended to apply it not to Americans and Britons alone, but to all peoples—they contemplated a progressive improvement in the condition of all men everywhere:

They meant to set up a standard maxim for free society, which should be familiar to all, and revered by all; constantly looked to, constantly labored for, and even though never perfectly attained, constantly approximated, and thereby constantly spreading and deepening its influence, and augmenting the happiness and value of life to all peoples of all colors everywhere.

The New York legislature adopted savagely condemnatory resolutions. After declaring that the Court had lost the respect and confidence of the State, it announced that New York would never permit slavery within its borders in any form, under any pretext, or for any space of time. Any slave brought to New York would instantly become free, and any person trying to hold a slave, even in transit, would be liable to imprisonment for two to ten years.[57] A committee of the Pennsylvania legislature reported that the decision was a gross misconstruction of the Constitution, inoperative on any point save Dred Scott's own status.[58] John A. Andrew assailed the Court in a speech to the Massachusetts legislature which became famous; and the Massachusetts, Maine, Connecticut, and Rhode Island houses all acted to condemn the decision. So did the Vermont legislature, a committee terming the majority judges "tyrants." Much of the press and pulpit did not hesitate to hit below the belt. The New York *Tribune* called Taney jesuitical, thought it fitting that he sunk his voice to a whisper, and spoke of his "atrocious" doctrine that Negroes had no rights which white men were bound to respect—though what he had actually said was that before 1787 this doctrine was universal.[59] Personal liberty legislation received a strong impetus.

Copies of Benton's book, his final testament to the American people, were soon sown broadcast. "I will die upon the truth and justice of what I wrote," exclaimed the old Roman, who confessed that the annulment of the Compromise "is the heaviest political blow that ever fell upon my heart." Another telling indictment was presented by George Robertson, former chief justice of Kentucky, who had been a Congressman when the Compromise passed. In three articles in the *National Intelligencer* he arraigned the majority decision and rebuked the Court. Such a tribunal, he wrote, could retain public esteem

57 *National Intelligencer*, April 11, 1857.
58 *Idem*, May 5, 1857.
59 The N. Y. *Tribune* issued in July a compact pamphlet "The Case of Dred Scott," containing the full dissenting opinions of Curtis, vital portions of the other justices' opinions, an analysis, and the legislative resolves of New York. It sold large quantities. For Dr. Cheever's sermon see N. Y. *Express*, March 16, 1857.

only by showing rare learning and complete impartiality—"and by never tampering with political questions or any others which its duty does not require it to decide." [60]

This antagonism to the judgment of the Court never subsided. It soon crystallized, for Republicans and Douglas Democrats alike, in a simple refusal to accept the decision as binding upon anyone save the poor black man whose plea had evoked it. Lincoln, speaking for Western freesoilers, declared that he would refuse to obey it "as a political rule." Benton crisply remarked that such political decisions could not be enforced. "No mandamus can be directed to Congress and the people; no process of contempt can issue against them." This was true. When the Republicans took control of the government, the decision was set aside quietly, completely, and forever.

[VI]

Events soon made it clear that Chief Justice Taney and his associates felt themselves upon the defensive. His half-inaudible decision had been very imperfectly reported by the press, and early and complete publication of the judgment was impatiently awaited. The custom was that judges should file their opinions with the clerk immediately after the delivery, whereupon they became accessible to anyone who applied and paid the costs of copying. The press soon carried reports, however, that Taney's judgment was being drastically revised.[61] The New York Assembly committee, in reporting its condemnatory resolutions, stated that it had been unable to obtain authenticated copies of any of the majority decisions.

Meanwhile, behind the scenes, a remarkable controversy was taking place between Taney and Justice Curtis. Filing his opinion with the clerk, Curtis gave a copy to a Boston journal for publication, and left for his vacation in Pittsfield. Learning there that Taney's opinion had been revised and materially altered, he wrote the clerk for a copy. This was refused him, the clerk stating that Taney had directed that nobody should be allowed to see his opinion until it was published in *Howard's Reports*. The fact was that three majority judges, Taney, Wayne, and Daniel, had agreed on a rule, after their colleagues left Washington, which sealed up the Court's judgment on Dred Scott until published in the term volume.

Curtis then applied directly to the Chief Justice for permission to see the opinion. He received a reply tinged with acerbity. Taney censured Curtis for the publication of his opinion, which, along with McLean's, had been widely

60 *National Intelligencer*, October 24, 29, November 3, 1857.
61 *National Intelligencer*, June 18, 1857.

used by assailants of the Court; he spoke of the use of such documents by "political and partisan newspapers, for political and partisan purposes"; he objected strongly to a proposed pamphlet issue of Curtis's and Taney's opinions,[62] implying that Curtis would take the profits "for his own emolument"; and he showed himself hurt because Curtis had announced from the bench that he regarded Taney's judgment on Congressional power as extrajudicial and not binding. Curtis made a vigorous rejoinder. He denied any connection with the scheme of pamphlet publication, censured the arbitrary rule laid down by the three judges, and deplored the delay in publication. Above all, he implied a strong criticism of Taney's course in revising his opinion after its delivery. Stung by this, the Chief Justice affirmed that he had not altered one statement of fact or principle in his opinion, but had merely inserted some new proofs and authorities. When Curtis saw the document, however (*19 Howard* appearing at the end of May),[63] he took a different view, commenting that Taney had added at least eighteen printed pages, with new factual and theoretical matter, in rebuttal of Curtis's dissent.[64]

Filled with disgust, Justice Curtis announced his resignation in September. His ostensible reason was the inadequacy of his salary; his real compulsion sprang from the fact that he could not again feel that confidence in the Court and that willingness to labor harmoniously with its members which were essential to a just discharge of his duties. He should have sat through one session more, declared his friends, to prove that no intimidation by slave State members could shake the firm seat of a judge of the Supreme Court.[65]

The significance of Taney's tart replies to the more polite letters of Curtis lies in their revelation of the bitterness of the Chief Justice over the public reception of his decision. His feelings were lacerated by the hostile analyses of his argument, the Northern denunciation of the "pro-slavery judges," and above all, the painful fall in the prestige of the Court. He soon realized, moreover, that the majority opinions had not strengthened slavery in the Territories by one iota, that they were rejected as sharply by the Cass-Douglas wing of the Democracy as by the Republicans, and that they had thrown oil and not water on the flame of sectional dissension. Would not posterity arraign him as critically as had the mass opinion of the North?

The novelist G. P. R. James, British consul in Richmond, found Taney sunk in depression when in May the Chief Justice visited that city on circuit duty. The two, as old friends, spent a number of evenings together. Domestic affliction, in the recent death of his wife and the loss of a daughter by yellow fever,

62 C. P. Curtis, former partner and distant kinsman, had suggested this.
63 Publication of opinions began in *National Intelligencer*, May 30, 1857.
64 Swisher, *Taney;* Curtis, *Benjamin R. Curtis,* I, 211-230.
65 R. C. Winthrop, September 21, 1857; Kennedy Papers.

had contributed to the melancholy of the aged jurist. The sad state of the nation, however, weighed most heavily upon his spirits. He spoke of the evils of the spoils system and rotation in office, and of the bad effect of the frequent election of all officers, great and small, so that public servants became too timid to do their duty. He feared that a bloody national convulsion impended. As James wrote to Lord Clarendon of the Foreign Office:

He believes that the unity and power of the Democratic Party have alone saved the Union from being torn in pieces by two conflicting factions—North and South—and that the growing dissolutions in that Party must end in arraying North and South in actual hostility against each other.

The Chief Justice expatiated largely upon the anarchical tendencies evident in various parts of the United States—upon the organized riots in Baltimore, the anomalous condition of New York, the apathy of the Magistracy, the system of lynching, the Filibustering spirit in all Southern cities, the fanaticism of the North, the corruption in Congress—even, as he asserted, in the Senate; and the disregard of law, and want of respect for authority, evident everywhere.

This, he said, might all be amended, and probably would be, did not the evils arise from sources, not only still acting, but daily increasing in force, and so deeply fixed in the new constitutions of the various States, and in the minds of men, that there was no hope of their peaceful removal.

Their conversation touched upon the recent decision:

A war on the subject of Slavery between the North and South, he thought very probable, and not remote; and he spoke freely of his late decision in the Dred Scott case, saying that he was fully aware, at the time he pronounced it, of the dangerous consequences which might ensue, but that he was on the Bench to announce the law and the Constitution, and not to make them; he was disinterested, too; for nobody could either promote or displace him, and all his own slaves he had emancipated twenty years ago.[66]

Taney must undoubtedly be credited with high and patriotic motives; but no man is ever as impartial as he thinks, and he, as much as any Chief Justice in our history, had been shaped by a special environment and a distinct set of allegiances. He wrote ex-President Pierce late in the summer that he felt an abiding confidence that his decision would stand the test of time and the sober judgment of the country.[67] This statement, itself a disclosure of uneasiness, has not been justified by events. Instead, the verdict of history has been enunciated by one learned jurist and endorsed by another: "The Dred Scott decision cannot be, with accuracy, written down as a usurpation, but it can and must be written down as a gross abuse of trust by the body which rendered it." [68] The

66 G. P. R. James to Lord Clarendon. May 30, 1857; FO 5/677.
67 August 29, 1857; *Am. Hist. Review*, X.
68 E. S. Corwin, *Am. Hist. Review*, XVII, 52–69; cf. Warren, *Supreme Court* (1926 ed.), II, 316.

same authority remarks that its worst result was simply that it dealt a shattering blow to the influence of the judicial branch, so that during neither the Civil War nor Reconstruction did the Supreme Court play anything like its due role of supervision. But this is erroneous: the worst result was to appear in 1858–60 in the fateful Southern demand that the Democratic Party should be placed upon a Dred Scott platform. The party should be moved, that is, from the old position that Congress had no right to legislate slavery *out* of the Territories, to the new position that it must protect slavery *in* them.

Not one of the results expected from the decision appeared. It did not affect Dred Scott. It did not strengthen slavery in a single Territory. It did not unite the Democratic Party. It did not discomfit the Republicans. But it did give Southern extremists a judicial basis for that positive-protection demand which contributed so much to rend the Democracy and the nation in twain.

As for President Buchanan, he may have read with satisfaction the editorial in the Philadelphia *Pennsylvanian* which dogmatized: "There are certain points which are settled and beyond the reach of the fanatics of the nation. . . . The decision is a closing and clinching confirmation of the settlement of the issue." [69] He may have helped John Appleton or Jeremiah Black write the leader in the Washington *Union* which sang a requiem over the slavery quarrel: "We believe it is settled, and that henceforth sectionalism will cease to be a dangerous element in our political contests. . . . Of course, it is to be expected that fanaticism will rave and clamor against the decision of the Supreme Court. But fanaticism ceases to be a formidable enemy, when it seeks to measure strength with the Union-loving spirit of the people, sustained or confirmed by the great arbiter of constitutional opinions." How completely these statements misread the situation the next stormy year was to show. Taney, who knew his Milton, could have pondered over applicable lines:

> Chaos umpire sits,
> And *by decision more embroils the fray*
> By which he reigns; next him high arbiter
> Chance governs all.

69 Quoted in Warren, *Supreme Court* (1926 ed.), II, 311.

The First Months

THE SPRING SUN, first warm, then hot, shone down resplendently on the little capital sprawled along the Potomac. It shone on the long marble colonnade of the new Treasury Building and the gleaming front of the White House hard by; on the fantastic red towers of the Smithsonian Institution in its embowered grounds; on the truncated monolith rising to the memory of Washington, with inscribed stones piled about its base; on the handsome Post Office Building and yet incomplete Patent Office staring at each other across F Street. On the imposing lines of the Capitol, broken in the center by the unfinished dome, cobwebbed with scaffolding, the black arms of several cranes pendant from the rim, and on the surrounding waste of mud and sand, dotted with wooden shacks and huts, Greenough's conception of Washington as a half-naked Jupiter looming up on the east front. On the ailanthus trees along Pennsylvania Avenue, bursting into sudden foliage; on the National, Willard's, and other hotels, some dingy, some gaily decorated, but all crammed with politicians, lobbyists, and newspapermen; on the compact shopping center, putting out its awnings; and on the curious conglomerate of handsome big residences, little red-brick houses flush with the uneven sidewalks, and squalid wooden shanties. On the silvery Potomac, the dense woods lining Rock Creek, and the rim of high hills to the west.

Washington, though mainly unpaved, unsewered, slipshod, and dirty, grew livelier year by year. Steadily it gained better railroad facilities, more hotels, a larger number of wealthy residents, and a fuller stream of visitors. Till recently, said Senator Seward in 1858, it had been only the mockery of a capital, but now it had become a seat of magnificent public edifices and gardens. This was extravagant. Half a dozen buildings at most deserved the adjective magnificent, while the public grounds should have been much better kept. Washington seemed to lack focus and plan; it was all suburb and no city, observed W. H. Russell a little later.

Still, that it was interesting nobody could deny. Indeed, some aspects were almost fabulous in character. At Willard's, twenty-five hundred people sometimes dined in the main refectory, doubtless the largest assemblage of hotel guests to be found in any capital in the world. Slaves and free Negroes lent an exotic touch: liveried servants running errands, nursemaids proudly wheeling their charges, maids in bright cotton-print gowns and gay shawls marketing or attending their mistresses. Officers in uniform, back from western posts, strutted along. Hunters from beyond the Missouri lounged by in buckskin, with bowie knives at side. More rarely, a few Wyandottes or Sioux stalked the streets, their feathered headdresses setting off impassive copper faces and greasy black hair. Europe and even Asia lent color to the scene: a Frenchman with the now fashionable imperial, a ruddy Englishman, a Turk with a fez. Everywhere billowy crinolines, swaying singly along the pavement or clustering at shop doors; everywhere parasols lifted against the sun. By day, vehicles clattered over the cobbles. By night, under flaring gas lamps, the hotel doors sucked in and poured out streams of people; men with cloaks, canes, and starched linen escorted white-shouldered women to carriages, and if several parties were being given, wheels drummed over the few paved streets with a steady rumble.

Buchanan, who despite his years and dignity unbent enough to let friends call him "the old Squire," had social tastes. He loved a good dinner, good wines, the sparkle of pretty women, and the conversation of well-informed men. He himself was a good talker, for, if lacking in saltiness, he had sense, geniality, and a wonderful store of reminiscences. His niece, Harriet Lane, who had made a success in English society while he was minister, rose to her opportunities as mistress of the White House. A robust young woman of more than medium height, now in her late twenties, with golden-brown hair, deep blue or violet eyes, faultless complexion, and regular features, she was handsome rather than beautiful. As Nathaniel Hawthorne tactfully put it, she bore an English rather than American look, "being of stronger outline than most of our young ladies." [1] Extremely well poised, quietly conscious of her rank, and inclined to avoid small talk in favor of a close-textured exchange of ideas, she seemed to many observers a stately woman. But she liked gaiety, could be vivacious in small gatherings, and played whist well. Her elegance lighting up any room, she made the White House a brighter place than it had been since Dolly Madison's time.

Dingy and faded under Pierce, the thirty-one-room mansion was given enough redecoration and refurnishing to make it glisten. Miss Lane insisted upon adding an inviting conservatory. While Buchanan settled into his office on the second floor, with its black walnut desk, table, and sofas, and its mantel clock telling the day, hour, temperature, and barometric pressure, she placed more books in the library, the mahogany cases of which had been installed by

1　Nathaniel Hawthorne, *English Note Books*, January 9, 1855.

Fillmore. The President sometimes used this room for receiving visitors. Immediately, with the aid of Buchanan's private secretary, J. Buchanan Henry, a systematic mode of entertainment was instituted.

Once a week, some member or members of the Cabinet, with ladies and perhaps an extra guest or two, were invited to dinner; these were informal occasions marked by cheerful merriment. State dinners were managed with more formality than under President Pierce, Miss Lane and Mr. Henry issuing invitations and assigning seats with care. So liberal was Buchanan's hospitality that his expenses, despite savings in summer when he stayed at one of the cottages of the Soldiers' Home, exceeded his salary of $25,000. At receptions, the contrast between the tall, snowy-haired, black-garbed old President, standing with head slightly awry, and the statuesque, golden young woman by his side, was appealing. Guests were soon remarking that the chief executive had brought Washington a touch of the formal elegance of St. Petersburg and St. James's; while one observer long afterwards pronounced Miss Lane's regime as hostess the best combination of good cheer and good taste that the capital had thus far known.[2]

The punctilious courtesy of the President, a gentleman of the old school, was refreshing. He toiled hard. It was his custom, rising early, to breakfast, read the newspapers, and reach his desk by eight in the morning. Mr. Henry briefed all the letters received; Buchanan replied to a few of the most important, and the rest were answered by Henry or referred to the departments. Not until five was the President ordinarily through with callers and other business, then (if possible) going for an hour's walk before dinner. He lamented to a friend that the duties of the office had grown so heavy during the past twenty years that he scarcely had time, in his good Presbyterian fashion, to say his prayers.[3] Jeremiah Black complained that he deputed too little business to others. He had suffered greatly under the late hours of London society, and White House entertainments usually broke up at ten. But he tried to be as polite to Northern Republicans as to Southern Democrats, while he combined dignity with democratic frankness, saying that what he had seen of British class feeling made him more appreciative of the manly equality of American life. He liked a good joke —in London he and Lord Clarendon, the congenial foreign minister, had indulged in much jesting—and in Washington he delighted in facetious raillery with Howell Cobb or Jere Black. He liked rapid-fire conversation; once, when the wife of the Mexican minister, a handsome woman of rare intellectual gifts, was at table, a friend found that he was "perfectly kindled by her genius and fascinations, and indulged himself in a flow of spirits and anecdote very rare

2 Ben Perley Poore, *Sixty Years in the National Metropolis*; M. C. Ames, *Ten Years in Washington*, 175, 234; Louise Quitman, January 23, 1858, Quitman Papers; Buchanan-Lane Papers, *passim*.
3 October 8, 1858; Buchanan Papers.

for him." [4] On official matters, however, he was reticent. He had once written his niece, "Be quiet and discreet and say nothing," and this was his own rule.

Miss Lane at first followed this advice, studiously ignoring party strife. She was nationally popular. Clubs, cravats, and flowers were named for her, as was a small government vessel; the song "Listen to the Mocking Bird" (one of Lincoln's favorites) was dedicated to her. With suitors both American and British, she might have wedded a title. But Buchanan admonished her not to act in haste ("I have witnessed the long years of patient misery which fine women have endured from rushing precipitately into matrimonial connections without sufficient reflection"), and it was not until 1866 that she married a Baltimorean of wealth, Henry Elliott Johnston.

[I]

In the social life of the Administration, Southerners continued to play the chief roles. Not only was the South politically dominant, but Southern gentry found attractions in Washington which it lacked for Northerners of equal distinction. Itself a town of Southern atmosphere, it offered more entertainment and intellectual stimulus than any center farther south except New Orleans. Planters, merchants, and politicians from all over Dixie found it in winter a beguiling social and political metropolis. They brought troops of black servants whose use they counted the chief of luxuries; they regarded as the height of splendor balls and dinners which patrician New Yorkers thought rather tame. Strongly social in tastes, they enjoyed the variety given to Washington by the uniforms, manners, and ideas of the personnel from the various legations. It was not until the city cast off its semi-rural character, the Senate became a millionaires' club, and a large number of expensive residences were built, that Northerners were strongly attracted to Washington.

Of the Cabinet members, Howell Cobb gave the most elaborate parties. He and his wife were both wealthy, and their house at the corner of Fifteenth and I Streets cost $1,800 a year, while their furnishings represented a small fortune. They could seat nearly fifty guests at table, and their fine silver, monogrammed Bohemian glassware, and china adorned with the Georgia coat of arms attracted much attention. Five wine glasses were sometimes set for each place.

Cass and Floyd, whose homes were less than two blocks apart, entertained much. [5] The old Secretary of State, who had grown wealthy with the increasing

4 See Buchanan to Marcy, August 25, 1854, Buchanan Papers; Joseph Holt to wife, August 26, 1859, Holt Papers.

5 *Georgia Historical Quarterly*, VI, 233; N. U. Gannon, *Howell Cobb*, MS dissertation, University of California. By contrast many public men lived with great simplicity. Senator Zach Chandler, complaining of high living costs, was content with hotel rooms. In 1857 the Avenue House, where Senator Crittenden lived, offered Chandler a parlor and two bedrooms, commanding a fine view of the Smithsonian grounds, with board for four persons, for $200 to $300 a month. A. S. Kellogg, October 20, 1857, Chandler Papers.

value of a tract he owned near Detroit, possessed a fine library, and many curios and *objets d'art* gathered during his residence in Paris. He valued intercourse with scholarly people as well as politicians, for he had written historical and political essays of lasting value, while he showed a kindly interest in young men. His granddaughter, Miss Ledyard, was highly esteemed as a cultivated hostess. Secretary Jacob Thompson and Postmaster-General Brown, who had houses in the same block near the corner of Eighteenth and G Streets, also used their fortunes in generous hospitality. And if a New England chilliness clung about Secretary Toucey, his wife was socially popular.

Of necessity, many official entertainments were appallingly heterogeneous and crowded. Buchanan at his levees suffered under the necessity of pumping two thousand arms. The houses of Cabinet members, Senators, and such grandees as Speaker Orr, who had a place on Lafayette Square, often burst at the seams. At small parties, guests moved in increasing fear of some sudden explosion between Northerners and Southerners. Yet the contacts between the two sections were often pleasant. One of General Quitman's daughters tells us how, at a White House dinner, it was arranged that Senator Collamer of Vermont should take her in, and Senator Dixon of Connecticut, her sister. "I could not but think, What extremes!" she writes. "However, my partner seemed to be a man of information and intelligence, and made himself quite agreeable." [6] Her sister has amusingly described the crush which she encountered the same season at "Auntie Cobb's." Two of the Quitman girls, with escorts, were ready when the hacks arrived at half-past nine:

I, dressed in my best, with Father in his handsome new suit, took possession of one, while Tonie, dressed in her new blue silk, with lace berthe, pink bows, and her chenille headdress, stepped into the other, escorted by Mr. Wright, member from Tennessee, and our radiant young friend Cluskey. When we arrived at the lighted-up mansion of the Secretary, we were quite terrified at the tremendous crowd in the hall and on the staircase. It was a terrible business getting up those steps to the dressing room. I am sure we were blockaded on the stairs midway for more than half an hour. Mr. Wright and I went forward, while Tonie and her *glowing* friend followed. Finally, after making desperate exertions, we reached the top, and after due patience . . . succeeded in getting into the ladies' room, and divesting ourselves of mantles and hoods, set out to meet our gentlemen in order to go to the drawing room. Mr. Whitely and Mr. Wright seized upon us and just as I was entering the crowded reception room I spied [my sister] Louie in front of me, shawled and hooded, within a few feet of our hostess, Mrs. Cobb, hair tumbling down and altogether having quite a battered look. I immediately caught her and carried her back to the dressing room and arranged her troubled cheveux. At last we were ready and with our attendant beaux worked our way up the stairs to the drawing room, which was on the second floor. We were presented to the Secretary and his *dignified* partner as the daughters of General Quitman. The old gentleman would come

6 Louise Quitman, January 23, 1858, Quitman Papers.

under Old King Cole's category of being a "jolly old soul." We passed along or rather squeezed along through the rooms, Father presenting us every few steps to some of the dignitaries. We at length took up our stand at the opposite end of the room, where there was a small breathing-space. You cannot conceive what a crowd it was! There stalked the grave statesman, the fiery politician; then came the gallant officer and the quiet citizen. Many persons were brought to our corner and introduced, among them Mr. Orr, the Speaker . . . a fine old South Carolina gentleman. Father and General Scott promenaded arm in arm. The gallant old general nearly shook our hands off and said that he felt as if we were his daughters. . . . Unfortunately we did not reach the refreshment room.[7]

In the circle of old-time residents, including W. W. Seaton, Joseph Gales, Benjamin Ogle Tayloe, and George Washington Riggs, the most important place was taken by W. W. Corcoran and his daughter Louise. This retired banker, of Irish extraction, great wealth, and Democratic leanings, held such a position that when Lord and Lady Napier left London to take the British legation, Minister Dallas gave them a letter of introduction to him. Corcoran's house on Lafayette Square, rich in works of art, some good, some as dubious as Powers's "Greek Slave," was a favorite meeting place of diplomatists, national leaders, scientists like Joseph Henry and young Spencer F. Baird, and distinguished visitors. Their host was by no means generally popular, for he had a Dombeylike stiffness and showed poorer men a displeasing condescension. Nevertheless, William Appleton of Boston, Slidell of Louisiana, Hunter of Virginia, and Daniel S. Dickinson, all wrote him in terms of warm friendship, while Edward Everett, who frequented the house, assured Louise that an entertainment for Reverdy Johnson, which he attended, had been the most memorable event of his recent years.[8] Corcoran kept a French *chef*, and his dinners (which Jenkins of the New York *Herald* called banquets) were worth eating. Senators Bright and Hunter were among the numerous politicians who owed him financial favors. Jefferson Davis shared his interest in the improvement of Washington, and in 1857 they were exchanging ideas on the unfinished landscape work undertaken by A. J. Downing. The marriage of Louise Corcoran in April, 1859, to a member of the Eustis family of Louisiana, was one of the social events of the Administration.[9]

7 "Darling" Quitman, January 8, 1858, Quitman Papers.
8 Edward Everett to Louise Corcoran, May 30, 1857, Corcoran Papers.
9 Prior to this marriage Miss Corcoran had a blighted romance with a handsome attaché of the Spanish legation, Sr. Muruaga. The two fell in love, Corcoran interposed, and a dramatic episode resulted. While Corcoran was dining with Slidell, word was brought him that Muruaga, defying strict orders, had come to the banker's house to see his daughter. Corcoran rushed home. The luckless attaché, dragged from behind a piano, was literally kicked out of the house. The diplomatic corps, indignant over this affront to a member, met, deliberated, and sent Corcoran word that it would hold no social relations with him until the matter had been adjusted. The banker's partner, Riggs, of course took a stand with him.

Somewhat different was the status of ex-mayors W. W. Seaton and Joseph Gales, editors and owners of the staid *National Intelligencer;* men not so rich, public-spirited rather than philanthropic, and of Whig, not Democratic, connections. Buchanan liked to pay an informal call on Corcoran, but never appeared at the editors' houses. Yet they maintained all their old-time leadership in the life of the community. Both Seaton, member of an old Virginia family, and Gales, who was English-born though educated at the University of North Carolina, were now past seventy, and their journal had been a political landmark since the War of 1812. They liked to talk of the great times of Jefferson and Madison, while one of Gales's treasures was the original of Webster's reply to Hayne, full of erasures and corrections.[10] They worked side by side, attended the same Unitarian church, and maintained until death a common bank account. Mrs. Seaton, a sister of Gales, and a witty, cultured woman who had once translated Spanish documents for the *Intelligencer,* gave frequent small dinner parties at their home in the city. Mrs. Gales, a daughter of Theodorick Lee and a niece of "Light Horse" Harry, entertained at her husband's country estate, "Eckington," two miles from the center of town. Here Gales had his library (he was a good Latinist), cellar and hunting trophies. The two men threw all their influence on the side of moderation, compromise, and the Union.

Great had been the sensation among the old families, when in 1856 Stephen A. Douglas became engaged to Adèle Cutts, grandniece of Dolly Madison and niece of the talented Rose O'Neil Greenhow. Married on Thanksgiving Day, Douglas and his wife returned to the large stuccoed house at New Jersey Avenue and I Street before Christmas. Mrs. Douglas refurnished it in elaborate style and was at once recognized as one of the arbiters of fashion. Douglas, who since the death of his first wife, Martha Martin, had been careless of dress and bearing, suddenly grew well-groomed, sober in deportment, and correct in habits. The extent of Adèle's influence became evident when, despite the protests of political friends, she entered his two boys in a Jesuit school in the city. A portrait of Mrs. Douglas by the second Benjamin West soon adorned their

---

For a time the two mansions were boycotted; but the pleasures of the Corcoran and Riggs cuisine were too much to forego, and the corps soon forgot its grudge. N. Y. *Tribune,* July 21, 1858.

10 See biography of Gales, *Appleton's Cyc. Am. Biog.,* II. The press mirrors many social changes of the time. Beards were steadily coming in; chin beards, cheek beards, mustaches, and bushy beards that covered half the face. One correspondent deplored the way in which young women plucked their eyebrows and used rouge and powder as well as jewels. Hoop skirts were in their glory. Husbands, it was said, were requested to ride on the box with the coachmen so that wives might arrive uncrushed; but in crowded gatherings women were quickly reduced to natural size. The early winter season in Washington was always gay, but when Lent began, small dinners and receptions took the place of large balls. See N. Y. *Express,* February 14, 20, 24, April 5, 1857, and the Washington notes in *Harper's Weekly* under "Domestic Intelligence."

dining room, and one of Douglas by G. P. A. Healy another apartment. For a time, Mrs. Douglas, richly dressed, as gracious as she was beautiful, and with the prestige of old family connections, held her own in rivalry with Miss Lane. Her dances, dinners, and Saturday afternoon receptions were bright affairs, and her house was besieged by callers. In the gay winters of 1856–57 and 1857–58 she exercised a charm that was all her own.[11] Visitors knew not which was the more fascinating, the tall, chestnut-haired lady of the house, with her beautiful figure and expressive brown eyes, or Douglas himself, his abundant hair now touched with gray, but his domelike brow, glowing black eyes, and combative bearing as impressive as ever.

Though the French minister, the Comte de Sartigues, was dean of the diplomatic corps, and though his American-born countess made their house on Georgetown Heights a brilliant place, leadership among the legations was quickly assumed by Lord and Lady Napier, who arrived a few days after Buchanan's inauguration. They took Hamilton Fish's former residence at 245 H Street and greatly enlarged it. Napier, a descendant of the discoverer of logarithms, was connected with the Scottish family of military and naval renown and with the historian of the Peninsular War. Not yet forty, with diplomatic experience at Vienna, Naples, and Constantinople, he meant to make his Washington appointment a success. At the dinner of St. George's Society in New York on April 23, 1857, his intimation that Britain would look with favorable eyes upon further American expansion made many friends. "His Lordship," wrote Edward Everett's naval son-in-law, Henry A. Wise, after an evening with the minister, "seems to be a man of enlarged views, and with a pretty fair knowledge of what constitutes the real interests of this country. Withal he is very undiplomatic, and expresses his opinions freely and openly. I judge he has a strong slavery tendency; that is to say, he regards the institution as a necessity under the circumstances. Jamaica seems to have sickened him for any further yearnings toward negro philanthropy. I feel pretty well assured, too, that his lordship *advocates* the acquisition of Cuba by these United States."[12] At the same time, Napier won the heart of William H. Seward. Before he had been in Washington a month, the two were talking of Anglo-American cooperation in opening China to foreign commerce and bringing her into the family of civilized states. He associated so intimately with Seward, in fact, that some Democrats complained that he did not show them equal favor.[13]

At the minister's house, however, all parties stood on an equal footing. Lady Napier, a sturdy Scotswoman interested in educating her four chubby boys, disliked ostentation. Her gowns, carriage, and furniture were all simple; her

11 Milton, *Eve of Conflict*, 255–258; Johnson, *Douglas*, 336, 337.
12 Henry A. Wise to Governor Wise, May 23, 1857; Wise Papers.
13 Seward, *Seward at Washington*, II, 299, 345.

receptions were remarkable only for their informality and the frequent appearance of some good singer to help entertain the guests. The Napiers' dinners were marked by good company, good food, and good music.[14] On exceptional occasions the pair displayed splendor enough. Lady Napier could be superb in satin embroidered with pearls, and a Juliet cap of pearls or a diamond and emerald tiara; Lord Napier shone in court dress; dinner was served upon gold and silver plate; and the guests admired paintings brought from England.[15] But it was the homely good sense of the Napiers that made Cabinet members and Senators their fast friends, and their stay a long-remembered page in Washington history.

[II]

As North and South confronted each other with growing bitterness, social decorum was often difficult to maintain. The White House, the Cabinet parlors, and the homes of the old Washington families were theoretically neutral ground —yet the atmosphere in all became too Southern for many a freesoil man. Nobody knew when a burst of temper might rip through etiquette. Mrs. Greenhow, a friend of the President and other prominent men, invited Representative and Mrs. Charles Francis Adams to dinner just after John Brown's execution; and when Mrs. Adams tactlessly spoke in praise of Brown, the hostess angrily bit her lip and retorted that he was a scoundrel. The episode illustrated the fact that the ladies of Washington, both Northerners and Southerners, showed more incandescence than their husbands.[16]

Southern radicals had various meeting places. Slidell's house on H Street near Sixteenth and Senator Hammond's at Third and C were favorite resorts. Mrs. Slidell, once Mademoiselle des Londes of New Orleans, and Mrs. Hammond, once the South Carolina heiress Catherine FitzSimons, were hostesses devoted to the South. No one knows just how much intrigue clustered about the unscrupulous Slidell, but it was plenty. W. H. Russell later described him as one of the most consummate masters of political machination alive. "He is a man who unseen moves the puppets on the public stage as he lists, a man of iron will and strong passions, who loves the excitement of combinations and who in his dungeon . . . would conspire with the mice against the cat rather than not conspire at all." Three of the men who took the Southern Rights creed most fervently lived, bachelor style, in a private house at 148 F Street, near Twentieth: Representatives Lawrence Keitt, W. Porcher Miles, and Muscoe Garnett. In 1858–60 this trio used to meet, after the House adjourned, at the home of

14 Clay, *Belle of the Fifties*, 117.
15 Pryor, *Reminiscences of Peace and War*, 57, 58.
16 Leech, *Reveille in Washington*, 19, 20.

Roger A. Pryor on New York Avenue. Mrs. Pryor has told us how, following a supper of ham, oysters, biscuits, and tea, they and such other radical Southerners as Lamar, Boyce, Barksdale, and Hunter would hold midnight conferences in the study. Sometimes, with the aid of bourbon, hot water, and lemons, they would talk out the night, the dawn finding them "again and again with but one conclusion—they would stand together." [17] Two, Garnett and Keitt, ultimately stood together in giving their lives for the South.

At the other extreme, radical freesoilers continued to gather at the house of Gamaliel Bailey, editor of the *National Era*. This devoted abolitionist was used to breasting a storm. He had been a ship's doctor on a China voyage in the eighteen-twenties and hospital physician in Cincinnati during a savage cholera epidemic. Turning to antislavery journalism at the time of the revolt in Lane Seminary, he had thrice seen mobs in Cincinnati attack the office of his *Philanthropist*. His *National Era*, which since its publication of *Uncle Tom's Cabin* possessed a household fame, celebrated its tenth anniversary just before Buchanan entered the White House. Bailey, a man of wit, culture, and common-sense judgment, with a real literary gift, was a genial host. He made his Washington home a distinguished intellectual center, where freesoilers of all parties, and especially those whose views verged upon abolitionism, conferred with each other and with outsiders like Horace Greeley, Samuel Bowles, and Moncure D. Conway. Here, such former Democrats as Hannibal Hamlin and Salmon P. Chase mingled with former Whigs like Tom Corwin and Ben Wade, and veteran Free Soil Party men like Joshua Giddings. Many were social outlaws elsewhere. Great was the regret when Bailey's death in the late spring of 1859 put an end to his Saturday night receptions.[18]

Another and more moderate club for freesoilers was Seward's house, a roomy three-story brick mansion on F Street near the business center, with his study on the basement floor. The New Yorker was not one of those who "entertained lavishly." He had Webster's liking for small suppers of turkey, venison, or broiled shad with ham and eggs, a half-dozen friends passing the bottle. He enjoyed a game of whist and was ready to invite any comer to make a *parti carré* with himself, his wife, and his son or daughter. Naturally he saw most of his Republican colleagues. But as a moderate, even-tempered man, he remained on pleasant terms with the Southerners. However spirited his public response to attack, in private he was always kindly and good-natured. Hence it was that he often took the role of peacemaker between politicians thirsting for a duel. "Nobody can apologize for insults but I, who never give any," he once wrote. Within a single month in 1858, he reconciled Jefferson Davis with the

17 Pryor, *Reminiscences*, 102, 103.
18 Hamlin, *Hannibal Hamlin*, 275 ff.; Grace Greenwood, *Cosmopolitan Magazine*, February, 1890.

irascible Zack Chandler, and Henry Wilson with the hotheaded William M. Gwin. People had feared street encounters or a formal exchange of shots, but, by scurrying to and fro and writing enough notes to make a bonfire, Seward composed these quarrels.[19]

Yet in the first two years of the Administration the general gaiety was not greatly troubled by the rising political storm. One Jenkins, the New York *Herald's* social correspondent in Washington, rose to ecstatic heights in the winter of 1857–58. He wrote of Miss Lane in mourning for a brother, her purple silk gown trimmed with black velvet; of Attorney-General Black at a Presidential reception with his pleasant wife and pretty dark-haired daughter; of a dinner at Postmaster-General Brown's attended by "Prince" John Van Buren, Vice-President Breckinridge, and Colonel John T. Heard of Boston; of a ball given by Sir William Gore Ouseley, the Queen's special envoy to Central America, at which Miss Cass was magnificently attired in pearl-colored satin, while Mrs. Thompson was dressed in rich pink silk, with lace flounces, and a coiffure of pink flowers; of the crush at Senator J. R. Thomson's and of diplomats airing their French at Mrs. Slidell's. If the Republicans seemed on the fringe of the social swirl, they comforted themselves by reflecting that their time might soon be at hand.

[III]

The first stern problem before Buchanan's Directory, the disposition of offices, was attacked with resolution. These leaders decided that the rule of rotation should apply in most States of the North and West; that is, that men who had held place for four years should go out unless a Senator or other power specially interposed. For one entire week in March the Cabinet met daily at nine and sat till three, giving most of its attention to the mass of demands before it. People with public business complained that department heads, including even Attorney-General Black, neglected all routine work for the first month.[20]

It was not strange that they did. The spoils system was now at its apogee, and the city was crowded with applicants. From Pennsylvania alone came a devouring horde. The President was incessantly besieged; he could not stir from his desk without being assailed, and the press reported that his very bedroom was invaded. As May ended, some two hundred gentlemen were said to be settled in Washington seeking foreign missions. Greeley's *Tribune* seized the opportunity to call attention to the British Civil Service Commission, which had

19 Seward, *Seward at Washington,* II. Chs. 43–45. Seward's house in 1855–57 was at the corner of G and Twenty-first.

20 N. Y. *Weekly Tribune,* March 28, 1857.

begun work two years earlier, remarking that it was high time the United States followed this example.[21]

Though Buchanan was more adroit than his predecessor Pierce, the distribution of patronage inevitably made more enemies than friends. In New York, where harmony was essential if the State were to be regained from the Republicans, a half-dozen factions squabbled and grabbed. The brazen demagogue Fernando Wood, just reelected mayor of the metropolis, headed one; Augustus Schell, a highly successful lawyer and a director in important corporations, of late the national committeeman for the State, captained another; various silk-stocking leaders, including August Belmont, formed a third; while an up-State group was led by Dean Richmond and Erastus Corning of the New York Central, and another by that narrow, selfish veteran of politics, Daniel S. Dickinson.

All insisted upon places, and all descended upon Washington to get them. At the end of a month it was announced that the "Hards," who had supported Buchanan before the Cincinnati convention, had got the best of the struggle. Their chieftain Schell was made collector of the port, controlling the populous Custom House; the position of Naval Officer was given to George N. Sanders of "Young America" fame; while the Federal marshalship went to a whilom "Soft" of gangster affiliations, Isaiah Rynders.[22] From the point of view of the public weal, these were all wretched appointments. Schell, the ablest of the three, was presently caught in a shameless piece of spoils-mongering. He addressed a circular letter to the Administration Congressmen of New York City, asking each to furnish a list of persons in his district whom he wished given subordinate posts in the Custom House, or protected in existing jobs there.[23] From the political point of view, the important fact was that Buchanan's appointments left nearly everyone dissatisfied. James Gordon Bennett, editor of the *Herald*, called them "horrible." Fernando Wood was bitterly resentful. An acrid quarrel broke out between the mayor and his old friend Daniel Sickles. So general was the dissension that Buchanan's faithful servitor "Chevalier" Wikoff—that incredible dilettante of politics and diplomacy—stayed in hot New York most of the summer trying to arrange a truce.[24]

In dealing with Pennsylvania, the President naturally took the advice of Senator William Bigler, Representative Glancy Jones, and Jere Black. Here his task was less difficult. He filled the chief positions, such as the Philadelphia

21 *Harper's Weekly*, March 21, 1857; N. Y. *Tribune*, May 13, 1857.
22 Nichols, *Disruption of the American Democracy*, 84, 85; *Harper's Weekly*, April 4, 1857.
23 *National Intelligencer*, September 24, 1858.
24 Henry Wikoff to Buchanan, August 6, 1857, Buchanan Papers. Wikoff, who for a short time had been editor of the *Democratic Review*, had a connection with Bennett's *Herald* that was useful to Buchanan.

collectorship, postmastership, and marshalship, without arousing any burning jealousies. His great misfortune in his own State lay in a final rupture with John W. Forney. That resentful editor was not at all placated when Buchanan offered him the Liverpool consulship or the second place in the Philadelphia Custom House. Neither post was sufficiently important or well paid: the Liverpool office, now divested of its rich fees, would mean political exile, and the Philadelphia office would place him beneath a Lancaster nonentity who had been made collector. Declaring himself "utterly disenchanted" with Buchanan, Forney cast about for other employment. He thought of taking charge of the *Daily Pennsylvanian* if the President would guarantee that paper a profitable share of the public printing. But Buchanan hesitated, having greater matters to think about and supposing that he could ignore so helpless a person as Forney. Little did he think that the volatile and vindictive journalist would soon be in a position to deal him the heaviest blows; little did he reckon that the *Pennsylvanian*, kept alive only by subsidy, would soon be rendered more unprofitable than ever by a rival journal under Forney's alert management.

The foreign service, taken up with deliberation, was for the most part filled respectably. The conciliatory, dignified George Mifflin Dallas, who had succeeded Buchanan in London, was left there. He had his full share of foibles, including vanity, of which the secretary of the legation, Moran, sent Buchanan vivid accounts. But this former mayor, Senator, and Vice-President kept a personal following in Philadelphia which it was well to conciliate, while the President meant to manage all British negotiations himself. John Y. Mason was retained in Paris, to continue enjoying his table, sideboard, card games, and occasional colloquies with Napoleon III. The President had an indulgent fondness for him as an old associate in Polk's Cabinet and in the Ostend Manifesto affair. South Carolina was favored with the Russian post, which went in 1858 to Francis W. Pickens, a confirmed nullifier and secessionist. The more respectable of the two warring Democratic factions in Indiana was recognized by the appointment of ex-Governor Joseph A. Wright to Berlin. It was to Buchanan's credit that he continued the novelist Theodore S. Fay as minister to Switzerland. Still more to his credit was the appointment of the brilliant Virginia editor, John M. Daniel, the friend of Poe and the man who had made the Richmond *Examiner* famous, as envoy to the court of Victor Emmanuel at Turin. Daniel's unconventional ways and fiery Americanism rendered him a focus of controversy, but he made even the great Cavour respect his views.

Once more that sensitive capital, Madrid, was treated frivolously. August Belmont would have welcomed a transfer thither from The Hague. But circumstantial stories were afloat that Belmont had managed affairs in Holland to his own business profit, and that of his old employers, the Rothschilds. Buchanan kept Pierce's recent appointee, the rough-hewn A. C. Dodge, a son of the frontier who had lost his senatorship when Iowa became Republican. Dodge, who had boasted to the Senate that he sawed his own wood and did his own marketing in Washington, showed an ignorance which inspired Greeley to remark that whereas his predecessor Soulé, with all his faults, had spoken six languages, the new envoy could not even talk one correctly. However, he soon gave way to a cultivated scion of patrician stock, the Kentuckian William Preston. For the rest, the diplomatic appointments were remarkable chiefly for the favor shown to annexationists and newspapermen. One apostle of Manifest Destiny, John L. O'Sullivan, became minister to Portugal; another, Joseph W. Fabens, was planted as consul in Cayenne; and a third, Edwin DeLeon, was made consul-general at Alexandria. Courting the favor of Bennett's *Herald*, Buchanan appointed two of its staff members to minor positions. Beverley Tucker, whilom editor of the Washington *Sentinel* and printer to the Senate, became consul in Liverpool.

In his treatment of the patronage Buchanan did nothing to soothe the resentment of Stephen A. Douglas. Northwestern foes of the Little Giant had marked with glee his failure to obtain a Cabinet post for any of his lieutenants. "Lincoln and I," wrote William H. Herndon just before the inauguration, "are glad to death that Douglas has been crushed." [25] His feelings might have been assuaged by a few timely gifts. He had hoped that John A. McClernand, the Shawneetown lawyer who had served four terms in Congress and been a faithful leader of the Illinois Democracy for a quarter century, might receive a good ministership—but he got nothing. He had hoped that his friend W. A. Richardson of Quincy might get a handsome appointment—but he received only the governorship of empty Nebraska Territory. He had hoped that Henry M. Rice of Minnesota might have a position; he was passed over. With the Dred Scott decision in mind, Douglas had ground for concluding that the Buchanan Directory really wished to "crush" the Northwestern Democrats. Meanwhile, one of Douglas's friends was equally incensed. Senator David Broderick had expected to control most of the California appointments. The former stonecutter's apprentice and New York fireman, wresting a senatorial seat from John B. Weller, had extorted from his colleague William M. Gwin an agreement that he should manage the Federal patronage while Gwin controlled the State offices. Buchanan, however, was an old friend of Weller, whom he had known as an officeholder under Polk. He did not like the agreement. Gwin dexterously gained the ear of the Directory, swayed their Far Western choices, and shouldered Broderick out into the cold.

The two fundamental political emotions are jealousy and fear. As Douglas

25 Herndon to Trumbull, March 2, 1857, Trumbull Papers.

saw Jesse Bright enjoying Administration favor and Broderick watched Gwin bask in Administration sunshine, as they thought of their unrequited services, and as they looked to the perils of the future, their wrath smoldered.

[IV]

Meanwhile, the unsolved Kansas problem haunted the pillow of all thoughtful Americans and demanded Buchanan's immediate attention. The President and Cabinet took office to find a new crisis convulsing the long-racked Territory. A volcano was rumbling on those Western plains which made the ground tremble even in Washington. Fighting, to be sure, had virtually ended. No longer did panoplied bands of settlers and border Missourians make intimidating raids and forays; no longer were immigrants waylaid on lonely prairie trails or along cottonwood-shaded creeks. Nevertheless, the spirit of violence still reigned. It would continue until the two rival authorities — the irregular regime of the free State men with their Topeka constitution and legislature, dominated by honest "Governor" Charles Robinson, and the regular regime headed by blunt John W. Geary—were somehow replaced by a single administration.

Geary, sent out by President Pierce in the late summer of 1856, had arrived determined to show no favoritism to any faction and to make himself the governor of the entire people. He efficiently stopped the disorders. Meanwhile, he discussed a secret agreement with Robinson; they would try to effect a merger of the Topeka and Lecompton regimes, with Geary as governor and the Topeka constitution the basic instrument. But the proslavery extremists in the Territory had not wanted a governor who would act with even-handed firmness. Friends had warned Geary in advance of the dangers he ran. "What you say suits us first rate," said the free State leader Captain Samuel Walker, "but mark my words, you'll take the underground railroad out of Kansas in six months." [26]

The new crisis was produced by the effort of the proslavery forces in Kansas to gain two great objects. They had resolved, first, to force Geary, the strongest governor Washington had yet sent out, to quit office, and second, to arrange a constitutional convention which by hook or crook would bring Kansas into the Union, at least nominally and temporarily, as the sixteenth slave State. Radical freesoil men were equally ready to block a fair solution.

To understand the audacious and unscrupulous course of the proslavery leaders we must recall the atmosphere of emotion which enveloped Kansas, so

26 Malin, *John Brown and the Legend of '56*, 643–690; Spring, *Kansas*, 197–210; Robinson, *The Kansas Conflict*, 337 ff.

lately a land of robberies and ruffianism. Many settlers who came from Missouri believed that it would be disastrous to their State to have the new Territory colonized by "slave-stealers." If fugitives were to be helped to freedom east, north, and west, in Illinois, Iowa, and Kansas, slavery would not last long in Missouri. Not a few settlers from farther south believed that the Yankees of the emigrant aid societies had used unfair tactics. We must recall, too, that it seemed an apt moment to achieve the goal of a new slave State. The election had momentarily stunned the Republican Party. Southerners would dominate the incoming Administration. Buchanan, like Pierce, had hotly condemned the free State Topeka regime under Robinson. About realities in Kansas he knew little. He had been in England during the worst troubles, had come back to associate with men who denounced the emigrant aid companies and the Topeka regime, and had read the *Pennsylvanian, Union,* and other newspapers which gave colored accounts of territorial affairs. In a speech to his Lancaster neighbors in the fall of 1856 he had displayed a strong bias. The abolitionists of Massachusetts and Vermont, he said, must not be allowed to prescribe to the people of Kansas their course on slavery; he did not say that Missourians must not be allowed to interfere. "Abolition fanaticism," he declared, had made the Kansas question acute; he said nothing about border-ruffian aggressions. Condemning the Topeka government as a body of lawless men, he threatened the use of military force to sustain the regular authorities. A President of such views might well support extremely partisan measures in Kansas.

Leadership of the slavery forces in the Territory had passed into more desperate hands. While ex-Senator Atchison was now confining himself to Missouri affairs, three men had arisen who seemed ready for anything; ready, said Geary, for revolution. They were John Calhoun, the surveyor-general, L. A. Maclean, his chief clerk, and A. J. Isaacs, lately district attorney. The land offices were natural citadels of power in Kansas. Calhoun, with several hundred employees, could exert a powerful influence on the settlement and development of the Territory. All settlers came to the offices to have preemptions confirmed; all speculators eyed them hungrily. Calhoun and Maclean could hold out an attractive bait; they could say that once Kansas was admitted, Indian titles to new tracts would be extinguished, and liberal grants of land would be made to the new State for schools, colleges, asylums, and railroads—especially a Pacific Railroad. These men expected to manufacture future governors and Senators, and shape State policy.

That they, and their Southern backers in Washington, expected to keep Kansas a slaveholding State for long is unlikely. But even a few years would be of practical help to the South; it would enable Southern politicians to save face;

and it would humiliate the free State men whom proslavery Democrats detested. Calhoun and Maclean were born fighters and speculators. The former had long dwelt in Springfield, Illinois, where Lincoln and Douglas knew him well and where he rose to be mayor; the latter was a tall, tough, hot-tempered frontiersman. Isaacs was a schemer. The trio worked in close cooperation with Chief Justice Samuel Lecompte—"Jeffreys" Lecompte, the free State press called him—and Judge Sterling G. Cato, who controlled the courts. They were pleased when Buchanan gave office to such men as J. W. Whitfield and Daniel Woodson, connected with old proslavery frauds in the Territory.

The expulsion of Governor Geary was a deplorable occurrence. If ever an executive deserved full support it was this Pennsylvania engineer and soldier who, after helping shape the new governments of San Francisco and California, had answered Pierce's call to duty. Arriving when partisan gangs scoured the country, towns were fortified like medieval strongholds, and agriculture was half abandoned, he had quickly grasped the situation. Kansas was the daughter not of New England, but of the Ohio Valley. The great majority of the small farmers who made up the population did not want the negro (the Topeka Constitution men had voted three to one to exclude free negroes), and hence did not want slavery. Geary restored peace. Finding the courts idle, the laws disregarded, and the government almost paralyzed, he put energy into the administration. The treasury was bankrupt, and Kansas, without adequate Congressional appropriations, seemed to lack financial resources; but partly from his own purse, partly from other channels, he supplied funds. A man of action, he made rapid, sagacious decisions; a hard worker, he toiled until even his strong frame broke down. At the outset he had naturally leaned toward the proslavery groups which upheld the regular government, but intercourse with the settlers and shrewd observation quickly brought him to an impartial course.

Not all the credit for the pacification could be assigned to him. Some of it belonged to the Federal troops under Persifor F. Smith, some to the growing strength of the freesoil elements, some to Democratic Party necessities in 1856, and some to a general desire to get on with peaceful industry. Nevertheless, he had succeeded—and he should have had the consistent help of Washington.[27]

But beneath the surface ran heady currents. The Free State Party had resolved to maintain its policy of watchful non-cooperation. Immediately after the Presidential election in 1856, "Governor" Robinson, A. H. Reeder, and other leaders, conferring with Amos A. Lawrence and various Easterners, had decided that, while they must avoid a conflict with Federal authority, they would never surrender to the regular territorial government and accept its proslavery legislature. They would gather support in the North, continue

27 Gihon, *Geary and Kansas, passim.*

passive resistance to the obnoxious code of laws still in force, and bide their time. On Christmas Day, Robinson had resigned his office to serve the cause of freedom in a private capacity. One large section of the population, therefore, regarded Geary with watchful coolness. Another section, as he became impartial, grew rancorously hostile. The proslavery men, seeing in his strength and honesty an insuperable obstacle, resolved to pick a quarrel and drive him out. John Calhoun, late in 1856, removed his office from Wyandotte to Lecompton to direct the campaign. He and his associates filled the Lecompton *Union* with venomous articles. A considerable group (Geary later thought fifty sworn men) were ready if necessary to murder the governor.[28]

As a result of these machinations, hardly had 1857 begun when Geary was involved in a desperate series of struggles. He had demanded the removal of Chief Justice Lecompte, accusing him of neglect of duty, for he had held court only two or three weeks in six months; of partisan entanglements which destroyed the standing of the court; of dealing harshly with freesoil prisoners while neglecting the cases of proslavery men; and of releasing an indicted murderer on straw bail. Beyond doubt, Lecompte had been lazy and inefficient, while his party sympathies made him an agent of the proslavery interest. A small, fair-complexioned man, keen-eyed, indolent, and kindly, he was later to find his proper place as a routine attorney.[29] But he struck back on January 9, 1857, in a letter of thirty-five closely written foolscap sheets, defending himself and assailing Geary. And he naturally found support in Washington. While Secretary Marcy called on the governor for further explanations, the Senate failed to confirm Pierce's half-hearted nomination of a successor to Lecompte.

The fact was that President Pierce, irritated by the extralegal Topeka government, moved by Southern influences, and soured by failure, turned a hostile shoulder toward the governor who had served him so well in Kansas. His lukewarm course in nominating a successor to Lecompte without removing that judge had simply invited senatorial obstruction; and though Geary on January 12 sent him a convincing exposition of his policies, Pierce paid no attention to it. Naturally Judges Lecompte and Cato did all they could to thwart and weaken the governor. Geary wished to keep on amicable terms with the free State legislature which met early in the year in Topeka, and with whose leaders he had an understanding that it would transact no business. His hopes for general peace and amity were dashed, however, when a deputy marshal appeared with a writ from Judge Cato and arrested seven of the legislators.[30]

28 Gihon, 158–162; Geary to Pierce, January 12, 1857, Pierce Papers; N. Y. *Weekly Tribune, Herald, Times*; Topeka *Kansas Tribune*, January-March, 1857.
29 Gladstone, *Englishman in Kansas, passim*; Holloway, *History of Kansas*, 409, 410.
30 *National Intelligencer*, January 15, 1857; N. Y. *Weekly Tribune*, January-March, 1857.

Worst of all, the recognized territorial legislature, chosen the previous fall in a one-sided poll, came into open conflict with the governor. It met in Lecompton on January 12, ready for a desperate series of acts to maintain Kansas as fighting ground for slavery. Geary had prepared recommendations for a statesmanlike course. The time had come, declared his message, to purge the statute books of the intolerant laws which, denounced throughout the North, had been admitted wrongful even in the South. Specifically, he recommended the elimination of all test oaths; reform of the election laws with due safeguards for the ballot; repeal of the provisions which entrusted the choice of county officers to the legislature instead of to the people; and removal of all pretexts for the use of the militia against settlers. In fact, he wanted a wholesale overhauling of statutes which were full of inconsistencies, intolerance, and injustice. Let men forget the bloody clashes of the past year, he urged. "The dead, whom the madness of partisan fury has consigned to premature graves, cannot be recalled to life; the insults, the outrages, the robberies, and the murders, 'enough to stir a fever in the blood of age,' in this world of imperfection and guilt, can never be fully atoned for." The legislators should look solely to the future. They should cultivate a jealous regard for the sanctity of the ballot box, for the principles of self-government guaranteed in the organic act, for the election of all officers by the people, and for unqualified submission to the will of the majority.

Unhappily, the Lecompton leaders had determined to strike boldly and lawlessly for a slave State. Calhoun, Whitfield, Lecompte, and others were in touch with such national leaders as Senator Slidell, Speaker Orr, and Jacob Thompson. A slight gesture was made toward modification of the obnoxious statutes, not because Geary requested it, but because it was feared that Congress would act if the legislature did not. But it was very slight; the abolition of the test oath was the only important reform effected. All the legislation protecting and fostering slave property, all the inhuman penalties prescribed for writing, printing, or speaking against the institution of slavery, were kept intact.[31] Having made this gesture, the leaders turned to their plan for a census of inhabitants, a registry of voters, and an adroitly controlled constitutional convention. Action had to be expedited, for the incoming migration would soon swamp the proslavery element. On February 14, the legislature finished its work and sent Governor Geary a bill which horrified him and all other fair-minded persons.

A bill which made a mockery of democratic self-government, its purpose was to guarantee the proslavery forces a thoroughly packed and partisan constitutional convention. It must be remembered that nearly all county officers, having been chosen by the dishonestly elected legislature, were proslavery men. The measure provided that the county sheriffs and their deputies, predominantly

31 See Topeka *Kansas Tribune*, February 16, 1857.

proslavery agents, should enumerate in March the white residents, including all free male citizens of the United States over twenty-one. Thereupon the sheriffs should file in the office of the probate judges complete lists of qualified voters in the various counties. Following this, the boards of county commissioners, also mainly proslavery men, should choose judges of election. Then, on the third Monday in June, delegates should be chosen to the convention; and, finally, this body should sit at Lecompton in September. Everybody knew that the provision that none but men resident on March 15 could vote would exclude a multitude of new settlers, mainly antislavery, who were expected that spring. Everybody knew that the sheriffs who enumerated the settlers, the probate judges who helped prepare voting lists, and the county commissioners who chose election judges were for most part Democrats who wanted to see Kansas a slave State.

Most objectionable of all, perhaps, was the fact that the convention was to be given a completely free hand; for the measure made no provision for submitting the constitution to the people. Indeed, when the bill was passing through the Council, one member admitted that the design was to avoid submission; for he suggested a clause to provide for the contingency that Congress might return the constitution for a popular vote.[32]

In this and other legislation the proslavery men showed their eagerness to flout Geary's wishes. Their speeches were full of defiance and insult. When in mid-February the governor paid a visit to the house, one excited sheriff, W. T. Sherrard of Douglas County, a florid young man of reckless character, waylaid him in the antechamber, cursed him, and, when Geary, ignoring his presence, walked past, spat twice on his back. Had the defenseless governor, who was unaware of the indignity until told of it, showed resentment, Sherrard would have killed him. Citizens of Lecompton promptly held a meeting to denounce the insult offered to Geary. Sherrard attended and grew violent. Suddenly he and others began firing, and, when the smoke cleared, he was dead. "I saw Sherrard leap into the air as a bullet struck him in the forehead," said one spectator. Next day Geary vetoed the convention bill.

The governor's arguments against it were unanswerable. He declared the whole movement premature. For twenty-five or thirty thousand Kansans—burdened with heavy debts, their public buildings unfinished, their schools, courthouses, and jails mere blueprints, the very title to their lands in great part insecure—to cast off the fostering care of the national government, ready to furnish financial and military assistance, was folly. Though Minnesota had become a thriving Territory of 180,000 people, it was only in recent weeks that her governor had urged steps to form a State constitution. Michigan had re-

32 The text of the bill and of Geary's veto are in the N. Y. *Tribune*, March 14, 1857. See also files of St. Louis *Missouri Democrat*, January-March, 1857.

mained a Territory for five years after she gained a population equal to that of a Congressional district. Why the haste in Kansas? And even if the movement for statehood was accepted, the pending bill was flagrantly defective. It left all the preliminary activity to county officers who were chosen by and subservient to one party. It contained no such precaution as the provision in the Toombs bill that five impartial commissioners should correct the census of voters and take additional measures to secure a fair election of delegates. Its failure to authorize a popular vote on the constitution was unforgivable, for, with scarcely an exception, State constitutions which had been made in controversial circumstances had been submitted to popular ratification.

The legislature quickly passed the bill over Geary's veto; and as it did so, the atmosphere in the frowsy, muddy river town of Lecompton, its streets full of rough men, grew more threatening than ever. Tough rowdies with bowie knives and revolvers profanely boasted that if the governor remained they would take his life. Citizens laid bets that Geary would be assassinated within forty days.[33] As the Lawrence *Herald of Freedom* said, the fire-eating leaders of the pro-slavery party, anxious to be rid of so troublesome an obstacle, "coveted his life's blood, and sought every opportunity to take it." The alarmed governor had written General Persifor F. Smith at Fort Leavenworth on February 9, requesting two additional companies of dragoons to meet a conspiracy to breach the peace. But Smith, who regarded Geary with jealous antagonism, and who at the moment bubbled over with gratitude to President Pierce for his recent promotion to brigadier, thought that his orders gave him discretion to deny armed support, and did so. In a sharp letter, he scoffed at Geary's fears. Thus left without Presidential support or proper military assistance, the governor felt powerless. Overwork and overstrain had brought him to the verge of collapse, and on March 4 he mailed his resignation to Washington.

Though some observers thought that Geary should have stood his ground, the more sensible view is that he did well to think of his safety and return east to arouse public sentiment to the critical situation in the Territory. He penned a manly farewell address to the citizens of Kansas.[34] Then, gathering his books and papers, and accompanied by his secretary, Dr. Gihon, he set out for Washington. On March 21 he was at Willard's, where he found himself the lion of the freesoil element in the city, his room thronged with visitors. He had paused in St. Louis to give the *Democrat* an interview, and that journal promptly sounded the tocsin in a widely reprinted warning to the nation. Proslavery intransigence, it declared, had undertaken to pack the approaching convention, and to drag a manacled Kansas before Congress with a slavery constitution:

33 N. Y. *Weekly Tribune*, March 28, 1857.
34 *National Intelligencer*, March 21, 1857.

Every contingency is provided for in this compact and complicated scheme. From the taking of the census by the county sheriffs to the organization of the convention, through the graded surveillance of election judges, probate judges, etc., the felon legislature has provided as effectually for getting the desired result as Louis Napoleon did for getting himself elected Emperor. . . .

In our humble judgment, the Kansas question has never worn the ominous aspect and the colossal proportions which it is now beginning to assume. It is impossible to conceive that the people of the North will acquiesce in the final triumph of a system of fraud, violence, and ruthless tyranny—equally impossible to conceive that the slavery extensionists will forego their purposes; and therefore the prompt and vigorous intervention of the President is demanded by the most serious considerations.[35]

[V]

During late March, excitement ran high in Washington over Geary and his revelations. The proslavery leaders of the South, delighted to have him out of the way, treated him with cool contempt. Buchanan, who knew that he was a political liability and who had already determined to send out a new governor, was pleased to have his resignation. But Republican members of Congress, free-soil journalists, and not a few old Democratic friends made the most of him. The Kansas ordeal, they noted, had laid a heavy imprint upon the man. A heavy brown beard covered his face; his high forehead and sharp-cut, handsome features were blanched with a pallor which told of overwork, worry, and confinement; he complained of ill-health.[36] Secretary Cass gave him a cordial private interview. On March 23, he sat with the Cabinet for two hours, making a detailed report on Kansas affairs. His antagonists, Calhoun, Maclean, and others, however, had hurried from Lecompton to give the Administration a different view, while Lecompte and Cato were busy writing letters to their Southern friends.[37]

Although Geary made no impression on the Directory, his repeated interviews did tell heavily with Northern opinion. He reiterated that the great majority of Kansans were conservative, peace-loving folk; that small combinations of crafty, passionate, unscrupulous men had deliberately fomented discord; that the fieriest proslavery leaders were actual foes of the Union; and that their scheme to use Kansas to disrupt the nation, while thwarted for the time being, was still alive and dangerous. General Smith, who had agreed with this, had written Buchanan on February 3 that the disunion plot had been laid in the capital: "A plan was organized in Washington to force Kansas to be a slave

35 St. Louis *Missouri Democrat*, March 18, 1857. The editor, declaring that the main features of the new constitution had already been devised in the proslavery Blue Lodges, urged honest Kansans to boycott the convention.
36 N. Y. *Evening Post*, March 23, 24, 1857.
37 N. Y. *Weekly Tribune*, March 28, 1857.

State, but if the effort to do it in the manner there proposed failed, it should at least produce a civil war ending in prompt dissolution of the Union." [38]

President Pierce, added Geary, had promised to support him with the Treasury and the army. Instead, Geary had been compelled to pay $12,000 from his own pocket to maintain his government; his request for two cavalry companies to meet an emergency had been scornfully denied; the judges had been allowed to thwart him at every step; and his life had been in constant jeopardy. Even his mail had been opened by proslavery officials, and letters to him frequently destroyed. Calhoun's liege-tool Maclean had boasted of suppressing two bushels of correspondence! Geary related that his letter of resignation, a profound secret between himself and his secretary, had not been in the post office an hour before its contents were the gossip of every Lecompton barroom. He warned hearers of the grave danger that Kansas, before snow flew again, would have a slavery constitution.[39]

These statements made Geary appear to most Northerners a deeply wronged man, and to most Southerners a prejudiced, malicious foe. Dr. Gihon's vividly written book on their joint experiences was shortly selling briskly. His denunciations of the Calhounite plot to dominate Kansas were the more telling because he had gone to that Territory with his sympathies on the slavery side. A fresh wave of alarm spread across the free States. It was nowhere felt more strongly than among Geary's fellow Pennsylvanians, who knew enough of him to respect his honesty. Even staunch Democrats are irritated, wrote one of Jere Black's correspondents. "It is manifest that unless 'order reigns in Kansas' we may soon add Pennsylvania to the domains of Northern fanaticism." [40]

Nobody was placed in a more difficult predicament by the new Kansas crisis than Senator Douglas and his squatter sovereignty allies. Their doctrine had been made a judicial nullity by the Dred Scott decision. Was it now to be made a practical absurdity by Calhoun and his schemers? This was a question of burning import to Douglas, for with a new election for his Senate seat coming on next year, his political future depended on the answer.

Inevitably, Douglas and his school had received the Dred Scott opinions with outward complaisance but inward irritation and antagonism. The principle subsequently termed the Freeport doctrine, the doctrine that the local police must control any system of labor, was already widely accepted by Northern Democrats. Geary had espoused it. In a letter of January, 1857, defending his record, he remarked that, the disunionists having been foiled, "the people here will soon be in the complete enjoyment of their sovereign rights, and 'sovereignty of the

38 Smith to Buchanan, February 3, 1857; Buchanan Papers.
39 N. Y. *Weekly Tribune*, March 28, N. Y. *Evening Post*, March 28, 29, 1857.
40 J. R. Jones to Black, March 26, 1857, Black Papers.

people' will hereafter be . . . the brightest jewel of the Democratic crown."
He had added that from a thorough acquaintance with every part of Kansas, he
knew that at least three-fourths of the actual settlers wished Kansas to be a free
State.[41] Buchanan's friend William Bigler had also enunciated the Freeport idea.
Writing Buchanan as 1856 closed, he had declared that sooner or later the popular will would decide the slavery issue in the Territory, and that the longer the
decision was deferred, the more certainly it would be for freedom.

Then, again, whatever diversity of opinion may exist as to the right of a
territorial legislature to reject or embrace the institution, all concede that there
is no power on earth to make a territorial legislature pass laws, or make police
arrangements for the protection of slave property—and that without such protection it cannot exist. . . . Hence I have said that I believe the people can *control* the subject. I have never used the terms *establish* or *abolish.*[42]

If, however, Calhoun, Maclean, and Lecompte packed a convention and
foisted a proslavery constitution on unwilling Kansas without a referendum, how
could Douglas ever talk of popular sovereignty again? How could he hold up
his head before the Illinois voters?

Douglas was therefore deeply alarmed by the reckless course of the Kansas
legislature. He had wished to see the obnoxious laws on the statute book repealed, and had made this plain to Calhoun as an old Springfield friend, long
under his influence. Calhoun had sent him an explicit promise that it would be
done, yet some of the worst laws were left untouched.[43] Again, Douglas had
been in no hurry to see Kansas write a constitution and apply for statehood. He
believed the population as yet insufficient for this step. When the proper time
came, the instrument should be drafted by a truly representative body, and
submitted to the people. Instead, the legislators, rushing into premature action,
had driven a forty-mule team through all representative principles. With much
uneasiness, Douglas felt himself betrayed by Calhoun. This headstrong fellow,
after going to Kansas as a moderate, and taking some sensible steps to procure
the abandonment of a slavery party in favor of an Administration party which
should include freesoil Democrats, slavery Democrats, and former Whigs, had
yielded to his associates and rapidly grown violent and vindictive.

For the Senator to aid and abet such defiance of the popular will would be
political suicide. He had staked his future on the Kansas-Nebraska Act; he had
given the North a solemn pledge that the voice of the people would be held
sacred; he had warned the South that Kansas would almost certainly become
free. He was the last man in the world to let himself be duped by Calhoun and

41 Geary to Buchanan, January, 1857, Buchanan Papers.
42 William Bigler, December, 1856, Buchanan Papers; Bigler had just toured Kansas.
43 John Calhoun, January 26, 1857, Douglas Papers; he wrote that the legislature "has the
subject in hand."

Lecompte, or to be made the tool of the Southern leaders advising them from Washington.

While Geary boldly placed his views before the country, Douglas and his fast ally, Senator Charles E. Stuart of Michigan decided that the legislature's work ought to be repudiated. Congress should take charge anew, pass an enabling act, and scrupulously supervise the whole process of State-making. Stuart, visiting New York late in March, was impressed by the exasperation of intelligent Democrats in the metropolis. If the scheme for a packed convention went through, multitudes of them would turn to the Republicans. Kansas could probably never be admitted under a constitution framed by such a body, but whether it was admitted or not, the outcome would be disastrous. Utter destruction awaited the Democratic Party in the North and Northwest unless his and Douglas's plan for heading off Calhoun and his crew by an enabling act was carried. The wisest and most prudent men in New York, wrote Stuart, agreed on this:

> You and I can do this thing. We can bring our party in the Senate to the support of this ground, if we unflinchingly stand by it ourselves.
>
> There are two reasons why I shall do it. The first is that it is right in itself, which ought always to be reason enough. And the other is, that *it is the only mode in which, what is left of the party in the northwest*, can be saved. The success of this measure, or our political burial, will be the certain result.
>
> I have seen several from our section, and they all say that the excitement is increasing both in amount and intensity in consequence of the . . . inaugural and the Dred Scott decision. . . . I know there is strong feeling in certain quarters of the great strength of the Administration. I hope it may prove so. But at the same time I am forced to the opposite conclusion by past and passing events. My wish is otherwise, but my *opinion* is, it cannot sustain itself, throughout its term. . . .
>
> But, sir, it will prove true as holy writ . . . on one side there is salvation, on the other inevitable ruin.[44]

Immediate action, however, was beyond Douglas and Stuart. Congress was not in session—the Senate, held for confirmations, adjourned March 13. Would the proslavery men in Kansas stay their hand? Douglas, returning to Illinois, had to content himself with a speech at Springfield (June 12) in which he interpreted the Dred Scott decision in his own way. A master's right to take slaves into any Territory was now unassailable, he said. Yet "it necessarily remains a barren and worthless right unless sustained, protected, and enforced by appropriate police regulations and local legislation, prescribing adequate remedies for its violation. These regulations and remedies must necessarily depend entirely upon the will and wishes of the people of the Territory."

44 Stuart to Douglas, March 29, 1857, Douglas Papers.

Alas for Douglas! In this same speech, for partisan reasons, he declared that the law under which Kansans three days later were to elect a constitutional convention "is believed to be just and fair in all its objects and provisions." [45]

[VI]

The new President, many men were saying, could write a bold and honest record in Kansas. But would he and his Cabinet insist on fair measures, or would they accept the scheme for a fraudulent census, a one-sided election, and a controlled convention?

Before Geary reached Washington, the President had found his successor in Robert J. Walker of Mississippi, the man who had almost been made Secretary of State. Doubtless Jacob Thompson, remembering the suppressed letter, grimaced over the appointment. This versatile, ambitious, skillful man, always restlessly self-assertive, accepted the governorship with some reluctance. Kansas was a political graveyard where three governors had failed; the meagre salary was less than Walker could make from a single legal case; life on the Kansas border was uncomfortable and risky. Mrs. Walker, of a prominent Pennsylvania family, related to the Baches and Dallases, was equally inclined to shrink. Buchanan held out the prospect, however, that Walker could perform a great national service, could soon return to Washington as Senator from Kansas, and could even gain laurels which would enhance his claims to the Presidency. Douglas and others seconded the plea. Finally, after making several conditions, Walker—who had a truly patriotic zeal in public service—accepted on March 26. One stipulation was that his friend, former Representative F. P. Stanton of Tennessee, should be made territorial secretary, and that General William S. Harney, then in Florida, should be placed in command in Kansas, to remain while disorder threatened. Another, of the first importance, was laid down in his letter of acceptance; he took office on the understanding that Buchanan and the Cabinet "cordially concur in the opinion expressed by me, that the actual bona fide residents of Kansas, by a fair and regular vote, unaffected by fraud or violence, must be permitted, in adopting their State Constitution, to decide for themselves what shall be their social institutions."

No better man could have been chosen. Most people liked Walker's personality: an indefatigable, wide-awake, nervous little man, he had a soft-spoken, ingratiating address that was almost feline and that lent itself to his gift for finesse. Though sometimes fussy and excitable, when aroused he had the heart of a lion. Nor did anybody ever question his abilities. The precocious son of a well-known Pittsburgh jurist, head of his class at the University of Pennsylvania,

45 Milton, *Eve of Conflict*, 260; N. Y. *Times*, June 23, N. Y. *Tribune*, June 25, 1857.

and a leader at twenty-two in the convention which placed the Keystone Democracy behind Jackson in 1824, he had once seemed destined to a career in his native State. Then in 1826 he had followed a brother to Mississippi. Combining law, land speculation, and politics, he had quickly made his mark in that still untamed State. He was a strong Union man in nullification days. In the middle thirties, by virtue of President Jackson's endorsement, the astute campaign management of William M. Gwin, and his own magnetism, he won a seat in the Senate. A tireless worker and a ready speaker, unafraid to cross blades even with Clay, he had achieved national prominence before Polk lifted him to the Treasury. Despite chronic ill-health, he had proved his ability to solve difficult problems. Nobody had done more to make Polk President; nobody had labored more shrewdly for the annexation of Texas. The principal author of the tariff bill which bore his name, he had penned in its defense the best state paper on commerce and revenue since Gallatin's day. He had devised astute measures to finance the Mexican War.

It was too much to expect that radical freesoilers would welcome the appointment of a Mississippian of such marked expansionist views. The New York *Tribune* grumbled because all of the territorial officers—the governor, secretary, and judges—would now be Southerners. Schuyler Colfax believed that Walker would accept the Calhoun scheme and send a slave State constitution to Washington, while Amos A. Lawrence was certain that his real aim was to let Kansas go and to create a new slave State south of it.[46] Objective comment, however, approved of the choice. As a Northerner by birth, a Southerner by adoption, and a Union man by conviction, Walker seemed as likely to take statesmanlike views as anybody. The ever-fearful freesoilers should have remembered that Southern radicals had barred his appointment to a high Cabinet place because he had always been a strong nationalist and a believer in gradual emancipation. The Washington correspondent of the New York *Times* printed an accurate estimate:

He is a thinking machine which works badly sometimes, and which has once or twice been turned to awkward uses; but his power, industry, and discrimination, keen insight into the motives of men, and laudable ambition to stand well before the country cannot be questioned. I urged in conversation today with a gentleman who stands high in Mr. Buchanan's confidence his identification with the ultra-Southern interests. . . . "You do not know," said he, "of whom you are talking. I predict that if Mr. Walker goes to Kansas, he will unravel the whole Atchison web, and pave the way for the admission of Kansas as a free State in such a manner that the mouths of those who have hitherto sympathized with border ruffianism will be effectually and forever stopped."

46 Colfax, April 8, Lawrence, May 16, 1857, Robinson Papers, Univ. of Kansas. For a succinct appraisal of Walker, see H. Donaldson Jordan, "A Politician of Expansion: Robert J. Walker," *Miss. Valley Hist. Review*, V (1918), 158–189.

Mr. Walker disowns all partisanship with Davis and men of that clique and calibre. He has professed a determination, since November last, as I am told by his intimate associates and friends, to sustain the Administration in its endeavors to build up a Union party in antagonism to the *per se* secessionist doctrinarians, who have flourished so gloriously under the regime of President Pierce.[47]

As a matter of fact, before his appointment Walker had placed on record his belief that Kansas was certain to become a free State. In his widely circulated *Appeal for the Union*, a campaign pamphlet dated six weeks before election day in 1856, he had based this prediction on several distinct grounds. Soil, climate, and production favored free labor. So did the flow of population, the North possessing superior numbers, greater human mobility, a steady European immigration, and freedom from any apprehension as to the safety of its property. Finally, he wrote, slavery could not long persist in any State against the constant agitation of even a powerful minority. It was also an important fact that a special tie existed between Walker and Douglas.

"You must go, Bob," Douglas had said, in effect. "I feel intensely on this. The whole success of the Kansas-Nebraska Act in that Territory is to a great extent dependent on your consenting to go. I beg it of you." [48]

Nor could Walker's emphasis in his letter of acceptance on the right of Kansans to decide their institutions by fair popular vote be overlooked; an emphasis which was echoed by Buchanan in the instructions he gave to the new governor. "The institutions of Kansas must be established by the votes of the people of Kansas," wrote the President, "unawed or uninterrupted by force or fraud." All alien voters must be excluded. When the new constitution was submitted to the people, "they must be protected in the exercise of their right of voting for or against that instrument, and the fair expression of the popular will must not be interrupted by fraud or violence." [49]

Meanwhile, in Kansas a free-state gathering on March 10 had adopted a policy on non-cooperation with the regular territorial government, which meant abstention from the polls in territorial elections; although some conservative freesoil men inside and outside Kansas condemned this decision. The Lawrence *Herald of Freedom* declared that the gathering should at least have waited to see how the course of the Administration would develop. It believed that the freesoil men would have done better to fling their full strength into the elections, rigged though they were. The opposite course gave the proslavery conspirators a clear field; "a proslavery constitution will be submitted to Congress as a result of that action, when, had a different policy prevailed, a different result might

47 Washington corr. N. Y. *Times*, March 26, 1857.
48 Walker's testimony, Covode Committee; 36th Cong., 1st Sess., House Report No. 648, pp. 105, 106.
49 Walker's instructions received May 17, published *National Intelligencer*, July 16, 1857.

have been attained." But in view of the way in which proslavery leaders had ridden roughshod over Geary's veto, and in view also of their patent determination to manipulate both the census of voters and the election of convention delegates, the refusal of most freesoil men to participate had been inevitable.

Summer heat and humidity closed down on the Potomac. Congress had gone home; most of the great houses were shuttered; the President and Cabinet toiled on with appointments and routine business. After the thunderclap of the Dred Scott decision, the season promised to be quiet. Most people forgot about the dark plot of Calhoun, Maclean, and Lecompte, and the outraged protests of Geary. The New York *Herald* and *Times* were busy praising Buchanan's Kansas policy, and together with the Washington *Union* were predicting its success. Only the doubters waited anxiously for news from the valley of the Missouri.

6

Melodrama in Kansas

HUNDREDS of people, a tense, expectant throng, had gathered in front of the Cincinnati House in Lawrence. The sun, just sinking in the west, threw its level rays on grimy farmers, wagoners, and blacksmiths in checked shirts and blue jeans, on storekeepers wearing aprons, on black-coated doctors and lawyers, and on women in sunbonnets holding children by the hand. Many stalwart fellows had knives in their belts or revolvers strapped to their waists. An impatient murmur arose, until "Governor" Robinson emerged upon the hotel steps with a portly, dignified gentleman of middle age—Frederick P. Stanton, former Congressman from Tennessee, now secretary and acting-governor of Kansas. He had preceded Robert J. Walker to the Territory, coming by steamboat to Kansas City and Lecompton. Thence he had ridden down to Lawrence, taken tea with Robinson, and let it be known that he would make a speech. With the ease of a practiced orator, he began talking of Walker, the Union, and the territorial government.

Suddenly a fierce shout burst from the crowd: "Never! Never!" Stanton faced them defiantly. He had said that he meant to enforce the laws of the much-hated "legitimate" legislature (to free State men the "bogus" legislature) and to collect the taxes it had levied. Tactfully retreating a little, he remarked that what he really had at heart was the enforcement of Federal law and Federal authority. An assenting murmur arose. "We're ready to obey the United States," shouted some. "Always have been," came other voices. But a few minutes later Stanton declared again that they must accept the territorial laws, and again a thunderous clamor checked him: "Never! Never!"

Then Stanton began to recite an appropriate passage from *Hiawatha:* the speech of the Great Manitou exhorting the Indians to cease their battling, wash the war paint from their faces, carve pipes from the redstone quarry, smoke the calumet of peace, and live together as brothers. Halfway through it, his memory failed and he broke down. Mrs. Gates, keeper of the hotel, hastily brought forth her copy of Longfellow. She held a candle to the page, and he went on:

I am weary of your quarrels,
Weary of your wars and bloodshed,
Weary of your prayers for vengeance,
Of your wranglings and dissensions;
All your strength is in your union,
All your danger is in discord;
Therefore be at peace henceforward,
And as brothers live together.

At nine o'clock Stanton sat down with the free State men to a bounteous meal, and the rest of the evening passed harmoniously.[1]

Stanton represented as happy a choice as Walker; shrewd, alert, courageous, he had just been described by a group of Tennesseans recommending him for a Cabinet post as the most prompt, reliable, and skillful attorney in the State. An honest man, he believed in the right of Kansans to a free and fair charting of their own course. Like Walker, he meant to insist on a square deal. Even more than Walker, he was ready to fight a crooked deal. Though he supported slavery and had voted against the abolition of slave-trading in the District of Columbia, he had often said that the institution could never flourish on the Kansas plains. Even while he was explaining that Governor Walker and he would enforce territorial laws, he declared that he would protect the ballot box as the remedy for all evils and would demand that both sides grant a political amnesty. Calhoun and Maclean had returned in a truculent frame of mind from Washington, where they had conferred with Jacob Thompson, Jefferson Davis, and other Southerners; but Stanton faced them coldly—he meant to be neutral and fair.[2]

Taking up quarters at Lecompton in the building formerly occupied by Governor Geary, Stanton began to urge free State voters to take part in the June election for a constitutional convention. His arguments were promptly challenged by "Governor" Robinson and fourteen other free State leaders in a letter explaining how unfair that election would be. The census and registry of voters already carried out had omitted large numbers of free State settlers, while including many names of non-residents. The freesoil men would participate in the election, therefore, only if certain conditions were met. First, in each township or district, two persons, one chosen by the free State and one by the slavery party, should act together in correcting the registry. Second, in each precinct,

1 MS address, J. C. Horton, December 2, 1903; Lane Papers, Univ. of Kansas; *National Intelligencer*, May 7, 1857; N. Y. *Tribune*, May 9, 1857.
2 Stanton reached Kansas on April 15. See his letters, Sen. Exec. Doc. 8 (35th Cong., 1st Sess.); L. W. Spring, *History of Kansas*, 210 ff.; *Missouri Republican*, April-June, 1857. Stanton and Maclean had a conference on April 24. Maclean justified the interference of Missourians in the spring election of 1855, demanded that the free State men be made to submit to the regular or "bogus" legislature, and intimated that Walker and Stanton should be guided by Calhoun and himself. Lawrence correspondence, N. Y. *Evening Post* dated April 24; *Missouri Republican*, May 5, 1857.

four election judges should act, two named by the free State and two by the slavery party; and at least three must sign the election certificate of every delegate to the convention. Stanton replied that as acting governor he had no authority to meet these conditions. He had no power over the probate judges who alone were authorized to correct the voting lists, and he could not appoint four election judges, for the law provided that the county commissioners should name three. Admitting that the registry was defective, he blamed the free State men for boycotting it, and called upon them to help correct the lists by sending in sworn statements.[3]

In this attitude Stanton agreed with Senator Douglas, who, after saying at Springfield that the election arrangements seemed fair, added that if any group of voters avoided the polls, the responsibility must rest "on those who, for partisan purposes, will sacrifice the principles they profess to cherish." Both men later rued their hasty statements. They had reason to learn just how grossly unjust the census and registration were. What were the facts? Kansas then had thirty-eight counties. The partisan officers deputed for the task took no census at all in nineteen counties, so that no apportionment of delegates could be made for them. In fifteen counties they made no registry of voters, so that these areas, including some of the oldest organized counties in Kansas, were entirely disfranchised.[4] No voting precinct was established in the town of Lawrence. Any citizen of that free State center who wished to follow Stanton's advice would have to ride twelve miles to vote. In such places as Leavenworth, prominent free State men were left off the registry lists. To be sure, radical freesoilers helped to block a proper enumeration; but the proslavery men were chiefly to blame.[5]

Walker soon followed the secretary westward. On his way, he stopped in New York long enough to attend a dinner given by Henry J. Raymond of the *Times*, George N. Sanders, and other friends. He told them he was determined that Kansas should have a full, free, and solemn referendum upon any constitution that might be framed, after a fair census of all the true inhabitants of the Territory at the time; and to this he pledged himself both as an officer conscious of his duty, and as a gentleman sensitive of his honor. Any attempt by a special group to impose upon the Territory a constitution unsanctioned by popular vote would be a usurpation and wrong which could not be tolerated for a moment. His statements got into the press and were applauded.[6] At the end of May he reached Kansas and made his first important public appearance there in strange company. He had landed at Leavenworth. Clattering into Lawrence with his staff on May 26, he rejoined in that town three New Englanders who had been

3 Kansas correspondence in N. Y. *Weekly Tribune*, May 16, 1857.
4 See details in Walker's letter of resignation, December 15, 1857.
5 Quindaro correspondence, *Missouri Democrat*, April 24, 1857.
6 *National Intelligencer*, May 16, 1857.

on his steamboat coming up the Missouri—Senator Henry Wilson, the venerable poet-preacher John Pierpont, and the abolitionist and philanthropist Samuel Gridley Howe. All three were to speak in the Unitarian Church, and some two thousand men and women, with a band, gathered to do them honor. Governor Walker consented to attend and spoke briefly, saying that his Kansas policy would be outlined in his inaugural next day.

That inaugural address, long, well-written, and conciliatory, was delivered at Lecompton. Walker necessarily recognized the enactments of the regular legislature, and said that all of them that were constitutional would be enforced. Urging participation in the imminent election of a constitutional convention, he expressed confidence that its handiwork would be submitted to the people for a fair vote. He pointed out the importance of removing the slavery issue from Congress and the Presidential elections. Most striking of all, he declared that the entry or exclusion of slavery would ultimately be determined by climatic law, for an isothermal line, regulating labor, productions, and profit or loss, seemed to have made Kansas unsuitable for slavery. If it was found that the institution could not exist there, Kansas must nevertheless recognize that she had a constitutional duty to other States, and particularly Missouri; she must yield up their fugitives. The address had been prepared with patient care (parts of it being rewritten many times), and had been shown to numerous friends. Buchanan had seen at least some sections of it, and Walker had let Douglas read it as he passed through Chicago.[7] This fact lent special significance to his emphatic warning

7 N. Y. *Weekly Tribune*, June 6, 1857; Nichols, *Disruption of Amer. Democracy*, 108.

that "in no contingency will Congress admit Kansas as a slave state or free state, unless a majority of the people shall first have fairly and freely decided this question for themselves by a direct vote on the adoption of the Constitution, excluding all fraud or violence."

[I]

Governor Walker's main intent was simple and logical: to bring Kansas by peaceful steps to the position of a freesoil but Democratic State. He rapidly confirmed his impression that climate, crops, and conditions of immigration made slavery impossible. As he wrote Buchanan, perhaps four hundred slaves had been held there the previous fall, but, since the severe winter with its icy gales and temperatures of twenty below zero, about half had been taken away. The permanent existence of slavery was preposterous; a very large majority even of settlers and investors from the South were against it because it would reduce the value of their holdings.[8] Walker hoped, however, that Kansas would become as heavily Democratic as California. Thus it might forge a strong link between the Northern freesoil Democrats and the Southern slavery Democrats, and thus Missouri would escape the calamity of finding an aggressive new abolitionist State as neighbor. He knew that Douglas shared his views, and believed that Buchanan did so.

His immediate aim, therefore, was to create a middle party of "national Democratic principles," neither ardently proslavery nor bitterly antislavery. This was a sensible aim, which harmonized with actual conditions. The great majority of Kansas settlers, drawn from the border and middle States, were freesoil on an anti-negro rather than antislavery basis; they did not want black men in Kansas. They were naturally conservative in temper.[9] Such a middle party would stand equally against the Calhoun-Lecompte faction who wanted to make Kansas slave soil, and the Jim Lane men who talked abolitionism and defied Federal authority. Upon this party, wrote Walker's private secretary to the New York Times, the destiny of Kansas must ultimately rest.[10] Talking with citizens and shrewdly appraising the situation, Walker found the prospect encouraging. A month after his arrival, he sent Buchanan a perceptive sketch of the political forces:

That a vast majority of the people of Kansas are with me is certain, but there are restless men on both sides who desire revolution. . . .
There are several parties here: First, Free State Democrats composed of men who supported your election; second, Proslavery Democrats who supported

8　June 28, 1857; Buchanan Papers.
9　See Malin, Legend of '56, Ch. 30, on the conservative triumph.
10　Dated Lecompton, June 3, 1857.

your election; third, Slavery men (a small party, mostly Know-Nothings) who opposed your election and supported Fillmore; fourth, Republicans who supported Frémont. With me, are, first, all the Free State Democrats, constituting a plurality of the settlers; second, a majority of the masses of the Proslavery Democrats, but a considerable portion of the leaders are against me, on the point of submitting the Constitution to the people. The Proslavery Know-Nothings [are] against me generally. The Republicans [are] against me generally, but three of their papers including the most influential are against the Topeka movement if the convention will submit the constitution to the people.

The relative strength of the respective parties is: First Free State Democrats, second Republicans, third Proslavery Democrats, fourth (very small) Proslavery Know-Nothings. Supposing the whole number of settlers to be 24,000, the relative numbers would probably be as follows: Free State Democrats 9,000, Republicans 8,000, Proslavery Democrats 6,500, Proslavery Know-Nothings 500.[11]

His initial success in handling the free State men encouraged Walker in his undertaking. On June 9, their "legislature" was to meet at Topeka under the guidance of Robinson and reckless Jim Lane. Governor Walker visited the town three days earlier to deliver a warning speech. If this pretended legislature should pass laws and try to put them into force, he said, the upshot would be a direct collision with the national government. If the free Staters behaved sensibly, peace would be preserved, and he would see to it that actual residents of Kansas managed territorial affairs—that is, he would exclude Missouri interlopers. In particular, he promised that if the constitutional convention tried to evade a popular vote on its work, he would take spirited action. "I will join you, fellow citizens, in opposition to their course. And I doubt not that one much higher than I, the chief magistrate of the Union, will join you." [12] But for this fresh pledge of popular submission, Walker assured Buchanan, the Topeka "legislature" would assuredly have passed a complete code of laws, and put them into operation in a large majority of counties. This would have united the freesoil Democrats and Republicans, and brought on a sanguinary civil war between them and proslavery Democrats.[13]

As it was, the free State "legislature" took a lenitive course. It met on a lovely spring morning, the sun flooding the rolling prairies and turning the little Kansas River to silver. Robinson delivered a long message, reviewing events since the pillage of Lawrence a year earlier, answering the governor's inaugural, and pointing out that no isothermal line could stop the machinations of infatuated slavery propagandists.[14] Jim Lane made an astoundingly conservative

11 Lecompton, June 28, 1857; Buchanan Papers.
12 Spring, *History of Kansas*, 213; George W. Brown, *Reminiscences of Gov. R. J. Walker*, 42–44.
13 Walker to Buchanan, June 28, 1857; Buchanan Papers.
14 For complete text see N. Y. *Weekly Tribune*, June 27, 1857.

speech. The gathering then passed resolutions denouncing the approaching constitutional convention, and adjourned. Nothing was done to harass Walker, who, with a carriage full of aides and ladies, bustled diplomatically from group to group on the initial day, trying, said critics, to emasculate the freesoil cause with wily cunning.[15]

Even without Walker's tactful mixture of promises and warnings, the free State men would not have dared to erect their government to full stature. They knew that they would have met implacable hostility from the Executive and Congress. They knew, too, that since Frémont's defeat, opinion among their Republican supporters in the east had altered. As Schuyler Colfax wrote Robinson, a multitude of Northerners believed that if two-thirds the people of Kansas were freesoilers, they should rely upon their own strength, try voting at least once, and attempt to capture the regular machinery of government. You will be playing against loaded dice, declared Colfax, but most Republicans do not know it, and will hesitate to act as auxiliaries to a Topeka government in defying Washington.[16] A collision might fatally weaken the free State cause.

Such New England conservatives as Amos A. Lawrence took this view. Raymond vigorously expressed it in his New York *Times*. While old Whig organs like the *National Intelligencer* and Boston *Courier* scolded the free State leaders for their contumacious non-cooperation with the Federal government, the redoubtable Whig leader Thomas Ewing denounced them as actuated by folly and ambition. If they provoked civil war, they would be overthrown by Federal arms. They had nothing to do but take possession of the government in legitimate fashion, he wrote, but this would not suit Horace Greeley and others who wished to capitalize on continued trouble-making. In Kansas itself, a majority of free State newspapers were against efforts to put the Topeka government into active operation.[17] The strongest journal in the Territory, the *Herald of Freedom*, which claimed a weekly circulation of about 8,000 copies, wanted to drop the free State or Topeka constitution in favor of determined action to take control of the regular government; and it declared that at least five-sixths of the free State settlers north of the Kansas River favored this conservative policy.[18]

While the fiery Lane and stubborn Robinson were not yet ready for cooperation with the regular government, they knew they had to stop short of obstruction. They must not resist the regular authorities. Their program was to wait and see. Walker nevertheless deserved credit for the firmness and skill with which he had brought their irregular legislature to its milk-and-water conclusions.

The governor's real difficulty lay with the other extreme—the proslavery

15 Topeka correspondence, N. Y. *Tribune*, June 9, 10, 12, 1857.
16 April 8, 1857; Robinson Papers, Kansas State Hist. Soc.
17 Thomas Ewing to his son, July 23, 1857; Ewing Papers.
18 Lawrence *Herald of Freedom*, July 18, 1857.

men. He had written Buchanan that some restless leaders desired revolution; and this meant Calhoun, Maclean, and Lecompte as much as Jim Lane and other violent freesoilers. He had written that a considerable number of leaders were against him on popular submission of the new constitution; and this was stating the situation mildly.

Actually they were belligerently defiant, and they meant to have their own way. The evening after Walker read his inaugural in the straggling village of Lecompton, placed on the bluffs looking north over the Kansas River, a banquet had been held for him at the best hotel. He sat at table with Calhoun on one side, Maclean on the other, and a roomful of proslavery Democrats in front of him. Whiskey-drinking, which had filled the day, continued. When toasts began, Calhoun spoke courteously. Maclean, however, was of the quarrelsome Highland breed, another Glencairn or Lochiel. He had heard with anger Walker's statement that he believed Congress would not admit Kansas until a majority of the people had fairly passed the constitution. To him the governor was simply a frail, bald, red-eyed little politician who could be kicked back to Washington like Reeder and Geary. Gigantic in stature, he glowered down at Walker:

"And do you come here to rule over us?—you, a miserable pigmy like you? You come here with ears erect, but you will leave with your tail between your legs. Walker, we have unmade governors before; and by God, I tell you, sir, we can unmake them again!"

So runs the report of an auditor.[19] Maclean even bade Walker tell the President to mind his own business—they cared not a fig for Buchanan. This might have been passed over as bibulous bluster but that on June 11 a formal deputation of "law and order" Democracy trooped into the governor's office in Lecompton with an ultimatum. Declaring that they were not going to let the people pass on the constitution, they demanded that he stop talking of a vote. They had their plans and meant to carry them out. At first Walker was aghast. "Gentlemen," he said, "today for the first time I have learned what is your real course and policy, and you have taught it to me." But with fire in his eye he showed his Jacksonian mettle. "Gentlemen," he declared with quiet determination, "you cannot force *me* into that policy." Freesoilers heard of the collision without surprise. The inevitable crisis had come a step nearer. Walker would have to face the political crookedness, corruption, and threats that had been too much for his predecessors. "He is getting into the breakers," wrote one observer, "and it is to be seen whether such a crafty bark can ride out the storm in so rough a sea." [20]

19 J. H. St. Matthew, *Overland Monthly*, December, 1870; A. B. Morris, "R. J. Walker in the Kansas Struggle," MS Dissertation Univ. of Chicago.
20 Topeka correspondence dated June 12, N. Y. *Weekly Tribune*, July 4, 1857.

[II]

With the western land boom at its height this spring, migration to Wisconsin, Minnesota, Iowa, and Kansas eclipsed all precedent. Beginning a month earlier than usual, the tide was flowing strongly by March 1. Week after week it swelled. During April, May, and June, newspapers published along the travel routes described a veritable torrent of humanity. The country seemed swarming with groups and individuals excited by the rich, virgin land available at low prices. "Yesterday morning," noted the Cleveland *Herald* early in April, "the train from Buffalo numbered thirty-four cars, and this morning twenty-six, all crowded. Our hotels are full; the second class even filling their floors full every night." It told of emigrant wagons rolling in long, white-topped files down every turnpike. Railroad men estimated that a fourth of the people passing through Cleveland were bound for Kansas, and the remainder for the West generally.[21] The Toledo *Commercial* spoke of hundreds daily pouring through that city. Many were from New England, with a solid, go-ahead, Bunker Hill look about them; many from the Pennsylvania German country with plenty of baggage; and many from Europe, clutching their savings.[22] Though more steamboats were running on the Ohio, Mississippi, and Missouri than ever before, every night dozens of passengers slept on the cabin floors. "Still they come!" exclaimed the Keokuk *Whig*:

By railways and steamers, the flood of immigration continues pouring into the great West. The lake-shore roads are crowded to their utmost capacity. . . . The Ohio River steamers are crowded in the same way. On Friday last, two steamers brought into St. Louis some six hundred passengers. And "still they come," from Pennsylvania, from Ohio, Indiana, and other States, until, by the side of this exodus, that of the Israelites becomes an insignificant item.[23]

Kansas, with land warrants selling for eighty to ninety cents an acre, and new Indian holdings about to be auctioned, got more than its share of the spate. People seemed converging from all parts of the map, but chiefly from the middle and prairie States. In Ohio, a veritable fever of speculation in Kansas lands was raging, men selling homes, giving up well-paid positions, and even borrowing money at ten percent to purchase farms.[24] Seeing trains of the Chicago & Alton and Ohio & Mississippi disgorge hundreds of prospective settlers in St. Louis daily, the Missouri *Republican* was almost ready to believe men who expected Kansas to increase by seventy thousand people that year. All the old sense of risk and experiment was passing away; men now came with families and imple-

21 Quoted in *National Intelligencer*, April 16, 1857.
22 Quoted *idem*, April 7, 1857.
23 N. H. Parker, *Iowa As It Is in 1857*, 60.
24 Cleveland *Herald*, Warren *Chronicle*, quoted in *National Intelligencer*, March 18, 1857.

ments. Railroads from the eastern seaboard to Chicago and St. Louis were advertising a reduction of one-fourth in rates, and promising settlers a safe, easy transit across Iowa or Missouri. A considerable number of emigrants winterbound in Illinois and Iowa the previous fall had resumed their march as soon as roads and rivers were passable. Teamsters swore and pushed on every muddy road; Missouri River towns marvelled to see every boat struggling upstream crowded till its decks were black.[25]

Between the opening of river transportation and the end of March, it was estimated that seven thousand settlers had arrived in Kansas City, and nearly as many more in neighboring towns. The Leavenworth *Herald,* boasting early in May that the population of that city had leaped to almost four thousand, told of seeing a hundred houses completed within the past fortnight. Indeed, Leavenworth grew with fairy-book rapidity. By midsummer it had seven or eight thousand people, lots that had been valued at $500 the year before were fetching $4,000, and many merchants had sold out and replenished their stock four times since early spring. Plans were afoot for a railroad to connect with the Hannibal & St. Joseph.[26] While the *Herald of Freedom* estimated in April that settlers were arriving at the rate of a thousand a day, the Kansas City *Enterprise* predicted that the Territory would have a population of one hundred thousand by October.[27] In areas recently known only to the prairie dog, crow, and cottontail, villages leaped into existence. "Four months ago," said the Emporia *Kanzas News* of August 15, "there was not a house where Emporia now stands, and from the town site none were to be seen. Now . . . as far as the eye can reach in every direction, every quarter-section is occupied. In every bend of the Neosho and Cottonwood is a dwelling, and one or more fields of grain. . . . The country around this is as thickly settled as many parts of the West that have been open for years." [28]

25 N. H. Parker, *Kansas and Nebraska Handbook, 1857,* 24 ff., 27; Leavenworth *Herald,* May 9, 1857. "Everybody is full of hope," E. B. Whitman had written Samuel Gridley Howe on December 6, 1856. "Real estate is rising rapidly. If peace continues there will be life and vigor beyond precedent. Land! Land! is the cry. . . . I am maturing some land operations of great importance, and hope to interest you and some of your friends in them." Howe Papers. Thomas Ewing, Jr., descended on Kansas late in 1856, and invested $11,300 for the family in lands near Leavenworth, declaring the property worth $100,000. E. L. Pierce, later the biographer of Sumner, wrote letters to the N. Y. *Evening Post* predicting that the huge spring migration would make Kansas a free State. See letter of Thomas Ewing, Sr., January 1, 1857, in Ewing Papers; Pierce to J. Q. Adams, September 10, 1886, in Charles Sumner Papers, Kansas State Hist. Soc.
26 Leavenworth *Herald,* May 9, 1857; N. Y. *Evening Post,* July 6, 1857.
27 Lawrence *Herald of Freedom,* April 11, 1857; Kansas City *Enterprise,* April 16, 1857. Actually the census of 1860, three years later, showed 107,206 people in Kansas, of whom 627 were Negroes.
28 A number of freesoil Kansans had lectured or written in the East during the winter of 1856–57 to stimulate emigration. For the activities of one former New Yorker, O. C. Brown, who induced "hundreds" to meet him in Buffalo this spring, see G. G. Smith, *Spencer Kellogg Brown,* 102–107.

Settlement continued to follow the streams, not for transportation but for alluvial soil and timber. With the Kansas River valley the principal attraction, Lawrence and Topeka became two of the liveliest bases for newcomers. The roads leading into them had a blithe holiday air, for they were filled with rattling stages, white Conestogas, buggies, carry-alls, lumbering oxcarts, and travellers afoot and horseback. Lawrence had rapidly repaired all the damage suffered in the previous spring; Topeka had become the third town in size (led by Kansas City and Leavenworth), and boasted a society of refinement and hospitality.[29] Three main government-protected highways opened up the interior. One was the Fort Leavenworth-Laramie road in the north; a second the Fort Riley-Bridger's Pass road near the center; the third, the Santa Fé road in the south. Along the eastern boundary a passable north-south highway ran from Leavenworth to Fort Scott. While the earliest settlers had flocked to the northeast corner of Kansas, many now pushed far to the south. Indeed, men hunting desirable claims had scattered over half the Territory.

With the whole country standing this spring at the apex of a precarious boom, Kansas had its full share of promoters, gamblers, and their get-rich-quick dupes. New towns were being laid out, with paper churches, opera houses, city halls, and colleges; ambitious railroads and factories were being projected; lots in cities only four years old sometimes brought $10,000. Attractive Indian lands, suitable for farming and dairying, were going on the market—some two hundred and fourteen thousand acres of Wea holdings, and some two hundred and forty-five thousand acres of the Delaware Trust property. The Neosho Valley lands, still distant from any market but pronounced by some the best in the Territory, had become preemptible, and settlers were turning eagerly to them. Everywhere, with prices rising, money seemed easily made. Senator Bigler of Pennsylvania had a partner in Fort Scott who beat the big drum with the ardor characteristic of his kind. Invest! invest! was his cry—by which he, like others, meant speculate. "I wish you would hunt up *money*," he exhorted Bigler. "It is sad to see so many chances—fortunes—passing into other hands because I need the 'stinko.' There will be a glorious opportunity here to get timber lands etc. with warrants if you could make arrangements with Drexel, Clark & Co., or some of the Washington City men. Timber lands here will be worth from $20 to $100 in a few years." One of his friends had purchased for $650 a quarter-section claim on which stood timber worth $16,000. This partner was interested in town lots, and had bought the principal Fort Scott hotel; in railroad building, for he thought the city would become the principal railway center of southwestern Missouri and northwestern Arkansas; in banking, for money could be lent at high rates;

29 Leavenworth correspondence, N. Y. *Evening Post*, dated March 29, 1857; M. J. Parrott et al., *Kansas*, 1856.

in furs and buffalo skins, which he got from the Indians in winter; and in mining, for he shipped Fort Scott coal to Westport at 35–45 cents a bushel.[30] Kansas was alive with such eager, pushing men.

As the boom grew, only a few observers saw the true facts. One was shrewd Amos A. Lawrence, who wrote "Governor" Robinson that spring: "There must be a collapse in the land speculation all over the West. Now is the time to sell a large half and lend the money to those who think differently." [31]

Most newcomers, however, were hard-working farmers, craftsmen, and merchants, vigorous, primed for hardship, and determined to establish prosperous homes. They meant business, even if many were greenhorns. The cost of settlement staggered poor men. To break the raw prairie cost $2.50 an acre; lumber for houses was $20 a thousand feet; fencing was often needed to keep out cattle, and that meant posts and rails; wells had to be dug down from twenty to fifty feet to reach water. Tools, horses or oxen, seed, all cost money.[32] Stoves were landed at Leavenworth and Kansas City in hundred- or two-hundred-lot consignments. Already one distinctive feature of the Kansas landscape was appearing— the windmill. Winter or summer, the plains nearly always had a breeze or a gale, and windmills were advertised to furnish from one to a hundred horsepower in a moderate wind.[33] The bright hope of most arrivals was that a single good crop year would pay for the initial investment.

The freesoil ascendency in this Great Migration to Kansas (not unlike the Great Migration of Puritan days to Massachusetts) was marked. The correspondent of the New York *Evening Post* thought that at least nine-tenths of the

30 G. A. Crawford, June-August, 1857; Bigler Papers. One of Thomas Ewing's sons was in Leavenworth when the sales in the spring of 1857 began. These sales, he writes, "attracted speculators and settlers by thousands from all parts of the Union. All the Indian reservations had been broken up and divided into sections and subdivisions of sections down to forty acres. The treaties solemnly promised the Indians that the lands would be sold at auction to the highest bidders for cash and the entire net proceeds should be placed to the credit of the tribes respectively. But the doctrine of squatter sovereignty had not been taught to the white settlers in vain. They organized in settlers' societies to secure the several selections at the appraised values; and to prevent speculators from forcing up prices on them at the public auction sales. The Indians protested and appealed to Commissioner Manypenny, a man of ability and courage who assured them that every acre of their lands should go to the highest bidder." Regular army troops were present, with cannon shotted and primed. So were a host of speculators loaded down with money. So were a thousand squatters armed to the teeth. Norman Eddy, the Federal Land Agent, appeared at ten, and announced that the first bidder would be expected to bid the appraised price, and that higher bids would then be received from others. The first quarter section was called. The settlers' representative then announced that John Doe was settled on that tract and that he bid the appraised price. As the auctioneers called for other bids, the squatters, glowering at the speculators, significantly fingered their revolvers. No bid came. "So the sale went on—one bidder to each quarter-section, and he the settler; and then the indignant and despairing speculators left the scene." Unsigned, undated memorandum in Ewing Papers, Vol. XI.
31 May 16, 1857; Robinson Papers, Univ. of Kansas.
32 Atchison letter in Warsaw, Illinois, *Bulletin*, August 4, 1859.
33 Lawrence *Herald of Freedom*, January-August, 1857.

spring settlers were from the free States; the correspondent of the Missouri *Democrat* said almost all; and the proslavery correspondent of the Missouri *Republican* put the proportion at fifteen freesoil emigrants to one slavery man. All observers agreed that they were a superior body, with a higher average of brains, character, and physical strength than could be found in old communities.[34] It was significant that the "border ruffians" had given up all attempt to interfere with the flow of population. For one reason, the very numbers of the freesoil men compelled respect. For another, the partial stoppage of Missouri River traffic in 1856 had cost various interests large sums, the steamboat owners alone reckoning that they had lost half a million; and western Missouri, suffering from a shortage of money, hoped for friendly relations with Kansas buyers of flour, meat, and other goods.[35]

Most proslavery men on the spot now knew that they had lost all hope of a preponderant voice in Kansas affairs. Ex-Senator Atchison wrote a significant letter this spring to the mayor of Columbia, S. C. Some of our Southern friends in Kansas have become apathetic and despondent, he wrote, while others have turned their attention to money-making. "I would therefore suggest that no more money be raised in South Carolina. The people of that State have been liberal above all others of the Southern States. Yet I fear that the North has and will raise and expend in Kansas, to effect their unholy purposes, ten dollars where we can raise one." [36] Actually subsidized emigration was but a small part of the whole. The National Kansas Committee, meeting early in the year in New York, had disclosed receipts of about $90,000 since the previous June, but it had sent out only about two thousand emigrants. Its chief usefulness had been in getting transportation rates reduced, selling low-cost tickets (fares from the eastern seaboard to Kansas City were now only $20–$25), and furnishing food and clothing to needy settlers. At the South, Captain A. B. Biland of Alabama was leading a new company to the Territory.[37] It was the volunteer efflux from the free States, spontaneous and unorganized, the same human torrent that had already given Iowa half a million people, that was determining the future character of the land.

Representative William Barksdale of Mississippi, sadly admitting to a British tourist that Kansas would probably be a free State, put his finger on one reason. While true settlers poured out from the North with their families, the South sent young adventurers who went for the frolic, and came home when they got tired. Men who wanted to take their slaves to new lands kept farther south. From Missouri itself a considerable migration of men, slaves, and cattle

---

34 Leavenworth correspondence, N. Y. *Evening Post*, dated March 29, 1857; Parker, *Kansas and Nebraska Handbook, 1857–58*.
35 Lawrence *Herald of Freedom*, January 10, 24, February 21, 1857.
36 Columbia *Times* quoted in *National Intelligencer*, July 7, 1857.
37 *Alabama Journal*, April 11, 1857.

was reported, but it was moving into Arkansas and Texas.[38] One token of the times was the sale of that stalwart proslavery journal, the Atchison (Kansas) *Squatter Sovereign*, to men who made it an antislavery newspaper. Of eighteen weekly sheets published in Kansas in the summer of 1857, thirteen were free-soil, and some of the others neutral.[39]

Yet the new freesoil immigration sweeping into Kansas all spring and summer would have no voice, under the law, in determining the State constitution. That privilege was confined to the voters registered in March. And unfair as this arrangement was, the proslavery element had stolen other advantages. The lands of the Shawnee Reserve were not yet legally open, but early in the year an association of men from Jackson County, Missouri, invaded them and pre-empted large tracts. They were divided among some two thousand seven hundred claimants, many of whom merely drove stakes and laid down four logs, while others left no token of ownership at all. Most of these bogus settlers at once went home, but many made a special return trip for the census and the election of delegates. Week by week, as summer came on, evidence accumulated of the gross injustices which had accompanied the census-taking, carried out by sheriffs' deputies paid four dollars a day. It was easy to understand why Calhoun, Maclean, and Lecompte wanted no fair referendum on the constitution. The rigged convention, arbitrarily foisting its handiwork on the people, represented the last hope of making Kansas a slave State.

[III]

The election of the convention took place on June 15 amid the scoffs and jeers of such antislavery citizens as took time from field and shop to look up. A little more whiskey-drinking than usual in Lecompton, a few more Missourians than ordinary riding into boundary-towns—these were the only signs of activity.[40] At least half of the antislavery men could not vote, and most of the

38 London *Daily News*, January 24, 1857; *National Intelligencer*, July 9, 1857. Yet some Southern spokesmen maintained their confidence. "That Kansas will be a slave State is now near to a settled question," declared Henry Clay Pate, publisher of the Westport, Mo., *Star of Empire*. He expected the coming Lecompton convention to deliver a slave State constitution. Then the South would say, "Let Kansas come in, and we shall not keep Minnesota out." Some men feared that even if admitted as a slave State, it would not remain so long. But, declared Pate, "the history of slavery in the United States goes to show that it is not so easily uprooted." Quoted in *Kanzas News*, June 6, 1857.

39 One slavery center after another, in fact, was either dying or being conquered. Douglas and Benicia had perished; Tecumseh had been taken over by freesoilers; and now many believed that Lecompton itself contained a majority of free State men. Lawrence *Herald of Freedom*, May 9, 1857.

40 Lawrence *Republican*, June 19, 1857; St. Louis *Democrat*, June 22, 1857. The free State men had issued an address to the nation (*National Intelligencer*, May 7) saying they would take no part because thousands of freesoil men had been disenfranchised, and other frauds committed.

remainder would not. They felt abundantly justified in boycotting an election so unfair. Though there were probably twenty thousand adult males in Kansas, only nine thousand two hundred and fifty-one had been registered—and a goodly number of these were outlanders. Moreover, the delegates had been apportioned on a basis of brazen gerrymandering. Of the sixty members, the three river counties of Doniphan, Atchison, and Leavenworth, easy of access from Missouri and supposed to be strong in slavery sentiment, were given twenty-four. Johnson County, which held the Shawnee Reserve and had not fifty legal voters, was allowed three delegates. Linn, Lykins, Bourbon, and McGee counties were given ten in all. Thus eight river and border counties were allotted thirty-seven of the sixty delegates; the other thirty counties, including thickly populated freesoil areas, were granted twenty-three.[41]

As an expression of territorial opinion the election was a farce, for only about twenty-two hundred men, out of the nine thousand two hundred and fifty-one registered, cast ballots. In Douglas County, containing the town of Lawrence, only two hundred and forty votes were polled; it had been announced that a voting place would be open in the Lawrence post office, but reporters searched every nook and cranny without finding it. Leavenworth County recorded only about five hundred votes.[42] No free State candidates had been put up. But certificates were immediately issued to the sixty proslavery men; and the Calhoun faction, now showing open enmity to the governor, hailed them as fit agents of the sovereign people of Kansas.

When this election took place, the Southern press and politicians were already savagely denouncing Governor Walker for a course much too impartial to please them.[43] On what ground? He was toiling hard at his duties, inquiring into a murder at Leavenworth, visiting land sales at Paoli, and urging the whole people to join in a new territorial election in the fall. The Washington Union, in an editorial which Jere Black wrote, was defending him and maintaining that his advocacy of popular submission of the constitution was just and statesmanlike.[44] Why was he bitterly assailed?

He had offended Southerners when, in his inaugural, he had said that if the instrument were not submitted to the people, he believed it would be and should be rejected by Congress. What right had he to dictate to the convention? This was "intervention." What right had he to prescribe what Congress should or should not do? This was more "intervention." He had likewise outraged many Southerners when he seemed to prejudge the result. His talk of an isothermal law, his statement that the "elevated plains" and "chilling blasts" of

41 *Kanzas News*, June 6, 1857; this paper was edited by Preston B. Plumb.
42 Lawrence correspondence, June 25, in N. Y. *Weekly Tribune*, July 11, 1857.
43 N. Y. *Express*, quoted in *National Intelligencer*, June 25, 1857.
44 Washington *Union*, July 7, 1857; Black Papers.

Kansas, reducing the average temperature nearly as low as that of New England, might well make slavery impossible, was another bit of "intervention." He was taking sides. Keitt of South Carolina accused the little governor of treachery. John A. Quitman thought this a misnomer, for Walker, more Pennsylvanian than Mississippian, had never been a proslavery man. "Like most Northern politicians, he desired Kansas to come in as a 'free State.' They esteem the ascendency of the party of more importance than the rights of the South, and believe the former would be best served by Kansas coming in as a free State. When Walker was selected, I anticipated some ingenious plan to effect that object. Even the inaugural of Buchanan squinted at it. Neither of these gentlemen have deceived me." [45]

By mid-July the entire Southern Rights press had opened fire on Walker. The New Orleans *Delta* raked him as the pet and tool of the North. The Jackson *Mississippian* declared that he now stood unveiled before the outraged South, a self-convicted traitor to her constitutional rights. The Richmond *South* was equally violent. The Augusta *Constitutionalist* published a letter suggesting assassination; his conduct "makes one think of the dagger of Brutus and the axe of Cromwell." The Montgomery *Advertiser* adopted a threatening tone, saying that the Administration must repudiate the governor, or the South would turn against the Administration: "Southern hopes in Kansas shall not be easily dashed; Southern efforts in that Territory shall not be easily defeated." [46] Dozens of Southern editors took the view that Walker was trying to cheat their section in order to keep the Northern and Southern Democrats united. This was the opinion of Quitman, who expected an effort to proscribe State Rights men. "When the war opens, how many will have the courage to stand and fight?" he demanded of Keitt. "The test struggle is before us and nigh us. It will soon be seen whether we will maintain our equality, or sink into a degrading subserviency to political masters." [47]

Both the anger and fear of the South, feeding on many supposed grievances, were rising steadily. It must be remembered that, with sixteen free and fifteen slave States in the Union, Southerners saw the balance tipping heavily against them. Minnesota and Oregon must soon enter as free States. Indeed, six or seven new free States loomed on the horizon, each with two Senators and a lengthening list of Representatives; whereas Kansas was the one Territory which *might*

45 To Keitt, July 23, 1857; Quitman Papers, Univ. of N. C.
46 All quoted in Lawrence *Herald of Freedom*, July 11, 1857. Many Southerners said that they did not object to a decision by the constitutional convention to submit its work; they did not even object to seeing Kansas become a free State. But they did object to intervention by the Federal government, or the governor it appointed, to compel submission. This, they said, violated popular sovereignty even as Douglas understood it. See Mobile *Daily Register*, June 17-26, 1857.
47 Quitman to Keitt, *ut supra*.

becon:e siave. Many believed Republicans had made a test case of Kansas, vowing that on no account must an additional slave State be admitted, anywhere, anyhow, anytime. If the South lost Kansas, it would feel that a seal had been placed on this decree. Innumerable Southerners had now been led to believe that the freesoil inundation of Kansas was a bought emigration, an influx of hirelings, an artificial maneuver which might fairly be fought by any weapon. "I will venture to say this much," fulminated Senator Mason, "that if African slavery be ultimately excluded from Kansas, it will be effected by the numerical force of organized majorities, operating against the usual laws which govern emigration, and will present a new and most instructive lesson to the Southern States." [48]

Another potent consideration was the manifest peril in which Missouri, the northwestern bastion of slavery, now stood. Early this spring an avowed emancipationist, John M. Wimer, was elected mayor of St. Louis over a proslavery candidate by a plurality of one thousand seven hundred and twenty-eight votes. The issue had been clearly stated and the result was decisive. It had long been evident that the growing German and Northern-born elements were converting St. Louis to an antislavery sentiment. For a variety of reasons—popular sensitiveness, old Southern ties, the desire of newcomers to behave tactfully, fear of isolating the city from the rest of the State—little had been done to assert a policy of doubtful strength. Now, however, the blow had been struck. For the first time in the nation's history an emancipationist party had given overt battle in a slave State and made conquest of its chief city. The lesson to hardy leaders in Wilmington, Louisville, Baltimore, western Virginia, and eastern Tennessee could not be missed. In Kansas, cried the St. Louis *Intelligencer*, "the effect will be strikingly manifest, no doubt. The Free State party will grow doubly strong in moral courage, and the proslavery party must cringe under such an 'attack from the rear.'" [49]

But most of all, the election result seemed to threaten the loss of Missouri to slavery men. A freesoil Whig, James S. Rollins, was entering the lists this summer for governor. He stood a good chance to win. If Kansas, Iowa, and Illinois surrounded Missouri on three sides by free soil, if St. Louis became a freesoil fortress, and if more Germans and Yankees rolled in, how long would the State stand firm? For immediate abolition, to be sure, there was little sentiment. But this was largely because many believed with Edward Bates that, since force of circumstances must soon extinguish slavery in the State, it was unwise to force the pace.

Many Southerners were in a mood of defiance—they had always meant to gain Kansas, and they would not be cheated of it; many were in a mood of

48 Letter in Richmond *South*, quoted in N. Y. *Weekly Tribune*, August 8, 1857.
49 St. Louis *Intelligencer*, April 8, 1857.

apprehension—the free States were growing too strong; many were in a mood of recklessness—Buchanan's victory and the Dred Scott decision had made them arrogant. Disunionists had sown their seed broadcast in the campaign of 1856, and it had taken root. An ebullition of wrath, verging on hysteria, swept

This will help explain why slaveholders in Missouri and southerners in general worried over the situation in Kansas. (Kentucky and Tennessee are colored black without reference to the density of slave population.)

the Lower South in particular as editors pictured Walker handing Kansas over to the abolitionists. The South Carolina *Times* agreed with the New Orleans *Crescent* that the governor was "probably the most unscrupulous, heartless, and unprincipled man in the United States."

Georgia was the first State to speak. Her Democratic convention, meeting at Milledgeville late in June, showed a radical temper, nominating Joseph E. Brown, Southern Rights lawyer and judge, for governor. Turning to Kansas, the members emphatically condemned Walker's course. They stigmatized the popular-submission section of his inaugural as "a presumptuous interference in matters over which he has no control"; declared his isothermal doctrine "a gross departure from the principles of non-intervention and neutrality"; and demanded that Buchanan recall him. Even the moderate Alexander H. Stephens was filled with indignation. Toombs felt the same. Walker was not expected to give advice, he wrote; much less to utter his insolent and arrogant threat that unless Kansas carried out *his* will, Congress would not admit the State. "It is this which so much aroused the South. The condemnation of him is as universal as just."

In Florida, Governor Perry was declaring that, unless the Northern Democrats upheld the rights of the South, the Union was ended. Mississippi took the same line. Of the leaders there, Jefferson Davis aspired to Calhoun's baton as field marshal of the Southern Rights host, while Jacob Thompson hated Walker with the rancor of his inveterate feud. Extremists ruled the Democratic Convention. They laid their malison on Walker's conduct as a discrimination against the just rights of the proslavery party in Kansas and the nation, and they demanded his removal. The American Party of Mississippi, meeting July 13, likewise condemned the governor in savage terms. Forthwith all the Southern Rights journals caught up the cry: Walker must go. As early as July 11 the New York *Evening Post* concluded that Buchanan would find the cotton kingdom implacable against him unless he recalled the governor. Not since the nation began, wrote R. B. Rhett, had any question brought the South into more complete union than Walker's course.[50]

The sudden bellicosity of the South amazed those who did not realize the sad fraying of slaveholders' nerves, the intensity of their conviction that freesoilers were practically abolitionists and mortal enemies, and the passionate hopes many had held for Kansas. (Even Stephens had said in 1855 they were about to get a slave State there.) It was their Brenner Pass, their Alsace-Lorraine. All had been going well there. Why should Walker interfere so suddenly and wantonly to their disadvantage?

Albert Gallatin Brown told a crowd on July 4 that if Buchanan suffered Walker to remain governor, the South would rise up against the President as false to the principles of the Nebraska Act. Judge T. W. Thomas, a Georgia lawyer-editor, seized his pen the moment he read Walker's inaugural. "If the document I have seen is genuine," he wrote Stephens, "it is clear that Buchanan has turned traitor." A crisis was upon them; "if Kansas is admitted as a free State we are ruined"; and unless the governor was dismissed within a month, they must repudiate the Administration. Toombs declared that ruin faced the government. It was the concern of the delegates alone whether the convention submitted its work to popular vote. His threat of hostile action if no referendum

50 N. Y. *Evening Post,* July 11; *National Intelligencer,* July 28, 1857; Toombs to W. M. Burnell, July 11, 1857, Toombs Papers, LC; Stephens in Augusta *Constitutionalist,* August 18, 1858.

were permitted should have emphatic answer: "The convention ought never under any circumstances to comply with his demand that it be submitted to all the people who happen to be in Kansas when the ratification takes place, and I trust they will give him a chance to carry out his threat and join the freesoil traitors." [51]

For Charleston fire-eaters the *Mercury* was declaring that Buchanan, Walker, and all the national spoilsmen might go to perdition together. In Virginia the Hunter faction caught up the agitation as a possible means of crushing Buchanan's friends Wise and Floyd, using Pryor's Richmond *South* as an organ. Their splenetic attacks on Walker were part of an effort to align the Old Dominion with the Lower South. The Jackson *Mississippian* and New Orleans *Delta* were vitriolic. That summer the Springs, always a favorite resort of irritable aristocrats, hummed with execrations of the Administration. George Sanders's son, prowling about White Sulphur, concluded that the States of Georgia, Alabama, Mississippi, and Virginia were in open arms against Walker— and his letter went to Buchanan's desk. H. W. Pickens at the same resort found sentiment insistent that Walker must be recalled, or at any rate that the Administration must disavow his utterances; otherwise the South would believe that he had been sent out to overawe the convention just as President Taylor had sent T. B. King to California to help mold its constitution. He wrote Buchanan warningly:

Since my arrival here I have seen and conversed with gentlemen from all parts of the South and West, not politicians only but planters and private gentlemen, and I find there is universal condemnation of Gov. Walker's extra-official conduct and speeches. I thought at first some weeks ago the extreme feeling against him was perhaps more stimulated by the partisan press than otherwise, but I now think there is a settled and deep feeling of disappointment and distress. It is a great mistake to suppose that the democracy of Virginia even sustains him, and the feeling in Georgia and Mississippi is running into excitement against the Administration too. . . .

I am sure that no moderation or conciliation on your part will ever appease your opponents of the free soil party or black Republicans of the non-slaveholding States. However much they may appear to acquiesce in your course, whatever it may be, they in reality intend war to the knife. With the loss of sympathy in the South your Administration would lose half its moral power to resist them and to mould conservative measures, so essential to save the Constitution, and preserve the real power and integrity of the Democratic Party for the future! [52]

51 N. Y. *Weekly Tribune*, August 1, 1857; *Toombs, Stephens, Cobb Correspondence,* 400–404.
52 Pickens to Buchanan, August 5, 1857; Buchanan Papers. See the Richmond *South,* July 28, 1857, for an excoriation of Walker.

The President's intimate friend Slidell, too, lounging away some August days at the Virginia Springs, found their Southern habitués unanimously castigating Walker, and he thought they took it for granted that Buchanan equally disapproved of the governor's foolish speeches and was only biding his time to reveal his condemnation. Slidell intimated, in a letter to the President, that he shared this view of Buchanan's duty.

[IV]

To a strong Executive the situation would have presented few difficulties, but to so weak a man as Buchanan it offered a cruel dilemma. On the one side he had to think of his recent pleas to Walker to go to Kansas, his pledge of support, and his written assurance that "the institutions of Kansas must be established by the votes of the people," and that when the constitution was submitted "they must be protected in the exercise of their right of voting for or against that instrument." He had to think of the fact that Governors Reeder and Geary had been broken because they stood up against what they deemed outrageous proslavery frauds and threats, and that it would produce the most painful impression if Walker were broken for the same reason. He had to think of Cass, Douglas, and the uneasy Northern Democrats. On the other side, he had to think of the pressure from the Southern majority in his Directory, from Slidell, Davis, and other Senators, and from the State conventions. He had to think of the peril to his legislative program. Above all, he had to think of threats of Southern secession.

Senator Bigler, who could speak with authority, for he had lately returned from a visit to all the principal towns of Kansas, exhibited unusual zeal—even impassioned feeling, the more impressive because he was a phlegmatic man—in trying to stiffen the President's backbone. The bad temper of the South, he assured Buchanan, sprang from a misunderstanding of the real state of Kansas parties. All probability of Kansas becoming a slave State had long since vanished; the leading proslavery men from St. Louis to Leavenworth had confessed as much; even Stringfellow, Whitfield, Jones, and others once so active for Kansas slavery now admitted that they did not have one-third the votes. It would be outrageous, declared Bigler, to let two thousand out of twenty thousand or twenty-four thousand voters make a constitution. The real question on which the South should fix attention was whether Kansas should come in as a Democratic or a Republican State. "Let Gov. Walker be sustained and all will be well," exhorted Bigler.[53]

At first Buchanan, while maintaining a Delphic silence in public, seemed

53 Senator Bigler to Buchanan, July 9, 1857: Buchanan Papers.

inclined to take this sensible attitude. On July 12 he was still firm—at least in the letter he wrote Walker that day. He told the governor that he had read the latter's long account of the party situation to the Cabinet, and that they hoped for the best in making Kansas a Democratic State. "The point on which your own success depends is the submission of the constitution to the people of Kansas; and by the people I mean, and I have no doubt you mean, the actual bona fide residents, who have been long enough in the Territory to identify themselves with its fate." He thought three months might be a reasonable period. "On the question of submitting the constitution to the bona fide residents of Kansas, I am willing to stand or fall. It is the principle of the Kansas-Nebraska Bill, the principle of Popular Sovereignty, and the principle at the foundation of all popular government." If it were applied, all would be settled harmoniously. "The strictures of the Georgia and Mississippi conventions will then pass away and be speedily forgotten." [54] This was at almost the same time as Attorney-General Black's editorial in the *Union*, supporting Walker's demand for submission. It was about the same time that ex-Senator Henry S. Foote, the staunch Mississippi Unionist, who visited Washington full of indignation over the wild talk in Georgia, Mississippi, and South Carolina, was assured by one Cabinet member that the President would never waver. Alas, that Buchanan did not nail his colors to the White House flagpole by a few public hammerblows! [55]

For almost at once he began to waver. The consideration which counted most heavily with Buchanan was fear of Southern secession, and the wish uppermost in his mind was to end his Administration with the Union intact. Throughout his later political career he had identified himself with the South. He agreed with Southern leaders that their section stood in genuine danger and should be supported and sheltered. The threats which came from the Lower South—threats pronounced by some of his correspondents to be the beginning of a new secession movement—terrified him. During the late summer he continued to hear such warning voices as Slidell's and Reid Sanders's. He continued to get vehement letters from such Southern Rights leaders as Governor Robert G. Wickliffe of Louisiana, who tartly censured any delay in dealing with Walker.[56] He continued to see the new shibboleth "nonintervention" bandied through half the Southern press, with a growing implication that Buchanan himself was guilty of intervention if he countenanced the governor's interference with the Kansas convention. Doubtless he heard the report that Jefferson Davis had drawn up the Mississippi resolutions. How far were Davis, A. G. Brown, Pickens, Rhett, Wickliffe, and their like going in the organization of the

54 This letter was first published in the N. Y. *Tribune*, April 21, 1860.
55 Foote, *Casket of Reminiscences*, 114 ff.
56 August 21, 1857; Buchanan Papers.

Southern Rights men? Quitman had written Keitt that they *must* organize.[57] How far would they go toward secession?

Great new forces were at work in the South, making much of it a one-party area. In August the Democrats swept three States, Kentucky, Tennessee, and North Carolina, in which the Whigs had long been dominant, carried Missouri (though narrowly), and made a net gain of ten House seats. The opposition, whether Whig, American, or what not, seemed collapsing throughout the slavery area. Buchanan might feel more than ever that the party's whole strength lay in maintaining Southern confidence.

Above all, as his Directory moved, so moved Buchanan. From Howell Cobb's letters we can gain some knowledge of what was occurring in Cabinet circles. Cobb himself was so hopeful of Southern victory in Kansas that he at first supposed that Walker's inaugural was simply intended to make her admission as a slave State more palatable to the North. He tells us that Jere Black *wanted* Kansas to be a slave State. The Cabinet, he informs us, thought Walker a selfish opportunist, a man who, strongly backed in New York, was playing a bold game for the Presidency. He also states that the Cabinet and Buchanan had discussed the propriety of submitting the constitution, that they had agreed on this, but without any view of "affecting the result," and that they had planned no action if the convention did *not* place its work before the voters. He believed that the President did not want Walker or any other official to use his position to affect the decision on the slavery question one way or the other. Buchanan, he thought, was really indifferent to that decision, so long as it was fairly and honestly made by the people of Kansas; and this was the position of all members of the Cabinet. Cobb's writings suggest that the Directory had a rather high opinion of the convention elected on so preposterous a basis.[58]

And as the summer passed the animus of the Cabinet against Walker became marked. Jacob Thompson, who had long detested him, was affected by the angry upheaval in Mississippi, and Cobb by that in Georgia. Jere Black's position was shaped in part by his narrowly legalistic mind, which rejected everything beyond the letter of the law, and was hence quick to condemn any bold action by Walker on behalf of the law's spirit; in part by his venomous hatred of all Republicans. Ever since he had fought the Wilmot Proviso he had regarded freesoilers much like rattlesnakes. Addicted even more than Floyd to intemperance of thought and utterance, he spoke of the free State men in Kansas as "abolitionists," who had "insulted and blasphemed the laws" made by the legitimate territorial government. All adherents of Robinson and the

57 Quitman to Keitt, July 23, 1857; Quitman Papers, Univ. of N. C.
58 *Toombs, Stephens, Cobb Correspondence*, 401–408. Cobb says that one of the Northern members of the Cabinet wished to see Kansas adopt slavery, and this must have been Black, not Toucey.

Topeka legislature he regarded as rebels and even traitors. Republican critics of the Administration he dismissed as "miserable hypocrites" who resorted to "vulgar abuse and brutal vituperation," their editors penning "daily slanders" packed with "lies." [59]

The three most active, vigorous spirits in the Directory could hardly reconcile themselves to the thought of a Republican conquest of Kansas. Calhoun, Maclean, and Isaacs, in their spring visit to Washington, had consulted at great length with Cobb, Slidell, and Jacob Thompson, and it is quite probable that letters (which have since disappeared) were now exchanged. It was common talk in Kansas that the Calhoun group were urging the Administration to dismiss Walker, and it was to Cobb and Thompson that they would naturally write.[60]

When, in mid-July, Walker fell into a controversy with the people of Lawrence, Cabinet feeling against him was plainly manifested. The dispute concerned an independent municipal government which a minority of voters, drawing up their own charter, had rashly instituted. To Walker, always given to excitement and melodrama, this attempt to organize the city in defiance of the regular territorial authorities was incipient rebellion. After issuing a proclamation against the movement and marching dragoons to a point near the town, he informed the President that he wanted a total force of two thousand men (more than twice the number on hand) to keep the peace in the Territory. At the moment Buchanan was resting at Bedford Springs, Pennsylvania. The Cabinet held two meetings, decided that no new force was necessary, and wrote the President in sharp terms about Walker's acts.

"We do not like Governor Walker's letter," declared Cass, "and I am satisfied this will be your opinion. . . . We all fear that Governor Walker is endeavoring to make a record for the future." Floyd was blunter. The Cabinet had concluded, he wrote, that the governor was alarmed by the Southern denunciation of his course, wished to retrieve lost ground, and desired to throw the blame for his "failure" upon either the Administration or the War Department. "I doubt, now, whether the investment in Gov. Walker is going to turn out very profitable, notwithstanding we all thought, and I in particular, that his mission to Kansas was to prove a perfect political California for the Administration." [61]

Walker had become such a political liability that when Buchanan returned from Bedford Springs, he found several Cabinet members ready to advocate dismissal. Jere Black in particular was in a violent frame of mind about the

59 All quotations are from Black's letters, 1857; Black Papers.
60 Lawrence correspondence, N. Y. *Weekly Tribune*, July 9, 1857.
61 Both letters July 31, 1857; Buchanan Papers. For the situation in Lawrence, see G. W. Brown, *Reminiscences of R. J. Walker*, 53–68.

whole Kansas situation. His advice to the President was to take drastic measures to crush the free State opposition to the existing territorial government. War, unfortunately, could not be levied against these traitors and murderers. But what the President could do was to arrest the ringleaders, bring them to trial, sentence them to jail, and thus force a crisis; the free State men would have to fight, with the certainty of being whipped, or give up forever.[62] This was dangerous counsel which Buchanan was too wise to accept, and which nobody heard about. It showed that the Attorney-General wanted the freesoil organization of Kansas smashed, and was not at all queasy about the means so long as they had a veneer of legality.

Ex-Senator Foote had meanwhile gone to Memphis, Jackson, and other Southern cities to speak in favor of what he thought was the Administration policy in Kansas. When he returned to Washington at the end of summer he got one of the shocks of his life. He found that Buchanan had "already become thoroughly panic-stricken." The firm policy had been abandoned.[63]

[V]

While the cotton States thus boiled with excitement, the hour for the constitutional convention was approaching. No man in Kansas or Washington knew whether Calhoun and his associates would yield to Walker's demand, or force a constitution on an unwilling people without a vote.

The Democratic "State" convention, which had met in Lecompton in July, had leaned strongly toward popular submission of the instrument. Amid tumultuous cheering, it rejected a resolution pledging support of the constitution even if *not* laid before the voters; and the correspondent of the St. Louis *Republican* thought that this made a referendum certain. The delegates-elect to the constitutional convention talked of an instrument modeled loosely on one of the Southern constitutions, with a section sanctioning continued ownership of

---

62 See Black's draft letter, proposed instructions to Walker, August 1, 1857; Buchanan Papers.

63 Foote, *Casket of Reminiscences*, 114 ff. In Memphis, writes Foote, his earnest plea to a large crowd to support Buchanan in this perilous conjuncture had elicited many evidences of public approval. He sent Buchanan newspapers showing what a cordial reception he had met. In Jackson he answered Senators Davis and Brown, who had just denounced Buchanan unmercifully; and again he obtained many testimonials of approval of the President and his supposed policy. All the greater was his astonishment to find that the President had abruptly surrendered. "The howlings of the bulldog of secession had fairly frightened him out of his wits, and he ingloriously resolved to yield without resistance to the decrial and villification to which he had been so acrimoniously subjected." Foote became deeply alarmed. "I knew well that a scheme for the destruction of the Union had been long on foot in the South. I knew quite as well that the leaders of the movement were only waiting for the enfeebling of the Democratic Party in the North, and the general triumph of Free-soilism as a consequence thereof, to alarm the whole South into acquiescence in their policy." See also D. Harmon, "Buchanan's Betrayal of Governor Walker," *Pa. Mag. of Hist.*, 1929, 51 ff.

the two hundred-odd slaves in the Territory, but forbidding the entry of more negroes whether free or slave. They talked, too, of providing for rigid execution of the Fugitive Slave Law, for the right of appeal to the Supreme Court in all constitutional cases, and for strict oaths of allegiance to the Federal Constitution by all officers. This would please the South. According to the *Republican* correspondent, the constitution would probably not be submitted entire to popular vote, but the section authorizing or forbidding the future introduction of slaves would be presented separately. Governor Walker, however, wrote Cass in midsummer that submission of any type was still uncertain.[64]

The nation's eyes were upon the delegates when they met at Lecompton on September 7 for a brief preliminary session. John Calhoun, who was elected president, made a speech notable for its avoidance of any explicit statement on the vital issue. They must present to Congress, he said, a constitution so framed and endorsed that they could not merely petition for admission, but demand it. Committees were appointed to draft various sections of the constitution, and the delegates adjourned until October 19.

Before that date arrived, a new demonstration of the recklessness of the proslavery leaders in Kansas startled the North. The very important election to choose a new legislature (and a Congressional Delegate) was held on October 5 and 6. Everyone expected this election, coming just as it did before the final convention session, to be decisive of the slavery issue. Accepting Walker's promise of a fair poll and eager to prove their overwhelming strength, the free State voters, both Democratic and Republican, turned out en masse. With a dismal rain to damp excitable men, and with Federal troops in troublesome precincts, the day passed with nothing worse than a few fistfights.[65] Returns came in slowly over the muddy roads. When all were counted, they showed an amazing outcome: the Republican candidate for Delegate had won by a majority exceeding four thousand, but the legislature was apparently proslavery. Careful inspection revealed that McGee County, in the extreme southeastern portion of Kansas, made up of Cherokee Indian lands not yet open to preemption and hence one of the most sparsely settled of all the counties, containing fewer than a hundred qualified voters, had returned 1,266 proslavery ballots! Still more remarkable was the showing of Johnson County, where the six-building hamlet of Oxford on the Missouri line reported 1,628 votes! Walker and Stanton visited both areas, made certain of the impudent frauds committed, and threw out the returns. If their action stood, the legislature would have a clear free State majority.[66]

64 July 15, 1857; Cass Papers. See also full Walker-Cass correspondence in *Kansas Hist. Colls.*, V, 321 ff.
65 N. Y. *Weekly Tribune*, October 17, 1857.
66 F. P. Stanton's "Letter to the People of the United States," January 29, 1859. Walker's proclamation is in *Kansas Hist. Colls.*, V, 403.

In two prompt and forcible proclamations, Walker presented full evidence of the illegalities, and pointed out that a victory gained by frauds so monstrous would be more fatal to the Democratic Party than any defeat. On his return from Oxford he halted at Lawrence, and, taking out of his portfolio a large roll of paper, told the crowd that he would exhibit a curiosity. He then unrolled the Oxford returns, consisting of sixteen hundred and one names all in the same handwriting on a roll fifty-four feet long, nearly fifteen hundred of them copied in consecutive order from Williams's Cincinnati Directory.[67]

Stanton and Walker felt a burning resentment. They had been put in the position of having to expose their whilom political associates, or of rendering themselves accomplices in a disgraceful trick. They had been compelled to face a revival of the dangerous party excitement of former days—for the freesoilers quivered with anger. They saw their hope of collecting the moderate groups into a dominant free State Democratic Party struck down, and hosts of voters so outraged that they would turn their faces toward the Republican fold. The governor took care to explain the validity of his action. "In rejecting these papers, *we do not go behind the returns*, because no legal or valid returns were made."[68]

Once more the fat was in the fire, which blazed up furiously. When Walker and Stanton took their decisive action, they knew that a storm would ensue. The immediate sequel was a furious mass meeting of proslavery Democrats, a mandamus (happily futile) from Judge Cato, and an effort by the hotheaded Sheriff S. J. Jones of Douglas County to obtain his legislative credentials by threat of violence. The governor's chagrin over the death of his hopeful plan for a strong "middle party" was intense. That had been the principal object of his mission, and his whole policy since his inaugural address had been designed to promote it. But he was a man of spirit, and by now was utterly sick of the machinations of the proslavery extremists. When he heard of Jones's gross outrage on the law, he caught up a pistol, bade Stanton follow him to beard the "Bengal tigers," and, visiting the saloons and gaming dens scattered along Lecompton's single straggling street, denounced the border ruffians there with all the expletives he had learned on the Mississippi frontier.

In Washington, Southern leaders were filled with consternation and anger. There and in Kansas, a long wrangle over returns, certificates, and forgeries, with control of the legislature in the balance, loomed up. The episode heightened sectional feeling throughout the nation. Walker wrote that he did not doubt that this disreputable assault on honest government would meet the reprehension of honest men of all parties. This was certainly true of the North, where repre-

67 *National Intelligencer*, November 5, 1857.
68 Proceedings, October 22, 1857; *National Intelligencer*, November 5, 1857.

hension was a mild word for the condemnation loudly expressed. In much of the South, however, a different response was visible. Multitudes, swayed by the prevalent excitement, concluded that Walker was again acting unfairly, and the clamor for his recall was simply accentuated.

Meanwhile, the final session of the Lecompton convention was beginning. As delegates gathered for it, a peremptory warning came from the great voice of the Democratic Northwest. Stephen A. Douglas had been profoundly affected by the emphatic free State vote. He knew well that if chicanery thwarted the will of the true residents of Kansas, he and his party were lost in Illinois, while the future of the Democracy throughout the North would be ruined. Speaking through the Chicago *Times*, he declared that the late Kansas election proved that the voters wanted a freesoil State; "that nothing less than a constitution which shall exclude and prohibit slavery will be accepted by the people of this Territory." In terms read as an ultimatum throughout the land (for half the press republished the editorial),[69] the Douglas organ went on:

What that Convention will do or what it will not do we have not the means of knowing. But we know that any attempt to force a pro-slavery constitution upon the people without an opportunity of voting it down at the polls will be regarded, after the recent expression of sentiment, as so decidedly unjust, oppressive, and unworthy of a free people, that the people of the United States will not sanction it. It would add thousands to the vote of the Republican party in every State of the Union. . . .

As Kansas must be a free State, even those persons in the Territory who are known as pro-slavery men must recognize in the late election a decision which must not be slighted or put at defiance. To that expression of the popular will there should be a graceful, if not a cheerful submission. Kansas is to be a free State. That fact being ascertained, let the Convention frame a constitution to suit her best interests, upon all other questions, and let *the prohibition of slavery be put into it*, clearly and without quibble, plainly, without disguise, explicitly, broadly, and firmly. Let the Convention then submit that constitution to the people.

But we have outrun part of our story. While the political skies were growing stormier, those of the financial and commercial world had also suddenly darkened.

69 Quoted in *National Intelligencer*, October 22, 1857.

7

Panic and Recovery

ON THE morning of August 24, 1857, the financial community of New York was horrified by the announcement of president Charles Stetson that his city branch of the Ohio Life Insurance & Trust Company had suspended payments. Men quickly learned that the house, which did a heavy business in western investments, had liabilities of from five to seven millions—and that its assets had been largely embezzled by the cashier. The economic situation had been uneasy. A panic now struck, sudden and devastating as a tornado. Stocks fell to incredible levels; commodity prices sank; bankruptcy followed bankruptcy.

This panic of 1857 ranks among the lesser financial convulsions of our history. Yet it may be doubted whether any other, in its implications and consequences, was so fateful. The most important of its results were psychological, and were felt during the next three years throughout both North and South. The eve of the panic had seen the North striding toward almost irresistible strength. Railroads were being hammered down, factories were rising, new cities were springing up, old cities were doubling in size. While immigration streamed in through the ports, British, Dutch, and German capital was being freely invested. The morrow of the panic saw railroad building stopped, factory doors locked, blast furnaces cold, and immigration almost paralyzed. The Northern giant had been brought to his knees—he was but a Goliath after all, and the pebble of a few bank failures had almost slain him. It was now the agricultural South, relatively but by no means absolutely unharmed, which appeared the stronger. How profound an effect this seeming revelation had upon the Southern leaders was quickly made evident in pamphlets, newspaper articles, and political speeches.[1]

[I]

The roots of the panic ran deep into the period of expansion and prosperity which had opened in 1846–47 with the repeal of the British Corn Laws, the

1 Cotton prices of eleven and twelve cents or better, which had softened the discontent of the cotton kingdom in 1850, accentuated Southern self-confidence after 1856.

victories in Mexico, and the discovery of California gold. Already the operation of the business cycle was partially understood. The *National Intelligencer* quoted an English economist on the periodic oscillation: "First quiescence, next improvement, then growing confidence, then prosperity, then excitement, then overtrading, then revulsion—followed in turn by pressure, stagnation, and distress, until the equilibrium of quiescence is again attained." [2] All these phenomena, in a long rising and falling curve, could be found in the exuberant era of the eighteen-fifties. Happily, the panic (the only one in our nineteenth-century history on a currency of approximately specie value) never struck deep into the productive powers of the nation.

The ten-year boom, beginning with the Corn Law repeal and our own liberal Walker Tariff of 1846, had gained impetus when the Irish potato famine of 1846–47 and the continental revolutions of 1848 had started heavy waves of emigration to America. The growing web of railroads in both America and Europe stimulated production and commerce. Steam navigation on ocean, lake, and river was rapidly increasing. The broad new conquests in the Southwest fed a spirit of confidence. When gold was discovered in California and Australia, small armies of adventurous men migrated to both lands, new cities arose, a speculative export trade to San Francisco and Sydney developed, and in return large quantities of the yellow metal flowed into the world's reservoirs of capital. New credit institutions to help handle the transfer of capital sprang up in all the Western nations. The St. Louis *Prices Current*, in its review of the year 1851, remarked upon the way in which California bullion and the multiplication of new banks in the North had made money and credit abundant. "Loans and banking facilities were obtained readily. The bankers and banking institutions were anxious to do business and make money." So rapid was the expansion of banks and banking operations, in fact, that in 1848–56 the credit resources of the country (in banknotes, loans, and deposits combined) rose from $538,000,000 to $1,042,000,000. [3]

California gold for a time seemed an Aladdin's lamp with which Columbia could make any coveted object her own. The new State, according to the Secretary of the Treasury in 1852, was producing at least seventy-five and probably one hundred millions annually, and the government had warrant for believing that this total would not diminish for many years to come. His estimate proved exaggerated. The five-year product for the first half of the eighteen-fifties was slightly under $300,000,000, while for the second half it was about $250,000,000. Even this output, however, then seemed immense. It inspired Americans with dreams of vast national wealth, and led multitudes to

2 *National Intelligencer*, October 22, 1857.
3 Cochran and Miller, *Age of Enterprise*, 82, 83.

believe that the currency system possessed such a strong metallic basis that it could not be seriously shaken. These notions were quite erroneous. The fact was that a large part of the gold was immediately exported to meet the unfavorable balance of trade, and more than the whole of it would have been required for that purpose had it not been for the sale of many million dollars' worth of railroad and other securities in Europe. Such large issues of State bonds were marketed overseas that the Treasury, replying to a Senate inquiry, estimated that on June 30, 1853, about $73,000,000 in State obligations was held by foreigners. Other estimates ran much higher; Winslow, Lanier & Co. of New York placed the true figure at more than $110,000,000.[4] By 1857, about $400,-000,000 in American securities of all types were held in Europe.[5]

The United States, in short, from 1850 to 1857 was laying railroads, opening factories and mines, and buying large quantities of manufactured staples and luxuries by the combined export of gold, farm products, and securities. The balance of trade was unfavorable in 1850, when the country's total exports, including specie, were $151,898,000, well below the total imports of $178,-138,000. The next year imports and exports almost balanced. The margin was slightly unfavorable in 1852, and very heavily so in 1853 and 1854.[6] Then in 1855 and 1856, thanks to the Crimean War, it became favorable again. If specie is excluded, however, the balance of trade was unfavorable in every year.[7] Borrowing abroad on stocks and bonds met the deficiency, and of course built up a huge mortgage on the future production of the country.

The sharp check administered to the boom in 1854 had turned out to be temporary and unimportant. With banks closing and stocks cascading, the recession was bad enough for a few months. Many men who owed money suffered severely. Horace Greeley, for example, lost good Pennsylvania lands which had cost him $5,000 because he was unable to raise one-tenth that amount.[8] The European demand for cotton and foodstuffs, however, remained high, railroad earnings on the main trunk lines were much better than in the previous autumn, and the steady supply of four or five millions a month in California gold furnished a basis for bank credit.[9] It soon became evident, too, that the Crimean War would heighten, not lessen, American prosperity. Throughout 1855–56, therefore, the flush times continued. Orders for grain, livestock, textiles, and metals rolled in from embattled France and Britain, filling the pockets of farmers, planters, and mineowners. Under rolling factory smoke, wages and profits rose.

4 *National Intelligencer*, March 4, 1854.
5 W. G. Sumner in *First Century of the Republic*, 254.
6 *Statistical Abstract*; E. R. Johnson et al., *Commerce of the U. S.*
7 See table in Van Vleck, *Panic of 1857*, 9.
8 James Harrison Wilson, *Dana*, 128.
9 *Journal of Commerce*, quoted in *National Intelligencer*, November 23, 1854.

As prices of foodstuffs and cotton touched high levels, speculation in land naturally increased. The Graduation Act of 1854, reducing the charge for some classes of unclaimed lands as low as twelve and a half cents an acre, helped persuade investors to buy large tracts. The Kansas-Nebraska Act, of course, lent its impetus to western settlement and speculation. The great land boom reached its peak in 1855–56, the government in each of these years parting with title to more than seventeen million acres, an area absolutely unprecedented. While the greater part of this was sold for cash, a good deal was purchased with military bounty and other warrants, which anybody could buy up cheaply.[10] As colonizers swept westward by train and steamboat, town-planners unrolled more gorgeously imaginative maps and sold wilder dreams of the future. Illinois, Iowa, Kansas, and Minnesota positively swarmed with promoters, who laid out more cities than already existed in the eastern and middle States, and sold "choice locations" at prices higher than good lots brought in Boston, Philadelphia, or Cleveland. By June 30, 1857, the outstanding railroad bonds totaled about $400,000,000 in face value, and the stocks about $500,-000,000. How much had been sunk in land was anybody's guess. A shrewd British observer, D. W. Mitchell, estimated that by 1857 more than $800,000,000 had been invested in idle western land and lots, held for a speculative rise, and but one-quarter paid for.[11]

At its apogee, this era of expansion, gambling, and lavish consumption of luxuries was as spectacular as all such periods are. The spend-and-splurge years under Buchanan did not differ essentially from the similar frenzies of boom-and-bust in the Jackson, Grant, and Coolidge-Hoover eras. In the North, moralists bewailed the heavy importations of diamonds, laces, silks, and fine wines. In the South, William Gregg protested against similar extravagances. "Ladies are seen dashing about the streets and watering places again with their $500 dresses and $1,500 shawls; merchants are seen pulling down princely buildings to vie with each other in the erection of stores, at an expense of three to five hundred thousand dollars; men are seen running to and fro, to find employment for money that has been borrowed at ten to fifteen percent premium; every railroad project, however visionary, may make bonds and find purchasers."[12] These were the years of Miss Flora M'Flimsey of Madison Square, who made three journeys to Paris, and on each

> Spent six consecutive weeks, without stopping,
> In one continuous round of shopping. . . .
> For bonnets, mantillas, capes, collars, and shawls;

10 The rapid disappearance of the public domain in parts of the West naturally heightened the demand for homestead legislation. In Illinois the westernmost land office, at Quincy, was closed in the summer of 1855. Cole, *Irrepressible Conflict*, 116–118.
11 Mitchell, *Ten Years in the United States*, 328.
12 "Speech in the South Carolina Legislature, 1857," pamphlet.

> Dresses for breakfasts, and dinners, and balls,
> Dresses to sit in, and stand in, and walk in;
> Dresses to dance in, and flirt in, and talk in;
> Dresses in which to do nothing at all;
> Dresses for Winter, Spring, Summer, and Fall—
> All of them different in color and shape,
> Silk, muslin, and lace, velvet, satin, and crepe.

And yet this same Miss M'Flimsey:

> The last time we met was in utter despair,
> Because she had nothing whatever to wear!

These were the years of Mrs. Fitzdazzle, who did her own "expanding" in diamonds at Tiffany's, laces at Stewart's, bonnets at Ferrero's, and a summer tour at Newport: "like a watch, she ran on tick, until her husband found himself wound up." [13] They were the years in which fashion and gaiety ran riot at Saratoga, Cape May, and the Virginia Springs. They were the years of the new marble Fifth Avenue Hotel, of W. W. Corcoran's resplendent entertainments in Washington, of the "nabob turnouts" of Commodore Vanderbilt, Robert Bonner, the Grinnells, and other lovers of fast trotters, of the height of antebellum luxury in Charleston and New Orleans. They were the years in which Emerson expressed a fear that the swift increase of great fortunes might "upset the balance of men, and establish a new, universal monarchy more tyrannical than Babylon or Rome." [14]

[II]

No feature of the boom had excited more comment than the novel vogue of speculation in securities. Stock-gambling, scolded the *National Intelligencer*, has grown to "an incredible extent" in the chief cities; "the parties to it are called the Bulls and the Bears." [15] Society, grumbled the New York *Evening Post*, must comprehend the dangers of a system that throws the faro table into the shade. While numerous journals printed sharp exposures of nefarious operations of brokers,[16] the New York *Observer* defended them. The public, it argued, had an incorrect estimate of the New York Stock Exchange. "It is not a gambling-house; and although many desperately risk their all on the rise and fall of the market, yet a large part of the business is as legitimate as any other commercial transactions." [17]

13 *Belle Brittan on a Tour* (Anon.), 60.
14 *Journals*, V, 285, 286; and see essay "Manners" for condemnation of a moneyed aristocracy.
15 August 18, 1857. The New York Stock Exchange dated from 1817.
16 An old topic; cf. O. G. Villard, *Early History of Wall Street*.
17 N. Y. *Observer*, quoted in *National Intelligencer*, May 12, 1857.

More than sixty years old, the New York Stock Exchange still conducted its business on the "call system" of trading. Members were elected, any person who had been a stockbroker for a year, or a clerk to a broker for two years, being eligible; seventeen votes sufficed to elect, though three blackballs might exclude; and the entrance fee was but $400. Brokerage charges were strictly regulated, fictitious sales were forbidden, and brokers who could not surrender a responsible principal were held personally responsible. The members met twice daily, the quarters in 1842–54 being in the Merchants' Exchange on Wall Street, and thereafter in Beaver Street near William. Their morning session, which all were expected to attend (though many members commuted fines for absence on a yearly basis) lasted from ten-thirty to a little after noon; the afternoon session opened at two-thirty and closed at three. Each member had a regular chair, whence arose the practice of referring to a "seat" on the exchange, while at the end of the long room the officers and secretaries sat on a dais. The method used was to call the roll of stocks and bonds, the sellers naming their prices and the buyers offering bids. Transactions in bank and insurance stocks were usually sedate, but railroad shares often produced a wild hubbub. The presiding officer would call out "Erie Railroad" or "Illinois Central":

First broker, "At 41⅝, seller 3" [that is, an offer to sell]. Second broker, "I'll give 45⅝, buyer 60, for 100." Third broker, "I'll sell 100 at 41⅝; I'll sell 100 at 41½." Broker, "Done!" Second broker, "Another hundred." Fourth broker, "I'll take 'em." Second broker. "Fifty more." Fifth broker, "Here, here, done!" By this time twenty voices are going at once; "I'll give 41½ regular"; "41¼, seller 10"; "43⅜, seller 3"; "done"; "take 'em"; "sell 'em"; "seller 10, 5 up"; "fifty more"; "one hundred more"; "I'll take your lot, buyer four months." A dozen men are on their feet, their arms swinging above their heads . . . and the scene is a perfect Babel to the uninitiated.

The Vice-President has seen everybody; heard everybody; above the din has distinguished the peculiar expressions denoting the closing of sales, and has rapidly repeated them, so that the secretaries have recorded them.[18]

To John Bigelow, the sale of more than $22,000,000 worth of stock in one fortnight of 1857 seemed ample basis for an *Evening Post* editorial denouncing "A Growing Evil"—overspeculation. The mania for playing the market had attacked everybody, he wrote; lawyers, merchants, doctors, and even clergy were abandoning a safe seven percent to gamble for twenty.[19] If the speculation was deplorable, the secret manipulation of stocks by insiders was far more reprehensible. Michigan Southern in the summer of 1857, at the apex of the boom, was a bone of contention between bulls led by the Litchfields and bears captained by young Leonard Jerome. Having learned the power of the press in

18 *Ibid;* cf. J. E. Meeker, *The Work of the Stock Exchange.*
19 N. Y. *Evening Post,* August 3, 1857.

Rochester, Jerome began an attack in the *Herald* on Wall Street security prices in general and the Michigan Southern stock in particular. Exhuming old railroad reports, he found facts which undermined public confidence. He was soon joined by Bigelow, who forced an admission from the railroad that it had printed and pledged several hundred thousand dollars in shares for a bank loan, trusting to future profits for a quiet retirement of the stock.[20] The immediate drop in the value of its securities cost the Michigan Southern a loss of about half a million.[21]

Commodity speculation was equally reckless. The press in 1856 and 1857 was studded with items on fortunes quickly conquered by bold Napoleons of the market. Chicago wheat brokers who bought at $1.40 and sold at $1.85, pork dealers who secured prime mess at $16 a barrel and parted with it at $20—these men were objects of admiration so long as prices rose.[22] Guano speculations, sugar speculations, even poultry speculations enlisted thousands. By midsummer of 1857, declared the New York *Herald*, commodity prices had increased forty percent in four years. Ignoring the effects of gold production, the Crimean War, and rising population upon prices, the *Herald* laid this disastrous rise to speculation. It made a particular point of cotton. Despite an estimated American crop in 1856–57 of about three million bales, with a large carry-over in European warehouses, raw cotton had gone so high that textile interests were being crushed between excessive costs and an overladen market.[23] Within a year, declared the *Herald*, speculators had forced it up nearly forty percent, while sheetings and other goods had risen only twelve to fifteen percent.

There was manifest truth in this statement. By mid-August in 1857, before the panic began, about six thousand looms had been stopped in New England because of the high price of raw cotton and the low price of goods, and orders had been given to stop many more as fast as the yarn was exhausted. In England, meanwhile, thirty thousand looms had been halted.[24] In other fields, commodity prices remained exorbitant while finished products were falling. The British consul in Chicago thought that grain speculation had become a mania. "The great increase of the exports of cereals both in quantity and value during the years 1855, 1856, and 1857, over the aggregate of the seventeen preceding years since Chicago had become an exporting port," he wrote his government, "produced a state of prosperity which ended in speculative excitement somewhat akin to

20 *Idem*, August 12, 18, 1857.
21 Margaret Clapp, *John Bigelow*, 111 ff.; J. K. Medbury, *Men and Mysteries of Wall Street*, 174, 175.
22 *National Intelligencer*, May 14, 1857.
23 July 18, 1857; quoted in Van Vleck, 35.
24 Providence *Journal*, N. Y. *Journal of Commerce*, quoted in *National Intelligencer*, August 18, 1857.

that which existed in Australia and California during the early development of the Gold Fields." [25]

Speculative ventures in lands, railroad building, and slaves kept pace and were closely interrelated; the rise in grain, meats, and cotton, and the westward movement of the population, maintaining all three. The "negro fever" was now rife in the South. Cotton planters found that the cost of hands soared out of all proportion even to rising prices for their staple. Prices in the Lower South were rising to $1,800 and even $2,000 for prime field workers. The two possible remedies were a reopening of the African slave trade, and a utilization of cheap lands.[26] Since the former could not be attained except after prolonged agitation, if at all, planters bought lands in Arkansas, Texas, and unsettled parts of the older States with avidity. If they could only get the labor, they might pay for their holdings with one or two crops. Similarly, in the Northwest, where McCormick's reaper and other machinery made labor a minor problem, high prices for foodstuffs and meat turned prosperous farmers and immigrants into land buyers, while speculators crowded in eagerly upon their heels. The Graduation Act of 1854, reducing the price of public land in proportion to the length of time it had been fruitlessly offered for sale, played into the hands of would-be monopolists; for it placed no limit on the amount of land one purchaser might take. Some bought large areas.

The London *Economist* in the summer of 1857 predicted a money panic as a consequence of this attempt by speculators to obtain a partial monopoly of the soil.[27] Banks were ready to lend large sums on land mortgages which, grossly overvalued in boom days, collapsed utterly when the panic came.

At the height of the inflation, town lots in nascent western cities might pass through a dozen hands within sixty days, rising in price with every sale. Unbroken farm lands in the Northwest were sold and resold in great tracts, neither buyers nor sellers having precise facts about location, fertility, or transportation facilities.[28] The land speculation in Kansas, conducted with Northern money, affected national history.[29] Greeley distrusted "Governor" Robinson because he was too much a speculator; Eli Thayer's Emigrant Aid Company was half an enterprise in land speculation; and Reeder owed his downfall as governor to his

25 R. Wilkins, April 30, 1859; FO 111/216.
26 Cf. Bancroft, *Slave Trading in the Old South*, 339–364.
27 London *Economist*, July 4, 1857.
28 For three years large sums of money had been sent into the West to buy land; for a similar period great numbers of young farmers had poured westward. A rational demand for land would have kept close to ten millions of acres a year; half again as much was being sold by the government, including land warrants. When it came to town lots, the speculation was fantastic. The Cincinnati *Railroad Record* in the spring of 1857 protested against the craze. The bursting of the bubble, it warned, was at hand. Quoted in *National Intelligencer*, May 19, 1857.
29 Malin, *Legend of '55*, 177.

inability to resist a chance on land. One of Walker's first concerns on going to the Territory was to oppose the grabbing of the best tracts, especially along projected railroad routes, by greedy monopolists. By the panic, half the people East and West had a share of God's earth which they fondly hoped was rising in value by twenty to one hundred percent yearly.[30]

Satire on land speculation: An imaginary town promotion scheme. About 1857.

[III]

Another element in producing the crash of 1857 was the grave weakness of the country's banking system. Its excessively rapid expansion, as State after State passed general banking laws, was alone a source of peril. In 1850 the United States had eight hundred and twenty-four banks, with an authorized capital of $217,000,000; in 1855 it had one thousand three hundred and seven, with an authorized capital of $332,000,000. This rate of growth far exceeded that of the population and far outpaced industry. The aggregate immediate liabilities of the banks in 1855, according to the Secretary of the Treasury, were about three times their aggregate immediate resources: $422,500,000 to $155,000,000. Their

30 Mitchell, *Ten Years in the United States,* 328.

total specie resources fell short of $54,000,000.[31] The general belief that profits would be large had much to do with the rapid multiplication of banks. One writer declared in 1856 that the net annual profits on the banking capital of the land averaged at least ten percent,[32] which was far more than railroad stocks paid. As Secretary Guthrie had pointed out, the profits of banks in the large cities were derived principally from the creation of deposit accounts through loans to merchants, industrialists, and country banks; while the profits of rural banks were gained chiefly from the substitution of their banknotes for money—that is, from circulation. In Wisconsin, for example, anybody could set up a bank by investing $25,000 or more in State or Federal bonds, and depositing them with the bank controller. He received banknotes equivalent to the market value of his bonds; and these banknotes he could lend to clients. A banker who bought $25,000 worth of Missouri State bonds got seven and a half percent on them, while on his $25,000 of banknotes he got ten percent more; a total of seventeen and a half percent without any real commercial service.[33]

Most incorporated banks were prohibited by law from engaging in any business other than banking. Unincorporated banks, however, were free to employ part of their capital in outside operations, and frequently did so. They sometimes made prodigious temporary gains at the sacrifice of safety. Banks of large capital were likely to have a more prudent management than lesser institutions, for they could employ more skillful and experienced officers, and command better means of credit investigation. Yet even large, incorporated banks were sometimes grossly misconducted. Much indignation was aroused in New York when in 1855 the cashier of the Mechanics' Bank, who had been forced to resign after a quarrel with the president, published a pamphlet containing amazing disclosures. It showed that the bank had contributed to political parties out of a secret drawer, that it had paid "assessments" by the City Chamberlain without keeping any account of them or making any report to the directors, and that it had permitted other shocking laxities in expenditure and bookkeeping.[34]

The banking heart of the nation was New York. "Every beat of this great financial organ is felt from Maine to Florida, and from the Atlantic to the Pacific," said the Louisville *Courier* on October 14, 1857. By 1855 the metropolis had fifty-three banks, of which seven were specially chartered, and the others established under general law; the aggregate capital falling just short of fifty millions. Boston, which as the center of industrial New England received most of the accumulations of capital in that section, fell into second place, with forty banks in 1854 capitalized at about thirty-seven millions. Her banking business,

31 Secretary of the Treasury, *Annual Report*, December, 1855.
32 "State Rights" in *National Intelligencer*, January 5, 1856.
33 Secretary of the Treasury, *Annual Report*, December, 1856.
34 "Defense of F. W. Edmonds, Late Cashier, Mechanics Bank"; pamphlet.

like that done in insurance, was actually not far behind New York's, a city four times as populous and enjoying about three-fourths of the import trade of the country. The Middle Atlantic States in 1855 had four hundred and sixty-four banks with a paid-in capital of $120,750,000; the New England States had four hundred and forty banks with a paid-in capital much larger, $191,804,000. Other areas lagged far behind.[35]

Far behind!—a reason for much heartburning. The Southern States had only one hundred and twenty-four banks in 1855, with a paid-in capital of about fifty millions, and the Southwestern States but ninety-six banks, with a capital of about forty-six millions. The Western States had one hundred and eighty-three banks, with the low capital of less than twenty millions. In short, the Eastern States possessed about nine hundred banks with a capital of $312,000,000, while all the rest of the country had but four hundred banks with a capital of $116,000,000. New York City in particular was already regarded as a financial tyrant. "Look at its functions," exclaimed a Virginia editor. "It regulates stocks, determines the value of produce, estimates the worth of State bonds, elevating or depressing them in the public estimation, without regard to their intrinsic value, and thus regulating the monetary affairs of the United States. The great heart of American commerce becomes diseased from a plethora of trade or a stagnation in the arteries of traffic and speculation, beats in unhealthy throbs, and every State in the Union . . . instantly feels the effects of its morbid action." [36]

In most new, fast-growing countries, and most flush periods, interest rates are high. Millions of Americans in the fifties, paying heavily for capital, thought that New York and the East were profiteering in the most exorbitant fashion. Though the year 1855 was not one of exceptional stringency, the United States loan maturing in 1862 at six percent a year stood in the autumn at only 112 and 113. The six percent bonds of Virginia sold at 96–97, and the seven percent bonds of California at 86–87. The six percent loans of a long list of cities, such as Pittsburgh, Cincinnati, St. Louis, and New Orleans, were well below par. As for railroads, despite the high profits of the Baltimore & Ohio its six percent bonds maturing in 1885 sold at 83–85.

With the West and Southwest hungry for capital, borrowers there had to pay from ten to twenty percent a year. State usury laws were utterly inefficacious. When Ohio in 1851 made the experiment of relaxing hers to allow a ten percent interest rate, that figure became practically the minimum, and in Cincinnati during 1852 money fluctuated upwards to twelve, sixteen, twenty and

35 *Special Report* of Treasury Department on Banks, February 27, 1855; *National Intelligencer*, April 11, 1854, October 25, 1855.
36 Bedford, Virginia, *Sentinel*, October 16, 1857.

even twenty-four percent. Yet in New York, distant hardly two days' travel, the ruling rate for good borrowers was only five percent. In semi-frontier areas, the demand for cheaper credit was always emphatically expressed. In Wisconsin, the Whig convention in 1852, for example, called for "a sound, specie-paying home currency" which would give farmers and merchants capital "without a resort to loans at exorbitant rates" from Eastern banks and brokers.[37]

Nothing irritated the West and South more than unexpected fluctuations in the money market, with the frequent sudden tightening of credit and interest rates. In 1851, for example, the year opened with flattering prospects of an easy supply of money. In St. Louis, loans were made on first-class security at five and six percent. Then the heavy imports of European goods made it necessary during the spring and summer to ship increasing quantities of specie to Europe. The New York bankers took alarm, and at the beginning of August determined to arrest the shipments of money by curtailing discounts and accommodations. This sudden contraction of the money market produced a wave of public apprehension. Confidence in all financial circles became impaired. For a time, eastern banks feared a suspension of specie payments, and interest rates in St. Louis and other outlying centers rose to eighteen and twenty-four percent. Gradually the country recovered from the shock. But the interior snarled resentfully. The mischief had been done, it said. The West had been robbed of the capital and credit it needed, while losses on the great Southern staple, cotton, had been so enormous that many firms in New Orleans had failed.[38]

Viewing the banking system of the country as a whole, men could see that it contained too many new and immature units; in the ten years preceding 1857, no fewer than six hundred and seventy-eight new banks had been set up. They could see that ready assets were much too small in proportion to liabilities; in 1856, deposits and circulation came to $407,000,000, while specie was only $53,000,000.[39] They could see that bank management was sometimes dishonest, often incompetent, and still more often reckless. The ablest bankers of New York, Boston, and Philadelphia, eager to increase their deposits, fell in with an unfortunate trend. Not content with being mere passive recipients of funds from country banks, they actively solicited deposits, even sending out circulars. On the floating capital thus obtained, they paid as much as four percent for sums up to $5,000, and as much as five percent for sums beyond that amount. These funds they then lent to brokers and others, often on dubious security, at profits of one to three percent a year. The brokers then used the money in ventures of a more or less speculative hue. As the nation's load of debt from railway con-

37 *National Intelligencer*, May 15, 1852; N. Y. *Tribune*, October 4, 1851.
38 *St. Louis Prices Current and Commercial Record*, January 10, 1852.
39 William Gregg, Speech in S. C. Legislature, January, 1857; pamphlet.

struction, the expansion of mills, factories, and stores, town promotion, and speculation in commodities rose, the sums owed to banks, brokerage houses, and private lenders became more and more disproportionate to the supporting assets.

The banking system was the weaker, moreover, because it was subject to great seasonal strains. At certain periods—chiefly late summer and early fall— the importers and country bankers were likely to bring heavy pressure on the large city banks for cash, and, if a crisis developed, their joint pressure might become catastrophic. Year after year the importers needed money to meet the unfavorable balance of trade. Their needs were likely to be greatest from midsummer on. Exports of cotton, wheat, and other agricultural products in winter and spring sufficed to square the accounts. In August, September, and October, however, before cotton-picking began and while the grain was merely being harvested and moved to elevators, the insatiable gulf had to be filled. Importers therefore drew many millions in coin or bullion. The movement of crops, meanwhile—the payment of farmers and planters at primary markets—caused country bankers in the West and South to make exigent demands upon the East. They had placed large deposits there, partly for the four percent interest, partly because eastern bankers refused to take and hold their bank notes at par unless such deposits were maintained. The annual strain was serious enough in good times; in a crisis it would become far worse. For the country banks were chronically short of cash; they based their circulation not on specie but securities, and when securities fell, their reserves were mainly in the East. These reserves were their most liquid assets, and, the harder the times became, the more frantically they demanded them.[40]

New York—much used, much hated New York—was certain to be hardest hit in a crisis. There were the chief importing interests, the stock speculators using borrowed funds, the busy land agencies and commodity markets. The city was the main money reservoir of the country—its money subject to calls which might make it dry up like a lake when the dam goes out. When debt reached the saturation point, the dam began to tremble.

[IV]

Still another factor in ending the boom and bringing on depression lay in foreign strains and stresses which originated, for the most part, in armed conflicts. The Crimean War, like all wars, was an international calamity. While it scattered gold among American farmers, planters, arms-makers, cloth manufacturers, and others, its long-term results were unfavorable. By its heavy costs, the shock it gave European production and trade, and the tax loads it imposed, it

40 Kettell, *Southern Wealth and Northern Profits, passim*; N. Y. *Tribune*, October 4, 851, for description of the system.

drained European funds from the American market. Huge quantities of specie had to be shipped from Western Europe to the Near East during the Crimean operations. The military campaigns of the British in China and Persia in 1856–57, the French operations against the Kabyles in Algeria, and the Indian Mutiny of 1857 also required large expenditures. From the spring of 1854 to the summer of 1857 Europe exported an estimated $700,000,000 in specie to the Near and Far East, much of which stayed there. The Bank of France, in the four years preceding 1857, lost more than $200,000,000 in specie, while the Bank of England, its reserves ebbing, had to raise its discount rate in 1856–57 to six and at times seven percent.[41]

By the fall of 1855, American observers in Europe were expressing fears of a financial crisis. The Bank of France was drawing large sums of gold from London; the Bank of England, irritated by the drain, was unable to stop it. Silver was growing steadily scarcer in France, where it was the legal tender. "There is a sort of war between the two great banks of London and Paris," wrote one American from the French capital.[42] When the Bank of England raised its discount rate to seven percent, other London banks began to charge borrowers eight. European capitalists who could get up to eight percent on good British mortgages, or five percent on Indian railway bonds guaranteed by the East India Company, felt little incentive to invest in American securities. Not merely did the flow of capital to the United States dwindle; as European interest rates advanced, many holders of American stocks and bonds sold them and called home the money. These sales did much to force a decline in the winter of 1856–57 in the price of American obligations—and a steady weakening of the banks, insurance companies, and other firms which relied on them as assets.

Nor was Western Europe herself guiltless of speculation and overexpansion. In France the Crédit Mobilier bubble was blown up to portentous size. That reckless trading bank, which under the encouragement of Napoleon III collected the savings of peasants, workingmen, and shopkeepers, using them to build railroads in Austria, to work mines in Spain, to dig canals in Belgium, and to carry on multiform enterprises in France, had for a time enjoyed a grandiose success.[43] Its stock had risen to dizzy levels. Its semi-annual reports, penned in bombastic language, had intoxicated the French public. It had whipped up a spirit of speculation which led British onlookers from Lombard Street to conclude that the French public was half mad. Even before the American crash, two large defalcations had created alarm, caused a rapid fall in shares, and forced most of the governing board to resign.[44]

41 A slight reduction took place in the summer of 1857; London *Economist*, June 20, 1857.
42 *National Intelligencer*, November 8, 1855; letter dated October 18, 1855.
43 In 1855 it declared a profit of 44 percent, and in 1856 of 25 percent.
44 Clapham, *Econ. Hist. of Modern Britain*, II, 367–372; *National Intelligencer*, October 1, 1857; London *Economist*, September 26, 1857.

[V]

The history of the panic itself, a world-wide convulsion, may be briefly dismissed; it is the results which concern us. During the spring and summer of 1857, talk of an imminent financial crash had spread throughout the country. Bankers and tradesmen discussed it; the press was full of it. "A Coming Crash" —such was the title of an editorial in the New York *Tribune* of June 25. The London *Economist* echoed the dark prognostications of the New York *Shipping List.*[45]

Yet to most Americans, confident in their resources and energy and encouraged by favorable crop reports, the blow that fell in August was stunning. Till the middle of the month the stock market remained fairly vigorous. At home, hopes of peace in Kansas remained high; abroad, the only serious trouble was the Sepoy revolt. On August 11, one of the oldest flour and grain houses of New York, N. H. Wolfe & Co., failed. Then came the Ohio Life & Trust crash, and alarm became universal. The largest purchaser of uncurrent bank notes in the city immediately failed. On the twenty-sixth, men learned that Jacob Little, prince of speculative investors, could not meet his debts, and that several important railroads were bankrupt. Stocks fell precipitately, distress spread like a cloud of poison gas, and money grew so tight that New York bank loans dropped by four millions in a week. The panic was on.

As merchants, factories, and country banks closed their doors, the universal cry was, "Who goes next?" A brief rally took place at the beginning of September; then the panic worsened. On the ninth a run on the banks for note redemption began, and on the thirteenth depositors came in crowds to demand their money. Before the fifteenth, all the New York banks but one had suspended specie payment, while those of New England and Pennsylvania, with many in the West and South, had fallen or were tottering. Credit was reduced to a minimum; bank loans in New York City, which stood at $120,000,000 on August 22, were down to $67,000,000 by October 17. During the autumn the situation became steadily darker. The seven hundred and four-mile Illinois Central, whose stock had recently sold at $140, and whose last yearly return had shown net receipts exceeding a million, went down—a staggering blow. Other great roads confessed bankruptcy. As security prices collapsed, financial houses toppled. John Murray Forbes wrote that William Appleton and W. Sturgis—the two best names in Boston—could not raise $100,000 within forty-eight hours at three percent a month.

British and American interests were so closely connected that a blow to one

45 London *Economist*, July 4, 1857.

struck the other with almost equal weight. More than a fifth of the British exports in 1856 had gone to the United States, while more than a third of the foreign government securities ordinarily listed on the British exchanges were American. When business with America was half paralyzed, American stocks and bonds dropped to abysmal levels, and New York paper became unsaleable, then British merchants, bankers, and investors were hard hit. In October and November a dismal succession of failures was chronicled by the British press. Scottish banks were smitten as by a plague. One London brokerage house failed for five million pounds. In France the Crédit Mobilier bubble was pricked. French failures in the autumn of 1857 were even more numerous and calamitous than British. Norway, Sweden, and all the Baltic ports suffered heavily. Hamburg, one of the principal trading links between North Europe and America, was brought to her knees. As far east as Poland and Austria, the battering impact of the panic was felt.[46]

As Disraeli said, the business mismanagement of half Europe was suddenly exposed. "All the bubbles, blunders, and dishonesties of five years' European exuberance and experiments in credit were tested or revealed." [47]

In the United States, the successive strokes of the panic left many businessmen utterly bewildered. As their notes were thrust in their faces, they tried to sell assets at half price and failed. Their feet became sore with running about town for unobtainable loans; their friends were out on the same errand—all borrowers, no lenders. Neighbors failed, banks failed, customers failed. They gazed sadly at drawers full of bills receivable (all worthless), attempted in desperation to sell their paper at any price, and went home sick with despair. The blackest rumors flew about every city. Talk of dishonesty was rife, and some of it was true.[48]

"Conceive," wrote Amos A. Lawrence from Boston in mid-October, "conceive of the rate of interest here being fifty per cent, and for large sums! Our manufacturing interest is for the present completely broken down and discredited." Two months later he reported that Boston was still prostrate. "Many men who have possessed handsome properties for thirty or even fifty years have become dependent on friends." [49] In Washington, Seward, for the first time in years, was unable to pay his current bills on demand, and ended the year more deeply in debt than he began it. "Money is a mere name," wrote a well-known Virginian, R. K. Crallé. "No one can safely sell anything except for specie—and there is no specie to be had." [50] Propertied people in Philadelphia were at first

46 *National Intelligencer*, November 17, 1857; London *Economist*, November-December, 1857.
47 Clapham, *Econ. Hist. of Modern Britain*, II, 370.
48 *Hunt's Merchants' Magazine*, XXXVII, 462.
49 A. A. Lawrence, October 19, December 17, 1857; Robinson Papers, Univ. of Kansas.
50 Frederic Seward, *Seward*, II, 327; R. K. Crallé, October 19, 1857, Brock Collection, HL.

sanguine, and the Bank of Philadelphia gave generous aid to distressed commercial houses. But on September 25 a sudden run forced this institution to close its doors. The news, spreading as on a gale, brought people thronging from every part of town into Third Street, which became jammed. Lines radiating from this vast but orderly mob poured into every downtown bank; the banks soon ceased paying on deposits, and their heads, hastily consulting, announced their suspension. Most banks of Pittsburgh, Reading, Baltimore, and various Jersey cities followed suit, and money rates were soaring.[51]

The chief western centers—Cleveland, Chicago, Milwaukee, St. Louis, and other cities—displayed the same distress and ruin. Western merchants had made large purchases of goods on notes which they expected to pay when the crops went forward. This year the western grain crops were good and the quality high. Wheat was just pouring freely to market, when the panic forced a heavy contraction in rediscount operations and prevented any large remittances from New York, Philadelphia, and other seaboard centers on produce account. By the end of September, harassed western merchants had to pay eight to twelve percent for sight exchange on New York, and a fortnight later could hardly get it at any price. Market quotations on grain and livestock dropped with a crash.[52] By November, western red and mixed wheats were selling at the seaboard for ninety-eight cents to $1.27 a bushel, while the general average for beeves in New York was eight cents a pound. In many Mississippi Valley communities, money disappeared so completely that little business was done save by dicker.

"You can have no idea of the troubles here," William Tecumseh Sherman wrote from St. Louis early in the fall. "We have correspondents as far up as Omaha City and all through Iowa who say the money has quit and gone they know not where." His neighbor, Frank Blair, bore the same testimony, though he believed that Benton's sound-money views had saved them from the suffering encountered in other cities. In Illinois, the stringency caused many people to cry for a special session of the legislature and a debt moratorium. "The most of us are determined to stand firm," wrote Lincoln's partner Herndon.[53]

One of the many who suffered from dire hardship in the St. Louis area was a former army officer who, after serving in the Mexican War and the Northwest, was living in pinched fashion on a small farm near the city. Two days before Christmas he realized that he was without money to buy gifts for his small children. He possessed a gold hunting-case watch. Placing it on a pawnshop counter, the shabby farmer took $22 from the pawnbroker's hand and signed his name on the ticket—U. S. Grant. He little thought that this ticket, with all its

51 N. Y. *Weekly Tribune*, October 3, 1857.
52 Report of Brit. Consul, Chicago, September 30, 1857; FO 5/678.
53 W. T. Sherman, September 22, 1857, Ewing Papers; F. P. Blair, Jr., October 16, 1857; Blair-Lee Papers; W. H. Herndon, October 5, 1857, Trumbull Papers.

associations of poverty and struggle, would in time become a cherished possession of the State of Illinois.

Within a few months, however, the storm had largely died away. "There never was a more severe crisis nor a more rapid recovery," observed the London *Economist*.[54] Before Christmas the New York banks voluntarily returned to specie payments, and with them up-State and New England banks. Those of Philadelphia and Baltimore resumed at the beginning of February, 1858, while all other banks not hopelessly insolvent were operating again by midsummer. Wise measures by New York financial leaders had helped the country banks accumulate funds which were in large part redeposited in the city coffers. Meanwhile, a steady flow of gold from California and Europe had reached the eastern centers—though the loss of the *Central America* off Cape Hatteras with more than four hundred passengers and $2,000,000 in treasure was one of the heavy blows of this dark year. These circumstances, which had made redemption possible sooner than had been expected, encouraged many to believe that the economic fabric of the nation was essentially sound and possessed a healthy recuperative power. The strong State banks of Indiana, Ohio, and Kentucky had stood erect throughout the tempest. The national credit was less shaken than might have been expected from the diminution in revenues.

But if the panic was over, the inevitable aftermath of depression had to be faced. It closed down over the country like a chill mist, filling the next two years with slowly diminishing misery and discontent. A painful readjustment in values had to take place. The price of land, for example, sank to a level bearing a far closer relation to tillage returns. Not merely speculators, but farmers who had mortgaged themselves to buy excessive tracts, paid a sad penalty. As late as 1860 Greeley wrote from Prairie du Chien: "The West is poor. The collapse of the railroad bubble . . . has spread desolation over the land." [55] Consumers' goods were a drug on the market. Europeans, estimating that they had lost hundreds of millions of dollars in worthless securities bought during the previous five years, were in a morose mood, and it gave them little comfort to think that Americans had lost more.

Buchanan wrote an inadequate analysis of the panic into his message of 1857, dwelling upon the stale theme of vicious systems of paper currency and bank credits. He said nothing about extravagant railroad construction, reckless speculation in land and commodities, or swollen imports. The London *Economist* characterized it as "a cloud of dust to cover a disgraceful retreat—a great scapegoat for the rash and impudent speculations—and in some cases, we regret to say, for the impudent frauds practised upon the too-gullible and too-avaricious

54 London *Economist*, January 2, 1858.
55 N. Y. *Weekly Tribune*, February 4, 1860.

people of the Old World." No action was expected of the general government in dealing with the depression, and except for certain palliative measures by the Treasury, nothing in particular was done.[56]

[VI]

The social misery of the winter of 1857–58 was even greater than that following the panic of 1837. Throughout the country, railway construction halted. In New England, textile mills stood lifeless amid scenes of poverty and discouragement. In Cincinnati, of some twenty-five thousand employees in clothing establishments fully half were discharged. More than half of the furnaces and iron mills of the country were idle, those of Pennsylvania being especially hard hit. The lumbermen of Wisconsin and Michigan, discharged with hardly a day's warning, were soon on the verge of starvation. In St. Louis, more than a mile of smokeless funnels lay frozen at the wharves. While New Bedford whalers and Gloucester fishermen commiserated with each other on the failure of their markets, Boston reported that two hundred and fifty ships were tied up. Frightened immigrants turned homeward in such numbers that the outgoing Boston and New York packets were soon full.[57]

The situation gave its opportunity to demagogues. Mayor Fernando Wood of New York lost no time in sending the Common Council a message which, mingling good proposals with bad, might have had a friendlier reception from the press but for its violent language. Pointing out that two hundred thousand New Yorkers depended directly or indirectly on manual labor, and that midwinter would find fifty thousand men out of work, he suggested a resort to public projects. Central Park needed improvement; a new reservoir had to be built; enginehouses were needed; and streets required paving. The city might well buy fifty thousand barrels of flour and corresponding quantities of corn meal and potatoes to be used in part payment of wages. This would be better than placing the unemployed on pauper relief. The proposal was sound, but unfortunately Wood made a venomous appeal to class feeling, and seemed to the propertied classes to be inciting men to violence. Multitudes, he wrote, "labor without in-

56 London *Economist*, December 26, 1857. Secretary Cobb began using some of the gold in the sub-treasuries to redeem government bonds, thus furnishing the banks with much-needed specie, while he speeded the mints to increase the circulation of coins. Government revenues fell, and when Congress met in December, 1857, a deficit clearly impended. Under emergency legislation, Treasury notes were issued, while later a loan of twenty millions was floated. Government expenses were somewhat reduced; indeed, Buchanan thought that Cobb and Jacob Thompson had done marvels in this direction. Buchanan, *Works*, XI, 243.

57 N. Y. *Times*, *Tribune*, October-December, 1857; Providence *Tribune*, October 23; Chicago *Journal*, November 7; Boston *Transcript*, November 9; Nevins, *Hewitt*, 171; Cole, *Era of the Civil War*, 203.

come while surrounded by thousands in selfishness and splendor who have income without labor."

Throughout the land, observers noted that workingmen did not bow to summary discharges and cruel pay reductions with the spiritless docility they had exhibited after the panic of 1837. They had learned fast in the interim years; the ideas of Owen, Fourier, and George Henry Evans, the writings of Leggett and Greeley, had taught them much. Philadelphia had its "hunger meetings," where thousands passionately implored Mayor Vaux to provide public works. "We will loan our labor, and our labor is capital," they declared, "if you will assure us that the scrip of the city, which we are willing to accept, will be taken for bread and butter, tea and sugar." In New York, noisy demonstrations were staged in City Hall Park and Tompkins Square, while long processions marched under banners inscribed "Work" and *"Arbeit"* to present the authorities with petitions declaring that work was a right. These ebullitions were orderly. When sharp pay cuts were imposed by some New England textile mills, the employees struck. Nor did they stay quietly at home; they thronged the streets, jeering their comrades who remained at the looms. New York, Philadelphia, Chicago, and other cities undertook some special municipal enterprises. But they were inadequate, and a defiant spirit was shown by workers all winter.[58]

The depression was most severe in the Northern industrial areas, and in the Middle West where an indifferent crop year in 1858 prolonged its effects. Of course a considerable part of the losses in the deflation of western land values fell upon the East. The border States, and particularly the tobacco kingdom, were also hard hit. Tennessee and Kentucky tobacco-growers found that, as most of the banks serving them suspended, they could not sell their product at all, and, when the eastern ports resumed buying, it was at halved prices. Many a trader went down and many a fortune melted away. Seven-eighths of the Virginia manufacturers of tobacco had to give up operations for the winter, for, with their drafts on the banks returned unpaid and with prices of cigars and plugs falling heavily, they could not meet their running expenses. Many of the factories returned their hired slaves to the owners. It was a dark season which followed in large parts of Virginia and North Carolina.[59]

The cotton kingdom suffered least of all. It by no means escaped scot-free, for the staple suffered a gradual but in the end a serious fall. Cotton quoted in September at sixteen cents a pound had dropped by Christmas to nine cents. While the largest crop yet known was being gathered, it became clear that both New and Old England would furnish a lighter demand than usual. The South, however, had not run into debt in the reckless fashion of the North. It had not

58 Pleasants, *Fernando Wood, passim.* At Chicopee this winter, women operatives earned an average of only $1.40 a week; Vera Schlakman, *Econ. Hist. of a Factory Town,* 143.
59 W. P. Titus, *Picturesque Clarksville,* 388, 389; J. C. Robert, *Tobacco Kingdom,* 227, 228.

imported so many luxuries, built so much railroad mileage in excess of need, or speculated so much in stocks and commodities. "In no respect are we the worse off than we were twelve months ago," boasted the Lynchburg *Virginian*.[60] The weak price of cotton might worry some planters as they sat down to their Christmas turkey. But, as various leaders assured them, they had only to store their bales under their own sheds and wait until prices grew better—as they did by spring of 1858.

The Southern banking system, moreover, stood up more sturdily than that of the North. The important houses of New Orleans came through the ordeal almost unscathed. In this busy commercial center the specie reserve against liabilities was one-third, or more than twice as great as in the country at large. Then, too, Louisiana law limited credit operations of each bank to twice its capital, prohibited banks from paying out at their counters any but their own notes, and laid down strict requirements as to the security basis for loans. Charleston banks which had suspended made a rapid recovery. Even where the banks stopped specie payment, as in North Carolina, the blow was less felt because the South depended less on specie. In Mississippi, for example, all the banks suspended. But there were only two of them; and as Governor McRae told the legislature, they had but small capital and circulated only a moderate amount of notes.[61]

Proud Southerners lifted exultant voices. The North is tottering with paralysis, declared Herschel V. Johnson of Georgia; but the South, with three million cotton bales, "stands calm and unmoved, poised upon the consciousness of her capacity to outride the tempest." [62] Our wealth, boasted *De Bow's Review*, is permanent and real, while that of the North is fictitious.[63] Senator Hammond called attention to a circular from a New York commercial agency, Tappan & McKillop. Listing the failures of 1857, it computed that the free States, with one hundred fifty-five thousand, five hundred and twenty-six business firms, had lost 3.24 percent, while the slave States, with sixty-one thousand, four hundred and ten business establishments, had seen only 1.21 percent go under. This agency estimated the total loss to the commercial community in the free States, after allowing for probable payments, at $142,000,000, and that in the slave States at less than $17,500,000. The liabilities of failed banks and mercantile houses in Massachusetts during 1857–58 were $6,115,000 against only $3,800,000 in Loui-

60 Quoted in *National Intelligencer*, October 3, 1857.
61 Annual Message, November, 1857. The admirable Louisiana law, which grew out of the depression of 1837–42, is discussed in W. O. Scroggs, *A Century of Banking Progress*, 132–135. Loans of capital had to be separated from loans of deposits; deposit loans were restricted to ninety-day paper; and a large specie reserve was required against all liabilities. A State supervisory board was created, which had to examine each bank four times a year. Louisiana pointed the way to other States, which in time followed her example.
62 N. Y. *Weekly Tribune*, November 7, 1857.
63 *De Bow's Review*, December, 1857.

siana. Similar liabilities in Virginia were lower than those in Michigan, while in Georgia they were less than half the Ohio totals.[64]

By the spring of 1859, the whole country seemed fast recovering. Pennsylvania iron mills and New England textile plants, though still depressed, were resuming activity. The South, with crops abundant and prices high, was notably prosperous—perhaps more prosperous than ever before. Railroad stocks were rising and railroad construction was being restored. Settlement and trade were flowing briskly into the West, where only the poor harvest had prevented a rapid liquidation of debt. Imports had fallen off so steeply that in 1858 they were little more than three-quarters of their value the previous year; and as a result the balance of trade favored the United States. The three chief elements in the nation's recovery were the rich revenues from cotton, the keen foreign demand during 1858 for foodstuffs (European harvests in 1857 having been poor), and the continued flow of California gold into world markets. Many communities, however, were still debilitated.

The psychological, social, and political consequences of this swinging economic blow were certain to be important. Some had been foreseen at once. A check to immigration; a marked accentuation of social discontent and radical agitation; a drop in the prestige of the Administration, were all immediately noted. As government revenues fell, without any effort to tap important new sources of revenue, the national debt was rising fast; it went from about twenty-nine millions in 1857 to almost sixty-five millions in 1860. As the American correspondent of the London *Times* wrote, many signs indicated that this financial deficit would be the groundwork of an attempt to revive the policy of protection.[65] "I look now to see matters of finance, the tariff, and so on become the leading topics in Congress," predicted Frank Blair, Jr. Most important of all, however, was the increased self-confidence of the South, its faith in its economic impregnability, its belief that its products were indispensable to the world.

64 See letter of J. M. Leitch, March 17, 1858, Hammond Papers, LC; table, *Bankers' Magazine*, XIII, 641–643.
65 Quoted in London *Economist*, August 21, 1858.

New Wine in Old Bottles

ALL MEN, according to an old maxim which rests on ample authority, derive a subtle pleasure from the misfortunes of their associates. While we would wrong the South to say that it was pleased by the heavy stumble of the industrial North in the panic of 1857, nevertheless many Southern people did feel that the event justified some of their criticisms. To understand the psychological effects of this economic disaster, we must realize that the waters of social and political controversy were boiling furiously, and that each section was assailing the fundamental basis of the others' civilization. No Communist of 1950 could have seized more eagerly on an economic depression in Western Europe as proving the vulnerability of democratic institutions than Southerners seized on the depression of 1857–58 as proving Northern weakness. Seldom in our history have two parties flung at each other weightier polemics—books, pamphlets, review articles—than the slave State and free State publicists were discharging in these years. Inevitably, any major social disturbance would be interpreted in very different fashions on the two sides of the Potomac.

[I]

Already, Southern writers had stated in both verse and prose the thesis that Northern wage-earners toiled in constant danger of that misery which actually filled the streets of Boston, New York, and Chicago in the winter following the panic. In 1854, William J. Grayson, postmaster of Charleston, a man in his middle sixties, had issued through the press of his friend John Russell a ninety-page poem in heroic couplets, after the style of Pope, called *The Hireling and the Slave.* Running through two small editions, it was republished with additional verse in 1856. The author threw his exposition into two parts. The first contended that the state of the slave and that of the hireling were substantially identical in that each was compelled to labor, and each got the same reward, a subsistence:

How small the choice, from cradle to the grave,
Between the lot of hireling and of slave!
To each alike applies the stern decree
That man shall labor, whether bond or free;
For all that toil the recompense we claim—
Food, fire, a home, and clothing—is the same.

But the hireling, declared Grayson, could not always find the employment he sought, nor obtain the subsistence, whereas the slave never lacked food and care. The versifier paused to explain how slavery had improved the lot of Africans lifted out of the cannibalism and idolatry of Africa.[1] He passed into invective against the meddlesome abolitionists who would ruin the South as their British brethren had ruined the West Indies:

There, chief and teacher, Gerrit Smith appears,
There Tappan mourns, like Niobe, all tears,
Carnage and fire mad Garrison invokes,
And Hale, with better temper, smirks and jokes;
There Giddings, with the Negro mania bit,
Mouths, and mistakes his ribaldry for wit. . . .
There supple Sumner, with the Negro cause,
Plays the sly game for office and applause.

In the second, longer, and better part of his poem, Grayson contrasted the comforts, sports, religious enjoyments, and security of the slave with the precarious position of the industrial hireling. Turning to the rural life he knew so well, he presented scenes of hunting, fishing, and picnicking with a gusto worthy of Cowper or Thomson. What worker would not choose the bounties of Carolina—the fruits, the game, the wholesome toil amid moss-bearded oaks over the squalid city slum? So, too, wrote the poetess Millie Mayfield:[2]

Your laborer is white, *and your equal*—yet he
Is a sufferer in a much greater degree

1 Wrote William J. Grayson later: "The question of negro slavery in the United States had been discussed for many years. It had assumed all garbs except the garb of verse. I thought the subject possessed aspects both of argument and description which admitted a poetical dress. In a broad view of the transfer of the African to America it may be regarded not merely as an act of commercial enterprise or avarice but as an emigration of the Black to a new country. It was an emigration hardly more forced than that of the starving Irish peasantry and not attended perhaps with greater suffering. The negro was brought to a country where he could be trained to those habits of industry which alone constitute the foundation of civilization and make it possible for a people to improve. The advancement of the Black in all relations, civil, social, or religious, must come from the white race. The negro has never been able to originate a civilization. The white man cannot live in the negro's country. The negro must therefore be brought to the home of the white. This has been accomplished by slavery only. The benefits bestowed on the negro are obvious. The slaves of North America are the most civilized of the African race." William J. Grayson, MS Autobiography, edited by Robert Duncan Bass, South Caroliniana Library.

2 Millie Mayfield, *Progression; or, The South Defended*, 199.

Than his ebony rival . . . tho' this till doomsday
Perhaps you'll contend; but I've this much to say:
Let 'crises,' 'panics,' 'suspensions,' invade
And break down the barriers guarding all trade;
Let banks go to ruin and stocks sink to naught,
The whirlpool, to one class with misery fraught,
Glides light past the other as singing brooks play
In the beams of the sun on a calm summer's day . . .

Simultaneously, George Fitzhugh of Virginia had likewise carried the war into Northern territory with the contention that free society was a monstrous growth, the natural result of whose competitive cruelties was the corruption of public morals, the sapping of domestic affections, the oppression of the laboring poor, and the accumulation of a mass of pauperism and crime. His *Sociology for the South; or, The Failure of Free Society*, issued from Richmond in 1854, admitted that slavery had its imperfections, which as far as possible should be corrected—and the South would correct them if the abolitionists would let the section alone, or advise with it as friends, neighbors, and gentlemen. But he concentrated his attention upon the defects of the free labor system of Europe and the North. In proof of their gravity, he quoted the *Latter Day Pamphlets* of Carlyle, who had influenced him, and the writings of Fourier and Robert Owen. The white slave trade, he declared, was far more cruel than the black slave trade, for it exacted more from its slaves without protecting or governing them. The irresponsible capitalism of free society, exploiting its hands as factory fodder, pursued the hireling from the hovel to the poorhouse, the prison, and the grave. He characterized free society as a bag of cats tied up together; and he, too, contrasted the safety, comfort, and solidarity of the Southern slaves with the disintegration of Northern communities which followed the old maxim of the devil take the hindmost.

While Grayson used *Russell's Magazine* for vigorous press attacks on industrialism and defenses of slavery,[3] Fitzhugh continued to press his ideas in essays for the *Southern Quarterly Review* and *De Bow's Review*.[4] In the year of the panic, he published *Cannibals All!; or, Slaves without Masters*, an expansion of the earlier book and a bolder statement of its principles. One feature of the work was a rough eviction of Jefferson from his pedestal.[5] Fitzhugh frankly declared his belief that slavery suited the masses; that the duty of protecting the weak always involved the necessity of enslaving them; and that Northern com-

3 See especially "The Dual Form of Labor," *Russell's Magazine*, VI.
4 See his "Centralization and Socialism," *De Bow's Review*, XX.
5 Fitzhugh's most direct contradiction of Jefferson is his statement: "Men are not born entitled to equal rights. It would be far nearer the truth to say that some were born with saddles on their backs, and others booted and spurred to ride them; and the riding does them good. They need the reins, the bit, and the spur." See Harvey Wish, *Fitzhugh, passim*.

munities might be much better off if they adopted slavery as a form of communism. Let men look realistically at the cruelties of Northern society, he declared, and they must see how inferior it was to the kind paternalism of the Southern institution, which he termed the oldest, commonest, and best type of socialism:

Capital exercises a more perfect compulsion over free laborers than human masters over slaves; for free laborers must at all times work or starve, and slaves are supported whether they work or not. Free laborers have less liberty than slaves, are worse paid and provided for, and have no valuable rights. Slaves, with more of actual practical liberty, with ampler allowances, and constant protection, are secure in the enjoyment of all the rights which provide for their physical comfort at all times and under all circumstances. The free laborer must be employed or starve, yet no one is obliged to employ him. . . . His wants and other men's capital make him a slave without a master, or with too many masters, which is as bad as none. It were often better that he had an ascertained master, instead of an irresponsible and unascertained one.

Fitzhugh's proposals for the universal establishment of some form of slavery were justly derided,[6] but his picture of the cannibalistic tendencies of raw industrialism—which anticipated Marx's chapters on capitalist production—did not lose force in the months of depression and unemployment.[7] This middle-aged, self-taught Virginia attorney had really convinced himself that the competitive life of mankind, when not mollified by human servitude, tended toward degradation. He had seen little of free communities. His only visit to the Northern States took place after he had gained some reputation by his writings, when he lectured in Boston, went to see his kinsman by marriage, Gerrit Smith, and met Harriet Beecher Stowe. Alas that we have no record of the conversation of these hostile authors! Fitzhugh clearly owed much to those earlier panegyrists of slavery as a positive good, Calhoun, T. R. Dew, and William Harper, but he had hammered out some notions all his own.

The chief of these ideas was that the free labor system had never been more than an experiment, and had already proved a dismal failure. The ordinary workingman, he wrote, with insecure employment, no fixed abode, and few if any savings, was almost certain in the end, through disease, accident, or old age, to come to penury. Such hopeless men had few incentives to virtue and many to

6 See the long review in *National Intelligencer*, June 9, 1857. For Congressional attention to him see Harvey Wish, *George Fitzhugh*, 275–288.

7 Thomas Carlyle ("Ilias Americana in Nuce," *MacMillan's Magazine*, August, 1863) wrote that the difference between North and South was simply this, that Northerners wanted to hire their labor by the day, Southerners by the lifetime. Karl Marx, in *Das Kapital*, Pt. II, quotes the London *Times* of July 2, 1863: "Very many of us think that, while we work our young women to death, using the scourge of starvation instead of the crack of the whip, as the instrument of compulsion, we have scarcely a right to hound on fire and slaughter against families who were born slave-owners, and who at least feed their slaves well, and work them lightly."

vice and crime; life gave them little happiness and abundant misery. Mankind must reorganize itself on a positive gradation of human levels. The State must compel the idle to work, assigning every person his or her place in the labor field; it must place toilers under the most rigid discipline and direction. In Old England, New England, and other industrial areas, unskilled hands ought to be converted into slaves of the capitalists, forbidden freedom of movement, and kept efficiently busy. At the same time the State should guarantee them what they had hitherto lacked, ample food, shelter, and old-age care. In the West, broad tracts of land might be granted to an aristocratic class under entail, and landless, unemployed men might be attached to these estates as life tenants or serfs, again under guarantees of full security. Thus the nation would become one great family, while idleness, poverty, and social strife would disappear.

It will be seen that Fitzhugh's dream had a distinct resemblance to that of subsequent totalitarian theorists in Nazi Germany and Soviet Russia: freedom and poverty would vanish together. While the dream was both absurd and vicious, the writer's explicit criticism of capitalist recklessness and *laissez faire* toleration of poverty had a trenchancy which gave it wide influence in the South. He and many of his readers exaggerated the evils incident to freedom of contract and personal liberty, underestimated the benefits, and ignored the evidence that free society was steadily restricting *laissez faire* for the general good. Like the future totalitarian leaders, Fitzhugh made his ideas more palatable by drafting a constructive program for the benefit of the ruling class. He urged better public education, more diversification of industry, and a protective tariff to foster Southern manufactures. Altogether, his books and his articles in *De Bow's* gave comfort to many Southerners who, facing the rising storm of world disapproval of slavery, wanted some answer, however flimsy, to the increasingly searching attacks made upon their system by able Northern and British writers.

[II]

Some of these attacks linked themselves with the great economic changes of the time. That could not be said, of course, of such polemic works as Frederick Douglass's *My Bondage and My Freedom*, Solomon Northup's *Twelve Years a Slave*, or Benjamin Drew's *The Northside View of Slavery; the Canadian Refugees' Own Story*, which had appeared in 1855. It could not be said of Mrs. Stowe's *Dred*, or C. E. Stevens's *Anthony Burns: a History*, or the numerous books on the Kansas struggle, all brought out in 1856. It could not be said of Harriet Martineau's *Manifest Destiny of the American Union*, or the Rev. G. B. Cheever's *God against Slavery*, issued in 1857. But it could emphatically be said of the writings of Frederick Law Olmsted, who did more than any other man of the time to make the discussion of slavery realistic by examining in detail its practical workings, and describing all its concomitants in the life of the people.

Few books of economic and social observation ever written in any land possess the enduring interest of Olmsted's *A Journey in the Seaboard Slave States*, published in 1856, and *A Journey Through Texas; or, A Saddle-Trip on the Southwestern Frontier*, issued in 1857. In due course a third title was added: *A Journey in the Back Country* (1860). Olmsted was exceptionally well equipped for his work. A son of Hartford, Connecticut, he was of adventurous tastes, as he had shown in his boyhood wanderings all over the Connecticut countryside, in four early journeys with his elders of more than a thousand miles each, and in shipping before the mast for Canton at twenty-one. By vocation he was a farmer, though he had taken courses at Yale, and had served for a time with a mercantile house in New York. He had managed a small place in Connecticut and a much larger farm on Staten Island, and he had written a book called *Walks and Talks of an American Farmer in England*. Only thirty when he accepted a commission from Raymond of the *Times* to explore the South and report on its condition, he had a shrewd, flexible mind, a tolerant outlook, and an intense sincerity.

It should be added that he belonged to the moderate school of Northern thought, being quite untouched by abolitionism. He resented and opposed all talk of political interference by the North to extinguish Southern slavery. Regarding slavery as an unfortunate circumstance for which the Southern people were in no way to blame, and an institution which could no more be summarily abolished than prisons or hospitals, he rejected the Garrisonian abuse of slaveholders as highly mischievous. It was his opinion that Southerners possessed certain peculiar virtues. But he did think that a thoughtful demonstration of the economic disadvantages of slavery and a tactful encouragement of Southerners to move toward a free labor system might be useful. The first step was to analyze slavery on the spot; and he resolved to scrutinize the situation "carefully and fairly, but cheerfully and kindly." [8]

Equipping himself for his horseback expedition with a general letter of credence from the governor of New York, and with supplies ranging from emergency rations to gunpowder, from quinine to pocket classics, Olmsted in his first journey traversed Virginia, the Carolinas, Georgia, Alabama, and Louisiana.[9] He took careful notes on every aspect of life, white or colored: dress, diet, rural scenery, inns, barrooms, religious conditions, methods of making tar, hoeing cotton, and rolling tobacco, slave-hunting, Christmas jollities, Creole balls.

8 Olmsted, preface to *Back Country;* Mitchell, *Frederic Law Olmsted*, 45.
9 Mitchell, 84–86; Olmsted, *Seaboard Slave States, passim.*

land values, crimes of violence, the sand-hillers and other poor whites, roads, overseers, and the prevalence of malaria. He even recorded the songs of river roustabouts and the inscriptions on slave tombstones. Innumerable scraps of conversation are set down verbatim. Frequently, Olmsted supplemented these notes with material drawn from newspapers, farm journals, or books. When he described the diet of slaves, he collected facts on the fare of Eastern and European laborers by way of comparison.

The second book, that on the Texan journey, contains more of the Western frontier, wild and rough to a degree, and less of the tame, settled South. Olmsted and his brother, after traversing Kentucky, on which he wrote a valuable chapter, explored about one-third of the huge State, covering the region east and south of a line drawn from Nacogdoches through Fredericksburg to Eagle Pass; a region embracing ranching country, farming areas of good soil, the old American settlements of central Texas, the main sugar district, the town of Houston, and the German or half-German counties around New Braunfels. A novel range of topics demanded description: frontier military posts, Indian camps, Mexican towns, the character of the peons, the Alamo, cattle drives, Kendall's famous sheep ranch, deer and bear hunting, vigilance committees, alligators, and organized emigration. Again he missed nothing, from the price of wild turkeys to the number of mechanics in New Braunfels and the make-up of a California cattle-train.

Had Olmsted written systematic treatises instead of travel journals, he would have conveyed scantier information and produced books of far less human interest. The charm of his *Seaboard Slave States* and *Texas*, like that of his subsequent *Journey in the Back Country*, lies in the constant flow of diverting incident, the spirited dialogues, and the brisk alternation of scene-painting and human sketches, all interspersed with bits of vigorous analysis. On one page we find an account of a stage-coach journey over muddy North Carolina roads, on another a report of a talk with a Louisiana slaveholder about *Uncle Tom's Cabin*, on a third the story of his dangerous predicament when his horse stampeded and disappeared on a boundless Texas prairie. He could etch a little picture with expert touch, as in his night-study of some wagoners near Fayetteville:

I walked out, about eleven o'clock . . . and found, upon the edge of an old field, near the town, a camp of wagoners, with half a dozen fires, around some of which were clustered groups of white men and women and negroes cooking and eating their suppers (black and white from the same kettle, in many cases), some singing Methodist songs, and some listening to a banjo or fiddle-player. A still larger number appeared to be asleep, generally lying under low tents. . . . There were thirty or forty great wagons, with mules, cattle, or horses, feeding from troughs set upon their poles. The grouping of all among some old sycamore trees, with the fantastic shadows and wavering lights, the free flames and black brooding smoke of the pitch-pine fires, produced a most interesting and attractive spectacle, and detained me long in admiration.[10]

He could report a conversation with Borrow's fidelity. On a river boat he fell in with a tall, thin, awkward planter, with a knife hilt protruding from his waistcoat:

"Stranger," [the planter] asked me once, "did you ever come up on the *Leweezay*? She's a right smart pretty boat, she is, the *Leweezay*; the best I ever see on the Alabamy river. They wanted me to wait and come down on her, but I told 'em time was in the objective case to me. She is a right pretty boat, and her capting's a high-tone gentleman; hain't no objections to find with him—he's a high-tone gentleman, that's what he is. But the pilot—well, damn him! He run her right out of the river, up into the woods—didn't run her in the river at all. When I get aboard a steamboat, I like to keep in the river, somewar, but that pilot, he took her right up into the woods. It was just clairin' land, clairin' land and playin' hell ginerally, all night; not follerin' the river at all. I believe he was drunk. . . . They hev good livin' aboard of her, too. Haan't no objections on that score, weddin' fixins all the time; but I won't go in a boat war the pilot's drunk. I set some vally on the life of two hundred souls. They wanted to hev me come down on her, but I told 'em time was in the objective case." [11]

And while he was so exact that he sometimes halted to measure the precise distance between cornstalks or the inches in a ploughshare, he could also impart a picturesqueness to his narrative which verged upon the poetic. On the Cumberland River:

As we lay quiet one evening in the fog, we heard and listened long to the happy wordless song of the negroes gathered at firelight work, probably corn husking, on some neighboring plantation. The sound had all the rich and mellow ring of pure physical contentment, and did one good to hear it. Like the nightingale, the performers seemed to love their own song, and to wait for its far-off echo. It was long before we discovered that this was artificial, and came in response from the next plantation. No doubt, had one the tender and ubiquitous ear of a fairy, he might hear, of a fine evening, this black melody, intermingled with the whippoorwills' notes, all the way from Carolina to Kansas, resounding, as the moon went up, from river to river.[12]

The fundamental preoccupation of Olmsted, however, was with the economic condition of the South. As he wrote later, he found the position of both white and black races worse than he had anticipated, and the more thoroughly he studied the section the darker did the picture appear.[13] White mastership over the Negroes he believed a necessity, and emancipation undesirable for the exist-

10 Olmsted, *Seaboard Slave States*, 357, 358.
11 *Ibid.*, 562, 563.
12 Olmsted, *Journey through Texas*, 34, 35.
13 Olmsted, *Back Country*, preface.

ing generation. But on economic grounds alone eventual emancipation was highly desirable, and the way should be prepared for it by organized action. He constantly emphasized a few cardinal economic doctrines. "Servile labor must be unskilled labor, and unskilled labor must be dispersed over land, and cannot support the concentrated life nor amass the capital of cities." [14] Slavery meant ignorance—in fact, a vast apparatus was set up to keep slaves ignorant. The result was constant misapplication of labor, constant waste and breakage, constant exhaustion of the land. He saw stock maimed, crops ruined, topsoil swirling down rivers, because of the enforced ignorance of the labor corps. On Carolina rice plantations the Negroes would dislike and break any improved implement; they were happiest with a clumsy iron hoe. "It is a common thing, I am told, to see a large gang of negroes, each carrying about four shovelsful of earth upon a board balanced on his head, walking slowly along on the embankment, so as to travel around two sides of a large field, perhaps for a mile, to fill a breach—a job which an equal number of Irishmen would accomplish, by laying planks across the field and running wheelbarrows upon them, in a tenth of the time." [15] Lack of capital accumulations, skilled tillage, machines, and factories was tragically retarding the South, and these benefits could be obtained only through free labor.

At no point did Olmsted condemn the slaveholder as a type; at every point he deplored the slaveholding system. Of cruelty he saw little. The contentment shown by many slaves pleased him, and he was quick to praise the paternal kindliness of numerous masters. He found the slaves in general not merely well fed but more abundantly fed, in all probability, than the proletarian class in most other parts of the world. But the social and economic effects of the slave system upon the Southern community as a whole he thought extremely pernicious. It kept the millions of Negroes far below their potentialities for usefulness; it banished free white labor, discouraging the artisan, the mechanic, and the manufacturer; it numbed the ingenuity, skill, and enterprise of the white population; it applied to the land a slovenly, ignorant labor force; and too often it depended on a ruinous exploitation of the soil. [16] He attacked the slaveocracy which defended this scheme of things. "The present agitation of the country," he wrote in the preface to his *Back Country*, "results less from the labors of abolitionists than from the conceit, avarice, and folly of wealthy owners of slaves. These

14 Olmsted, *Journey through Texas*, 37.
15 Olmsted, *Seaboard Slave States*, 481.
16 *Idem*, 146-148, 286 ff., 195 ff., 208 ff., etc. It should be added that Olmsted did condemn the typical slaveholder of a few areas, such as Eastern Texas, where he met special brutality. These Texas planters, he writes, seemed to wish to work the "damned niggers" with a sole eye to cash profits; they constantly said, "Damn 'em, give 'em hell," as if they meant it; and they were determined to make the slaves' life infernal if they did not submit abjectly. *Journey through Texas*, 123.

constantly, and by organized action, endeavor to reverse the only line of policy by which safety and peace can, in the nature of things, be secured to the people of the South; for there are moral forces, as well as material, in nature, and there is the same folly in expecting to overcome the one as the other."

The system also struck him as hostile to democracy, fostering the sway of small patrician groups, restricting education, and in many places (most notably South Carolina) inculcating among the superior caste a contempt for the masses.[17] The large body of poor whites, a group whom he defined as those who brought nothing but their labor to market, he regarded as economically and politically the victims of the slave system.

Olmsted was in fact deeply depressed by the squalor, ignorance, and social degradation which he found in large parts of the South. The great mass of Southern whites he described as ill-clothed, ill-fed, and uneducated. Talking with everyone as he jogged along the roads and put up at night at farmhouses, he found that most common people did not know the elementary facts of geography: they thought Virginia south of Carolina, and Indiana somewhere between Georgia and Texas; they believed New York, then a city of seven hundred thousand, a town in which Olmsted must know everybody and see every Southern visitor; they talked in 1856 of the recent annexation of Nebrasky, which they thought as large as the original thirteen States. Many of them read nothing and knew nothing outside the affairs of their locality. He found their tables spread with coarse, ill-cooked food. He travelled almost the length of the South without finding a farmhouse which boasted of two sheets to a bed. He saw white women and children laboring in the fields, often beyond their strength. The scattered homes of the large planters of course bespoke prosperity, and sometimes elegance; but the great majority of Southerners dwelt upon a level of poverty. Indeed, he declares in *A Journey in the Back Country* that he honestly believes that the average free Negro in New York or New England lived in greater comfort than the average white man of the Lower South.

This does not mean that Olmsted failed to perceive the variegated class structure of the South, or to note that many families which lived in discomfort really had considerable capital. He was aware that a large part of the Southern population was composed of small slaveless farmers who owned land, houses, and implements, and that another large part was made up of farmers and small planters each of whom held from one to twenty or thirty slaves. Indeed, in his *Back Country* he states that nine-tenths of the planters were small planters and small slaveowners. What struck him was that many families which possessed a capital that Northerners would have thought substantial had a standard of living that the Northern farmer or mechanic would have despised.

17 *Seaboard Slave States,* 500 ff.

What was the cause of this low standard? In the hilly areas it was attributable to physiographic circumstances: poor land, inaccessibility of markets, and like factors. In Texas, frontier conditions played their part. In the old cotton area, however, Olmsted found the root of bad living standards in the institution of slavery. This region, which had the most favored soil, in the most favored climate, with the cheapest natural facilities of transportation to market for that product which commanded the most urgent commercial demand, should have been far richer than it was. Slave labor was by no means always unprofitable. To many individuals it yielded a very high return indeed, making the great planters opulent. But to the South as a whole, he wrote, it was a relatively unprofitable form of labor. It produced gains only in the sense in which the practice of rolling tobacco a hundred miles to market in casks had once yielded gains in Virginia, and only in the sense in which the harvesting of wheat with sickles and threshing it with flails had once yielded gains. Slave labor was in itself inefficient; the necessity of investing most of the free capital of the South in it, so that funds could not be used for better buildings, livestock, roads, bridges, and increased soil fertility, was calamitous to the section. The constant increase in the slave investment arose largely from the special feature of the Southern economy —its dynamic, expanding character. As Southerners viewed slavery, it was not merely a labor system but a system of colonization as well.

In the distant future Olmsted looked forward to the abolition of slavery as an unprofitable, anachronistic institution. Meanwhile, as the best step for the immediate amelioration of the South, he advocated its restriction to a definite territorial area. The result would be beneficent. The natural increase of the negroes would make them more abundant within this area and provide more and cheaper labor. Land would then rise in productiveness. This rise would bring about better transportation facilities; and, as more goods were exported, so a richer assortment of wares would be imported. Articles of use and comfort, including tools and machinery, would become more accessible, and with them the methods of agriculture would improve. Mines would be opened, textile mills be built, and other factories established—and thus poverty might slowly give way to prosperity. At the same time, the South ought to take some immediate steps toward ultimate emancipation. That is, it should educate the Negro; give him an incentive to perform larger tasks and more skilled work by compensating him for unusual achievement; let him save money, and respect his family relationship:

When he desires to marry, and can persuade any woman to marry him, let the two be dealt with in partnership. Thus a young man or woman will be attractive, somewhat in proportion to his or her reputation for industry and providence. Thus, industry and providence will become fashionable. Oblige them to purchase food for their children, and let them have the benefit of their children's labor, and they will be careful to teach their children to avoid waste and to honor labor. . . . When any man has a balance to his credit equal to his value as a slave, let them constitute him a free man. It shall be optional with him and his employer, whether he shall continue longer in the relation of a servant.[18]

Olmsted was as eager to see the South assimilate its society to a free labor system as Fitzhugh was to convert the North to a rigid caste system based on servile labor; and Olmsted really knew both sections well, while the untraveled Virginia theorist knew neither. The Northerner, who includes facts on the earning power (expressed in food, shelter, and comforts) of the Yankee wage-earner, tells us frankly his opinion of those writers who believed slavery a "positive good." Virginia in 1832 had come near to emancipation; in 1857 she was further from it than ever. "Like a poor man rendered prematurely imbecile by his long endurance of pain, and who, conscious that every pretext against the application of the surgeon's relieving knife has long since been exhausted, finally, in unconquerable cowardice . . . throws himself, in a flood of grateful tears, into the embrace of some contemptible, bragging quack, who pretends that his disease has hitherto been entirely misunderstood . . . ; so Virginia now insultingly spurns from her counsels all who suggest that slavery is *ever* to be eradicated, and not one man is allowed to enter her legislature who dares to declare and demand 'the rights of the middle class.' "[19]

[III]

Another attack upon slavery, this time from the pen of a Southern-born journalist, Hinton Rowan Helper, was still more intimately connected with the economic changes of the time. It let some light—of dubious quality, to be sure —into a dark situation. Such Southern apologists as Harper, declared Olmsted, persistently ignored the poorer class of the white population.[20] As a practical student of all sides of Southern life, Olmsted paid close attention to them, and was distressed by their ignorance, indigence, and helplessness. Intelligent representatives of the underprivileged whites voluntarily told him that slavery laid a heavy incubus upon their folk. The sand-hillers of South Carolina, gaunt, cadaverous, and listless, living in shanties on rice and milk, their women sometimes working at hand looms for a wage of sixteen cents a day; small subsistence-farmers on the Congaree, superstitious and idle, their dress the coarsest

18 *Seaboard Slave States,* 444. For a brief account of the complex social structure of the South and the predominance of the small farmer and small planter of substantial capital see *Ordeal of the Union,* I, 468, 469.
19 *Idem,* 287, 288.
20 *Idem,* 357.

cloth, their chief sustenance a porridge of cow-peas;[21] the illiterate folk of the frontier regions of Louisiana and Arkansas, the wretched starvelings and wild men of the pine woods in Georgia, the backward hillbillies of north Alabama— these were all victims of slavery.[22] He noted that white artisans were constantly made to feel themselves engaged in a degrading competition with slave labor. He commented upon the lack of educational facilities for the poor in most slave-holding communities.[23]

Unexpectedly in 1857 appeared a forcible appeal to that great majority of Southern whites who possessed no slaves. "The Resurrection of the Dry Bones" was the title which the New York *Tribune* placed above its eight solid columns of summary and comment, for if Helper's *Impending Crisis* were read, Ezekiel's prophecy of an exceeding great army risen from the valley of skeletons might be realized. The book soon picked up with enhanced interest because of the concern with all economic subjects generated by the panic.

The few who had heard of Hinton Rowan Helper knew him as author of a disillusioned, prejudiced book, *The Land of Gold*, on a three years' unprofitable sojourn in California. A North Carolinian, the son of a poor blacksmith named Helfer, he had from boyhood reflected upon the pernicious effects of slavery on the white race, and his residence in the North and Far West had crystallized his convictions on that subject. He had no interest whatever in the moral aspects of slavery, and no feeling for the colored people but dislike. To the end of his life he regarded Negroes, Indians, Chinese, and other colored folk as obviously inferior races of mankind; in his work on California he had lumped the Digger Indians and the blacks together as degraded groups, and had attacked the abolitionists.[24] His family had possibly owned slaves (he mentions three by name), and he was convinced that the Negroes could not exist in the United States without becoming subordinate to the will of the whites, or else dropping to a very low level of life.[25] He believed fervently in a white America. The coexistence of these other peoples was a calamity on any terms, but he thought it particularly a calamity when fostered by the crippling institution of slavery, which enriched a few white men and injured all the others. What he had seen of the rapid progress of the North and West had convinced him that the South was being tragically outdistanced, that the blindness of its own citizens to its terrible handicaps was appalling, and that the non-slaveholding majority must be awakened to the evils from which they were suffering.[26]

21 *Idem,* 505, 506, 507.
22 Olmsted, *Journey through Texas,* 61, 62.
23 Olmsted, *Seaboard Slave States,* 296, 297.
24 Helper, *The Land of Gold,* 276; T. V. Theobald's MS Life of Helper, Columbia Univ.
25 In *Nojoque: a Question for a Continent.*
26 Southerners had frequently uttered precisely Helper's sentiments. C. J. Faulkner had told the Virginia House of Delegates on January 20, 1832, that the once fertile Common-

Helper resolved to address a warning not to the illiterate "poor whites" in the specialized meaning of that unscientific term, but the great body of self-respecting, thoughtful small farmers, artisans, shopkeepers, and clerks of the South—the millions who had no slaves but held a deluded loyalty to the de-vitalizing slavery system. If the more primitive whites of the hill-billy type heard his arguments, all the better; but he had sprung from the yeoman and mechanic groups himself, and knew they constituted the real strength of his section.

He was shrewd enough to realize that he must buttress his argument at every step with facts, figures, and influential testimony. Though only in his mid-twenties and mainly self-schooled (he speaks of getting his early education from some half-dozen old books which had found their way into his Davie County neighborhood, and which he read by the light of pine knots at his father's hearth), he was master of a clear, vigorous English style. His *Land of Gold* proves that, and so do his surviving letters of the period.[27] Spending about two years in study, travel, and writing, he completed his manuscript in Baltimore early in 1857. When he sought a publisher there, he was shown a Maryland law which made it a criminal offense to print anything that tended to excite discontent among colored people. The disgusted Helper caught a train to New York. Established publishers like Harper and Appleton rejected his volume, for they had no mind to anger their Southern customers. Finally, after Helper had guaranteed costs of paper and printing, A. B. Burdick of Nassau Street issued the 420-page volume in midsummer. It was at once reviewed far and wide, even in England.[28]

"Non-slaveholders of the South! farmers, mechanics, and workingmen, we take this occasion to assure you that the slaveholders, the arrant demagogues whom you have elected to offices of honor and profit, have hoodwinked you, trifled with you, and used you as mere tools for the consummation of their wicked designs. They have purposely kept you in ignorance, and have, by moulding your passions and prejudices to suit themselves, induced you to act in direct opposition to your dearest rights and interests." So cried Helper, emphasizing the fact that among the six million one hundred eighty-five thousand whites of the slave States in 1850 there had been only three hundred fifty thousand slaveowners or slave-hirers. His book contained much denunciation of "the bloodhounds of slavery." Speaking of the necessity for uprooting

wealth had become "barren, desolate, and seared," and that the change was to be attributed solely to the withering effects of slavery; to that unfortunate state of society in which free-men regarded labor as disgraceful, and slaves shrunk from it as a burden tyrannically imposed on them.

27 Notably those in the Blair-Lee Papers.
28 Greater part of N. Y. *Weekly Tribune*, July 4, 1857.

the institution, he wrote that men who wished to perpetuate it were on a level with the basest criminals. At one point he suggested that slaveholders might become the objects of vengeance from non-slaveholders by day and of attacks by the negroes at night. At another he remarked that it was for the poorer

THE

IMPENDING CRISIS

OF

THE SOUTH:

HOW TO MEET IT.

BY

HINTON ROWAN HELPER,

OF NORTH CAROLINA.

Countrymen! I sue for simple justice at your hands,
Naught else I ask, nor less will have,
Act right, therefore, and yield my claim,
Or, by the great God that made all things,
I'll fight, till from my bones my flesh be hack'd!—*Shakspeare.*

The liberal deviseth liberal things,
And by liberal things shall he stand.—*Isaiah.*

FIFTIETH THOUSAND.

NEW-YORK:
A. B. BURDICK, No. 145 NASSAU STREET.
1860.

whites to decide whether they should gain justice from the oligarchs, the "slaveocrats," peaceably or by violence. He accused "the slave-driving Democrats" of "almost every brutal outrage that ever disgraced our halls of legislation." This rhetoric defaced the book and was to make trouble for its sponsors. But the main tenor of the volume was sober to the point of dullness.

Negrophobe though Helper was, he did not make the tactical mistake of ignoring the moral and humanitarian argument against slavery. He devoted nearly a hundred pages to showing how Washington, Jefferson, Madison, Marshall, Randolph, and Monroe had condemned or deplored it; how eminent Northerners like Franklin and Jay had bewailed it; how England and other nations bore testimony against it; and how Catholic and Protestant leaders had long regarded it with aversion. Much the greater part of the text, however, was given to economic and social data. With the inflaming scalpel of sectional comparison Helper probed beneath the Southern skin. By census reports, State figures, and letters from mayors he tried to show the vast superiority of the free North in wealth, trade, production, libraries, education, churches, and literature. Slavery, he exclaimed, was ruining the South. Particularly was it ruining the poorer whites, a people who in "deplorable ignorance and squalid poverty" seemed to him below the serfs of Russia.

To what end did Helper print his arid rows of statistical tables, his dull facts on books, schools, and factories North and South? To arouse the non-slaveholding whites to thrust aside the "slaveocrats," to convince them that the Negro must be emancipated, and to urge the nation to transport the blacks back to Africa. "Why will you not see realities?" Helper demanded in effect. "Why will you yeomen and artisans not throw off your thraldom? Do that and you can insist on emancipation followed by African resettlement; the preludes to Southern progress, wealth, and cultural distinction." Essentially, he was appealing to the small farmers and laborers of the South to conduct much the type of revolt which, when great political and economic changes had prepared the way, Ben Tillman, Cole Blease, Huey Long, and others led a generation or two later.

Always specific, Helper laid down an eleven-point program for the slaveless whites. They should begin by a thorough organization for independent political action. Then they should move forward to exclude slaveholders from office, to boycott slaveholding merchants, hotelkeepers, and professional men, and to stop proslavery newspapers. They should end by taxing owners $60 for every slave, the money to be used to carry negroes to Africa, Latin America, or some distant part of the United States. Once the yeomen gained control, they should enforce a general liberation within a reasonable time. "Then let us charter all the ocean steamers, packets, and clipper ships that can be had on liberal terms, and keep them constantly plying between the ports of America and Africa." It was a program as harsh as it was impracticable.

The immediate impact of Helper's book was considerable in the North, but very slight in the South. While Northern journals caught it up, sometimes critically but more often with elation, Southern newspapers tended to ignore it. Gradually, however, it gained sufficient Southern currency to make some notice imperative. Edmund Ruffin early in 1860 was reading it for the second time, and marvelling over Helper's delusion that any real hostility existed between slaveholders and non-slaveholders in the South.[29] Senator James H. Hammond devoted a speech in the spring of 1858 to its blunders, the least of which,

29 Edmund Ruffin, MS Diary, March 1, 1860.

he remarked, was the omission to point out that the three hundred fifty thousand slaveholders represented not individuals but families, and must be multiplied by five or six.[30] Hostile publicists gave it prolonged scrutiny, and in such books as Samuel M. Wolfe's *Helper's Impending Crisis Dissected*, and Gilbert J. Beebe's *Review and Refutation*, contended with many apt illustrations that the poor man enjoyed a better chance in the South than in the North, and insisted that the Negro, stamped with a permanent mental and physical inferiority, held precisely the place where he was most happy and useful.

The non-slaveholders whom Helper specially addressed read the book least of all. Nevertheless, Southern leaders manifestly dreaded the spread of its arguments. The small farmers and poorer whites had so many real grievances in unfair taxation systems, uneven representation, wretched schools, and other social and economic injustices that the call to a class war—the war that Ben Tillman, Jim Ferguson, and Huey Long subsequently led—was dangerous.[31] The race issue could as yet be used to maintain solidarity. Albert G. Brown of Mississippi, representing those rough frontier planters who particularly valued slavery as the quickest means to wealth, sounded the already familiar note of warning. Slavery equalized all white people by assigning to slaves the degrading labor, he wrote. If the slaveless whites let themselves be misled by Helper, they would sink to a lower level. While the rich saved themselves, the poor man would have to submit to Negro competition:

The negro will intrude into his presence—insist on being treated as an equal —that he shall go to the white man's table, and the white man to his—that he shall share the white man's bed, and the white man his—that his son shall marry the white man's daughter, and the white man's daughter his son. In short, they shall live on terms of perfect social equality.[32]

Yet if a really serious and protracted economic depression ever overtook the South, the suffering yeomanry would be unlikely to remain insensible to some of the arguments which Helper used. These would be expounded with greater force by more skilful men. It was significant that 1858-59 witnessed

30 *Cong. Globe*, March 4, 1858. See *National Era*, July 23, 1857, on impact of the book.
31 See the fiction of Faulkner and Erskine Caldwell for pictures of the gulf between the poor whites and aristocracy of the South—and the ill-feeling.
32 A. G. Brown, "Letter on the Interest of Non-Slaveholders in the Perpetuation of African Slavery," 1860 (pamphlet). Most non-slaveholders feared abolition even more than slaveholders. They believed they would suffer the most. The wealthy classes could lift themselves above the harsh results of emancipation; the poor would have to bear the competition of the liberated Negroes and adjust themselves to the new equality. They would have to live in a country delivered back to barbarism—so at least some of them reasoned. What an appalling fate would be theirs, wrote Daniel R. Hundley to the *Southern Advocate* (December 12, 1860): "What social monstrosities, what desolated fields, what civil broils, what robberies, rapes, and murders of the poorer whites by the emancipated blacks would then disfigure the whole fair face of this prosperous, smiling and happy Southern land."

the rise in the border States, including Virginia and North Carolina, of power-ful "Opposition" movements, which we shall describe later; movements based largely on the inequalities in taxation, representation, education, and other matters from which the small farmers of few or no slaves suffered. The keen-eyed journalist E. L. Godkin, after travelling widely on horseback in the South in 1856–57, wrote that the world had long rung with the wrongs and miseries of the Irish peasant and the Turkish rayah; that he had seen much of both classes; and that he believed the poorest whites of the South were worse off than either. Some kind of revolt could not forever be prevented.

[IV]

An inevitable result of the depression was the heightening of economic and class antipathies. The old, deep-seated animosity of the frontier toward the metropolis, the suspicion the West always held of eastern banking and trading interests, were touched to new life. "Who but Eastern jobbers and speculators are responsible for the panic?" demanded the Chicago *Press and Tribune*.[33] Farmers from Ohio to Kansas, suffering from frozen markets and beggarly prices, laid the blame on the manipulations of Boston, New York, and Phil-adelphia. The many settlers who lost their land through the foreclosures of eastern mortgages were filled with resentment. The hardship imposed by high interest payments to lenders, and by the refusal of railroads to make any material reduction in freight charges, brought down many a curse on the head of Boston plutocrats and New York Shylocks. Farmers of Central Illinois in 1858 held a convention which passed severe resolutions against "trading combinations," banks, and railroads for depressing prices and lifting interest rates and transporta-tion levies. They urged that every community form a Farmers' Club to strengthen the economic position of the tillers of the soil, and give them that class equality which they had lost by their own neglect. A Farmers' Congress at Centralia later in the year went further. It was angrily convinced that stock-yards and grain-market rings were robbing the agriculturist. Resolutions were passed, declaring that the producing class should assert not merely its equality but its supremacy, condemning rules for trading made by non-producers, and calling for the establishment of cooperative buying and selling agencies. This was plainly a forecast of the Granger movement.[34]

Even in Cleveland, Chicago, and Milwaukee, surly mutterings were heard over the ten or fifteen percent which these cities had to pay for New York exchange; a cruel imposition, thought many. Throughout the upper Mississippi

33 Chicago *Tribune*, quoted in N. Y. *Tribune*, November 4, 1857.
34 Beveridge, *Lincoln*, II, 569, 570, fn.

Valley, too (as in the South), an intensified demand for home manufactures was heard. Five-sixths of the Wisconsin and Iowa farmers wore shoes made in Massachusetts and hats made in New York; and this gear was paid for by corn which the Iowan sold for twenty-five cents a bushel and which cost the eastern workman seventy-five. Why not bring the shoe factory to Burlington and the hat factory to Oshkosh, saving freight both ways?

Even if manufacturing could not be transplanted in a hurry, the commercial system certainly might be modified to bring its center of gravity farther west. Horace Greeley, visiting Davenport, Iowa, the winter after the panic, prophesied that fewer merchants would thereafter make semi-annual pilgrimages to the seaboard for goods. Why should five thousand men take a costly journey of two thousand miles when two hundred agents could buy for them more judiciously? An expansion of jobbing businesses into the thriving western towns —into Dubuque, Racine, Burlington, Rock Island, Quincy, Springfield, Peoria, South Bend, Jackson, and Kenosha as well as Chicago, Milwaukee, and Indianapolis—would benefit everybody. Local merchants, replenishing their stocks more frequently, could pay for smaller and more numerous orders in cash or short-term notes; the goods would be fresher; and the east would have a more stable business.

Indeed, Westerners manifested a widespread feeling that henceforth they ought to stand more sturdily on their own feet, and pay less heed to eastern speculators, land sharks, railroad promoters, and boomers generally. (They forgot how many of these breeds were their own.) We need fewer dream cities, fewer surveyors, lithographers, and auctioneers, wrote Illinois and Iowa editors. But, they added, never has such an opportunity existed for Easterners to come out with a few thousand dollars and buy good prairie farms at rock-bottom prices.

Many poor men, caught in the depression, turned wistful thoughts to the old idea of free homesteads. Farms, in the boom days, had cost altogether too much. An Iowa correspondent of the New York *World* declared that the government's stubborn insistence on selling its land at high prices had been the primary cause of the northwestern depression.[35] It was a quaintly fallacious view, but not a few adopted it. Similarly, a demand arose for more competition in the transportation field. Was it not exorbitant rail charges that made wheat sell in the West for seventy cents when it brought $1.20 in New York? asked farmers. The government should develop rivers, canals, and harbors. On these points, said midlanders, the East and South must give way.[36] If the industrial

35 Iowa correspondence, N. Y. *World* quoted in *Weekly Illinois State Journal*, July 25, 1860.
36 Madison Kuhn, "Economic Issues and the Rise of the Republican Party in the Northwest," MS dissertation, Univ. of Chicago.

East was to receive the benefit of higher tariffs, then the agricultural West must have homestead legislation, and western shippers must have internal improvements.

A bargain on this basis could obviously be struck within the new Republican Party; but such a compact would just as obviously be regarded by the South as a hostile movement. Appropriations for internal improvements, A. G. Brown had told the Senate in 1856, are "a tribute levied upon the labor and wealth of one part of the country for the benefit of the other!" [37]

[V]

The most unfortunate of all results of the depression was the deepening of the chasm between North and South. Angry sectional recrimination began at once. Herschel V. Johnson laid the troubles of the Georgia banks to "the assaults from the commercial centers of the North." Greeley retorted with a peremptory summons: "Pay Up!"—if Georgia would only meet her commercial debts, the North would be more solvent.[38] The fact that the South escaped the worst evils of the depression strengthened the arrogant self-confidence of the Hammonds and Slidells. It was *our* cotton, Southerners were soon boasting, which when shipped abroad at good prices lifted the prostrate North Atlantic region to its feet. When the North and West began demanding reform and readjustment, the South, complacent in the rich yield of its main staples, was content to maintain the *status quo*. Its labor system, its steady expansion of cotton production, its well-tested principles, said Southerners, gave it economic, social, and political stability; why alter them? Only its excessive dependence on the Yankee manufacturer, banker, and shipper needed to be changed. Will the South, asked Johnson, "break the only chain that now fetters her giant limbs?"

More than ever, after 1857, the South chafed under the burden of its real and fancied tribute to Northern capitalists and middlemen. When the Boston *Post* estimated that New England sold sixty million dollars' worth of merchandise annually to the South, editors below the Potomac asked how much profit the Yankees extracted. When New Englanders boasted that their large fleet was the common carrier of the South, cotton shippers inquired just how much wealth it had taken from Southern pockets. Above all, Southern producers denounced Northern factors, bankers, jobbers, and exporters as leeches battening upon their hard-earned income.

The panic helped convince cotton-growers that their sales had become altogether too heavily dependent on eastern financial interests. Whenever Wall

37 Debate of May 6, 1858; *National Intelligencer* report. Cf. *Cong. Globe*, 34th Cong., 1st Sess., 1118, 1119.
38 Both quotations in N. Y. *Tribune*, November 4, 1857.

Street so mismanaged its affairs (as by delaying to pay its just debts to Europe) that no demand for sterling bills existed, then the cotton market sagged. And not merely did Southern staples pay a large profit to legitimate agents through whose hands they passed; they yielded—so the complaint ran—another large

SOUTHERN WEALTH

AND

NORTHERN PROFITS,

AS EXHIBITED IN

STATISTICAL FACTS AND OFFICIAL FIGURES:

SHOWING THE

NECESSITY OF UNION TO THE FUTURE PROSPERITY

AND

WELFARE OF THE REPUBLIC

BY

THOMAS PRENTICE KETTELL,

LATE EDITOR OF THE DEMOCRATIC REVIEW.

NEW YORK:

GEORGE W. & JOHN A. WOOD,
LAW BUILDING, 59 NASSAU-STREET.
1860.

profit to mere speculators and manipulators. Before long, Thomas Prentice Kettell, former editor of the *Democratic Review*, was bringing out his effective book on *Southern Wealth and Northern Profits*, which set forth in some one hundred and seventy pages of text and tables the thesis that, while the South produced vast wealth, the North grabbed most of it.[39] His argument boiled down to the old physiocratic doctrine that all profits of manufacture and trade come out of the land; and he estimated the annual Northern profits taken from the South at $231,500,000.[40] Like Helper, he made careless and emotional use of

39 New York, George W. and John A. Wood, 1860.
40 Kettell, *Southern Wealth and Northern Profits*, 127.

statistics. At one point he compared the wealth of New York and New Orleans, implying that the Northern city had a bloated prosperity, when his figures actually showed that their ratio of wealth to population was about the same.[41] The inevitable rejoinder promptly came in Samuel Powell's *Notes on Southern Wealth and Northern Profits*.[42] But Kettell found a public already burning with indignation.

Here, said some slaveholders, was the answer to Helper's fallacious analysis. In early days, Virginia and South Carolina had been busy, opulent States, boasting a vigorous leadership. Now wide areas were in decay, once-smiling farms were used for cattle ranges, and stately mansions were falling into ruin. Why? It was nonsense to point to slavery as the reason. The Tidewater South had possessed slavery at the height of its power and glory; Brazil and Cuba, possessing slavery, yet flourished. The true reason, wrote Richmond and Charleston editors, was that the North placed unequal burdens on the Southern people. The protective tariff, the fishing bounties, the charges of brokers, bankers, and shippers, all wrung a vast tribute from the South. The national system, wrote E. A. Pollard, has been "made a conduit of wealth and power to the North, while it drained the South of nearly every element of material prosperity." [43] The same view was expounded with still greater vigor in the articles, lectures, and letters of George Frederick Holmes, an omnivorous scholar of English parentage who became professor in the University of Virginia in 1857.

The South, according to its leaders, was wealthy and powerful, but might be far stronger if the North would but do it economic justice. Events of 1857–58 seemed to prove how completely dependent the world was on the great Southern staples. In Great Britain cotton manufacturing stood third in the list of occupations, employing more than half a million people directly and hundreds of thousands more indirectly. Shipments of cotton goods and yarn in 1856 had constituted one-third the value of the kingdom's exports. The welfare of countless British families and the prosperity of the country seemed bound up with the cotton-textile business; and the South supplied about four-fifths of the entire British consumption.[44] Fear that war might suddenly cut off this supply haunted the pillows of innumerable Britons, and spurred Manchester men in 1857 to form an association to promote cotton in other parts of the globe. India, where American seed had been planted, was the chief hope of British mill owners; but nobody pretended that Surat cotton approached in quality the

41 *Ibid.*, 132, 133.
42 Philadelphia, C. Sherman and Son, 1861. See also Wolfe, *Helper's Impending Crisis Dissected.* I have treated Kettell in another connection in *Ordeal of the Union*, I, 470, 471.
43 In *The Lost Cause*, echoing many early editorials.
44 London *Economist*, April 25, June 20, 1857.

"Uplands," "Bowed Georgia," or "New Orleans" grades from the South.[45] Lancashire had built on American fibres one of the most remarkable industrial edifices in the history of mankind; her two thousand factories, with twenty-one million five hundred thousand spindles and three hundred thousand power looms, had filled England with fortunes and raised Lancashire workers to the head of the European laboring class.[46] How could Lancashire exist without the South? For that matter, what could the cotton industry of the North, with nearly five million spindles, do without Southern production? And how would the world fare without Southern sugar and tobacco? [47]

While the panic increased the confidence of Southerners in their resources, it sharpened their resentment over tariff burdens which Kettell estimated at forty millions a year. Secretary Cobb, Senator Hammond, A. Dudley Mann, and others labored to establish direct trade with Europe and direct mercantile and banking connections with England, as the one way to lift the South to economic independence. Our drawbacks, declared Hammond, have not been inferior energy or intellect, and certainly not slavery, but our shallow bars, yellow fever, want of capital (for we use our money to settle fresh lands and thus clothe and feed the world)—and Northern exactions. Give the South direct trade, give it a fair tariff, land, and taxation system, and it will yet lead the world.[48] As Northern workers clamored for free homesteads and Northern manufacturers for higher tariffs, Southern opposition became more determined. "We must separate," Edmund Ruffin was writing in 1857, "and the sooner it is done, the greater will be the relative strength of the Southern party, and the more sure will be the success of the movement." [49]

[VI]

The tariff—this, on the morrow of the stinging blow from the panic, suddenly became a party and sectional issue. With the object of cutting down an unwelcome surplus,[50] Congress had just finished (in the last month of Pierce's Administration) a slight reduction of the rates of 1846, passed almost without debate, without visible relation to sectional interests, and without arousing any popular feeling. Now, however, the sleeping tiger of tariff controversy awakened, to ramp and roar his way through the next three generations of history.

45 *Ibid.*, May 23, 1857.
46 Henderson, *The Lancashire Cotton Famine, 1861–1865.*
47 Clark, *Hist. Manufactures in U. S., 1807–1860.* 552–558.
48 James Hammond to Cobb, March 29, 1859; Hammond Papers, LC.
49 Edmund Ruffin, February 2, 1857; C. C. Clay Papers, Duke Univ.
50 Stanwood, *Amer. Tariff Controversies in Nineteenth Century,* II, 83–109.

As a matter of fact, the tariff had been a subject of occasional contention in the press and in local politics, for the old Whig demand for increased duties had been inherited by a powerful wing of the Republican organization. Until now, however, the debate had been languidly intermittent, for most Whigs had been as moderate as sucking doves. Such men as Tom Corwin, J. J. Crittenden, and even Horace Greeley stood not for head-high but merely breast-high protection. The United States, they declared, ought industrially to be more self-sufficient, and less a British appanage. They quoted the words of the London *Times* in 1851: "For all practical purposes the United States are far more closely united with this kingdom than any one of our colonies, and [with us] the United States keeps up a perpetual interchange of the most important good offices; taking our manufactures and our surplus population, and giving us in return the materials of industry, of revenue, and of life." [51] A moderate, well-graduated set of import duties, helping the nation's nascent industries attain strength, would be the shortest road to genuine free trade; for with maturity these industries could fearlessly meet world competition.[52] To this postulate, such low-tariff statesmen as Robert J. Walker, supported by editors like William Cullen Bryant and Henry J. Raymond, had replied that the Treasury did not need more revenue, that it would be iniquitous to tax the many to benefit the few, and that our industries were already great and growing. "What has a giant to do with swaddling clothes?" [53]

The basic argument of the Whig-Republican protectionists was that the United States ought to produce its own iron, cloth, and most other manufactured commodities; that this could not be done while European wares came in unchecked floods; and that, when home manufactures once gained vigor, they would benefit American producers of raw materials far more than any European markets could. No nation, they argued, had ever grown rapidly in wealth, power, intelligence, and arts while exporting raw materials and importing finished goods. On the contrary, such nations had always been impoverished.

The United States, many said, had rolling mills, but they were very poorly utilized; for, without a tariff, profits were impossible. Yet one great iron mill in Chicago would open a market for more Illinois foodstuffs than ten such mills in England. Look at Germany! By a wise policy of protection she had created a textile industry which supplied her with cloth more cheaply than any other nation in the world. Before 1820, German cloth was seldom seen in America, but by 1850 it sold in New York on equal terms with British

51 London *Times*, June 4, 1851.
52 N. Y. *Weekly Tribune*, June 28, 1851.
53 Robert J. Walker quoted in N. Y. *Tribune*, June 26, 1851.

cloth. On the other hand, Italy had no protection and, except for silks, almost no manufactures; and the poverty of her people was proverbial. Not even in Ireland, another unprotected country, was there a more irregularly employed, wretchedly paid, shabbily clad population. The United States was exporting grain, meat, cotton, and lumber; it was importing rails, clothing, china, and hardware; and it had to redress the adverse balance of trade by pouring California gold into British pockets, and in addition filling them with bonds and stocks.[54]

In the spirit of Hamilton, the moderate Whig-Republican protectionists had pleaded for a balanced economy; and Henry Carey, who wrote many of the New York *Tribune's* editorials on the subject in the fifties, entitled one of his most effective volumes *The Harmony of Interests, Agricultural, Manufacturing, and Commercial*. Protection had benefited the German farmers, declared Carey, for not only did the industrial population of Germany consume large quantities of food, but the mills furnished agriculture with implements, garb, and household wares at prices as low as those in Manchester, Sheffield, and Leeds. The seaboard merchants of the United States were assured that tariffs, while not lessening foreign commerce, would greatly increase domestic trade. On every hand the protectionists found facts to illustrate their views. Certain Fall River manufacturers in 1850 made nearly half a million shawls, supplying the Canadian as well as American market; and this was held to prove the value of the thirty percent duty—the American shawl industry had become sturdy, and was furnishing goods at lower cost than if no duty had ever been laid.[55] Charles A. Dana, making a vacation tour of the Adirondacks, found that the Saranac Valley, which under the tariff of 1842 had promised to become a thriving ironmaking area, had been blighted by the low rates of 1846. Out of sixty-six furnaces and bloomeries, only three were left running, and they at only one-third their capacity.[56]

But the great body of Americans had seemed content with the Walker Tariff. Why not, when the national revenue was rising to unprecedented heights and furnishing a broad Treasury surplus? Why not, when in the first seven years of the fifties the nation's exports rose from $137,000,000 to $338,000,000; the imports from $178,000,000 to $360,000,000; and the shipping in foreign trade from one million four hundred thousand tons to two million three hundred thousand? When business in nearly every field was expanding, and with it banking and credit? To protectionists demanding a balanced economy, Douglas for the West and Walker for the South replied that a steady, healthy develop-

54 N. Y. *Tribune*, September 24, 1851.
55 N. Y. *Tribune*, August 8, 1851.
56 N. Y. *Weekly Tribune*, September 6, 1851.

ment was providing it. A forced growth of manufacturing at the expense of agriculture and the consumer was rejected by men satisfied with the existing system. "The result of that system," wrote Walker in 1853, "has been to double our exports and imports, and also our revenues; whilst the taxes imposed on our people have been diminished one-half. At the same time the increase of our tonnage, foreign and coastwise, has been unprecedented. These are great results, but I assure you, the good work is only fairly begun." [57]

But now, in 1857–58, to many the results seemed apples of Sodom. "That an efficient Protective Tariff would have kept our country out of the vortex of this mad whirlpool . . . we most earnestly believe," declared the *Tribune*.[58] Most Republican journals in the East opened fire on the low tariff breastworks, with the *National Intelligencer* and other Whig journals joining the bombardment. Friends of Seward recalled that in a speech of March 1, 1855, on iron rail duties, he had foretold the panic, and even the year of its occurrence, with signal precision. The government was stimulating importation, he said, when it should stimulate production, and the result would be a disastrous revulsion in 1857 or soon after.[59]

In the debates which filled the winter of 1857–58 the Democrats found the readiest scapegoat for the panic in banking errors. Buchanan told Congress that such calamities were inevitable so long as the amount of paper currency and the management of loans and discounts were left to fourteen hundred irresponsible State banks; and Nathan Appleton of Boston, echoed by a thousand voices in the South and West, laid the principal blame on the New York bankers, greedy manipulators who had expanded too much in fair weather, and contracted too harshly when the tempest lowered.[60] Most Republicans, however, found the scapegoat in the Walker Tariff of 1846, and the more recent tariff reductions.

Their demand for higher duties was posited on two main grounds. Pointing to the sudden stoppage of iron mills, textile factories, and other establishments under sharp European competition, they showed that these businesses suffered doubly from foreign goods when falling prices made the *ad valorem* duties a weaker defense than ever. Again, they argued that the country had imported too lavishly, spending its money recklessly for foreign merchandise, and letting an adverse trade balance drain off gold bullion and specie sorely needed at home. We have indulged in wild luxuries, said the Cincinnati *Times*; only California gold saved us from earlier disaster; yet a prudent tariff would have

57 Robert J. Walker, February 7, 1853; Cushing Papers, LC.
58 N. Y. *Weekly Tribune*, January 30, 1858.
59 *Cong. Globe*, March 1, 1855.
60 N. Y. *Weekly Tribune*, October 24, 1857; see Appleton's *Remarks on Currency and Banking*, enlarged edition, 1858.

made us the richest people in the world.[61] The foreign exchange brokers, lamented the *National Intelligencer*, have shipped money abroad in floods:

During the last fiscal year ending June 30, 1857, these brokers have sent out of the United States to pay for drygoods, cotton, and woolen cloths, hardware, glassware, cutlery, jack-knives, and domestic wares; saws, gimlets, axes, and chisels; rolled iron, hammered iron, bar iron, railroad iron, and other like things which should have been made by our own people, the sum of $69,136,922 in solid gold and silver.

Yet the *South* naively wonders at the scarcity of *specie*.[62]

With a Democratic Congress in power until at least March 4, 1859, and a Democratic President until at least March 4, 1861, no merely spasmodic demand for higher tariffs could accomplish anything. A sustained crusade was needed. Were any economic constituencies sufficiently strong and earnest to make a ten-year uphill fight? The answer lay primarily with the iron and textile industries.

Little by little, a compact, able, and well-to-do body of ironmasters had arisen in the East—and 1857 found them bitterly incensed. The United States was obviously suited to a great iron industry. It had iron ore, coal, and the necessary fluxes in close juxtaposition; it had capital, skill, and labor. Iron was demanded in ever-greater quantities for rails, farm implements, and articles of popular use. Inevitably, ironmasters and consumers of cheap British iron had clashed along a widening front. Walker, James Guthrie, and other low-tariff leaders believed that a just balance could be struck between the two interests, with iron manufacture growing steadily but slowly under moderate duties as the national needs increased. Production of iron, steel, and articles made from them was greater in proportion to population in 1850 than in 1840; greater in 1855 than in 1850. Secretary Guthrie had written in 1856 that considering this growth, the rising cost of freights from abroad as the interior population moved westward, and the constant home improvements in iron and steel manufacture, "Americans would be justified in expecting home supply for their own consumption before the year 1870 was reached." [63]

This slow, low-profit growth, however, often interrupted by setbacks and losses, did not suit aggressive industrialists. The *ad valorem* duty on iron, they declared, offered an inadequate protection. Fixed under the Walker Act at roughly thirty percent of the invoiced value of foreign iron, it fell whenever prices were lowered, giving lessened assistance to American mills just when they needed it most. When the Act was passed, a ton of railroad iron had paid

61 Cincinnati *Times*, October 7, 1857.
62 *National Intelligencer*, October 24, 1857.
63 Secretary of the Treasury, *Annual Report*, 1856.

about $15 in duty, and domestic production seemed rapidly overtaking consumption. But the British ironmasters in various ways reduced costs and prices, so that by 1850 the effective duty had fallen to half what it was in 1846; and many American furnaces were sold under the sheriff's hammer. A period of rising prices, under the influence of gold from California, then began. Iron quotations rose, and the duty went up once more to the point of protection, so that in 1852–54 American iron output steadily increased.[64] Railroad building was active not only in the United States and Britain, but all over Europe, in India, and in South America. The rolling mills of the entire globe in 1852 could produce enough rails for only some six thousand miles of track. Under the eager American demand for rails at $70–$80 a ton, the domestic mills (which of course added the duty to their charges) prospered. But a new era of cruel competition was at hand. British geologists found extensive ore deposits in the Cleveland area of Yorkshire, where fifty or sixty new mills instantly sprang up.[65]

By the end of 1854, plethoric imports had dispelled what Abram S. Hewitt called "the delusion that Great Britain could not supply all the iron required by the world at the present time." British rails had fallen in a year from $70 to $50, the *ad valorem* duties dropping with them. Stocks of iron were accumulating in every market in the world, and a majority of American mills had closed. As they faced ruin, the agonized ironmasters had once more raised a clamorous demand for higher duties.[66]

Yet in the South and West, the great Democratic areas, this demand still met the sternest opposition. Much of the press teemed with articles insisting that *all* duties on railway iron be abolished forthwith. Every railroad, declared one writer, must pay at least $1,500 a mile in tariffs, a hardship felt by new sections struggling to reach an ordinary standard of prosperity.[67] Why, demanded another, should hard-working communities, intent upon improving their transport facilities, pay tribute to selfish eastern millowners? Let the easterners show enough efficiency to meet the British price for rails, and let them build new mills in the West, where they would find abundant materials and an eager market.[68] In 1852, Hewitt, lobbying in Washington for better duties on iron, wrote a friend that no tariff bill could be passed without Southern and Western votes, and that concessions on railway iron would have to be made to obtain higher rates on other shapes. When the tariff of 1857 actually reduced iron duties, the struggling mill owners were deeply resentful.[69]

64 N. Y. *Tribune*, July 10, 1854.
65 Nevins, *Hewitt*, 108–111.
66 *Idem*, 112.
67 "Memphis" in *National Intelligencer*, May 6, 1856.
68 "Indiana" in *National Intelligencer*, May 17, 1856.
69 Nevins, *Hewitt*, 154, 155.

Textile manufacturers insisted as loudly as ironmasters that the Walker Tariff was grossly unfair, and indeed disastrous. Most woolen mills had been reduced to utter ruin, one observer complained in 1857. A steep duty on raw wool, and a lack of any correspondingly high duty on finished woolens, had placed them at the mercy of British competitors. Either raw wool should be made free (and free raw materials was classic Democratic doctrine, often stated by Guthrie), or satisfactory tariffs should be imposed on woolen goods; and though some sheep-growers might protest against the former step, efforts to increase sheep-farming by tariffs had accomplished nothing.

As for cotton textiles, manufacturers grumbled that Walker's abolition of "minimums" had stopped all efforts to make the finer fabrics and invited a torrent of British goods. In ten years, 1846–56, the imports of British printed and dyed cottons had leaped from thirteen million yards to one hundred fourteen million; those of plain calicos from ten million to ninety million. By partial use of cheap Bengal fibre, Lancashire was able to produce low-priced goods more cheaply than Lawrence and Lowell. These plaints fell on deaf ears.[70] The tariff of 1857 slightly reduced cotton duties, and placed only the lowest grades of raw wool on the free list, while reducing the duty on finished woolens. Textile manufacturers, too, were sullenly indignant.[71]

All these resentful interests had money to fight their battle. The capital invested in cotton manufacturing by 1860 approached a hundred millions. Woolen manufactures, situated mainly in New England and the Middle States, by that year had an annual value exceeding sixty millions. Northwestern Pennsylvania and northeastern Ohio alone then counted sixty-six furnaces.[72] And ironmasters and textile men found potent allies in other industries. Even the South had one important group of tariff claimants—the sugar growers. Competing with the West Indies and Brazil, they too grumbled over the *ad valorem* system. In the spring of 1857, a spokesman for the Louisiana planters asserted that the thirty percent levy upon the high valuations then ruling was double the amount needed to satisfy sugar producers if made a permanent and specific duty. It came to two and a half cents a pound on fine sugar, which was at least a cent more than growers wanted. What they did ask was a fixed protection against heavy imports when a large home crop (as in 1853–54) brought prices to a ruinously low level. It is significant that J. D. B. De Bow, editing his *Review* in the sugar metropolis, and wishing to see industries developed in the South, held that protection was frequently desirable.

All the manufactures of the country taken together in 1860 had an invested

70 *National Intelligencer*, January 29, 1857.
71 Dewey, *Financial Hist. U. S.*, 262, 263.
72 Eighth Census, Vol. III (Manufactures); Clark, *Manufactures, 1807–1860*, I, 498, 499.

capital exceeding a billion. The iron men had already learned the value of a regularly employed lobbyist, John L. Hayes, in Washington. In the period of depression, many industrialists rallied to wage a determined campaign.

They knew that they had a hard struggle ahead of them. Intermittent and lackadaisical effort had accomplished nothing against the insistence of the rural South and West upon cheap rails to extend their trackage, cheap implements for farms, and cheap cloth for yeomen and slaves. It could accomplish nothing, so long as a host of merchants, railroad builders, and land speculators took sides with the agricultural interests. The opening-up of the Mississippi valley and the Southwest seemed more important, for the nonce, than developing the seaboard industries by artificial stimulants. In the debates on the tariff of 1857, Representatives from three sections, Norton of Ohio, Boyce of South Carolina, and Bennett of New York, had agreed that the great mass of the American people should not be required to pay an indirect tax in favor of the manufacturers, while every Massachusetts member had voted for the downward revision. Garnett of Virginia had expressed the hope that America, the greatest democracy in the world, would take the leadership in a grand movement for unfettered commercial intercourse among all nations.[73] The same hope was expressed by Raymond in the New York *Times*. It was an alluring ideal, closely connected with some of the most idealistic currents of the time. Many of those who espoused the low-tariff policy were obedient to the bright vision of a freely interconnected world, first painted by Adam Smith and now eloquently defended by John Stuart Mill.

It would take time, labor, and money to make headway against these convictions. But the campaign was at once opened. While the *Tribune, National Intelligencer*, and Philadelphia *Press* pleaded for higher duties, members of Congress from industrial districts began to raise their voices. Senator Simmons of Rhode Island was quick to answer Buchanan's message blaming the State banks. Not so, he said; productive home labor had been unable to compete with foreign dumping, and an upward revision of the tariff would both fill the Treasury and revive industry.[74] Certain circumstances favored the protectionists. The old obstacle of the constant Treasury surplus was gone. New York was now a Republican State, while Pennsylvania, with her iron interests prostrate, had become doubtful.

[VII]

New wine had been poured into old bottles, and they were cracking. Through all the political movements after the panic, disputation on economic

73 *Cong. Globe*, February 10, 1857.
74 *Idem*, December 18, 1857.

issues ran as a deepening undertone. The South, more confident than ever of the superior toughness and resiliency of its system, and more sharply critical of Northern flaws, was determined to make a stand against tariffs, bounties, and land donations which hurt its interests; the West was more convinced than before that a rapid distribution of land to actual tillers would strengthen the foundations of the nation—a conviction which was deepened when Buchanan ordered the sale of large tracts under conditions seemingly favorable to speculators; while half the East was eager to shelter its industries from excessive foreign competition. Happily, the sections had great complementary interests, and the bonds of interdependence were still powerful.

The Sixteenth Slave State?

ANY CRITIC of democracy who wished to indict its American workings would have done well to attend the constitutional convention which sat at Lecompton in the fall of 1857. Destiny waited upon this body. The fate of the Administration, of the Democratic Party, and of the nation itself was to be mightily affected by its acts. And what was it? The sixty delegates, forty-eight of them from slave States, had been chosen by a small minority of voters in a rigged election; they met under the shadow of fresh election frauds committed by their supporters; they were regarded with open hostility by the majority of citizens. Four-fifths of them were ignorant, semi-illiterate, and prejudiced men, totally unrepresentative of the Kansas population. One of President Buchanan's correspondents wrote that he had not supposed such a wild set, with hardly six fit debaters in the lot, could have been found even on that frontier.[1] They began with three days of struggle to get a quorum, and ended with a shout from one prominent member: "Now, boys, let's come and take a drink!" [2]

Newspapermen from far and near had gathered in the picturesque hamlet, beautifully situated on a low bluff above the Kansas River, the hills and valleys bright with autumn foliage. They watched the evolutions of the several hundred Federal troops, horse, foot, and a brass field-battery, who had pitched their tents and stood ready to keep order. They examined the two hotels, the American and National, the heavily stocked barrooms, and the three shops—a hardware store, drugstore, and Leamer's general store. They lounged about the office of the weekly *National Democrat,* and some had their pictures taken by the ambrotype artist who had come in for the convention.[3] They climbed the steps of the two-story, clapboarded hall as the delegates gathered, and collected

1 Findley Patterson to Buchanan, November 10, 1857; Buchanan Papers.
2 Lecompton Correspondence, dated November 7, 1857, N. Y. *Weekly Tribune,* November 28, 1857.
3 See files of Lecompton *National Democrat,* October, November.

opinions on the vital issue: Would the constitution be submitted to popular vote? [4]

When debate began, the Northern correspondents could hardly believe their ears. If any fact in Kansas was plain, it was that an overwhelming majority of residents wanted a free State. Yet a preponderance of the convention was resolved to adopt a proslavery constitution and send it direct to Congress for acceptance. And if this preponderant body was, in the words of the Emporia *Kanzas News,* a set of "broken-down political hacks, demagogues, fire-eaters, perjurers, ruffians, ballot-box stuffers, and loafers," they had some shrewd leaders. Their managers included J. H. Danforth of Georgia, a tall, well-built man of piercing eye and stern countenance, who spoke little but showed consummate skill in maneuver; the dashing and persuasive young Colonel W. H. Jenkins, of South Carolina origin; and A. W. Jones, a lawyer from Virginia who was an accomplished wire-puller. At times they were reinforced by Lucius S. Bolling, an attorney from Georgia, who had oratorical force, and by Captain J. W. Martin of the reckless band called the Kickapoo Rangers. They gained encouragement from the Southern press, now in full cry for direct transmission of the constitution to Congress. Some of them exhibited letters from important Southern leaders, R. M. T. Hunter of Virginia having written two widely published arguments for this course.[5] Both leaders and followers knew that the one last chance of a slave State lay in writing an adroit instrument and avoiding any popular vote. All were influenced by hatred of Governor Walker—grown greater since his denunciation of the recent frauds.[6]

The moderate minority in the convention, who knew that some type of popular submission was almost imperative, were led by John Calhoun, Rush Elmore, and John D. Henderson; supported, of course, by Governor Walker, who was absent, and Secretary Stanton, who was present. Unfortunately, they lacked the single-minded determination of their enemies. Calhoun, with his record of activity among Illinois Democrats and his personal friendship with Douglas, was an honest believer in popular sovereignty. But his limited moral stamina had been weakened by whiskey—the Chicago *Tribune* reporter wrote of his

---

4 The Cincinnati *Gazette,* N. Y. *Tribune, Herald,* and *Times,* St. Louis *Republican,* and *Missouri Democrat,* all had correspondents present. According to Dr. Gihon, Lecompton had been a sort of moral plague spot, shunned by good citizens. The personnel of the convention was not unlike that of the regular Lecompton legislature. Gihon in his book on Geary in Kansas tells of a stage-driver who, falling into bad company in a Lecompton barroom, slept off his excesses in a shed. Roused the next morning by a man who wanted his vote for a bank charter, he flew into a passion, ejaculating: "It is bad enough to get drunk and make a fool of myself, but no man shall insult me by mistaking me for a member of the Kansas legislature!"

5 Nichols, *Disruption of the American Democracy,* 122.

6 See full characterizations of convention membership, Emporia *Kanzas News,* November 7, 14, 21, 1857.

florid face, swinish eyes, and Bardolph nose—and by association with proslavery Kansas politicians. He gave battle, but not with the temper demanded by the crisis. When the struggle ended the freesoil citizens bitterly indicted him as villain and traitor.[7] Rush Elmore, of a distinguished Southern family, had been appointed Federal judge by Pierce and was now esteemed the ablest attorney in the Territory. A stalwart six-footer of massive frame, his large head set squarely on his shoulders, his jaw firm, he was vigorous, conservative, and unscrupulous.[8] He spoke effectively for submission. Henderson was editor of the Leavenworth *Journal*. The trio were given assistance by Hugh Moore, vice-president of the convention, a former Georgian living in Leavenworth and a stump speaker full of Union-saving oratory, who after some hesitation came over to their side.

Sundry speakers for the majority made it plain that they still hoped to see a Southern type of society dominate Kansas. John W. Randolph of Atchison, a stonemason out of Kentucky, proposed that the upper age for militia duty be fixed at forty. "I think," he said, "that a man of forty-five is too old to be run about over the prairies at the will of some boy of eighteen who mought be captin. I expect we air goin' to make a slave State, and if we air most of the spectators will be children and niggers, and I object to makin' such a spectacle of an old man jist to make laughin' for niggers."[9] Warmer debate was evoked by a proposal that the legislature be empowered to stop the importation of slaves for sale. This paralleled the statutes of Georgia and some other Southern States. The object, said Randolph, was to prevent negro-traders from bringing in the scrapings of the Southern communities: "all the old, blind, halt, and lame niggers, so that they would get all the mean niggers. It would be so if the African slave trade was opened. The country would be filled with mean niggers." On motion of Bolling, who wanted no interference whatever with slavery, the restriction was eliminated.

The convention really began work, taking up draft sections prepared by various committees, on October 28. Most of the instrument, conventional in form and based on older State constitutions, was readily disposed of. The critical points were the slavery article and the issue of submission or non-submission; and the culminating battle took place November 6–7, the convention finally adjourning at one o'clock Sunday morning, November 8.

This final battle was a tensely exciting contest. As the convention for two days debated into the small hours, newspapermen reported bitter wrangling and the gloomiest uncertainty as to the outcome. The radical non-submissionists were determined to win, and fought like tigers. They were united behind the

7 Leavenworth *Times*, January 9, 1858.
8 Elmore family papers, University of North Carolina; Emporia *Kanzas News*, November 21; N. Y. *Weekly Tribune*, November 14, 28, 1857.
9 N. Y. *Weekly Tribune*, November 14, 1857.

demand that the constitution be sent direct to Washington as the will of Kansas, while the submissionists were divided on various schemes of reference. At one moment the ultras seemed to have won completely. On the night of November 6, taking advantage of dissensions in the opposition and the absence of a few moderate delegates, they passed a clause sending the constitution straight to Congress, with no popular vote whatever. The utmost excitement ensued. Moderates at once gave notice of a motion for reconsideration. The anti-submissionists, denouncing it, resolved not to adjourn until they had finished the text of the constitution and won the final vote. The battle then waxed violent. At last, early in the morning, the radicals gave way, permitted an adjournment, and trooped wearily to bed. But the moderates gathered at once in caucus, organized more firmly, and when the convention reopened later on the morning of the seventh, were able, 26 to 25, to reconsider the vote for direct transmission to Congress.[10]

In the final clash, an important part was played by an agent sent West by two Southern members of the Cabinet. Howell Cobb and Jacob Thompson, anxious to make their views known, first tried to enlist L. A. Gobright, a Southerner connected with the Associated Press, and then sent out a land-office clerk, Henry L. Martin of Mississippi.[11] His ostensible errand was to investigate charges of land-office corruption, his real mission to help guide the convention. It need not be said that Cobb and Thompson wanted Kansas to become a slave State. Just what instructions they gave Martin we do not know. At a later date when Governor Wise of Virginia, hearing sinister rumors, queried Buchanan about it, Thompson was evasive.[12] But we do know that Secretary Cobb wished the constitution to say nothing about slavery (which would leave it in existence); that he, like Thompson, wished the instrument submitted to the voters; and that he wished the voting list confined to those who recognized the existing government, which would leave out a great body of free State men. This, he wrote Alexander H. Stephens on October 9, "presents the only fair mode that I see of making Kansas a slave State, a result most desirable if it can be brought about on the recognized principle of carrying out the will of the majority." [13]

10 Lecompton correspondence dated November 7, 1857, N. Y. *Weekly Tribune*, November 28, 1857; some observers gave the vote as 27 to 24.
11 L. A. Gobright, *Men and Things*, 170.
12 See letter of C. J. Wise, December 17, 1857; Buchanan Papers.
13 Cobb to Stephens, *Toombs, Stephens, Cobb Correspondence*, 424. In the Covode Investigation of 1860, Martin, Thompson, and Cobb all testified. Their evidence shows that the two Cabinet members were in favor of submitting the constitution to popular vote, and asked Martin to make representations to that end in Lecompton. It also shows that the two men were by no means rigid in the matter. Martin quoted Jacob Thompson's words to him: "We are in favor of the submission of the constitution, when made, to the popular will of Kansas for ratification or rejection; but I am not willing to take the converse of that proposition; that is, I am not prepared to take ground against the admission of Kansas if a pro-

Probably Martin was instructed in this sense. He took up his quarters in the basement of the convention hall, where the land records were stored. He conferred with John Calhoun; and both supported Hugh Moore, chairman of the committee on the subject, in demanding a referendum. However, Martin wished this vote taken in a fashion which would allow a strong chance for the State to preserve existing elements of slavery; and he conveyed this idea to Calhoun.

Out of the conferences of Martin with Calhoun, Elmore, Moore, and others in the final two days emerged a compromise plan. The constitution proper would not be submitted to the people, but they would be allowed to vote on a separate section permitting a choice between "the constitution with slavery" and "the constitution without slavery." Moreover, the constitution would preserve existing slave ownership. The scheme, matured by November 6 and brought forward on the seventh when direct transmittal to Congress was barely defeated, was hailed with satisfaction by proslavery observers. One Southerner pronounced it the best proposition yet offered for making Kansas a slave State, while the correspondent of the proslavery St. Louis *Republican* praised it with a tribute to Calhoun's "profound talents." [14] It was open to two strong objections: first, that it was a transparent device for preserving the shreds of slavery already in the Territory; and second, that it fell far short of the full and fair submission promised by Buchanan and demanded by Walker and Stanton.

Calhoun should have realized that it would never satisfy his friend Senator Douglas. But his drink-fogged mind was not what it had been; he had written Douglas for advice but received no answer; and what caution he possessed was overborne by Martin, Isaacs, and other associates. He read the Chicago *Times*

---

slavery constitution should be made and sent directly to Congress by the convention. I am not prepared to say that the convention have not the right to make a constitution and demand admission under it." When Martin reported this in Lecompton, as he must have done, he doubtless encouraged the radicals. Martin also quoted Jacob Thompson as taking up the question of the future status of slavery in the area, it being generally agreed that no reasonable hope existed of making Kansas an out-and-out slave State. The Secretary "made several suggestions as to how the constitution might be shaped to protect the rights of owners of the slaves then there, and their natural increase, and indicated that all fair-minded men ought to be willing to go a step further than this; that young men from the southern States had gone there in considerable numbers and established themselves homes for the future; they may *inherit* negroes, family servants that they would not be willing to dispose of, and all just men ought to be willing to allow them to bring such servants to Kansas and keep them rather than force them to abandon their homes or sell them." Howell Cobb testified that he asked Martin to press upon the convention the propriety of submitting the constitution. He awaited the event eagerly. Then, "when the news was received it was considered that, as the only question at issue—the slavery question—had been submitted, the material point had been attained; and it was regarded as virtually carrying out the policy of submission." Covode Report (36th Cong., 1st Sess., Report No. 648, pp. 157–171, 314–323).

14 See long letter dated Lecompton, November 7, in Jackson *Mississippian*, November 27, 1857; Dispatch of November 6, 1857, in St. Louis *Republican*.

editorial of October 14, and thought he found warrant there for a separate vote on the mere question of slavery. Had he read it more carefully, he would have seen that it said in conclusion: "Let them, if they desire to vote in favor of a slave State, have the opportunity; but let the constitution be submitted to the popular vote, and at an early day." This plainly meant the whole constitution.

On the last day the compromise plan was carried. A few radical slavery men, struggling to the last for direct transmittal to Congress, resigned rather than take it. On the final passage of the whole constitution the vote was 28 for, and about a dozen against.[15] The convention, returning from dinner, remained in session to deal with some last items of business. As midnight arrived, the smoke-filled hall, dimly lighted by a dozen guttering candles, presented a strange scene. Some delegates stood, some sat with feet cocked at an angle of forty-five degrees, and some who were half intoxicated stretched themselves on the cloth-covered tables. Rough horseplay interspersed the last resolutions and complimentary speeches. Outside, the gloom was relieved only by the twinkling lights of the scattered grogshops, from which now and then came a boisterous shout.[16] As President John Calhoun brought down his gavel and proclaimed the termination of the convention, few would have thought that such a cheap, disorderly assemblage had carried the nation a long step nearer to civil war.

[I]

What kind of a constitution had been drawn up? And who would be allowed to vote on the separate slavery question? The North was eager for news on these points.

Vital parts of the instrument at once aroused the hot indignation of free-soil circles. They represented an attempt to fasten at least partial toleration of slavery upon an antislavery population. The preamble of the first section declared: "The right of property is before and higher than any constitutional sanction, and the right of the owner of a slave to such slave and its increase is the same and as inviolable as the right of the owner of any property whatever." The legislature was forbidden to emancipate slaves already in Kansas

15 Forty-five members signed the engrossed document. Nichols, *Disruption of the American Democracy*, 124. Martin relates (Covode Report, 163) that after he and Calhoun had fought to the last for out-and-out submission, and been defeated, they feared that all was lost and the constitution would go straight to Congress. "Colonel Isaacs and myself induced Mr. Blair, who had voted with the majority, to move a reconsideration, on the assurance that if we could get a reconsideration, the plan of partial submission, for which he had expressed his willingness to vote, should be brought forward. . . . They voted for a reconsideration, which was carried. The plan finally adopted was then brought forward and carried by a majority of three votes."
16 Lecompton correspondence of N. Y. *Weekly Tribune*, November 28, 1857.

without the consent of the owner and payment of a full money equivalent. Stringent enforcement of the Fugitive Slave Law was required. Still other parts of the constitution seemed objectionable on general grounds. Know-Nothing influence appeared in a provision that governors must have been citizens for twenty years before election, while radical agrarian influence was evident in a stipulation that the State might have only one bank, with not more than two branches, to be incorporated only after popular consent. Free negroes were excluded. A peculiar provision forbade amendment of the constitution prior to 1864—this apparently to prevent any change of the clauses upon slavery.

And what of the vote? By an outstanding "schedule" attached to the constitution, the convention ousted Governor Walker and other Federal office-holders on December 1, 1857, and devolved their authority upon a provisional government. The head or "regent," John Calhoun, was to order an election for State officers and legislators. He was to appoint all judges of elections until the legislature took jurisdiction, was to have charge of the counting of returns, and was to decide who was entitled to legislative seats, issuing certificates of election. He was also to convene the legislature by proclamation. As the New York *Express* remarked, this was a Parisian *coup d'état*. On December 21, the special referendum was to be held on the "constitution with slavery" or "constitution without slavery." Calhoun was to appoint three election commissioners for each county, who were to name three judges for that county, with power to establish precincts and open polls. This gave the regent complete authority over the referendum—and the Oxford and McGee frauds were in recent memory!

But how much real choice would be permitted in even a fairly conducted election? If the "constitution with slavery" carried, the institution would be planted in Kansas with no possibility of eradication prior to 1864, and then only if two-thirds of each house submitted the question of a new convention to the people, and a majority of qualified voters (not merely of those voting) approved the call. If "without" carried, even then some two hundred slaves might remain in the State. Would their progeny also be held in servitude? Many believed that they would; that this servile population would facilitate the smuggling of new slaves across the border; and that Kansas would have a slavery atmosphere. True, the number of slaves would be small. But then the number in Delaware was small, and yet Delaware was a most tenaciously slave State. True, again, the importation of slaves would be illegal. But various slave States had laws prohibiting any such importation, and yet somehow large numbers were fetched in. This conditional and partial choice was a trick, declared free State men. The question was, *Heads I win, Tails you lose;* you may vote for slavery unlimited or slavery limited, but you may not vote for freedom. As one Kansan expressed it, the doctor had said: Vote to take this arsenic with bread and butter, or without bread and butter.

An angry outcry instantly arose throughout Kansas. "The Great Swindle," trumpeted the Emporia *Kanzas News*.[17] "Act or Be Slaves" was the caption over an editorial of the Topeka *Kansas Tribune*. As Governor Walker presently stated, only one of the twenty Kansas newspapers supported the instrument. Charles Robinson and "Jim" Lane were ready to lead an organized resistance. Meetings were soon being held all over the Territory, with freesoil Democrats prominent in many of them, expressing their indignation at this latest trick. Leaders like young Preston B. Plumb, fearful that all was lost and that the constitution would be rapidly carried through Congress, called upon the people to rise in their wrath, let the country know of their condemnation, and if necessary resist by force.

Particularly impressive was the protest of the Democratic editors. The pending scheme is an infringement of the people's rights, an outrage upon the spirit of republicanism, and a violation of the intent of the Nebraska Act, said the Kickapoo *Pioneer;* it has not only done the Democratic Party great harm, but the injury is of a permanent nature, declared the Leavenworth *Journal*.[18] These papers accurately reflected public sentiment. Intense excitement reigns, a friend wrote President Buchanan. "The instrument itself, the manner of its submission, and the means by which it was adopted, are the subject of emphatic condemnation all over the Territory, and none but the ultras, most of whom are Know-Nothings from the South, endorse it. The true Democracy both from the North and the South repudiate it." [19]

As was to be expected, the Republican press throughout the North echoed this Kansas uproar. One plot follows another, the editors declared; outrage is piled upon outrage. The columns of the Chicago *Tribune*, Cleveland *Leader*, Albany *Evening Journal*, Springfield *Republican*, and the newspapers made famous in New York by Bryant, Greeley, and James Watson Webb, with dozens of less prominent dailies, blazed with denunciation. The *National Intelligencer*, for surviving Whigs, pronounced a more measured condemnation.

What was hardly more surprising, but profoundly significant, was the instant verdict of the popular sovereignty organs of the Northern Democrats.

17 Emporia *Kanzas News*, November 7, 1857.
18 Leavenworth *Journal*, November 27, 1857.
19 J. F. Schroder, November 22, 1857; Buchanan Papers. Arkansas in 1836 had been the last State to adopt a constitution without popular vote. Her people were homogeneous, no sharp issues existed, and the constitutional convention was trusted. Beginning with Massachusetts in 1780, and ending with Ohio, Iowa, and Minnesota in 1857, twenty States had adopted or amended their constitutions by popular vote. As Douglas said, those which had not resorted to popular submission were States where the utmost harmony prevailed.

Their chagrin was natural. Here was a constitution which, apart from slavery, was studded with controversial provisions. The bank restriction, the twenty-year residence clause for the governor, the bar against free negroes, the provision for a tax system which had been tried and abandoned in Illinois, were all debatable. To put such a constitution into force without a general vote was to make popular sovereignty a farce. As early as November 18, the Chicago *Times*, Douglas's mouthpiece, recalling the solemn promises of 1854, declared that all action by the Democratic Party must have in view the faithful redemption of that pledge. The Quincy, Illinois, *Herald*, speaking for Douglas's friend W. A. Richardson, termed the Lecompton stand an insult to all intelligent Kansans and all honest Democrats. The Columbus, Ohio, *Statesman* called for rejection of the constitution, a flagrant outrage which could not be tolerated without disorganizing the Democratic Party. The Detroit *Free Press*, the leading Democratic journal of Michigan, predicted that any Northern Democrat who lent himself to this scheme to evade the popular will would be visited with political annihilation. The Northern wing of the party, it announced, "will not recede one inch from the preservation of the integrity of the great principle of the Kansas-Nebraska Act." [20] Equally emphatic was the Milwaukee *News*, leading Democratic organ of Wisconsin.

And in Pennsylvania a defiant new voice was lifted. John W. Forney, bitterly resentful of Buchanan's neglect, had returned to Philadelphia, collected a fund from his many friends, and on August 1 launched the *Press*. This independent Democratic journal scored an astonishing success. Within a short time it had a larger daily circulation than any other Philadelphia paper except the *Ledger*, and was distributing thirty thousand copies of its weekly edition. Animated by a trenchant fighting spirit, it lost no time in declaring that the Lecompton convention had shown a cool disregard of the people, an impudent deceit, and an utter shamelessness, which made it unique among representative bodies. Congress should reject its work by unanimous vote; and "we trust that the Senators and Representatives from Pennsylvania will boldly and at once put their feet upon it, and spurn it as it deserves to be spurned." [21] It kept up its fire. Its vehement words created a sensation. "The streets of Philadelphia this morning are filled with people speculating on the course of the *Press*," wrote J. C. Van Dyke to the President on November 21. [22]

All over the North, in hotels, barrooms, clubs, stores, and where farmers met on country roads, men were shaking their heads: "A dirty piece of work!" Did the Kansas gang really think they could get away with it? Forney shortly

20 Quotations in Phila. *Weekly Press*, December 5, 12, 17, 1857; Lawrence *Herald of Freedom*, December 12, 1857.
21 Quoted in N. Y. *Weekly Tribune*, November 25, 1857.
22 J. C. Van Dyke to Buchanan, November 21, 1857; Buchanan Papers.

listed fifteen local Democratic papers in Pennsylvania which roundly denounced the Lecompton plot, while a longer roster might have been made in New York. A suggestion of the Chicago *Times* that Congress should authorize the Kansans to assemble a new convention and write a new constitution was widely echoed. The handful of Democratic newspapers which sustained the Lecompton scheme in the North were viewed with suspicion. Two were the Albany *Argus* and Rochester *Union*, whose editors were said to hope for postmasterships; two were Pittsburgh papers; and one was the Dubuque *Northwest*, whose head had been promised the clerkship of a Senate committee.[23]

In the South, however, the story was different. The editorial fire against Walker as a traitor and renegade had never slackened, and now the convention's work was greeted as the richly deserved defeat of the governor. Inflamed with a suspicion and hatred which drew little distinction between freesoilers and abolitionists, most Southerners believed that the freesoil pronouncements against any new slave State were a challenge which must be emphatically answered. Many of them regarded Kansas as rightfully their own. Did the North think itself entitled to take every trick in the game? to seize Kansas as well as California, Iowa, Nebraska, Minnesota, and Oregon? to allow the South nothing? If the Yankees had placed more settlers in Kansas, it was by the forced and unfair measures of the emigrant aid societies. To Southerners, the Lecompton delegates were not ruffians but dauntless paladins, making a gallant last-ditch stand. The Yankees declared their tactics were fraudulent; this was not so—they were entirely legal; but if some sharpness did appear, it was a just answer to the chicane and arrogance of the North.

Even the sober Richmond *Enquirer* greeted the Lecompton constitution as the promise of a final settlement of the Kansas troubles, predicting that of course Congress would accept it. The Washington *Union* was jubilantly confident of the future. "The vexed question is settled—the problem is solved—the dead point of danger is passed—all serious trouble about Kansas affairs is over and gone," it rejoiced. "Kansas comes into the Union on the principle of the great act which organized her and Nebraska as territorial Governments. Another star is added to the republican constellation." Not a hint was breathed in half the Southern editorials that the constitution would ever be called into question. Yet some journals were frank as to its central design. "You see," wrote a Lecompton correspondent to the Jackson *Mississippian*, "that while it seems to be an election between a free-State and proslavery constitution, it is in fact but a question of the future introduction of slavery that is in controversy."[24] And the Charleston *Mercury* proclaimed:

23 J. W. Sheahan to Douglas, November 30, 1857; Douglas Papers.
24 Jackson *Mississippian*, November 27, 1857.

We do not think that the question of slavery or no slavery is submitted to the vote of the people. Whether the clause in the constitution is voted out or voted in, slavery exists, and has a guarantee in the constitution that it shall not be interfered with; whilst, if the slavery party in Kansas can keep or get the majority of the legislature, they may open wide the door for the immigration of slaves.[25]

The Northern and Southern wings of the Democratic Party were openly at odds. To add to the suspense, news came that Governor Walker, his health and his personal affairs both needing attention, would leave Kansas on November 17 for a visit to the East. The Northern public had applauded his firm stand against the Oxford and McGee frauds; the South had denounced this tampering with election returns as another piece of "intervention." What authority, Southerners asked, had *he* to go behind the returns? None whatever.

Walker was going east on what he considered a vital mission. He had never been confirmed as governor, and he realized that Southern extremists would give him no quarter. He could explain that he had not gone behind the Oxford-McGee returns, but had thrown them out because the judges had not taken the proper oaths, the poll books had not been sent to the territorial secretary in proper form, and the votes had been recorded in an impossibly brief period of time. He could place the Kansas situation before the President and the entire country.

[II]

Seldom in the history of the nation has a President made so disastrous a blunder as Buchanan was about to commit. Within a few weeks, Pierce's old secretary, B. B. French, was to write: "I had considerable hopes of Mr. Buchanan—I really thought he was a statesman—but I have now come to the settled conclusion that he is just the d——dest old fool that has ever occupied the Presidential chair. He has deliberately walked overboard with his eyes open—let him drown, for he must." It is misleading, however, to speak of his policy. It was rather the policy of the Directory; of the Cabinet junta (Howell Cobb, Jacob Thompson, and Jere Black), and of the gray-eyed, thin-lipped Slidell, persevering, subtle, and in W. H. Russell's words, "full of device." [26]

From the moment the Lecompton gathering adjourned, these men began to exert a tremendous pressure on Buchanan. Secretaries Cobb and Thompson were committed to the Kansas scheme by their wishes and the work of their agent Martin. Jere Black was filled with detestation of freesoilers everywhere

25 Quoted in Phila. *Weekly Press*, December 26, 1857.
26 B. B. French, December 17, 1857, to brother, French Papers; Russell, *My Diary North and South*, Ch. 30.

but particularly in Kansas, the men who controlled the extra-legal Topeka "government." He hated the Black Republicans, and he specially hated those who had been ready to defy the recognized territorial legislature. His manuscripts contain a draft paper in which, defending the Lecompton instrument, he wrote: "Lane and the godless crew of fanatics and knaves that followed him have lived in open rebellion against the laws, and not one of them has yet been punished. The convention that framed the constitution was threatened by the tools and hirelings of the abolition aid societies and was saved from their attack only by a military force." He tried to imbue Buchanan with these passionate and distorted views. Floyd and Toucey lent their aid. The President knew that Jefferson Davis and other Senators were ready to open a raking fire on the Administration if Governor Walker were not forced to resign; and even before the Lecompton result he was privately condemning the little governor.[27] Buchanan's pliability in Southern hands was a matter of jest. It was reported that Howell Cobb, on being asked once why he bore a transiently worried air, replied: "Oh, it's nothing much; only Buck is opposing the Administration." [28]

Buchanan knew that the hot blood of the South was up; he knew that the more rabid politicians of the cotton States were denouncing him along with Walker as a turncoat. Threats of secession were growing more numerous. Believing that party discipline would hold the Northern Democrats in line, he regarded the South as the prime point of danger. He was affected by his old Southern bias, his deep dislike of freesoil agitation, his belief that popular sovereignty was a delusion, and his personal antipathy for Douglas. Above all, however, he was swayed by timidity: he quailed before the Southern menaces transmitted to him by Cobb, Thompson, and a hundred others—before the jealousy and resentment which for the time, as the Columbia *South Carolinian* remarked a year later, "seemed to have inflamed the whole South." [29] Appeasement appeared the best course.

Undoubtedly, when Governor Walker left for the East he believed that, inasmuch as Buchanan had pledged himself to a popular submission of the

27 Undated paper, end of 1857, Black Papers; N. Y. *Express,* November 2, 4, 1857.
28 Greeley, *Recollections,* 335, 356.
29 Quoted in *National Intelligencer,* November 18, 1857. Southern extremists were partly influenced by political reasons. The Washington *Republic* declared, just before the convention adjourned, that nothing was so vital to the union of the Southern Democracy as a proslavery victory in Kansas. "In truth, it is not merely the union but the very existence of the Southern Democracy which is staked upon making Kansas a slave State. . . . If Kansas comes in as a free State, the black Democratic ascendency at the South is ended, and the next House will be overwhelmingly in opposition to the Administration. From whatever motives Mr. Buchanan was voted for at the North, he was supported at the South simply and solely from the belief that his election would fix slavery upon Kansas." Quoted in Chicago *Tribune,* November 11, 1857.

constitution, instructing Walker that the people must be protected in their right of voting for or against that instrument, he could bring the President to take a stand against Lecompton. The doughty little governor was deeply exasperated. He regarded Calhoun, Isaacs, Elmore, and the other ringleaders as a set of scoundrels who had ruined all hope of Democratic ascendency in Kansas, had tried to ruin him, and might yet ruin the Democratic Party throughout the North. He believed that his own career, the future of Kansas, and above all, the vital Democratic principle written into law by Douglas, were at stake. He would tell the President what all fair-minded Kansans knew, that the people of the Territory would never submit to Lecompton. He would confer with Cass, Douglas, and others on means of vindicating the great rule of popular sovereignty upon which they had staked their honor. He would remind Buchanan how explicitly he had promised a full and fair vote on the institutions of Kansas. He would fling his defiance in the teeth of his old enemy Jacob Thompson and the other Southern ultras.

Walker did not know that on the very day he left, November 17, the Administration organ, the *Union*, had come out with its complete endorsement of the constitution. Nor did he know that in Virginia the moderate Henry A. Wise had just withdrawn from the senatorial contest, apparently under pressure from the Directory, in favor of the radical R. M. T. Hunter. This was an ominous event. Wise was a warm friend of the President. The Directory had overruled Buchanan, and the event was interpreted as making the Senate's rejection of Walker almost certain.[30]

Amid fervent farewells from admiring friends, Walker strode up the gangplank of the steamer *Oglesby* at Leavenworth. "The Governor leaves here," the former Pennsylvanian John F. Schroder wrote Buchanan, "with the endorsement of nineteen-twentieths of the friends of the Administration, and of all the good people of the Territory."[31] But he took all his books and papers, well boxed, and his other movable property. Cheerful but determined, he talked with fellow passengers, as the boat swung downstream, in a vein which showed that he did not anticipate returning.[32] Like Reeder and Geary, he had been worsted by the proslavery fanatics of the border.

Arriving in Washington, Walker on November 26 had a long talk with the President. After several hours they parted in friendly spirit. Immediately thereafter the governor appeared before the Cabinet and stated his position emphatically. Word quickly spread about Washington that irreconcilable differences had appeared. Southern Senators, arriving for the new session, heard with pleasure that Walker's resignation or dismissal seemed a certainty. Dozens

30 N. Y. *Evening Post*, November 19, 1857.
31 J. F. Schroder, November 22, 1857, Buchanan Papers.
32 Chicago *Tribune* correspondent aboard *Oglesby*, November 20, 1857.

of newspapermen, avid for news, were soon able to tell the country what had happened behind the White House doors.[33]

Walker had sworn the oath of John Hampden against the Lecompton constitution; the Cabinet majority and the President were immovable in its defense. Walker declared that the Administration was bound by the Nebraska Act, and by solemn pledges the previous summer, to see the entire instrument submitted to a popular vote. The Directory replied that the convention was at liberty to submit its whole work to the people or send it direct to Congress, as it pleased; and that they had not deemed submission advisable, chiefly because of the feverish state of opinion in the Territory. A fundamental principle is involved, said Walker. Not at all, rejoined the Directory; for the convention is submitting that part of the constitution which bears on slavery, the only serious question at issue. All that was required by the principles of the Nebraska Act, the Cincinnati platform, and the President's inaugural was that the problem of slavery should be submitted to popular vote; as this is done, no ground for objection exists. The attempt to jam through such a constitution will cause bloody strife, explained Walker. "I doubt if three hundred men wish to fasten slavery on Kansas; no party stands for slavery; the people will fight before they let this cheating document, which means slavery both ways, go through." So much the worse for them, declared Cobb and Black. If these lawless freesoilers fight against a legally drawn and legally adopted constitution, we shall quell their resistance. "They will not submit, and they ought not to submit," exclaimed the governor.[34]

The Southern wing of the Democrats, having Buchanan's ear, placed him under an adroit and insistent pressure to drop Governor Walker, forget his pledges, and make a fight for Lecompton. "The people are so tired of Kansas that they will sustain your settlement," wrote Robert Tyler, in effect. "If you can convert Walker, well and good; if not, I trust you will remove him without hesitation."

Leading Southern politicians, crowding into the capital, saw a golden opportunity to check the Presidential aspirations of Walker and Douglas and suppress the freesoil elements in the party. They talked earnestly with the President.[35] A hasty canvass indicated that five Northern Senators—Bright,

33 The N. Y. *Herald, Times, Evening Post* accounts are good; November 28–December 5, 1857. The *Herald* quotes Walker as telling Buchanan in their first interview that slavery was no longer the issue in Kansas—that was settled; but all the questions respecting their government were involved in the constitution, and the people would resist at all hazards the attempt to force it upon them. So intense was the feeling that he could not influence a single man to vote for it. He suggested that Congress should pass a bill similar to the Minnesota Enabling Act.

34 Wash. correspondence, *Express, Herald*, November 28, 30, 1857.
35 Wash. correspondence, N. Y. *Tribune*, dated December 1, 1857.

Bigler, Fitch, Thompson, and Wright--would support the Administration's Kansas policy, and that some Northern members of the House would follow their lead. Senator Slidell lost no time in carrying this news to the White House. Bigler was anxious to see a vigorous policy pursued. If you will put the full power of the Administration behind Lecompton, he wrote the President, the people of Kansas will knuckle under, vote quietly on December 21, and thus end all our troubles. J. C. Van Dyke lent his strong personal influence to the same end. And two soldiers with some claim to expert standing (both Southerners) put in their word. General Persifor Smith was for admitting Kansas forthwith under the Lecompton plan. General Harney assured Buchanan that he need not worry about disturbances in the Territory, for winter was coming on, troublemakers on both sides would be kept busy getting fuel to burn and food to eat, and the existing forces could meet any contingency; moreover, many Northerners, after a bad crop season, were going home from sheer necessity.[36]

Most important of all were the continued threats from the South. The well-informed Washington correspondent of the New Orleans *Picayune*, "Tiber," later described just how aggressive this *démarche* was:

The President was informed in November, 1857, that the States of Alabama, Mississippi, and South Carolina, and perhaps others, would hold conventions and secede from the Union if the Lecompton constitution, which established slavery, should not be accepted by Congress. The reason was that these States, supposing that the South had been cheated out of Kansas, were, whether right or wrong, determined to revolt. The President believed this. Senator Hunter, of Virginia, to my knowledge, believed it. Many other eminent men did, and perhaps not without reason. The President determined in November, four or five months after his famous letter to Gov. Walker, to submit the Lecompton constitution to Congress, and recommend its acceptance. . . .

I was myself at the time [November, 1857] disposed to go with Governor Walker, Mr. Douglas, and others, but became convinced, from facts presented to me, that the course of the President was expedient, and I supported him in it. It was not worth while, as I thought, to provoke a quarrel with the South, or any part of it, upon a matter of opinion, which was of little practical importance. Everybody knew that the danger in Kansas itself had passed over. It remained to concede an abstract question to the South.[37]

Since the Cabinet had now taken Buchanan's measure, its bolder spirits—Cobb, Thompson, Floyd—were growing arrogant in their treatment of him. A few episodes indicated just what the relation of the Directory to the weak Executive was. Early in September, weeks before the Lecompton decision, the

36 J. C. Van Dyke, November 29, Persifor Smith, December 14, W. S. Harney, November 29, 1857; Buchanan Papers.
37 "Tiber" in New Orleans *Picayune*, April 29, 1860.

President, anxious to shield himself against Southern attacks, had asked two Kansans in Washington, General Whitfield and Dr. Tebbs, to send the *Union* a letter explaining that Walker's policy pleased the people of Kansas, a majority of whom favored a free State. The letter was in type, with an editorial endorsement of Tebbs as a veracious observer, when a Southern member of the Cabinet ordered its suppression. Howell Cobb had countermanded the President's action.[38]

A little later the accurate head of the Associated Press in Washington, L. A. Gobright, who was on intimate terms with Cobb and Thompson, heard from a Cabinet member that Walker and Stanton would be removed or forced to resign. He sent out an A.P. dispatch to this effect, reporting that the governor's rejection of the Oxford and McGee returns had been condemned, that the Cabinet believed the legislature alone was competent to pass on the election of its members, and that both the offending officers would soon be ousted. This was published under date of October 30, just as the Lecompton drama was nearing its climax. Buchanan, taken aback, wrote a paragraph denying the story, and had the contradiction telegraphed over the country. Summoning Gobright to the White House, he unavailingly tried to learn who had supplied the information. Then he questioned the Cabinet about the leakage. At once the Cabinet officer responsible (doubtless Cobb or Thompson, though Gobright does not say) boldly avowed his responsibility. He did this, as he told the journalist, not merely to protect the Associated Press, but to remind Buchanan of their previous understanding upon the removal of Walker! The incident unpleasantly illustrates two facts—the President's malleability and the whip-cracking attitude of the Southern Cabinet members toward him.

Even Jere Black, who combined his attorney-generalship with editorial writing for the *Union*, now did not hesitate to override Buchanan. The private papers of that bitter partisan contain a note which he received just after the Lecompton convention ended, a distinct indication of Presidential weakness.

My dear sir: In reading your article this morning which was excellent in its original form, I deeply regret to observe that the notice of Governor Walker has been stricken out, whilst the praises of the Convention remain. What is the reason for this? It will give just cause for offence to Governor Walker's friends; and I confess I am much worried myself at the omission.

Your friend, very respectfully, James Buchanan.[39]

Several Southern governors in their annual messages were calling for the admission of Kansas under the Lecompton scheme. Governors Perry of Florida

38 See N. Y. *Weekly Tribune*, November 6, 1858, for Stanton's story of this incident.
39 Buchanan to Jeremiah S. Black, November 18, 1857; Black Papers.

and Wickliffe of Louisiana rumbled threats against the Union. Other politicians in the South were predicting that the party there would go to pieces unless Buchanan forced the scheme through Congress. We have quoted the statement of a Washington newspaper that if Kansas came in as a free State, Democratic ascendency at the South would be ended, and the next House would be overwhelmingly in opposition to the Administration. Day after day the leaders and articles of the Washington *Union*, controlled by the Cabinet, fixed a semiofficial stamp of approval on Lecompton.[40]

In vain did George Bancroft, as a fellow-Jacksonian, send the President an eloquent plea. You occupy a position which is inexpugnable if you choose to make it so, he wrote. Pierce's Administration had died of Jefferson Davis and Caleb Cushing, and you should not listen to similar men. "I entreat you, as one who most sincerely wished honor and success to your Administration, not to endorse the Lecompton Constitution." That document, he continued, had not been submitted to the people because it was obvious they would reject it. He should put aside this arrogant usurpation, and ask Congress for an enabling act and a new convention. "Justice, the peace of the country, the present strength of your Administration, its standing with posterity, all point to the same policy. Jackson resisted the nullifiers when they had a real ground of grievance from the excessive tariff of the day; now the nullifiers rally on a ground which, if they are resisted with firmness, will sink under them and compel them to fly to you for shelter." [41]

But what of his explicit pledges to support Walker in insisting on popular submission? Clamorous voices assured Buchanan that Walker lusted for place and power. The governor was acting in bad faith, Robert Tyler declared; he had chosen a line which he thought might make him a great man, "and this outside the Democratic Party perhaps." [42] Roger A. Pryor brought the same accusation against Walker in the Richmond *South*, alleging that the governor was scheming to revolt and put himself at the head of an opposition party in the North. "He thinks he holds the Administration by the throat." [43] Far out in Leavenworth, the wily A. J. Isaacs had caught up the same insinuation. The governor, he assured the President, has been "against your friends, and he is doing all in his power to secure the Northern support for 1860." [44] While

40 Washington *Union*, November–December, 1857. The message of Governor Allston of South Carolina spoke of Kansas in moderate terms, while Governor Winston of Alabama made no reference whatever to the subject. But the Alabama legislature passed resolutions attacking Walker, deploring the failure of the government to remove him from office, and endorsing the convention system of adopting a State constitution. N. Y. *Herald*, December 2, 1857.
41 George Bancroft, December 5, 1857, Buchanan Papers.
42 Robert Tyler, November 16, 1857, Buchanan Papers.
43 Quoted in Chicago *Tribune*, November 10, 1857.
44 A. J. Isaacs to Buchanan, November 16, 1857.

Buchanan knew the honest, hard-working, loyal Walker too well to accept these malicious insinuations, he may have let them color his mind. At any rate, that mind was now made up—as the Southerners desired.

The error of Buchanan was in not clinging to principle. He had enunciated a wise principle—the people of Kansas must have a full, free, and fair opportunity to pass on their constitution; a true statesman would not have abandoned so just a line. Of course, it was easy (as he soon did) to cite all kinds of expedient arguments. The Lecompton convention was quite legal; the country, struggling out of a depression, needed peace; a Southern uproar would hurt business; if Kansas voted for the constitution "without slavery," the institution would gradually wither there as in other free States; and once in the Union, Kansans could change their constitution and laws as they pleased. Such pleas had a plausible ring. But for all that, they represented an abandonment of a clear public pledge and of the high ground of principle.

That the President knew this is evident from an interview with Forney, who called at the White House to expostulate. Relations between him and the President were now strained. While getting his *Press* upon its feet, Forney had penned the harshest letters upon Buchanan. After spending two years and sacrificing $150,000 to make his old friend the Chief Magistrate, he wrote, he had found the man an utter ingrate. Buchanan had first tried to balk the new journal; now that it had made a dazzling success, he was patronizing a gang of men who, with the *Pennsylvanian* office as headquarters, were systematically attacking the *Press*.[45] Forney had sent some of his bitter letters to Jere Black, who was just the man to show them to the President. No doubt the talk took place in a tense atmosphere. Its date is uncertain, and the details rest only upon the editor's recollection nearly a year later, perhaps overdramatized.

"Mr. Buchanan," he said, "for the first time in our lives we are at variance. I find myself standing by one principle, having followed your lead—and you have deserted it."

"Well," Buchanan rejoined, "cannot you change too? If I can afford to change, why can't you? If you, Douglas, and Walker will unite in support of my policy, there will not be a whisper of this thing. It will pass by like a summer breeze."

Forney replied that he could not go back to Pennsylvania to eat his own words, and that he possessed a conscience. He suggested that Buchanan ought at least to let dissenting Democrats have their own way: Jackson had tolerated large differences of opinion, while Polk had suffered Buchanan to remain in the Cabinet despite his objections to the Administration's tariff policy. But

45 J. W. Forney to Black, July 24, 30, August 2, 1857; Black Papers.

Buchanan was angry with the *Press* for fomenting dissension among the Pennsylvania Democrats.

"Sir," he grimly avowed, "I intend to make my Kansas policy a test."

"Well, sir," rejoined Forney, "I regret it; but if you make it a test with your officers, we will make it a test at the ballot box." [46]

[III]

That Buchanan's surrender to Lecompton would precipitate a terrible schism in the Democratic ranks was clear to all observers. The Washington correspondent of the *Evening Post* was quick to prophesy "a bitter contest between the two wings of Democracy"; that of the *Times*, "open hostility"; and that of the *Herald*, a warfare involving "disaster to the country and perfect annihilation to the Democratic party." Why did not Buchanan see this? For one reason, never understanding the freesoil sentiment of the North, he naturally underrated its force. For another, as a thick-and-thin party man, always talking about unity and well remembering how Jackson and Polk had outridden temporary factional storms, he believed that the Administration could quell any revolt. As he had no nerve, so he had no imagination. And the fact was that he had so completely placed himself in the hands of the Cobb-Thompson-Slidell group that he was their prisoner. He had let them encourage instead of quell the Southern storm; he had allowed them to commit the Administration to a false policy by condemning Walker's rejection of the Oxford-McGee ballots and by sending Martin to Kansas; he could not turn back. Timid and vacillating, he feared the wrath of the strong men about him more than the calm judgment of the people. A truly courageous man, a President with the courage of John Adams in 1798 and Grover Cleveland in 1887, might have stood on principle—but not Buchanan.

"If the back-track is taken—if the Administration reconsiders its decision, and sides with Walker and Douglas—the South will justly feel humbled and trifled with," wrote one of the ablest Washington observers. "There are men in the Cabinet, too, who will hardly consent to such a course. It is well known that a portion of the Cabinet have incessantly labored to check and thwart Mr. Douglas, and they are not likely, except from sheer necessity, to allow him such an advantage as the credit of guiding the policy of the Democratic Party in the just and liberal direction, and of compelling a reluctant Administration to follow him." [47]

Congress fully organized itself on Monday, December 7. The Senate elected

46 See Forney's Tarrytown Speech, September 2, 1858; N. Y. *Weekly Tribune*, September 11, 1858.

47 Washington correspondence, N. Y. *Weekly Tribune*, December 5, 1857.

an Alabaman of ability and high integrity, Benjamin Fitzpatrick, its President *pro tem*; the vote of 28 to 19 over Hannibal Hamlin accurately indicated the party strength.[48] The House chose the Democratic caucus slate for its various offices, James L. Orr of South Carolina becoming Speaker. A large, powerfully built man, Orr was well equipped for his post. Not yet forty, he had graduated from the University of Virginia, from newspaper work, and from a leisurely career as lawyer in the upland town of Anderson, center of a Scotch-Irish population. His frank, ruddy countenance, his straightforward, business-like air, his common-sense, logical speeches in debate, had inspired general confidence. He was far removed in opinion from the fire-eating radicals. In fact, his whole career was to demonstrate his moderation, for in Reconstruction days he was to become a Republican governor, and he was to die in St. Petersburg as President Grant's minister to Russia. He was familiar with the rules, patient but authoritative, and gifted with a loud ringing voice (like a locomotive whistle at a crossing, somebody said) which could instantly quiet confusion on the floor.

Next day Buchanan's message was read to the intent Houses. It contained some excellent recommendations, including an espousal of the Pacific Railroad and a condemnation of filibustering. But on the Kansas issue Buchanan showed a subtlety in word-juggling which was all his own, combined with a bold defense of the "dodge" which smacked of Cobb and Thompson. He upheld the Lecompton arrangement, urged the voters to go to the polls on December 21 to choose between "with" and "without," and scolded the country for its excessive preoccupation with the Kansas question. Trying to slip adroitly over his instructions to Walker, he declared that when he had written that the voters must be protected in a full and fair expression on the constitution he was thinking only of a vote on the slavery question! The Nebraska Act, he argued, had not provided for a popular vote on the entire constitution; it had merely declared that the people should be free to "regulate their domestic institutions" in their own way. Since the phrase "domestic institutions" had a meaning "limited to the family," wrote Buchanan, it embraced the relation of master and slave, but no other institution whatever. This word-juggling was worthy of the worst of sophists. As if the tax system, or banking, or the mode of elections were not domestic institutions in the time-honored sense!

Buchanan declared that citizens of Kansas had been "fairly afforded" an opportunity to register and vote for convention delegates, which was simply not true. He asserted that the election of December 21 would give the inhabitants a "fair" opportunity to decide the slavery issue, which was also false. He remarked that the only alternative to the protection of slaves already in

48 Hamlin voted for Seward.

Kansas was their confiscation, ignoring the fact that they might be taken else-where. Finally, he failed to state that, under the Nebraska Act, Congress had given the people a right to decide on the immediate existence of slavery, whereas the Lecompton convention gave them only a right to decide whether additional slaves should or should not be introduced.

As the gauntlet was thus thrown down, nobody could doubt that Douglas would pick it up. The climactic years of his career were opening. He was about to find his true role on the national stage. Hitherto, compromising with the Lower South, he had appeared in a dubious light to most freesoil North-erners; now, standing up to give battle for principle, he was to take on heroic stature. Two parts politician and one part statesman, he found in this new crisis a challenge to powers previously unknown even to himself. Always an essen-tially honest man, he thought no longer of the main chance but of the public weal. Anger at the malice of his Southern assailants, scorn for Buchanan's cowardice, apprehension for the future of party and nation, abhorrence of disunion schemes, all united to give him a stern determination. He had been a great Democratic chieftain; now he was to be a great American leader.[49]

49 Albert J. Beveridge, in a curiously myopic passage (*Lincoln*, II, 533), assumes that Douglas had a choice between supporting the Administration's Lecompton policy and break-ing with it; and writes that if Douglas had stood with Buchanan probably no resistance would have been made to Lecompton by any but Republicans, and it would have been adopted with little difficulty. He is wrong on both heads. The fact is that Douglas had no choice. His political future was bound up with the Northwestern Democracy, and the Northwestern Democrats were instantly in arms against Lecompton. The newspapers and Douglas's personal files, full of letters urging him to act, show this. Had Douglas played the part of Dr. Trimmer, the vengeance of Illinois would have fallen upon him in the Senatorial election of 1858 and the Presidential election of 1860. But no man was less likely to be a trimmer than Douglas. And what if Douglas had broken with his popular sovereignty vows, with principles, and with the Northwestern Democrats? Would only the Republicans have opposed Lecompton? Walker and Stanton were against it; Senator Stuart was against it; Forney and the Philadelphia *Press* were against it; George Bancroft and many like him were against it. These Democratic spokesmen would have made a fight even without Douglas; and while they were being defeated, a host of plain Northern Democrats would have moved *en masse* into the Republican ranks.

10

Douglas in Revolt

THE DISRUPTION of a great party, as the Whigs could have told any inquirer in 1857, is a pitiable spectacle. To keep a victorious party harmonious and unified is, for obvious reasons, a severer test of leadership than to maintain the integrity of a defeated party. Had the Buchanan Administration possessed statesmanlike attributes, it would have realized that the very life of the republic might depend upon meeting this supreme test; for the Democracy was the one great organization left which united the North and South with tenacious bonds. But how accurately did Buchanan read the omens of Kansas?

As Douglas in late November packed his bags to return to Washington, word that he was determined to resist the Lecompton scheme was spreading far and wide. He made no public announcement, for he had seen no copy of the constitution and did not wish to speak hastily on the basis of mere newspaper reports, but his private utterances were emphatic. The intention of Buchanan and the Cabinet to support what the Senator called "treachery and juggling" filled him with contempt. "We must stand on the popular sovereignty principle," he wrote his old friend John A. McClernand, "and go wherever the logical consequences may carry us, and defend it against *all assaults* from whatever quarter."[1] To a caller, he stated his resolve to maintain the fundamental principle he had laid down. "I will show you that I will do what I promised. By God, sir, I made Mr. James Buchanan, and by God, sir, I will unmake him!"[2]

Upon the issue of justice against fraud, said his organ the Chicago *Times*, the Northern Democracy will offer an undivided front. Douglas's mail was full of assurances of this fact. From every northwestern State during November came pledges of support. J. D. Eads wrote from Iowa that the party pledges were

[1] November 25, 1857; McClernand Papers. A Representative in Congress 1843-51, McClernand had just removed from Jacksonville to Springfield, where he worked hard for Douglas. As early as 1850 he had thought that the Southern radicals were trying to break down the Democratic Party, and he insisted sternly on the popular sovereignty doctrine. Milton, *Eve of Conflict*, 40, 41.

[2] C. H. Ray, November 24, 1857; Trumbull Papers.

sacred, and that all true men looked to him as the champion of squatter sovereignty. Four-fifths of our people, declared Samuel Crawford of Wisconsin, oppose nonsubmission as a violation of the Nebraska Act. "You alone," asserted Daniel Mace of Indiana in essence, "have the power to vindicate popular rights in Kansas, and you will stand forth with the fearless boldness which is your nature." "We do not doubt your course," exclaimed W. N. Coles of Urbana, Illinois, "and every Democrat in Champaign County will sustain you." A stream of such letters, soon augmented by eastern mails, poured in upon the Little Giant.[3]

Douglas knew that with the Old Democracy of the South and the New Democracy of the West at a complete rupture, he had a fight to the finish before him. He knew that proslavery politicians were making a tool of the pliant Buchanan, and he believed—with Henry S. Foote of Mississippi and other Southerners—that many of these politicians hated free government and meant to break up the Union. For politic reasons he made no public threats. He intended, as soon as he reached Washington, to try to persuade the President to drop Lecompton, ask Congress for an enabling act modelled on the old Toombs bill, or the Minnesota bill, and thus bring into existence a new and fair constitutional convention. To the Federal Attorney in Kansas, William Weer, who was resigning in disgust, he wrote that while he would battle for all his well-known tenets, "I shall do this in a kind spirit towards the Administration and all my friends." [4] Actually, however, he knew that a kind spirit would be impossible. He told Chicago friends that one object of Cobb, Thompson, and other Southerners in the Kansas proceedings was to ruin him, that Buchanan was too pusillanimous to interfere, and that the conspirators hoped to run Buchanan again as their tool in 1860. As for himself, he would never rest content with less than a fair vote on the whole Kansas constitution: "Depend on me to carry out the principle or fall in the attempt," he exclaimed.

With his eye for strategy, he instantly saw how vital would be the question of Republican aid or passivity. He knew that the party which had been defeated just a year earlier would watch the civil war in Democratic ranks with incredulous joy; that they would ask whether they could make the most of it by alliance with Douglas or by cheering from the sidelines. He knew that in Illinois, where most freesoilers regarded Douglas as an adroit and unscrupulous politician, and where the glittering prize of the senatorship would be contested in 1858, the Republicans were all suspicion. Douglas took pains to call a number of leaders to his house and tell them how implacably he meant to fight the

3 J. D. Eads, Fort Madison, November 19, Samuel Crawford, Mineral Point, November 28, Daniel Mace, Lafayette, November 28, 1857; Douglas Papers.
4 November 22, 1857; Wyandotte, Kansas, *Western Argus*, October 22, 1860.

Administration. He sent a friend to C. H. Ray's office at the Chicago *Tribune* to protest that the paper ought to desist from its attacks now that he was doing just what it wanted done. Several of the Northern Illinois chieftains were impressed by his bellicosity. "He really made some of their eyes stick out at his zeal," Norman B. Judd reported to Senator Trumbull. The general view among Illinois Republicans, however, was that Douglas bearing gifts was nearly as dangerous as Douglas bearing arms, that he could not gain forgiveness for past blows by an act which after all was one of political self-preservation, and that the party should cheer on his assault but stick to its own banner. If they relaxed their discipline, some of their recruits from the former freesoil Democrats would drop away and disorganization ensue. Hearing Douglas talk of an enabling act for Kansas similar to that of Minnesota, several Republicans urged Trumbull to get in first with such a bill.[5]

While still in Chicago, Douglas talked with the irate Governor Walker, and, en route to Washington, tarried briefly in New York to confer with adherents. He perhaps saw George Bancroft there. That honest Jacksonian, who had sat in Polk's Cabinet alongside Buchanan, was intensely aroused. The trickery in Kansas seemed to him abominable; the path out of the difficulty, an enabling act in the words of Douglas's Minnesota Act, was so simple that the President could hardly miss it. If they did talk, Bancroft urged the Senator to try persuasion first and then offer relentless battle, the advice he shortly put into a letter full of historical instances.[6]

Reaching the capital on December 2, Douglas was received with huzzas, bonfires, and a serenade. He found the city filling with Congressmen, office-hunters, and newspapermen, and hotel lobbies buzzing with speculation on the impending fray. Votes were already being counted. Coincident with Douglas's arrival, the combative secretary of Kansas Territory, Stanton, withdrew the resignation which for business reasons he had recently offered. Since Walker was battling for justice and right, he wrote, he would stand with his chief. The Cabinet that day once more discussed Kansas, and gossip reported that it once more resolved to support Lecompton.

On December 3, Douglas called at the White House. His bosom was filled with fresh anger, for friends had told him that Southerners were spraying Washington with venomous attacks on his and Walker's "lies," "contumacy," and "treason," and uttering dire threats of ruin. The Northern Democrats, he felt, were being pushed toward the abyss and must struggle for their lives.

5 E. Peck, N. B. Judd, C. S. Wilson, M. W. Delahay, November 26–December 1, 1857; Trumbull Papers.
6 George Bancroft, December 2, 1857; Douglas Papers.

[I]

One of the historic scenes of the period was enacted as Douglas confronted the tall, white-haired President. They had never liked each other, and doubtless shook hands in frigid fashion.

The Senator advised Buchanan, as a friend, not to recommend acquiescence in the Lecompton constitution. He gave his reasons for a new enabling act. Buchanan, whose message—the Directory's message—lay written in his drawer, declared that he would urge acceptance. "If you do," Douglas replied, "I will denounce it the moment your message is read." Despising Buchanan, he was probably at little pains to conceal his contempt, while the President responded to his dark scowl with ill-restrained resentment. At last, Buchanan terminated the interview with an abrupt threat. Glaring down at the short, powerful, defiant Senator, he exclaimed: "Mr. Douglas, I desire you to remember that no Democrat ever yet differed from an Administration of his own choice without being crushed." This was inaccurate, for John Randolph of Roanoke, William H. Crawford, and Calhoun had all dared to differ, and none had been crushed. On the other hand, the Barnburner revolt had actually crushed Cass in 1852. Buchanan added: "Beware the fate of Tallmadge and Rives." Opposing Jackson's policies, N. P. Tallmadge and William C. Rives had been forced to take refuge with the Whigs.

But Douglas was not to be read out of the Democratic Party by a man he regarded as a pigmy. He tossed his mane of black hair angrily:

"Mr. President," he said, "I wish you to remember that General Jackson is dead."

To that doughface member of the Cabinet, Toucey, the Senator was still more scornful. With bland assurance, Toucey urged upon Douglas the evils of a split in the Democratic Party; a calamity which would sink the combatants so deep that it might take a generation to raise the party again. Douglas declared that this was quite true. "Why, my dear sir," cried the delighted Secretary, "you agree with me in everything—I don't see how we can disagree at all."

"Certainly not," said Douglas, wringing Toucey's hand with excruciating grasp. "We *can't* disagree, Mr. Toucey; it's impossible; for you are always right on a constitutional question, and while the Constitution declares that *Congress* may admit new States, it hasn't a word in it about *Cabinets* admitting them!" [7]

7 N. Y. *Express*, December 9, 1857. Douglas later wrote that Southerners at this time were threatening that unless Lecompton passed, four States would immediately secede. *Cong. Globe*, 35th Cong., 1st Sess., 1865.

As Douglas stalked out of the White House, the President knew that a terrific internal upheaval awaited the party; but he believed it would be short. His faith in party discipline was always great. The fall elections had just shown that despite Dred Scott, the Kansas troubles, and the panic, the Democratic Party was well organized and vigorous in the North.

New York, which the Republicans had swept in 1856, now ran up a Democratic margin of nearly twenty thousand for minor State offices, while the Republicans lost control of the legislature. Wisconsin, which the previous year had given Frémont a plurality of more than thirteen thousand, was almost recaptured. The Republicans elected a governor by only a few hundred votes, and saw the impassioned Carl Schurz defeated for secretary of state. In Ohio, another Republican stronghold of the previous autumn, the Democrats carried the legislature and almost placed an able young Cleveland leader, Henry B. Payne, in Chase's chair as governor. In Pennsylvania, the Democrats had nominated for governor an exponent of the coming industrial order, the railroad organizer William Fisher Packer, against the doughty Republican champion David Wilmot. In a three-cornered contest Packer overwhelmed both Wilmot and the American or Know-Nothing nominee, getting more votes than the two combined.[8] Kentucky elected eight Democrats to Congress, and only two Americans; Tennessee similarly filled eight of her ten Congressional seats with Democrats. In both States the legislatures were Democratic, with the result that Kentucky would soon elect one and Tennessee two Democratic Senators. North Carolina, too, witnessed a Democratic sweep.[9]

The Know-Nothing Party was manifestly going to pieces, and the Democratic organization seemed the chief beneficiary of its breakup. It was true that the Americans could take some comfort in Maryland, where they elected the able and popular Thomas H. Hicks governor, while the Republicans could rejoice over the victory of N. P. Banks in Massachusetts. But on the whole, the results tended to increase Democratic confidence. They indicated to many that the Republican effort in 1856 had been spasmodic and impermanent, that any third party was certain to be short-lived, and that the ingrained conservatism of the American people favored the Administration. Various Democratic newspapers trumpeted their hope of the approaching dissolution of the "Black Republican" gang, and the New Orleans *Bee* expressed the hope of many old Whigs for a revival or reincarnation of their truly national and patriotic organization.

Buchanan's faith in party strength and party discipline, however, was shortsighted. No matter how favorable the result of the fall elections, everyone knew

8 Packer's vote was 188,890; Wilmot's 146,147; Hazelhurst's, 28,132.
9 Andrew Johnson and A. O. P. Nicholson were the two Tennessee Democratic Senators.

that the Democrats could not win in 1860 without important Northern States, and close observers were aware that these States would respond sensitively to the new Kansas issue. The Lecompton game was not understood when voters went to the polls; it was a burning topic of discussion by the opening of Congress. Douglas was not a mere Rives or Tallmadge, but one of the most powerful leaders the Democratic Party had ever produced; he had an appealing principle on which to stand; and he was the fiercest and most tenacious fighter since Jackson himself.

Most important of all, many Northern Democrats were increasingly irritated by Southern domination, increasingly aware that doughface policies would mean loss of power to the Republicans, and increasingly jealous of their own rights. Despite the Dred Scott decision, most Northwestern Democrats clung to popular sovereignty; and if the Administration tried to ram Lecompton down the throat of a gagging Kansas, popular sovereignty would seem more than ever a weapon against governmental injustice. Party discipline as Jackson had interpreted it meant the will of the Administration against a small, well-scattered economic minority; party discipline as Buchanan was interpreting it meant the will of Southern Democratic leaders against the great majority of Northern Democrats. Jackson had always used party discipline in behalf of national cohesion; Buchanan was doing the precise opposite. He was risking the division of the Democratic Party into hostile Northern and Southern wings. He was risking, that is, the worst possible threat to the Union, for such a schism would overthrow the last barrier to a disruption of the nation itself.

Douglas was right. In more senses than one, Andrew Jackson, the President who had said, "Our Federal Union: It must be preserved!" was dead.

"The Lecompton Constitution will pass both Houses, though after a terrible fight," predicted Laurence Keitt of South Carolina.[10] So Buchanan and the Directory thought—perhaps sharing Keitt's faith that Douglas would return to the fold after the battle. In the Senate the Democrats had an easy majority, counting 39 members against 20 Republicans and 5 Americans. Their House majority was similarly substantial—131 Democrats against 92 Republicans and 14 Americans. With a majority of fourteen in the Senate and twenty-five in the House, the President believed that the use of the whip with one hand and some office taffy with the other would produce an early victory.[11] By the hour Congress opened, he knew that at most only four Democratic Senators would stand against the Lecompton constitution; after defeating Douglas in his own chamber, he hoped to carry the House with a rush.

It was quickly evident that the Directory meant to force the fighting. The

10 Keitt to Hammond, December 18, 1857; Hammond Papers, LC.
11 John G. Nicolay and John Hay, *Abraham Lincoln*, II, 127.

tone of Buchanan's message was uncompromising. Immediately after sending it to Congress, he removed Stanton, the acting governor of Kansas, and nominated General J. W. Denver, Commissioner of Indian Affairs, in his stead. Stanton's offense was that, yielding to the demands of the great majority of Kansans, he had called the newly elected legislature to meet at Lecompton on December 7, four weeks in advance of its regular date, so that it might give legal direction to the resistance to the Lecompton constitution. The Senate at once confirmed Denver, who was hurried west with all speed. In the secret-session debate, according to one correspondent, "the tone and manner of the Southern Senators indicated unmistakably that they felt they had full possession of the government, and meant to put down with the strong hand Walker and Douglas, and all who dissent from their policy with regard to Kansas." Jefferson Davis was declaring that he would mangle Douglas in the Senate debate.[12]

Already it was evident that the Administration would use its patronage to keep men in line. Douglas reported that in their conversation Buchanan had threatened to decapitate every friend of his who held office. One of those friends, the Ohio editor James B. Steedman, called at the White House with reference to an appointment. If a newspaper story can be believed, Buchanan frostily remarked, "Sir, you did all you could against me at the Cincinnati Convention." Steedman retorted: "True, sir, I *did* support Judge Douglas in that convention because I believed him the ablest and fittest man presented. I am of the same opinion still. I wish you good morning." [13] The tale was probably invented. It is certain, however, that when Douglas was asked if he had counted the cost of the battle, he replied: "I have taken a through ticket and checked all my baggage!" [14]

[II]

Since Administration control of the Senate was incontestable, the decisive struggle would be waged in the House; but the effect of the Senate speeches and of events in Kansas might prove of critical influence. Douglas intended to appeal to Northern sentiment, to effect a temporary alliance with the Republicans, and, in unison with Walker and the free State delegate from Kansas, Marcus J. Parrott, both of whom he called into protracted conference, to encourage the resistance of Kansas settlers to Lecompton and the regency government of John Calhoun. He meant to force a long delay. By the time the House voted, he hoped to have the North fully aroused.

12 Washington correspondence, N. Y. *Tribune*, dated December 10, 14, 1857.
13 N. Y. *Weekly Tribune*, December 12, 1857.
14 Washington correspondence, N. Y. *Evening Post*, May 10, 1858.

The day after Buchanan's message was read, Douglas rose for one of the most honest, impassioned, and therefore greatest speeches of his life. A skillful dissection of the tricky Lecompton scheme, its inconsistency with Democratic promises, and its impolicy on national grounds, the address had a compact force that was masterly. While his language was courteous, his manner was haughty and defiant, the mien of a man who meant to brave all the consequences of his perilous stand. Even the hostile Washington *Star* called the speech the ablest forensic effort Douglas had ever made in Congress.[15]

His first thrust pierced a weak spot in Buchanan's armor. With irrefutable evidence, he denied the President's assertion that the Nebraska Act had carried merely an obligation to submit the slavery question, and not the whole constitution. "Sir, permit me to say, with profound respect for the President of the United States, that I conceive that on this point he has committed a fundamental error—an error which lies at the foundation of his whole argument on this matter." He showed that during the debates of 1854 he and others had argued that the people of a Territory should decide for themselves their type of judiciary system, school system, tax system, and banking system. The Nebraska Act did not make a stipulation in behalf of slavery alone in giving the people a free and full voice on their institutions; it abolished the old stipulation in order to make self-government universal and complete. Douglas corrected a widespread misapprehension when he pointed out that the Lecompton convention had never been recognized by Congress as legal, for on the contrary, Toombs's enabling bill for a convention had been defeated. The only authority behind the convention was a territorial enactment. It had no legal power to establish a government—indeed, no power, except to petition Congress for a redress of grievances; and while this petition might take the form of a draft constitution, it ought not to be endorsed by Congress unless it expressed the popular will.

Douglas pointed to the President's own pledges on popular submission, to Governor Walker's repeated assurances on the point, and to the fact that numerous delegates had been directed by the people to lay the constitution before the voters. The election now arranged, he said, offered Louis Napoleon's choice: Vote *yes* and be protected, vote *no* and be shot. Those in favor of the instrument could vote for it, and those opposed could not vote at all. Why?

I have asked a very large number of gentlemen who framed the constitution —quite a number of delegates and a still larger number of persons who are their friends—and I have received the same answer from every one of them. . . They say that if they allowed a negative vote, the constitution would have been voted down by an overwhelming majority, and hence the fellows shall not be allowed to vote at all. [Laughter]. . . . I believe it would have been voted

15 Washington *Star*, December 10, 11, 1857; N. Y. *Tribune*, December 10-12, 1857.

down by a majority of four to one. I am informed by men well posted there—Democrats—that it would be voted down ten to one; some say twenty to one.

In conclusion, he proposed a return to the Toombs bill, on which all Democrats had agreed at the previous session. Discard both the Lecompton and Topeka constitutions, he urged; attach to the Toombs bill a clause providing for a general submission; or take the Minnesota Enabling Act, which contained such a clause, and apply it to Kansas. This course would give Kansas and the nation peace within ninety days. "But," exclaimed Douglas with solemn emphasis, "if this constitution is to be forced down our throats, in violation of the fundamental principle of free government, under a mode of submission that is a mockery and insult, I will resist it to the last." [16] As he sat down, the crowded galleries burst into applause so loud that Mason of Virginia angrily moved they be cleared.

The twenty-five Southern Democratic Senators listened to this speech with grim hostility. Already it was known that at least eight of their Northern colleagues would stand with them. Douglas's inveterate enemy, that Kentucky slaveholder Jesse Bright who had been elected from Indiana, would take sides against him, and so would his associate Fitch. John R. Thomson and William Wright of New Jersey (though Thomson might better be called Senator for the Camden & Amboy Railroad, of which he had been a director some twenty years) were sound Administration men. Gwin, formerly of Alabama and now of California, George W. Jones of Iowa (a college mate of Jefferson Davis at Transylvania) whose term had little more than a year to run, and Allen of Rhode Island, also near the end of his term, were equally regular. Both Jones and Allen hoped for diplomatic posts from Buchanan. Bigler of Pennsylvania was closely attached to Buchanan. The only two allies on whom Douglas could count were Charles E. Stuart of Michigan and David Broderick of California, neither very effective in debate. For a short time the position of George E. Pugh of Ohio was doubtful. He belonged to the popular sovereignty school, knew that Lecompton would cost the Ohio Democrats dear, and had a warm personal liking for Douglas. But, a conservative of staunch party feeling, he could not yet support a factional revolt. It was not strange that Slidell and Jefferson Davis counted on humiliating and crushing Douglas, and that Buchanan said openly that the Illinoisan had ruined himself.[17]

Yet the Administration front was by no means the unfaulted granite it seemed. The party was splitting not into two, but three or four groups. Such Southern extremists as Toombs, Davis, and Hammond assailed Douglas with

16 *Cong. Globe,* 35th Cong., 1st Sess., December 9, 1857.
17 Washington correspondence, dated December 9; N. Y. *Courier and Enquirer,* December 11, 1857.

epithets of which traitor and scoundrel were the mildest; excommunicating him
and his followers, they hailed the breach as final. To them, he was as hateful 'as
Seward and Chase. A very different tone prevailed north of the Potomac. While
Buchanan and Jeremiah Black showed intense bitterness, old-time leaders like
Cass were saddened and taciturn. Pugh would have preferred to follow Douglas,
and when he bowed to expediency it was with deep regret and foreboding. Bigler was uneasy, while even Fitch, no such minion of slavery as Bright and well
aware of Indiana's feeling, would have inclined toward Douglas's standard had
he not needed Administration support to hold his contested seat. It was quickly
noted that two prominent up-State New Yorkers, Horatio Seymour and
Daniel B. Dickinson, were exceedingly reluctant to express themselves on the
painful question. Seymour, in fact, said he could make no statement until he
consulted his friends.[18] Not a few old eastern Jacksonians, men of George Bancroft's stamp, who had long distrusted Douglas, decided that he was essentially
right and that they must either go with him or cross into the Republican camp.

The short interval between the opening of Congress and the Christmas recess on December 23 witnessed a hot running debate between Bigler, Fitch, and
Green of Missouri on the Lecompton side, and Douglas as a one-man opposition.
Not until December 23 did Stuart and Broderick speak, and then unimpres-
sively. But Douglas was in superb fighting form. Repeatedly he harried Bigler as
an Elizabethan ship-royal would outsail and harry a Spanish galleon. The slow,
clumsy Pennsylvanian was helpless against his charges. On the twenty-first,
after summarily disposing of both Mason and Bigler, he let off a sudden broadside against his Southern enemies and the newspapers they controlled; newspapers like the Montgomery *Advertiser* for W. L. Yancey, the Jackson *Mississippian* for Jefferson Davis, and the Richmond *South* for R. M. T. Hunter:

> There are men here personal enemies of mine—men who would be willing
> to sink an Administration if they could kill off northern men, and get them out
> of the way in the future; such men are getting their tools to denounce me as
> having abandoned the party. Why? Because I do not desert my principles as
> freely as the masters of these editors desert theirs. I have seen this attempt—not
> sanctioned by the President; he scorns it; but there are men under him busy
> at work to convince every one that I have betrayed my party and my
> principles, in order to see if they cannot crush me among my Democratic
> friends. That every press which can be controlled, is thus controlled, is beyond
> denial or dispute. Nineteen twentieths of all independent Democratic presses—
> those who do not depend on certain departments of the government for support
> —are with me in sustaining the credit of the Democratic party. . . .; but the
> few who are not allowed to speak for themselves are endeavoring to drive me
> where they cannot drive me—to desert the [party] principles. . . .

18 Daniel Sickles, December 21, 1857; Buchanan Papers.

Next day Fitch of Indiana drew another destructive volley. He had delivered an elaborate defense of Lecompton, combined with a harsh attack on the Topeka faction; his discourse being distinguished by malignant, personal innuendoes against Douglas. He held up *in terrorem* a picture of the tragic fate of Burr and Van Buren when they treacherously attacked the Democratic Party. During the latter part of the speech, the Little Giant lay perfectly motionless in his chair, his back to the orator; but he knitted his brows angrily, and his deep-set eyes took on smouldering fire. When Fitch sat down and Douglas rose slowly to his feet, a murmur of expectation ran through the hall. His rejoinder was magnificent in itself. It was compressed, epigrammatic, and forcible. And its effect was doubled by the proud, fierce energy of the speaker, who presented a striking picture of physical and intellectual strength as, pacing to and fro across the Senate floor, tossing his shaggy locks, and indulging in dramatic gestures, he threw out his arguments in a ringing voice. Several times he turned with sudden fury toward his assailant. Stamping his foot, he demanded what Fitch had meant when he compared him with Aaron Burr? What did he mean by accusing him of a selfish ambition to destroy the Democratic Party? What was behind his dark insinuations and vague innuendoes? "What if I do differ from the President? I have not become the servile tool of any President to receive and obey his instructions against my own judgment and sense of right." [19]

This was no teapot tempest; this was a party earthquake. Nobody who listened to Douglas's speeches could doubt that he would fight to a Waterloo end. His manner, his tone, his promise that he would repel every blow struck, bespoke irrevocable determination. He showed a bitterness toward his former brethren, too, which animated gestures and bearing. When he mentioned the "returns" of Kansas votes, it was with scorching contempt; when he spoke of the men behind Lecompton, it was with a mingled venom and disgust which proved that he would never again strike hands with Southern radicals. He accused the Administration of sending agents west by express to snatch the slavery clause out of the constitution so as to win doubtful Congressional votes. Walker showed the same temper. Returning to Washington on December 11, he shortly met Jeremiah Black, and the fire flew. He came to Douglas after that talk with a firm conviction that the Cabinet were determined to ruin both of them politically and financially. As for the Southern "ultras," they knew that they must conquer or forever lose control of the party which they had dominated, except for Cass's brief summer of candidacy, since 1840.

The Administration had used its light guns first. It reserved its heavy artillery until after the Christmas recess: Davis, Slidell, Hammond, Hunter, and Toombs.

19 N. Y. *Weekly Tribune*, December 23, 1857; for a slightly different version see *Cong. Globe*, 35th Cong., 1st Sess., 140.

But the Republican chieftains were now ready to move reinforcements to the aid of Douglas. As Seward, Fessenden, Lyman Trumbull, and others polished their weapons, the outlines of a strange alliance emerged. Douglas began talking confidentially of a Constitutional Union party to save the nation from Southern secession, such a coalition of Union Democrats and Republicans as actually appeared in 1864.

[III]

The Illinoisan was quick to renew in Washington the overtures which he had made to Republicans in Chicago. On December 14, he called Schuyler Colfax and Anson Burlingame to his house for a long conference.

"I believe," he said in effect, "that Jeff Davis and other Southern ultras are ready for disunion. I believe they want an opportunity to break up the nation. If they go on, we must form a grand Constitutional Union party to stop them. I confess, I never expected to meet such opposition to the simple demand for justice that I made on behalf of the people of Kansas. I shall stand my ground inflexibly; I shall uphold the principle of popular sovereignty even if this means my enemies will drive me from public life." He was confident that he could keep the bulk of the Northern Democracy behind him and that, if the Republicans gave full aid, he could defeat the Southern radicals.

"Our strategy is clear," he told Colfax and Burlingame. "The Administration will try to rush Lecompton through. They will say that Kansas must come in at once. If they succeed, all is lost. We must fight a delaying game. We must insist that Minnesota, with her unanimously adopted constitution, be admitted first. Let the South resist that if they dare! If they oppose Minnesota, we can block the appropriation bills in the House, and stop Cobb's Treasury note issue there. After Minnesota comes in, we must press for the admission of Oregon. As for Kansas, I shall present the Toombs bill with a hard and fast clause for popular submission added." When Colfax pointed out that many Republicans were so committed against the Toombs bill that they could not change front, Douglas said he would be glad to use a copy of the Minnesota Enabling Act. "I will go for any measure of any kind that provides for a full and fair vote of the people of Kansas on the whole constitution." He agreed to meet Banks to arrange a joint plan of action.

"Our true policy," continued Douglas with a far look into the future, "is to put the disunionists in their real light before the country. We must put them in such a position that when the break comes, as come it must, they will be in the position of insurgents; instead of letting them create a situation, as they wish to do, in which *we* must revolt. We will let them be the rebels. Then the army and the power of the nation will be against them." [20]

The Republican leaders, exultant but suspicious, were ready to effect a temporary alliance on the clear understanding that it involved no permanent commitment. Ben Wade, who had hailed Douglas's initial speech as "the first slave insurrection I ever saw," gladly went to his house for a friendly talk. He would concert plans with alacrity. Nevertheless, he thought Douglas actuated only by selfish motives, for the man knew that if he followed Buchanan's lead, Illinois would defeat him for reelection to the Senate. "You are driven into our port like a ship by stress of weather," he crowed to his host.[21] Lyman Trumbull was equally distrustful. At first he thought the Democratic schism mere shadowboxing; Douglas would be allowed to vote against Lecompton if his ballot was not necessary to carry it, and would then quietly return to the fold.[22] Even after hearing the Little Giant's angry speeches, he was uncertain how far the revolt would extend. Trumbull would neither embrace nor assail the new ally, but simply accept him so long as his course was right. "Douglas does not mean to join the Republican Party, I presume," he wrote Lincoln, "and yet if the Kansas question should be kept open for a few months, he may be forced into that position." [23] Seward, too, was for a cautious, mistrustful alliance. Douglas could never be consistent, he wrote. "After making a bold stroke for the defense of Kansas, we shall soon see him making a demonstration for the acquisition of Cuba." [24]

This cautious position suited Douglas; he, too, wanted only an emergency coalition. Colfax, anxious to encourage him in the fight, bade him look to the distant future. He probably underestimated the power of the Administration, which by use of patronage, prestige, and party press could wear down and defeat any rebel; but he must remember that defeat within the party was not defeat in the nation. "You have an opportunity," said Colfax in essence, "to place yourself in the most commanding position held by any statesman in the country; you can make yourself the Silas Wright of your party and conquer the prejudices of your old freesoil opponents." Colfax could promise nothing for the Republicans if Douglas was forced into their fold; he could not pledge Republican support for the senatorship in 1858, much less the Presidency in 1860. But he could say that the Republicans agreed that popular sovereignty in Kansas was the ques-

20 Schuyler Colfax, "Memorandum of Interview," December 14, 1857; Colfax Papers, Ind. State Lib.
21 December 20, 25, 1857; Wade Papers. "We must treat him with friendship, but not hunt him."
22 Trumbull to Lincoln, December 5, 1857; Trumbull Papers, Ill. State Hist. Lib.
23 *Ibid.*, December 25, 1857.
24 Frederic Seward, *William H. Seward*, II, 322; December 22, 1857.

tion of the hour, and would cooperate in maintaining that principle wherever it protected free men on free soil.

"You are right," responded Douglas, "I ask no support except in this present contest. If this issue is settled aright, new issues will come up hereafter, and we shall divide again. If it is not settled rightly, and remains the dominant question, we can let the future determine our duties and positions." Douglas introduced his bill to give Kansas a new enabling act on December 18, and the same day N. P. Banks for the Republicans offered a new enabling bill in the House.[25]

Spending the Christmas holidays with his wife in New York, Douglas was received by Democratic leaders, Republican editors, and the public with a hearty good will which elated him. He found members of Greeley's staff cordial. Greeley himself, delighted that the Senator had "broken the backs of the Democrats," was writing leaders to say that the Little Giant had the popular side, that he must win, and that the Administration could never turn him out of the party. Douglas found the *Herald* conducting a mere sham fight against him, which helped rather than hurt his cause; he found Raymond and the *Times* strongly on his side. Many Federal officeholders in New York were secretly with him. Talking freely, he told John Bigelow and Parke Godwin of the *Evening Post*, whom he met in N. P. Banks's room at the St. Nicholas, all about his plans. He was confident of defeating the Administration by preventing a House vote on Lecompton until late spring or summer, meanwhile mobilizing public sentiment and marshaling his Congressional forces so that he could either force an adjournment without action or destroy the measure. He left no doubt of his earnestness. Banks thought that he was almost ready to become a Republican convert—that he realized that no halfway house could be found between the Administration and the Republican Party. This was wishful thinking. But, testified Bigelow in a note to Bryant, his bitterness was extreme:

"Douglas does not disguise his conviction that he can never be forgiven by the South if he were ever so much disposed to ask forgiveness, and I thought I could perceive by the way in which he talked abundant evidence of an old hostility rankling in his bosom of which this outbreak about the Lecompton Constitution was as but the flash of the priming to the discharge." [26]

Republican suspicion of Douglas went far deeper in Illinois than in New York and the East generally. Let the party profit by the treason without taking the traitor to its embraces, recommended Illinoisans; Douglas may be capable of

25 *Cong. Globe*, 35th Cong., 1st Sess., 65, 84. The Washington correspondent of the *Herald* wrote of the Republicans, December 19, that "the case is by no means settled whether they will work for him [Douglas] or merely avail themselves of his labors to advance themselves and their interests." N. Y. *Herald*, December 23, 1857.
26 John Bigelow, December 28, 1857; Bryant Papers.

good, but his long fellowship with wrong and outrage should inspire misgivings.[27] Greeley, Preston King, Bigelow, and N. P. Banks, however, began to cherish hope that Douglas would follow in the path of the Blairs and Lyman Trumbull. A Democrat asked Banks if the Republicans would take the Little Giant into the party.

"Yes, sir," replied Banks, whom Massachusetts friends liked to call "the little iron man." "We will take all who want to come; the church is large and the door wide."

"Very well," rejoined the Democrat, "but are you willing to make him your leader?"

"We are willing, after they all get in," replied Banks, "to let the smartest man lead the column." [28]

Events played into the hands of Douglas in his struggle for delay. When Congress resumed work after New Year's of 1858, it was deemed wise to await the result of the January elections in Kansas, while financial problems, the arrest of the filibuster William Walker by Commodore Paulding of the Navy, and the Mormon question all urgently demanded discussion. February found the able Republican platoon in the Senate—Seward, Trumbull, Fessenden, Collamer, Doolittle, Wade, Henry Wilson—all alongside Douglas on the firing line. "You are great and strong," cried Seward to the Southern members, "but you can never, never conquer Kansas."

[IV]

That Territory was furnishing proof of the statement, and helping arouse precisely the Northern feeling that Douglas desired. In a series of dramatic moves, the free State settlers of Kansas defied the regency government of John Calhoun, provided for a plebiscite on the entire Lecompton constitution, and showed that the people overwhelmingly repudiated the instrument. These acts sealed the fate of Lecompton in the national House.

Much evidence exists that the Administration hoped to sweeten the Lecompton pill by having the constitution accepted at the December 21 election "without slavery." We have noted Douglas's charge that agents were hurried west to arrange this. Schuyler Colfax learned, early in December, that a dozen men had been sent to Kansas to insist that the slavery clause be voted out, or taken out by a falsification of the returns.[29] Buchanan, indeed, told his friends that he was sure the "constitution without slavery" would triumph. Most Senators seem to have supposed this.

27 C. S. Wilson of the Chicago *Journal*, December 14, 1857; Trumbull Papers.
28 N. Y. *Evening Post*, December 19, 1857.
29 Colfax, "Memorandum," December 14, 1857; Colfax Papers.

But the Administration erred in two respects. It failed to realize how completely free State voters would boycott the Hobson's choice election. Still more egregiously, it failed to comprehend that the little proslavery faction in Kansas, hardly a thousand men out of sixteen thousand voters, were determined to get the "constitution with slavery" even if the heavens fell. As Thomas Ewing, Jr., wrote his distinguished father, this group under John Calhoun were utterly reckless. "They are composed of those of the Ruffians who figured conspicuously in the arsons and murders of the past two years, and who have not yet died of delirium tremens. That is, honestly, the character of the men who are likely to have the control of the State government and to have the power of the General Government to back them in subjugating the people. But Kansas cannot be forced like a bastinadoed elephant to kneel to receive the paltry riders." [30]

The Administration failed, also, to reckon with the intrepid Stanton, secretary and acting-governor of Kansas until supplanted by Denver. The Oxford and McGee frauds, and the Lecompton convention, had incensed this former proslavery man. He had discovered, as he put it later, why the great mass of the Kansans were so dissatisfied with their government that they were ready to rebel to throw it off. [31] The Territory naturally boiled with indignation after the convention broke up. Settlers in scores of communities swore that they would fight to the death before submitting. A call went out for a free State convention in Lawrence to determine what action should be taken to meet the new contingency. Demands poured in upon Stanton to convene the recently elected legislature that it might deal with the situation. He sympathized with the popular feeling, for he regarded the whole convention scheme for a regency government as outrageous. This regency government, under the Lecompton "schedule," was to reign supreme until a new legislature and other officers were chosen on January 4, 1858. In view of the unjust apportionment clause which gave a heavy preponderance to counties on the Missouri border, of the special powers conferred on Calhoun to manage the new elections, and of the grant of suffrage in these crucial elections of December 21 and January 4 to every white male "in the Territory on that day," fair balloting was impossible.

"It was apparent," Stanton later wrote, "that all the machinery had been artfully prepared for a repetition of gross frauds, similar to those which had been attempted in November." While Congress fastened the Lecompton constitution on the new State, a rigged election would furnish a new Lecompton legislature which would prevent any interference with the obnoxious instrument.

Stanton cut through the regency scheme with his call of December 1 for a

30 Leavenworth, January 18, 1858; Ewing Papers.
31 F. P. Stanton, Philadelphia speech, February 5, 1858.

special session of the recently chosen legislature. He acted none too soon. The next day the Cabinet dispatched a messenger westward with that part of Buchanan's forthcoming message which related to territorial affairs. Cobb, Thompson, and Floyd wished to paralyze Stanton. That next day, too, the free State convention opened in Lawrence, with "Governor" Robinson and Jim Lane in charge. The delegates, meeting in soft Indian summer weather, filled the town to overflowing. Angered as never before, they pledged the freesoil majority to implacable resistance to Lecompton. Eighteen thousand men, said Lane, were ready to shoulder arms. If Stanton had not given the people due legal means for protecting themselves from imposition, the elections of December 21 and January 4 would doubtless have witnessed a reopening of civil war. As it was, when the legislature convened December 7, the acting-governor laid before it a message which not only spoke of the "profound agitation" and the "sense of wrongs and injustice," but recommended definite action. He asked for legislation to punish election frauds. But above all, he urged the legislature to fix an election date when qualified citizens might vote for the constitution in either of the forms provided by the convention, and also might vote against it *in toto*. He believed that Congress could not disregard the voice of the people, thus legally expressed.[32]

The legislature immediately took this sage advice. It was anxious to fortify the freesoil settlers before Washington could send out a new governor to harass them. While the members had promised Stanton that they would not try to set the Topeka government in operation, they were nevertheless able to inaugurate a new era. Hitherto the free State men had acted extra-legally; now they wielded a legitimate authority. They provided for an investigation of the Oxford and McGee frauds, and prescribed effective penalties for such acts—with the result that some offenders fled the Territory. They also submitted the Lecompton constitution to popular vote on January 4. Ballots might be cast "For the constitution with slavery," "For the constitution without slavery," and "Against the constitution."

Three elections were now impending: the partial plebiscite on December 21, the full plebiscite January 4, and the election of a new legislature and other officers on the last-named date. It was thus possible for Kansans to prove themselves overwhelmingly against the instrument in all its parts. Republican leaders in Washington kept in close touch with "Governor" Robinson and other free State leaders. Using B. Gratz Brown of the Missouri *Democrat* as intermediary, they advised that the legislature stay in session to await Washington events, repeal the act authorizing the Lecompton convention, and make preparations

32 Full message in Emporia *Kanzas News*, December 19, 1857.

for regaining full possession of the Territory if necessary.[33] No rash steps, however, were taken.

Beyond question, Stanton's call of the special session was a statesmanlike act. It diverted public attention from schemes of violent resistance, substituted debate and investigation for angry personal collisions, and enabled representatives of the people to devise methods of counteracting the wrongs planned against them.[34]

The Administration was taken aback by the acting-governor's spirited course. The Cabinet, in sending him an advance copy of part of Buchanan's message, had instructed him to follow the President's views.[35] He was to encourage voters to accept the Lecompton formula; instead, he had assisted them to reject it! His instant removal came too late. Long before Denver could arrive to take his place, the legislature had completed its work, passed a militia bill over Stanton's veto, and adjourned. For a few days, Administration leaders were fearful lest Walker make a hurried trip to Kansas to supersede acting-governor Denver. But Walker thought he saw a more effective mode of helping the Territory than by beginning a contest which would end in his swift decapitation. After hurried conferences with Douglas and other friends, he spent several days composing a long appeal to the country. Under date of December 15, he sent this to Cass as a letter of resignation which the freesoil press gleefully published in full. It produced a public sensation, brought about an extra session of the Cabinet, and gave Lecompton a heavy new blow. He should not have resigned—he should have gone down with his flag nailed to the mast; but his parting shot did heavy execution.

Disgust, chagrin, and burning resentment mingled in the letter. Abandoned by the Administration, stigmatized by Southern epithets, laboring under a sense of betrayal, Walker spoke with devastating frankness. He branded "my Southern opponents" as cheats. He reiterated the familiar facts showing that the Lecompton convention had not represented one-tenth of the people. He warned Congress that an attempt to force the constitution upon Kansas would require coercion of an overwhelming majority, would settle nothing, and would, "I fear, be attended by civil war, extending, perhaps, throughout the Union." He declared that he would not play the part of a mute in a pantomime of ruin. Most stingingly of all, he told the nation that the President had been victimized by a Southern conspiracy. All had been going smoothly; the peaceable entry of Kansas had seemed assured—and then "my Southern opponents interfered . . . and by denunciation, menaces, and otherwise, aided at a critical period by several Federal officeholders in Kansas, including the Surveyor-General, and the Presi-

33 N. P. Banks and F. P. Blair, Jr., telegraphed B. G. Brown thus December 14; Brown to Robinson, December 15, 1857, Robinson Papers, KHS.
34 F. P. Stanton, "To the People of the Union," January 29, 1858.
35 Cass was the mouthpiece; *Senate Exec. Docs., No. 8*, 35th Cong., 1st Sess., 112, 113.

dent of the Convention with his immense patronage, embracing many hundred employees, intervened, and as I believe without the knowledge or approbation of the President of the United States, produced the extraordinary paper called the Lecompton Constitution."

Ex-Secretary Stanton was ready to add his voice to Walker's. In a long letter, written as soon as his hands were free, he laid bare the frauds in the Territory, defended his own conduct there, and warned Congress not to force upon the Kansans an instrument which four-fifths of them condemned; not to commit the supreme folly of defending "so wicked and dishonest a contrivance as the Lecompton Constitution." His detailed speech in New York on the subject was soon being sold by the *Tribune* as part of an eight-page extra.[36]

The men who had gone out as proconsuls of the Directory to make Kansas a Democratic State had come back as surrogates for the freesoil settlers who were soon to make Kansas one of the most rock-ribbed Republican States of the Union. Walker was concluding his service under Buchanan; his next great public role would be under Abraham Lincoln.

Meanwhile, all eyes were fixed upon the three Kansas elections. The Administration accepted the *fait accompli* of the legislature's arrangement of a plebiscite on January 4, instructing Denver to see that the election was held as freely and fairly as the two ordered by the convention. Just before Christmas, therefore, the new acting-governor issued a proclamation in which he certified to the legality of the plebiscite and also recognized the validity of the law passed to punish election frauds. While Denver was not so strong a man as Geary and not so able as Walker, he was honest and impartial. A Virginia lawyer who had made a sterling record in the Mexican War and in California, and who had lived on the Missouri border before Kansas was opened to settlement, he was resolved to yield no improper ground to any party or group. Announcing that he would carry out Walker's policies in good faith, he soon won the regard of conservative freeholders.

The first election, the "with slavery" or "without slavery" contest of December 21, followed the old farcical pattern. An alleged vote of 6,226 was cast for the constitution with slavery, and 569 for it without. Proof was later adduced that many ballots were fraudulent, a legislative committee which inspected them declaring that at least 2,720 should be annulled.[87] Most free State men of

36 Priced at $15 per thousand; N. Y. *Tribune*, February 25, 1858.
37 Spring, *Kansas*, 228, 229. President C. W. Babcock of the Council, present at the counting of the votes, believed that about 4,000 of them were fraudulent; see Douglas's report for the Committee on Territories, 1858. Walker also declared about 4,000 of them invalid. This was the conclusion reached by the State officers elected January 4. They pointed out that 3,012 of the votes for the constitution "with slavery" were polled in three sparsely settled districts on the Missouri border, Oxford, Shawnee, and Kickapoo; and from personal knowledge of these settlements they knew the great bulk of the vote to be fictitious. They believed that not more than 2,000 true citizens cast their vote for the Lecompton constitution on December 21. See text of their protest, Phila. *Weekly Press*, February 13, 1858.

course ignored the election. In the contest for officers on January fourth, 6,545 votes were allegedly cast, of which 2,458 were later pronounced fraudulent. Freesoil settlers largely boycotted this, too. Once more the proslavery element perpetrated grave frauds, and the result was uncertain, both sides claiming the victory. The referendum on the constitution as a whole, held without disorder on the fourth of January, was much more impressive. No fewer than 10,226 voted against the constitution, while 138 were ready to accept it without slavery and 24 with slavery. This emphatic result, proving clearly how Kansas stood, brought John J. Crittenden's influential voice in the Senate over to Douglas.

Most Southerners accepted the vote of December 21 as final; Kansas had asked for entry with a slave State constitution, and must be admitted. Most Northerners accepted the vote of January 4; Kansas had rejected slavery, and must be allowed to write a new constitution. Acting-Governor Denver felt no doubt whatever that the free State men had carried both the election of State officers and the only valid test on the constitution. On January 16, he wrote Buchanan that Congress would commit a vital error if it accepted Lecompton. The free State men constituted a large majority; feeling was high—an organization had been formed sworn to kill every man who took office under the Lecompton constitution; and the people simply would not submit to that instrument. Denver recommended that Congress pass an enabling act and let a new constitutional convention be held. "As for the Democratic party here it cannot be worse off than it is at present, and this course will afford them an opportunity to organize a strong conservative party which will be able to control the Territory."

Bitter it would have been for a truly sensitive President to review the events of these six weeks in Kansas; to see how Stanton had outmaneuvered him, to read of the overwhelming repudiation of the constitution by more than ten thousand voters, and to find the new acting-governor recommending substantially Douglas's proposal. But no one doubted that Buchanan would prove obedient to the voice of his masters. He pressed forward with the tenacity not of courage but of timidity. Having chosen his path, he felt it would cost him too much to make honest confession of error; while he was afraid to turn against the Directory.

The Cabinet had discussed a compromise plan, under which Congress would approve of Lecompton with a solemn stipulation that the first State legislature must submit the whole constitution to popular vote. Buchanan, Cass, and Toucey, three Northerners, had favored it—and the time had been when a President backed by his Secretary of State would have had his own way; but Cobb, Floyd, Brown, and Jacob Thompson were sternly opposed, and Buchanan yielded to the strong men about him.[38] When Denver's letter was brought to

38 H. Von Holst, *United States*, IV, 204; Nichols, *Disruption*, 156.

him by Rush Elmore, a former judge and a man who, although the largest slave-holder in Kansas, held moderate, sagacious views, the President was ready to renew his championship of Lecompton. He was ready, that is, to tell Congress that the burlesque vote of December 21 constituted good ground for accepting Kansas as the sixteenth slave State.

What he said to Elmore we do not know. He had the effrontery to write Denver that he regretted he had not received the information sooner, for having prepared a special message re-espousing Lecompton and having shown it to several Senators, he could not withdraw it.[39] On February 2, 1858, he sent the Lecompton constitution to Congress with a long message urging immediate admission of Kansas—"at this moment as much a slave State as Georgia or South Carolina." He knew that more than 10,000 Kansans had voted against the constitution and not more than 3,000 for it. The peculiar features of the message were two: a vitriolic denunciation of the Topeka organization under Robinson and Jim Lane as treasonable, disloyal, and revolutionary, its very existence consti-tuting "a state of rebellion"; and an argument that if Kansans did not want slavery, they need only enter the Union, and then they could remake their government immediately. But could they really do so? A constitutional clause would forbid it; and even if this were disregarded, the accomplished fact would be hard to reverse.

[V]

The important fact was that the course of events in Kansas, with the vigorous letters of Walker and Stanton, had greatly strengthened Douglas and his Repub-lican allies. Another broad ebullition of public sentiment, akin to that of 1854, was visible from the Kennebec to the Kaw. The moral position of the Douglas-Seward coalition was invulnerable, for only the most extreme Southerners denied that the constitution should have been submitted to popular vote, and Buchan-an's instructions to Walker had placed the President in a role where he must eat his words. The political position of the coalition was also strong. The entire Republican Party, almost the whole Know-Nothing Party of the free States, and a heavy majority of Northern Democrats, stood behind Douglas on this issue. In the Northwest in particular, Democratic newspapers seemed ten to one on his side.[40] The ablest editors of the land were embattled against the Administra-tion. In all the larger cities from Boston to Chicago, and in country districts everywhere north of the Ohio, public meetings testified to the groundswell of feeling. The fighting power of Douglas, Walker, and Stanton, their defense of popular rights, their dramatization of a bold cause, aroused general admiration.

39 *Kansas State Hist. Publs.*, I, 170.   40 N. Y. *Weekly Tribune*, December 26, 1857.

They were for the New Democracy against the old; they were the people's men against privilege and power. Douglas, wrote Greeley, "would carry this State for President tomorrow, as against Buchanan, Dickinson, or anybody that could be started to compete with him in the Democratic convention." [41]

Day after day, a snowfall of approving letters from every free State whitened Douglas's desk. Many were from prominent men. Governor Henry A. Wise was with him, declaring that this legerdemain scheme, if Buchanan pushed it through, would raise the Black Republican flag above Capitol and White House; George Bancroft applauded him, writing that every student of history knew that Lecompton must leave the Administration helpless with the people.[42] It pleased Douglas to receive from the owner of the Gloversville, New York, *Standard* a belligerent anti-Lecompton editorial with the assurance that it yielded but a faint indication of the feeling in that area.[43] He was still better pleased by word from Lanphier of the *Illinois State Register* that a Democratic convention in Springfield, representing all parts of the State, had shown almost complete unity and a belligerent spirit.[44] Humble party workers sent their testimony as to popular support. A citizen of Reading, Pennsylvania, who circulated five thousand German translations of Douglas's anti-Lecompton argument, declared that if Governor Packer's inaugural had not been sound on Kansas, he would have been left without a Cabinet twenty-four hours after he took office.[45] A lieutenant in Scioto County, Ohio, wrote that he did not know a Democrat in that region who was not heartily behind Douglas's party. Another in Lawrence, Massachusetts, declared that the Senator was on the floodtide of popular enthusiasm. A third in Trenton, New Jersey, sending a fiery speech by a local politician, estimated that nine hundred and ninety-eight voters in every thousand were with the Little Giant.[46]

Particularly striking were the expressions welling up from the border States. Virginians sent numerous letters: R. H. Glass of Lynchburg, father of a future statesman, for example, praised Douglas's courage and fairness.[47] A Marylander

41 December 20, 1857; Greeley-Colfax Correspondence.
42 Bancroft to Douglas, December 2, 1857; Douglas Papers.
43 January 24, 1858; Douglas Papers.
44 C. H. Lanphier, January 22, 1858; Douglas Papers.
45 G. M. Sanman, January 23, 1858; Douglas Papers.
46 J. Enslow, January 24, G. W. Harland, January 26, F. F. Patterson, January 22, 1858; Douglas Papers.
47 R. H. Glass, January 21, 1858; Douglas Papers. Some Southerners of course wrote their disapproval. J. J. Quarles of Carthage, Texas, informed the Senator that if he did not drop his fight against Lecompton he would not get a corporal's guard to support him in Texas for the next Presidential nomination. But such letters are comparatively few, and the impression to the contrary given by A. L. Venable in his article "The Conflict between the Douglas and Yancey Forces" in the Charleston Convention (*Southern Hist. Review*, May, 1942) is misleading.

wrote that Ogle County gave the Senator strong adherence.[48] A citizen of Mt. Vernon, Kentucky, who had hoped to see Kansas a slave State, declared that his section was against any constitution not popularly approved. Simon B. Buckner, destined for a distinguished career, wrote that a majority of Louisville people gave Douglas their full approbation. Another Kentuckian put local sentiment crisply: "We would rather Kansas would come into the Union as a slave State. But we are opposed to trickery and all such abominations as the Lecompton Constitution." [49] The Louisville *Democrat*, oldest and ablest Democratic paper of the State, thought that Lecompton would fare worse there than in Kansas.

Early in 1858, the legislatures of New Jersey, Rhode Island, and Michigan passed resolutions denouncing Lecompton; the New York Assembly invited Stanton to address it; and the Ohio legislature instructed Pugh to vote against admission. In Buchanan's own State, Governor Packer said that he believed he expressed the conviction of the people in declaring that if the people of a new State wished to vote on their constitution after it was framed, they should have an unqualified right to do so. Forney's *Press* and George W. Child's *Public Ledger* were attacking Buchanan in every issue, while the *Pennsylvanian* offered but weak resistance. An anti-Lecompton meeting in Philadelphia on February 8, where Forney presided and Stanton made a rousing address, elicited letters from a long roll of Democrats—Douglas, Walker, Stuart, Representatives T. L. Harris of Illinois and S. S. Cox of Ohio, and Governor Wise. Characterizing Lecompton as undemocratic and oppressive, Wise contradicted Buchanan's assertion that admission would speedily end the agitation outside Kansas. Instead, he wrote, it would have the worst effects. It would create a border war, arouse Northern bitterness, drive multitudes of honest Democrats from the party, and ensure Republican triumph—thus raising the last dread issue of disunion.[50] Only by heroic efforts, using officeholders present and expectant, did the Administration prevent the State convention at Harrisburg early in March from passing hostile resolutions.[51]

Walker and Stanton, throwing their private business aside, were maintaining an effective crusade. They were able orators. Both spoke at an anti-Lecompton gathering in New York. Stanton addressed another in the capital of Ohio for three hours,[52] while in Philadelphia he caustically arraigned Buchanan's timidity. It was the well-understood design of certain Southern leaders in Washington, he said, to break up the Union if Lecompton failed. Their threats had caused

48 J. A. Ettinger, January 25, 1858; Douglas Papers.
49 W. R. Thompson, January 24, 1858; Douglas Papers.
50 *National Intelligencer*, February 11, 1858.
51 N. Y. *Weekly Tribune*, March 13, 1858.
52 *Idem*.

the President to surrender, when, if he had only defied them, the true-hearted Democracy of Tennessee, Kentucky, Virginia, North Carolina, Louisiana, and possibly other Southern States would have rallied to the national standard, and he could have crushed the conspirators.[53] If any man knew the upper South, it was Stanton.

In Michigan, Wisconsin, and Iowa, no less than Illinois, most Democrats were reported for Douglas; the Detroit *Free Press* (still regarded as Cass's organ), the Columbus *Statesman*, Cincinnati *Volksfreund*, Milwaukee *Wisconsin*, *Illinois State Register* and Chicago *Times* heading the roll of anti-Lecompton papers. Senator-elect Shields of Minnesota was doubly indignant, because he thought the admission of his State was being made dependent on the passage of the Lecompton scheme. In California the party was rent asunder, Broderick as head of the San Francisco machine and close friend of the Illinois leader fighting tooth and nail against Gwin, who had executive patronage to aid him. Governor Weller was on Douglas's side, while the Democratic *Globe* and *Herald* in San Francisco, with the well-edited *Alta California* and Sacramento *Union*, took the same position. California had good historic reasons for believing in popular sovereignty.[54] When the legislature instructed Broderick to support Lecompton, the Senator defied it, saying he was satisfied that four-fifths of the people of the State repudiated the Lecompton fraud.[55]

The most remarkable evidence that the tide was running against the Administration was furnished by the revolt of the Indiana Democrats—a "majestic uprising," as the New York *Tribune* called it, against which the two Senators fought in vain. Bright and Fitch believed that they could use the postmasters, Federal marshals, swamp-land commissioners, and other officeholders to maintain the line against Douglas. They were aided by Governor A. P. Willard, one of Bright's lieutenants. The State convention had been fixed for January 8, 1858, and for weeks beforehand the Administration machine promised offices right and left, strained every sinew to pack the county conventions, and even when those bodies condemned Lecompton, tried to choose Buchanan delegates. The result was that despite fairly plain evidence of popular sentiment, the convention was so closely divided that the outcome was uncertain.

The Bright-Fitch faction, blanched but determined, played all its best cards. By nominating Willard for president of the convention, they gained the vote of counties which would have rejected any other Lecompton man, and the gover-

53 Philadelphia *Weekly Press*, February 13, 1858.
54 *National Intelligencer*, March 4, 1858. Every Democratic newspaper but one in Iowa was on Douglas's side. J. D. Eads, Des Moines, December 12, 1857; Douglas Papers. Of the fifty-nine Democratic newspapers in Illinois, only four supported Lecompton; Lewiston (Illinois) *Fulton Democrat*, March 13, 1858.
55 Jeremiah Lynch, *A Senator in the Fifties: David C. Broderick of California*, 180.

nor then shut out all Douglasites from the platform committee. Bright, so apprehensive that he trembled, made a speech which even his supporters pronounced a failure. When his faction by desperate exertions averted a flat condemnation of Lecompton and passed inconclusive resolutions on Kansas, the body was thrown into a perfect bedlam. It broke up in an uproar, many delegates swearing that not a constable or justice of the peace could be elected on such a platform. The dissenters at once launched a movement for a new mass gathering of Democrats in Indianapolis the following month. Fresh county conventions were held and delegates chosen. "In no other way can the State be saved," wrote one leader; and many agreed that feeling was so intense that unless the party was brought over to the right track, the State would go Republican.[56]

When the mass convention crammed into Masonic Hall, it represented every part of the State. Letters from Walker and Henry A. Wise were cheered. Henry B. Payne of Ohio spoke. Resolutions passed arraigning the Lecompton movement, thanking Douglas for his exertions, and proposing a convention of Northern Democrats. From end to end of Indiana, it was clear that candidates for Congress must take an anti-Lecompton stand or face almost certain defeat.[57]

And Indiana was typical of a long list of Northern States where the Administration had the party machinery but the anti-Lecompton men had public sentiment. When the Connecticut convention, after stormy scenes, adopted a straddle endorsing both Buchanan and popular sovereignty, the chairman of the platform committee uttered a blunt warning. The party had met defeat ever since the Nebraska Act, he said; it had been decimated in the past five years; if it now passed a Lecompton resolution, it would sink in ruin. In Rhode Island, a collision between Federal officeholders and anti-Lecompton spokesmen resulted in similar predictions.[58] Most ominous of all was the spring election in New Hampshire. The Democrats went down with a crash. Again, said the Concord *Patriot*, leading Buchanan organ of the State, the Kansas question has crushed us with its blind ponderous weight. "Before the Lecompton constitution question was brought before the country, our prospects for success were highly flattering: our triumph seemed to be certain; that matter, with the course of the Administration upon it, fell like a wet blanket upon the rising courage and earnest zeal of our friends, and from that day we were doomed." [59]

Nowhere did Democrats look to the coming elections with more dread than in New York. The Administration forced to heel every adherent it could; not only good party mastiffs like Dan Sickles and D. S. Dickinson, but the more

---

56 A. May, December 1, 1857, Ezra Reed, January 21, 1858, to Douglas; Douglas Papers.
57 Indianapolis *Journal*, February 24, March 1, 1858.
58 *National Intelligencer*, March 6, 1858.
59 Concord *Patriot*, March 10, 1858. The Boston *Herald* and the Augusta, Me., *Age*, both supported Douglas.

independent John A. Dix, who told a Tammany mass meeting that, while he had at first condemned Lecompton, he now supported it on the ground that admission of Kansas would leave that State free to remake its constitution immediately in freesoil form. This easy reasoning was rejected by Bancroft and other former Barnburners, by Raymond of the *Times,* and by a great body of Know-Nothings led by the Brooks brothers of the *Express.* Representative John B. Haskin of Westchester, a staunch anti-Lecomptonite, became a popular hero. The Democrats here, too, adopted a preposterous straddle by declaring for both Buchanan and popular sovereignty—and their candidates made as much of Douglas and as little of Buchanan as possible.[60]

[VI]

It was a perplexed, harassed Buchanan who thus saw revolt sweep the North and Northwest, corrode the border States, and find voice even in the New Orleans *Delta,* which spat contemptuously on Lecompton. Alexander H. Stephens was touched to find the President worn out with official cares. "He is now quite feeble and wan," reported Stephens on February 3. "I was struck with his physical appearance; he appears to be failing in physical health." [61] The Directory, however, quite undaunted, was beginning to use the patronage to enforce its will. Forney, visiting Washington early in March, found the capital full of gloom and apprehension. "What is the aspect now?" he exclaimed. "One wide Reign of Terror." A test had been erected, and those who would not crawl through it went to the guillotine. He described a typical piece of discipline: Maxwell McCaslin of western Pennsylvania, who had worked for Buchanan's advancement during fifteen years, who had been given an Indian agency in Kansas by Pierce, and who had discharged his duties capably, was summarily dismissed when it was found that he agreed with Walker instead of Jacob Thompson. "An army of spies are on the alert, hunting for victims," warned Forney.[62]

The outcome in the Administration-controlled Senate was certain. Had Douglas and Seward possessed the logic of Burke and the eloquence of Cicero, they would have made no converts in that chamber. About fifty set speeches were delivered, which changed not one vote in Congress and not a thousand outside. Southern leaders delivered attorney-like pleas on the legality of the Kansas convention; Douglasites reiterated their defense of popular sovereignty; and Republicans proclaimed their freesoil views.

60 N. Y. *Express, Tribune;* D. S. Alexander, *Pol. Hist. New York,* II, 248–250.
61 R. M. Johnston and W. H. Browne, *Alexander H. Stephens,* 329.
62 Phila. *Weekly Press,* March 20, 1858.

A handful of Senators, however, made contributions of some originality to the debate. Jefferson Davis uttered a plaintive defense of disunionist tendencies in the South while avowing his own love of the Union. A stranger in the Senate gallery, he said, might suppose that he was watching a conference of representatives of two belligerent nations. The South was being arraigned day after day as an aggressive power. Yet what aggressions had it committed? The sum of its offense was a wish to let slavery expand into those parts of the common territory where the people wished to have it. Why should the South care about such expansion? "Simply because of the war that is made against our institutions; simply because of the want of security. . . . You have made it a political war. We are on the defensive. How far are you to push us?" So long as the Southern people were violently denounced, and so long as institutions which they inherited and intended to transmit were being undermined, he added, the Union was truly in danger.[63]

Peculiar weight was given to John J. Crittenden's speech on March 17 by his venerable years, high impartiality, and position as spokesman for the borderland. For two hours he held the attention of one of the largest audiences of the debate. Lord Napier, Baron Stoeckl, and many Representatives were given seats on the floor. The question, he said, was whether Lecompton was the constitution of the *people* of Kansas. He described the chicanery in the writing of the instrument, the election frauds, and the popular disgust. He scoffed at the idea that Kansas could first accept and then immediately rewrite the instrument: "It cannot be abolished, except in the manner prescribed and pointed out in the constitution itself, if any manner is prescribed." Better take twenty votes, better hold twenty elections, than force a misshapen, ill-begotten fundamental law upon a resisting people.

In Clay's spirit, the aged Senator appealed for a decision above bitter sectional antagonisms. "Look at our great country, and the great subjects which claim our attention as her legislators; look at them in all their majesty and their magnitude, and then say how little, how pitiful, in comparison, is the question about which we are making so much strife and contention."[64] With the aid of anti-Lecompton Representatives, Crittenden shortly framed a substitute for the Lecompton bill. It provided for the admission of Kansas on condition that the Lecompton constitution should *first* be submitted to the voters in a carefully guarded election; a new constitution to be drawn up if the old one were rejected.

63 Robert McElroy, *Jefferson Davis*, 176. The N. Y. *Herald* in an editorial of February 4, 1858, pointed out that Southerners who thought that Lecompton would permanently give them a slave State were deluded. But, it declared, the South is frightened by the growing preponderance of free States in Congress, and by the concurrent increase in antislavery sentiment in the North. Appeasement of Southern fears, it argued, was merely common sense.
64 *Cong. Globe*, 35th Cong., 1st Sess., 1153–1159.

This substitute was to be brought forward in the House as soon as the Senate bill was taken up there.

Extremists on both sides made the Senate walls resound with their challenges. Toombs paid tribute to the "sublime spectacle" presented by Buchanan and Black in defending Southern constitutional rights. James H. Hammond, the wealthy grandee of "Redcliffe" in South Carolina, a quiet-mannered but impetuous man, made his famous "cotton is king" speech, which bore only slightly upon the questions in hand. It provoked the angriest rejoinders from Republican seats. Altogether, the long debate was lively—but it altered no opinions.

Throughout the struggle, Douglas by physical and mental force dominated the scene. A host in himself, he was always ready to meet any onslaught, to answer any argument. The incessant strain bore heavily on him. He was harassed by financial worries (for he had overextended his realty purchases and suffered cruel losses in the panic); he was exhausted by sixteen hours of labor a day without exercise, and anguished by his wife's illness. But, determined to protract the contest until national feeling was fully aroused, he was always in the thick of the battle. An able new Republican Senator, scholar, poet, and lawyer in one, James Dixon of Connecticut, expressed his admiration for the Little Giant:

Douglas is quite unwell. He came into our night session about midnight on Monday, but we sent him home. He was not fit to be there. He is very nervous, though he does not show it at all in his looks or appearance. His wife was dangerously sick for some days—say about three weeks ago; and from this cause and the anxiety natural to his position, he became nervous and sleepless. For ten days and nights he did not sleep at all, and for four days last week he was confined to his bed. He now wishes to be able to speak on Monday next. The design of the majority was to force the Kansas bill to a vote on Monday night—but they found the minority determined and resolute. About half-past six on Tuesday morning they gave up the effort. . . .

I am more and more impressed with admiration for the man. I see more and more what a struggle it cost him to sever all personal and political ties, and take his stand on the foundation of eternal truth and justice. All sorts of blandishments and fascinations were applied in vain—and when promises proved unavailing, resort was had to threats. He could have had the assurance of fifteen States at the next Presidential election, with a good prospect of Illinois, Pennsylvania, and perhaps others. But he was decided and resolute. He is now calm and hopeful—and says he has no personal wishes; is willing to throw his influence for the cause.

The South never made a greater mistake than in provoking his opposition. He will prove a terrible foe.[65]

The best single contribution by Douglas lay in his minority report from the Committee on Territories; one of three, for Green brought in the majority

---

65 James Dixon to Gideon Welles, March 17, 1858; Welles Papers, LC.

Lecompton report, and Collamer and Wade the Republican report. Douglas refuted Buchanan's contention that the Kansans could forthwith revise their constitution. It is only when public sentiment approaches unanimity, he stated, that constitutions and governments can be radically altered without violence. Did the character of John Calhoun's gang of slavery men furnish any prospect that, once they had put the constitution in force, unalterable until after 1864 and then only by two-thirds vote, they would "permit it to be subverted and abrogated by a revolutionary amendment, when they will have acquired the right under the Constitution of the United States to demand of the President the use of the Federal Army, to . . . protect the State 'against domestic violence'?" [66]

The Little Giant was never more combatively irresistible than in his final speeches. The admission bill he termed a deathblow to State rights and popular sovereignty. "Reverse the case," he challenged the Southern Senators. "Would Southern men, if a convention of freesoilers should make a constitution, and allow you to vote for it, but not against it, and then attempt to force that constitution on a slaveholding people against their will, would you Southern gentlemen have submitted to such an outrage?" He scornfully attacked the Washington *Union* and the editorials that Attorney-General Black was writing for it. With savage defiance, he warned the Administration that its proscriptions were forcing the party to ruin. Every officeholder was being asked if he were Douglas's enemy, and if he said *no*, off went his head. Men might vote as they liked on the Pacific Railroad bill or Army bill, but on Lecompton no tolerance was extended. Did Cobb, Thompson & Co. intend to expel from the party every man who did not vote for admission? If so, "how many will your Democratic Party number in Pennsylvania? How many in New York? How many in Ohio? How many in any other Northern State?"

Dramatic scenes attended the final debate on March 22. Long before the Senate met at ten o'clock, hurrying crowds, anxious to hear Douglas, had blocked the corridors and gallery. Stuart spoke for three hours. Broderick indulged in scathing language; the attempt to carry this indefensible measure sprang, he said, from the petulance, failing intellect, and trembling dotage of an old man on the verge of the grave. Still Douglas reserved his fire; he would be heard at the evening session. As this drew near, the crush became greater than ever. Veteran observers thought the crowd unprecedented in Capitol history. To rescue many ladies, a motion was carried to admit them to the floor, and in a twinkling the aisles were jammed. Messengers trying to carry copy from the

66 Full text in Phila. *Weekly Press*, February 27, 1858. His wife's illness had delayed Douglas in composing his report. Receiving notice from Green that it was needed at once, he toiled for two days and two nights, pausing only to snatch three hours' sleep and a little food. Two clerks copied the sheets as they came from his hand.

press correspondents to the telegraph offices were unable to fight their way through. As Douglas took the floor, he looked worn and ill. Yet he spoke for three hours with unsurpassable resolution and vigor. When Toombs replied with arrogant insults, even terming Douglas's supporters hypocrites, Stuart rebuked him with the statement that his language and manner befitted a barroom, and moved adjournment.

Next day, only a few desultory exchanges preceded the vote, on which Lecompton carried 33 to 25. Houston reluctantly yielded to the instructions of the Texas legislature and voted *aye;* Pugh, who had a futile compromise plan of his own, followed those of the Ohio legislature by voting *no.* Administration men hailed the victory as decisive. The Douglas-Seward forces pointed out that, if Allen of Rhode Island and Jones of Iowa had obeyed *their* instructions, if Wright and Thompson of New Jersey had followed the clear wishes of their constituents, and if Indiana had been represented by truly elected men instead of Bright and Fitch, the bill would have been defeated. Some Republican comment, following a still more caustic line, recalled that it was almost four years to a day since the Kansas-Nebraska Act had passed Congress; that the fruit of this legislation was now implacably opposed by Douglas himself; that the seats of eight Senators who had voted for the Nebraska bill had been filled by men who were antagonistic to Lecompton; and that not a single Senator who had voted against the bill had been superseded by a Lecompton supporter—though Pugh, chosen by a legislature elected before the Lecompton issue arose, was half hostile to the manifest sentiment of his State.

But the real battle lay ahead. The House offered the crucial test—and the House was more responsive to tides of public feeling than the Senate.

11

"Yield Not One Inch"

BURKE'S REMARK upon "the mischief of not having large and liberal ideas in the management of great affairs" might well have been remembered by the chief officers of the nation early in 1858. When the Lecompton bill passed the Senate, the most fateful crisis in the history of the Democratic Party since the rivalry of Jefferson and Burr was nearing its climax. The next few weeks would see momentous and irrevocable decisions taken. Would Douglas be crushed, or would the South be beaten and humiliated, or would some final face-saving compromise be arranged? It must be repeated that since the party was the last powerful link binding North and South together, the impending decisions might involve the life of the Union itself.

Senator Crittenden was right when he said that the situation of the republic was fantastic. Although the panic had confronted the country with complex economic difficulties, and although a dozen other problems, from the contumacious Mormons to public lands legislation, demanded attention, the government was half paralyzed by the slavery issue; and no less paralyzed because the disproportion between the immediate quarrel and its effects was ludicrous. Because a few score slaves dwelt in the wide, empty spaces of Kansas, the nation was in an uproar. Their presence was repugnant to four-fifths of the thirty or forty thousand white people dwelling with them; climate and products were hostile to their stay; sensible men knew that these faint dewdrops of slavery would swiftly evaporate under the western sun. A little realism, a little readiness to accept the equities of the situation, would apparently cut through the mesh, for the nation seemed a Hercules entangled in packthread.

To contrast the hundred slaves of Kansas with the frenzied commotion in Washington was, in one sense, to demonstrate what trifles control history. A few words in a treaty, a disputed mile in a boundary, or a bullet in an archduke's body can detonate mighty human explosions. Actually, of course, the hundred slaves were but symbols; and ghostly armies fought in the clouds above Kansas, while legions with flaming swords stood in her red sunrises and purple sunsets. Both North and South, millions had now entered the sphere of hysteric emotions; prejudice warped and passion inflamed their minds; they were influenced by the memory of old affronts and the fear of future wrongs. Above all, fear actuated them. Because each section imputed aggressive designs to the other, every proposal became a plot and every act a menace. Northerners saw the "slave power" already in control of the Presidency, Congress, and Supreme Court; saw it ready to grasp Kansas, cut Texas into five States, and send ten new proslavery Senators to Washington; saw it scheming to annex Mexico, Cuba, and Central America; saw slavery, in short, dominating the continent. Southerners, meanwhile, conjured up a vision of equal perils. They saw Oregon, Kansas, Nebraska, and Minnesota all coming in as free States, Northern population and wealth gaining with ten-league strides, a sectional party taking control of the government, and arrogant majorities rewriting the Constitution to extirpate slavery.

As fear, antagonism, and irrational hostility grew, only statesmanlike action could keep the Northern and Southern wings of the Democratic Party in patient collaboration; and how much statesmanship was at hand in the early months of 1858?

[I]

When Buchanan sent Congress his special message in support of Lecompton, Southern opinion had almost completely solidified. In the Lower South particularly, the arguments of Buchanan, Jefferson Davis, and Alexander H. Stephens (the two latter managing the cause in Senate and House) were accepted at face value. The South was convinced that the Kansas convention, legally elected, possessed full power to form a constitution and prescribe how it should take effect; that interference by any officer of the national government was intolerable; and that so long as the constitution was republican, Congress must accept it. Nor was this all. The South also believed that the Northern assault on Lecompton was in effect a proclamation that no new slave State, anywhere, should ever be admitted. It believed the Republican Party had declared in 1856 that it would never consent to another slave State; Kansas was demanding entry as one; and therefore all who opposed her were upholding this Republican dogma. Sooner than consent to any such prohibition, the cotton States would leave the Union.

It was useless to point out to incensed Southerners the flaw in their syllogism. They did not listen even to Crittenden when he declared that, readily as he would assent to a new slave State, he would never force a constitution on Kansas which three-fourths of her people abhorred. As for the Douglas Democrats, many already half identified them with the Republicans. Linton

Stephens expressed the view of a multitude of Southern men when he declared with passionate energy that if Kansas were excluded, it would not be because of any flaws in the process of constitution-making, but because the canting, holier-than-thou North considered her unworthy company. "The true issue is, and Congress ought to be held to it, and it ought to be so proclaimed to them with a united defiance, whether a State with slavery is fit to be admitted into the Union. If it be decided against us, honor leaves us but one course, and that is, for all the slave States to walk out of the Union, and fling their defiance behind them; and if no other will, I hope Georgia will do it, solitary and alone."[1] The pride of the slaveholders, deeply wounded by Northern utterances on the moral degradations of the peculiar institution, was too hotly inflamed to let them make nice distinctions. Many of them failed to distinguish between a "Black Republican" and an abolitionist; both were enemies, and that was that. Many were hostile, moreover, to arguments based on an appeal to the rights of popular majorities. Preferring government by an elite, they attached no weight to mere numbers in Kansas or elsewhere—to an irresponsible mob or a despotic democracy, as they put it.[2]

It must be remembered that the South was ill-informed. It was not addicted to newspapers, magazines, and books like the North; illiteracy was commoner, and travellers like Olmsted not only found homes bare of reading matter but were thunderstruck by the ignorance of farmers and shopkeepers. The semi-organized campaign against Walker's policies in the summer of 1857 had diffused a general idea that Kansas was being prevented from realizing her desire for slaves only by the plots of emigrant aid men and antislavery governors. "Our people here, and especially the Democrats," wrote F. P. Stanton's brother from Maysville, Kentucky, "are kept in lamentable darkness in regard to the facts and principles involved in the Kansas question"—and this could have been said of many areas.[3] Being more and more on the defensive respect-

1 J. D. Waddell, *Biog. Sketch of Linton Stephens,* 138.
2 *Ibid.*
3 February 17, 1858; Douglas Papers. And not the South only, but Washington as well. Democratic newspapers North and South, including the Washington *Union,* had suppressed much news about Kansas and distorted more. The *National Era* had told the truth, but while it had a wide Northern circulation it was little read in Washington and never seen in the great hotels. The *National Intelligencer* was honest in what it did print, but timid in publishing news that would offend the mass of Washington, Maryland, and Virginia subscribers. In consequence, Southern Senators and Representatives (who would as soon pick up a rattlesnake as a *Tribune*) actually did not know what was going on in Kansas. When the "law and order" foray against Lawrence took place late in 1855, Administration Democrats were as much taken aback, one of them remarked, as if they had heard that a Russian fleet had occupied San Francisco. Not a single Democratic newspaper in the free States had maintained a regular correspondent in Kansas throughout the eventful years 1855–57. The N. Y. *Tribune* of August 20, 1857, declared that if the Philadelphia *Public Ledger* had only stationed an honest reporter there and printed his letters, Pennsylvania would have sent Frémont to the White House.

ing slavery, the South was also more and more intolerant—and no intolerant community, applying restrictions and censorships, can face realities clearly.

It must also be remembered that not a few men both North and South, desiring and planning disunion, hoped that Kansas would furnish an adequate pretext. If they could bring on civil war in Kansas in such fashion that the other side would seem the aggressor, so much the better.

In the South, Robert Barnwell Rhett, W. L. Yancey, William Gilmore Simms, and other private citizens could count now on the cooperation of such Congressional radicals as Keitt, Porcher Miles, Milledge L. Bonham, and Alfred Iverson. To be sure, it was only a small minority as yet who delighted in the idea of party disruption as leading up to national disunion; but their ideas had infective quality. A good many men talked about separation with apparent revulsion but secret attraction. "We cannot remain with honor in the Union if Kansas is thrown out as the issues are now made," exclaimed Senator Hammond. "I have given my ear to every suggestion for a peaceable arrangement of this rotten business that would not compromise the South. I now say Lecompton or Separation, and I will go out, if we can do no better, with South Carolina, Georgia, Florida, Alabama, and Mississippi—three and a half million people and two and a half million cotton bales."[4] Simms, to whom he sent this statement, knew just how much weight to give to Hammond's talk of a peaceable arrangement. The Senator, he informed his fellow conspirator, Porcher Miles, is friendly to Buchanan and will aid him while he is useful. "In brief, Hammond will support the Democratic Party only while it is tributary to the interests of the South."[5] There were an increasing number of Hammonds.

The forces behind this rising disunionist sentiment were numerous. Bright as the vision of the ancient Athenian democracy, so rich in poets, historians, philosophers, and scientists, the dream of a separate Southern nation floated before the eyes of thousands. Casting off the shackles of the dour, jealous, commercial-minded North, they would erect a republic as opulent, as confident of the future, and as full of great men as Virginia and South Carolina just after the Revolution. Others thought of practical commercial advantages. The South produced the wealth of the nation, and the North wrung it from her. Once separate, Southerners could keep the vast sums exacted by Yankee jobbers, manufacturers, bankers, export merchants, and shippers; could use it to fill the land with plenty. Still other Southerners believed that the only hope of peace, of a cessation of the constant antislavery agitation, lay in secession. The very churches had divided on the subject; how, then, could publicans

4 To W. G. Simms, February 7, 1858; Hammond Papers, LC.
5 December 28, 1857; Miles Papers, Univ. of N. C.

and sinners cease to quarrel while tied hand to hand? "No, sir, there is no hope of peace, for there is no peace now—nor will there be until we separate," wrote one Georgian to Alexander H. Stephens.[6]

More and more, however, one feeling dominated all others: the feeling of inevitability. We must eventually separate, men reasoned; the sooner the better, for we are far stronger now than we shall be hereafter. The South was actually in the midst of a revolution, declared Judge Magrath of South Carolina, and it must be hurried on lest the Southern mind become distracted.[7] "The issue will come sooner or later," wrote James H. Taylor of Montgomery, "and the sooner we stand to arms the better for the South." [8] W. H. Trescot spoke for the most thoughtful of these inevitable-secessionists when he told his friends that since disunion was coming, the quicker it came the better, and they should maneuver to throw the onus on the North. If Kansas were admitted under the Lecompton constitution, if Dred Scott were maintained, and if party discipline were enforced in the North, they could carry the election of 1860. This was not important as a mere Democratic victory. It was important "as a means to force the great Republican party into open antagonism with the government and compel them to threaten dissolution etc. when if circumstances favor we can take them at their word or force them to put their principles into the extremest practise. With such a state of parties I think the next four years would give us a good practical issue and one made by the opposition." [9] This was truly Machiavellian.

Honest Quitman was proposing a much more direct procedure. He wrote, as the vote on Lecompton approached:

We are now on the eve of the solution of the great questions: 1. Whether the Northern Democrats will stick to the principles laid down on the slave question in the Cincinnati platform? and 2. Whether any new slave State can ever be admitted? These are the issues involved in the vote on the Kansas constitution. All other questions are mere pretences, flimsy as the mazy sophistries by which they are attempted to be sustained. . . .

Well, suppose we carry the constitution! National democracy will almost cease to exist in the free States. Every man who votes with us will be swept off in the next election. The Black Republicans, or the anti-slavery party under some other name, will sweep every free State at the next contest for President. Parties will become purely sectional, and no remedy [be] left to us of the minority, but separation.

On the other hand, should the constitution be rejected, the South must regard the plighted faith of the Northern Democracy [as] violated. It will assure us that no more reliance can be placed on them to aid us in protecting

6 M. C. Fulton, March 30, 1858; Stephens Papers, LC.
7 To W. P. Miles, February 18, 1858; Miles Papers, Univ. of N. C.
8 To Hammond, March 23, 1858; Hammond Papers, LC.
9 To Hammond, March 20, 1858; Hammond Papers, LC.

our rights; that National Democracy is worthless. We must also see in the act, a fixed and inexorable determination on the part of the majority never to admit another slave State, to stop forever the extension of slavery, and thus to bind the South to the triumphant car of an antagonistic majority.

, Who can doubt what under such a state of things the South ought to do? If she waits for the border States, Virginia, Maryland, Kentucky, and Missouri, or either of them, to move, she will never act, but gradually become the willing slave of an insatiate master. The cotton States must move first. . . .

Let but five States determine upon secession, and separate to preserve their social systems, and all the other States having similar systems must sooner or later unite with them.[10]

The most striking single speech of the Senate debate, Hammond's "cotton is king" address, was essentially a bombastic piece of disunionist propaganda, the full flower of Southern nationalism flaunting its petals more gaudily than ever before. Hammond was one of those grotesque figures, like Wade, Sumner, and Wigfall, who if transferred to the pages of Dickens would have been pronounced incredible. Short, plump, with a domelike brow and pleasing manners, this master of broad reaches of rice and cotton, herds of blooded stock, and four hundred slaves, was as temperamental as Randolph of Roanoke, as inflated with vanity as Thomas Hart Benton, as crotchety as John Tyler. He actually dreamed of a Presidential nomination; as if any party could nominate a man who declared that "God created negroes for no other purpose than to be the subordinate 'hewers of wood and drawers of water,'" and who expressed the hope that slaves would populate every spot on earth where their labor would benefit the whites.[11] He preened himself on all his public utterances. Withal, he was kind, shrewdly independent (he disliked the Lecompton constitution because it demanded an exorbitant body of public land, some twenty-three million acres in place of the four millions that would normally be allowed, while he believed the slavery clause worthless), well-read, and able. He was a brilliant novice in politics. As he wrote to the Charleston *Mercury*, he had never acquired much practical experience of public service, had lived for thirteen years immersed in plantation affairs exclusively, and had felt no desire for political battle.[12] But now, suddenly elevated to the Senate, he meant to strike a heavy blow for the South and slavery.

Why, he asked the Senate, should his section not become a great independent power? The slave States covered eight hundred and fifty thousand square miles, an imperial domain, rich in every natural product; their population was four times that of the colonies when America had become independent; a million brave men, familiar with the arts of war, were registered on their muster rolls.

10 February 1, 1858; Quitman Papers, Mississippi Dept. Arch. and Hist.
11 J. H. Hammond, *Letters and Speeches*, 338 ff.
12 Letter dated October 2, 1857; Hammond Papers, LC.

Athwart the South ran the mighty artery of the Mississippi, holding in tributary affiliation the rich Northwest. It was idle, he declared, to talk of checking the spread of slavery throughout the valley of the Mississippi and along its affluents. Above all, he boasted of the impregnable economic strength of the South. That region had a monopoly of two or three staples which controlled the commerce of the world; above all, a monopoly of cotton. Cotton could bring Europe to its knees; for, cut off the supply, and within three years Britain would topple headlong from her seat of power. Cotton had just rescued the North from bankruptcy. When in the great industrial cities a speculative bubble burst and business sank in ruin, the South, selling her cotton crop for $65,000,000, had saved the country. Inasmuch as, but for the panic, she could have gotten a hundred millions, she had put $35,000,000 into her charity box for the textile lords and merchants of the North. No power on earth dared make war on the fleecy bolls. Cotton *is* king, said Hammond. It was far stronger than that other potentate, the Bank of England.

The greatest strength of the South, however, he continued, lay in the harmony of her social institutions. Every society required a menial class, characterized by strength, docility, and recognition of its own lack of skill; those menials upbore the class which led progress and civilization; they were the mudsill of society. The South had a race happily adapted for that very end. Did the North boast that it had abolished slavery? "Aye, the *name*, but not the *thing;* all the powers of the earth cannot abolish that." [13] Naturally, this sally infuriated many Northern champions. Hannibal Hamlin pointed out that the value of Northern manufactures far exceeded the hundred millions in cotton annually exported by the South. Ben Wade drew a scathing contrast between Northern democracy and Southern aristocracy. Henry Wilson, stung by the mudsill image, declared that his father had been a manual laborer all his life; that for years he himself had been farmhand and shoemaker; and that he gloried in the sturdy character of the Northern workers. But Hammond's speech etched a proud impression on the Southern mind. "The rank and file of Southern men are delighted," the Senator informed his brother; "over twenty-five thousand copies have been subscribed. . . . I have changed the programme." [14]

Many Southerners held with Hammond that cotton was king; that as Simms put it, the North, boasting perpetually of its prosperity, owed everything to the South. Southern officials continued to rumble threats of secession. The Alabama legislature spoke; the governor of Texas penned a scolding message. In Washington, a shrewd Representative, T. L. Harris of Illinois, thought the atmosphere alarming. "There is a worse state of feeling here than there was in 1850,"

13 *National Intelligencer*, April 13, 1858, full text differing slightly from *Cong. Globe.*
14 To Colonel M. C. M. Hammond, March 9, 1858; Hammond Papers, LC.

he wrote McClernand. "There are less open outside threats than were made then—but there is in fact a more sullen hostility and bitterness than I ever saw before. The truth is that there are many earnest disunionists in the South who see no obstacle to their wishes but the destruction of the Democratic Party—and they think the passage of Lecompton will effect that." [15]

[II]

Because the House was the crucial arena, much of the bitterness was concentrated there. Everybody knew that the contest would be close. At the outset, Administration leaders boasted they would carry the bill by ten or fifteen votes, but impartial observers doubted that. By the time the Senate acted, Buchanan's supporters had lowered their probable margin to five.

The tempers of Southerners in the House had been strained by Commodore Hiram Paulding's sudden seizure of William Walker (who, overthrown in May, 1857, had returned to Nicaragua with a new expedition late in the year) for violating the neutrality laws of the United States. When Walker and his fellow prisoners were landed at Norfolk on January 1, 1858, the South buzzed like a mutinous ship. Chairman Clingman of the House Foreign Affairs Committee called on the President for information; Quitman demanded a special committee to revise the neutrality laws; and Stephens made a speech in which he used the word "outrage" eight times. The South was not mollified when Buchanan, in a special message to the Senate, declared that Paulding had committed a grave error, but also expressed the Administration's hostility to filibustering. Stephens wrote his brother on January 20 that the whole ground for Buchanan's opposition to Walker in Central America was the fear that "if successful he would introduce African slavery there." To such an unreasonable pitch had even this calm man's emotions led him! Many Southerners were more determined than ever that, if they could not have Central America, they should at least have Lecompton.

The tempers of Northern Democrats, too, were wrought up to a high pitch. A caucus of twenty-three anti-Lecompton members had sent a deputation of three, Haskin of New York, S. S. Cox of Ohio, and James B. Clay of Kentucky, to expostulate with the President. They had found Buchanan courteous but firm. He knew that the Northern Democrats faced ruin if the bill passed—but he insisted on passage. When he sent his special Lecompton message to Congress, his opponents tried to refer it to a select committee with power to investigate, while Stephens moved to refer it to the Committee on Territories. A gruelling struggle that lasted until two in the morning ensued. The Republicans, seeing

15 February 16, 1858; McClernand Papers.

that they had a temporary majority, attempted to force a vote. The Administration leaders, sending out urgent calls for men absent at dinner parties, used every tactic of delay. Nerves began to snap. Finally, when Galusha A. Grow stepped over to the Democratic side, an affray began.

Keitt of South Carolina shouted at Grow: "Go back to your side of the House, you Black Republican puppy!" Grow retorted with a sneering defiance of "nigger drivers." They grappled, Grow knocked Keitt down, and excited members rushed into the melee. For two minutes, about thirty Representatives engaged in a free-for-all fight. Finally order was restored. Though nobody was hurt, the damage to tempers was serious. Remarking that this was the first sectional fight in the House, Stephens wrote that if weapons had been at hand blood would probably have flowed. "All things here are tending to bring my mind to the conclusion that the Union cannot or will not last long."

Others took the shindy more lightly. It had a droll look, commented one reporter. "There were some fifty middle-aged and elderly gentlemen pitching into each other like so many Tipperary savages—most of them incapable, from want of wind and muscle, of doing each other any serious harm." [16] *Punch* did the event justice. In a long poem beginning, "Sing, O Goddess, the wrath, the untamable dander of Keitt," it told how the debate had raged long and late; how "plugs were becoming exhausted, and Representatives also"; how Keitt the clear grit, Reuben Davis the ra'al wild hoss of Mississippi, and others lunged at their enemies; how "fiercely they gathered around Grow, catawompously up as to chaw him"—

But without Potter they reckoned, the wiry from woody Wisconsin,
He, striking out right and left, like a catamount varmint and vicious,
Dashed to the rescue, and with him the Washburnes, Cadwallader, Elihu . . .
Well was it then for Barksdale, the wig that waved o'er his forehead,
Off in Cadwallader's hands it came; and the wearer releasing,
Left to the conqueror nought but the scalp of his worthy opponent!

On the question of reference to a special committee, the anti-Lecomptonites won, 114 to 113. Their majority comprised ninety Republicans, twenty-two Douglas Democrats, and one Know-Nothing, Henry Winter Davis. The select committee of fifteen, however, did the opposition no good. Speaker Orr gave it eight men opposed to any investigation; Alex Stephens, as chairman, directed the majority astutely, and it brought in a report, eight to seven, endorsing the Lecompton constitution. The anti-Lecomptonites lost that skirmish.

With every vote precious, both sides lobbied frenziedly, while the Administration used patronage and pressure. Strange scenes were enacted in Washing-

16 N. Y. *Weekly Tribune*, February 13, 1859. The long night sessions were conducive to disorder, for the exhausted Congressmen resorted to stimulants.

ton as spring came on. The city seemed full of Kansas men, come partly to argue for Lecompton and partly to beg for offices; an *Evening Post* correspondent counted about a hundred who made the Kirkwood Hotel their headquarters.[17] John Calhoun was brassily laying siege to Congress, for if Kansas were admitted, he hoped that a proslavery legislature would elect him Senator. Judge Cato seconded him, while J. J. Clarkson, who had fetched the constitution to Washington and wished to be made Superintendent of Indian Affairs, buttonholed unwary members. Calhoun had with him the returns of the election of January 4 for State officers and a legislature. By virtue of the extraordinary powers given him under the Lecompton schedule, he was entitled to hold these returns; and as yet he had not decided whether the free State or proslavery tickets had been elected! It was evident that he would manipulate the result in whatever manner best suited his own interests and those of the Administration.

To impartial onlookers it seemed preposterous that one man, the agent of a discredited convention, should have arbitrary power to determine the complexion of the Kansas government. "Why Does He Not Decide?" demanded the *National Intelligencer* in an unwontedly belligerent editorial.[18] In Kansas itself, no doubt existed that a free State legislature and State officers had been chosen. Citizens swore to numerous depositions of proslavery fraud. The president of the council and speaker of the house, who had assisted at the counting of the votes, proclaimed the victory of the free State forces. Calhoun, however, rejected some votes which these men declared valid, while he stated that late returns from the Delaware Crossing precinct seemed to elect the whole proslavery ticket. At once a blaze of publicity was fastened upon Delaware Crossing, Kickapoo, and other points where the free State men alleged fraud. Calhoun spoke of several hundred votes from Kickapoo; the judges of that precinct testified that only forty-three had been cast. Still, Calhoun kept his strategic seat astride the fence; he would decide in his own good time.[19]

Soon after reaching Washington, Calhoun was ushered into Douglas's handsome mansion. The two had been close Illinois friends for years; now they were enemies. The Senator, receiving his guest coldly, chatted about general matters. Then he suddenly fixed his intensest gaze on the visitor. "What about Delaware Crossing?" he demanded. Calhoun stuttered out that the return had been properly certified. With quick step Douglas crossed to his desk, drew out the depositions of fraud, and slapped them on Calhoun's knee. "Then how about this evidence?" he thundered. Calhoun turned pale and left the house.[20]

Not since the great Bank war of Jackson's time, if then, had Federal patron-

17 Letter dated February 14, 1858.
18 February 16, 1858.
19 *National Intelligencer*, February 9, 13, 16, *et seq.*, 1858.
20 Washington correspondence dated February 9, 1858, Phila. *Press.*

age been used so brutally as Buchanan's Directory used it now. The President himself may have averted his gaze and stopped his ears; but he unquestionably knew that contracts, jobs, perquisites, and even army commissions were being traded for much-needed votes. In the name of discipline, Douglas's friends were struck down right and left. J. W. Gray, editor of the Cleveland *Plain Dealer*, was postmaster of his city and a warm friend of Douglas. Caught by his dilemma, he wriggled lustily for a time but finally gagged over the Lecompton bolus. Off went his head. The Chicago postmaster was a Douglas Democrat named William Price. He was summarily dismissed, and Isaac Cook, a particularly tough-hided liquor dealer, land speculator, and machine politician, was reappointed in his stead despite the fact that during Pierce's regime Cook had allowed subordinates to steal several thousand dollars. In fact, special efforts were made by the Directory to weaken Douglas in Illinois. The efficient mail agent for the State was removed, and Dr. Charles Leib, another liquor dealer and machine hack who had flirted with Mormonism, was installed in his stead. Leib, traveling freely on his railway pass, was able to twist the screws on postmasters. The marshal for northern Illinois lost his place, and a Lecompton man seized it. By the middle of March, Cook, Leib, and Nye were busy organizing Lecompton demonstrations and plotting against the Little Giant.[21]

All over the North, officeholders were put in terror of their poor livings; editors of papers like the Pittsburgh *Union* were rewarded with government advertising; Congressmen deemed approachable were told of position and pelf which might be theirs. Cornelius Wendell, with his large revenues from the public printing, was called upon to finance weak newspapers like the *Pennsylvanian*, and to put up money for still more dubious purposes. Evidence exists that he offered one capable Ohio lobbyist $5,000 for every Ohio Congressman whom he won over to the Lecompton side.[22] Representative Montgomery of Pennsylvania was assured that he could have almost anything he desired if he would sell out his constituents.[23] Because the New York *Sun* denounced Lecompton, the publishing of lists of letters was taken from it and given to the more amenable *Herald*.[24] In Indiana, decent party leaders protested publicly against the despotism of the Administration and its use of what one disgusted man called a venal press, and a horde of dirty officeholders or expectants.[25] Postmaster-General Brown made lists of all the Douglas postmasters he could find, and had letters sent them of which the following is typical:

21 Cleveland *Leader*, index for 1858, *passim;* Havana, Illinois, *Democrat*, March 13, 20, 1858.
22 Covode Report, 120 ff.
23 J. L. Dawson to Jeremiah S. Black, May 12, 1858; Black Papers.
24 N. Y. *Express*, February 3, 1858.
25 W. W. Wick, April 2, 1858; English Papers.

Sir: Complaints are made against you that you are unfriendly to the present Administration, and circumstances are detailed in confirmation of this fact. An opportunity is now offered you to present such evidence as you may deem proper in refutation of the charges.

Respectfully, etc.

Horatio King, First Assistant Postmaster-General.[26]

Buchanan's opponents charged, late in March, that several million dollars in army contracts for the Utah expedition, let at prices that would make a dozen fortunes, had been awarded by Secretary Floyd himself to men whose political aid was needed. They charged, with evidence, that Cobb was using the rich patronage of the Treasury in the most shameless way; that Jacob Thompson was even more shameless with the benefits of the Interior Department; and that Toucey was letting politics creep into his contracts for new naval vessels. They accused Representative Burns of Ohio, originally an anti-Lecompton man, of coming to a new perception of his duty under a pledge that his son-in-law should remain postmaster of Keokuk and that he himself should be made marshal of northern Ohio when his term ended. Greeley's *Tribune* declared that, if Lecompton passed the House, it would be only because a sufficient number of members had been paid directly or indirectly to support it. Everyone knew that, as was proved by the current case of Orasmus Matteson, a New York Republican expelled for corruption, a few Representatives were venal.[27]

[III]

Despite all this pressure, together with the blandishments of Administration hostesses in as lively a social season as Washington had seen, the anti-Lecompton Democrats held their House lines almost intact. Five Illinois members led by T. L. Harris, six Ohioans led by S. S. Cox, and three Indianians led by William H. English constituted the solid Middle Western heart of the phalanx. Pennsylvania supplied three men of unshakeable fiber, and New York two. At the beginning, this block counted twenty-four members. If it could keep at least twenty, and could gain the support of half a dozen or more Know-Nothings, then, with the ninety-two Republicans, it could win the day. The group organized in caucus, with Harris as chairman and John B. Haskin of New York as secretary. Douglas conferred steadily with the members; Forney's *Press* and the Washington *States* applauded them heartily; and Greeley wrote editorials

26 Phila. *Press*, March 13, 18, 1858.
27 N. Y. *Tribune*, February 11, March 28, 1858; *Cong. Globe*, March 4, 1858; Nichols, *Disruption*, 165, 166. It was said that Glancy Jones was armed with blank invitations to White House dinners which he was empowered to use in enlisting doubtful Congressmen. London *Daily News* (American correspondence), January 11, 1859.

assuring them that, if they stood firm, they would have wide Republican support for reelection in the fall.

All efforts to arrange a compromise between Lecompton and anti-Lecompton Democrats broke down. The Crittenden plan was unacceptable to most Administration supporters. As taken up and slightly amended by the anti-Lecompton caucus (becoming the Crittenden-Montgomery amendment), it provided that Kansas should be admitted on condition that the constitution was submitted to the voters in its entirety, at a carefully controlled election, and approved by them; but that if they rejected it, a new constitutional convention should be called. Toombs helped sponsor another proposal which was quite unacceptable to most anti-Lecompton men. Declaring that nothing in the act of admission should be construed to abridge the right of the people of Kansas at all times to alter, reform, or abolish their form of government as they thought proper, it fell far short of the positive provision for a popular vote which the opposition demanded. But could not a formula be invented midway between the two extremes? [28]

As March drew to an end, Stephens, floor manager for the Lecomptonites, made a supreme effort, enlisting William H. English in the formation of a conference committee. English, still in his middle thirties, was precocious, adaptable, and cultivated. The son of an Indiana pioneer, a graduate of Hanover College, he had been admitted to the bar at eighteen and to practice before the Supreme Court at twenty-three, and had held a variety of minor posts in Indiana and Washington before being chosen for Congress in 1852. While a loyal Douglas man, his residence in southern Indiana and friendship for Bright gave him a moderate outlook. On March 27, the Democratic Representatives held a night caucus. Stephens made a speech imploring the anti-Lecompton men to be reasonable, and English moved that each side appoint ten men to a conference committee. When this body met on the twenty-ninth, the anti-Lecomptonites brought forward what they thought a generous offer. They would vote for the Senate bill if it were amended to declare that the people of Kansas then had, and might at all times exercise, the right of altering or rewriting their constitution at will.[29]

28 See Toombs to Buchanan, March 2, 1858; Buchanan Papers.
29 Washington correspondence, N. Y. *Tribune*, March 28, 29, 30, 1858. Buchanan evidently talked the situation over with English soon after the middle of March; for on March 22, Buchanan sent him a memorandum "according to promise," saying that it might contain some ideas useful to him. He buttered up English: "I repeat that I consider the present occasion the most fortunate of your life. It will be your fate to end the dangerous agitation, to confer lasting benefits on your country, and to render your character historical." English Papers. The feeling of southern Indiana came out strongly in English's subsequent statement that he and his friends believed Negroes "inferior by nature," had no "sickly sentimentality" upon slavery, and regarded free Negroes as "a great pest." *Cong. Globe*, January 3, 1860, 312 ff.

Garnett of Virginia and other Southerners, making no proposal of their own, instantly objected to this as a Federal intervention in State affairs. A large body of Southern Senators and Representatives, in fact, had consistently opposed any weakening of the slavery clauses in the Lecompton constitution, and had deplored Buchanan's suggestion that Kansas might immediately amend that instrument. Thirty-five men had agreed in conference to stand against any dilution. Iverson had been vehement on the subject; Keitt had proclaimed that the Kansas instrument could not be altered before 1864. The committee of twenty broke up in dispute, and thereafter the Douglas bloc was more determined than ever to kill the measure. This deadlock, they and their Republican allies exulted, sealed its scroll with defeat. They believed that many Southerners did not care if they were beaten so long as they could keep their records straight for the fall elections—and that some actually courted defeat as a step toward disruption of the party.[30]

Even yet, it was with great difficulty that Buchanan and the Directory reconciled themselves to a fiasco. They had hoped to the last to hew their way through. With fully a hundred Democratic votes in their pockets, they had counted on buying or bullying a dozen members and on gaining most of the fourteen Know-Nothings from Southern districts. They remembered how effectively Stephens, in 1854, had beaten down the House opposition to the Kansas-Nebraska bill. Day after day, Howell Cobb appeared in the House lobby, rotund, smiling, and talkative, expending charm and promises on doubtful men. Night after night, Jacob Thompson feasted Congressmen at his sumptuous table. Buchanan invited dozens of Congressmen to the White House, where he argued, expostulated, and, as the outlook grew darker, even pleaded. By last-minute solicitation, following the advice of George Sanders to change his bill-of-fare from lemon salad to orange, and from vinegar to champagne, he won the votes of Dewart and Reilly of his own State, being somewhat assisted in this by a timely endorsement of Lecompton at Harrisburg.[31] The experienced Sanders labored with such Know-Nothings as Marshall of Kentucky, Campbell of Ohio, and Harris of Maryland—as it turned out, in vain. The eve of the final House vote found almost the entire Cabinet sitting up with doubtful cases and trying to nurse them into compliance.[32]

In this uphill struggle the Administration suffered from the antics of John Calhoun. Had that marplot stayed in Kansas, made a fair count of votes in the

30 Washington correspondence Phila. *Press*, March 29, N. Y. *Express, Herald*, March 31, 1858.
31 Sanders to Buchanan, March 25, 1858; Buchanan Papers. The Washington correspondent of the N. Y. *Express* wrote April 2 that Buchanan had in one instance shed tears, salt tears, to get a member to change his vote.
32 N. Y. *Weekly Tribune*, April 10, 1858. Campbell called himself a Whig.

January election, and given prompt notice of the free State victory, he might have contributed much toward the success of Lecompton. Northern Democrats would have been readier to vote for admission if assured of a free State legislature and State officers to interpret the new constitution. Having come to Washington, however, Calhoun lingered with the undecided election totals in his breast pocket. The East was much impressed by news of flagrant frauds unearthed by a Kansas investigating committee; in one issue, the *National Intelligencer* spread before its readers full columns of depositions on the subject.[33] Proof of the irregularities was clinched when the committee, hearing that bogus returns had been secreted, obtained a search warrant, went to the suspected spot, and found the Delaware Crossing vote in a candle box under a wood pile.[34] At first, Calhoun did nothing except declare through the Washington *Union* that he awaited full evidence and would sanction no frauds. But after a Kansas investigator brought to Washington sworn copies of proof that the returns had been crooked and that Federal officers in Kansas had connived at the cheating, Calhoun had no choice. On March 19, he announced that he would certify the choice of a free State Republican majority in the legislature—but said nothing about the other State offices.

If we may believe Calhoun's brother, he had been under intense pressure to deliver the election to the proslavery ticket. When he announced his decision, writes the brother, it "gave great umbrage to the Democratic party, and to President Buchanan in particular. That functionary gave him the cold shoulder at once; and very soon afterward evinced his disapprobation by superseding him in the office of Surveyor-General. . . . It was well understood that he was to have been reappointed, and had he connived at the fraud . . . no one doubted that his name would have been sent to the Senate." [35]

The Charleston *Mercury*, Richmond *Whig*, and other newspapers exploded in denunciation of Calhoun, terming him a traitor who had invalidated proslavery votes while accepting fraudulent free State ballots. His decree, they agreed, made Kansas a thoroughgoing abolitionist State, and there should be no hurry about admitting it to send Jim Lane and some equally rabid Black Republican to the Senate.[36] Senator Iverson declared that the decision was a cheap political trick, forced by Cobb, Toombs, and Stephens in a desperate final effort to gain over a few anti-Lecompton Democrats. Whether Cobb & Co. had intervened or not, many passion-blinded Southerners agreed with R. B. Rhett that Northern fanaticism, placing an intolerable sectional pressure

33 February 9, 1858.
34 With other returns; for details see Ewing Papers, February, 1858.
35 A. H. Calhoun, MS "Vindication of John Calhoun," Kansas State Hist. Lib.
36 Quoted in *National Intelligencer*, March 27, 1858.

on the party and Administration, had pushed Calhoun into a base betrayal of the South.[37]

The decisive factor in the final Congressional vote was certainly Northern sentiment. No experienced politician could mistake the trend of opinion. Every weathervane—newspapers, pulpit, mass meetings, letters—pointed in the same direction. Shrewd Congressmen forecast the result shortly announced in the spring elections. The Republicans carried New Hampshire in April by some five thousand majority, electing governor, council, and legislature. Franklin Pierce, who viewed Buchanan with jaundiced eye, found something to please him in this overturn in his State. They similarly swept Connecticut in the largest vote in years, electing William A. Buckingham in opposition to a popular and active Democrat who had handled Lecompton as gingerly as he could. They confirmed their grip on Rhode Island. Still more significant were certain western decisions. The Republicans again carried Chicago, where *both* parties were anti-Lecompton. They seized Toledo from the Democrats, won a large majority in Michigan towns, and with a People's ticket carried Dubuque, usually Democratic two to one. In Cincinnati an anti-Lecompton opposition overthrew the Democrats, while St. Louis chose a freesoil Democratic ticket by about twelve hundred majority.[38]

Douglas's tactics of delay had succeeded; the popular will had made itself felt. As the final test of April 1 approached, many Northern Democrats knew that a Lecompton vote meant political suicide.

At a little past noon, the galleries jammed, every member was in the House but two: Caruthers of Missouri and Harris of Illinois, the latter gravely ill. Administration lobbyists, among whom Senator Bigler was prominent, were urging a last word. Speaker Orr had to rap thunderously and threaten to call members by name if they did not come to order. Still the buzz continued; knots of Lecompton men gathering for final instructions about Stephens, anti-Lecomptonites about Montgomery, Republicans about Grow, and Know-Nothings about Gilmer of North Carolina. Only Joshua Giddings gazing contemplatively from his seat, Quitman reading quietly as usual, and Eli Thayer with hands in pockets, seemed unperturbed. As business commenced, Harris, pale as death, was carried in and assisted to his seat. This hero of Cerro Gordo, who would not outlive the year, was determined to vote against the bill if it

37 Rhett to W. P. Miles, April 7, 1858; Miles Papers, Univ. of N. C. It appears that Stephens and Toombs did advise Calhoun to make his announcement. They saw that it would have to be made some time, and they thought it would be best to let the South know the true state of affairs before the vote on Lecompton, so that if the bill were defeated radical Southerners would take the disappointment more calmly. See a letter dated Milledgeville, April 6, illegibly signed, in Stephens Papers, I.C.
38 Summaries in N. Y. *Weekly Tribune*, April 10, 17, 1858.

killed him. Stephens moved to take up the Senate measure, and the grapple began.

First, a majority of Administration men voted to strike out an amendment originating from Senator Pugh and guaranteeing Kansas the right to change its constitution immediately. Then a vote was taken on the Crittenden-Montgomery amendment, which, providing a popular vote on the constitution, was really a substitute measure. Men totalled the names one by one. The amendment passed, 120 to 112. A wild shout rang through the galleries. Keitt rose, shaking with rage, to move that they be cleared, but was mollified. The amended bill was put on its final passage and carried by the same vote. A coalition of ninety-two Republicans, twenty-two anti-Lecompton Democrats, and six Know-Nothings had defeated Lecompton.

"This Crittenden substitute," said Douglas, "carries out those principles to which I have given my life, and it should now pass the Senate." Forney called the vote a magnificent Democratic triumph. Republicans struck a fuller note of joy. The oppressor's rod is breaking, wrote Greeley. "Champions of Freedom and Honest Rule—Let us rejoice and take courage!" In New York a great crowd, gathering at the Battery to celebrate, heard a hundred and twenty guns fired—one for every vote.[39]

[IV]

The Administration was now in a dilemma. It could not possibly accept the Crittenden substitute. Southern pride would not swallow it; while Buchanan, though willing to acquiesce in the clause which provided for submission of the Lecompton constitution, would not agree to the other section which authorized a new convention if the popular vote were unfavorable. This he deemed unconstitutional, and he said he would veto it. Yet some kind of admission bill had to be passed. It had become a political necessity. Upon Stephens fell the unhappy task of arranging a face-saving measure—Stephens, discouraged, disillusioned, disgusted. The able Georgian, who knew well that Buchanan was

39 The elder Blair called on the dying Thomas Hart Benton on the morning of April 6, finding him unable to talk above a whisper. They spoke of the compromise of 1850. Benton dwelt on the immeasurable service Clay had then rendered in preventing disunion. According to a record which Blair set down that very day, the great Missourian was intensely aroused by the new crisis. "In energetic whispers," wrote Blair, "he told his visitor that the same men who had sought to destroy the republic in 1850 were at the bottom of this accursed Lecompton business. Among the greatest of his consolations in dying was the consciousness that the House of Representatives had baffled these treasonable schemes and put the heels of the people on the neck of the traitors. Few events in our history had given him so much satisfaction as the defeat of Lecompton. He warmly praised the intrepid and incorruptible Douglas Democrats who had resisted the power and the wiles of a corrupt and deluded Administration." N. Y. *Semi-Weekly Tribune*, May 28, 1858; W. E. Smith, *Blair Family in Politics*, 1, 435, 436. Blair's report aroused a violent controversy, but it rings true.

weak and Howell Cobb shortsighted, and who had begged both not to make war upon Douglas, had now to help them out of the pit they had digged.[40] He was vexed at his fellow Congressmen of the South. Half a dozen slave State men had voted against Lecompton, others would have done so if they had dared, and still others had been so drunken, disorderly, and lazy that it took herculean labor to keep them in the House for a vote. Even before the defeat, Stephens had concluded that he was wearing his life out for nothing. He desired nothing so much as to get home to peaceful Liberty Hall and stay there.

Yet he resolutely set to work; indeed, foreseeing the defeat, he had laid some plans before it took place.[41] The Administration majority in the Senate of course refused to heed Douglas's plea for a swift passage of the Crittenden substitute, thus (Douglas suggested) ending the Kansas excitement forever and letting the Kansas people shape their own institutions. The Senate rejected the substitute, and a deadlock between the two chambers ensued. Both the Republicans and anti-Lecompton Democrats were quite ready to let Buchanan languish in his self-made predicament. When the Senate requested a conference committee, the House majority was loftily reluctant. Buchanan, the Directory, and the Administration whips in Congress had to use every conceivable form of magic—more offices, more contracts, more army commissions, more money—to gain over the three or four anti-Lecomptonites they needed to save the President from utter humiliation. They suggested that two Ohio regiments might be included in the expedition to Utah; they promised that when the conference took place, they would accept some modification of the Crittenden substitute. William H. English, genuinely anxious to repair the broken Democratic unity, lent efficient aid. Two other Representatives joined him. One was Lawrence W. Hall of Ohio, and it was later shown that Wendell, as party bursar, paid Hall's roommate $5,000 just before he came over.[42] The three men sufficed; the vote for a conference stood 108 to 108; and Speaker Orr turned the balance for the President.

The way was thus open for a juggle, masking the Administration's defeat. Green, Hunter, and Seward acted for the Senate; Stephens, English, and Howard of Michigan for the House; four Democrats and two Republicans. Within a week the ingenious Stephens and the brilliant English had a scheme ready.

This so-called English bill, reported to the two houses on April 23 with Seward and Howard dissenting, had one all-important provision: it gave the people of Kansas a chance to vote upon the Lecompton constitution in its entirety. It did so, however, under very curious conditions. The greedy authors

40 Johnston and Browne, *Stephens*, 329, 428.
41 Nichols, *Disruption*, 168.
42 *Idem*, 170.

of Lecompton had asked for land grants larger than had ever been given a State on admission—23,592,160 acres, or nearly 37,000 square miles, about the area of Indiana. The English bill (substantially a bill, though in form it was an amendment) cut the grant to 3,988,868, the same proportion of land given to all the States recently admitted and the same amount named in the Crittenden substitute. If the people of Kansas accepted the Lecompton constitution, they were assured of this amount, and, in addition, of five percent of the net proceeds from about two million acres which were to be sold by the government at the beginning of July. If they rejected the land grant and constitution, Kansas might not enter the Union until a census had proved that she possessed the population required of a Congressional district, about ninety thousand. The probability was that she would thus be kept waiting for at least two years longer. A curious measure, and made the more curious by the fact that Stephens, Hunter, and Green, asserting that the vote would be primarily upon the land grant, denied that any popular submission of the constitution lurked in the measure.[43]

Actually it did submit Lecompton to popular vote, and for this reason alone the Administration expected to be able, with an immense renewal of pressures and cajoleries, to carry it. Henry Wilson attacked it as carrying a bribe in one hand and a threat in the other. To a limited extent this was true; a minor cash reward was held out on one hand, and a penalty of delay offered on the other, to a poverty-stricken, uneasy, ambitious frontier community. It was also true that if Kansas was fit to come in under a slave State constitution with but forty thousand people, she was fit to come in under a free State constitution with that many.

The vital fact, however, was that the bill allowed Kansans a fair opportunity to crush the Lecompton iniquity; and only a few deluded men doubted that they would seize it. Do not worry over the measure, Greeley wrote Colfax. "It is a vicious blunderbuss, and will kick over those who stand at the breach. Of course the earnest anti-Lecomptonites must all oppose it, but if it is passed I shall not shed a tear. The Kansans will dispose of it." [44] This view was confirmed by all experts on Kansas sentiment. The Leavenworth *Daily Ledger* declared that the English proposal had the chance of a snowball in a prairie heat wave; the government did not own land enough to buy up the Kansas people, who would rather live in eternal poverty than be the instruments of their own degradation.[45]

43 Nominally, the land grant alone was submitted to the people, with the implication that if it were accepted, the Lecompton constitution would go into effect; if it were rejected, Kansas would remain a Territory and Lecompton would pass into oblivion. The collateral consequences were infinitely more important than the direct question. Five percent on public land sales had been given to other States on admission; see statement by Senator Green, *Cong. Globe*, 35th Cong., 1st Sess., 1824.
44 April 21, 1858; Greeley-Colfax Correspondence.
45 May 7, 1858.

The exciting question was whether Douglas would come around to support so disagreeable a measure. Once more the Administration exerted every ounce of its strength. It was later shown that from $30,000 to $40,000 was spent in helping wavering members see the light; three men, including a government clerk and a newspaperman, being almoners of the fund. It was not denied that from $10,000 to $15,000 was paid for a single vote.[46] The honest anti-Lecompton member from New York, Haskin, was put to the trouble of rejecting a proffered grant of a township of land.[47] Cobb, Thompson, and other Cabinet members used their personal influence unstintedly. So did Slidell, who felt no scruple in offering bribes. One by one, for good reasons or bad, the House anti-Lecompton Democrats fell away until only twelve remained. Pugh of Ohio endorsed the bill. So did Robert J. Walker, declaring that it laid Lecompton before the people and that the odious constitution, baptized in forgery and perjury, would be slain by an overwhelming vote. F. B. Stanton also, while declaring some features very objectionable, wrote that he was willing to accept it.[48] After all, party unity was worth a mass—particularly just before an election.

Still, Douglas held out. He was torn between detestation of the shabby expedients of the bill, and realization that after all it would permit a popular vote; torn between his hatred of Buchanan and the malicious Directory, and his honest desire for Democratic harmony; torn between apprehension that in the impending Senatorial election in Illinois the freesoil Democrats would turn against him if he acquiesced in the bill, and fear that Administration men would knife him if he did not. He was torn, in short, between conflicting ideas of duty and expediency. In his agony of mind he wavered. For one brief day he seemed about to yield. Stephens and Slidell expected to carry the bill through the House on Wednesday, April 28, and to take it up in the Senate immediately. On the previous Saturday evening, Douglas held a conference with Forney, Stanton, and Walker. Their influence had just weight with him: all three were men of great ability and high patriotism, who had suffered heavy indignities from the Administration and had battled courageously against injustice. When Walker argued persuasively for compromise and was supported by Stanton, the Illinois

---

46 Covode Report, 138–159, 184–197. Wendell testified that he had several interviews about carrying the Lecompton bill; that "I paid some money to outsiders to aid" in that process; that he drew checks "pay to politics," "pay to Kansas," and "pay to bearer"; that using sums up to $20,000, "it was a matter that I tried to banish from my mind as soon as possible, and I intentionally disguised my books." He did not deny that he might have authorized a payment of as much as $15,000 for a vote.

47 Wilson, *Rise and Fall of the Slave Power*, II, 565.

48 May 2, 1858; to *National Intelligencer*. Representative Harris of Illinois wrote Lanphier that nobody liked the miserable English scheme; that they could beat it by twenty votes but for Administration pressure; and that Southern men were alarmed by Buchanan's stubborn folly. When the bill passed, he reported that the Administration had bought men "like hogs in the market." April 20, 29, May 7, 1858; Lanphier Papers.

Senator was reluctantly moved by their pleas. Finally he assented, and agreed to advance $100 to have a statement of their position and reasons telegraphed over the country.[49]

But next day he had to break the news to the irreconcilable anti-Lecompton Democrats; to Senators Stuart and Broderick, and to Representatives Montgomery, McKibbin, Haskin, and their associates. He met a group at Broderick's rooms in the Kirkwood House. They received his statement with stark hostility. As he proceeded, the atmosphere grew heated. Broderick, a man of intense feelings, was furious. Passion was running high in California on several political issues, Senator Gwin and Representative Scott taking the Southern side while Broderick and McKibbin assailed the Administration machine. Feeling wronged by Buchanan's use of the patronage, and resenting the haughty airs of Southern aristocrats, Broderick was athirst for revenge. He had replied to Hammond's remarks about mudsills and white slavery with the proud statement that for five years he had been an apprenticed stonecutter, that his father had been a stonecutter, and that he never looked at the beautiful capitals supporting the Senate roof without thinking of his father's talent. All his Irish temper inflamed, he stormed at Douglas: [50]

"I can't understand you, sir. You will be crushed between the Administration and the Republicans. I shall denounce you, sir. You had better go into the street and blow out your brains!"

Others present said nearly the same. Simultaneously, Douglas's mail was filled with appeals to stand firm. "Yield not one inch," wrote an Illinois friend. "For God's sake, put your foot on every proposition looking that way," implored an Ohioan. To the State Democratic Convention in Illinois on April 21, ninety-seven of the ninety-eight counties represented had sent anti-Lecompton delegates; and the convention had adopted resolutions of the most spirited character on Kansas. How would these delegates feel if Douglas let them down? He turned back decisively.

On April 27, Crittenden opened the brief Senate debate, and next day Douglas followed. Many of his friends had besought him to compromise, he said; he desired no personal triumph over the Administration; but he could not sanction a measure which made admission contingent on a set of unfair conditions and offered only an indirect popular submission of the constitution. Stuart and Broderick attacked the bill. While these three Democrats stood out to the last in the Senate, thirteen party associates did the same in the House. On the thir-

---

49 See memorandum in the Buchanan Papers stating what Walker had told Gwin of the meeting.
50 P. G. Auchampaugh, "The Buchanan-Douglas Feud," *Ill. State Hist. Soc. Journal*, XXV, 5-48; "Journal of Milton S. Latham," *Calif. Hist. Soc. Quarterly*, XI, 14 ff.

tieth, however, the English bill carried by 112 to 103 in the lower chamber, and 31 to 22 in the upper.[51]

In effect, Kansas had been thrust back into territorial vassalage, with Buchanan's nominee Denver as governor, and Pierce's nominees Cato and Lecompte as judges. But the Republicans and Douglas Democrats rejoiced in the certainty that the people would now show their utter scorn of Lecompton, a lethal blow. They did. When the vote was taken August 2, it stood 11,812 to 1,926 for rejection of the constitution. Most of the people of Kansas were willing enough to continue in territorial status if only they could have peace, security, and fair elections. The troubles of the land now practically ceased, for though slavery was permitted under the Dred Scott decision, it was practically excluded by force of determined freesoil control.

Buchanan showed heartfelt relief at the partial measure of face-saving that he had achieved. He wrote English that it was painful even to think what would have been the alarming condition of the Union had Congress adjourned without passing his compromise, and that he wished he had a thousand votes to cast for the reelection of the Indiana Congressman. Southern men exhibited mixed feelings.[52] Stephens, who justly claimed most of the credit for the scheme, having prompted English and managed the passage, was in a triumphant frame of mind; out of defeat he had snatched a cup of balm. Not a few associates were pleased to reflect that Kansas, which had manifestly been ready to send two Republican Senators and one Representative to Washington, would be kept on the doorstep indefinitely. The most radical Southerners, however, felt mingled grief and anger over the loss of the one new slave State that might have been theirs.

[V]

The dark Kansas chapter in the chronicle of intersectional conflict was now closing. As the country looked back upon it, a number of lessons were distinctly visible. Foremost among them, the most glaring and the most painful, was the lesson of the gross miscalculations involved in the Kansas-Nebraska Act. Intended to quiet sectional antagonisms, it had increased them; designed to furnish a relatively quick, automatic, and natural solution of the slavery issue, it had produced delays, artificial interventions, and endless conflicts; presented as the embodiment of justice, it had fostered fraud, chicanery, and outrage. The gallant role of Douglas in the final scenes of the drama could not conceal the fact that it would have been infinitely better for Kansas, for the Democratic

51 Senator John Bell of Tennessee also voted against the bill, defying instructions from his State.
52 July 2, 1858; English Papers.

Party, for the South, and for the nation, had he insisted in 1854 on respecting the Missouri Compromise. He could say that he was not to blame for the raids of the border ruffians, the heated propaganda of the Kansas aid societies, the frontier clashes, the stuffed ballot boxes, the trickery and tyranny; certainly not. But he could be blamed for not foreseeing the false arousal of Southern hopes, the Northern sense of outrage, and the angry contest on the western plains.

Almost equally evident was the failure of two successive Presidents to show candor, vision, and above all courage in dealing with Kansas affairs. Pierce and Buchanan had appointed a succession of good governors—Reeder, Geary, Walker, Denver. These men had all grappled with their problems manfully and reported upon them honestly; they had tried to punish fraud and extirpate violence. The betrayal of Geary by President Pierce was a tragic episode. Still more inexcusable was the betrayal of Walker by President Buchanan. After making every effort to entice this able and highly experienced man to accept the governorship; after giving him explicit promises of support, in which the Cabinet joined; after endorsing and underlining his insistence upon fair elections and a popular submission of the new constitution, Buchanan had abandoned him and let his enemies drag him down.

The one excuse that can be made for Buchanan was that he became terrified in the summer of 1857 under Southern threats, and thought the sacrifice of the sturdy little Kansas governor preferable to the risk of a cotton-State secession.[53] But a President should not become terrified. Georgia, Mississippi, Alabama, and South Carolina had no ground for disunion in the admission of Kansas as a freesoil State. The business of the President in that crisis was to stand by his pledges and his governor; to use every possible means (even a speechmaking tour would have been warranted) of driving home to the Lower South the fact that a heavy majority of Kansans were freesoil men and had fairly won the right to a freesoil constitution; to force Cobb, Thompson, and Floyd to join him in stating the true facts, and to await the result. If the four States had tried secession, which is highly improbable, they would have been brought up short. We cannot doubt how a Washington, a Jackson, a Cleveland, or a Theodore Roosevelt would have acted that fateful summer.

But a still deeper failure was involved—the failure of the American people. Both North and South, Republicans and Democrats, had at critical moments shown deplorable partisanship and excitability. The feverish beating of tom toms by the emigrant aid societies and the editors and politicians back of them

53　Henry S. Foote writes: "But he had, in some way, learned to dread the fierce audacity of the Southern fire-eaters, as he was accustomed to call them, and it several times became obvious to me, long before he fell under their domination in 1860, that his fear of the leaders of this boisterous and menacing faction was not wholly unmixed with something of a respectful admiration." *Casket of Reminiscences*, 113.

was as needless as it was provocative. As events proved, the freesoil settlement of Kansas was effected not by artificial inducements but by a natural flow of small farmers, artisans, and shopkeepers from the Middle Atlantic, Border and Middle Western States. Many Republican leaders were anxious to keep the Kansas excitement alive to strengthen their party. Had they accepted the Toombs bill in the summer of 1856, the subsequent embroilments might have been avoided and Kansas quietly brought into the Union as a free State. The Republicans and abolitionists who extolled Jim Lane and John Brown incurred a heavy responsibility. On the other hand, Southerners who cheered on Atchison, Stringfellow, Sheriff Jones, and the border ruffians were equally culpable. The willingness of proslavery men to profit by the brazen swindling of John Calhoun and his fellow delegates at Lecompton was saddening. Southern Cabinet members were *particeps criminis* in that shabby juggle; Southern Senators abetted it by hollow arguments; even Stephens, admitting that Lecompton was a cheat, regretted its failure because he thought the South entitled to another slave State.[54] Had the level of political morality in America been higher and that of political excitability lower, the worst Kansas pages would never have been written.

If Kansas ceased to haunt the dreams of the nation, it left a sinister general heritage in the enhancement of sectional ill-will, and a specific legacy of evil in the Democratic schism. The refusal of Douglas to assent to the English compromise had hardened the hearts of Buchanan and the Directory against him. Even had he acquiesced, many Southerners would have been reluctant to pardon him. Now that he had stood recalcitrant to the last, Cobb, Jacob Thompson, Floyd, and the fire-eaters of the Deep South were implacable. They meant to ruin him even if this meant party ruin. Some hoped to ruin him, the party, and the Union together. "We shall treat Judge Douglas," said the Nashville *Union* on June 24, "just as we should treat any other Democrat who, in an emergency, abandoned his principles and made common cause with the enemy."

How great the change in the short fifteen months since Buchanan was inaugurated! The Democrats were broken, leaderless, bitter; the Republicans were filled with confidence. Frank Blair, actively organizing his party in Missouri, threw out an exultant prophecy: "There is now no earthly doubt of the overthrow of the Administration party in the next Congress and Presidential election." [55]

Meanwhile, it became evident to Americans that the rapid growth of Kansas was but one chapter in an astonishing story of trans-Mississippi development. In this magical tale, unmatched at the time in any other part of the globe,

54 R. M. Johnston, *Autobiography*, 151.
55 April 19, 1858; Brodhead Papers.

several elements require examination: the creation of populous new communities by mining rushes; the optimism with which settlers looked forward to State-building; the steps taken to integrate Mormon Utah into the national structure; the increasing demand for capital in Western mining, lumbering, and cattle-raising; and the steady improvement of communications. This new West, as many saw, was a land quite unsuited to the economy of slavery; this unexhausted athletic West, with its scorn of fetters and conventions, was a veritable stronghold of individualism and freedom. Yet its future could not be assured until the contest over slavery was settled.

12

And Still the Country Grew

ONE LATE summer day in 1858, an unusual stir was noticeable in the streets of Leavenworth. A roughly dressed man named E. Y. King, an Ohioan turned prospector, had arrived from the Rockies with important news. He had accompanied a party of Kansas men led by John Easter, a Lawrence butcher, who had gone to the Pike's Peak region some months earlier to investigate stories of gold brought by two Delaware chiefs. Though reticent to strangers, King told his friends that the group had found pay dirt.

"It is on Cherry Creek," he said in effect, exhibiting a little store of dust and nuggets. "You go west along the South Platte, up and up; Cherry Creek forks to the south. Long's Peak is almost in front of you, and Pike's Peak away off to your left."

He was certain of gold in that region. A party of Georgians under one Green Russell, equally positive, was remaining there. It was seven hundred miles from Leavenworth, but King was going back in the spring.[1] And in the ensuing months, other prospectors arrived in eastern Kansas bringing reports which filled the towns with a glow of interest and were speedily telegraphed east. While some of the returning men were disillusioned and intended to take up Kansas farming, others set to work to form companies, buy tools, and launch systematic operations. Any man, they said, could make five to ten dollars a day, and with luck twenty, in panning gold; but capital, skill, and some organization were desirable.

Iowa and Missouri quickly caught the fever, while workless men in Atlantic cities listened hopefully to the reports. Kansas City, Lawrence, and Omaha were soon full of adventurers planning a spring expedition to the mountains. Thousands, all the way from Maine to Illinois, were eager to join the search. "Never," wrote a lad who was lifted out of a dull general store in Iowa, "have a great boom, a fabulously wealthy mining district, and a new civilization been started on slimmer realities. It was all talk and dream, and yet in Iowa we were hotter about it than a prairie fire." [2]

---

1 King reached Leavenworth September 10; *National Intelligencer*, September 18, 1858.
2 Robert Claiborne Pitzer, *Three Frontiers*, Ch. 3.

Don't go if you have a job or a farm, exhorted Greeley's *Tribune*. But if you have neither, possess strength and grit, and can gather $50, we do earnestly advise you to set out *toward* Pike's Peak. You can reach Chicago, St. Louis, or Lawrence before winter, can find work somewhere, and when spring comes can decide whether to get your gold riskily along Cherry Creek, or safely and easily by farming, trading, or hauling in the West.[3] Some bold gold-hunters pushed through to Cherry Creek during the winter of 1858–59, and the first bakery, carpenter shop, watchmaker's, and saloon were opened, along with the Eldorado Hotel. As spring came, lines of Conestogas rolled across Iowa and Missouri, while the boats up the Missouri River were thronged with adventurers. The stampede, irrational and irresistible, was on.[4]

Minnesota had been admitted to the Union on May 11, 1859, with a population stated by the last territorial census at about one hundred and fifty thousand. Oregon stood knocking at the door, to be admitted February 11, 1859. Now the future Colorado was being born. The star of fortune rising over the Rockies attracted a swarm of those whom Henry Villard called masters of the ready Anglo-American art of town-making.[5] Near the site of the future Colorado Springs, a hamlet named El Paso sprang up and withered. Boulder City was laid out and survived. Central City (at first Mountain City) and Golden City were established. But a preeminent place was taken by the two settlements on Cherry Creek—that on the west bank called Auraria after a Georgia mining town, and that on the east Denver after the recently retired governor of Kansas. By the first snowfall of 1858, the two had about a hundred and twenty-five cabins, dugouts, and tents, and by May the habitations had increased to two hundred. Denver-Auraria became the commercial center of the gold-hunting district. The principal founder of the Denver Town Company, William Larimer, had arranged with W. H. Russell, planner of the Central Overland California & Pike's Peak Express Company, to make it a terminus of the stage line. Goods from the East were trans-shipped at Denver-Auraria to all the mining camps about.

The situation was superb. More than five thousand feet in altitude, Denver-Auraria lay within fifteen miles of the eastern base of the Rocky Mountain chain, visible through the crystal atmosphere for two hundred miles. Bold bluffs rose abruptly from the sandy bed of Cherry Creek which flowed into the South Platte hard by; the countryside was dotted with little lakes; cottonwood groves lined the streams. The first settlers lived in rude comfort, sleeping on buffalo robes and rising to a breakfast of antelope meat, trout, and flapjacks.

3 N. Y. *Tribune*, September 16, 30, 1858.
4 Henry Villard, *Past and Present of the Pike's Peak Gold Regions* (L. F. Hafen, ed.), Ch. 2.
5 *Op. cit.*, Ch. 11.

San Francisco had not risen much more lustily than did the Colorado metropolis. The spring rush of fortune seekers arrived in 1859 to find a discouraged population, for the placer deposits were quickly depleted. Then, on May 8,

W. H. Russell and Alexander Majors' Link
Colorado with the East.

news reached Denver that John H. Gregory had made a splendid find of lode gold—and hope was reborn. Miners swarmed to the Gregory Gulch diggings and spread out through all the mountain valleys and pockets. Fresh discoveries were made, ensuring the future of the region. By midsummer, fifty or sixty thousand treasure-hunters had arrived and Denver-Auraria had become a thriving city of fully five thousand, its buildings alone representing an outlay of $700,000.

This Colorado population, drawn from all parts of the nation and half the outside world, was remarkably industrious and orderly. Town governments were established, and a vigilance committee repressed lawlessness, warning undesirable men and women to leave. Stagecoaches furnished regular transit from the Missouri River to Denver-Auraria in six days. By the end of 1859, this city had twelve wholesale-retail and twenty-seven retail establishments dealing in all kinds of merchandise, five commission and shipping houses, eight hotels, eleven restaurants, an express office, a newspaper (the *Rocky Mountain News*), four lumberyards, two theatres, two schools, and a plentiful array of doctors, lawyers, architects, and ministers. Sawmills and all kinds of mechanics' shops were to be found. Henry Villard was struck by the "considerable accession of capitalists" during the summer and fall. In August, a so-called constitutional convention of about one hundred and sixty delegates, many self-appointed, drew up a framework of government; and a hotly contested election resulted in sending two rival delegates to Washington to ask the formation of a new Territory of Jefferson. Horace Greeley came to see the country for himself, accompanied by Albert D. Richardson of the Boston *Journal*. On one memorable night, the editor, worn out by his travels, in pain from a wounded leg, and angered by the din of the bar and gambling den which occupied half of the Denver House, suddenly appeared, called the drinkers to order, lectured them on their vicious ways, and actually produced a temporary reformation.[6]

Greeley, Villard, and Richardson united in a favorable report on the mining developments and the prospects of the region. Ultimate results bore out their predictions, but the immediate harvest was far smaller than prospectors, dreaming of a new California, had anticipated. The placer miners found little. Vast treasures of precious metal lay in the Rockies, but they were locked in quartz and galena and could be extracted only by corporations assembling engineers, chemists, and costly machinery. A refluent tide of disappointed men spilled across the Missouri in the autumn of 1859. "The rush got as thick coming as going," writes one participant. The whole mineral yield of the Pike's Peak region that year did not reach three-quarters of a million—far less than the capital sunk in outfits and travel. Yet enough people remained to make Denver, Boulder, and other towns prosperous centers, and in the closing days of Buchanan's term (February 28, 1861) the Territory of Colorado came into existence.[7] The mining thenceforth was of a type which required large investments for machinery and transportation.

6 Villard, *Memoirs*, I, 115–130.
7 Fisk Stone, ed., *History of Colorado*, I, Ch. 6.

[I]

Realms of gold, silver, and copper, of cattle, timber, and fisheries, this trans-Mississippi West opened vistas of strength and daring to the American people. Men's blood flowed faster as they took draughts from the stream of newspaper stories, magazine articles, and books portraying the exuberant life and manifold opportunities of this domain of forests, peaks, and plains. Home-staying youth, to be sure, had plenty of chances. But what hardy young man would not like, in imagination at least, to be a prospector on Cherry Creek? Who would not like to be the pilot who brought the steamer *White Cloud* up to the Omaha landing on April 15, 1857, finding himself overwhelmed by a crowd hilarious over the first arrival of the season? What young fellow worth his salt would not delight in cracking the whip over the six-horse team of Butterfield's Overland Mail as, fording the Arkansas at Fort Smith, it straightened out on the short-cut trail through the Choctaw reservation toward Texas? What young woman would not (in dreams) leap at the chance to spend ten years in pioneering at the Falls of St. Anthony, amid such experiences as Harriet E. Bishop described in *Floral Home; or, First Years of Minnesota*—with lumbermen, hunters, and fur traders as friends, a schoolroom of Sioux children to teach, and a fast-developing frontier community to watch?

The Western adventurer might choose his place and vocation at will. He might be an Indian fighter under Will Harney or Jeb Stuart, anywhere from Fort Pierre to Tucson. He might be a missionary on Puget Sound. James G. Swan portrayed the allurements of that region in *The Northwest Coast*, telling of mines of coal, lead, and gold, incredible forests of fir, spruce, and pine, a soil that produced grain and fruit in perfection, woods filled with elk, deer, and antelope, and rivers almost choked with salmon and sturgeon. He might be a ranchman in Texas, or one of the cattle-drivers now bringing herds of many hundred beeves at a time to cross the Mississippi between Quincy and Rock Island, bound for Chicago. He might be a lumberman floating one of the giant rafts down the Wisconsin, a stream carrying annually a hundred million feet of boards. To form one of these rafts, from fifteen to thirty cribs, each containing from fourteen to twenty tiers of close-packed inch lumber, were fitted together, with spring poles in front to lift the edges of the rafts as they rushed down over foam-mantled rocks, and a heavy oar behind for steering. To shoot the perilous dalles of the Wisconsin just above the sturdy new town of Racine, where the river for half a dozen miles was compressed into a boiling gorge, the rafts were broken up into what were called "rapid-pieces," each consisting of five to seven well-secured cribs. Once out on the smoother Mississippi, the rivermen would gather together an extensive flotilla, on which they erected cabins and cookhouses for the trip to cities downstream. Log rafts, too, were not uncommon.[8]

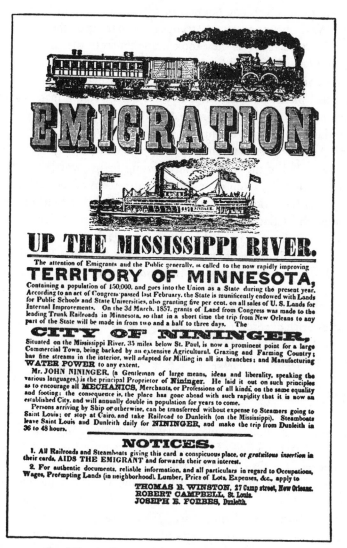

Real Estate Promotion for Minnesota, 1859.

News of the trans-Mississippi West formed a great part of the intelligence in the American press. Some of it was dreary enough: the eternal Kansas bickering, the murders and vigilante lynchings, the incessant Indian hostilities, or

8 Racine Correspondent, N. Y. *Weekly Tribune*, September 5, 1857, gives a full description.

the riot over slavery in Oregon's constitutional convention of the summer of 1857. Much more of it was constructive. The older sections were constantly being bombarded with statistics exhibiting the wonderful growth of cities and States, railways and factories, banks and colleges. Let a reader open any newspaper in those months in which the Lecompton scheme was hatching, for example, and his eye would light on a story describing some new phase of regional development. He would read Governor Robert M. Stewart's inaugural address at Jefferson City, Missouri, declaring that the coal of the State was inexhaustible, that within a few miles of Iron Mountain and Pilot Knob were ores enough to furnish two hundred million tons of finished iron, and that the lead and copper mines were tremendously rich; or a prediction from St. Croix, Wisconsin, that the town's river trade, new railroad, and farm and timber resources must soon make it one of the largest manufacturing and commercial cities in the Northwest; or a statement upon the swelling commerce of Santa Fé; or a letter from a tourist describing how Omaha, where the first house was built in 1854, had sprung into a city of two thousand, with schools, churches, banks, and newspapers.

The growth of the West was indeed fabulous. It seemed marvellous that Chicago more than doubled its population between 1852 and 1855, leaping from thirty-eight thousand people to eighty thousand. It was marvellous to hear that Milwaukee, which probably counted a greater proportion of foreign-born inhabitants than any other American city, had more than trebled in size within a decade. It was remarkable to find that railroad crews were briskly laying down lines from Chicago and Milwaukee to St. Paul, and that by 1857 no fewer than three railroads were being planned to traverse Minnesota from east to west.[9] Easterners were astonished to learn that, beyond Minnesota, the still inchoate region of Dacotah had settlements. When Congress passed in 1857 an enabling act fixing the western boundary of the State in part along the Red River, news came of a county and town of Pembina left out in the cold and needing some specific government.[10] It was another marvel to find the Oregon legislature in 1856 not only boasting of fifty thousand people, but declaring them the wealthiest fifty thousand on the face of the globe. As for California marvels, they were innumerable. In the mid-fifties that land of gold had ceased to import breadstuffs and was shipping wheat, oats, and barley in increasing quantities to Australia and the Atlantic ports; it had its own paper mill, furniture factories, and large machine shops; and it was erecting a sugar refinery intended to meet the entire West Coast demand.[11]

9 *National Intelligencer*, March 24, 1857, quoting Andrews's recent work on Minnesota and Dacotah.
10 *National Intelligencer*, June 30, 1857.
11 *Ibid.*, May 9, 1857.

The whole West grew like a young giant fed on some magic food of the gods. Down to the panic of 1857 it was a land of speculation—and by 1859 the speculator was again ready to pluck up hope of rich booms. As population flowed outward, the glittering lure of the unearned increment in new cities appealed to investors as better than a gold mine. Douglas was a speculator in farmlands and city lots. R. M. T. Hunter, John W. Forney, and John C. Breckinridge were all involved in real estate transactions at the western end of Lake Superior.[12] Caleb Cushing at the beginning of the fifties owned a seventh part of "Rock Island City" in Illinois. Daniel Webster at an earlier date had held part of this same tract, but, neglecting to pay taxes, had lost possession.[13] Land speculation was one of the motors that drove forward the rapid development of Kansas. Throughout the Middle West, government policies which gave speculators almost unlimited opportunities to buy land fostered the swift rise of tenant farming.[14] Everyone who traveled beyond Ohio was impressed by the materialistic spirit pervading the air. A keen-eyed German, J. G. Kohl, who came over in 1856–57, was struck by the universal preoccupation with business openings, investments, prices, and profits. Traveling up-river from Dubuque to St. Paul in a handsome steamboat, he thought that some of his fellow passengers would take time to look at the enchanting scenery. Not at all; everybody was talking of the cost of farms and the turnover on lots.

The optimism that was a general American trait swelled higher in the West than anywhere else, catching its tempo from the tub-thumping of the boosters. For such men in Wisconsin, Governor Bashford was speaking early in 1857: [15]

Our soil is rich, productive, and easily cultivated; our climate as salubrious and healthy as any on the continent; and with our rapidly increasing facilities for internal communication at home and our direct railroad and water communication both with the Atlantic States and those bordering on the Gulf of Mexico, the cause of our swift advancement and present prosperity, as well as the earnest of their continuance, are alike apparent. . . . The day seems not

12 Douglas Papers, *passim;* Henry Harrison Simms, *Life of R. M. T. Hunter,* 100, 101. Douglas obeyed principle in his speculations. "When I became chairman of the Territorial Committee of the Senate, twelve years ago," he wrote August 29, 1857, "I determined never to purchase, or own, or become interested in any land, town lots, or other property in any of the Territories of the United States, whilst I held that position, for the reason that I would not allow an enemy even a pretext for saying that my public interest was influenced or stimulated by my private interest. I have never departed from this rule in any one instance." He visited Minnesota in 1857 to obtain information on that Territory useful to him in his Congressional duties; he was forthwith accused of some connection with the sale of the Fort Snelling military reservation; and he indignantly denied that he had an inch of land in Minnesota or any other Territory. Chicago *Times,* August 30, 1857.
13 William Brackett, Rock Island, July 20, 1850; Cushing Papers, LC.
14 Paul W. Gates, *Frontier Landlords and Pioneer Tenants, passim.*
15 Message of January, 1857.

far distant when, in agricultural and mineral wealth, in commercial advantages, in educational facilities, and all that tends to make us truly great and prosperous as a State, we shall be among the first in the Union.

For realty promoters in western Texas, the San Antonio *Sentinel* was lustily beating the drum:

We have a climate unsurpassed even by the far-famed Italy. . . . The scenery of Western Texas, we venture to say, in point of variety and beauty

BRING OUT THE BIG GUN

GLORIOUS NEWS!!

MINNESOTA A STATE!!!

100 GUNS FIRED AT WINONA:

GENERAL REJOICING,

Minnesotans Exult Over Their Admission,
May 11, 1858.

is second to that of no other country in the world; from the cold and rugged mountain steeps, where the cool clear waters gush from living fountains, interspersed with rich valleys, teeming with luxuriant growths, to the wide-extended prairies, with their gentle undulating surfaces covered with a rich dress of living green. . . . Stock of all kinds are very prolific, and disease among them is almost unknown. We have a varied soil. . . . More produce of almost every kind can be raised in Western Texas with a less amount of labor than in any other State in the Union.

Equal enthusiasm animated the correspondent of the New York *Tribune* in Minnesota: [16]

The new State will very probably number half a million at the census of 1860. No part of the West is receiving a more intelligent or valuable class of

16 Quoted *National Intelligencer*, January 31, 1857.

immigrants than Minnesota. The climate is the delight of the New Englander, the soil is extremely fertile, the beauty of natural scenery is not surpassed in any portion of the Union. The natural productions embrace all the valuable grains, grasses, vegetables, and fruits grown in Wisconsin. Waterpower abounds in every direction, and timber is comparatively abundant. Twenty years hence Minnesota will be gridironed over with railroads, dotted with towns and cities, and will hold upwards of two millions of sober, industrious, intelligent, freedom-loving inhabitants.

Much of this proved true, though the census of 1860 gave Minnesota only one hundred seventy-two thousand people, and that of 1880 only seven hundred eighty-one thousand. Detailed prophecy is risky, as Senator Weller should have remembered when, speaking in Congress for a Pacific Railroad, he boasted of California:

In 1856 there was imported into San Francisco merchandise to the value of one hundred millions, more than the whole amount of goods imported into the United States fourteen years ago. In point of commerce that city is ranked as third in our Union. . . . Although five times destroyed by fire, [she] will now compare favorably with any other city of the republic. In her schools, her churches, her public institutions, in all that dignifies and ennobles human nature, she has made more rapid advances during the last five years than any other city in the world. . . . San Francisco, the greatest city on that coast, before the lapse of a quarter of a century, if this road is constructed, will become the formidable rival of New York. Indeed, I venture the prediction that, within the lifetime of some who now hear me, the American commerce on the Pacific will far exceed that on the Atlantic.

[II]

As the country grew, national authority was necessarily extended over de-tached and neglected areas of the West. The so-called Mormon war was an episode in this extension. It fell to President Buchanan to write a stern adminis-trative chapter in that Mormon chronicle which had hitherto been so out of keeping with the nineteenth century that, despite its grotesque and ugly sides, it had a touch of romance.

What an epic it was: the brilliant woodland vision seen by the farm lad Joseph Smith in western New York one autumn eve in 1823; the revelation of the buried plates of gold by the angel Moroni; the translation of their engraved contents by the aid of Urim and Thummim; the publication of the Book of Mormon, and the organization of the church; the successive transfers of the devoted adherents to Kirtland, Ohio, to Jackson County, Missouri, and Nauvoo, Illinois; the building of their prosperous church and massive temple on the banks of the Mississippi; the murder of the prophet and his brother, and the accession to power of Brigham Young; the winter flight across the river at the cannon's mouth in 1846; the journey of the intrepid saints, Young like a second Moses at their head, up the arid valley of the Platte, through Echo Canyon and over the Wasatch Range, stoically enduring heat, cold, hunger, thirst, and Indian peril; the triumphant arrival in July, 1847, at their Pisgah, whence they greeted with a shout the spectacle of the gleaming inland sea and fertile Salt Lake Valley—"The Land of Promise! The Land of Promise, reserved by God for the resting -place of his saints!" All the errors and follies which had marked some activities of these unconventional enthusiasts could but slightly mar the splendid chronicle of devotion, heroism, and resourcefulness.

Nor could anyone well deny that Brigham Young was the most command-ing single figure of the West. This rugged Vermonter, who had been given only eleven days' formal schooling before he set to work as carpenter, glazier, and painter, possessed an inexhaustible energy, a domineering temper, and a rocklike will which made him seem truly the Lion of the Lord. The visionary Joseph Smith had been a prophet; he believed in his dreams—he could not have persuaded thousands to accept them had he not possessed a burning faith, even though it was the faith of self-delusion. Young, with only rare flashes of the prophetic spirit, was a masterly organizer, policy-maker, and ruler. Though his sermons were childish, his other writings were shrewd, while his apt practical sagacity, inflexible resolution, and courage against any odds gave him the pro-portions of a statesman. From the moment he took the helm he had never faltered. He had ordered the harassed Nauvoo colony to seek a home in the wilderness, had directed the exodus, fixed upon the goal, and laid out the new metropolis. He had chosen spots for the settlement of Mormon companies sent out from Salt Lake City to various parts of Deseret, the land of the honey-bee. He had made plans for agriculture and industry. He it was who in 1852 announced the doctrine of polygamy, which though to many an abominable institution nevertheless temporarily served a sound purpose in the develop-ment of the colony.

For years, the national government had recognized Young's leadership. Kearny had called on him in 1846 for five hundred men to fight the Mexicans. "You shall have your battalion at once," replied Brigham, and the service of the detachment won him the gratitude of the Polk Administration. Upon the establishment of Utah Territory in 1850, President Fillmore immediately ap-pointed Young as governor, commander of the militia, and superintendent of Indian affairs. In short, he confirmed Young's dictatorship. Visitors to the region were impressed by the business acumen of the theocrat, who estab-lished industries, cooperative stores, banks, and transportation agencies to the prosperity of both the church-state and himself. Mormons chuckled with pride over his personal wealth, for though he lived in simple fashion (except for his costly establishment of wives in the "lion house") he piled dollar upon dollar. As far-flung missionaries sent home recruits, Utah steadily grew. Converts trickled in from Scandinavia, Switzerland, Germany, and above all Great Britain, until the eleven thousand struggling people of the Territory in 1850 were forty thousand ten years later.

Pages of heroic endurance were written into the Mormon record. Crops having failed in 1855 so disastrously that retrenchment was imperative, Young decided to encourage the incoming immigrants of 1856 to make the journey from the Iowa border not with specially despatched wagons and teams, as formerly, but on foot, pushing handcarts. This was simple, ingenious, and feasible, but it gave hostages to fortune. Of five companies which pushed across the plains in this fashion, the first three were successful. The two others met disaster. About five hundred in number, they started late, were crippled by dysentery, a stampede of their cattle and other misfortunes, and finally encountered heavy storms. With inadequate food and clothing, all would have perished had not relief parties reached them on the Sweetwater and near South Pass. As it was, about one-sixth died, while many of the remainder lost toes, feet, or hands. Efforts by the Mormon authorities to put a good face on the situation, and by their enemies to exaggerate the losses, made it difficult to obtain the true story. It was certain that many converts had endured dire sufferings gallantly, that they had complained little, and that the church heads were anxious to conceal their miscalculations. Brigham Young, saying that some members of the handcart companies had expired while singing hymns, and that others, when succor arrived, died while trying to eat the bread in their hands, remarked that nobody should feel a misplaced sympathy; he would be glad if he finally died without a groan or struggle, and with a keen appetite for food! [17] Next year the handcart migrations were resumed with better planning.

Despite his coarse and brutal vein, his egotism, and his frequent pettiness, Brigham Young was popular. He treated his own people with affability, throwing his arm over any Mormon's shoulder and asking cordially about his wives and children. His rough and ready manners, provincialisms of speech ("leetle," "beyond," "disremember," and "they was"), his kindness, and his justice in business dealings, were all assets in that primitive community. Subject as he was to the Quorum of his church, he had to rule by persuasion rather than fiat, and in accordance with the general discipline of the Latter Day Saints; and his policies showed an astute combination of tact and firmness.

17 Deseret *News* quoted in *National Intelligencer*, April 30, 1857.

No man of less strength could have succeeded; he had taken a heterogeneous people, foreign and native, skilled and unskilled, and moulded them into an industrious, orderly, devoted, and homogeneous community. Visitors from the East were struck by the contrast between his meagre intellectual attainments and his indomitable force of personality. They saw, in a house almost destitute of books, pictures or other tokens of refinement, a broad-shouldered, burly, powerful man of more than medium height, his face fringed in wavy hair and adorned with short chin-whiskers. His heavy jaw, tightly shut lips, and suspicious gray eyes proclaimed him a master, and, if need be, a cruel master. He was doggedly determined to remain autocrat of his church state. "I am and will be the governor," he had remarked, "and no power can hinder it, until the Lord Almighty says, 'Brigham, you need not be governor any longer.'" This attitude was the more strongly approved by the Mormons when they found President Pierce appointing political hacks of bad personal character, prejudiced and quarrelsome, to executive and judicial offices in the Territory. Indeed, nearly all the Territories had reason to complain of unfit and rapacious Federal officials. In Utah just before Buchanan entered the White House the friction between the people and the agents of the national government had become even hotter than in Kansas and New Mexico, and the charges and countercharges even angrier. Most Mormons believed they were threatened by an intolerant tyranny.

Several Federal officers, on the other hand, loudly accused the people of criminal and rebellious acts. Is the authority of Washington to be utterly flouted by Utah? they demanded.

This was the question that Buchanan believed he must test. Thunders of the national government, he was told, were rolling unheeded over the heads of a people who wanted total autocracy and were frankly intolerant of the rights of minorities; a people who, after long persecution, desired to be let alone and could not comprehend that they must be incorporated in the national fabric. President Pierce in 1854 had offered the governorship to Lt. Colonel E. J. Steptoe, who was in Salt Lake City with a small body of soldiers; but Steptoe had deemed it imprudent to accept the post, and after a quiet winter he betook himself and his little force to California. Various other civil officers who received commissions from Pierce, arriving after Steptoe departed, were overawed by the hostile aspect of Young, Heber C. Kimball, J. M. Grant, and other Mormon leaders, and found it wise to leave. An act of the Mormon-controlled legislature declared that no law should be valid except those enacted by the governor and assembly, and those of Congress *when applicable*—which meant when sanctioned by Brigham Young. Another act gave the probate courts an authority rivaling that of Federal courts, so that, in effect, one set of courts existed for Gentiles and another for the Mormons.[18] H. H. Bancroft in his *Utah*, which is favorable to the Mormons, quotes Young as saying after Steptoe left that "if they play the same game again, so help me God, we will slay them."

Just before Buchanan was inaugurated, the official Mormon newspaper pealed its defiance of the government. If a majority in any Territory preferred a state of vassalage, it remarked, well and good. But when practically the entire community were known most persistently to prefer officers of their own election to those foisted upon them by arbitrary power, and laws of their own enactment to statutes dictated by unconstitutional authority, then tyranny was intolerable. "How long, think ye, can such oppression be quietly endured? How long, think ye, will any people submit to the dictates, slanders, corruptions, and abuse of officers whom they have no voice in electing, and whose efforts are constantly put forth to the utmost for the destruction of the people?" [19]

This was a challenge which no President could ignore. Nor could Washington ignore the passionate protest of Judge W. W. Drummond of the Federal court in transmitting his resignation on March 30, 1857. Drummond had charged a grand jury in Carson County the previous summer to deal sternly with polygamy under the territorial law against lewdness and adultery.[20] He now posed as hostile to a dictatorship which paralyzed all Federal authority and recoiled not from murder to accomplish its ends; and he appealed loudly to the country. He declared that the judiciary was treated as a farce in Utah; that the infatuated Mormons bowed to but one law, the church law emanating from Brigham Young; that officials were insulted, thwarted, and even slain if they administered any other; and that as the Territory had been governed by Young ever since Fillmore's time, it was noonday madness to try to brook this autocrat's sway. He asserted that after careful investigation he had concluded that his predecessor, Judge Leonidas Shaver, had been poisoned by the Mormons; that the late secretary of the Territory, A. W. Babbitt, had been slain by Indian marauders instigated by the church; and that Captain John W. Gunnison and his party of eight surveyors had been killed in 1853 by savages under Mormon direction. He charged that Young had controlled the action of grand juries on indictments, connived at the destruction of court papers, thrown Gentiles into jail without warrant, and pardoned atrocious murderers simply because they held the Mormon faith.

18 Richardson, *Beyond the Mississippi*, 353; McMaster, VIII, 374, 375; Stenhouse, *Rocky Mountain Saints*, 280 ff.; H. H. Bancroft, *Utah*, 494.

19 Deseret *News*, January 28, 1857.

20 Full text of charge is in *National Intelligencer*, December 23, 1856. Critics of Drummond declare that he was a venal, dissolute gamester, who openly insulted the Mormon community, and whose misrepresentations completely misled Washington; Bancroft, *Utah*, 490, 491.

Another Federal judge, George P. Stiles, whose writs had been defied, who had been threatened with personal violence, and whose office had been sacked, arrived at Leavenworth in May, 1857. With him came Surveyor-General D. H. Burr, who with his clerks had fled under threat of death. Both reported robberies and murders unpunished by law, insolent rebuffs by Young when they asked for protection, and a general defiance of the national government.[21] No Federal officers except two Indian agents remained in the Territory. Meanwhile, a lurid work by an apostate, F. G. J. Margetson's *Horrors of Mormonism*, together with other wildly exaggerated tales, excited popular antagonism. A wave of excited feeling rose against Young and his peculiar people. At least half the charges made by Drummond and Stiles, including all their allegations of murder, were baseless, while the other half were overcolored; but the American people were ready to believe anything of the polygamists.

[III]

Buchanan was prepared to act vigorously. He appointed as governor a capable, courageous Georgian, Alfred Cumming, who had been superintendent of Indian affairs on the upper Missouri; named a new chief justice, two associate justices, a secretary, and a marshal; and deputed a body of twenty-five hundred troops under Colonel Albert Sidney Johnston to accompany Cumming to his post. No man in the army was more highly regarded than Johnston. A West Pointer, he had shown quickness of mind, courtesy, daring (he once killed a puma with his clubbed rifle), and endurance. In the Mexican War, Zachary Taylor called him "the best soldier I ever commanded." When in 1855 he was made colonel of a new regiment of cavalry (with Robert E. Lee as lieutenant-colonel and George H. Thomas a major), Winfield Scott declared the appointment "a godsend to the army and the country." Part of Johnston's troops gathered at Fort Leavenworth and in midsummer of 1857 began their march.

The news of the President's determined action filled Young, Kimball, and their associates with mingled fury and apprehension. It must be remembered that the Mormons had good reason, recalling riot, pillage, assassination, and expulsion, to fear American violence. They were a rigid, earnest, ignorant, and prejudiced people, moulded by sermons, speeches, and newspaper articles which exalted their peculiar system and denounced the American government and people bitterly. Facing an ignorance and prejudice even greater than their own, for few men in the East tried to understand the Mormon outlook, they

21 *National Intelligencer*, June 6, August 1, 1857. Chief Justice Stiles, a former Mormon and onetime counsel for Joseph Smith, has also been assailed as a man of bad character; Bancroft, *Utah*, 488, 489. For the official charges by Drummond and others and the reply of the Mormon authorities, see 35th Cong., 1st Sess., *House Exec. Doc.* 71.

were frightened at the prospect of outrage and subjugation. Their leaders, see-ing their own authority endangered, whipped up the popular emotion.

Why, demanded the *Deseret News*, should Federal troops come to prey upon the industrious, sober Mormons when they were needed to halt the riots which reddened the streets of Baltimore, Washington, and New York? Why should a horde of Federal officials, the scourings of grogshops and gambling dens, be thrust upon people who wanted their own paternal governors?

Young poured forth a rhetorical incitement to resistance. "I don't profess to be such a prophet as were Joseph Smith and Daniel, but I am a Yankee guesser, and I guess that James Buchanan has ordered this expedition to appease the wrath of the angry hounds who are howling around him." He had sworn in Nauvoo to send any future aggressor to hell across lots, and he would now muster three hundred men who could lap water and help him whip the Midianites. Woe to meddlers! The Mormons would fight to the end ("in the mountains, in the canyons, upon the plains, on the hills, along the mighty streams, and by the rivulets," ran his anticipation of Winston Churchill's phraseology) for their homes and their religion.[22]

Armed resistance was soon a .reality. The beginning of October found Colonel E. B. Alexander's forward command of about five hundred cavalry approaching Fort Bridger, a hundred and fifteen miles by direct road from Salt Lake City. The rear of the expedition had not yet reached South Pass and Johnston was hurrying to join the little army, which, all told, hardly numbered fourteen hundred men. At this moment, three supply trains com-prising seventy-four wagons equipped by Russell & Waddell of Leavenworth, contractors for the transport of stores and provision of beef, were seized by Mormon bands, pillaged, and burnt. Young had issued an audacious procla-mation forbidding armed forces to enter his Territory, mobilized the Mormon militia, scattered parties through the mountains, and fortified Echo Canyon. These events crystallized eastern indignation. Johnston's forces were compelled to go into winter quarters on the Green River near Fort Bridger, which the Mormons had destroyed; and the country echoed with demands that the mod-ern Sodomites, as one editor called them, be brought to terms—though many people began to wonder if Buchanan had chosen the right method.[23]

As infantry and dragoons dragged out the winter, they spoiled for a fight. Johnston roughly declined Brigham Young's gift of salt. Some men, he wrote his family, think the Mormons will submit, but I disagree. "I think their fanati-

22 Long speech in *National Intelligencer*, September 17, 1857. See O. G. Hammond, ed., *The Utah Expedition, 1857–58, passim;* John L. Sinn, *The Utah Expedition of 1857.* Harney had originally been asked to lead the expedition, but his duties kept him in Kansas.
23 Full account of bringing trains from Fort Laramie by correspondent, N. Y. *Weekly Tribune*, November 21, 1857.

The March of the Army of Utah, and the Beale Survey.

JOHNSTON'S MARCH BEGAN SEPT. 16, 1857

MINN.

IOWA

MO.

ARK.

Ft. Smith

UNORGANIZED TERR.

UNORGANIZED TERR.

Missouri R.

TERR.

Ft. Leavenworth

Ft. Kearney, SEPT. 24

Platte R.

SEPT. 29

Platte R.

NEBRASKA TERR.

KANSAS TERR.

Arkansas R.

Washita R.

Red R.

Canadian R.

TEXAS

OCT. 13

Ft. Laramie, OCT. 4

N. Platte R.

S. Platte R.

Pecos R.

OCT. 15

Sweetwater R.

OCT. 13

South Pass, OCT. 13

Rio Grande

Zuni

Albuquerque (Ft. Defiance). AUG. 26, 1857

Green R.

Camp Scott NOV. 30

WASHINGTON TERRITORY

Black Fork

Ft. Bridger WINTER

Salt Lake City

Provo

Ft. Utah

Colorado R.

NEW MEXICO TERRITORY

NEW MEXICO TERRITORY

Little Colorado R.

Verde R.

Gila R.

GREAT SALT LAKE

Cedar Valley, APRIL, 1858

Camp Floyd

UTAH LAKE

OREGON

UTAH TERRITORY

CALIFORNIA

Colorado R.

Los Angeles

PACIFIC OCEAN

Tscherley

Legend box:

.... March of Albert Sidney Johnston's force from Ft. Leavenworth to Great Salt Lake. 1857-58

———— E. F. Beale's survey
    1857, from Ft. Defiance to Colorado River and California with camels
    1858-59, from Ft. Smith to Albuquerque

Miles
0   100   200

cism and villainy will lead them to try one encounter at least; and I think our government ought to desire it, as affording a simple solution of a difficult political question. If they resist, a final settlement would be on the basis of a conquest. We could then dictate to them the terms of adjustment." D. R. Eckels, accompanying the force as new chief justice for Utah, shared this lust for battle. For their part, the excited Mormons were guilty of unhappy acts. In September, a party of one hundred and thirty-seven California-bound emigrants passing through southern Utah had been all but wiped out by a Mormon-Indian attack in the Mountain Meadows massacre.[24]

If war was to begin, obviously a larger force might have to be thrown across the plains. Exaggerated western reports declared that the Mormons could raise eight to twelve thousand armed men, and credited them with a powder mill, a rifle and pistol factory, and a foundry capable of casting cannon. The Utah roads abounded in opportunities for ambuscades and guerrilla fighting. Brigham Young's agents might also enlist vengeful Indian allies.[25] When Congress met, Buchanan therefore asked for ten new regiments, of which five might be used against the Mormons. Because of the popular distrust of military establishments, however, together with the demand for economy to meet the Treasury deficit and Republican irritation over the use of troops in Kansas, the Administration bill failed; Congress merely authorized two new volunteer regiments for quelling disturbances in Utah and fighting Indians.

Actually neither Washington nor Salt Lake City wanted a war. The Mormons knew that their militia, ill-armed and ill-trained, were no match for regulars. Their crops had been poor in recent years, and despite a better harvest in 1857 they still suffered from scarcities. Their powder factory turned out only an inferior type of coarse ammunition.[26] Brigham Young confessed their weakness when he declared that if the army marched into their towns he would put the immovable property to the torch, and go with the remainder to some distant haven, perhaps Sonora, perhaps British America. Industries were stopped, elders called home from Europe, and Mormons in what is now Nevada and in California ordered to concentrate in Salt Lake, ready to move elsewhere at command. As spring in 1858 began, Young directed the people of the capital and all the northern settlements to leave home and march southward. Roads by mid-April were filled with herds, wagons, and perhaps twenty-five thousand people. Salt Lake and the neighboring towns would be deserted except for men left to guard property and if necessary to fire it. The anguished

24 Johnston's letter December 12, 1857; *National Intelligencer*, February 18, 1858. See C. W. Penrose, *The Mountain Meadow Massacre, passim.* Neither Young nor the Mormon Church approved this murderous attack on the Missouri emigrant train.
25 Sacramento *Age*, October 16, 1857.
26 N. Y. *Tribune*, May 5, 1858.

Mormons apparently looked forward to the obliteration of their laboriously built state. Fortunately, the Administration had no appetite for costly guerrilla warfare ending in the dispersal of a prosperous and useful people.

At the last moment, one of the few strokes of statesmanship exhibited in this period brought about a happy ending. Although the credit went mainly to Buchanan, it belonged primarily to Thomas L. Kane, brother of the Arctic explorer, and to Governor Cumming. Kane was a vigorous, adventurous man in his middle thirties whose published letters reveal his warm-hearted idealism. Born the son of a Philadelphia judge, he had been educated largely in France, where he knew Auguste Comte, and returning home, had been admitted to the Pennsylvania bar. In 1847 he had gone west to visit the Mormons, had assisted them in their flight to Utah, and had won their enduring friendship. His book on them (*The Mormons*, 1850) was well known. When he heard that the wrath of the government was aroused and that fire and sword were about to be carried into their country, compassion impelled him to try to avert bloodshed. He wished neither office nor salary—merely an opportunity to be useful.

Buchanan consented to his proposal for mediation. Leaving by sea for San Francisco in the first days of 1858, Kane made his way to Salt Lake City, conferred with Brigham Young, reassured him, and reached a tentative agreement. While in temporal matters Washington must be supreme, he said, in church affairs the Mormons would not be molested. Then he hurried on to the dugout quarters which Cumming had been occupying at Black's Fork, arriving after a forced ride in a state of utter exhaustion. Cumming, who desired a peaceful solution, received him cordially. The upshot was that the two men, to the chagrin of army officers thirsting for cheap glory, set off for the Mormon settlement and for new conferences with Young.[27]

In doing this, Cumming, who knew that he would be bitterly assailed by military men and misrepresented in Washington, played a fine part. He realized that force would settle nothing, whereas, if fighting with the fanatical church leaders began, many on both sides would perish, and honest farmers and artisans would suffer most. He had been ready to hurry on as soon as the road was clear of snow, without any military escort or any assurances of a safe reception.[28] Leaving camp on April 5, he was in Salt Lake City on the twelfth. The placated Mormons had kindled bonfires to illuminate his night journey through Echo Canyon; they greeted him everywhere as their governor; Young at once paid him a visit of courtesy; and the territorial seal was immediately delivered to him.

27 Oscar L. Winther, ed., *The Private Papers and Diaries of Thomas L. Kane, a Friend of the Mormons.*
28 J. Forney, Camp Scott, April 18, May 1, 1858; Black Papers.

One of the dramatic scenes of the time was the great public meeting in the Tabernacle on April 25, when Young introduced the governor, and Cumming explained to three or four thousand people his purposes. He was tactful but firm. He had seen the pathetic preparations for general flight. He knew that if the Mormons were driven from their homes by terror the event would be remembered like the expulsion of the Acadians. He was aware that many of his auditors were embittered by the thought of old wrongs, some real, some fanciful; he knew how deeply all English-speaking peoples object to the quartering of troops in their midst. To the respectful audience he said that he had come to vindicate the national sovereignty, and would exact an unconditional submission to the Constitution and the laws. He also said, however, that he had no intention of stationing troops in immediate contact with their settlements, that he would not use military power until all other means had failed, and that he would see that any indicted citizen was tried by a jury of his peers. Above all, he would not interfere with the Mormon religion. When he invited citizens to respond, the scene became uproarious. Speaker after speaker, laboring under marked emotion, dwelt upon their persecutions, the want of national gratitude to the Mormon Battalion, their toils in creating their Western home, and their resolve never to be overrun by a brutal soldiery. Cumming remained temperate, and after the meeting more than one Mormon apologized for his own vehemence.[29]

Already, adverse public opinion and the protests of Kane and others had caused the President to alter his policy. On April 6 he signed a proclamation which, though declaring Utah in rebellion, promised a full pardon to all who would submit to the government. A large additional force had been assembled at Fort Leavenworth for use if needed; but in June two Federal peace commissioners reached a complete agreement with the Mormon leaders. It was arranged that Johnston's little army should march through Salt Lake City, which it found almost entirely deserted, and encamp some distance beyond. In due course it established its post at Cedar Valley, about thirty-six miles south of the city. A disastrous conflict had been narrowly avoided. In this bloodless Mormon War the army had made a demonstration which cost the depleted Treasury millions, which terrified and demoralized the hardworking citizens of Utah, and which accomplished no constructive object that peaceful means could not have attained. Cumming and Kane, supported by a far smaller force, could have brought Brigham Young and his associates to the same terms they now made. This grandiose military display, costly and provocative, could and

29 Cumming, May 2, 1858, to Cass, N. Y. *Weekly Tribune*, June 19, 1858. The governor traveled about the Territory, talked with the people, and tried to reach a mutual understanding. Most people were only too glad to be on good terms. J. Forney, May 6, 1858, to J. Black; Black Papers. For additional matter on the Mormon War, see Appendix II.

should have been avoided. Blame for it rested in part on the Mormons, guilty of unwise words and acts, in part on an excitable public opinion in the East, and in part on the Administration.

Of course nothing could shake the imperious temper of Brigham Young, reduce his prestige as leader of the church, or alter the loyalty of most Mormons to his authority. As church head, he remained chief potentate in the Territory. But from this time forward, the civil governor was given due obedience in his restricted sphere, the laws were respected, and a growing Gentile element was protected in its pursuits. Mail, goods, and emigrant trains could again flow freely from the Missouri to the Pacific, and the development of the West could go on.

[IV]

The mining frontier, the Indian frontier, the cattlemen's and farmers' frontiers, all were fast being transformed. All had to adapt themselves to a nation with a lengthening and thickening network of railroads, a maturing set of business institutions, a shifting balance between agriculture and industry, and a stronger social sense.

No more individualistic figures ever existed than the placer miners who had flocked to the Sierra foothills in 1849–50. Men worked alone, or with but one or two partners. A group might band together to build a dam or ditch, but so long as placers paid handsome returns, the semi-solitary digger predominated. Of the first half-billion dollars in gold taken from California, much the greatest part was recovered with the placerman's simple tools of pick, shovel, pan, and cradle. Even after more elaborate and costly operations were instituted, it was often difficult to find hands for them because men preferred trying their luck as prospectors along bars, riffles, and gulches.[30]

Astute miners quickly perceived, however, that much the richest concentrations of gold occurred in rock veins or in Tertiary "high gravels"—that is, the beds followed by streams in the Tertiary era. The quartz veins along the "mother lode," which runs irregularly through Mariposa County to Amador, were in many instances fabulously large; and capital and associated effort quickly appeared. When tempting outcrops were found in Grass Valley, on Frémont's Mariposa holdings, and at other points, Californians with access to capital began to make large investments.

A Los Angeles company was selling stock as early as the summer of 1850.

---

30 In the period of greatest productiveness, 1850–53, the California placer mines yielded about $65,000,000 a year. If an average of 75,000 miners were at work, they made an average of $8 a day. Some think the average the first year was $20 a day.

Even though none of the quartz mines by 1852 had gone below three hundred feet, the drilling, blasting, and ore-crushing stamps cost more than most individuals could afford. A few early stamp-mills were erected for from $5,000 to $10,000, but this was exceptional. In 1852 California had one hundred and eight mills, representing an investment not far short of six million dollars. As time proved, this was a false dawn for quartz mining. Because the early stamps did not grind the ore to sufficient fineness, because the process of chemical amalgamation to extract the gold was at first inefficient, because for a decade no means of reaching the gold locked up in sulphides was known, because, in short, good engineering knowledge and good apparatus were lacking, most of the metal was lost—sometimes four-fifths of it; while the high costs and low returns quickly ruined companies possessing inadequate capital. Nine in ten of the early plants for extracting rockbound gold failed. Men became so skeptical of quartz mining that the number of mills fell in 1854 to thirty-two. Although the industry soon grew vigorous again, not until after 1860 did it reach significant proportions.

While the Tertiary gravels were more easily dealt with, they too required large investments in labor and capital. They might be covered by hundreds of feet of earth and detritus, together with lava, basaltic crust, or other semi-rocklike material which the miners called cement. To reach the deeper gravel deposits meant tunneling into a slope, timbering and shoring at every step. To wash the gold out of the gravel, rock, and dirt often required the construction of huge dams and flumes. In a rich district, a single hill might have dozens of tunnels sunk into its sides. Where gold deposits lay nearer the surface and were not covered by too indurated a layer of cement, a stream could frequently be diverted to erode the covering and bring the pay dirt into the sluices. That is, water was turned in to strip off the useless layers of the hillside. Somebody quickly perceived that a hose could bring the water more expeditiously and cheaply than a flume; then somebody else placed a nozzle on the hose, got a high pressure, and bored down faster and harder than ever. Bigger and stronger hose came in, fitted with iron collars. Before long, the Sierra foothills were being bombarded with hydraulic artillery which demolished grass, trees, soil, sand, and loose rock, shattering and shearing everything down to the ancient bedrock, and creating havoc with the landscape.

As the fifties wore on, more capital was collected, more companies were formed, and larger bodies of engineers, tunnel-blasters, flume-builders, and hosemen were brought in. The hydraulic operations became gargantuan. Blasting, to loosen refractory rock or cement, was combined with the use of water, and ingenious combinations of tunnels and hydraulic monitors made it possible to wash the very bowels out of seemingly unconquerable mountains. Placer miners downstream complained angrily of the waste washed from the upper slopes. Millions of tons of rubble were dumped into the Sierra streams; sand, gravel, and rocks choked many valleys and ravines; and when spring floods came, the offscourings were carried down to overwhelm valuable farmlands. The once-clear Sacramento flowed yellow. In time, the silt closed the upper channel to navigation and became perilous to steamboats even on the lower reaches. Finally a levee system had to be built to protect the capital city. Passage of legislation to check the grosser mining abuses, however, did not come for another generation.

Until the beginning of 1858, quartz mining had produced only a tiny fraction of California's gold—probably not one percent; the Tertiary gravels had yielded but a modest share; and placer mining remained dominant. But the wheel was turning. Quartz mining required technical expertness for success; and, as it had failed at first for lack of good machinery, experienced technicians, and sound business managers, so in the later fifties it began to revive when these were applied. In Grass Valley in 1856 several rich veins were developed, one yielding more than $400 a ton.[31] Better machinery was landed at San Francisco and Sacramento to be carried into the interior. A convention of quartz operators met at Sacramento in June, 1857, to draw up a code of regulations and to set forth the attractions of their mines to eastern capital.[32] These men believed the "science" of extracting rockbound gold would quickly advance and would make their method supreme. Early mills had been worked by horses or mules attached to an abrasive apparatus, an arrastre or "raster"; later mills were run by steam or waterpower.[33] Butte City in 1856 boasted of a dam and overshot wheel which drove twelve heavy stamps. The Amador County *Sentinel* then predicted that ore-crushing establishments in California would soon employ more capital and labor than the woolen mills in any eastern State.[34] This faith in the future was well founded, for more than three hundred stamp-mills were busy by 1861. If the second half of the first billion of California's gold was furnished chiefly by hydraulic mining, the second billion came mainly from quartz.[35]

After 1858, indeed, the annual output of placer deposits diminished rapidly,

31 *National Intelligencer*, April 26, 1856.
32 *Ibid.*, July 16, 1857.
33 Borthwick, *Gold Hunters*, edited by Horace Kephart, 235, gives a description of the methods.
34 Quoted in *National Intelligencer*, January 19, 1856.
35 John W. Caughey, *Gold is the Cornerstone*, 266, 267. The San Francisco *Bulletin* in its annual review of mining operations for 1856 spoke of five water companies in Columbia County, with canals 27 to 60 miles in length, and capital of $250,000 to $550,000. Placer County had 24 canals. The value of all the canals and ditches in the State at the end of 1856 was placed at $11,000,000. Quoted in *National Intelligencer*, March 3, 1857. Cf. R. G. Cleland, *From Wilderness to Empire*, 255 ff.

falling to $24,000,000 in 1864, while the yield from hydraulic mining rose with spectacular speed, and quartz production increased steadily if slowly. A basic change in the economic pattern of mining ensued. The multitudinous adventurers who had made such places as Hangtown famous—the ravines for eight or ten miles about filled with diggers, the shorn hillsides strewn with buckets, picks, and "long toms," the village stores and gambling houses crowded each Sunday with boisterous young fellows eager for diversion after a week's toilsome isolation—gradually disappeared. Individual effort waned. A few hydraulic mines, and a number of small quartz crushers, were worked by a group of proprietary partners, but in general the corporation took control. The biggest quartz mines soon represented an investment of millions for shafts, railroads, batteries of stamps, and workers' houses. Frémont, who had in Mariposa an estate conservatively estimated to be worth ten millions, lost it to the greedy capitalists he called in to finance his work. Gravel mining also demanded larger amounts, until one twelve-hundred-and-fifty foot tunnel dug into Table Mountain in the middle fifties cost $80,000. Absentee owners, plant superintendents, and companies of wage-hands replaced the versatile and resourceful emigrants who had made immortal "the days of old, and the days of gold, and the days of '49."

Such, in fact, was the story of mining throughout the West. When silver and copper were found in the Gadsden Purchase, not individuals but mining corporations took control. By 1857, the Arizona Copper Mining Company, the Gila River Copper Mining Company, and the Sonora Exploring and Mining Company were busy in the region.[36] A survey of 1861 listed more than a dozen mining corporations in the Arizona country, of which the Santa Rita and the Sapori companies were capitalized at a million dollars each, and the Arizona Land and Mining Company at two millions. Most of this capital came from eastern cities. The sum thus far expended in developing the so-called Heintzelman Mine alone was $230,000.[37]

Colorado was found to be designed not for the creek-trotter but the capitalist. The influx of 1858–59 soon exhausted the limited gulch or surface washings. Attention was then turned to "blossom rock" or disintegrated quartz; the rich strikes of 1859 near Central City and other points, where men found beds of rotten quartz, nuggets, and gold scales, loosed a tremendous rush, with mining camps as feverish as those of California a decade earlier. Yet at the height of the furore Greeley, Villard, and Richardson in their public statement warned enthusiasts that "gold mining is a business which eminently requires of its votaries capital, experience, energy, endurance"—and this was manifestly true.

36 *National Intelligencer*, April 18, 1857.
37 Sylvester Mowry, *Arizona and Sonora, passim*.

Principal Early Mining Camps of the Colorado Rockies.

The storehouses of precious metals in the mountains were locked in stubbornly difficult receptacles, most of the gold being found in combination with copper and the silver with lead. Tunnels had to be driven deep into the mountains and heavy machinery installed to crush and smelt the ores. Colorado's future, until the day of irrigation and semi-arid farming, was mainly a mining future, and the mining of necessity fell into the hands of corporations.[38]

So it was in the Nevada country. The sensational gold and silver discoveries there in 1859 brought a torrent of Californians pouring eastward through the Sierra passes, all bound for the barren flank of Davidson Mountain a mile and a half above sea level. Four thousand reached the district before snow choked the trails, and ten thousand more poured in during 1860. The fortunate few who staked claims on the Comstock and other paying lodes shipped out gold and silver in incredible quantities. Excited prospectors checkered the districts about Washoe with claims and camps, naming their chief settlement Virginia City. Several amazing strikes were made in the Esmeralda Mountains to the south and the Humboldt Mountains to the northeast.

Everywhere, however, loose surface deposits were quickly swept up, and the extraction of the gold from the deep quartz veins required organization, money, and science. The formation of companies, drafting of incorporation papers, and peddling of shares became a brisk industry. While nobody would call such fabulous adventurers of the Comstock Lode as William Sharon, James G. Fair, and John W. Mackay anything but individualists, they were less representative of the development of Nevada than the banker William Ralston, owner of mines, mills, steamships, and politicians, or the tunnel builder Adolph Sutro. Capital flowed in from San Francisco and the East to build roads, erect quartz mills, and sink shafts. Within a few years, Virginia City, boasting newspapers, schools, churches, banks, fine mansions, and theatres, was an opulent backdrop for the exploits of Mark Twain, Artemus Ward, Adah Isaacs Menken, and William M. Stewart. In 1863, the Gould & Curry Mine, crushing daily $8,000 to $10,000 worth of ore, had two thousand people on its payroll.

[V]

In short, western mining quickly became a field for big business, and so did transportation, lumbering, and some forms of agriculture. The successive frontiers east of the Missouri had all been, in overwhelming degree, farmers' frontiers; the frontiers west of that river were to be more varied—the miners' frontier, the lumbermen's frontier, the ranchers' and sheep-herders' frontier, the bonanza-farmers' frontier. For half a dozen reasons, united planning and capital

38 Bayard Taylor, *Colorado* (1887), Chs. 7, 8, 9.

counted for more, and individual effort for less, than in the trans-Missouri region.

First, the scale of the land was greater; transportation, a key factor, required more organization and a larger investment.

Second, the surface mineral wealth so quickly garnered in California, Colorado, and Nevada, created towns and cities, with accumulations of capital, almost overnight. Tremendous social power, such as once required decades to create, was generated within a few years. One early arrival in San Francisco was shocked by what he called "the high pressure principle" in evidence everywhere; another wrote that he found everything on a monstrous and perverted scale. As the California historian Hittell remarks: "It seemed impossible that a wealth greater than that of the Indies should flow through such a narrow channel; that such prodigious power should be confined in . . . such an awkward, shambling city." [39]

In the third place, as soon as the loose surface wealth was skimmed off, the remaining riches of the land were found in more refractory form than in the East. Mining required more machinery, lumbering larger sawmills and longer transportation, cattle-raising larger acreages, than in the past.

As a fourth consideration, farming on the great plains and in the San Joaquin Valley faced entirely new conditions; fencing, water-supply, defense, and the processes of seeding, cultivation, and harvesting demanded new inventions (barbed wire, windmills, light rapid-fire weapons, and improved farm machinery) which in many instances meant a heavy outlay.

In the fifth place, labor was costlier in the Far West than it had been on the other frontiers, and the demand for labor-saving machinery was proportionately strong.

Finally, the industrial revolution had now advanced further in America, and improved transportation and communication brought it closer to the frontier. Quite apart from the need for such essential products as mining tools, windmills, and harvesters, the taste of Westerners demanded many of the comforts and conveniences which industrialism was producing. The bales and boxes of merchandise that crowded the Kansas City or San Francisco wharves represented a higher standard of living than the old-time eastern pioneers had known, and one which the population of the trans-Missouri area was determined to maintain.

The romance of the covered wagon with the pioneer family inside can hardly be celebrated too often. But an equally romantic story might be written upon the adventures of a stamp-mill, manufactured in New York, sent around

39 James L. Tyson, *Diary of a Physician,* 51; *Golden Dreams and Leaden Realities,* 74, 75; Hittell, *California,* III, 347.

Cape Horn, uncrated at Sacramento, laboriously carted into some remote mountain valley, and painfully assembled beside a shaft. Nor was it long before good stamp-mills were being manufactured in California. The exploits of the cowboy will never pall. But what of the exploits of a man like T. V. Smith—an enterprising artisan who migrated from Baltimore to Oregon City in Washing Territory, established himself as foundryman and engine-builder, and in 1853 constructed an iron steamboat, *Belle of Oregon City*, which was wholly an Oregon product from the plates of her ninety-foot hull to her boilers and walking-beam engines? The small farmer of Kansas or Nebraska was often a heroic figure. But so were the lumbermen of Oregon and Washington who, cutting cargoes of spars and boards, sold them during the decade to California, the Mexican coast, Hawaii, and China. Indeed, the most lucrative occupation of Puget Sound settlers was lumbering, a type of enterprise requiring considerable capital. By 1858, nineteen sawmills on the Sound had a combined capacity of more than two hundred thirty thousand feet of lumber daily, the two largest steam mills, at Teekalet and Port Madison, producing seventy-five thousand feet a day. The Teekalet establishment, hiring about one hundred and fifty men at $2 to $4 a day with board included, did a general mercantile business and carried a stock of goods worth from $15,000 to $25,000.[40]

Bold men were laying the foundations of large-scale ranching in various parts of the West long before 1860. We have noticed the early cattle drives from Texas to the upper Mississippi between Quincy and Rock Island, and before the war the Morgan steamship line was cramming cattle into its vessels plying from Galveston to New Orleans and Mobile. Some shiploads were even sold in Cuba for the plantations.[41] On the northern plains the western migration quickly created a few large herds. A cattleman near Fort Hall had six hundred head in 1856; and three years later Horace Greeley encountered in the Wyoming country another, whose steers, horses, and other property were worth $75,000. In Washington Territory, one Ben Snipes was in a position to sell cattle to the miners of British Columbia during the Fraser River rush at $100 a head, giving him the money on which he later amassed three large ranches and a hundred thousand beeves. Other bold men were laying the foundations of great timber fortunes. Philetus Sawyer, destined to be a powerful Wisconsin magnate, joined some partners in 1853 in purchasing a sawmill at Fond du Lac, while the elder Weyerhaeuser seized his opportunity after the panic of 1857 to take over, in conjunction with his brother-in-law, the Rock Island Lumber Company of Illinois.[42]

40 *Cong. Globe*, 35th Cong., 2nd Sess., App., 210, 211; San Francisco correspondence in N. Y. *Weekly Tribune*, November 27, 1858.
41 Osgood, *The Day of the Cattleman*, 26, 27.
42 Greeley, *Overland Journey*, 195; Washington Department of Social Security, *Told by the Pioneers*, 155, 195, 211, etc.; R. S. Lillard, *The Great American Forest*, 180 ff., 197 ff.

Capital, in fact, found fertile fields in a hundred directions: in forming the San Francisco Gas Company to light the Western metropolis after 1854 with coal gas; in bringing cargoes of oysters and other shellfish from Puget Sound to Pacific Coast ports; in a huge business of freighting and supply for Indian-fighting troops; in Sacramento's thriving manufactories of California saddles, carriages, and wagons; in the production of California wine and Oregon cider; in the newspapers that sprang up everywhere—Kansas listing thirteen pros-perous sheets by the spring of 1858; [43] and indeed, in everything from theatrical troupes to cemetery companies. Congress in 1858 authorized the publication of a digest of manufacturing statistics. As presented soon afterward, the report showed that California on June 1, 1856, had more than a thousand manufac-turing establishments, employing almost four thousand hands, and with an annual product worth almost fourteen millions. Her manufactures were already of greater value than those of any Southern (not border) State except Vir-ginia. Even Oregon had fifty-two manufacturing establishments with an annual production much greater than those of Texas, and not far below Mississippi's; even Utah and New Mexico had together thirty-seven manufactories. [44]

Was Minnesota exclusively agricultural? "Two years ago," wrote her first commissioner of statistics in 1860, "Minnesota imported flour to supply the deficiencies in her own product. She has now probably one hundred and forty grist mills." Some of these mills were large, their shipments were growing, and the quality of the flour rivaled the best eastern brands. The new State had plough factories, whiskey distilleries, and breweries. On the St. Croix alone, twenty sawmills cut nearly seventy-five million feet of lumber. The commis-sioner included a section on the beneficial results of the panic of 1857. Chief of these, stemming in part from a reduction of prices and interest rates and from the stoppage of useless speculation in town lots, was an increase in the active capital of the region. As living costs had declined, the relative profits of industry had increased. [45] And was Utah exclusively agricultural? In the Christmas Day edition of the Deseret News in 1852 Brigham Young had writ-ten of new pottery and leather works, of an iron industry getting under way in Iron County, of a woolen mill already running, and of plans for a sugar factory. Sugar-making machinery was bought by the Deseret Manufacturing Company in England, landed in New Orleans, and sent by steamboat to Leav-enworth. There it was loaded on fifty special wagons drawn by two hundred yoke of oxen. Though five months were needed to drag the equipment to Salt

43 N. Y. Herald, April 25, 1858. The Portland Oregonian was begun December 4, 1850.
44 For the remarkable water-power development of the fifties in Wisconsin, operating grist mills, sawmills, a sash and door works, and an ironworks, see Joseph Schaefer, Wisconsin Magazine of History, December, 1934. The Sacramento Union for July, 1858, has a series of articles on manufacturing in that city.
45 Report, Chs. 8, 12.

Lake City, before the end of 1853 the factory was ready. Beet-sugar making, at first a failure, became eventually a basic industry of Utah.[46]

Above all, the West required transportation. Even California by the end of 1861 had built three hundred and forty-three miles of railroad, a good deal more than Illinois had possessed ten years earlier. The Pacific Mail Steamship Company had been organized in 1847-48 with an outlook that many businessmen thought dubious. Could its steamers find an adequate annual traffic? While the first, the *California*, was on her way to the West Coast, full news of the gold discoveries arrived. The vessel had no sooner reached Panama going northward than she found a clamorous multitude of gold-seekers waiting to get aboard; and the *Oregon* and *Panama*, following her, were equally crowded. The service had to be rapidly expanded. Late in the fifties, the ships *Adriatic*, *Atlantic*, and *Baltic* of the Collins Line, bought jointly by the Pacific Mail and the Panama Railroad from Brown Brothers & Co., were used to establish a line between New York and the Isthmus. As Brown Brothers took payment in Pacific Mail stock, the company secured the backing of one of the strongest banking houses in the country. Its capital was increased to four millions in 1860. By that date it was a political as well as commercial power, looking forward to the opening of a rich trade with the Orient.[47]

Western river steamboating on the Sacramento, Columbia, and lesser streams was another field for enterprise and investment. Here were conditions far different from those of the slow-rolling Mississippi and placid, well-settled Ohio. The Columbia in particular, fed by Canadian snows and the turbulent Snake and Salmon, offered a new setting for adventure: its majestic gorges, its white rapids and deep dark stretches, its thunderous falls and the solid green of its pines, inspired many rivermen with a lifelong passion. The angry conflicts of rival steamboat owners, the Indian uprisings, the lawlessness attendant on the abortive gold rushes into the upper valleys of the Snake and Clearwater, and the perils of flood and forest broke many a man; but the steamboat was indispensable to the rise of Portland, Dalles City, and other towns.[48]

One of the features of the industry was its tendency toward monopolistic practices. A combination of steamboat owners plying San Francisco Bay and the inland rivers organized early in 1854 the California Steam Navigation Company, which controlled passenger and freight business—despite many attempts to institute competition—for the ensuing fifteen years.[49] Its profits were nat-

46 Nels Anderson, *Desert Saints: the Mormon Frontier in Utah*, 135. The first California refinery was opened by the San Francisco & Pacific Sugar Company, with a capital of $800,000 in 1855. T. F. Cronise, *National Wealth of California*, 608.
47 F. N. Otis, *Isthmus of Panama and Its Commercial Connections*, 149 ff.
48 See the vivid novel by Nard Jones, *Swift Flows the River* (1940).
49 Hittell, *California*, III, 49, 426, 427; H. D. Hubbard, *Building the Heart of an Empire*.

urally enormous. During the eighteen-fifties, the Columbia River was the scene of strenuous activity by numerous small vessels. Then in 1860 the Oregon Steam Navigation Company, pooling a dozen steamboats, was established. Next year it carried some ten thousand five hundred passengers and nearly six thousand three hundred tons of freight between Portland and Dalles; and Indian wars and Idaho mining soon increased its business. It, too, long had a monopoly and made handsome profits—but service was good and its rates did not seem exorbitant.[50]

On the Missouri and its tributaries, as elsewhere, the great days of steam-boating lasted until the Civil War. As for the Mississippi, the traffic on the upper reaches of the river, sustained by immigrant travel, quite rivalled that on the lower. The number of steamboat arrivals at upper ports in 1860 almost equalled those of the lower Mississippi, Missouri, Ohio, Illinois, Tennessee, Cumberland and Arkansas rivers combined.[51]

When the whole story of the West is reviewed, much can be said for the thesis that after 1850 its fundamental conditions developed corporate activity on an equal footing with individual effort, and favored the capitalist rather more than the poor man. Mining, whether of iron, coal, copper, silver, gold, or lead, was most profitably carried on by well-financed companies. Railroad-building across the broad plains and into mountain fastnesses was impossible without capital resources, experienced technical skill, and astute business management. Government land policies gave the speculator a fertile opportunity. Ranching in the Southwest offered young Hotspurs a life in which they might find freedom and fortune; but even here the corporation could be a profitable device, as eastern and British capitalists would shortly recognize. The lands beyond the Missouri, full of untouched wealth, beckoned to the hardy farmer, cattleman, and prospector. They beckoned quite as vigorously to the mining-company organizer, town projector, lumber magnate, railroad entrepreneur, and manufacturer in primary industries.

[VI]

As Kansas moved toward statehood, as Oregon and Minnesota entered the Union, as Colorado and Nevada valleys filled with treasure-hunters, and as California in 1860 reached a population of nearly four hundred thousand, the problem of Western communications grew urgent. Until the end of the decade, the Pacific Railroad debate continued sterile. Four routes, examined in detail by expert Federal surveys, had been pronounced practicable. Each had its sedu-

---

50 Randall V. Mills, *Stern Wheelers up Columbia*, Ch. 4.
51 W. J. Peterson, *Steamboating on the Upper Mississippi 1823-1861*.

lous proponents, and but for sectional rivalry and the slavery issue agreement might easily have been reached on one or even two. The northernmost ran from St. Paul to Puget Sound, the southernmost from New Orleans along a line near the Thirty-second parallel to the Gila River and San Diego. Putting them both aside, Congress could well have fixed upon either the line from the Platte River by way of Great Salt Lake and the Humboldt Valley into California near the Forty-first parallel, or the line from Memphis and Fort Smith through Albuquerque to the coast near the Thirty-fifth parallel. But the lion of sectional jealousy stood in the way.

While men waited, mining discoveries helped to tip the balance. The Nevada gold rush threw a pier of population eastward from central California toward Salt Lake City. More importantly, the Pike's Peak fever threw another pier into central Colorado. The freight and passenger business with Denver-Auraria would obviously help any transcontinental line pay its way. Henry Villard wrote that the prime consequence of the Rocky Mountain rush of 1859 was its influence upon the choice of a railway and telegraph route. "The result of the mining season of 1860 in the Pike's Peak gold regions will definitely settle the long-mooted question of their location and construction. In less than twelve months, no sane mind will doubt the certainty that the first chain of iron and wire, that will render the circulation of the life-blood of our great Republic through the agricultural, industrial, and commercial systems of all its parts, possible and perfect, will be strung across that portion of the Rocky Mountains that has lately been found to abound in mineral wealth." [52]

Only lesser projects could as yet be pushed to fruition, but several were spectacular. Wagon roads became more and more important. The Santa Fé Trail and Oregon Trail, with various alternatives and cut-offs, grew into busy highways. Freighting firms sprang into existence. The largest—Russell, Majors & Waddell—was from 1855 to the Civil War perhaps the most important single business agency in the trans-Missouri West. It sprang to greatness when the government awarded the partners contract after contract for transporting military supplies. Thus, early in 1855, they gained a two-year monopoly of carrying all such stores beyond the Missouri, built offices, warehouses, and shops at Leavenworth, opened a sawmill, lumberyard, and meat-packing plant, and hired a small army of employees. By summer they had five hundred wagons (which alone represented an investment of nearly $400,000), with seven thousand five hundred oxen, and one thousand seven hundred workers. A renewal

---

[52] Villard, *Past and Present of the Pike's Peak Gold Regions*, 147. This statement may be regarded as part of a well-planned propaganda campaign. Actually, when the first transcontinental was built it passed a hundred miles north of Denver, through Cheyenne; though Denver leaders quickly constructed a line connecting with the Union Pacific (1870). See Herbert O. Brayer, "History of Colorado Railroads," in L. R. Hafen, ed., *Colorado*, II.

of the contract early in 1857 gave them a monopoly on the carriage of up to five million pounds of military goods that year. Then, when the expedition against the Mormons took shape, the military authorities served notice that they would have to carry three million extra pounds of supplies to Utah. This was a low estimate. When the army left for Utah, forty-one trains (normally twenty-six wagons each) were scheduled to accompany it with more than four and a half million pounds of supplies.[53]

By 1858 the firm employed four thousand men, and used forty thousand oxen in hauling its three thousand five hundred covered wagons. Army posts, mining camps, and trappers were all dependent on its exertions. The light, strong vehicles, made of white oak, iron-tired, and covered with white osnaburg stretched over hickory bows, could carry five thousand pounds over rough country. Regulations for the bull-whackers stated bluntly (and the rule was enforced), "Swearing, gambling, and intemperance will not be allowed, either in camp or on the plains." Trains moved on a rigid time schedule. Sabbath was observed. At nightfall the wagons formed a circular corral, within which the oxen were turned loose. It is not strange that the "empire on wheels" which Russell, Majors & Waddell built up was treated with great respect. The notes and drafts of the firm were regarded as the equivalent of gold. In Missouri, Kansas, and Nebraska, farmers and stockmen blessed them for their purchases of cattle, hogs, grain, and other products. In every plains fort or mountain camp their wagons were hailed as indispensable to life and comfort. They made Lexington, their first depot, and Leavenworth and Kansas City, their subsequent eastern headquarters, important centers of retail and wholesale trade. It was natural that when the Cherry Creek discoveries brought population flocking into Colorado, William H. Russell should organize (February, 1859) the Leavenworth & Pike's Peak Express Company, with a thousand Kentucky mules and fifty new Concord coaches to operate between the Missouri and Denver. His store and office in the new settlement were the most important business places in Colorado. Alas for the venture! When the surface gold was exhausted, traffic to and from the mountains sank below profitable levels, and as in their work for the army in Utah, the partners suffered heavy losses.

Other firms, while not comparing with Russell, Majors & Waddell, did useful transport service. In 1860, according to the *American Railway Times*, sixty-eight thousand oxen, eight thousand mules, six thousand nine hundred wagons, and about twelve thousand men were employed in freighting in the Far West.[54] Demand for a direct mail road to California, with enough way

53 M. L. and R. W. Settle, *Empire on Wheels*, 17 ff.
54 January 21, 1861.

stations to change horses frequently, became clamorous. Once more sectional jealousy arose. The South stood adamant against a central highway through South Pass as likely to draw the Pacific Railroad after it. A compromise had to be arranged, and Congress appropriated money for various bits of road-building. The War Department in 1858 pushed work on a military road from Fort Smith through Albuquerque to the Colorado, and, in connection with the Mormon operations, greatly improved the roads from Fort Bridger into central Utah. The Interior Department in 1859 completed a road from Fort Kearny through South Pass to Honey Lake, which emigrants found highly useful.[55]

One road survey involved a long-remembered experiment with camels. Lieutenant Edward F. Beale, a Mexican War veteran, was deputed to explore the ground for a wagon road from Albuquerque (Fort Defiance) due west, or nearly so, to California; and he decided to test the desert animal. The idea was an old one; Congress had sanctioned action, and a number of camels had been landed in Texas in 1856–57. Beale picked up twenty-odd camels, with three dromedaries, at San Antonio, loaded them with grain for mules, and covered the thousand miles and more to Albuquerque in forty-five days. Thence he set out (August 28, 1857) for the coast. His journey took him across grassy plains, along the bottom lands of the Little Colorado, over the forested San Francisco Mountain, and across the Colorado River, which the camels swam with ease. Traversing desert sands to the Mohave, and threading more mountains, they reached Los Angeles. Beale was enthusiastic. The camels, he reported, had walked unhurt over ground covered with sharp volcanic rocks, had borne heavy packs up precipitous stretches which unladen mules found difficult, and had carried water for a week at a time without swallowing a drop. They could live on herbage too coarse and scanty for mules, oxen, or horses.[56] In the end, however, most of the camels went to circuses and zoos.

Mail service to the West, too, could be improved. Californians had been glad since 1850 to get monthly mails by way of Independence and Santa Fé, or later through Independence, Salt Lake, and Placerville. They had also rejoiced in semi-monthly mails via Panama, Nicaragua, or Tehuantepec, and the signal gun announcing the mail steamer brought thousands flocking to the San Francisco wharves. During the Mormon War the Independence-Salt Lake-Placerville mail was put for a time on a weekly basis, and then reduced to semi-monthly status.[57] Meanwhile the hearts of Californians were brightened by the announcement of semi-weekly overland mails. At a late hour of the session which expired with Pierce's Administration, Congress provided $600,000

55 Report, Secretary of War, 1858; Report, Secretary of the Interior, 1859.
56 N. Y. *Tribune*, January 24, 1858; House Exec. Doc. 124, 35th Cong., 1st Sess.
57 Report, Postmaster-General, 1858.

The Pony Express, the Overland Mail and the Great Trails.

yearly for the carriage of high-speed mails from the Mississippi to San Francisco by coach in not more than twenty-five days.

Seven men comprising the Overland Mail Company, with John Butterfield as president and William G. Fargo a member—two of the leading expressmen of the country—were the successful bidders. The contract was signed September 16, 1857, and precisely one year later four-horse stages started simultaneously with pomp and ceremony from St. Louis and San Francisco. Postmaster-General Brown had persuaded Buchanan to accept an extreme southern route. From St. Louis (or rather Tipton) the coaches ran to Fort Smith, Arkansas, and thence southwest to Sherman and Gainesville in Texas, on to El Paso, up the Rio Grande and through the Gadsden Purchase to Tucson, along the Gila Valley and across the Colorado into Los Angeles.[58]

The enthusiasm which greeted the first mails in San Francisco was prodigious; at least so the New York *Herald* correspondent, the only passenger, reported. An artillery salute, a procession, and a public meeting with a vote of thanks to the government marked that tenth of October. The whole distance from St. Louis to San Francisco, two thousand seven hundred and thirty miles, was covered in half an hour under twenty-four days, while the mail moving the other way reached St. Louis on October 9 in just over twenty-three days. Only letter mail was regularly carried; the space for six passengers was not always filled, especially westbound. Indeed, as the stages ran day and night, as the line was poorly equipped with eating stations, and as Comanche hostility was feared, many preferred another mode of travel. Much Northern criticism was directed at the "oxbow route" as an obvious attempt to lay the foundation for a Southern Pacific railroad. Postmaster-General Brown was accused of choosing an indirect, perilous, and unduly expensive line, long stretches of it without water or hay, in the hope that the military guards, the station corrals, and the temptation to emigrants to accept the road would build up towns and give Southern railroad promoters an artificial advantage.[59] While such accusations were perhaps ungenerous, the oxbow detour did leave the more direct central route temptingly open to private enterprise.

58 Roscoe P. and Margaret B. Conkling, *The Butterfield Overland Mail, 1857–1869, passim.*
59 *Harper's Weekly*, December 11, 1858. The N. Y. *Tribune* held that the overland coach service should have been started much sooner. For ten years after the discovery of gold, it declared, about a million a year had been expended on transport of mails by the Isthmus. Had this money been spent on mail service by the most direct overland route, it would have developed a great natural highway across the continent, with settlements and stations. Groups of speculators, including men high in office, had been intent in squandering appropriations on the Panama, Nicaragua, Tehuantepec, and other routes; whereas from 1849 on, mails should have gone direct from St. Louis to San Francisco. Had this been done, a telegraph would have been laid, a safe wagon road constructed, and stages set running daily for two-thirds of the year. And how much would have been saved to the pioneers! Many men in Wisconsin and Illinois had travelled a thousand miles east before undertaking the seven thousand mile sea voyage. N. Y. *Weekly Tribune*, October 16, 1858.

The Overland Mail continued with almost clocklike regularity, its great Concord coaches, staunchly built and swung on leather thoroughbraces instead of springs, with four to six sturdy horses or mules to draw them, sometimes making a hundred miles in twenty-four hours. When winter came on, the El Paso-Tucson route unquestionably had its advantages. But men West and East were irritated by Postmaster-General Brown's assertion that the southern road was alone feasible for all-season travel. Californians doubted this; so did Kansans; and Senator Gwin found it easy to persuade William H. Russell to prove the practicability of the central route. The result was the launching of the Pony Express. In the hope of gaining a lucrative mail contract, Russell and his partners set to work, began hiring fleet horses, riders, and agents, and announced that on April 3, 1860, they would begin a fast service between St. Joseph, Missouri, and Sacramento. They were as good as their word. On the appointed day a rider in the Missouri town sprang into his saddle after the mayor had fastened to it a pouch with forty-nine letters and five telegrams. Amid wild cheers he galloped off to the westward, while far away in San Francisco another mail was started east.[60]

For the eighteen months that the Pony Express continued in operation it was an institution which touched the imagination of the American people. Stations were equipped at fifteen-mile intervals; some one hundred and fifty wiry Indian ponies were kept in readiness; hardy light-weight riders, in darkness or daylight, in storm or sunshine, in peace or amid hostile savages, covered each his stage of seventy-five miles. At first weekly, the service soon became semi-weekly. At every junction point, a fresh rider had just two minutes to fasten the mailbag to his saddle and be off. If a carrier failed to come through, his replacement pushed on empty-handed with the news, which was carried from point to point to the ultimate destination. Fort Kearny, Fort Laramie, South Pass, Fort Bridger, Salt Lake City—this part of the route kept close to the familiar Oregon and California Trail. Then from the southern end of Great Salt Lake the riders pushed through Fort Churchill, Carson City, and Placerville to Sacramento. Americans thrilled to learn of the speed records set. News of Lincoln's election was carried from Fort Kearny to Fort Churchill in six days. The dauntless determination of the riders to get the mail through impressed the nation.

[VII]

If in its practical aspects the Pony Express experiment left something to be desired (for it cost Russell, Majors & Waddell a ruinous sum, while no demon-

60 G. D. Bradley, *The Pony Express*; Leroy Hafen, *The Overland Mail, 1859-1869*.

stration of the feasibility of the central railroad route was needed), in its exemplification of the spirit of the expanding West it was a memorable undertaking. It expressed the enterprise that was converting so much of empty plain and savage mountain into populous and wealthy communities, and that within a dozen years after the peace with Mexico brought four rich trans-Mississippi States into the Union. It was saddening to turn from the boundless constructive energy shown in the West to the dreary quarrel over slavery; a quarrel which, in its failure to achieve any forward constructive steps, contrasted so markedly with the vigorous nation-building beyond the Missouri. And yet it was impossible to look at the West without seeing that its conditions threw light upon the sectional conflict.

For three salient facts stood out in any survey of the Far West. First, this land of plain and peak was natural soil for a free-spirited and highly competitive society, demanding of every resident skill and intelligence. It was, therefore, even in that Gadsden Purchase country which had been bought at the behest of the slave States, a country naturally inhospitable to slavery. Second, when so much energy was steadily flowing into western expansion, and such wide outlets for more effort existed there, it was impossible to think of the country turning to Caribbean areas for a heavy thrust southward. Its main forces moved naturally toward the sunset, where rich opportunities were hardly yet sampled. The cotton kingdom, which realized that the West gave little scope for its peculiar culture, might plan grandiose Latin American adventures; but it would get little support from other regions. And in the third place, conditions in the West demanded capital and organization on a broad scale; if it was a land for individualists, it was even more a land for corporate enterprise—a land for the businessman. Those who pondered these three facts could see that they held an ominous meaning for the South. The nearer Northwest had already done much to upset the old sectional balance, and the Far West, as it filled up, would do still more. Here was a population fronting the future:

Fresh and strong the world we seize, world of labor and the march.

13

Douglas Under Challenge

EARLY IN August of 1858 Americans felt a thrill of pride to learn of the latest triumph of their inventive genius, the laying of the Atlantic cable. An American and a British warship, the *Niagara* and the *Agamemnon*, had met in mid-ocean the previous month. After dividing the huge coils, they had proceeded in opposite directions; and one end was soon ashore in Newfoundland, the other in Ireland. While there was credit enough for both nations, the inventor Morse and the indomitable organizer Cyrus W. Field deserved special honor. Surely, wrote Benjamin Moran of the American legation in London, "those who accomplished the work of uniting at a throb people divided three thousand miles by ocean have done more for mankind than Alexander and Napoleon." On August 16, President Buchanan and Queen Victoria exchanged congratulations. Alas, service was soon interrupted—but men knew that human ingenuity would shortly perfect this abbreviation of time and space.

This peaceable achievement was the more welcome because, but three months earlier, the United States and Britain had seemed uncomfortably near a breach of relations. British vessels in the Caribbean, commanded by officers excessively eager to stop the slaving business, had begun to board and search vessels flying the stars and stripes. "These aggressions are intolerable," Seward had told the Senate on May 17. "Already eleven vessels have been fired upon in the Gulf of Mexico." Toombs and Stephens, incensed by the first reports, had gone to the White House and urged Buchanan to send a squadron to hunt down the British offenders and seize or sink them. The President, keeping quite cool, had said that he would ask for reparations and then act if they were denied. "Let England have the onus of asking explanations," exclaimed Stephens. "Our flag is insulted and it ought to be resented on the spot. . . . This is the time to act." He and Toombs, staying until near midnight, had made it clear that they actually wanted a war with England. Stephens believed that such a war would stop the sectional quarrel—as Seward was to believe in 1861. "I thought it the most fortunate thing that could have happened to unite the heart of the entire people of the United States and to put down all sectional parties," he wrote his brother Linton. But Buchanan had wisely insisted on a peaceful course, and had easily achieved a complete victory, Lord Malmesbury at the Foreign Office assuring the United States that Great Britain accepted all the principles laid down in the American protest.

The President was able to leave for a short vacation at Bedford Springs without fear of foreign embroilments. Senator Seward, returning to his beloved Auburn, meanwhile diverted central New York by entertaining Lord and Lady Napier and Count Sartiges there, while Jefferson Davis, his health impaired, pleased New Englanders by sojourning amid the cool Maine breezes.

Surely the country, with prosperity returning and the foreign skies clear, could sit down in hope and serenity. Farsighted men, unfortunately, did not think so. They knew that without some change in the spirit of both North and South, the lull was but a truce. Slavery and freesoil, Governor Adams of South Carolina had said, can never be reconciled. We must separate, Edmund Ruffin kept writing his friends—and the sooner we do it the greater the relative weight of the South. Garrison, Theodore Parker, and Wendell Phillips were publicly stating that a bloody termination of the struggle was at hand.[1]

In view of all the trends of nineteenth century civilization, the terrible problem of slavery could be given a final solution only upon the principle which Washington, Jefferson, and Clay had espoused: the principle of gradual emancipation. Obviously, this settlement could not be reached at one stride. It must be achieved by degrees. The first step was to stop the expansion of slavery, and to confine that institution within the fifteen States it already possessed. Such a decision would be equivalent to a decree that slavery was marked for gradual evolution into a higher labor system. Slavery contained would be slavery under sentence of slow death. The second step would be the termination of slavery in the border States. Missouri by 1859 stood near the verge of emancipation. Every advance in the industrialization of the State, every wave of German, British, and eastern immigrants, brought the step nearer. Delaware should soon be a free State. Kentucky had a strong body of ultimate emancipationists. Once the number of slave States was reduced to twelve, and that of the free States proportionately augmented, the fate of slavery would be clear.

The great hope was that if the South could be educated to accept the principle of friendly containment, it would be willing to consider plans for gradual compensated emancipation. When it was ready to entertain such plans, surely a Northern party would arise to offer them. Webster's proposal for using the entire proceeds of the public lands; Clay's hope that emancipation might be

1 N. Y. *Tribune*, September 22, 1858; J. H. Adams, Message No. 1, November 24, 1856; Garrison, *William Lloyd Garrison*, III, Chs. 14-18. For Stephens's course above, see his letters to Linton Stephens, June 1, June 10, 1858; Stephens Papers, Manhattanville.

combined with some measure of colonization abroad; Olmsted's plan for letting the best-equipped Negroes earn their freedom; the Stafford House suggestion that the South educate the Negroes, sanction marriages, and protect slave families——all had elements of statesmanship. Most Northern Democrats would be willing to support a constructive scheme; such moderate Republicans as Hamilton Fish, Lyman Trumbull, Edward Bates, and Abraham Lincoln would certainly do so. But would the South ever ask for aid in giving its peculiar institution a progressive character?

Two groups were aligned against this hopeful possibility that slavery might first be immobilized, then subjected to attrition at the margin, and finally helped by money and migration to evolve into a free labor system. They stood at opposite poles.

One group was the abolitionists and radical Republicans, who wished emancipation attained in a hurry—and many of whom, men of malicious temper, wanted to hurt the South. They thought that the Negro could step from slavery to equality as a man steps from a dungeon into a bright parlor. They did not realize what a dim maze of corridors, anterooms, and halfway apartments lay between. Ever since Birney and Garrison began their intemperate crusade, the abolitionists had accepted a fearful responsibility before history. Now Garrison, Phillips, Higginson, and Theodore Parker seemed positively exulting in talk of disruption, battle, and bloodshed. These men neither knew nor cared anything about the vital question of race adjustment. To most of them it did not exist. The black man, once emancipated, would almost instantly become in all but color a white man; so the *Liberator* and *Independent* implied.

The other group were the Southern extremists, the fire-eaters represented by Yancey, Keitt, Rhett, Porcher Miles, A. G. Brown, Slidell, and Jacob Thompson —a group every month more numerous and influential. They were strongest where Negro population was densest; not so much because slavery was most profitable there as because the problem of race adjustment was most difficult and Negro subordination seemed most imperative. These two groups of extremists were reinforced by politicians whipping up fear and prejudice for votes, editors mongering hate for subscriptions, and millions of devotees of Drift.

The tragic fact was that extremists always possessed the power to catch up the ball and carry it into scrimmage. When the Kansas ball failed, some other would do. Garrison at Framingham on July 4, 1854, burning the Constitution and exclaiming, "So perish all compromises with tyranny!"—Wendell Phillips writing that the Union must sever, and "It is now with nine-tenths only a question of time"—were apparently harmless except to irritate. But John Brown was to give violent application to their preachments upon blood. If the development of the West proved anything, it was that American capital and energy found such broad fields for activity there that Caribbean adventures seemed preposterous. Yet Southern extremists demanded Caribbean grabs and forays. If the growth of the West proved another fact, it was that free institutions must dominate the Terrories of the region and that slavery could never take root in them. Yet the Charleston *News* and Richmond *Enquirer* were raising the sinister demand for a Federal slave code in the Territories and declaring that it must be made the issue in 1860.

Congressional debates had done little to turn men's minds toward a constructive solution. If hope for reason, common sense, and imagination existed anywhere, it was in the Northwest, with its mingled Southern and Northern stocks, practical temper, divorcement from fettering traditions, and idealism. On the prairies of Illinois this summer, a resounding debate on national issues was to take place. Would it point to some road out of the labyrinth, away from the youth-devouring Minotaur of civil war?

[I]

The Douglas of 1858 was a different man from the Douglas who had visited Europe in 1853 to shake off his grief over the death of his first wife. Since in personal affairs he was reticent, writing few letters and confining them to politics and business, we know little of his inner life. But it is evident that his bereavement had been a heavy blow, throwing him for a time into dissipated ways; evident also that his love for Adèle Cutts was an elevating influence and that his marriage restored a lost harmony to his existence. His ambition had been at low ebb in 1855–56; it reawakened when in 1857 he found his wife ready to dispute with Harriet Lane the social primacy of Washington.

His political experience during these years, too, had done much to mature him. With him, the line between rapid decision and recklessness was thin; he had crossed it in 1854, and from the ensuing storm he had emerged with a deeper respect for the convictions of the people of Illinois. Fighting heavy battles in the Senate and on the prairies, he had gained education from the blows he took. If his ambition was to be gratified, he could not flout the sentiment of the growing body of freesoil Democrats in the North.

Above all, Douglas had found his experience with the Southern Democrats a maturing and disillusioning process. How confident he had been in 1854 of a mutually profitable partnership—how sanguine two years later of a friendly alliance—how nonplussed to find Buchanan taken prisoner by Cobb, Thompson, and Slidell—how shocked to discover behind the Lecompton imposture a game of rule or ruin!

Still a young man, only forty-five in the spring of 1858, still using his gifts to educate himself, the Chicagoan was steadily becoming less of a politician and more of a statesman. He had always had a statesmanlike eye to large objects. Only two weeks after he had obtained his license to practice law in Jacksonville, Illinois, he had risen before a large Democratic meeting to fling forth his defense of Jacksonian principles: government by the people, and the expanding role of the republic. The enthusiasm had been intense. He had spoken with heat, and he awoke next day to find himself famous in his prairie world. From these first-enunciated principles he had never deviated. Popular government and national expansion had remained his Arcturus and Aldebaran. He instinctively trusted the people he saw about him. And why not? Some of them were Yankees like himself, some were Southerners, and many were from the Middle States, but they made up a folk of hard sense and sturdy character. The Illinoisans were a self-reliant, honest-minded stock which in one generation developed Lincoln, Douglas, Grant, Trumbull, Yates, Koerner, McCormick, Ogden, Logan, Medill, and David Davis—a proud record for a raw new State.

Let the voice of the people rule! Douglas had never believed that less than the boundless continent could suffice as a theater for American energies. Opposing settlement with England on the Forty-ninth parallel, opposing Trist's peace with Mexico, opposing the pledge in the Clayton-Bulwer Treaty never to annex or colonize any part of Central America, incessantly calling for an honorable acquisition of Cuba, he had made it plain that he wished to see all North America under the starry banner. Make new Territories, carry the flag forward, build railroads, improve harbors, homestead the land, preserve liberty, free the Western Hemisphere from the Old World, and trust to the people—this was his national plan.

As he grew older, he thought less of expediency and more of principle. Looking back, he could see that his championship of the Compromise of 1850 had been based on principle—and it had been a resounding success; his championship of Kansas-Nebraska had been based on expediency—and it was a many-sided failure. Undoubtedly this strengthened his instinctive feeling that principle, in the long run, paid. Yet he was also becoming devoted to principle for its own sake. Some opponents declared that he had fought Lecompton because he saw that otherwise he could never be reelected to the Senate. They did Douglas an injustice. Too powerful to be downed by one blow, he did not overvalue his Senate seat. What he did value was his honor; and Lecompton dishonored the basic doctrine of his political faith—popular sovereignty. He was now showing an increasing adherence to the Jacksonian principle of the Union. As secession lifted its head among Southern extremists, he was to stab and hack at what he considered a dangerous monster.

By the late spring of 1858, he could feel that as a champion of honesty and democratic principle he had won a memorable triumph over the Directory. The Lecompton constitution was as dead as the Yazoo Fraud. His victory was a moral triumph not the less sweet because it was his first thoroughly creditable success since, in the fall of 1850, he had forced the Chicago city council to turn about-face on the Compromise.

But what of the Democratic future? The party had won the narrowest of victories in 1856 when fully united. With Republican strength rising and with the last vestiges of the Whig and American parties slowly disappearing, the Democrats faced certain defeat in 1860 unless they healed their schism. Unfortunately for the party, Douglas and the Administration regarded the problem of unity from divergent standpoints. To Douglas, reconciliation on the basis of popular sovereignty and expansion seemed logical. Let him return to the Senate for six years, let old quarrels be forgotten, and let the party march forward under the banners of Manifest Destiny so popular with most Southerners, and popular control over local institutions so dear to Northern Democrats. To Buchanan and the Directory, however, discipline was the watchword. The Washington *Union* laid down the doctrine that every Democrat must acquiesce in party decisions on great questions, such as the Bank of the United States under Jackson, Texas under Polk, and Lecompton and the English bill under Buchanan.[2] The way to restore the unity of the party was to purge it of traitors and to crush all ideas conflicting with the Dred Scott decision.

The divergence was ineluctable and vital. Douglas had to stick by his principles, not only because they were his breath of life, but because if he did not, half the Northern Democrats would desert to the Republican banner. Cobb, Thompson, Floyd, and Slidell, controlling the President, could not yield to Douglas because that would make him master of the party and logical candidate for 1860; because, too, his type of popular sovereignty meant the containment of slavery, so far as existing American territory went, just as surely as the Republican platform meant it. The breach was unavoidable.

As always in such affairs, personal antipathies deeply tinged the quarrel. Buchanan knew that Douglas regarded him with contempt; Cobb, Thompson, and Floyd knew that Douglas thought them potential traitors. For his part, the Illinoisan was aware that aloof Southern leaders mistook him for a bumptious, ill-mannered upstart. Their talk of him as a recusant, a Benedict Arnold, rankled in his mind. If Jefferson Davis or R. M. T. Hunter could get elected to the Presidency, either man would give Douglas and his friends short shrift. If Douglas were elected, everyone knew that he would make an imperious, self-willed President, that he would fight disunion as Jackson had fought it, and that while he might favor Wise, Stephens, Breckinridge, and a few others who had treated

2 September 1, 1858.

him fairly, the Southerners about Buchanan would walk the plank without mercy. Senator Green of Missouri wrote a friend that Slidell had burned during the winter of 1857–58 to drive Douglas from the party, and that "the Slidell clique" controlled Buchanan and the Senate caucus.[3]

Meanwhile, Douglas had to think of his own seat and his own State, where political war was raging. It was the Directory which had begun the war. It did not have any really compelling reason to oppose his reelection by the Illinois legislature, which would be chosen in the fall and would select a Senator the ensuing January; yet all spring it had been busy trying to undermine him.[4]

The Administration adherents in Illinois, nearly all men presently or prospectively fed from the public crib, were a crew that Douglas detested. Chief among them was Isaac Cook, postmaster of Chicago, who dispensed postmasterships, mail contracts, and postal advertising for political effect, kept in close touch with Washington, and wrote frequently to Buchanan. We have mentioned his associate (and later rival), Charles Leib, Federal mail agent for the State, whose talent for intrigue roused Douglas's special scorn. Leib, a jack of many trades, sometime doctor, lawyer, liquor dealer, Mormon, and an adherent of Jim Lane in Kansas, was a Dugald Dalgetty of politics; Douglas knew that he had been busy for months helping organize the Buchanan machine, getting perquisites for his friends, and making furtive approaches to Republicans for an alliance against the Senator. The notorious John Calhoun, revisiting Springfield, lent the Buchanan men his hand, and so did lesser figures—ex-Governor John Reynolds, John Dougherty, and R. B. Carpenter, who handled large Federal building contracts. These *condottieri* had labored like mad, tempting local politicians with petty offices, trying to buy country editors with printing contracts, and putting every jobholder to work.[5]

They had done him some harm, Douglas knew; but none that he did not feel confident of repairing. The main body of Democrats, especially outside of "Egypt," had remained loyal to the Senator. When the State convention met in Springfield on April 21, just as the English bill was being whipped into shape,

3 Green's letter of September 29, 1858, to Judge Samuel Treat, throws light on the plot. He describes how Slidell had frequently reproached him the previous winter and spring for not joining the movement to oust Douglas. Slidell, Cobb, and Bright, he writes, were leagued together for the purpose. Representative Harris of Illinois had been informed in May that Floyd wanted peace because he feared the Douglas Democrats would join in the Republican hue and cry over his incapacity (or worse) in sale of army property at Fort Snelling and Wills Point. He heard too that Toucey and Black, who knew Northern sentiment, were for peace. "But Brown, Cobb, Thompson, and 'Old Obliquity' are for war." He added for the Douglas bloc in Congress: "We are quite indifferent which is chosen, and so tell them." As it would be stupid of the Administration to levy war, he expected them to do it. Green's letter is in the Treat Papers; that of Harris (May 8, 1858) in the Lanphier Papers.

4 For its course see H. S. Foote, *Casket of Reminiscences*, 135.

5 *Cong. Globe*, 35th Cong., 1st Sess., 3055–3058.

nine-tenths of the delegates were for Douglas. The Buchanan men, jeered and denounced, had fled from the hall. Peter Cartwright, roaring like a backwoods exhorter, had choken with the anger of his invective against the Administration tools. John A. McClernand, about to reenter Congress, had been made chairman of the platform committee, and his planks that upheld Douglas, the five anti-Lecompton Representives, and the popular sovereignty cause were carried with a shout. Amid unfeigned enthusiasm, the Senator had been renominated—and of the fifty-nine Democratic newspapers of the State, fifty-five had come down like an avalanche on his side.[6]

This had been a heartening event; and there had been nothing in subsequent Buchananite maneuvering in Illinois to alarm Douglas. To be sure, from the moment the Senator voted against the English bill early in May, Buchanan's weakly resentful attitude had been fixed. He had thought the Senator's course ruinous both to party and country. Had the measure been defeated, he wrote, the country would have been left in a terrible condition; national integrity would have been shaken to its center.[7] The Washington *Union*, in a broadside on May 27, had announced that the Administration would regard Douglas as an outcast.

Perhaps one element in fanning the anger of the Directory was a spiteful story which a Missouri politician, Isaac Sturgeon, a Treasury official in St. Louis, had sent to Washington on May 5. He asserted, with circumstantial detail, that Douglas had assured Frank P. Blair, Jr., that he intended to join the Republicans in 1860. The story was absurd. Douglas meant to bend the Democratic Party to his principles, not abandon it; and the loquacious, bibulous Blair was noted for his ability to garble facts. Nevertheless, gossip regarding this alleged engagement soon filled Washington and Illinois. All summer and fall the question was to be hurled at Douglas: "What about your promise to Blair?" The *Union* charged that he was playing the same part in trying to hamstring the Democratic Party that Van Buren had played in 1848; and during June the tokens of Administration implacability had increased.

Douglas knew that the Administration—through Cobb, Thompson, and Brown—had pulled the strings for the Punch-and-Judy convention of National Democrats which, representing about half the counties of Illinois, met in Springfield on June 9 to organize an opposition. A full ticket for State offices had been nominated. John Dougherty, selected for State Treasurer, had told Lincoln that the Buchanan forces would run a man for every office in every county and district. "If you do this, the thing is settled—the battle is fought," exclaimed Lincoln. The clear evidence that some Buchanan men and some Republican

6 *Fulton Democrat* (Lewiston, Illinois) March-April, 1858.
7 July 31, 1858; Buchanan, *Works*, X, 224–225.

leaders were plotting to exchange advice, labor, and even votes, gave point to a bitter invective which Douglas uttered against Cook, Leib, and their aides just before Congress adjourned. What was this June convention of dissenters? he asked. The true Democratic Convention had been held in April. The cheap Federal placeholder Leib had been touring the State to say that the Administration authorized him to denounce every Democrat who had opposed Lecompton as false to his party. False to his party! Yet this agent Leib had been a member of Jim Lane's reckless Republican gang in Kansas, had done his best there to defeat the Democrats, and had embraced Buchanan's cause only when paid for his dirty work. By assiduous effort, said Douglas, he and his fellow conspirators, after having been voted down twenty to one, had gotten up their convention of jobholders and lickspittles. Their aim was to split the Democratic vote and throw the next Illinois legislature to the Republicans.

Douglas, journeying homeward as the summer of 1858 began, was sanguine that he could prevent this calamity. With all his latent pugnacity aroused, he was prepared to fight desperately for return to the Senate—for popular vindication. Heavy expenses had to be met: travel, campaign quarters, posters, pamphlets, fireworks, marching-clubs' regalia, newspaper advertisements, speakers. Though financially straitened, with many notes outstanding and little income but his salary, he plunged yet deeper into debt. He mortgaged his Illinois property for $100,000, of which $40,000 went to discharge maturing debts, and the rest was for immediate use; according to some reports, he sold his Washington house; he borrowed $13,147 from a friend.[8] At the same time, he mustered all his energies. His health had suffered from the incessant anxieties and exertions of the past four years, from late hours, from occasional drinking, and from neglect of exercise, so that repeatedly he had confessed to the Senate that he was ailing. Fessenden had said at the close of 1856 that he was a dying man unless he mended. While this was exaggeration, onlookers had been struck by his weary if undaunted look.[9] But his fame, his national power, his hope of the Presidency were all at stake, and he intended to sacrifice every dollar and every ounce of strength rather than fail.

The Little Giant's arrival in Chicago on July 9 was a memorable event. All along his route he had met ovations. In Buffalo, followers gathered at the station; in Cleveland they cheered him lustily, with Rhodes, Payne, and Vallandigham in the reception committee, and Governor Salmon P. Chase seeking him for

8 Springfield *Republican*, July 27, 1858; Milton, *Eve of Conflict*, 307. The lien on his Chicago estate in 1864 exceeded $64,000; Johnson, *Douglas*, 383. In the first five months of the Congressional session of 1857–58 Douglas franked out 198,600 copies of his speeches, nearly twice as many as any other Senator, and three times as many as Seward. At a cost of $20 a thousand, this meant a bill of about $4,000. N. Y. *Weekly Tribune*, May 22, 1858.

9 Horace White, *Lyman Trumbull*, 89.

a conference; Ohio, Indiana, and Michigan Democrats kept his car crowded. Mrs. Douglas, with her charming smile, enchanted everybody.

His Illinois supporters intended to outdo all rivals. Hiring a special train, four hundred delegates, representing nearly every county and accompanied by a brass band, climbed aboard to meet him at Michigan City, sixty miles to the east. Here a huge crowd of Indianians halted the Senator for a speech. It was late in the afternoon before the special started back. From stations, farmhouses, and fields where men worked, shouting people waved flags and hats. As the train passed slowly along the Chicago waterfront, women shook handkerchiefs from the houses, thousands of men swarmed about the cars, a militia company fired a one-hundred-and-fifty-gun salute from Dearborn Park, and answering guns boomed from the North and South Divisions. The station was filled with a jubilant mob. Douglas, placed in an open barouche drawn by six horses, was escorted by Montgomery Guards and Emmet Guards along Wabash Avenue and Dearborn Street, heavily beflagged, to the Tremont House. Here, two hours earlier, a crowd had begun to form. As the crash of artillery announced the Senator's arrival, others poured in until thirty thousand packed the streets and every roof and window ledge within hearing distance. Chicago had never before witnessed such enthusiasm. As the barouche ploughed through the crowd, the surge and roar were like those of the sea. A moment later, in the fast-gathering dusk, Douglas appeared on the balcony to be greeted by a deafening yell of welcome. Bands blared, fireworks soared, and bonfires threw a ruddy glare upon the scene.

Into his first sentences he threw a note of defiance. This reception, he said, "so great in numbers no human voice could be heard by all the countless thousands who participated in it," was not so much a tribute to him as to the basic American principle which he fought to vindicate. He recalled how he had pledged himself to battle for popular sovereignty. "Have I not redeemed that pledge?" he demanded. And he declared that he would resist to the last the unnatural combination of Buchanan Democrats and Republicans. "I intend to fight that allied army wherever I meet them."

[II]

It was time that Douglas returned home, for already his Republican opponent had been chosen and had opened his campaign with a speech that arrested national attention. Three weeks earlier, when Congressmen were streaming out of Washington to their homes and the country was reading Douglas's final Senate blast against the Administration cabal, a Republican convention had met in Springfield and nominated Abraham Lincoln for the senatorship. Of all rival party leaders, Douglas feared him the most.

Lincoln had fairly earned the honor. Illinois Whigs had respected him ever since he had sat in Congress for their party. His cordiality in stepping aside in 1854 to permit the election of Lyman Trumbull to the Senate was appreciatively remembered by anti-Nebraska Democrats. For nearly three years now he had been the leading forensic champion of the new party in the State, his close-knit arguments against the Nebraska bill, the Dred Scott decision, and Lecompton making him known from Galena to Cairo. Professional politicians liked his humor, his fraternal kindliness, his unfailing sagacity, and his integrity, while they saw in his grasp of ideas and trenchant logic the promise of a doughty champion—the only man in the State capable of meeting Douglas in full onset.

Though almost unknown in the East, Lincoln was in fact as clearly the head of the party in Illinois as Seward was in New York or Cameron in Pennsylvania; and that position he had earned in a way all his own. At a later date, a more tamed and settled American society found a romantic attraction in his rise from backwoods poverty and ignorance. It caught eagerly at certain poignant elements in a story reflecting so many facets of western development—the grandfather slain by Indians while clearing the forest; the father building his slab-roofed log cabin in the Kentucky woods; the work-worn, unnursed, dying mother calling little Abe and his sister Sarah to her bedside for a parting admonition; the removal of the bereaved family to another ill-finished cabin on an Indiana creek, where they lived in the squalor of poor shelter, coarse clothing, shoeless feet, bad water, and ill-cooked food; and the rescue of the children by Thomas Lincoln's new wife, who washed, combed, and fed them, brightened the cabin, and installed good home-made furniture. Americans of later days thrilled to a boyhood of struggle: the hard toil of the bony, fast-growing youth, in homespun trousers and deerskin shirt, helping to till the stumpy acres; his introduction to his first books—the Bible, *Pike's Arithmetic*, the *Kentucky Preceptor*, Noah Webster's *Spelling Book*, *Robinson Crusoe*, *The Pilgrim's Progress*, *Aesop's Fables*, Grimshaw's *History of the United States*, William Scott's *Lessons in Elocution*, and the *Revised Laws of Indiana;* the work of stockdriver, ferryhand, and (in 1828) flatboatman journeying to New Orleans with pork, meal, and other produce. Then came the renewed migration, this time to a better settled area in Illinois, the second river trip to New Orleans, the Black Hawk War, the experience in surveying and storekeeping, the hard study of a few lawbooks, and admission to the bar. In the pioneer West such a story was fairly common, yet there, too, it commanded attention.

Lincoln's neighbors at New Salem and later in Springfield had found his appearance as arresting as a circus poster. The spare muscular frame of six feet four inches, the rugged features, the deep-set, widely spaced gray-brown eyes, and the mobility of the countenance, all melancholy one moment and all mirth the next, caught every eye. But the man's brain and character soon attracted them more. His mind was a countryman's mind; slow, careful, serious, and intensely tenacious; sagacious rather than shrewd, clear rather than clever; given to flashes of humor chiefly because its profound earnestness would have been insupportable without some break. Its quintessential quality was as plain to the unlettered rustic as eventually it became to Lowell and Bryant: it was a dogged desire to learn the exact truth about everything and anything, and a delight in the reasoning process as a means of apprehending truth.

Through his early fascination with Euclid, Kirkham's *Grammar*, and two writers marked by exceptional perspicuity of style, Thomas Paine and Blackstone; through his grappling with the mind of Mentor Graham; through his study of Congressional debates and the editorials of the *National Intelligencer*, both of which he read regularly from his early manhood, ran an intense pleasure in the logical processes of truth-seeking. He accepted no truth at second hand, but reasoned it out for himself; and once it was found, he tried to set a lucid vision of it before others. In seeking a statement of truth, he slowly gained the finest grace of style, a simple accuracy in diction and a logical progression in sentence arrangement which gave everything he wrote the beauty of perfect clarity. One biographer tells us that precise truthfulness and meticulous honesty were his most striking characteristics.[10] This statement pertains to his character, yet it illuminates the fact that the honesty of his mind was of one piece with the honesty of his nature, that a truthful spirit lay back of his intellectual operations and personal acts alike. Being so intensely a truth-seeker, so happy in the task of getting his mind exactly right on every problem, he was also a singularly consistent man. His mind seldom leaped to inspirations or intuitions; his slowness irritated his effervescent law partner Herndon, his fellow politicians in Springfield, and, in the end, half of his Cabinet and more than half of the editors of the North. But once he had laid hold of a truth, stripped it of non-essentials, and fixed it in shining perfection before him, he clung to it.

Next to this delight in truth and logic as a guiding trait was his humanity. Intellect and temperament were often at war in him, for he had the intellect of a cold logician, the temperament of a warm humanitarian. The mast-fed lawyer, as he called himself, took a rich pleasure in Shakespeare, who opened before him a broad world of human nature. He was almost abnormally gregarious in the sense that he loved small social gatherings (not crowds, which he avoided), was an unmatchable funmaker though never without a certain reserve of dignity, and felt instantly at home with men of all sorts—preachers, lawyers, politicians,

10 Beveridge, *Lincoln*, I, 113.

farmers, boatmen, mechanics, newspapermen, anybody with a touch of comradeship in his disposition. Himself simple and good-hearted, he was ready to be
a friendly neighbor to any man worthy of esteem. Out of his delectation in
human society sprang his kindliness, magnanimity, and spontaneous democracy,
which made no account of social distinctions and little even of intellectual differences. He remitted the widow his legal fee; he was the same man to Governor
Bissell and the governor's coachman; *Lear* and the Sangamon County will
litigation illustrated the same values to him. Of the hustling spirit which the
frontier engendered he showed very little; he loved the people about him too
much to like combat or self-assertion; yet in the management of men he had a
skill invaluable to his political advancement. Withal, as his partner Herndon
well knew, he was ambitious of political honors. Brought up in an environment
where political campaigns were personal, he never faltered in his understanding
of the electorate from the time he won two hundred and seventy-seven of the
three hundred New Salem votes for the legislature until he was running
for the Presidency. In his social thinking he was a Jeffersonian, emphasizing
equality and justice; in his economic thinking he accepted the ideal of a free
laissez-faire competitive society.

In the years after Lincoln had formed his law partnership of 1841 with
Judge Stephen T. Logan, and that of 1844 with William H. Herndon, he became
recognized in the West as one of the leaders of the Illinois bar—an attorney who
had built his reputation slowly and soundly on hard work, grasp of the principles of equity, and dexterity in fair-minded appeals to a jury. He was not
widely read in law, nor deeply grounded in precedent. In dealing with most
cases he followed a method both congenial to him and natural under the hard
conditions of circuit practice, where few lawbooks were available and no time
or facilities existed for briefing analogous cases—he based his argument upon
broad considerations of abstract justice, presenting the issues so luminously that
the application of these considerations was plain to the dullest juror.[11] It followed that when his case was bad—when justice lay on the other side—his plea
was listless and feeble. When it was good, however, and when it involved interesting human issues, his logical power, understanding of character, and moral
fervor rendered him almost irresistible. He liked to have time to think his cases
through; he never believed himself fully prepared unless he had gotten up his
opponent's side nearly as fully as his own; and he was thus at his best only
when his mind, as deliberate as it was sure, had time for reflection and study.
The more intricate a case, the more brilliant would seem his lucid presentation
of its elements. Beginning with the kind of litigation that abounded in a rough
new country—land titles, debt collection, tax suits, cattle trespasses, disputed

11 A. A. Woldman, *Lawyer Lincoln*, Chapter X.

boundaries, quarrels over wills—he and the State grew up together, their business becoming more complex, difficult, and important.

As industrial development began, Lincoln became counsel for rich railroad and business corporations; as municipal and State affairs increased, he was called upon for legal opinions on governmental acts. He represented banks, insurance companies, merchants, a gas-light enterprise, and manufacturing concerns. Some of his cases were important. In the famous *Effie Afton* suit of 1857, which grew out of the wreck of the steamer of that name against the bridge built across the Mississippi at Davenport by the Rock Island Railroad, Lincoln joined Norman B. Judd of Chicago and Joseph Knox of Rock Island in arguing the railroad's case. His closing plea was masterly—and the disagreement of the jury was in effect a victory for his side.[12] In the same year he defeated the St. Louis, Alton & Chicago Railroad in a far-reaching case which held the road responsible for the acts of its duly authorized agents, thus establishing a rule cited in many subsequent cases.[13] He was engaged by the Illinois Central Railroad in a still more important case; its resistance to the attempt by McLean County to levy a tax on the railroad's property within the county limits. If the McLean officials succeeded, other local governments would imitate it, and the Central would be thrown into utter bankruptcy. Arguing the constitutionality of the charter exemption of the Illinois Central from taxation, and the interdiction of local as well as State levies by this exemption, Lincoln won his case. Compelled to bring suit for his fee, he easily won a verdict (June, 1857) for $5,000. The sum was important, for it enabled Lincoln the next year to drop his law business for the senatorial campaign. Still other important cases might be mentioned.[14]

Any student of Lincoln's legal career must be struck by the immense variety of cases which he pleaded, the acquaintance his circuit practice gave him with the whole central belt of his rich State, his unvarying industry and competence, and the steadily widening fame of his talents. He appeared in all the State and Federal courts of the area. He dealt with constitutional law, admiralty law, patent law, common law actions, and bills in equity. He was at least once offered an advantageous opening in Chicago. Several State departments, a number of counties, and various towns retained his services. The very month before his

12 Summarized in Beveridge, *Lincoln*, I, 600–604.
13 Woldman, *Lawyer Lincoln*, 164.
14 Douglas was quick to attack Lincoln for his connections with the railroad. "Can you Republicans deny that this day and this hour your candidate, Abraham Lincoln, is the agent and attorney of the Illinois Central Railroad, making stump speeches on its money? . . . Can you deny that he received from the company a single fee of $5,000 for procuring a decree releasing its property from taxation in McLean County, thus taking the side of the company against the people whose votes he is now asking?" Speech at Henry, Chicago *Daily Times*, October 5, 1858.

nomination for Senator, he conducted with brilliant success the defense in one of the most renowned murder trials in the history of Illinois: the trial of Duff Armstrong, son of an old friend and benefactor, whose acquittal he obtained by incisive logic, abetted by an almanac which proved that a witness could not have seen by moonlight the acts which he swore he had seen. His friend David Davis, judge of the State circuit bench, sometimes called upon Lincoln to hold court in his place, and Lincoln always did so to general satisfaction. In all his work as lawyer, his two ruling traits appeared: his earnest, deliberate, inexorably logical search for truth, which when found he presented in luminous terms, and the warm interest in plain humanity, which made him so kindly in administering justice, so modest in his successes, so magnanimous in all his dealings.[15]

His nomination was not untouched by drama. But one rival had appeared, and that a worthy figure—"Long John" Wentworth, just chosen mayor of Chicago by a resounding majority, the first Republican head of any great American city. A scion of the famous New Hampshire family, a graduate of Dartmouth, one of the moulders of the early destiny of Chicago, long editor of its principal newspaper the *Democrat*, an associate of Douglas in obtaining the Illinois Central land grant, a lawyer and politician of shrewd address, Wentworth was a formidable candidate against any man. The morning after the Kansas-Nebraska bill passed the House, he had joined other anti-Nebraska Whigs and Democrats at Crutchet's boardinghouse in Washington, and, then serving his fifth term, had forsaken the Democratic Party to help form a new freesoil organization. People could well respect his versatile abilities and progressive temper. But the imperious will and biting pen of the "Chicago autocrat" had made enemies, and, when the test came, he proved unable to carry the northern counties. Men in and about Chicago, led by State Chairman Norman B. Judd and Charles L. Wilson, editor of the Chicago *Journal*, were determined to defeat him and they made thorough preparations. On April 21 a conference of editors, including C. H. Ray of the Chicago *Tribune*, William Bross of the *Democratic Press*, and George T. Brown of the Alton *Courier*, met in the State library at Springfield to complete their plans. On the appointed day the city delegates marched into the convention hall under a banner reading, "Cook County is for Abraham Lincoln." Still more important than the activities of the leaders just named was a grass roots movement for Lincoln in the county gatherings, where the plain voters demanded his selection. Ordinarily the convention would have

15 Woldman, *Lawyer Lincoln*, Chapter XIII. Not merely did Lincoln travel widely. His home in Springfield was a strategic situation for a lawyer-politician, for the legislature brought scores of his friends there every year, while the session of the State supreme court and Federal court attracted lawyers from all over the State. These attorneys held many informal meetings which Lincoln attended. Cf. John G. Nicolay, January 9, 1858, to Trumbull; Trumbull Papers.

nominated men only for State offices, leaving the senatorial preference to be settled later. But to make Wentworth's defeat doubly sure, his opponents and Lincoln's supporters resolved upon the unprecedented step of riveting into the platform a declaration that Lincoln was the party nominee.

Enthusiasm for the freesoil cause and confidence in Republican destiny animated the thousand or more delegates and alternates who met that beautiful June 16 in the little Illinois capital. They gathered in jubilant knots under the maples, elms, and catalpas. They wandered about the Square, with the handsome little Capitol framed in its midst, the post office on the north, and two six-pillared stone structures in the classical style—the courthouse and an insurance building—on the east. They gazed at the new governor's mansion with its cupola, its high windows set in heavy brick walls, and its wide rear porches. When the hour struck, they poured into the Representatives' Hall. Ninety-five counties were represented, and all but five had passed resolutions for Lincoln. Richard Yates pounded for order, launching forthwith into a vigorous prophecy of national triumph. Our party this very hour, he proclaimed, is the most powerful on the continent of North America. Gustave Koerner, the able graduate of Heidelberg who had risen to be lieutenant-governor, was made president of the gathering.

Well might these Illinois Republicans face the future jauntily. Theirs was the united party of hope and fervor, the guardian army of moral progress! So they believed, as they cheered Koerner's ringing predictions of victory, and adopted the platform which Lincoln's friend, Orville H. Browning of Quincy, had drawn up. A little caucus of leaders in the State Library the night before, Lincoln among them, had deputed him to execute the task. It was a platform remarkable for its economic content. Slavery was of course mentioned, with a demand that it be kept out of all Territories; the Dred Scott decision and Lecompton constitution were suitably denounced. Emphasis fell, however, upon the propositions that public lands must be wrested from speculators and corporations and granted to actual settlers; that rivers and harbors must be improved; that the Pacific Railroad must be built; that the rights of free labor must be maintained; and that the national expenses must be reduced. A bold and constructive platform—but it omitted all mention of tolerance, for the Know-Nothing vote had to be won if the party were to achieve its goals.[16]

After naming two men for State offices, the convention passed by acclamation a resolution declaring Lincoln its first and only choice for Douglas's seat. Dislike of "Long John" and wholehearted approbation of the equally long Springfield attorney found vent in cheers which made the State House quiver.

16 Beveridge, *Lincoln*, II, 570, 571. B. Gratz Brown of Missouri had sent Browning the draft of a free labor plank. June 10, 1858, Browning Papers.

Then the convention adjourned, to meet again at eight in the evening to hear its champion deliver the first speech of the campaign.

[III]

Having long known that he would be designated, Lincoln had determined to make his address a memorable appeal to all thoughtful citizens. Thus far he was known (apart from his "spot" resolutions) for only three or four public utterances. He had delivered in 1852, in the Capitol at Springfield, a eulogy upon Henry Clay, commonplace enough except for a glowing endorsement of the purposes of the American Colonization Society. It showed that he still believed in the possibility of ridding America of slavery and restoring the Negro to Africa—"and this too so gradually that neither races nor individuals shall have suffered by the change." [17] He had made his famous reply to Douglas at Peoria in 1854 on the Kansas-Nebraska issue, striking with deadly aim at the central point: the assumption in the Nebraska Act that no moral issue was involved in the spread of slavery. Four months after the Dred Scott decision, he had presented in a Springfield speech a scathing analysis of its moral fallacies, and a telling indictment of the idea that the black man's bondage should be universal and eternal.[18] These three speeches, with a few fragments like the post-election address at the Republican banquet in Chicago in 1856, constituted his contribution to the thought of his time. And he was now almost fifty.

To his new address, Lincoln gave a more careful preparation than to any earlier effort of his life. For weeks, he had been filling stray envelopes and scraps of paper with jotted ideas, throwing them into that wonted receptacle, his hat; and of late he had carefully combined these fragments and had rewritten and polished his argument.[19] The time had come, as he saw, for the Republican Party to take more advanced ground. The hour had struck when, no longer content with an interdiction of slavery in the Territories, the party should assert that even in the South the "peculiar institution" must be viewed as a temporary and transitional system, bound in the course of generations to give way to a better regime. Only by a wise acceptance of this idea could the country be brought to devise bold measures for slavery's ultimate termination.

Lincoln therefore decided to throw into the first paragraph of his speech a flat assertion that a house divided against itself cannot stand; that the nation must in time become all slaveholding (which was unthinkable), or all free. The Biblical phrase, perhaps unconsciously borrowed from Edmund Quincy, had

17 Speech, July 16, 1852.
18 Speech, June 26, 1857.
19 Nicolay and Hay, *Lincoln*, II, 136.

long been in his mind. The fundamental idea he had thought of using earlier that year in a Bloomington speech, but he had discarded it when some conservative friends argued that it would encourage extremists North and South and embitter the sectional struggle. It had been partially stated by George Fitzhugh, but then Fitzhugh was an eccentric radical. Now, convinced that the time was ripe for its enunciation, or at least that the truth ought no longer to be suppressed, he had fixed upon his course.[20]

Just before the convention, he called a dozen or more friends to the library of the State House and read the speech to them. Herndon's recollection was that everyone, as his opinion was asked, condemned the utterance until Herndon himself spoke up: "Lincoln, deliver that speech as read and it will make you President." [21]

Whether this is accurate or not, there is a ring of authenticity in Herndon's report of Lincoln's rejoinder to the group: "The time has come when these sentiments should be uttered; and if it is decreed that I should go down because of this speech, then let me go down linked to the truth—let me die in advocacy of what is just and right."

Lincoln was thinking of Illinois, not the nation, when he made this statement; thinking of the Senatorship, not any larger office; and yet thinking, too, of what the whole country ought to know. From the prairie chrysalis, a winged creature was being born. The speaker who mounted the platform that night appeared to be only the plain circuit lawyer of uneven education and limited reading that his fellow-citizens knew—a provincial figure who, but for one inconspicuous term in Congress, knew nothing of the older sections and had left his State only once since 1849. He seemed to be only a State leader who would now become known to the East, not through his own incontestable merits, but because his opponent was the most redoubtable Democratic chieftain of the nation. Of crudities and limitations, indeed, he still had all too many.

Yet ever since 1849 Lincoln had been steadily taking on stature. Returning from Congress, he had temporarily put aside political ambition, and for five years had devoted himself to self-improvement in general culture, the law, and thought by sustained study and hard desk work. In 1854, when he rose to the challenge of the Nebraska Act, some fruits of that discipline had appeared. Now more were to be revealed. Few in the crowd which sat shirtsleeved, perspiring, and restless in the Capitol hall that hot June night could have had much perception of his still undisclosed intellectual and moral greatness. But all, even the least

20 Harvey Wish, *George Fitzhugh*, 150 ff. Fitzhugh had written in the Richmond *Enquirer*, May 6, 1856, that either slavery or free society must be very wrong. "The war between the two systems rages everywhere; and will continue to rage till the one conquers and the other is exterminated."

21 Herndon and Weik, Angle ed., *Lincoln*, 325.

perceptive, could appreciate the courage and the sinewy logical power of his discourse. Without a word of rhetorical embellishment, he drove home in the opening sentences a thesis to whose elaboration most of the remainder of the speech was devoted:

We are now far into the fifth year since a policy was initiated with the avowed object and confident promise of putting an end to slavery agitation. Under the operation of that policy, that agitation not only has not ceased, but has constantly augmented. In my opinion, it will not cease until a crisis shall have been reached and passed. "A house divided against itself cannot stand." I believe this government cannot endure permanently half slave and half free. I do not expect the Union to be dissolved—I do not expect the house to fall— but I do expect it will cease to be divided. It will become all one thing, or all the other. Either the opponents of slavery will arrest the further spread of it, and place it where the public mind shall rest in the belief that it is in the course of ultimate extinction; or its advocates will push it forward until it shall become alike lawful in all the States, old as well as new, North as well as South.

From this courageous beginning, Lincoln had an opportunity to move forward to a statesmanlike examination of the necessity for facing all that was implied in "ultimate extinction." But one radical step was enough; he deemed it wise not to go further. Instead, he made a strictly partisan appeal to the rising fear among freesoilers that slavery would be made lawful everywhere, arguing that the Republican Party must be strengthened as a bulwark against that dire possibility. Slavery, he affirmed, was an aggressive force. Its champions, abetted by Douglas, who cared not whether it was voted up or down, had gained one victory after another in a program of shrewd, unsleeping expansion. First, they had forced through Congress the Nebraska Act opening all the national domain to slavery. Second, they had gained in 1856 what they declared was a national endorsement of this step. Third, they had then obtained from the Supreme Court in the Dred Scott decision a three-headed engine to batter down further walls in their path. One head, declaring that no slave or descendant of a slave could ever be a citizen, was designed to deprive the Negro of any possible benefit from the constitutional guarantee that citizens in each State shall be entitled to all the privileges and immunities of citizens in other States. Another head, asserting that neither Congress nor the local legislature might exclude slaves from a Territory, was intended to facilitate the colonization of the public domain with slaves and thus enhance the chances of permanency for the institution throughout the future. The third head, stating that the Federal courts would not decide whether the transfer of a slave into a free State made him into which the Negro might be forced by his master, had a still more sinister free, but would leave that to be determined by the courts of any slave State intention. Not pushed forward immediately but left to fix itself slowly in the public conscience, it was to be used to sustain the logical conclusion that, as Dred's master had taken him as a slave to Illinois, every other master might take one or a hundred slaves to any free State.[22] This succession of measures, said Lincoln, might not be the fruit of a conspiracy:

> But when we see a lot of framed timbers, different portions of which we know have been gotten out at different times and places by different workmen— Stephen [Douglas], Franklin [Pierce], Roger [Taney], and James [Buchanan], for instance—and we see these timbers joined together, and see they exactly make the frame of a house or a mill, all the tenons and mortices exactly fitting, and all the lengths and proportions of the different pieces exactly adapted to their respective places, and not a piece too many or too few, not omitting even the scaffolding—or, if a single piece be lacking, we see the place in the frame exactly fitted and prepared to yet bring such a piece in—in *such* a case, we find it impossible not to *believe* that Stephen and Franklin and Roger and James all understood one another from the beginning, and all worked upon a common *plan* or *draft* drawn up before the first lick was struck.

A fourth step remained, said Lincoln. If the Court decided that the Constitution did not permit a State to exclude slavery (and Judge Nelson had hinted at constitutional restraints upon State power over slavery), then the institution would indeed become national. "Put this and that together, and we have another nice little niche, which we may, ere long, see filled with another Supreme Court decision" of just this purport. This was especially to be expected if Northern voters turned from their Republican guardians to men like Douglas, indifferent whether slavery was voted up or down.

This partisan conclusion, in the eyes of posterity, was pitched on a disappointingly low plane. To be sure, it had some merit as an exhortation to Northerners to maintain a sleepless vigilance lest worse than the Nebraska Act and Dred Scott decision should befall them, and as an appeal to Republicans to stand firm. But its theory of a conspiracy among Douglas, Buchanan, Pierce, and Taney was unfounded. The charge gave Douglas an opportunity—in a speech at Clinton on July 27—to fling at Lincoln the words "infamously false," declaring that he had never exchanged one word with Taney or Pierce on the Dred Scott decision and had not spoken of it to Buchanan until long after it was made.[23] Lincoln's prediction that "we shall lie down pleasantly dreaming that the people of Missouri are on the verge of making their State free, and we shall awake to the reality instead that the Supreme Court has made Illinois a slave State," was an absurd bogey; no court would have dared such folly. He would

22 The Washington *Union*, November 17, 1858, published an article asserting the doctrine that slaves could be brought as slaves into the free States, and kept there. Douglas in his own words, "Branded it at once, and denounced it." Toombs said in the Senate that not a man in any slave State held such a doctrine. See Lincoln, *Works*, II, 454.

23 Carthage *Republican*, August 5, 1858.

have done well to confine himself to the simple facts that Douglas's Nebraska Act, Taney's Dred Scott decision, and Buchanan's championship of Lecompton all outraged the convictions of men who opposed the extension of slavery, and that such outrages would continue unless the voters stood firm behind the Republican Party. Lincoln might have pointed to two very real perils. One was the peril of forcible annexations; the other was the peril of the rising Southern demand for giving slavery positive Congressional protection within the Territories. He did point to the danger of plans for the revival of the African slave trade.

It was not the partisan temper of the speech, for this was a party occasion, but its lack of constructive elements which made it disappointing. Lincoln bravely insisted on the great truth that the nation could not permanently remain half slave and half free; he called for vigilant action to prevent it from becoming wholly slave; but he said nothing as to the means of making it wholly free. This, he plainly implied, had to be done. But how? How much patience, wise counsel, and self-sacrificing help might the South expect from the North in that agonizing process? Nearly three years earlier, he had written a Kentucky leader that no peaceful extinction of slavery seemed in sight. "So far as peaceful, voluntary emancipation is concerned, the condition of the negro slave in America, scarcely less terrible to the contemplation of a free mind, is now as fixed and hopeless of change for the better, as that of the lost souls. . . . The problem is too mighty for me—may God, in his mercy, superintend the solution." This vague hopelessness could not be maintained. From such western moderates as Lincoln and Bates, if from anyone, a constructive attitude might be expected.

The speech was a ringing prologue. Lincoln took characteristic care that it be printed correctly. Giving the manuscript at the end of his address to Horace White of the Chicago *Press and Tribune*, and requesting him to go to the *Illinois State Journal* office and read proof, Lincoln soon followed to con the text himself. He explained that he had taken great pains with it and wished no errors to creep in. Not only the *Journal*, but the Chicago *Press and Tribune* and other western sheets published it. A pamphlet edition was soon issued in Illinois. Would he follow this prologue by a fuller definition of his views?

[IV]

Douglas lost no time in replying. The "house divided" speech was published throughout the East before the Senator left Washington. Printing it in full, the New York *Tribune* and *Weekly Tribune* carried it to millions of readers, with an editorial calling it compact, forcible, and admirable: "Mr. Lincoln never fails to make a good speech, when he makes any, and this is one of his best efforts." [24] The Philadelphia *Press's* Washington correspondent, terming it very ultra, intimated that Douglas would quickly demolish it. At his Chicago homecoming, Douglas shook hands with Lincoln who sat behind him on the Tremont House balcony. His speech, too, had been carefully prepared; and though he delivered it under the exhaustion of two nights' loss of sleep, it was distinguished by the vigor with which it assailed both the Lecompton Democrats and the doctrines that Lincoln had advanced.

The attack upon Lecompton, to be sure, named not a single person, spoke of principles only, and avoided the remotest allusion to the President. Throughout the Senate debates of April, May, and June, in fact, Douglas had uttered not a harsh word (in public) about Buchanan. His Springfield organ, the *State Register*, had essayed during these months (as Lincoln observed to Elihu B. Washburne) to reduce its readers to a drowsy forgetfulness that the two chieftains had ever quarreled.[25] To this extent Douglas was yet holding the door open for reconciliation. But he softened no words in his fiery vaunt of triumph over that "fraud" and "monstrosity" termed Lecompton. He had felt bound in honor to resist, and, with the aid of Crittenden and Bell, of a staunch band of Know-Nothings, and of the manful Republicans, he had won what he boldly called a great moral victory. "We forced them to refer that constitution back to the people of Kansas, to be accepted or rejected as they shall decide at an election which is fixed for the first Monday of August next." While the mode of submission under the English bill did not meet his approval, Douglas was sure that the voters of Kansas would resist its penalties and inducements. "Hence, my friends, I regard the Lecompton battle as having been fought and the battle won, because the arrogant demand for the admission of Kansas under the Lecompton constitution unconditionally, whether her people want it or not, has been abandoned, and the principle which recognizes the right of the people to decide for themselves has been substituted in its place." [26]

Then, turning to the coming campaign, Douglas trenchantly defined his two vital differences with Lincoln and the Republican Party. First, he sharply rejected the "house divided" doctrine, which he stigmatized as an effort to set section against section, and hammer a tyrannous, grinding uniformity of institutions down upon the blessed breadth, variety, and freedom of the American scene. Why should the Union be all free or all slave? Why should its customs and practices not be as diverse as the climate and physiography of the rich domain that stretched from frosty Maine to opulent Louisiana? Tolerance of

24 N. Y. *Weekly Tribune*, July 3, *Daily Tribune*, July 1, 1858.
25 Lincoln to Elihu B. Washburne, May 15, 1858; Ill. State Hist. Lib.
26 Full text, Phila. *Weekly Press*, July 17, 1858.

local differences meant peace; the "house divided" thesis meant war between North and South. In the second place, Douglas emphatically condemned Lincoln's refusal to abide by the Dred Scott decision. He would support the Supreme Court in all matters within its jurisdiction; he regarded a crusade against the highest judicial tribunal in the land as a threat to liberty and security. Moreover, he condemned Lincoln's main ground of complaint (as Douglas misdefined it) against the Court. Lincoln, he said, stood for negro equality; he was against it. He was opposed to every step that recognized the negro or Indian as the equal of the white man; he would give these dependent races every right, privilege, and immunity consistent with the safety of the superior race; but he would stand adamant against equality, political, social, or whatnot.

Readers of this adroit speech could hardly doubt that it was the opening gun of Douglas's contest for the Presidency in 1860. It was written with an eye not only to his senatorial seat but to the White House. He knew well that the Directory—Cobb, Slidell, Thompson, Black—would fight until their thirst for revenge was slaked by defeat or choked by victory; he despised them. He knew that he could expect no votes from those Republicans of rigid principle represented by Seward, Chase, Wade, and Lincoln. But moderate Northern Democrats (with many in the South) would cling to him, while not a few moderate Republicans and Know-Nothings, lovers of the Union and believers in peace, might well join them. The next two years would certainly be a period of political upheaval. Might he not, as a leader who had striven since 1850 for median policies and a natural, unforced solution of problems, rally all those who were tired of perilous extremes? That the Southern radicals led by Slidell and Yancey were a menace to the republic most Northern and border Democrats agreed. That Seward and Chase, with their rejection of Dred Scott, insistence on containing slavery, and higher-law doctrine, were likewise dangerous, conservative Republicans would grant. The nation as a whole, which had voted in 1852 and 1856 for rest and safety, distrusted agitators and wanted a moderate leader in the Presidency. Could not Douglas thrust both sets of radicals aside, and carry the country as a strong, hopeful man typifying the old Jackson-Polk ideas of Union, expansion, and reform?

A fighter who like Sheridan or Patton loved the attack, Douglas was happiest when carrying battle into the enemy lines. To him the foe lay on two flanks. On one side, the more flamboyant men of the cotton kingdom, addicted to juleps, feuds, and gasconade, had shown that they would stop at nothing. They meant to draw an advanced line on slavery and meet any violation of it with secession. On the other side, Seward, still esteemed the almost inevitable nominee of the Republicans two years hence, denounced slavery as a curse, assailed expansion, and hoped to erect a sectional administration. Douglas struck at both. In hailing the downfall of Lecompton he was exulting over the humiliation of Southern fire-eaters. In denouncing the "house divided" dogma and the resistance to Dred Scott he was aiming not so much at Lincoln, who seemed a transient foe, as at Seward. Already Douglas foresaw the triple contest of 1860, with radical Republicans on one side, radical Democrats on the other, and his moderate popular-sovereignty party in the middle. His vision was accurate. He erred only in overestimating his power to take votes away from the radical wings; erred in not foreseeing John Brown's raid, Buchanan's folly, and the impetuous rush of Yancey and Rhett.

From Chicago, Douglas moved to carry the contest down-State, and since "Egypt" was clearly his own, especially into the central counties from Quincy on the west to Danville on the east. He addressed a German delegation in Chicago, boasting that he had made the first speech in the county against the system which proposed to humiliate men on account of birthplace or religion.[27]

Then, on July 16 he stepped into a private car, decorated with bunting. A gay party, including his wife, the young sculptor Leonard Volk, the shorthand expert James B. Sheridan, and various political leaders, took their seats, and the regular train to Bloomington carried them southward. En route, a flat-car with a twelve-pounder cannon was attached, and its boom at every stop reverberated across the flat prairies. At Joliet, the Senator acknowledged the cheers of a throng with dancing banners and blaring band. At Bloomington, a strongly Republican town, he found a drum-and-fife procession, and every preparation for a huge audience. His speech in the midsummer dusk lasted until ten o'clock, when amid flaring torches he and Mrs. Douglas were tumultuously escorted back to the Landon House. He went on to Springfield, where thousands braved a heavy rain to gather about his platform, and thence to Clinton, where he made another long address.

In all these speeches he elaborated upon his Chicago address. He reemphasized his doctrine of white superiority, and repudiated what he called Lincoln's doctrine that the negro should be given equal social and political rights, rights leading to suffrage, officeholding, lawmaking, and in the end racial amalgamation. He reiterated that a division of the American house upon the slavery question was logical and proper; so variegated a nation needed variegated institutions. Very significantly, he restated at length his belief that the Dred Scott decision did *not* mean that slavery would go into all the Territories. Slavery was completely dependent on local support; it would spread just as far as the people wanted it; it could never be forced on an unwilling community. In his Bloomington speech, distributed in eighty thousand copies throughout the State, he quoted a Southern Senator as having said that, without affirmative

27 Phila. *Weekly Press*, August 7, 1858.

legislation to foster it, slavery could no more exist in a hostile community than a newborn infant could survive on a Sahara rock. The local police power would be decisive, declared Douglas: "Slavery will never exist one day, or one hour, in any Territory against the unfriendly legislation of an unfriendly people."

[V]

Both parties had entered the Illinois contest divided. In both, desperate efforts were made to close up the ranks, and in neither was complete success attained. Unity would have been achieved in both had the State been left to itself. But the eastern Republicans and the Cobb-Thompson-Slidell Democrats wished to subordinate party success in Illinois to their own aims.

The position of Greeley, N. P. Banks, Henry Wilson, and others who deluded themselves into thinking that Douglas might take up Republican principles was by no means incomprehensible. Watching the Senator's battle against Lecompton with admiration, they believed that if the Illinois Republicans made no contest against him, a hundred thousand Illinois Democrats might be won over to the Republican cause in 1860. With them would come a host of other Northwestern Democrats—and perhaps Douglas himself. Reject a joint stand against the flagitious Administration, however, and the hundred thousand would be driven back into alliance with the slavery forces.[28] All during the spring, Greeley's *Tribune*, Bowles's Springfield *Republican*, the Hartford *Courant*, and other eastern journals had exhorted Republicans to support the reelection of such anti-Lecompton Democrats as Hickman of Pennsylvania, Adrian of New Jersey, Haskin and Clark of New York, and John G. Davis of Indiana. Douglas seemed to belong in that category. Anson Burlingame was warm for the return of the Little Giant to the Senate, but so were many eastern abolitionists. Be it remembered that the new Republican Party was made up primarily of freesoil Democrats and freesoil Whigs.

Senator Trumbull warned Lincoln on January 3 that the laudation of the Little Giant by seaboard Republicans threatened the success of the party in the Illinois campaign. "Some of our friends here act like fools in running after and flattering Douglas," he wrote. "He encourages it and invites such men as Wilson, Seward, Burlingame, Parrott, etc., to come and confer with him and they seem wonderfully pleased to go. I have had no conversation with him about his course. . . ." This statement was unjust to Seward, who, as his editorial friend James Watson Webb took pains to explain to Lincoln in a long letter, believed

---

28 N. Y. *Daily Tribune*, July 1, 1858. The Robert Todd Lincoln Papers contain many letters to Lincoln on this peril. They indicate that John H. Bryant of Princeton, Illinois, may have done much to keep his brother the editor-poet in line against Douglas.

in Republican men and Republican principles, and was not going to meddle in the Illinois contest. But it was accurate as respected others, and particularly some onetime Democrats who had joined the new party. As David Davis wrote Lincoln this spring, the Republican organization still remained a confederated and not a consolidated party.

Yet this eastern movement seemed to the Illinoisans who knew Douglas best, not only infidelity to principle but the worst kind of practical folly. From the outset, many western Republicans had doubted the sincerity of Douglas's stand, for they deemed his motives selfish. They thought he realized that unless he attacked Lecompton he could never go back to the Senate and never obtain any Northwestern support in 1860; that, as Governor Bissell wrote Lyman Trumbull, his course was dictated solely by fears for his political future. In this they were wrong, but on other points they were right. While it was indeed important to rebuke the Administration, it would be more pointedly and damagingly rebuked by Republican victory than by Douglas's reelection. There was never the slightest chance that convinced Douglasites would embrace Republican tenets, for between them and the new party yawned two impassable gulfs. Douglas had labored for years, as Lincoln said, to prove it a sacred right of white men to take slaves into any new Territories where they were welcome; the Republican Party had been born as a protest against permitting slavery in the national domain. Douglas saw no moral issue in the slavery question; all Republicans did.[29]

Only a few Republicans in Illinois had been infected by the new eastern love affair with Douglas. Jonathan Blanchard, the Vermont-born president of Knox College, who had learned his abolitionism under Theodore Weld at Lane Seminary, had veered early in the year to the Douglas forces. Elihu Washburne of Galena, a former Whig now in the House as a Republican, for some time played an equivocal part. The early spring found him reputedly on Douglas's side; then he wrote a letter to Lincoln's partner Herndon which indicated that he was an honest party adherent; and finally he was reported in Springfield, just before the Republican convention, urging delegates to drop Lincoln and endorse Douglas in his stead.[30] A few other western men were seduced. In

29 Multitudes of Republicans felt with George A. Nourse, who wrote Trumbull January 1: "His course on the Kansas-Nebraska bill is unatoned for, he is just as far off as ever from Republicanism, and is just as big a political scoundrel as ever." They felt with D. L. Phillips, who wrote January 3: "I have no faith in the sincerity of his movements. He is looking to a reelection to the U. S. Senate. We have been cheated enough from that quarter, and when we remember his unstinted abuse, I am willing to let him retire without following him." D. L. Phillips to Lyman Trumbull, January 3, 1858; Trumbull Papers.

30 Washburne sent Lincoln strong protestations of his loyalty. "I have here and in all my letters hence," he wrote May 2 from Washington, "invariably taken the ground that the republican party in Illinois must stand by their principles and their men—that for Senator I was for you against the field—that the party was bound by every obligation of honor and

Indiana, Schuyler Colfax played with the idea that it might be wisest to ensure the Little Giant's return to Washington, and in Missouri Frank P. Blair, Jr., did the same. But the great mass of prairie Republicans had no intention of playing into the hands of the man they had fought for years.

As they marshalled their lines for the campaign, they took steps to put their eastern brethren right. Not only did Joseph Medill's Chicago *Press and Tribune*, Charles L. Wilson's Chicago *Journal*, and other sheets expostulate with Greeley and Bowles, but C. H. Ray and other editors wrote them argumentative letters. From Washington, Lyman Trumbull let his anti-Douglas views be emphatically known. Greeley replied in May with a ringing eulogium of the Little Giant, saying that "no public man in our day has evinced a nobler fidelity and courage," and, while admitting that his future course was unpredictable and that he might soon espouse filibustering and free trade, declaring that Illinois Republicans should at any rate never ally themselves with Buchanan's base cohort of hirelings.[31]

Inasmuch as Greeley's *Weekly Tribune* had about five thousand Illinois subscribers, his stubborn position gave Lincoln pain. Why does he wish the Senator reelected? asked Lincoln. "It is because he thinks Douglas's superior position, reputation, experience, ability, if you please, would more than compensate for his lack of a pure Republican position." [32] Herndon, early in March, had gone east to look at Revolutionary scenes, to make the acquaintance of the New England abolitionists he so much admired, Garrison, Parker, and Wendell Phillips, to get a first-hand view of the Lecompton battle, and to talk with Douglas. Primarily this was a pleasure trip. Perhaps as an additional motive, he was stirred by Lincoln's complaint that "Greeley is not doing me right." More probably a political object did not develop until he reached the East. In Washington he smoked a cigar with Douglas, who wanted him to tell Lincoln that he had crossed the river and burned his boats. He chatted with Trumbull, who expressed his belief that neither the Republicans nor anybody else could put any confidence in the slippery little Senator. In Boston, he saw Governor Banks, Theodore Parker, and several others—cold and rather repellent men, thought Herndon. They inquired whether the Illinois Republicans would accept Douglas, and looked astonished when the vehement response came, "No, never!"

Most important of all, Herndon bearded Greeley in his den and resentfully asked if the editor really wished to see Douglas ride into power with the aid

---

fair dealing to elect you, if it had the strength to elect anybody." Lincoln had already written him on April 26: "I am satisfied you have done no wrong, and nobody has intended any wrong to you." Robert Todd Lincoln Papers. See John M. Palmer in McLean Co. Hist. Soc. *Transactions*, III, 123.

31 N. Y. *Weekly Tribune*, May 15, 1858.
32 Lincoln to C. L. Wilson, June 1, 1858, *Works*, I, 238, 239.

of freesoilers whom he would certainly betray. Do not worry about his future course, responded Greeley. "Douglas is a brave man. Forget the past, and sustain the righteous." Writing to Springfield, Herndon repeated this to Lincoln with a snort: "Good God, righteous, eh?" [33]

Altogether, Herndon's visit probably did a little to enlighten the temporarily bemused easterners as to the real situation in Illinois; and he doubtless used his opportunity to tell Greeley, Parker, and others of Lincoln's true stature. Resentful editorials and letters from the West also had their influence. But what completed the general conversion of eastern Republicans was Douglas's Chicago speech. When Greeley, Bowles, and Bryant read that deliverance, they rent it to shreds.

After Lincoln's formal nomination and Douglas's early speeches, Republicans East and West fell into line. The New York *Tribune*, finally admitting that this was no duel of Hamlet and Laërtes, gave clear if lukewarm support to the party in Illinois. In a succession of editorials it denounced Douglas's squatter sovereignty principle, his expansionist views, his hostility to a broad program of civil rights, and his readiness to let slavery grow. Elihu Washburne made speeches for Lincoln. But, to the very end, nobody knew how many of those anti-Nebraska Democrats who had voted as Republicans in 1856 would turn back to their old hero Douglas, as Napoleon's veterans turned to the Emperor after the landing from Elba. Sheahan of the Chicago *Times*, analyzing the situation early in the contest, believed that while no important leaders could be won over, many of the rank and file would support a Democratic legislature; and Representative T. L. Harris agreed.[34]

If the Republican divisions were largely healed, those in the Democratic ranks rather grew worse. The Senator remained ready for a reconciliation; he had in fact sent explicit word to Buchanan, through James May of Philadelphia, that if the Administration would sustain his Illinois candidacy he would let bygones be bygones. A large body of regular Democrats expressed the view that it would be shameful to rive the party in two on issues that were now as dead as the Continental Congress. Alexander H. Stephens, Vice-President Breckinridge, and Henry A. Wise were among the prominent slave State leaders who hoped ardently for a reconciliation. The St. Louis *Republican*, Memphis *Appeal*, Mobile *Tribune*, New Orleans *Delta*, Richmond *Enquirer*, and Vicksburg *True Southron* advocated mutual forgiveness and forbearance in the cause of party success. Some of these men and journals were thinking of imperiled national union as much as party union.

---

33 Herndon to Trumbull, April 12, 1858; Trumbull Papers; W. H. Herndon and J. W. Weik, *Lincoln*, II, 390–396. According to Greeley, Herndon also praised Douglas.
34 Milton, *Eve of Conflict*, Ch. 20; David Donald, *Lincoln's Herndon*, 112 ff.

But Buchanan, who knew that reconciliation would be construed as defeat, and who called Douglas just what George III called Chatham—"that perfidious man"—made no move. Not for him the statesmanlike tact with which President Jefferson had sought to heal the schism of John Randolph. And the implacable Directory lost no time in taking matters into its own hands. They seized on the Chicago speech as text for a violent editorial in the *Union* of July 16, written without Buchanan's knowledge and padlocking the gates which barred Douglas out of the party. The *Union*, in fact, was now the organ not of the President who feebly disavowed it, but of the Directory ruling in his name. It was members of the Directory who speeded an agent, Francis J. Grund, to Chicago to organize the opposition to Douglas more firmly than ever.

As Douglas continued his heavy work of speechmaking, the National Democrats put forth every effort to defeat him. District-Attorney Henry S. Fitch, one of the most venomous agents, informed Buchanan in mid-August that they were doing better than they had expected. Money had been collected from Slidell and others; nine new Administration papers had just been established in the State; a full speaking program had been arranged. With hundreds rallying daily to the Administration standard, Douglas, knowing defeat was certain, "is becoming desperate in his denunciations and intrigues." [35] Ex-Governor John Reynolds, ex-Judge Sidney Breese, and C. N. Pine of Chicago were helping direct the warfare. The tactics of the National Democrats were to fight on the sly, as the Illinois phrase went. Before long the guillotine was working mercilessly. The Senator's friends were decapitated wherever the patronage-managers could reach them. Postmasters of Springfield, Rock Island, Peoria, Bloomington, Belleville, Galesburg, and many smaller places were summarily removed for no offense but loyalty to Douglas. The Little Giant at times felt as desperate as Cicero proscribed by Octavius at the behest of Antony. When an old friend, Usher F. Linder, proffered his services, an urgent telegram came back: "The hell-hounds are on my track. For God's sake, Linder, come and help me fight them." [36]

This war of the Directory, relentlessly prosecuted by Cobb, Brown, Slidell, Thompson, and Jere Black while Buchanan took refreshment at Bedford Springs, was waged in defiance of the majority will of the party. As the Springfield *Republican* pointed out, most politicians wished harmony restored; and the generality of Democratic newspapers not only ceased their attacks on the Senator but manifested a decided friendliness.[37] James Gardner, editor of the Augusta, Georgia, *Constitutionalist*, voiced his disgust that a test of orthodoxy

35 Henry S. Fitch to Buchanan, August 17, 1858; Buchanan Papers.
36 Linder, *Reminiscences*, 78.
37 Springfield *Daily Republican*, July 27, 1858.

had been laid down upon a question which most voters were willing to regard as extinct. Continuance of the vendetta against Douglas, he wrote, would show a factious and vindictive spirit, and would entail upon its prosecutors the responsibility for all the consequences which would follow division of the party. Perhaps he dimly foresaw how awful those consequences would be! [38]

But the Directory halted at nothing. It acted to found an anti-Douglas newspaper in Chicago. It aroused a wave of resentment in Ohio by dismissing Douglas's friend J. W. Gray, city postmaster and editor of the Cleveland *Plain Dealer*.[39] Veteran politicians expressed amazement at the venom of the Washington *Union*, which spewed epithets and tirades against all Douglas men. Cook, Fitch, and other placeholders scurried about over Illinois, bullying officeholders, arranging meetings, and using Federal printing to bribe newspapers or start new sheets. The whole panoply of Administration influence was set in motion. "For three years," Douglas was to say in 1860, "no friend of mine has been permitted to hold a crossroads postoffice, or even to circulate the public documents under my frank, as a general thing, in my own State." [40]

Alexander H. Stephens, anxious to arrange a compromise, visited Illinois for nearly a fortnight in August, talked with leaders, and came away resolved to use what influence he had with the Administration. He seems to have arranged a brisk peace movement in Chicago. Colonel R. B. Carpenter of that city, who had gotten $500 from the National Democrats for a speaking tour, suddenly gave up his opposition and hurried to Washington. David Stuart, a former member of Congress from the Detroit district and now a prominent attorney in Chicago, whom some regarded as the principal leader of the Douglas forces in Illinois, also visited the capital, his reputed object being to work upon his old friend Cass and others to bring about a friendly readjustment. In alarm, Isaac Cook, Pine, and others hastily appealed to Buchanan to stand firm.[41] They need not have worried. The President had forgiven Representative Montgomery of Pennsylvania his anti-Lecompton course only after the Congressman had written a letter of Uriah Heep 'umbleness. He would get no letter from Douglas, and the Directory would not forgive the man if he did. An earlier effort by George Sanders to patch up a peace had been emphatically rebuked by the President, who bade Sanders withdraw a conciliatory telegram which he had dispatched to Chicago.[42] While expert observers concurred in the view that the Directory had taken the bit in its teeth, they agreed that Buchanan felt

---

38 Augusta *Constitutionalist*, July 7, 1858; see New York Correspondent, London *Daily News*, October 2, 1858, on Southern protests, Virginia, Tennessee, and Kentucky.
39 N. Y. *Weekly Tribune*, June 26, 1858.
40 *Cong. Globe*, May 17, 1860; 36th Cong., 1st Sess., 2156.
41 Isaac Cook, August 16, C. N. Pine, August 17, 1858; Buchanan Papers.
42 G. F. Milton, *Eve of Conflict*, 327.

a bitter and unrelenting hatred for the man who had defied and defeated him.[43] On this point the Administration would meet no trouble from the President!

The hard-beset Senator could take comfort in the number of national leaders who called for his return to Washington. Senator Green of Missouri, after much wavering, was so impressed by the sentiment of his State that, as summer waned, he frankly declared his willingness to come to Illinois to speak for Douglas.[44] The Democratic candidates for Congress in Iowa, Indiana, and Ohio were, with few exceptions, compelled to declare their support of the Senator, while from Ohio came news that the only way to save the party was to put it back on the Douglas platform.[45] Vice-President Breckinridge finally wrote an open letter (October 4) in which he stated that, while he could not leave home to enter the campaign, he could never forget the courage and ability with which Douglas had repeatedly defended the Union and the rights of the State, and that he wished for his success in the election. Henry A. Wise not only reexpressed his adherence to Douglas, but sternly rebuked the Administration for its course. Could folly be greater? he asked. Douglas's success in Illinois would be the Administration's rebuke; his defeat there would be its death. Buchanan would eventually have to let Kansas enter, wrote the Virginia governor; he might as well have done so on fair terms, for he would lose the Southern Lecomptonites anyway on the issues of the tariff and Pacific Railroad.[46]

It would be the hottest, the closest, the most momentous senatorial campaign in decades; and the announcement that Douglas and Lincoln would engage in a series of joint debates seized the attention of the country.

43 J. P. Heiss (ed. Washington *States*) to Douglas, July 15, 1858; Douglas Papers.
44 Milton, *Eve of Conflict*, 347.
45 Phila. *Weekly Press*, July 21, 24, 1858.
46 Henry A. Wise, October 12, 1858; Buchanan Papers.

14

The Douglas-Lincoln Debates

"WE TRUST," remarked Greeley's *Tribune* in mid-July, "Messrs. Lincoln and Douglas will speak together at fifteen or twenty of the most important and widely accessible points throughout the State, and that the controversy will be prosecuted . . . at every county seat and considerable town. Such a conflict of principles of the gravest public consequences tends to purify the political atmosphere and ennoble the strife of parties."

At first it had seemed that this joint discussion would take place on a purely informal basis. Lincoln spoke in Chicago on the night following Douglas; he sat on Douglas's platform at Bloomington, but kept silent; and in Springfield he followed Douglas's afternoon discourse at Edward's Grove with an evening address in the Hall of Representatives.[1] When Douglas's managers issued a program of engagements covering a long list of towns, the Republican State Committee laid plans to place Lincoln at many of the same points on the same day or the day following. Simultaneously, on July 24, Lincoln challenged Douglas to "divide time and address the same audiences, the present canvass." The Senator reluctantly replied, agreeing to joint debate at one prominent point in each Congressional district save those of Chicago and Springfield, already covered; and he suggested Freeport, Ottawa, Galesburg, Quincy, Alton, Jonesboro, and Charleston. Lincoln assented. It was agreed that the first debate should take place at Ottawa on August 21 and the last at Alton on October 15; that one man should speak for an hour, the other reply for an hour and a half, and the first then conclude in half an hour. Douglas, as the challenged party, seized the advantage of four of the seven openings. Illinois newspapers were quick to appreciate the significance of the encounters.

The arrangement, which followed a pattern familiar in the South and West, was sensible. It conserved the time of busy rural voters, assured both candidates of larger audiences (including Whigs and Know-Nothings) than they might

---

1 For this speech the hall was crowded with what Herndon called "a most enthusiastic gathering of the intellect, and heart, and soul of our town"; and Lincoln's speech was "a whaler." Herndon to Trumbull, July 22, 1858; Trumbull Papers. For the Republican organization in Springfield, see Paul M. Angle, *Here I Have Lived*, Ch. XII.

otherwise reach, and facilitated a true clash of arguments. To Douglas's partisans, the contest seemed to give Lincoln, as the less famous and important man, some artificial benefits. They declared that he could never have collected large crowds of his own, and would gain a spurious prestige from Douglas's renown. They consoled themselves with the belief that the champion of mighty Senate debates would shake this provincial attorney, in full sight of the nation, as a mastiff shakes a terrier. Lincoln, predicted the *State Register*, "will get enough of debate and discomfiture to last him the rest of his life." [2]

Douglas, however, knew well that he had entered upon no light undertaking. Before leaving the East, he had told John W. Forney that he would face the most formidable antagonist to be found in Illinois. To Chicago associates he said frankly that in clarity, force, and dexterity Lincoln was the doughtiest opponent who could be brought against him. At an evening party among friends in the city, just before the debates opened, he betrayed an uneasy preoccupation; when a guest asked if he could entertain any anxiety over his combat with the Springfield lawyer, he replied that he felt deep uneasiness.

Three August weeks remained between the compact of Douglas and Lincoln and their first debate. The Senator spent them in active campaigning, while Lincoln gave the first ten days to preparation and letter-writing at home. On August 11, Douglas spoke at Beardstown, beautifully situated on the Illinois. He had been angered by Lincoln's charge in the "house divided" speech of a conspiracy of Stephen, Roger, and others to thrust the Dred Scott decision on an unsuspecting country; a charge which Lincoln had repeated with emphasis in another Springfield speech on July 17. This accusation was not the less dangerous for being false. At Beardstown, Douglas exploded that it was "an infamous lie." With equal heat he attacked Senator Trumbull for charging that he had been partly responsible for the Lecompton constitution. "The miserable, craven-hearted wretch would sooner have both ears cut off than to use that language in my presence, where I could call him to account." Hardly had Douglas departed, accompanied by his queenly looking wife, than Lincoln arrived on August 12, met at the wharf by two bands and forty horsemen. Speaking for two hours, he once more repeated the conspiracy charge.

The informal contest then moved up the Illinois valley, its broad cornfields basking in the heat. On August 13, Douglas spoke at Havana (center of the Spoon River country which Edgar Lee Masters was later to immortalize). Lincoln in high spirits boarded the steamer *Editor* to follow him. "Several of his old Whig friends were on board," Horace White later recalled, "and the

2 For preliminaries of the debate see Beveridge, *Lincoln*, II, 641 ff.; Baringer, *Lincoln's Rise to Power*, 11 ff.; and Milton, *Eve of Conflict*, 328 ff.

journey was filled up with politics and storytelling." His stories were always apropos of some event or idea, and were told with a "facial expression so irresistibly comic that the bystanders generally exploded in laughter" before he reached the point. At Havana, Douglas again lost his temper, called Lincoln a liar, coward, and sneak, and said something about fighting him. Replying the next day, Lincoln remarked that his opponent had been a little excited, and humorously deprecated any idea of a fistic battle. It would prove nothing; besides, "he and I are about the best friends in the world." The judge, he added, was merely trying to stir up political excitement, and "as I find he was tolerably successful in this, we will call it quits." [3]

The two moved on northward, their audiences growing in size. The turn-out for Douglas at Lewistown was especially impressive. Both men found elaborate receptions in Peoria, where they used again the arguments of their Chicago and Springfield speeches. And so, on August 21, they came together at Ottawa.

[I]

This pleasant town of six thousand people at the junction of the Illinois and Fox rivers, eighty-four miles southwest of Chicago, filled up that day with nearly fifteen thousand visitors. Long special trains—decked with banners, their seats packed and one car vibrant with a band—ran in from Chicago and La Salle. Special boats churned down the canal. Towers of choking dust rose from roads which since early morning had been alive with spring wagons, buckboards, carriages, buggies, and horsemen, each vehicle with a plump food basket under the seat. Military companies drew into lines under the bark of impatient officers; peddlers cried their wares; farmers talked of crops and politicians of votes; urchins popped an occasional firecracker. The town had scythed its lawns, dressed its store windows, and flung mottoed strips of canvas across the main street. All morning, citizens were hurriedly tacking flags and bunting to their porches. As the throng thickened, men, women, children, and dogs made Ottawa "one mass of active life"; it became difficult to force a passage through the crowd. Horses neighed, drums thudded, fifes squealed, and knots of men bore transparencies aloft.

Excitement among Democrats rose to a climax as a long cavalcade of horse-men with flags and inscribed ensigns, streaming out on the La Salle highway, met Douglas's four-horse carriage and brought him into town with music, cannon, and resounding cheers. The fervor of Republicans rose in a similar crescendo as Lincoln came in by train from Chicago and was placed in a car-

3 Horace White, quoted in Herndon and Weik, *Lincoln*, 1892 ed., II, 102, 103.

riage decorated with evergreens to be escorted to the home of the mayor. Shortly after one o'clock rival processions formed, and, with much marching and counter-marching, carried the candidates to the treeless public square. Here the crowd was so tightly packed that it took half an hour of rough-and-tumble pushing to get the speakers, committees, and reporters to the platform; and they were no sooner there than a section of the wooden awning, laden with men and boys, collapsed on the heads of the Douglas committee.

Intense feeling was shown. As the candidates took their seats, each was wildly cheered by his followers as the apostle of principles that would save the nation, the preacher of truth that would usher in a bright new era. These hard-headed men of the West, drawn from every section, from Britain and Germany, young in average years and in outlook, had a shrewd realization that the republic indeed stood at the crossroads; that it was girding itself to take mighty decisions; and that the issues under discussion involved the welfare of generations yet unborn.[4]

Never in our history have orators stood in more dramatic contrast. "Everybody knows Douglas," wrote the correspondent of the New York *Evening Post*, "a short, thickset, burly man, with large round head, heavy hair, dark complexion, and fierce bulldog look." As Douglas spoke for an hour, recalling the days when he had been schoolmaster in Winchester while Lincoln was a Salem grocery-keeper, and striving to identify the Republican Party with abolitionism, the crowd frequently interrupted with approving shouts. Then Lincoln rose, getting a long roar of applause. "Built on the Kentucky type, he is very tall, slender, angular, awkward even, in gait and attitude," wrote the *Post* reporter. "His face is sharp, large-featured, and unprepossessing. His eyes are deep set under heavy brows, his forehead is high and retreating, and his hair is dark and heavy." In short, he was ugly. "But stir him up and the fire of his genius plays on every feature. His eye glows and sparkles, every lineament, now so ill-formed, grows brilliant and expressive, and you have before you a man of rare power and of strong magnetic influence. He *takes* the people every time, and there is no getting away from his sturdy good sense, his unaffected sincerity, and the unceasing play of his good humor, which accompanies his close logic and smoothes the way to conviction." The correspondent thought Lincoln the more fluent of the two.[5] As a matter of fact, each candidate had his special virtues and defects as an orator.

4 E. E. Sparks, ed., *The Lincoln-Douglas Debates*, 85–147. In the Ottawa district, radical Republicans were numerous and feeling over Kansas had run high. The district was represented in Congress by the abolitionist Owen Lovejoy, of Princeton, Illinois, a man whose strong convictions, powerful physique, and personal magnetism made him popular. He was renominated and reelected this year, lending strength to Lincoln—who would later clash with him. See Isabel Wallace, *Life and Letters of W. H. L. Wallace*, 73 ff.

5 Chester P. Dewey of the *Evening Post* in Herndon and Weik, *Lincoln*, II, 105–107.

At Ottawa and other points, the advantages of prestige, personal force, platform experience, and intellectual dexterity were all with Douglas. For years he had been one of the most famous of Americans; he had a peculiar magnetism, compounded of dignity, energy, and strength; as he stood up to speak, the victor in a hundred senatorial duels, his square shoulders, broad chest, and leonine head making men forget his shortness, he seemed the very embodiment of thrust, combativeness, and staying power. The defiance, audacity, and restless belligerency of his port irresistibly appealed to the rougher element in every crowd. His well-tailored broadcloth, shining linen, and broad felt hat, his prominent friends and the deference of influential office-holders all over the State who lost no opportunity to lionize him, deepened the impression that a great man had returned home to his people. His voice rolled forth in a fierce if monotonous bulldog bark, never carrying to the outskirts of a large crowd, but effective wherever heard.

By contrast Lincoln, ludicrously tall, angular, and awkward in gait and gesture, was at first glance unprepossessing. His clothes fitted badly; his stovepipe hat accentuated his height; his face, sharp, yellow-leathery, and wrinkled, with heavy nose, jaws, and forehead, had a backwoods homeliness; he seemed unsure of himself. It was not until some minutes passed that the audience appreciated the keenness of his gray eyes, the breadth of his forehead, the strength of his chin. He shambled when he walked. His principal movements when talking—clasping and unclasping his hands, first behind and then in front of himself, an uncouth swing of his long arms, or a sudden dip at the knees followed by a sharp upward jerk with much gesticulation of the head—were often indescribably gauche. Three attributes of value, however, he did possess. When he became aroused by his theme, as the *Post* correspondent noted, his face lighted up, his deep eyes glowed, and his uneasy diffidence gave way to a profound earnestness. His voice, always shrill in moments of excitement and sometimes rising to a high treble, had a remarkably penetrating quality, so that the most distant auditor could hear it. Above all, he combined a patent sincerity and common-sense logic with better self-control than his antagonist. When Douglas was angered, his features became distorted, his voice deepened, and he looked like a man in an intense rage. But Lincoln never lost his simple, self-possessed blend of honesty and good humor, which lent persuasiveness to his clear, compact arguments.

The debate under the broiling sun in the treeless, seatless Ottawa square held the audience for three hours. At the end, enthusiastic Republicans carried the embarrassed Lincoln away on their shoulders. Newspapers treated the bout with the partisanship of the time. "Lincoln's Heart Fails Him!—Lincoln's Legs Fail Him!—Lincoln's Tongue Fails Him!" ran part of the headline of the

Chicago *Times*. We think that "since the flailing Senator Douglas received at Ottawa," his friends should "address him as the late Mr. Douglas," declared the Chicago *Journal*. Actually both had spoken well, and with a genuine clash of views.[6]

Douglas had attacked Lincoln's position on two fronts. Up to 1854, he said, the Whig and Democratic Parties, both national, had affirmed the right of the people of each State and Territory to decide their own local and domestic institutions for themselves, subject only to the Constitution. Then, in 1854, Lincoln, Trumbull, and others had brought as many former Whigs and Democrats as possible into a Republican Party which was essentially abolitionist and sectional. Lincoln now declared that the nation would not endure permanently half free and half slave; and he also asserted that he would not submit to the Dred Scott decision because it deprived the negro of the privileges of citizenship. On both heads he was wrong. Touching his first statement, the founders of the nation had willingly seen the country divided into free States and slave States, while it had endured half slave and half free for seventy years. Why should it not continue to exist with the diversity of institutions which fitted a land so huge and varied? Touching Lincoln's second statement, it was plain that the government had been made by white men for the benefit of white men and their posterity. "Do you desire to turn this beautiful State into a free negro colony, in order that when Missouri abolishes slavery she can send one hundred thousand emancipated slaves into Illinois, to become citizens and voters, on an equality with yourselves?" No, the path to concord and progress lay in acceptance of the Supreme Court decision and of Douglas's popular sovereignty doctrine.

Lincoln counterattacked with vigor. First, he cleared up certain misconceptions. The Republican Party was in no sense an abolitionist party. "I have no purpose, either directly or indirectly, to interfere with the institution of slavery where it exists. I believe I have no lawful right to do so, and I have no inclination to do so. I have no purpose to introduce political and social equality between the white and the black races." Nevertheless, the natural right of the negro to life, liberty, and the pursuit of happiness must be respected. He might not be the equal of the white man in mental and moral endowment. "But in the right to eat the bread, without the leave of anyone else, which his own hand earns, he is my equal, and the equal of Judge Douglas, and the equal of

6 Sparks, ed., *Lincoln-Douglas Debates*, 124–147, reprints much press comment. Lincoln was getting a taste of the scurrilous abuse that was to follow him the rest of his life. The Chicago *Times* continued to call him a scarecrow, declared he was so illiterate he could not utter five distinct sentences in succession, and pictured him as utterly discomfited after the principal debates. "Poor Lincoln!" it exclaimed after the Galesburg encounter; October 9, 12, 1858.

every living man." Having made this position clear, Lincoln turned his guns on Douglas.

He agreed that a variety of local institutions was necessary and wholesome in America; but slavery was not one of these desirable variations. It had ever been an apple of discord, and so long as it survived would continue an element of division. The fact that the nation had existed for seventy years in spite of this baneful element could be explained by the position in which the fathers had originally placed slavery. They excluded it from new Territories, and cut off its source in the slave trade, so that the public mind rested in the belief that it was in course of ultimate extinction. But, since of late years Douglas and others had placed the institution on a new basis, looking to the nationalization and perpetuity of slavery, the national discord had become greater than ever. The proper course was to arrest the spread of slavery and place it where Washington, Jefferson, and Madison had placed it—on the way to death. Then peace would come. "The crisis would be past, and the institution might be let alone for a hundred years—if it should live so long—in the States where it exists—yet it would be going out of existence in the way best for both the white and black races." As for the Dred Scott decision, it was no more eternally binding than any other court pronouncement. Had not Douglas once helped add five new judges to the Illinois supreme court in order to reverse one of its decisions?

[II]

The second debate, that at Freeport, might be called the question-and-answer discussion; for here Lincoln replied to certain interrogatories which Douglas had put at Ottawa, and propounded four questions of his own which Douglas answered on the spot. Historically, this was the most momentous of all the debates.

Freeport, close under the Wisconsin line in the Rock River valley, drew an even larger crowd than Ottawa—fully fifteen thousand. The three railroads had offered excursion rates and special trains, one of which, with sixteen coaches, brought a thousand passengers. Spectators poured in from Chicago, Galena, and Beloit. Douglas, arriving the night before, was received with an enthusiastic torchlight procession. Lincoln came in by train the next morning from Dixon, to be greeted by a dense crowd which formed in parade line to escort him to the Brewster House. The weather was cloudy and cool, with an occasional fine drizzle. A grove on the outskirts of town had been chosen for the occasion. For Douglas, a fine carriage had been provided; but when Lincoln clambered into a homely prairie schooner with an escort of weather-beaten farmers, the Senator decided to prove his kinship with the common people by walking to the grounds. Once more the crowd had so closely packed the area that a battering-ram rush was required to get the debaters on the platform. Lincoln was to open. But as he was about to begin, while Douglas sat coolly smoking his cigar, a friend stopped him. "You can't speak yet," he said. "Hitt ain't here"—and they waited until Robert R. Hitt, the Chicago *Tribune's* short-hand reporter, was ready.[7]

Lincoln began by answering a series of Douglas's queries. He had never asked the repeal of the Fugitive Slave Act, for he believed the South entitled to such a law. He was not pledged against the admission of more slave States, for if the people of a Territory on fair vote wanted slavery they would have to be admitted with it. He was not pledged to the abolition of slavery in the District of Columbia, or to the prohibition of the domestic slave trade. But he did believe in the right and duty of Congress to exclude slavery from all Territories. He favored the abolition of slavery in the District of Columbia on condition that it should be gradual, effected with majority consent, and accompanied by compensation. Once more, he declared that he wished slavery put in such a position that it might be regarded as on the road to ultimate extinction. He then turned to Douglas with his own set of questions, of which the second was crucial. How could the Senator reconcile popular sovereignty with the Dred Scott decision?

Lincoln knew well what the answer would be. He had written a Quincy friend, Henry Asbury, two months earlier that it might be hard work to get Douglas to deal directly with the point whether a territorial legislature had the power to exclude slavery. "But if you succeed in bringing him to it—though he will be compelled to say it possesses no such power—he will instantly take ground that slavery cannot actually exist in the Territories unless the people desire it, and so give it protection by territorial legislation. If this offends the South, he will let it offend them, as at all events he means to hold on to his chances in Illinois." Lincoln knew, in fact, that Douglas had already answered. But it was worth while to put Douglas on the defensive; it was worth while to hold up his position plainly in sight of the South. Talking with Medill of

7 Sparks, *op. cit.*, 147–212; Sandburg, *Lincoln, the Prairie Years*, II, 142. It was evidence of the importance of the debates that a corps of newspapermen accompanied the principals. Chester P. Dewey represented the N. Y. *Evening Post;* Henry Villard the Phila. *Press;* Horace White the Chicago *Press and Tribune.* Robert R. Hitt of the *Press and Tribune* furnished a good shorthand report of Lincoln's speeches; and two experts, James B. Sheridan and Henry Binmore, did the same for Douglas in the Chicago *Times.* Various editors, including C. H. Ray and Joseph Medill of the Chicago *Tribune*, appeared at times. David R. Locke, the Ohio journalist later known as Petroleum V. Nasby, talked with Lincoln at Quincy, and Charles F. Browne (Artemus Ward) interviewed him at Springfield for *Vanity Fair.*

the *Tribune* and others on the train, Lincoln had insisted against their objections on posing the question.[8]

The Little Giant answered all four of Lincoln's queries promptly. Three were minor. He would vote to admit Kansas before she had ninety-three thousand people; he believed it impossible for the Supreme Court to commit such "moral treason" as to hold that a State could not exclude slaves; and he would have the United States acquire more territory whenever needed, leaving the inhabitants of each new area to settle the question of slavery as they pleased. Coming then to the major query, Douglas unhesitatingly affirmed that the people of a Territory could, by lawful means, shut out slavery prior to the formation of a State constitution. Despite the Dred Scott decision, the people had the right to admit or exclude slavery, for it could not exist a day or an hour unless supported by local police regulations. "These police regulations can only be established by the local legislature, and if the people are opposed to slavery they will elect representatives to that body who will by unfriendly legislation effectually prevent the introduction of it into their midst." Thus, no matter what the Supreme Court said on the "abstract question," still "the right of the people to make a slave Territory or a free Territory is perfect and complete under the Nebraska bill."

In thus pinning the Senator down, more sweepingly and dramatically than ever before, to the doctrine of control by local police legislation, the Freeport debate caught the nation's attention. Various other men had stated this idea. Speaker Orr had enunciated it in the Kansas debates in 1856. Alexander H. Stephens had asserted it. Senator Cass in his Detroit speech of September 4, 1854, had explained just how at all times "the fate of slavery in these new regions must depend upon the will of the people." But now, forcibly reiterated at a time when men's emotions were keenly sensitive, the doctrine had the naked, quivering, eye-compelling quality of a brandished sword.

[III]

Nearly three weeks elapsed between Freeport and the third debate on September 15 at Jonesboro, a period spent by both men in active campaigning. At Clinton on the 2d, Lincoln perhaps said: "You can fool all of the people some of the time, and some of the people all of the time, but you cannot fool

8 When Medill, shown the question, protested on the train, Lincoln declared that he would "spear it at Douglas" that afternoon. Arriving in Freeport, Medill told Norman B. Judd and Elihu B. Washburne of Lincoln's purpose. They too protested, but Lincoln could not be moved. See Medill's story in Sparks, ed., *Lincoln-Douglas Debates*, 203–206. Cf. Randall, *Lincoln the President*, I, 124, 125. As a matter of fact, Douglas had asserted the doctrine of "unfriendly legislation" in his Bloomington and Springfield speeches, July 16–17; *Illinois State Register*, July 19.

The Seven Douglas-Lincoln Debates

Black lines indicate Congressional Districts; numerals the points and dates of debates.

all the people all the time." He was thinking of Douglas, for he remarked to a lawyer of the place that the Senator would "tell a lie to ten thousand people one day even though he knows he may have to deny it to five thousand the next day." At Carlinville, Lincoln shared a platform with John M. Palmer. He spoke also in Bloomington and Monticello, and at Paris was joined for a day by the eloquent Owen Lovejoy, who, knowing his own ill-fame as an abolitionist, invited timid hearers to come up and feel his horns and examine his cloven foot and forked tail. At Edwardsville, Lincoln delivered a memorable denunciation of the spirit which did not care whether slavery was voted up or down. "Our defense is in the spirit which prizes liberty as the heritage of all men, in all lands everywhere," he said. "Destroy this spirit and you have planted the seeds of despotism at your own doors." [9]

The Jonesboro debate, deep in hilly "Egypt" only thirty miles from Cairo, drew a crowd of hardly fifteen hundred. The country was poor. Most of the farmers came into town on decrepit wagons drawn by ox-teams, and stunted oxen at that. Douglas arrived from Cairo with a trainful of supporters; but he aroused no enthusiasm, for Union County was a fortress of Buchanan Democrats. It is not strange that the discussion was lackadaisical, full of personalities, and lacking in ideas. Much of it was concerned with futile efforts by Douglas to forge a bond between Lincoln and the abolitionists, and equally futile stage-thunder by Lincoln in trying to shore up his theory of a plot among Stephen, Roger, James, and Franklin. Douglas added nothing substantial to his old arguments; Lincoln added only an attempt to refute the Freeport Doctrine. He declared that history proved the falsity of the idea that slavery could not enter a new country without friendly police legislation; for it had entered the colonies without such aids, and Dred had been held a slave in Minnesota without them. Moreover, the Federal courts in all Territories would have to meet any infringement of property rights with such remedy as was necessary.

At one point they did push into fresh ground. Lincoln raised the vital question of an attempt by the South to obtain Congressional protection of slavery in the Territories—a slave code—asking if Douglas would support it; and the Senator replied emphatically that he would not.[10]

At Charleston, the attendance swelled again—ten or twelve thousand people gathering. The flat prairie town was gay with flags and emblems, while a banner eighty feet long across the main street depicted "Old Abe Thirty Years Ago"

9 Sandburg, *Lincoln, the Prairie Years*, II, 142; Baringer, *Lincoln's Rise to Power*, 27, 28. It was not until after 1900, when the epigram about fooling the people had long held popular currency, that several men who had heard the Clinton speech declared that Lincoln had used the words quoted. Our only contemporaneous summary of the speech, a partial report in the Bloomington *Pantagraph* of September 9, 1858, does not contain the epigram. But it sounds like Lincoln and has gained a qualified acceptance as his by good students.
10 Sparks, ed., *Lincoln-Douglas Debates*, 213–266.

driving three yoke of oxen harnessed to a Kentucky wagon. Excitement over the campaign seemed now at its peak. Delegation after delegation rolled in. One train discharged eleven carloads of interested Indianians. The *Evening Post* correspondent wrote that the popular interest in politics was astonishing. "Over long, weary miles of hot, dusty prairie, the processions of eager partisans come on foot, on horseback, in wagons drawn by horses or mules; men, women, and children, old and young; the half-sick just out of the last shake, children in arms, infants . . . pushing on in clouds of dust under a blazing sun . . . talking, discussing, litigious, vociferous, while the roar of artillery, the music of bands, the waving of banners, the huzza of crowds . . . combine to render the scene one of commotion and confusion." Lincoln and Douglas had spent the previous night at Mattoon, and were escorted ten miles along the highway by lines of carriages, wagons full of young people, and prancing horsemen. In Lincoln's procession was a chariot with thirty-two young women, representing as many States.

Both candidates by this time had found the campaign physically gruelling, for it meant lost sleep, bad food, heat, dust, and incessant strain. Douglas suffered the more, though he traveled much of the time in a private car which both impressed voters with his dignity and saved his strength; while on some journeys his wife accompanied him. She was "without exception the handsomest woman I have ever seen," recorded one observer; her charm, good sense, and tact were invaluable politically; and she guarded her husband's diet and rest. But his drinking and his poor physical condition told against him. Mrs. Douglas complained that he lost half his clothes. "I got him four dozen shirts last spring, and two or three sets of studs; he lost all his shirts but two, with one that doesn't belong to him, and all the studs but four, which belong to four different sets."

Lincoln snatched some sleep wherever he could. Traveling by night in a dirty day-coach from Springfield to Clinton, he promised to rouse Horace White of the Chicago *Tribune* at Decatur, where they had to change cars; but both fell fast asleep. Lincoln awakened barely in time to scramble off, and White was carried on to Indiana. Herndon gives us a vignette of Lincoln after the Jonesboro speech: sitting hot, dust-stained, and exhausted in a packed railroad station, still harassed by politicians as he waited for the midnight train north, and worrying over his Charleston speech the day after; then jammed into an overcrowded coach; and finally obtaining a few hours' slumber when a stratagem got him into an empty car.

At Charleston, most of the debate was on the low level of accusation and counter-accusation. The invented conspiracies, that of Lincoln and Trumbull to convert freesoil Whigs and Democrats into abolitionists, and that of Buchanan, Taney, and Douglas to spread slavery over the whole Union, received preposterous attention. This shadowboxing was unworthy of such men. At one point, Lincoln snatched his former colleague O. B. Ficklin by the coat collar to the front of the stand, to testify that in Congress Lincoln had not refused to vote supplies for the Mexican War. Ficklin's astonishment was so comical that the audience burst into a roar of laughter. Douglas vigorously reiterated his old positions. Lincoln, however, did present his conservative views on the racial question at some length. Douglas had accused the Republicans of lacking consistency on the subject. In northern Illinois, he said, their principles were jet black, in the center a decent mulatto, and in "Egypt" almost white. A house divided cannot stand—well, what of the Republican house?

To this witty hit Lincoln answered that he believed the negro must hold an inferior status. "I am not, nor ever have been, in favor of bringing about in any way the social and political equality of the white and black races. . . . I am not, nor ever have been, in favor of making voters or jurors of negroes, nor of qualifying them to hold office, nor to intermarry with white people, and I will say in addition to this that there is a physical difference between the white and black races which I believe will forever forbid the two races living together on terms of social and political equality." Ultimate emancipation, he thought, would take a century or more; but slavery must be put in a position where ultimate emancipation was in prospect. Meanwhile, though Lincoln believed that the States had power to make negroes citizens, he was opposed to the exercise of such a right by Illinois. By the standards of 1950 these utterances lacked courage; by those of 1860 his general stand seemed advanced, and his reservations accurately reflected the views of the vast majority of Illinois free-soilers, who did not want negro equality—or the negro at all.[11]

Nearly three weeks elapsed before the next debate. Douglas spoke in Sullivan, Danville, and Urbana—Lincoln following him. Then Lincoln turned west while Douglas went on north.

[IV]

They met again at Galesburg on October 7, in the most picturesque and impressive of all the debates. The town, founded just over twenty years earlier under the inspiration of the Rev. George W. Gale, who planned it as seat of a

[11] This emphatic utterance against racial equality at Charleston brought down on Lincoln's head the abuse of abolitionists. The *Congregational Herald*, edited in Chicago by four clergymen, assailed him (September 30) because he did not go far enough in defense of the negro. "Our standard-bearer has faltered thus soon, while the contest has only begun," it lamented. More than a vague sympathy with freedom was needed from him: "He must adopt its radical principles and stand by them in victory or defeat." This was a foretaste of the Radical attacks which Lincoln would meet in Civil War days.

theological seminary and a rallying point of freesoilers, could boast not only of five thousand people but of some intellectual distinction. Knox College, coeval with the settlement, flourished there. Henry Ward Beecher's brother, Edward, was pastor of the Congregational church. White houses and fine lawns under rising elms gave the town a neat, quiet New England look; but it was also an important rail junction, a line from Burlington and another from Quincy joining here to run northeast to Chicago, and a foundry and farm-implement factory were busy. In the Frémont campaign, Knox County had voted two to one for the Republicans. After a heavy downpour the previous day, the weather was damp and chilly. Nevertheless, twenty thousand people gathered under the snapping flags and bunting and they showed genuine enthusiasm. One delegation carried a great poster depicting Douglas and a flimsy platform labeled "Dred Scott" collapsing together. The Macomb Lincoln Club bore aloft another which gave the answer of Illinoisans to Hammond's mudsill speech:

SMALL-FISTED FARMERS, MUD SILLS OF SOCIETY, GREASY MECHANICS, FOR A. LINCOLN.

This, wrote Horace White later, was Lincoln's best speech of the campaign. Nor did Douglas fail to keep his argument on a high level. Standing on the platform in front of Knox College's "Old Main," they held public attention for three hours in the cold northwest wind, as they had held it elsewhere in blazing heat. Once more Douglas boasted of his fidelity to the banner of popular sovereignty; once more he chided Lincoln for believing in negro equality; and once more he asserted his Freeport Doctrine. Lincoln, responding, again declared that the negro was equal to the white man in his right to life, liberty, and the pursuit of happiness; he again said that while this principle could not be thrust too roughly against the necessities springing from the actual presence of black people and slavery in America, it should be applied to new areas; and he again asserted that the Union would be safe only when slavery was placed in the path to ultimate extinction.[12]

Never had Douglas shown greater intensity of feeling. He taunted the Republicans with their sectional character. "Permit me to say," he thundered, "that no political creed is sound which cannot be proclaimed fearlessly in every State of this Union where the Federal Constitution is the supreme law of the land." Is it a true test of the soundness of a doctrine, rejoined Lincoln, that in some places people will not let you proclaim it? At one time Chicagoans would not let Douglas preach his favorite doctrine. "I ask his attention to the fact that by the rule of nationality he is himself fast becoming sectional. I ask his atten-

---

12 At Galesburg, Lincoln wore a long cloak instead of his usual shawl, and when he rose to reply to Douglas he handed it to a friend, saying: "Hold this while I stone Stephen." Earnest Elmo Calkins, *They Broke the Prairie*, 277-295.

tion to the fact that his speeches would not go as current south of the Ohio River as they have formerly gone there." Douglas accused Lincoln of infidelity to the Constitution. But Lincoln answered that the Supreme Court followed the election returns. "The Dred Scott decision, as it is, never would have been made in its present form if the party that made it had not been sustained previously by the elections." The grand future of the nation, declared Douglas, lay with the broad principles of the Democratic Party. Yes, responded Lincoln, Douglas stood for annexations, and if Democratic policy were followed, a grab would be made for large parts of Latin America. And as neither the whole people nor the whole government of the United States—merely President and Senate—would have a voice in these annexations, the policy was dangerous.

At Galesburg both men disclosed for the first time a gleam of eloquence. Douglas's contrast between the high national mission of the Democratic Party and the bigoted sectionalism of the Republicans was eloquent. So was Lincoln's echo of one of Clay's finest passages. "I do think," proclaimed Lincoln, "that Judge Douglas and whoever, like him, teaches that the negro has no share, humble though it may be, in the Declaration of Independence, is going back to the era of our liberty and independence, and, in so far as in him lies, muzzling the cannon that thunders its annual joyous return; that he is blowing out the moral lights around us, when he contends that whoever wants slaves has a right to hold them; that he is penetrating, so far as lies in his power, the human soul, and eradicating the light of reason and the love of liberty, when he is in every way possible preparing the public mind, by his vast influence, for making the institution of slavery perpetual and national."

Quincy, too, where they met on October 13, had a New England aspect, though Adams County had been almost equally settled by Yankees and former Virginians and Kentuckians. Here, on the fine bluff overlooking the Mississippi, near some old Indian mounds, was a city well known to young Mark Twain and young John Hay, who had grown up close at hand. The brilliant Carl Schurz, traveling to Quincy for a speech of his own, was on a Chicago train when Lincoln climbed aboard, and has left us a vivid impression of the man. The whole car broke into glad shouts of "Hello, Abe! How are you?" Amid much back-slapping, Lincoln greeted the politicians by their first names. "There he stood," writes Schurz, "overtopping by several inches all those surrounding him." He wore a rusty black dress-coat with inadequate sleeves, black trousers which fell far short of his large feet, and a battered stovepipe hat. His long neck projected from a soft white collar encircled by a black string tie. While his left hand clutched a cotton umbrella and scarred black satchel, and his left arm bore a gray woolen shawl, he kept his right hand free for the endless hand-shaking. When Schurz was introduced, he treated the awed German like a lifelong friend. He explained the points he intended to make at Quincy and asked advice; he told quaint stories to illustrate his ideas; and he talked so simply and familiarly that Schurz soon felt as if they had known each other always.

The day of the debate was fine. Twelve thousand people came by river boat, rail, and highway from Iowa, Missouri, and Illinois; banners and bands were as exciting as ever; and both orators got a rousing reception. Lincoln spoke so persuasively that Schurz, while not crediting him with any distinction of thought, did not see how he could be answered. But when Douglas stood up, natty in well-fitting broadcloth and white linen, the horizontal wrinkle between his keen eyes deep and scowling, the German soon learned. Douglas's baritone voice was hoarse and rough; his tone was angry, dictatorial, and insolent; he used offensive language. "But his sentences were well put together, his points strongly accentuated, his argumentation seemingly clear and plausible." As he sat down, his followers burst into jubilant applause. Lincoln then made the final half-hour speech, and in Schurz's opinion carried off the palm. His arguments were so forcible, his thrusts so piercing, his illustrations so apt, "that the meeting again and again, broke out in bursts of delight by which even many of his opponents were carried away, while the scowl on Douglas's face grew darker and darker." [13]

At Quincy, much old straw was lustily rethreshed, yielding little grain. The most striking passages were those in which the debaters assailed each other for proposing no constructive action regarding slavery, and exchanged divergent views of the Freeport Doctrine. Lincoln asserted that the Republicans did have a plan. Whenever they could get the country to stand and act with them in regarding slavery as a wrong, "then, and not till then, I think, will we in some way come to an end of the slavery agitation." Douglas declared that this "plan" was barren. Lincoln would simply hem slavery into the areas where it existed; and what did this mean? The natural increase of the negroes would soon exceed the capacity of the soil to support them. "He will hem them in until starvation seizes them, and by starving them to death he will put slavery in the course of ultimate extinction." Lincoln pronounced the Freeport Doctrine a fraud. How could a member of a territorial legislature swear to uphold the Constitution and then deny a slaveholding settler rights which Douglas said the Constitution gave him? But Douglas retorted that the Freeport Doctrine was entirely valid, and that such Southerners as Speaker Orr, A. H. Stephens, and Sam Smith of Tennessee said so.

The seventh and final debate at Alton, however unoriginal, was one of the most creditable of the series, pitched throughout on a high level of reason. The crowd was small, but both men knew they would be well reported in Missouri and Kentucky as well as the North. Douglas was in his best fighting trim, though a St. Louis journalist, John F. Hume, who had come on an excursion steamer, was impressed by the painful huskiness of his voice. Lincoln, according to this observer, stood stiff and straight, his countenance immobile; Douglas's countenance was leonine and full of expression, while his manner was excited and he emphasized his speech by almost continuous movement of hands, feet, and face. This auditor was disappointed that Lincoln, standing almost on the spot that had drunk Elijah Lovejoy's blood, spoke without any touch of fiery inspiration.[14]

Douglas showed courageous energy before an audience mainly of Southern sympathies by denouncing the English bill as unjust and assailing Buchanan for following a vengeful course against him. He was full of contempt for the Administration lackeys in Illinois. Appealing for party unity, he said that the life of the nation depended on avoiding a sectional schism. Once more he enunciated his Freeport position, refusing to cringe or evade on the issue. His speech rose to a fervent climax. No principle on earth, he said, was more sacred than that of popular sovereignty. "I will never violate or abandon that doctrine, if I have to stand alone. I have resisted the blandishments and threats of power on the one side, and seduction on the other, and have stood immovably for that principle, fighting for it when assailed by Northern mobs, or threatened by Southern hostility. I have defended it against the North and the South, and I will defend it against whoever assails it, and I will follow it wherever its logical conclusion leads me." That was Douglas's finest hour. However mistaken some men might deem his Nebraska Act, he had shown magnificent consistency in defending its principles.[15]

Lincoln, too, brought his campaign to a telling climax. His speech was full of witty points. He referred to Douglas's old promises that the Nebraska Act would see them at the end of the slavery agitation. "The last tip of the last joint of the old serpent's tail was just drawing out of view." Once more he pointed out that the Republicans, without desire to touch slavery in the States, wished to exclude it from the Territories; and he rehearsed their two chief arguments. One was that the people of the whole nation had a stake in the kind of institutions set up in the common domain. How many men about Alton had left slave States and came to Illinois to get rid of the institution of slavery? A voice shouted: "A thousand and one!" The greater argument was that slavery ought to be placed in the course of ultimate extinction. He quoted Henry Clay. He pointed to the care with which the fathers of the nation had excluded the word "slavery" from the Constitution; for they hoped that, when

14   John F. Hume, *The Abolitionists*, Ch. 12.
15   Sparks, ed., *Lincoln-Douglas Debates*, 449–510, covers Alton in detail.

it was read by patriotic men after slavery had passed away, nothing on the face of the great charter of liberty would suggest that human servitude had ever existed in the republic. Then, adverting to Douglas's refusal to treat slavery as a wrong, he uttered a dozen sentences which indicated why he, rather than his rival, held title-deeds to greatness. That is the real issue, he declared:

> That is the issue which will continue in this country when these poor tongues of Judge Douglas and myself shall be silent. It is the eternal struggle between these two principles—right and wrong—throughout the world. . . . The one is the common right of humanity, and the other the divine right of kings. It is the same principle in whatever shape it develops itself. It is the same spirit that says, "You toil and work and earn bread, and I'll eat it. . . ." [A clarification of this issue] will hereafter place with us all men who really do wish that the wrong may have an end. And whenever we can get rid of the fog which obscures the real question—when we can get Judge Douglas and his friends to avow a policy looking to its perpetuation—we can get out from among them that class of men and bring them to the side of those who treat it as a wrong. Then there will soon be an end of it, and that end will be its "ultimate extinction." Whenever the issue can be distinctly made, and all extraneous matter thrown out, so that men can fairly see the real difference between the parties, this difference will soon be settled, and it will be done peaceably, too. There will be no war, no violence. It will be placed again where the wisest and best men in the world placed it.

[V]

Obviously, the debates had shown little logical progression. Had the speakers left slavery and devoted some attention to other topics in the Republican platform—free lands, opposition to monopolies, internal improvements—they might have achieved more freshness. For three reasons this was not done. First, slavery was so much the burning topic of the hour that the public really wanted exclusive attention paid to it. In the second place, Lincoln and Douglas were in rough agreement on most economic topics. Douglas believed in free homesteads; he had been one of the first to introduce a measure on the subject, granting one hundred and sixty acres to any settler who cultivated the land for four years. Douglas believed in internal improvements, and he had been ingenious in plans to finance them by land grants and tonnage taxes. Neither Douglas nor Lincoln was much interested in the tariff, or understood its intricacies, or believed that his supporters cared much about it. In the third place, slavery was the topic best suited to hold disparate elements in the two parties together.[16]

16 Douglas confessed his ignorance of the tariff; *Cong. Globe,* 36th Cong., 2d Sess., 953; Lincoln ignored the subject. Obviously, Lincoln could unite old-time conservative Whigs, old-time freesoil Democrats, and even abolitionists on his freesoil platform; Douglas could unite pro-Southern and pro-Northern elements on his popular sovereignty doctrine.

Yet, for both nation and State, the debates, which were at first over-estimated in value and later underestimated, did contribute to a clarification of issues. Though Douglas had long before stated the essence of the Freeport Doctrine, the debates dramatized it in a way which for the first time arrested the attention of millions. "There was a great deal of sympathy felt for Douglas throughout Kentucky," wrote a Covington man to Alexander H. Stephens, "until his speech at Freeport, where he put forth squatter sovereignty in all its monstrosity. That speech cooled the ardor of our people." [17] Republicans also seized on it. Horace White suggested to Senator Trumbull that the Kansas legislature be incited to put the doctrine of unfriendly legislation in force by abolishing slavery and nullifying the Fugitive Slave Act; these measures were to be based on the Freeport speech in an effort to ruin Douglas at the South. Thus, he wrote, they might put Douglas out of the running at Charleston.[18]

Lincoln's speeches, read from the Kaw to the Kennebec, had driven home with memorable distinctness his salient conclusions. What were they? First, that slavery was the one great divisive issue which constantly threatened the disruption of the Union. Second, that it had not been such a threat in earlier times because the nation's founders, by restricting its sphere, cutting off its African source, shamefacedly avoiding any direct description of it in the Constitution, and in numerous instances denouncing it, had led men to believe that it would ultimately perish. Third, that ever since Douglas and others had adopted a new attitude, treating slavery as national and perpetual, the fever aroused by the issue had deepened. Fourth, that the only salvation was to return to the old path, restricting slavery and convincing Americans that it was on the way to disappearance. Finally, that once this new attitude was adopted, its ultimate abolition might take a century or more, but could be achieved without war or bloodshed.

Historically and economically, his argument was subject to sharp emendations. The fathers had not forbidden the expansion of slavery into areas to which it was manifestly suited; the Southwest Territory had been opened to it while the Northwest was closed. Their *expectations* regarding its termination had been much more equivocal than their hopes. The agitation had grown dangerous when the nation had first annexed areas in which it seemed an open question whether slavery would be pecuniarily advantageous to settlers, long before Douglas had dealt with Kansas.

17 J. W. Stevenson, October 8, 1858, Stephens Papers, LC. Southerners at the Charleston Convention in 1860 had the Freeport speech with them to use in bombarding Douglas's followers. Murat Halstead, *Caucuses of 1860*, p. 3.

18 December 8, 1858, Trumbull Papers. "A similar broth might be put to boiling in Nebraska," wrote White. For a full account of the indignation which the Freeport Doctrine aroused in the South, see Judah P. Benjamin's speech in the Senate in May, 1860; *Cong. Globe*, 36th Cong., 1st Sess., 2241.

GRAND RALLY
OF THE
LINCOLN MEN
OF
OLD TAZEWELL!

WE   THE

HONOR   ABRAHAM   LINCOLN.   HONEST!

The opponents of those twin cherries on a split stem, BUCHANAN and DOUG-
LAS, in TAZEWELL and adjoining counties, are requested to assemble in

GRAND COUNCIL!
AT PEKIN, ON TUESDAY, OCTOBER 5TH, 1858.

ABRAHAM LINCOLN!

Will address the People at 2 o'clock, P. M. on the Political Topics of the day. Let good men of every name and
tongue who love the patriotic principles of the Father of our Country, come together and sustain the man who represents these principles. When Presidents, Senators
and Supreme Courts decide to make the constitution carry slavery, all over our free states and territories, it is time for the people to rise in their might and maintain our Glorious Union upon the cherished Republican Principles of Washington, Jefferson, Clay and Lincoln.

WM. KELLOGG!

candidate for re-election to Congress, will also address the meeting.

HON. LYMAN TRUMBULL

is expected to speak in the evening.

President of the day, DAVID MARK, Esq.

VICE PRESIDENTS.—Washington JOHN L. KING. Greenfield JOHN BAILY &c. Tremont JOEL H. CLARK. Tracy town JOSEPH GRIFFITH. Fremont JOHN S. ANDO. Mackinaw JOHN SMALLEY. Dillons A. G. NEVILLE. Groveland G. W. HYDE. Elmwood SAML. I. WAGENSELLER. Sprngfield J. SNOTT. Sand Prairie M. M. MANN. Deer Creek NATHAN SMITH. Boynton P. BROADFOOT. Hopedale P. MILLER. Pekin B. JAMES WEBB. Delavan F. W. CROSSLAND. Dunn JAMES ALLSBUFF. Malone I. P. HURLEY. Fort Mardel D. SMITH &c.

     FARE ON STEAMERS NILE AND DELTA
HALF PRICE.

B. A. PICKETT, T. KING, Jr., J. WAGENSELLER, B. A. CHEESEKGE, C. GROVENBERG, J. G. HAWLEY, TE IS SMITH, Committee of Arrangements.
Printed at Pickett & Dowdall's Job Office, Flints' Hall, over Bergstresser's store, Pekin, Illinois

A Typical Lincoln Meeting in 1858
(Tazewell County lay on the Illinois just north of Springfield.)

393

His thesis was also subject to a more vital criticism. The phrase "ultimate extinction," disregarding all questions of *when*, and *how*, and with what *aids*, was too vague to be helpful. Why did he not speak of compensated emancipation, of some broad scheme of colonization, of the Northern obligation to share the expense and to give homes to many of the freedmen? Not, we may be sure, because he had not pondered these matters. He might have said that one step at a time was sufficient. Politically, it was sound policy not to speak of these social costs until public opinion had been prepared; his party had to gain power first, and unfold its practical program as circumstances allowed. His vagueness was regrettable—but the core of his position remained irrefutable.

"I am glad I made the late race," Lincoln wrote a friend on November 19. "It gave me a hearing on the great and durable question of the age, which I could have had in no other way; and though I now sink out of view, and shall be forgotten, I believe I have made some marks which will tell for the cause of civil liberty long after I have gone." For the immediate purpose of winning votes, Douglas's speeches had been as good as his. In any larger view, however, Lincoln had decidedly come off the better; and it was significant that the Republicans, not the Democrats, presently issued large editions of the joint debates and publicized them persistently.[19]

[VI]

The issue remained doubtful to the end of the campaign. Throughout the State the American Party was breaking up, most members in the northern area apparently joining Lincoln, and those in the southern districts, Douglas. The closest struggle took place in the central belt, both sides straining every sinew. Douglas labored almost to exhaustion there; for example, in the single week September 28–October 4, he spoke at Hennepin, Henry, Pekin, Oquawka, Burlington, and Monmouth, giving set addresses at every point but one. Some of his friends toiled devotedly. Charles H. Lanphier of the *State Register* not only filled his paper with campaign arguments and distributed bales of documents, but visited personally every precinct and almost every voter in the

19 The Ohio Republican Committee printed a large edition of the debates early in 1860, before Lincoln was regarded as a probable candidate for the presidency. It went through numerous editions, the second announcing that fifteen thousand copies had been sold, and the third that thirty thousand copies had been sold. The price was fifty cents a copy, $250 a thousand, paper bound; $350 a thousand, cloth bound. Follett, Foster & Co. of Cincinnati took care of distribution. The N. Y. *Tribune* and other Republican papers solicited purchases. Douglas's protest, June 9, 1860, that the text of his speeches, as reported by the Chicago *Times*, had been altered and mutilated, does not seem to have been justified. Cf. Sparks, ed., *Lincoln-Douglas Debates*, 592–595; N. Y. *Weekly Tribune*, June 2, 1860. Lincoln, early in 1859, had suggested to Johnson and Bradford, Springfield printers, that they bring out an edition of the debates, but they refused in a letter of March 21, 1859; Lincoln Papers.

counties surrounding Sangamon.[20] Lincoln spoke with as much assiduity as his rival. Sometimes he dropped from his high moral level to score a swift hit. For example, late October brought him into Hancock County, speaking to large crowds at Carthage, La Harpe, and other points. One Republican wrote:

I took Lincoln to Dallas on Saturday 2000 persons there he was interrupted often in his speech one Tom Gates called him a liar Lincoln requested him to stand up he done so, great God how Lincoln scored him you could have heard the boys shout a mile. Fitch and others painted a large Negro on a canvass 12 feet square and wrote in a circle over the head Equality this was swinging to a line stretched across the street and we marched under it. Lincoln said in his speech that the democrats had honored them with their favorite banner, that it had been a peculiar favorite banner ever since they had elected Col. Richard M. Johnson to the Vice Presidency and that the motto surrounding the head was certainly his for Col. Dick had shown proof of the fact. [Johnson had lived openly with a Negro woman by whom he had a family of children.] [21]

In a contest of this kind, Douglas was no less in his element than in the senatorial melee, and his inborn gifts of political appeal gleamed brightly against the Illinois cornfields. His unaffected warmth of heart, frank ingenuousness of speech, and bonhomie of demeanor won friends in myriads. With a marvelous gift for names and faces, a genuine interest in the personal welfare of others, and a deep vein of talkative companionship, he addressed Joe and Tom, Squire Rice and Parson Hickham, in just the way which touched their self-esteem; recalled old episodes—the misspelled indictments in McLean County, the reception at Governor Carlin's back in '38, the day the first train ran into Peoria—with just the right felicity of touch; rattled off Washington anecdotes in a fashion which gave little knots of hearers the sense of being on the inside of national politics; inquired after an ailing child or an aged parent. He inspired young men with a feeling of partnership in his great cause. One remembered for decades how he had placed his hand upon a flattered shoulder, saying: "I count very much on your help in this campaign." His boyish appearance, his wonderful memory, the pleasant smile and kind words with which he threaded every crowd, left all those he momentarily touched with a pleased sense that he was their personal friend.[22]

In speaking to his hard-working, hard-living rural audiences, Douglas did not fail to recall his days of boyhood poverty. "I made as good a schoolteacher as I could, and when a cabinet-maker I made a good bedstead and tables, although

20 Chicago *Times,* October 1–9, November 7, 1860.
21 Alexander Simpson to John C. Bagby, October 25, 1860; Bagby Papers.
22 Allen Johnson, *Douglas,* 319. His tremendous industry also aroused admiration. The Washington correspondent of the Baltimore *Sun* wrote (August 23) that several Illinoisans had come East full of wonder over his endurance: "He makes two or three speeches a day, and, by reason of the heat, is obliged to change his clothes three times a day at least."

my old boss said I succeeded better with bureaus and secretaries than anything else." In cities, he was adept at making the Germans and Irish feel his goodwill. It was no accident that the Emmet Guards had escorted him to his Chicago platform. Everyone admitted that the Catholic vote would be a unit on Douglas's side.[23] Sheahan's Chicago *Times* appealed vigorously to all foreign-born groups, publishing on election day a long final editorial headed "A Word to Irishmen." The Democratic campaign made the most of the racial issue, contending that Lincoln advocated negro equality, and that the Democrats were the only bulwark against the entry of colored men into Illinois to compete with white farmers and laborers. Beyond doubt this racial appeal had potency in special areas.

By his skillful fight, Douglas made the unremitting attacks of the Buchanan Administration seem impotent spleen. The officeholding gang exhibited more fury than ability, and were little helped by such imported speakers as Daniel Voorhees of Indiana, who called the Douglas men white-livered traitors. The executive blade continued to fall on Douglasite postmasters until the Chicago *Tribune* remarked that only one or two were left.[24] In their desperation the Buchananeers adopted outrageous tactics. When Douglas spoke to a large crowd at Hennepin, Fitch and Hoyne appeared with a brass band that played noisily within a hundred yards of the platform; while at Henry the audacious Hoyne mounted a stand about fifty yards from Douglas and began shouting at the top of his voice.[25] Such acts infuriated Douglas.[26] But the Buchananeers faced one insuperable obstacle; they could not meet the argument of loyal Democrats that to defeat Douglas meant electing Lincoln. This ground was much strengthened by the letters of J. J. Crittenden, Breckinridge, and Reverdy Johnson in favor of Douglas, and the speeches of Paine and Steedman of Ohio. A multitude of old-time Whigs in southern Illinois heeded Crittenden's voice. By election day it was evident that the contest was essentially one between Douglas and the Republicans, with the Administration out of the running.

The result was practically a dead heat. On November 2, the Republican legislative ticket polled 125,275 votes; the Douglas Democrats 121,090 votes; and

23 See letter of a Jewish gentleman of Quincy, December 26, 1858; Trumbull Papers. He wished to put fifty thousand Jewish votes behind the party in 1860 by getting the Republicans to push a Senate protest against Jewish persecution abroad.
24 Chicago *Tribune*, quoted in Indianapolis *Journal*, October 20, 1858.
25 Chicago *Times*, October 1, 5, 1858.
26 James May to Buchanan, October 23, 1858; Buchanan Papers. "The Washington *Union* by its injudicious assaults has created a strong sympathy for Douglas. He is a hero in Ohio." J. W. Stevenson, Covington, October 8, 1858, Stephens Papers, LC. This was true. The Cincinnati *Enquirer*, Cleveland *Plain Dealer*, and Columbus *Statesman* all expressed sympathy for Douglas and deprecated the idea of his defeat. Congressman Burns, the only Democratic Representative in Ohio who had voted for Lecompton, was a special object of attack. Madison Kelly, Cleveland, September 15, 1858; Buchanan Papers.

THE DOUGLAS-LINCOLN
CONTEST OF 1858

VOTE FOR CONGRESSMEN
IN ILLINOIS, 1858

Counties that voted Democratic

Counties that voted Republican

the Buchanan Democrats the pitiful figure of 5,071 votes. The Republican plurality, however, did not carry control of the legislature. An unfair apportionment of seats, which took no account of the rapid growth of population in northern Illinois since 1850, gave the Democrats in joint session a clear majority. The Republicans, who had spared no expenditure and who emerged (after Lincoln had subscribed $500) with a debt of about $2,500, could comfort themselves with their superior showing.[27] Probably a letter from Crittenden in favor of the Republicans, or a larger Know-Nothing vote for them in central Illinois, would have elected Lincoln. Douglas could exult in his return to the Senate, and could point out that his vote combined with that of the National Democrats overtopped the Republican figure.

Although a few voices, notably those of the Chicago *Press and Tribune*, and of Wentworth's Chicago *Democrat*, suggested Lincoln for the Presidency, Douglas emerged the hero of the contest.[28] While almost the entire North had gone against the Democrats, he had held his State; he had turned the Buchanan faction into a fleeing rabble. The cost was high: he had worked to exhaustion, had spent sums that almost ruined him, and had made new enemies. But his triumph was as brilliant as it was hard-won, and, as congratulations poured in, he might well feel happy. The natural impulse of friends and foes alike was to declare him the inevitable party choice in 1860—though he tactfully discouraged all talk of the Presidency. When the legislature met in January, it gave him fifty-four votes on joint ballot against Lincoln's forty-six. The devoted Lanphier telegraphed the result to him in the East, adding that Springfield was wild with excitement, guns booming, bands playing, and whiskey flowing. From Douglas came the laconic reply: "Let the voice of the people rule." [29]

Immediately before the election, the Richmond *South* had published an eleven-point summary of Douglas's doctrines, drawn from the debates.[30] Sheahan's Chicago *Times*, doubtless with the Senator's approval, promptly corrected this summary.[31] The first three points, thus revised, affirmed the natural inferiority of the negro, asserted that he was not a citizen, and denied that the Declaration of Independence applied to him. The last two points were mere

27 To pay off the party debt Lincoln had to dive into his pocket for $200 more, while a general tax was levied on Republicans of means. O. M. Hatch, November 22, 1858, in miscellaneous papers, Chicago Hist. Soc.

28 Chicago *Tribune*, November 19, 1858; *Colls. Ill. State Hist. Soc.*, III, 581. The story that a massmeeting in Mansfield, Ohio, had proposed Lincoln for the Presidency seems to have been a fiction invented by the Sandusky *Commercial Register* of November 6. But a letter-writer in the Cincinnati *Gazette* of November 10 did propose Lincoln for the White House. "You are like Byron," a friend wrote him, "who woke up one morning and found himself famous."

29 Lanphier Papers.

30 Richmond *South*, October 30, 1858.

31 Chicago *Times*, November 11, 1858.

statements of fidelity to Democracy. The remaining six were more important. Douglas, according to the *Times*, maintained the possibility of a harmonious union of free and slave States. He asserted the absolute sovereignty of the States with respect to their domestic institutions. He called for a policy of noninterference between free and slave States, and between the Federal government and slave States. He upheld all constitutional guaranties of the rights of the South. He would vindicate the independence of members of Congress against executive encroachment. Not least important, he and his followers upheld the Freeport Doctrine:

They support the decision of the Supreme Court in the Dred Scott case, in the sense that it guarantees the owners of slave property an equality with the owners of other property in introducing it into the Territories; contending, also, that as slave property is thus placed on an equal footing with other property, it, like all other property, must be subject to all such local laws of the Territory as do not infringe upon the Constitution of the United States; that slave property being thus placed on an equality with other property, if it require higher and further affirmative legislation for its protection and security than is afforded to other property, and the legislature of the Territory should decide not to discriminate in its favor to that extent, then the failure to obtain the higher protection than is afforded to other property is a misfortune attending that description of property for which the Democratic Party have no remedy and are not responsible.

A labored statement! A statement obviously chocolate-coated, too, with the half-dozen conjoined affirmations sweet to the South. The tortuous clauses about "that description of property" and the accompanying emphasis on absolute State sovereignty, non-interference, and constitutional guaranties, pointed to a deep-seated uneasiness on Douglas's part. He might have added a twelfth article of faith. He had said during the debates that the rapid growth of population made it necessary to envisage further annexations, intimating that this might well mean a marked extension of the slaveholding area.

Despite this last article of faith, which he was not anxious to emphasize in Chicago but was soon expounding lustily on a Southern tour, it was far from certain that the cotton States would take kindly to the clarification of Douglas's opinions. When they studied this statement of the impossibility in some Territories of affording slavery the special protection it needed to exist, how would they treat it? Would they not see that it meant containment just as much as the Republican position? In short, what would they think of the Freeport Doctrine? The answer to this question was given with speed and emphasis.

15

Steps Toward Secession

ON THE evening of October 14, 1858, James Buchanan was host at a small bachelor dinner party, his niece, Harriet Lane, being out of town. The private dining room of the White House was cheerful with flowers from the conservatory. Three congenial guests were present—Jeremiah Black, James C. Van Dyke, and James P. Anderson, a courtly Mississippi colonel in the Mexican War who would soon be a Confederate general. This was the night following the crucial Pennsylvania election. As the men dined, telegrams were handed around; and although the President had anticipated losses, they showed an unexpectedly stinging reverse. Nevertheless, the *chef* had provided a good menu; wine circulated freely; and next day Buchanan wrote Miss Lane, "We had a merry time of it, laughing among other things over our crushing defeat. It is so great that it is almost absurd." [1] Seldom if ever has a President taken so sharp a discomfiture with such levity.

Indeed, the early elections proved to be nothing less than a rout for the Administration. In Indiana, an historic fortress of Democracy, seven Representatives would be Republicans, two would be Douglas Democrats, and only two supporters of Buchanan. The next legislature would be Republican. In Pennsylvania, also traditionally Democratic, but two of the twenty-five Representatives chosen were Lecompton men. One of them succeeded in Philadelphia only after his party had mobilized about seventeen hundred "colonized" hands in the Navy Yard.[2] Buchanan's foe, Hickman, was sent back to Congress in triumph.

Particularly bitter to the President was the downfall in the Berks County district of his old friend Glancy Jones, chairman of Ways and Means, and Administration floor leader. Violently attacked for his support of the Lecompton and English bills, the servile Jones had been renominated by a more than servile placeholders' convention. A passionate revolt of the voters had ensued. Despite the use of large sums from Washington, the opposition can-

1 To Harriet Lane, October 15, 1858; Buchanan-Johnson Papers.
2 So F. P. Blair, Sr., learned in Philadelphia; letter October 20, 1858, Cameron Papers.

didate was sent to Congress. Buchanan's immediate appointment of the discomfited Jones to be minister to Austria excited indignant comment among those who regarded it as an excessively plain way of setting popular opinion at defiance.[3]

In Ohio, the Republican upsurge left the Democrats with only four Representatives out of twenty-two—and three of them, S. S. Cox, Vallandigham, and George Pendleton, had endorsed Douglas. In upper New England, the Republicans swept Maine and Vermont. In the Northwest, they carried the Minnesota legislature (which would give them a new Senator) and elected the two Congressmen from that State and the two from Iowa. Altogether, October closed in a hubbub of Republican rejoicing. The party was particularly pleased to return to public life a pair of Whig veterans too long out of office: Tom Corwin of Ohio, humorous, shrewd, and eloquent, and Thaddeus Stevens, called by Greeley's *Tribune* the ablest man in Pennsylvania.

And if the October elections staggered the Administration, those of November left it prostrate throughout the North. The remaining New England States chose solid Republican blocks of Representatives. In Massachusetts, the vote was overwhelming. N. P. Banks was reelected governor with a clear majority over both the Democratic and Know-Nothing parties, while only a corporal's guard of Democrats was left in the legislature. Eli Thayer, Anson Burlingame, and Henry L. Dawes went back to Congress, and in the historic Third District Charles Francis Adams, who had just declared that the current issues touched the very essence of free government, was chosen.[4] New Jersey filled its five Congressional seats with three Republicans and two anti-Lecompton Democrats. In Illinois, the victory of Douglas was worse than gall to the Administration, but that was not all. Of the nine Representatives, the Douglas Democrats chose five including John A. Logan and T. L. Harris, the Republicans four. Michigan and Wisconsin kept their places in the Republican column.

To make the result decisive, the Administration lost nearly all its remaining entrenchments in New York. Here the factional quarrel between the Hards under Daniel S. Dickinson and the Softs under Horatio Seymour, together with the personal feud of Fernando Wood and Dan Sickles in the metropolis, had weakened the Democrats. The Republicans nominated a strong man for governor in the merchant Edwin D. Morgan, and the trend of the hour proved irresistible. Morgan gained a decisive plurality over his opponent Amasa J. Parker; his party swept the Assembly; and of the thirty-three Congressional seats, the Republicans or anti-Lecompton Democrats took twenty-nine. In the

3 E. L. Godkin's correspondence, London *Daily News*, November 9, 1858.
4 For Adams's letter, dated October 12, see N. Y. *Tribune*, October 21, 1858.

Westchester district, the President's arch enemy, John B. Haskin, won a smashing victory. Utica sent to the House a tall, handsome young Republican of whom more would be heard—Roscoe Conkling.[5]

The catastrophe, costing the Administration eighteen House seats in all, meant that the Directory had lost control of the House, where the ten or twelve anti-Lecompton Representatives would hold the balance of power.[6] It meant a heavy diminution of Administration prestige. Toucey and Black, who knew Northern sentiment at first hand, were alarmed by the omens for 1860. And what were the causes of this slaughter, heavy enough to choke Scamander?

The central impulse behind the popular uprising was unmistakable; as the Albany *Argus* said, "a Kansas swell" had submerged every other consideration. The North was condemning Lecompton and the English bill. It was significant that nearly all Northern Congressmen who had supported the bill at the Directory's behest had run pell-mell for cover as soon as they faced the voters. English himself had been compelled by Indiana sentiment to promise to vote for the admission of Kansas as soon as the Territory framed and popularly ratified a constitution, without regard for the ninety-three thousand population test. Almost every other Democratic candidate in Indiana, Ohio, Pennsylvania, and New York had been equally explicit.[7] Wherever Lecompton was a direct issue, the popular vote was decisive. In Buchanan's own State, for example, ten Lecompton Representatives went down; two beaten for renomination, eight for reelection. Tremendous enthusiasm attended the victories of Haskin, Hickman, and Harris.[8]

In a few areas, the tariff and homestead issues had played significant roles. In lower New England, the Middle Atlantic States, and Ohio, protection was a popular Republican plank. While Thaddeus Stevens demanded higher iron duties, Yankee candidates called for assistance to textiles. The Northern Democrats, however, did not let their rivals have exclusive use of the tariff issue. Forney told a New York audience that he was for protecting industry in its whole length and breadth, while Ben Butler, running for Congress in the Lowell district of Massachusetts, denounced the low duties of 1846 and 1857 and asked for legislation to save the country from cheap European labor. He proposed a light tariff on the necessities of life and raw materials not produced at home, heavier duties on such raw materials as coal and iron, and an adequate revenue tax on luxuries. Since he also condemned the English bill, critics re-

5 See N. Y. *Tribune* editorial, "Our Elections," November 4, 1858.
6 Nichols, *Disruption of the Amer. Democracy*, 220, 221.
7 So Douglas taunted Buchanan men at Galesburg, October 7, 1858.
8 For John Van Buren's laudation of popular sovereignty see Alexander, *Pol. Hist. N. Y.*, II, 250.

marked that his platform was more Republican than Democratic.[9] The *National Intelligencer* noted that the New England Democrats desired tariffs on textiles, Louisiana Democrats on sugar, Kentucky Democrats on hemp, and Pennsylvania Democrats on iron and steel.

Party lines were similarly crossed on the homestead issue. While the Republicans thought themselves the most active friends of free land grants to settlers, and inveighed against the hostile attitude of the Deep South, many western and border Democrats stood for a rapid disposal of public holdings under a homestead law. For that matter, not a few eastern Republicans continued to pick flaws in the free land program.

Above all, the election was an emphatic Northern condemnation of the Administration's policy in trying to jam Lecompton through Congress and crush Douglas; and, exultant as the Republicans were, the popular sovereignty Democrats were happier still. Forney's *Press* gleefully pointed out that every anti-Lecompton Democrat who sought reelection had been sustained. The party might have won in State after State had it accepted Douglas's policy. If it still clung to the Administration's course, it would be completely wrecked. "Dearly as tens of thousands of honest men love the Democratic party . . . they love the vital principles of free government better, and if the bands of mercenary politicians are not quickly made sensible of their folly, they will be buried deeper than plummet ever sounded." [10] Many Democratic journals remarked that the success of Douglas in Illinois pointed the way forward.[11] Indeed, the general view of impartial men was that the party had two alternatives: they could unite on the Senator's platform with good hope of success in 1860; or they could go forward divided to sure defeat. The *Union* was quick, however, to declare that true Democrats could never surrender to Douglas and to a platform which it pronounced hardly distinguishable from that of the Free Soil Party in 1848.

The amazing fact was that the White House group took the defeat lightly. Behind the *Union's* utterance lay something more than Buchanan's weak vindictiveness, and the arrogant temper of Cobb, Thompson, and Slidell. The Directory believed that mere transient causes had produced the defeat. The economic depression, the mid-term restlessness of voters, exaggerated tales of bleeding Kansas, and the eastern belief that Republican Congressmen would furnish more tariff benefits than such a good friend of industry as Glancy Jones—these were factors which time would erase. Buchanan complacently informed Harriet Lane that he would present Congress, when it met in Decem-

9 *National Intelligencer*, October 28, 1858.
10 Phila. *Weekly Press*, November 6, 1858.
11 For example, Providence *Journal*, November 6, 1858.

ber, such a record of success as had seldom been equalled.[12] The *Union* remarked that the party always survived disasters, "and gathers new power and strength from each recurrence of them."

But such utterances could not mask the appalling condition in which the election left the country. A feeble President, the captive of a self-willed faction of his party, now repudiated by the North; a divided Congress which faced a certain deadlock on any important legislation; a Supreme Court discredited in half the nation—such would be the government in the next two years. And civil war was already on the horizon. Had the United States possessed a ministerial constitution, this election would have turned Buchanan out and brought new leaders and new policies forward to meet the crisis; but the American system had all the defects—as well as the occasional merits—of rigidity.

[I]

In one area, however, the blow was not underrated. It rendered the South more conscious of its exposed position, and hence more defiant. Radical slavery men had discounted it in advance; and they understood two great facts—first, that the Republican movement for containment could not easily be checked, and second, that the Northern Democrats were ceasing to be a shield for "Southern rights." All year, a steady rise of intransigence had been visible in the South. This did not spring primarily from the loss of Kansas, the party schism, and the refusal of Northern Democrats to accept Dred Scott at face value. Rather it came from a realization that the balance in area, population, wealth, and power was tipping ever more heavily against the South. This realization gave birth to a sense of angry desperation in many Southerners. The resentment aroused by Douglas's Freeport Doctrine, and the upflare of secession talk which followed the election, cannot be understood unless this alarm of the slaveholding region over the strategic weakness of its overall position is clearly grasped.

The moment the Lecompton quarrel became implacable, radicals of the cotton kingdom had seen their opportunity. With one accord, the fire-eaters had turned their faces toward the annual Southern Commercial Convention opening in Montgomery on May 10, 1858. A. P. Calhoun cf South Carolina was chosen

12 October 15, 1858; Buchanan-Johnson Papers. A sufficient commentary on this was furnished by the Columbia *South Carolinian*, which expressed its deep regret that Southern radicals had pushed the wavering Buchanan into support of Lecompton. "Madly we rushed on under the impulse of this ultra sentiment, which for the time seemed to have inflamed the whole South, until, finally, we found ourselves arrayed against the vast majority of the people of Kansas, a majority of Congress, a majority of States, and a vast majority of the popular vote; and . . . we found ourselves butting with violent collision against our own principles." Quoted in *National Intelligencer*, November 18, 1858.

president, and the usual committees were appointed. The gathering was interested in but two subjects, however: the African slave supply and disunion. L. W. Spratt brought forward a demand for reopening the foreign slave trade which provoked bitter debate, Yancey and others defending it against the attack of such men as Pryor and Preston of Virginia, Hilliard and Harper of Alabama. Although the disagreement was an obstacle to bold action, Rhett, Yancey, and Ruffin privately agreed that the time had come to push their disunion program.[13] The convention showed that the temper of the Lower South, which supplied most of the three hundred delegates, was changing; revolutionary shibboleths were on many tongues, and hatred of the North charged the air. "If you were in this region," a moderate Charlestonian, George S. Bryan, had just written John P. Kennedy, "you would not be considered entirely safe unless you would advocate the slave trade, and declare boldly that you held every man who *worked* at the North as no better than a slave." [14]

The natural center of any disunionist movement would lie in South Carolina, Georgia, Mississippi, and Alabama; the natural leaders of agitation were three nervous, hot-tempered, intractably independent men, Edmund Ruffin, Robert Barnwell Rhett, and W. L. Yancey. They were not young war-hawks. Ruffin was sixty-four this year, Rhett was fifty-eight, and Yancey was forty-four. Not one of them had made a notable mark in politics. Yancey had spent some fitful, unprofitable years in Congress; Ruffin had left the Virginia legislature in disgust with political chicanery; and Rhett, succeeding to Calhoun's seat in the Senate, had resigned it when, after the Compromise of 1850, the secessionists were defeated in his State.

All three, however, were gifted in propagating and organizing sectional sentiment. Ruffin was a proficient journalist and pamphleteer. His defenses of slavery and indictment of Northern aggression were skillfully brought before Southern intellectuals in *De Bow's Review*, the *Southern Literary Messenger*, and the Virginia and Carolina newspapers. Rhett was an able journalist who made the Charleston *Mercury* (of which his son became editor in 1857) an effective organ. He was also a passionately earnest speaker. Yancey, the most striking figure, was *par excellence* the orator of Southern independence. This talented Montgomery attorney, educated at Williams College, who had turned

13 Henry W. Hilliard wrote Buchanan from Montgomery that the Commercial Convention had gone wild on the slave trade, and that the Southern radicals were as bad as the Republicans; May 20, 1858, Buchanan Papers. Edmund Ruffin and Robert Barnwell Rhett had held a long conference on secession a year earlier, May 12, 1857. They then agreed that what was needed was leadership. Rhett, wrote Ruffin in his MS Diary, "despairs of any easy or efficient action by any of the Southern States—and mainly because there are no proper leaders—men who have the will and the ability, and also the necessary influence with the people." Now, in 1858, they thought the omens better.

14 April 10, 1858; Kennedy Papers.

from Jacksonian Unionism when he married into a wealthy planting family and fell under the spell of Calhoun, combined grace of person and melody of voice with logical force. He made hundreds of speeches to audiences always loath to have him close. Beginning in conversational style, he would rouse himself to climaxes worthy of Patrick Henry. All three believed that Southern independence was a necessity, that the Southern people must be awakened to their peril, and that the great hope of secession lay in a Republican victory in 1860.

In midsummer, a letter by Yancey, running through the press and evoking a fusillade of editorial comment, revealed to the nation the fierce intolerance which animated a large body of Southern zealots. In his principal speech at the Montgomery convention, the eloquent if long-winded Alabamian had arraigned the North for its injustice, and told the delegates that unless their enemies showed a change of heart, they must ere long assemble to devise measures for placing their industrial, social, and political relations on the basis of an independent sovereignty. While Ruffin was critical of Yancey's wordiness and dependence on alcoholic inspiration, he had seen that the man's torrential eloquence could be used. He suggested that Yancey organize a spearhead body, called "The League of United Southerners," to apply pressure to leaders, legislatures, and parties. The orator, eagerly assenting, brought out the proposal in the Montgomery *Advertizer and Gazette*. Ruffin forthwith explained it in the Richmond *South* and the Charleston *Mercury*, and began drumming up support in Virginia and North Carolina. Their basic intentions were revealed in the unauthorized publication of Yancey's letter of June 15, 1858, to James H. Slaughter of Atlanta, demanding immediate organization to meet the next aggression:

It must come in the nature of things. No national party can save us; no sectional party can do it. But if we could *do as our fathers did*, organize "Committees of Safety" all over the Cotton States (and it is only in them that we can hope for any effective movement), we shall fire the Southern heart—instruct the Southern mind—give courage to each other, and at the proper moment, by one organized concerted action, we can precipitate the Cotton States into a revolution.[15]

In speeches during July at Benton, Bethel Church, and Montgomery, Alabama, Yancey wrought his hearers up to such a pitch that they forthwith formed bodies of "Leaguers." Their object was to establish local leagues, State leagues, and finally a league of all the slaveholding States; to nominate no candidate, but to vote for such men as would serve their objects; and to inculcate a new Southern motto, "A republic is our only safety." The idea slowly spread. Most Southern comment was dubious or disapproving, most Northern opinion

15 For text and comment see *National Intelligencer*, July 20, 1858.

sneering, but here and there groups took the crusade seriously. Some border men complained that the Alabamian wronged their area by terming it unde-pendable.[16]

In a second and even more extraordinary letter to Pryor of the Richmond *South*, Yancey dealt with these complaints. It was true that he placed but slight trust in the border region, he explained, but he did expect Virginia to play an indispensable role first in protecting, and later in joining, the Southern Confed-eracy. In Delaware, slavery was but a nominal institution; in Maryland, the free-soiler Henry Winter Davis had been chosen to Congress; in Kentucky, Henry Clay's support of emancipation was bearing fruit in a strong antislavery move-ment; and in Missouri, where Thomas Hart Benton had so long opposed any extension of slavery, St. Louis was the center of a powerful freesoil agitation. As for Tennessee, one of her Senators, Andrew Johnson, was essentially a free-soiler; the representatives of Tennessee Methodism had opposed striking the antislavery clause out of the church discipline; and the State maintained as judge in its supreme court and professor of law in its university a man who openly declared slavery a moral, social, and political evil. Altogether, Yancey believed that the border States offered little hope to the architects of Southern inde-pendence. Virginia, however, could place herself at the head of a buffer tier in defending the nascent Southern republic:

A well-conducted Southern policy (a policy which has been digested and understood and approved by the ablest men of Virginia, as you yourself must be aware), would seem to demand that, when such a movement takes place by any considerable number of Southern States, Virginia and the other border States should remain in the Union, where, by their position and their counsels, they would prove more effective friends than by moving out of the Union, and thus giving the Southern Confederacy a long abolition, hostile border to watch. In the event of the movement being successful, in time Virginia, and the other border States that desired it, could join the Southern Confederacy, and be pro-tected by the power of its arms and its diplomacy.[17]

16 Yancey's organization presumably borrowed its name and part of its spirit from the old-time League of United Irishmen. Already the South had its Southern Rights Associa-tions. Richard K. Crallé of South Carolina, editor of Calhoun's works, was in touch with the Central Southern Rights Association of Virginia. It had been suggested late in 1857 that delegates of all the associations meet in Richmond sometime in 1858 to consult on measures of redress. Floyd, of Buchanan's Cabinet, was to issue the circular call. Meanwhile, a memo-rial was to be presented to Congress demanding "reparation for the past and security for the future." Crallé, December 4, 1857; Hammond Papers, LC.

17 DuBose, *Yancey, passim;* Yancey's "Speech in Dem. State Convention, 1860," pamphlet. Ruffin's old classmate P. Carr, living in Pike County, Missouri, wrote the Virginian that freesoil St. Louis was a cancer in the body of the State. "I foresee that we may be the Flan-ders of the Union, and if not of the Union, then the advance guard of the South. There are no truer men than the slaveholders of Missouri." December 16, 1857; C. C. Clay Papers, Duke Univ.

Should this Machiavellian letter be taken seriously? That the proud Old Dominion should play a dissimulant role, that Maryland, Kentucky, and Tennessee should likewise act a double-dealing part to give the cotton principality a buffer zone, that the political heirs of Jefferson, Clay, and Jackson should enter into such tortuous schemes—these assumptions aroused much disgust. Yet, as evidence that a disunion plot was being matured, the letter was important. Whom did Yancey mean by "the ablest men in Virginia"? Readers guessed be meant Wise, Hunter, and Ruffin. Pryor's *South* had often spoken hopefully of dissolving the Union, but it had deprecated any premature step. The iron was to be struck when hot, and not before.[18] When Yancey's first local units of the League of United Southerners sprang into existence, Pryor's journal ridiculed them.

Other radical voices were raised during the summer of 1858. Representative Milledge L. Bonham of South Carolina, speaking at Edgefield on September 2, bewailed the loss of Kansas and saw but one remedy—separation. If the Republicans elected such a man as Seward, Chase, or Hale to the Presidency in 1860, he believed the dignity and safety of the South would demand her departure. "The electric spark which conveys that intelligence ought to be and will be the silent death-signal of the confederacy, come when it may." Bonham made it clear that he thought most Northern Democrats little better than the Republicans. Nine days later an even more defiant speech was delivered by A. G. Brown at Hazelhurst, Mississippi. He was for acquiring Cuba, annexing Tamaulipas and other Mexican states, and taking possession of Central America. All the new territory was to be devoted to slavery; and he would treat a Northern refusal to assist in this aggrandizement, or to admit a new State because it had slavery, as ground for disunion. Congress should pass a territorial slave code. Brown larded his harangue with insults to the North. "That slavery is a blessing to the masters," he shouted, "is shown by simply contrasting a Southern gentleman with a Northern abolitionist. One is courageous, high-bred, and manly. The other is cowardly, low-flung, and sneaking."[19]

As Bonham and Brown spoke, so did others. A strong current of secession talk was running through the general speechmaking of Southern members of the two houses. The time had been when such leaders as Howell Cobb and Alexander H. Stephens fulminated aggressively in Congress so that they might return home to speak moderately to the voters. Those days were past; Southern champions now uttered more radical doctrines at home than in Washington. A competent observer for the New York *Tribune* believed that the disunionists

18 Quoted in N. Y. *Weekly Tribune*, September 11, 1858.
19 Bonham's speech, *National Intelligencer*, September -16; Brown's speech, *idem*, September 23, 1858.

were gaining fast in numbers and power.[20] The Richmond *Enquirer* spoke with irritation of the gallant but excessively radical men who would never be satisfied until slavery was extended to the North Pole.[21] One such figure was Lawrence M. Keitt. In a speech at Whippy Swamp, South Carolina, on October 2, demanding secession if Kansas were admitted with less than ninety-three thousand people or if a Republican were elected President, he sounded the clarion:

Like mildew and blast, like pestilence and famine, abolitionism has swept through the free States, and girdled them round with a belt of deadly influences. If there be any power to stay the ravages of this moral sirocco it has not been exerted. . . . I have seen the Whig Party die; its legions dissolve, its glories melt away, and its proud banner . . . folded over the grave of its great leader; and the Black Republican party, an amalgam of isms, a base conglomerate of opposing elements tied together by fanaticism, step into the field, instigated by hatred to the South, and greedy of sectional power. . . . It has formally announced its intention to abolitionize every department of the government and use them to the overthrow of slavery.[22]

[II]

The Southern feeling thus whipped up during the campaign was intensified when, early in autumn, Seward lifted his voice in an indiscreet interpretation of the crisis. Campaigning for Morgan, the Senator spoke at Rochester on September 25. He wished to define the basic distinction between Republicans and Democrats in a fashion which would bring wavering Know-Nothings and abolitionists into the party. The same unhappy afflatus which had produced the higher-law doctrine descended upon Seward. America, he said, had two radically different systems of labor, one free and one slave, which, as population grew and communications thickened, were brought in some areas into jarring collision. "Shall I tell you what this collision means? . . . It is an irrepressible conflict between opposing and enduring forces, and it means that the United States must and will, sooner or later, become either entirely a slaveholding nation, or entirely a free-labor nation." His phrase "irrepressible conflict" leaped into the nation's consciousness.

In this phrase it was the word "conflict" which rang like a bell, alarming many and angering some, for it bore a connotation of armed strife. To avoid this construction, Seward expressed his belief that the United States would yet in peaceful ways become a land of universal freedom. It would do so through some cooperative action of the several States with the national government, in

20 Washington correspondence, N. Y. *Weekly Tribune,* October 9, 1858.
21 July 30, 1858.
22 Phila. *Weekly Press,* October 30, 1858.

strictly constitutional fashion. In short, his irrepressible conflict was merely a cold war. But other passages had a less irenic tone. Declaring that the sole hope of making a free-labor system national lay in the Republican Party, he seemed to predict a series of drastic measures. The party could not lay down a detailed blueprint, he remarked. "Who would ever have joined even the Whig Party of the Revolution, if it had been obliged to answer, in 1775, whether it would declare for independence in 1776, and for this noble Federal Constitution of ours in 1787?" This had a disturbing ring. Did the Republicans, then, contemplate the possibility of revolutionizing the country within a year after coming to power, and of writing a new instrument of government within a dozen years? Seward's peroration, too, seemed alarming.

"I know, and you know, that a revolution has begun," he asserted. "I know, and all the world knows, that revolutions never go backward. Twenty Senators and a hundred Representatives proclaim boldly today in Congress sentiments and opinions and principles of Freedom which hardly so many men in even this free State dared to utter in their own homes twenty years ago." Under the Democrats the government had surrendered post after post to slavery. But meanwhile the Northern people had been marshalling their hosts to recover these lost forts, "and to confound and overthrow, by one decisive blow, the betrayers of the Constitution and Freedom forever." What did he mean by this one decisive blow?

Although Seward's biographers have compared his "irrepressible conflict" speech with Lincoln's "house divided" address,[23] the New Yorker obviously took the much more radical stand. Lincoln attacked slavery as an institution; Seward also attacked the slaveholders. Whereas Lincoln declared slavery immoral, Seward termed it inhuman as well, and in saying that its legitimate fruits were the poverty, imbecility, and anarchy of Latin America, implied that these traits were being stamped on the South. Lincoln believed that the question would be agitated until a crisis had been reached and passed. He hoped that this would fix territorial bounds to slavery and restore the old view that it was but a temporary institution; whereupon the agitation would cease, and a solution could be left to time. Seward, however, envisaged a conflict intensifying until it reached a climax which would abolish slavery rather than merely put it on the road to extinction. The current strife, he said, marked the inevitable ripening of the conflict; and he spoke not merely of revolution, but of a rising demand that the Republicans, when victorious, should act as the interest of justice and humanity should require.

Lincoln considered the dominant idea of the Republican Party to be the exclusion of slavery from the Territories; Seward declared that its dominant idea

23 Bancroft, *Seward*, I, 461, 462.

was the equality of men before human tribunals and laws. In fine, Lincoln was a Fabian reformer, while Seward stood much nearer the root-and-branch abolitionists. When he spoke of trade in the bodies and souls of men, his phrasing had an abolitionist twang.

That Seward had gone too far was proved by the instant protest of responsible Northern opinion. Gideon Welles published in the New York *Evening Post* of November 15 a criticism which his friends regarded as able even for Welles. The Springfield *Republican* deplored the speech,[24] the Boston *Courier* raised such an uproar that young Henry Adams pronounced it and the conservative Bostonians incredibly terrified, and Raymond's New York *Times* sternly deprecated the utterance.[25] Bennett's *Herald* described the speech as a brutal and bloody manifesto, declared that Seward meant to plunge the country into war, and predicted that if he were elected in 1860, the South would secede. The address was in fact a characteristic piece of impetuosity. Horace Greeley that very spring had written Colfax that, while he liked Seward very much as a man, he was repelled by his selfishness, self-conceit, reluctance to ask the advice of associates, and ingratitude; and that he had ceased to trust the Senator's judgment as a politician. This was the feeling of one of Seward's associates in Washington, the moderate Dixon of Connecticut, who, pronouncing his speech indefensible, said that he was honest, talented—and untrustworthy.

The Senator, distressed by the Nothern outcry, attempted four days later at Rome, New York, to soothe the lacerated feelings of the South. Slaveholders, he declared, were intelligent, reflective men who understood that they could not make America a land of slavery, and who, being a propertied class, were inclined toward moderation; it was only the incitements of Northern Democrats which had led them to take intransigent positions! This was not only absurd, but wholly inconsistent with his previous speech. Having blown too hot, he tried to blow too cold. The inconsistency revealed Seward's greatest weakness, his want of any compelling sense of principle. He would take advanced and even reckless positions with an air of Hotspur courage, but he lacked the profound convictions of Lincoln and Sumner, Jefferson Davis and Stephens. His partial retraction did not mitigate the shock of his Rochester blast. The irrepressible conflict speech frightened many New Yorkers that autumn into voting Democratic, and led many Republicans to feel that Seward was too extreme to lead their presidential battle.[26]

24 Merriam, *Bowles*, I, 243.
25 Adams, Berlin, December 22, 1858, to Sumner; Sumner Papers.
26 Bancroft, *Seward*, I, 464. Greeley was irritated by Seward's self-sufficiency. "That he never said 'I thank you' is very well; but I cannot remember that Gov. Seward ever in his life said to me, 'What do you think of the present aspect of affairs? What is our true course in this emergency?' Do *you* happen to know of his ever consulting and counselling with anybody on terms of equality?" February 5, 1858; Greeley-Colfax Corr.

The Southern uproar over the speech was naturally tremendous. Governor Adams of South Carolina had said the same thing, but Adams was not the leader of a great party. Southern editors never forgot it. Many journals, like the Washington *Union* and its successor the *Constitution*, thenceforth treated it as an avowal of Republican intent to attack Southern institutions in every way possible. Senator Iverson of Georgia, calling it a proclamation of war against slavery, said that it was proof the Southern people would shortly be forced to choose between their special way of life and the Union.[27] After the speech, nervous Southerners felt less safe. The fire-eaters, of course, rejoiced that their antagonist had done so much to unite the section. Senator James H. Hammond had lately made a signally moderate speech at Barnwell Court House, the burden of which was that if the South but stood united it could probably continue to control the government.[28] At the same time, he had declared that, if the Republicans won in 1860, it might be the duty of the South to dissolve the Union. He now read Seward's speech with elation. "It is glorious," he wrote William Porcher Miles. "We have got them dead." Seward had clarified the Republican position for every Southern voter; Hammond had not expected that it would be done so rashly:

> But the true issue is now made. The South is to be Africanized and the elections of 1860 are to decide the question. In other words it is emancipation or disunion after 1860, unless Seward is repudiated. If he is not we shall make jelly of him and his party in 1860, if we promptly accept and fight the battle right through on the issue tendered; or, failing in that, we are consolidated, organized, and trained for a Southern Republic.[29]

27 *Cong. Globe*, 35th Cong., 2d Sess., 243.

28 Hammond's speech had largely been realistic in tone. European immigration to the North, he said, was sufficient to form one or two new States every year, while to the South it was negligible. Nor could the South expect to gain much if anything from expansion southward. Slavery seemed to have failed in Mexico and Central America; and what could be done with the millions of Indians and Spaniards in those lands? Calhoun had said that Cuba was forbidden fruit unless plucked in war, and even if it were acquired, it would not restore Southern equilibrium with the North. But the South should not undervalue herself. "She has been lamenting her weakness and croaking about the dangers that beset her when she might glory in her strength and hurl defiance at her enemies." Thirty years earlier the South had been menaced by the tariff, the Bank, the internal improvement system, and abolitionism, all of which had advocates within her own borders. She had united her forces against them; and now the high protective tariff, the Bank, and the brigandage of internal improvements were dead. Why not trust the future? The South had nearly always held control of the general government; "and our history proves that no man and no measure has yet been strong enough to stand against the South when united." But he nevertheless gave warning that the South would accept disunion rather than an abridgement of its constitutional rights. If fanaticism and brute force rode down the slaveholders, the Southerners "will carry with them the pillars of the temple of civilization, and force a common fate on all mankind." That is, they would deprive the world of cotton. The speech, delivered October 27, is largely quoted in N. Y. *Weekly Tribune*, November 20, 1858.

29 November 5, 1858; Miles Papers, Univ. of N. C. Punctuation corrected.

When on the heels of Seward's speech came news of Republican success in the elections, Southern apprehension and defiance rose together. The loss of Kansas, the squatter sovereignty position of the Douglas Democrats, and the growing strength of the Republican Party made it clear that slavery *would* be contained. Hemmed in on the north and west, what chance would it have to expand southward? Very little; and once immobilized, it would begin to die. Adams of South Carolina repeated in a public letter that if the Yankees gained control in Washington, the Southern States would become degraded provinces. Their only safety lay in secession; and it would be more than safe, for the North would soon learn its dependence on the South, and would turn on the Sewards and Giddingses to devour them.[30] With many radicals, the only question now was of ways and means.

Quietly, persistently, efficiently, Ruffin, Yancey, and Rhett were diffusing their ideas (they were primarily Ruffin's) as to a *modus operandi*. Any three coterminous Southern States, acting in unison, could unite to form a new independent nation, safe from Northern aggression. Other States would gradually join these three. It would even be preferable, asserted Ruffin, to dissolve the Union by a series of secessions. If it were done by one general and spontaneous movement, the North might be stung to take up arms, and blood would flow. If, however, a broad belt of slaveholding States were left legally within the old Union, they would serve as a barrier and a safeguard, impregnable against any warlike movement. In time they, too, would secede, for the border States could not hold their property at the mercy of the sixteen or more antislavery States; but the secession would be peaceable.[31] The staid *National Intelligencer* was profoundly shocked at the spectacle of Roger Pryor's Richmond *South* and the *Enquirer*, Wise's organ, debating with impassioned vigor the question whether Virginia would stick to the old Union or join the new Southern Confederacy in that grand breakup which both journals thought at hand. Seaton and Gales published a horrified front-page editorial on the subject.[32] But Ruffin was not in the least disturbed by the debate, for he thought it would be well if Virginia hung back a little before her inevitable decision.

After his sojourn on the Maine coast, Jefferson Davis, returning south in mid-October, halted in New York to speak at Palace Garden. A responsive crowd, largely Tammany men, heard him describe the current crisis as a contest over State Rights and local home rule. Appealing to the Irish and Germans, he declared that Federal encroachments were equally a menace to slaveholders in the South and the alien-born in the North. He was actually cheered as he

---

30 November 13, 1858; N. Y. *Weekly Tribune*, December 4, 1858.
31 Ruffin's MS Diary, May 12, and his article in Charleston *Mercury*, May 13, 1857.
32 *National Intelligencer*, July 10, 1858.

threatened secession. If one section gained such a predominance that it could override the Constitution and legislate for the other section, he said, the subjugated population would be placed in a colonial position; and they would merely show the spirit of their sires if they struck down this tyranny by revolution. Franklin Pierce had once assured Davis that, if ever a Northern army assembled to march for the conquest of the South, it would have to fight a battle at home before it reached the border. Some New York Democrats now gave him a similar assurance, declaring that the freesoil army would probably be defeated.[33] Another bit of evidence that secession would be safe!

On November 16, Davis addressed the Mississippi legislature on the dangers confronting the South. Much personal vanity and not a little vituperative temper appeared in the speech. Denouncing Seward as a dangerous and powerful man, attacking the irrepressible conflict speech as a threat to amend the Constitution and destroy slavery, lauding Buchanan (with whom he had just talked) as a true friend who would not only maintain his ground but would move another step in advance, Davis gave every sentence a ring of defiance. Repeatedly he threatened secession. If a Republican were elected President in 1860, he said, disunion would be a necessity; and he would tear Mississippi's star from the American flag, "to be set even on the perilous ridge of battle as a sign round which Mississippi's best and bravest should gather to the harvest-home of death." [34] Splendid rhetoric, wildly cheered! There were many thousands of brave, handsome lads in Mississippi at that moment who would rot underground within six years because of such rhetoric, and whose weeping parents would find "the harvest-home of death" an iron and pitiless phrase.

[III]

As radical leaders in the South talked of imminent disunion, they required a fresh issue as a rallying point. Kansas was now as useless for their purposes as for those of the Northern extremists. Particularly did the chieftains of the Southern Democracy need some hurricane demand with which they could confront and defeat Douglas.[35] Within a few weeks after the elections of 1858 they

33 *Works*, III, 332–339; for the Democratic assurances, p. 358.
34 *Works*, III, 339–360.
35 "Take any view of the picture," M. J. Crawford of Georgia wrote Alexander H. Stephens, "and our condition is not flattering for the next race and the next presidency. . . . There is nothing upon which we can go to our own people and rally them, and unless we can *get up* something we are 'done for.' We have made all out of niggers that is to be made, there's nothing left. We have made all out of Kansas that was in it, in fact it was a great investment; it paid handsome dividends to all the Southern stockholders. The charter has expired, however, and all the debts due to and from it are extinguished." September 8, 1858; Stephens Papers, LC. Punctuation corrected.

found it in a sudden revival of the idea of positive Congressional protection of slavery in the Territories, which was a complete rejection of Douglas's Freeport Doctrine. Considering the needs of Davis, Cobb, Thompson, Yancey, and other radicals, this issue was ideal. It would furnish a war cry to "fire the Southern heart," for only aggressive action would keep their ranks intact. At the same time, it would stop bold Douglas. Flushed with his victory in Illinois, and more the idol of most Northern Democrats than ever, he would seize the leadership of the party unless Southern men struck at him instantly. This weapon suited their double purpose completely.

So swiftly did Southern revolutionaries adopt it, and so sharply did some of them change front in doing so, that allegations of a conspiracy were soon bruited about. Very significantly, these allegations were first presented by Southern Unionists. The Nashville *Patriot* presently identified the leaders of the plot as Yancey and Davis.

It declared that Yancey, Ruffin, and other disunionists had conferred at the commercial convention in Montgomery; that the first result had been Yancey's letters to Slaughter and Pryor, and the formation of the Southern Leagues; that he had perceived that his secession scheme must have some immediate basis; and that, knowing that the reopening of the slave trade had too little popularity for the purpose, he had turned to the Congressional protection scheme. The scheme was broached early in September, 1858, in the editorial columns of the New Orleans *Delta*. After the elections, Yancey and his associates disseminated it vigorously, said the *Patriot*. "The calculation was to break up the Democratic Party (as Mr. Yancey intimated in his Slaughter Letter), to excite violent sectional antagonism, to unite the South against the North, and thus to insure the election of the Republican candidate." Governor Wise immediately had the Richmond *Enquirer* espouse it. "But a short time previously he had approved the course of Mr. Douglas in his split with the Administration, and the sudden change of front of his organ shows an undoubted understanding that the doctrine of Congressional protection was to be made, for the first time, an *issue in party politics*." Meanwhile Jefferson Davis also adopted the new issue.[36]

In the eyes of the Columbia *South Carolinian* and the Mobile *Daily Register*, the leaders in the conspiracy were Governor Wise and Senator Albert G. Brown of Mississippi. Within a year, the *South Carolinian* was stating bitterly, and John Forsyth of the *Register* was repeating, a formal indictment:

36 Nashville *Patriot*, "The Conspiracy to Break Up the Union," pamphlet, 1860, HL. John Minor Botts of Virginia also accepted the conspiracy theory; *The Great Rebellion*, 68 ff. Wise stated his position in a letter in the Richmond *Enquirer*, October 28, 1858, demanding "Protection in the Territories and *everywhere*, to all rights of persons and of property."

When Judge Douglas made his famous Lecompton "dodge," it will be remembered that Gov. Wise followed him. Mr. Hunter and his party sustained the Administration. Gov. Wise lost ground fearfully, both in the South and in his own State. It was necessary, therefore, that something be done to effect a restoration of his Southern strength. His dilemma was one of desperation.

In this unpleasant state, Mr. Brown, of Mississippi, happened to hit upon the idea of invoking Congressional intervention to protect slavery in the Territories. Immediately Gov. Wise was up for action. Here was his opportunity. True, the South had been contending for non-intervention. True, she had been demanding of the Federal Government simply to be let alone, to have no restrictive laws against slavery. True, she had never asked for a Territorial slave code, as no one had ever asked for a Territorial horse code. True, there was little territory left to be settled, and therefore no advantage to be derived from such a code. True, under the past history of the country, Alabama, Louisiana, Mississippi, Arkansas, Texas, Tennessee, Kentucky, and Missouri had all been made slave States without a special slavery code, thus demonstrating the uselessness of any such Congressional protection. True, the South when her population was much smaller, both in whites and blacks, than at the present time, had succeeded in colonizing every foot of ground in the confederacy which was adapted to the production of her staple. True, therefore, that the remedy of Congressional protection was being prescribed after the necessity for it was passed. Still, notwithstanding all these practical facts, a Congressional slavery code was an exciting measure which could keep up agitation, and thus keep up politicians.[37]

It is certain that both Wise and Jefferson Davis made a complete *volte-face* on the subject of Congressional protection, and that Davis's change of front was embarrassingly sudden. While in Maine, he was called upon by the Portland Democrats for an address, which they thought needed to dispel the belief of many Northerners that the South was determined to force slavery into the free States. Indignant Yankees were repeating the story that Toombs had boasted he would yet call the roll of his slaves on Bunker Hill; and though Toombs denied it, his disclaimers were treated with incredulity by radical antislavery men. Davis accepted the invitation, and his speech received nation-wide attention.[38] He asserted the familiar Southern dogma that the people of the States had a right to carry their property, including slaves, into any Territory; and this right endured, he said, until the Territory became a State and took the subject entirely under its own control. However, even a Territory could not be compelled to accept slavery if the people did not want it:

If the inhabitants of any Territory should refuse to enact such laws and police regulations as would give security to their property or to his [another migrant's], it would be rendered more or less valueless, in proportion to the difficulty of holding it without such protection. In the case of property in the

37 Mobile *Daily Register,* August 11, 1859.
38 *Cong. Globe,* February 20, 1860; Davis, *Works,* III, 295 ff.

labor of man, or what is usually called slave property, the insecurity would be so great that the owner could not ordinarily retain it. Therefore, though the right would remain, the remedy being withheld, it would follow that the owner would be practically debarred by the circumstances of the case, from taking slave property into a Territory where the sense of the inhabitants was opposed to its introduction. So much for the oft-repeated fallacy of forcing slavery upon any community.[39]

This was the doctrine of Orr, of Cass, of Douglas. At Freeport, Douglas said that if the people of a Territory disliked slavery they would adopt unfriendly legislation, thus excluding it. At Portland, Davis declared that if the people disliked slavery their legislature would withhold laws giving it security, and thus it would "be practically debarred." The one envisaged a positive course, the other a passive course. This was a distinction without a difference. Davis went on to say that the South never asked Congress to extend slavery into the Territories, but instead denied that Congress had any right to do so. Indeed, it held that the general government had no constitutional right to establish or prohibit slavery anywhere. "Hence it is their policy not to interfere on the one side or the other, but, protecting each individual in his constitutional rights, to leave every independent community to determine and adjust all domestic questions as in their wisdom may seem best." Despite the weasel-clause about "protecting each individual in his constitutional rights," this again was substantially Douglas's opinion.

But when Davis reached Mississippi; when he found the Republicans victorious; when he saw Northern Democrats exalting Douglas as the one rock of hope in 1860—then he swung abruptly about. At Jackson, he adverted angrily to Douglas's recent use at Alton of a quotation from the Portland speech. The Illinoisan had no right to treat him as an ally, said Davis. They had differed for years; for while both believed that all property requires protection by the society in which it is held, Douglas thought that this fact conferred a right to destroy, while *he* believed that it "rather creates an obligation to protect." Indeed, Davis added that he found little difference between Douglas and the Republicans. The Republicans asserted the power of Congress to deprive the South of a constitutional right; Douglas denied that Congress held such power, but would confer it on a territorial legislature. Mississippi could tolerate neither position.

Now Davis had not said a word about Congressional protection at Portland —he had disclaimed it. He had not said a word for it in his previous speeches inside and outside Congress. He knew that it was a practical absurdity. He knew that the idea would divide Northern Democrats from Southern Democrats as by a sword of fire. Why did he suddenly adopt it? Why was it so suddenly enunciated by Wise's organ, the Richmond *Enquirer*? Why was it at once taken up

39 Davis, *Works*, III, 299.

throughout the South? It was natural that Unionist journals like the Nashville *Patriot*, Columbia *South Carolinian*, and Mobile *Register* should leap at the word conspiracy, for this seemed the obvious explanation. The word was significantly used by a very different and more important journal, the Washington *Union*. This Administration paper within a few weeks warned the country that some persons unknown were circulating alarmist tales in the South for mere purposes of agitation. "They are only a part of many contemporaneous circumstances, which reveal to the country an important fact. They warn it of a widespread and dangerous conspiracy in the Southern States against the authority of the laws, Constitution, and government, the continuance of the Union, and the integrity of all existing institutions, not only in the Southern States, but in every quarter that can be reached from the Southern States. We see evidences of this movement in the effort to revive the African slave trade against the wish and conviction of nine-tenths of the Southern people." [40] When the *Union* asserted the existence of "a widespread and dangerous conspiracy" in the South, the accusation was startling.

That Davis, A. G. Brown, Yancey, Wise and others actually conspired together to use Congressional protection to check Douglas, split the Democratic Party, and bring about disunion, is nevertheless an exaggerated concept. They had different ideas and aims, they were not personally harmonious, and we have no evidence that they met or corresponded. Yancey, who had more of the conspirator in his blood than the others, later explicitly denied that he had planned to split the Democratic Party and precipitate disunion. He called the charge "an infamous calumny." [41] What had happened was that a long-dormant idea, by a combination of circumstances, was suddenly lifted to prominence in the minds of numerous political leaders and party editors, and spontaneously seized upon by them to achieve certain emergency ends. No conspiracy was required. The times demanded a certain weapon, it lay at hand, and men grasped it. They acted together but without preconcert. What were the main objects which suddenly made the Congressional protection of slavery an ideal engine? They were two. One was to keep the South united on a definite demand. The other was to halt Douglas and his associates—to prevent them from taking control of the party.[42]

40 Washington *Union*, January 6, 1859.
41 Memphis speech, August 14, 1860. But he had declared at Columbia, South Carolina, in 1859, that he had no hope of remaining in the Union, and bided his time only until Southern unity in secession was obtained. If not a secessionist *per se*, he was a unionist only under terms that he knew could never be met. See his "Speech in the Dem. State Convention, 1860," pamphlet. He, Rhett, Ruffin, and Slidell were secessionist intriguers.
42 Judah P. Benjamin told the Senate on May 22, 1860, that the Freeport Doctrine was "the explanation of the sudden change that has been wrought in the relations of the Senator from Illinois with the rest of the Democratic Party." It was not the explanation. But it was made the pretext when a handy pretext was needed; and the natural counter to it was the Congressional-protection idea. *Cong. Globe*, 36th Cong., 1st Sess., 2237.

[IV]

Two overlapping bodies of Southern voters had now determined never to accept Douglas's leadership or adopt the final implications of his popular sovereignty principle. The larger body believed simply that Douglas had betrayed and humiliated them in Kansas. He had first held up to the anxious, harried South a light which proved an *ignis fatuus*. Then in the test on Lecompton, when the section was stumblingly hunting a way by which it might emerge from the situation with credit, he had basely thwarted the Southerners. Even when the English bill offered an easy bridge, he had refused to rejoin his party. A smaller but growing party believed that the Northern Democrats were untrustworthy on the tariff, on the public lands, and on the issue of Caribbean expansion; and that the rupture of the party, as a prelude to disunion, was inevitable. The Cincinnati *Gazette*, just after the election, had pointed to the realities of the day. To the Democratic Party the election was a turning point, it said —for good, if the entire party could reconcile itself to the dictatorship of Douglas as it had once accepted that of Jackson; for evil, if it could not. "*And they cannot. The party is henceforth rent in twain and hopelessly ruined.*" [43]

What of Douglas himself? He could afford now to be magnanimous. His first thought after his victory was to conciliate his late opponents.

Turning southward as November ended, he planned to pay a friendly visit to his slave State friends, and to make a series of speeches emphasizing his regard for the welfare of that area. The eleven-point program published by the Chicago *Times* had really been intended to reassure the South. Taking passage at Alton on the *City of Memphis*, he might have pointed to a symbolic element in his passage down the Mississippi. He had done what he could to keep intact the alliance of South and Northwest, of which the great river constituted the binding chain stronger than steel. The waterway was still black with commerce; it was for the South itself to say whether the link should be snapped in twain. At every landing crowds cheered him.

Reaching Memphis on a Sunday, he stayed to address an immense concourse in Exchange Hall the following afternoon. It did not please him to see in a Memphis slave-pen some miserable blacks newly run in from Africa. Introduced by Senator Jones as a friend of the South, he assured his audience that his principles were the same in Tennessee as in Illinois; and he proved it, for his compact, vigorous speech restated the main points made in his debates with Lincoln. The Almighty, he said, had drawn a line across the continent on one side of which

43 November 5, 1858.

the soil must be cultivated by slave labor, on the other by free labor. The peoples of each State and Territory must decide the question for themselves. Once more he reiterated his Freeport Doctrine. "Whenever a Territory has a soil, climate, and production, making it the interest of the inhabitants to encourage slave property, they will pass a slave code and give it encouragement. Whenever the climate, soil, and production preclude the possibility of slavery being profitable, they will not permit it." It was visionary to talk of planting slavery where it was not wanted, and folly to attempt to exclude it where it was desired.[44]

Continuing his southward journey, Douglas met a reception sometimes frigidly polite, sometimes cordial, sometimes enthusiastic. Going ashore at Vicksburg, he found more wretched African savages cowering in the slave-pens—one account says three hundred; a sight which, with current rumors that more slaves had been imported the previous twelvemonth than in any year of the legitimate slave trade, awakened him to the menace in the demand for revival of the traffic. At New Orleans, the followers of Slidell (who called Douglas "the King of the Thugs") and Judah P. Benjamin were openly hostile, but the opposing faction under Pierre Soulé had arranged an imposing reception. Cannon barked as the steamer slid to the wharves; flags and bunting fluttered in the breeze; a brass band poured out music, and a clattering military company escorted Douglas's carriage through dense lanes of cheering people to the St. Charles. On December 6, the Senator delivered another address, reiterating his political creed with an additional article—the acquisition of Cuba. This rich island belonged by nature to the continental power which it flanked, he said; it must be acquired; but the acquisition must be on terms honorable to all. He did not go as far as the slippery Caleb Cushing, who, in a recent address in Richmond, had urged the annexation of both Cuba and Mexico with no fastidiousness about methods; but he did prove that he still held the expansionist views of Young America.[45] Obviously, he was not for popular sovereignty in Cuba, for he did not suggest for a moment that the will of the people should be consulted upon the transfer.

The Senator was anxious to avoid any appearance of pressure upon the party or of discourtesy toward the South. Far from letting his followers press his name for the Presidency, he was boldly stating that the South was entitled to the next Chief Executive. Of course he had no use for Cobb, Slidell, or Davis among the Southern aspirants, but he spoke in high terms of Breckinridge.[46] All the Ad-

44 Memphis *Avalanche*, November 30, 1858. Before leaving Chicago, Douglas had told friends that he would take decided ground against a territorial slave code; Weck to Lyman Trumbull, November 22, 1858, Trumbull Papers.

45 A. Dudley Mann wrote Buchanan: "Those supposed to be most in the secrets of Judge Douglas give out *sotto voce* that during the first days of the session he will make a peace offering demonstration, with respect to Mexico and Cuba, which will be cordially accepted by the slaveholding States." November 29, 1858; Buchanan Papers.

46 And also of Wise; Chicago *Tribune*, November 13, 1858.

ministration regulars and the Southern extremists, however, believed that if they met him as a friend he would quickly establish his domination. They had assailed him as a traitor, they had said repeatedly that the breach with him was final, and they feared him too much to take his extended hand.

Hence it was that, while he pushed down the Mississippi and proceeded to Cuba, some Southern leaders who knew perfectly well that the Freeport Doctrine was an old story and who had accepted it without protest from the mouths of Cass, Douglas, Orr, and Stephens, suddenly turned about, denounced it with seeming anger, and proclaimed the Congressional protection dogma. The breach between Northern and Southern Democrats was to be made total. Scores of editors dipped their pens in the ink furnished by Davis, Brown, and the Richmond *Enquirer*. That journal, which was Wise's organ, stated that Congressional protection was an issue raised above the platforms of parties, that it could not and must not be compromised, and that the South could take nothing less than the legislation needed to validate its rights under the Constitution—"rights sanctioned and judicated by the Supreme Court." [47]

The response to this extraordinary demand was certain to come with vigor. Northern Democrats would no more submit to it than Republicans; that is, all Democrats except those represented by the New York *Day-Book*, a proslavery sheet which echoed the *Enquirer* and the Charleston *News*. Even many Buchanan men, predicted the New York *Tribune* on September 22, 1858, will raise the indignant inquiry: Is thy servant a dog that he should do this thing? While Davis's speech and the ultimatum of the *Enquirer* were still being reprinted, Governor William F. Packer of Pennsylvania, who had supported Buchanan's nomination two and a half years earlier, was writing his annual message. He denounced the new dogma as a menace to the Union. It "will shake the very pillars of our constitutional fabric," he declared. "It would compel every Territory to elevate property in slaves above every other description of property, and to establish a slave code in its early municipal regulations, or else it would convert the Congress into a theatre of crimination and confusion, and fill the country with strife; and all this without securing a single advantage to the North, or protecting a single right of the South." [48] Great numbers of hitherto moderate Northern Democrats began to think that much truth attached to Republican talk about the aggressions of slavery.

If ever there was a pernicious abstraction, it was this new Southern demand. The history of Kansas, Nebraska, Oregon, and Minnesota had illustrated anew the truth that slaveholders would never migrate to any region where slavery was unprofitable. These Southerners were uniting in a preposterous appeal

47 November 11, 1858.
48 Packer's full message is in *National Intelligencer*, January 9, 1859.

which they knew would never be granted, and some of them were plotting secession once it was refused.[49]

[V]

It was one of the heavy misfortunes of the nation not merely that it elected small Presidents, but that the potentialities of the Presidency as an instrument of democratic leadership were so little recognized. The Chief Magistrate executed the laws; now and then he proposed one; but he knew little about rallying public opinion behind some great new policy. The value of the Presidential speechmaking tour in arousing sentiment, the use of interviews or public letters in focussing attention on an issue, the feasibility of appointing an executive commission to investigate and report—all this remained to be discovered. The discovery did not lie far in the future. Lincoln was to employ the public letter and interview with great effect; Andrew Johnson was to make a momentous speechmaking "swing around the circle," and to use special investigative agents. Had Buchanan possessed more imagination, energy, and elevation of outlook, he might have used them to divert the nation's attention from jarring quarrels to constructive tasks.

The message which he laid before the new session of the Thirty-fifth Congress when it met on December 6, 1858, evinced a desire to place the country upon new roads. An upward revision of some tariff rates, with a substitution of specific for *ad valorem* duties; Congressional action for a Pacific railroad; a national bankruptcy law; and a bold series of moves in Mexico, Central America, and the West Indies—these made up a program argued in several thousand words. At the same time, Buchanan rejoiced that the Kansas question had been settled—as it had. The republic could turn to new questions. A fighting President with a talent for dramatizing his views might have persuaded it to do so; but not a President who was widely despised, who made but a single limp statement without following it up, and who confessed that he had not an ounce of pugnacity. He remarked, for example, that his tariff suggestions were "the fruit of my own observations, to which Congress, in their better judgment, will give such weight as they may justly deserve."

Had he been an aggressive President who meant to enforce his ideas, his statements on foreign policy would have created an angry international sensa-

49 Nor would a Congressional slave code work. The Louisville *Democrat*, staunch warrior journal of the Douglas clan, remarked: "No act of Congress or decision of the Supreme Court will make or unmake the institution of slavery anywhere. The local public sentiment will always dispose of the case. . . . If any other party than the Democrats has power in a Territory they will legislate slavery out somehow if its advocates are in a minority; and there will be found no practical remedy. The power is complete and uncontrollable." Quoted in *National Intelligencer*, November 25, 1858.

tion. What he said of Cuba was essentially outrageous. Spain and Mexico had recently been on the brink of hostilities. Filibustering circles had talked of using a Spanish-Mexican war as an excuse to grab Cuba; the Washington *States* had asserted that the last chance of acquiring the island was at hand; August Belmont had written Slidell that the hour for action was approaching; and during November the Cabinet had held protracted sessions on foreign relations.[50] Buchanan now announced that our relations with Spain were highly unsatisfactory. Spanish officials in Cuba, he said, had insulted our flag, injured the persons and property of our citizens, and refused redress. He asserted that Cuba in its colonial condition was a standing threat to all trade issuing from the Mississippi, and a constant source of injury to the American people. We should like to acquire that island peaceably, he declared, but circumstances might so shape themselves that it would have to be taken by force.

Equally extreme were his statements regarding Mexico. The President described the civil war which was again raging in the republic; the war of Benito Juarez and other liberals against the dictator Comonfort, who, supported by the large landholders, the church, and much of the army, had suspended the constitution. The struggle was destined to continue for three years before the forces of reform triumphed. Meanwhile, the reactionary regime in Mexico City had treated Americans and other foreigners with arrogant brutality. Buchanan said flatly that abundant cause existed for a resort to hostilities against it, and that, if Comonfort crushed Juarez, all hope of a peaceful settlement would be gone. The frontier, too, was so disorderly that the President requested Congress to let him send the army into Chihuahua and Sonora, to set up a temporary protectorate supported by military posts. This came close to a proposal for war and seizure. It was reinforced by another urgent recommendation that Congress authorize him to use forces on the Isthmus of Tehuantepec, blockading the coast and moving troops into the interior for the protection of transit rights. This would mean placing American bayonets in other Mexican states.[51]

The President likewise dealt unmercifully with Nicaragua. This little country he assailed on the ground that, early in 1856, the Rivas government had summarily revoked the grant and charter of the Transit Company, though he knew that the regime was but a facade for William Walker and his filibusters. Since

50 Belmont's letter, June 5, 1858, was forwarded to Buchanan; Buchanan Papers.

51 Senator Judah P. Benjamin had been interested in the Tehuantepec Company, which planned the construction of transit facilities. Our minister, John Forsyth, had been instructed to demand full transit rights, but made no headway. He remained in Mexico City until June, 1858, when with Buchanan's approval he first suspended and then broke off diplomatic relations. No intercourse existed until the spring of 1859, when Buchanan sent down Robert McLane of Maryland, with authority to recognize the Juarez government if he thought proper. Buchanan, *Defence*, 267 ff.; Bemis, *Amer. Secretaries of State*, VI, 324-347.

then, the government had failed to ratify a treaty signed by its minister in Washington guaranteeing to all nations the use and protection of the Transit Route, for it objected to a provision empowering the United States to keep the line open if Nicaragua ever failed to perform that duty. Under the circumstances, Buchanan recommended that Congress allow him to employ the army and navy to prevent obstruction of the route, and to safeguard American travellers. The same proposal was made with respect to the Panama route, traversing the territory of New Granada (Colombia). Finally, a sharp cause of quarrel was specified with Costa Rica. A party of unarmed Americans had been fired upon there in 1856 by Costa Rican troops, with some casualties.[52]

Three views might be taken of these aggressive proposals. The first was that armed invasion and occupation all around the Gulf were the only proper answers the nation could make to intolerable injuries. If Buchanan held such an exaggerated opinion of our sufferings and the proper remedy, he stood almost alone in doing so. The second was that, as four years earlier the Nebraska bill had been brought forward partly to end Democratic dissensions, so now the President's expansionist program had the same object. But his hostility to Douglas jarred with such an interpretation. The third and likeliest view was that the Southern annexationists, eager to gain new lands and just now anxious to out-Douglas Douglas, were guiding the President's pen.[53]

Jacob Thompson, according to press reports, had been insisting in Cabinet on an extreme policy with respect to Mexican and Central American affairs.[54] For some time, with the Southern press commenting resentfully on the movements of foreign warships in the Gulf, a stir of hope had been visible in expansionist circles. One of the largest American fleets ever sent out had just gone southward to help persuade stubborn Paraguay to make amends for an attack on the warship *Water Witch* and other offenses. Some observers supposed that this squadron might arrive home at an opportune moment to assist in gaining territory in the Caribbean or Gulf.[55]

Moreover, it was now or never with the expansionists. Congress was still briefly Democratic, but after March 4 the House would be in hostile hands. It was now or never, too, with any Democratic-sponsored scheme for a Pacific railroad.

52 Buchanan had asserted his intention of enforcing the neutrality laws of the United States. Nevertheless, a certain sympathy seemed to exist between his Administration and William Walker, as was shown in the rough treatment of Commodore Paulding after his arrest of Walker. R. P. Meade, *Hiram Paulding;* Bemis, *op. cit.,* VI, 356, 357.

53 "This is in my judgment the worst and most dangerous document ever originating from a President of the United States," observed Ben Wade. It "would make the people of the United States no better than a nest of Pyrates." December 8, 1858; Wade Papers.

54 Wash. correspondence dated November 30, 1858, N. Y. *Tribune.*

55 See Edward Bates's letter, N. Y. *Weekly Tribune,* April 23, 1859. For additional material on foreign affairs, see Appendix III.

[VI]

Public attention was instantly snatched from the President's forcible-feeble utterances to a melodramatic episode: the deposition of Douglas from his chairmanship of the Senate committee on Territories. Both governmentally and politically, this was one of the three most important committees of Congress. With Kansas waiting outside the door, with Colorado and Dakota requiring nurture, with Arizona's ten thousand people demanding a separate territorial government, it had highly important work on hand. Everyone knew that it had been the scene of Douglas's hardest work, and the theater of some of his greatest achievements. Year after year, since 1847, he had been reelected by unanimous vote in caucus. The position was the one in which he had taken the keenest pride, for it identified him with the growth of the West, where his heart had always lain.

Not since the Senate had defeated Martin Van Buren's appointment as minister to England had such a blow been struck in the face of a Democratic leader. Douglas, resolved not to take his seat in Washington until after the Illinois legislature had reelected him, had proceeded with his beautiful wife to Cuba. His enemies had arrived in Washington determined to cast both him and Senator Broderick into outer darkness. They were encouraged by the Directory, and cheered by news that the Virginia Democratic convention had administered a rebuff to his friends by tabling a resolution congratulating the Illinois Democracy on their victory. The nomination of John Letcher for governor of Virginia was also regarded as a victory for Buchanan-Hunter forces against the Wise-Douglas group. Jefferson Davis and Slidell placed themselves at the head of the cabal against the absent Illinoisan.[56]

On Thursday, December 9, the caucus handed down its vindictive decree: Green of Missouri was to be chairman in Douglas's place. Over all opposition, Davis, Slidell, Hunter, Iverson, and the other radicals had ridden implacably. Bigler had opposed the step because he thought it unfair to attack Douglas in his absence; Toombs had denounced it as dictated by vengeful hostility toward an individual; A. G. Brown had objected that it was impolitic and ungenerous. Douglas's close friends, Shields and Stuart, had made indignant protests, terming the action suicidal. Besides these men, Clingman and Green had voted against any change. This made seven opponents in all, Broderick not having been asked to the caucus. The debate, beginning at ten-thirty, had raged until noon. Then, after being adjourned for a brief session of the Senate and for lunch, upon its resumption it had grown steadily more acrimonious until the final vote late in the afternoon. At the height of the battle Toombs walked out in disgust. As

56 N. Y. *Weekly Tribune*, December 11, 1859.

word of the decision flew around Washington it created intense excitement and its significance was instantly grasped.[57]

The extreme proslavery wing of the Democratic Party was determined not only to overthrow Douglas but the principle for which he stood. It meant to take the advanced step which Davis had said Buchanan was ready to support: it intended to force the demand for a territorial slave code, and this implied the destruction of the Freeport Doctrine, to which all anti-Lecompton men would subscribe. A leading Southern Senator declared that the South had temporized long enough and would tolerate no halfway position.[58]

The response among Douglas's followers was immediate. Rumors had been current that he had prepared, and would soon issue, a declaration that he would not be a candidate for the Presidential nomination in 1860. If this were true (and he certainly had said that the South was entitled to the nomination), the Cobb-Thompson-Slidell-Davis group had taken the one step that would force him to make a desperate and indomitable battle for the nation's leadership.

As for the Republicans, they were openly exultant. Seward grimly remarked that the truth of his statement about an irrepressible conflict between slavery and freedom was now evident. To such impartial observers as yet existed in Washington and the country, the caucus blow indicated a most alarming refusal of proslavery Democrats to tolerate any diversity of opinion upon the measures they wanted, including their inordinate demand for the Congressional protection of slavery in unwilling Territories.

From that fateful December day, the lists were cleared for the onset; the combatants, in three groups, took station; the trumpeters prepared to blow their signal. The Southern irreconcilables maintained an air of sullen determination. The Douglas group burned with pent-up resentment; and those who had complained of late that their chieftain had been too conciliatory would now have no reason to doubt the savage energy behind his blows. The Republicans, seeing their star in the ascendant, were ready to fight hard and seize fast every gain that fortune threw into their grasp. Their own Senate caucus had decided unanimously against falling in behind Douglas in his contest with his fellow-Democrats. With the great prize now in full view, the Republican Party was resolved to battle its own way to victory.

57 Senator Green of Missouri wrote that the "chief worker" (probably Slidell) expressly said he regarded Douglas as still a Democrat, and that he justified the move on other grounds: "That the Territorial Committee was the great leading committee of the Senate, and that to satisfy the majority, they must elect one without doubt or suspicion." Green warned that the change would excite public indignation. To Samuel Treat, December 14, 1858; Treat Papers. 58 The man is not named; Wash. correspondence dated December 9, 1958, N. Y. *Tribune.*

16

Deadlock in Congress

THE GATHERING of Congress, always a diverting spectacle, was rendered more interesting in December, 1858, by the fact that except for the dome, the Capitol was at last practically completed. This would be the first full session which Senate and House could spend in their handsome new quarters. After the British raid in 1814, Benjamin H. Latrobe had supervised the rebuilding of the old central portion of the Capitol, with its freestone walls and small Bulfinch crown. From the Administration of J. Q. Adams to the death of Zachary Taylor, the legislative and judicial branches had been satisfied with that quaintly attractive structure. Then, in 1851, the great north and south wings of New England marble, designed by Thomas U. Walters, had been begun and were rapidly pushed forward. In 1856, the larger dome, adapted from the immortal creations of Michelangelo and Wren, had been undertaken. Senators and Representatives had been elated to leave their outworn chambers. Thirty years later, S. S. Cox vividly recalled the gaiety of the House as it marched from the old shadowy and murmurous hall into the new apartment with its ornate gilding, lights shining through the varicolored escutcheons of thirty-one States in the roof, and richly carved oaken furniture.

Year by year now, the House seemed to gain upon the Senate in ability and influence. To be sure, it had only a few veteran leaders. On the Democratic side James L. Orr resumed the gavel as Speaker, while Galusha A. Grow and Joshua Giddings among the Republicans were rich in experience. But both sides of the chamber exhibited young men of brilliant promise. The Republican roster included John Sherman, Elihu B. Washburne, F. P. Blair, Jr., Schuyler Colfax, and Henry Winter Davis. Among the Democrats were J. L. M. Curry, L. Q. C. Lamar, S. S. Cox, a weatherbeaten Texan named John H. Reagan, and a quick-witted, somewhat boisterous North Carolinian, Zebulon B. Vance.

Yet, if by a diminishing margin, leadership still rested with the Senate. The Nestor of that body was John J. Crittenden, who had entered it on the day Monroe was inaugurated. His bushy eyebrows, stern countenance, and severely earnest speech gave a misleading impression of his personality, for he was eminently a man of peace. In ability no one compared him with Clay, whose mantle he had inherited. He was an acute and learned but not profound lawyer, a forcible but not eloquent orator, a political tactician always patriotic but often clumsy. His negligent dress and rustic manners pointed the contrast with the elegant Harry of the West. Nevertheless, he was loved for his affability, and heard with respect for his sense and moderation. With him could be ranged a few other temperate men. The judicial-minded John Bell, a wealthy slaveholder who hated proslavery extremists and who had opposed the Nebraska Act and 'Lecompton bill, was conspicuously national-spirited. Sam Houston, the hero of Texas history now mellowed by years, was not so much a moderate as a nationalist; for on sectional issues he was a roughly eloquent battler for the Union. But circumstances threw him into the compromise group. Pugh of Ohio could fairly be termed moderate in temper and tenets.

By general agreement, the most brilliant Southern speaker was a man of alien birth and Jewish blood, Judah P. Benjamin of Louisiana. At first glance no member was less prepossessing. His short body, thick and ill-proportioned, his heavy-jowled, swarthy face, shrewd and even cunning rather than intellectual, his excessively suave manner—all this told against him until he began to speak. Then his deeply musical voice, the grace of his delivery, his exquisite diction, and the keen plausibility of his argument produced an irresistible impression. As the bar, first of America and later of Britain, was to testify, he was an admirable advocate. The Senate gallery stirred with expectation when he rose, and sighed with regret when he sat down.[1]

Equally a type, but antipodean in character, was the fine old Virginia aristocrat, James M. Mason. Brought up among large slaveholders, this grandson of George Mason looked down upon middle-class folk without pretense or snobbery but in the manner of a genuine patrician. Elegant in shining broadcloth and white linen (though later he turned to Virginia homespun), he had natural distinction of manner; even in taking a chew of tobacco he lifted it from a velvet pouch with Attic gesture. Though without oratorical power, he was heard with attention, for he had sound judgment; his rigid integrity was admired (something which could not be said of the gamester Benjamin); and he was a man of principle.[2] He had been too proud of his standards to say a word for Lecompton, or to vote for the claim of Bright and Fitch to Senate seats. Members equally respected R. M. T. Hunter, a Virginian of commonplace parts but tireless industry, who was a conservative in natural temper and a radical in his attachment

[1] Buchanan on August 31 had offered Madrid to Benjamin, who declined it because he could not afford the expense and preferred the Senate. Benjamin to Buchanan, September 7, 1858; Buchanan Papers.

[2] G. M. Towle, *Continental Monthly*, II, 156 ff.; C. F. Adams, Jr., *Autobiography*, 59, 62, 82.

to Calhoun's memory and Southern Rights ideas. Rather shrill and awkward in speaking, he could display, when really interested in a subject, a clear logical power. Because of his natural moderation and grasp of finance he was now often mentioned for the Presidency. That far more brilliant debater, Robert Toombs, whose grasp, terseness, and salty wit were almost worthy of Charles James Fox and who was equally a watchdog of the Treasury, was too extreme and capricious to inspire any such trust.

Next to Douglas, of course, the two strongest Senators were Seward and Jefferson Davis. The personalities of both, long familiar to the country, were becoming better understood every year—yet neither was genuinely popular in a national sense. Neither had much eloquence or epigrammatic force. Seward adopted a conversational, monotonous delivery, and when he took his favorite stand, leaning against a Senate pillar, his left hand twirling his glasses while his right delivered occasional brief gestures, he might have been talking to a drawing room. His coolness, mental alertness, and balance won admiration, but of a restrained kind. Then, too, he continued to display an impish, mocking, ironic vein, which alternately delighted and enraged his friends but which the public did not understand. Few saw that beneath it lay a calm, patient nature, too philosophical to be capable of unflinching combat, too reasonable to treat any issue as having but one side. As for Davis, his chief fault was an excessive severity and nervous tension. Now at fifty just rising to the height of his powers, he was growing moodier, harder, and more austere. He was almost the beau ideal of a Southern leader—but he lacked the requisite imagination, warmth of heart, and faith in the people. His chiseled features, unaffected courtesy, and fluent conversation masked a proud reserve. In debate he was increasingly apt to give way to sharp sarcasm, and to betray his fanatical devotion to the slaveholding culture. If only he were less polished and rigid!

It was Douglas who had wonderful gifts of popularity; and he returned to the Senate flushed with his recent honors. In Cuba, the Spanish authorities had shown him great deference. When he reached New York, a civic reception was tendered him at City Hall, and, despite a cold rain, throngs gathered outside to cheer him. In Philadelphia, he spoke to five thousand people; Baltimore gave him another ovation; and a crowd at the Washington station roared its welcome.[3] No other political figure in the country could have aroused such enthusiasm. When he entered the Senate chamber, however, he was treated coldly by most Southern leaders. Slidell was insolent, Davis loftily frigid, and Toombs frankly hostile.

The backdrop of the Congressional session was again a busy social season.

3 N. Y. *Herald*, January 1, Philadelphia *North American*, January 4, *National Intelligencer*, January 6, 8, 1859.

Once more Miss Lane and Mrs. Douglas were the two reigning hostesses. Prominent among the foreign visitors were Sir William Gore Ouseley and his wife, London friends of the President, and the prima donna Piccolimini, who created a sensation at a White House levee on the arm of the Sardinian minister. Daniel Sickles was at that levee with a beauty (not his wife) at his side. The President came in, escorting Mrs. Gwin; he had aged and his head drooped more perceptibly, but hostile observers thought his eye as shrewd as of old. Four roughly dressed Pottawatomie Indians attended, emitting an aboriginal odor. The White House was scarcely an adequate setting for the sparkle and color of these personalities. Its faded frescoes and gilding, threadbare curtains and rugs, and worn-out chairs looked increasingly shabby, while it lacked enough pictures, bric-a-brac, and other ornaments to make it attractive. But although Congress was being asked to pay for a renovation, many members were cool to the project. Buchanan was unpopular throughout the North, the South wondered who would be the next occupant, and some critics grumbled that the President had used the White House not for a national hospitality, but for the gathering of votes.[4]

The Cabinet group still made a cheery, congenial circle, which despite thickening troubles gave its rather insouciant tone to the capital. Governor Cobb, as everybody called him, was fond of a good dinner and an evening at cards, and as Mrs. Cobb stayed in Georgia with her babies a good deal ("she knows her duties," wrote Jeremiah Black), he was often a house-mate of the President. Everyone liked Jacob Thompson and still more the sprightly Mrs. Thompson, with her gay laugh and warm, frank manner. It was "Jere" Black, however, who was the life of Cabinet gatherings. He wrote Hattie, as Miss Lane was affectionately termed by her intimates, notes touched with delightful humor, addressing her as "Most Excellent and Thrice Illustrious," and signing himself the humblest of her servants. Once when he, Cobb, Gwin, and a few others accompanied Buchanan on an excursion to Baltimore, they had an amusing day. "We spent the morning shopping and sightseeing," Mrs. Thompson reported to Hattie. "We had dinner at three o'clock, and a very good dinner it was. We sat at table a long time, eating, drinking, telling jokes, etc. I never saw the President in better humor, and Governor Cobb was more than himself on this occasion—and you can account for it when I tell you they had some old wine they said was worth $10 a bottle." The group, sometimes enlivened by John Appleton and that courtly Virginian, Ambrose Dudley Mann, enjoyed their drives, receptions, and suppers. Cass, to be sure, was something of a problem, but Buchanan's letters showed a fondness for him, praising his benevolence, his ability, and his readiness to forget his dangerous fainting

4 *Harper's Weekly,* February 19, 26, March 5; N. Y. correspondence January 11; London *Daily News.*

attacks. Both men liked a brisk morning walk, and a Southern journalist depicts them encountering each other:

As I pass to my breakfast every morning about nine o'clock, I meet an old gentleman in a suit of black, with white hair and white cravat, and a gold-headed consequential walking-stick; his countenance, generally austere, is rendered doubly so on these occasions by an air of troubled thought; his step is firm and rather decided, and anon the pompous cane plumps testily into the gravel promenade which connects the executive mansion with the Department of State, for here I always fall in his way. The old gentleman is the President, full of weighty matters of government. . . . As he enters the portico in front of the State Department he meets another old gentleman, and they salute each other with a ceremony befitting the days of the *ancien régime* in France. This second old gentleman wears a rusty old suit, with a tough old stick and an old brown wig. He is chunky and robust, and walks erect as a soldier. He once was one, for it is General Cass, the Nestor of American politics.

A minor ripple rolled through the press when Buchanan made James Gordon Bennett and his wife (ignored in the best New York society) his guests at dinner and the last White House reception. This was well-earned pay for valuable services. Bennett's *Herald* had been so fulsome in praise of Administration policies that Republicans called it the New York organ. Another minor ripple emanated from Mrs. Douglas's last ball of the season, crowded with select guests from the eastern cities as well as Washington. Douglas stood beside her as she received seated, for she was indisposed. Half a hundred Southern members of Congress attended—but not a single Cabinet member or presidential intimate.

By common consent, the greatest social event of the season took place on February 17, 1859, when friends of Lord and Lady Napier, the retiring British minister, gave them a ball. No foreign envoy had ever been more popular than the young Scot and his wife. The gathering in the one hundred and fifty-foot ballroom at Willard's drew groups of guests from distant cities, and twelve hundred people kept up the gaiety and feasting until early morning. Secretary Cass escorted Lady Napier into the room, Lord Napier following with Mrs. Justice Wayne. Everybody of importance seemed present under the flashing chandeliers and the portraits of Washington and Victoria. Seward was seen dancing a quadrille; Sam Houston stepped forth with a Massachusetts belle; Burlingame of Massachusetts and Keitt of South Carolina stood *vis-a-vis* in a set. The armed services were represented by dozens of officers, from General Jessup and Commodore Kearny down; the press, by such sages as Seaton of the *National Intelligencer* and Schouler of the Boston *Atlas;* the diplomats, by Sartiges escorting his Boston-reared countess, by the bachelor Spanish minister so attentive to a Western belle that some thought he favored annexation after all, and by dozens of lesser figures. If in part distinguished, the company was also mixed, and one guest long remembered James Gordon Bennett, Jr., capering through a set with Dan Sickles. Yet the newspapers were no doubt right in saying that no earlier Washington gathering had beheld so many beautiful women, costly toilettes, and important men.[5]

Then fell upon Washington the shock of the murder of Philip Barton Key—district attorney, son of the author of "The Star-Spangled Banner," and nephew of Taney—by Congressman Sickles. Washington was an enlarged village, busy with gossip; it had gossiped much about the dashing Sickles, the vivacious and feather-headed Italian girl, Teresa Bagioli, whom he had married (she then only seventeen) in 1853, and the attentions shown her by the handsome, fine-mannered "Phil" Key. The smitten pair carried on their intrigue so openly that they seemed never to have entered their place of assignation on Fifteenth Street without a cloud of admiring witnesses at the windows of neighboring houses.

A melodramatic climax was inevitable. In March, the whole country was reading of it: The quiet Sunday afternoon in Lafayette Square; the emergence of Key from the Washington Club house; his sudden confrontation by Sickles, drawing his derringer; the three shots; the retreat of Sickles, as Key's body was borne away, to the residence of Attorney-General Black; and the rapid ventilation of the whole sordid story. Equally inevitable was Sickles's acquittal, a crowd carrying him on its shoulders to his carriage. He was a favorite of Buchanan, Black, and Slidell, but many people had thought it unseemly for the President of the United States to visit him in his cell.

One happier incident received less notice from the press. On the last evening of the session, the Senate galleries noticed a tall, distinguished-looking gentleman entering the eastern door of the chamber. Members hurried to greet him. First Mason, then Douglas, took his hand, while Seward, Hammond, Clay and others clustered about. Someone brought up Simmons of Rhode Island, who had begun life as a farm-and-factory boy—for the stranger was Richard Cobden, who had gone from the Manchester factories to Parliament. Next morning the Liberal statesman, after breakfasting with Senators Hunter and Mason, hurried off to talk with Gamaliel Bailey of the *National Era*, and to accompany Robert J. Walker to Brady's gallery, where they had their photographs taken. That evening Cobden dined with Lewis Cass, and the following day breakfasted with the President, who asked him to stay at the White House when he returned to Washington. His impressions of Buchanan are interesting. "Found him looking much older, and apparently out of spirits, and not so happy as when I knew him in London. Having attained the highest object of his worldly ambition, he is disappointed with the result."

Cobden, disposed to think the best of American democracy, was a friendly

5 *National Intelligencer*, February 19, 1859; Mrs. C. C. Clay, *Belle of the Fifties*, 118.

observer. After visiting Chicago, he was soon on the *War Eagle* descending the Mississippi to Cairo, and pleased both with crew and passengers:

The company on board the boat comprised a great many rough bearded men with coarse dresses of uncouth fashion, some with loose trousers tucked into their dirty boots, others with their pantaloons rolled up above their shoes like our "navigators." These men, most of them young and full of animal spirits, were on their way to the new gold mines at Pike's Peak, all of them carrying the baggage and provisions and small firearms required for a journey across the plains to the foot of the Rocky Mountains. I was struck with the orderly sober and forbearing demeanor of these men. Not a rude or boisterous word fell from any one of them. This I attribute to the sobriety of all on board. With only one exception I observed that nothing but water was drunk at the table.[6]

[I]

The Congressional session had begun amid gloomy omens of rising sectional irritation. Southerners were exasperated by the sale of Helper's *Impending Crisis*, which went from printing to printing and continued to inspire editorials and speeches. Republicans were of course aware that it reached few of its intended audience, the slaveless whites of the South. Whether they would respond to Helper's thesis if it were brought to their attention was a moot question. J. F. H. Claiborne, a Mississippi editor, had written that although the poor whites were regarded as the vulnerable bastion of the Southern fortress, he thanked God that they were thoroughly republican, well educated, and sensible of their superior position in the existing order.[7] At the same time, he admitted that the efforts of the abolitionists to incite the slaveless majority against the slaveowning minority were of necessity closely watched, and year by year that watch had to be sharpened. Republicans, anxious to sow Helper's seed, realized that few could pay a dollar for it. Frank P. Blair, Jr., Cassius M. Clay, Lewis Clephane, William H. Anthon, and others therefore arranged to print a hundred thousand copies of a pamphlet compendium costing only sixteen cents each. This two-hundred-page version contained all the essential matter in the regular edition, and the Republican press was soon giving umbrage to the South by calling for subscriptions.

The North, meanwhile, found new provocation in the clandestine slave trade. While Buchanan was berating Cuba for maintaining the traffic, the Southern clamor for reopening it was growing, slave-ships fitted in American ports were being captured off the African coast, and worst of all, Southern juries were refusing to enforce the national laws.

6 Richard Cobden, MS Journal, March 5–28, 1859, Midhurst, Sussex.
7 Undated memorandum, Claiborne Papers, Univ. of N. C.

Late in the summer of 1858, the brig *Echo*, captured in Cuban waters by the U.S.S. *Dolphin*, was brought into Charleston. She had cleared from New Orleans, shipped about four hundred and fifty Negroes at the Guinea port of Kabenda, and recrossed the Atlantic in a painful forty-seven-day voyage which cost about one hundred and forty blacks their lives. The survivors, landed at Castle Pinckney wharf, presented a pitiable sight. Some were in a dying condition, others were walking skeletons.[8] While arrangements were made to convoy the negroes to Monrovia as wards of the Colonization Society, the Federal authorities undertook to prosecute the motley crew—Spaniards, Portuguese, and other nationalities. These sixteen desperate-looking scoundrels were guilty of the deaths of nearly ten times their own number.[9] Under the law of 1820 the crime was piracy, its penalty death; and severity was obviously more than justified. South Carolina sentiment, however, condemned the law. Pronouncing it despicable, the Charleston *Evening News* expressed a hope that the grand and petit juries would do their duty and then ask for executive clemency. When the grand jury did bring in an indictment, resolutions were introduced in the State Senate declaring the law unconstitutional, null, and void, and members roundly applauded the assertion that the slave trade was as innocent and legitimate as any other.[10]

The result was the complete breakdown of the case. The jury in the Federal circuit court in Charleston, sitting under Justice Wayne and Judge Magrath, brought in a verdict of not guilty. While the *Mercury* showered them with compliments, Senator Hammond proudly told the Senate that South Carolinians were unconquerably opposed to enforcement of the statute. The government then brought Captain Townsend of the *Echo* to trial at Key West in the spring of 1859. Here the Southern judge interposed every possible obstacle. The Federal attorney proved that the *Echo* was a slaver, that she was an American ship, that Townsend was her master, and that he was an American citizen. But the judge held it necessary to prove, in addition, that the vessel was owned or fitted out by an American. When the prosecution produced from the New Orleans custom house a certified copy of the ship's registry, representing Townsend to be the owner, the judge decided first that, being a copy, the document could not be admitted as evidence, and second, that it did not really prove Townsend the owner. The prosecution then offered in evidence the original bill of sale of the *Echo* to Townsend. This the judge rejected because the handwriting of the men

8　*National Intelligencer*, September 2, 1858.

9　See the interesting diary of officer of the *Niagara*, N. Y. *Weekly Tribune*, October 27, 1858.

10　Charleston *Evening News*, August 30, Charleston correspondence, N. Y. *Tribune*, November 26, 1858.

who had executed it was not proved. At this point, Northerners concluded that judges and juries in the South were acting to nullify the laws against the slave trade.[11]

The heinous case of the ship *Wanderer*, caught bringing slaves not to Cuba but the United States, went far toward proving this true. Her story was one of the most extraordinary of the time. The *Wanderer* was a one-hundred-and-four-teen-foot yacht built at Setauket, Long Island, in the winter of 1856–57, remarkable for speed and seaworthiness. Sailed southward, she gained admiring attention in Charleston and Savannah, particularly attracting a young businessman, interested in planting, banking, and the cotton trade, named Charles A. L. Lamar. Returning to Long Island, the yacht was sold, nominally to a recently elected member of the New York Yacht Club, "Captain" William C. Corrie of South Carolina, but actually to Lamar. From that moment the craft began to arouse suspicion. Corrie shipped a hard-looking crew, installed huge iron water tanks, and made curious interior changes. Federal Marshal Rynders of New York, apprised of her queer character, had her stopped by a revenue cutter in Long Island Sound and searched; but the captain talked so plausibly that she was not detained. The yacht then proceeded to Charleston. Here no secret was made in select groups that she was intended for the "trade," and that Lamar was her principal owner. Before long she made for the African coast; fell in with one of the British fleet watching for slavers; entertained some of the naval officers, Corrie laughingly asking them what sort of a slaver they thought the *Wanderer* would make; anchored at a well-chosen spot; took aboard an estimated six hundred slaves; and cracking on all sail, turned about for a Southern port. Many of the negroes were buried at sea.

Reaching Cumberland Island below Brunswick, Georgia, on a night in late November, 1858, the *Wanderer* landed about three hundred surviving negroes at the Du Bignon estate on Jekyll Island, where preliminary preparations had been made. Thence they were hastily distributed to customers in the interior. Since news of the episode could not long be suppressed, the Federal marshal from Savannah was soon on Jekyll Island searching for evidence. Early in December the yacht was seized, and, while the North expressed indignation, the Department of Justice took steps to prosecute. Lamar wrote a friend that "things are in a hell of a fix," that the yacht "will be lost certain and sure," and that it would be necessary to bribe witnesses. Half a dozen ailing slaves had just died. "I think the whole of them now sick will die," he wrote; "they are too enfeebled to administer medicine to." The character of the business may be inferred from the fact that he later admitted that he had lost two out of three negroes. He

11 N. Y. *Weekly Tribune*, June 4, 1859.

did attempt bribery, offering two of the chief witnesses five thousand dollars not to testify.[12]

The grand jury in the Charleston district refused to find an indictment against Captain Corrie, popular in that area. When the government instructed the Federal attorney to enter a *nolle prosequi* with a view to removing Corrie to Georgia where the slaves had been landed, Judge Magrath refused to permit such action. He offered three arguments. First, he said, although the slaves had touched soil in Georgia, Corrie had been found in South Carolina where process was served on him, and was therefore answerable to the South Carolina tribunal. Second, the President had no power to interfere with the course of the law, or to use his discretion as to discontinuing a prosecution when once begun. Finally, the offense of carrying off a negro who had been a slave did not amount to piracy, the law of 1820 being applicable only to the abduction of a negro who was a freeman when taken! Corrie's detention in the Charleston jail thus served merely to prevent his trial in Georgia. Federal law ought to be enforced, wrote Magrath privately to Hammond; but could it be? "Why in South Carolina the jurisdiction of the U. S. does not prevail in the Court House itself!" [13]

In Savannah, the Federal attorney and judge were represented by the press as men determined to permit no child's play; yet here too the issue was farcical.[14] A Savannah jury which found indictments against the owner, captain, and others accomplished nothing. Indeed, the jurors shortly recanted. They published a protest saying that they had acted under compulsion of the court, for they regarded the law against the slave trade as a gross injustice. "We feel humbled, as men," they asserted, "in the consciousness that we are freemen but in name, and that we are living, during the existence of such laws, under a tyranny as supreme as that of the despotic governments of the Old World. . . . Longer to yield to a sickly sentiment of pretended philanthropy and diseased mental aberration of 'higher law' fanatics . . . is weak and unwise." [15] Nobody was tried. The *Wanderer* was sold by government order on March 12, 1859, at Savannah, but only one other person had the courage to bid, and Lamar got the vessel for $4,000. He was determined to go ahead with the trade. "To be sure," he wrote another Georgian, "at first I knew nothing of the business. I have learned some-

12 See "A Slave Trader's Notebook," *North American Review*, November, 1886; articles in *The Rudder*, Vol. XV, February–March, 1904; W. M. Thompson, "The Slave Ship Wanderer," *National Intelligencer*, January 4, 1859; Savannah *Republican*, December, 1859.
13 Robert Bunch to Lord John Russell, May 3, 1860; FO 115/230. Pamphlet, "Slave Trade Not Declared Piracy by Act of 1820; United States vs. W. C. Corrie, Opinion of Hon. A. G. Magrath." Magrath to Hammond, January 21, 1859; Hammond Papers, LC. Magrath wrote that a plot was afoot to defy the nation by giving an imported African to certain desperate men, widely publicizing the fact, and then supporting these lawless characters.
14 Savannah *Republican*, December 30, 31, 1858.
15 *Harper's Magazine*, 1859, p. 255.

thing since, and I hope can put my information to some account. I have been in it for 'grandeur,' and have been fighting for a principle. Now I am in it for the dollars." [16]

Other men, too, regarded the slave trade as a matter of principle. Judge Magrath presided in the Federal district court at Charleston when, early in 1859, the case of the captain and crew of the ship *Brothers*, captured off Africa under suspicious circumstances, came up. The Federal attorney presented evidence and asked for indictments. Magrath responded with a charge which, while calling for enforcement of the law, consisted largely of laudation of slavery with an allusion to the rapid change of Old World opinion in its favor. Naturally the jury, after retiring for an hour, refused the indictments. [17] The British consul was an alert observer of the proceedings on the *Echo* crew and Captain Corrie of the *Wanderer*. Judge Magrath's conduct in the latter case he thought "a melancholy instance of that which in this country is too common, the overwhelming power of public sentiment." [18] The jury in the *Echo* trial, he reported, paid no attention to the evidence, and had the defense asked them to do so, would have declared that not one of the accused had ever been aboard the *Echo*. He also reported that plenty of money for the defense came from Havana; that the pilot of the captor ship, the U.S.S. *Dolphin*, was shortly murdered; that a man ready to turn state's evidence was threatened with assassination; and that everybody in the trade was assured that those who got into trouble would be safeguarded. The Federal attorney said privately that the failure of the case would give a fresh impetus to slave-running. [19]

[II]

The question of the proportions reached by the slave trade we treat elsewhere; but it may be said here that what most alarmed Northerners was that the long-hesitant movement to make the traffic legal was now reaching full-blown proportions. Originally, its advocates had appealed chiefly to the large planters who found their labor supply too costly. Some Southern leaders still frankly advocated it as certain to benefit wealthy landholders and foster an aristocratic culture. Thus William H. Trescot assured Porcher Miles that the trade would lead to the development of a hierarchical Southern civilization in contrast with the Jeffersonian theory of government. [20] But now the movement was

16 June 29, 1859; *North American Review*, November, 1886, "A Slave Trader's Notebook."
17 *National Intelligencer*, January 15, 1859.
18 Bunch to Lord John Russell, May 3, 1860; FO 115/230.
19 Bunch to Lord Malmesbury, April 21, 1859; FO 115/216.
20 W. H. Trescot to W. P. Miles, February 8, 1859; Miles Papers, Univ. of N. C.

pressed on two very different lines: as an appeal to a democratic diffusion of slavery, and as a contribution to Southern defiance of the North.[21]

John Mitchel in his *Southern Citizen*, just established in Washington, adopted what he called the honest human flesh program, declaring that the trade would soon reduce the price of a robust fieldhand from $1,000 to $100, enabling every Southern farmer to buy one. No longer would a line be drawn between nabob and poor white; the monopolist would be put down; every citizen could belong to the grand family of slaveholders. Daniel Lee preached the same doctrine in his *Southern Cultivator*.[22] John J. McRae, who succeeded to Quitman's seat, espoused this plan for equalizing the dignities of Southern citizenship. Some estimates of the number of slaves needed if they became a "democratic" possession were extremely high. A Texan wrote the New York *Express* that half a million of the "black rascals" were wanted in his State, while Daniel Lee computed that it would take a million Africans to till the seven hundred thousand square miles of unimproved land in the South. Then, too, talk of heavy slave importations was coupled with talk of territorial annexations. Martin J. Crawford of Georgia told Congress that unless the war upon slavery was stopped, within fifteen years the South would have reopened the trade and extended its dominion as far as Guatemala or farther.[23]

A similar defiance of the North was expressed by other men. Such leaders as A. G. Brown of Mississippi emphasized State sovereignty;[24] the South had a right to meet its own labor problem, declared Davis, and Federal intervention was improper if not unconstitutional.[25] To many Southerners, the phraseology of the Act of 1820, terming the importation of slaves "piracy," seemed to throw a slur on the whole institution. They forgot that the law so stigmatizing the trade had been advocated by President Monroe, with the support of such Cabinet members as Calhoun and W. H. Crawford, and that the measure, introduced by Mercer of Virginia, had received the vote of the whole South Carolina delegation, including Poinsett and McDuffie. Since then, the sensitivity of slaveholders had increased.[26]

21 And other reasons as well. Three had been brought forward in the Southern Commercial Convention at Savannah just after Buchanan's election. They were (1) that abundant negroes would overflow into the Territories, expanding the institution; (2) that cheap slaves would safeguard the cotton kingdom against Brazilian and Indian competition; and (3) that it was more humane to bring negroes from Africa than to break up families in the border States by purchasing them there.
22 *Southern Citizen*, December 4, 1858, *et seq.; Southern Cultivator*, August, 1858.
23 Amer. Anti-Slavery Society, *Annual Report* year ending May, 1859, pp. 40–42; *De Bow's Review*, October, 1858, "African Slavery Adapted to the West and Northwest."
24 A. G. Brown quoted in New Orleans *Picayune*, July 3, 1859.
25 Speech of July 6, 1859; *Letters, Papers, and Speeches*, IV, 61–88.
26 Jefferson had called the slave trade "an execrable commerce"; Madison had pronounced it "infernal"; Hayne had said in 1826 that any South Carolinian concerned in it "would be indignantly driven out of society." Yancey to A. Alison, August 11, 1861, Yancey Papers.

It was true that, as Slidell said, the great mass of Southerners condemned the foreign slave trade. In Texas, for example, despite some planters who wanted cheap hands, Sam Houston assailed any revival, while John H. Reagan after attacking it was reelected to Congress by an unprecedented majority.[27] In Louisiana, many citizens expressed a sense of shock when early in 1858 one house voted for the importation of twenty-five hundred Africans to be indentured for not less than fifteen years; and the *Picayune* declared that the movement would meet the utter repugnance of five-sixths of the population.[28] Albert Pike of Arkansas had said that he would be torn apart by wild horses before he would consent to renewing so cruel a traffic.[29]

Yet it seemed to be true that the movement was growing, and that many, like Ruffin, were confessing a conversion to it. Had not the majority of the South Carolina legislative committee to which Governor Adams's message was referred reported in favor of it? Had not one prominent figure after another taken it up? Did not eighteen Mississippians advertise in the spring of 1858 that they would pay $300 a head for a thousand Africans landed between Pensacola and Galveston?[30] It seemed also to be true that much of the opposition rested on grounds of mere expediency. Many men did not want slaves made cheaper. Many held that importation would not pay, for too many blacks would die before being acclimated. Many thought the agitation ill-timed because it divided Southern sentiment in the face of Northern menaces.[31]

To Northern reproaches over the nullification of slave-trade laws, the South could reply with reproaches over Yankee nullification of the Fugitive Slave Act. It could point to such episodes as the mob disorders in the neighboring towns of New Albany, Indiana, and Brandenburg, Kentucky, when the seizure by slaveholders of an alleged underground railroad agent, Horace Bell, and his rescue from a Kentucky jail, caused whole communities to rush to arms. For a week, parts of southern Indiana and northern Kentucky seethed with mutual hostility.[32] Of course the danger of a reopening of the African slave trade was small. Of course the actual loss of the South (and especially the Deep South) from runaway slaves was easily bearable. But dread of future peril does most to harrow men, and North and South had grown deeply apprehensive of each other's policy. Misunderstanding made fear, fear made hatred, hatred made hysteria. Helper, the *Wanderer*, the Bell riots, were but indications of a

27 *National Intelligencer*, August 25, 1859.
28 New Orleans *Picayune*, March 5, 1858.
29 Southern Commercial Convention, 1856, *Proceedings*.
30 Enterprise *Weekly News*, April 14, 1859; *De Bow's*, August–November, 1858.
31 *National Intelligencer*, October 30, 1858; Ruffin to Mitchel, June 14, 1859; Ruffin Papers, Univ. of N. C.
32 October, 1858; New York, Louisville, and Cincinnati press.

massive trend. "What is Kansas or any similar question," Representative Wil-loughby Newton of Virginia asked, "but the drift on the surface of the stream over which politicians are madly contending, regardless of the steady current that is steadily sweeping them to destruction?" [33]

[III]

It was again in an atmosphere of emotional unreason that Congress began its deliberations. Lecompton was no more; the pending questions were nearly all economic—the Pacific Railroad, the homestead bill, the tariff, and internal improvements; yet they too tended to arouse sectional passion. For one reason, the old issue of local rights and State activity against centralized national power was involved. For another, all the proposed economic legislation seemed likely to take dollars out of Southern pockets and put them into Northern. Above all, however, the pending bills threatened to upset the sectional balance more violently than ever. The South desired to bind the Northwest to itself in continued enjoyment of a low tariff and cheap European goods, in the use of the Mississippi as a grand North-South artery of trade, and in the production of complementary agricultural staples. All the pending proposals tended rather to bind the Northwest to the East.

Buchanan, as everybody expected, had renewed his Pacific Railway recommendations in emphatic terms. He suggested a route traversing a temperate latitude, where trains would not be impeded by the ice and snow of winter, or the tropical heats of summer. This left a wide field of choice open, for towns all the way from Dubuque to Baton Rouge would naturally assert that they enjoyed a beatifically ideal climate. Time had not lessened the rivalry of cities and sections. Men of Chicago and St. Louis found the extreme southern route, which Jefferson Davis had favored when Secretary of War, incredibly repulsive; men of New Orleans and Memphis viewed a road through Minnesota and Dakota with stupefaction; while a route west from St. Louis would receive few Southern votes and very grudging Northern support. Nobody liked the idea of having to pay for three railways to get one, but nothing less seemed likely to satisfy all areas.[34]

Debate was opened by the hopeful Gwin of California as soon as the session began. The pending measure, held over from the previous session, provided that the western terminal should be in San Francisco and the eastern at some point between the Big Sioux and the Kansas rivers as they emptied into the Missouri,

33 Va. Military Institute speech, *National Intelligencer*, July 24, 1858.
34 Cf. Foot of Vermont, *Cong. Globe*, 35th Cong., 2d Sess., 75; N. Y. *Weekly Tribune*, December 4, 1858.

the contractors being required to make their choice on grounds of feasibility, directness, and economy. The government was to grant alternate sections of land in a strip twenty miles wide on each side, and to lend $12,500 a mile for every section of twenty-five miles completed, the loan to be repaid with interest in mail service and military transportation. Gwin, Douglas, Harlan of Iowa, and many others were satisfied with this plan. The contractors, they said, would know best. They might decide to push their line from the Missouri southwestward to Texas and New Mexico; they might follow the Thirty-fifth parallel (roughly the Memphis, Fort Smith, and Albuquerque line); or they might push northwest up the Missouri River and then across to Puget Sound. Any attempt to restrict the choice could readily exclude the best route of all. Whatever the eastern terminal, it could easily be connected by radiating lines with many cities North and South. And why should Congress delay? The broad West awaited communications and development, while British competition by a Canadian transcontinental was all too possible.[35]

But enthusiasts for the bill were taken aback by the formidable strength of two opposition elements. The larger was a Southern bloc which urged that the road would tax the whole nation and deplete the national domain for the benefit of Northern interests. The smaller was a group of hard-headed realists, chiefly New Englanders, who declared that the pending scheme would attract irresponsible speculators, line the pockets of crafty promoters, and, after tens of millions had been expended, result only in throwing a half-built road upon the government. This second group might have been placated by a few safeguarding amendments, but the Southern dissenters would run no risk of a northern or central line.

Jefferson Davis objected that a terminus between the mouths of the Kansas and the Big Sioux would be a terminus on the borders of the Great American Desert. Within a hundred miles, the railroad would enter a region of arid and utterly worthless land, and it would remain isolated unless it turned sharply south to strike the road which Texas was constructing westward. While he denied any sectional bias in the matter, he made it clear that he thought the southernmost route (from Fulton, Arkansas, to San Diego near the thirty-second degree and then to San Francisco) much the most practical, and doubly desirable because of the readiness of Texas to build the line to the Rio Grande.[36]

Iverson of Georgia, in a stirring speech, also attacked the central route on the grounds of its injustice to his section. This contractors' bill, he said, would rob the South to benefit the North. The two prizes of twenty-five million acres of public land, and twenty-five million dollars to be taken out of a quarter-

35 *Cong. Globe*, 35th Cong., 2nd Sess., 49–56; 333, 334, etc.
36 *Ibid.*, 72–78.

century mail contract, would be irresistible to Wall Street. The moneyed interests which were financing the northern and western roads would seize the new opportunity. They would infallibly adopt a northern route, pouring all the freights of the Far West over the Pennsylvania, New York Central, Erie, and other lines into the Northern cities and States. What Northern capitalist would invest in a Southern railway? It was notorious, said Iverson, that hardly a Yankee dollar had gone into any enterprise in the slaveholding area; if Senator Hammond tried to raise ten thousand in New York on his half-million-dollar estate in South Carolina, he would be refused. I protest, said the Senator, against any scheme of government aid which will heap untold benefits upon one section, and give hardly sixpence to the other.

Other Southerners, such as Brown of Mississippi and Mason of Virginia, argued against both the constitutionality and the necessity of the proposed Federal-aid scheme. Not a few slave State members felt that they could hold out for the El Paso-San Diego line or nothing—for by government surveys it was the shortest and cheapest of all routes. Texas proposed to subsidize her own road for six or seven hundred miles across the State, and, at the moment, the prospects of this Texas Pacific Railway seemed bright. The charter had been granted; a generous State subsidy (no less than 10,240 acres of land and a loan of $6,000 for every mile built) had been promised. Efficient officers had been elected, who, late in 1858, persuaded J. Edgar Thomson, widely regarded as the best railroad engineer in the land, to take charge of construction. The bi-weekly government mail service along the projected route had done much to clear the way for builders. Efforts were being made to induce some eminent Southerner (William C. Rives was approached) to take the presidency.[37]

The objections of Fessenden, Henry Wilson, and other New Englanders were very different from those of the South. They wanted a railroad built; they favored the north-central route; but they deplored the financial arrangements of the pending measure. On the one hand the bill offered too little incentive to responsible capitalists, and on the other held out too easy a prize to thieves and charlatans. It would be easy for speculators, these Yankee realists declared, to build that part of the road which ran through fertile land, collect the government bounties, and, when the semi-arid region was reached, stop short. Dishonest contractors would need only to raise half a million as security, set to work at Sioux City or Council Bluffs, construct the line through six hundred miles of the best country within reach, take six millions in cash and six or seven million

---

37 *Ibid.*, 242–244, for Iverson; *De Bow's* July, 1858, contains Beale's favorable report to the War Department on the survey of a wagon road from Fort Defiance to the California line near the Thirty-fifth parallel.

acres of fertile land, and when they touched the rattlesnake and prairie-dog belt, abandon the road to the government.

Wilson's own plan had great merit—as the history of the Credit Mobilier later taught. The government itself, he argued, should forthwith build a central railroad as a grand national enterprise, reserving all the adjacent lands as a sinking fund to pay off the bonds sold for construction purposes. If, subsequently, Southern interests wished to build along the Thirty-second parallel and Northern interests near the Forty-ninth, he would give them adequate land grants; but these roads could wait. The initial railway was a national necessity, while those which followed it would be commercial enterprises, dependent for their prosperity upon the growth of population.[38]

Advocates of the Pacific Railway bill had counted, as Harlan of Iowa plaintively remarked, on the twelve New England Senators. They had counted, indeed, on all the Northern Senators except those of New Jersey, and on the eight Senators of Missouri, Iowa, Minnesota, and California. This would give them thirty-four votes, a clear majority. The defection of Wilson, Fessenden, and others was a heavy blow. In vain did Douglas expend his most forcible arguments on the question; in vain did Bigler and Green reason with their Southern colleagues; in vain did the California Senators lobby with frenzied energy. John Bell was ready to submit to any ordeal of prolonged hours to reach a vote. But the combination of New England and the South sealed the fate of the bill. It was a disappointment all the bitterer to Douglas, Gwin, and Harlan because they had cozened themselves with dreams of a large majority.[39]

It was soon evident that the debate had merely thrown a searchlight from a new angle into the widening chasm of sectional animosity. Jefferson Davis remarked that he had foreseen from the beginning that they would finally run into the poverty-stricken sectional quarrel, a thing from which he always turned with loathing. With visible rancor, Henry Wilson accused the Southerners of a secret plan to place the western terminal at Guaymas on the Gulf of California, where it would serve a coming Southern Confederacy. This was untrue, and was hotly denied. But, with equal acerbity, Iverson avowed an attitude which gave some ground for Wilson's suspicions. "Sir," he exclaimed. "I believe that the time will come when the slave States will be compelled, in vindication of their rights, interests, and honor, to separate from the free States, and erect an independent confederacy; and I am not sure, sir, that the time is not at hand. . . . And, sir, it is because I believe that separation is not far distant . . . that I am unwilling to vote so much land and so much money as this bill proposes, to build

38 *Ibid.*, 35th Cong., 2nd Sess., 304–315.
39 *Ibid.*, 333, 334.

a railroad to the Pacific, which, in my judgment, will be created outside of a Southern confederacy, and will belong exclusively to the North." [40]

As Wilson and Iverson spoke in these terms, Sam Houston delivered the finest single utterance of the debate. He naturally wished to see the railroad hammered down in Texas, traversing the fertile trough (as he called it) from the mouth of the Red River to El Paso. But, spurning sectional name-calling and secession doctrines, he denied the right of any man to talk of disunion. "Disunion, sir! You might as well tell me that you could have a healthy patient and a whole man, if you were to cut the main artery of his life. Have gentlemen ever reflected as to when, where, and how they are to begin disunion; and where it is to end? Who will cut the great Mississippi in two? Who is to have the mouth of it? Who is to command its source? Will it be those who agitate the subject, or who are ultra upon it? Never, never! Look at the great West, rising like a giant." To this outburst Iverson replied with new threats of disunion. [41]

Amid jeers and laughter on one side, reproaches and lamentations on the other, the bill failed as on January 27, 1859, the Senate by the overwhelming vote of 38 to 20 carried an amendment which reduced it to nullity. Party and sectional lines were thrown into confusion as Fessenden voted *no* with Slidell, and Preston King *aye* with Hammond. Gwin, red with anger, moved that as the Senate had turned six weeks' labor into a farce, it should adjourn for the day; and it did so, the members aware that the transcontinental railroad was dead until after the election of 1860. The victory lay with the South.

[IV]

Would homestead legislation, which the previous session of the Senate had postponed by a vote of 30 to 22, fare any better? Its advocates hoped so. Since the bill of 1854 had been slain outright in the Senate, the situation had radically changed. While Southern opposition had solidified, most of the old Northern antagonism had melted away. The long struggle of Greeley, Galusha A. Grow, Andrew Johnson, and others was achieving some of its ends. Originally, the seaboard States had stood in the main against the Ohio and Mississippi valleys. [42] But logical argument, Republican Party solidarity, and the results of the panic of 1857 had told in favor of the measure until only a conservative Northern minority, with the New York *Herald* as chief mouthpiece, was against the bill. Seward of New York professed as much ardor in the cause as Richard Yates of Illinois, or Doolittle of Wisconsin.

40 *Ibid.,* 242-244.
41 *Ibid.,* 334.
42 Helene Zahler, *Eastern Workingmen and National Land Policy, 1829-1862,* 178, 179.

The panic had taught the North a manifold lesson. It had shown manufacturers that apprehension of a future labor shortage arising from migration westward was exaggerated. Burning the fingers of land speculators, it had taught these gentry that they would do well to give small holders a better opportunity. It had placed before eastern cities the spectacle of unemployed multitudes crowding the breadlines and soup houses, when (theoretically) they might be growing food. Above all, it had suggested to industrialists and traders that nothing was more important than the rapid development of Western markets for goods—and homesteaders would furnish markets and fat profits.

Since House passage of the bill was certain, Southern Senators would have to fight against it with their backs to the wall. They were aware that the rapid colonization of the West by small farmers would stimulate Yankee industrialism, that it would hasten the emergence of more Northwestern States dedicated to free soil, and that it would strengthen the Republican Party. But some Southern leaders hesitated to avow a naked sectionalism, while nearly all were reluctant to emphasize the old cry of unconstitutionality, which John Bell had recently told a Nashville audience was too sophistical to impress anybody.[43] It was necessary to fall back upon other staple arguments. Senators from slaveholding States contended that the grant of free homesteads would destroy land values in the older areas, and would soon result in glutted crop-markets and ruinous farm prices. They predicted that it would swell the immigration from European slums. They argued that it would penalize the slaveholder, for he found it so difficult to remove to the common domain that he would get nothing out of the law. Above all, they declared that it would throw the door wide open to class legislation, for a government which gave land to the landless might soon vote money to the moneyless.

Making a sudden bold thrust, Grow and his friends on February 1, 1859, carried the bill through the House by a vote of 120 to 76, with thirty-seven Northern Democrats among the majority.[44] It was significant that only three slave States cast any votes for it, and only seven free States any votes against it. The hopes of friends of the measure rose with this House passage. Let Congress press on, wrote Greeley, to give the nation this new Declaration of Independence, emancipating and elevating the poor but industrious worker.[45]

Hardly had the struggle opened in the Senate, however, than it became inextricably involved in another and fiercer battle over the pending bill to appropriate thirty million dollars for Buchanan to use in negotiating the purchase of Cuba. The South was almost a unit against the Homestead bill; the North was

43 Speech of July 18 in *National Intelligencer*, August 6, 1857.
44 Roy Nichols, *Disruption*, 232.
45 N. Y. *Weekly Tribune*, February 12, 1859.

almost unanimously against the thirty-million grant; and as they came up simultaneously, sectional feeling was certain to spin a connection between them. Buchanan, with Slidell, Belmont, and other expansionists prodding him, had set his heart upon making the annexation of Cuba the grand achievement of the Administration. Thus he would placate the South, appeal to the nationalist feeling of Young America, and place his name beside those of Jefferson, Monroe, and Polk as leaders who had broadened the national domain. Immediately after his inauguration, he had begun secret negotiations with an American financial agent of the Spanish Queen-Mother, one Christopher Fallon. The two men revived the old scheme of Belmont for combining bribery, banking influence in Europe, and the pressure of Spain's hungry creditors upon her half-bankrupt government, to bring about a sale of Cuba at a good round sum—say one hundred millions. Fallon hastened to Europe, where he devoted some busy weeks in Paris, Rome, and Madrid to conferences and intrigue. Among others, he saw the avaricious Queen-Mother Christina. Although vexatious delays ensued, the grand plan was kept alive. In accordance with it, Buchanan, late in 1858, had sent William Preston, lawyer, former Representative, and scion of a wealthy Louisville family, as minister to Madrid, and Slidell had arranged the bill for dangling before Spain this initial bait of thirty millions.

So preposterous was the idea of any immediate purchase of Cuba that nearly everybody regarded the thirty-million scheme as a device for the campaign of 1860 rather than for serious negotiations. To persuade Spain to part with the rich island in which its pride, its easiest revenues, and its hopes of power were centered would be difficult to achieve, even by the nicest combination of solicitation, cajolery, secret pressure, and weighty financial inducements. Cuba was the brightest remaining jewel of a nation which had all the haughty jealousy of a decayed grandee. The melange of insult, abuse, and bullying in Buchanan's December message had been resented by Madrid as a blow in the face. That message was intended primarily for expansionist elements at home, and Slidell's bill was meant to satisfy the desires of Southern annexationists and perhaps give the Democrats a unifying issue in 1860 as Texas had given them one in 1844. Caleb Cushing, writing Franklin Pierce of the utter demoralization of the party, had declared that the problem of rallying it seemed baffling. "We may have to intervene in Mexico. In fine, I live in hope that something will turn up to animate and justify the party"—and now Micawber Cushing could see Cuba turning up.[46]

---

46 April 9, 1858; Pierce Papers, LC. Buchanan thought that if Slidell would go as minister to Paris, where he might be far more effective than Mason, he could help get Cuba; but Slidell was reluctant to go unless he saw a strong chance of success. See their correspondence, May–June, 1858; Buchanan Papers. Cf. Sears, *Slidell*, 152.

Spanish resentment over Buchanan's affront was expressed by all parties of the Cortes on the last day of 1858, in a debate whose dignity and moderation contrasted with the rodomontade often heard in Congress on foreign affairs. The colonial minister referred scornfully to the philanthropic pretensions of Buchanan's passages on the slave trade, strange enough from a country where slavery was preserved in a harsh form and Negroes were punished for the crime of getting a little instruction. Spain, he said, would confront the Americans defiantly: "If you want Cuba, come and take her!" The leader of the opposition predicted that the nation would stand as a single phalanx in defense of Spanish rights all over the globe. Before rising, the Cortes voted unanimously to defend the integrity of the empire against any assailant. The Spanish press would have been more scorching but that, like the European press in general, it connected the President's outburst with the coming elections.[47]

Spain was no longer the faction-torn, decrepit nation she had been when Buchanan helped draft the Ostend Manifesto. Marshal Leopold O'Donnell, a former governor-general of Cuba, was now at the helm and giving the country fresh optimism and strength. If Spain was not strong enough to menace others, he told the Cortes, the nation could at least defend its own name from stain.[48] Demonstrations of loyalty also broke out in Cuba.[49] Needless to say, they were largely inspired by the authorities, and one Havana observer wrote Preston that among the numerous groups which had spirit enough to resent the tyranny of the regime, Buchanan's proposals had made a most favorable impression.[50] A great part of the Cuban population, however, actually did spurn the message, for the efforts of officials during recent years to prejudice the people against American annexation had met with considerable success. Among the Spanish-born elements, perhaps a fifth of the people of the island and half those of Havana, few would support any scheme of purchase.[51]

The general belief that the thirty-million bill was nine-tenths politics found reflection in Washington gossip. Edmund Ruffin spent some time in the capital, as 1859 opened, quietly preaching secession. He was there when the Democratic caucus on January 15 gave three or four hours to the bill, with opinion much divided. Hunter and Shields thought the proposed action impolitic, while Douglas, though willing to place the money in Buchanan's hands, believed the prospects for gaining Cuba gloomy. He declared that only one chance of success existed; if another *Black Warrior* affair took place, the island should instantly be seized. Ruffin regarded the President's message as ill-advised, for it had

47 London *Times, Daily News*, December, 1858.
48 *National Intelligencer*, January 25, 1859.
49 *Ibid.*, January 22, 1859.
50 G. W. Madan, December 24, 1858; Buchanan Papers.
51 C. J. Helm, January 1, 1859; Buchanan Papers.

not only angered Spain but aroused apprehension in Britain and France. He entered in his diary:

> January 17.—At night went to see Hammond. He thinks that neither the President nor others of the members in Congress, are sincere in their proposed measures to acquire Cuba—but that each wants only to cultivate popularity by pretending to be foremost in the move—that all of them would be horrified if the bill should, by possibility, be enacted. Hammond thinks that war would certainly be made on us by France and England, if we were to acquire Cuba, even by purchase. He ascribes this evil political move, and most others, to the aspirants to the Presidency, of whom he enumerated and named eighteen in the Southern States, as understood by the public (and among whom he counted himself), and of them eleven who were active in the pursuit. They were Hunter, Wise of Virginia, Breckinridge and Crittenden of Kentucky, Orr of South Carolina, Bell and Johnson of Tennessee, Toombs of Georgia, Houston of Texas, Davis of Mississippi, and Slidell of Louisiana.[52]

Yet the real basis of the move lay not so much in Presidential ambitions as in a desire to anneal the party—a commendable desire—and give it a winning issue. As such, and as a means of avoiding a national crisis in 1860–61, it met the covert hostility of determined secessionists. They now saw clearly that Democratic unity must be shattered before the Union could be rent in twain. "Don't touch Cuba," William Gilmore Simms exhorted Porcher Miles. "It is the bait which the Democratic Party holds out to the South. Beware how you enter this field. The Democratic Party has but one chance left for life, that of involving us in foreign war. It is a mere delusion to suppose that our chances of getting Cuba are less, if we separate, than as a whole. *If separate, we can control the whole commerce—all the shipping of the North! It is better to be separate before we take Cuba.*"[53]

Altogether, the thirty-million bill was utterly unrealistic, and, since it could not possibly pass the House, no statesmanlike reason existed for pressing it. Southern speakers, tacitly admitting its worthlessness for diplomacy, tried to justify it as an instrument for arousing expansionist sentiment. The President, remarked Mallory of Florida, had touched a popular chord, and the spirit that had given the country Louisiana and Texas was reawakening.[54] Others adopted the argument that if the United States exhausted peaceable negotiation, it could more easily justify summary measures if they became necessary. At a later date, Jefferson Davis gave his own complete rationalization of the annexationist case. In the first place, he said, the moral effect of the Senate's passage of the thirty-

52 Edmund Ruffin, MS Diary, LC; abbreviations spelled out. Yet John A. Dix wrote the President of strong feeling even among Republicans for the Cuban bill; January 22, 1859, Buchanan Papers.
53 W. G. Simms to W. P. Miles, February 3, 1859; W. P. Miles Papers, Univ. of N. C.
54 *Cong. Globe*, 35th Cong. 2nd Sess., 1189.

million bill would have fortified the Executive in his negotiations. In the second, the Administration would have been put in a better position to fish in troubled European waters; for the war of Napoleon III against Austria was about to begin, and Spain might be involved. Finally, a victory for the bill would have rebuked British meddling in Cuba, and warned Victoria's government to cease its demand for measures of emancipation.[55] Actually it may be doubted whether it would have achieved any one of these very dubious ends.

It was easy for opposition Senators, supported by the whole freesoil press, to riddle the bill. As Seward said, it was not a giant in armor but a crazy windmill. They argued that for Buchanan to pledge thirty millions in negotiating for the island, at a time when the national revenue had sunk to fifty millions, would be reckless extravagance. If he gave the thirty millions as advance payment on a treaty promising $250,000,000, said Seward, then the Senate must either ratify the bargain or lose the money. And what other promises might Buchanan not make in his negotiations? Would he agree to make Cuba a State, or several States? What status would he assign to the two hundred and fifty thousand free Negroes and four hundred thousand slaves in the island? Wilson, Collamer, Doolittle and others ridiculed the idea that annexation would help in the suppression of the slave trade; they expatiated on the difficulty of assimilating a half-million Spanish creoles; and they prophesied that other annexations would necessarily follow—Jamaica, Santo Domingo, Central America. Toombs, said Collamer, wished to annex the whole tropical belt of the Western Hemisphere; and Toombs interjected, "It is true; the whole of it!" [56]

[V]

By the last week of February, a variety of events had wrought Congressional tempers to a savage pitch. The expansionists were angered by the taunts of the Republican press, daily reiterating that the Buchanan regime was bankrupt, that the Cuban bill was the last desperate dice-throw of unscrupulous gamesters, and that the South, having failed to extend slavery in the Northwest by fraud, was trying to push it in the Caribbean by force. They were angered also by the refusal of many Republicans to debate the merits of annexation. Many leaders

55 Speech of July 6, 1859, Mississippi Democratic Convention. Open aggression was preached by several Southern leaders. Governor Wickliffe of Louisiana had said in his annual message that if this mode of freeing the island should fail, he hoped "some more potent one will be used." Judah P. Benjamin was for three steps: first to support Buchanan's offer of purchase; second to offer Spain a large sum to make Cuba independent; and finally to inform Madrid that whenever an opportunity should occur the United States would give Cubans the same aid that Great Britain had lent to other revolting Spanish colonies. *Cong. Globe*, 35th Cong., 2nd Sess., 960-964, 1186. A. G. Brown made a swashbuckling speech in Tammany Hall; he was ready to fight Spain, Britain, and France all at once for Cuba.
56 *Cong. Globe*, 35th Cong., 2nd Sess., 1187.

of the new party carefully refrained from saying that the United States should *never* acquire Cuba; they simply opposed the Buchanan-Slidell method. Seward, Fessenden, Dixon, and others took the view that they would not discuss the question whether new Caribbean areas (say Cuba with the Wilmot Proviso applied and Catholicism disestablished) were not desirable; they should merely denounce the infamy of the pending scheme. To Slidell and Toombs this was dishonest.[57]

Republicans for their part were irritated by Buchanan's veto, February 24, of the long-desired measure to grant public lands or land scrip to the States for the support of colleges of agriculture and the mechanic arts. The general idea of this legislation had been in the air for years, taking a wide variety of forms: Greeley's grandiose project for a People's University; the plan of Jonathan B. Turner of Illinois for industrial universities founded on land grants; the proposal of the Massachusetts legislature in 1855 for a national agricultural college, and so on. It was fitting that Justin S. Morrill of Vermont, the son of a horny-handed blacksmith who had often lamented the lack of more than six weeks' schooling, should crystallize these current ideas into a practical measure. It was also better strategy to put the bill in the hands of an easterner than in those of (say) Trumbull of Illinois, for many people felt that the western States had already gotten too much of the common domain. Behind the bill rallied an impressive array of Northern farming, labor, and professional supporters, while two border Senators, Crittenden and Pearce, lent their aid. Opposition came from various groups —from people who distrusted book-larnin', from enemies of class legislation, from Westerners who feared land speculation by absentee scrip-holders, and, most stubborn of all, from Southerners who stressed the constitutional argument and who saw that, since the lands would be distributed in proportion to Congressional representation, the measure would benefit one section more than the other.[58]

Something like a farm bloc seemed arising—and it would yet be aligned with the Republican Party. An Agricultural Congress meeting in Washington under Patent Office auspices helped supply pressure. The bill had passed the House the previous session 105 to 100; it now passed the Senate 25 to 23. Slidell, who had reason to know, predicted that the President would veto it. Despite the fact that even Toombs said that no veto could be justified "by a damned sight," despite Dan Sickles's intervention for it, and despite protests from loyal Pennsylvania Democrats, Buchanan killed it. Federal aid to agricultural education could never

57 James Dixon to Welles, January 24, 29, 1859; Welles Papers.
58 See W. E. Sawyer, "Evolution of the Morrill Act of 1862," MS doctoral dissertation, Boston Univ., 1948. No connection has been found between Jonathan B. Turner's bill and Morrill's, but it is not impossible that it existed; Mary T. Carriel, *Turner*, 152–165. State agricultural colleges were still extremely weak.

become law while he sat in the White House. In a futile vote on reconsideration, Morrill kept his House strength intact, 105 to 96.[59]

Though Buchanan was undoubtedly sincere in his constitutional objections, his veto message irritated many Northern commentators. To his arguments that the public lands should be safeguarded, that the States should not look to the Treasury for gifts, and that the grant would probably not benefit agriculture or mechanic arts, they replied that the bill did not donate one-sixth as much land as that given in the previous decade for railroad and military bounties, that it was merely a plan for dividing a small part of the common domain, and that experts had offered impressive evidence of its benefits. Actually, in the existing state of agricultural science, a delay of a few years was not harmful. Politics and sectional jockeying had probably motivated Morrill quite as much as an interest in scientific education. But the veto gave Greeley an opportunity to berate the President as a "Slave Power tool." Another veto, that of the bill for eliminating the dangerous shoals in the St. Clair channel connecting Lakes Huron and Erie, aroused the ire of Northwestern commercial interests, for the cost was trifling and the prospective benefits were immense. Again Buchanan's constitutional position was tenable, and doubtless taken in all sincerity. But Michigan and Wisconsin politicians, reacting to public sentiment, swore to support any Presidential candidate who would promise river, harbor, and lake improvements. Some even said that this would be the cardinal issue of 1860 in the Northwest.

Meanwhile, the quarrel between the Douglas Democrats and the Administration men had broken into the debates like the regular eruption of Old Faithful geyser. Since his arrival, the Illinois Senator had suffered contumely and insolence. While some Southerners were haughtily freezing, others sought a personal quarrel. Again we have to remember the venoms of the period. In mid-January, Slidell published a provocative card in the *Union*. He had denounced Douglas, on the authority of some talebearer, as a calumniator; Douglas had replied that he was nothing of the kind; and now Slidell repeated that he *was*, for the Illinoisan had inspired anonymous attacks upon him. Rumors spread in Washington that a Southern plot had been formed against Douglas's life. Men even said that Slidell had agreed to insult him in the Senate bar, force him into a duel, and kill him.

On the advice of a Washington correspondent, Douglas sent for a well-known Kentucky marksman, Tom Hawkins, to be his bodyguard. The Senator was nearly maneuvered into an encounter with Fitch of Indiana, but managed to avoid it. When Buchanan, still determinedly hostile, sent the Senate another

59 W. B. Parker, *Justin S. Morrill*, 267. John A. Norton, February 22, 1859, wrote Buchanan that in a recent Southern tour he had found much sentiment for the bill, that Philadelphia feeling strongly favored it, and that his signature would soften the antagonism of many Pennsylvanians who had condemned his Lecompton policy; Buchanan Papers.

list of Danite appointees for Illinois, Douglas attacked many of them as corrupt. Fitch's son held a place on the list, and the Indiana Senator chose to resent the speech as an affront; but in the end he withdrew his challenge.[60] Seven notes passed between the two men in four days! [61] The dudgeon of Douglas's followers was intense. After he was murdered, they declared, the Southern fire-eaters planned to assassinate other opponents! [62]

It was impossible to keep this flaming quarrel between Northwestern and Southern Democrats confined to committee rooms, lobbies, and newspaper offices. On February 23, Senators Hale, Seward, and Chandler adroitly tossed the issue of slavery protection in the Territories into the tiltyard of the full Senate. Instantly the two Democratic factions rushed into battle. All the more resolute Southerners—Jefferson Davis, A. G. Brown, Gwin, C. C. Clay, Judah P. Benjamin—repudiated popular sovereignty, and demanded an efficient protection of slavery in the Territories by enactment of Congress. Under the Dred Scott decision, they contended, slavery had a right to obtain the shield and buckler of Federal law in all instances in which a Territory denied it a proper defense.[63] These tenets were ferociously (the word is not too strong) rejected by Broderick, Stuart, Pugh, and above all by Douglas, as ever a host in himself. Congress, thundered the Illinoisan, has never yet enacted a criminal code or a property code for any organized Territory of the United States; why should it begin with slave property? I am obliged to the Senator from Mississippi, he remarked with an ironical bow to Davis, for assuming that I would never vote for fastening a slave code upon a Territory; "and I have yet to learn that there is a man in a free State of the Union, of any party, who would." [64]

The debate, running on till midnight, committed the opposing groups to positions which they declared they would never surrender. The schism was fundamental, and could end only in the total defeat of one side. Davis, Brown, and other Southerners served notice, in effect, that if the party convention which had already been fixed for Charleston in May, 1860, should adopt Douglas's Freeport doctrine, they would leave the hall in revolt. With equal intensity of conviction, Douglas and his associates made it plain that if the convention were forced to adopt the slave-code demand, they would attack that black flag.

60 Milton, *Eve of Conflict*, 364. In Illinois the Buchanan men were hostile as ever to Douglas; and Isaac Cook, losing no opportunity to assail and besmirch him, reported regularly to Buchanan. In Missouri, Isaac Sturgeon and others were equally vindictive, and also kept in close touch with the White House. Meanwhile, Douglas's organ the Chicago *Times* continued to castigate the Directory (Cobb, Slidell, Black, Jacob Thompson) as "political hucksters" who made Buchanan their "tool." This group, it said, had stooped to acts from which Bomba of Naples would have turned in disgust.
61 *National Intelligencer*, January 27, 1859.
62 Washington *States*, January 26, 1859.
63 *Cong. Globe*, 35th Cong., 2nd Sess., 1241, 1242.
64 *Ibid.*, 1244.

In some of the exchanges on that fatal February day, Davis and Douglas snarled at each other like panthers. Moderate Democrats perceived that the party was being torn in two. The sober, canny, somewhat timid Hunter, occupying a seat midway between the two chief combatants, was almost ludicrous in his dismay. His afflicted visage, as he turned during the four-hour battle, first to the bellicose Illinoisan and then to the icily cutting Mississippian, seemed to one observer to recall poor old Adam in the quarrel of Orlando and Oliver: "Sweet masters, be patient; for your father's remembrance, be at accord." [65]

The Union no less than the party was involved, and everybody knew it. Davis, Mason, and Brown uttered their hot words in behalf of an abstraction; but some of the bloodiest pages of history have concerned abstractions, which are peculiarly unsusceptible of compromise. If Douglas was resolved to follow his Freeport road, said Davis, "I wish him godspeed and a pleasant journey"; but, "not the breadth of one hair would I follow the Senator." [66] With like finality, the Little Giant retorted, amid applause from the galleries: "Allow me to inform him [Davis] that I stand on the platform, and those that jump off must go out of the party." Each side warned its opponents that they would receive no votes in the opposite section. No party embracing the popular sovereignty creed could carry a single Southern State, for this meant containment. No party clinging to the slave-code doctrine could win one electoral vote north of the Ohio, for this meant a coercion of freedom. The drama of the encounter was enhanced by an interruption:

Mr. Greene. Will the Senator permit me to give him a little information I have just received?
Mr. Davis. Certainly.
Mr. Greene. The legislature of Kansas has passed a law, declaring that from and after the passage of the act, slavery shall cease to exist in Kansas. [67]

So Horace White's scheme to give the slavery-protection question practical shape, and thus make the Freeport Doctrine more divisive, had succeeded! Republicans did not conceal their elation over the Democratic quarrel. The differences are so vital, trumpeted Greeley's *Tribune*, as to forbid all hope of Democratic unity in 1860. [68]

With tempers sharpened by these events, Republicans and Buchanan Democrats on February 25 flung themselves into the final battle on precedence for the

65 N. Y. *Weekly Tribune*, July 2, 1859.
66 *Cong. Globe*, 35th Cong., 2nd Sess., 1247.
67 *Ibid.*, 1255. It is significant that Douglas's friend James W. Singleton of Quincy, a man of Virginia origin, wrote him that public sentiment in Illinois required a firm stand. "We are not in a condition to carry another ounce of Southern weight, and I say so with the most painful reluctance." February 25, 1859; Singleton Papers, Ill. State Hist. Lib.
68 N. Y. *Weekly Tribune*, March 5, 1859.

Cuban grant or the Homestead bill. Slidell declared that since all argument on Cuba had been exhausted, before the Senate adjourned that night he meant to get a vote or have an hour fixed for one. The Democratic caucus had aligned itself behind him. Republicans, however, persisted in obstruction; they urged that while it was admittedly impossible to get the Cuban bill through the House, the Senate might within ten minutes send the Homestead bill to Buchanan's desk. Douglas, who supported both measures, was in despair. Let us, he said, agree to act on each of them, the Cuban bill first, before we take up the indispensable appropriation bills. Very well, rejoined Lyman Trumbull: we shall permit a vote on the Cuban proposal if Senator Hunter, who always has an appropriation bill ready whenever any measure comes up to which he is opposed, will promise not to block us.[69] Hunter, his eye upon Southern support for a Presidential nomination, refused.

It was now past nine o'clock: the Senate, which had sat the two previous nights until twelve, was weary; nerves were ready to snap. Seward, remarking bitterly that this was the last hour of the last day on which a motion could be made to take up the Homestead bill, arraigned the South for preferring Cuban adventures to a great constructive enactment. Toombs, flushed with anger, took the floor. His seat being near those of Seward and Wade, he directed his declamation full in their faces, betraying his passion by gestures and language. He smote his own desk and that of Seward; he thrust his chair against Wade's; he waved his fist. I despise the paltry tricks of tuppenny demagogues to prevent a vote, he shouted; they use their cry of land for the landless to evade a plain issue; shivering in the wind, they are afraid to take up a great national policy which appeals to the patriotism of the whole American people.

The instant he sat down, Seward, Wade, Fessenden, and Wilson were on their feet. Blunt Wade obtained the floor. "Skulk, eh? Shiver, do we?" he ejaculated as he brought his fist crashing down on Toombs's desk. He threw the Georgian's reproach for obstruction back in his teeth. It was the South which was obstructing the most glorious measure that had ever come before Congress. "The question will be, shall we give lands to the landless, or niggers to the niggerless?"[70]

As the debate thus reached a paroxysm of sectional passion, both the Cuban and Homestead bills failed. Other men spoke. Toombs, returning to the fray, said that Georgians were proud not to ask a single favor from the government: not land, not tariffs, not fishing bounties, not steamship subsidies. At one in the morning, Slidell and Brown gave up their fight. They won a hollow victory on a test motion to lay the Cuban bill on the table, which its adherents defeated 30 to 18.

69 *Cong. Globe*, 35th Cong., 2nd Sess., 1352.
70 *Ibid.*, 1354; pieced out by N. Y. *Times, National Intelligencer.*

While they could point to this as evidence that the Senate favored the bill, the measure was left just where it had been. It was clear, in fact, that while the Democratic Senate would have passed the Cuban bill, the Republican and Know-Nothing vote in the House would have killed it. The Senate would have defeated the Homestead bill, for the decisive motion for taking it up, made by Pugh of Ohio, was beaten 29 to 26. Only two members from the slaveholding States, Bell and Andrew Johnson, voted for the motion, and only six members from the free States against it. Sectional lines held firm.[71]

Even as these bills died, the heritage they left was all too evident. Buchanan's message, the Senate debate, and the newspaper discussion had imbued many Southerners with a stronger determination to expand the national domain toward the tropics. When the thirty-million proposal was denied even a clear-cut vote, radical proslavery men saw fresh evidence that the North was determined never, under any circumstances, to allow slavery another rood of land. The contest had meanwhile excited in countless Northern minds a new suspicion of Southern aims. Henceforth many Northern publicists constantly drove home their suspicion that the South intended to annex Cuba, Mexico, and Central America, spreading its own type of slavery throughout this domain; and that its leaders would not hesitate, once the scheme was consummated, to break away from the North and form a separate nation.[72]

[VI]

The tariff, meanwhile, had thrust a new lever into the widening sectional chasm. Never, said Simon Cameron early in 1858, had there been such distress among the ironworkers of Pennsylvania. Wide parts of that State were dependent directly or indirectly upon iron, for when furnaces went out of blast, coal mines, railroads, and canal boats felt the blow. Luzerne County, for example, a principality in itself, had thousands of miners, blacksmiths, woodcutters, machinists, hardware merchants, and railwaymen who responded to the pleas of ironmasters for more tariff protection. While the cost of making rails was at least $45 a ton, the spring of 1858 found fifty thousand tons of English rails offered in New York at $41. A parallel situation existed in textile areas of New England. Wool manufacturers grumbled that the existing tariff on raw wool was practically a bounty to the English manufacturer, who got his wool free. They pointed to idle mills and hungry workmen. The recent elections had shown

71 *Ibid.*, 1363 ff. Earlier the vote had stood 28 to 28 to take it up, and Vice-President Breckinridge had cast the deciding negative; pp. 1074–1076. Republicans knew that Buchanan would veto the bill, but they believed that if they could force it to a veto their chances in the campaign of 1860 would be improved.

72 N. Y. *Weekly Tribune*, April 16, 1859.

Northeastern Democrats that if their party was to survive, it must adopt the cry for greater protection. Particularly were the Keystone Democrats, who had just lost ten seats in the House, determined to insist on a revision.[73] They wholeheartedly approved of Buchanan's proposals for new schedules. But Secretary Cobb was for keeping the *ad valorem* duties, and once more was quoted as saying: "Old Buck is opposing the Administration." [74]

The struggle began on the opening day of the session, when Representative W. M. Dewart of Pennsylvania moved to instruct the Ways and Means Committee to report a bill increasing the coal and iron duties. Although this failed of the required two-thirds vote, various tariff measures were immediately tossed into the hopper. The most important were three: a bill prepared by the Pennsylvania Democrats, another written by Chairman Phelps of the Ways and Means Committee in consultation with Secretary Cobb, and a bill of Justin S. Morrill of Vermont, spokesman for the Republicans. The Pennsylvania group proposed a general return to the rates of 1846; the Phelps bill slightly increased the schedules of 1857; and the Morrill bill was a fairly strong protectionist measure. Though the committee strove earnestly to reconcile conflicting views and bring out a measure commanding general support, it fell into hopeless disputes.

Everyone knew, meanwhile, that the Senate would almost certainly block any tariff increases, for its Southern bloc would stand immovable. The Democratic caucus, on January 29, determined that it was inexpedient to raise duties or put them on the specific basis—a rebuff to Buchanan. Even yet, however, House revisionists did not despair. They brought renewed pressure to bear on the Ways and Means Committee. In that body, three Southern Democrats wanted no increases whatever; three Republicans wanted generous increases; and two members stood in a median position. The protectionist Democrats now threatened to join hands with the Republicans.[75] They threatened, too, to block vital appropriation bills unless the Southern members consented to some increases. Montgomery of Pennsylvania tried to tack an amendment for specific iron duties to the post office appropriations. At every point, Southern Representatives, using ingenious modes of delay, blocked these efforts.[76]

73 "I cannot see how you are to get Pennsylvania back in rank and file by 1860 unless this Congress will give them protection for coal and iron." Rev. John Chambers to Buchanan, Philadelphia, November 8, 1858; Buchanan Papers. Between Harrisburg and Columbia, eleven out of fourteen furnaces had shut down, throwing a thousand men and their families into poverty. Officers of the Phoenix Iron Companies, Paxton Furnace, and other corporations were bombarding Congressmen; see Cameron Papers, 1858.
74 Nichols, *Disruption of the American Democracy*, 234. For the demands of wool manufacturers see the anonymous pamphlet, "Free Trade in Raw Materials Considered in Its Effect upon All Classes of the People," New York, 1855.
75 N. Y. *Weekly Tribune*, January 29, 1859.
76 Nichols, *op. cit.*, 235, 236.

Greeley was vigorously scolding the Republican dissenters on the tariff. At least fourteen members of the party, and perhaps nineteen, he thought, were at heart free traders; they included Nichols, Mott, Edward Wade, and Bingham of Ohio, Leach of Michigan, Curtis of Iowa, Lovejoy of Illinois, Potter and Billinghurst of Wisconsin, and Frank Blair of Missouri. "I do think," he burst out at one point to Colfax, "you fifteen bolters ought to be whipped." The sectional alignment was thus, in large part, the Northwest and South against the East. In the end nothing was done. On February 26, with the end of the session at hand, Chairman Phelps moved a suspension of the rules to let him introduce a bill for reinstating the Walker tariff of 1846—with its duties higher than the existing schedules—for a limited period. His motion received a heavy majority, 128 to 88, but failed for want of two-thirds. The slave State members voted 66 to 17 against it, and the free State members were 111 to 22 in its favor.[77]

The irritation of Northern industrial areas over the failure of revision was trenchantly expressed. Pennsylvania manufacturers declared that a failure of Congress to act would give their State to the Republicans in 1860.[78] At a meeting of the Iron Masters Association in Philadelphia on New Year's Day, James Cooper of Pottstown had significantly called for united action to control the next Presidential election in various States. Proper organization in Pennsylvania, New Jersey, Maryland, Ohio, and other States, he declared, would suffice to secure a large majority for adequate protection to the iron interest and other manufactures. It had often been said that Buchanan had carried Pennsylvania only because of a vague but universal impression that he sympathized with the iron industry, and Cooper repeated the statement. "A glance at the election returns of 1856 will show that the general election in October of that year, which controlled the presidential election a month later, was carried by this interest without organization." Already Simon Cameron, John Covode, and other Pennsylvania Republicans were making the most of the tariff issue; already the New York *Herald* was slyly boosting Cameron for the Republican nomination in 1860 as a conservative man of Democratic antecedents for whom the Pennsylvania coal and iron districts would pour out a vote that would surely elect him.[79]

[VII]

Once more, members could look back on an utterly barren session, spent mainly in wrangling. The whole Thirty-fifth Congress, to which men said adieu

77 *Cong. Globe*, 35th Cong., 2nd Sess., 1409–1412; Greeley, February 4, 14, 1859, in Greeley-Colfax Corr.
78 N. Y. *Weekly Tribune*, February 12, 1859; J. M. Hopkins, November 24, 1858, Buchanan Papers.
79 *National Intelligencer*, January 22, 1859; N. Y. *Herald*, June 24, 1858.

on March 5, 1859, had been a Congress of deadlock and fission. Apart from the passage of the English bill, the admission of Minnesota and Oregon were the only forward steps of consequence. Even the making of these new States was a compromise process; for if both were freesoil, both were also initially Democratic, and sent Democratic Senators to Washington.

Superficially, the deadlock in Washington merely expressed the old antagonism of slavery and freesoil interests. The progress of the inexorable revolution, which in both sections was replacing moderate men by radicals, was dramatically revealed when the Senate of the Thirty-sixth Congress met for a short special session. Nineteen members had been newly elected or reelected. Tennessee, Kentucky, and Texas had replaced three conservative nationalists, John Bell, J. B. Thompson, and Sam Houston, with three proslavery sectionalists, A. O. P. Nicholson, Lazarus Powell, and J. W. Hemphill. Rhode Island, Michigan, and Iowa had dismissed three moderate-minded Democrats to fill their seats with radical-minded Republicans, Henry B. Anthony, the slashing owner-editor of the Providence *Journal*, Kingsley S. Bingham, who had won his spurs as a freesoil Representative, and James W. Grimes, who, like the others, had been an early organizer of the Republican Party. The reelected Senators were without exception men of granite opinions and belligerent energy: Fessenden, Henry Wilson, and Douglas among the Northerners; Toombs, A. G. Brown, and Judah P. Benjamin among the Southerners. The Senate would hear less, in the next two years, of the cooings of the dove of peace.

In a less superficial view, the session showed that a new element had intensified the old hopes and fears regarding slavery. A third section was involved, the teeming Northwest. Its destiny was not yet firmly settled. It was still linked with the South by the busy Mississippi, by Southern markets for its corn and pork, by the common interests of two agricultural regions, and by the ties of sentiment binding countless thousands of settlers to their ancestral homes in Virginia, Carolina, Kentucky, and Tennessee. It was linked with the Northeast by equally powerful ties. While it could no more give up either set of bonds than it could give up its life, a preponderance of interests would always express itself in lines of political preference; and that effort would sway the balance between the North and the South. The session also showed that economic issues were becoming more prominent. They were not dangerous in themselves, and the fact that such Northwestern men as Nichols of Iowa, English of Indiana, and Hodges of Illinois voted with the South on the tariff proved that they were not clearly sectional; but they might seriously reinforce the central element of cleavage.

Half-way mark for the Buchanan Administration! One misfortune had followed another: the Dred Scott decision, irritating millions and settling nothing; the Lecompton struggle, dividing the Democratic Party; the costly and needless

Mormon War; the panic and the depletion of the Treasury. The temper of both North and South had grown worse. At this eleventh hour, could the conservative forces of the nation be awakened? It did not seem likely. The country might yet regain the partial concord won in 1850—or it might slip swiftly toward disunion and war.

Index

INDEX

Abolitionists, oppose gradual emancipation, 345

Adams, Charles Francis, on dangers of slave power, 14–15; elected to Congress, 401

Adams, James H., 13

Alabama, Southern Leagues organized in, 406

Alton debate, 389–391

American Party, break-up of in Illinois, 394

Anglo-American relations, disturbed by British vessels searching American vessels, 343–344

Anthony, Henry B., elected to the Senate, 458

Appleton, John, confidential assistant of Buchanan, 68; qualifications as aide to Cass, 71; in Washington social life, 430

Athenaeum, The, 33, 34

Atlantic Cable, laying of, 343

Atlantic Monthly, 55

Bailey, Gamaliel, and radical freesoilers, 128

Baldwin, Henry, votes for Missouri Compromise, 92

Baldwin, J. G., 41

Bancroft, George, as historian of democracy, 42; pleads with Buchanan not to endorse Lecompton, 245; anger over Lecompton, 252; backs Douglas on Kansas issue, 271

Banking, state of in 1857, 185–188

Banks, N. P., sees Douglas late in 1857, 263, 264; attitude toward Douglas, 367; re-elected governor, 401

Barbour, Philip, vote on Missouri Compromise, 92

Bashford, Coles, Governor, praises Wisconsin, 312–313

Beale, Edward F., 338

Beebe, Gilbert J., author of *Review and Refutation* (commentary on Helper's *Impending Crisis*), 214

Bell, John, Senator, favors Pacific Railroad scheme, 443; votes for Homestead bill, 455; replaced in Senate, 458

Belmont, August, advocates annexation of Cuba, 446

Benjamin, Judah P., as brilliant Southern Senator, 428; demands protection of slavery in the Territories, 452

Bennett, James Gordon, 431

Benton, T. H., denounces Dred Scott Decision, 113

Bigler, William, Senator, characteristics of, 68; opinion on Kansas, 168; supports Lecompton, 243

Biland, A. B., Captain, leads Southern company into Kansas, 160

Bingham, Kingsley S., elected to Senate, 458

Bishop, Harriet E., 309

Black, Jeremiah, appointed Attorney-General, 72; character of, 77–78; advises Buchanan on Kansas, 172; policy on Lecompton, 239; as popular Cabinet member, 430

Blair, Frank P., Jr., and Douglas's relations to Republican Party, 350; as member of House, 427

Blair, Montgomery, in Dred Scott Case, 85 ff.

Bolling, Lucius S., as member of Lecompton Convention, 230

Bonham, Milledge L., 408

Border States, 407

Botts, J. M., 54

Breckenridge, John C., Vice-President, backs Douglas in fight for Senate, 373

Bright, Jesse O., as enemy of Douglas, 74; characteristics as friend of Buchanan, 68; attacks Stanton and Walker, 274

Broderick, David, Senator, as friend of Douglas, 132–133; rejects protection of slavery in Territories, 452

Brown, Albert G., Senator, defends slavery against Helper's arguments, 214; favors annexation of Cuba, 408; charged with conspiracy against Union, 415–418; and advocacy of slave trade, 458; and Pacific Railroad, 442; repudiates popular sovereignty, 452

Brown, A. V., Postmaster-General, appointments of, 72; threatens pro-Douglas postmasters, 290–291; and trans-continental mail service, 340, 341

Brown, John, influence of, 345

Browning, Orville H., author of program adopted by Republican convention of 1858, 358

PART II

The Emergence of Lincoln

PROLOGUE TO CIVIL WAR

1859–1861

ABRAHAM LINCOLN IN 1858

(From an ambrotype taken by Mr. T. P. Pierson on August 25, 1858, at Macomb, Illinois)

CONTENTS

ILLUSTRATIONS

1

1

Plotters North and South

A RAINBOW of resurgent prosperity was now bent against the storm clouds of sectional dissension. Indeed, the Manichean dualism of the period was never better illustrated than during the summer and fall of 1859. On every hand a restoration of economic activity was visible. Although the depression had continued with slowly lessening force until the beginning of the year, and though the flour-milling, coal-mining, and ironmaking industries continued to suffer severely, spring had brought a steady brightening of business prospects. The New England cotton, woolen, and shoe factories began running almost full time; lumbering showed a revival in Michigan and Wisconsin; railroad traffic increased, and a midsummer agreement by leading roads upon more remunerative rates was hailed with pleasure in financial circles.[1] As French, Austrians, and Italians fought in Lombardy, agriculture found a stimulant in the new war.[2] Wages of laborers rose, securities sold at quotations which made their low level just after the panic seem incredible, and real estate in the large cities found a brisker market. When importers and exporters cast up the totals of the year, they found them larger than in any twelvemonth of the nation's history except 1857.[3]

Yet all the while the sectional quarrel, like a cancer gnawing at the viscera of some outwardly healthy man, furnished constant spasms of pain and fever. When Congress was in session the inflammation was at its worst, but it never quite ceased. In the very issue in which Greeley's *Tribune* hailed the return of good times, it declared that no soft words could annihilate the fact that the predominant sentiments of North and South were irreconcilably hostile, and the chasm between them was inexorably widening.[4] It was even so. As summer brought news of Magenta and Solferino, as the demand for cotton and grain increased,

1 *Bankers' Magazine*, August, 1859, p. 159.
2 Greeley, travelling 270 miles from Chicago to Quincy in 1859, found Illinois steadily growing. "There are new blocks in her cities, new dwellings in every village, new breakings on this or that edge of almost every prairie." N. Y. *Weekly Tribune*, May 28, 1850.
3 *Wages in U. S. From Colonial Times*, 254; *Statistical Abstract*.
4 N. Y. *Weekly Tribune*. May 7, 1859.

3

as smoke thickened over industrial towns and money jingled on the planter's desk, citizens began looking ahead to the Presidential contest. Republicans scanned the future with confidence. But thousands of Southerners declared, with John Cuningham of Charleston, that if such a man as Seward were elected, the Union would become intolerable for the cotton States and all that was dear to them would best flourish under a separate nationality.[5]

One of the fundamental tasks of reviving business was to knit the country together by rail and steam. John W. Garrett, the young Baltimore businessman who was made president of the Baltimore & Ohio late in 1858, was drafting plans for expansion. In the West, he meant to acquire the railroads between Marietta and St. Louis, and throw a branch into Pittsburgh; in the East, he intended to construct splendid port facilities in Baltimore.[6] John Murray Forbes, supported by Baring Brothers and wealthy New Englanders, had made possible the completion of the Hannibal & St. Joseph across northern Missouri in 1859.[7] J. Edgar Thomson was strengthening the Pennsylvania and its allied line the Pittsburgh, Fort Wayne, & Chicago; Forbes gave the Chicago, Burlington & Quincy complete control of the roads linking the three cities of its name; the railway from Chicago to Fond du Lac was completed in 1859; and in Alabama, Mississippi, and Louisiana men were making plans to utilize the Congressional land grants of 1856–57.[8] The thickening network of railroads, their mileage practically doubling in 1855–61, was creating a national market for manufactures in place of the old myriad of local markets.[9,10]

But while unity was being promoted by economic forces—while textile production was demanding larger and larger central mills;[11] while the patents of Lyman Blake and the enterprise of Gordon McKay foreshadowed the day when great central shoe factories would replace local shoemakers; while dozens of American products, from pens to pianos, gained trade names known all over the country—unity was being undermined by political forces. And while economic forces moved slowly, political forces moved with terrible speed.

Certain clouds hardly larger than a man's hand appeared on the horizon early in 1859. Ominously, the name of John Brown of Ossawatomie had cropped up again in the news from Kansas. He had left that Territory in the fall of 1856, shocking old friends in the east by his gray, gnarled look and his intense mental

5 Cuningham to Hammond, April 18, 1859; Hammond Papers, LC.
6 Hungerford, *Baltimore & Ohio*, I, 345.
7 J. W. Starr, *One Hundred Years of Amer. Railroading*, 181; H. G. Pearson, *An Amer. Railroad Builder*, 92, 93.
8 *Bankers' Magazine*, February, 1859, pp. 606, 607.
9 The fateful meeting of Cornelius Cole, Judah, and others above the hardware store of Huntington & Hopkins in Sacramento to organize the Central Pacific took place early in 1861. Cornelia Phillips, *Cole*, 111.
10 Oscar Lewis, *The Big Four*, Ch. I; N. Y. *Weekly Tribune*, June 9, 1860.
11 Clark, *Manufactures in U. S. 1607–1860*, pp. 560, 574.

fixity. In the next three years his actions were destined to affect American affairs profoundly.

[I]

John Brown was fifty-nine years old in May, 1859. He was no ordinary man. All who saw him, whether friends or foes, were struck by his iron will, his consuming inner fire, and his intense though erratic devotion to causes outside himself. Great as were his faults, he united a certain elevation of character with the traits of a born leader. His intimates—members of his family, employees, his picked Kansas band, the eastern conspirators soon to befriend him in a desperate venture—regarded him with deferential admiration. His business partners (who all rued the partnership) knew that it was hopeless to argue with his stubborn convictions. Proslavery settlers in Kansas, upon whom his murder of five men on the Pottawatomie had created a deep impression, breathed more easily when he left the Territory. He was the product partly of inheritance. He came of stern Puritan stock, but of unhappy immediate antecedents. His father Owen, a man of strong religious and abolitionist convictions, was an industrious, respected citizen of his chosen Ohio community for more than fifty years, becoming a trustee of Oberlin and accumulating a substantial estate; but his mother Ruth Mills Brown, like his maternal grandmother, died insane. John Brown was the product also of a peculiarly hard, failure-ridden life.[12]

A man of scanty schooling, speculative, of nomadic tastes and marked business incapacity, he made repeated migrations in a fruitless effort to better himself. From northeastern Ohio, where he made his start in life, he went for ten years to northwestern Pennsylvania; then back to Ohio again; then to Virginia, to look into the possibility of settlement; then to Springfield, Massachusetts, on wool business; and then to upper New York. He tried calling after calling; managing tanneries, land speculation, breeding racehorses, surveying, selling cattle and sheep, wool factorage, and farming. Once he even contemplated winemaking. His large family—for his first wife bore him seven children, his second, thirteen—were reared in hand-to-mouth fashion. His character seemed full of contradictions. Usually rigidly honest, he sometimes showed a financial irresponsibility that approached dishonesty; a man of principle, he could be a provoking opportunist; kindly and philanthropic, he had a vein of harsh cruelty. All this,

---

12 Oswald Garrison Villard's *John Brown Fifty Years After* is exhaustive and judicious. Hill Peebles Wilson relentlessly states the adverse case in *John Brown, Soldier of Fortune: a Critique*, while Robert Penn Warren in *John Brown, the Making of a Martyr* attempts a balanced view. Of the older biographies Richard J. Hinton's *John Brown and His Men* is much the best. F. B. Sanborn's biography is not only inaccurate but suppresses vital particulars and mangles documents. James C. Malin's *John Brown and the Legend of '56* is indispensable. I have used collections of papers relating to John Brown in at least a dozen libraries from Boston to Topeka.

with his self-righteous stubbornness and utter intractability, pointed to some psychogenic malady.

All our evidence on his early years shows that he was an exemplary husband, father, and citizen, public-spirited and industrious though incompetent in affairs.

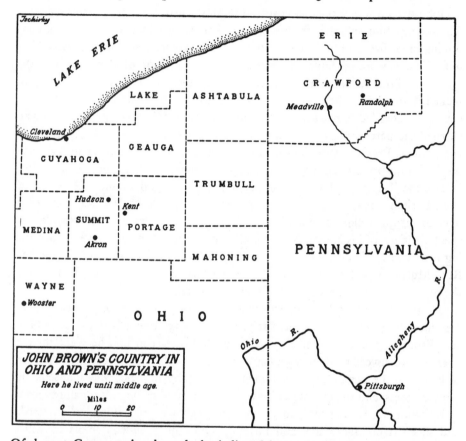

JOHN BROWN'S COUNTRY IN
OHIO AND PENNSYLVANIA
Here he lived until middle age.

Of devout Congregational stock, he believed in predestination, foreordination, and providential interpositions, and prayed daily with family and apprentices. He had cherished in youth, he said later, a strong desire for death—doubtless a wish to be united with God. He showed a rigid probity. A journeyman who lived with him in Hudson, Ohio, for some years, testifies that he was stern in ferreting out dishonest employees, but with an eye to reformation rather than punishment. He took pride in good workmanship. A customer might come ten miles for five pounds of sole leather, yet if Brown detected the least particle of moisture in his stock, he sent the man home empty-handed. He was highly charitable. Once he learned that a neighboring family was destitute; he sought out the neighbor, struck a bargain with him for work the following summer, and made him take food and clothing as pay in advance. He studiously kept the Sabbath, but on other days he toiled hard. He abhorred fishing and hunting as a waste of time. His conversation was often jocose and mirthful, but never vulgar, and always studded with Biblical texts. He liked to argue stubbornly with others, and was eager to gain information from all comers. He despised any man who agreed with him at all points, respecting only those who had ideas of their own. On certain principles, however, he was unyielding. If a stranger entered the community, his first questions were whether the man observed Sunday, supported the gospel and common schools, and opposed slavery. If he failed on any point, Brown regarded him with suspicion.

His own early record on slavery was that of a moderate abolitionist. As a boy he had been shocked and grieved by a Northern innkeeper's maltreatment of a Negro lad his own age. In early manhood he had frequently concealed fugitive slaves. Indeed, a friend who knew him well in Ohio testifies that he repeatedly saw Brown come in at night with several blacks whom he had piloted all the way from the Ohio River; and a woman neighbor thought that he spent time and money on fugitives that might better have gone to the neglected education of his own children. In 1834, he proposed to his brother Frederick that the two enlist helpers and start a school for Negro children in Randolph, Pennsylvania, but the scheme came to nothing. While at first Brown seems to have been a nonresistant of the Garrisonian type, in 1850, helping some free and fugitive Negroes of western Massachusetts organize a League of Gileadites for mutual protection, he preached them a fighting doctrine.[13]

As he grew older, as the world gave him hard buffets, as his lack of business system and foresight plunged him into failure after failure, and as his sceptical temper weakened his religious dogmas, his character changed. One disaster was especially severe; the crash of the Franklin Land Company (1837), in connection with which he had made excessive realty purchases near Franklin Mills, Ohio. His affairs in 1837–41 (which were gloomy depression years after the panic of 1837 anyhow) fell into utter confusion. Struggling in a morass of debt, he lost his reputation for probity. In 1839, he persuaded an agent of the New England Woolen Company of Connecticut to let him have $2,800 for buying wool in Ohio. He converted the money to his own uses, and escaped punishment only because the corporation was lenient—perhaps also because he gave pledges of payment which he never wholly carried out. To reimburse some Ohio sureties who had put their names on one of his bonds or notes, he pledged them his rights to a certain piece of property; then, when this property was conveyed to him,

13 The *Ohio State Arch. and Hist. Quarterly* has printed valuable articles on Brown in Vol. XXX by C. B. Galbreath; in Vol. LXVII by Mary Land; and in Vol. LVIII by Louis Filler. Other aspects of his career are examined by Floyd C. Shoemaker in *Missouri Hist. Review*, XXVI, and by Ernest C. Miller in *Pennsylvania History*, XV.

he secretly recorded the deed and raised money on it by a mortgage. In 1840, he made an abortive effort to obtain a thousand acres in a tract of Virginia land belonging to Oberlin College. His business misfortunes, combative temper, and failure to meet clear legal obligations had resulted in one controversy after another, so that between 1820 and 1845 he figured in twenty-one lawsuits in Portage County, Ohio. One case was specially embarrassing; the Bank of Wooster, suing him for a check which he had drawn on the Leather Manufacturers Bank of New York when he had no account there, recovered $917.65.

It was thus as a failure, a man who had lost part of his early integrity as well as his faith in organized Christianity, a soured, hardened reformer who took refuge from his own deficiencies in fighting the wrongs of others, that Brown in 1855 reestablished his family on the farm at North Elba in the Adirondacks that he had obtained from Gerrit Smith, and saw his sons off to Kansas, himself soon to follow. His purpose was not to resist border ruffians, but to engage in farming and surveying. The Browns migrated to the frontier, like countless other families, to get a fresh start in life. It was only when the sons reported that many Missourians were hostile that John Brown collected arms and money for possible battle. That incisive Kansas historian, James C. Malin, tells us that Brown was not an idealist longing to liberate the prairies; that through years of toil, error, and frustration he had rather become a restless trader moving from place to place in one business after another, constantly pursuing that will-of-the-wisp, a spectacular stroke which would make his fortune. He tells us that Brown's murder of five men on Pottawatomie Creek in May, 1856, probably had nothing to do with slavery, but was an act of political assassination.

This may be true, and yet not all the truth. Brown apparently remained a convinced hater of slavery, who had steeped himself in abolitionist literature and who regarded slaveholders as criminals. He remained, also, a man with a sense of mission—one on whom the finger of the Lord had been laid for some great object. Such a man was easily kindled by the heroic struggle of the free State men in Kansas.

The old veins of Puritan idealism and reformative zeal were still to be found in his nature; but a vein of the ruthlessness peculiar to fanatics, and especially fanatics gnarled by failure, had asserted a dominant place. The cranky scepticism which now kept him from any formal church allegiance perhaps chiefly concerned the New Testament. It is significant that in the many religious letters of his last year he makes but one reference to Christ, and none to Christian mercy. His belief in the harsh, implacable Jehovah of the Old Testament, however, remained unchanged. Charity and forgiveness had no place in his creed. When executed, he refused to let a Virginia minister go to the scaffold, for these ministers believed in slavery, and (said he) "my knees will not bend in prayer with them while their hands are stained with the blood of souls." He left a final injunction to his children to be good haters—to abhor that sum of all villainies, slavery. To him, the Missourians who mustered along the Kaw in 1856–57 were as the Philistines who camped between Sokoh and Azekah; he was as Gideon against the Midianites; he was like the Samson who slew thirty citizens of Asca-lon. The scarred, warped, self-tortured man who supervised the murders on the Pottawatomie told Mahala Doyle, whose husband and sons he killed, that if a man stood between him and what he thought right, he would take that man's life as coolly as he would eat breakfast.

"Always restless," wrote poor Mahala Doyle. "With an eye like a snake, he looks like a demon."

We are thus brought to the question of mental aberration, a subject on which much evidence is available. Most of it lies in affidavits in the papers of Governor Henry A. Wise of Virginia, sent him by people who knew Brown well. It can be summed up in a sentence written by Dr. W. W. Durbin of Canfield, Ohio, whose acquaintance was of long standing and who wrote emphatically: "I am fully satisfied he is and has been a crazy man for years." These affidavits are supplemented by other evidence. The word "monomania" is used with sig-nificant frequency. When Brown paid his last visit to Boston in May, 1859, that shrewd businessman John Murray Forbes noted "the little touch of insanity" about his glittering gray-blue eyes, an impression not lessened by Brown's loud insistence that only bayonets and bullets could settle the Kansas issue—though Kansas was then at peace. A correspondent of the Chicago *Tribune* declared in 1860 that many who knew Brown in Kansas believed that the slaying of his son Frederick had "made him a monomaniac on the subject of slavery"; and that, denying any motive of revenge, he labored under "a religious hallucination to the effect that he was the appointed instrument for putting an end to human slavery." [14]

In the parlance of the day, he had a tendency toward monomania. Endowed with a narrow, intense, dogmatic mind, he fastened it upon one subject with a fervor which shut out all other considerations. But how early did this tendency appear? Was it upon slavery alone that he was a monomaniac? If so, we might doubt the analysis, for by 1860 the country had a multitude of monomaniacs upon slavery. But evidence appears of inordinate preoccupation with one topic after another before he turned to slavery. He was subject to extravagant religious fixations. In 1852, worried because his son John did not exhibit piety, he spent

14 For testimony from many sources relating to Brown's sanity see material in the Villard Collection, Columbia University Library; John Brown Papers, LC; and State Executive Docs., Va. State Library. For a modern treatment of pertinent medical questions see Charles Berg's *Clinical Psychology;* E. H. Williams, *The Doctor in Court.* The author has been advised on this subject by Dr. Joseph Collins of New York and Dr. Bradford Murphey of Denver.

an entire month writing a letter of pamphlet length to him, composed largely of scriptural quotations. We might question the sanity of a nearly penniless man with a large family who devotes a month to such an exhortation—which proved futile. He seems in 1836–37 to have shown a similar fixity of interest in land speculation. And while no final judgment is possible, his wool ventures may also point to psychogenic disorders amounting to mental disease.

That they did so was the belief of Aaron Erickson, a shrewd, well-educated wool dealer of western New York who saw much of Brown in the years when he engaged in sheep growing and wool selling. Brown in 1844 had gone into partnership with Simon Perkins, Jr., of Akron, in the sheep business. Two years later, Perkins & Brown had established an agency in Springfield, Massachusetts, for the sale of wool, with Brown in charge. In August, 1846, a Springfield meeting issued a call for a wool-growers' convention in Steubenville, Ohio, the following year. It was duly held, with Alexander Campbell, founder of the Campbellite sect, as chairman. Brown was present, and delivered a shrewd, practical address on the preparation of wool for the market. He had gained a standing among farmers and stockmen by contributions to the *Ohio Cultivator* and other publications, and by a well-esteemed cure for bots in sheep. The Steubenville meeting adopted a report complaining that textile manufacturers and dealers generally did not properly grade wool, but paid for fine and medium qualities on a low-grade basis; thus endorsing a crusade long carried on by Brown.

Erickson had heard of this crusade; he had heard of local meetings in Ohio at which Brown had declared with rhadamanthine unction that his great mission in life was to right this wrong. Believing the existing system fair, Erickson concluded that the man was some unscrupulous sharper imposing on the farmers' credulity. After Brown had opened the Springfield agency, Erickson had taken pains to meet him. He had been instantly disarmed of his suspicions. Instead of a swindler, he found a man whose frank character, simple manners, and childlike ignorance of his great project stamped him a Dr. Primrose, a deluded visionary. He had convinced himself, Erickson writes, of a total fallacy.

Sometime later, Erickson called again at the Springfield headquarters, finding Brown in high elation. The Perkins & Brown agency, designated as an eastern depot by the Steubenville meeting and supported by the *Prairie Farmer*, had received large consignments of wool from its western friends. Once more Brown showed intense fervor in proclaiming his mission of doing justice to the growers. Once more he praised his own grading system, which Erickson thought manifestly bad. The visitor seized an opportunity, when Brown's back was turned, of transposing three fleeces; and when he pointed to them, Brown emphatically maintained the accuracy of his classification. The reformer, writes Erickson, had valued the finer grades about fifty percent above true market quotations, and the coarser grades about twenty-five percent below. He was deaf to warnings that he had underestimated these lower grades, which would be snapped up by buyers. When he persisted in his course, they were quickly bought at ruinous prices, while the finer fleeces remained a drug on the market. Some farmers interposed before the wool was all sold, states Erickson, bringing a lawsuit which cost Perkins & Brown heavy damages.

Talking of a manufacturers' conspiracy, Brown in 1849 decided to ship his best grades to England. Fine British wools were then being imported despite the tariff; and Brown no sooner shipped two hundred thousand pounds abroad than a Massachusetts manufacturer who had unsuccessfully offered sixty cents a pound at home brought a consignment back from London at a cost, freight and duty included, of fifty-two cents. The loss on this venture may have reached $40,000, and Perkins & Brown went into liquidation. "These," Erickson writes, "were the acts of an insane man." This whole wool agency business constitutes an intricate chapter. Much evidence on it has been lost, and Brown's supporters thought his general position sound. But that at least one astute judge believed him a monomaniac on wool grades and prices is certain.[15]

Medical science has long since discarded the term monomania. It might now classify Brown's aberrations under the head of reasoning insanity, which is a branch of paranoia; that is, of mental disease marked by systematized delusions, but accompanied in many instances by great logical acumen. Such a man may mingle with others and most people will never suspect his disorder. One form of the disease is called litigious paranoia, the victim engaging in many lawsuits; another form is ambitious paranoia, in which the subject feels called to exalted missions. On all subjects but one the patient may appear eminently sane. It is perhaps significant in this connection that a son of one of Brown's partners states: "J. B. saw everything large; felt himself equal to anything; . . . and would accept no suggestions, advice, or direction from anyone." If Brown was a paranoiac, he had moved by 1857 to a feverish absorption in the idea of guerrilla warfare upon slavery. As he did so, the sectional crisis reached a pitch which rendered the acts of such a cool, determined, fanatical leader potentially dangerous.

And Brown intervened in precisely the way that was calculated to do the gravest damage to sectional concord. The steps leading toward his intervention may be briefly exhibited in a series of scenes, all dramatic enough.

15 Brown's wool ventures deserve a separate monograph. While his business mismanagement was deplorable, much may be said for his effort to protect the wool growers. Many papers on the subject are in the Brown collections of the Boston Public Library, Columbia University Library, and Ohio Arch. and Hist. Society. Files of the *Prairie Farmer* are useful.

[II]

Scene First: Concord, Massachusetts, on a February night in 1857. The Town House is ablaze with lights. A hundred citizens and more stamp in, taking off scarves and mittens in the grateful heat from the big stove. They glance curiously over their shoulders as tall lanky Frank B. Sanborn, a young Harvard graduate whom Emerson had brought to the town as head of the academy, escorts down the aisle a worn but wiry man of medium height, with clean-shaven face, burning eyes, and grimly set mouth. Some townsfolk know that John Brown had come by the noon train, had lunched at Mrs. Thoreau's house with Henry and the boarders, and later had chatted with Emerson, who called on an errand. He begins to speak in a metallic, clipped voice, with positive gestures, about the Kansas troubles. He tells of the outrages committed by the border ruffians, of the murder of his son Frederick, and of the interference by Missourians in elections. Attacking the peace party in Kansas, he declares that the Territory needs men who will fight, and needs money too—for war is expensive where food, clothing, and arms must be carted for long distances. He shakes the chain that his son John wore when dragged for miles by Federal dragoons under a hot sun to prison. He also utters some telling epigrams. When he says that the proslavery marauders "had a perfect right to be hanged," Emerson and Thoreau exchange appreciative glances. His declaration that he and his five remaining sons will never stop battling against slavery brings a murmur of approval, and the townspeople march out into the chill night air manifestly impressed.[16]

This Concord address is one of many which Brown makes in his fund-raising tour of New York and New England in late winter and spring of 1857. Naturally, he says nothing of the coldblooded murders which he had instigated on the Pottawatomie the previous May; nothing of other homicides by free State men, and nothing of the fact that the volunteer company he left in Kansas had (under his instructions) made a horse-stealing raid into Missouri.[17] It is only the crimes of proslavery men that he lists. The time is well chosen for his appeal. The Dred Scott decision, the appointment of Walker as governor, the publication of

16 Authorities differ on details. Emerson's *Journals*, followed by Townsend Scudder in *Concord: American Town*, fixes the date of this meeting in February; F. B. Sanborn's *Recollections*, I, 108 ff., followed by Villard, places it in March. Edward Emerson's note to the *Journals* obviously confuses some parts of John Brown's two appearances in Concord. Scudder says Sanborn was on leave in Boston, while Sanborn says he was living in Concord. Such details are inconsequential. As evidence of the impression Brown made, see Thoreau's "Plea for Captain John Brown." Mr. Boyd B. Stutler, owner of valuable John Brown material, believes that the Concord meeting took place about February 18.
17 Villard, *Brown*, 261.

TO THE FRIENDS OF FREEDOM.

The undersigned, whose individual means were exceedingly limited when he first engaged in the struggle for Liberty in Kansas, being now still more destitute and no less anxious than in time past to continue his efforts to sustain that cause, is induced to make this earnest appeal to the Friends of Freedom throughout the United States, in the firm belief that his call will not go unheeded. I ask all honest lovers of *Liberty and Human Rights, both male and female,* to hold up my hands by contributions of pecuniary aid, either as counties, cities, towns villages, societies, churches or individuals.

I will endeavor to make a judicious and faithful application of all such means as I may be supplied with. Contributions may be sent in drafts to W. H. D. CALLENDER, Cashier State Bank, Hartford, Ct. It is my intention to visit as many places *as I can* during my stay in the States, provided I am first informed of the disposition of the inhabitants to aid me *in my efforts,* as well as to receive my visit. Information may be communicated to me (care of Massa-soit House) at Springfield, Mass. Will editors of newspapers friendly to the cause kindly second the measure, and also give this some half dozen insertions? Will either gentlemen or ladies, or both, who love the cause, volunteer to take up the business? It is with *no little sacrifice of personal feeling* that I appear in this manner before the public.

JOHN BROWN.

John Brown's Circular Preceding His Eastern Tour of 1857

13

Geary's attacks on the slavery party, have excited widespread Northern apprehension. Brown meets one important rebuff. He and Sanborn spend an afternoon with ex-Governor Reeder at Easton, Pennsylvania, trying to persuade him to go

for being suspected of favouring free State men   Page 4th
He is known as Ottawa Jones, or John T Jones.

In S.M.A.Cort   free State called Stonton
I visited a beautiful little town, on the North side of the Osage
or Meriderine as sometimes called; from which every inhabitant
had fled for fear of their lives after having built a strong Block house
or wooden fort at a heavy expence for their protection. Many of
them had left their effects liable to be destroyed or carried off
not being able to remove them. This was a most gloomy sene &
like a visit to a vast Sepulchre

Deserted houses, & Cornfields were to be found in almost every direction
South from the Kansas river.   by a boddy 400 Ruffians
I saw the burning of Osawatomie, Aug 30th & of Franklin after
Gov Geary had been some time in the territory; & might have easily pre-
-vented it. It would not have cost the U S. One Dollar to have saved
Franklin.
*   I saw three mangled bodies two of which were dead*
& one alive with twenty Buck shot & Bullet holes in him; after the
two murdered men had lain on the ground to be worked at by Flies
for some 18 Hours. One of those young men was my own Son.
*   saw   about the head*
I,a Mr Porter who I will know; all bruised & with her Throat partly
cut, after being draged sick from the House of Ottawa Jones, & thrown
over the bank of the Ottawa creek for dead: about the first of Sept

From John Brown's Notes for A Speech

to Kansas as agent of the Massachusetts Kansas Committee, and to take the Kansas leadership away from moderate Charles Robinson. "I will serve as commander of field forces in guerrilla warfare," promises Brown. Reeder warily declines. Elsewhere, however, the fanatical leader has better success.[18]

18 Brown had issued a well-printed circular, of which the Chicago Historical Society has a copy. It states that he intends to visit as many places as possible in his tour of the East

Wherever he goes—Philadelphia, New York, Syracuse, Worcester, Boston—the gaunt, weather-beaten warrior pleads for money and arms; everywhere he denounces the Kansas peace party and predicts that war will again burst forth on the plains.[19] He induces the Massachusetts Kansas Committee (which includes the manufacturer George L. Stearns, the reformer Dr. Samuel Gridley Howe, and Sanborn) to give him custody of two hundred Sharps rifles at Tabor, Iowa, with four thousand ball cartridges and thirty-one thousand percussion caps, and to vote him $500 for their care. The same body grants another $500 to him for the relief of Kansas. The National Kansas Committee in New York appropriates $5,000 to him in aid of defensive measures, but this results in an actual transfer of only $150 to his pockets.[20] In Boston, various men, including Amos A. Lawrence and Wendell Phillips, give him $1,000 to complete the purchase of the farm at North Elba, New York, where his wife and some of the children reside. While the total of monetary donations falls far short of his goal of $25,000, it is nevertheless considerable.[21]

Scene Second: A village drugstore in Collinsville, Connecticut, one February morning in 1857. A group are gathered about Brown, congratulating him on his Kansas lecture the night before, and asking for additional information. He launches into the story of his encounter at Black Jack with a little force led by Henry Clay Pate, captain of Missouri militia and deputy Federal marshal. Brown, boasting that with nine brave followers he had captured twenty-odd well-armed border ruffians, draws a vivid picture. "We came up at daylight to those blackjack oaks at the spring," he says. "It is on the Santa Fé trail. I ordered my men to get ready to attack. Pate and his crew were lurking in a ravine; plenty of bushes and trees for cover. I moved around to their flank, and drew in to close quarters. The sun was well up then and getting hot. The grass was dry; I remember thinking how it would look spattered with blood. Suddenly one of those border ruffians stood up with a white handkerchief on a long rod."

The listeners gape. Then they draw back as Brown whips from his bootleg a handsomely mounted bowie knife. "Look—this was Pate's. His Virginia friends gave it to him when he left for Kansas." Several men, including a blacksmith named Charles Blair, feel its keen edge. "If I had a lot of these blades fastened to poles about six feet long," says Brown, ruminatively, "they would make good weapons for our freestate settlers to keep in their cabins." The group chorusses

"provided I am first informed of the disposition of the inhabitants *to aid me in my efforts.* . . ." He was so pressed for money that he wrote H. N. Rust offering to sell a captured sabre, for "I am literally driven to beg: which is very humiliating." Brown Papers, Chicago Hist. Soc.
19 Sanborn, *Recollections*, I, 117.
20 Villard, 274–276; Sanborn, I, 118, 119.
21 R. J. Hinton, *John Brown and His Men*, 143–145.

assent. With an air of sudden decision he turns to Blair. "You're a forge-master," he remarks. "You can make good edge tools. What would you charge to make five hundred or a thousand of these pikes?" Blair considers a moment. "Well," he ventures, "I could probably make you five hundred at a dollar and a quarter apiece, or a thousand at a dollar apiece." "I want them made," says Brown in his terse way; and a little later a contract is signed.[22]

Obviously, this order for pikes has curious aspects. With rifles and revolvers so abundant in Kansas, why an order for a thousand spears? They might be useful for men who could not handle firearms—say colored men, but not for hardy frontier folk. Why give the order to a Connecticut blacksmith, when an Iowan could fabricate them just as well? Delivery is to be made July 1, 1857, but Brown is able to supply only $500 on the contract, and though Blair buys the materials, no weapons are shipped this summer.

It is also curious that Brown holds conferences this spring and summer with an Englishman now resident in New York, Hugh Forbes, who, at one time a silk merchant in Siena, had taken up arms with Garibaldi in the disastrous campaigns of 1848–49. A middle-aged man of considerable ability as linguist, drill-master, and military engineer, Forbes is a radical idealist of the Mazzini school, loves conspiracy, and is hungry for better employment than his odd jobs as fencing-master and translator and reporter for the *Tribune*. He and Brown talk eagerly of methods of guerrilla warfare. In fact, the two exchange ideas, and if we may believe Forbes, hammer them together in what they call "The Well-Matured Plan." The Englishman agrees to serve at $100 a month instructing a volunteer company which Brown intends to raise, providing a handbook of tactics (*The Manual of the Patriotic Volunteer*, based on an earlier book), writing a tract to persuade American soldiers never to support wrong against right, and doing other work. When authorized to draw upon one of Brown's supporters for $600, he does so within the month.[23] Partly as a result of his talks with Forbes, Brown is making some curious notes in his memorandum book. For example, he writes of the "valuable hints" for guerrilla warfare in a life of Wellington, adding: "*See also* same book Page 235 these words Deep and narrow defiles where 300 men would suffice to check an *army*." [24]

22 *Mason Report* (36th Cong., 1st Sess., Senate Rept. No. 278), 121–199; Sanborn, I, 104. Brown made final payment for the pikes by a draft from Troy, N. Y., June 7, 1859; Brown Papers, Chicago Hist. Soc.

23 A Hartford gentleman, W. H. D. Callender, supplied this sum; Villard, 286.

24 All statements by the adventurer Forbes require verification. He arrived in New York in 1850, and in 1851 delivered anti-Catholic lectures in the city. His tactical handbook was based on his *Manual of the Patriotic Volunteer* published in one volume in New York in 1854 and in two volumes in 1856. That with his military experience (treated in G. M. Trevelyan's volumes on Garibaldi), versatility, and dash he made an impression on Brown's thinking is indubitable. Hinton in *Brown and His Men*, 146–152, treats him rather favorably; Villard, 285, 317 ff., very unfavorably.

In truth, Brown's talk to certain eastern supporters of defensive operations in Kansas is a blind. He is contemplating offensive activity, not merely in Kansas but in some part of the Southern Appalachians; perhaps the Shenandoah, perhaps further south. He believes that hundreds of slaves will rise at the first blow. He intends to place the thousand pikes in their hands, and to use the two hundred revolvers which Stearns bought for him from the Massachusetts Arms Company in hand-to-hand fighting.[25] Perhaps already he is scheming a dash at the Harper's Ferry arsenal, destroying what arms he cannot carry off.

How long he has revolved his plan for moving a well-armed force into the Appalachian country, making raids into slave areas, and destroying slavery by rendering it unsafe, we do not know. If we may credit the autobiography of Frederick Douglass, he had confided to that Negro leader in 1847 his belief that he could put a well-trained force into western Virginia, support them there, run off large numbers of slaves, keep the bravest while sending the weaker north by the underground railroad, and thus so undermine the institution that it would topple in ruins.[26] Once seized with an idea, he is not the man to let it go. Early in August, 1857, he reaches Tabor, Iowa, where two days later Forbes arrives. They agree that their volunteer company will need a school of instruction. Forbes presently goes back east to choose a place; Brown goes on to Kansas to raise recruits and money.

Scene Third: A blazing campfire at night on the open prairie near Topeka in November, 1857. Chill winds howl about, as Brown piles fuel on the embers. Four roughly dressed men sit near, their knapsacks and blankets affording partial shelter. These first recruits of Brown's irregular company are fairly typical of the whole lot, a body of reckless, adventurous young drifters with a few true idealists. Physically the most striking is Aaron D. Stevens, a six-footer with magnificent chest and limbs and handsome face. He had run away from a Massachusetts home to fight in the Mexican War, had got into a drunken riot at Taos and struck an officer, and had been sentenced to three years in jail at Fort Leaven-

25 Villard, *Brown*, 289.

26 Frederick Douglass, *Life and Times* (London, 1882), 238–240. Brown knew how to dissemble his purposes. When the National Kansas Aid Committee, sitting in New York in January, 1857, showed some inquisitiveness, he pretended to take offense. The secretary, H. B. Hurd, asked what he thought a pro forma question: "If you get the arms and money you desire will you invade Missouri or any slave territory?" Brown replied with asperity: "I do not expose my plans. No one knows them but myself, except perhaps one. I will not be interrogated; if you wish to give me anything, I want you to give it freely. I have no other purpose but to serve the cause of liberty." The committee, which had previously understood that Brown intended to arm some Kansas settlers who would not be called out except to protect the free State population, became suspicious. He got his vote of $5,000 only for defensive purposes. At the same time Brown was giving his abolitionist friends a fuller view. Gerrit Smith, Frank Sanborn, and T. W. Higginson knew that he intended violence, and that this violence might aid their disunionist schemes. H. B. Hurd, March 19, 1860, to Stearns; Stearns Papers, Kansas State Hist. Soc.

worth, whence he escaped to join the free State men. The most talkative, an incessant chatterer, is John E. Cook, an impulsive Connecticut Yankee in his late twenties, one-time law clerk in Ogden Hoffman's office in New York. Fresh-faced and youthful looking, he has never quite grown up. Intellectually the most distinguished is John Henry Kagi, an Ohioan of Swiss-English descent, whose speech gives evidence of a quick mind and superior education. Only twenty-two, this ardent young man, a devoted abolitionist, has been a schoolteacher, is proficient in Latin, French, and mathematics, has studied law, and has helped report the debates in the recent Kentucky constitutional convention. He talks with the skill of a trained debater.[27]

The four treat Brown with deep respect. They know that he has other recruits, but they wish to learn his plans; and they inquire where they are to serve.

Brown tells them that the whole company is to go back east to drill. The Territory is quiet, and winter campaigning is impossible anyhow. His sons, with various other volunteers—Realf, Parsons, Tidd—will travel with them. He hands Cook a draft for $82.50. "Get this cashed in Lawrence tomorrow. We'll all meet again at Tabor in Iowa. Then I'll tell you just what we are going to do. If you want hard fighting you'll get plenty of it."

And at Tabor, as ten men gather about him, Brown's face wears a look of awakened resolution. "Our ultimate destination," he says, "is Virginia."[28]

Scene Fourth: The town of Chatham in Upper Canada, not far from Detroit, on a Saturday in May, 1858. It is a bustling city of six thousand, with one long shopping thoroughfare, King Street, wharves on the Thames from which ships ply to all the Great Lakes ports, and prosperous industries—flour mills, wood-working establishments, iron foundries, wagon shops. It is also a center for refugee slaves, who constitute one-third the population. The streets are full of them; and, as even unskilled Negroes earn $1.25 a day, while many are artisans and farmers, they seem well dressed and happy. At least one colored man has a bachelor's degree from Oberlin.[29] On this May 8, a number of Negroes and whites are at a Negro schoolhouse in Princess Street, where they say they are organizing a Masonic lodge.

Inside the schoolhouse, as ten o'clock strikes, the eyes of the eleven white and thirty-four colored men present are fixed on John Brown. He nods to a delegate named Jackson, who raps for order. The first business is the election of officers. A colored minister from Detroit, W. C. Munroe, is made president, and Kagi, an impressive figure with his long dark hair, large eyes, and fine forehead,

27 Hinton knew these recruits and in *John Brown and His Men* gives excellent sketches; for fuller material see Villard, 678-687.
28 See Cook's pamphlet "Confession" published in November, 1859.
29 Chatham is fully described in the N. Y. *Weekly Tribune*, October 24, 1857.

is chosen secretary. A colored physician, Dr. Martin R. Delany, later to hold in the Civil War the highest rank, that of major, given to any colored man, moves that John Brown address them on the purpose of the meeting. Rising, the fiery-eyed leader begins to talk. He remarks that for more than twenty years the idea of giving freedom to the slaves has obsessed him. He describes how, when he visited Europe in 1851, including Waterloo, he inspected fortifications and especially earthworks.

"I have formed a plan of action," Brown asserts. All over the South, he explains, slaves are eager to escape from bondage. He wishes to strike a blow from some point in the mountain chain which thrusts diagonally down from Maryland and Virginia into Tennessee and north Alabama. He believes that slaves will rise all over the South and struggle to reach his standard; he will welcome them and put arms in their hands; they will entrench themselves, and make sudden descents into the plantation country on each side.

"But what if troops are brought against you?" asks one listener.

A small force will be sufficient to defend these Thermopylae ravines, responds Brown. We shall defeat the green State militia if they march against us. If United States troops come, we shall defeat them too. I hope, however, that little bloodshed will be necessary. If the slaveholders resist us, we shall carry them back as hostages, holding them to guarantee proper treatment of any of our own men who may be taken prisoners. We shall soon be too strong to attack, for I expect the able-bodied free negroes of the North to flock to my banner, and all the Southern slaves who can escape will do the same. Gradually we shall build up a powerful state. Our freedmen will go to work tilling farms and running workshops; they will organize schools and churches. We shall not molest slaveholders who do not interfere with us, but of course we shall treat all enemies who attack us alike. I am confident that we can maintain ourselves, and can defy any enemy. John Brown draws himself more erect and gesticulates more emphatically. Thus, he concludes, the slave States will finally be compelled to emancipate the people they are holding in bondage, and we shall put an end to that accursed institution. That done, we shall reorganize our mountain state on a new basis, and elect a fresh set of officers.[30]

The next business is the adoption of a constitution for the proposed state, and the choice of a commander-in-chief, secretary of state, and secretary of war. Brown has his document ready, and after an oath of secrecy is taken by every member, it is read. "Whereas," its preamble began, "slavery throughout its entire existence in the United States is none other than a most barbarous, unprovoked, and unjustifiable war of one portion of its citizens upon another portion . . ." On motion of Kagi, the provisional constitution is adopted, and that

30 See Realf's report of the speech, Villard, 331, 332; *Mason Report*, 96, 97.

afternoon, with congratulatory speeches, is signed. At an evening session Brown is elected commander-in-chief and Kagi secretary of war, while the next day a white recruit named Richard Realf is named secretary of state.

Monomania has reached its climax, for this Chatham gathering marks a full crystallization of Brown's plans. In every feature the scheme is preposterous: the idea that slaves are ready for wholesale revolt; the idea that State and national forces can be resisted; the idea that a temporary new commonwealth can be created. Yet there is method in Brown's madness. The preamble of his constitution is a declaration of war which justifies the killing of slaveholders, the liberation of slaves, the confiscation of other property, and the ravaging of enemy lands. It does more than justify the fomenting of slave insurrections; it assumes that a universal and incessant slave insurrection is under way, and that only brute force is restraining it within bounds. Rejecting the American Constitution, Brown is establishing his own government and laws, under which he will be free to commit any act of belligerent violence. As he wages war against the slaveholders, the States, and the nation, his robberies will be called the confiscation of enemy property, his kidnappings will be termed the seizure of enemy hostages, and his murders will be denominated legitimate military operations. His knowledge of what had happened in Haiti when a war of races began does not daunt him, for he believes that without the shedding of blood there can be no remission of Southern sins, and that, as he has told Emerson, it is better that a whole generation of men, women, and children should pass away by violence than that slavery should endure.

[III]

By the spring of 1858—and this fact is of cardinal importance—a group of New England and New York abolitionists approved Brown's mad plan for an attack, at some unnamed point, upon the South. In February, staying with Gerrit Smith at Peterboro, New York, he had unfolded his scheme to that wealthy reformer and his wife, to his old friend Frank Sanborn, and to Captain Charles Stewart, a veteran of Wellington's army in Spain. When they protested that failure was certain, Brown made it clear he would go forward whether they aided him or not. Sanborn tells us that they decided to lend assistance rather out of their regard for the Kansas fighter than from any hope of immediate success; but this, as we shall see, by no means covers their motivation. They were thinking of a remote success rather than of any immediate victory. Proceeding to Boston, John Brown early in March communicated his scheme in outline to Theodore Parker, Samuel G. Howe, and George L. Stearns. Thomas Wentworth Higginson at Worcester knew all about it, and so did Frederick Douglass. What they did not know was just where Brown would "raise the mill," as he put it. But they formed a secret committee of six which advised Brown and raised a considerable sum of money for him.

Why did these abolitionists lend their aid to the fanatic who, fatuously over-rating his strength and underestimating that of the South and the nation, intended to hurl himself against the Gibraltar of slavery? Partly, because the stalwart courage of the man awed them. He loomed up in their vision like another William Tell or Robert Bruce. Holding the conviction they held upon the wickedness of slavery, they could not let him rush into desperate battle without a helping hand. Partly, too, because they believed that he did have one chance in a dozen of instant success. The abolitionists constantly exaggerated the intellectual capacity and fighting power of the slaves; they constantly deluded themselves that widespread slave insurrections were possible in the South. Above all, however, they helped him in the hope of achieving a remoter object; he would fail, but in failing he would start a civil war in which slavery would perish.[31]

For years, many of the abolitionists had wished for civil war—we have quoted Wendell Phillips and Theodore Parker in wishful predictions; even the pacifist Garrison had predicted civil war. Some abolitionists had not merely hoped that it would start in Kansas, but had labored to blow the spark into flame. Just after Frémont's defeat in 1856, Thomas Wentworth Higginson had written Gerrit Smith that he desired "to start a *private* organization of picked men, who shall be ready to go to Kansas in case of need, to aid the people against *any* opponent, State or Federal." It would not be expedient to form a large organization in the East because of the cost of transportation. "But it is essential to involve *every* State in the war that is to be." His plan therefore would be to enlist a hundred men in Massachusetts and perhaps fifty each in the other New England States; drill and organize them; and then, when trouble began in Kansas, use them as "a nucleus of an Army of Reinforcement." As his movement grew he would extend it to other States. He had talked his plan over with "all the best men," who approved it but were disposed to leave the leadership to him:[32]

Some of us here (Republicans and Garrisonians) are planning a *Convention* to be held here, which shall consider the idea of Disunion between Free and Slave States, *as a practical problem which the times are pressing on us.* . . .

31 Sanborn had read a lecture on John Brown before the Concord School in March, 1857, the MS of which is in the Chicago Hist. Soc. He declared that if the country was to have a war over slavery, it needed such old men and young men as Brown. Many abolitionists wanted slave insurrections. The abolitionist and disunion convention which met at Cleveland in the fall of 1857 adopted a resolution declaring that the slaves ought to strike down their masters by force whenever the blow could be effective. *Ann. Rept. Amer. Anti-Slavery Soc.*, 1858, pp. 181, 182.
32 November 22, 1856; Gerrit Smith Papers, Univ. of Syracuse.

Garrison, Phillips, and others see the time is come for such a movement, and will gladly cooperate on a common platform, with all who believe that the time is come for resisting the U. S. Government in Kanzas, and sustaining such resistance everywhere else. . . .

Half the people I meet are within an inch of Disunion, and I wish to keep them there; so that when the fight begins, whether in Iowa or Washington, they will be ready to act themselves and *drive* their politicians.

This letter throws a broad beam of light upon one phase of the hysteria of the time. In other communications, Higginson declared that men were ready for revolution, that blind superstitious loyalty to the national government was declining, and that in Kansas he had found the free State men just as ready to fight the United States forces as the Missourians. He wished several Northern governors to agree that in the event of another Missouri invasion of Kansas, or renewed interference by Federal officials with the constitutional rights of free State men, they would issue a call for volunteers. He had talked with Governor Fletcher of Vermont, who was willing to join such a group. Companies of volunteers should be gotten ready to respond immediately to such a call. Hysteria readily embraces monomania. Civil War had failed in Kansas; now John Brown might be the firebrand to set the conflagration roaring in Virginia.[33]

A conspiracy had sprung up behind Brown. He might have pushed his plan rapidly forward, but suddenly a delay became necessary. Hugh Forbes, whose ideas of practical action differed widely from Brown's, who saw the man's touch of insanity, and who felt that he himself had been exploited only to be cast aside, wrote a series of letters to abolitionist leaders attacking Brown as a reckless, dangerous man who ought to be disarmed. Selfish though he was, he stated sound practical objections. Visiting Washington, he partially exposed Brown's wild designs to Henry Wilson and others. He informed Seward that the Kansan was an utterly untrustworthy and vicious person who ought to be restrained. None of the secret committee (Sanborn, Parker, Gerrit Smith, Stearns, Howe, and Higginson) knew just how much he had revealed. Senator Wilson wrote Dr. Howe in alarm (May 9, 1858) that the men who had contributed to Brown's very foolish movement ought to get the arms they had given him out of his hands, and keep clear of him for at least the time being.[34] This was the month

33 November 1, 1856; Gerrit Smith Papers, *ibid.* "I think perhaps you do not realize how much better men are prepared for revolution now than they were six months ago," Higginson wrote Smith.
34 Forbes acted with fairness. He first appealed to Stearns, Sumner, and others sympathetic with Brown; when they did not act, he turned to Wilson and Seward. Hinton, *op. cit.*, 160. Brown's return to Kansas was partly a successful ruse to shake off suspicion; Villard, 396. If we had the full text of all Forbes's letters (H. P. Wilson asserts they have been partly suppressed) we could better assess his motives. To Brown's admirers he has always been a blackmailer who, if he were not paid for more work, was willing to betray Brown. But he had a military sense that Brown lacked.

of the Chatham convention. In a panic, five of the secret committee met at the Revere House in Boston and decided that the raid must be postponed. The absent Higginson was violently opposed to this, saying that postponement for a year was postponement forever, but he was overruled. These lion-hearted abolitionists were willing to see a blow struck, but it must be at a time and in a way that would not imperil their own skins.

Stearns, as chairman of the Massachusetts Kansas Aid Committee, sent Brown an official missive warning him not to use the arms collected for Kansas in any other area. Then, by a distinctly sharp piece of evasion, he saw to it that the arms (two hundred rifles) were given to the leader only on condition that he went to Kansas for the next few months, but were thereafter left to his discretion to use anywhere. Various conferences between Brown and the committee members took place in Boston. The grim warrior, at first peevish over the timidity of his eastern associates, was finally brought into an acquiescent mood. It was agreed between him and the abolitionist conspirators that, as Higginson put it in a memorandum, he should visit Kansas "to blind F[orbes]"; that he would get $500 at once, with a promise of $2,000 or $3,000 in the spring of 1859; that his main operation should be postponed until then; and that the arms should be transferred to him "so as to relieve them [the conspirators] of responsibility—and they in future not to know his plans."

Truly, these Yankee abolitionists were a valorous group! They hoped to provoke war, but not one offered to stand by Brown's side as he invaded the South; they took arms that the Massachusetts Aid Committee had bought for use in Kansas, and by a subterfuge encouraged him to use them elsewhere; they egged him on, but with a stipulation that they should be kept uninformed so that they could not be prosecuted.

On June 3, 1858, Brown left Boston in good spirits with his $500 in gold, and on the twenty-fifth he was back in Lawrence.

[IV]

He found Kansas in what he regarded as a deplorably quiet condition. Conservatism had triumphed; the population, drawn from the broad border area of moderate outlook, rejoiced in the moderate solutions at last reached. Conservative eastern friends like A. A. Lawrence rejoiced with them. No issue existed to create dissension. Since the defeat of the English amendment it was universally agreed that Kansas would in due course enter the Union as a free State. The most populous area, the northeastern district embracing Leavenworth, Lawrence, and Topeka, was enjoying almost complete peace, the sharpest quarrels being those between rival free State factions. Only in the southeastern area, about Fort Scott and Trading Post, did sporadic troubles between proslavery men and freesoilers ("jayhawkers") continue. They had reached a climax in the late spring of 1858, in the horrifying Marais des Cygnes massacre, in which a hotblooded Georgian named Charles A. Hamilton, heading a band of border desperadoes, marched eleven prisoners into a ravine, drew them up in line, and opened fire, killing five and wounding more. Fortunately, an attempt at retaliation by the principal jayhawker chieftain, James Montgomery, resulted in nothing worse than a little incendiarism at Fort Scott. Thereupon, Governor Denver undertook a pacificatory tour through the region, making speeches and using his personal influence to compose old feuds. By July, a period of comparative repose had opened. Freesoilers who desired to see it prolonged heard of Brown's arrival with uneasiness and dread.[35]

Inevitably, Brown swung to any area of fever and violence as the needle swings to its pole; inevitably, he exaggerated whatever trouble existed; and inevitably, he preached an eye for an eye and a tooth for a tooth. On July 23, he wrote his family from a poor, narrow, hot little cabin at Trading Post near the Missouri line, where for a week he and about ten of his men had stayed on the same quarter section where the Marais des Cygnes murders had been committed. Every few days, he inaccurately declared, some new murder was committed; deserted houses and farms lay in every direction; the atmosphere was one of uncertainty and fear.[36] A fortnight later, he boasted to his son John of the consternation which his arrival had created among the Missourians. "Which of the passions most predominated, fear or rage, I do not pretend to say." A prolonged attack of malarial fever helped keep him inactive until autumn. Recovering with the cool weather, he was ready, as he wrote Kagi, to take the field with Montgomery in a renewal of guerrilla operations; and he soon validated this statement by going far beyond anything that Montgomery had contemplated.[37]

First, he joined Montgomery and about a hundred others in a descent upon Fort Scott to liberate a free State prisoner there, the attack ending in the death of a storekeeper and the seizure as loot of about $7,000 worth of goods. Montgomery later declared that he had taken the leadership of this expedition because Brown was bent upon burning the entire town to the ground, and killing anybody who resisted. Immediately thereafter, Brown executed a raid into Missouri to free all the slaves he could reach. One object in this, according to his follower

35 Spring, Kansas, 244–251; Robinson, The Kansas Conflict, 391–395.
36 John Brown Papers, Ohio Arch. and Hist. Soc.
37 Charles Robinson later wrote with bitterness that while his forces took great care to commit no crimes, Brown's murders and thefts had "put all our people under suspicion." By lies and disguises he escaped unhurt; innocent men suffered the penalty. "While our free state colonies were trying to convert the whites from the South and make them sound free state men, John Brown thought it better to murder them." Undated fragment, Robinson Papers, Kansas State Hist. Soc.

Cook, was to illustrate the feasibility of his grand scheme so that it would be easier to raise in the East the funds that he needed.[38]

This raid, an indefensibly lawless outrage upon inoffensive citizens, created a sensation North and South. On the night of December 20–21, Brown invaded Missouri with two bands; he leading eight or nine men, while the former dragoon Stevens headed eight. Brown's group attacked the homes of two planters, seized their slaves, stole some watches and personal trinkets, and carried off livestock, harness, clothing, and miscellaneous articles. Stevens's expedition forced entry into a house, looted it, stole livestock, and carried away a slave. Worst of all, Stevens shot the owner of this house dead. The morning of December 21 found Brown safe in Kansas again, with eleven Negroes, two white prisoners, and a large booty of spoils. Sheltering his force that day in a heavily wooded ravine, he moved northward as soon as darkness fell. On Christmas Eve the Negroes were at Ossawatomie, to which point Brown, after delaying near Fort Scott for a time, followed them on January 11. Late that month, he and the slaves set out on their long journey to Canada. He might have lingered in Kansas if the warfare for which he hoped had broken out along the Missouri border; but although the countryside sprang to arms, and for a time general bloodshed was feared, the frantic efforts of Montgomery and other responsible leaders to preserve the peace proved successful. He had good reason for leaving, in that he found his outrage emphatically condemned by the very settlers whom he had hoped to excite to battle. He had miscalculated sentiment.[39]

The opinion of decent Kansans, in fact, was registered in no uncertain terms. A correspondent of the Lawrence *Herald of Freedom* expressed consternation at finding free State men guilty of the same villainies for which they had arraigned the border ruffians. Montgomery, whom Brown urged to fight, turned the other way. A prominent free State settler, William Hutchinson, sought out Brown near Trading Post to expostulate. "We are settlers—you are not," he said. "You can strike the blow and leave; the retaliatory blow falls on us. We are at peace with Missouri. Our legislature is a free State legislature; even in the disturbed counties of Bourbon and Linn free State men are in the majority. Without peace we can have no immigration. No Southern immigrants are coming, and your agitation only keeps out our Northern friends." This man found, as did others, that Brown was engrossed in the monomania of "my work," "my great duty," "my mission." Another settler and old friend of Brown's, Augustus Wattles, also took him to task. Brown replied that he had considered the matter

38 Villard, 367; Cook's "Confession" (pamphlet).
39 A few Kansans took the view that, as one wrote the N. Y. *Tribune*, the raid was needed to punish Missouri crimes, give free State settlers confidence, prevent further flights from the country, and teach border ruffians to stay at home. Dated Moneka, Kansas, December 22, 1858.

well and would now leave Kansas. "I consider it my duty to draw the scene of excitement to some other part of the country." [40]

Yet the fact that as Brown carried his slaves into free soil he found ready helpers did not escape the Southern press, which resounded with denunciation of his act. To the law, he was a dangerous felon. President Buchanan offered a reward for his capture; the Missouri governor rumbled threats; the newly appointed governor of Kansas, Samuel Medary, not only did the same but asked the legislature to take some action. Nevertheless, as Brown and his charges worked their way across the north-central states to Ontario, he met with no real obstacle. At one point in Kansas, his band successfully charged through a posse from Atchison, and at another evaded a larger force. In Iowa, his party stopped at various underground stations; at Des Moines, the editor of the *Register* paid their ferriage across the river; at Grinnell, three Congregational ministers led the townsfolk in extending succor, while the founder, Josiah B. Grinnell, provided an ample store of supplies and money and hired a boxcar to carry them to Chicago. In that city, the detective Allan Pinkerton raised more than $500 for them, and procured a well-stocked car to Detroit. In short, although every reader of the press knew that Brown had organized a robbery and been party to a murder, and although the presidential reward of $250 for his capture was an attraction, he crossed State after State with impunity. Such was the public sentiment upon Kansas and the protection of escaped Negroes that no officer of the law cared to touch him.[41]

John Brown's self-confident sense of a special mission could not but be increased by the applause which he met outside Kansas. He made two speeches at Grinnell, and moved freely about Chicago; he and Kagi lectured in Cleveland, where Artemus Ward praised his pluck in the *Plain Dealer;* and on March 12 he saw his colored wards marshaled aboard the Detroit ferryboat to Windsor. Proceeding to Rochester and Boston, he was petted as a hero. The Northern press had published a self-exculpatory letter in which he weirdly distorted the facts of his raid, and most Northern editors accepted it at face value.[42] Gerrit Smith told an applauding audience that, of all men, he thought John Brown the nearest approach to a perfect Christian. The South found something more than

40 Villard, 373, 375.

41 The oft-made statements that Missouri posted a reward and that all rewards aggregated $3,500 have no basis. Brown wrote an exultant letter to his son from Winterset, Iowa, on December 13, 1857, mentioning that he had nine young men whom he was placing in the military school at Springdale, Ia.

42 The perversions were egregious. He wrote that he heard that a family of Negroes was to be sold, and had gone to liberate them; the sale was a fiction. We "took certain property," he confessed; they took a great deal. He declared they had returned some property, the owners denied. His force had killed one white man "who fought against the liberation"; this man was slain defending his cabin. For text of letter see N. Y. *Weekly Tribune,* February 12, 1859.

Northern insolence in the protection of such an assailant of its peculiar institution; it found a threat to its safety. It noted, too, that the effort of the free State legislature to outlaw slavery in Kansas and the use of Kansas as a base for raiding a slave State, occurring almost simultaneously, could be cited as arguments for a Federal slave code in the Territories.

The threat to slavery was greater than the South realized, for it knew nothing of the plan of Brown and the abolitionist committee for a direct blow. The eastern conspirators were deeply impressed by their hero's success. While Gerrit Smith pledged him $400, the Boston group raised more than $4,000, nearly all of it given with a clear knowledge that it would be used in a new and larger effort. Dr. Howe delightedly wrote John Murray Forbes that Brown was staying at a hotel in Beach Street, and that any man who wanted $3,500 had only to go and try to take the old fellow. "He knows more about the question of practical emancipation than anyone whom I have seen." The emotional hysteria of those abolitionists, who totally disregarded both the property rights of Southerners and the tremendous difficulties of race-adjustment bound up in any plan of emancipation, had always been dangerous. Now a cabal of them had found in this implacable Puritan warrior from the Kansas border, robbed by his exalted mental state of all ability to calculate risks or observe ordinary canons of right and wrong, a fearfully dangerous instrument.

[V]

Such was the antagonism between North and South that perils and irritations now came not as single spies, but in battalions. While John Brown was spiriting his captured slaves off to Canada, the South was watching with anger the movement to circulate in vast numbers a free, or nearly free, edition of Helper's *Impending Crisis*. Regarding the book with abhorrence, Southern leaders did not fail to note the prediction of the New York *Tribune* that its general circulation would lead to a speedy extinction of slavery, at least in the border States. Just how, asked slaveholders? By setting class against class, by firing all the materials for a social conflagration, by arousing the slaves to a bloody revolt? The fund required was raised with considerable difficulty. A long list of Northern freesoilers contributed $100 apiece, while an anonymous Southern clergyman gave $250 through Cassius M. Clay. Copies were soon passing from hand to hand in the North and border area.[43] Nor did the South fail to find other provocations.

43 The main aim of Republican leaders was to convert Northern Democrats rather than to reach border men. We agree, one wrote Lyman Trumbull, that arduous labor will be required to carry Pennsylvania, Illinois, and Indiana in 1860; the book will help. W. M. Chace, October 19: 1857; Trumbull Papers.

This spring brought on the much-advertised trials of the "Oberlin rescuers," which proved again that the Fugitive Slave Law could no more be enforced in northern Ohio than in New England. The previous September, two Kentuckians had appeared in the college town of Oberlin, an abolitionist center since the middle thirties, in search of a runaway.[44] They would have encountered trouble anywhere in the Western Reserve, but in this particular community they struck a hornets' nest. The fugitive was no sooner captured than a body of excited citizens from Oberlin and the neighboring town of Wellington seized him and hurried him off to Canada. The frustrated Kentuckians appealed to the Federal authorities. Indictments were found against thirty-seven of the rescuers, and the ensuing trials in the Federal court in Cleveland proved one of the *causes célèbres* of Ohio history. A counterattack was opened on the Kentuckians, the grand jury of Lorain County indicting them under State law as kidnappers. Since they were indispensable as witnesses in the Federal case, the Federal Marshal locked them up to prevent their being arrested and detained elsewhere. Rival county and Federal posses glared at each other in the courthouse grounds; a great Cleveland massmeeting on May 24, with the venerable Joshua Giddings presiding and Governor Salmon P. Chase (full of Presidential ambitions) the chief speaker, cheered resolutions declaring the Fugitive Slave Law null and void; and a tumultuous procession marched through the streets to demonstrate in front of the jail. The rescuers were continuously feted; visitors thronged to their cells, letters of sympathy and funds for expenses poured in, and they were showered with presents.[45] The first sentences were ridiculously light, all the Wellington defendants gaining release in April with fines of $25 and costs apiece, superadded to a day in jail. Only by a narrow vote of three to two did the State Supreme Court decide against releasing the Oberlin prisoners on a writ of *habeas corpus*.

By late spring, despite the earnest attitude of the Federal authorities, it was plain that the case against the rescuers still in jail could never be pressed to a successful termination. The extreme penalty thus far meted out was sixty days in prison and $600 fine. When the Kentucky "kidnappers" were put upon trial, their counsel, fearing that the court would sentence them to heavy terms, proposed a compromise. In virtue of this arrangement, the men still under Federal indictment were freed by a *nolle prosequi*, while the State proceedings against the Kentuckians were dropped. Northern Ohio held gay celebrations. While the Cleveland *Leader* announced that the rescuers of Oberlin were returning home in triumph, a hundred guns were fired on the public square.

44 Many antislavery students and some teachers had migrated to Oberlin from Lane Seminary in Cincinnati. Arthur Tappan and other abolitionists had made gifts; the college admitted colored students; and it scattered antislavery lecturers through the region. Henry Howe, *Hist. Collections of Ohio*, II, 126.
45 Cleveland *Leader*, May 25–28, 1859.

Manifestly, this episode was certain to excite Southern indignation. The national government, with law, justice, and the facts on its side, said slaveholders, had been mocked by Ohio's higher-law fanatics. Nobody denied that John was a fugitive slave, that the Kentuckian legally owned him, or that the Federal statute of 1850 applied. But, since the spring of 1857, Ohio had a law which made it an indictable misdemeanor to arrest, imprison, or forcibly carry away any free person of color. The spirit in which the Western Reserve would interpret this law was suggested by Judge Carpenter of the Lorain County court: "The constitution of Ohio inhibits slavery and regards all persons as free and equal except criminals." Various Ohio newspapers termed the Federal law wicked, abominable, and anti-Christian; and the *Leader*, threatening with the halter all "men-thieves who dare to pollute our soil," remarked that it would save trouble if they would bring along some Kentucky hemp in addition to their manacles.[46]

Throughout part of the North, the Fugitive Slave Act was now largely unenforceable, for State after State had passed laws making recovery difficult or impossible. The obstructive areas with "personal liberty" statutes eventually included all New England, Pennsylvania, and the four Mid-Western States of Ohio, Indiana, Michigan, and Wisconsin. When the first conflicts occurred between the Federal and State authorities, Northern sentiment proved defiant. In Wisconsin, the State Supreme Court declared the Fugitive Slave Act unconstitutional and discharged an editor named Sherman M. Booth for helping to rescue a runaway black. The Federal Supreme Court then took jurisdiction, and Taney pronounced its unanimous judgment in one of the most powerful of all his opinions. The central issue did not concern slavery or the enforcement of a particular statute on fugitives, but the supremacy of the national government within its own sphere. Taney pointed out that unless Federal jurisdiction were sustained in Federal areas, the general government could not meet the grand and indispensable purposes for which it had been established; and impartial journals commended his stand.

Yet extreme Republican sheets assailed it as an encroachment on the reserved rights of the States, even Bryant's *Evening Post* taking this view; and the Wisconsin legislature responded with a *brutum fulmen*. On March 17, 1859, only ten days after Taney spoke, it accused the Supreme Court of an arbitrary act of power, and declared that the several States, being sovereign and independent,

46 Cleveland *Leader*, July 7, 1859, *et seq.*; W. C. Cochran, *Colls. Western Reserve Hist. Soc.*, 1920, pp. 118–157, 197–207; J. R. Shipheard, *History of the Oberlin-Wellington Rescue*, *passim*. The press of northern Ohio reviled the prosecution in the harshest terms. It termed the presiding judge a Jeffreys, the jury a set of broken-down party hacks, and the Federal attorney a man of infamous character. See the *Ohio State Journal*, Cleveland *Leader*, and *Portage County Democrat* for April–July, 1859.

had the right to judge of infractions of the Constitution. It was a State's duty, said the legislature, to offer a positive defiance to all unauthorized acts done under color of constitutional interpretation. This was the very doctrine of 1798. Nor did the quarrel of State and nation stop with mere words. The Federal authorities once more arrested Booth; the editor once more asked the State courts for a writ of *habeas corpus;* and they once more liberated him. Thus, in fighting the Fugitive Slave Law, the Republicans went to the verge of nullification, even while their leaders were denouncing the Southerners as the arch-nullifiers of the country.[47]

The fanatic never sees his own inconsistencies. Though antislavery journals continually arraigned Southerners for their intolerance, no more dishonorable example of political lynching could be found than the removal of Judge Edward G. Loring in Massachusetts in 1858. An upright, capable magistrate, he was forced from the Suffolk County bench by the legislature because he had sat as Federal Commissioner in the Burns rendition case of 1854; "in defiance of the moral sentiment of Massachusetts," ran the address. In fine, he was removed because, in the face of angry public antagonism, he had faithfully done his duty as a Federal officer. Enlightened editors of Massachusetts, without regard to party, condemned the action as arbitrary and vindictive. The Boston *Traveller* and the *Journal*, for example, termed it disgraceful. In other parts of the North comment was scathing, the *National Intelligencer* remarking that the Bay State should have given Loring not a stigma but a statue. A later generation of New England historians was to admit that even South Carolina, which always honored the dissident J. L. Petigru, had placed no such stain upon her escutcheon.[48]

The press throughout Buchanan's administration was full of stories of Northern defiance of the law for recovering fugitive property. In Indianapolis, a slave belonging to a Kentuckian became the center of spirited legal clashes between a State judge and Federal commissioner, incidental to which the owner was arrested on the familiar kidnapping charge. At New London, Connecticut, a fleeing Negro was seized to be returned South; a police magistrate at the head of a mob asked the man if he wished to reenter slavery, and bade him go on his way. At Ottawa, Illinois, in the fall of 1859, a slave who had fled from Missouri was brought before Judge John D. Caton, on a writ of *habeas corpus.* Caton, pleading with a hostile crowd not to violate the law, remanded him to the custody of the Federal deputy marshal of the southern district of Illinois. He might as well have spoken to the Mississippi in flood-time; the mob seized

---

47 Arthur C. Cole, *The Irrepressible Conflict*, 274; Warren, *Supreme Court* (1926 ed.), I, 336; Carl Schurz, *Reminiscences*, II, 105 ff.; *National Intelligencer*, April 2, 1859; N. Y. *Weekly Tribune*, June 4, 1859.
48 See press quotations in *National Intelligencer*, March 23, 1858.

the fugitive and carried him to safety. Later a Federal marshal appeared in Ottawa, arrested the ringleaders, and lodged them in jail in Chicago, where they were tried, found guilty, and sentenced; but this did not restore the slave. That same fall, William Dennison, a Miami University graduate, made a successful run for governor of Ohio. He declared that if elected he would permit no slave to be returned South, "and if I cannot prevent it in any other way, as commander-in-chief of the military of the State I will employ the bayonet—so help me God!" [49]

These were galling injuries which the South suffered in Brown's triumphant slave-stealing foray, in the preparations for scattering Helper's attack upon slavery broadcast, and in the occasional breakdown of the Fugitive Slave Law. All the while, the radical Northern press augmented its fire upon the special Southern institution. Scores of journals seldom mentioned slavery without opprobrious epithets, or slaveholders without a sneer. When Henry Wilson was reelected early in 1859, Edmund Quincy rejoiced, not because he was a good Senator but because "it gives vexation and rage to the enemy." Enemy! Some Southern Congressmen, as Charles Francis Adams shortly observed, were spoiling for a fight; but so were Northerners like Wendell Phillips, who said he would thank God if the South would defy Massachusetts to the sword and the musket. Greeley, visiting Kansas early in 1859, denounced the "slave power" with stinging epithets. Carl Schurz, delivering an oration in Faneuil Hall, assailed the slaveholding system for despotic tendencies and termed the Fugitive Slave Law an abomination. Southerners noted that few Northern journals ever spoke of

49 *National Intelligencer*, December 8, 1857; N. Y. *Weekly Tribune*, October 9, 1858; Washington *Constitution*, October 21, 1859. In April, 1859, the arrest of a colored man in Pennsylvania as the property of a Virginian precipitated the movement to carry a personal liberty bill through the legislature, then in session. It should in all fairness to the North be added that newspaper accounts gave an exaggerated impression of the number of rescues. They reported all escapes; they seldom reported recaptures. Douglas said in 1860 that nine-tenths of the Southern complaints were unfounded. "As far as Illinois is concerned, I am prepared to say that in nineteen cases out of twenty where a fugitive slave enters Illinois, he is arrested and returned without any judicial process whatever. Those portions of the State which border on the Kentucky and Missouri lines are in harmony with their neighbors on the other side, and a fugitive slave is returned as regularly as a stolen horse." He added that in the Northwest it was seldom that a rescue was not followed by penalties of the law. "And then civil suits are brought to pay for the slave, and not only the damage, but smart-money granted." *Cong. Globe*, December 11, 1860. The exaggerated impression was eagerly accepted, however, in the Lower South.

A Kentuckian who wrote an able pamphlet on the subject ("South Carolina, Disunion, and a Mississippi Valley Confederacy") pointed out that the Lower South lost very few slaves; he doubted if South Carolina had lost ten in as many years. It was the border States which suffered, and their sufferings had been greatly overstated. "A slight application of the *lex talionis* would soon compel Ohio to repeal her obnoxious legislation. She is the only one of our three near neighbors who has resorted to such statutes. Indiana and Illinois have habitually performed their duty to us in this particular. A large majority of our recaptured fugitives have been taken by their owners or by the citizens of those States, without the aid of any officers of the law." See Appendix V of this work.

the beneficent side of slavery; but when early this year Pierce Butler held his sale of more than four hundred slaves at the Savannah race course, the detailed description penned by a correspondent of the New York *Tribune* was quoted far and wide.[50]

It is not strange that the South now believed the North incapable of a fair attitude toward an institution which Southerners had inherited, of justice to Southern fears, or of helpfulness. A passenger on a Potomac steamer in 1859 heard a Virginian address a newsboy who had New York *Tribunes* for sale. "Don't you know better than to sell that paper here? Take it and put it in the stove. If you don't I'll cut the heart out of you!" It is not strange that moderate men in both sections began to feel genuine despair. Washington Hunt wrote from northern New York to his friend William C. Rives: [51]

It becomes a very important practical question, which cannot be long postponed, by what means the honest and conservative men of the North and South can be brought together so as to unite their strength in the approaching Presidential election. Many of the leading politicians in both sections are evidently disposed to prolong the strife and inflame the people, by adhering to extreme issues on the slavery question. . . . There must be an end of this unnatural and hateful warfare between the North and the South.

[VI]

If the South found solid ground for suspicion and resentment, so did the North. The Southern demand for territorial expansion in the Caribbean seemed made for the strengthening of an eventual Southern Confederacy; the crusade for reopening the slave trade and importing hordes of barbarous Negroes seemed made for capturing western Territories with an expanding slave population; the demand for a Congressional slave code seemed made to fortify territorial slavery against any adverse majority. If the North was nullifying the Fugitive Slave Act, the South was nullifying the law against the foreign slave trade. If the North seemed bent on expanding freesoil institutions all over the West, the South seemed bent on expanding slavery throughout Gulf and Caribbean. If the North took a one-sided view of slavery, so did the South; and while Virginia officers arrested men on the charge of circulating Helper's book, a Kentucky mob sacked the *Free South* office in Newport on the Ohio.

"Is it not already clear," demanded the New York *Tribune*, "that the 'irrepressible conflict' affirmed by Mr. Seward is . . . a sober and present reality?

50 Quincy Papers, January 17, 1859; Schurz, *Works*, I, 48–72; London *Times*, April 13, 1859. The account of the Butler sale (*Tribune*, March 9, 1859) was a masterly report, whose accuracy was never impugned. All such sales were blots on American civilization—but slavery had less repugnant aspects.
51 May 19, 1859; Rives Papers.

Is it not plain that we are already in effect two nations, held together by the ties of tradition and interest, but at heart and in life as hostile as the Romans and Carthaginians of old?" [52]

While the agitation for reopening the African slave trade seemed growing, Northern sentiment was aghast at the thought that the traffic might already reach significant proportions. In this spring of 1859, the Southern Commercial Convention, meeting at Vicksburg, significantly reversed its stand on the subject. It voted three to one for the repeal of all laws prohibiting the foreign slave trade, State or Federal, and some members were hot for a declaration that the Federal prohibitions ought to be flouted as unconstitutional.[53] The convention had no sooner adjourned than an African Labor Supply Association, with the tireless De Bow as president, was organized to conduct a crusade for repeal.[54] Additional journals, such as the Richmond *Whig*, were demanding a renewal of the trade. Yancey and De Bow, in a widely publicized correspondence, called for the removal of the Act of 1820 from the statute books; for the government, declared Yancey, should have no concern with slavery except to protect it.[55]

Although part of this might be bravado, a deeper significance had to be attached to speeches of the most eminent Southern leaders. Alexander H. Stephens, retiring from Congress and, as he thought, from all public life, was tendered an impressive dinner at Augusta this summer. In his carefully prepared speech he asserted that the revival of the slave trade might be considered a necessity if the institutions of the South were to expand. States could not be made without people, and slave States could not be made without Negroes; unless the South had more Africans, it could not colonize more territory and might as well give up its race with the North. In the same month (July, 1859) Jefferson Davis made a defiant address to the Democratic State Convention at Jackson, Mississippi. He pronounced the law of 1820 insulting to the South, and added that he deemed it unconstitutional. It would be best, he thought, to leave the importation of Africans to the decision of the various States; he would oppose it for Mississippi, but other States might do as they pleased. What had been the result of the Federal law? "It has magnified the horrors of the middle passage; it has led to an alliance with Great Britain, by which we are bound to keep a naval squadron on the deadly coast of Africa . . . under the false plea

52 N. Y. *Weekly Tribune*, May 7, 1859.
53 Moderate Southerners complained that these conventions had ceased to be commercial and had become political. The Vicksburg gathering was convoked by a committee of radicals including De Bow, J. J. McRae, and Yancey, and was sharply attacked by such conservative journals as the New Orleans *Picayune* and Savannah *Republican*. See quotations in *National Intelligencer*, April 9, 1859, H. Wender, *Southern Commercial Conventions*.
54 Vicksburg *True Southron*, May 14, 1859.
55 Correspondence, N. Y. *Weekly Tribune*, August 13, 1859.

for humanity; it has destroyed a lucrative trade for ivory, oil, and gold dust . . . and transferred it to our commercial rivals, the British." [56]

To be sure, the Administration maintained its strong opposition to the slave trade, and, under constant British proddings, even increased its measures of enforcement. During the fall of 1859 it strengthened the squadron off the African coast to a total of one hundred and sixteen guns, borne by four sloops and four steamers. The latter, being of light draught, could penetrate shallow coastal reaches and were therefore specially useful in pursuit. Simultaneously, the African base was removed from Puerto Praya to São Paulo de Loando, much nearer the main seat of the slave traffic. Four armed cruisers were on station in the vicinity of Cuba to pick up slavers which escaped through the African cordon. But the Administration was so feeble in most respects, so sensitive to Southern opinion, and so frigid in its attitude toward British requests for cooperation, that Northerners placed little reliance upon its continued vigilance. Moreover, if such a man as Jefferson Davis entered the White House in 1861, the trade might well flourish.

And how great were the clandestine importations already? Some thought them large. The New Orleans *Delta*, an advocate of the trade, had announced early in 1858 that a depot had been established on Pearl River in Mississippi, where cargoes of Africans were landed and sold. The slavers, it added, generally used the French flag. The Richmond, Texas, *Reporter* in the spring of 1859 carried an advertisement, signed only by initials, of four hundred likely Africans, lately landed on the Texas coast, and to be sold on reasonable terms. That summer, a correspondent of the New York *Herald* declared that the running of African cargoes into secluded inlets and bays was reaching wide proportions, and the New York correspondent of the London *Daily News,* without corroborative data, made the same assertion. The *Herald* quoted Senator Douglas as saying that within a year and a half seventy vessels, with more than fifteen thousand slaves, had reached the Florida coast, and as predicting that a dozen more would discharge Africans between Pensacola and Key West during the summer. This latter prediction he had made on the authority of an interested Southern Senator. [57]

Such statements were supported by John C. Underwood, a large Virginia landowne who had lately removed to New York. A graduate of Hamilton College and an attorney and scientific farmer, Underwood had many Southern connections. Returning in early summer from an extended Southern tour, he declared that the slave trade was so brisk that the arrival of cargoes of blacks in unguarded Southern waters had become a frequent event. Why, then, was so

56 Rowland, IV, 61–88.
57 N. Y. *Herald*, September 3, 1859.

little known of the traffic? Because, Underwood explained, many Southern journals were attached to the trading interest; editors of others feared the brutal men engaged; and public sentiment favored the crime wherever planters were hungry for cheap labor. Many people in the Gulf States were denouncing the law as a protective tariff which enabled the slave-breeders of Virginia and the borderland to grow rich by charging $1,000–$1,500 for slaves who might be brought from the Congo for $100–$300. Then, too, sectional loyalty and the omnipresent hostility to the North made many observers keep still.[58]

Actually, these reports of clandestine shipments seem to have been decidedly exaggerated. No clear evidence exists that Douglas made the statements attributed to him, and if he did, he was deceived. The Pensacola *Tribune* called the *Herald* report a Munchausen absurdity. The Federal marshals for both the northern and southern districts of Florida, vigilant men with watchful deputies throughout the State, believed that not a single African had been landed there.[59] The New York *Journal of Commerce*, taking pains to inquire into the reports, published letters from three independent and informed sources in Florida, each declaring the stories of importations false. From other Southern intelligence, the *Journal* found good reason to conclude that the only ship which had landed negroes in the country during the past thirty years was the *Wanderer*, and that the Africans whom Douglas had seen were from this vessel.[60] President Buchanan had detective work done by a special agent in Florida, who found no basis for the tales of importations. Yancey, writing just after the opening of the Civil War, stated his belief that not more than five hundred Africans had been brought into the United States since 1807, and that these had been imported during 1859–61 rather as a political than a commercial transaction.[61]

Majority opinion in the South as a whole, moreover, was unquestionably against any revival of the trade. W. L. Yancey admitted as much. Even in South Carolina, we have the testimony of Judge Magrath that only a small minority were agitating for a revival, that the overwhelming majority of citizens were opposed, and that it was the noisy violence of the advocates that made the State seem greatly divided. Governor A. B. Moore of Alabama, running for re-election, condemned the movement both on grounds of public policy and as a cause of division among the Southern people. So did Robert Toombs, speaking at

58 Underwood in N. Y. *Weekly Tribune*, July 23, 1858.
59 Washington *Constitution*, September 20, 1859.
60 Quoted in *Idem*, August 30, 1859.
61 August 11, 1861, to A. Alison; Yancey Papers, Ala. State Lib. On the other hand, John S. Kendall, in his article on "New Orleans' 'Peculiar Institution'" in *La. Hist. Quart.*, XXIII, 864–866, declares that contraband slave traffic with Cuba, and less extensively, with Africa, was "heavy," slave ships slipping into quiet bayous on the Gulf coast to discharge their cargoes. And William H. Russell in *My Diary North and South*, I, 270–272, describes newly imported Negroes whom he saw in Alabama.

Augusta soon after the dinner to Stephens; and he added that prohibition was in harmony with the judgment and sentiment of the country. When Buchanan paid a visit to Raleigh, Secretary Jacob Thompson took occasion to condemn the scheme as the work of a class of reckless men, which would prove an evil for the South "in the Union or out of it." Houston, Wise, and all the border State leaders were resolutely antagonistic. Meanwhile, a finer voice than that of any politician had fallen upon the South, grave, melodious, and inspiring, when Justice Campbell of the Supreme Court, in charges to Federal grand juries in Louisiana and Alabama, reminded citizens that the suppression of the slave trade had enlisted the most enlightened, humane, and just men of all the nations of Christendom. He told them that in every civilized state the laws condemned this foul traffic, and that the people of the nation would take no backward step from a policy so right and high.[62]

Nevertheless, a large body of Southerners agreed with De Bow, Keitt, Hammond, and A. G. Brown that determined effort could in time effect a repeal of the Federal prohibition. In repeated speeches these men called upon the small farmers who wanted Negroes to join hands with the large planters who desired to widen the base of slavery; arguing that with a rich expanding supply of slaves they could consolidate their hold upon the border States, and win new Caribbean realms for their cherished institution.

Beyond doubt, a considerable number of extremists went further. Their aims could be summed up in a sentence: They meant to have explicit Congressional sanction for obtaining slaves from Africa and placing them in all the Territories. What A. G. Brown said bluntly, the adroit A. H. Stephens suggested by indirection. Antislavery newspapers this summer sounded the alarm. No careful scrutinizer of the times, they warned, could doubt that Democratic success in 1860 would be followed by a double *coup de main;* the legalization of the foreign slave trade, and the enactment of a territorial slave code. These measures might not be expressly incorporated in the Charleston platform, for the Lower South still preferred to finesse its cards until it could make sure of winning the rubber —but they were being planned by determined leaders.[63]

Frenetic as this program seemed, Senator A. G. Brown informed Douglas that in the Charleston convention the South would insist upon precisely these demands. Our section, he wrote on September 10, will call for "a platform explicitly declaring that slave property is entitled, in the Territories and on the

<hr>

62 Magrath to Hammond, July 21, 1859, Hammond Papers, LC; Moore's letter in N. O. *Picayune,* July 2, 1859; Toombs's speech, Washington *Constitution,* September 22, 1859; Campbell's charges of July 30, 1858, and April 12, 1859, in *National Intelligencer,* January 11, August 25, 1859. Though Wise was against the slave trade, he was for the territorial slave code; *Harper's Magazine,* 1859, p. 555.
63 N. Y. *Weekly Tribune,* July 23, 1859.

high seas, to the same protection that is given to any other and every other species of property. Failing to get it, she will retire from the convention. The South will demand of the Congress that it afford protection to her people in their lives, liberty, and property. If Congress refuses . . . we will as our right resist the Government and throw off its authority." [64] Nor was this the bluster of an isolated Sir Lucius O'Trigger. Shrewd observers knew that behind at least half of Brown's program, and in many instances all of it, stood Rhett, Miles, and Pickens of South Carolina, Jefferson Davis, John J. McRae, and J. J. Pettus of Mississippi, Mason, Pryor, and Muscoe R. H. Garnett of Virginia, Howell Cobb and Senator Iverson of Georgia, C. C. Clay and Yancey of Alabama, and Slidell of Louisiana. They knew that these men were supported by such influential journals as the Charleston *Mercury* and *Standard*, New Orleans *Delta*, Mobile *Tribune*, Montgomery *Advertiser*, and Jackson *Mississippian*. Some of these sheets were steadily proclaiming their readiness to break up the Union if Congress refused to enact a territorial slave code.

We have seen that Yancey and Rhett had conferred in detail early in 1858. Now, in midsummer of 1859, after an exchange of letters, they carried their campaign into a more active phase. In an Independence Day speech at Grahamville, South Carolina, his first public appearance in half a dozen years, Rhett urged the South to make the coming Presidential campaign a final struggle against Northern tyrannies, demanding its full rights in the Territories or an end of the Union. Yancey spoke at Columbia and other towns, laying down a defiant program. Southern men should go to the Charleston convention, he said, prepared to quit it and organize a new party unless full protection were promised slavery in the Territories; and if a Republican were elected, the South should withdraw before he could be inaugurated. While Rhett promulgated these ideas in his Charleston *Mercury*, Yancey turned homeward to subsidize the Montgomery *Advertiser* and begin his struggle for control of the Democratic Party in Alabama.

This double-barreled ultimatum of Southern radicals, the slave trade and slave code, seemed so preposterous that many sober observers North and South quickly concluded that it must cloak an ulterior motive. Behind it, they said, lurked a desire for disunion or at least a readiness to accept it. Jefferson Davis seemed extreme enough when, in his before-mentioned address to the Democratic Convention of Mississippi on July 6, 1859, he said that if the existing laws did not protect slavery in the Territories the South must insist on special legislation; argued for the acquisition of Cuba; and called for the dissolution of the Union if any President were elected on Seward's "irrepressible conflict" plat-

64 Milton, *Eve of Conflict*, 371.

form. Altogether, his chip-on-shoulder speech was full of ultimatums to the North. Still more reckless were the Rhett-Yancey-Ruffin group, steadily speaking and laboring for secession. The time has come, Yancey said at Charlotte, North Carolina, this summer, to strike for independence. "We have eight millions of people educated to the use of arms, trained to self-reliance, with a thorough knowledge of governmental principles, with as much real spirit and manhood as was ever possessed by any people. We have unity of production, unity of institutions, and a compact country. We have the great product without which the world cannot do. We are rich in all the elements of prosperity." If three millions had won freedom from Britain, demanded Yancey, could not eight millions win freedom from the North? [65]

The Buchanan Administration, anxious now to pursue a middle-of-the-road course, temporarily opposed both demands of the Southern radicals. It had a new voice in the Washington *Constitution*, successor to the *Union*. Under pressure from the Directory, George W. Bowman, a Pennsylvania journalist who had become superintendent of printing, had bought the paper in March, 1859, changed its name, employed William M. Browne, an English-born writer for the New York *Journal of Commerce*, as leader-writer, and invigorated its editorial policy. The *Constitution* became a steam calliope with five keys: economy, administrative reform, protection of the people against special privilege, expansion, and suppression of the "dead" slavery question. "Constitution" Browne plied a lively pen and received assiduous help from the heads of the Directory, Black, Cobb, and Thompson. The paper scored the slave-trade movement. As for a territorial code, it argued that new legislation was unnecessary, for the Federal courts would apply the same laws to slave property as to other possessions; that it was unwise to draw any distinction between different sorts of property; and that if one demand for special laws were carried through, others would arise. Some grumbler would allege that the territorial laws against murder were too lenient to afford protection; somebody else would call the laws against arson weak. Congress would soon be intervening along a broad ambit. The proper course was to look to the judiciary for aid—and if necessary, the courts could ask for Federal troops.[66] A sagacious stand; but would Buchanan maintain it, once Howell Cobb and Jacob Thompson yielded to the Southern thrust?

No Northerner was more emphatic in pointing to the spectre of disunion which lurked behind the "slave-trade, slave-code" demands than were certain Southern watchers on the Union battlements. Yancey's neighbor, Benjamin

65 Yancey's Columbia speech, Charleston *Mercury*, July 14, 1859; Du Bose, *Yancey*, 439–441; Yancey to Samuel Reid, July 3, 1861, on the *Advertiser* subsidy, Yancey Papers, Ala. State Lib. South Carolina moderates attacked the program, Senator Chesnut declaring a slave code unnecessary. Laura White, *Rhett*, 155–157.
66 Washington *Constitution*, August 20, 1859 and ff.

Fitzpatrick, pronounced the idea of "positive protection" a baneful abstraction.[67] In Yancey's home city, the Montgomery *Confederation* spoke of a dissembled purpose. "Is there any sane man living in this broad land who believes that the laws prohibiting the African slave trade can be repealed? That Congress will intervene and discriminate in favor of slavery and slave property in the Territories, and pass a system of laws specially designed for its defense and protection? No man would be so wanting in candor as to pretend that he had any such idea. Then, are we to stake the existence of the Union upon the issue of these two propositions, that we admit at the outset are foregone propositions?" [68] Sam Houston wrote the Galveston *Union* this summer that the very existence of the country was threatened by the three dogmas of Nullification, Secession, and Disunion, "which are in vogue with many men who claim to be friends of the South, but are in reality demagogues, who live on agitation, hoping to be elevated by the confusion of the times." The men who urged revival of the slave trade were trying to fasten on the land a horrible piece of barbarism. "In my opinion, all these devices are intended to bring about disunion." [69] Senator Hammond, who blew alternately very hot and very cold, penned a denunciation of the South for countenancing the *Echo* verdict and the *Wanderer* importations. His section had put herself in the same lawbreaking category with the North.[70]

Then she has demanded, what may in a very abstract sense be her right, but what practically is as absurd to ask for as a railroad to the moon (and everybody knows it), a Congressional slave code for the Territories. This is *sheer faction.* Another suicidal stab, and all in six or eight months. She seems to have surrendered—*prostituted* herself all at once to every sort of adventurer—Cuban filibusters, slave trade felons, and political aspirants of the basest and *silliest* order. Who would have thought it? *I am ashamed of her.* I have constantly blushed for her during the late session. Such folly—such madness—I never expected from the South. It makes things look very blue. It is insuring Seward's election on the Rochester platform.

Nevertheless, the radicals held their ground. In the autumn of 1859 an avowed disunionist, John J. Pettus, was chosen governor of Mississippi. Another, the wealthy, cultivated, and implacably secessionist William Henry Gist, had the previous year been made governor of South Carolina. A third, Andrew B. Moore, who had sat for two years in the governor's chair in Alabama, was now chosen for his second term. Scattered all over the South, men who openly or covertly wished to see a great slaveholding republic come into existence looked toward 1860 as their year of opportunity. As they thought of the boiling

67 August 30, 1859; C. C. Clay Papers.
68 Quoted in Washington *Constitution*, August 3, 1859.
69 Quoted in Warsaw, Illinois, *City Bulletin*, July 25, 1859.
70 To W. G. Simms, April 22, 1859; Hammond Papers, LC.

excitement of the Presidential campaign, the prospect that a Republican might be chosen to the White House, and the certainty that in that event many would say "Now or never," their spirits rose.

The country was coming back to prosperity. It was also moving inexorably toward disruption. Yet two final hopes remained. One was that the Democratic Party, the only great organized bond of union not yet parted, would somehow place a strong leader, respected by all sections, in the Presidential chair. The other was that a new Union party, composed of the Whigs, the remaining Know-Nothings, and moderate Democrats and Republicans, might organize to elect such a man as Crittenden of Kentucky or Bates of Missouri. The time has come to examine a party situation as interesting as any in the history of the nation, and to see how a bright possibility of strengthening the Union was raised to view just before an unpredictable catastrophe took all conservative men by surprise.

2

The Last Hope of Adjustment

IF THE Democrats were to win again in 1860, they must quietly ignore the demand for territorial protection of slavery which would hurry the party to a yawning grave. Voters of every Northern State would flock to the Republican guidons if the slaveholding radicals dictated such a requirement. But who would lead the party along a safe path that would hold Northern votes without repelling those of the South? It would not be Buchanan. In September, 1859, he wrote a letter avowing his final determination not to be a candidate for reelection. His high office beckoned to a number of ambitious politicians. While people followed with intent gaze the new gold rush to the Pike's Peak region, while they watched Napoleon III gather his Italian garlands, while they saw Palmerston overthrow the Derby ministry, while they read George Eliot's *Adam Bede*, and while industry and employment revived, newspapers were busy "hoisting the flag" of various aspirants, and politicians were forming committees and raising funds. It was the Democratic organization which provided most of the drama.

Observers were struck by the fact that Southern leaders were far hotter than Northerners in pursuit of the Democratic nomination. Since Polk, the party had named no man from below the Potomac, but now word had traversed the slave States that it was their turn. Though Howell Cobb was widely regarded as a failure in the Treasury, his Georgia followers were planning to send to Charleston a delegation that would give him devoted support. If most politicians thought Jefferson Davis too much a martinet, too moody and metaphysical to be a good candidate, he too had his loyal band. A. H. Stephens was publicly issuing disclaimers but he was privately receptive.[1] Yancey and Houston, both impossible, had their eyes on the prize. The temperamental James L. Hammond, who under happier circumstances would have made a good Vice-President, believed he had a chance for the White House. "If I had the stomach and nerves and muscle of Cobb or Toombs I would get it easy enough," he wrote. "By common consent, I am universally regarded as *dignus imperate*."[2] In brief, as

1 Von Abele, *Stephens*, 179, 180.
2 To M. C. M. Hammond, April 10, 1859; Hammond Papers, LC.

Hammond put it, there were at least twenty men in the South looking for the nomination, and forgetting their public duties in their anxiety to get it.[3]

Some of them were put out of the running this summer by their enemies or their own indiscretions. Henry A. Wise, brilliant and erratic, permitted the New York *Herald* to publish a letter to a friend which made his opponents rub their hands with glee.

He indulged in a baseless fling against the President as secretly a candidate, using the patronage to promote his fortunes. He assailed Tammany, and proposed steps to force a factional split in the New York delegation. He took up the "positive protection" cry. Above all, he proclaimed a remorseless vendetta against Douglas, whose platform he described as a short cut to all the ends of Black Republicanism. The South would not tolerate the Little Giant's ideas, declared the Virginia governor. "If he runs as an independent candidate, and Seward runs, and I am nominated at Charleston, I can beat them both." If Douglas got the regular nomination and the South named an independent candidate, the election would go to the House. "Where, then, would Mr. Douglas be? The lowest candidate on the list. If I have the popular strength you suppose, it will itself fix the nomination. Get that and I am confident of success." [4]

At one stroke Wise had heightened the active enmity of the Administration, the Tammany men, and the Douglas Democrats, while the rank egotism of his epistle offended everybody. "He has written one letter too much," remarked the St. Louis *News.* "Smothered by his own gas," was the verdict of the Pittsburgh *Post.*

Slidell, meanwhile, had been put out of the contest in different fashion. This unscrupulous intriguer, always close to the ear of Buchanan, had made countless enemies by his crafty ways and malignant temper. While all Douglas men hated him for his implacable warfare on their chieftain, the Soulé faction in his own State lusted for his political life. The spring of 1859 gave them their chance. Slidell rested under the stigma of the Houmas Grant scandal, and Northern journals never ceased to attack him for the juggle by which he had gotten this Louisiana grab through Congress to his alleged personal profit, under the dark cover of a bill relating to Missouri lands. He met the Yankee assaults stoically. But when in April the New Orleans *Delta* published a mass of letters relating to the subject, and other Southern newspapers took them up, he emitted a groan of agony. At the same time, Soulé organized a thrust against his dictatorship. A great mass meeting in New Orleans, with eighty-seven prominent organizers, heard Soulé declare that the time had come for revolt against Slidell's "unprincipled gang of political speculators and blacklegs"; that his contemptible oli-

3 To W. G. Simms, March 13, 1859; Hammond Papers, LC.
4 N. Y. *Herald*, August 4, Washington *Constitution*, August 6, 1859.

garchy, "incrustated on all sorts of Federal and State spoils," must no longer be allowed to make legislatures and party conventions open marts for the sale of votes; and that men who smuggled through laws for their own pecuniary interests must be forced out of public life.[5] The revolt was carried into the State convention at Baton Rouge near the end of May. Slidell, staggered in his own State, was more discredited than ever in the nation at large.

Three Democratic leaders stood well in advance of all others as possible nominees at Charleston. The least able, R. M. T. Hunter, was in some ways the most available, for, if he was a mediocrity, he was a hard-working, likeable man of fairly moderate views who had offended few outside of Virginia. Though when Southern institutions were under fire he would fly to their defense as readily as the proud Davis or the blustering A. G. Brown, his nature was essentially cautious and conciliatory. In guiding the tariff of 1857 through the Senate, he had made many Northern friends. Moreover, he had long experience, for he had been in Congressional life since the late eighteen-thirties. Vice-President Breckinridge, who modestly insisted that he was not a candidate but was obviously as willing as Barkis, possessed still wider popularity. An urbane, polished gentleman, with plenty of common sense backed by moderation and tact, he had been fittingly chosen, though a Democrat, to deliver the funeral oration over Clay, and had easily carried Clay's Ashland district for Congress. In presiding over the Senate he had shown judicial poise. When, at the beginning of 1859, the Senate had moved to its new chamber, he injected into the farewell address a stirring appeal for the Union.[6] Greatest of all, looming head and shoulders above other aspirants in intellectual power, energy, fighting edge, was Douglas, the storm center of the Party. The Democratic South had many sons; the Democratic North had an Achilles with no helping Patroclus and no rival.

Since his deposition from the Territorial Committee, Douglas was more than ever a fighting leader. Returning to Chicago from a late spring visit to inspect some family properties in Mississippi, he determined to utter a plain warning to the Southern fire-eaters. As he journeyed on to Washington, he shaped a letter which, dated June 22 and addressed to the editor of a Dubuque newspaper, created a national sensation. He announced that he would be a candidate for nomination on a platform embodying the principles of the Kansas-Nebraska Act and the Cincinnati Convention, but would repudiate the party if it adopted extreme dogmas. If the Charleston gathering should reject time-honored Democratic principles and substitute "such new issues as the revival of the African slave trade, or a Congressional slave code for the Territories, or the doctrine that the Constitution of the United States either establishes or prohibits slavery

5 See *National Intelligencer*, April 14, 1859, for details.
6 *Cong. Globe*, 35th Cong., 2d Sess., 202–204, January 4, 1859.

in the Territories beyond the power of the people legally to control it as other property, it is due to candor to say that in such an event I could not accept the nomination if tendered to me." Nor, obviously, could he support any candidate who did accept it.

This display of manly independence won the applause of most Northern Democrats and many Republicans. The New York *Times* praised it warmly, declaring that if Douglas had small chance of nomination it was because he was too strong a man; the Philadelphia *Press* said that, while doing no injustice to the South, the letter offered the party a prospect of victory in every free State.[7] Greeley's *Tribune* hailed the statement as a proclamation of independence from the tyranny and assumed infallibility of national conventions.[8] It was much more than this, however. It was an announcement that the Northern Democrats would flatly refuse to follow the lead of the Southern ultras in 1860. A few friends of Douglas believed that he had committed a tactical error. Pugh of Ohio, for example, one of his staunchest aides, then and later asserted that he had played into the hands of his enemies; that he had given the whole pack of anti-Douglas men an opportunity to make a rush upon Charleston with the intention of placing the denounced doctrines in the platform, and thus preventing his selection.[9] Actually, the pack needed no pretext; they had already gathered for their manhunt. Douglas had said what the party crisis demanded, vindicating with promptness the moral position of the millions of Democrats north of the Ohio—and many below that river, for his mail was filled with vigorous letters promising support even in the Deep South.[10]

In great part, the letter was an attempt to appeal over the heads of the Southern radicals to the sober-minded rank and file of the party in the slave area. Though the Charleston *Courier* called it an insult to the South, and the Administration organ deplored it as a blow to party unity, actually it was but a courteous statement of the only terms on which continued party unity was possible. Even in Alabama and Louisiana, in eastern Tennessee and northern Georgia, many of the rank and file were with Douglas.[11] Could they assert themselves against the Slidells, Rhetts, and Davises? As part of his propagandist campaign, the Little Giant issued his speech on popular sovereignty in the debate of February 23 as a pamphlet, with an appendix of statements by Davis, Brown, Quitman, and others praising the principle. It was circulated by hundreds of thousands—with such effect, indeed, that a rumor sprang up that A. G. Brown had prearranged the debate in order to give Douglas a triumph over his opponents.[12]

7 Both editorials in Phila. *Weekly Press*, July 2, 1859.
8 N. Y. *Weekly Tribune*, July 2, 1859.
9 *Cong. Globe*, 36th Cong., 1st Sess., 2246; May 22, 1860.
10 Milton, *Eve of Conflict*, 372; Douglas Papers, *passim*.
11 John W. Womack, Eutaw, Alabama, 1859, n.d., in McClernand Papers.
12 Milton, *Eve of Conflict*, 379.

The response of the Southern ultras and of the Directory associated with Buchanan was prompt. These men had put themselves in a position where they could not yield to Douglas without a fatal loss of prestige. The old ambiguity on popular sovereignty had become impossible; the party had to accept or reject the Freeport Doctrine; and Douglas's letter dramatized the fact that a vital issue of principle must be resolved before a candidate was chosen. Had the radicals been acting on a non-political plane they might have ignored abstractions, accepted the situation in the Territories where the Kansas settlers *had* proved their power to exclude slavery, and cloaked their defeat in a mere readoption of the platform of 1856. A wise and courageous President would have supported such a compromise with the Dred Scott decision; compromise alone could avert party disaster in 1860. Unfortunately, the Southern radicals were acting on a plane of practical politics. They had aroused popular fears and prejudices which they must satisfy or their political careers would be forfeit. In Mississippi, for example, Jefferson Davis and A. G. Brown were at bottom eager rivals, bidding against each other with defiances of the North.[13] As for the President, his virtues included neither sagacity nor bravery. His confidence in Cobb, Floyd, and Jacob Thompson was undiminished, and he constantly corresponded or talked with Slidell, who saw the only safety of his section in a Southern Rights leadership of the party.

Throughout the summer and early fall of 1859, the Administration's attacks on Douglas were as flagitious as in the previous year. Slidell spurred Buchanan on with charges that the Illinoisan was intolerably arrogant, a would-be party dictator.[14] Floyd, going to the Virginia springs for his health, consorted with the wealthier type of Southerner and reported to the President their faith that the Administration was completely right and that the squatter sovereigns of the prairies were utterly impossible. The Southern people are behind you, wrote Floyd. "You have only to dictate your policy and to excommunicate all who fail or refuse to sustain it, to organize the party, and assure harmonious action sufficient to carry whatever their united strength can accomplish."[15] The Washington *Constitution* was tirelessly abusive. Republishing every misrepresentation or criticism uttered by Northern marplots or Southern fanatics, it maintained its own stream of denunciation; and other pensioned newspapers throughout the country followed this lead. Still, month by month, the heads of officeholders friendly to Douglas or lukewarm in the Administration cause continued to roll.

The grand object now was to deprive Douglas of every possible Northern delegate at Charleston. In New England, where the party had little strength except as it was nourished by Federal offices and contracts, the Administration

13 S. P. McCutchen, "A. G. Brown," MS Dissertation, Univ. of Chicago.
14 John Slidell, July 3, etc., 1859; Buchanan Papers.
15 From Red Sweet Springs, September 5, 1859; Buchanan Papers.

ruled with an iron hand. Such lieutenants as Caleb Cushing, B. F. Hallett, and Isaac Toucey kept the party file leaders on the alert. Jobholding or jobhunting Democrats ran the newspapers, staffed the post offices, and manipulated State committees and conventions. In the Middle Atlantic States the Administration grip was weaker. Such willing agents as Daniel S. Dickinson and William Bigler could transmit orders to thousands of placemen, but the organization leaders were conscious of a groundswell of public opinion in opposition to Southern domination. Revolt against the Directory had progressed far in New York, where Dean Richmond of Buffalo, vice-president of the New York Central and chairman of the State committee, agreed with Henry J. Raymond that Douglas alone could carry the North. It had progressed far in Pennsylvania, where Forney's *Press* daily cheered on the struggle against the Buchanan regime. Freest of all from Washington controls was the Middle West. From Ohio, where Senator Pugh and Henry B. Payne upheld Douglas's hands, to Iowa, where Augustus Caesar Dodge and other moderate Democrats relied on him to recapture the State from the Republicans, the Administration was in low repute.

Yet everywhere the Directory exerted itself mightily. Even in Illinois, the bolters of the previous year were instigated to raise a clamorous opposition, and to call a convention to send anti-Douglas delegates to Charleston. Many conservative Democrats saw that this attempt to kill Douglas's chances by machine manipulation—by efforts to wheedle, bribe, and threaten, particularly effective in New England and the border region—was a costly luxury for the Southern wing of the party; that if he were implacably assailed for now holding opinions which he had entertained without change for at least ten years (and opinions well understood when a majority of Southern delegates voted for him at the Cincinnati convention), the effect on Democratic fortunes would be calamitous. But Slidell, Cobb, Floyd, and Thompson had imbued the President with their vindictive hostility. Defending his removals, Buchanan wrote a friend:

I cannot retain in an important position any man who preaches rebellion against the Supreme Court of the United States. A party founded on this principle is purely revolutionary. Let a territorial legislature confiscate the property of an American citizen;—such a law has been already declared unconstitutional by the Judiciary and must of course produce a collision between Federal and Territorial authority. Never before in this country has there been a general party founded on the principle of repudiating a judgment of the Supreme Court. The attempt to resist such a decision was made in individual States, as in the case of Olmstead in Pennsylvania; but was indignantly put down. Now Seward and the Black Republicans resist this decision on the ground that Congress has the right to prohibit slavery; and Douglas and his followers resist it on the ground that a Territorial Legislature possess this right.

If the power existed the latter would be the worst mode in which it could be exercised. In Congress it could be debated by Representatives from the whole country and might be successfully resisted. Not so before a territorial legislature on the frontiers. Besides, one legislature might prohibit and another might introduce slavery and so the people be kept in a state of constant excitement on this subject.[16]

A singularly prejudiced statement this, in its unfounded talk of rebellion and confiscation; a singularly confused statement in its suggestion that the way to get rid of "constant excitement" over slavery was to let slaves into all the Territories. And Buchanan added a singularly inept prophecy. "The issue in 1860," he wrote, "beyond all question will be between the Republicans who refuse to yield obedience to the decision, and the Democrats who sustain it and in doing so will sustain the cause of law, property and order. *On this line we shall win.*" He actually thought the North could be swept for the Dred Scott decision!

Buchanan, in fine, was with the radical proslavery men on every issue except revival of the slave trade. He was with them in opposing any bar against slavery in the Territories, any bar against expansion in Cuba and Mexico, any bar against new slave States. In a letter to Slidell on June 24, 1859, he even intimated his support of a Congressional slave code, if needed for "the rights of property consecrated by the Constitution of the United States."[17] He was against the principal Northern Democrat with all his power, sneering at him as a man who would not condescend to accept a nomination unless the party first erected just the platform he wanted. As the agitation for a slave code continued to overspread the South, making progress even in the border States partly as a "logical" deduction from the Dred Scott decision and partly as promising new territorial markets for slaves, the anti-Douglas front gained solidity.

[I]

The Little Giant, spending most of the summer in Washington, saw that organization of his forces was imperative. Before autumn, a group of friends led by A. D. Banks had opened headquarters for him in New York. A committee which included Moses Taylor, John Jacob Astor, Dean Richmond, August Belmont, and Walter Sherman, with other wealthy men, began raising an initial campaign fund. George Sanders besought Douglas to cultivate the good will of Senator Green of Missouri. James B. Steedman was active in Ohio, with Washington McLean and the Cincinnati *Enquirer* taking a friendly attitude; Lanphier and Sheahan were busy as ever in Illinois; and that staunch Unionist, John Forsyth, made the Mobile *Register* an efficient exponent of Douglasite doctrines. As the Douglas forces picked up delegates here and there in New England, and

16 To M. Johnson, September 19, 1859; Buchanan Papers, NYHS.
17 June 24, 1859; Buchanan Papers.

in New York despite the opposition of Dickinson took forty-five of the seventy delegates, they gathered confidence. The Illinoisan could count on most of the Middle West, and his hopes grew.[18]

To help rally his forces and give Democrats of the South a fair exposition of his doctrines, Douglas astonished the country by publishing in the September issue of *Harper's Magazine* a copyrighted twenty-page discussion of "Popular Sovereignty in the Territories: the Dividing Line between Federal and Local Authority." [19] It became the sensation of the hour. Written in a heavy, involved style quite unlike Douglas's lucid, hard-hitting speeches, and loaded with erudition, it was hard reading for most politicians; yet no other article of the decade was so widely discussed. It had been prepared with a thoroughness which would have done credit to Lincoln; Douglas had borrowed from the Library of Congress the works of Calhoun, the *Federalist*, five volumes of Bancroft, Elliott's *Debates*, Carey's *Slave Trade, Domestic and Foreign*, and other treatises. Ostensibly directed against both Republicans and positive-protection Democrats, it concentrated its fire on the latter. Widely summarized in newspapers and issued in pamphlet form, it attained national currency. "You have made the most of a bad cause," A. G. Brown wrote the author.[20]

Douglas began by describing the various schools of Democratic thought upon the issue of slavery in the Territories. He then launched into an argument, mainly upon historical grounds, for his own view that the people of a Territory were free to form and regulate their own institutions. He did not go into the vital questions of precisely *how* and *when* the people should act upon slavery, but implied that they had the power to do so from the moment that they became "a distinct political community." One passage, as Lincoln noted, indicated a rough guess that the number of inhabitants needed to deal with slavery lay between ten and twenty thousand. He did not restate the Freeport Doctrine, but strongly implied his faith in it. He did not say precisely what the functions of the courts touching slavery should be, but he plainly intimated that the popular will should be the court of last resort.[21] Altogether, the article politely renewed his defi-

18 Milton, *Eve of Conflict*, 384, 385.
19 William A. Seaver of New York had given a dinner party in the summer of 1859 where Douglas met Fletcher Harper, Park Benjamin, Paul Morphy, J. W. Forney, and others; the article followed. Douglas tried to keep the paper a secret, but word of its preparation leaked out. He took pride in it, and was pleased by its national circulation in the magazine. Douglas to Seaver, July 17, 1859; Douglas Papers, Ill. State Hist. Library.
20 Milton, *Eve of Conflict*, 389.
21 Kellogg of Illinois had introduced a bill at the previous session for what he called genuine popular sovereignty. It provided that the people of the Territories should elect their governors, secretaries, judges, marshals, and all other officers; and that Congress should put its legislative power in the Territories in abeyance in favor of popular rights. This recalled Chase's amendment to the Nebraska bill. The Chicago *Tribune* termed the bill "Republican Popular Sovereignty—the pure metal, with a clear and always recognizable ring!" June 28, 1859.

ance of the Administration and the South. In its historical portions, it traced the dividing line between local and central governments from colonial days down to the Dred Scott decision. At every stage since Jamestown, Douglas argued, the planters and shapers of the nation had insisted that the people should make their own local laws and mould their own institutions, subject only to the Constitution, first of the British Empire, and later of the United States. He quoted the admission of Taney himself in the Dred Scott decision: "No word can be found in the Constitution which gives Congress a greater power over slave property . . . than property of any other description"—and property in the Territories had always been controlled by local legislatures and sentiment.

Argument of this sort was open to forcible rebuttal, and Republican editors, led by Bryant, Greeley, and Bowles, had no difficulty in citing history to their own purpose—to show Congressional supremacy over the question.[22] Lincoln, too, summed up Douglas's inconsistency in an epigram: "Slavery may be legally excluded from a Territory in which it may legally remain." The main quarrel of the Senator, however, was with his Democratic colleagues. His article evoked sterner attacks than ever from such journals as the Jackson *Mississippian*, Richmond *Enquirer*, Charleston *Mercury*, and Memphis *Avalanche*, all declaring that the South could never accept him. And since the Administration could not afford to keep silent, its readiest writer, Jere Black, was chosen to fire an immediate salvo in reply.

The five-column article of the Attorney-General, published in the Washington *Constitution* on September 10, was simultaneously issued as a pamphlet, while many Administration newspapers reprinted it in full. Black's arguments were constitutional, not historical, and as such were familiar. His main thesis was simply that the Constitution regarded as sacred all the rights which a citizen might legally acquire in any State, and if a man gained property in a State and carried it into a Territory, he could not then be deprived of it. What was most notable in his legalistic presentation was its strong proslavery tone and its virulently anti-Douglas trappings. Black spoke of slavery precisely as Howell Cobb and Jacob Thompson spoke of it, as a positive good. "Here, then, is a species of property which is of transcendent importance to the material interests of the South—which the people of that region think it right and meritorious in the

22 For example, Douglas had written that in Jefferson's plan for the Northwest, the article prohibiting slavery after 1800 was rejected by the Continental Congress. True; but the States had voted 6 to 3, the delegates 16 to 7, in favor of it, and it failed of the required majority of seven States only because neither New Jersey nor Delaware had enough delegates present to cast a ballot. The Ordinance of 1787 did exclude slavery from the Northwest Territory, and the first Congress under the Constitution accepted the Ordinance. Republicans reiterated their familiar contention that as Congress would estop the transportation of explosives, harmful drugs, and intoxicants into a Territory, it could forbid the entry of property so dangerous to peace, order, and prosperity as slaves.

eyes of God and good men to hold—which is sanctioned by the general sense of all mankind among whom it has existed—which was legal only a short time ago in all the States of the Union, and which was then treated as sacred by any one of them—which is guaranteed to the owner as much as any other property is guaranteed by the Constitution"; such was his language.

Acrid and contemptuous references to Douglas studded the essay, which accused the Illinoisan of raising a new issue and stirring up the bitter waters of strife. In making this accusation, Black did not mention the attempt to foist Lecompton upon Kansas in which the Administration had been so signally defeated. He did not speak of the Southern demand for positive protection which was now rending the party asunder, nor did he take any Southern extremist to task for opinions far less defensible than Douglas's.

Other pamphlets appeared on both sides. By far the ablest came from the pen of Reverdy Johnson, who was heard with the more interest because as counsel for Sanford he had helped bring about Taney's decision upon Dred Scott. In his "Remarks On Popular Sovereignty," he unequivocally took Douglas's side.

What would be the consequence of accepting Black's view that the territorial legislature had no power to shape local institutions? asked the former Attorney-General. The cards, dice, and roulette wheels used in gambling were legal property in some States; was the legislature of a Territory to have no power to exclude gambling? Polygamy might be legal in one State; could the husband take ten wives into a Territory? And then, as to slavery itself, how absurd would be the result of the doctrine that the statutes of the State of origin controlled that species of property! "An emigrant from one State might sell each slave single, whilst one from another could not sell at all, or sell if the sale separated man and wife, parent and child. In one case slaves would be liable to execution for debt in the lifetime of the owner, in the other not. In one the children of a slave might belong to her owner, in the other not. . . . In one the mode of feeding, working, and clothing might be prescribed, in the other not." Adopt Black's interpretation, remarked Reverdy Johnson, and the statute book of a Territory would be a singular volume. Its title would be, The Statutes and Other Laws of the Territory; open it, and readers would find the enactments of Massachusetts, Virginia, Georgia, and other States, with a note that they applied respectively to the citizens who had emigrated from each State.

Johnson also argued that if the Dred Scott decision meant anything, it was that Congress had no power whatever over slavery in the Territories; neither power to prohibit nor to establish it. And if Congress had no authority to prohibit or establish, how could it legislate to protect slave property? When Buchanan had told Congress that, under the Dred Scott decision, slavery existed by virtue of the Constitution, he made an unfounded assertion, for no such doctrine was to be found in the decision either in words or by fair inference. "All that the court decided . . . was that the Constitution did not prohibit the institution, and that it gave no power to Congress to prohibit it." This was the opinion of a man whose reputation in constitutional law far exceeded Jeremiah Black's.

As the debate continued, it became acrimonious. Douglas was incensed by passages in Black's article bearing upon his public conduct, and especially by the charge that he had completely revolutionized his political opinions in the course of eighteen months. An important election was at hand in Ohio; handed Black's argument when traveling to Wooster, he made a vituperative reply. At Columbus and Cincinnati he spoke more calmly. Once more, he said, the Administration was endeavoring to drive him from the party. Attorney-General Black had been the agent of the cabal about Buchanan when, in 1858, he had sent letters abusing Douglas to Democrats all over Illinois. Now he was its catspaw again. This effort to thrust him into exile would fail; "the thing cannot be done." Returning east, he began to write a full-length rejoinder to Black, but was prostrated first by inflammatory rheumatism and then by bilious fever. His illness rapidly became so alarming that friends and opponents alike besieged his door to express sympathy, while several times rumors of his death flew about Washington. Happily, by mid-November he was recovering.[23]

The Ohio speeches provoked a fresh clamor of denunciation in the South. Douglas, declared Representative Eli Shorter of Alabama, was great in talent, in oratory, in ambition—and in treason to the South and the party. Numerous Southerners swore they would just as soon vote for Seward or Joshua Giddings as for the Illinoisan. The Democrats of Noxubee County in Georgia announced their rejection of Douglas, even if the Charleston convention nominated him. If the Dred Scott decision is to be trampled into the dust, wailed the Memphis *Avalanche,* for heaven's sake let the infamous outrage be committed in the name of Black Republicanism instead of the Democracy. The Mobile *Tribune,* Montgomery *Advertiser,* and Atlanta *Intelligencer,* spurning the Northwestern wing of the party, and branding Douglas as a hypocrite and marplot, demanded every jot and tittle of territorial rights. If the South should fail of full protection for slavery when asked, declared the *Intelligencer,* "she will then fall back upon her own resources, seize the sword of independence, and fight for the laws of the land and our rights." [24]

It was Douglas against the field—but Administration enmity and Southern rejection of the Freeport Doctrine made his chances dubious. Nor was his

23 Washington *Constitution,* September 10–27; Phila. *Press,* November 25; Mobile *Register,* November 23, 1859, etc.
24 *National Intelligencer,* quoted in N. Y. *Weekly Tribune,* October 15, 1859.

candidacy without other elements of weakness, rooted in his personality and record. In the border area, he had never been much liked by thoughtful, conservative men like Bayard, Letcher, and Guthrie. While he had many friends in New England, shrewd politicians of the Caleb Cushing-B. F. Hallett stripe were affected not merely by Administration pressures but by a sense that he was unsafe, and so took an adverse stand. Throughout the rest of the North he possessed immense power, the main body of Middle Western Democrats positively idolizing him. Even there, however, many sober men had always distrusted his flamboyant attitudes, bellicosity, and impetuosity. The main body of the Northern party still hoped that he might carry everything before him, and believed that in any frontal collision with the Southern wing his forensic power and personal force would be irresistible. But the chance of Democratic success more and more depended on the choice of some such trustworthy if uninspiring compromise nominee as Hunter.[25]

[II]

On the Republican side, Seward and his aide Thurlow Weed, as efficient a political combination as any in American history—as Jackson and Van Buren, or McKinley and Hanna—were actively at work for the nomination, Weed pulling wires, enlisting editors, keeping in *rapport* with such New York leaders as E. D. Morgan and Preston King, and planning the capture of State delegations. Seward spent the summer in Europe. Before going abroad, he visited Cameron at Harrisburg, shook hands with the whole legislature, dropped encouraging words on the tariff, and departed with some half-promises of support. The little Senator, with his careless rural dress, bubbling loquacity, and burning ambition, was hailed in New York City with music, cheers, and feasting—"the next President." Far down the bay he was accompanied by a vessel full of friends, waving, huzzaing, and singing.[26] He stood preeminent among aspirants for the nomination—but half a dozen powerful elements distrusted or disliked him.

The Ohio governor was equally ardent and equally hopeful. Chase, like Seward, had been talked of in 1856, and he too belonged to the radical antislavery wing of the party. Carl Schurz spent the night at his house, breakfasted with him and his pretty daughter Kate, and heard him express a frank desire to be the next President. "You will be a delegate to the convention, Mr. Schurz," he said in effect. "What do you think?" And Schurz replied with

25 Cf. John Appleton's letters to Buchanan on political situation, September 1859; Buchanan Papers.
26 Thurlow Weed, *Memoir*, 256, 257; R. H. Luthin, *The First Lincoln Campaign*, Ch. 2; Frederic Bancroft, *Seward*, I, 493-495.

blunt candor: "If the Republican Convention at Chicago have courage enough to nominate an advanced antislavery man, they will nominate Seward; if not, they will not nominate you." But Chase was not abashed; he could not see why antislavery men should not place him ahead of Seward. What of his long labors for the Liberty Party and Free Soil Party? What of his ten years' experience as Senator and governor? Throughout the fall of 1859 and the ensuing winter, he and his friends, with the *Ohio State Journal* as organ, were ceaselessly busy.[27]

As in the Democratic Party many were turning to the hope of some compromise figure, so a growing number of Republicans began to study Edward Bates of Missouri. The staid, white-bearded, mild-eyed old jurist, past sixty-five but still vigorous, had never identified himself with the new party. In principle he was still an old-line Whig; but he was ready to accept a Republican nomination on terms that would permit other Whigs, freesoil Democrats, and moderate Know-Nothings to join hands behind him. The three Blairs believed that they might rally an irresistible coalition around him. Their platform would embrace the containment of slavery, a homestead bill, internal improvements, the colonization of negroes outside the United States, and a Pacific railroad.

In the spring of 1859, Frank Blair and Schuyler Colfax, dining with Bates, ascertained that he would stand firm against any expansion of slavery and that he sympathized with Blair's hope to abolish slavery in Missouri. They assured him that Seward could not get the nomination. Bates rose to their proposals, which contemplated not so much a Republican as an Opposition Party—a People's Party, for which, wrote Gratz Brown, the Republicans, Whigs, Americans, and Honest Democrats could all vote.[28]

The immediate result was the publication of a long letter by Bates (written before the dinner conference, but now first brought forth) assailing Buchanan's policies, expounding old Whig doctrines on the tariff, river and harbor improvements, and railroad aid, and deprecating the agitation of the slavery issue. The question of slavery extension he did not discuss. Greeley's *Tribune*, praising the letter as just and sagacious, intimated that if he *had* treated this issue, he would have taken a correct stand. Bates's candidacy had two great and obvious weaknesses. It assumed that the slavery agitation *could* be stopped—and all those who saw that it could not distrusted his stand; and it involved the practical creation of a new party, from which radical Republicans would be certain to depart with wrath and clamor. Nevertheless, the Blairs, laboring diligently, enlisted Orville H. Browning, Henry Winter Davis, and Tom Corwin in at least tentative support. Browning shortly talked to his friend Lincoln in Springfield on the subject:

27 Pike, *First Blows;* Schurz, *Reminiscences,* II, 171 ff.; Hart, *Chase,* 179–181.
28 Bates, *Diary* (ed. Howard K. Beale), 11; Luthin, *op. cit.,* 55.

February 8 (1860). . . . At night Lincoln came to my room and we had a free talk about the Presidency. He thinks I may be right in supposing Mr. Bates to be the strongest and best man we can run—that he can get votes even in this county that he cannot get—and that there is a large class of voters in all the free states that would go for Mr. Bates, and for no other man. He says it is not improbable that by the time the national convention meets in Chicago he may be of opinion that the very best thing that can be done will be to nominate Mr. Bates.

Of the less prominent aspirants for the Republican nomination, Lincoln displayed the shrewdest type of activity. Having stated the issue of slavery-restriction so forcibly in the Douglas-Lincoln debates that all influential free-soilers began to watch him carefully, he intended to maintain the position he had won. As his comment on Bates indicated, this old-time follower of Henry Clay believed that a moderate rather than radical candidate was needed in 1860. At the same time, he realized that the party must win essentially on its Northern strength without regard to the South, and that if it sacrificed freesoil principle in order to woo border votes, Cotton Whigs, and weak-kneed Democrats, it would meet well-merited defeat. On such a basis, he wrote Nathan Sargent, the Republicans would probably carry Maryland—and would certainly lose every other State. They would gain nothing in the South and fail in the North.[29] Or, as he put it in another widely publicized letter of May, 1859, he would support a fusion of Republican and other opposition elements only if it could be had on Republican terms. In the selection of a candidate, compromise was possible. He would even go to the South for an able, patriotic man who would stand on Republican ground.

"But," Lincoln declared, "I am against letting down the Republican standard a hair's-breadth." [30] Bravely spoken! At the same time, while privately making modest assertions that he was unfit, he was keeping his name and views before the voters and cultivating political friends.

He bought title to a German newspaper in Springfield, the *Staats-Anzeiger*. He abandoned his distaste for social formalities to give parties for politicians. He made an Independence Day speech at Atlanta, Illinois. He corresponded with Schuyler Colfax, giving sagacious advice; the party must not campaign in one State for some idea popular just there, but unpopular in other States and divisive in the national convention.[31] In midsummer of 1859 he made a nine-day trip to Iowa and Kansas on business, delivering by request a political speech at Council Bluffs. Here, discussing the slavery question at length, he again insisted that the Republican Party retain its definite principles and national organiza-

29 Gilbert A. Tracy, *Uncollected Letters of Abraham Lincoln*, 111-113.
30 To Theodore Canisius, May 17, 1859; *Works*, I, 534, 535
31 To Schuyler Colfax, July 6, 1859; *Works*, I, 535.

tion.[32] The friendly *Nonpareil* termed his speech masterly and unanswerable, while even the hostile *Bugle* admitted that he had been quite a lion in western Iowa. Invited by Republican leaders to speak in half a dozen States from Minnesota to New York and New Hampshire, he agreed to make addresses in Ohio (replying to Douglas) and Wisconsin.

The Ohio speeches were of sufficient importance to obtain wide notice. In Columbus, where the *Ohio State Journal* had announced Lincoln as a man of "great renown and national reputation," he spoke on September 16 from the steps of the capitol for two hours. Next day in Dayton he made a speech of similar length at the courthouse, even the Democratic *Daily Empire* admitting that he "is a very seductive reasoner." At a rally that night, ex-Representative Robert C. Schenck called him the proper man for the Republican Presidential nomination. On his arrival in Cincinnati, where he spoke on Saturday evening, the seventeenth, he met an enthusiastic reception. His audience, according to Murat Halstead's *Commercial*, was three or four thousand. The hostile *Enquirer* carried a good Sunday morning report of the speech, and the *Gazette* on Monday printed its full text. Facing his Cincinnati hearers, he had modestly remarked: "This is the first time in my life that I have appeared before an audience in so great a city as this. I therefore make my appearance under some degree of embarrassment." It was evident to thoughtful readers, however, that the State was entertaining one of the most vigorous political thinkers of the time. And of readers he had a great many. Robert Hitt of the Chicago *Press and Tribune* accompanied Lincoln to report his utterances in shorthand; the New York *Times* paid careful attention to his tour; and the New York *Tribune*, to which Greeley now returned from California, printed nearly a column of matter from the Columbus address.

Taking the Ohio speeches together, Lincoln made a number of forcible points. (1) He insisted that the central purpose of the Republican Party was eminently conservative; it proposed only to bring slavery back to its original place in the American scheme and keep it there, asking for no other change than that which the framers of the government had anticipated with respect to it. (2) He brilliantly exposed the logical weakness of the Freeport Doctrine, pointing out again how it declared that an institution might lawfully be driven from a place where it might lawfully exist. (3) Douglas, he said, assumed that slavery was one of the little, unimportant matters, of no more consequence in a Territory than the question whether men should grow tobacco or raise horned cattle; a matter of dollars and cents, with no moral implications. The Little Giant assumed that the first comers to a Territory might properly plant there something which the millions who came thereafter could never dig up; some-

32 Baringer, *Lincoln's Rise to Power*, 90–93.

thing which deeply affected the family of older States. It was not so. (4) This non-moral view of slavery, he remarked in Columbus, was a sapping and mining operation, breaking down public opinion. Once men were converted to the view that no wrong inhered in slavery and that whoever wanted it might have it, then both territorial expansion and fresh importations would become possible. Men would be ready for Jeff Davis, Stephens, and their friends to sound the bugle for revival of the slave trade, pouring a flood of slavery over the free States. (5) In Cincinnati he appealed to the freesoil Democrats to come into the Republican Party as their only ark of refuge. He did so by ostensibly speaking to Kentuckians, telling them that if they wished to make slavery permanently safe and extend it over new lands, they should hasten to nominate Douglas.

In their homely, lucid combination of logic with historical citations, the Ohio speeches were the best refutation of the *Harper's* article which had yet appeared. As in all of Lincoln's utterances, however, appeals to principle dominated mere debating points. All his arguments were woven about two main themes. One concerned ideas:

Mr. Clay many, many years ago . . . told an audience that if they would repress all tendencies to liberty and ultimate emancipation, they must go back to the era of our independence and muzzle the cannon which thundered its annual joyous return on the Fourth of July; they must blow out the moral lights around us. . . . I call attention to the fact that in a preeminent degree these popular sovereigns are at this work: blowing out the moral lights around us; teaching that the negro is no longer a man, but a brute; that the Declaration has nothing to do with him; that he ranks with the crocodile and the reptile; that man, with body and soul, is a matter of dollars and cents. I suggest to this portion of Ohio Republicans, or Democrats . . . that there is now going on among you a steady process of debauching public opinion on this subject.

The other theme concerned action:

This government is expressly charged with the duty of providing for the general welfare. We believe that the spreading out and perpetuity of slavery impairs the general welfare. . . . I say that we must not interfere with the institution of slavery in the States where it exists, because the Constitution forbids it, and the general welfare does not require us to do so. We must not withhold an efficient fugitive-slave law, because the Constitution requires us, as I understand it, not to withhold such a law. But we must prevent the out-spreading of the institution. . . . We must prevent the revival of the African slave-trade, and the enacting by Congress of a territorial slave code. We must prevent each of these things being done by either Congresses or courts. The people of these United States are the rightful masters of both Congresses and courts, not to overthrow the Constitution, but to overthrow the men who pervert the Constitution.

Moncure D. Conway went to the Cincinnati meeting, held in a public square in bright moonlight. He listened to the steady battering flow of logic from the gaunt, hollow-cheeked, sad-eyed Illinoisan, whose strong features wore such a bronzed, thought-carved, kindly look that he seemed to fit Robert Browning's description of a German savant—three parts sublime to one grotesque. Conway was struck by Lincoln's voice, every intonation expressing liveliness, earnestness, and shrewdness. He thought the man's personality charming in its total lack of pretense—simple, direct, and humorous. When Lincoln said, "Slavery is wrong!" Conway heard the Kentuckians in the audience murmur and hiss. Lincoln instantly elaborated: "I acknowledge that you must maintain your platform just there, if at all. . . . But your hisses will not blow down the walls of justice." [33]

As the New York *Tribune* printed its quotations from the Columbus and Cincinnati speeches, and the Chicago *Press and Tribune* and *Illinois State Journal* published both in full, Lincoln tarried in Indianapolis on his way home to deliver a two-hour address to an enthusiastic audience.[34] Again, using the Ohio arguments, he produced a notable impression. The end of September found him in Milwaukee, addressing the Wisconsin State Agricultural Society; a non-political discourse remarkable chiefly for the vigor with which he demolished the mudsill theory of society. Who were the mudsills? In the free States, he said, most people were neither exclusively hirers nor hired, but a mixed body working partly for themselves and partly for others; no hired laborer was fixed to that condition for life; and free labor was deemed compatible with the highest education attainable.[35] He made another impromptu speech in Milwaukee, and on his return addressed audiences at Beloit and Janesville. The *Gazette* of the last-named town, admitting that his oratorical style was plain and his gestures were awkward, added that the power of his intellect made itself felt not only while the speech was being delivered, but afterward; that his arguments and hits would be long remembered; and that his audience would retain "a vivid recollection of that tall, gaunt form, stooping over towards his hearers, his countenance full of humor or frowning with scorn, as he lays bare" the absurd positions of his opponents.[36]

Of all the speeches delivered in 1859, Lincoln's showed the shrewdest thought, the most irrefutable logic, and the greatest moral power. That fact did

33 Conway, *Autobiography*, I, 317, 318; "Personal Recollections of Abraham Lincoln" in *Fortnightly Review*, I (1865), 56 ff. Lincoln's written version of his speech makes no reference to hisses, but does contain his flat statement to the Kentuckians: "I think slavery is wrong, morally and politically."
34 N. Y. *Weekly Tribune*, September 24, October 1, 1859.
35 Lincoln, *Works*, I, 576–584.
36 Quoted in Baringer, *Lincoln's Rise to Power*, 110.

not escape some party leaders who recalled his similar primacy in 1858. He kept in touch with Norman B. Judd and Secretary Jesse Fell of the Illinois Republican organization. Content with a dark-horse position, he took pains to praise Seward, Chase, Cameron, Bates, and other leaders, sought no delegates outside Illinois, allowed the impression to grow that he might be content with a Vice-Presidential nomination, and labored for party harmony on a platform genuinely embodying principle. He was far from being a prominent figure. When the Philadelphia *Press* this fall listed forty-five men who had been named for the Presidency, he was not among them. Yet the Chicago *Tribune*, asserting its preference for him, declared that the Northwestern Republicans would insist upon placing him at the head of the ticket.[37]

[III]

Douglas was a moderate leader—his popular sovereignty position was an effort to reconcile Northern and Southern views and keep the Democratic Party national. Lincoln was a moderate leader—he was ready even to accept a Southern candidate in order to make the Republican Party less sectional. The groping attempt of the Blairs, Gratz Brown, and Schuyler Colfax to lift Edward Bates to leadership of a Republican-Opposition Party was a moderate movement. The great mass of reflective Americans, at least outside New England and the cotton kingdom, were in apprehensive mood; only moderation, they believed, could save the country. Throughout the border States, meanwhile, a vigorous attempt was being made to organize moderate men behind a more realistic, generous, and patriotic approach to State and national problems. Dark was the outlook in areas dominated by slave-code men in the Deep South and radical antislavery men in the North; but a gleam of sunshine lighted up the broad region from Maryland to Missouri.

"Recent political results in Virginia, Kentucky, North Carolina, and Tennessee," exulted the Mobile *Register*, John Forsyth's moderate paper, "conclusively show that at least in these important central States of the Union, which constitute the northern division of the slaveholding section, the prevailing sentiment of the people is sound, wholesome, and true to those broad national principles which look to the peace and harmony of the Confederacy, and to the sinking of the slavery agitation." [38]

The attempt to create an Opposition Party in this region was half a movement against fanaticism and disruption, half a movement for long-overdue attention to internal reform and development. The resources of the borderland

37 Phila. *Press*, November 28, 1859; Chicago *Tribune*, November 19, 1859.
38 Quoted in *National Intelligencer*, August 24, 1859.

were wasting away while men quarrelled over slavery instead of planning more railways, more canals, better seaports and river ports, a fairer tax system, and free public schools. As historic friends of internal improvements and business enterprise, the old-time Whigs could best take up the demand for new attitudes. This rebirth of the opposition in the upper slave States began with the Lecompton schism. The hope for some effective Southern front against the triumphant Democrats, slight just after the election of 1856, had revived when the Democrats quarrelled and the Administration became demoralized. A strong body of Southern Whigs and Know-Nothings disapproved of the attempt to force the Lecompton constitution on Kansas. The speech of Crittenden of Kentucky against it, and the still more spirited denunciation by Bell of Tennessee, terming it fraught with evils tending to the destruction of the Union, were lustily applauded.

Leaders began to confer and exchange letters. Nathan Sargent of Washington (remembered for his graphic memoirs of the long era from Monroe to Fillmore) and A. H. H. Stuart of Virginia (Fillmore's Secretary of the Interior, now a Know-Nothing member of the State Senate) were especially active in shaping plans for a new party—a conservative, national, Union-exalting party, which should thrust aside the slavery issue, denounce all secessionists, push a broad program of internal improvements, and on constructive grounds overthrow the Democrats. These two men talked or wrote to Bell, Crittenden, Washington Hunt, Tom Corwin, ex-Senator W. A. Graham and George E. Badger of North Carolina, and such former Representatives as Kenneth Rayner of North Carolina, Henry W. Hoffman of Maryland, and L. M. Kennett of Missouri. William C. Rives of Virginia, heartily sympathizing with the movement, used his pen to forward it.[39]

So rapidly did the project of an Opposition Party develop that, by the winter of 1858–59, an impressive group of leaders believed that they might combine the disjointed conservative elements of the nation, displace the Republicans as the chief anti-Democratic Party, head off the "radical" Seward, and elect a statesman of nationalist convictions.[40] Theirs must be a new party; it could not be the Republican Party reorganized, for the Republicans could hardly carry a Northern State *without* a slavery-containment plank, while the Opposition could not carry any border State *with* it.[41] In the closing days of 1858, representative Opposition men of thirteen States met, canvassed their prospects, and resolved to nominate a moderate Union leader in 1860.

39 A. C. Cole, *The Whig Party in the South*, 330 ff.; Rives Papers, 1859.
40 Nathan Sargent, October 31, 1858; Stuart Papers, LC.
41 George D. Prentice of Louisville wrote Orville Browning that the Southern Opposition could never support the Republican Party on a platform forbidding any further extension of slave territory. January 9, 1860; Browning Papers.

Many thought that if they held an early convention the Republicans would have to fall in behind them. Sargent was especially sanguine. Suppose we name Crittenden and Washington Hunt, or Edward Bates and Senator Solomon Foot of Vermont, he asked; what can the Republicans do but ratify the ticket? The early months of 1859 found the new gospel converting followers. In February, the State Council of Maryland Know-Nothings congratulated voters on the prospect for a union of all conservative elements, and called for a national Opposition convention in 1860. In March, the Whig General Committee of New York City applauded letters from William A. Graham and D. D. Barnard explaining the need for a great Opposition Party. A. H. H. Stuart was organizing Virginians, and proposing an Opposition newspaper of national range.[42]

In several States the crusade gained strength from a demand for internal reform and development. Virginians of the Shenandoah and the West still had serious grievances against the Tidewater. The State constitution, as revised in 1850, showed a decided favoritism to slaveholders, for it exempted from taxation all slaves under twelve, while upon others it placed an average valuation of $300 which was notoriously too low. Because of insufficient revenues, and the high cost of improvements which benefitted chiefly the Tidewater region, the State debt had reached a disturbing level. It was necessary to raise more money. Western Virginia wished the slaveholders taxed more heavily; the Tidewater discussed instead a tax upon wages and salaries—that is, upon free workers. Senator Hunter had just said that "the master at the South, who owns the labor, wields the power of the government, and does justice to all." To freemen of the western counties it seemed plain that while he did wield the rod of power, his justice was something less than even-handed.

In North Carolina the Opposition, with Rayner, Badger, and Graham as spokesmen, meanwhile declared for internal improvements, a better support of education, and—most appealing of all—a just system of State taxation. At last, many North Carolinians were awakening to a realization that the revenue system grossly favored the wealthy slaveholders. Negroes paid nothing but a poll tax, which varied from county to county but was always low. Land taxation, by contrast, might reach one percent of real value. In the Fayetteville area, land worth $2,400 was taxed $24, while two slaves worth that amount bore a burden of only $5.82. Inasmuch as the eastern part of the State contained a heavy majority of the Negroes, the issue aroused sharp sectional feeling. The Tidewater counties, protesting that they already paid two-thirds of the State levies, declared that if slaves were taxed by value, the burden would become intolerable. The western spokesmen, estimating that the three hundred thousand slaves were worth $600 on the average, or $180,000,000 in all, contended that

42 February 18, 1859, Stuart Papers, LC; *National Intelligencer*, March 17, 1859.

the chief slaveholding districts paid nothing like their due share. Newspapers on both sides of the *ad valorem* proposal mentioned Hinton Rowan Helper's suggestion that the slaveless majority in the South should tax Negroes to the point where they became unprofitable. Beyond question, a good many small farmers were growing restive and critical as they looked at their slaveholding neighbors. The system of representation, too, seemed unfair to the upland counties; it had a mixed foundation, resting upon taxation and Federal numbers, and a few hardy reformers proposed a pure white basis. The Democrats were for maintaining the existing socio-economic system, and the Opposition was hot to change it.[43]

In Kentucky, the Opposition held its convention in Louisville February 22, 1859, with the venerable Robert P. Letcher in the chair. Nominating candidates, it drew an indictment of the Democrats as essentially a disunion party, who embraced many avowed secessionists, and many of whose national leaders had threatened rebellion if Frémont were elected in 1856. Ample proof exists, declared the resolutions, of "the general diffusion of the disunion sentiment within the great body of the party at the South." A week later, the Tennessee Opposition met in Nashville. Ex-Governor Neil S. Brown presided and John Bell, who had just left the Senate, spoke. The ten-plank platform constituted an attempt to combine old Whig tenets with the more legitimate Know-Nothing doctrine. It called for stern maintenance of the Union; a tariff with specific duties wherever applicable, discriminating in favor of American industry; the acquisition of Cuba whenever this was consonant with national honor; a stiffening of the laws on naturalization and voting; and such a disposition of the public lands as would give Tennessee and other old States a proportionate share with the western States and Territories. This platform, on which John Netherland stood for governor, was widely published East and West.[44]

Meanwhile, in Virginia the Opposition under A. H. H. Stuart, John Minor Botts, and W. C. Rives was gathering its forces to defeat the radical Democrats under Henry A. Wise, Roger A. Pryor, James A. Seddon, and Edmund Ruffin. For several reasons the contest attracted national attention. It would indicate whether Virginia would favor extreme or moderate action in the Charleston convention, would show whether the Shenendoah-Western Virginia or Tidewater-Piedmont sections were likely to dominate the State, and would throw light on the question whether the proslavery pamphleteering of Ruffin and George Fitzhugh had affected public sentiment. The Opposition convention, held August 22 with Stuart in control, adopted resolutions which followed the principles of Clay and Webster. Calling for a revenue tariff with incidental

43 See Wilmington *Weekly Journal*, March–April, 1860; Fayetteville *Observer*, 1859–60.
44 *National Intelligencer*, March 15, April 5, 1859.

protection to industry, it assailed the Democratic Party for permitting factories and furnaces to close, crops to lie unsold, and labor to languish for want of action to stimulate manufactures and afford a home market for products of the farm. It declared against any disposition of the public lands not general in character and equal in benefits to all the States. It also demanded a livelier prosecution of internal improvements. Why should the trans-Allegheny region remain isolated from the rest of the State? Why should Norfolk not be made a port rivaling Baltimore and Philadelphia? The convention pronounced its inflexible antagonism to the reopening of the slave trade. Attacking the Democratic Party for measures which had irritated sectional feeling, it appealed for an end to the whole dolorous slavery quarrel.[45]

The leaders of this Opposition movement were men of character and some intellectual eminence. Crittenden, a veteran champion of conservatism and the Union, was beloved wherever known. His repugnance to the slave-trade and slave-code demands was shared by most Kentuckians. Bell's retirement from the Senate had been widely deplored as removing a pillar of moderation. A wealthy slaveholder, a loyal Tennesseean whose life paralleled the history of the State, this old-time Jacksonian turned Whig had always detested extremists both North and South. He had never failed to fight for his convictions. In Tyler's Cabinet he had opposed a spoils appointment so implacably that the President, giving way, had remarked: "Bell, I know you are honest, but I think you are obstinate." Combating Douglas's Nebraska bill as the violation of a compact to which Southern honor had been pledged, he had predicted with prophetic force the calamities flowing from its passage. He had assailed Lecompton in defiance of instructions from the Tennessee legislature. His final Senate speech, opposing Buchanan's Cuban scheme, showed all his grasp and prudent outlook, many deeming it the best argument made on the subject. Stuart, too, was a leader of principle; and John Minor Botts had been a rugged fighter ever since 1836, when, a young Congressman from the Richmond district, he had supported J. Q. Adams in battling against the gag rule. Later he had denounced the annexation of Texas.

It was not true that, as many Southerners said, Crittenden, Bell, and Stuart were harlotting with the Republicans. It was not true that, as the Nashville *Union* bitterly alleged, many leaders of the border Opposition had a positive dislike for their proslavery brethren of the South, and that the Kentucky and Tennessee elections would decide whether the Opposition in these States could move forward to a coalition with the Republicans in 1860.[46] Actually, the

45 C. H. Ambler, *Sectionalism in Virginia*, Ch. 10; H. T. Shanks, *Sectionalist Movement in Virginia*, Chs. 3, 4; Richmond *Whig*, July–September, 1859.
46 Nashville *Union*, July 31, 1859.

marshals of the Opposition hoped to found a party midway between Republicans and Southern Democrats.

Their object was to force an abandonment of extreme proslavery or antislavery positions in national affairs. They did believe, however, that a multitude of conservative Republicans, Democrats, and Know-Nothings might throng to this bright new standard. Even in the Deep South not a few men cried them Godspeed. In Alabama, for example, James H. Clanton of Montgomery, an attorney, legislator, and militia officer, sprung from a wealthy planting family and sometimes called the Chevalier Bayard of his State, took precisely the Opposition point of view. Like John Forsyth of the Mobile *Register*, he constantly denounced secession, but unlike Forsyth, he had no antagonism to protective tariffs, internal improvements, and centralization of power. In due course he was to become an elector on the Bell-Everett ticket. The Selma *Reporter* called for an Opposition convention. In Louisiana, fourteen members of the legislature signed an appeal in March for a revival of the Whig Party on the principles of Clay.[47]

Moderation made the Opposition a powerful aggregate in Kentucky, Tennessee, North Carolina, and Virginia. Moderation made Edward Bates an imposing figure in Missouri, the St. Louis *Evening News* declaring him its candidate for the Presidency (with Crittenden or Everett second choice), and the St. Louis *Democrat* asserting that he and Bell alone of the Southern Opposition could be elected. Moderation led the Virginia Democracy to select John Letcher for governor who, a dozen years earlier, had expressed strong views on the evils of slavery. Moderation inspired Senator Green of Missouri, wrung by the quarrel within the Democratic ranks, to propose a plan for uniting the Buchanan and Douglas wings: Douglas to be reinstated in the party, all discussion of intervention or non-intervention in the Territories to be dropped, and Kansas to be admitted by the next Congress. That a decided majority of the American people wanted such compromises and adjustments as would assure general peace, there could be no question.[48]

Naturally, Republicans of the radical type, believing in the milk of the word, denounced the movement for a union of the Northern and Southern Opposition. Bryant's *Evening Post*, declaring that the basic issue was slavery in the Territories and the basic tenet was antagonism to slavery extension, assailed the idea

47 William Garrett, *Reminiscences of Public Men in Alabama*, 632–645.
48 Bates, *Diary*, 41–45; Washington *States* quoted in *National Intelligencer*, May 12, 1859. Secretary Floyd recognized the strength of the moderates. "You have power in the South," he wrote Buchanan, September 5, 1859; "and this was never stronger than it is today. The efforts to form extreme parties even this summer have signally failed. Nothing could be more pitiable than the abortive efforts of Governor Adams on the slave trade question. . . . So too with a movement gotten up for the peaceful colonization of Sonora, a sort of varioloid form of filibustering." Buchanan Papers.

of any fusion. Who would dilute our tonic medicine to dishwater, it demanded? Naturally, the few true-blue Know-Nothings left were sceptical. The New York *Express*, their chief eastern organ, thought that the slightest aroma of Republicanism would kill Bell, Bates, Botts, and their friends in the South. It was evident that, as the Know-Nothing organization continued to disintegrate, many slave State members—including half a dozen Congressmen—were joining the Democratic ranks. But commercial elements were catching at the new hope. The Philadelphia *North American*, a mercantile journal, recommended that Republicans, Whigs, and Know-Nothings, uniting in a spirit of forbearance, frown down the men who wished to prescribe rigid platform tests.

[IV]

The October elections in 1859, watched with interest as forecasting the trends in 1860, had two spectacular results. They were another stinging repudiation of the Administration, suggesting that the people were disgusted with President, Cabinet, and policy. They were also a demonstration of the strength of conservatism, North and South.

The Republicans carried Ohio by seventeen thousand majority, taking control of both branches of the legislature. The Democrats had known they were beaten before they began. Senator Pugh had disgustedly written in the spring that his own county, which once gave the party forty-five hundred votes above all opponents, was going the way of Berks in Pennsylvania: "Buchanan has lost, for us, these famous strongholds which the enemy was never able to storm—to what taunts is he not entitled?" [49] In Iowa, the Republicans carried the governorship, legislature, and other offices. They swept Minnesota, electing both Representatives and making sure of a Senator in place of Shields. Their most telling triumph, however, was in Pennsylvania. Here a coalition which was predominantly Republican, though it included Know-Nothings and anti-Lecompton Democrats, won Philadelphia, Pittsburgh, and most other cities, seized the legislature, and piled up a majority of nearly eighteen thousand in the State. So much for Buchanan's dream of winning Pennsylvania on the Dred Scott issue! In New Jersey, the Democratic candidate for governor was defeated.

These elections meant that the Republicans in the Senate would be strengthened by James W. Grimes, Salmon P. Chase, and M. S. Wilkinson, shortly sent thither by Iowa, Ohio, and Minnesota. They meant more Republican governors controlling the State Houses in the critical days to come. Above all, they meant that the party possessed a bright opportunity in the campaign

49   June 5, 1859; C. C. Clay Papers, LC.

of 1860. The national platform was largely written this year in various State platforms. In Minnesota, for example, the Republicans declared against any expansion of slavery into the Territories, and any reopening of the slave trade, denounced the Administration for the defeat of the Homestead bill, called for efficient national aid to a Pacific railroad, and favored rivers and harbors improvement. In Pennsylvania, the coalition emphasized the tariff so heavily that such newspapers as the New York *Herald* and *Journal of Commerce* traced its victory to that demand. Though this interpretation was challenged by the *Tribune*, which pointed out that the Wilmot-Grow district, never much interested in the tariff, had been swept from its old Democratic moorings, Greeley too declared the tariff a potent factor. The Republican Party had numbers, it had the spirit of victory, and it had appealing new doctrines.

Upon the question whether the Republican gains were a blow to Douglas, opinion was much divided. His friends of the New York *Times* put the best face upon the situation by contending that as the Democrats could not win in 1860 without Pennsylvania, Ohio, and Illinois, and that as Douglas alone could reverse the tide in these and other Northern States, his nomination was therefore imperative. But could even he change the current? In Iowa, Minnesota, and Ohio, the Democrats had stood squarely upon a popular sovereignty platform, striving to cast off the dead weight of Buchanan's unpopularity— and yet they had met defeat. Both Southern Democrats and Republicans asserted that Douglas had been repudiated in his own section. "The truth is," remarked the Warsaw (Illinois) *Bulletin*, "all this talk about Douglas's popularity in the West and Northwest is sheer gammon, and the result of the elections proves it most conclusively." [50] Judicious observers might conclude that internecine war had almost fatally weakened the Democratic Party, that only a restoration of unity under Douglas's leadership could save the critical Northern States, and that the march of freesoil Democrats into the Republican Party was so strong that even the Little Giant would have to fight his hardest battle to hold the Northwest.

In parts of the cotton kingdom the current of intransigence flowed strong. The Democrats carried Mississippi three to one, doubled their majority of two years earlier in Georgia, and swept Florida. This area was becoming a one-party region. Yet, taking the slaveholding States as a whole, the surprising fact was the strength of the conservatives.

A strong Opposition showing had been foreshadowed by the early election in Virginia. John Letcher's nomination by the Democrats was itself a victory for moderation, bitterly disappointing Wise and his radicals. The Opposition Party named for governor a Tidewater man, W. L. Goggin, who had opposed

50 Warsaw *Bulletin*, October 17; Washington *Constitution*, October 19, 1859.

the admission of Texas, supported the Compromise of 1850, and aligned himself since with Stuart and Botts. By a close vote Letcher won, losing every Congressional district but two east of the Blue Ridge and carrying all but one west of it.

No doubt could exist that despite a recent recantation of his criticisms of slavery, he owed his margin to his refusal to extol the institution or support its extension and to his fervent attachment to the Union. While antagonists accused him of warring on the foundation interests of the State and trying to abolitionize western Virginia, the Wheeling *Intelligencer* denied that slavery was a foundation and appealed to the white workingmen and farmers of the uplands to reject such an assumption. The geographical cleavage in the election foreshadowed the future partition of the State. A victory for Goggin himself, popular in the slaveholding counties, would not have been a more emphatic rebuke to the fire-eaters. The Richmond *Whig* pointed out that after nominating a man of former freesoil views, strong in freesoil districts, the Democratic Party had won by a margin of only 5,570 as against Buchanan's majority of nearly 26,000, three years earlier.[51]

The election of Alexander R. Boteler to Congress especially heartened the Virginia Opposition. The scion of an aristocratic family which owned "Fountain Rock" at Shepherdstown, a graduate of Princeton, united by marriage with the Stocktons of New Jersey, he had moved from the Whigs through the Know-Nothings into the Opposition. His success gave the Union an eloquent defender, destined to make for it within two years what S. S. Cox pronounced one of the two most eloquent speeches ever delivered in Congress.[52] The journalist "Porte Crayon" (D. H. Strother), a son of the district, congratulated him on overthrowing a despicable regime, while William C. Rives was delighted at the prospect of having a sterling old-time Whig in Washington to maintain communications between the Virginia Opposition and their brethren in other sections. If the moderates of the border kept their ranks firm, and if the Opposition in the North showed a true national spirit, prophesied Rives, Virginia might well be won back to her ancient principles in 1860.[53]

In Kentucky and Tennessee, the Opposition made an equally impressive showing. Sensible men in these States realized that if secession precipitated war, the border would find brother fighting brother, and would be trampled under contending armies. Though the Democrats elected Beriah Magoffin (himself a moderate man) governor of Kentucky with 76,187 votes, the Opposition nominee, Joshua F. Bell, was close behind him with 67,271. In Tennessee, a

51 Ambler, Ch. 10; Shanks, Ch. 4.
52 S. S. Cox, *Three Decades*, 93.
53 Rives, June 4, D. H. Strother, June 15, 1859; Boteler Papers, Duke Univ.

radical proslavery Democrat, Isham Harris, ran against the Opposition leader, John Netherland. Here the result was still closer; Harris polled just over 76,000 votes, Netherland just over 68,000. Between them, Kentucky and Tennessee elected eleven (some said twelve) Opposition Congressmen. At least two of them, Francis Bristow and Emerson Etheridge, both former Whigs, were men of ability. The party did particularly well in Tennessee, where it chose seven out of the ten members of Congress; and jubilee meetings in Nashville and Memphis celebrated the result. John Bell's star rose higher than ever.[54]

While the New Orleans district elected a Know-Nothing of staunch Unionist views, John Edward Bouligny, to Congress, and the Opposition polled a respectable vote elsewhere in Louisiana, in Texas the moderates swept the board. With State officers and two Representatives to be elected, the Democrats were soundly trounced. Sam Houston, running for governor as an Independent Democrat, defeated the regular party nominee, 33,335 to 27,500. One of the Congressional seats went to A. J. Hamilton, another Independent Democrat of rigid Union views. The regular Democrat, John H. Reagan, was reelected in the first district after proclaiming his unflinching enmity to all proslavery extremists. He denounced filibustering. He attacked the slave-trade proposals. He called the disunionists of the Lower South wanton troublemakers. They ranted about the evils of Northern aggression and the violations of the Fugitive Slave Law, he said, ignoring the fact that it was the border States alone which really suffered. Yet from Maryland to Missouri the border people, proud and courageous as they were, opposed disunion, filibustering, and the foreign slave trade, and labored for peace and concord. "These facts show that it is for revolution and conquest, and not merely for the resistance of Northern aggression, that our agitators are at work." He would labor staunchly for the preservation of Southern rights. "But I will not advocate a destruction of our government as a matter of policy, or those revolutionary measures, based upon crime, which look to such a result. It is time that we should all see where we are drifting, to what the times are tending, and determine whether we are ready for revolution, with all its attendant insecurities to life and property, and with all its hazards to civil and religious liberty." [55]

Altogether, the Opposition vote in the border region, the Southwest, and

54 Election figures from N. Y. *Tribune Political Textbook for 1860*. The Washington *Union* (August 11, 1859) viewed the Tennessee battle as John Bell's fight. "Whatever influences large wealth, high social distinction, extensive and powerful political and family connections, elevated personal character, and the *prestige* of associations in public life with the most illustrious statesmen whom this country has produced, could exert in favor of a presidential candidate, have been thoroughly employed for many months for the purpose of carrying the State for the opposition."

55 J. H. Reagan, "Address to the Voters of the First Congressional District."

parts of the Lower South showed an impressive antagonism to extremist ideas.[56] It was obvious that the Republican victories in the Northwest and Pennsylvania were attributable to the revolt of freesoil Democrats against Buchanan and the appeal of new economic ideas. At least three-quarters of the nation opposed radical proslavery or antislavery ideas. Only in a few States of New England had abolitionist principles taken deep hold, and only in a few States of the cotton kingdom could State Rights extremists claim a majority. If the Opposition Party was given effective organization and leadership, it might play a decisive role in the coming campaign. Douglas, as reported by Nathan Sargent, told Democratic friends that if moderate voters united on Bates, he would defeat any man the other parties put into the field. As yet, Bates, Bell, Stuart, and Sargent had ground for hoping to capture the whole moderate wing of the Republicans. They were encouraged by such Republicans as two former Congressmen, S. F. Vinton of Ohio and S. A. Purviance of Pennsylvania.[57] As yet, Pugh, Green, and other Democrats had grounds for hoping to effect a reunion in their party.

Much depended on unforeseeable events. It was a time for generosity. If some national leader suddenly caught men's imaginations as Clay had known how to do! If some bright act lifted men's gaze above that sullen abstraction of slavery in the Territories! Then the crisis of 1860 might be passed. If, on the contrary, the nation's luck was bad, if ill-temper exploded into violence, then all hopes might be dashed.

[V]

Violence was an American tradition. In mid-October the country was startled by news that, for the first time in its history, a Senator had been slain in a duel. The victim was one of Douglas's ablest lieutenants, David C. Broderick.

California had just witnessed a campaign of alarming bitterness, the most passionate ever known on the Pacific Coast. Broderick was leader of the popular sovereignty Democrats, and Gwin of the Administration forces. Dozens of orators stumped the land from the Sierra to the sea. The two antagonists stooped to savage recriminations. On September 7 the election brought more than a hundred thousand voters to the polls. The Administration Democrats won, but by a closer margin than they liked. Broderick still had four years to serve in the Senate, and his abilities and prestige were both growing. His enemies

56 In Alabama, according to the Mobile *Daily Advertiser*, good leadership might have made a strong battle. If the Opposition had fought on old Whig principles, it might have carried Mobile, while in Montgomery an excellent chance for victory "was literally thrown away—sacrificed at the shrine of ultraism."

57 Nathan Sargent, February 18, 27, August 28, 1859; Stuart Papers, LC.

marked him for destruction. David S. Terry, a hot-tempered man of Southern origin, challenged the Senator to a duel; they met before a crowd of spectators; and Broderick fell, mortally wounded. California and the Douglas forces were deprived of a talented, aggressive leader. As a free State, California should have stood with the Northwest, but now she would send delegates to Charleston to support a proslavery candidate on a slave-code platform. "They have killed me," Broderick gasped on his deathbed, "because I was opposed to the extension of slavery and a corrupt Administration." [58]

Would further acts of violence occur? Would some unforeseen accident interrupt the growing movement for moderation and reconciliation? "Nobody who has watched history in the making," wrote Harold Nicolson after the second World War, "can doubt the immense part played in human affairs by the element of chance." America was a land of the unexpected, and the situation was one in which some blind stroke of fate, falling on excited nerves, might have malign consequences.

For the moment, in the autumn of 1859, the state of the country seemed fairly serene. Crops were excellent; wheat, corn, and cotton were bringing high prices; and business continued to improve. The iron mills were finding Western and Southern customers as railroad-building revived. On August 30, Edwin F. Drake struck oil at Titusville, and the ensuing rush to Pennsylvania's fields of black gold gave instant vigor to the petroleum industry. Businessmen everywhere were laying plans which assumed a peaceful national future. Nobody anticipated that a catastrophic lightning bolt might fall upon the land.

One of the most energetic of these businessmen, as we have seen, was John W. Garrett of the Baltimore & Ohio, planning an integrated trunk line from the Atlantic to St. Louis and extending the use of sleeping cars and other innovations. October 17, 1859, found him and other officers busy with their usual tasks. A telegram, filed at Monocacy at 7:05 A.M., brought them news which some at first thought incredible. It came from a conductor:

"Express train bound east under my charge was stopped this morning at Harper's Ferry by armed abolitionists. They have possession of the bridge and of the arms and armory of the United States. Myself and baggagemaster have been fired at. . . . They say they have come to free the slaves, and intend to do so at all hazards." [59]

58 Jeremiah Lynch, *A Senator of the Fifties*, 199–226; A. E. Wagstaff, *David S. Terry*, *passim;* N. Y. *Weekly Tribune*, October 15, 1859. Terry had previously wounded a vigilante agent (1856) with a bowie knife. Later he entered the Confederate army and fought bravely. In 1889, assaulting Justice Field of the Federal Supreme Court, he was shot dead by Field's bodyguard. Quite a chapter in American morals and manners is bound up in his career.
59 Edward Hungerford, *Story of the Baltimore and Ohio RR.*, I, 332–336.

3

John Brown at Harper's Ferry

WORDS MAY excite mankind, but it is the violent act which raises emotions to fever heat. Newspaper polemics and party broadsides can never crystallize popular sentiment like a dramatic blow—the Boston massacre, the destruction of the *Maine*, the sinking of the *Lusitania*. In both the North and South by 1859, feeling was deeply stirred, nerves were tense, and anger lay near the surface. Any sudden clash—the quick frenzy of some street mob, or a new Brooks-Sumner affair in Congress—might fall on latent passions like a spark on tinder. What would kindle Northern emotions most quickly? The slaying of some devoted man in an effort to liberate a slave. What would enrage the South to an implacable temper? Any attempt to foment, arm, and support a slave insurrection, with its peril to property, wives, children, and the entire social fabric for whose safety many Southerners felt a sharp and sleepless apprehension.

[I]

From Maryland Heights, just north of Harper's Ferry, a strikingly beautiful landscape extended to the south and west. Jefferson, in his *Notes on Virginia*, had called it "stupendous," adding: "This scene is worth a voyage across the Atlantic." In the foreground flowed the silvery Potomac, studded by islets, its high banks green in summer with foliage, its current rippling and boiling as it poured southeastward through its cleft in the Blue Ridge. It was flanked by a canal along which, now and then, lazily passed a horse-drawn barge. Here was the river highway which Washington had dreamed of making a link between the Atlantic and the Ohio-Mississippi system. Looking across it to the southward, an observer on the Heights could see the narrower Shenandoah winding through its rich valley to join the Potomac. The two streams enclosed a high, narrow neck of land, a hill or bluff, its sides washed by the converging waters, its crest dotted with houses, and the brief stretch of level ground at its toe occupied by a village and some workshops. The village was Harper's Ferry. The substantial shops, looking like factories, were the Federal armory for arms

70

manufacture, the arsenal for housing military stores, and, some distance away, the rifle works. Among them they usually employed several hundred hands and could fabricate ten thousand stand of arms a year.

SCENE OF THE
HARPER'S FERRY RAID
1859

At this point, the Baltimore & Ohio Railroad crossed the Potomac on a bridge about nine hundred feet in length, a sturdy structure supported by five heavy piers and covered by a strong wooden roof. The glistening tracks of a little branch railroad led up the Shenandoah Valley to Winchester. Harper's Ferry was only about eighty miles from Baltimore by rail, and a little less than sixty miles from Washington by turnpike, but its mountain setting gave it an air of remoteness. The village itself, with its railway offices, hotels, stores, cheap eating-houses, frame cottages, and gaunt national shops, was not attractive. All the buildings lined two confluent streets, Potomac Street beside one river and Shenandoah Street along the other. The effect was drab and straggling. But the village seemed negligible in the beautiful panorama of swift streams, white sand-spits and islands, and richly wooded hills.

To this district, a chosen base of operations, John Brown, two sons, and a friend had come on July 3, 1859, the taciturn leader calling himself Smith and letting men believe that he was a land-seeker and cattle-buyer.[1]

After a brief search, he had rented a rough two-story farmhouse owned by the heirs of Dr. Booth Kennedy about five miles from town on the Maryland side of the Potomac, a rickety cabin across the road affording additional shelter. Here the men of the little force he had recruited trickled in, until by early fall he had twenty-one followers in all. Of his principal lieutenants, the able, high-minded John H. Kagi remained most of the summer in Chambersburg, Pennsylvania, where he had useful tasks to perform; the reckless former dragoon, Aaron D. Stevens, who had killed a Missouri farmer in a former raid, was at the farmhouse; and the boyish, loose-tongued John E. Cook took up quarters in Harper's Ferry. The sons, Owen and Oliver, were soon joined by their brother, Watson.

Great pains had to be taken, as the band increased, to keep them concealed. Two quick-witted girls of Brown's family, his daughter Anne and daughter-in-law Martha, each in her seventeenth year, arrived to keep house and divert suspicion. Both were delightfully ingenuous and observant. Anne, who showed a vein of poetic feeling, later wrote appealing sketches of some of the company, notably Kagi, whose idealistic temper pleased her, and the adolescent William Thompson, with his yellow hair, innocent blue eyes, and diffident yet affectionate manner. "My evenings," she recorded, "were spent on the porch or sitting on the stairs *watching*, and listening to the katydids and whippoorwills. I used to enjoy watching the fireflies, and looking at the lights and shadows on the fine old trees and the mountain ridges on fine moonlight nights." Late in September, fifteen heavy boxes of "tools" were brought down to the farm from Chambersburg, containing one hundred and ninety-eight Sharps rifles with appurtenances, and nine hundred and fifty pikes. As the men occupied themselves studying tactics under Stevens upstairs, browning the rifle barrels, making belts and pistol holsters, playing checkers, reading the Baltimore *Sun* and a thumbed copy of Paine's *Age of Reason*, and arguing, the girls mounted sentinel. If a

---

1 Brown, wiry and alert as ever, had grown a long beard, largely because his quarrel with Forbes and the approach of his scheme to its climax made a disguise desirable. See pencil note by R. J. Hinton in G. W. Brown's *Reminiscences of Old John Brown*, Hinton Papers.

caller approached at mealtime, he was detained outside until the men, seizing dishes, food, and tablecloth, could vanish upstairs.[2]

The fierce-eyed, iron-jawed chieftain, adjuring everyone to constant caution and vigilance, awaited the best hour to strike. When he arrived, he had almost completely matured his plan. It was not what many writers have stated. He did *not* intend to make a sudden raid and then retreat to some mountain bastion. He meant by a sudden blow to take Harper's Ferry, thus (as his daughter put it) striking terror to the slaveholders about; to send agents among the surrounding plantations, rallying the slaves; to hold the town for at least a short time, expecting as many helpers, white and black, from the district as assailants; to prepare for rapid movement *southward*; and, as he moved, to continue sending out armed bands to free more slaves, secure provisions and hostages, and destroy slaveholding morale. He would follow the Appalachians into Tennessee and even Alabama, the heart of the South, making forays into the plains on either side. He had told Forbes that on the first night of the stroke he thought he might get from two to five hundred Negro adherents. As for the militia and regular army, he contemptuously judged them by the specimens he had seen in Kansas. His daughter writes that he deemed them "an inefficient lot." A crazy plan? At any rate, he believed in it intensely. An Ohio friend had expostulated with him in 1858:

He replied that with a hundred men he could free Kansas and Missouri too, and could march them to Washington and turn the President and Cabinet out of doors. . . . He seemed unable to think of anything else or talk of anything else. This affiant attempted to quiet him and get him into conversation upon other matters, but without success. The Kansas difficulties, the death of his son, and slavery were the only things of which he could be induced to speak. His whole manner and conversation was that of a monomaniac, and upon matters in regard to which he held the conversation, this affiant regarded him as altogether insane; such was his opinion at the time.[3]

News of his proposed attempt to deal a bloody stroke at some Southern community and set a slave revolt ablaze was being awaited with varying degrees of knowledge by his abolitionist backers: Gerrit Smith, George L. Stearns, Theodore Parker, Frank B. Sanborn, Thomas Wentworth Higginson, S. G. Howe, Frederick Douglass, and others. Visiting New England in May, Brown had held frequent meetings with the secret conspiratorial committee; had spoken again in Concord Town House, where he impressed Bronson Alcott and Rockwood Hoar as well as Emerson; and had received a little more than $4,000, of which Sanborn says that at least $3,800 was given with a clear understanding of its

2 Undated MS, Hinton Papers; Warren, *John Brown*, 323–325.
3 James W. Weld, Richfield, Ohio, undated affidavit of 1859; Villard Papers, Columbia Univ. See also Realf's testimony, *Mason Committee Report*, 96 ff.

future use. Indeed, he intimated frankly to all his intention of levying a blow for freedom, running off as many slaves as he could, and making slavery insecure. Higginson and Douglass knew that he intended to strike at Harper's Ferry.[4]

Servile insurrection, armed strife, wide and continued bloodshed—these were inherent elements of Brown's wild scheme, and he and his fellow-conspirators of the North knew it. In an effort to delude others (and perhaps himself) he had tried to confuse the issue. He had said that his well-controlled blow would *forestall* an inevitable, uncontrollable, and horribly vengeful revolt in the future. He had also told Higginson that he would not foment a slave rebellion at all, but merely get together families and bands of fugitives who would then defend themselves. This was a distinction without a difference. Any widespread attempt by slaves to escape would be insurrection, would be treated by masters and government as such, and would involve fierce combat. What Brown called defensive warfare by slave bands would be called offensive warfare by all Southern whites. According to his follower Realf, Brown spoke of killing no slaveholder, and yet in the same breath talked of fighting off individual opponents, militia, and the Federal army—which meant general killing. It was not for nothing that he had given careful study to the tactics of Toussaint l'Ouverture and Garibaldi. If Gerrit Smith, Sanborn, and the rest did not comprehend that his enterprise would bring on an implacable conflict and a heavy effusion of blood, they were much less acute men than the world esteemed them. The greater Brown's success, the bloodier would be the fighting of whites and blacks, raiders and troops.

The fact was that Higginson and some others actually wanted civil war, and hoped that Brown's raid would precipitate it. For a clergyman, young Higginson had a bloodthirsty mind; for while visiting Kansas in the spring of 1856 he had approved of the killings on the Pottawatomie, and he now avowed himself ready to see slavery extinguished in gore. Brown had told Gerrit Smith, Sanborn, and Higginson how many weapons he had and how he meant to use them. He had written Sanborn: "I expect to effect a mighty conquest, even though it be like the last victory of Samson." Of the conspirators, Parker, Stearns, and Howe knew less about the details of the scheme, and Parker, mortally stricken, had departed for Europe. They were aware, however, that he planned shortly to launch his great scheme of slave-liberation.

For the selection of Harper's Ferry as the point of attack, Brown alone was responsible. He had hesitated as to the place of his stroke, for a time believing that it should be in the Deep South—Anne Brown says that he mentioned Baton Rouge. But he had rejected this idea on grounds of humanity, believing

---

4 Sanborn, *John Brown*, 423; Alcott, *Journals*, May 8, 1859.
5 Sanborn, *Recollections*, I, 150; Higginson, *Cheerful Yesterdays*, 207.

that the "ferocity" of the slaves in the Lower South might prompt them to a wholesale massacre. His notion of the fierce rebelliousness of slaves in the cotton kingdom had been derived from abolitionist publications. Moreover, Harper's Ferry seemed a better point in that he hoped for helpers from Pennsylvania and western Maryland and Virginia. Frederick Douglass had vehemently protested against the choice on strategic grounds, declaring that the town would prove a perfect trap where concentrating forces would swiftly recover the arsenal, cut off the raiders, and kill or capture them. But Brown was immovable.

Members of the attacking party expressed similar fears when Brown first explained the plan to them after they had gathered at the Kennedy farmhouse. Until then, they had believed that he intended merely to repeat on a more ambitious scale the slave-running coup executed in Missouri the previous year. Hearing the leader announce that they were to take the town, garrison the arsenal, armory, and rifle works, and hold them, the men were aghast. A majority, including Brown's three sons, protested that failure was inevitable. The dispute grew heated. "In September it nearly broke up the camp," Charles P. Tidd, a Maine lad who had shared in the Missouri raid, later testified. But the sanguine Cook, busy familiarizing himself with the town, supported the plan; Kagi accepted it, believing they would get out of the pent-up village before troops could be mobilized; and Stevens acquiesced. When Brown told the men that since a majority opposed him he would resign and they could choose another leader, this ultimatum brought them to his side. Several, however, believed they were going to certain death—and one described his own end.[6]

John Brown's whole course showed that, despite statements made by some biographers, he had given up the idea of a swift retreat to some mountain fortress. In the first place, no impregnable eyries, no deep hidden fastnesses, exist anywhere near Harper's Ferry. The district bounded by Winchester, Hagerstown, Frederick, and Fairfax is everywhere passable; it contains no steep cliffs, no chasms, no swamps, no unknown caverns; troops could move through it at will. During the Civil War they did quarter it in every direction, and stormed Maryland Heights opposite the Ferry with ease. Three expert topographical engineers, writing a dozen years later of the mountainous country of Maryland between the Potomac and Pennsylvania, stated that it, "so far from being wild and uninhabitable, contains some of the finest roads and most desirable farms in the State, much of the region being characterized by hills of moderate height whose rounded summits are covered with verdure." The two Virginia and two Maryland counties which environ Harper's Ferry were a rich grain country with

---

6 Higginson, *op. cit.*, 228, 229; Hinton, *John Brown*, 258, 259; Sanborn, *Recollections*, I, 182–184; letter by Charlestown, Virginia, correspondent in N. Y. *Weekly Tribune*, November 12, 1859.

a combined population in 1860 of one hundred twelve thousand, three hundred people. No real hiding places were available.[7]

In the second place, Brown never even made a reconnaissance of the surrounding country to familiarize himself with hidden paths and spots of refuge. He knew the road north to Chambersburg, and that was about all. And thirdly, he made no effort in advance to stock or fortify any hill area. To retreat to the Allegheny ridge, some twenty-five miles to the west, without food and water, would have been madness. Any leader contemplating a stand in some recess there would have made a cache of arms and provisions. It is significant that, just before his attack, Brown moved his main stock of weapons—to what point? Not to the hills, but to a schoolhouse about a mile from the Ferry.

Obviously, this military tyro believed that he could hold Harper's Ferry for some time. He expected to be successful in gaining widespread support, and to push forward down the Appalachian chain. If by any chance he was unsuccessful, he might retreat northward into Pennsylvania.

Two factors gave him a certain amount of confidence. He knew upper Maryland and Virginia to be full of people who disliked slavery, the citizens who later held Maryland firm in the Union and who detached West Virginia as a new State; and he believed many would flock to his aid. He was deceived by his Kansas experience into thinking that any border country was a region of sharp antagonism between slaveholding and freesoil elements. At an early date he had taken some steps to inform himself about the antislavery families of Bedford, Chambersburg, Gettysburg, and Carlisle in Pennsylvania, of the Hagerstown district in Maryland, and of the Martinsburg area in Virginia. As the second factor, he believed great numbers of slaves would flock to him. Here he was deceived by abolitionist literature, which represented the negroes as a highly intelligent body, chafing under their yoke and eager to rise. He knew that the lonely Allegheny chain was a favorite route for escaping slaves, much used by the intrepid underground leaders of rescue work. He knew that in Jamaica and Guiana runaway blacks, the Maroons, had maintained impregnable settlements in upland valleys and plateaus not for decades but for generations, treating with the Crown officers as an independent power. Abolitionist literature was full of accounts of these heroic Maroons.[8]

Once established in Harper's Ferry, he thought he could arm a large number of white and colored recruits from the arsenal. He could destroy or barricade

7 S. J. Martenet, H. F. Walling, and O. W. Gray, *New Topographical Atlas of the State of Maryland and District of Columbia* (1873), 5 ff.

8 See letter of Anne Brown (Adams), May 23, 1893, to Hinton; Hinton Papers. Brown's instructions for collecting data on antislavery families are in his letter of April 8, 1858, to his son John; Brown Papers, Ohio Arch. and Hist. Soc. For articles on the Maroons see Henry Brougham, *Edinburgh Review*, II, 376 ff., and T. W. Higginson, *Atlantic*, V, 213 ff., 549 ff.

the two bridges; taking hostages, he could use them in negotiating with attackers, and when ready, he could move forward. He later told one of the prisoners he took just why he chose Harper's Ferry: "I knew there were a great many guns there that would be of service to me, and if I could conquer Virginia, the balance of the Southern States would nearly conquer themselves, there being such a large number of slaves in them." One of his men, Jeremiah Anderson, wrote a brother late in September that they expected to win a victory at Harper's Ferry and push through Virginia and on southward, inciting the slaves to rise and carrying them forward in a growing body. When himself captured, Brown told Governor Wise that he had expected ample assistance once he put the ball in motion. From what States? asked Wise. "From more than you'd believe if I should name them all," replied Brown, "but I *expected* more from Virginia, Tennessee, and the Carolinas than from any others." [9]

Here, perhaps, lay the paranoiac flaw in John Brown's mind, the key to his type of reasoning insanity. On all subjects but one—slavery and the possibility of ending it by a sudden stroke which would provoke a broadening wave of slave uprisings as a rock thrown into a pond sends forth widening ripples—he was sane. (An admirer was later to call him the stone tossed by God into the black pool of slavery.) He talked and acted with great coherence and even acuteness; he laid ordinary plans rationally; he maintained his domination over his followers, and was later to impress Governor Wise as exceptionally clear-headed and logical. But on this special question of the readiness of slavery to crumble at a blow, his monomania, as Amos A. Lawrence termed it, or his paranoia, as a modern alienist would define it, rendered him irresponsible. This it was that made him seem to some observers increasingly speculative and impulsive, a gambler on chance; from this paranoia, too, sprang his sense of a God-given mission, in which Providence would carry him to success even through seeming failure. When his confident blow met a sharp check, he was certain to grow confused. Hence the conclusion of his ablest biographer that he seemed to be losing the power of quick, effective decisions.[10]

That his fanaticism and violence of speech on slavery had increased is unquestionable. Speaking in Kansas the previous March, he declared that his son had been shot down like a dog for no reason save that he was a free State man. The killing of Frederick Brown was certainly murder but it had not been without provocation, for he had helped to slay the five men on the Pottawatomie, and he was tending stolen horses when he was assassinated. Brown had boasted to his Cleveland audience how he had taught his young men to dispatch adherents

9 *Mason Report*, 1–12; Sanborn, *Recollections*, I, 184, 185.
10 Villard, *John Brown*, 424. Brown's Negro follower Osborne P. Anderson writes in *A Voice From Harper's Ferry*, 36, of the raid: "Capt. Brown was all activity, though I could not help thinking that at times he appeared somewhat puzzled."

of slavery, and had said that, if necessary, he would execute more of them; he would drive them into the ground like fence stakes, where they would remain permanent settlers. He felt that he was *at war* with slaveholders, and that his private war justified shootings and confiscations. To his recent Missouri raid he pinned an exaggerated significance. The fact that it had spread alarm far and wide, had sent some slaveowners fleeing into Arkansas and had led others to mount a close guard, convinced him that a stroke in some more strategic quarter might bring slavery down in ruins. He had forgotten how glad free State men were to see him leave, and how quickly peace had descended upon the Kansas-Missouri border as soon as he departed.

Not a figure out of Cromwell's time, as some have said, a warped religious fanatic; not one of the old Puritans or Covenanters, ready to harry for conscience's sake and to hold with Clarendon's hero that stone dead hath no brother. Let us say rather that he had the strength and weakness, the sincerity and cunning, of a gnarled Western pioneer who through inheritance and prolonged hardship had fallen prey to reasoning insanity. Such a man was certain to move forward relentlessly.

As September ended, the two young women went home. A late recruit arrived, F. J. Meriam of Boston, whose gift of $600 in gold to the treasury ended all financial embarrassments. The last arms were fetched in. On October 10, Kagi quitted Chambersburg for the farm. All was in readiness.

[II]

About eight o'clock on the night of Sunday, October 16, Brown ordered his troop to march upon the Ferry. Two by two, armed with a Sharps rifle and two revolvers apiece, seventeen men swung down the lonely road, while Brown himself drove a one-horse wagon with some pikes, a crowbar, and a sledge hammer. Three men were left at the farm. The moonless gloom, the chill damp air, the sombre silence of the column, broken only by the creaking of the vehicle and the rustle of dead leaves and grass underfoot, gave some of the marchers a funereal impression. As they came within sight of the town lights, nerves grew tauter. Cook and Tidd turned aside to cut the telegraph wires; the others pushed on.[11]

With a brisk rush, the force deployed across the railroad-and-wagon bridge,

11 Had Secretary of War Floyd exercised due vigilance the march would never have begun. On August 25, he had received an anonymous letter of warning dated Cincinnati, August 20, saying that Brown would invade Virginia at Harper's Ferry in a few weeks. Text of letter in *Mason Report*, 250. Its author was David J. Gue, who had received secret information; Gue, *History of Iowa*, II, 26–30. Floyd dismissed it as a hoax. The night of the attack was overcast, ending in rain. Anderson (*A Voice from Harper's Ferry*, 28 ff.) says the company "marched along as solemnly as a funeral procession."

seized the bridge watchman, and left two men as guards. The end of the Shenandoah bridge was similarly secured, and two sentinels were posted. Turning up Potomac Street, the force pinioned the watchman at the armory gate and quickly took possession of both armory and arsenal. Brown and others then hurried to the rifle works, half a mile up the Shenandoah, took possession, and placed Kagi and two privates in charge. Here another watchman was captured.

All the Federal property, including several million dollars' worth of arms and munitions, was now in John Brown's hands. His next step was to send a detachment of six men about five miles into Virginia to seize as his first hostage Colonel Lewis W. Washington, great-grandnephew of the President and a prosperous planter. That gentleman was forced to surrender a sword which Frederick the Great had reputedly given to General Washington, his carriage, wagon, and horses were taken, and four of his bewildered slaves were collected. Another farmer, John H. Allstadt, his son, and six of his Negroes were similarly aroused from sleep. The whole body were brought down to the arsenal, where the slaves were given pikes and told to guard Washington and the Allstadts. Telegraph wires had now been cut both east and west of town.

At about one o'clock in the morning, the express train from Wheeling to Baltimore arrived at Harper's Ferry, stopped, and was ready to proceed across the bridge when Conductor Phelps learned that the track was obstructed. The engineer and another employee walked forward to investigate, were fired upon, and hastily backed the train to the platform again. At this point the first bloodshed occurred. Hayward Shepherd, a free Negro working as station baggage master, went to the bridge to look for the night watchman there, was fatally wounded by Brown's men, and was carried inside the station to die. The shots, the long delay of the puffing train, the hum of the bewildered passengers (who guessed some labor trouble was afoot), the noise of the Washington-Allstadt cavalcade, and the unusual bustle about the arsenal, attracted attention. Citizens began to stir, and as dawn broke, one of them, Thomas Boerley, was also fatally shot. A number of employees, innocently entering the armory yard for the day's work, were added to the list of prisoners.

Meanwhile, John Brown was waiting for Negro and white recruits to pour in; "when I strike the bees will swarm," he had told Douglass, and Cook had given him misleading assurances of a rising. Slaves from the Maryland side were supposed to report to Owen Brown at the schoolhouse and take arms there; slaves from the Virginia side were to report to Oliver Brown at the Shenandoah bridge and Kagi at the rifle works, receiving arms from the arsenal. Had the bees swarmed, had a large-scale insurrection begun, Brown expected to establish a commanding position at the armory, holding both ends of the Potomac and Shenandoah bridges; to parley with any assailants, demanding an exchange of slaves for his hostages; and as he gained force, to go on. Only if an overwhelming force came up would he retreat northward. But he had done nothing to prepare defenses out of town, and the rapidity with which troops arrived left him utterly nonplussed.

For as day broke cold and gray, the alarm was spreading swiftly. A slow-witted physician of the town, brought out by the shot that wounded Shepherd, first attended the dying man and then waited till dawn to act. But he finally saddled a horse, roused the outlying parts of Harper's Ferry, set the Lutheran churchbell clanging, hurried a messenger to Shepherdstown, and himself rode with all speed to Charlestown. On the alarm of this tardy Paul Revere, the Jefferson Guards of Charlestown fell hastily into line with any weapons they could pick up. Meanwhile, before five o'clock that morning Brown had foolishly let the Baltimore express push on. It quickly carried news of the raid to Monocacy. Thence word was hurried to Frederick, where shouting men by about ten o'clock mustered a volunteer company into line. Farmers from all the surrounding area caught up firearms and clattered toward the Ferry. In Baltimore, the telegram which the train conductor sent from Monocacy was at first treated with incredulity. When in midmorning Garrett saw it, however, he immediately notified President Buchanan, Governor Wise, and the commander of the Maryland militia that a slave revolt, with whites assisting, was under way.

Before eleven o'clock, general firing began at Harper's Ferry, townsmen and farmers engaging the raiders. Noon saw the Jefferson Guards seizing the Potomac bridge, while a swiftly mustered volunteer company from Charlestown, accoutered with muskets, shotguns, and squirrel rifles, occupied the heights back of the Ferry, and swept down from them to capture the Shenandoah bridge. The celerity with which these farmers and villagers moved was as creditable as the skill with which they seized the key points. Brown was now trapped.

Seeing that his position was hopeless, he determined to negotiate a truce. But the first man he sent out for the purpose was taken prisoner, held for a time at the Galt House, and soon afterwards killed by the excited mob. A little later, Watson Brown and Stevens were sent out under a flag, but were promptly fired upon; Watson dragged himself back to shelter mortally wounded, while Stevens, also hurt, was taken prisoner. Early in the afternoon the rifle works on the Shenandoah were stormed by a small party. Of the little garrison, the brilliant Kagi was killed, another man mortally wounded, and the third seized.

All that day and night the alarm spread through Maryland, northern Virginia, and the District of Columbia. In Baltimore, a half-dozen militia companies were ordered under arms. A special train was assembled, thousands poured to the Camden Station, and in midafternoon it pulled out amid deafening cheers of the populace. Along the line of the B. & O., crowds were gathering to hear the news. In Martinsburg, a company formed chiefly of railway employees was hurriedly mustered. It reached Harper's Ferry about four o'clock, just after the beloved mayor of that town, Fontaine Beckham, had been killed by one of Brown's men. Deploying through the armory yard from the rear, it drove the remaining raiders, with a handful of prisoners, into the small fire-engine house. Forces from Sheperdstown were at that moment arriving on the Shenandoah side of Harper's Ferry to join the Charlestown men on the bridge. Other companies were on their way from Frederick and Winchester. As night fell, the arriving troops thronged the town. John E. Cook, of the small rear guard of raiders left in Maryland, looking down from a hilltop, saw John Brown's party closely beleaguered and under constant fire. Summoned to surrender, the bewildered and desperate Brown offered to liberate his hostages if he were allowed to escape across the Potomac bridge, but these terms were of course rejected.[12]

While the Maryland and Virginia militia thus sprang to arms, Federal troops were on their way. Nowhere was the excitement that Monday afternoon greater than in Washington. The mayor put the whole police force on duty, stationed guards on every road into the capital, and conferred with citizens who thronged his office. Before one-thirty, President Buchanan ordered three companies of artillery from Old Point Comfort to the scene of action, and then directed the ninety-odd marines at Washington Barracks to move. Garrett, learning of these measures, told the White House they were inadequate, for his information indicated that seven hundred determined whites and Negroes held the arsenal. First reports in Baltimore had put the insurrectionists at several hundred, who were gaining reinforcements from the surrounding district, and rumor magnified the figures. The President, duly impressed, held a hurried conference with Secretary Floyd, Brevet-Colonel Robert E. Lee of the Second Cavalry, and Lieutenant J. E. B. Stuart of the First Cavalry. These officers were instructed to proceed at once to Harper's Ferry, where Lee would take command. Late that night they reached the town, took charge of the newly arrived company of marines, and deployed them to strengthen the militia surrounding the engine house. Lee would have attacked at once but for fear of killing some of the hostages.

Headlines were blazing that night throughout the East. "Negro Insurrection at Harper's Ferry!" ran the typical caption. As yet the outside world did not know the identity of the leader. No dispatch published on Monday in Washington, Baltimore, or New York bore Brown's name. Instead, one Anderson or Andrews, a gray-bearded stranger, was reported in charge. Not until evening

12 This account is based on the books of Villard, Hinton, Sanborn, H. P. Wilson and R. P. Warren on John Brown; on reports in the Baltimore *Sun*, N. Y. *Herald* and *Tribune*, and Washington *Constitution;* on the *Mason Report;* and on statements by J. T. Allstadt and others in Villard Papers, Columbia Univ.

did Harper's Ferry dispatches reveal that the raiders had rendezvoused at a farm rented by Captain Brown of Kansas notoriety, and thus make it possible to spread his name in Tuesday's journals.[13]

Brown's losses during the day had been severe. His sons Oliver and Watson had been mortally wounded. The reckless ex-dragoon, A. D. Stevens, had been wounded and captured, "Captain" W. H. Leeman had been slain, and others killed or taken. The free Negro, Dangerfield Newby, had been the first of the raiders to die. He had a greater object in fighting than anyone else, for his wife and seven children were in bondage in Virginia, and feared sale farther south. "Oh, Dear Dangerfield," his wife had written, "come this fall without fail, money or no money I want to see you so much: that is one bright hope I have before me." Shot twice, he expired instantly. Cook and the rear guard, including Owen Brown, had gotten away—at least for the time being.[14]

Inside the engine house that night, pitch dark and intensely cold, Oliver Brown died in great agony; a young Canadian, Stewart Taylor, lay dead; and Watson Brown drew his last heavy breaths. Three unwounded raiders with their leader and eleven prisoners watched the hours drag by. The gaunt, haggard old man, exhausted by a day of fighting without a morsel of food, fingered the sword which the Prussian monarch had given Washington, the mocking symbol of a very different attempt at revolution. He listened impassively to the clank of arms outside. He bade Oliver to bear up and to die like a man. This long vigil in the gloomy building with its three great barred doors, the forces of the land gathering for his doom, was the Gethsemane of Brown's life. Small wonder that, momentarily giving way, he essayed a few words of lame self-justification to his hostages. "Gentlemen," he said, "if you knew of my past history you would not blame me for being here. I went to Kansas a peaceable man, and the pro-slavery people from Kentucky and Virginia hunted me down like a wolf. I lost one of my sons there." It was the last time in his life that he would take an unheroic attitude.

Lee had resolved to carry the engine house at dawn at the point of the bayonet, not firing lest he injure the hostages. At five o'clock on Tuesday morning, chill and misty, all the military companies were ordered under arms, an imposing display. The soldiers cleared spectators from the streets surrounding the government buildings, and the ninety-odd marines, who had encircled the engine house all night, were drawn up inside the arsenal enclosure. Storming parties, armed with heavy sledges, were formed. The engine house, perhaps thirty-five feet in length and thirty in depth, was a heavy brick structure with

13 Baltimore *Sun,* Washington *States,* N. Y. *Times, Herald, Tribune,* October 17, 18, 19, 1859.
14 Villard, *John Brown,* 415.

three large double doors in front, each of strong oak planking, girt with iron and studded with nails. Arched windows high above the doors afforded light but no means of ingress. Brown had barricaded and loopholed the doors, inside one of which stood a fire engine. As the sun rose, Lee beckoned Jeb Stuart to his side. A son of the Shenandoah, a West Pointer, this tall, bearded young man, not yet twenty-seven, was already an experienced Indian fighter. He was to take a note, said Lee, to the raiders. If they came out and surrendered, they would be protected from harm and handed over to the proper legal authorities. If they refused, the marines would come in and take them. Stuart was to demand an answer, yes or no; he was not to parley; if it was no, he was to leap aside, and the two storming parties, twenty-four of the biggest, strongest leathernecks at hand, would charge at a run.[15]

A moment later Stuart was at the right-hand door. It opened a crack, and the white beard and fierce troubled eyes of John Brown (whom he recognized from Kansas days) appeared. Reading the note deliberately, Brown began to talk; he would surrender only on terms that would allow his party a safe head start from pursuers. One of the men inside and perhaps others wished to give up, while several prisoners begged for Lee to parley. But cutting Brown short, Jeb Stuart leaped from the door and gave the signal by waving his cap.

Instantly the storming parties sprang forward, some men battering at the doors with sledges while others pried at them with hammers. The little garrison inside fired with carbines, the smoke wreathing through loopholes and cracks. Seeing that hammers were useless, Lieutenant Israel Green ordered a double file to attack with a heavy ladder. A few powerful efforts shattered the right-hand door at the bottom, the planks buckling upward. As the troops and spectators raised a wild yell, Green threw himself through the opening, and with marines at his heels rushed inside. Colonel Washington coolly pointed to Brown, who knelt firing, and said, "This is Ossawatomie." Two marines fell, one shot through the body and the other in the face. A general melee followed. One raider was pinned to the wall by a bayonet, and another, cowering under a fire engine, was run through; both were mortally wounded. Green aimed a blow at Brown with his light dress sword which did little harm. Then, plunging, he almost lifted him from the floor by a savage thrust which failed, as his weapon struck a belt or buckle and bent double. As the leader fell, Green beat him with the hilt until he sank unconscious. A minute later, the dead and wounded were all lying on the grass outside, while Lee gave orders for their attendance.

Within thirty-six hours after it commenced, Brown's attempt to detonate a slave revolt, enlist and arm a force of colored men, and establish a base to which hundreds of adherents could flock, had been utterly defeated. Ten of his crew

15 John W. Thomason, Jr., *Jeb Stuart*, 47-57.

had been killed or fatally injured, five were prisoners, and the others had escaped, some temporarily, some for good. He himself, less seriously hurt than was at first believed, was lodged in Charlestown jail, whither Governor Wise and others repaired to interrogate him. He had only himself to blame for the swift debacle. He had made no thorough plan of action, had hesitated at the crucial moment, and had miscalculated the time required to mobilize a sufficient force to pin him down.

In any event, however, his rash scheme would quickly have failed. One historian has suggested that he might have fared better in an area containing more slaves. This is erroneous, for in any Southern district the whites would have risen with instant power, while the blacks would have been both unwilling and unable to aid him. Another has written that if after taking the arsenal he had fled to the mountains, he could have placed his force in a position where starvation alone could have conquered them.[16] The quick efficiency of the marines shows that this is a wild overstatement. Though he could have resisted longer, his men would have been dislodged by mortar and bayonet within a few days; no mountains near Harper's Ferry were wild enough to afford safety, and the larger the body of slaves in his train the greater would have been his vulnerability —for the slaves had to be fed, and they were too ignorant and undisciplined to make fighters. Ignorant of military science, he had never learned that guerrilla bands succeed only with the help of mobility, celerity, compact unity, surprise, and numerous fit hiding places or strong points.

Is it not evident that he knew he would probably fail, but that his very failure would deepen the antislavery sentiment of the North as no success could? He had written of dying for the cause, and had told Sanborn that God had honored him with a chance for mighty and soul-satisfying rewards.[17] This much is certain: he believed that his attempt, victorious or defeated, would bring the struggle over slavery to a crisis. It would test the ripeness of the slaves for rebellion; it would show the South that at least a few Northerners were ready to die in striking at the institution; it would give antislavery men everywhere an example of desperate action. It would thus succeed even while failing. In so far as he grasped these ideas, Brown was making no mad attempt. He was quick to see the possibilities opening from Lieutenant Green's failure to kill him on the spot. Dying on the scaffold, in full national view, he would meet the end of a martyr. Except in the one respect in which systematized delusion flawed his mind, he retained a piercing vision; the foresight of a man "cool, collected, and indomitable," as Governor Wise of Virginia was soon to write.

16 Allen Johnson, *DAB*, III, 133, 134; Channing, *United States*, VI, 222.
17 Sanborn, *Recollections*, I, 150. Brown had often said to his men: "We have only one life to live, and one to die; and if we lose our lives it will perhaps do more for the cause than our lives would be worth in any other way." Owen Brown, quoted in Sanborn, 183.

[III]

The excitement and anger of the South were proportionate to its belief that many Northerners thirsted for an uprising of the slaves. Exaggerated reports of the power and ramifications of the conspiracy filled the press. Having accepted the early stories of an attack by hundreds of armed men, Virginians and Marylanders clung to an exaggerated notion of the outbreak. While Lee immediately withdrew his marines, the surrounding region remained in a state of deep apprehension. Many feared that a force of Yankee invaders—from Pennsylvania, from Ohio, from other points—was about to rescue Brown. Rumors flew about of confederate bands and clandestine shipments of arms. While citizens improvised local defense companies, scouts were sent into the mountains to hunt escaped raiders and look for other troublemakers. Strangers were eyed with suspicion and sometimes arrested. Farther South, men looked to their arms, tightened the slave patrols, and drilled the militia companies. On large plantations the discipline became stricter. The raid of twenty-two men on one Virginia town had sent a spasm of uneasiness, resentment, and precautionary zeal from the Potomac to the Gulf.

Although this alarm was largely irrational, it was not wholly so. It is true that slaves about Harper's Ferry showed no disposition to accept Brown's invitation to revolt, and that many negroes felt the warmest loyalty to their masters. *Harper's Weekly* spread on its front page a sentimental picture of a Southern planter arming his slaves to resist invasion. The Civil War was to show that amid the stress of battle slave risings were almost unknown, and practically no violence was offered the white folk by their dependents. But the South believed it was living on volcanic soil—and in one sense it was right. We cannot too often repeat that slavery was not only a labor system but a mode of racial adjustment; that the Southern majority had resolved to freeze this adjustment as it stood; and that countless Negroes secretly opposed this determination. Should news of a Northern attempt at slave liberation be diffused by the efficient grapevine telegraph, it might have a profoundly disturbing effect. Slaves might feel little impulse to rebel; they *would* feel disposed to question their status. They would feel the emotions of a prisoner who, half-resigned to his walls, suddenly catches the faint sound of men battering on the outer gates. Since the news of Brown's raid could not be stifled, it had to be met by disciplinary measures.[18]

18 Evidence of widespread restlessness among slaves in 1856, verging on revolt, is abundant. The Northern and Southern press printed numerous stories on the upheaval. Robert Bunch, British consul in Charleston, wrote in December that plans had been discovered for a great slave insurrection, with Nashville as headquarters, embracing Kentucky, Tennessee, Louisiana, and Georgia. To prevent alarm and avoid unfriendly Northern comment, Southern news-

From the hour of the raid, the South denounced it as not merely a crime involving robbery, murder, and treason, but a fearful effort to cut the ligaments of society in fifteen sovereign States.[19] Much of the North viewed it very differently. It was a crime, assuredly—but a crime with extenuating circumstances, committed by a man holding a noble purpose. A hundred journals agreed with Bryant's *Evening Post* that Brown had been driven to madness by the outrages of proslavery men on the soil of Kansas. A hundred others agreed with the New York *Tribune* that he and his men "dared and died for what they felt to be right, though in a manner which seems to us fatally wrong."

Inevitably, the trial of Brown and his associates commanded the eager attention of the whole nation, and gave him an opportunity to arouse the sympathy of millions by a display of heroic firmness and devoted self-sacrifice. From the first, he acted in the knowledge that he stood upon a great stage. Not once did he exhibit any weakness. He was questioned by bystanders when first laid on the lawn in front of the engine house; questioned again in the paymaster's office by Governor Wise, Senator J. M. Mason, Representative Vallandigham of Ohio, Jeb Stuart, and others; questioned once more at a preliminary examination in the magistrate's court of Charlestown on October 25; and then, after being indicted on the triple charge of conspiracy with Negroes to produce insurrection, murder, and treason to the Commonwealth, was brought to trial in the Circuit Court of Virginia.[20] His statements showed general consistency (we cannot be sure that apparent inconsistencies are not attributable to bad reporting) and unbroken composure.

All his words breathed conviction that whatever he had done to free slaves was right, that he deserved credit for the humane treatment of townsmen and hostages, and that he should be given the respect due a prisoner of war. At the same time, he displayed a basic confusion as to his central object. His first utterances when taken doubtless contained less rationalization of his course than those made later. To Governor Wise, Representative Vallandigham, and others

---

papers had said little, but Bunch learned that many Negroes had been executed and several whites arrested. The consul in Richmond, G. P. R. James, sent word of the same movement. He believed that it was vague and disjointed but general, extending from Delaware to Texas, and that its wide diffusion and the implication of some whites indicated a Northern origin. He, too, heard that many Negroes had been executed, and one white man had been flogged to death. Foreign Office dispatches, November, December, 1856, January, 1857.

19 Yet many Southerners found their condemnation tinged with another feeling. Edmund Ruffin wrote of Brown on October 26: "It is impossible for me not to respect his thorough devotion to his bad cause, and the undaunted courage with which he has sustained it, through all losses and hazards." MS Diary.

20 The Virginia law of treason covered the levying of war against the State, the giving of comfort to its enemies, and the establishment of any other government within its bounds, the punishment being death.

he said that he did not intend to excite a slave revolt, but did intend to gather up large bodies of slaves and set them free; he did not intend to fight, burn, or destroy, but did intend to fight off resisting Southerners. As if this did not mean insurrection and bloody warfare! He let out one statement that frankly implied his expectation of a widespread servile rebellion—his before-quoted remark to Wise that if he could conquer Virginia, the other States "would nearly conquer themselves, there being such a large number of slaves in them."

Judge Richard Parker, presiding over the Charlestown courtroom in which Brown's trial began on October 25, combined dignity with a judicial spirit. Two capable attorneys were assigned to defend the prisoner, and others came from the North to assist them. From first to last, Brown had five different lawyers at his command. Order was strictly preserved—the courthouse yard bristled with bayonets. Though Brown, who at first seemed weak and haggard, complaining that his wounds enfeebled him and impaired his hearing, asked for a brief delay, the court ordered the case to proceed forthwith. On the second day, one of the defending counsel read a letter from a citizen of Akron, stating that Brown and his family had lived in that county for years, that insanity was hereditary in their line, that his mother's sister had died insane, and that two nephews and a niece of his mother were at that moment under restraint. The raider, while admitting that his mother's family was tainted with insanity, was incensed. Raising himself from the cot on which he lay, he told the court that he regarded the move as a miserable artifice on the part of friends who ought to treat him as responsible for his actions. He believed himself of perfectly sound mind—and the court dropped the matter.

The seven-day trial, moving with efficient speed, brought out much interesting testimony. Colonel Washington declared that although Brown had complained of the mortal wounding of his son Watson under a flag of truce, he had made no threats to the prisoners and uttered no vindictive word. Another prisoner, J. A. Brua, said that once only during the night vigil had Brown seemed to show temper. Allstadt described the listlessness and indifference of the Negroes, passive pawns in the game played for their future. He believed that in the final struggle it was Brown's shot which had killed a marine, while Lieutenant Green thought that this bullet had gone wild.[21] Conductor Phelps of the midnight express train and Armistead Ball, master machinist at the arsenal, testified that the leader had told them that his object was to free slaves and destroy slavery, not to hurt the whites. According to Ball, Brown had spoken of his determination to seize the arms and munitions of the government to enable the negroes to defend themselves against their masters, and had called on the officers

21 Full testimony on this point in N. Y. *Weekly Tribune*, November 5, 1859.

of the armory to give up their stored weapons. A. M. Kitzmiller, in charge of the arsenal when it was attacked, heard the raider say that his object was to free the slaves and, if necessary, fight the proslavery men for that purpose.

From this and other evidence it was plain that Brown had been both deluded and confused. He had clung to the delusion that large numbers of slaves would peacefully flock to his standard, that many antislavery whites in western Maryland and Virginia would come to his aid, and that Southerners would let themselves be kept at bay by his imposing force and by fears for the safety of his hostages. He had held the confused idea that war is not war when waged against a bad institution, that an attack is not an attack when called a defensive action, and that wholesale slave liberation could be distinguished from wholesale slave insurrection. On slavery his mind was distorted. Yet throughout the trial he gave every impression of composure, shrewdness, and balance. Lying wrapped in a blanket, his eyes often closed, from time to time he started up, grim as a cornered wolf, to snap out a sharp question or deliver a curt, dry speech. He never lost his coolness, never offered an apology, and was defiant only when deeply aroused, manifesting in general a civil, courteous demeanor. When questioned he spoke frankly, and when granted small favors expressed his gratitude.[22] He interrupted the proceedings several times, but only to speak to important points. Given the unusual privilege of helping cross-examine witnesses, he used it sagaciously.

No one could deny that the prisoner received a thoroughly fair trial. Of the three Northern counsel, George H. Hoyt of Athol, Massachusetts, who arrived the third day, took the leading place. When defense attorneys moved that the prosecution be confined to one of the three counts, Judge Parker's adverse ruling was in accordance with legal procedure, and was later upheld by the Virginia Court of Appeals. On the murder charge, Brown's counsel tried to show that he had been free from malice aforethought and had killed only in self-defense. On the treason charge, they argued that since he had never sworn allegiance to the Commonwealth of Virginia, he could not be held guilty of treasonable action. On the charge of fomenting insurrection, they declared that he had merely abducted slaves, a very different matter. Of the two prosecuting attorneys, only one counted. Andrew Hunter, an able, aggressive Virginian of distinguished bearing, pushed his case with relentless energy, fighting for every possible advantage. Sharing the exasperation of the Southern people, he called for justice at double-quick time, expressed fear that the prisoner Aaron Stevens, who had suffered terrible wounds, might die before he could be hanged, and was disappointed at the end when the case had to be continued over Sunday.

22 *Harper's Weekly*, November 12, 1859.

Before pronouncing judgment on November 2, Judge Parker (the jury having held Brown guilty on all three counts) asked the prisoner if he had anything to say. This was Brown's culminating opportunity. He had seized every chance of protesting that he had merely done the will of God, obeying the Biblical injunction to remember them that are in bonds as bound with them. Now, rising slowly and speaking with distinct utterance, he addressed himself not so much to the court as to a vast unseen audience beyond. In a five-minute discourse he made a truly noble statement:

I see a book kissed, which I suppose to be the Bible, or at least the New Testament, which teaches me that all things whatsoever that men should do to me, I should do even so to them. . . . I endeavored to act up to that instruction. I say I am yet too young to understand that God is any respecter of persons. I believe that to have interfered as I have done, as I have always freely admitted I have done, in behalf of his despised poor, I did no wrong, but right. Now, if it is deemed necessary that I should forfeit my life for the furtherance of the ends of justice, and mingle my blood further with the blood of my children and with the blood of millions in this slave country whose rights are disregarded by wicked, cruel, and unjust enactments, I say, let it be done.

He also made three statements as to his purposes: that he had intended only to carry slaves off to Canada, that he had not designed any slave insurrection or bloodshed, and that he had never tried to induce men to join him, merely accepting them as volunteers.

Millions in the North took these words at their face value. Emerson was later to compare Brown's speech with Lincoln's Gettysburg Address. A modern biographer has asserted that it must forever remain on the list of great American utterances.[23] The fact was, however, that all three statements contravened the truth. Brown had not intended quietly to push north with a small group of slaves; he had intended to induce large bodies of slaves to join him, to arm them, to push south, to organize them into a state, if possible, and to make this state impregnable. His constitution for his proposed state of liberated slaves could not be explained away. His Missouri raid had not been bloodless, for one man had been slain; and this Virginia undertaking was not simply a larger raid for spiriting slaves northward—it was an entirely different kind of enterprise. Had he intended to repeat his Missouri venture he would have fled with his handful of captured slaves at dawn on Monday. Finally, his assertion that all his men had joined of their own accord was false. He had recruited most of them with various inducements, among them the chance of station and rewards in his provi-

23 Emerson, *Works* (Concord ed.), VIII, 125. Emerson's two addresses on Brown are more admirable as expressions of his idealism than as accurate essays. Calling Brown the founder of liberty in Kansas, he contributed mightily to the legend of the man. Villard's statement (*John Brown*, 497) is more just. Brown's parting words will be remembered along with Vanzetti's, and for much the same reasons.

sional government; he had led them (largely impulsive, pliable young fellows) from step to step; and he had finally precipitated them into criminal acts from which they would originally have shrunk.[24]

The full measure of Brown's distortion of truth can be illustrated by comparing his courtroom appeal with what he had privately told Frederick Douglass early in 1858. He denounced slavery "in look and language fierce and bitter," writes Douglass; he "thought that slaveholders had forfeited the right to live"; he believed that neither moral suasion nor political action would ever abolish the system. While he did not wish an insurrection, "his plan did contemplate the creating of an armed force, which should act in the very heart of the South." He was "not averse to the shedding of blood"; he thought that the practice of carrying arms would give colored people a sense of their manhood; they must "fight for their freedom" in order to gain self-respect. When Douglass suggested that the slaveholders might be converted, he angrily replied that these proud folk "would never be induced to give up their slaves, until they felt a big stick about their heads." Nearly three weeks after his courtroom statement, he wrote a letter to the public prosecutor to explain the discrepancy between a statement he had made in the paymaster's office that he did not intend to carry off slaves and free them, and his subsequent statement that his whole object was to carry off slaves. The latter assertion was true, he wrote, but required more explanation. He meant to place the slaves in a condition to defend their liberties, if they would, but not to run them out of the slave States. That is, he meant to carry them into his new state. But this brings us back again to the fact that what Brown called defensive fighting would have seemed to any slaveholding community an aggressive operation; and that to organize liberated slaves in some grand defensive body was essentially to take them out of the slave States.

John Brown, no doubt partly self-deluded, was striking the pose of a blameless as well as heroic figure for the benefit of his unseen audience of Northern millions. If he could not be the Spartacus of a new freedmen's state, he could be the martyred Stephen of a new gospel. Given a month in prison between sentence and execution, he made the most of it in eloquent letters and interviews. He *was* heroic—but not blameless.

24 Brown contradicted himself on several points in his last weeks. He insisted that he did not value the armory weapons, having plenty of his own. But Armistead Ball, master machinist at the Ferry, and one of Brown's prisoners, testified that Brown had said he was determined to seize the arms of the government to enable the slaves to defend themselves, and had called on him and others to deliver up the government stores. At his first examination Brown was asked respecting the slaves: "Your intention was to carry them off and free them?" He replied: "Not at all." Later he insisted that he *did* mean to carry them off. As a commentary on his statement that his followers had come to him voluntarily, see his daughter Anne's admission: "Father had hard work to induce a few men who did follow him to go there." Undated MS. Hinton Papers. But of the man's fundamental sincerity in wishing to help the poor and oppressed there is no question whatever.

[IV]

Was putting him to death expedient? Reflective men, North and South, saw that the consequences of making him a martyr might be highly unfortunate for the Union. Numerous letters fell upon Governor Wise's desk begging him on humanitarian grounds to spare Brown's life, and with them came many which urged him to deny the abolitionists any opportunity to canonize a saint. Amos A. Lawrence, who now repented the aid he had given Brown, advised the governor to deal leniently with the man. "From his blood would spring an army of martyrs, all eager to die in the cause of human liberty." Following the trial, Lawrence wrote "Governor" Robinson of Kansas: "If they hang old Brown, Virginia will be a free State sooner than they expect." [25] Mayor Fernando Wood of New York informed Wise that his firmness was highly applauded. "Now, my friend, dare you do a bold thing, and 'temper justice with mercy'? Have you nerve enough to send Brown to the State Prison instead of hanging him? Brown is looked upon here as the mere crazy or foolhardy emissary of other men. Circumstances create a sympathy for him even with the most ultra friends of the South."

Many antislavery leaders, contrariwise, were eager for a scaffold scene which they could exploit with revivalist fervor. While the trial proceeded, Henry Ward Beecher admonished his flock not to pray for Brown's release. "Let Virginia make him a martyr. . . . His soul was noble; his work miserable. But a cord and gibbet would redeem all that, and round up Brown's failure with a heroic success." [26]

Quite aware of the perils of the situation, knowing as well as anybody that "glorious is the martyr's gore," Wise also knew that he could assign plausible grounds for his staying a death sentence in the evidence of Brown's dementia. The traits the leader exhibited at the trial—his intense egotism, his belief in his providential mission, his display of a persecution complex when he denounced his Virginia attorneys, his distortions of fact—pointed to the "monomania," the reasoning insanity, of which various observers had accused him. His behavior in Kansas pointed as strongly to an irrational element in his nature. Amos Lawrence gave the governor his emphatic conviction: "Brown is a Puritan whose mind has become disordered by hardship and illness." John Brown's brother, Jeremiah, certified in writing that after talking with John about two years earlier, "I had no doubt he had become insane upon the subject of slavery, and gave him to understand this was my opinion of him." Jeremiah had such

25 William Lawrence, *Amos A. Lawrence*, 134, 135.
26 Warren, *John Brown*, 415–417.

"knowledge of him, when once intensely absorbed in any one subject," as made him sure that the Harper's Ferry raid was an insane act. We have spoken of the similar affidavits by reputable, informed people, chiefly relatives and former neighbors. Brown's attorney, Hoyt, collected no fewer than nineteen.[27]

But Virginia paid the penalty in this hour for having elected a hopelessly erratic governor. Most States now and then put men devoid of judgment into their gubernatorial chairs; but they seldom suffer as the Old Dominion was to do from its error in electing the learned, the patrician, the eloquent, and the brilliant fool (a man, writes Forney, who "rioted in the eccentricity of his genius") now directing her affairs. Wise's folly combined with Brown's mania to make the raid a great turning point in American history. On one side, he magnified the event to whip up excitement all over the South, firing men's fears and tempers. On the other, he insisted upon an execution which gave the North an antislavery martyr.[28]

Wise, believing it just possible that 1860 might see him elected President, did his utmost to dramatize both the raid and his own dauntless resourcefulness in meeting it. He helped give currency to alarmist reports of fresh Northern invasions. He repeatedly mobilized bodies of militia, marching and countermarching troops to sustain the excitement. He did everything to foment a legend that the raid sprang from a portentous Northern conspiracy, probably with organized Republican support behind it, and offered a dire threat to the South. At the same time, he gave the Northern legend of martyrdom its opportunity to expand into a pillar of fire by night and of smoke by day. Confinement of Brown in an asylum for the criminal insane would have satisfied the demands of justice, protected public safety, and prevented any idealization of the man and his offense. Instead, Wise placed him on a pedestal for the ages.

The governor momentarily wavered. Eight days after sentence was pronounced he instructed Dr. Stribling, the expert superintendent of the State

27 Brown's attorney, Hoyt, visiting Washington, talked with Montgomery Blair, who told him that he thought Governor Wise would probably welcome a demonstration of Brown's insanity. An article which had appeared in the Richmond *Inquirer* looked to Blair like an inspired invitation for affidavits. At once Hoyt went on to Ohio to see what could be gathered up in the shape of statements. Blair was positive that Senator Mason and other fire-eaters would make every effort to use the affair to break up the Union, and was anxious to block their schemes. See letters of Hoyt November 14, 16, 1859, to J. W. L. Barnes, Hinton Papers.

28 One measure of Wise's folly is found in his statement of 1856 that, if Frémont were elected, he would arm and equip 50,000 men the next morning ready for revolution. L. G. Tyler, *Life and Times of the Tylers*, II, 523. Another is found in his belief that "a preparation of the Southern States in full panoply of arms," and "a prompt, bold, defiant, armed attitude," in 1860–61, "would have prevented war." Wise, *Seven Decades*, 250. Wise declared in his message to the legislature on December 5, 1859, that imprisonment would have been martyrdom no less than hanging; that Brown's state of health would have been heralded weekly from the jail, visitors would have come with affected reverence to see him, and the work of his hands would have been sought as holy relics. To this the answer, as Villard states (pp. 505, 506), is that prison rules could have been adopted to block publicity and visits.

lunatic asylum at Staunton, to examine Brown and report before the date of execution. Then, on reflection, he cancelled the order. For one reason, before Hoyt's affidavits reached him the Court of Appeals had confirmed the sentence, thus closing the door to a legal presentation of the plea of insanity. For another, Wise convinced himself that the prisoner was exceptionally quick, logical, composed, and shrewd mentally. "Did I believe him insane," the governor told a caller just before the execution, "if I could even entertain a rational doubt of his perfect sanity, I would stay his execution even at this hour. All Virginia should not prevent me. I would sooner sever this arm at the shoulder than permit his execution. But I have no such belief, no such doubt." It can be said that Wise did not have the benefit of modern knowledge of mental derangement. It can also be said that an important legal precedent would have supported him in refusing to treat Brown as insane. In 1843, the private secretary of Sir Robert Peel had been murdered by a paranoiac named McNaghten. The appeal judges, passing on McNaghten, made a famous deliverance in the House of Lords on criminal responsibility in this type of insanity. They held that since the man might be regarded as quite sane except on the subject of his "monomania," he should be held accountable for his acts. This was precisely the line Wise followed in deciding that Brown knew the quality of his acts and should therefore be hanged. Modern science, however, holds that the paranoiac is not partially but wholly insane and should be so treated. And on grounds of mere expediency, as the New York *Journal of Commerce* counselled, Wise should have seized the opportunity of depriving the antislavery fanatic of the martyrdom for which he longed.[29]

As John Bigelow wrote, it was much easier to put John Brown upon a scaffold than to get him down again.

[V]

The fact that skillful management by the Virginia authorities might have reduced John Brown's attempt to the level of a reckless, crazy adventure was demonstrated by the conduct of the Northern conspirators abetting him. Almost

---

29 One fiery Virginian, Roger A. Pryor, believed that imprisonment would have been the wiser course. Wise's statements show that he was not (as some have said) influenced by public clamor in his decision. Yet plenty of public clamor there was. "The miserable old traitor and murderer belongs to the gallows," declared the Richmond *Whig*. That Wise had no qualifications for passing on Brown's sanity is clear. Writes Dr. E. H. Williams in *The Doctor in Court*, p. 100: "Insanity is a complex disease, the most difficult of all diseases to understand; so much so that even a regular medical education simply lays foundation knowledge for special study of this condition. The amount of knowledge about it that any layman can acquire, even from the Bench, is limited." Yet Wise made his judgment on the basis of some brief conversations.

with one accord they broke for cover. The pusillanimous behavior of Samuel G. Howe, Gerrit Smith, and others placed them in lamentable contrast to the iron strength of their champion. They had hoped for some easy, resounding success; instead, when news came of the killing of innocent men, the seizure of Federal property, and the arming of slaves, all terminating in surrender, they realized that they faced hard penalties. The rich Gerrit Smith, enjoying the role of abolitionist so long as it meant simply the expenditure of money, time, and talk to gain applause, had never done anything that called for Garrisonian courage. Now, as clamor broke out in the press, he fell into a panic, hastily burned all letters bearing on Brown's plans, sent his son-in-law to Boston and Ohio to destroy evidence there, talked wildly of impending ruin, and suffered a physical and nervous collapse. He was well past sixty. Sleepless nights of excitement and fear culminated in temporary insanity. Five days after Brown's trial ended he was removed to the State asylum at Utica, where he stayed nearly two months. When discharged, he was too ill to appear before any investigating committee, but not to pour out lying denials of his connection with any conspiracy.[30]

The equally terror-stricken Howe fled to Canada, accompanied by the half-reluctant George Stearns. According to Mrs. Stearns, Howe was "possessed with a dread that threatened to overwhelm his reason"; he came to Stearns, declared he would go insane if they did not both go North at once, and persuaded his friend to take care of him. "How well do I remember his agitation, walking up and down the room," writes Mrs. Stearns, who calls her husband's consent an act of heroic self-abnegation.[31] Howe had given Brown a Smith & Wesson revolver to use in fighting.[32] Frank Sanborn heard with alarm that a number of his letters had been captured at the Kennedy farm. He instantly destroyed compromising papers, and picking up Stearns at Medford, drove into Boston to consult the abolitionist lawyer John A. Andrew. Andrew told them they might be suddenly arrested and extradited to Virginia. Late the next day Sanborn was in Quebec, where he stayed for a week. When he heard that Andrew had revised his opinion, and believed that if indicted he would be tried in Massachusetts, he returned to Concord—only to make a new flight to Canada some weeks later, when the United States Senate voted his arrest. By November 10, three weeks before the date set for the execution, he was urging that something be done (by other men) to effect Brown's escape.

Edwin Morton, who as Sanborn's classmate and Gerrit Smith's household companion knew the inside of the conspiracy, hastily took refuge in England. Frederick Douglass, after seeing to the concealment of his papers, hurried by

30 Harlow, *Gerrit Smith*, 421–425.
31 Undated MS in Hinton Papers.
32 Sanborn, *Recollections*, I, 182.

way of Canada to the same haven. It can be said in his behalf that he had never believed in the Harper's Ferry raid, that he had for some time intended an English trip, and that he sent a letter to a Rochester newspaper with a frank confession: "I have always been more distinguished for running than fighting, and tried by the Harper's-Ferry-Insurrection test, I am most miserably deficient in courage." The only important conspirator who stood his ground was Thomas Wentworth Higginson. Rejoicing in his mistaken view that Harper's Ferry was the most formidable slave insurrection in our history, this militant minister remained in Worcester, joining Wendell Phillips, John A. Andrew, and others in providing counsel for Brown.[33]

An inglorious record! Several conspirators, notably the religious Gerrit Smith, must have felt that a heavy responsibility for the death of innocent men at Harper's Ferry lay on their souls, but none admitted it. Not one, except Higginson, had the manliness to express regret that the conspirators were not at Brown's side when he fought. Nor were the attempts of these safe-distance helpers to organize Brown's rescue at all creditable. Hoyt, sent from Boston ostensibly as Brown's lawyer, was actually a spy and plotter. One of his objects was to get hold of the raider's papers lest they incriminate the Yankee group. He made a nervous search for these "relics," and tried to snatch them and other property of Brown's from under the eyes of the Virginia authorities—unavailingly as regarded the "records." He also tried to arrange a jail delivery. This rescue would have involved more bloodshed, including the possible slaying or wounding of the sheriff and jailor, both kindly, humane men.[34] Brown himself had the good sense to reject the scheme. My death, he declared again and again, is worth infinitely more for the cause than my life. It was with good reason that Hoyt was compelled to leave Charlestown by the excited citizens of that place. Going to Washington, he characteristically urged his friends to stir up a newspaper clamor over his expulsion.

[VI]

In his last weeks John Brown rose to a height of moral grandeur which went far toward redeeming his name from the terrible blots which he had placed upon it. Caught up by exaltation of spirit in his confidence of a vast posthumous influence, he displayed neither grief for the two sons killed at his side nor fear of approaching death. Moving as a man who fulfilled a mighty destiny, he impressed all observers by his unshaken courage and serene equanimity. He believed that he had done right; he felt certain that God reigned and would yet

33 *Letters and Journals of T. W. Higginson*, 84–88.
34 George H. Hoyt, November 11, 13, 14, 16, etc., to Barnes *et al.*; Hinton Papers.

overmaster all opposition to his divine decrees. He realized that he was now holding the center of the stage in a historic scene watched by the nation and millions overseas. "Already," he wrote his family during the trial, "dear friends at a distance with kindly sympathy are cheering me with the assurance that *posterity* at least will do me justice." [35]

The Virginia authorities generously permitted him to write anyone he pleased, and he displayed in his letters a spiritual power, couched in a style as simple and forcible as Bunyan's, which was destined to impress multitudes of readers. His only suffering was lest his kindred should feel humiliated by his scaffold death. The burden of his message, the same in all his epistles, may be summed up in two sentences addressed to his wife. "I will say here that the sacrifices *you;* and I, have been called to make in behalf of the *cause we love,* the *cause of God; and of humanity*: do not seem to me as at all too great. I have been *whipt* as the saying *is*; but I am sure I can recover all the lost capital occasioned by that disaster; by only hanging a few moments by the neck; and I feel quite determined to make the utmost possible out of a defeat." [36] Remembering his ancestor Peter Brown, who came over in the *Mayflower*, and his grandfather, who died in the Revolution, he was anxious to display a fortitude worthy of his sires. On his last Sunday he wrote his sisters that he had experienced a perfect consolation and peace. In great part, beyond doubt, this arose from a belief that his death would aid "the crushed Millions who 'have no comforters.' " [37]

At eleven o'clock on the morning of December 2, a bright, warm day, Brown was brought out of his Charlestown jail. Drawn up on the street were the glittering ranks of six companies of Virginia infantry and a troop of horse, commanded by Major-General W. B. Taliaferro with his entire staff. At the door stood an open wagon with a pine box containing a heavy oak coffin. Brown climbed into the vehicle, seated himself beside his jailor on the box, and surveyed the soldiery with interest. Closely flanked by two files of riflemen, the wagon creaked slowly off to the forty-acre field chosen for the execution. Here were additional troops, massed in a hollow square with cannon commanding the scaffold, a precaution against any attempt at rescue. From the field, the beautiful undulating country and distant Blue Ridge were in full view, the

35 Villard, *John Brown*, 537. As early as November 24, the New York *Independent* was urging that special ceremonies be held all over the East to make the day of the execution memorable. "What is it that will be hung up on the gallows in the gaze of all men?" it asked. "Not John Brown, but Slavery!"

36 *Ibid.*, 540.

37 November 22, 1859, to Mary and Martha Brown; Brown Papers, Chicago Hist. Soc. Brown on the morning of his execution handed a jail guard his famous prophecy, now also in the Chicago Hist. Soc. It announced: "I John Brown am now quite *certain* that the crimes of this *guilty land:* will never be purged *away;* but with Blood. I had *as I now think:* vainly flattered myself that without *very much* bloodshed; it might be done."

mountain crests bright in the sun, while through several lower valleys the night mists were still pouring like slow silvery torrents. Clusters of spectators were to be seen on various eminences about the grounds. When Brown reached the spot, he inquired why none but the military were allowed there, saying: "I am sorry citizens have been kept out."

He had refused to permit any minister who approved slavery to accompany him to the gallows, and no friend was allowed at his side. Several notable figures were scattered through the concourse. One, accompanying the detachment of cadets from the Virginia Military Institute, brave in their uniforms of gray trousers and red flannel shirts, was Professor Thomas J. Jackson; one, a militia-man from Richmond, was the actor John Wilkes Booth; one, a newspaper editor in the same city, was a son of Governor Wise who would soon lay down his life on the battlefield. Another, given place among the V.M.I. corps, and carrying his musket with soldierly erectness, was the agricultural reformer and disunionist agitator Edmund Ruffin. Fixing his eyes intently on the doomed man, Ruffin was impressed by his firmness, dignity, and impassive silence.[38]

The prisoner climbed the scaffold with readiness and even alacrity, the first man on its platform. Shaking hands with the jailor and sheriff, he bade them farewell, and stood erect as a large hood of white linen, with an aperture for the halter, was drawn over his head. The rope was knotted about his neck. When the jailor asked him to step on the trap, he replied, "You must lead me—I cannot see," and was properly placed. All seemed ready. Then occurred an awful delay as the last-arriving troops marched and countermarched to take their appointed places. It was a striking sight, as eight long minutes ticked away, to see the old man straight and unmoving on the trap, his dark clothing in contrast with his blood-red slippers and the long white hood. To him, as to onlookers, those minutes must have seemed an age. The jailor asked if he were tired. "No, not tired," came the answer, "but don't keep me waiting longer than is necessary." Then, as the soldiery came to a stand, the sheriff brought his hatchet down upon the rope sustaining the trap. In the preternatural stillness which had settled upon the field, the screech of the hinges and thud of falling planks struck heavily on all ears.

The voice of Colonel J. T. L. Preston of the V.M.I. rang out: "So perish all such enemies of Virginia! All such enemies of the Union! All foes of the human race!"

38 Ruffin, MS Diary, December 2, 1859; letter of December 4, 1859, Ruffin Papers, Univ. of N. C. An important duty of the V.M.I. cadets was to guard the arsenal at Lexington. Their vigilance had been increased when in December, 1856, a request was received from Buchan, about twenty-five miles away, for arms to meet an anticipated slave revolt. W. Couper, *One Hundred Years at V.M.I.*, I, 318, 319.

4

"Drifting into Destruction"

WHILE John Brown was being hanged; while the noonday sun shone down upon the far-sweeping Blue Ridge, the two winding rivers, the immobile lines of riflemen and horse, and the grim gallows; while the commanding officer proclaimed that the majesty of Virginia law had been satisfied, a mounting emotion swept the whole land from St. Croix to the Florida keys. Next day, the telegraph told how deep an imprint Brown's act and fate had laid upon the feeling of millions.

In many Northern communities, such as the Concord of Franklin Pierce and the Chicago of Douglas, bells were tolled at the hour of execution; in some, minute guns were fired; in still others, crowded public meetings were held. In Philadelphia, a gathering offered prayers for Brown, heard the Rev. W. H. Furness read letters from him, and applauded a speech by Lucretia Mott. In New York, Dr. George B. Cheever, author of *God Against Slavery*, addressed an audience at his Church of the Pilgrims. A crowd filling Tremont Temple in Boston heard a discourse by William Lloyd Garrison. In Albany, while a hundred guns were fired, meetings continued all afternoon and evening; in Syracuse, the city hall was packed with citizens who met for three hours of speechmaking; in Cleveland, buildings were hung with black, and a leading minister spoke to five thousand people. Newspapers everywhere appeared in augmented editions.[1]

Had Wise acted foolishly in making a martyr? He must have been prepared for the instant voice of the abolitionists. Emerson termed Brown a new saint in the calendar; Thoreau described him as an angel of light; Longfellow, on the day of execution, entered in his diary, "The date of a new revolution, quite as much needed as the old one." Dr. Cheever's sermon the following Sunday treated Brown as an incarnation of God's protest against slavery. But the significant fact

---

[1] In Oberlin citizens erected a monument to three negroes: Lewis Leary, killed in following Brown, and Shields Green and John Copeland, who had been hanged. Copeland's letters to his family made a great impression in the North. He would rather die a rebel than live a slave, he declared, and hoped his name might be preserved with that of Crispus Attucks. "Believe me when I tell you, that though shut up in prison and under sentence of death, I have spent some very happy hours here." Hinton Papers.

was that men whose opinions fell far short of abolitionism spoke in similar terms. Wrote William Cullen Bryant: "History, forgetting the errors of his judgment in the contemplation of his unfaltering courage, of his dignified and manly deportment in the face of death, and of the nobleness of his aims, will record his name among those of its martyrs and heroes." Young William Dean Howells, writing his father from the capital of Ohio, predicted for the raider a great place in history: "Brown has become an idea, a thousand times purer and better and loftier than the Republican idea." Charles Eliot Norton, explaining to an English friend how the bitterness of the Virginia press, the hurry of the trial, the noble manliness of Brown under condemnation, his speech, his letters from prison, the visit from his wife, and, at last, his death, had wrought up popular emotion to the highest pitch, predicted that it would not die away: [2]

I have seen nothing like it. We get up excitements easily enough . . . ; but this was different. The heart of the people was fairly reached, and an impression has been made upon it which will be permanent and produce results long hence. . . . The events of this last month or two (including under the word events the impression made by Brown's character) have done more to confirm the opposition to slavery at the North . . . than anything which has ever happened before, than all the antislavery tracts and novels that ever were written.

A great legend had been created in the North; a legend that was to place its mark on political thought, influence multitudes at the ballot box, and within two years send armies into battle singing "John Brown's Body." In the aura of that legend the real man was transfigured, and his crimes were palliated by his favorite text: "Without the shedding of blood there is no remission of sins." To be sure, conservative men in thousands denounced his raid. Washington Hunt termed it an infernal performance; Edward Everett confessed himself disgusted and alarmed; Richard Henry Dana, Jr., spoke of the man's insanity. Even Henry Wilson wrote that he knew of no Republican who did not condemn the John Brown blow, or at least regret it. Whittier, as a non-resistant Quaker, a believer in moral warfare alone, of course deplored such violence. Yet most Northerners believed that the man's character was noble, that his errors were those of a fanatic, and that if his act condemned himself, it also condemned slavery. It is the heaviest blow yet struck against the institution, said some; it brings the end of slavery ten years nearer, said others.[3]

Within a few weeks, Brown was being canonized. In Kansas, the *Herald of Freedom* disgustedly commented that his conduct in the Territory was being gilded and garlanded, his murders on the Pottawatomie were being praised, and his unreal "victories" over proslavery men were being grossly exaggerated;

2 Mildred Howells, *Life in Letters of W. D. Howells*, I, 26; Norton, *Letters*, I, 197, 198.
3 Winthrop Papers, November 13, February 8, 1860.

that, in short, his erratic and often vicious course was being treated as splendid. In the East, the most powerful of editors wrote that though his acts were lawless, they were not really criminal. The essence of crime, Greeley argued, is selfish gratification; but Brown had sacrificed his life and those of his sons to benefit a despised race and deliver from bitter degradation those whom he had never seen. This was also the verdict of the Springfield *Republican.*

"We can conceive of no event," it remarked, "that could so deepen the moral hostility of the people of the free states to slavery as this execution. This is not because the acts of Brown are generally approved, for they are not. It is because the nature and spirit of the man are seen to be great and noble. . . . His death will be the result of his own folly, to be sure, but that will not prevent his being considered a martyr to his hatred of oppression, and all who sympathize with him in that sentiment will find their hatred grow stronger." [4]

Swiftly the legend grew. Lithographed portraits were soon circulated all over the North. One weekly magazine gave its subscribers free copies of a large nine-color chromo depicting five of the most crucial scenes in Brown's life. [5] James Redpath hurried a popular and highly mendacious biography through the press, and compiled a five-hundred-and-fourteen-page volume of the better speeches, poems, and other effusions following Brown's death (*Echoes of Harper's Ferry*), which sold widely at $1.25 a copy. [6] Within six months, more than $6,000 was raised by popular subscription for Brown's family. After the burial of the body at North Elba, New York, where Wendell Phillips spoke eloquently, his grave became an object of pilgrimage. On the next Independence Day, nearly a thousand people assembled there to hear speakers reaffirm Brown's principles. [7] His deed had caught the attention of Europe. Britons paid their tribute, and Victor Hugo proposed an epitaph: "Pro Christo sicut Christus."

For many, a great movement of the age had found in Brown its Arnold of Winkelried, its Hampden, its Nathan Hale—a more spotted hero than these but one as ruggedly devoted. To abolitionists, to many freesoilers, and to radicals of all types, countries, and future times, his was now a name which raised spirits

4 *Herald of Freedom,* December 15-30; N. Y. *Weekly Tribune,* December 3, 1859; Merriam, *Bowles,* I, 252, 253.

5 *The Philadelphia Weekly;* critical of Brown in general effect.

6 Redpath was assisted in writing his biography by Richard J. Hinton, who had lived in Kansas, and who later produced a superior biography himself. The book was being advertised before Brown's execution and quickly sold thirty-five thousand copies. It outrageously falsified the Kansas story, declaring that Brown had nothing to do with the Pottawatomie murders, and treating him as one of the liberators of Kansas. Until F. B. Sanborn issued his equally distorted *Life and Letters of John Brown* in 1885, Redpath's book was the chief vehicle of the Brown legend, which was more fable than truth. Three British publishers brought out editions.

7 Thaddeus Hyatt, N. Y. *Tribune,* July 28, 1860.

from the vasty deep.[8] Like Cranmer and Algernon Sidney, men said, he had been executed because he embodied a sublime idea. Nor should we forget that to another group, destined to grow important, his services were unforgettable— the Negroes. When his remains reached Philadelphia on the way north, the city

JOHN BROWN

PAR

VICTOR HUGO

Oh! va, nous te ferons de belles funérailles!
V. H.

PARIS

E. DENTU
Éditeur
PALAIS-ROYAL, GALERIE D'ORLÉANS.

DUSACQ ET Cⁱᵉ
Éditeurs
RUE DE LA VICTOIRE, 46

1861

Victor Hugo's Tribute to John Brown Contained an Imaginative Sketch of the Execution by the Poet.

was astonished to see the station choked by a spontaneous outpouring of free colored people, poor, meanly clad, and ignorant, but showing the deepest emotion and frantically eager to lay their tributes on his coffin.

8 In 1948 the author, after lecturing to a group of German editors, chatted with them about American history. Did they know the name of Charles Sumner? Nein. Had they ever heard of William H. Seward? Nein. Of Stephen A. Douglas? They were doubtful. Of John Brown? "Oh, ja! ja!" they exclaimed with eager smiles; his name was famous.

[I]

It was just as inevitable that a very different legend of John Brown should spring up in the South. The bitter resentment aroused by his raid, felt by slave-holders and slaveless alike, embraced all Northerners suspected of being his helpers and abettors.

Suspicion fell not merely upon Gerrit Smith, Higginson, and other actual conspirators, but upon numerous Northern politicians. A Virginian advertised in the Richmond *Whig* that he would be one of a hundred men to pay $10,000 for the delivery of Joshua Giddings dead, or half that sum for his head.[9] At first, many Southerners were reluctant to believe that any but the more malignant abolitionists would express sympathy for treason, servile insurrection, and murder. Then, when they learned that Emerson, Longfellow, and Bryant had penned panegyrics of their assailant, that leading newspapers and hundreds of ministers were apotheosizing him, their tempers hardened. An observant young Tennesseean, John W. Burgess, found that a revolution in sentiment occurred during the month after the raid. The tolling of Northern bells and half-staffing of Northern flags for Brown's execution were accepted as evidence of a wicked desire to destroy the South. Governor Wise's son noted the same change in Virginia. People of the Old Dominion began to look upon the Yankees as men who hated them, who were willing to see them assassinated at midnight by their own slaves and who were ready to support still more formidable invasions of Southern soil.[10]

The activities of Wise in giving credence to wild rumors of fresh Northern invasions, in deploying large bodies of militia, and in temporarily suspending travel on certain railways, had done much to whip up an artificial antagonism. John Minor Botts condemned his policy in scathing language. It had struck blows which cracked the fabric of the Union, he wrote. "Whether designed or not, it has exasperated and frenzied the public mind—it has begotten an ill-feeling, antipathy, and hostility between members of the same political community, that every good man and patriot must deprecate, and that it becomes

9 That is more than my head is worth, said Giddings, who added that he would let the Virginians have it at that quotation—after he was through with it. He at once added a lecture on Brown to his repertory. Joshua Giddings to his children, November 9, 25, 1859; Giddings Papers.
10 Burgess, *Civil War and Constitution*, I, 36; John S. Wise, *End of an Era*, 135. Ruffin, a shrewd observer, thought that Wise gained strength from his errors and follies. "Before the Harper's Ferry affair, he had but little support in Virginia (and none elsewhere) for the presidency, which he was seeking so boldly and shamelessly. But his conduct in and since the affair, though very blameable for indiscretion, has given him more popularity than all he ever acquired for his real worth and ability, or his praiseworthy public services." *Diary*, February 6, 1860. One of Robert Toombs's closest friends believed that Harper's Ferry turned the scale with him, convincing him that secession was a necessity. Reed, *Brothers' War*, 264.

the . . . representatives of the people to do all in their power to smooth down and rectify."

That wealthy Calhounite Democrat and former Congressman, James A. Seddon, who was spending the winter in Louisiana, believed equally that Wise had done tremendous mischief. Instead of treating the Harper's Ferry affair as the work of a few fanatics or the crime of a squad of ruffians, he had elevated the perpetrators to the station of political offenders and had done his utmost to make them appear champions of Northern sentiment. Throughout the South, others, taking their cue from the Virginia executive, had joined him in trying to convert the squalid foray into a grand political transaction and to arouse hostility toward all Northerners. In short, wrote Seddon, the foolish governor, mad for the Presidential nomination, "has conjured a devil neither he nor perhaps any other can lay, and, arraying the roused pride and animosities of both sections against each other, has brought on a *real crisis* of imminent peril to both." Seddon did not deplore this, as Botts did, from love of the Union. He deplored it because he thought the raid should have been used to strengthen the Democratic Party both North and South, bringing Northern members into better comradeship with Southerners, and because he feared that this premature cry of "Wolf! Wolf!" would leave disillusionment in its wake, rendering the South more apathetic toward the "practical disunion" which Seddon wanted.

It was natural that a great part of the Southern press should interpret John Brown's raid as evidence that the abolitionists would arm new bands of assailants, and that their section must now live under daily menace of attack. The scope of the conspiracy was vastly exaggerated. When maps of several Southern States were found in Brown's baggage, with marks indicating certain counties in which the colored people exceeded the whites, many jumped to the conclusion that abolition agents had been sent to these areas or would soon go thither.[11]

Indeed, the captured papers indicated that Brown had dispatched an emissary, one Lawrence Thatcher, to make a Southern tour and determine the best places for blows against slavery; and that Thatcher had reported, early in October, that Tennessee and Arkansas were exceptionally favorable ground, for the slaves were ripe for action and few whites were strongly attached to the institution. Governor Isham Harris of Tennessee regarded the report as proof of a widely ramified plot.[12] It was easy to quote—or misquote—statements by the abolitionist leaders. Garrison had written in the *Liberator* three years earlier that it was far more important to send Sharps rifles to the Southern slaves than to Kansas. "If every border ruffian invading Kansas deserves to be shot, much more does every slave-

11 *De Bow's Review*, XXIX, 71.
12 *National Intelligencer*, November 16, Baltimore *Weekly Sun*, November 19, 1859.

holder, by the same rule; for the former is guilty only of attempting political subjection to his will, while the latter is the destroyer of all human rights, and there is none to deliver. Who will go for arming our slave population?" [13] Giddings had declared that he looked forward to the hour of servile revolt, "when the torch of the incendiary shall light up the towns and cities of the South, and blot out the last vestiges of slavery."

Unfortunately, the Republican Party was now widely misidentified with the abolitionists. Though most Republicans reprehended Brown's deed, the South was no longer in any mood to make the vital distinction between those who wished to contain slavery and those who wished its immediate extirpation. Howell Cobb, declining in a letter of October 31 to speak in New York, called the raid a practical result of Republican abuse of the South and talk of an irrepressible conflict. Much of the Democratic press in both sections took up the hue and cry.

Thus the Administration organ, the Washington *Constitution*, which could have raised a moderating voice, burst out in a series of articles on Seward's responsibility for the raid. It remarked in the first article that while the South had accepted the irrepressible conflict speech as a declaration of war upon its equality, peace, and safety, nobody had supposed that the initial blow would be struck so quickly. The anonymous letter of warning to Secretary Floyd was construed as evidence that widespread arrangements had been made for the outbreak. Later articles quoted Giddings and others, declared that the Republican Party was the implacable enemy of the South, and accused Seward of doing more than anyone else to consolidate antislavery feeling into a political organization pledged to war upon the rights of fifteen sovereign States.[14] The New York *Herald*, reprinting Seward's "bloody and brutal" speech entire, saw a connection clear as sunlight between it and the bloody and brutal acts committed on the Potomac.[15] The New York *Daily News* spoke in similar vein. A Democratic group in New York City, the Fifth Avenue Hotel Committee, even circulated the accusation that Seward had known in advance of the raid and kept silent about it.[16] The *Democratic Review* in its October issue arraigned Seward along with Wendell Phillips, Giddings, and Gerrit Smith as more guilty than Brown himself for the Harper's Ferry murders.

The unhappiest single result of the raid, in a practical sense, was this intensification of Southern hatred and suspicion of the Republican Party. It was uni-

13 Garrison, *Garrison*, III, 439. A non-resistant, Garrison was against arming anybody.
14 Washington *Constitution*, October 20, 21, 22, 1859.
15 N. Y. *Herald*, October 19, 1859.
16 N. Y. *Weekly Tribune*, December 10, 1859. A slight basis of fact existed for the story of the Fifth Avenue Committee. Brown's associate Forbes declared that he had discussed Brown's general scheme with Seward; but we cannot trust Forbes.

versally called the Black Republican Party, its leaders were increasingly characterized as enemies of Southern institutions, and its doctrine of non-interference
in the States but exclusion of slavery from the Territories was vituperatively distorted into a doctrine of warfare upon slavery everywhere. A resident of
Plaquemines, Louisiana, wrote Lyman Trumbull that absurd misrepresentations
of Northern feeling were being daily and weekly thrown before the Southern
people in an inflammatory phraseology which could not but work mischievous
results.[17]

When the mild Amos A. Lawrence (an old Cotton Whig, an enemy of abolitionists, a man shocked by Harper's Ferry) wrote Wise to ask mercy for Brown,
he received a sharp rebuke. The governor expressed the view that Brown's folly
was the fruit of the excited preaching and arms-shipping which Lawrence and
other Yankees had used to sway the result in Kansas—that Lawrence and his
friends had instigated John Brown to his crime.[18] Jefferson Davis was typical of
hundreds of Southern leaders now proclaiming that Republican hostility knew
no limit. At first, he said, the antislavery agitation had been a thrust for political
power; then it had assumed a social form; and now it had reached the pitch of
revolution and civil war. He asserted that Brown's raid represented an attempt
"by extensive combinations among the non-slaveholding States" to levy war
against Virginia and stigmatized the Republican Party as one "organized on the
basis of making war" against the South.[19]

In an effort on the part of some to reassure the South, and of others to turn
public sentiment against the Republicans, Northern conservatives hastily arranged Union meetings in many cities. Such gatherings, however, simply confirmed the South in its fears and prejudices, while irritating honest-minded
Northerners. Many orators took an apprehensive view; John A. Dix told the
New York meeting that Brown's invasion was the product of a "vast" conspiracy
that was but scotched, not killed. Many speakers cried encouragement to Southern disunionists; Charles O'Conor said that if the North continued to elect
fanatics to Congress, he would not blame the South for seceding.[20] Franklin
Pierce sent a letter to the Portsmouth meeting which laid unfortunate emphasis
on the continuing nature of the peril. The Republicans, he wrote, had long been
ready to scuttle the Union, and now seemed prepared to condone murder and

17 Paul Selby, former Illinoisan, November 28, 1859; Trumbull Papers.
18 Anon., *William Winston Seaton*, 321–323.
19 *Cong. Globe*, 36th Cong., 1st Sess., 1942.
20 N. Y. *Weekly Tribune*, December 24, 1859. The effort in many Union meetings, and
in such newspapers as the N. Y. *Herald*, Washington *Constitution*, and Boston *Courier* to
hold Republicans responsible for the raid cost the party few votes in November. N. P. Banks
was reelected governor of Massachusetts on the Republican ticket by more than twenty
thousand plurality, while in the election of minor state officers in New York the party made
marked gains.

treason. "The amazing, dangerous, and unconstitutional aggression on the part of the North against the people and institutions of the South which has been kept up through so many years . . . must cease, or the relations which have been the basis of our prosperity, power, and glory must be terminated." [21] No Southern agitator could have been more alarming as to the future. A wealthy Philadelphian was writing William C. Rives: "I cannot think the South can endure many such attacks; I can hardly hope the North will protect them from them"—as if attacks were to become a regular feature of national life.[22]

The Union meetings gave no reassurance because they could give no guarantees. They demonstrated what was obvious, that right-thinking Northerners deplored any outrage; but who could check wrong-thinking Northerners? The conservative Senator Dixon of Connecticut was struck, in talking with Hunter of Virginia, usually the calmest of men, by his perturbed words and despondent manner. When, asked the Virginian, would the growth of radical abolitionism stop? Would Garrison and Wendell Phillips ultimately win all Northern opinion to their views? Was the irrepressible conflict not at hand, and in a shape more violent than Seward had envisaged? Communicating these inquiries to Gideon Welles, Dixon warned him that disunion, long dreaded, might be near now that Southern leaders were holding it up not as an evil to be deprecated, but as a good to be desired.[23]

Outwardly, the Faneuil Hall meeting, addressed by Caleb Cushing and Edward Everett, was impressive; so was the Academy of Music meeting in New York, with speeches by Mayor Tiemann, John A. Dix, and Washington Hunt; so were meetings in other commercial centers. They struck many Southerners, however, as ridiculous. Men who had sowed the wind were now affecting astonishment at the whirlwind harvest. They struck other Southerners as insincere: if Brown's insurrection had succeeded, would not Everett and Hunt have sung a different tune? Their effect on Northern freesoilers of principle was equally bad. The willingness of some Democratic speakers to defend slavery as morally right created disgust. When the eminent attorney O'Conor said that slavery was benign in its influence on whites and blacks, was a necessity created by nature herself, and must be perpetuated, he exacerbated the feeling he should have quieted. Republican editors were quick to declare these Union-saving assemblages a double hypocrisy. On one side, they were a partisan attempt to use John Brown's irresponsible raid to besmear the Republican organization. On the other, they were an effort of Northern merchants to truckle to the Atlanta *Daily Confederacy* and other agencies which had gotten up blacklists of offen-

21 December 26, 1859; Pierce Papers, LC.
22 J. L. Fisher, November 29, 1859; Rives Papers, LC.
23 December 17, 1859; Welles Papers, LC.

sive Yankee firms, and to keep slaveowners in a mood to buy A. T. Stewart's silks and Ben Whitlock's extended brandy.

In short, emotion North and South had now passed the point at which moderate utterances could have an emollient influence. If they pleased one side they seemed provocative to the other.[24]

As the wave of anger and fear, throwing up its surf of hysteria, rolled across the South, it had a variety of unpleasant immediate effects. Intolerance was accentuated. From this hour it became treason in most Southern areas to breathe a word against slavery. Newspapers far and wide published warnings that the section was infested by abolitionists, trying to imbue both races with their doctrines. The Montgomery *Mail* was especially fearful of peddlers and colporteurs, slipping about among the plantations to corrupt the slaves. The safest course, it said, was to arrest such men and hang them upon conviction of anything like sedition. Forsyth's Mobile *Register* protested against such dangerous teachings —behind every bush a Catiline!—but they had their effect.[25] The publication of letters from Brown's valise which indicated that he had considered operations at various Southern points brought Wise a flock of agitated inquiries. We have several abolitionists near here, wrote citizens of Center, North Carolina, including a Wesleyan minister from Ohio; is he one of Brown's agents? We have a Yankee schoolteacher named Forbes, stated people of Cold Spring, Louisiana; he looks suspicious; does he belong to Brown's gang? Two Northern book agents, one selling a volume on the Indians and the other a treatise on Christ and his apostles, were seized at Salisbury, North Carolina, threatened with tar and feathers, and driven from the State. "Do you know Old Brown?" demanded the mob.[26] To be sure, underground agents did exist—but they were few.

24 Philip S. Foner, *Business and Slavery*, 156–164. The Southern blacklists, an attempt at commercial proscription, lent themselves to blackmail. Various offices calling themselves Southern business agencies were opened in Northern cities, and invited patronage on an implied-threat basis. William P. Gilman & Company of Richmond, for example, proposed to publish a directory of sound Northern firms, which could get their names entered by paying not less than $50. The Atlanta *Confederacy* published black-and-white lists for the benefit of Georgia merchants, while the Charleston *Mercury* threatened to list all Charleston merchants doing business with a New York firm whose partners attended Beecher's church. The alacrity of many Northern merchants to attend Union meetings, and to get their names signed to the printed call for such gatherings, was attributed by unkind folk to business considerations. *Annual Report, Am. Antislavery Society, 1860*, 197–199.

25 Mobile *Register*, November 29, 1859. The idea that they might have to defend their women and children against slaves armed by the North made many Southerners savage. T. J. Jackson, the future "Stonewall," said that in dealing with any new raiders they should raise the black flag of no quarter, for in the end that would prove true humanity and mercy. Mary Anna Jackson, *Life and Letters of T. J. Jackson*, 308–310.

26 Hartford *Press*, December 12, 1859. Newspapers were soon chronicling scores of instances in which well-behaved residents of Southern communities had been forced to flee; innocent book venders and notions peddlers had been threatened and even attacked for no offense but speaking with a Yankee twang; schoolteachers, intent only on teaching, and ministers devoted to the gospel had been warned to leave because their education had been

For some weeks the panic and anger grew. The protests of such responsible Unionists as Herschel Johnson, John Minor Botts, and B. H. Hill seemed unavailing. The British consul in Charleston reported on December 9 that a veritable reign of terror had opened in the Lower South. Suspect men were being torn from their homes, tarred and feathered, ridden upon rails, or cruelly whipped; and, as a result, Northern businessmen, drummers, and tourists, finding their letters opened in the post offices and all talk about slavery sternly prohibited, were leaving for home.[27] More than one person, added the consul, had been hanged for uttering obnoxious sentiments. The consul in New York complained of the hard case of a Scotch-Irishman in Augusta, Georgia, who, after suing a local firm and obtaining judgment, was warned out of town as an abolitionist, and at two in the morning seized by a mob and thrown into jail. As he had done no wrong, a courageous lawyer released him—but he had to leave. In Virginia, various postmasters, such as R. H. Glass of Lynchburg, informed the New York *Tribune* that they would no longer distribute the journal. In Arkansas, after reports spread that the John Brown conspirators intended to stage another raid from some point on the Arkansas River, and after panic-stricken inhabitants arrested various abolition agents and shot one alleged Negro-

---

gained at Northern colleges; mechanics of British or New England origin had been tarred and feathered on some groundless accusation. In December, it was stated that thirty-two men, agents of New York and Boston houses, had arrived in Washington on one day, reporting sentiment in the South so hostile that it was no longer safe for them to pursue their work as commercial travellers. The temper of Southern communities is illustrated by two newspaper utterances. "We regard every man in our midst an enemy to the institutions of the South," declared the Atlanta *Confederacy*, "who does not boldly declare that he believes African slavery to be a social, moral, and political blessing." When a meeting was held at Boggy Swamp, S. C., to expel two Northern tutors from the district, the Kingstree *Star* commented: "Nothing definite is known of their abolitionist or insurrectionary sentiments, but being from the North, and, therefore, necessarily imbued with doctrines hostile to our institutions, their presence in this section has been obnoxious, and, at any rate, very suspicious." Quoted in *Annual Report Am. Antislavery Society, 1860*, pp. 167, 168.

27 "The time has come," wrote the Washington correspondent of the New Orleans *Picayune*, "when no Northern man, whatever his business, can safely travel in the Southern states, unless he has means of showing that his objects are not unfriendly. Many who have business in the South come here to obtain credentials. A proper passport system must be devised and adopted, in order to secure the South from Abolition intruders and spies." New Orleans *Picayune*, January 11, 1860. Many old friendships were now feeling a severe strain. Philip St. George Cooke of Virginia and A. J. Davis of New York, for example, both interested in art, had seen each other whenever possible and maintained a genial correspondence. But just after Christmas Cooke warned his friend that the South was in earnest. "If your Conservative Party at the North does not *put down* and *put out* the accursed and pestiferous abolition faction, they will speedily bring about a dissolution of our hitherto glorious Union! Able men of all parties have come to this conclusion at the South, and as we see no hopes of such a result at the North, we are arming . . . as rapidly as possible." He expected to turn his peaceful lawn into a drillground for soldiers. What hellish madness!—but the South must defend itself against this insane crusade, led by the vilest of the Northern population. A. J. Davis Papers, Metropolitan Museum, N. Y.

stealer, a plot for a general slave escape was discovered in Washington County and some white men were seized as participants.[28]

One of the unhappiest episodes occurred in Kentucky. Here, at Berea on the fringe of the bluegrass district, Cassius M. Clay had established an antislavery community, and through the activities of an abolitionist minister, John G. Fee, and others, the Berea School had been founded for the education of white children and Negroes. Just before Christmas, a mob which included prosperous and influential men, riding from house to house, ordered Fee and his associates to leave Kentucky within ten days under threat of death; when the governor refused to interfere, a dozen families were stripped of their property and lost their means of livelihood.[29] Fee's offense was that, being in New York at the time of the raid, he had delivered a sermon in which he said (like Whittier in "Brown of Ossawatomie") that the country needed more John Browns, armed not with guns but spiritual weapons. The slaveholders of the county, hearing of this, had met, appointed a committee, and passed resolutions warning the antislavery folk of Berea to quit the State.[30]

One unfortunate result of the Southern furore was a heightened rigor in the treatment of the Negro. It was a bitter irony that Brown's effort to aid them should have made their lot harsher. The tension that caught at the nerves of slaveholders found expression in stricter patrols, a closer watch on recreation and much petty tyrannizing. Legislatures of various States hastened to debate bills (which we summarize later) to hedge free Negroes within narrow bounds, or drive them back into slavery; the theory being that, as the Montgomery *Mail* put it, "their anomalous position is an eyesore to the slaves and an annoyance to the white population." [31] British consuls were shocked by the passions of the hour. In Louisiana, Consul William Mure, under instructions from the Foreign Office, prepared to expostulate against the new law requiring that all free Negroes on ships arriving from abroad must be held in jail until the vessel was ready to depart. When he spoke to two legislators who had opposed the law, however, they advised him not to offer any petition while such excitement reigned, for a protest might retard repeal for years. In Georgia, a British sailor, a Negro named Brodie, was thrown into jail on a charge of enticing a slave to run away, tried before the mayor's court at Darien, illegally sentenced to be sold into slavery, and hurriedly sent to unknown western points. It was impossible to

28 See John Bunch, January 25, 1860, F.O. 115/230; E. M. Archibald, January 16, 1860, F.O. 115/230; Little Rock *True Democrat*, November–December, 1859; E. L. Harvin, "Arkansas and Crisis 1860–61," M.A. Essay, Univ. of Texas Lib.
29 Cincinnati *Commercial*, December 31, 1859, gives full documents.
30 Fee, *Autobiography*, 147, 148; Coleman, *Slavery Times in Kentucky*, 112, 321, 322.
31 *Annual Report Am. Antislavery Society*, 1860, 206–225.

find him. On a trumped-up charge, he had been enslaved for life. Worse still was the case of a colored British seaman at Charleston. A runaway slave hid himself in this man's berth; the sailor denied any knowledge of him; but Judge T. J. Withers of General Sessions sentenced him to death. When J. L. Petigru persuaded the governor to commute the sentence, the judge evinced great chagrin.[32]

Amid this general fever, disunionist excitation blazed up with renewed vigor. Such leaders as Ruffin, who got a consignment of Brown's pikes from Harper's Ferry and distributed them as evidence of what he termed the fanatical hatred in the North, plucked up hope. Talking with Letcher in Richmond on December 17, Ruffin, after finding that even the moderate governor-elect thought it impossible any longer to preserve the rights of the South within the Union, urged him to call a convention in Virginia and to propose a general convention of all the Southern States. Rhett and Yancey were jubilant over the outlook. "Never before, since the Declaration of Independence, has the South been more united in sentiment and feeling," rejoiced the Sumter (South Carolina) *Watchman* the day before Christmas. Ruffin was for immediate secession by any State that could act, but most radicals thought this premature. The first step, they held, was to effect a firm alliance of the Southern States for future action.[33]

Various leaders and legislatures expressly formulated the idea of Southern solidarity. The Georgia house resolved that any blow at slavery in a sister State vitally affected the interests and honor of Georgia, and that the Southern people were bound by such a close community of feeling that they must stand or fall together. The State senate, in language shaped by the moderate Benjamin H. Hill, contented itself with praising the energetic action of Buchanan and Wise.[34] In Louisiana, the brilliant Henry W. Allen, who had studied at Harvard and traveled widely in Europe, presented resolutions declaring that the universal sympathy manifested by the Black Republican Party for the murderers of Harper's Ferry gave evidence of deep-seated hostility to all the slaveholding States, and if a Black Republican were elected to the Presidency, Louisiana

32 William Mure, February 16, 1860, F.O. 115/230. E. Molyneux, March 8, 1860, F.O. 115/230. John Bunch, January 7, 1860, F.O. 115/230.
33 Edmund Ruffin, *Diary*, December 16, 1859–January 4, 1860. A significant letter appeared in the N. Y. *Express*, Know-Nothing organ. Signed R. S. P., it quoted a conservative lover of the Union who had just arrived in Washington from New Orleans, traversing Alabama, Georgia, and South Carolina, and visiting Montgomery and Columbia while the legislatures were in session. "He says in his whole route he has not met a single individual who does not advocate an immediate secession, and the formation of a Southern confederacy. He says all attempts to reason or argue are useless; they will not listen. For once, and the first time, he says, in his life, he almost despairs." Quoted in N. Y. *Tribune*, December 10, 1859. This was exaggerated—but it was perhaps possible for a man seeing only restricted circles to get this impression.
34 *House Journal; Senate Journal*, November 5, 1859, p. 47.

would consider this a ground for dissolving the Union.[35] Though not passed, the resolutions were widely supported. Alabama, affirming the right of any State to secede and declaring she would take part in a convention of slaveholding States, provided for calling her own convention if a Republican were elected President —for she would never submit to the foul domination of a sectional Northern party. Florida, too, resolved that the choice of a Republican President, committed to interfere with slavery, would justify the rupture of the Union.[36]

It was natural for South Carolina and Mississippi to go farthest of all. The States of Calhoun and Rhett, A. G. Brown and Jefferson Davis, hold the leadership in disunion sentiment.

Governor William H. Gist of South Carolina, a wealthy lawyer-planter, hot-tempered (he had killed his man in a duel), rigid (an ardent Methodist and prohibitionist), and hostile to the Union (he had demanded separate secession in 1851), was quick to see his opportunity. He told the legislature that the whole North was arrayed against the slaveholding area, that Harper's Ferry had marked the crossing of the Rubicon, and that it was hopeless to look to the Democratic Party for protection—it was a pasteboard ship tossed by ocean storms. Resolutions were introduced by Christopher G. Memminger, lawyer and financial expert of Charleston, now turning from conservatism to radicalism. They recalled that South Carolina by her ordinance of 1832 had affirmed the right to secede, asserted that the assaults upon Southern rights had continued with increasing violence, called upon the slaveholding States to meet for concerted action, and directed the governor to send a commissioner to Virginia to press for joint measures of defense. These resolutions were received with acclaim. Already, many public gatherings had been called to organize local vigilance committees, while a number of previously cautious newspapers had become extreme. A vote on still more radical resolves indicated that not less than fifty-three percent of the senate and forty-three percent of the house stood for disunion. As Memminger's proposals passed, and the governor named him commissioner to Richmond, Mississippi accepted the plan for a Southern convention, suggested that delegates meet in Atlanta early in June, and sent a commissioner of her own to Virginia.[37]

Forthwith, the governors of South Carolina, Alabama, and Mississippi began exchanging letters. Where, Gist asked Moore of Alabama, shall our convention

35 New Orleans *Picayune*, January 21, 1860.
36 *Acts of Alabama* 1859–60, 685–687. The Alabama legislature, immediately after the raid, authorized the organization of a volunteer corps in each county to the total of eight thousand men and set aside $200,000 for equipping them. Denham, *Secessionist Movement in Alabama*, 77. Letter of mother of E. Kirby Smith, St. Augustine, January 11, 1860; Smith Papers, Univ. of N. C.
37 Harold Schultz, "South Carolina and National Politics, 1852–60," Ph.D. Dissertation, Duke Univ.; Ames, *State Documents*, 69, 70; Capers, *Memminger*.

be held?—as our three States alone seem ready, must it not be within our borders? [38] Forthwith, too, the radicals in Congress began conferring as never before, talking, planning, and spurring each other on. Representative Porcher Miles of South Carolina gave special attention to the Virginia members. "If," he wrote Memminger, "you can only urge our Carolina view in such a manner as to imbue Virginia with it . . . we may soon hope to see the fruit of your addresses in . . . a Southern Confederacy." [39]

Some strange scenes marked the startling shift of public sentiment in both sections as 1859 closed. In the North, pulpits were still resounding with laudation of John Brown, hawkers were selling John Brown biographies, and halls were vibrating with antislavery oratory. In border cities, pathetic bands of free Negroes, exiles from harsh Southern laws, were succored by private charity as they passed on their way to Canada. In Southern towns and cities, people were meeting to adopt rules for boycotting Northern merchandise, young men and women were agreeing to wear nothing but homespun, and vigilance committees were warning commercial travellers to turn home. In Richmond, a tumultuous crowd gathered at the station to welcome one hundred and sixty medical students, who had left Philadelphia in a body upon assurances that they could receive training in the medical colleges of the South. "Let Virginia call home her sons!" exclaimed Governor Wise. On many a Southern field, militia and volunteers were training; for Alabama this winter appropriated $200,000, Mississippi $150,000, and South Carolina $100,000 for military contingencies. Everywhere, men found excitement pervasive, emotion mounting, and premonition rising of momentous events just ahead. [40]

[II]

The opening of Congress on December 9, 1859, brought no reassurance to the nation, for many shared the fear of ex-President Tyler that a contest over the speakership and the debates of both houses would only add fuel to the general blaze. This first session of the Thirty-sixth Congress, destined to last until the summer heat of 1860 smote the capital, found Minnesota and Oregon added to the American constellation. Each had sent eastward a man of whom more would be heard, Minnesota giving William Windom a place in the House, and Oregon awarding Joseph Lane, an able secessionist orator of North Carolina birth, unscrupulous and imperious, a seat in the Senate. While the upper chamber

38 March 29, 1860; Governor's Papers, Alabama Dept. Archives and History.
39 January 10, 1860; Memminger Papers, Univ. of N. C.
40 Clement Eaton, "The Resistance of the South to Northern Radicalism," *New England Quarterly*, VIII, 215.

was safely Democratic, the House was closely divided. The Republicans counted one hundred and nine members, the Democrats one hundred and one, and the Know-Nothings and Whigs, chiefly from the South, twenty-seven. It would require one hundred and nineteen votes to organize the House. This meant that either the Republicans, who wanted John Sherman for Speaker, or the Democrats, whose caucus nominated Thomas S. Bocock, would have to engineer an alliance with the American-Whig group to succeed. Battle and stratagem lay ahead.

The Senate had profited from some recent losses of the House, for it now had the brilliant oratory of Toombs and the sturdy force of Andrew Johnson. There were giants still in the upper chamber—Douglas, Trumbull, Seward, Davis, and Crittenden; there were lesser men of impressive stature—Wilson, Wade, Chandler, Fessenden, and Benjamin. There were intellectual grotesques, commanding in some ways, absurd and dangerous in others—Sumner for the North and Hammond for the South.

And some striking new figures appeared in the Senate. Iowa, as we have noted, sent James W. Grimes, a Dartmouth graduate and man of culture. While active as farmer, lawyer, and railroad promoter, he was a skillful politician who had done more than anybody else to make his State Republican.[41] From Rhode Island came Henry B. Anthony, charming, kindly, and cultivated, who for twenty years had edited the influential Providence *Journal*. South Carolina gave a seat to James Chesnut, Jr., a quiet-mannered attorney, educated at Princeton and in the law office of J. L. Petigru, who displayed a persuasive gift of speech. From Texas an alarming newcomer strode down the aisle, Louis T. Wigfall. Before Harper's Ferry, the Texans had seemed securely under the control of such unionists as Sam Houston and Reagan. After the raid, however, the legislature met in an ugly mood, seized upon Wigfall as the most advanced Southern Rights man in sight, and, knowing that he was peculiarly obnoxious to Houston, sent him to Washington. The change which had placed A. O. P. Nicholson in John Bell's seat was equally significant.

Republican newspapers could boast that in the House, at least, their stripling party already had a greater intellectual strength than the Democrats. The Northwestern group were particularly strong. Here was Tom Corwin, who had sat in the Senate and held the second office in the Cabinet; despite his sixty-odd years and ripe experience, a man still vigorous. Here were Owen Lovejoy and Elihu B. Washburne of Illinois, Schuyler Colfax of Indiana, and Cadwallader C.

---

41 Grimes became a boon companion of Fessenden of Maine, and Justin S. Morrill heard them in their rooms repeat Shakespeare, Pope, and Burns to each other almost by the hour. Parker, *Morrill*, 115.

Washburn of Wisconsin. Before long, William A. Howard of Michigan would arrive from the Detroit district. The New England delegation contained nearly as many able men. Eyes turned expectantly to Charles Francis Adams, who had spent most of the interval since his Free Soil campaign editing the ten volumes of John Adams's papers and writing a biography. He owed his nomination and election largely to the personal aid of Charles Sumner. Massachusetts had returned Anson Burlingame and Henry L. Dawes to the House, while Maine had sent back Israel Washburn, making three brothers from one yeoman Androscoggin Valley family. Vermont had reelected Justin S. Morrill. From New York came Roscoe Conkling, all fire, party zealotry, and well-preened vanity; from Pennsylvania, Galusha A. Grow and "honest" John Covode; and from New Jersey, William Pennington.

The member from the middle States who carried most weight, however, was Thaddeus Stevens, club-footed, shaggy-haired veteran of old renown. "I am old and lazy," he wrote his friend Giddings, when actually he thirsted for battle.[42] Two rough witticisms in this session became famous. Smarting from interruption in an argument, he snorted: "I yield to the gentleman from Virginia for a few feeble remarks." Entering the House while an election contest was being debated, and being told that both men were rascals, he commented as he reached for a ballot: "Yes, but which is *our* rascal?"

On the Democratic side, Alexander H. Stephens, Orr, and the generous-hearted John A. Quitman were all missed sorely. The place of the much-lamented Harris of Illinois, Douglasite leader in the fight against Lecompton, was taken by the clever, flippant John A. McClernand. Some striking Southern figures compelled notice. William W. Boyce of South Carolina extorted even from the New York *Tribune* a handsome compliment—"a thinker, a reasoner, a scholar"; J. L. M. Curry of Alabama, who had vision and heart as well as intellectual power, was the brains of the Alabama delegation; L. Q. C. Lamar was an exceptional parliamentarian as well as a man of philosophic depth; and Roger A. Pryor of Virginia, youthful and self-confident, brought a reputation as a fiery editor. The impetuous, lovable Keitt was conspicuous.

On both sides, the extremists were in the saddle. How could it be otherwise? Before Harper's Ferry, moderate doctrines had seemed in the ascendant; the Opposition Party, basis for a future Constitutional Union Party, had shown astonishing strength in the October elections; and Crittenden, Bell, Rives, and Everett hoped for a rapidly growing body of followers. Now in Virginia worried groups were talking of Wise's military measures; on Charleston drill grounds gray-haired men were clattering arms alongside boys who thirsted for action; amid the Alabama cottonfields, officers were selecting two young men

42 November 4, 1859; Giddings Papers.

from each county to attend at State expense the private military academies. In the North, an editorial writer for the *Tribune* was declaring that the Seventh Regiment alone could conquer the Old Dominion; Edmund Quincy was sneering at Louisiana and South Carolina as militarily helpless; the Republican press was ablaze with stories of Southern intolerance. "The Reign of Terror" was a headline which some editors kept standing for items of violence or repression.

With defiant mien, Southern members in hotel lobbies unfolded the *Union*, the *Mercury*, or the *Picayune* to accounts of Yankee provocations. As days passed into weeks, they had plenty to read. The annual convention of New York antislavery forces, held at Albany early in 1860, surpassed itself in vehemence. Slaveholders were denounced as robbers, adulterers, pirates, and murderers. The first resolution declared that in the irresistible conflict being waged against despotism, men could find a glorious assurance that the deliverance of enslaved millions drew nigh. Wendell Phillips was soon telling a Brooklyn audience that slavery should be destroyed, law or no law, Constitution or no Constitution; and that if a Democrat were elected President, war would break out along the Southern mountains.[43] Tokens multiplied that the Fugitive Slave Law had become unenforceable. A runaway Negro who reached New York smuggled aboard a Norfolk schooner had the help, in making his escape to a safe area, of attorneys and magistrates.

Meanwhile, Northern members with equally defiant mien opened the *Evening Post*, the *Republican*, or the *Press* to stories of Southern misdeeds. They, too, had plenty to read. They could study tales of lashing and lynching. Cassius M. Clay, defying the Kentuckians who chased Fee and other Berea men from the State, was asserting that, if necessary, he and his family would flee to some natural stronghold and sell their lives dearly. In North Carolina, Daniel Worth, a minister of fine character and imposing presence, was sentenced to a year in jail on a charge of circulating incendiary books; and onlookers lamented that he was not publicly flogged, as the law permitted. "We shall stripe him yet!" one exclaimed.

On the opening day in the Senate, after prayer and the swearing in of new members, Mason of Virginia arose with his usual stiff dignity. He offered a resolution, he said, which the clerk would read. From the desk came a voice: "Resolved, that a committee be appointed to inquire into the facts attending the late invasion and seizure of the armory and arsenal of the United States at Harper's Ferry, in Virginia, by a band of armed men."

Assuredly, there was truth in what Thoreau had written of John Brown after the execution: "I meet him at every turn. He is more alive than ever he was."

43 N. Y. *Weekly Tribune*, February 4, March 24, 1860.

[III]

In keeping with his character, Buchanan in his annual message of December, 1859, treated the Harper's Ferry affair in admonitory but soothing terms. The raid, he remarked, was important only because it excited Southern fears (which he did not share) that still more dangerous outrages would follow. Good citizens in both sections, he urged, should cultivate mutual forbearance, and allay the demoniac spirit of internecine strife. As an old public functionary, he appealed to the spirit of the wise statesmen of the preceding generation, under whom he had commenced his service, declaring that his dearest earthly wish was to leave the country tranquil, united, and powerful.

A happy sentiment! Yet the light of patriotic generalities paled when brought beside the deep red flame kindled by clashing material and political interests. In one part of the message, Buchanan declared that the Supreme Court had established the right of every citizen to take slave property into the Territories "and to have it protected there under the Federal Constitution." An interesting phrase, whose authorship could probably be traced to Cobb and Jacob Thompson. Just what did Buchanan mean by "have it protected?"—protected by a slave code passed by Congress? Douglas Democrats would have something to say on that. At this very moment, the Republican national committee, calling the party convention at Chicago in May, declared that it would oppose to the last the doctrine that the Constitution of its own force carried slavery into all the Territories.[44]

At once, the House plunged into a convulsive two months' battle over the speakership. The contest began on the first day when, as Republicans rallied behind John Sherman, Representative J. B. Clark of Missouri brought forward a resolution declaring that no man who had endorsed the insurrectionary doctrines of Helper's *Impending Crisis* was fit to be Speaker. Sherman was among the sixty-eight Representatives who had signed a circular asking for funds to scatter a hundred thousand copies of the compendium of that volume throughout the land. In vain did he now assert that he had never read Helper's book. In vain did he offer a letter from Francis P. Blair, Sr., explaining why many leading Republicans had joined in recommending the compendium before it was printed. Helper had brought the book to Silver Spring for examination. After ploughing through it, Blair had told the author that it was objectionable in many passages, and had obtained his written promise to excise or modify the harsh language. On the strength of this pledge, many Representatives had signed the circular—

44 Buchanan's phrase deeply angered Republicans and outraged Douglas's followers. Representative John A. McClernand called the message "a national calamity"; January 3, 1860, Lanphier Papers.

READ! READ! READ!

In the year 1857, an individual named Hinton Rowan Helper, who had been forced to leave his native State, North Carolina, in disgrace, published a book, of which he was the reputed author, entitled "The Impending Crisis." The book recommended *direct* warfare on Southern society, "be the consequences what they might." It was so extravagant in tone, and so diabolical in its designs, that it was at first generally supposed to be the work of a fool or a madman. No one could believe that any sane or civilized person really entertained any such devilish purposes as it professed.—

What, however, was the surprise of the public when the book was actually adopted by the Republican party as a campaign document, and its atrocious principles endorsed by SIXTY-EIGHT Republican members of Congress and *all the influential members of the party!* Below will be found an abstract of the principles it advocated, taken from the large edition of the work, published by A. B. BURDICK, No. 145 Nassau street, N. Y., 1860, and the names of their endorsers, &c:

1. We unhesitatingly declare ourselves in favor of the immediate and unconditional ABOLITION OF SLAVERY.—*Page 26.*

2. "We cannot be TOO HASTY in carrying out our designs."—*Page 33.*

3. "No man can be a true patriot with-

The Mottoes on Our Banner.

1. Thorough organization and independent political action on the part of non-slaveholding whites of the South.

2. Ineligibility of slaveholders; never another vote to the trafficker in human flesh.

3. No co-operation with slaveholders in politics, no fellowship with them in religion no affiliation with them in society.

4. No patronage to slaveholding merchants; no bequest to slave waiting hotels; no fees to slaveholding lawyers; no employment to slaveholding physicians; no audience to slaveholding parsons.

5. No recognition to pro-slavery men, except as ruffians, outlaws, and criminals.

6. Immediate DEATH to SLAVERY, or if not immediate, unqualified proscription of its advocate during the period of its existence.—*Pages 155 and 156.*

7. Thus, terror engenderers of the South, have we fully and frankly defined our position: we have no modifications to propose, no compromises to offer, nothing to retract, Frown, sirs, fret, foam, prepare your weapons, threat, strike, shoot, stab, bring on civil war, dissolve the Union, nay, annihilate the solar system if you will—do all this, more, less, better, worse, anything—do what you will, sirs, you can neither foil nor intimidate us; our purpose is as firmly fixed as the eternal pillars of Heaven; we have determined to ABOLISH SLAVERY, AND SO HELP US GOD, ABOLISH IT WE WILL.—*Page 187.*

to me a work of *great merit,* rich, yet accurate in statistical information and logical analysis, and I do not doubt that it will exert a great influence on the public mind, in favor of *the cause of Truth and Justice.*

I am, gentlemen, very respectfully,
Your ob't servant,
W. H. SEWARD.

We, the undersigned, members of the House of Representatives of the National Congress, do cordially endorse the opinion and approve the enterprise set forth in the foregoing circular:—

Schuyler Colfax,	Anson Burlingame,
Owen Lovejoy,	Amos P. Granger,
Edwin B. Morgan,	Galusha A. Grow,
Joshua R. Giddings,	Edward Wade,
Calvin C. Chaffee,	William H. Kelsey,
Wm. A. Howard,	Henry Waldon,
John Sherman,	Geo. W. Palmer,
Daniel W. Gooch,	Henry L. Dawes,
Justin S. Morril,	I. Washburn, Jr.
J. A. Bingham,	Wm. Kellogg,
E. B. Washburne,	Benjamin Stanton,
Edward Dodd,	Cydnor B. Tompkins,
John Covode,	Cad. C. Washburne,
Sam'l G. Andrews,	Abraham B. Olin,
Sidney Dean,	Nath'l B. Durfee,
Emory B. Pottle,	DeWitt C. Leach,
John F. Potter,	T. Davis, (Mass.)
J. F. Farnsworth,	C. L. Knapp,
R. E. Fenton,	Philemon Bliss,
Mason W. Tappan,	Charles Case,
T. Davis, (Iowa)	James Pike,
Homer E. Royce,	Isaac D. Clawson,
A. S. Murray,	Robert B. Hall,

Greeley, Horace, New York city,	100
Greenleaf, R. C. Boston, Mass.	50
Harris, Edward, Woonsocket, R. I.	100
Henrick, Benjamin S. New York city,	50
Helper, H. R. New York city,	25
Hurlbut, F. Brooklyn, N. Y.	100
Jay, John, New York city,	10
Ketcham, Edgar, New York city,	10
McCauley, Wm. Wilmington, Del.	10
Marble, Nathan, Port Byron, N. Y.	10
May, Samuel, Boston, Me.	100
Morgan, Edwin D. Albany, N. Y.	100
Nesmith, John, Lowell, Ma.	100
Norton, John T. Farmington, Ct.	100
Parsons, J. C. New York,	10
l'inner, M. Kansas City, Mo.	10
Plumly, Benjamin Rush, Philadelphia, Pa.	20
Randolph, Evan, Philadelphia, Pa.	
Republicans of Pottsville and N. Coventry, Pa. $40.	51
Republicans of Shawnee Mound, $20. South Bend, Ind. $10,	30
Roberts, W. S. New York city,	30
Robinson, Hanson, New Castle Co. Del.	10
Byerson, David, Newton, N. J.	20
Sherman, S. N. Ogdensburgh, N. Y.	64
Smith, Gerrit, Peterboro, N. Y.	33
Spring, Marcus, Eaglewood, N. J.	20
Stoner, John A. Smyrna, N. Y.	100
Stranahan, J. S. T. Brooklyn, N. Y.,	10
Tappan, Lewis, Brooklyn, N. Y.,	100
Thompson, Wm. B., Philadelphia, Pa.,	100
Tweedy, Edmund, Newport, R. I.,	10
Wadsworth, James S., New York City,	100
Wakeman, Abram, New York City,	100
Weed, Thurlow, Albany N. Y.,	10
White, Aaron, Thompson, Conn.	19
Wright, E. N. and James A., Philadelphia, Pa.	30
Wood, Bradford R., Albany, N. Y.,	100
A. A., $50; B. B., $50; C. C., $10; D. D., $10; E. $20; F. F., $25, North Carolina,	165
S. F. M. Wilmington, Del.,	10
A friend, by S. E. Sewell, Boston, Mass. $10; E. B., Brooklyn, N. Y., $25	35
Total,	3,518

Democratic Propaganda Against the Republican Endorsers of Helper's Book.

and then some deplorable paragraphs slipped through. This explanation did not mollify the Southerners. We are entitled to know, declared Leake of Virginia, whether we are to select a Speaker who, whilst we are discharging our public duties in Washington, is inciting our slaves at home to apply the torch to our dwellings, and the knife to the throats of our wives and children.

The Southern uproar over a book which probably few members had seen, much less read, was somewhat exaggerated. We have seen that the original volume contained much indefensible billingsgate directed at "slaveocrats," and a few suggestions of violent action.[45] But in general it was a dry, statistical, and factual body of comparisons between the results of free and slave labor. It was as exciting as Euclid, and as fiery as a ledger. Moreover, it was addressed wholly to the whites—the non-slaveholding whites—of the South. Not being intended for Negroes, it would not interest even those who could comprehend it, while its plan of Negro deportation would anger them and their abolitionist friends. It was unfortunate that the compendium contained offensive matter, including a passage headed "Revolution Must Free the Slaves." But all attempts to connect it with John Brown and slave insurrections were wide of the mark.

House debate had been disorderly for years, but never with the deep, searing hatred which now manifested itself. On the second day, Thaddeus Stevens accused the South of trying to intimidate the free States; you have succeeded fifty times, he said, but now you will fail. Crawford of Georgia strode forward to confront him. Your Union meetings are hypocrisy, he said; you pretend to respect our rights, yet continually plan war; when will you let us alone? As excited groups collected behind each champion, a collision seemed imminent.

Next day the House met in a chastened spirit. "A few more such scenes as we had on this floor yesterday," exclaimed Morris of Illinois, "and we will hear the crack of the revolver, and see the gleam of the brandished blade." Tempers soon grew edged again, however, and on December 9 an affray was barely averted. Logan of Illinois was understood by Kellogg of that State to use the expression "a spaniel coward"; the two rushed at each other, and amid general uproar were parted with difficulty. Both on the floor and in the lobbies, talk of civil war was now frequent. Try to stir up insurrection in our midst, or to force us back into the Union once we decide to secede, said Bonham of South Carolina, and we shall welcome you Yankees to bloody graves.

More was at stake in the speakership contest than a mere question of prestige, for the make-up of the committees depended upon the choice. Having won the advantage in the elections of 1858-59, Republicans felt entitled to make the most of it. No mere expert in rules will do, insisted Thaddeus Stevens; the Speaker must have nerve and iron fidelity to *our* principles. Democrats could not face

45   Helper, *The Impending Crisis*, 128, 139, 149, 158.

with indifference the threat that their opponents would set up committees to investigate the situation in Kansas, the foreign slave trade, Federal expenditures, and, most painful of all, accusations of departmental mismanagement.

Yet it was certainly true that, in organizing the Senate, Southern Democrats had set an example of flagrant partisanship. The sixty-six members of the Senate represented eighteen free States with a white population of about twenty millions, and fifteen slaveholding States with about seven million white inhabitants. Of the twenty-two standing committees among which business was distributed, however, the chairmanships of sixteen went to slaveholding States, and of the six others to Northern Democrats politically sympathetic with the South. Not one really important Senate committee was allowed either a Northern chairman or a majority of Northern members. This sectional partisanship was denounced by no less prominent a Northern Democrat than Pugh of Ohio, who warned his Southern brethren that if they wished to put down the agitation over slavery, they must forego such transparent tactics. If the South is to rule the Senate, said Republicans, the rich and populous North has a right to rule the House.[46]

Partly because committee control would be so important during the Presidential campaign and afterwards, and partly because of heightened sectional animosities, this eight weeks' struggle differed sharply from the speakership contest of 1855; it was more desperate, more violent, and, above all, more clearly stamped as the effort of a minority to coerce the whole House and make obstruction a political weapon. The slave State Democrats were willing to block the wheels of government until March 4, 1861—until a new House had been elected and seated—if they could not have their way. Their strategy came nearer to an introduction of Latin American methods into Washington affairs than any previous event in our history. Even Jefferson Davis was ready for an indefinite paralysis of Congress, writing a friend that as the South had little to hope and much to deprecate from its action, no legislation at all might be their best estate.

46 See Cleveland *Leader*, December 23, 1859, for typical comment. The Foreign Affairs Committee in the Senate was presided over by James M. Mason, old-time messmate and disciple of Calhoun, and a firm believer in the necessity for Southern separation. The chairman of the Territorities Committee was Green of Missouri, whose name was gall and wormwood to Western Democrats who could never forget how he had planned and executed the overthrow of Benton and stepped into Douglas's place as head of this key group; tall, spare, intellectual looking, he was an incisive spokesman for the Buchanan Democrats. Clay of Alabama was head of the Commerce Committee, Yulee of Florida of the Post Office Committee, Bayard of Delaware of the Judiciary Committee, Brown of Mississippi of the Committee on the Federal District, Mallory of Florida of the Naval Affairs Committee. Why, Republicans asked, should the South complain that one chamber was led by its opponents? The slaveholding States still controlled the Presidency, Vice-Presidency, Supreme Court, and machinery of the Senate. A single county in Ohio—Hamilton—had more voters than all Florida, yet Florida boasted of two important Senate chairmanships and Ohio had none. The Democrats of the Northwest had once been a powerful body; they could now declare that because of such Southern measures as Lecompton, they had lost most of their members in both Senate and House.

Some Northern sympathizers believed that a deadlock might frighten their section into surrender. "Don't organize," George Sanders telegraphed the secessionists Keitt and Porcher Miles on December 16; "earnest revolution going on all over the North adjourn Congress until after holidays and all come here." [47]

Representative Clark's resolution for the exclusion of any person who had endorsed Helper's book was unprecedented in character, a breach of parliamentary practice, and in violation of the Act of 1789. When it was dropped, a substitute of somewhat similar tenor was offered and lost by a tie vote. Democratic members thereupon claimed unlimited freedom of debate. They obstructed a resolution to shut off all discussion until after the election of a Speaker. They obstructed a proposal to take at least three ballots daily; even one ballot. They obstructed a plan for limiting each speaker to one thirty-minute utterance on any pending question. They flatly refused to permit adoption of a rule for electing the Speaker by plurality, which had twice before been accepted to break a deadlock, and which for weeks seemed to offer the only escape. Meanwhile, the Administration Democrats made long and vituperative speeches, offered endless chains of dilatory motions (to adjourn, to be excused from voting, to call the *ayes* and *nays*, and so on), and did everything in their power to create confusion. Fifty-eight of them, all from slaveholding States, signed a pledge of mutual union in resisting by every weapon of parliamentary tactics the adoption of a plurality rule. This rule-or-ruin group constituted an iron-bound body to prevent the strongest party from taking effective action. With 114 or 115 votes usually needed to elect a Speaker, Sherman could muster 110 or 111, but no more.

The obstructionists thus held the House at a standstill, permitting votes only when they believed them perfectly safe. In the first week, they allowed three ballots for Speaker; in the second, seven; in the third, when they were trying to make combinations with other groups, eleven; in the fourth, when these combinations failed, three; in the fifth and sixth, five each; in the seventh, none; and in the eighth and ninth, again five each. Altogether, they permitted forty-four votes in forty days of actual session. During a similar period in 1855, no fewer than one hundred and thirty ballots had been taken. With good reason, McPherson of Pennsylvania later said that the Administration men, organizing a conspiracy, had approached the verge of revolution.[48] The Republicans, meanwhile, showed a praiseworthy moderation. They held no caucus meetings, displayed little discipline, and were so ready to let their most conservative men do nearly all the talking that the radicals chafed. An Iowa member, Samuel R. Curtis, found the taunts of the Southerners almost insupportable and longed to retort

47 Jefferson Davis, January 1, 1860, De Leon Papers, South Caroliniana Library; Sanders, December 16, 1859, Miles Papers, Univ. of N. C.
48 *Cong. Globe,* 36th Cong., 1st Sess., February 24, 1860.

in kind. "But our friends generally advise a cool, quiet indifference," he wrote in his journal, "believing the [Southern] object is to keep up such a feeling as will drive stragglers into the Democratic lines." [49] Tom Corwin's good-natured utterances had a mollifying effect.

Restraint was imperative, for at times a spark would have set loose an explosion. The Clerk, his indecision approaching imbecility, was utterly unable to control the vociferous assemblage. Again and again, when he declined to put motions that would have restored discipline, members longed for another John Quincy Adams to arise, as Adams had done in the deadlock of 1839, to take control and lead the House in self-organization. Henry A. Wise's ejaculation of that time might have been reechoed: "Now we are a mob!" Until its constitutional officers were installed the House *was* a mob, and an inflammable one.

On the floor, angry harangues, denunciations, and charges, emphasized by bursts of hand-clapping, foot-stamping, and raucous laughter. In the galleries, applause and hissing from the motley crowd of onlookers—loafers, clerks, politicians, handsomely dressed ladies and gentlemen. In the lobbies, a seething, murmuring, ugly-tempered mass of hangers-on; everywhere, at times, language that would have disgraced a barroom. Recurrently, speakers lashed out in passages that threatened to precipitate a general affray. Once, two Indianans, Dunn and Davis, exchanged the lie amid a general uproar; once, Haskin of New York ridiculing McRae of Mississippi as a circus rider brought on an approach to mob fighting. Roger A. Pryor made insolent speeches in polished language; Keitt turned on his stage thunder; and Reuben Davis declared that he was for hanging Seward and others who avowed what he called murderous sentiments. "The Capitol resounds with the cry of dissolution," wrote Senator Grimes to his wife, "and the cry is echoed throughout the city."

Practically all members were now armed with deadly weapons. In both chambers, Senator Hammond said, "the only persons who do not have a revolver and a knife are those who have two revolvers." For a time a New England Representative, a former clergyman, came unarmed, but finally he too bought a pistol. A Louisiana Congressman threatened to fetch his double-barrelled shotgun into the House. Supporters of both parties in the galleries also bore lethal weapons, and were ready to use them.[50] A single shot or blow might have brought on a melee which would have shocked the civilized world and perhaps have dissolved the government.

One Southern spectator wrote Alexander H. Stephens that he expected to see bloody fighting before the House was organized. A good many slave State members, he declared, "are willing to fight the question out, and to settle it

48 MS Journal, December 8, 1859; Illinois State Hist. Library.
50 *Cong. Globe*, 36th Cong., 1st Sess., December 7, 8, 1859, January 5, 12, 1860, etc.

right there; and some are even anxious. Deplorable as this is, it is nevertheless true. I can't help wishing the Union were dissolved and we had a Southern confederacy."[51] These were the Southerners who impressed Charles Francis Adams, Jr., as spoiling for a war; but this was a mistaken interpretation, for their temper was much less aggressive than it seemed. Fear—honest fear of the future—was really at the root of much of the bluster. The Southerners had a general fear of losing their rights, a deadly fear of servile rebellion, and a growing fear of Northern onslaughts. A few subtle men, listening to the speeches, thought that their brave words concealed a gnawing apprehension.[52]

However compounded of resentment, aggressiveness, braggadocio, and fear, the current temper made some kind of violent denouement all too possible. Reports circulated that Governor Wise had promised, if fighting began, to send Virginia troops to seize the capital and impound the national funds and papers. The impetuous governor had certainly used Brown's raid as an excuse to arm and drill the militia, spending more than $250,000, quartering large bodies of soldiery on the inhabitants, and enforcing martial law. "More than fifty thousand stand of arms already distributed," ex-President Tyler had written on December 6. Wise's alarmist inflation of the raid had done much to place Virginia on a military footing—and, had fighting broken out in the capital, he might have been foolish enough to march on the city.[53]

It is certain that another governor, Gist of South Carolina, promised armed support to the Congressmen of his State if they offered forcible resistance to the seating of such a Speaker as John Sherman. Declaring that, though he preferred a peaceable solution, he was prepared to wade in blood rather than submit to a degrading inequality, he privately assured them: "If . . . you upon consultation decide to make the issue of force in Washington, write or telegraph me, and I will have a regiment in or near Washington in the shortest possible time."[54]

The country was perhaps nearer to bloodshed in these tense weeks than it knew. In the South particularly, popular feeling rose as the press published reports of the speeches. Just before Christmas, the Virginia legislature passed resolutions extending sympathy to the Representatives of the State in the struggle in which they were engaged, and recommending, in view of the public danger, a union of all elements opposed to the Black Republicans.[55] As January dragged on with Congress still deadlocked, business became alarmed. Men directing the large financial houses predicted that, unless early organization of

51 J. Hanly Smith, January 14, 1860; Stephens Papers, LC.
52 S. R. Curtis MS Journal, December 6, 1859.
53 See J. M. Botts, "Letter to Opposition Members" (pamphlet); *Hunter Corr.*, 281.
54 To W. P. Miles, December 20, 1859; Miles Papers, Univ. of N. C.
55 Printed circular, December 23, 1859.

the House restored confidence, the country would suffer a panic worse than that of 1857.[56]

[IV]

Then, at the end of January, to the nation's intense relief, the paralyzing contest terminated. With only 109 Republicans and 86 Administration men in a House of 230 sitting members, neither side could elect a man without gaining a considerable number of Know-Nothings or Whigs. At one moment, on the thirty-ninth ballot, it seemed that the Democrats were about to triumph. Joining hands with the "South Americans," they mustered one hundred and twelve votes for William N. H. Smith, a North Carolina Know-Nothing. As last-minute pledges on the popular sovereignty issue were given, some Douglas Democrats changed their votes to place themselves in Smith's column: Pendleton of Ohio, Montgomery of Pennsylvania, Morris of Illinois, and others. Amid cheers over their decision, pages raced down from the Clerk's desk to report that Smith had a majority of one and was elected! Triumphant Democrats placed the news on the House telegraph.

The Republicans, however, still had a card to play. Instantly, the tall, slender form of John Sherman rose above the clamorous groups. For seven weeks, while his name led the balloting, he had cast no vote. "Mr. Clerk," he said calmly, "call my name." The Clerk did so. Sherman responded, "Mr. Corwin!" The vote was tied. As several members again changed their votes, the Clerk announced the final result: Smith 112, Sherman 106, scattering 10, with no choice.[57]

It was now the turn of the Republicans to strike a blow. On January 30, Sherman withdrew to clear the track for a coalition nominee. It was unfortunate that he had to do so, for he would have made an excellent Speaker. A quiet, moderate, businesslike man, who since entering the House in 1855 had devoted his main attention to financial subjects, he no more sympathized with abolitionism than his brother William Tecumseh, who wrote him from New Orleans that abolitionist ideas would mean disunion, war, and anarchy. "You ask why I signed the recommendation of the Helper book," John wrote his brother. "It was a thoughtless, foolish, and unfortunate act."[58] During the debates, Sherman had reemphasized his opposition to any interference with slavery inside the States, and had assured his Southern colleagues that the Republicans had come to Washington filled with condemnation of the John Brown raid.

56 J. W. Bryce, Phila., January 20, 1860; Boteler Papers, Duke Univ.
57 *Cong. Globe*, 36th Cong., 1st Sess., January 28, 1860; N. Y. *Herald, Tribune*, Washington *Constitution*, January 29, 30, 1860.
58 *The Sherman Letters*, 78, 70.

Now, as he gave way, a coalition slate comprising William Pennington of New Jersey for Speaker, John W. Forney for Clerk, and Thomas H. Ford of Ohio for printer, was brought forward. Pennington, a new member of hazy political affiliations, long a Whig, had been elected to his seat by a People's Party. On the forty-fourth ballot, taken February 1, he obtained one hundred and seventeen votes and a majority. He was to prove one of the worst-equipped and most incompetent Speakers in the nation's history.

Both sides could take some satisfaction in what one member termed a dogfall result. The Democrats could boast that they had blocked Sherman and forced their opponents to turn to an old-time Whig who supported the Fugitive Slave Law just as it stood. The Republicans could say that they had chosen a determined upholder of Congressional exclusion of slavery from the Territories. The major advantage, however, lay with the Republicans.

Pennington, aligning himself with that party, accepted with little change the roster of committees which Sherman had drawn up in anticipation of his own election. He made Sherman chairman of the powerful Ways and Means Committee, and placed Justin S. Morrill in that key group to write new tariff legislation. He made Owen Lovejoy, a champion of homestead legislation, chairman of the Public Lands Committee. He named the veteran Galusha A. Grow head of the Committee on Territories. Well might Republicans give the new Speaker a serenading party, with champagne flowing freely at Willard's Hotel. Well might John Sherman stand up there to assert that, since the decisive vote, stocks had advanced, cotton ruled firm at eleven cents, slave property was as valuable as ever, and the public mind was serene. The Republicans had elected a Speaker, and the Union was safe. So will it be, he predicted, when they have elected a President.[59]

Nevertheless, passionate scenes were still enacted on the floor. Early in April, a violent speech by Lovejoy aroused the anger of Southerners to a high pitch. Pryor interrupted him; friends of the two men sprang forward to support them; and for a moment a battle seemed imminent. Crawford, who declared that not a dozen overseers in Georgia would submit to such language as Lovejoy used, was minded to shout: "Gentlemen will take parties for a cotillion." By a mighty effort he kept calm. "I never said a word to anybody," he wrote Stephens, "but quietly cocked my revolver in my pocket and took my position in the midst of the mob, and as coolly as I write it to you now, I had made up my mind to sell out my blood at the highest possible price." For several days the excitement constantly threatened an explosion. If some member had lost his self-control, the ensuing melee might have precipitated civil war.

59 N. Y. *Weekly Tribune*, February 11, 1860. Elihu Washburne was made chairman of the Commerce Committee, Schuyler Colfax of Post Offices, and Corwin of Foreign Affairs.

[V]

The currents of sectional antagonism which flowed from the House were reinforced by similar impulses from a quarreling Senate. Mason's resolution for an inquiry into Harper's Ferry had no sooner been offered than Lyman Trumbull was on his feet to demand an investigation into the pillaging of the arsenal at Liberty, Missouri, in 1855, by a band arming for the invasion of Kansas. This was a gratuitous gesture, for the facts of the Missouri episode were well known. After Trumbull had irritated Southerners by alluding to the "shrieks" of Virginia, Hale of New Hampshire deepened their resentment by declaring that some judges of the Supreme Court were base tools of the slave power, that Federal trials under the Fugitive Slave Law were the most monstrous perversions of justice in the history of the English-speaking peoples, and that Northern forbearance had been stretched to its utmost limits. If the first attack in the House had come from the South, in the Senate it came (with far less provocation) from the North.

Republican spokesmen, one after another, spiritedly denied any connection with or sympathy for John Brown. Trumbull, for example, declared that no man who was unprepared to destroy the government and society itself could justify such a criminal act. Yet even as these men spoke, Jefferson Davis, Chesnut, Yulee, C. C. Clay, and other Southerners insisted that the raid was the logical result of Republican teachings. They scornfully rejected the idea that a few pale words of Republican censure could weigh against the memorial meetings and minute guns which had honored Brown on the day of his death. What had given birth to his violence and Helper's incendiarism? It was the nefarious spirit of multitudes of Northern Republicans, who, shouted Chesnut, are constantly scattering firebrands among us. Southerners harked back not only to the irrepressible conflict address, but to Seward's speech of 1855 in which, pointing to three million slaves as a sullen, half-hostile force, he had said that a servile rebellion is always the most hideous form of war, and that the outside world always sympathized with slaves in revolt.[60]

Conditional threats of secession were taking on increased emphasis in Senate as well as House, and were all too plainly an expression of hardening sentiment. It was not difficult to detect the note of apprehension underlying these utterances. We say, declaimed Chesnut, that we can no longer tolerate the present dangers; "we will sunder the Union, pull it to pieces, column, base, and tower, before we submit to be crushed by a government which is our own as well as yours." Clay of Alabama predicted that few if any Southern States would sub-

60 *Cong. Globe*, 36th Cong., 1st Sess., 129.

mit to the installation of a Republican President. Senators Toombs, Iverson, and Clingman all asserted that the triumph of a Northern party would mean the disruption of the Union. Hunter, always inarticulate, voiced his emotions in an absurd figure of speech. The Union was a mighty arch, held together by the concentrated strength and mutual support of its parts—"and the very keystone of this arch consists of the black marble cap of African slavery; knock that out, and the mighty fabric, with all that it upholds, topples and tumbles to its fall." In the House, Albert Rust was declaring that the people of Arkansas loved the Union. "But, sir, when it is perverted and prostituted into an instrument of wrong, injustice, insult, and oppression, . . . we will oppose and resist it, though it should be rent into as many fragments as there are States composing it." Jefferson Davis expressed the feeling of radicals: "The power of resistance consists, in no small degree, in meeting the enemy at the outer gate." [61]

That there was no danger of immediate action, however, was demonstrated by the failure of Memminger's mission to Virginia. The agent of South Carolina, received with due ceremony, delivered a four-hour address to the Richmond legislature on January 19, 1860. He urged the Old Dominion to join other States in a convention to discuss means of protecting their rights and property. South Carolina, he said, would abide by the will of her sisters. "If our pace be too fast for some, we are content to walk slower; our earnest wish is that all may keep together." While the address was heard with attention, and the legislature voted to publish and distribute ten thousand copies, no strong disposition to act appeared. Not wishing to embarrass the deliberations, Memminger returned to South Carolina on February 10. He reported to Governor Gist that the Virginians were hesitant because they felt that Southern rights might yet be preserved within the Union, and feared that the proposed convention would prove precipitate.

In the end, the Virginia legislature resolved that it was inexpedient to appoint deputies to a conference. Most other Southern States showed a similar reluctance (Mississippi alone selecting delegates), and the gathering vanished into oblivion. On this point, conservatism still won the day. Gist, indeed, had to write Governor Hicks of Maryland that he never desired secession so long as the rights of the South in the Union were respected and her equality was recognized.[62]

61 *Idem*, 37, 124, 272, etc.
62 A group of former Whigs and other Opposition members of the Virginia legislature addressed a letter to John Minor Botts, January 14, 1860, declaring themselves disturbed by the manifestation of a design to prepare Virginia for Civil War, and to use the John Brown raid as a pretext for early hostilities. Botts replied to the group in a pamphlet of fifteen pages of fine type, denouncing the efforts of Wise and the Virginia radicals to exaggerate current difficulties. In Richmond, he wrote later, these men had created an uproar that had rarely been paralleled even in Paris and that had spread all over the State. See Botts. *The Great Rebellion*, 177, 178; Shanks, *Secession Movement in Virginia*, 62 ff.,

In the running Congressional debate, the repercussions of the John Brown raid happily counted for less than had been anticipated. The investigating committee under Senator Mason, sitting behind closed doors, accumulated a mass of evidence but none of it implicated the Republican Party. Gerrit Smith, T. W. Higginson, George L. Stearns, and the others involved were abolitionists pure and simple. The committee failed to make any deep impression on public opinion. When Frank B. Sanborn and several others whom it summoned to Washington to testify refused to move, the Senate voted their arrest as contumacious witnesses.[63] Early in April, a deputy Federal marshal and deputy sergeant-at-arms of the Senate, acting under a warrant issued by the Vice-President, appeared in Concord to seize Sanborn. As they tried to force the struggling young man into a carriage, a menacing crowd gathered, while Judge Rockwood Hoar hurriedly wrote out a writ of personal replevin. The case promptly came before the State supreme court under Chief Justice Lemuel Shaw. That tribunal held unanimously that no authority existed for the arrest, and that Sanborn should be discharged. All spring, vehement disclaimers of John Brown by most Republican chieftains continued, and a repudiation of his acts was shortly to be written into the Republican platform.

Yet the fact of a powerful change in Southern feeling since the raid could not be ignored. It was not founded on any growing desire for disunion *per se;* it was not attributable—far from it—to any rising response to the demands for a territorial slave code and a reopening of the foreign slave trade. It was a change founded on fear; fear, since Harper's Ferry and the Northern response thereto, of assaults from without and uprisings from within which would undermine their precarious social and economic system and initiate a series of revolutionary changes. The best Southerners knew in their hearts that the system was full of objectionable features. Thoughtful men were well aware that they could no more hold the system frozen and changeless than they could immobilize the Mississippi River. Committed to the pretense that slavery was untouchable and unchangeable, they saw the tides of world-wide social progress surging at their bastions. They realized that Harper's Ferry, unimportant in itself, was a symbol; that John Brown's pikes were so many flaming glaives brandished in the heavens. They were afraid; afraid of the future, which down to the night of the

---

85 ff. For Memminger's mission, see Charleston *Courier*, February–March, 1860; "South Carolina Mission to Virginia," *De Bow's Review*, IV, 751–777; Miles Papers, Univ. of N. C. Gist's letter is in the Charleston *Mercury*, February 17, 1860.

63 Stearns more courageously appeared before the Senate committee on February 24, 1860, and did not mollify Southerners by his outspoken statement that he believed John Brown the representative man of the 19th century as Washington was of the 18th. "The Harper's Ferry affair and the capacity for self-government shown by the Italians in 1859 were the great events of the age," he remarked. N. Y. *Weekly Tribune*, March 3, 1860.

raid had still seemed far away, but which the morning after was knocking imperiously at their gates. How could they forget those levins of a coming tempest, and how arrest the future? Only by forsaking the Union—only by isolation. A tie with the North and the world was a tie with irresistible social progress.

This widespread fear, struggling with the deep-seated love of the Union and with the hope that some rational adjustment could yet be worked out (for optimism was one of the cardinal traits of American life), produced a seething maelstrom of ideas and emotions. How far even the more radical States yet stood from any desire for an irrevocable break was illustrated by the course of Alabama.

Outwardly, the Alabamians seemed bent on militant action. The State Democratic convention, meeting in Mobile on January 11, 1860, with Yancey its leading spirit, passed with a remarkable approach to unanimity resolutions declaring that the South should maintain the principles of the Dred Scott decision, that the delegates in Charleston should present these resolutions, and that if they were not accepted in substance, the delegation should withdraw. Yancey, after a struggle of twelve years, had succeeded in committing the Alabama party to support of Calhoun's resolutions of 1848. On February 24, the Alabama legislature adopted resolutions—and here again Yancey's master hand was visible—directing the governor, in the event of a Republican victory in November, to call an immediate State convention to determine what steps Alabama should take to protect herself.[64] Yet these steps did not point to a general intention to break with the Union if a Republican were constitutionally elected President; they did not even point to a general desire to break with the Douglas Democrats.

Many voted for the conditional instructions to withdraw at Charleston simply as a threat, believing that the fear of Democratic ruin would bring about concessions by the Douglas men to the demands of the South. If the threat failed—well, the delegation might disregard its instructions. Much the same threat had been made by the Alabama State convention in 1848, but the delegates had meekly fallen into line behind Cass. Many also believed that even if the Alabama representatives did bolt at Charleston, this would break up neither the party nor the Union. In some fashion or other the party would reunite before the

64 A desperate struggle had been under way in Alabama between the forces of Yancey and of Douglas. The chief Yancey organ was the Montgomery *Advertiser*; the chief Douglas organ, John Forsyth's Mobile *Register*. The Montgomery *Confederation*, which wished the Lecompton issue forever buried, was ready to support Douglas on the Cincinnati platform and a noncommital reassertion of the Dred Scott decision. John J. Seibels, editor, to Douglas, January 17, 1860, Douglas Papers. The *Southern Advocate*, published in North Alabama, took the same stand. The Yancey wing stood for the slave-code doctrine; the Seibels-Forsyth wing for a reassertion of the Cincinnati platform. As we shall see later, the Yancey forces won. Murphy, *Alabama and the Charleston Convention of 1860*, 245 ff.

campaign got well under way; and if it did not, the fact that three or four parties were in the field would mean no electoral majority for anybody, a choice of President by the House, and a probable Southern victory. As for the legislative resolutions providing for a State convention to decide upon the question of secession, here too defiance of the North was more apparent than real. "Many who voted for the call," testifies an Alabamian familiar with the spirit of the time, "were ready to deny that occasion existed for extreme action, and in the event of the meeting of a convention, would be ready to resort to any delay by which the passions of the hour could be assuaged and the dreaded spectre of disunion be exorcised." [65]

Nobody, in fact, as 1860 opened, could predict how far the South would go in the fateful months just ahead. The men most uneasy were those who realized that, in a time of revolutionary crisis, the extremists always gain ground at the expense of the moderates. Crittenden, Bell, Rives, Botts, and other border State men of the Opposition were trying hard to rally and organize the conservative groups. Declaring the country on the verge of ruin, carrying on an active correspondence with Washington Hunt, Letcher, John P. Kennedy, Amos A. Lawrence, and others of their type, Crittenden led in issuing a January call for the establishment of a national constitutional party to combat both the Democrats and Republicans. He implored Alexander H. Stephens to aid him in the movement, which he thought was favored by the feeling of the whole country.[66]

At the same time, Southern radicals made no concealment of their determination to push forward as fast and far as circumstances permitted. Another correspondent of Stephens, Representative Martin J. Crawford of Georgia, asserted that his fellow-Southerners in the House were prepared for decisive measures. "All the members say that they have no doubt their people are ready to dissolve, not only extreme men but men from the border States, in fact they talk stronger than we do." [67] The South, declared Pryor of Virginia, "is bracing her energies for the inevitable struggle." The more intransigent governors—Moore of Alabama, Perry of Florida, Joseph E. Brown of Georgia, Gist of South Carolina, McWillie of Mississippi—continued to issue exhortations to resistance.

Everywhere in the South, men were torn between old loyalties and new fears. From letters and diaries significant testimony of their agony of spirit can be disinterred. Typical of innumerable others is the statement of a North Carolina Unionist, William A. Walsh, that, long as he had stood by the national cause, the Northern applause for John Brown and Helper had shaken him, and that unless the slaveholding areas were made safe from further assaults, he was

65 Hodgson, *Cradle of the Confederacy*, Ch. 15.
66 January 13, 1860; Stuart Collection, 1860.
67 Washington, December 13, 1859; Stephens Paper, LC.

willing to take the chance of every probable evil that might flow from disunion. A majority in his county, he believed, would still accept an honorable compromise, but a large minority was already determined upon secession by fair means or foul.[68] In the South Carolina senate, another staunch Unionist, E. J. Moses, announced that while he had never expected his feelings to change, he was at last ready for secession; for he did not believe that peace, safety, or honor could longer be found in a yoke with the North. Only one Unionist newspaper was now left in South Carolina, Benjamin F. Perry's *Southern Patriot* at Greenville; and only two effective speakers in the legislature, Perry and M. P. O'Connor, took the Unionist side in debate.[69]

The passions of the hour were strongly affecting the emotions of Southern women. Though that good soldier, E. Kirby Smith, serving in the West, was still a hearty nationalist, his mother wrote him from St. Augustine in terms used by countless others:

The whole country is in a state of fearful agitation—disunion! disunion! is the cry with our Southern friends, it is boldly spoken of by the fireside, in public, in all places it is the absorbing subject. The aggressions of the North and the insults to which we are subjected in their papers their treasonable acts how can it be otherwise if our rights as guaranteed by the Constitution are trampled under foot defiantly—disunion must follow. Southern men and Southern women will not sit down with folded hands if the masses elect a Black Republican President. There are no doubt noble Patriots, lovers of Country and respecters of law among them, but they are as sprinklings in the multitude. These are fearful times. What will be the end I know not. . . . I feel confident that your sword will be offered to the land of your birth—was not the stampede of the Southern students from Northern colleges a beautiful thing—how I honor those youths—I have the blood of a soldier of the Revolution in my veins, and it warms up as I think how the noble fabric of this building has been desecrated.[70]

It is not remarkable that Caleb Cushing, whose legal work took him to Washington, used New Year's Day to make a gloomy report to ex-President Pierce. "We seem to be drifting into destruction before our eyes, in utter helplessness. The Administration is utterly depopularized; the President is embarrassed with insoluble questions; Congress is paralyzed by party spirit; and everybody seems to despair of any help from man, though many are looking vaguely for they knew not what interposition from Providence."[71]

We have spoken of the Southern realization that a tie with the North and the world was a tie with irresistible social progress. A good many Americans

68 December 12, 1859; L. C. Branch Papers, Duke Univ.
69 Kibler, *Perry*, Ch. 16; M. D. O'Connor, *Life of M. P. O'Connor*.
70 January 11, 1860; E. Kirby Smith Papers, Univ. of N. C.
71 January 1, 1860; Pierce Photostats, LC.

were now hearing of *The Origin of Species*, just published in England. The Darwinian age, not only in biology but in the social sphere, was opening. Faith in evolution was henceforth to be mightily reinforced. Slavery could not be detached or shielded from the forces of the time; and how, in the year of grace 1860, did slavery look against the background of an evolving world civilization? For beyond all question, beneath the issue of union or disunion, war or peace, lay the complex problem of slavery.

Slavery in a World Setting

IN THE summer of 1860, Augustus Baldwin Longstreet, former judge, author, and head of South Carolina College, drove to Somerset House in London, scene of the Fourth International Statistical Congress, to which Secretary Cobb had appointed him a delegate. The American minister, Dallas, was present. They had just applauded Prince Albert's opening address when a voice abruptly addressed the chair. Lord Brougham was saying in an ironical tone that as a veteran reformer he wished to call the attention of Mr. Dallas to the fact that one delegate was a Negro, Dr. Delany, born in the United States but now a resident of Canada. As the audience clapped, Delany got up, thanked Brougham, and begged to assure the congress that he was a *man*.

Thereupon, as Dallas glowered, Longstreet stalked out of the assemblage with affronted dignity. A great commotion followed. The venerable Brougham, wishing to soothe Dallas's feelings, called on the minister but was turned from his door. Lord Lansdowne, for the government, tendered regrets. The greatest reformer of all, Lord Shaftesbury, wrote that Brougham's conduct had been foolish and unwarranted. Though friends urged Longstreet to return to the congress, he sternly refused. Before leaving London, he not only sent Cobb a long letter of explanation but published in the *Morning Chronicle* a paper upholding slavery and pouring out against the free society of Britain the same arguments that Southerners often used against the North.[1]

The infirm, eccentric Brougham had offered the American representatives a sad insult; but then the United States was in a sad position before other lands.

[I]

It was all too true, as Bryant wrote and Lincoln said, that slavery placed American principles in a false light to the outside world. "How it moves the pride and curls the lip of European despotism!" wrote Bryant. "How it strikes

---

1 Wade, *Longstreet*, 325, 326; *Diary of G. M. Dallas*, 407–410.

down the power and crushes the hopes of the struggling friends of freedom all over the world!" [2] In 1859, Lord John Russell brought out the first volume of his life of Charles James Fox. Although in treating the Revolution he paid tribute to the founders of the republic, he noted certain defects of the American system; above all, slavery—a blot which oceans could not wash away. No boasts of wealth, literary power, and refinement of manners, he wrote, could make men overlook the vices and crimes which American slavery begat.

Fortunately, declared Russell, this blot must vanish. "Neither the philosophical dogma of the authors of the Constitution, nor the strict pedantry of law, can stifle the cry of outraged humanity, nor still the currents of human sympathy, nor arrest forever the decrees of Eternal Justice." Such moralizing stung many Americans like a whiplash. So did the Earl of Carlisle's introduction to *Uncle Tom's Cabin*. So did the news in 1859 that citizens of the Swiss canton of Vaud were raising money to purchase freedom for American slaves. And so did word early in 1860 that an emancipation committee had been formed in London, addressed at its first meeting by the Haitian minister, to put Britain on guard against proslavery visitors, protest against any communion between British religious bodies and American proslavery churches, and diffuse information on slavery.

The fact that the antislavery movement, as a world force, was bound up with the world-wide struggle for democracy, was clear to all who studied European opinion. In Britain, France, and other lands the eighteenth-century aristocracy, with some philanthropic exceptions, had been relatively indifferent to slavery; titles and wealth had long protected the slave trade. In France, the Revolution, an uprising of the masses, had given birth to a powerful if short-lived emancipationist movement. The British crusade which outlawed the slave trade and brought about abolition in the colonies had been organized mainly by middle-class Quakers, Methodists, other Dissenters, and Radicals. Taken up by artisans, tradesmen, and writers, it had finally become an overwhelming mass movement before which the government gave way. Few national acts in history have exhibited such a disinterested benevolence as British emancipation; and it, like the stoppage of the slave ships, had been forced upon the governing class by an irresistible pressure from below.

Whatever friendliness to slavery remained in Britain, France, Holland, and other European lands was found chiefly in aristocratic circles, and in wealthy trading groups connected with the old West Indian planting interest. It was no accident that in France such students of democracy as Tocqueville and Edouard Laboulaye were emancipationists. The liberal elements in England represented by Bright, Cobden, Forster, and John Stuart Mill, by the London *Daily*

2 Nevins, *Evening Post*, 253.

News and the *Spectator*, were keenly absorbed in the antislavery movement in America. An address of "Democrats of England," nearly two thousand in number, had been sent in 1853 to "Democrats of the United States":

Brace up your hearts to extinguish slavery as soon as it can be done *with safety*, and you will at once have double resolution, double moral power, to reanimate the swooning liberties of Europe. Fail us not, we pray you! but urge your government to all active aid which can be prudently and wisely given, and that without delay. Strengthen your own liberties, fulfill your providential destiny, and earn the glory of rescuing fallen Europe—a glory which *our* government does not know how to appreciate or achieve.[3]

The voice of one great European democrat claimed attention on the morrow of John Brown's execution—Victor Hugo. The fame of the French poet was now at its height. From his exile under the British flag, he had protested against the tyranny of Napoleon III and every other form of European oppression. The day Brown died, he wrote the London *Daily News* a letter which was republished in every nation of the civilized globe, even Russia. As was his habit, he grew over-rhetorical. "There is something more terrible than Cain slaying Abel," he declared; "it is Washington slaying Spartacus." But, expressing the devotion of freedom-loving Europeans to the transatlantic republic, his letter was moving in its appeal from the America of 1860 to the America of the Founders. The transaction just closed, he wrote, took place not, alas, in Turkey, but in the brightest free community of the globe:

Such things are not done with impunity, in the face of the civilized world. The universal conscience of mankind is an ever-watchful eye. . . . At this moment the gaze of Europe is fixed on America. . . . The more one loves, admires, reveres the Republic, the more heartsick one feels at such a catastrophe. No matter how intense may be the indignation of the generous Northern States, the Southern States associate them with the disgrace of this murder. All of us, whosoever we may be, for whom the democratic cause is a common country, feel ourselves in a manner compromised and hurt. . . . When we say to ourselves that the republic is a glory of the human race, that she is the queen of an entire world, and that she bears on her brow a radiant light of freedom we affirm that John Brown will not die, for we recoil, horror-struck, from the idea of so great a crime committed by so great a people.

3 N. Y. *Tribune*, September 20, 1853. The *Edinburgh Review*, discussing slavery and the slave trade in its issue for October, 1858, emphasized the fact that in proportion as the South placed restrictions on the press, and discouraged free thought and speech, it must grow less liberal. In the North, meanwhile, the lower type of mercantile spirit was inimical to public service. "No consideration, however, is more plain than that of the high merit and hopeful greatness of the genuine republicans throughout the Union." The British and Americans must stand together for democracy. "Never were we and they more bound to each other in a common duty and a common sentiment than now. . . . We are thinking of the free millions who regard labor and social organization in the light of the century in which they live."

American slavery was one of the stubborn obstacles to the progress of democracy throughout the world. Harriet Martineau had said so in the eighteen-thirties, James Silk Buckingham said so in the eighteen-forties, and Alexander Mackay said so in the eighteen-fifties. Laboulaye and Fredrika Bremer were emphatic in this assertion—the latter adding, however, that the curse of slavery might eventually be made a world blessing if large numbers of American-taught Negroes could be returned to Africa to give that land freedom and progress. Every reactionary abroad, even admitting the need of home reforms, could ask whether it was well to discard existing institutions for the ideas of a slaveholding America; for the practices of a democracy which, as one Englishman put it, sold wives and children into perpetual exile from distracted husbands and mothers. As slavery was defended in the United States by men who pointed to the slums of Lawrence, Manchester, and Lyons, so social and political ills in Europe were defended by men who pointed to the evils of Southern slavery. By simple logic (as the Civil War soon proved), European liberals and American freesoilers were partners in a grand common cause.

Intelligent British opinion (better informed than Continental criticism) recognized the complexity of the American problem, the fact that slavery was inherited from the era of European domination, and the defensibility of the system as a transitional status. The *Westminster Review*, in various articles, reminded Britons that they had done much to fasten slavery upon the South; that an immense part of Southern wealth was invested in slave labor; that if four million black people dwelt in England the British would feel differently about the race problem; and that the apprehension of the Southerner for his property, the lives of his family, and all that made existence comfortable and honorable, was excusable. It accused the North and Europe of complicity with the slaveholders in accepting profits from forced labor.[4] The *North British Review*, too, was aware of the many difficulties attending emancipation. Much, in its opinion, would depend on the gradual advance of the Negro. He had arrived in America with only a barbaric culture, but already climate, religious instruction, and intercourse with the whites had made him entirely different from his African congeners. His intellectual curiosity, above all, had been aroused; nothing that America could do would prevent him from acquiring knowledge, and knowledge must ultimately mean freedom.[5]

This magazine had little faith in compensated emancipation. While Britain

---

4 Vol. 59, p. 153; January–April, 1853, 127, 128, 140 ff.
5 Vol. 27 (1857), 442 ff. As early as 1854, *Fraser's Magazine* warned the South not to count on British support in secession. The *Quarterly Review*, three years later, predicted that if war came the South would be defeated—and defeated in part by global sentiment; for "a bad cause cannot prevail against the sympathy and reason of the whole civilized world."

had been able to afford it because her slaveholders were a small body, Northerners could not and would not buy up the slave rights of fifteen States. Nor had the review any faith in colonization schemes. The problem, it believed, would be solved by gradual elevation of the Negro in association with the white, by the influence of industrialism, always incompatible with brutish slave labor, and by the force of world opinion.

Olmsted's proposals for the gradual extinction of slavery made a sharp impression in Britain. Dickens praised his book in *Household Words*, urging a return to Jefferson's doctrine of gradual emancipation.[6] The *Westminster Review* pointed out that Olmsted's plan was far more constructive than Helper's proposals for a vindictive class warfare. Articles in the *Spectator*, *Saturday Review*, *Fraser's*, and other periodicals indicate that Olmsted's ideas were more widely accepted than those of any other student. As the years passed, a rising note of impatience crept into liberal British commentaries.[7] Let the Southern planters put aside their exaggerated fears, urged many critics. A writer in the *Westminster Review* pointed to West Indian experience as disproving their predictions of impoverishment, black supremacy, racial amalgamation, and ceaseless social strife. In Jamaica and other islands, the immense colored majority had made no vengeful use of its preponderance; the Negroes were more prosperous and enterprising than before emancipation; strife had diminished. As for amalgamation, the author—who urged a gradual liberation in America—thought that less of it would occur under freedom than under slavery. Unprincipled whites would not have such easy access to colored women; religion would do more to elevate morality; and the marriage bond among Negroes would be respected.[8]

Other British writers suggested that the first step toward emancipation, after restricting slavery within existing bounds, would be to abolish the internal slave trade—the very life of the system. If the sale of slaves from border States were forbidden, the Lower South would be deprived of about thirty thousand Negroes annually. Already the cost of Negro labor had cut into plantation profits; and without new hands, the cotton kingdom would have to turn toward a more variegated agriculture, demanding better-skilled labor. The next step would be to stop all dealings in slaves. The odious conception of human property would be eradicated, the Negro would become a man instead of a chattel, and a

6 *Household Words*, Vol. 14, August 23, 1856.
7 The London *Times* was reckoned particularly tolerant of slavery. But its editorial comment on the New York *Tribune* report of Pierce Butler's sale of slaves at Savannah on March 2–3, 1859, which it reprinted, was scathing. The whole melancholy drama of slave life, it remarked, was here exhibited; the ruin of a speculative Southern gentleman, the woe of the slaves, the grasping character of their buyers. "If anyone wishes to see how low the white man can be brought by unlimited power to use human beings for gain, let him read the lifelike description of the Southern planters, and see into what a class the increase of the cotton trade has changed the gentlemen of the Carolinas and Georgia."
8 *Westminster Review*, January–April, 1853, 152 ff.

scheme could be worked out by which the Negro could be paid for unusual exertions and given other opportunities to earn money, his savings being appropriated to buy his freedom. The more diligent, intelligent Negroes would gain liberty first, while the stupid and lazy continued in a state of serfdom. Thus the difficulty of dealing with a horde of semi-civilized Africans would gradually disappear. So ran the argument of various Britons.[9]

Of two important British books on slavery in the late eighteen-fifties, that of William Chambers was pessimistic, that of James Stirling hopeful. Chambers, depicting the institution in *American Slavery and Colour* as both a social wrong and a wasteful, inefficient economic arrangement, feared there were but two remedies: insurrection or war. Stirling, whose *Letters From the Slave States* was fairer, believed that rising economic forces would overthrow the system. As trade and industry grew and one-crop agriculture declined, slavery would be abolished as unprofitable. Both men thought slavery doomed. So, indeed, did all British writers. And all liberals continued to express a hope that the republic would soon vindicate its moral position. Calling slavery a pestilential marsh which infected the world air, the *North British Review* declared: "America will see reflected in European opinion the coming doom of the accursed evil, and will be ashamed of the foul blot that makes Europe point the finger of scorn at her professions of liberty." [10]

French opinion, too, oversimplifying the problem, manifested a growing impatience. The geographer Elisée Reclus, who had traveled in America, contributed a denunciatory essay to the *Revue des Deux Mondes* just after Lincoln's election, attacking slave law in particular. Cucheval Clarigny, a French librarian and essayist who had been horrified by radical Southern pronouncements on the perpetuity and expansibility of slavery, wrote a more burning attack in the same review. He was specially severe on Southern censorship and terrorism.[11] Sir Willoughby Jones, who translated Clarigny in a widely circulated pamphlet, was equally critical of the Southern attitude. It was safer for a Frenchman to profess sympathy with Louis Capet in 1793, he wrote, than for a citizen of Charleston to take the side of a maltreated Negro in 1860.

[II]

Many fair-minded men, looking at the clock of the world, hoped that it might be telling the last decades of slavery in western lands. In half a century

9 *Westminster Review*, Vol. 75 (1861), 166, 167; *North British Review*, Vol. 27 (1857), 435 ff.
10 Vol. 27 (1857), 435 ff. Marshall Hall's *Facts of the Twofold Slavery of the U. S.* (1856), which proposed a scheme of self-emancipation, also attracted notice.
11 Clarigny in *Revue*, December 1; Reclus, December 15, 1860.

MEXICAN TERR.

OREGON TERR.

C A N A D A

UNITED

ATLANTIC

STATES

PACIFIC

MEXICO

CUBA (SP)

HAITI, 1793
DOMINICAN REP.
PUERTO RICO (SP.)

BR.
HONDURAS

JAMAICA

GUATEMALA
SALVADOR
NICARAGUA
COSTA RICA

HONDURAS

VENEZUELA

GUIANA

COLOMBIA

ECUADOR

PERU

BRAZIL

BOLIVIA

OCEAN

PARAGUAY

CHILE

ARGENTINA

URUGUAY

OCEAN

SLAVERY IN THE
WESTERN HEMISPHERE
1820

Slave states

Tschirky

138

CANADA

UNITED
STATES
1863

ATLANTIC

BAHAMA IS. *(BR.)*
1834

HAITI, *1793*
DOMINICAN REP.
PUERTO RICO, *1872*

CUBA
1886

MEXICO
1829

BR.
HONDURAS
1834

PACIFIC

HONDURAS
1823

JAMAICA, *1834*
(BR.)
NETH., *1863*

GUADELOUPE *(FR.), 1848*
MARTINIQUE *(FR.), 1848*
BARBADOS *(BR.), 1834*
TRINIDAD *(BR.), 1834*

GUATEMALA, *1823*
SALVADOR, *1823*
NICARAGUA, *1823*

COSTA RICA, *1823*

VENEZUELA
1854

GUIANA
BR. *1834*
1863
FR. *1848*

COLOMBIA
1852

0

ECUADOR
1854

0

PERU

1855

BRAZIL
1888

BOLIVIA
1851

OCEAN

1843
PARAGUAY

1846
URUGUAY

CHILE
1823

ARGENTINA
1853

OCEAN

SLAVERY IN THE
WESTERN HEMISPHERE
1860

Slave states

Tschirky

139

the clock had registered a sweeping change. Men still living in 1860 could recall the time when slavery or serfdom had seemed the rule throughout most of the globe. Chief Justice Taney might well remember a day when the British, French, Dutch, Portuguese, and Danish combined had forty factories on the African coast for the shipment of slaves; when Yankee slave ships dotted the Atlantic; when Spanish America and the Portuguese, Dutch, and French colonies, with many under the British flag, were strongholds of slavery; and when the institution yet existed in considerable parts of the North—for New Jersey, the last State, did not act until 1804. But stroke by stroke, the bell of the world clock had rung the knell of slavery and the slave trade as institutions which the Western World could tolerate.

Two strokes had rung out in 1780, when Massachusetts by the memorable words in her constitution declaring all men "born free and equal" extinguished slavery, and when the Pennsylvania legislature provided that all children born thereafter to slave parents should be free, though holding the position of servants until twenty-eight.[12] Another stroke sounded when, in 1787, Congress passed the Ordinance forbidding slavery northwest of the Ohio. The negroes of Haiti gained freedom and independence in 1804.

Then, as the South American colonies broke away from Spain, slavery (never strong except on the northern and northeastern shores of the continent) was abolished in one new republic after another. Chile had only a handful of negroes. Her struggle for independence began in 1810, and the first Congress decreed emancipation. In Buenos Aires, the more numerous colored population was signally versatile and energetic, carrying on many crafts; and the state no sooner gained practical independence than it provided that all children born to slaves after January 21, 1813, should be free.[13] Colombia, which had more than two hundred thousand blacks and mulattoes, took similar action, decreeing that all children born after July 16, 1821, should be liberated on attaining their eighteenth year. In Mexico, negroes were comparatively few. In view of her nearness to the United States, however, her abolition of slavery in 1829, eight years after independence, was another telling stroke on the world bell.[14]

Immediately afterward came a more resounding peal when on August 28,

12 Emory Washburn, *Mass. Hist. Soc. Proc.*, May, 1857; *Laws of Pa.*, II, 246.
13 Sir Woodbine Parish, *Buenos Aires and the Provinces of the Rio de la Plata;* F. A. Kirkpatrick, *A History of the Argentine Republic.* For Latin American slavery in general, see the *Hispanic American Historical Review*, XIII, 151–196, and XXIV, 363–431, 547–559. Light is thrown on the matter by Charles E. Akers, *A History of South America*, and A. Curtis Wilgus, ed., *South American Dictators.* It must never be forgotten that Latin American humanitarians did much more for the negro than for the impoverished and maltreated Indians and *mestizos.*
14 Bancroft, *Mexico;* Priestley, *The Mexican Nation;* and Ralph Roeder, *Juarez and his Mexico.* On slavery in Colombia, see Eduardo Posada, *La Esclavitud en Colombia, o leyes de manumision;* J. Fred Rippy, ed., Hennar and Arrubla's *History of Colombia.*

1833, as a result of the long crusade of Clarkson, Wilberforce, Zachary Macaulay, and others, the law abolishing slavery in all British possessions received royal assent. Originally, a seven-year transitional period was fixed but it was soon abbreviated, so that all slaves became completely free in 1838. The disappearance of slavery in Jamaica, Trinidad, Barbados, and neighboring islands with a dense black population, in Guiana, South Africa, Mauritius, and other areas, was important not only in itself but as making similar action in the French, Dutch, and other colonies eventually certain.[15] Slavery had lingered on in Paraguay. A law of 1842 for gradual emancipation struck it at the root, and it rapidly withered away. France, unable to lag far behind Britain, moved just after the revolution of 1848, when her provisional government decreed immediate colonial emancipation. Next came Venezuela, where negroes and mulattoes composed nearly a third of the people; perhaps more. The land of Bolivar, by a law of March 24, 1854, conceded liberty and equal rights to all inhabitants. Once more the world clock struck in 1858, when Portgual enacted that all slaves in her possessions should be placed in a system of tutelage, and become free in twenty years. In Macao and Angola, the Lisbon authorities abolished slavery outright.

Thus in half a century many living Americans had seen slavery wither away on three continents. In civilized regions of the globe it had been driven back into four redoubts: Brazil, Cuba and its neighbor Puerto Rico, Dutch Guiana and adjacent islands, and the American South. In the South itself, down to 1830 and even afterward, large elements had responded generously to the tendency of the age. Slavery was sternly criticized. The debates on it in Virginia showed a potent opposition; in Maryland and Virginia the number of free negroes increased faster than that of slaves, reaching eighty-four thousand in Maryland and fifty-eight thousand in Virginia by 1860; and many slaves were permitted broad privileges. But the Southern impulse ebbed.

Year after year, the two great antislavery societies, those of Britain and America, chronicled the progress of a movement that went forward fitfully but seldom slipped backward. Two parts of the globe that in 1858–60 attracted hope-

15 On slavery in the Guianas see James Rodway, *Guiana: British, Dutch, and French*, especially Ch. 6; J. F. H. Mourie, *La Guyane Française*, 280 ff.; Anthony Trollope, *The West Indies and the Spanish Main* (1859). Much was made by proslavery men in America of the introduction of African and East Indian apprentices or indentured workers into the British and French colonies after the abolition of slavery; and the French system in especial permitted gross abuses. But Rodway declares that the coolie improved his lot in America, and was well protected. "Having thrown off the fetters of caste, he has become more independent than he once was at home. The system may be a five years' bondage in one sense, yet in another it is such freedom as was never before known by these people." P. 205. On slavery in Venezuela, see Miguel Tejera, *Historia de Venezuela*, 231; J. M. Spence, *The Land of Bolivar*, I, 142. See also Charles H. Washburne, *History of Paraguay*, I, 348, 349; Harris G. Warren, *Paraguay;* Eduardo Acevedo, *Manuel de Historia Uruguaya;* Luis Goldames, *Chile.*

ful attention were the Dutch West Indies and Russia. The Netherlands held about forty thousand slaves in Surinam (Dutch Guiana) and a few thousand in Curacao, St. Eustatius, and St. Martin. Emancipation, backed by a growing sentiment in Holland, had been discussed for years. Inspired by *Uncle Tom's Cabin*, some young men of Amsterdam in 1853 had formed an abolition society. For a time, the planters and their mercantile friends had obstinately resisted the pressure. But after French emancipation, many landholders, seeing that with free British Guiana on one side and free French Guiana on the other slaves would constantly desert, themselves called for action. By the late fifties, the ministry was ready to move, and for several years presented the States-General with plans for compensated emancipation. Though in 1860 the project still hung fire, it was certain of success—which actually came in 1863; the only question was of details. Meanwhile, in 1859, slavery was abolished outright in the Dutch East Indies. Many slaveholders, according to the Hong Kong *Register*, refused compensation, while others accepted it only to transfer the money to the freedmen.[16]

As for Russia, her press reported that by the summer of 1858 thirty-eight governments, containing about ten million male serfs, had commenced the formation of committees of emancipation; and the Czar was speeding the nobility forward in a reform which, he said, must come peacefully from above lest it come bloodily from below.[17] Russian serfdom was a very different system indeed from American slavery—but to strike one kind of shackle from toilers in the Muscovite domains was to hearten those who wished to strike fetters from the bondsmen of the New World.

[III]

Why was it that the South, as its own antislavery energies flagged after 1830, stood in such evident contrast with the remainder of the world, and especially with Latin America? Some of the reasons have already been indicated, but others require a brief explanation. The Southerners, many of whom were sensitively concerned with Northern and British opinion, had certain defensive considerations to urge. If pressed by critics, they replied that the slavery problem had unique features in the United States, where special reasons existed for continuing the institution.

That they were correct, and that slavery in the United States differed

16 *Anti-Slavery Reporter* (London), March 1, 1855. On Dutch emancipation, see Ackersdyck, "Mouvement des Idees Economiques; Progres des Reformes; État de la Question Coloniale et de l'Esclavage en Hollande," pamphlet, Utrecht, 1861. See also N. Y. *Tribune*, October 17, 1857; *Report*, Paris Anti-Slavery Conference, 1867, pp. 75–78. In Dr. Morton E. Kahn, *Djuka: the Bush Negroes of Dutch Guiana* (1931) readers will find much on the culture of a primitive people who received comparatively little from the whites.
17 *Ann. Report Am. Antislavery Soc.* 1858–59, p. 129–132.

sharply from slavery in Mexico, Venezuela, or Peru, is unquestionable. In those countries, the Indian and *mestizo* (that is, mixed Indian and white) populations far outnumbered the pure whites.[18] Indeed, the largest single element in Mexico and Venezuela was the *mestizo* element. So it was, also, in Colombia. In Peru, the largest single group was the pure-blooded Indians, with the *mestizos* next. In all three republics, as in the Guianas, people of Indian or part-Indian blood felt no reluctance to intermarry with Negroes or mulattoes. Economically, socially, and culturally, the Indian, *mestizo*, and negro were all on a fairly even footing. For that matter, even the pure-blooded Spaniard of the lower classes was often ready to take a Negro or mulatto woman in marriage. It was therefore natural to make the road to manumission easy, and widespread manumission led to general emancipation. The freedman became a freeman.

Why should a Mexican Indian, still following his ancient way of life, his possessions few, his education tribal, his social status lowly, hinder the liberation of a black slave? Aside from a small white ruling class, society in the greater part of Spanish America was comparatively level and devoid of racial antipathies; the intermarriage of different stocks was natural, and the transition from slavery to freedom could be accomplished without friction. Formal abolition of slavery was also facilitated in various Latin-American countries by the fact that great masses remained in peonage, midway between slavery and freedom. This was notably the situation in Mexico, where the Spanish conquerors had instituted a system of forced labor, and in Peru, where the *mita* served the same purpose. J. Fred Rippy writes of Latin America as a whole: "Debt peonage or some other system differing from serfdom was prevalent in the majority of nations until after 1900."

Inherited Latin traditions and legal and religious concepts, moreover, simplified the processes of manumission, intermarriage, and emancipation.

Long before the Moorish conquests, before even Hannibal's invasions, the people of what are now Spain and Portugal had been familiar with their African neighbors, had intermingled with them, and had learned to attach no excessive importance to the color line. The burnished livery of the sun carried little if any stigma. The peninsular peoples shared, too, in the ancient Greco-Roman concept of the slave; a concept based on the fact that in the ancient world most slaves were white, that they fell into slavery through conquest, economic misfortune, or some other accident, and that servile status implied no natural infe-

---

18 The term *mestizo* usually meant a half-breed of white and negro, or white and Indian, parents. The term *zambo* was applied to the issue of negro and Indian unions. But no exact and unvarying meaning can be attached to any of the names applied to persons of mixed blood, whether mulatto, *mestizo*, *zambo*, *zambo preto*, *chino*, or *cholo*. A table of these names with some of their general meanings may be found in A. Wyatt Tilby, *Britain in the Tropics, 1527–1910*, 59.

riority.[19] The codification of Spanish traditional law under Alfonso the Wise (1263–1265) accepted the principle that men are naturally equal and that slavery is contrary to the law of nature. Slavery in the ancient world was cruel beyond any comparison with the American system; the picture of it given by Cato, Juvenal, Seneca, and Caesar (who after the capture of the Aduatuci sold fifty-three thousand prisoners into slavery on the spot) is revolting in the extreme. Tacitus states that the Romans lived in constant fear of slave revolt. But it was primarily white slavery. Many slaves possessed talent and skill; friendships between master and slave were often close—Cicero's letters were edited by his manumitted slave Tiro; and when a slave was admired, loved, or pitied, he could be freed without the slightest difficulty.[20]

Spain, Portugal, and the Latin-American lands had largely inherited this Roman tradition of slavery. The two leading facts in the legal position of the Roman slave had a potent influence on Hispanic-American thinking. One was that the slave was absolutely under the control of his master, who possessed a power of use, punishment, and life or death without accountability to any higher authority. The other was that the slave, if capable, well-behaved, or appealing, enjoyed a fair prospect of liberation, and, when manumitted, often achieved Roman citizenship with all accompanying civil rights. Spanish and Portuguese law mitigated the first principle, though on Cuban sugar plantations in the eighteen-fifties countless slaves were treated with a brutality that might have shocked Tiberius, and many were callously worked to death. Spanish and Portuguese law preserved and extended the second principle, holding open the road to freedom. We must, however, be on our guard against accepting written codes as representing social realities. The evidence is strong that in parts of Latin America the laws were ignored or violated.[21] Nevertheless, the statutes did

19 Tannenbaum, *Slave and Citizen: the Negro in the Americas*, 45. Negro slaves had become common in Spain and Portugal by the close of the fifteenth century, and very numerous by 1650. Lisbon, indeed, at that date had more negroes than whites. H. Morse Stephens, *Portugal*; Tannenbaum, *Slave and Citizen*, 44. Marriage between whites and negroes had taken place from the beginning without hindrance. Elizabeth Donnan, *Documents Illustrative of the Hist. of the Slave Trade to America*, I, 29.

20 Fowler, *Social Life at Rome in the Age of Cicero*, 204–236.

21 *Journal of Negro Hist.*, VI, 183 ff.; XXIX, 7 ff. Cruelty of slavery in Cuba and Puerto Rico is proved by a mountain of evidence. On paper, the Spanish laws were relatively good; in practice, slavery was much harsher than in the South, was attended by a much heavier mortality (placed by some writers at five percent a year), and left the slaves in a much more barbarous condition. The Cuban and Puerto Rican abolitionists who wrote *The Abolition of Slavery in Cuba and Puerto Rico* (N. Y., 1865; p. 34) declare the better laws a dead letter. They state of Cuba that "were it possible to make public all the data existing in the offices of the *Sindicos*, the Christian world would be horrified at such an enormous sum of cruelties committed against that poor and defenseless class." Puerto Rico in 1860 had 41,736 slaves against 300,430 whites and 241,015 free colored people. Cuba in 1862 had 368,550 slaves, as against 764,750 whites, 221,417 free colored people and 34,050 slaves. In Brazil, however, slavery was milder than in the Lower South. Lord Brougham was correct when he told Dallas's clerk that negroes had a better status in Brazil than in the United States.

facilitate manumission, social custom encouraged it, tax gatherers imposed no obstacle, and a procedure was developed by which slaves might buy their freedom in installments. Once liberated, the slave mingled with the Indian, *mestizo*, black, or mulatto population on terms of full equality.[22]

The church, too, accepting the traditions of its environment, lent aid to assimilation. It would be erroneous to say that Catholicism *per se* was more hostile to slavery than Protestantism, for much evidence can be adduced for an opposite conclusion. In Britain and the United States the antislavery crusade was a child of Protestantism. The Catholic Church was not more friendly to the Negro in Maryland or Louisiana than the Protestant sects; it was a slaveholding church (Southern monasteries owning bondsmen), which the Protestant churches were not. A Catholic historian writes that the slave system among American Catholics reflected on the whole the patterns of thought prevalent in the community, and that the church condemned the principles of Garrisonian abolitionism as conflicting with Catholic ethics and ideals.[23] In Latin America, however, the church threw itself on the side of forces that labored for manumission, social equality, emancipation, and intermarriage. Emphasizing the spiritual integrity of every individual, teaching that all human beings are children of God, urging that marriage and the family be held sacred, and instituting religious fraternities among slaves, the church made full use of its favorable social environment. The Indians, Negroes, Caucasians, and people of mixed blood were taught to regard each other as brethren in Christ.

Very different, and much more difficult, was the situation in the South. The population had but two elements, white and colored, master and slave. Since the aborigines had died out or disappeared beyond the Mississippi, no large Indian or half-breed population existed to break down lines of color and caste and act as a racial solvent. The norms of education, intellectual discipline, comfort, skill, and social responsibility attained by the whites were a pole apart from those to which the Negro, in Africa or America, had been used; no such flattening-out of standards had occurred as in Latin America. No system of peonage existed (at any rate outside New Mexico) as a halfway house between slavery and freedom. One might be developed, but that would require time. The whole tradition of the white American respecting slavery was not merely alien to the Greco-Roman tradition, but antipathetic toward it. It was the tradition of a stock which, whether among the folk of the ancient Teutonic forests, the Danish and Norse sea rovers, or the modern English-speaking peoples, had always regarded slavery as a badge of degradation. To sink into servitude, in the opinion of this stock, was the ultimate humiliation; to raise Gurth or Sambo from it required a heroic effort.

22 Tannenbaum, *Slave and Citizen*, 53, 54.
23 Rice, *American Catholic Opinion in the Slavery Controversy*, 60, 85.

It was the tradition, too, of a people which associated slavery almost exclusively with the Negro race, and which—however mistakenly—found it natural to think of that race in terms of natural inferiority. In the United States the line of slavery coincided with a marked color line, a line of apparent substandard capacities, a line drawn by inherited beliefs respecting the baseness of any people who let themselves become enchained—and hence an almost impassable social line. In Latin-American countries no such coincidence existed. The Indian, *mestizo*, Negro, and mulatto recognized no important differentiation as regarded color, capacity, attainments, or traditional dignity. The ordinary Spaniard or Portuguese, with perhaps a Moorish pigmentation, founded his immense pride of race on other considerations.[24]

The Southerner was hostile to large-scale manumission and emancipation because he felt that racial equality might end in race mixture; the Latin American felt no such hostility because he accepted racial amalgamation. A South Carolinian or Mississippian would have said that his view proved him a better man than the Mexican or Venezuelan. The Venezuelan would have said that *his* view proved him the better man. The fact was that they were different men, made so by an immense complex of inheritances and pressures. The special character of society in the United States made the problem of slavery incomparably more difficult than in Latin countries.

How great a gulf existed, again, between the Southern States and the typical West Indian colony! The English and Dutch planters felt as sharp a racial exclusiveness as the Southern slaveholders. But in most islands they were a handful of men lost in a black sea. These tropical holdings never built up distinctively white civilizations which required protection and perpetuation as such. Once Jamaica was filled with slaves, the whites never represented much more than two percent of the inhabitants. In Barbados and St. Kitts, which of the British islands had the largest white elements, the figure was usually six or seven percent; elsewhere it was below five percent. Emancipation, therefore, involved no great social or cultural revolution. Its effects, disastrous at first but later beneficent, were primarily economic. The Dutch islands were from eighty to ninety percent colored, while in Martinique and Guadeloupe the French amounted to but two or three percent of the whole. Where the disproportion of races was so great, there could be no such grim problem of race adjustment as that which appalled the South.[25]

24 G. Freyre, *The Masters and the Slaves*, 11, 40, 185–277.
25 Cf. W. W. Macmillan, *Warning from the West Indies*. Oceans of ink were spent on the controversy whether Jamaica had benefited or suffered from emancipation. The best conclusion is that a decline in prosperity had been incipient before emancipation, attributable mainly to the one-crop system and to absentee landlordism. Under the new order a hundred thousand negro farmers successfully tilled their own holdings, rejecting the long hours of

No, Southerners might well assert that the question of liberation was far more difficult in the fifteen slave States than in any other part of the globe; so perplexing that it demanded the utmost caution. The successive strokes of the world clock registered the trend of the age. In the long run, the spirit of modern industrial society, liberalism, and the humanitarian movement must prove irresistible. But then why not a little patience? And nothing was to be learned from superficial comparisons with simpler lands. The extreme difficulty of the Southern situation arose in part from the advanced nature of Southern civilization; the high pride of Southerners in their inheritance and achievements accentuating the gap between the races. "The question," as Robert Toombs said, "is not whether we could not be more prosperous and happy with these three and a half million slaves in Africa, and their places filled with an equal number of hardy, intelligent, and enterprising citizens of the superior race; but it is simply whether, while we have them among us, we would be more prosperous with them in freedom or in bondage." [26] More prosperous, that is, spiritually, culturally, socially, and materially.

What *was* the Southern feeling about slavery? Most Southerners had a sense, to begin with, that this was *their* problem; that they had to live with it and plan for it; that it was their business and nobody else's; and that they could deal with it better if they were not hectored and reproached by ignorant onlookers. They had a belief, in the second place, that, while they might do much voluntarily to improve slavery, they would do nothing under compulsion. No self-respecting individual or community cares to be driven to any course of action. As the Northern and foreign clamor grew, Southern obstinacy grew with it.[27] The South felt a strong conviction, in the third place, that Northern emphasis on the moral aspects of slavery distorted the problem, insulted the Southern people, and gave the critics an air of ethical superiority as false as it was offensive.

Liberal-minded Southerners did not deny that slavery had moral implications. But they knew that its social and economic aspects were as important as its moral

toil for low wages offered on the white plantations. John Bigelow, *Jamaica in 1850*. The termination of the protection which British sugar-planters had enjoyed in the home market, effected by the free trade legislation of 1846, was most damaging to the island industry. A. Wyatt Tilby, *Britain in the Tropics, 1527–1910*, 60, 61.

26 Phillips, *Toombs*, 165.

27 This was well expressed by W. L. Yancey. The South, he wrote, had at first viewed the warfare upon its rights and institutions by Europe and the North with contempt; then with indignation. "The inevitable effect of this moral warfare upon slavery, has been to force the adoption of a more rigid police over the intercourse of the slaves and a strict watchfulness over the movements of strangers through the slave population. Insulated from the world by their peculiar institution, denounced by the world as a degraded and corrupted race on account of his connection with it, the Southerner brightly rejects all opinions and schemes relative to it, which the world may proffer. Such a disposition is the natural consequence of insult, contumely, and wrong, long endured by our section." Undated essay, Yancey Papers, Ala. Dept. Arch. and Hist.

aspect, and that, in any scientific study of labor systems, Northern and European industrialism had dark moral blots which should be weighed against the evils of slavery. They resented the tendency of abolitionists to treat the moral issue as if it alone counted, or could be detached. Such an approach obscured the fact that the two cardinal goals in a proper race relationship—the best economic use of the Negro, and the establishment of the Negro on a plane where he could better himself and yet not break down the barriers to racial union—were more important than the satisfaction of an abstract moral demand.

Most intensely of all, even liberal Southerners felt that terrible dangers to their whole future might lurk in hasty action upon slavery. They saw that many Northerners wished to free the slaves and raise them (hundreds of miles from their own homes) to equality with the whites. They believed that such equality would lead in the immediate future to a breakdown of the plantation system, to harsh competition between the Negro and the small white farmer or artisan, and to a thousand social frictions. They believed it would lead in the distant future to that nightmare, wholesale racial amalgamation and the birth of a negroid South. Even to ameliorate slavery by hasty steps involved, in the Southern view, the risk of frightful evils. Much was to be said for legislation to legalize slave marriages and prevent the forcible break-up of families (though Southerners believed that such break-ups were less frequent than under Northern industrialism); much was to be said for tuition in reading, writing, and the mechanic arts; and much was to be said for letting industrious slaves earn their freedom, as the New Orleans merchant John McDonogh had done. Once this process of amelioration was started, however, how could it be prevented from rushing forward with accelerated speed? Where would it stop? Northern pressure and Negro demands would double-quick the march to complete freedom. Plans might be made for an intermediate tutelage, but, as in the British colonies, this would be cut short. Once let the camel get his head into the tent, and the whole animal would lunge inside.

From the prospect of these dangers, Southerners sprang back affrighted. Small farmers, clerks, and laborers, owning not a single slave, felt the perils of race adjustment quite as keenly as their richer neighbors. In most instances, they did not uphold slavery because they hoped to become slaveholders; they upheld it, rather, because they were appalled by the dangers of a premature forced march toward racial equality. And gradually many Southerners arrived at a conviction which in older days would have horrified them: If they could not persuade the North to let them alone in facing the problem, they would set up an independent Southern republic which could deal with slavery according to its own interest and conscience. Meanwhile, they would do what they could to strengthen their social system against its enemies.

[IV]

As slavery was increasingly menaced, so it must be increasingly buttressed. As the knocking on the prison gates became louder, more stringent precautions had to be taken against efforts to respond. The history of all forces of occupation is the same; while secure they can afford to be mild, but when menaced they become severe. The world movement against slavery produced a sense of crisis in the South, and, with it, panicky restrictions.

Already the slave was helpless. His status, a Southern historian writes, had been fixed to the satisfaction of masters by legislation in the years 1829–1835; the Negroes were prostrate, restrained at every point by law.[28] The institution, however, might be weakened in various ways; by benevolent owners, by the growth of industry and trade, by population changes, and by the spread of education. At various points, slavery by 1858 seemed crumbling away. In Delaware it was manifestly dying. Of the three counties, Sussex alone had many slaves, and lands there were worth only a fraction of their value in Kent and Newcastle. Exponents of gradual emancipation, led by the Milford *News*, were urging the legislature to pass a law freeing all slaves born or brought into the State at the ages of eighteen for women, twenty-one for men; this, they said, would attract a rush of immigration, stimulate industry, and raise realty by five millions at once. The chief argument against such a law was that slavery would soon perish without it. As prime field hands became worth $1,500, it paid better to smuggle them southward than to keep them.

The situation was not very different in Maryland, where nearly half the negroes had gained their liberty. At the slaveholders' convention in 1859, one planter declared that, if the existing trend continued, the State would glide into freedom within a quarter-century. Another asserted that it was impossible to hold slaves in the northern counties, for they would not do forced labor while Pennsylvania was a night's journey away. These counties *could* not keep negroes; and, while slaves were worth $1,500 in New Orleans, *would* not. The tone of the convention led the Richmond *Argus* to predict that Virginia's northern neighbor would be lost. "We shall soon cease to regard Maryland as a slave State practically. Politically, she has been dead to the South for a long time past."

In Missouri, freesoil population and ideas were growing apace. For every hundred thousand whites, the State in 1850 had fifteen thousand two hundred and nine colored people; in 1860 it had only eleven thousand one hundred and forty-three. The *Missouri Democrat* fought continuously for the free labor

28   Bassett, *Slavery in the State of North Carolina*, 108, 109.

cause, and John F. Hume's editorials, collected in a pamphlet entitled "Hints Toward Emancipation in Missouri," were widely distributed. B. Gratz Brown told the legislature in 1857 that a system of graduated emancipation was already

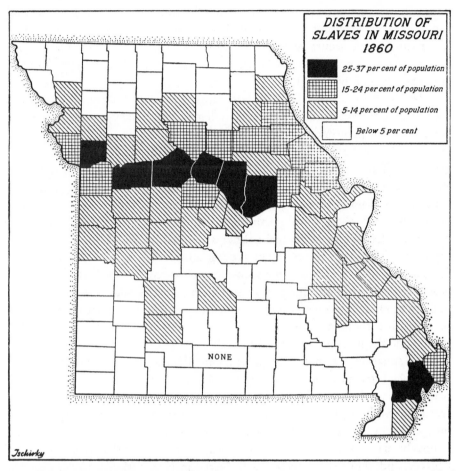

One Weak Point in Slavery. White population in Missouri more than trebled 1840–1860, rising from 322,000 to 1,063,500. Slave population failed to double, rising only from 58,000 to 115,000.

in effect; that every census showed the whites gaining steadily over the slaves; that a few years would find ninety-five largely slaveless counties pitted against a dozen heavily slaveholding counties; and that Missouri, marketing three-fourths of her exports through Northern cities and drawing two-thirds of her imports thence, had far more in common with the North than the South. James S. Rollins was almost elected governor that year on a free labor platform, declaring that emancipation might be left to the laws of latitude, climate, immigration, and production.[29]

Other danger points existed—in northern Kentucky; in western Virginia; in New Orleans, where the varied occupations of the port required intelligent labor, free Negroes thrived and the attorney George M. D. Hahn dared to denounce the institution; and in the German area of Texas. The astonishing rise in the value of Negroes was placing a heavy strain on slavery in some novel areas. Consul Bunch in Charleston noted that many rice planters were selling hands. "During the past winter," he wrote Lord Clarendon on March 4, 1857, "nearly all the slaves sold in the Charleston market have been purchased by Negro Traders from or for Mississippi and the Southwestern States; an entirely novel proceeding here, where Publick Opinion has, hitherto, been opposed to the removal of slaves from their own neighborhood." [30] In Mississippi, Texas, and other new States a $1,400 Negro could earn twelve percent or more on his value; in South Carolina, as in Missouri and Maryland, he might earn but three or four percent. Hence the tendency to dispose of hands to the richest cotton-growing districts; and hence the continued decay of slavery in the upper Carolinas from Greenville and Spartanburg to Asheville, where slavery did not pay at all. As these perils and stresses appeared, even before Harper's Ferry legislators set their pens to protective bills.[31]

Much of the restrictive legislation we have already reviewed. Louisiana went as far as any State. In 1857, it provided the death penalty for murder, rape, attempted rape or murder, insurrection, arson, or violent robbery by a slave. Any slave who struck any member of his master's family (or an overseer) hard enough to bring blood might be put to death. No slave was allowed to testify for or against a free Negro, except in cases involving servile insurrection. In 1859, free Negroes not native to the State were compelled after September 1 to choose between exile and reduction to slavery. No free Negro might keep billiard tables, coffee houses, or any establishment where spirits were sold; and free Negroes on vessels reaching Louisiana ports were to be kept in jail until the vessel was ready to leave. Slaves were forbidden to hire their own time in four

29 Wright, *The Free Negro in Maryland, 1634-1860*: Merkel, *The Anti-Slavery Controversy in Missouri, 1819-1865*; Hume, *The Abolitionists*; Brown, "Speech on Gradual Emancipation in Missouri" (pamphlet St. Louis, 1857); *Ann. Report Am. Antislavery Soc.*, 1860, pp. 209, 210.

30 FO 5/677.

31 In the western slave area of Texas many runaways escaped to Mexico. Texas slave laws were stringent, and in Washington on the Brazos, planters banded together to discourage the practice of letting slaves hire their own time. M. H. Ellis, "Social Conditions in Texas About 1850," MS, Univ. of Texas. The Charleston correspondent of the N. Y. *Tribune*, writing under date of November 7, 1860, states that a South Carolina slave cannot earn at home three percent interest on the high price he fetches; if he is sold, the money invested in State bonds or bank stock will earn eight or nine percent.

parishes where the practice had been common. Arkansas took equally harsh steps. Months before Harper's Ferry, in 1859, it prohibited any future emancipation of slaves, gave free Negroes the choice after January 1, 1860, of leaving the State or going into slavery, and forbade steamboats in Arkansas waters to carry or employ any free negro. Another law abolished imprisonment for criminal slaves, substituting up to one hundred lashes.[32]

Other States responded to the apprehensive movement. The free Negro was a menace to the institution of slavery, and must go or be kept in social fetters. The Alabama legislature in its session of 1859–60 forbade any manumission of slaves by will or bequest, or the removal of slaves from the State for the purpose of freeing them. It enacted another law permitting free persons of color to select a master or mistress, if the choice were made free from any undue influence, and become slaves.[33] The Montgomery *Mail* proclaimed it the universal sentiment of Alabamians that within two years not a single free Negro must be left. In Mississippi, the lower house carried an exile-or-slavery bill which was halted in the senate. In Georgia, both chambers voted a similar measure but the governor refused his signature. A widespread clamor for such action in North Carolina might have resulted in legislation but for the fact that a very respectable elite existed among the thirty thousand free colored folk. As it was, the increasing hostility to this so-called third class encouraged mob violence, and deterred kindly whites from helping them.[34] The Georgia legislature made it possible to indict any free Negro leading an idle, immoral, or profligate life, and to sell his labor; at the first offense for not more than two years, and, at the second, for life.

Even in the border States this attempt to rivet new armor upon the institution yielded some detestable proposals. The Missouri legislature, in March, 1860, laid before the governor a bill which prohibited the emancipation of any slave unless he or she were removed from the State within ninety days, and provided that all free adult Negroes who remained after the following September should be reduced to slavery. Special provision was made for free colored persons under eighteen. The governor, declaring that the measure was unconstitutional because it deprived persons of liberty without due process of law, and that the enforcement of any such law would cause a strong revulsion against slavery, vetoed it.

The Tennessee legislature debated a similar measure for banishing or enslaving the free Negroes. It gave Judge Catron of the Federal Supreme Court an opportunity to utter the same home truths spoken by the Missouri executive. Such an enactment, he asserted, would be cruel, shameful, and unconstitutional.

32 *Louisiana Acts of 1857,* No. 232; *Acts of 1859,* Nos. 16, 87; *Arkansas Acts of 1859,* Nos 151, 195, 225.
33 *Acts 1859–60,* Nos. 36, 71.
34 Johnson, *Ante-Bellum North Carolina,* 581, 611, 612.

FREE NEGROES, 1860

Areas without free Negroes, or unsettled
1-10 free Negroes per county
10-100 free Negroes per county
100-1000 free Negroes per county
1000 free Negroes per county and over

No Returns

Tschirley

The number of free colored people sturdily if slowly increased. In 1850, it stood at 434,000; in 1860, at 488,000, of whom about 250,000 were in the South.

The sight of the wretched exiles begging for bread would be the most forcible of all antislavery arguments. "In what nook or corner of the State," he demanded, "are the principles of humanity so deficient that a majority of the whole inhabitants would commit an outrage not committed in a Christian country of which history gives any account?" [35] The bill failed.

In the fall of 1858, a gathering of Marylanders of the Eastern Shore (where slavery was strong) not merely called for a State convention to deal with the regulation of the colored race, but suggested that all free Negroes should be given a choice between expulsion or enslavement. The convention duly met in Baltimore in June, 1859, and debated this suggestion for two days. One group of planters vehemently urged that the free colored population was a nuisance and an injury; that it ought to be abolished on terms advantageous to the whites; and that such Negroes as would not consent to leave should be sold on easy terms, thus enabling citizens of limited means to become slaveowners. Happily, most delegates were against any such heartless policy. The census of 1850 had shown that free Negroes constituted about forty-five percent of the colored population, and many were conspicuously industrious and enterprising. The convention majority decisively rejected the demands of extremists. In fact, it passed resolutions condemning the proposed action as cruel and oppressive and declaring that expulsion would be a heavy blow to the State. Removal of the free Negroes, it declared, would nearly cut in half the agricultural and household labor furnished by the colored inhabitants, produce great inconvenience to thousands of householders who used them as servants, and largely destroy the property of many landowners. Moreover, public sentiment would not tolerate it. Such a scheme, said one delegate, would damn forever those who adopted it.[36]

Yet a majority of delegates pronounced any increase in the free Negro population pernicious, and recommended that the legislature either forbid emancipation entirely, or compel the prompt migration of all persons liberated. And when the legislature met after Harper's Ferry, an attempt was actually made to pass an expulsion-or-enslavement bill. The movement was sufficiently formidable to alarm many Negroes and whites. The Baltimore *American* warned its advocates that they were playing with explosives, for they would arouse a public anger which might deal slavery a heavy blow. While the measure failed, others were passed reflecting the passions of the time. One forbade owners to liberate slaves unless they were transported out of Maryland, and allowed free Negroes to choose masters if they liked. Another created a commission to supervise the free Negroes in eleven counties, required them to provide homes for themselves,

---

35 *Ann. Report Am. Antislavery Soc.*, 1860, pp. 215, 216.
36 N. Y. *Tribune*, June 9–12, 1859; *National Era; Ann. Report Am. Antislavery Soc.*, 1860, 205–212.

and provided that those incapable of self-support, with their minor children, should be hired out. This regulatory law, however, was to be submitted to popular vote in the fall of 1860.[37]

These hard enactments produced a horrified impression in the North. They were the work not of excited mobs, but of gentlemen in glossy broadcloth and snowy linen, sitting at their desks in handsome marble capitols. "Barbarism Rampant" was the caption which the American Antislavery Society placed over a partial summary in its yearbook for 1860. The South seemed not merely unwilling to go forward; many leaders wished to move backward. Jefferson Davis was saying that the law against the slave trade in the District of Columbia was not only unconstitutional but abominable. Did he wish to see auctioneers again selling human chattels near the White House, as A. G. Brown wanted to see slave ships again plying the Atlantic?

So enlightened a leader as Edmund Ruffin was now denouncing manumission in any form, assailing the Virginia law which gave the Colonization Society $50 for every free Negro sent to Liberia, calling for the reduction of many free colored persons to bondage, and insisting that slaves be placed under a tighter discipline. He wished the emancipation of slaves by kindly masters (one, he wrote in 1858, had recently set three hundred free) completely stopped. He wished laws passed requiring that all free Negroes guilty of major crimes to be sold into slavery; that all who committed minor offenses should be hired out temporarily as slaves, and if the offense was repeated, be sold into lifelong slavery; and that all free Negroes leading an idle, improvident, and dissolute life should similarly be placed in bondage, to be made perpetual if they did not reform.[38]

The result, he believed, would be to remand at least three-fourths of the free colored folk of the Old Dominion to slavery. In addition, Ruffin argued for laws which would completely block all self-redemption from slavery. That is, he would terminate what he called the abusive system, in cities and towns, of giving slaves a money allowance in lieu of food and lodging; and the equally abusive practice of letting slaves hire themselves and act as if free. He recommended the entire exclusion or effectual punishment of all "abolitionist agents" operating within the borders of Virginia. In fine, Ruffin would convert slavery in Virginia (a State where Seward noted that slaves were well treated, and that many masters refused to call them anything but servants) into a system with Dante's legend, "All hope abandon," inscribed over its gate.[39]

37 *Ann. Report Am. Antislavery Soc.*, 1860, pp. 211, 212.
38 During the summer and fall of 1857, large meetings had been held in Virginia to pray the legislature to authorize a sweeping sale of all free negroes by auction. *Cong. Globe*, 35th Cong., 1st Sess., 294.
39 Cf. Ruffin's articles in Richmond *South*, 1858, *passim; Diary*, January 28, July 2, 1858.

Lincoln said at Springfield on June 28 that the condition of the Negroes in the United States had deteriorated sharply since the era of the fathers, "and their ultimate destiny has never appeared so hopeless as in the last three or four years."

And yet harshness was no real part of the temper of Americans of the South, who differed no whit from Americans of the North. The main excitant impulse was fear, and they wanted to protect the *institution,* not to penalize the individual. It was because the free Negro menaced the institution, because manumission undermined it, because all self-help systems for the slave corroded it, that proslavery men urged new legislation. Their object was not to surround slavery with an atmosphere of terror. It was to shore up an institution built on quicksand and battered by all the forces of world sentiment and emergent industrialism. Ruffin was personally the kindliest of masters. The unhappy fact was that it had become impossible to safeguard slavery without brutal violence to countless individuals; either the institution had to be given up, or the brutality committed. The legislators of Louisiana and Arkansas, of Alabama and Georgia, with humane men like Ruffin and the Eastern Shore planters of Maryland, had faced this alternative. They had chosen the institution. The Richmond *Examiner* stated their choice in unflinching language:

It is all an hallucination to suppose that we are ever going to get rid of slavery, or that it will ever be desirable to do so. It is a thing that we cannot do without; that is righteous, profitable, and permanent, and that belongs to Southern society as inherently, intrinsically, and durably as the white race itself. Southern men should act as if the canopy of heaven were inscribed with a covenant, in letters of fire, that the negro is here, and here forever—is our property, and ours forever—is never to be emancipated—is to be kept hard at work and in rigid subjection all his days.[40]

This has the ring of the Richmond publicist Fitzhugh, and would have been repudiated by many Southerners. But Jefferson Davis said, July 6, 1859: "There is not probably an intelligent mind among our own citizens who doubts either the moral or the legal right of the institution of African slavery." Senator A. G. Brown said September 14, 1858, that he wanted Cuban, Mexican, and Central American territory for slavery: "I would spread the blessings of slavery . . . to the uttermost ends of the earth." Such utterances treated slavery as permanent, and assumed that it must be defended at every point.

[V]

Terrorism was not the object; and yet, as the danger to the institution grew, terrorism came to be practiced. "There exists, at this moment," declared the

---

40 *Quoted in Ann. Report Am. Antislavery Soc.,* 1855, p. 128. Toombs had said in the debates of 1850: "This is a proslavery government. Slavery is stamped on its heart!"

New York *Tribune* in 1860, "throughout the Southern States, an actual Reign of Terror. No Northern man, whatever may be his character, his opinions, or his life, but simply because he is a Northern man, can visit that region without the certainty of being subjected to a mean espionage over all his actions, and a rigid watchfulness over all his expressions of opinion; with the risk of personal indignity, and danger even to life and limb."

The wave of apprehension that rolled across the South after Harper's Ferry naturally brought into activity the most reckless and violent members of ill-organized communities. Already, large Southern groups had been conditioned to yield an emotional response to activating shibboleths and signs. "Abolitionist," "Black Republican," "nigger-lover," and "slave-stealer" were terms which, loaded with bitter feeling, were applied with little discrimination to all Northerners. The Southern press had for years assailed "Yankee incendiaries" and "Garrisonian fanatics" in terms which made multitudes ready to believe that the North was filled with them. It is a basic principle of social psychology that mob action readily appears in situations in which two or more opposed races, or social classes, or religious or political elements, stand in uneasy equipoise—the resulting prejudices and fears quickly generating an explosive hatred. That situation existed in large parts of the South in 1859. Tension, conflict, and alarm were ready, on a slight impulse, to create a pathological state of mind—in many places, actual hysteria. Inhibitions of custom and reason would go down; mob action would come to the front. John Brown's raid supplied the requisite stimulus. When Governor Wise set his evil example, how would weaker men act?

In some Southern communities, the committees of safety and vigilance committees which sprang up in hundreds provided an orderly control; but in others, they acted as agents of a mob, usually of a confused and erratic rather than purposeful type. To the mob any Yankee was suspect, and any suspected man at least half guilty. A New Yorker, Dr. Meigs Case, who arrived in Salem, Alabama, in the late summer of 1859 to reorganize a female college there, was run out of the community when the Harper's Ferry excitement surged. In the same State a Connecticut minister named Alberton, an innocent book agent, was imprisoned, threatened with hanging, and frightened into mental derangement. In Arkansas, an Illinois schoolteacher was given thirty-six hours to depart. From all over the South, as we have seen, scores of drummers, evangelists, itinerant mechanics, and notion peddlers fled northward. Men were tarred and feathered, and a few were hanged.[41]

Fundamentally this was not, as the New York *Tribune* suggested it was, an expression of sectional antagonism; a hatred of the Northerner "simply because

41 *The New "Reign of Terror" in the Slaveholding States, 1859–60* (Anon. 1860). Beyond doubt the terrorism was exaggerated; but it was sufficient to deepen the Northern belief that the South was engaged in a sweeping denial of civil liberties. Cf. Russell B. Nye, *Fettered Freedom: Civil Liberties and the Slavery Controversy, 1830–1860, passim.*

he is a Northerner." Nor was it an expression of brutal proclivities, of which the South had no more than the North. It was an attempt to defend the institution of slavery as the one tolerable solution of the race problem which the South knew. For a generation, the Southern public had been made increasingly responsive to certain stereotyped stimuli. The terms slavery, abolition, freesoil, Southern rights, servile revolt, and popular sovereignty had been filled with a deep emotional content. For ten years, the Southern masses had been interconditioned to the psychology of a crisis. Ever since Calhoun said that he knew but the South, and the South in danger, the section had taken on an increasing fixation of interest. It had become, like publics of all nations at such times—like Americans in 1775–76, when New England saw plenty of mob action—more credulous, excitable, and primitive. It would be easy to make too much of the hundreds of instances of Southern violence. What was really significant was the social psychology beneath them. It was a psychology which was erecting an iron wall around the special Southern institution, as Spain, Japan, and Russia have at various times tried to erect iron walls around equally special ways of life.

By the beginning of 1860, Republican newspapers—the New York and the Chicago *Tribune*, the Springfield *Republican*, the Cleveland *Leader*—were being stopped in Southern post offices. Even *Harper's Weekly*, full of compliments to the South, was being excluded in some communities because of the private antislavery views of its editor, George William Curtis. In Virginia, a Doddridge County postmaster asked Governor Wise what he should do with such journals as Greeley's. The governor replied on November 26, 1859, that when mail reached its local destination, Federal control over it ceased; the State alone could determine whether citizens should receive it; and postmasters were bound under heavy penalties to obey a State law which required them to extract from the mails any publication or writing which incited negroes to rebel or inculcated resistance to the rights of masters. Postmaster-General Holt accepted this doctrine, writing another Virginia postmaster that Wise had correctly stated the facts. Inevitably, Southern postal officials were soon halting a great variety of Northern publications. Even religious periodicals were stopped, and *Frank Leslie's* innocuous pages were impounded.

The embargo on newspapers, books, and magazines spread so rapidly that by 1860 the Springfield *Republican* observed that nearly all Northern journals had been excluded except the New York *Herald* and New York *Observer*, "the one the organ of proslavery diabolism and the other of proslavery piety." [42] The Montgomery *Mail* suggested, early in 1860, an *auto da fé* of the sermons of the

42 *Ann. Report Am. Antislavery Soc.*, 1860, 192 ff.

English divine Charles Spurgeon, and, when a pile of his books had been duly burnt, it commented approvingly that if the pharisaical author should ever find his way into central Alabama, the editors hoped that a stout cord would speedily be placed around his eloquent throat.[43]

On many points Southerners would have denied, quite correctly, that they were a static community. They had progressive leaders in agriculture, in political thought, in letters, and in industry. But dominant elements insisted that the slavery system must be static and even retrogressive; and to maintain the status, they countenanced tendencies which fettered progress in many departments of Southern life. Their intolerance was akin to that later created in totalitarian states of one overruling dogma. They stood for something approaching a one-party system; for an increasingly rigid control of all implements of education, publicity, and propaganda; for police agencies of patrol and espionage; and even for the use of violence against dissenters. The faster the Western world in general marched, the closer had to be the Southern lock-step. E. L. Godkin, traversing the South, found a former governor of Mississippi, a grave, wise gentleman, ready to use the halter to stop discussion:

. . . He could see no harm in lynch law when directed against abolitionists or Frémonters. He considered it a necessity of the case. He declared that he looked upon the freesoil party as more dangerous and objectionable than the rank abolitionists, because more harmful and insidious. To restrict slavery within certain limits looked a more harmless proposition than to abolish it outright, but in reality was just as fatal. Room for the expansion of the "institution" was, he said, an absolute necessity for the South. If the slaves became massed together, insubordination would be the result, and it would be impossible to keep them in subjection. Even now, he declared, many men could not lie down quietly at night, though the blacks were scattered over a wide extent of territory, and though they still bore a reasonable numerical proportion to the whites. What would it be if the whites found themselves in a miserable minority; and if the blacks, crowded together in a confined area, began to discover the strength which lay in numbers? This day, he knew, would come some time or other, even if the South had it all their own way; but it would not, and should not, come in his own time; and as to the future, it should take care of itself. If each generation did its duty, it might be staved off for a long time.[44]

[VI]

As the South thus lowered its portcullis, locked its gates, and manned its battlements, hope that really constructive proposals would be received for solv-

---

43 February 17, 1860.
44 London *Daily News*, January 29, 1857.

ing the combined problems of slavery and race adjustment died away. The North had been gravely remiss in failing to make such proposals. Down to the Kansas struggle, perhaps down to Harper's Ferry, a statesmanlike plan, solidly supported, for compensated emancipation combined with such a diffusion of the negro population as would have reduced the tensions of racial readjustment, might gradually have enlisted a large Southern allegiance. John Brown's raid coffined all hope of such a happy consummation.

Did the hope ever really exist? Probably hundreds of thousands of Southerners, in the aggregate, took a realistic view of slavery, believing it a social curse and an economic handicap. Though most of them kept quiet, every traveler in the South found these men. Olmsted conversed with them in Virginia, Alabama, and other States.[45] Godkin talked in Louisiana with a slaveholder who feelingly described the incubus which the institution laid upon farmers and small planters. He expatiated upon the fact that if he could use the capital which he was compelled to put into slaves, he could till a farm three times as large as the one he held, using free labor—if it was to be had. Because cotton required Negroes and the price of Negroes was exorbitant, he predicted that all the rich level lands of the lower Mississippi Valley would soon fall into the hands of the great planters, the small holders being driven to the hills where they would live by growing corn and livestock. He knew, as Godkin knew, that this tendency meant social retrogression. In large areas, the whites would almost disappear, the land would be given over to slaves and their overseers, all importation of goods beyond the scanty fare and clothing of negroes would end, and education, cultural pursuits, good morals, and religion in all its higher characteristics would disappear before the advance of a blind exploitation of soil and slaves. In one Mississippi county the Negroes numbered six thousand, the whites two hundred and fifty, and in some other localities of the cotton kingdom (by no means all) the disproportion between the two races was growing.[46]

Hundreds of thousands of Southerners, too, knew in their hearts (and not a few said openly) that slavery was doomed, that it could not survive much longer except as a transitional institution, and that it must therefore be ameliorated. The ideas of Washington, Madison, and Jefferson were not so easily eradicated as the positive-good school supposed. When the Southern Central Agricultural Society was established in 1846, it avowed as one of its purposes the cultivation of the negro's aptitude for Christianity and civilization, so that by the time slavery had fulfilled its beneficent mission in the South, the social condition of

45 *Seaboard Slave States*, 210 ff., 572, 573, etc.
46 London *Daily News*, March 25, 1857. The census of 1850 did show one Mississippi county where 93 percent of the people were slaves; another with 91 percent. But Blanche Clark in *The Yeoman Farmer of Tennessee* proves that the small farmer in that State was quite holding his own; and see Frank L. Owsley, *Plain Folk of the Old South*.

the race might permit of a system which would relieve the colored race from servitude, without sinking it to the sad condition of free negroes in the North. The society lasted until 1857.

In 1855 some unidentified reformers in North Carolina—the State of Helper, B. S. Hedrick, Daniel R. Goodloe, and a large Quaker group—offered a plan for a triple change in the institution. They called for legal protection of marriage among slaves, preservation of the parental relation by outlawing all sales of minor children, and repeal of the statute forbidding the education of slaves. Their project received noncommital notice outside the State. In Mississippi, the Port Gibson *Reveille* remarked that most planters of that area had at least partially adopted the main features of the program, which was worth serious consideration. It weakly added, however, that evils might lurk in the scheme.[47] Robert Toombs, in his address on slavery in Boston in 1856, declared that to protect marriage and other domestic ties by laws forbidding the separation of families would be wise, proper, and humane. He, too, however, added the weak reservation that the evil of separation was much exaggerated, for Negroes in Africa knew no marriage, and more families had been separated by migration from Ireland than by the Southern slave trade.[48]

Other Southerners of prominence advocated amelioration. The sociologist Henry Hughes, insisting on the progressive character of the Southern labor system, declared that it should be called not slavery but warranteeism, the principle of which was justice; and he advocated a diminution of "the accidental abuses of our system." [49] J. F. H. Claiborne, editor, historian, and Unionist politician, penned an undated memorandum declaring that if the South were let alone, slavery would conform to the liberal ideas of the age by steadily improving its character. How? "Not towards the abolition of slavery, but towards its gradual improvement—to servitude—field labor—domesticity—mechanical apprenticeship—city drudgery. A steady progress, first physical, next mental and moral, is the upward tendency of a sound social policy." [50]

The very fact that many masters allowed slaves to purchase their freedom was a tacit acknowledgment of the weakness of the institution; since, as Booker T. Washington pointed out, the slave who could purchase his own freedom was one whom it was less profitable to hold in servitude. Even in the eighteen-fifties, many slaves, particularly in towns and among the skilled or semi-skilled, continued to buy their liberty.[51] Negroes sometimes earned their freedom in ingenious ways; one by hawking poems in manuscript, and one by migrating to California, with his master's sanction, where he made enough money to redeem

47 Quoted in *National Intelligencer*, June 7, 1854.
48 Brewton, *The Son of Thunder*, 243, 244.
49 November 5, 1858; Claiborne Papers, Miss. Dept. Arch. and Hist.
50 Claiborne Papers, Univ. of N. C.; probably between 1851 and 1855.
51 Matison, "Manumission by Purchase," *Journal Negro Hist.*, XXXIII, April, 1948.

his whole family. The majority simply showed unusual enterprise as carpenters, blacksmiths, shoemakers, and the like. As industrialization increased, opportunities for self-purchase should have multiplied. But the reactionary wave of 1830–60 interfered. John H. Russell, in *The Free Negro in Virginia, 1789–1865,* estimates that before 1800 the Virginia slave had about ten chances in a hundred of manumission in any of its forms; from 1800 to 1832 four or five chances; and after 1832 about two chances.

Another weak spot in slavery: western Virginia.

Many Southern churchmen felt like W. H. Barnwell, rector of St. Peter's in Charleston, who in 1848 earnestly desired two changes in the laws of his State: a repeal of the act prohibiting emancipation, and repeal of the law which severely punished anyone who taught a slave to read and write. Barnwell, who knew well "the old half-brute native Africans, of whom a few survive," saw that the difference between their lot and that of the healthy, lively, cheerful slaves who enjoyed Charleston life was a testimonial both to the educational value of slavery, and to the Negro's improvability. He recognized that some South Carolina legislation was bad—though he believed that the chief obstacle to its removal was the reckless agitation of the abolitionists. Many churchmen, like Alexander Campbell, boldly taught their slaves to write. When a Massachusetts clergyman wrote a pamphlet decrying colonization and advocating the amelioration of the lot of slaves where they were held, he received favorable answers from clergy-men as far South as Natchez and New Orleans.[52]

Before the Southerners hardened their minds and spirits; before Governor Thomas Moore of Louisiana wrote that the institution of slavery had been com-pletely vindicated and its perpetuity proved desirable; [53] before W. L. Yancey, reading Olmsted's pages, declared that if retrogression in the treatment of slaves had taken place, it was the fault of the abolitionists; [54] in short, before the middle fifties, a bold scheme for gradual compensated emancipation might have won, not a majority of Southerners, but a considerable minority. It might have been a minority sufficient, in alliance with a generous body of Northern opinion, to turn the scale in 1861 in favor of a new compromise and some improved scheme.

[VII]

The ablest, most passionate, and most industrious proponent of a plan of gradual emancipation was Frank P. Blair, Jr., on whom part of Benton's mantle had fallen. He rose to prominence in Missouri, where the movement for gradual emancipation had grown strong; where an emancipation candidate had been elected mayor of St. Louis in 1857, and where Carl Schurz would dare in 1860 to deliver an eloquent address on the imminent doom of slavery. Such leaders as Blair, Gratz Brown, and James O. Broadhead, a Unionist of Whig antecedents, emphasized both the moral and economic arguments for turning Missouri into a free State. Slavery was wrong; slavery was also unjust to white workers who had to compete with forced black labor. Blair held a noteworthy interview with Lincoln in Springfield, early in 1857. Entering Congress in December, 1857, he introduced a resolution to inquire into the expediency of acquiring territory in Central or South America for the colonization of free Negroes and liberated slaves; and he supported it in a careful speech which F. P. Blair, Sr., and Montgomery Blair had approved.

52 Letter to J. G. Palfrey, Charleston *Mercury*, August 11, 1848; W. W. Jennings, *Short Hist. Disciples of Christ*, 158; Everett MS Diary February 27, 1857. Colonization in Liberia was more and more regarded as a failure. Reports from Monrovia were discouraging. One Southern naval officer, who visited the capital in 1858 on the U. S. S. *Marion*, was horrified by the hardships suffered by Negroes from the United States in that unhealthy climate, and amused by the pompous talk of President Benson and other high officials at a state dinner. "I imagined myself among a collection of house-servants who were closely imitating their masters." June 19, 1858; C. C. Clay Papers, Duke Univ. The American Colonization Society lived to issue its sixtieth report in 1877; but by that time it had become largely a missionary society.
53 Address to Leg. 1860; Moore Papers, Univ. of La. Archives.
54 Yancey Papers, undated, Ala. Dept. Arch. and Hist. Frank Blair, Jr., wished early in 1857 to bring forward in Congress a bill granting to Missouri all the public lands in the State, amounting to about fifteen million acres, to be sold and the proceeds used to buy slaves and colonize them abroad. March 25, 1857, to his father; Blair-Lee Papers.

The background of Blair's speech was the raging debate on Lecompton, and the angry discussion of Commodore Hiram Paulding's seizure of Walker. He had been depressed by the wave of reactionary legislation on slavery in the South. He had also been struck by the proposal of Earl Grey, as Colonial Secretary, for importing into Trinidad large numbers of free colored people from America. He had learned that Honduras was anxious to enlist American capital in mining, railroad building, and commerce. African colonization was a failure, for climate, distance, and the barbarous state of society were against it. Central American colonization, however, as Britain had shown in sending Jamaican blacks to help develop Belize, was feasible. The time had come to realize Jefferson's great dream of so directing the process of emancipation and deportation that slavery would gradually disappear and the place of the negroes be *pari passu* filled up by whites.[55]

The voluntary removal of free Negroes to parts of Central America where the United States could establish homes for them, argued Blair, would benefit the emigrants, the people receiving them, and the United States. Central America was inhabited already by mixed races. Honduras, for example, had one hundred and forty thousand people called Negroes and mulattoes, one hundred thousand called Indians, and fifty thousand called whites—all showing great mixture of blood. Many Negroes and mulattoes had risen high in politics, commerce, and the church. Honduras and Guatemala, indeed, had been ruled by *mestizo* dictators. Poverty and insurrection fermented in Central America; but let the United States buy lands there for hundreds of thousands of Christianized, English-speaking, industrious negroes, and the little republics would make rapid progress toward wealth and stability. As Great Britain had colonized land after land, throwing a chain of dependencies around the globe, so the United States could colonize this neighboring region. Once Central America was thus opened up, benevolent masters in the temperate slave States would liberate their chattels, accepting a due recompense. The benefits would be immediate:

What a change would soon be wrought in the position of Maryland and Virginia, Tennessee and Kentucky, and in my own State, Missouri, if a smooth way were opened into the heart of the tropics—prodigal of wealth in the soil, in the mines, and in the forests; where the labor of the robust and skilful freedman, assisted by the capital and instruction, and inspired by the energy of enterprising American merchants, miners, or planters, would start everything into life. The mixed condition of the four different classes which, in our grain-growing States, obstruct each other; the masters dependent on the slaves, the slaves on their masters; the free negroes hanging on the skirts of both; while the great mass, the free white laborers, are cast out, in a great measure, from employment and all ownership in the soil; would be succeeded by the most useful of all the tillers of the earth, small freeholders and an independent tenantry. The influx of immigrants from Europe and the North, with moderate capital, already running into Maryland and Virginia, would, as these States sloughed the black skin, fill up the rich region round the Chesapeake bay, the noblest bay in the world.

To proslavery Congressmen, Blair's proposal was a draught from the bitter waters of Marah, and they turned from it with revulsion. Lucius J. Gartrell of Georgia spoke for those who wanted slavery, more slavery, and slavery forever. The institution, he said, was not what Washington, Jefferson, Madison, and John Randolph had imagined it; the South now knew better. It was right in principle and practice; it was sanctioned by Holy Writ; it was a blessing to the colored man; it had developed the resources of the nation, and by its conservative influence had elevated Southerners in morality, wealth, enterprise, and intelligence to a point never attained by any other people.[56] Southern Democrats ranked Blair among the traitors to his party. Northern freesoilers, who had no faith in colonization, refused to come to his aid. Only one member gave him support, and that indirectly—Eli Thayer, who wanted to see Central America colonized by white Americans rather than blacks. His resolution did not come to vote.[57]

Yet the Blairs continued their drum-beating. The *Missouri Democrat*, Gratz Brown, and Frank Blair insistently pressed the demand for gradual emancipation in Missouri. With his brother Montgomery, Frank enlisted Senator Doolittle of Wisconsin in an effort to rally the Northwestern governors to the cause of colonization in Central America. The Blair family believed that if the Northwest spoke out boldly for such a policy, the border slave States, at least, could be brought into line; and they wished Governors Dennison of Ohio, Kirkwood of Iowa, and Randall of Wisconsin to press the subject simultaneously upon their legislatures. Let these governors come boldly up to their work, wrote Montgomery to Doolittle; let them say that the national government must provide passage for such free Negroes as will go voluntarily to some land where their capacities may be developed; let them give a vigorous leadership to Northern opinion. This would do more than ten thousand speeches to convince the great body of Southerners that the Republican Party did not wish to set the negroes free to be the equals of the Southern people, and hence their rulers in areas where they were more numerous than the whites.[58]

Frank Blair spoke for his plan during 1859 in various parts of the Northwest, in Missouri, and in New England. His most noteworthy address, delivered in Boston on January 26, was heard by Emerson, Governor Banks, and other distinguished men. To deal with slavery by emancipation and colonization, he said,

56 *Ibid.*, 391–393.
57 Smith, *Blair Family*, I, 405, 406; *Cong. Globe*, 35th Cong., 1st Sess., 227–229.
58 Smith, *Blair Family*, I, 443 ff.; *Mo. Hist. Rev.* XI, 136.

would require the joint action of State and Federal governments. Some Latin-American area should be acquired for a free negro state, dependent on the United States. Freedmen and their families should be persuaded to migrate thither by the same inducements which had persuaded settlers to move westward: financial aid, moral encouragement, and political protection. Why should the enterprise of Boston not take the lead in this new crusade? And why should the plan not be the principal undertaking of the Republican Administration to be elected in 1860? But he made few converts.[59]

"Has any person, of any party or opinion," inquired Edward Everett just after Harper's Ferry, "proposed, in sober earnest, any practicable method of wholesale emancipation?" Apart from Webster and Blair, the answer was no. "Has any person . . . ever undertaken to sketch out the details of a plan for effecting the change at once, by any legislative measure that could be adopted?" Not even Blair had done that. Everett pointed out how much emancipation would cost the South: a billion dollars in slave property, the outfitting of the emancipated millions for self-support, the derangement of the labor system, and an immense social turmoil. What contribution would the North make toward footing this bill? [60] Lyman Trumbull was suggesting the purchase of a great tract somewhere for the resettlement of the liberated colored people of both North and South; but he was careful not to speak realistically of costs, and his Illinois followers assumed that his main object was to exempt Republicans from the reproach that they wanted a large Negro body in the North.[61]

The fact was that all suggestions for compensated emancipation, whether in Elihu Burritt's plan of heavy taxation to buy slaves en masse,[62] or Webster's plan

59 Blair, March 1, 1859, Dana Papers; Smith, *Blair Family*, I, 448–450. Senator Doolittle believed that if the Republicans had embraced this scheme of Latin-American colonization, the hope it held out of ending the evils of slavery would have prevented John Brown's raid. Frank Blair, Jr., to his father, November 2, 1859; Blair-Lee Papers.

60 "Union Meeting in Faneuil Hall," December 8, 1859. Pamphlet.

61 McKibben, December 25, 1859, Wing, May 4, 1860, Trumbull Papers. See N. O. *Picayune*, August 18, 1860, for indignant comment on the unwillingness of Illinois to receive negroes while asking the South to set them free.

62 Elihu Burritt and others held a convention of friends of compensated emancipation in Cleveland on August 25–28, 1857, which scores of delegates attended. They resolved that it was highly desirable "that the people of the North should cooperate, in a generous and brotherly spirit, with the people of the South, and share liberally with them in the expense of putting an end to so great a moral and political evil as American slavery." Each slaveholder, they proposed, should be paid $250 for every slave freed, and each slave should be presented with $25; a sum which, the gathering hoped, would "go far toward supplying them with humble homes on this continent, or upon another, should they prefer so wide a removal." Abolitionists greeted the plan with hoots of derision. It received chilly disapproval from the N. Y. *Tribune*, which commented that while it was willing to devote the public lands to immediate emancipation, and to give twenty million dollars a year for fifty years from the Treasury for this purpose, it believed that it was both unjust and inexpedient for the country to pay the slaveholders for liberating their chattels. The slaves were entitled

for using the proceeds of the public lands, or Blair's plan of joint Federal-State effort, ran into three obstacles: radical opinion at the South, unwilling to part with slavery on any terms; radical opinion at the North, which held slavery immoral and therefore opposed paying slaveholders for giving it up; and the inertia of the majority, unwilling to do anything but drift. While national thought on slavery ran the gamut from Yancey to Garrison, most schools agreed on one thesis: that no drastic, costly, and painful plan need be made for the future. The abolitionists wanted no plan because they oversimplified the problem: free the slave, they said, and he will at once become an intelligent, self-governing citizen of high quality. The proslavery extremists wanted no plan because they believed that the *status quo* was the best possible situation. The Negro is just where he should be, said Charles O'Conor.[63] As for the great central mass of Americans, whether freesoilers or mildly proslavery, they were content to wait and hope. If slavery was doomed, they held, moral pressure and changing economic conditions would in time bring it to its appointed end.

The most thoughtful exponent of the policy of waiting upon time and economic change was Thomas Ewbank, English-born inventor, manufacturer, and author, who believed that the Age of the Machine would gradually conquer the Age of Slavery. Head of the Patent Office under Taylor and Fillmore, Ewbank returned to New York to write books and pamphlets on a wide variety of subjects. In the spring of 1859, he delivered a remarkable address before the American Ethnological Society of which he was a founder, entitled "Inorganic Forces Ordained to Supersede Human Slavery." His belief was that mechanical invention and industrialism would gradually extinguish all the baser forms of toil.

Neither the radical Northern nor the radical Southern attitude toward slavery seemed valid to Ewbank. He had no faith in the eradication of slavery by moral crusades or penal statutes; at the same time, he thought slavery an evil and rejected the doctrine of negro inferiority. The roots of the system, extending to the lowest depths of man's selfish nature, must—he declared—be deprived of nourishment before they would wither. As long as slavery paid in dollars, it would live. What would make it unprofitable?—the machine. Multiply machines, predicted Ewbank, and slavery would disappear; for a piece of fuel costing a

---

to freedom as a right, and by generations of unpaid labor they had earned it. This was the attitude of other freesoil journals. Southern newspapers, meanwhile, were hostile or contemptuous. The convention formed the National Compensated Emancipation Society, with Benjamin Silliman as president, Mark Hopkins as a vice-president, and Burritt as corresponding secretary. But the gathering was abortive, drawing fewer delegates and commanding less support than the radical abolitionist convention which met in Cleveland in the autumn. N. Y. *Weekly Tribune*, August 1, 1857; *National Intelligencer*, September 5, 1857; *Ann. Report Am. Antislavery Soc.*, 1858, 184.

63 Speech Academy of Music, N. Y., December 19, 1859 (pamphlet).

few cents would do the work of several rude hands.[64] Machine power, steadily advancing throughout the world, would eventually displace unskilled labor on the Alabama cotton plantation as it had done on the Illinois wheat farm. Already, machines ginned, spun, and wove cotton, "nor is there any insuperable obstacle to their planting and hoeing and picking it, or something equivalent to picking." Machines already ground the sugar cane; they would soon cultivate, reap, and transport it. When a proper combination of mechanical skills gave the South its needed inventions, predicted Ewbank, slavery would pass away amid the hosannas of proslavery as well as antislavery men. He might have quoted John Randolph's statement that once slave labor was proved unprofitable, the master would run away from the slave faster than the slave had ever run from the master. Societies to promote mechanical progress, said the lecturer, would achieve more than abolition societies. His pamphlet did not suggest, however, what was to be done with the displaced slave.

Lincoln had declared that if all earthly power were given him to deal with the institution, he would not know what to do with it. As a question of practical politics, Lincoln was right, for the subject bristled with difficulties which only a tremendous educational crusade could affect. The central perplexity had been stated long before by Jefferson: "Among the Romans emancipation required but *one effort.* The slave, when free, might mix without *staining* the blood of his master. But with us a second is necessary, unknown to history." The only place where the freed Negro could be colonized successfully was in the United States, North and South; and colonization at home by plan would cost the country far more in effort, money, and social friction than it had yet paid for any object— even independence. But the time had come when the country, however reluctantly, must face a plain fact: if the United States was really to be the last, best hope of mankind, it could not much longer remain a slaveholding republic.

[VIII]

While the American deadlock on slavery continued unbroken, the cause of human freedom was still advancing round the globe. Great Britain, in giving up her hold upon the Bay Islands, tried to stipulate that slavery should never exist in them. The Dutch colonies in America stood on the verge of emancipation. Year by year, outside Brazil and the Spanish possessions, the last vestiges of slavery died away in Latin America. And most impressive of all, the Russian movement for the liberation of serfs reached its climax.

64 Eli Thayer told the House in 1858: "Why, sir we can buy a negro power, in a steam engine, for ten dollars, and we can clothe and feed that power for one year for five dollars; and were we the men to give $1000 for an African slave, and $150 a year to feed and clothe him?" *Cong. Globe,* 35th Cong., 1st Sess., 229.

Provincial groups and an imperial commission had labored during 1859–60 on a practical scheme of emancipation. Finally, on the day before Lincoln was inaugurated, a decree of the Czar set all serfs free. With a stroke which rang throughout the globe, the hand on the world clock moved forward in a sudden leap. Nobody supposed that a white serf in Russia, his blood identical with that of the noblest families, occupied a position remotely comparable with that of a black slave in the South. Nevertheless, some circumstances connected with this emancipation were of direct significance to Americans.

The fact that the Russian authorities had enlisted the ablest men in the land, in a variety of national and local agencies, to work out a *plan*, was significant. So was the fact that Russia avowedly responded to a variety of pressures, among which world opinion, fear of a servile uprising, and a preference for long-term rather than short-term economic benefits were important. So, too, were the facts that once the reform was assured, land values rose; that when the spirit of idealism was given free rein, it proved unexpectedly powerful; and that the sobriety, industry, and ambition of the peasants immediately increased. The Czar paid tribute to the altruism of the landholders, actuated by Christian love of neighbor and philosophic respect for the dignity of man. From all parts of the realm came news of the opening of free schools, the progress of temperance, and the rise of a new social concord.

One incident of the emancipation seemed clothed with a certain meaning. John Brown's body lay mouldering in the grave. But far away in St. Petersburg, when the drafting of the final plan of emancipation was completed, the Czar's representative rose at a public dinner to offer four toasts: to the Czar; to the cause of emancipation; to the landholders; and to the memory of Emilian Pugatchev. Pugatchev was a serf who, heading a rebellion in 1774, had been caught and executed, his body being burnt. Now, by the changes of time, the work he had done was extolled by the very power which had put him to death.

The Russian emancipation, like John Brown's raid, was a lightning flash which illuminated the tragic predicament of America. While nearly the whole civilized world was moving in one direction, the South was moving in another. While even in Russia the movement for human freedom was scoring victories, *De Bow's Review* was announcing that no Southern movement had ever gained strength so fast as that for the revival of the slave trade. Abroad, believers in democracy looked to the shining principles of the Declaration of Independence. In Virginia itself the *Southern Literary Messenger* now repudiated those principles, and quoted Jefferson's statement that in any contest between masters and slaves, Divine Goodness must take the side of the downtrodden, only to stigmatize it as ignorant and erroneous. We may say that in setting the spasmodic Southern reaction against Northern attack 1850–1860 in contrast with the secular world movement 1776–1860, we do the slaveholding States a certain injustice. We may say that Southern retrogression was the natural outgrowth of a sense of peril. But these considerations do not exonerate a Southern leadership which might have clung to Jefferson's principles with that statesman's own vision and devotion; which might have appealed less to Southern fears and appetites, and more to Southern courage and idealism. The passion of John Brown, the patient, wise insistence of Lincoln that America must not evade its moral responsibilities, gained their deepest significance from a realization that the nation was losing its position of democratic leadership in the world. This realization that it was falling short of the objects of its founders was to give intensity to the final stand of the North for the restriction of slavery within its existing domain—a stand to which we now turn.

6

See the Front of Battle Lower

SOCIAL relations in Washington this winter of 1859–60 were sadly disrupted. "We shall *not* leave cards!"—so ladies from one side of the Potomac spoke of those from the other. In growing numbers, Southern and Northern Congressmen cut each other as they passed in the streets. Hostesses making up dinner lists had to bend with anxious care over the names. The feud between Buchanan and Douglas remained so bitter that the beautiful Adele Douglas never deigned to appear at a White House reception, and when she met Miss Lane on neutral ground they bowed with polite frigidity. Toombs and Henry Wilson had once been friends; now they glared frostily when their paths crossed.

To be sure, some accomplished hostesses counted good friends in both sections and among all party groups. The Pryors of Virginia, who loved to gather such fellow-Southerners as Lamar, Hunter, Muscoe Garnett, and Porcher Miles to their fireside, were also hospitable to Westerners and New Yorkers. Mrs. Horace F. Clarke, wife of a wealthy New York Representative, impartially entertained Yankees and men of the cotton kingdom. So did Mrs. Senator Thompson of New Jersey. The kindly intimacy between Seward and Jefferson Davis continued, while such border families as the Crittendens cultivated friendships in every quarter. As resentments deepened, however, even tactful matrons feared some sudden explosion.

Once, at the theatre, Mrs. Douglas entertained Mrs. Pryor in a box next that of Miss Lane. When Porcher Miles halted at the entrance, Mrs. Douglas turned upon him with glacial dignity: "Sir, you have made a mistake. Your visit is intended for next door!" And Miles haughtily retorted: "Madame, I presumed I might be permitted to make my respects to Mrs. Pryor, for whom my call was intended." [1]

Yet despite the tension, it was a busy social season. Never had more money been spent on dinners, receptions, and balls than in this year of returning prosperity. Even so plain a man as Seward felt it necessary, when he gave a dinner, to serve seventeen courses, changing the plates for each; and at the end, waiters

---

1 Mrs. Roger A. Pryor, *Reminiscences of Peace and War*, Ch. 7.

handed around pyramids of iced fruits, oranges, French sweetmeats, and nuts.[2] A correspondent of the Charleston *Mercury* complained that dinners were not what they had been in the days of Clay and Webster, with ducks, oysters, and terrapin from the Chesapeake, shad from the James, venison from Virginia, and wines from the best Charleston or Philadelphia merchants; but, at any rate, entertainments were costlier. Secretary Toucey's grand evening party in February, graced by wealthy New Yorkers, was considered especially brilliant. As always, a contrast was visible between the quiet entertainments of the old Georgetown aristocracy and the affairs held by Southern grandees like Senators Slidell and C. C. Clay, with liveried servants, banks of flowers, music, and a superabundance of comestibles.

An ingenuous view of Washington is afforded by the letters of Susanna Keitt, bride of the South Carolina Representative, who saw everything through unspoiled eyes. Lawrence Keitt, now in his middle thirties, had faults enough, being hot-tempered, bombastic, and egotistical. But he was a very likable person, warm-hearted, impulsively affectionate, quick-witted, and of iron courage, as he would prove in dying at Cold Harbor for his principles. His romance with Susanna Sparks had been tempestuous enough. From Washington, he had written her on her South Carolina plantation long letters full of politics, gossip, and above all his personal philosophy. The young girl had been difficult and changeable after the manner of Southern belles; they became engaged, but she broke off the engagement; finally she consented again and they were married. She had extorted the promise of a long stay in Europe, where she wanted to live, study art, and travel extensively. They made a grand tour—and then the deepening crisis recalled him to Washington. She came reluctantly, and took quick alarm at the currents of passion swirling about them. A touching note is struck in her cry to her brother in the midst of the speakership contest—one of her repeated expressions of real fear:

"Oh, Alec, we are having frightful times here—war any moment, and no knowing who may fall. Mr. Pryor, Clingman, and Mann have just left the parlor, saying that all hope for a democratic speaker is gone, and that the Southerners are resolved a black Republican shall not take the chair. They are armed and determined to fight to the knife there on the floor of Congress. . . . Governor Wise has ten thousand men, drilled and armed, that would march to the Capitol at the first sound of war. Oh, Alec, I am so uneasy I can write no more."[3]

This sensitive girl, terrified by the violent talk, bored by the bigwigs and wistful for the quiet pleasures of plantation life, found the receptions, dinners,

2 *Harper's Weekly*, March 24, 1860.
3 Susanna Keitt to Alexander Sparks, undated; Keitt Papers, Duke Univ.

and balls exhausting. "It takes all your time to return the visits and all your money for the hire of hacks, and all this for people who care nothing for you." The city had too many rowdy Congressmen, importunate office-seekers, fast young women, and insipid dancing men to suit her. (Charles Francis Adams, Jr., mentions the fast young women; he sometimes hardly knew where to look when they talked to him.) It was a great place for dilly-dallyings, flirtations, and quasi-engagements. The men had better times than the women; on one occasion, when Porcher Miles gave the South Carolina Congressmen a dinner, wives were indignant over husbands returning at two A.M. half-tipsy. Buchanan insisted on seeing Mrs. Keitt, for Slidell said she was the handsomest woman resident in Washington, and after her visit he gave a dinner party for her. But though she thought Miss Lane very agreeable, she was not impressed by the President. "He has one of the most quizzical faces I ever saw—head and mouth twisted to one side, and then the erratic performance of that famous eye!" Moreover, he was full of prosy reminiscences: "I have no fancy for the story-telling old man."

At the White House receptions Susanna eyed some famous figures with amazement: Madame Bodisco, for example, still in her mid-thirties and good-looking despite her corpulence, wearing a court dress the diamonds and laces of which were whispered to have cost thirty thousand. Sometimes the Washington atmosphere, with its sectional hatreds, social rivalries, and malicious gossip, seemed stifling. She turned to close friends like the Crittendens and Hammonds for companionship. Particularly did she like Mrs. Crittenden, a lively woman who, though at least sixty, wore low-necked, short-sleeved evening gowns with lace flounces and tossed her curls, adorned with pink roses, like any debutante.

Chief place among the diplomats was taken by the new British minister, Lord Lyons, a bachelor of wealth, sagacity, and easygoing manners whose legation dinners were of statelier type than Napier's. His advent aroused talk of possible matches, with unfounded rumors of an engagement to Harriet Lane.

"The American women are undoubtedly very pretty," wrote the amused envoy, who was forty-two, "but my heart is too old and too callous to be wounded by their charms. I am not going to be married either to the fascinating accomplished niece of the President, nor to the widow of a late Foreign Minister, or to any other maiden or relict to whom I am given by the newspapers." [4] He noticed that Americans were pleased by courtesies from a man of title, and prone to think themselves slighted if little favors were omitted; "this quality may be sometimes turned to good account," he wrote Lord John Russell. Like others, he took care to avoid sectional collisions. Senator Clay's wife, driving to a legation dinner with her husband and the Crittendens, was perturbed lest the inex-

4 Lord Newton, *Lord Lyons*, Ch. 2.

perienced minister assign some Black Republican to take her in to dinner. "I will refuse to accept him!" she exploded. Her fears did not diminish when various Southern gentlemen, talking with her, revealed that they had to escort someone else to table. She was looking nervously at the Republicans when the massive doors slid apart and a voice announced dinner. Then, to her astonished relief, Lyons stepped to her side and took her arm with, "I have the honor, madam!"

Winter had brought the usual minor events: lectures by savants at the Smithsonian, attended by two thousand people, an exhibition of Indian dancing at the Navy Yard, an invasion by the New York Seventh, reviewed in glittering lines on Pennsylvania Avenue, and so on. Clark Mills's equestrian statue of the *pater patriae* was unveiled on Washington's birthday with a short discourse by Buchanan and a long one by Representative Bocock. Like Mills's other work, the statue tried to be exciting. It showed the magisterial-looking general in full regimentals, sword in hand, spurring his horse up to the cannon's mouth as he rallied his broken troops at Princeton.

Happily, no murder took place this season. But the capital quivered for a time over two threatened duels, Pryor calling out Potter of Wisconsin, and Robert J. Walker demanding satisfaction from Jeremiah Black. In the end, both disputes were adjusted bloodlessly; for when Potter proposed fighting elbow-to-elbow with bowie knives Pryor rejected the terms as barbarous, while Black refused even to consider Walker's challenge.[5]

After Lent came the visit of Japanese ambassadors carrying the recently concluded commercial treaty, and charged with cordial messages from the Emperor to the President. Installed in a large suite at Willard's, they endured cheerfully the inquisitiveness of the crowds. They were received in the East Room by the President, the Cabinet, leading members of Congress, and other dignitaries. Secretary Cass gave them a ball, attended by Miss Lane, Mrs. Douglas, and so many other ladies that reporters wrote of being engulfed in surging waves of silk and muslin. Then they left to accept honors in New York.

Their diminutive stature, dark skins, and dignified restraint; their half-shaved heads, surmounted by a boxlike headgear; their flowing robes of silk and brocade, with wide sleeves and crêpe belts; their straw sandals; their heavy swords, in chased and jewelled scabbards; their fans, and the pipes they carried at their sides for frequent whiffs—all this was amusingly fantastic. "They looked for all the world," wrote Major Jack Downing, "like little old ladies dressed up to kill, with queer little things tied on their heads, and two swords stuck in every fellow's belt, which reared up when they bowed down like the tail-feathers of a cockerel." The Japanese must have been equally astonished by the tail coats and stovepipe hats of American dignitaries, and the voluminous garb of the ladies,

5 *Harper's Weekly,* February 25, 1860.

Studying the hoop-skirts, they were impressed by the insubstantiality of Western costume; and one visitor, when jostled by a very fat Congressman, prodded the man twice in the abdomen, ejaculating with surprise—"Solid!"

[I]

The speakership contest ended, Congress turned to neglected tasks. This seven-month session was remarkable for the constant emergence of economic issues through the crust of slavery disputation, boiling up like lava propelled by irresistible internal forces. Morrill's tariff bill of the previous session was dead, but the Ways and Means Committee was busy with another predicated upon it. A bill was drafted to abolish Robert J. Walker's warehousing system—a system held to encourage excessive importations. The House made Morrill's bill donating lands for the establishment of agricultural colleges a special order for the third Tuesday in March. Improvement of communications came up in varied forms: the perennial Pacific Railroad bills, Gwin's proposal for a Government telegraph to California, Yulee's suggestion of a postal money-order system, and a Senate inquiry into the expediency of semi-weekly mails to San Francisco and El Paso. Homestead legislation, internal improvements, and the government of the future Colorado Territory could not be denied debate, for they touched the immediate interests of many millions.

Compared with such issues, the slavery question seemed barren. As one after another the new economic measures passed the House, Southern leaders of the Senate grew alarmed; they saw the national balance tipping against them, and centralization growing. As one after another the measures were stopped by Senate or President, Northerners dominating the House became more irritated. The alarm and the irritation reacted upon the slavery debate, which everybody knew would underlie the imminent Presidential campaign—and which indeed was plainly coming to a new crisis.

Next to this thrust of new economic demands, the session was made dramatic by the determination of radical Southern Democrats to subjugate the Douglas faction. Washington, and especially the Senate, was now the forum of something like a conspiracy to split the Democratic Party. Davis, Slidell, C. C. Clay, Iverson, Mason, and Benjamin were determined to dictate party policy in advance of the convention. With Buchanan's aid, they committed the Democratic caucus to their demands. This was a busy winter of subterranean activity. Many Southern Rights men believed that the slaveholding area was already in the labor pains of delivering a new nation.

Senator A. G. Brown of Mississippi had served notice on Douglas late in 1859: "The South will demand at Charleston a platform explicitly declaring that slave property is entitled in the Territories and on the high seas to the same protection that is given to any other and every other species of property and failing to get it she will retire from the Convention." [6] Governor Moore's address to the Alabama legislature late in 1859 had insisted upon positive territorial protection. From the Peedee to the Arkansas, voices were echoing the demand. It was inevitable that it should be raised in Congress as soon as that body began deliberations.

Just how far the Southern extremists, taking their courage in their hands, wished to proceed—just how much they hoped for party schism as opening the way to national disunion—just how ready they were for war—it is impossible to say except by examining one individual after another; and difficult to say even then. Jefferson Davis hoped to avoid even a party schism, believing that some neutral candidate like ex-President Pierce might yet be accepted by both Northern and Southern Democrats.[7] Judah P. Benjamin declared that he had never felt such an utter sinking of his whole being as when he learned that the party was being rent in twain. Toombs, J. L. M. Curry, Slidell, and even Yancey, all still posed as friends of the Union. But was not the use of party disruption to achieve secession contemplated by these men when, demanding that the South flatly refuse to accept either the nomination of Douglas or the election of a Republican, they strove to screw their States up to the pitch of their own temper? [8]

To a multitude of Southerners the slave-code demand appeared moderate enough. Memminger, appealing for concert of action between South Carolina and Virginia, told the legislature at Richmond on January 19, 1860, that the perilous position of the South rendered four guarantees necessary. The section was entitled to ask for an equal share in the nation's Territories; for the disbanding of all antislavery societies; for the repeal of all laws obstructing the return of fugitives; and for a bar against any amendment of the Constitution with respect to slavery. What was the slave-code compared with such sweeping requirements?

Virginia's new governor, the reasonable John Letcher, who loved the Union and was ready to support Douglas for President, was urging the South to demand Seward's exclusion from the White House on pain of secession. The irrepressible conflict doctrine, he told the legislature in his message of January 7, 1860, was an open declaration of war against slavery, and the election of its author ought to be resisted by all slaveholding States. "The idea of permitting such a man to have control and direction of the army and navy of the United States, and the appointment of high judicial and executive officers, postmasters included, cannot be entertained by the South for a moment."

6 Percy L. Rainwater, *Mississippi, Storm Center of Secession, 1856–61*, 109.
7 Davis to E. De Leon; De Leon Papers, South Caroliniana Library.
8 R. D. Meade, *Benjamin*, 139–141; Phillips, *Toombs*, 176–182; Yancey's Memphis Speech, August 14, 1860.

Yet many who supported the slave-code ultimatum knew that Northern Democrats, as Douglas had said, could never accept it; that if pressed, it would break the back of the party; and that its direct result would be the election of a Republican. The Alabama Democratic convention laid down its ultimatum in January. Is it conceivable that those who wanted secession, like E. C. Bullock of Eufaula, did not associate cause and effect? Is it conceivable that Alabama secessionists in Congress, led by C. C. Clay and J. L. M. Curry, did not do so? Plainly an ill-organized but very determined conspiracy was coming into existence.

That cultivated secessionist, Porcher Miles, had been given advice on strategy by another polished enemy of the Union, W. H. Trescot. The direst misfortune possible, Trescot warned him, would be a lull in the slavery discussion. If any such calm was threatened, a few strong men might act in concert to keep the agitation alive. They could arouse Southern emotions by some new policy which, while it preserved the color of a national system, should be based essentially on Southern principles and look to sectional effect. "Such a policy, whether it assumes an administration or an opposition character, might be made to form a Southern party which would either succeed and thus govern the country or fail and thus form a compact Southern party ready for action. I submit this would require subtlety in the leaders, and great skill in their tactics, but I am sure it is practicable." [9] This was the very definition of the policy behind the demand for positive protection.

Most Northern Democrats from New York to Iowa could assent to a call for guarantees to the South against invasion. Douglas himself quickly introduced a bill for that purpose. But when the Southern hysteria after John Brown was directed against the Douglas Democrats, and voiced demands which most Northerners interpreted as an attack on the right of freemen in new communities to exclude a pernicious institution (an attack threatening to ruin the Northern Democracy), it became in the eyes of millions quite unreasonable. The new Southern ultimatum was intolerable to Pugh of Ohio, Tilden of New York, Representative William S. Holman of Indiana, and countless others. They thought bitterly of the ground the party had lost because of Buchanan's weakness, the Lecompton folly, and Southern Rights threats. They all felt angered by the President's declaration in his message that no power whatever could interfere with slavery in any Territory, a statement which had given direct encouragement to slave-code radicals in the South.[10] Congressman Holman

9 December 29, 1858; Miles Papers, Univ. of North Carolina.
10 Evidence of this lies in the letter of J. L. M. Curry to Governor Moore of Alabama urging that the Democratic State convention come fully up to the State Rights standard. "Since Buchanan's message, our Convention can hardly hesitate upon our right to the Federal protection of our property in the Territorities." January 3, 1860; Governors' Letters, Ala. Dept. Arch. and Hist.

wrote his Indiana friend, Allen Hamilton, that the Northern wing must make a stand:

The Charleston Convention will take the ground indicated by the Message unless there is a very decided popular expression to the contrary in the Northwest. . . . The chances are that we shall be compelled to face such a platform on the territorial question in 1860. And it is my private opinion (confidential) that we cannot carry a single Congressional district on that doctrine in the State. The South largely controls political sentiment here [in Washington], and the South can only be influenced by a bold and decided stand in the Northwest, the only part of the North for which they have any remaining regard.[11]

Not rule or ruin, but rule *and* ruin—such seemed the Southern demand to Northern Democrats. It appeared the more unreasonable because a slave-code, in the circumstances of the day, was a pernicious abstraction without the slightest practical value. Slavery was dead in Kansas; in Nebraska, Colorado, Utah, and other actual or potential Territories it had never been born or could not exist. Protected in New Mexico by a slave-code which many Northerners regarded as harsh, it had no real life there. Sensible Southerners admitted that a mere abstraction was not worth the sacrifice of Democratic unity.[12] Governor Magoffin of Kentucky, for instance, wrote sharply of the lack of realism in the demand. No individual in the Territories had yet complained of the want of legal protection or the impotence of the courts to protect slave chattels, he said; yet, though the issue would destroy the only national party in existence, it was suddenly dragged forth without any justifying grievance.[13] John Forsyth in the Mobile *Register* pointed out the the important distinction between the institution of slavery and property in slaves.[14] It might well be argued that Congress was bound to protect property everywhere under its jurisdiction. But was it bound to protect the institution of slavery? And if the Constitution enjoined any such duty, did it not apply to States as well as Territories?

These rational expostulations meant nothing to two groups: the small but resolute body which wished to destroy Democratic unity in order to clear the ground for a Southern Confederacy, and the great emotional mass of proslavery men eager to voice their irritations, injuries, and fears. This latter group was nettled when the lawmakers of Kansas and Nebraska, defying Taney and Buchanan alike, passed their bills to declare slavery forever abolished. Nebraska now had a capital town sprawling over the hills and ravines of Omaha, a population (such as it was, remarks one historian) of perhaps twelve thousand, and a new governor, Samuel W. Black, whose appointment had been opposed on the

11 December 28, 1859; Allen Hamilton Papers.
12 L. O. Branch in "Letters 1850–60," *N. C. Hist. Review*, X, 41 ff.
13 Beriah Magoffin in the Washington *Constitution*, February 10, 1859.
14 Mobile *Register*, December 4, 1859.

ground of intemperance, and who spent much time demonstrating that the charge was well founded. He vetoed the bill to abolish slavery, as Governor Samuel Medary did that in Kansas. In New Mexico, meanwhile, the legislature defeated a bill to wipe out slavery. These provocative Western nose-thumbings were probably intended by Republicans to emphasize the Freeport Doctrine, and in any event did so.[15]

The demands of the Southern radicals were quickly placed before Congress. On January 18, 1860, Senator A. G. Brown submitted resolutions declaring it the duty of that body, whenever any territorial legislature failed to pass adequate laws for the protection of slavery, to supply them.[16] A fortnight later, after more Southern conferences, Jefferson Davis introduced another set furnishing a more elaborate program. They declared that no State had a right, by itself or through a combination of citizens, to intermeddle with the domestic institutions of other States; that all attacks on slavery within the fifteen slave States were a breach of faith and a violation of the constitutional compact; that it was the special duty of the Senate to resist all discriminations with respect to property or persons in the Territories; and that the national government, through its courts and if necessary, Congress, should give slavery all needful protection in the Territories. His resolutions also asserted that the people of a Territory might not decide for or against slavery until admission; and finally, that all State laws interfering with the recovery of runaway slaves were hostile, subversive of the Constitution, revolutionary in effect, and, if persisted in, certain to lead to sharp counter-measures.[17]

Here was a grim sectional manifesto. At least five of its propositions were certain to be taken by all Northern Republicans as slaps in the face. Two—the demand for a slave-code and the denial of any right by territorial inhabitants to discourage slavery—were violently objectionable to all Douglas Democrats. It was given out that Buchanan supported them all.

This manifesto, the most aggressive step taken by any important Southern leader since Calhoun's day, stamped Davis as an aspirant for Calhoun's old position as the undisputed chieftain of the Southern Rights forces. Although he still believed himself an adherent of the Union, this was the platform of theories built to sustain the drama of secession. Davis asked for a full-dress debate, a rehearsal of the first lines of that drama, on February 8; but it was postponed and repostponed. The fact was that prescient Democratic leaders wished to avoid an irreparable party breach. Toombs, for one, sharply disapproved of the defiant demands of Brown and Davis; it was the very quintessence of folly to raise such

15 Morton and Watkins, *Nebraska*, 273–275; N. Y. *Weekly Tribune*, March 10, 1860. For denunciation of the antislavery bills see New Orleans *Picayune*, February 26, 1860.
16 *Cong. Globe*, 36th Cong., 1st Sess., 404.
17 *Idem*, February 2, 1860; 36th Cong., 1st Sess., 658.

issues on the eve of the election, he grumbled to Alexander H. Stephens.[18] Wigfall in his homely way derided the demand for a slave-protection bill applying to such Territories as Kansas. In the first place, it could not pass Congress; in the second place, if passed it could not be enforced—no territorial jury would sustain it. Then why cripple the Democracy on the eve of its great contest with the Republicans, whose victory would involve the destruction of the Union? [19]

Nevertheless, in March the Democratic Senate caucus voted that Davis's resolutions were the true interpretation of the Constitution. It was spurred to this action by the Directory, and that lesser part of the Administration, Buchanan himself. A year earlier, the President had been against the slave-code and for reliance on the courts; now he had moved forward to stand with Slidell and Davis. Naturally, Northwestern Democrats spurned the caucus action with contempt. Douglas declared that no mere Senate group could dictate party policy on any issue; only the national convention could do that. They must wait, he said, to see whether the Charleston gathering would abide by the Cincinnati platform or not. Davis retorted that no attempt was being made to prescribe a platform for the party, and that personally he would rather have an honest candidate on a rickety platform than an untrustworthy candidate on the best platform men could devise.[20]

Both wings of the party stated their position again and again, for the slave-code had a way of rearing its head in debate with disconcerting abruptness. At times, Davis, Mason, Curry, and others treated the issue as a matter of common honesty. If a man comes into a community avowing that he has a particular species of property which requires general aid for its preservation, they said, he has a right to get it. On other occasions they treated it as a matter of constitutional right, quoting Taney, and asserting that protection was the price paid by government for the support of its citizens.[21] On the other side, Douglas, Pugh, and their associates reiterated that if the people of New Mexico wanted slavery, they should have it; if the people of Kansas did not want it, it should not be forced upon them. Why these disruptive resolutions? Douglas demanded of Davis.

The Senator does not contend that there is any pressing necessity for them; he does not pretend that there is any great evil to be redressed; for, when asked by his colleague why he does not bring in a bill to carry out this right, he says there is no necessity for it. There is no necessity for legislation; no grievances to be remedied; no evil to be avoided; no action is necessary; and yet the peace of the country, the integrity of the Democratic party, are to be threatened by

18 February 10, 1860; U. B. Phillips, *Robert Toombs*, 184.
19 *Cong. Globe*, 36th Cong., 1st Sess., 1490.
20 *Idem*, p. 2155.
21 *Idem*, pp. 578, 1487, etc.

abstract resolutions. . . . The people will ask what all this is for; what it means; why it is so important to have a vote. . . . Why? There must be some purpose.[22]

[II]

Yet the main battle during winter and early spring was still between Republicans and Democrats, for most people believed that the Democratic Party would ultimately close ranks to meet its adversary. Wigfall's watchword, "Defeat them!" still seemed the natural rallying-cry as Lincoln and Seward defined the issues.

The New York Senator, returning from Europe in late December, had encountered a mixed reception. New York City and Auburn welcomed him with affectionate warmth. But powerful Democratic newspapers and Southern politicians were daily abusing him as the prime instigator of the John Brown outrage. The slave States seemed almost unanimous that his election as President would spell the end of the Union. Among the Republicans, his political future was poised in an uneasy balance, for many party members believed him too radical to make a good nominee. Received cordially in Washington by some and with icy restraint by others, he realized that weighty considerations, personal, party, and national, required from him a moderate and conciliatory course. As February ended, he delivered not so much to Congress as the country an eagerly awaited speech. Crowded galleries, a throng of House members, and a full corps of reporters heard a discourse of dulcet gentleness.

It would be an overwhelming source of shame and sorrow, he began, if thirty million Americans could not so combine prudence with humanity in dealing with the slavery question as to preserve their free institutions amid general harmony. He went on to expound Republican principles in the mildest terms. Not a hint of the higher law or the irrepressible conflict appeared. Instead, he declared that he knew of only one party policy, the exclusion of slavery from the Territories. And he invented placatory new terms to define sectional differences, speaking of the "capital States" of the South and "labor States" of the North.

No more slave States and free States; instead, capital States and labor States! Whereas moral considerations had long mingled with the distinction between slave and free, Seward now suggested that the difference in systems was merely economic. The capital States of the South were easy to unite, he said, while the labor States of the North stood dissevered. The capital States threatened disunion, while the labor States were devoted to the national fabric. But the capital States misunderstood the situation; they failed to distinguish between

22 *Idem*, p. 2156.

constitutional resistance to the extension of slavery in the Territories and unconstitutional aggression against slavery in the States. Seward condemned John
Brown's raid in language emphatic enough to suit Wise himself, terming it sedition and treason, justly punished by death. The South, he declared, misappre-
hended Republican policy, which was in no sense hostile. His party represented
simply a popular reaction against a measure fastened upon the nation by surprise (here Douglas's scowl deepened), the introduction of slavery into the new
lands of the West. It was merely defensive against that measure; it wished to save
the boundless plains from slavery or polygamy.[23]

At some points, Seward lifted his speech to the level of eloquence. It might
be inferred from circumstances, he remarked, that his party would protect freedom of speech and the press, favor speedy improvement of the public domain
under a homestead law, encourage mining, manufacturing, and internal commerce, and promote a Pacific railway. But free Territories being its prime aim,
it would meet other contingencies cautiously, for "already it feels the necessity
of being cautious in its care of the national health and life." And in a passage of
notable force, he repelled the charge that the party was sectional.

Come if you will into the free States, he invited, into New York anywhere
from Lake Erie to Sag Harbor, into my own Owasco valley. Hold your conventions, nominate your candidates, address the people as freely as at home; you
will have hospitable welcome and appreciative audiences, with ballot boxes open
for all the votes you can win. Are you less sectional than this? Extend us the
same privilege, and you will soon have as many Southern Republicans as we have
Northern Democrats. Suppose a Republican Congress and President elected, he
went on, they would be friendly to all sections; and how could they practice
tyranny under a Constitution so full of checks? Expressing incredulity at the
idea of disunion, he closed with an eloquence anticipatory of the peroration he
was soon to attach to Lincoln's first inaugural:

The earth seems to be heaving under our feet, and the pillars of the noble
fabric that protects us to be trembling before our eyes. But the appointed end
of all this agitation comes at last, and always seasonably; the tumults of the
people subside; the country becomes calm once more; and then we find that
only our senses have been disturbed, and that they have betrayed us. The earth
is firm as always before.

23 Douglas had an explanation for Seward's newly minted terms. Some strikes had occurred among Massachusetts shoemakers, and the New Yorker, he thought, was playing for
the votes of the laboring masses. Actually a great "free labor" movement was under way.
Men interested in it said that free labor was to be encouraged in the West by a homestead
law, and made prosperous in the East by tariffs. Bowles, Greeley, Medill, and other editors
chanted the praises of free labor. The Republican (People's) State convention in Pennsylvania was shortly to hail its candidate for governor, Andrew G. Curtin, as a man who
had "given a lifetime of earnest, untiring effort to the interests of Free Labor." *Cong. Globe*,
36th Cong., 1st Sess., 915; N. Y. *Weekly Tribune*, June 16, 1860.

A politic speech which, in its contradiction of Southern bogey-raising, was much needed. Many proslavery men in Congress were giving a wildly exaggerated picture of the Republican objects. Anderson of Missouri, for example, told the House that they embraced not merely the restriction of slavery, but its abolition in the District of Columbia, repeal or emasculation of the Fugitive Slave Law, prohibition of the interstate slave trade, and remodeling of the Supreme Court to sustain these acts.

The major Republican newspapers reprinted Seward's speech with editorial commendation, Raymond's *Times* declaring that it would remove unfounded prejudices from the public mind. The New York *Tribune*, boasting on March 1 that it had already printed two hundred and fifty thousand copies of the speech, prepared to sell a pamphlet edition of a million within the month. That the address strengthened Seward and his party in doubtful areas of the North and West, where both were feared as too radical, there could be no question.[24] It is unlikely, however, that it did much to diffuse reassurance throughout the South, which was in no frame of mind to accept it. And was the speech that of a man of firm principle? Might not the disclaimers of all aggressive intent have been combined with a certain constructive quality?

Very different in tone, and a far greater landmark in the thought of the period, was the speech which Lincoln had delivered two days earlier, February 27, in Cooper Union.

Despite his debates with Douglas, to most easterners Lincoln remained just what the New York *Times* called him, a lawyer of some local Illinois reputation. The *Tribune* had spoken of him as one of the secondary group of aspirants for the Republican nomination: "Banks, or Fessenden, or Dayton, or Cameron, or Lincoln." [25] The previous October, he had been invited to give a lecture in a popular course in Beecher's Plymouth Church in Brooklyn, with an offer of $200 and expenses. Advised by friends to seize the opportunity to speak on politics, he had obtained the consent of the church committee. At almost the last moment, the lecture was transferred to the Young Men's Central Republican Union of New York, and the place changed to Cooper Union. For several days in advance the speech was prominently announced in the metropolitan press, the *Evening Post* assuring readers that it would be a powerful assault upon the principles of the proslavery party and an able vindication of the Republican creed. The Young Men's Union was being adroitly used by Bryant, Greeley, Hamilton Fish, and David Dudley Field, opponents of the Weed organization, to bring forward important Republican alternatives to Seward; and it had already presented Frank P. Blair, Jr., and Cassius M. Clay to the city.[26]

24 Bancroft, *Seward*, I, 518, Merriam, *Bowles*, I, 301, 302; Pike, *First Blows of the Civil War*, 501 ff. Raymond's *Times* was now regarded as a Seward organ.
25 N. Y. *Weekly Tribune*, February 25, 1860.
26 Baringer, *Lincoln's Rise to Power*, 154.

Lincoln had prepared himself carefully. His discourse (and it is strange that this has never been pointed out) was in great measure a refutation of Douglas's labored historical article in *Harper's*, and was largely inspired by that performance. We can picture him, the previous fall, stretched on the sofa in his cluttered law office, absorbed in Douglas's essay; we can imagine the emphasis with which, talking to Herndon, he repudiated Douglas's thesis that popular sovereignty was a time-hallowed tradition of the republic; we can picture him, as he paced between house and office, resolving to make the eastern speech a demolition of Douglas's argument. Spending weary hours in the State Library, he had toiled over Elliot's *Debates on the Constitution*, early Congressional reports, and newspaper files, until he had an exhaustive reply ready.

Arriving on Sunday at the Astor House, he was doubtless somewhat astonished to find many Republican politicians seeking him out, and to learn that elaborate preparations had been made to give him a distinguished audience. Tuesday night came, chill and snowy. As yet Cooper Union, the building less than two years old, seemed fairly well uptown. But fifteen hundred people tramped through the massive doors and downstairs to the great, round, subterranean hall with its many pillars, long, square stage, and flaring gas lamps. William Cullen Bryant, spare, bearded, and dapper, presided; David Dudley Field escorted the speaker to the platform; Peter Cooper, radiating pride in his shining structure, was benignly attentive; and among others in the audience were Greeley, the publisher G. P. Putnam, Abram S. Hewitt, and ex-Governor John A. King. As the *Tribune* remarked, no man since the days of Clay and Webster had spoken to a larger assemblage of the city's brains and character. Lincoln knew that he was under inquest; the two great editors and others, remembering his house-divided speech and his skill in bringing Douglas into the Freeport net, regarded him as a Presidential spar and were eager to measure his stature.

Seldom has a speaker risen with such quiet mastery to his opportunity. His gaunt height, shaggy hair, and ungainly awkwardness in managing his long limbs and huge hands and feet, the bad cut and wrinkles of his new broadcloth suit, the shrillness of his voice, all combined at first to make a questionable impression.[27] Then, as he warmed to his theme, as the glow of his earnestness lighted

27 G. H. Putnam, *George Palmer Putnam*, 274, 275.

The passage shown in the illustration on the facing page illuminates Lincoln's basic attitudes. This fragment, the conclusion of his speech at Springfield, October 30, 1858, was not published until long after his death. The original was owned by Oliver R. Barrett. Paul M. Angle, printing it in "New Letters and Papers of Abraham Lincoln" (1930), writes that it is probably only a small part of what he said on the occasion. It is inserted here as defining the assumption on which he reared his Cooper Union Address.

Lincoln's Last Speech

In the Campaign of 1858

My friends, today closes the discussions of this canvass. The planting and the culture are over; and there remains but the preparation, and the harvest.

I stand here surrounded by friends – some political, all personal friends I trust. May I be indulged, in this closing scene, to say a few words of myself. I have borne a laborious, and, in some respects to myself, a painful part in the contest. Through all, I have neither assailed, nor wrestled with any part of the constitution. The legal right of the Southern people to reclaim their fugitives I have constantly admitted. The legal right of Congress to interfere with their institution in the states, I have constantly denied. In resisting the spread of slavery to new territory, and with that, what appears to me to be a tendency to subvert the first principle of free government itself my whole effort has consisted. To the best of my judgment I have labored *for* and not *against* the Union. As I have not felt, so I have not expressed any harsh sentiment towards our Southern brethren. I have constantly declared, as I really believed, the only difference between them and us, is the difference of circumstances.

I have meant to assail the motives of no party, or individual; and if I have, in any instance (of which I am not conscious) departed from my purpose, I regret it.

I have said that in some respects the contest has been painful to me. Myself, and those with whom I act have been constantly accused of a purpose to destroy the Union; and bespattered with every imaginable odious epithet; and some who were friends, as it were but yesterday have made themselves most active in this. I have cultivated patience, and made no attempt at a retort.

Ambition has been ascribed to me. God knows how sincerely I prayed from the first that this field of ambition might not be opened. I claim no insensibility to political honors; but today could the Missouri restriction be restored, and the whole slavery question replaced on the old ground of "toleration" by *necessity* where it exists, with unyielding hostility to the spread of it, on principle, I would, in consideration, gladly agree, that Judge Douglas should never be out, and I never *in*, an office, so long as we both or either, live.

up his craggy face, as men caught the force of his ideas and language, he carried his audience with him. The tenor of his speech was as soberly conservative as Seward's. It fell into two halves; the first addressed to Douglas and a refutation of his arguments, the second to the South and a correction of its misconceptions. Its spirit throughout was calm and philosophic, employing historic facts to meet the popular sovereignty fallacy, and a sweet reasonableness to allay Southern fears. But whereas Seward had tended to blur moral principle, Lincoln emphasized it.

Turning to the national record, he reviewed it far more searchingly than had Douglas. To show that the early leaders of the Union had legislated for the restriction and, wherever possible, exclusion or elimination of slavery, he carefully scrutinized the action of the Federal Convention, of the Continental Congress as it had drawn up the Northwest Ordinance, and of the early sessions of the Federal Congress. Nowhere, he showed, had they fixed any line dividing national from local authority in the Territories, or laid down any rule forbidding the national government to exercise authority over slavery therein. Douglas had said of slavery at Columbus: "Our fathers, when they framed the government under which we live, understood this question just as well, and even better, than we do now." Lincoln ironically declared, "I fully endorse this." The fathers of the republic had marked slavery as an evil to be halted and contained; they had tolerated and protected it only insofar as its actual presence in the nation made toleration and protection a necessity. To that attitude the country should return.

The Southern people, Lincoln remarked in the second and more important half of his address, were as reasonable and just as any. What were their accusations against the Republican Party? They termed it a sectional party, when actually it was the Southerners who made it so, for they would give it no hearing. They declared it revolutionary, whereas it merely clung to Washington's doctrine that slavery ought to be restricted. They accused it of stirring up slave insurrections; yet such revolts had been just as common before the Republican Party was organized—everyone recalled the Southampton rising. No Republican had been connected with Harper's Ferry, which Lincoln roundly condemned, and for aught the Republicans said or did, the slaves would scarcely know there was a Republican Party. How much would it really avail the South if that section could break up the party? The sentiment against slavery in the United States commanded at least one and a half million votes, and if the party disappeared, that feeling would simply break into new and perhaps less peaceful channels. Would destruction of the party lessen or increase the number of John Browns?

The South, continued Lincoln, was asserting through numberless speakers and newspapers that it would end the Union if a Republican President were elected. This, in effect, was holding a pistol at the head of the Northern voters and demanding that they give up their ballot. To such a threat no self-respecting men could yield. Nevertheless, he said in conclusion, the Republicans ought to concede to the Southern people as much as their sense of duty permitted. The difficulty was that duty forbade a surrender of principle:

All they ask, we could readily grant, if we thought slavery right; all we ask, they could as readily grant, if they thought it wrong. Their thinking it right and our thinking it wrong is the precise fact upon which depends the whole controversy. Thinking it right, as they do, they are not to blame for desiring its full recognition, as being right. . . . Wrong as we think slavery is, we can yet afford to let it alone where it is, because that much is due to the necessity arising from its actual presence in the nation; but can we, while our votes will prevent it, allow it to spread into the national Territories, and to overrun us here in these free States? If our sense of duty forbids this, then let us stand by our duty fearlessly and effectively. Let us be diverted by none of those sophistical contrivances wherewith we are so industriously plied and belabored—contrivances such as groping for some middle ground between the right and the wrong: vain as the search for a man who should be neither a living man nor a dead man; such as a policy of "don't care" on a question about which all true men do care; such as the Union appeals beseeching true Union men to yield to Disunionists, reversing the divine rule, and calling, not the sinners, but the righteous to repentance; such as invocations to Washington, imploring men to unsay what Washington said and undo what Washington did.

The crowd, which had grown steadily more enthusiastic, gave Lincoln an ovation, shouting, clapping, and waving hats and handkerchiefs. Noah Brooks, the *Tribune's* reporter, exclaiming that Lincoln was the greatest man since St. Paul, hurried to his office to write that no description could do justice to the tones, the gestures, the kindling eye, and the mirth-provoking look of the speaker; that the assemblage had frequently rung with cheers and shouts; and that "no man ever before made such an impression on his first appeal to a New York audience." Hiram Barney, a veteran politician, was equally enthusiastic. "The *Tribune* has a good report of the *words* of your speech," he wrote Lincoln. "What a pity it cannot give the *manner* of it."

Lincoln's and Seward's addresses went to most of the reading public at the same time. Greeley's *Weekly Tribune* carried Seward in six columns of fine print on its first page, Lincoln in five and a half columns on its second and third. Both speeches were promptly issued by various presses in cheap pamphlet form for wide distribution; both were commended by all Republican editors. Seward's speech had in certain passages a nobler eloquence. But in bold candor, intellectual vigor, and positiveness of moral conviction, Lincoln was clearly the superior. He brought forward more ideas. He stated the case of the South with more complete honesty. Unlike Seward, he did not treat the disunionist threats as so unnatural that no hand would execute them; he implied that the peril was real. He did not gloss over the great divisive issue, but explicitly defined it; and instead of appealing to an expedient patriotism which would ignore issues, he appealed to a patriotism of principle which would face them.

"It has produced a greater effect here than any other single speech," one young New Yorker presently wrote Lincoln. "It is the real platform in the eastern states and must carry the conservative element in New York, New Jersey, and Pennsylvania." [28]

[III]

Immediately before the Seward-Lincoln broadsides, the House had placed the first of the pending economic issues—the homestead bill—before the country. This measure was the work of Galusha A. Grow, who brought to it two principal impulses. One was derived from his early experiences in the Tunkhannock Valley, a semi-frontier region of northern Pennsylvania, where, first as a farm boy and later as an active lumber trader operating down the Susequehanna, he had observed the voracities of land speculators. The other came from the land-reform ideas of George H. Evans and similar writers.

When he entered Congress in 1851 as its youngest member, Grow had been full of fire for his cause. In his first important speech he had taken a ground very different from Andrew Johnson's. Repudiating all ideas of state help and state paternalism, he asserted that men who would occupy and work the common lands had an inborn right to own them. In the ten years that followed, he stuck to his own broad proposals: no more public land to be sold, all surveyed lands not reserved for special purposes to be opened to settlers, and no distinctions to be allowed among groups or classes. The stalwart Grow (he was six feet two, with muscles hardened by woodchopping and bark-peeling) made an ideal champion. He was indefatigable, combative, and all devotion to his grand object. Most cool-headed when dealing the hardest blows, he loved the rough and tumble of debate with hot-tempered Southern members. When he had risen in mid-February to reintroduce his bill, House passage was assured, and to obtain quick action, debate was almost entirely cut off. He made one speech interesting for its economic principles. Free homesteads, he said, would shut out from land-investment a great deal of capital which would then flow into industrial undertakings. The rapid colonization of the West would not only create agricultural wealth but furnish avid new markets for manufacturers.

---

[28] Once more Lincoln took pains to see his speech correctly presented, going late in the evening to the New York *Tribune* office to read proofs. Amos J. Cummings, who gave him the proofs, thinks that the original manuscript was tossed into the waste paper bin.

Thus farming, transportation, and industrial activity would all receive benefits. The measure passed the House early in March by a vote of 115 to 65.

Only one free State member, Montgomery of Pennsylvania, voted no, and he said he was for homestead legislation but wished the bill amended; only one slave State member voted yes. The alignment was completely sectional. At once the issue was transferred to the Senate, where debate that had crackled and sputtered on the slavery question swung to economic problems. Andrew Johnson, who represented the spirit of Jacksonian democracy as well as any man living, had said years earlier that the homestead issue would soon control elections; and it was now certain that it would play a great part in the campaign of 1860.[29] Petitions for passage rained upon the Senate table.

The Senate had its own bill, a substitute which Johnson proposed when it became evident that the House measure could not pass. It contained various conservative features. It gave homesteads only to heads of families, not to any man over twenty-one; it required a nominal payment of twenty-five cents an acre instead of granting the land free; it gave farms to the alien-born only when they became fully naturalized; and it was stricter than the House bill in its residential requirements.[30] Even in this modified form, however, the proposal aroused the antagonism of most Southern members. They were convinced that it would restrict slavery (for slaves were seldom profitable on a one-hundred-and-sixty-acre holding), encourage a flood of European immigration to the North and West, and increase the preponderance of the free States.[31] One Southerner alone, A. G. Brown, spoke warmly for the legislation. It was outrageous, he said, to compel the hardy pioneer to pay $200 within a year for the one hundred and sixty acres upon which he settled. The man and his toiling family reared a cabin, cleared some ground, and fenced it in; then if drought or flood ruined the crop, if sickness smote them, or if panic and depression brought prices to a ruinous level, they were without money, and lost everything to some land shark who possessed capital. Every settler taken from urban poverty to go and dwell upon a homestead would be lifted from the consumers and placed among the producers.[32]

The ablest of the slave State opponents, Green of Missouri, called the legisla-

29 *Cong. Globe*, 36th Cong., 1st Sess., 1114, 1115.
30 Robbins, *Our Landed Heritage*, 180; Winston, *Andrew Johnson*, 138.
31 When Doolittle of Wisconsin dropped an incautious remark that the homestead legislation was "a measure of empire," indignant Southerners caught this up as proof of a sinister intent. It reveals, said Mason, the Northern determination to take "command and control of the destinies of the continent." In the eyes of many Southern Senators, the North intended to fill the West with small farmers as a means of promoting abolition. They also arraigned the legislation as a political stroke, a baiting of the Republican trap for German, Irish, and Scandinavian voters. Mason called it a powerful political engine for battering down the last walls that protected Southern institutions. Cf. Matthews, *Grow*, 212, 213.
32 *Cong. Globe*, 36th Cong., 1st Sess., 1553.

tion unnecessary, because, under the graduation law, public land was already selling for as little as twelve and a half cents an acre. He argued that it was unwise because it would destroy an annual revenue of from two to two and a half millions from the sale of public lands, requiring a higher tariff revenue, and because it would cripple further land grants for railroads and thus impede the growth of transportation facilities. It was unjust because it would render worthless the bounty land warrants held by veterans, would encourage rich speculators to hire perjurers to go upon the public lands and swear to occupancy, and would take property belonging to all citizens in common and parcel it out to the very poorest, thus subsidizing the lazy and raffish. You cannot go to Richmond or Charleston and hire men to colonize the West, said Green; you might beat your drum and wave your flag for six weeks without getting five settlers. But go to New York and Boston, and men will flock forward by thousands. "Who are they? Men intent on destroying the institutions of the South—men determined to destroy the rights of the South." [33]

Green and such other Southern Senators as Wigfall would willingly give the public lands to the States in which they lay, letting Tennessee, Arkansas, or Minnesota pass homestead laws if they liked. Both frankly stated their sectional motive: We are under no obligation to provide for your paupers, they told the North. It was clear that the history of Kansas lay painfully in the Southern consciousness. The bill means more emigrant aid societies, growled Mason. On the other side, Douglas and Pugh, rehearsing familiar arguments for the measure, protested that opposition to it must not be made a test of Democratic regularity. The first men to bring such a bill into Congress had been Democrats; a homestead bill had passed the same Democratic House which enacted the Kansas-Nebraska bill. Andrew Johnson, pursuing a higher line of exposition, declared the measure essentially Jeffersonian and Jacksonian. The nation had a mighty patrimony of land, amounting to some seven million quarter-sections. It could give each of its four million voters a farm, and have a tremendous domain left over. It was sound Jeffersonian policy to build up the rural areas as a balance to the great cities, to fill these vacant spaces with virtuous, hard-working men of a type to sustain the government. Critics talked of encouraging radicalism, but who ever heard of a government being overturned by people having property? It was want of independence that created discontent. Rome had decayed because a few men had monopolized the land, shutting the poor servile masses out of all hope of prosperous homes.[34]

After much obstruction, the Senate bill came to a vote on May 11. It was then evident that no party which defeated it could carry critical Northern and

33 *Ibid.,* 1556.
34 *Ibid.,* 1650–1655.

border States. Passing 44 to 8, the measure went to the House. After two conference committees had failed, a third finally whipped a compromise bill into shape, which in mid-June passed both chambers by overwhelming vote: 115 to 51 in the House; 36 to 2 in the Senate. Political expediency made its passage a necessity.[35] The large number of abstentions told a significant story, however— and the South had its ace card still to play. The bill really suited nobody. It was a changeling, stripped of most of its homestead features. Abolishing the old price of $1.25, it allowed heads of families, after five years of occupancy, to purchase quarter-sections at twenty-five cents an acre. One reason it passed so easily lay in the universal expectation that Buchanan would kill it.

By this date the Presidential campaign had begun; and partly to strike a heavy new blow at Douglas and other Northwestern Democrats, partly to meet the wishes of the South, and partly to express his own strict-constructionist views, Buchanan vetoed the bill. The Constitution, he wrote, gave Congress no power to make such a huge donation; it would be unjust to earlier settlers who had paid $1.25 an acre and to veterans with bounty warrants; it would hurt the old States by reducing the value of their lands and tempting their people to emigrate; it would open a vast field for speculation, as rich sharpers settled poor men on the land under secret agreements to divide their homesteads; and it would diminish the public revenues and so increase taxation. These objections were succinctly riddled by Senator Harlan of Iowa, who had been reared in a log cabin on the Illinois prairie. They irritated Andrew Johnson, who recalled that Buchanan in his inaugural had promised lands to actual settlers at moderate rates. But the bill failed by three votes to pass the Senate over Buchanan's veto. The South, for the last time, had balked a measure which it saw would give enhanced population and power to the freesoil States.[36]

Homestead legislation had become enormously popular in the Northwest. A typical Illinois country newspaper, the Warsaw *City Bulletin*, published in the boyhood home of John Hay, dwelt in every issue upon its importance. It would cure the evils of the existing laws, under which vast tracts fell into the hands of speculators; would give work and shelter to the unemployed and homeless surplus population of the cities; would fill the West with a thrifty race of producers; would restore the equilibrium between capital and labor; and would bring a flood of Northern and European settlers to secure every mile of the West to freedom. If defeated in Washington, it would be a plank of the Republican platform and would win a multitude of voters to the party. Many a Northern farm youth at his plow, many a casual laborer—and many a land speculator too—cursed the interests that killed the homestead bill.

35 *Ibid.*, 3159, 3179.
36 *Ibid.*, 3267-3272; Brigham, *James Harlan*, 142-144.

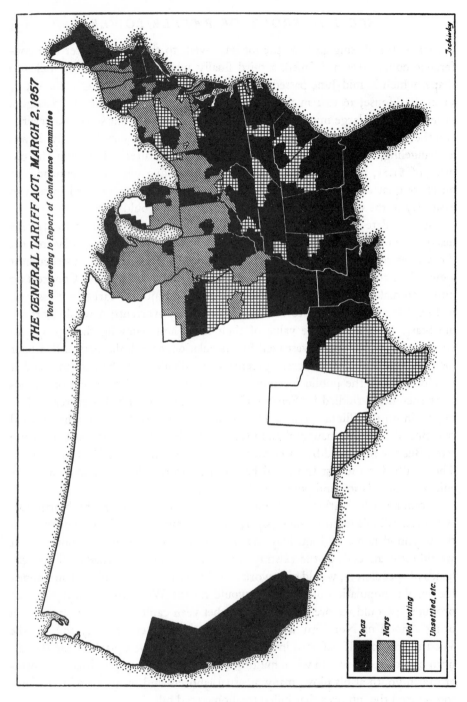

THE GENERAL TARIFF ACT, MARCH 2, 1857

Vote on agreeing to Report of Conference Committee

Yeas

Nays

Not voting

Unsettled, etc.

A different kind of legislation interested the factory owner nervously watching prices and profits. "While you, gentlemen of the South, are protecting your peculiar institutions," cried Simon Cameron in the Senate, "you ought, at least, not to forget that we of the North have a peculiar institution to protect and encourage—our free white labor." He pointed to the fact that the annual value of the manufactured products of Philadelphia alone was $250,000,000.[37]

The Republican House this spring, by rapid effort, carried a bill for a slight upward revision of duties. Justin S. Morrill, the sharp-eyed, sharp-nosed, sharp-witted Yankee at the head of Ways and Means, believed in protecting Vermont wool and much besides. The bill promised the country the means to meet its deficit, to ease the cramped departments, and to pay off nearly fifty millions of debt which the Administration had contracted. At the same time, it would stimulate the metal, textile, and other industries. Its friends declared that within four years it would double the nation's annual output of coal and iron. The measure passed the House by a nearly solid vote of Republican and Opposition members, with half a dozen Democrats concurring.[38] In the Senate, however, it was blocked by the South and the Democratic low-tariff tradition.

Southern antagonism was voiced in extreme terms. Senator Hunter, denouncing it as monstrous, suggested that it be engrossed on vellum and sent to the Tycoon of Japan as a suggested method of improving upon the historic exclusiveness of his nation. Toombs declared that the true basis of taxation was property, and that an indirect tariff tax would lead to gross extravagance, the government plundering the people without their realizing it. Yulee agreed that the measure was an effort to benefit the North at the expense of the South. Jefferson Davis pronounced for a system of free trade, applied not merely to raw materials but to the woodman's axe and the farmer's plow and scythe.[39]

In the final Senate vote, every Republican present cast his ballot against postponement, while every Democrat but two followed Hunter's leadership in deferring action. The dissenters were Bigler of Pennsylvania and Latham of California. An indignant chorus rose from the eastern press. Greeley's *Trib-*

37 *Cong. Globe*, June 15, 1860, 36th Cong., 1st Sess.
38 *Ibid.*, May 10, 1860; the vote was 105 to 64.
39 Stanwood, *History of the Tariff*, II, 99; *Cong. Globe*, 36th Cong., 1st Sess., 3013, 3188, 3189.

The map on the facing page shows how the low tariff bill passed the House in 1857 by a vote that was mainly non-sectional and non-partisan. The mildly protectionist bill passed in the spring of 1860 received a very different support. Every representative from Massachusetts, Connecticut and Pennsylvania present and voting supported it; every representative from Alabama and Mississippi present opposed it. The vote of Illinois and Indiana was divided.

une spoke for scores of other papers when it said that the issue was made up, and that a multitude of Northern Democrats would now be converted to the Republican Party.[40] As that party entered the campaign, it planned to scatter broadcast the incisive tariff speeches of Morrill, Thaddeus Stevens, and Senator Simmons. Dogberry's axiom, "When two ride a horse, one must ride behind," seemed to countless Northerners to apply to the situation created by the failure of the homestead and tariff bills. The rear rider, as the slave States guided the steed, was growing restive.

Two other economic issues aroused special irritation in the Northwest. One was the failure of legislation to improve the navigation of the Great Lakes. All commerce from the west into Lake Erie had to pass through the River St. Clair, at whose mouth lay extensive shoals. After the opening of the Soo Canal, these shallows were the chief impediment to a fast-developing inland commerce. Republicans complained bitterly that since 1857 the Senate Commerce Committee, a body of seven, had only two members to represent New England, New York, and the Northwest, the South completely dominating it. Chandler's bill of 1858 to deepen the St. Clair channel was first blocked in committee by the chairman, C. C. Clay, and then on the floor by Judah P. Benjamin. When he got an appropriation for $55,000 worth of work added to the civil appropriation bill, Buchanan threatened a veto and the item was removed. Never a patient man, Chandler was roused to intense wrath. In demanding a yea-and-nay call on the appropriation, he uttered a peal of defiance. "I want to see who is friendly to the great Northwest, and who is not—for we are about making our last prayer here. The time is not far distant when, instead of coming here and begging for our rights, we shall extend our hands and take the blessing. After 1860 we shall not be here as beggars." He returned home to Michigan with a blazing tale of wrong.[41] In the winter session of 1858–59 a renewed effort was killed by Buchanan.

Now, early in 1860, Chandler offered his St. Clair legislation once more. This time Buchanan met it with a special message explaining his previous pocket veto, his main ground being that the Constitution made river and harbor improvement the function of the States, and that Michigan and Upper Canada should jointly remove the obstruction. Jefferson Davis, Toombs, Wigfall, and other Southern Senators stoutly defended Buchanan's position. Northern Senators, with Critten-den of Kentucky, assailed it. As all of Chandler's efforts to lift the bill from the table met defeat, the debate aroused strong feeling. "Wait until after the election!" declared Republicans.

Some observers discerned a deeper peril in Buchanan's veto. He had adopted

40 N. Y. *Weekly Tribune*, July 14, 1860.
41 Detroit *Free Press* staff, *Zachariah Chandler*, 169, 170.

Calhoun's mischievous idea that every State and town on the inland waters might pay for their betterment by local tonnage dues, thus denationalizing these arteries (they said) and allowing State and local authorities to clog trade by a multitude of vexatious duties. "I see," exploded Samuel B. Ruggles of New York in a letter to Chandler, "that Mr. Slidell has introduced a bill giving the consent of Congress in advance to any tonnage duties any State adjacent to the Mississippi may lay for the improvement of the river, real or intended—in other words, a bill to denationalize that national river. It is the beginning of the end, and the greatest blow with which the Union has yet been menaced. . . . It should be resisted *to the death*." [42]

The Pacific Railroad was another point at which the South appeared to countless Northerners to be blocking the legitimate demands of a growing nation. Sixty thousand people were now going to the West Coast annually, and some military men estimated that a railroad would have saved ten million dollars in fighting Indian wars. Such an empire was rising beyond the Rockies that it was manifestly imperative to provide rail communications. A select House committee under S. R. Curtis of Iowa, fairly representing every section, reported in May a bill for the private construction of a railroad starting from two points, one on the western border of Missouri and the other on that of Iowa; the two converging lines bearing westward and uniting within two hundred miles of the Missouri River, thence proceeding by a single trunk line to the Sacramento or San Francisco. This was essentially a bill for a railroad on or near the forty-first parallel. A generous land grant and other aids were to be provided by the United States.[43] In vain did Phelps of Missouri, a member of the committee, continue his ten years' battle for a railroad following generally the thirty-fifth parallel. Once more opposition appeared, both to the route chosen and to the financial provisions. By a narrow vote, 101 to 87, the House, as May ended, sent the bill back to committee, while the Senate did nothing.[44]

The central route, however, had won a moral victory in the committee report. Public sentiment seemed swinging in favor of that line. While emigrants plainly preferred it, mineral discoveries were fortifying its position. We have noted that Denver was now plainly destined to become a Western emporium; and meanwhile the winter and early spring of 1860 beheld another tumultuous exodus to Virginia City and the silver camps of Washoe. These rushes, with the steady growth of Kansas, Utah, and San Francisco, appeared to establish the superiority of the central route. It was generally believed that the government could afford to assist only one railway; and if two were built, Minnesota stood

42 S. B. Ruggles, March 19, 1860; Chandler Papers.
43 See Curtis's discussion, *Cong. Globe*, 36th Cong., 1st Sess., 2439-2452.
44 *Cong. Globe*, 36th Cong., 1st Sess., 2452.

ready to argue that a St. Paul-Puget Sound road would find a shorter, easier, richer, and better-wooded route than a New Orleans-El Paso-Gila Valley road. The West was eager for action and impatient of Southern obstruction.

Nor would the Kansas question disappear. The settlers had elected a constitutional convention, which, sitting at Wyandotte during the summer of 1859, had drawn up a serviceable instrument. This had been ratified on October 4 by a majority of nearly five thousand in a total vote of about sixteen thousand, and just as Congress opened, Charles Robinson had been elected governor. The House quickly passed a bill for admission, but the Senate was adamant. Wigfall declared that virtuous Texas would never associate with such a State of outlaws and land pirates as Kansas would make. Meanwhile, Morrill's bill for aiding agricultural colleges was also doomed.

In short, the familiar deadlock of the Thirty-fifth Congress was extending itself into the Thirty-sixth. Legislation which increasingly powerful blocks of voters regarded as urgent was being defeated by a more or less rigid sectional alignment. As one after another these economic measures were hurried through the House, the Southern managers of the Senate became more incensed; for the South believed its position entirely defensible—a position in harmony with the older traditions of the republic. Southern leaders wanted the government of Jefferson and Madison: a government that would not overshadow and weaken the States, that would not expand its activities and its expenditures, and that would guard against conferring economic favors on one section at the expense of the others. They held that it would be fatally easy to build up a great centralized power in Washington, and that, once created, this power could readily be used against them. On grounds both of theory and practice they had forcible arguments. Yet as one after another the new economic measures were stopped by the Senate or President, the Northern Congressmen felt a deepening resentment.

[IV]

Meanwhile, a House committee under "Honest John" Covode, appointed under a resolution of March 5, was inquiring into the Executive use of money, patronage, or other improper means to influence Congress or the administration of the laws. The primary object was to expose the pressures notoriously used by Buchanan in behalf of Lecompton and the English amendment.

Covode, a big-boned, awkward Pennsylvania German, part owner of the Westmoreland Coal Company, had distinguished himself in the Keitt-Grow affray by his rush into the melee brandishing a heavy spittoon. Republicans hoped for campaign ammunition from the inquiry, while the chairman was vengefully eager to repay Buchanan for a charge of bribery in the Pennsylvania Congressional elections of 1858. The President, deeply wounded by the implied accusation, sent the House a solemn protest. "Amid all the political storms through which I have passed," he declared, "the present is the first attempt which has ever been made, to my knowledge, to assail my personal and official integrity." Though his friends tried to obstruct the inquiry, it was relentlessly pressed.

Indeed, Covode's friends extolled, and his foes denounced, the inexorable thoroughness of his work. Buchanan in a second protest to Congress declared that the committee was more tyrannical than the Star Chamber, while the Democratic minority report asserted that the chairman had usurped all its powers, summoned a weird variety of witnesses, and pursued every type of suspicion and allegation.[45] Hearings continued from March 22 until the beginning of June. The first witness, Cornelius Wendell, onetime owner of the *Union*, was discontented with the Administration because it had failed to let him keep most of his perquisites. He talked freely. He was followed by such politicians as Augustus Schell, James C. Van Dyke, and George Plitt, by Attorney-General Black, prominent Senators and Representatives, and two Democratic haters of Buchanan, Robert J. Walker and John W. Forney. The complete testimony filled eight hundred pages; but the gist of it was summed up in the final majority report of thirty pages which the Republican press spread broadcast before the end of June.

Seldom in our history has a Congressional investigation furnished material more damaging to a President and his coadjutors. Its most disturbing evidence was the disclosure of Buchanan's weak timidity, and of the consistent skill of Cobb, Jacob Thompson, Slidell, and Jeremiah Black in overawing him. Forney told how Buchanan had first promised him the editorship of the Washington *Union*, and then under Southern pressure had withdrawn the pledge. "Sir," Forney told him, "you have surrendered me." Buchanan rejoined: "I have been compelled to do so." Later Buchanan had been "compelled" to give way on Lecompton, the Directory coercing him by pointing to the threats of certain States to secede or fight. Evidence was introduced by Ellis B. Schnabel, a friend of Douglas and Walker, to show how directly Jeremiah Black controlled the Washington *Constitution* when it made its fight for Lecompton. His details angered Black, who sat in the committee room, and the two men left the hall exchanging epithets and threats of criminal prosecution.[46]

The inquiry brought out the full text of Buchanan's letter to Walker of July 12, 1857, fully endorsing the very Kansas policies which he shortly repu-

45 Buchanan, *Works*, X, 402, 438; 36th Cong., 1st Sess., H. Rept. 648, 29 ff. The hearings were nominally secret, but the best bits were published; *Covode Report*, 31.
46 *Covode Report*, 296.

diated. It made a profound sensation as Douglasite and Republican organs all over the land gleefully reprinted it. The rash Jeremiah Black had called a clerk a liar for certifying to the existence of the letter; Walker then humiliated both the President and Attorney-General by producing it. Buchanan had not only written that "the point on which your and our success depends is the submission of the constitution to Kansas"; he had repeated that on "the question of submitting the constitution to the *bona fide* resident settlers of Kansas, I am willing to stand or fall." [47] Why had he receded from this high ground? Walker's emphatic statement left no doubt as to the way in which the Southern group had manipulated Buchanan. Secretary Thompson's despatch of his clerk Martin to Lecompton at the time the constitution was being written in that town was thoroughly aired. Plainly, a great deal of subterranean intrigue had accompanied the drafting of that document and the effort to get it through Congress.

The Covode Committee also revealed how Buchanan had employed the patronage to gain support for controversial measures and to destroy Douglas. Forney related that, after he had founded the Philadelphia *Press*, Black had sent an agent to offer him printing contracts worth $80,000 if he would abandon his opposition to Lecompton. "You can get all that post-office printing," said the man, "if you will write an editorial article as long as your hand." [48] Evidence showed that the Administration had frequently interfered in local elections, particularly in Pennsylvania. Equally disturbing was the testimony as to the misuse of public printing in both Pierce's and Buchanan's day. The profits had been enormous. Wendell and others furnished data indicating that they had aggregated nearly two million dollars in six years. In return for liberal government contracts, Wendell had diverted part of these profits into the hands of men conducting Buchanan's State organ, the *Pennsylvanian*, and the official Administration paper, first the *Union* and later the *Constitution*. Another part had been used to help contest close election districts. At one point, corruption was exposed. Wendell testified that he had distributed between thirty and forty thousand dollars to obtain passage of the Lecompton and English bills; and much of this went in plain bribery, for he admitted drawing checks to bearer or to fictitious names and he had used much loose cash, employing two newspapermen as almoners.

While the committee was at work, the East was startled by a report of heavy defalcations in the New York post office; and on the heels of this came news that Postmaster Isaac V. Fowler had absconded leaving his accounts short by some $155,500. The episode presented mysterious aspects. Fowler, a genial, warm-hearted man, universally liked, had no bad habits, did not speculate, and

47 *Ibid.,* 112, 113.
48 *Ibid.,* 291-304.

was not extravagant. He had held for seven years a position which, with its perquisites, paid at least $15,000 a year; his place in the local Democratic organization could have been made to produce additional revenues; and he had borrowed about $50,000 from friends. One New York writer calculated that altogether during the past seven years he had received at least $400,000—and yet he had fled with only a few thousands. Where had the money gone? Why had he escaped arrest and why was so little effort made to pursue him? Years later it was revealed that his shortages had originated in heavy campaign contributions and party gifts and that promises of reimbursement had not been kept. While John A. Dix took over the post office to straighten out its affairs, the Republican press naturally played fortissimo on the theme of Democratic corruption.[49]

Equally shocking was the exposure of an incompetence amounting to betrayal of duty on the part of Secretary Floyd. Incapable of taking dishonest money himself, the Virginian was willing to protect men who did. At Fort Snelling, the government owned a beautiful military reservation of about eight thousand acres overlooking the junction of the Mississippi and the Minnesota. Floyd decided to sell it, even though it had recently been declared essential. Rapidly advancing in value, at auction it would probably have brought hundreds of thousands. Instead, the Secretary permitted a combination of Virginia friends and New York politicians to buy it through quiet inside bargaining for only $90,000. The purchasers defaulted after the panic, but proof of Floyd's carelessness remained, and even the Democratic majority of an investigating committee pronounced the management of the sale injudicious and improper. Just as malodorous was the Willett's Point affair. This Long Island peninsula was wanted by the government for a fortified post. As late as the summer of 1856 it was priced at only $45,000. The next spring, Floyd authorized Augustus Schell, the slippery Collector of the Port in New York, to ascertain its value. A group was hurriedly organized under Prosper H. Wetmore to get hold of the tract; Schell notified the Secretary that it was worth $200,000; and the government paid that sum. A House committee reported that Schell was the chief instigator of a fraudulent arrangement to cheat the government—with Floyd holding the door wide open.

Nor was this all. Floyd had treated contracts, pay rolls, and appointments with a disregard for economy, efficiency, and the public welfare, and a readiness to assist political and personal friends, which were sometimes positively illegal. The alarmed Democrats at one time thought of conducting an investigation themselves to forestall Republican inquiry.[50] His purchases for the army were bad enough; his management of the work on public buildings in Washington

49 N. Y. *Tribune*, May 19, 1860; Nichols, *Disruption of Democracy*, 313.
50 Nichols, 329.

was worse. The Capitol had to be completed; wings were being added to the Treasury and Interior buildings; a new Post Office building was going up; and the Great Falls aqueduct was being prosecuted. An admirable army engineer, Captain Montgomery C. Meigs, was in charge of these works. Since he was as vigilant as Floyd was lax, the two men came into sharp conflict; and early in 1860 Floyd actually tried to banish him to the Dry Tortugas, where some fortifications were being constructed. This was temporarily blocked. But the quarrel continued, and as Davis, Toombs, and other prominent Democrats came to Meigs's aid, the Secretary's shortcomings were brought before the public. It was shown that he had bought building materials from favorites in violation of statute, and had let an important contract for heating the Capitol to a Virginian who knew nothing of the business and was going to farm out his concession.

Floyd was disgraced. The Republican press, in impassioned editorials, connected his acts, Fowler's thefts, and Wendell's exploitation of public printing with other shady occurrences of the day. The sharp practice by which Indiana Democrats had seized a seat in the Senate, the election frauds of 1857 in Minnesota, the unfortunate act of Buchanan himself in helping a Philadelphia firm obtain a naval contract in order to secure its aid in an important local election— all this was lumped together. To a country which believed honesty a high Federal tradition, these revelations came as a heavy shock.

[V]

By mid-April, the eyes of the nation were bent upon Charleston, where the Democratic Convention was about to assemble. The whole weight of the Administration was being exerted against Douglas's candidacy. He reiterated again and again that he attacked no man, that he wanted party unity, and that he asked only for adherence to the Cincinnati platform. But deeply resenting the course of the Administration in promoting a convention at Springfield on January 10 which elected anti-Douglas delegates in Illinois, he spoke of Buchanan with a personal animosity which the President returned.[51] Howell Cobb and other Directory heads were assuring the Northern politicians who trooped into Washington on their way south that Douglas could get few votes in the slave States. Slidell, Jefferson Davis, C. C. Clay, and others were making it clear that they would accept no Northern Democrat whatever, save some impossible anti-Douglas figure like Dickinson of New York, who would ruin the party in the free States.

Had Douglas been more fairly treated in recent months by the Administration, he would probably have been willing to withdraw in the interests of

51 N. Y. *Weekly Tribune*, May 19, 1860. The Buchaneer convention in Springfield is described by an eyewitness in the Warsaw *City Bulletin*, January 16, 1860.

harmony. But his deposition from the Committee on Territories rankled; the venomous attacks by Jere Black and others seemed to him unforgivable; and he was not going to let proslavery men read him out of the party. He was the champion of the Northwestern Democracy, which was lost if he should be defeated.

January of 1860 brought Douglas an avalanche of Northwestern delegates. A heavy majority of the party in this region was devoted to him and his principles; and, quite apart from this, the leaders knew that his nomination would give them their best chance of carrying State and local offices. Ohio, Illinois, Indiana, Michigan, Iowa, and Wisconsin all chose Douglas men for Charleston and bound them to the unit rule. In several of these States the Administration groups suffered a humiliating debacle. In Illinois, everyone knew that the Douglas forces mustered all but a few thousands of the party membership. The Danite convention, with Isaac Cook as ringmaster and Federal pensioners largely furnishing the rank and file, was regarded from Chicago to Cairo as an absurdity. It talked of a State ticket, but did not venture to name one. The Douglas convention, on the other hand, was full and enthusiastic, speaking authoritatively for the State as it bound its delegates for the Little Giant. In Ohio, the convention declared unanimously for popular sovereignty, and by a vote of 242½ to 94½ instructed the delegation to support Douglas. Wisconsin and Iowa fell into line with enthusiasm.

The keystone of the Democratic arch in the Northwest was Indiana, and here the Buchanan men attempted a stubborn stand. According to the Washington correspondent of the Cincinnati *Enquirer*, nine prominent gentlemen who hated Douglas met, after visiting the White House, and subscribed $8,000 each to control the Indiana delegation. The money, said the *Enquirer* story, was to be used in buying up delegates to the State convention.[52] This body met in Indianapolis on January 11–12. A huge crowd of onlookers, tense with excitement, gathered in and about the Metropolitan Theatre. The Administration coterie, led by Senator Bright, Governor Willard, and Marshal J. L. Robinson, was on hand to threaten, cajole, and offer Federal jobs to the office-hungry. But the Douglas men immediately took control; they nominated a future Vice-President, Thomas A. Hendricks, for governor; and by a vote of 265 to 129, they instructed all delegates at Charleston to work for Douglas to the end. Senators Bright and Fitch were routed in their own counties. This was a blow to the Directory; and so was the action of the Minnesota convention, which expressed a warm preference for Douglas and adopted a popular sovereignty platform.

As spring approached, Douglas, toiling in Washington to strengthen his lines, sought the favor of the delegates who gradually thickened in the capital. He took the field in person, canvassing with his usual energy. "He may be seen in

52 Cincinnati *Enquirer*, Jan. 3, 1860.

the Senate lobbies, in the hotels, and on the sidewalks," reported Greeley's correspondent, "talking earnestly with his friends and by looks, word, and gesture stimulating them to action. Probably no other candidate for a presidential nomination ever played his hand so openly and boldly." [53] His hopes were high. Even in the Lower South he had his supporters. In Louisiana, Soulé was trying to organize anti-machine Democrats and Know-Nothings for him; [54] in Alabama, John Forsyth of the Mobile *Register* continued to laud his ability; in Florida, Senator Yulee was more than willing to make him the nominee. Even in South Carolina the Edgefield *Advertiser* laid down several reasons why his nomination might be desirable. He was the most available candidate, it argued; he was the only man upon whom Northern Democrats could effectively concentrate; his powers were unquestioned, and the South could be sure of just dealing from him.

As the date for the convention approached, however, all haters of Douglas redoubled their opposition. The Administration never rested; all over the land its officeholders abused the Senator and contrived plots to thwart his nomination. The incessant barking and snapping of even its meanest curs had some effect. But the harshest antagonism was that found among the radical slaveholders of the cotton kingdom. Since Jackson's day, no Democratic candidate had been named without their consent, and they intended to make their veto effective against the popular sovereignty leader. Slidell spun his webs with unresting, spidery skill. "Not a prominent politician of the North and West arrives here," wrote the *Tribune* correspondent early in April, [55] "but instantly he is approached by some emissary of the anti-Douglas cabal, of which the Louisiana Senator is the cogitating brain and the animating soul." Equally determined, if less bitter, was Jefferson Davis, a man who placed his opposition upon public grounds, and who labored adroitly to strengthen the Southern front against the Freeport Doctrine.

Like another Herne the Hunter, the shade of John Brown stalked the Windsor Forest of party affairs, frightening all peaceloving folk. The Harper's Ferry raid had gravely injured both Douglas's chances and the hope of Democratic harmony. Alarming large areas of the South, it had caused many citizens to take the view that safety demanded the nomination of a Southerner, and many more to assert that at any rate it required the selection of a man whose *friendliness* to slavery was more fervent and unbending than Douglas's. It had confirmed the hysteria now epidemic in much of the South, and thus strengthened the divisive demand for a slave code. As the convention opened, the Democratic Party was in a state of internecine war.

53 N. Y. *Weekly Tribune*, April 14, 1860.
54 Slidell to Buchanan, May 2, 1859; Buchanan **Papers**.
55 N. Y. *Weekly Tribune*, April 10, 1860.

7

The Democratic Rupture

CHARLESTON, heedlessly selected four years earlier as the scene of the Democratic convention of 1860, roused herself in April to write a new page in American history.[1] In this balmy season, perfumed with the last azaleas and first roses, the little city of some fifty thousand people offered many physical attractions. Perceptive Northern visitors were charmed by the eighteenth-century houses, prodigal of verandahs and piazzas; the old gardens, rich with tamarisks, camelias, and poppies, half-concealed behind wrought-iron gates and red-brick walls; stately St. Michael's, its tower lifting the four-faced clock that had told Charleston's time since George III ruled the Province, and the English chimes that had rung for so many great events; St. Philip's, guarding the plain brick tomb of Calhoun; the quaint shops of King Street, and the high sea wall of the Battery. They were delighted by the swishing palmettoes, the jargon of the Gullah darkies, the calls of street vendors, and the liquid accents of the citizens. Prosperity—the prosperity of King Cotton's subjects at the height of that monarch's pride and power—stamped the lineaments of the town: fine carriages in the ways, fine raiment on the women, fine silver and mahogany in the houses.

Those admitted to the more exclusive homes (many Southern but few Northern delegates had that honor) quickly realized that sharp social lines were drawn, and that the residents below Broad Street and along the Battery possessed a special distinction. They discerned, too, that this city of old English and Huguenot stock, with its memories of the Rutledges and Pinckneys, of Audubon and Alexander Garden, of the architect Robert Mills and the jurist Hugh S. Legaré, possessed a fine if slightly antique culture. The Charleston Hotel, where eight years earlier Thackeray had made a pencil sketch of colorful lobby scenes, the old Planters' Hotel whose courtyard had for half a century been the favorite resort of cotton and rice growers, and Russell's bookshop, were centers of cultivated talk. The college, the Citadel school, and the Society Library were proof that Charleston by no means neglected education.

1 In the Cincinnati Convention the special committee on national conventions had been headed by a New Yorker, T. C. McCreery. After considering New York and Charleston as meeting places, it chose Charleston as an incentive to party harmony. *Proceedings Reported for the Cincinnati Enquirer*, 42.

Nevertheless, the city was ill-chosen for the convention. It was difficult of access, and those who came by rail arrived exhausted. Already the heat was becoming uncomfortable. The hostelries, all too few and too small for convention crowds (though not so many spectators arrived as had been expected), had agreed upon the high rate of five dollars a day for bed and meals. At the best-known hotels, four or five delegates were sometimes stuffed into a single room. The Northwestern men supporting Douglas had hired Hibernian Hall, where the ground floor was equipped with chairs, writing tables, and campaign materials, including a large supply of Sheahan's life of Douglas, while the second story was crammed with several hundred cots. Fernando Wood's contesting delegation from New York had similarly taken St. Andrew's Hall, where a portrait of Queen Victoria looked down on a confusion of improvised beds. At night the visitors, tortured by noise, poor ventilation, and thirst, tried to snatch a few hours' sleep, and in the morning made rough toilets with washbowls, pitchers, and a few hand mirrors.

The atmosphere of the town was hostile to Northern men and ideas, and the tone of its press, parlors, hotel lobbies, and counting rooms was antipathetic to conciliation. Any large border city would have been a far better choice. The local hostility to Northerners was the more serious in that it was generally agreed that if the Democratic Party could remain united, its chances of victory were bright. The whole number of electoral votes would be 303, with 152 necessary to a choice. The Democrats would almost certainly carry the Southern States with 120 votes and Oregon and California with 7 more. Then New York alone (35 electors), or Pennsylvania alone (27), or Indiana and Illinois with any one of the less populous States, would be sufficient. It was obvious, however, that New York and Pennsylvania could never be carried on a slave-code platform. Neither could any other Northern State. Admit a slave-code plank into the platform, and defeat was practically sure.[2]

[I]

The delegates and their friends came in droves from Wednesday to Saturday, April 18-21, days bright, hot, and dusty. The Massachusetts men, with a brass band which began playing on the Battery every night, arrived by boat, as did the New York and Pennsylvania delegations. Barrooms, with bowls of iced punch and a weird variety of cocktails, did a rushing business; gamblers, unmistakable in their flashy dress and manners, were hard at work; pickpockets engaged the attention of the mounted and armed police.

Reporters mingling with the crowds were struck by the violent temper of

2 Cf. Chicago *Times*, March 13, 1860.

many delegates. While Illinois and Michigan men were denouncing Jeff Davis as a fire-eating fanatic, Alabamians were calling Douglas a traitor only less vicious than Seward. The Northwestern representatives made the Mills House their principal place of resort. Here, in the humming lobby and corridors, the principal Illinois leaders, John A. Logan, John A. McClernand, and William A. Richardson, a formidable trio, could be seen talking with such other adherents of Douglas as George Sanders, the burly, piratical-looking Navy Agent in New York who had placed his office in peril by coming to work for the popular sovereignty cause, and Pugh of Ohio, determined not to yield an inch to the demand for a slave-code. Most Southerners could be sought in the parlors of the Charleston Hotel. Waiting delegates enjoyed excursions up the Cooper and Ashley, or down to islands in the bay.

One by one, the great men of the party arrived.

W. L. Yancey, a compact, erect man of medium height, with a square head and face, his bland, quiet manner belied by his quick, expressive eyes, came with a cohort of Alabamians who predicted that his oratory would sweep the Douglas forces away like chaff. He kept aloof from the swirling crowds. But he was soon conferring with his fellow radicals on the ground, the A. B. Rhetts, father and son; men who hoped rather than believed that the party and the nation could be rent in twain, and who meant to work closely with other extremists.

Caleb Cushing, delegate-at-large from Massachusetts and supposedly a supporter of Jefferson Davis, impressed onlookers by his high, full forehead, straight, sharp nose, and strong jaw—a leader obviously of intellectual power, Lowell's "dreffle smart man," surprisingly youthful-looking for his sixty years. The best Charleston families threw open their doors to him. Everyone knew of his recent activities: his defense of the Dred Scott decision, his futile efforts to obtain a repeal of the Personal Liberty Act in Massachusetts, his attacks on the abolitionists as a band of drunken mutineers, his laudation of Davis in Faneuil Hall, and his candid avowals of a desire to annex not only Cuba, but all of Mexico. As a result of close association with Davis and other Southern leaders, he no longer believed that the Union must be preserved at all hazards; instead, he had written after John Brown's raid that if the Southern States did not receive guarantees that such offenses would not be repeated, it was their duty as well as right to form a separate republic. In fine, Cushing would support the Southern extremists.

Slidell arrived, his long, thin, white hair framing his cherry-red countenance, harder and craftier than ever. Among other Administration spokesmen were Ben Butler, short, bald-headed, cross-eyed, hook-nosed, his every movement showing his sleepless energy, and his harsh voice (like a file on a crosscut saw, wrote one reporter) suiting his combative temperament; Jesse D. Bright of Indiana, who wore the aspect of an oily businessman, a yellow vest setting off his portly frame; and Bayard of Delaware, a handsome patrician whose long, brown, curly hair parted in the middle.

The radicals of the Lower South included the aggressive Barksdale brothers, Ethelbert and William, two Mississippians of fiery temper (William had stood beside Brooks when he assaulted Sumner, and had lost his wig in the House fracas with Grew); and Leroy P. Walker of Alabama, who was Yancey's best aide. Of various spokesmen for business, the most conspicuous was Dean Richmond, vice-president of the New York Central, owner of Buffalo elevators and lake shipping, and head of his State delegation; a well-built man of bulging brow and shrewd eyes, who believed in moderation and unity.[3]

The captaincy of the Administration forces was in the hands of Senators Slidell, Bright, and Bayard, who had done so much to accomplish Buchanan's nomination at Cincinnati four years earlier. They had quarters (hired as in 1856 by S. L. M. Barlow) in an old Charleston mansion.[4] The diversity of opinion among Southern and Administration delegates, however, forbade their union on any single candidate. Senator Hunter, Vice-President Breckinridge, and former Secretary James Guthrie were all possible nominees, while many believed that Davis might make the best candidate. The opposed group of Northwestern leaders included Henry B. Payne and Daniel P. Rhodes of Cleveland; the former a lawyer and railroad-builder, the latter a successful coal and iron capitalist. They, with Pugh, Stuart, Logan, and McClernand, followed the general guidance of Douglas's veteran lieutenant, Richardson, whose robust physique, loud voice, and quick tactical eye made him a doughty floor leader.

Douglas himself professed great confidence. He had written Peter Caggner of New York on February 19: "There will be no serious difficulty in the South. The last few weeks have worked a perfect revolution in that section. They all tell me and write that all will be right if our Northern friends will fearlessly represent the wishes and feelings of the Democracy in their own States." [5] But if these professions were sincere, he was grossly mistaken.

The atmosphere of Charleston grew more bitterly hostile to Douglas and to any idea of union under his leadership as the delegates from the Lower South thickened. They gathered in knots to declare that they would permit no equivocation in the platform, such as the readoption of the hazy Cincinnati plank on the Territories, and that the nomination of Douglas would precipitate the dis-

3 Cf. portrait in Stewart Mitchell, *Horatio Seymour*, 246; Richmond favored Seymour.
4 Nichols, *Disruption*, 294.
5 February 19, 1860; Lanphier Papers.

ruption of the party.[6] They met in larger groups to make unavailing attempts to agree upon a candidate. In the lobbies of the Charleston and Planters' Hotels, men talked defiantly of secession and a new republic, and when any moderate Democrat tried to answer the Southern nationalists, he was jeered into silence. Douglas men were shocked by the black looks they encountered. The fire-eaters called them abolitionists, and told them they had better join their own kind at the Republican convention.[7] Even so warm a sympathizer with the South as Caleb Cushing was both shocked and alarmed, and resolved to use every resource to effect a compromise on some such candidate as Guthrie or Franklin Pierce.[8] But intransigence continued to grow. "There is going to be an explosion," said sagacious men.

Before the end of the week, word flew about that Yancey, who had induced the Alabama convention to instruct its delegates for withdrawal if they did not obtain a slave-code plank, had scored a major victory. A meeting of Southern delegations had been held. Those of seven States—Georgia, Alabama, Florida, Mississippi, Louisiana, Arkansas, and Texas—had agreed to withdraw in a body unless the platform pronounced for the Congressional protection of slavery in the Territories.[9]

[II]

The Douglas leaders, who had planned their strategy more shrewdly than the Administration elements, were hopeful that they could write an inoffensive platform and gain a two-thirds vote for their candidate. They were elated by their general success in inducing the Northwestern States to elect Douglas delegates, and to bind them to the unit rule. Each State had as many votes in the convention as in the electoral college; as the college now numbered three hundred and three, Douglas must have two hundred and two delegates to win

6 The readiness of Southerners to talk of Douglas as a disguised abolitionist (Stephen A. Douglas and Fred Douglass are just the same, said some) did not rest alone on Lecompton and the Freeport debate. Greeley boasted privately that the *Tribune's* praise of Douglas was injuring the man in the South. "Don't you see that they all believe already that he and I are in *cahoots*, as they say—secretly leagued to humble and ruin 'the South'?" February 28, 1860; Greeley-Colfax Corr. The fiercest hatred guided plans to stop the Little Giant. George W. Paschal of San Antonio had written Douglas that he knew on indisputable authority that the Texas delegates were secretly pledged to withdraw from the convention if they could not otherwise defeat the Little Giant's nomination. April 17, 1860; Douglas Papers. What another correspondent called "the clique at Washington" had been pulling wires to break up the convention rather than let Douglas win. I. I. Jones. Raleigh, April 18, 1860; Douglas Papers.

7 Milton, *Eve of Conflict*, 429.
8 Fuess, *Caleb Cushing*, I, 247.
9 Nichols, *Disruption*, 295.

the traditional two-thirds. But did not many Democrats hold that any man who attained a clear majority ought then to be given the requisite two-thirds as a matter of courtesy? And would not office-hungry delegates flock to the band wagon of a prospective victor? [10] The five States of the Old Northwest would furnish Douglas a solid bloc of fifty-eight delegates; Iowa and Minnesota would supply seven or eight more; of the nine Missouri delegates, shrewd observers thought he would have five.[11] This would give him at least seventy western votes, a good start. Ten or eleven from Pennsylvania and four from New Jersey would bring his column up to eighty-five, while Maryland, where Reverdy Johnson had labored devotedly for him, should add two or three.[12]

New York, after its habit, had sent two delegations to the convention. But here—though not as clearly as in Illinois—the Senator's group had the better title. Dean Richmond's body of Douglas men asserted that they had been regularly elected; they declared that Fernando Wood's anti-Douglas group had been chosen before the legal hour for the State convention by a minority of its members. The businessmen and politicians who clustered about Richmond— August Belmont of New York, Erastus Corning and Peter Cagger of Albany, Sanford E. Church of Albion—would stand behind the Little Giant as long as victory seemed possible. They included a former member of the Free Soil Party, John Cochrane, whose ringing voice, aggressive manner, and proficiency in parliamentary law made him a great asset in Charleston.[13] Douglas was strong also among the New Englanders. He could count on the fourteen votes of New Hampshire, Vermont, and Rhode Island, and would divide those of Massachusetts, Connecticut, and Maine with other aspirants. He knew, too, that nearly all the Southern delegations held members who, after an initial vote for favorite sons, would be ready to turn to him; some of them, like Joseph R. Bradley of Alabama and T. B. Flournoy of Arkansas, ready even to make a spirited fight for him.

Altogether, before the gavel fell in Charleston, the Douglas lieutenants— their chief remaining in Washington—were confident of a majority. This, they thought, should give them control of the platform, even though the resolutions committee, with one member for each State, might divide closely against them. After all, they asked only for a noncommittal stand; a reiteration of the Cincinnati platform or something like it. And from a majority they hoped that, like Buchanan in 1856, they could vault to two-thirds.[14]

---

10 Milton, *Eve of Conflict*, 430 ff.
11 Cf. Senator Rice in *Cong. Globe*, 36th Cong., 1st Sess., 2245.
12 Milton, *Eve of Conflict*, 415.
13 Alexander, *Pol. Hist. N. Y.*, II, 270–273.
14 Jefferson Davis had completely failed to gain strength. He recognized this himself, writing Edward De Leon: "My opinions as you know them would be sufficient to defeat

The Little Giant was resolved never to give up. His health was now poor. He was financially embarrassed. He was heartily tired of fighting on two fronts. But, stung by slurs upon his honor, he believed the fate of party and nation hung on his battle; only popular sovereignty and non-intervention could yet save the Democracy from destruction and the Union from disruption. "I do not intend to make peace with my enemies nor to make a concession of one iota of principle," he had written.[15] Pains had been taken to send considerable bodies of spectators from the Northwest, Douglas himself urging the appointment of consulting delegates; "the more the better." [16] Richardson and Stuart were prepared for a fight to get their New York and Illinois delegations seated. They had also laid plans to carry an astute motion: while the unit rule must apply to all delegations upon whom the State conventions had imposed it, in other delegations each member should have the right to cast his vote as he pleased. Because the Northwestern delegations were bound, and most of the border and Southern States were not, this motion would enable Douglas to pick up scattering votes. Finally, the Senator's managers were ready to offer Federal appointments right and left to ambitious men.

[III]

The strength, aggressiveness, and skill of the Douglas forces accentuated the readiness of the Lower South to use extreme measures. The senatorial triumvirate, Slidell, Bayard, and Bright, were at a heavy disadvantage for want of a single dominant candidate. From January onwards, attempts to place Hunter or Breckinridge in command of the stop-Douglas element had run into insuperable obstacles. Kentucky's delegates were for ex-Secretary Guthrie rather than Breckinridge. Tennessee was for Andrew Johnson. While Hunter could count on Virginia and most of North Carolina, with scattering votes elsewhere, he had never approached a clear preeminence. Hammond thought him the best candidate, and Bayard had predicted his nomination if the convention did not break up. But of late he had lost ground.[17] The South Carolina Convention had voiced a preference for ex-Speaker Orr, who was a Union man.[18] Had the oppo-

---

any efforts of my friends to nominate me at Charleston and should do so as they would impair the ability of the Democratic Party to succeed in the next presidential canvass." He thought that sentiment had moved toward the Southern Rights creed ("We are now all powerful at the South, but are still in a minority at the North"); it could best be promoted by someone acceptable to both sections, such as Franklin Pierce or Dallas. January 21, 1860; De Leon Papers, South Carolinian Lib.

15 March 31, 1859, Douglas Papers, Ill. State Hist. Lib.
16 Douglas to C. H. Lanphier, January 1, 1860.
17 Senator Hammond to Harry Hammond, April 27, 1860, Hammond Papers; James Bayard to T. F. Bayard, March 24, 1860, Bayard Papers.
18 Charleston *Courier, Mercury*, April 17–19, 1860.

sition to Douglas rallied about a single magical name, it might have taken strong ground—but no Merlin had found an Arthur. In talents, experience, and magnetism, the Little Giant loomed above all rivals.

The Gulf State delegations were in the main implacably hostile to Douglas. Nevertheless, many citizens of those States held that he had been traduced by Buchanan and the Directory; that the delegates had been unfairly elected; and that the people, if they knew his true character, would gladly support him. Soulé charged that the election for the Louisiana State convention had been controlled by placeholders, and that the delegates sent to Charleston were creatures of trickery and fraud.[19] In Texas, Douglas men described the Galveston convention as a pack of secessionists, totally unrepresentative of Union sentiment in the State. In Mississippi, wrote R. D. Shropshire, editor of the Aberdeen *Mississippi Conservative*, the delegation chosen to Charleston by no means voiced the real views of the State. It included fire-eaters of the most rabid description. They had been selected after the Buchanan Administration had done everything possible to whip up anti-Douglas feeling; after a violent campaign of deception by men who hoped that a break-up of the Union would give them prominence and office which they could never otherwise attain; after wire-pulling and manipulation. Yet he was sure that the Mississippians would cast an overwhelming vote for Douglas if he were nominated.[20]

Gideon Pillow of Tennessee described a similar campaign of calumny in part of the press of that State. Yet he too was sure that Douglas could carry every Southern State.[21] In Alabama, an observer thought that the voters who had chosen the Charleston delegates did not form one one-hundredth part of the population:

We all know how meetings of this kind are gotten up—one or two leading men in each county propose a call for a public meeting. A few youths, ambitious of distinction, and of their spouting qualifications, take the matter in hand. Chairmen, committees, and resolutions are manufactured beforehand. A few meet! The committee are formed, and as a matter of course withdraw to consider resolutions, long before cut and dried for the occasion. . . . Five or ten casual spectators, lolling over the railing of a dirty courtroom, are microscoped into a numerous body of the bone and sinew of the county. Resolutions are adopted; delegates, anxious to show off, are appointed. They attend the convention. They take to this or that aspirant for fame or office, as accident or favor influences. They vote for this or that set of resolutions, as this or that particular interest is to be served, or is in the ascendent. Here is the whole machinery of the plots by which national and State movements are regulated.
With respect to the late [State] convention, I have attended a great many

19 *State Rights Louisianian*, April 8, 1860, clipping in Douglas Papers, U. of Chicago Lib.
20 April 16, 1860; Douglas Papers.
21 April 3, 1860; Douglas Papers.

meetings for the appointment of delegates, and so far as the people are concerned, I could never discover but a single idea moving them; this was to appoint delegates to the Charleston Convention to join with the Democrats of the entire Union in nominating a President.[22]

And John Forsyth wrote that Douglas had not a few friends even in the Alabama delegation, though they were helpless; that he was a thousand times stronger than the superficial currents set in motion by the politicians would indicate; and that he had the sympathy of the entire Union feeling of the South, prodigiously strong both within and without the party. Bradley of Alabama actually thought of protesting to the credentials committee that his entire delegation had been improperly chosen and should be excluded.[23]

The one hope of defeating Douglas lay in using the resolutions committee to draft the type of platform which he had sworn he would never support. Of the thirty-three members of this committee, seventeen (the fifteen slave States and the Administration catspaws from California and Oregon) would bow to the wishes of the anti-Douglas leaders. A majority report on the platform might, by threats, bribes, and eloquence, be forced through the convention. If it were defeated, the Gulf States could withdraw. Before they would let Douglas be nominated on an equivocal platform, they *would* withdraw.[24]

For different reasons, the threat of a party schism did not terrify either the Northern or Southern delegates as it should have done. As Murat Halstead and other expert journalists soon reported, the Douglas men were not averse to a minor schism; if Alabama and Mississippi left the convention, it would be easier to roll up a two-thirds vote for their candidate. Many good Unionists in the South believed that two Democratic tickets, one headed by Douglas and one by Breckinridge or Hunter, would throw the election of a President into Congress and ultimately into the Senate, where the South could choose a trusted son. These men showed a singular myopia and levity in contemplating the disruption of the last great organization uniting the two sections. For a petty temporary advantage, for a chance of contingent benefits, they were willing to run the gravest risks not merely to the party but the nation. Far more penetrating was the vision of disunionists like Rhett and Yancey, who saw behind schism their goal of two American republics.

22 Letter by B. F. Porter of Sidney, Alabama, signed "John Smith" in *Southern Advocate*, n.d.; Douglas Papers.

23 April 5, 1860; Douglas Papers.

24 "There would have been no trouble about the platform . . ." wrote "Tiber," the Washington correspondent of the New Orleans *Picayune*, when the convention was over, "had the New York delegation offered to support any nominee selected by the South. But the South was and is determined that Douglas should not be nominated." *Picayune*, May 9, 1860. The New York delegation was in many ways the key group.

[IV]

On Monday, April 23, after a delightful eleven-o'clock shower had broken the heat and quenched the dust, the delegates trooped into the hall of the South Carolina Institute on Meeting Street. Though a spacious structure for Charleston, it was ridiculously inadequate for the gathering. A platform just large enough to hold the presiding officer and twenty or thirty others; a level floor set with plain wooden chairs, bolted by the half dozen to planks under the seats; narrow galleries on each side, occupied at first by male onlookers whose expectoration greatly troubled delegates beneath; high rounded windows of church-like aspect, admitting more than enough of the brilliant Carolina sunshine—such was the hall. Below the platform, and in front of the delegates, was an enclosure occupied by the press. When three thousand people crowded the room, it soon become so stifling that coats came off and palm-leaf fans were lustily plied.

The first two days proved not only that the followers of Douglas constituted a phalanx stronger than all the adverse groups, but that they enjoyed a superior leadership. Two committees were appointed, one on organization and one on credentials—New York and Illinois being excluded from the latter. Much cheering and excitement marked the discussions. The organization committee promptly selected Caleb Cushing for permanent chairman. Though he was hostile to Douglas, his qualifications were so preeminent (for he had prestige, force of personality, a quick mind, and a thorough training in parliamentary law) that he was accepted with general acquiescence. On taking the chair he delivered a spread-eagle speech in which, after referring to the eastern hills, the Mississippi basin, and other geographical glories, he denounced the Republicans for a traitorous conspiracy to set section against section.

A hot debate then began on the question whether uninstructed State delegations should vote as units or according to the individual preference of delegates. This was a matter of considerable moment, for a number of delegations whose majorities stood against Douglas contained men who wished to vote for him. Even Alabama, it was thought, had a member or two on his side, and North Carolina certainly had one. Several Southern delegates, with one angry Pennsylvanian, spoke against giving uninstructed individuals full liberty. When William A. Richardson responded with a personal indictment of the Pennsylvanian, a wild uproar ensued; but standing on a chair, his sleeves rolled above his elbows, his voice as cacophonous as the screech of a fire-engine, he finished his speech. By a heavy majority, the convention decided that votes might be cast individually unless a delegation was bound by specific State instructions; and thirty or forty

Douglas men were thus freed to act as they liked. To many Southerners the new rule, for which no strict precedent existed and which gave the popular sovereignty forces a decided advantage, seemed a bit of sharp practice.

As ill-feeling thus increased, the convention determined, practically by acclamation, that the platform should be adopted before balloting for candidates began. In this action, Yancey's extremists and the Douglas column for once agreed. The decision was not so nearly unavoidable as it seemed—and it contained the seeds of disaster.

To be sure, Douglas was pledged not to accept a nomination if the platform contained a slave-code plank, and the whole Northwest stood with him. To be sure, Alabama and some sister States were pledged to withdraw if the platform did not meet *their* demands. Superficially, the issues of the platform apparently had to be resolved before the convention could proceed. Whenever the desire for party unity is strong, however, platforms have usually been subordinated to candidates—who interpret them much as they please anyway. If in this instance a candidate (whether Douglas, Hunter, Breckinridge, or someone else) had been nominated, then no quarrel need have taken place over the platform; a compromise would have been possible. The decision to grant the platform priority gave the South and the Administration men every incentive to fight for a set of resolutions which would debar Douglas, and it gave the platform an unwonted prominence. From that moment all hope of unity disappeared.

On the night of the second day, reporters were sending word over the country that Douglas was certain of a majority of delegates, that the struggle to give him two-thirds would be tremendous, and that the convention, rent by irreconcilable feuds, was heading for disruption.

The third day, Wednesday the twenty-fifth, brought the South a new blow and Douglas a fresh victory. The convention, as good judges had predicted, excluded the Danite contestants from Illinois and the Fernando Wood group from New York. The first decision was certainly just, and the weight of evidence supported the second. Inevitably, however, it aroused deep feeling, for the New York votes were of almost crucial importance. Fernando Wood, emphasizing the riotous character of the Syracuse convention, had made out a case which impressed many. The South felt a deep injustice in the fact that although Dean Richmond's delegation contained thirty anti-Douglas men to forty Douglas men, under the unit rule the entire vote of the State would be cast for the Illinoisan.[25] Nine slave States, with California, had mustered fifty-five votes for dividing the New York seats between the two sets of claimants, but they were overwhelmed by two hundred and ten noes. The New Yorkers might vote, before the end, for Guthrie, Hunter, or some other slave State man, but they would

25 See Ben Butler's speech, N. Y. *Herald*, May 19, 20 or 21, 1860.

certainly stand as rocklike as the Illinois delegates against any slave-code demand. Once more, on this third day, Murat Halstead reported to his newspaper that an explosion was certain, and that the only question now was the extent of the Southern defection.

Marking time on the fourth day, for the platform committee was still at work, the convention waited breathlessly for the great battle on resolutions. It knew that the future of the party, perhaps even the future of the nation, was being decided in that committee room. As they waited, the delegates let their animosities break into the debate. Douglasites and slave-code men baited each other. Several Southerners offered motions favorable to their own radical position and made speeches which Northern Democrats regarded as threatening the ruin of the party throughout the free States. As night closed in, everyone agreed that the platform committee must bring forward either a subterfuge, or a bombshell.[26]

At ten o'clock on Friday morning the delegates (many shivering, for the weather had changed to cold rain and blustering wind) gathered anew, and after routine business recessed to give the platform committee additional time. Parts of the floor as well as the galleries were now occupied by women, whose merry laughter furnished an incongruous note. At about eleven-thirty the committee, pale and careworn, filed into the hall. Printed copies of minority and majority reports were being excitedly passed from hand to hand

The majority report, signed by the fifteen slave States, with Oregon and California, declared that Congress had no power to abolish slavery in the Territories, and that the territorial legislature had no power to abolish slavery, exclude slaves, or impair the right of property in slaves by any legislation whatever. It further asserted that it was the duty of the national government to protect, when necessary, the rights of persons and property on the high seas, in the Territories, or wherever else its constitutional authority extended.

The minority report stood in sharp contrast. It reaffirmed the Cincinnati platform of 1856, with a preamble declaring that, since differences of opinion existed as to the rights and duties of territorial legislatures and Congress with respect to slavery in the Territories, the party would abide by the decisions of the Supreme Court on the questions of constitutional law. W. W. Avery of North Carolina, speaking for the committee majority, made the first argument. He represented, he said, the seventeen trustworthy Democratic States of the nation. Inevitably, Mexico, Cuba, and Central America would become part of the republic; and if the popular sovereignty doctrine, as interpreted by the Douglas faction, were accepted, no slaveholder would dare to enter these an-

26 Murat Halstead, *Caucuses of 1860*.

nexed domains with his slaves. He appealed to the Northern Democrats to prove that they would stand courageously by the Southern slaveholders. It was an outrageous speech, which many border men would have repudiated; but the Lower South cheered it to the echo.

Thereupon H. B. Payne of Ohio, a man of distinguished bearing, rose to speak for the committee minority. His address, logical, clear, and beautifully phrased, was worthy of one of the leaders of the Ohio bar. All those who signed the minority report, he declared, were deeply impressed with the belief that upon the action of the convention probably hung the fate of the party and the destiny of the Union. They were convinced that the national government should not interfere with slavery in the Territories, but permit the people themselves to determine their institutions. He could show, he continued, that every eminent Southern leader since 1850 had at some time planted himself upon the doctrine of non-intervention by Congress. Hunter, Toombs, Mason, Calhoun—he quoted them all. The Northern mind was too thoroughly imbued with the principle of popular sovereignty to abandon it. Northern Democrats asked for nothing but what the Constitution allowed them, for they promised to abide by the decision of the courts, the interpreters of the Constitution. Why should the South for a mere abstraction, he asked, throw away the chance of party success? If the Northern Democracy were allowed to run its race unhampered, it would do its full duty in the contest. But the North would not be coerced: "We cannot recede from this doctrine without personal dishonor, and so help us God, we never will abandon this principle. If the majority report is adopted, you cannot expect one Northern electoral vote, or one sympathizing member of Congress from the free States." [27]

Ben Butler then took the floor to plead for his own report from a minority of one, which proposed that the convention simply reaffirm the Cincinnati platform. Before he sat down, he engaged in a brisk skirmish with a Maryland delegate who acridly remarked that his State had never encouraged resistance to the Fugitive Slave Law. Recalling the recent Baltimore mobs, Butler retorted that Massachusetts had never submitted to a regime which frightened men from the polls with bludgeon and knife. After a recess for luncheon, Barksdale of Mississippi made a violent ultra-Southern speech, to which Austin A. King, former governor of Missouri, replied that the slave-code platform carried the sting of death to the party; that it would lose them all the Northern electors and all the border States except Missouri itself. Then the convention turned to the two principal contestants of the day: Yancey for the South, Pugh for the Northwest, both eager for battle. The very crisis of the gathering had arrived.

27 Halstead, *Caucuses; Official Proceedings;* N. Y. *Weekly Tribune,* May 5, 1860.

[V]

Yancey, a truly great orator and nothing more—not a constructive legislator, not a party organizer, not an administrator, not an able writer—held views which require a discriminating assessment. While men like Rhett, Porcher Miles, and Ruffin believed in disunion as a benefit in itself, Yancey (at least ostensibly) demanded disunion only because he thought it no longer possible to obtain the constitutional rights of the South within the Union. Rhett and Ruffin gloried in the name of disunionist; Yancey, whenever that epithet was fastened upon him,

Mr. Yancey, through his friend, William Barksdale, asks for the floor in the Charleston Convention.

protested indignantly. He said repeatedly that loyalty to the Constitution was the lodestone of his policy. He talked in Calhoun's terms of the compact among the States and the compact between North and South. He held that the position of Douglas and that of the Republicans were substantially identical, in that both would abolish the sectional compact and abrogate the Constitution. In short, he was for maintaining the Union—if only the rest of the country would accept the extreme Southern position. Within a few months he was to appeal to voters to "save us from Lincoln and so save the Union." [28]

Already, his opponents were charging that he was the head of a conspiracy to break up the party as a prelude to disruption of the Union, but this charge he angrily repelled. The South, in his opinion, should stand firm; show first the Northern Democrats, and later the Northern Republicans, what would be the result of their folly, and then, if they persisted in tyrannous courses, act to protect itself. It was the opponents of the South who were disunionists! [29]

Rising amid a storm of applause, Yancey spoke with characteristic quiet geniality, uttering the most uncompromising sentiments in the most musical and

[28] Speech at Florence, Kentucky; Cincinnati *Gazette*, October 20, 1860.
[29] George Petrie, "W. L. Yancey," in *Transactions Ala. State Hist. Soc.*, IV, 307-312.

ingratiating tones. The Southerners, he declared, had come to Charleston to save their constitutional rights. If they lost and the popular sovereignty platform prevailed, they would be bankrupted. They must let the Democracy go down to defeat if necessary, for defeat on principle was glorious defeat. He upbraided the Northern Democrats for treating slavery as an inherited evil; they should boldly pronounce it a positive good! If they had taken the position that slavery was right by the laws of nature and of God, they would have triumphed. With more force than logic, he appealed to Southern emotions on the issue of basic rights. "Ours is the property invaded; ours are the institutions which are at stake; ours is the peace that is to be destroyed; ours is the honor at stake—the honor of children, the honor of families, the lives, perhaps, of all—all of which rests upon what your course may ultimately make a great heaving volcano of passion and crime, if you are enabled to consummate your designs. Bear with us, then, if we stand sternly upon what is yet that dormant volcano, and say we yield no position here until we are convinced we are wrong." [30] He charged the Southern delegates to stand true to their constitutional duties, for if recreant they would merit defeat and eternal ignominy.

The gas lamps had now been lit. The deep feeling of Southern delegates and of the throng of Charleston spectators, excited by Yancey's rolling periods, found expression in wild handclapping and shouting. It was in an atmosphere glacial with hostility that Pugh, at seven in the evening, began his reply. He was glad, he declared, to hear a Southern leader speak out so plainly and boldly. Reading the resolutions which Yancey himself had presented to the Alabama Democratic convention four years earlier in favor of non-intervention, he pointed out that Alabama did not then ask what she now demanded, and that Yancey's mind was not then what it was now. His remarks on Southern inconsistency and intransigency became scathing. Must the Democratic Party be dragged at the chariot wheel of three hundred thousand slave-masters? A more fearless speech had never been heard in any party convention. It was as if Douglas himself were confronting the angry crowd. This Southern demand that the long-suffering Northern Democrats should avow slavery to be right, and its extension to be desirable, Pugh pronounced intolerable. "Gentlemen of the South," he declaimed, "you mistake us—you mistake us! We will not do it!" [31]

The convention adjourned that evening in an uproar. Everyone knew that a party split would probably take place on the morrow. Delegates stalked the streets with dripping umbrellas, or huddled in anxious consultation. Some Douglas men, knowing that they could muster a majority but not a two-thirds vote, were still cheerful in facing a disruption. They would let three or four State

30 "Speech of W. L. Yancey of Alabama," April 28, 1860; pamphlet.
31 Halstead, *Caucuses*, 50; Charleston *Courier*, April 30, 1860.

delegations leave the convention—just enough to give them control! Many Southern Unionists, too, still hoped complacently that a break-up might throw the election into Congress. But the anxiety of reflective men was growing, and not a few Democrats were haggard with worry.

Telegrams flew between Washington and Charleston. Various Southern members of Congress were advising their State delegations to withdraw alongside Alabama. Robert Toombs wired the Georgia delegates that if they could not get a sound platform with a Southern man on it they should bolt. The South Carolina delegation, asking the advice of their Congressmen, were told to leave.[32] George Sanders in a long telegram (sent collect at a cost of $26.80) had already implored the President to intervene. After denouncing Slidell and Bright for trying to break up the convention, he declared that most of the Northern delegates, with half of those from Kentucky, North Carolina, Maryland, Missouri, and Alabama, and a number from Florida, Tennessee, Georgia, and Arkansas, had agreed to accept certain changes in the old Cincinnati platform. The two most important amendments left all questions respecting the rights of property in States and Territories, arising under the Constitution, to the Supreme Court. But Buchanan was in no mood to carry out a type of intervention that would probably result in Douglas's nomination.[33]

Dawn broke on Saturday with rain still falling, and the air chill and clammy. A grave calamity stared the Kentucky and Ohio delegations in the face; their private stock of whiskey was almost exhausted. Everybody growled at the weather, the high prices of hotels and restaurants, and the gloomy party outlook. The only persons who looked cheerful were the Rhett-Yancey extremists, and supporters of such secondary aspirants as Hammond, Andrew Johnson, and Franklin Pierce, who hoped that the confusion over the platform could be manipulated to their advantage.

A dozen different crosscurrents of ambition and sentiment swirled through the convention as it reopened. Once more the proceedings became tumultuous— but almost miraculously, an immediate break was averted. The platform was sent back to committee, and when late in the day it reemerged, the Southern delegates made a brave stand against the Douglas majority by staging a filibuster.

32 *Toombs, Stephens, Cobb Correspondence*, 468, 469; B. F. Perry, *Biographical Sketches*, 188. A letter had been exhibited on the third day from Jefferson Davis, advising Mississippi to withdraw if Douglas were nominated; Charleston *Courier*, April 26, 1860. Some other men in Washington had already decided for a breach. "The plan for breaking up the convention is said to have been formed here some weeks ago," wrote "Tiber" from Washington on May 1. "The scheme was first announced in the N. Y. *Leader*." New Orleans *Picayune*, May 9, 1860.

33 Sanders to Buchanan, telegram, April 27, 1860; Buchanan Papers. It was widely reported that Hunter telegraphed the Virginia delegation not to withdraw. W. H. Trescot, May 8, 1860; Miles Papers, Univ. of N. C.

At one moment the disorder became so great that Cushing threatened to leave the chair.[34] Finally, after weary wrangling, the assemblage adjourned over Sunday—a Sunday to be spent in plots, discussion, and efforts to negotiate a peace.

[VI]

For several reasons the New York delegates stood in the best position to effect a compromise. Their metropolis and State had an immense stake in the maintenance of the Union; the feeling of New York City was notoriously moderate; August Belmont and Dean Richmond had a host of Southern friends; and the persuasive John Cochrane had been prominent in national conventions for a quarter of a century. On Sunday, several New Yorkers, with at least one Southern peacemaker in the person of Richard Taylor, son of the former President, approached Slidell and Bright. These Senators assured them that under certain circumstances and conditions the unity of the party could be preserved. They sent for Yancey, and some evidence exists that he promised to try to persuade the other Alabama delegates not to bolt the convention immediately. Perhaps, in characteristic fashion, he merely uttered uncompromising words in such soothing tones that they seemed to suggest compromise. At any rate, while the conciliators labored, the Southern lines were actually being drawn tighter, and Virginia was coming to the side of the Lower South in insisting upon a slave-code plank. The New Yorkers went to bed that night hopeful. Richard Taylor, Slidell, Bright, and Bayard sat up till nearly dawn in the vain hope that Yancey would return with encouraging news. He never came. The border State men talked of concord and victory—but in reality the situation had grown worse.[35]

On Monday morning, the seventh day, it was evident that the atmosphere of Charleston had become implacable. The *Mercury*, edited by the younger Rhett, appeared with an eloquent plea for the vindication of Southern rights. Alabama and Mississippi were resolved to leave if their demands were ignored, said the journal, and the other slave States should follow. Greater crowds than ever pushed into the convention hall, and trains and boats having carried many Northerners back home, South Carolinians rushed into their seats.

At ten o'clock, the platform was taken up. The minority, or Douglas, version was swiftly carried, 165 to 138, but amid a clamor of voices raising points of order. The Douglas forces then consented to separate votes on the component planks. The first resolution, reaffirming the Cincinnati platform of 1856, was carried by a heavy majority—the border States and Virginia giving it sixty

34 Charleston *Courier*, April 30, 1860.
35 Richard Taylor, *Destruction and Reconstruction*, 11, 12; N. Y. *Weekly Tribune*, May 5, 1860; Alexander, *New York*, II, 274.

votes. Thereupon a member of the New York delegation moved that the remaining part of the Douglas platform be laid on the table so that the convention might proceed immediately to the nominations. But some of the Douglas leaders, anxious to show their strength and possibly ready to court a limited defection, shelved the motion. A vote was then in order on the second part of the minority platform, declaring that the party would abide by the Supreme Court's decisions. But a number of Southerners uttered impassioned warnings that if this plank carried their States would leave; they insisted on a slave code; and no fewer than seven Southern delegations refused to vote at all upon the plank.

As it thus became clear that a large-scale schism would follow adoption, the Douglas men became frightened. A wild din had broken out; Richardson of Illinois was on his feet bellowing to be heard; the New England delegates were plainly anxious not to drive out the Southern men; the Northwestern delegates were hurriedly conferring. Dean Richmond withdrew the New Yorkers to a rapid conclave, in which they decided to vote against the plank. They returned to find the Douglas column beating a disorganized retreat. The roll call showed a perfect rout, the second resolution losing, 238 to 21. It was a humiliating result for the Northwestern men.

The convention might now have contented itself with restating the Cincinnati platform, have left the slave-code abstraction to time, and have gone on to name a man satisfactory to both sections. Unfortunately, Southern passions had been too deeply aroused. As the tumult over the critical Douglas plank had risen to frenzy, Yancey had been observed smiling as happily as a child at a Christmas feast. He knew well what was coming next. Several speakers rose to make conciliatory remarks. Stuart of Michigan attempted an explanation of the concessions which the Douglas men had made in helping vote down the principal plank of their own platform, but he was so hurt by the forced surrender that his remarks became bitterly offensive. Various observers surmised that perhaps he wished to make sure that the slave-code men would leave the convention.[36] Had he been sweet as honey, however, that would have availed nothing. The Southern radicals now knew that they could keep a popular sovereignty plank out of the platform, but they also knew that they could never force a slave-code plank into it, and on this issue many were ready to revolt. The echoes of a sharp exchange between Stuart and Yancey had hardly died away when L. P. Walker, chairman of the Alabama delegation, gained Cushing's recognition and declared that he had an announcement to make. As he walked to the front, a profound hush fell upon the gathering. The fateful moment had come!

The Alabama convention at Montgomery, said Walker, had directed its delegates to withdraw if they could not obtain a slave-code resolution, and as

36 Charleston *Courier*, May 1, 1860; Halstead, *Caucuses*, 9.

their demand had been denied, they must now follow their instructions. As the Alabamians rose to leave, Barry of Mississippi was on his feet. He and his associates, he announced, were also departing. One of them insisted on a final speech; and D. C. Glenn, in a powerful valedictory, prophesied that within sixty days the world would see a united South—a statement hailed with resounding cheers. In quick succession, Mouton of Louisiana and Simmons of South Carolina announced that their delegations too were withdrawing—although in fact two Louisianians and two South Carolinians remained. Milton of Florida presented the protest and withdrawal of his State, and another spokesman did as much for part of the Arkansas representation. The Texas representatives left in a body. Of the cotton States, only Georgia remained undecided, and as her delegates retired to consult, their secession was certain.[37]

That night, excitement ran high in Charleston, its streets thronged with men not merely excited but jubilant. A great crowd, gathering at eleven o'clock in front of the courthouse to listen to Yancey and L. Q. C. Lamar, wildly cheered an independent Southern republic. The city was mad with a passion not felt since Nullification days. "Perhaps even now," declared Yancey, "the pen of the historian is nibbed to write the story of a new revolution"—and Charleston hoped so. The withdrawn delegates, among whom Bayard and his Delaware associate Whiteley took their places, hesitated over their action. After much discussion, they resolved not to adopt a platform or a distinctive party name, and to adjourn to Richmond on June 11 for separate action.[38]

Meanwhile, on Tuesday, May 1, the regular convention met again; this time in an atmosphere of dejection, for few could still hope for a Democratic victory. Theoretically, about two hundred and fifty of the original three hundred and four delegates should still have been present, but the heat, confusion, hostile atmosphere, and high expenses were driving many to the homeward trains. The first decision taken by the convention was that no man should be nominated

---

37 Dumond, *Secession Movement 1860–61*, 52; *Proceedings*, 118–125. Next day 26 of the 34 Georgia delegates, followed by the remaining Arkansas men, withdrew. Halstead, 76.
38 Fuess, *Caleb Cushing*, II, 254. The South Carolina delegation, a moderate body, had no instructions to withdraw. Public sentiment in Charleston forced its action. When the delegates arrived, wrote Rhett, they had no more idea of going out than of flying. "If they had not retired, they would have been mobbed, I believe." May 12, 1860; Porcher Miles Papers, Univ. of N. C. The fact was that Yancey, having taken out his extremists, did not know what to do with them. Trescot thought that if Hunter had not telegraphed the Virginia delegates to stay in regular convention, Yancey might have nominated him. May 8, 1860; Miles Papers, Univ. of N. C. Louisiana and Delaware delegates opposed any nomination or even recommendation, and Yancey and his Alabama delegation yielded to this. He thought that Davis was the favorite for the Southern nomination, though Lane, Guthrie, and Breckinridge were urged by some. At once, Yancey took steps to scatter copies of his speeches at Charleston throughout the South, and wrote C. C. Clay—and doubtless others—in Washington urging them to stand by the radicals. Prompt and efficient action was necessary to back up the bolters, he stated. May 4, 1860; C. C. Clay Papers.

without a two-thirds vote of all elected delegates. This was a blow to the Douglas men, who contended that two-thirds of the delegates present ought to suffice. But Caleb Cushing ruled against them; the remaining Southern delegates threatened to withdraw if he were not upheld; and he had the support of various Northern groups, including the powerful New York delegation, which did not wish to cut its members off from a possible Presidential nomination. One participant remarked that the ballot had the sound of clods falling on Douglas's coffin. From that moment, all hopes of a rapid victory for him at Charleston were dead, for he could never obtain two-thirds of all the seats. While this rule had not been followed in earlier Democratic conventions, it could be said that the circumstances this time were unprecedented.[39]

Six men were formally but briefly nominated for the Presidency: Douglas, Guthrie, Hunter, Daniel S. Dickinson, Andrew Johnson, and Joseph Lane of Oregon. With 202 votes necessary for a choice, the first ballot gave Douglas 145½; Guthrie 36½; Hunter 42; and 30 for other men. Twelve ballots were taken that day and forty-five more the next without result. Strive as they might, Douglas's followers were unable to push his vote above 152½. This was a clear majority of all the seats, and they were quick to point out that four years earlier he had withdrawn the moment he learned that Buchanan had attained a majority. His enemies contended, however, that his vote included many delegates bound by the unit rule who were really against him. The strongest rival was James Guthrie, but even after Andrew Johnson was formally withdrawn in favor of the Kentuckian, Guthrie obtained only 64½ votes. With the convention hopelessly deadlocked, nothing remained but to vote an adjournment. Cushing, whose encouragement of Southern intransigency in years past had contributed not a little to the catastrophe, closed the proceedings by a rhetorical appeal for a restoration of harmony. His words could not assuage the bitterness with which most of the delegates, and particularly the Northwestern men—some of whom had shed tears over Douglas's failure—turned their backs on the flowers and rancors of Charleston.[40]

Something more than the convention had come to an end when the delegates of the cotton kingdom walked out of the hall. The Democratic Party had been riven asunder, and the stage set for secession and disunion. The melancholy words which a veteran leader of the South, ex-Senator Foote, wrote decades later, were all too true; the Southern extremists who had declared that they would never tolerate a Republican President had taken the very steps to make

39 Charleston *Courier, N. Y. Tribune,* May 3; Halstead, *Caucuses,* 85; E. D. Fite, *Presidential Campaign of 1860,* pp. 110, 111.
40 *Official Proceedings;* Fuess, *Caleb Cushing,* II, 253; Milton, *Eve of Conflict,* 447–449.

Republican victory certain, and had thus deliberately sealed the destruction of the national fabric.[41]

The word "deliberately" requires a gloss; levity, hot-blooded precipitancy, a stupid confidence that party schism would soon be healed, and other factors played a part. But that Rhett, Yancey, and others substantially foresaw the main events of the next nine months can hardly be questioned, and Slidell, Bright, and Bayard coolly dealt cards that gave these men their trumps. Alas, that nobody looked further ahead than the next nine months! The cheers that grew thunderous when Glenn of Mississippi predicted a united South before midsummer were cheers for the closing of the bright page on which all the glories of the old fraternal Union were inscribed. The bright smiles and handclappings which Charleston ladies bestowed upon the receding delegates were applause for an irrevocable step toward war; the bouquets which they brought next day to fill the empty seats of the seceders were symbolic of the flowers soon to be cast upon multitudinous Southern graves.

[VII]

Before the convention adjourned, the stubborn South Carolina Unionist, B. F. Perry, who had remained when his brethren departed, insisted upon being heard. Refusing to let the hissing galleries be cleared, he stood until silence reigned; then, erect, with outstretched arm and warning finger, he combined an appeal for reconciliation with an indictment of Southern radicalism. It was suicidal, he declared, for the South to demand Congressional intervention, which it had been resisting so many years. The South should instead yield as much as possible to the Northern Democrats who had sacrificed themselves in protecting slave State rights. Why insist on a "mere abstraction" at the hazard of breaking up the party? The recent South Carolina Democratic convention, he correctly said, had been controlled by moderates, anxious for party harmony. It had mentioned no contingency which would justify the South Carolina delegation in leaving the national convention. He was confident that his colleagues had contemplated no such step when they came. They had been swept into folly by a storm of emotion carefully prepared by intrigue.[42]

No question can exist that the main responsibility for the disruption, both immediate and remote, lay with the Southern extremists and the Administration men. The program of the disunionists had been outlined months before by Rhett in a letter to Porcher Miles. Revolutions, he wrote, are made by deter-

41 H. S. Foote, *Casket of Reminiscences*, 121, 122.
42 Charleston *Courier*, May 2, 1860; Perry, *Biographical Sketches*, 145-150, 188, 602.

mined minorities.[43] The War of 1812 had been effected by a mere handful of patriotic, fearless Southern men when a cowardly spirit was rife throughout the land. The South must now dissever itself from the rotten Northern element. There was no hope that the State Rights men could control the Charleston convention. "Hence the importance of obtaining the secession of the Alabama and Mississippi delegations on the issue of squatter sovereignty and the construction of the Dred Scott decision. If they will but do it, the people I am sure will come up to the scratch, and the game will be ours." This was the fire-eaters' own plan to precipitate the Southern States into revolution.[44] It had been realized to the letter; some steps remained to be taken, but so far it had operated well. The Administration men under Slidell and Bright made their indispensable contribution to the debacle by refusing to accept Douglas as a candidate and using the slave-code demand to exclude him.

To be sure, if Douglas had withdrawn, the South would doubtless have yielded to a compromise candidate and compromise platform, and the party would have marched into the campaign with united ranks. But Douglas had three excellent reasons for not withdrawing. The first was that by every available index a majority of Democratic voters, and probably a heavy majority, wanted him as their candidate. The second was that after the Administration effort to force him, the champion of the Northwest, out of the party, and especially after the culminating blow of his deposition from the chairmanship of the Territorial Committee, honor required him to fight to the end. The third was that he represented a principle which Northern Democrats simply could not give up.[45]

What had happened was that a minority of the gathering, who spoke for a minority of the party, had undertaken to dictate to the majority what they should put into the platform. By decisive vote, after full discussion, the convention had pronounced against the slave-code demand. Few sane observers could doubt that two-thirds of the Democrats of the country were against such a plank. Yet the minority had tried to coerce the majority by threats of a bolt,

43 "The bolt at Charleston," wrote J. H. Clay Mudd to Alexander H. Stephens on May 22, "was the result of prearranged action outside of the delegates, in advance of the Convention. The struggle over the platform was a mere sham; the real contest was about the candidate. Douglas out of the way, and the platform was of no consequence to the central managers who combined for his destruction. Slidell and Bright openly confessed before they went to Charleston that their action was governed by personal hostility to the man. The Administration labored and still labors diligently to the same end." Stephens Papers, LC.

44 January 29, 1860; Miles Papers, Univ. of N. C.

45 Douglas in a Senate speech of May 15 made an explicit statement that his honor was involved. "My name never would have been presented at Charleston, except for the attempt to proscribe me for a heretic, too unsound to be the chairman of a committee in this body, where I have held a seat for so many years without a suspicion resting on my political fidelity. I was forced to allow my name to go there in self-defense; and I will now say that had any gentleman, friend or foe, received a majority in that convention over me, the lightning would have carried a message withdrawing my name from the convention."

and, when they achieved only partial success, had bolted. In the matter of a candidate, the position was equally clear. Had all delegations remained, Douglas would certainly have had a heavy majority, and might have approached two-thirds. After the split, he not only had a majority of the votes cast on every one of the fifty-seven ballots, but on several ballots had a majority of *all* delegates. His agents were accused of sharp practice in passing the rule for individual voting by unbound delegates. He could reply to this charge that although the votes of New Jersey, Delaware, California, Oregon, and nearly half of Massachusetts were cast against him, most Democrats of those States were heartily for him. The New York *Tribune* remarked that he assuredly had two-thirds of the Democratic voters of the Union behind him.[46]

Looking back over the unhappy sequence of events, we can fix upon certain crucial moments. The first was the deposition of Douglas from the Senate Territorial Committee; a notice that his political life was sought and that he must conquer or be slain.

The second was the adoption by the Alabama State Democratic Convention in January, 1860, of Yancey's program. In 1856, the delegates to the national convention had been positively instructed to withdraw if they did not obtain a plank stating the principle of Congressional non-intervention in the Territories; in 1860, they were positively instructed to withdraw if they did not obtain a plank making it the duty of Congress to protect slave property in the Territories.[47] This Alabama convention had been far from unanimous. While Yancey led the slave-code wing, John Forsyth and J. J. Seibels led a militant wing willing to leave the status of property in the Territories to the courts, and eager to nominate Douglas. Outvoted two to one, Forsyth and others contended that the convention expressed the views of the politicians rather than the people. Our best evidence indicates that it really did reflect the majority will, but with a large dissenting minority.[48] By the beginning of 1860, Douglas had thus been compelled to fight to the end for popular sovereignty; while one Southern State was committed to disruption of the party if it did not get a plank which made popular sovereignty into mincemeat. Another, Mississippi, was ready to follow. Jefferson Davis's resolutions had determined its course. The Texas delegation, too, according to word sent to Douglas before the Charleston gathering, had secretly determined to bolt if he were nominated.

46 Much evidence on the methods by which the choice of delegates in various States was controlled by Administrative officeholders is to be found in the Douglas Papers. See, for example, the letter by John D. Stranahan of Le Boeuf, Pennsylvania, on the way in which the customs collector and postmaster in Erie manipulated the county convention against the will of the people; May 7, 1860.
47 Denman, *Secession Movement in Alabama*, 80, 81.
48 Murphy, "Alabama and the Chicago Convention of 1860," *Transactions Ala. State Hist. Soc.*, 1904, V. 224 ff.

The third crucial turning point was the midnight conference of Southern delegates which, just as the convention opened, decided that Mississippi, Louisiana, Arkansas, Texas, and Florida, with the South Carolina delegates cooperating "in a certain contingency," would stand by the Alabama demand: a slave-code, or withdrawal. Our best account of this conclave is that given by the special correspondent of the New Orleans *Picayune*, who, returning from it at one A.M. April 24, dashed off a full dispatch.[49] The caucus met in the hall of the Meagher Guards, with Governor Alexander Mouton of Louisiana presiding. Resolutions upon Southern rights were reported by Milton of Florida as the basis for demands in the convention. Yancey sustained them in what the correspondent termed a most powerful argument, and was vigorously seconded by Glenn of Mississippi, who dilated upon the Jefferson Davis resolutions. Rousing speeches were also made by L. P. Walker of Alabama, an old Nashville Convention man, and Burroughs of Arkansas. When a North Carolina delegate expostulated, denying the right of Congress to legislate upon slavery in the Territories, the majority laughed at him. Resolutions were adopted by acclamation for a Southern ultimatum: The platform must be written before a candidate was nominated, and the platform must contain the essential features of the Jefferson Davis-Mississippi program, including a slave-code.

The final turning point occurred on the night of Sunday, April 29, when the effort of leaders to avert the now imminent bolt broke down. Slidell, Bright, Bayard, and others were frightened by the impending ruin of the party. They made a last-minute effort to hold the cotton kingdom delegates. Their plan was to reaffirm the Cincinnati platform, table the remaining minority resolutions, and proceed to ballot for candidates. They told Southerners that a careful nose count showed that without slave State votes Douglas could get little if any more than a majority; that New York, with a majority of Pennsylvania delegates, was ready to swing to Guthrie; and that if the South remained, Guthrie could be nominated. Richard Taylor's story that Yancey vainly tried to get Alabama to consent may be correct. Southerners thought the count too close for safety. They knew that some slave State men *would* vote for Douglas, and they hence refused to change front (as Northerners were willing to do) and take up nominations before the main part of the platform. Until the very end, however, the managers and mediators retained hope. When, on Monday, the convention by a large majority reaffirmed the Cincinnati platform, six border slave States (Maryland, Delaware, Virginia, Tennessee, Kentucky, and Missouri) voted for it. The Douglas men gave way on the next resolution leaving territorial property to

49 N. O. *Picayune*, April 28, 1860. The South Carolina delegates did not attend this caucus; the phrase as to cooperation in a certain contingency (later verified by events) is in a Charleston dispatch to the N. Y. *Tribune* of April 23, 1860.

the court. Then it was dramatically revealed that the midnight attempt at an arrangement had failed.

Why did it fail? "The seceding States came to the convention," wrote Robert H. Glass, editor of the Lynchburg *Republican*, in a letter from Charleston dated May 1, "with a deliberate purpose to break up the convention if they failed to get, as they knew they would fail to get, their extreme ultimatum, and their ultimate design is to break up the Union by breaking up the Democratic Party." We have noted that Virginia on that fateful Sunday temporarily came to the support of the cotton kingdom in insisting on a slave-code plank. Glass believed that if his State had stood staunchly by its original position and upheld the Cincinnati platform, it would have become the ruling factor in the convention and would have drawn all the Northern States to its standard. His fellow-delegate Barbour also believed that Virginia made a fatal error when it temporarily followed Yancey's lead. "For myself," concluded Glass, "I have no great admiration for the Union . . . but I have no idea of assisting in bringing about such a serious result by insisting upon a mere abstraction which is not worth the paper upon which it is proposed to be written." His general conclusions were supported by the Washington correspondent of the Cincinnati *Enquirer*, who wrote May 1: "The secession movement [that is, from the convention] is universally regarded as a concerted plan for the dissolution of the Union."

Essentially, as we have said, the disruption came because Southern extremists, abetted until too late by Slidell and other Administration men, tried to force into the platform a slave-code plank which the majority would not accept. The motive of some in this attempt was disunion; the motive of the majority was their wish to stop Douglas. They wished to stop Douglas because they realized that the Freeport Doctrine meant the containment of slavery (so far as the existing domain of the United States went) just as surely as Republican doctrine meant it. Yancey was absurd when he said that the position of the Northern Democrats might convert the South into a great heaving volcano of passion and crime. The refusal to enact a slave-code for Territories opposed to slavery would not excite servile insurrections. But Yancey was right when he said that basically two different assumptions were in conflict. The South contended that slavery was a good and should be protected in any possible expansion. Most Northern Democrats held that slavery was an evil and should be restricted. Republican restriction by Congress and Douglasite restriction by popular sovereignty came to the same practical result. The cotton States men would not accept either type of containment.

Containment—or disunion! It had at last come to this naked issue. This was the fundamental question which underlay the Charleston schism. The South had refused to let the Wilmot Proviso be applied to lands won from Mexico, for that would have meant containment. It had blocked the organization of Kansas Territory without the free entry of slavery, for that would have meant containment. It was now rejecting the Freeport Doctrine as another name for containment. When Yancey called upon Pugh, Stuart, and other Douglas leaders to accept his assumption that slavery was a positive good, he was appealing to the bar of history. When Pugh declared that the Northern Democracy would never do it, he too was appealing to the bar of history. No question whatever exists as to the verdict which history, in the light of man's advancing concepts of social morality, has passed upon the two rival assumptions.

But disaster and twilight for the Democratic organization spelled opportunity and morning radiance for its great rival the Republican Party.

Sunrise in Chicago

THE DELEGATES and spectators who poured into Chicago in the third week of May, 1860, came with a spirit and to a scene which stood in startling contrast with Charleston. The spirit was one of complete confidence. When the chairman of the convention lifted the gavel, made of oak from Commodore Perry's flagship at the battle of Lake Erie, he remarked: "All the auguries are that we shall meet the enemy and they shall be ours." The scene was typical of the rough, exuberant, progressive outlook of the West. A city of a hundred and ten thousand people, of a dozen busy railroads, of meat-packing plants, grain elevators, foundries, and farm implement factories, suddenly swarmed with literally tens of thousands of visitors, full of gaiety, energy, and enthusiasm. They had a Western earnestness, too. "What seems a brilliant festival," wrote one journalist, "is but the rally for battle; it is an army with banners."

Across the page of party history falls the light of a great name, illuminating every recoverable detail. We know much more about the Republican convention and campaign of 1860 than about any similar events of the era, for they brought into power one of the nation's immortal leaders. But to the delegations which arrived by special trains and Lake boats, to political clubs which paraded with flaring torches, to the crashing bands and excited throngs, Lincoln's name was only one of a dozen under consideration—and not the most important. One reason for the sanguine mood of the party lay in its wealth of chieftains— Seward well in front, but a group of strong men behind him. All that the host which met in Chicago knew at first was that this convention was unlike any thus far known in national history. It was greater in size, in enthusiasm, in noise, in wire-pulling, in self-righteousness, in lust for office, and in its blend of mass hysteria with idealistic fervor.

The gathering multitude—thousands from Wisconsin, from Indiana, from Ohio, six hundred on one train from Pennsylvania, as many on another from New York—could afford to be uncertain about the candidate. They were starting their campaign with many advantages. They could thank their foes for half a dozen great vote-winning issues; free homesteads, tariff revision, internal improvements, adequate Pacific communications, and departmental honesty. They could point to needed measures obstructed by Southern Democrats. They could assert that Buchanan's Administration was more inefficient and inept than even Pierce's. They could shake their heads over the corruption of Fowler and the laxity of Floyd. And, as a crowning gift, their opponents had torn the Democracy in twain! [1]

The Republicans, far better organized than in 1856, were ready to make the most of their advantages.[2] Delegates from every Northern State could tell of growing strength. They and their allies had twice swept Pennsylvania, where their doctrines continued to infiltrate Philadelphia and other populous centers. They had three times won the governorship in Ohio, where Salmon P. Chase, going to the Senate, was giving way to William Dennison. In Illinois, the party had not only put a Republican in the governor's mansion but had carried Chicago, Rockford, and Quincy, all normally Democratic, at the last city elections.[3] Indianians in Chicago recalled how Frémont might have carried that State in 1856 but for the votes of several thousand Irish railway workers, and predicted that the party would win in 1860. The national committee, led by Governor Morgan of New York, had learned much in recent years. It had displayed shrewdness in choosing Chicago as a salute to the West; in advancing the convention date to mid-May to yield an extra month for campaigning; and in raising money. In its official call it had included members of the People's Party of Pennsylvania and the Opposition Party of New Jersey, along with all others who were ready to uphold the Republican nominee.[4]

The party was fortunate, again, in that the Republican press was reaching the height of its influence. It possessed an array of editors—Bryant, Greeley, Bowles, Medill, Schouler—which the Democrats could not match, and it was steadily gaining adherents. Raymond's *Times* had veered to catch the Republican breeze. Bennett's *Herald* could seldom resist the temptation to choose the victorious side. Similar journals of the North, whether they felt the moral groundswell of the

1 An admirable general treatment of the convention is found in William E. Baringer, *Lincoln's Rise to Power*; see also Reinhard H. Luthin, *The First Lincoln Campaign*; P. O. Ray, *The Convention That Nominated Lincoln;* Murat Halstead, *Caucuses of 1860;* O. H. Oldroyd, *Lincoln's Campaign; or, The Political Revolution of 1860;* Thomas H. Dudley, "The Inside Facts of Lincoln's Nomination," *Century Magazine*, 1890, 477 ff.

2 Lyman Trumbull and Zachariah Chandler had been active during 1859 in an organized plan of Republican publicity, furnishing prepared articles to the press, and franking out large quantities of documents. For this work a Mr. Dodd had raised funds. Lyman Trumbull to Chandler, April 4, 1859; Chandler Papers. The chief authors of the articles, which dealt with the tariff, homestead, slavery, and Democratic extravagance and corruption, were Frank P. Blair, Montgomery Blair, and George M. Weston. Trumbull wrote friendly editors asking them to publish the articles, which were then reissued in pamphlet form. See Trumbull to Thurlow Weed, April 11, 1859; Stuart Collection, HL.

3 Cole, *Era of Civil War*, 182.

4 MS Journal, NYHS.

Friends of Republicanism:

This town is the County Seat, with about 1,400 inhabitants, and is destined to be a city of first rank. Upon the opening of the Illinois Southern Railroad, its natural advantages for manufacturing purposes, which are not surpassed by any place in our land, will be developed, and thus hasten a rapid growth. Capitalists predict this will be a Western "Lowell" in the "Eden," of our nation. All who are acquainted with Southern Illinois say that no part of the country offers such inducements to the enterprising emigrant as this. Ere long, this beautiful section of our Republic will be filled up with representatives of many nations.

The above facts as regards our town, are stated only to impress upon the reader that we are a centre of influence, and ought to be in a position to do all we would like to for the cause in the midst of "Egypt," and could, had we the pecuniary ability. It must be remembered that this is the District represented by John A. Logan in Congress, who claims it (and with truth) as the Banner Democratic District of the Union. Is any other statement necessary to prove that we are in great political darkness, when John A. Logan can boast of 13,000 majority? We will reduce it some four or five thousand this Fall, we hope. "Old Abe" has many friends in Southern Illinois, yet there is a great want of ordinary political intelligence among the masses. One specimen, of many I could give, will suffice to show who hurrah for Douglas and boast of their Democracy. A few weeks after the Chicago Convention a prominent person in the community (in a position to pre-suppose ordinary intelligence upon the current matters of the day,) asked who the Republicans had nominated? Abraham Lincoln, was the answer. Well, who is He? The man who contested the State in 1858 with Douglas? Well, who is Douglas?

I ask, how are we to overcome such stupidity except by constant, patient laboring—"Here a little and there a little," &c.

There are many Third Party men who will be with us in November, if we can reach them, meanwhile, by the Press and Documents, and School District laboring. The masses are honest, but often deluded by designing demagogues. Judge Bates' letter is doing much good where it is read; but is a fact that we have only three Republican papers south of the Ohio and Mississippi Railroad, with an aggregate circulation of not over 1,500. Now, of course does not know how to do, as we might wish our present Republican strength we have obtained within a year or two, and of course does not know how to do, as we might wish it would; so we must have the aid of outside friends—if we have it betimes, we shall, ere long, redeem "Egypt" to light and political purity.

For our encouragement, I will state that in this precinct, in 1856, we had but 8 votes, now we have over 150—in some of our counties not a vote for Fremont, now we can count over 400—and so on all over Southern Illinois. Is not this a hopeful field?

We ask that whoever can, will send forward all the documents possible pertaining to Republicanism and our Candidates. I earnestly request that every person who reads this, will at least send me a number of each paper published in his section, of every party, that we may, by reference to the enemies' organs, learn their fallacies, and use those of our party as campaign documents. It is astonishing how many will read a newspaper before it is worn out—often when we can reach our most bitter opponents by giving them a paper, when a document they will reject.

If you can do nothing more, send Fifty cents to George Harrington, Secretary of the Republican committee, Washington, D. C., and ask him to send its worth in documents, for "Egypt." Also, you may send to the Young Men's Republican Union, 659 Broadway, New York—Charles T. Rodgers, President—to forward the value of documents of their publications, to the amount you may remit them, as we would like to have at least,not less than 100,000 of the right documents.

You will see that unless we are aided by our friends, we will be greatly hindered in the good work. Any of the campaign documents published by the New York Tribune would be greatly received, as they are very good.

Induce your Republican Editors to send for the campaign a copy or more of their papers, and we will repay by correspondence from our field. Let it be known that this place is the largest in Southeastern Illinois, and about ten counties can be reached through us. If this be represented to Republican organizations where our cause is strong, they will feel inclined to subscribe for clubs of the Tribune, Evening Post or any good paper to enlighten "Egypt."

I have shown how any one who may wish to do something for "Lincoln and Hamlin," Free Press, Free Speech, Free Soil, and Liberty and Union, can, if he will.

We would be happy to have a personal reply from you, sir, in regard to the prospects in your field of operations. It will serve to encourage our friends here to hear from elsewhere the "Nation o'er."

GEORGE P. EDGAR, Corresponding Secretary.

A Republican Organizer Uses Greeley and Bryant to Convert "Egypt."

231

freesoil movement, or were disgusted with the Pierce-Buchanan record, or wished to stand with the winners, were enlisting with the party of the future. What gave power over opinion to the great Republican journals—the New York *Tribune* and *Evening Post*, the Springfield *Republican*, the Philadelphia *Press*, the Cleveland *Leader*, and the Chicago *Tribune*—was the homogeneity of their audiences, the vogue of their weekly editions in village and country, and the power with which they combined editorial argument and news-gathering vigor.

Typical of them all in some ways and uniquely distinguished in others, was Greeley's *Tribune*—a splendidly equipped fighting unit. It covered the events of each day thoroughly; its Washington correspondence, by Dana, J. S. Pike, or "H. G." himself, was expert, colorful, and stingingly antislavery; its western intelligence was full and firmly agrarian in tone; its editors displayed a keen instinct for events and documents—a Congressional affray, a Tammany demonstration, a London *Times* leader—which served their ends; and the editorial page, written by Greeley, Dana, George Ripley, C. T. Congdon, and others, was a magnificent combination of argument, invective, and news. The issue of the *Weekly Tribune* which opened its twentieth year (April 14, 1860) was a typical production. Its front page contained, along with Albany and European news, a three-and-a-half-column article on the antislavery excitement in North Carolina and the trial of Daniel Worth for circulating Helper's book. Other contents included a House committee report in defense of the Covode investigation, London comment on a speech by Seward, a manifesto of Cassius M. Clay to Kentuckians, a speech by Congressman Lovejoy, and a Washington letter on Douglas's effort to win delegates. The editorials ranged from foreign policy and the homestead issue to sarcasm at the expense of Pollard's book on the Negro, *Black Diamonds*. Miscellaneous news articles dealt with the Pennsylvania oil fields, the Nevada silver mines, the Japanese mission to Washington, Illinois farming, and the author James K. Paulding, just dead. Such a newspaper was valuable enough to be passed from hand to hand and read from end to end, and could not but influence opinion.[5]

Systematic efforts were made by party organizers to augment the circulation of Republican sheets, while many clergymen allied with the new party encouraged the reading of the *National Era* and the *Independent*, both now powerful organs. Lyman Trumbull's correspondence is sprinkled with letters

5 The N. Y. *Tribune*, April 10, 1860, boasted that more than twenty-five new Democratic campaign sheets had been started expressly to counteract its influence. The Philadelphia *Press* was still nominally a Douglas sheet; but Forney was confidentially advising Thurlow Weed, who sent his information on to Lincoln—as the Robert Todd Lincoln Papers show. The *Pennsylvanian* of October 2 spoke of the *Press* as in the Republican interest.

from adherents describing the growing strength of the press. One rural Illinois correspondent had boasted in the summer of 1857, for example, that he had obtained more than three hundred subscribers for the Chicago *Tribune*, with a telling effect upon county sentiment. "I asked a gentleman the other day who has been taking it for about six months, how he liked it, his answer was, 'about twice as well as I ever intended to,' and then further remarked that some of his [Democratic] neighbors had been reading his paper, and that it had converted them also." Another adherent wrote Trumbull that whereas in 1856 not a copy of the *National Era* had come to his county, the close of 1857 found forty-five or fifty being circulated. Still other workers in southern Illinois wrote of promoting that ably-edited freesoil journal the *Missouri Democrat*. Horace Greeley offered his *Weekly Tribune* to clubs of twenty or more subscribers, using one address, at a dollar a year each, and other editors imitated him. The late fifties, we repeat, saw the freesoil press at its very apogee of energy and prosperity. Raymond's *Times* moved in 1858 into a handsome new building on Park Row; Greeley's *Tribune* the next year passed the 200,000 circulation mark; the *Evening Post* was making John Bigelow and Bryant rich men; the Philadelphia *Press* had become the chief Pennsylvania daily, and the Chicago *Tribune* was soon to reach a quarter of a million readers. The German-language press, too, had become a potent force in New York and the Middle West.

Facing a divided enemy, supported by a broadening freesoil sentiment, possessing so much effective ammunition and such powerful batteries to discharge it, the Republicans felt sanguine. But it was essential to make no blunder in candidate or platform.

[I]

When the year opened, the primacy of Seward had been universally conceded. He was the first choice not only of New York and New England, but of Michigan, Wisconsin, and Minnesota.[6] His enthusiastic reception on returning from Europe, and the general praise for his politic Senate speech of late February, had strengthened the confidence of Weed and other managers. Cool, calculating, and realistically informed, Weed believed his nomination certain.[7] Even the hostile Greeley, writing from Davenport, Iowa, in January, declared

6 Chase could possibly wait for a nomination; Seward could not. "It is now or never with him," wrote John Bigelow, who thought a stronger man should be named. "He does not mean to return to the Senate and he is fast becoming an old man." Paris, January 25, 1860; Blair-Lee Papers. The elder Blair told a friend that Seward wished Frank P. Blair, Jr., to be candidate for Vice-President on his ticket, and it is possible that Seward did make such overtures to the great border family. J. D. Andrews, July 16, 1859; Banks Papers, Illinois State Hist. Library.

7 Bancroft, *Seward*, I, 522.

that Seward enjoyed the preference of the Northwest.[8] His claims to the nomination on grounds of governmental experience, long service to the freesoil cause, and tested ability, seemed to outweigh those of anybody else.

Nevertheless, the field was crowded with possible candidates, for the new party had appealed so strongly to idealistic young men and had drawn so heavily upon the best Whig and freesoil Democratic talent that it was rich in ability. In the Northwest, wrote Greeley, many wished Lincoln's name on the ticket; everywhere, the merits of Bates, Dayton, Cameron, Chase, Banks, and others were canvassed; and a few suggested Frémont. The editor, convinced that Bates was the strongest figure, labored to prove that he could carry the borderland as well as the North. The Blairs also continued supporting Bates, and with them stood Gratz Brown, Orville Browning, and Schuyler Colfax. Bates himself was sanguine. "The signs indicating my nomination are growing in number and strength every day," he wrote in his diary on February 26. He hoped to be the nominee of both the Republicans and Constitutional Unionists. Simon Cameron had the initial support of the fluctuating New York *Herald*, strong-stomached Pennsylvanians, and scattered protectionists elsewhere. While many New Englanders, including Samuel Bowles, gave lukewarm recommendation to Banks, most Ohioans stood behind the very smooth Chase or the very rough Ben Wade.

Had the nomination been bestowed for length and power of freesoil service or proved capacity in important office, only Seward and Chase would have been considered. Political expediency, however, had to be weighed. The party being young, in such States as Pennsylvania and New Jersey devotion to its principles was not yet well established; for these States were as conservative as New England and the upper Northwest were radical. Special predilections and antagonisms likewise had to be regarded: the dislike of many former Whigs for Chase as a former Democrat, the opposition of Greeley, Bryant, and Bowles to Seward, the belief of many German-Americans that Bates had once leaned toward the Know-Nothings, the desire of many Yankees for a radical antislavery man, and the insistence of most border men upon a moderate nominee. The Republican Party is beset with difficulties, wrote a brilliant young Connecticut Representative, O. S. Ferry. Without the radical Yankees and Germans of Michigan, Wisconsin, and northern Illinois it might lose the Northwest, while if it meets the wishes of this wing, it will repel voters in the Middle States.[9]

The more prominent the aspirant, the more numerous were the objections to him. Seward, as marshal of the Republican forces in the Senate, a longtime champion of the alien-born, and the leading advocate of internal improvements and higher tariffs, had a legion of friends. But he also had countless enemies. His

8 N. Y. *Weekly Tribune*, February 11, 1860.
9 To Gideon Welles, March 1, 1860; Welles Papers .

irrepressible-conflict speech still alarmed the conservatives.[10] His devious ways and fits-and-starts leadership had offended men of iron conviction. Former Democrats, remembering him as the principal lieutenant of President Zachary Taylor, distrusted him. Were he elected, prophesied Bryant, it would be a special favor of Providence if every honest Democrat in the new party were not driven into opposition within a year. His quarter-century partnership with Weed had long been hurtful, for everyone knew that Lord Thurlow's ostentatious show of unselfishness in declining office masked an insatiable appetite for other rewards. In the last legislative session, Weed had damaged the Senator fearfully by helping engineer the corrupt passage of six street-railway bills which grid-ironed half a hundred New York streets without conditions as to compensation, tenure, or fares. Raymond, Greeley, and Governor Morgan unsparingly de-nounced this scheme, the object being, Bryant wrote, to get the franchise-recip-ients "to furnish a fund of from four to six hundred thousand dollars, to be expended for the Republican cause in the next presidential election." [11] How could Seward be sent to the White House without sending Weed there too?

There was something deeply pathetic in Seward's position. He had toiled so long for the Presidency, first among the Whigs, then the Republicans. His expec-tations were so confident; he had spoken all spring as if his nomination were certain, throwing his house open in elaborate entertainments and keeping in touch with powerful economic interests in New York which desired his election. When he left the capital for Auburn on the eve of the convention, he told friends that he expected to return in a much higher capacity. The feeling among most Republican Congressmen was that he would almost surely be nominated—and that his nomination would be a disaster to the party.[12] It was not his fault that the legislature, with which he did not have even a Spenlow & Jorkins con-nection, had been corrupt. Yet many now believed that if the party nominated him it would lose the shining advantage which it drew from Covode's exposures of Democratic venality. Nor was it Seward's fault—altogether—that his radical-ism with respect to slavery was grossly exaggerated. While his higher-law and irrepressible conflict speeches had been indiscreet, his usual temper was moder-ate; indeed, many who were truly radical distrusted him as a trimmer. Yet some of the mud thrown after the John Brown raid inevitably clung to his garments.

10 Numerous expressions of conservative Republican feeling in southern and central Illinois against Seward may be found in the Lyman Trumbull Papers. Even Stephen T. Logan did not know whether he could vote for him. Our people, wrote a Peoria citizen, are generally moderate men, opposed to extremes—neither abolitionists nor nullifiers. Seward's nomination, declared a Collinsville citizen, would place success beyond hope. Trumbull Papers, April–May, 1860.
11 W. C. Bryant to John Bigelow, December 14, 1859, Bigelow Papers; Nevins, *Evening Post*, 261, 262; Van Deusen, *Weed*, 245–248.
12 J. S. Pike in N. Y. *Weekly Tribune*, May 26, 1860.

And those who opposed him for mistaken reasons were reinforced by a good many whose reasons were quite definite. As Hamilton Fish wrote, for twenty years Seward had sown innumerable seeds of selfishness which were now springing up to choke his hopes.[13]

The Republican victory in Connecticut in April, 1860, had the curious effect of injuring Seward's chances—simply because it was so close. The little State had seethed with excitement; both sides had spent money by the bucketfull. Observers called the contest a Presidential election in miniature. Governor W. A. Buckingham was reelected—but by a plurality of only 541. Had he been a man of more extreme views, he would have lost. In Rhode Island, simultaneously, a wealthy young Democratic manufacturer was chosen governor over a Republican whose tenets came close to abolitionism. The Hartford *Courant* expressed the hope that the Republicans of the nation would take warning, and turn away from any "ultra" leader.[14]

Salmon P. Chase, a man of intellectual vigor, spotless character, and commanding physique, had been one of the first of the nation's leading statesmen to identify himself with the Republicans, and had done so when the step took courage. He possessed a clear head, an inflexible will, and a cultivation which impressed young William Dean Howells. If, like Seward, he seemed somewhat devious, it was not from any lack of conviction, but because he had too keen an eye to the main chance. He had flirted with the Know-Nothings when that seemed advantageous and with the foreign-born when that appeared helpful. Cold, dignified, aloof, he had never attracted hearty allies nor constructed an effective personal organization. Though burning with Presidential ambitions, he had no party managers, no important editors, and no Congressional friends to push him forward. We have seen that he made no secret of his hopes, and that in March, 1860, Carl Schurz had frankly told him they were impossible. Undiscouraged, Chase traveled to Washington the following month to seek friends among the easterners and to urge Ben Wade to withdraw his troublesome candidacy. He was received frigidly, got nowhere with Wade, and heard his friend, Dr. Gamaliel Bailey, urge him to withdraw in Seward's favor. Nevertheless, he remained hopeful. The fact that as a former Democrat he was distrusted on the tariff question was not enough in itself to disqualify him, but he lacked any advantages sufficient to offset that handicap.

One of Lincoln's Washington friends, J. M. Lucas, sent him a vivid picture of Chase bustling about on the floor of the House to enlist support; his usual cold and stoic aspect was replaced for the nonce by the cheeriest and most genial smiles, and the friendliest and most obliging manner. This struck Lucas and

13 Nevins, *Hamilton Fish,* 78.
14 Springfield *Republican,* March 26–April 7, 1860; Hartford *Courant,* April 7, 1860; S. G. Buckingham, *William A. Buckingham,* 43 ff.

others as hypocritical, for they knew that Chase was by nature chill, calculating, and selfish, uniting a powerful intellect with still more powerful ambition. It was not in the man to make devoted followers. One Ohio observer defined his shortcomings bluntly: "Chase is too supremely selfish to be popular or to have any devoted personal friends among men of sense who know him thoroughly but this is not his worst misfortune. I will not say that he cannot distinguish between a sycophant and a friend but I will say that he ever preferred the former and every one of his entire political helpers that I know belongs to the class of cheats or nincompoops." It is not strange that Ohioans looked to other men for a Presidential nominee—not a few of them to Lincoln. The proud, sensitive Chase was deeply wounded by the divisions in his own State, and by the plain disposition of many politicians there to prefer Joshua Giddings, Ben Wade, or some rank outsider.[15]

The dapper, adroit N. P. Banks, with his somewhat commonplace mind, the wealthy, unprincipled Simon Cameron, the ignorant, profane Ben Wade, and the drab septuagenarian John McLean were all receptive and all impossible. Banks, by failing to oppose an amendment to the Massachusetts constitution which unreasonably deferred the grant of the ballot to naturalized citizens, had destroyed what little chance he had ever possessed. To nominate Cameron would have been to select a crass businessman, a turncoat politician, and the head of one of the most notoriously venal of State machines. McLean, a legalistic old fogy, was obviously standing on the edge of his grave. As for Wade, a self-made man whose blustering egotism had carried him into a Senate seat which might better have gone to Joshua Giddings, he had great force and genuine ability; but he would have required schooling of several kinds to make him fit for the White House.[16]

For a time, at the beginning of 1860, it had seemed that the only leader likely to be strong enough to defeat Seward was Bates of Missouri. A former Clay Whig, as hostile to slavery as his great mentor, he would command the votes of many border State citizens who wanted a safe, tactful, and sagacious Unionist.[17] John Minor Botts, naked-sword enemy of secessionist "conspirators," had said

15 Lucas, May 6, 1860, Robert Todd Lincoln Papers; J. M. Root, May 26, 1860, Chase, May 10, 1860, Giddings Papers, Ohio Arch. and Hist. Soc.

16 Frémont was never seriously considered, even the Blairs, once his closest political friends, having dropped him. A story of a sort all too commonly alleged against prominent political leaders and probably not true was sometimes mentioned; see Preston King, March 3, 1860, Gideon Welles Papers, LC.

17 Some influential men thought that the Republican Party was moving to the right and hence could well take Bates. This was the view of James S. Rollins of Missouri, who wrote J. O. Brodhead of that State: ". . . the truth is, as you remark, the Republicans have greatly moderated their views; in fact, they differ in no very essential particular, on the subject of slavery, from the Whigs; they entertain now, almost the precise view, which Henry Clay reiterated hundreds of times, whilst living." This could indeed be said of Republicans like Lincoln; not of Republicans like Wade, Chandler, or Sumner. J. S. Rollins, February 1, 1860; Brodhead Papers.

in Virginia's Opposition convention early in 1859 that if the Republicans should nominate Crittenden, Bell, or Bates, the candidate would actually poll a large slave State vote. This was true. Western Virginia, for example, now had three good weekly Republican newspapers and one daily, while Wheeling had enough Republicans to justify a proposal that the Republican National Convention be held there.[18] If Bell and Crittenden were out of the question, Bates was not. Charles A. Dana was typical of many ardent young Republicans who believed their best chance lay with the grave Missourian. "It is either Bates or Seward," he had written James S. Pike. "I can't see any third chance. The Northwest won't have Chase. With Seward we are dead, beaten. He can't carry Ind., Ill., Penn., or N. J. With Bates we can carry Missouri certainly; Maryland and Tennessee probably. He may be elected. No one else can. That is the beginning, middle, and end of the story." [19] When Greeley returned from his Far Western tour in the fall of 1859, the *Tribune* adopted Bates with earnestness if not precisely enthusiasm. A flattering sketch of the public services of the sage of Grape Hill (Bates's residence four miles outside St. Louis) blossomed in the paper early in February; and thereafter, though refraining from explicit endorsement, it gave more space to his claims than to those of any other candidate.[20] The Baltimore *Patriot* gave him early support.

One difficulty was that, since Bates had for years given all his energy to legal and judicial work, he was little known in the East. At the time of Botts's speech, the New York press had felt it necessary to identify him.[21] But as newspapers by dozens from Massachusetts to Oregon gradually placed his name at their mastheads, his personality became known. Another difficulty was that he had long treated the slavery issue as a mere exciting device of politicians to keep themselves in power. Seeing that it was necessary to rectify this position, he published a letter to Missouri delegates to the Chicago convention which had the right freesoil ring. He made it clear that he detested slavery, opposed its extension, denied that the Constitution carried it into the Territories, and held that the Dred Scott decision had no validity beyond affirming the incapacity of a Negro to sue in the Missouri courts. Going further, he pronounced in favor of the

18 J. C. Underwood to Welles, April 9, 1859; Welles Papers, LC. Underwood, an officer of the American Emigrant Aid & Homestead Co., wrote that the operations of this company had produced a marvelous change in Western Virginia in the previous two years. "Instead of my blood or banishment being demanded as in 1856 I have been feasted and serenaded and invited to make public speeches in the principal towns."

19 Charles A. Dana to Pike, August 25, 1859; Pike Papers.

20 Crawford *Journal*, quoted in N. Y. *Weekly Tribune*, February 11, 1860. "If Bates cannot be nominated," wrote Greeley, whose political judgment was often deplorable, to Schuyler Colfax, "I think our next man is Dayton." Greeley reported from the West that Banks would not do: "The odor of Americanism without the support of Americans." February 3, 1860; Greeley-Colfax.

21 Cf. N. Y. *Weekly Tribune*, February 26, 1859.

building of a Pacific railroad, the passage of homestead legislation, and the immediate admission of Kansas.[22] These sentiments, as the Blairs and other friends exultantly remarked, were as unequivocally Republican as those of any leader.[23]

Yet Bates, too, had his weaknesses, and opponents thrust fiercely at the joints of his armor. While most Missouri Germans knew that he had supported Fillmore in 1856 for reasons quite unconnected with the Know-Nothing platform, many foreign-born voters outside the State viewed his stand in that year resentfully. When the Missouri Republican convention met in March, a German-American demonstration against him disturbed observers in far-away areas. Inasmuch as we depend on the Germans to help carry the western States, wrote E. C. Smith to the economist Henry C. Carey, this ebullition of feeling ought to be conclusive against his nomination.[24] Lyman Trumbull heard from well-informed politicians in the West, such as Gustave Koerner in Illinois and John G. Stephenson in Indiana, that the Germans and Scandinavians would never accept Bates.[25] Germans of Davenport, Iowa, held a meeting in March which formally resolved that his nomination would imply such a desertion of principle that it would compel them to forsake the party. At the same time, the conservatism of the Missourian chilled ardent Republicans who pronounced him an old granny or a wet blanket.[26] Fitz-Henry Warren of the New York *Tribune* spoke for many young men when he said that to carry Pennsylvania, New Jersey, and Indiana he would go almost anywhere for a leader, but not into a cemetery or catacomb.[27] The Chicago *Tribune* warned the party that the selection of Bates would estrange its entire radical wing.[28]

Thus, although on the eve of the convention Seward appeared the leading figure, he lacked the vital quality of "availability" in the conservative States, and although Bates was the chief secondary aspirant, he was equally deficient in "availability" in the radical States. Seward's confidence continued undiminished. On the day that the Chicago convention began its balloting, his friends placed a cannon on his lawn to roar the expected news of his triumph. Bates's hopes ran almost as high. His diary shows that he believed that he was the only man who could carry Missouri and other border areas for the Republicans.[29] Yet no aspirant had a really commanding lead.

22 *Missouri Democrat*, March 21, 1860.
23 N. Y. *Weekly Tribune*, March 31, 1860.
24 E. C. Smith to Carey, March 14, 1860; Carey Papers.
25 J. G. Stephenson, March 25, Gustave Koerner, April 16, 1860; Trumbull Papers.
26 G. A. Nourse, May 13, 1860; Trumbull Papers. E. L. Pierce, April 20, 1860; Sumner Papers.
27 Pike, *First Blows of the Civil War*, 484.
28 Chicago *Tribune*, March 15, 1860.
29 Bates, *Diary*, 105, 106, 122, 127.

[II]

It was this fluidity of the situation which gave opportunity for a new standard bearer whose armor was tighter than that of Seward, Chase, or Bates, and
who stood midway between the radical and conservative wings of the party.
The Democratic schism in Charleston had helped to make the outcome of the
convention unpredictable. It opened up brilliant vistas of success, but it also left
visible some menacing dangers. Most cool observers expected, to begin with,
that the Democrats would reunite in Baltimore. In the second place, the Constitutional Union convention, meeting May 9, nominated John Bell and Edward
Everett on a platform which seemed certain to appeal to the broad belt of border
States. Obviously, the election might be thrown into Congress and thus lost to
the Republicans. They must find a leader who would minimize the chances of
such a catastrophe.

Without foreseeing the outlines of this situation, Lincoln throughout 1859
had done much to meet it. Although not flagrantly pursuing the nomination, he
had prepared the Party to give him serious consideration.[30] During the year, he
had traveled four thousand miles to deliver twenty-three political speeches,
every one of which he might easily have avoided. His friends' plan, in which he
acquiesced, was to make him the second choice of as many delegations as possible. He had written numerous letters to men of potential political usefulness.
In December, he had sent a group of influential Ohioans a carefully prepared
manuscript of the Douglas-Lincoln debates (mainly clipped and pasted reports)
for immediate publication. That same month he had written his short autobiography for Jesse Fell, corresponding secretary of the Illinois Republican Committee, to use in promoting his ambitions. He was gratified when a Pennsylvania
newspaper, the Reading *Journal*, declared that the West might successfully
bring Honest Old Abe forward as its candidate; and when an energetic young
newspaperman of West Urbana (now Champaign), William O. Stoddard, used
his four-page weekly, the *Central Illinois Gazette*, to boom Lincoln as the man
who could carry the Mississippi Valley in a rush of popular enthusiasm. As the
Illinois State Journal took up the cry, Springfield in January witnessed the
formation of a Lincoln Club.

The last week of that month found a number of the best lawyer-politicians
of Illinois in the capital to plead before the Supreme Court and Federal Court.
Under the guidance of Jackson Grimshaw of Quincy, a dozen of them, including secretary of state O. M. Hatch, Leonard Swett, and State Chairman Norman
Judd, who had just returned from Washington, met with Lincoln to discuss

30 Baringer, *Lincoln's Rise to Power*, 159.

plans for gaining him the nomination. After a night and day of reflection, for modesty made him hesitate, he authorized them to place him in the field.[31]

It was significant of Lincoln's sagacity that, when Grimshaw asked if his friends might, on finding the Presidency unattainable, press him for the Vice-Presidential nomination, he replied emphatically: "No!" He thus set his face firmly against the kind of dicker that might end in a Seward-Lincoln or Cameron-Lincoln ticket. It was the highest type of strategy to insist on first place or nothing.[32] Actually, he was not very hopeful. He wrote Norman Judd early in February: "I am not in a position where it would hurt much for me not to be nominated on the national ticket; but I am where it would hurt some for me not to get the Illinois delegates." [33] He meant that it would hurt his prospects for a future senatorial seat. He was anxious to keep his path open in either direction; to the Presidency if possible, to the Senate if not. Judd, conferring with him, suggested an avoidance of controversial local efforts to get delegates distinctly pledged to him, leaving it to State pride to carry resolutions of instruction through the Decatur convention.

While Buchanan was letting the Democratic Party be disrupted, Lincoln had been worrying over the problem of maintaining Republican unity. "Massachusetts Republicans," he had written, "should have looked beyond their noses, and then they could not have failed to see that tilting against foreigners would ruin us in the whole Northwest. New Hampshire and Ohio should forbear tilting against the Fugitive Slave law in such a way as to utterly overwhelm us in Illinois with the charges of enmity to the Constitution itself. Kansas, in her confidence that she can be saved to freedom on 'squatter sovereignty,' ought not to forget that to prevent the spread and nationalism of slavery is a national concern and must be attended to by the nation."

On February 16, the powerful Chicago *Tribune* came out editorially in Lincoln's behalf, as a man equal in ability to any yet named, and more nearly certain than anybody else to carry Illinois and Indiana. Moreover, the *Tribune* urged careful organization; Lincoln clubs should be formed in every precinct, township, and city ward in the State.[34] Though belated in its championship of the Springfield attorney, the newspaper quickly struck some hard blows for him. Young Joseph Medill, part owner and at this moment Washington correspondent, wrote a long letter from the national capital, published February 27, in which he argued that as a leader midway between the radical Seward and the conservative Bates, Lincoln could hew his way to party victory. The journalist

31 *Idem.*, 142, 143.
32 Jackson Grimshaw in Herndon-Weik, *Lincoln*, II, 366.
33 Lincoln, *Works*, I, 598; February 9, 1860.
34 Baringer, *Lincoln's Rise to Power*, 140, 150.

showed it to Republican politicians in Washington, and Seward, seeing it, expostulated vigorously.[35]

Then came the Cooper Union address, already described. The accident of its delivery immediately after Seward's long-studied Senate speech made it (in a sense) a trial of strength with him, as the debates of 1858 had been a trial of strength with Douglas. The millions—for literally they were millions—who read Seward's and Lincoln's efforts together could have no doubt that the prairie statesman, as Seward condescendingly called him, had the more sinewy mind, the surer touch on political realities, and the stronger moral impulse.

In the New England tour which followed, undertaken primarily because he wished to see his son Robert at Phillips Exeter Academy in New Hampshire, Lincoln made speeches in New Haven, Hartford, Providence, Concord, and other towns. At Manchester, New Hampshire, he was presented as the next President of the United States; at Norwich, Connecticut, as the next Vice-President. All his speeches were effective, and that at Hartford was very able. Gideon Welles was much impressed by Lincoln on his visit to the Connecticut capital. After talking with him for an hour in the *Evening Press* office, Welles wrote editorially that Lincoln had been caricatured—that if not Apollo, neither was he Caliban. "He was made where the material for strong men is plenty, and his huge, tall frame is loosely thrown together. He is in every way large, brain included, but his countenance shows intellect, generosity, great good nature, and keen discrimination. He is an effective speaker, because he is earnest, strong, honest, simple in style, and clear as crystal in his logic." That the New England speeches assisted the Cooper Union address in making the Illinoisan much better known in the East than before is unquestionable. Whether they did anything more—whether, for example, a New Hampshire writer is justified in stating that the Concord speech did much to mould sentiment throughout the State in Lincoln's favor—is dubious.

These New England speeches were devoted exclusively, as Lincoln's audiences expected, to the slavery issue. To be sure, he adverted to current troubles in the shoe industry, defending labor's right to strike. Even this, however, bore upon the problem of slavery: "I like the system which lets a man quit when he wants to, and wish it might prevail everywhere." More emphatically than ever before, he spoke of the economic importance of the Southern institution. Involving at least two billion dollars' worth of human property, he remarked, it naturally aroused a strong protective instinct among slaveholders. He also dwelt upon both the magnitude and the irrepressibility of the issue. With one-sixth of the population of the land held to forced labor, how could so great a problem

35 Philip Kinsley, *Chicago Tribune*, I, 105-110; H. I. Cleveland in *Saturday Evening Post*, Vol. 172, pp. 84, 85.

be ignored? Southerners said that if they were just let alone, they would quickly solve it. But essentially they *were* let alone, and they did nothing. Since the system touched the vital future of the nation and its standing in the world, the North simply had to discuss it. "If slavery is right, it ought to be extended; if not, it ought to be restricted—there is no middle ground." All previous efforts to deal with the issue, said Lincoln, had proved failures—partly because they had been small efforts, a plaster too tiny to cover the sore. The Republican plan of restriction, he implied, would be adequate.

Once more, fault could have been found with Lincoln for not saying what he wished done with slavery once it had been bound within an immovable ring— for he certainly hoped for some gradual type of national action. And once more, Lincoln could have replied that one step at a time was enough, and that if the South agreed to restriction it would by implication agree to reasonable further measures. He said he would not act rashly. If he saw a venomous snake crawling in the road, he declared, he would seize a club and kill it; but if he found the snake in bed with his children, that would be a different matter.

Even before Lincoln's eastern appearances, his swelling correspondence showed that he had become a national figure. Particularly after his speeches of 1859 in Ohio and other States, letters had come from political leaders all over the North. Tom Corwin wrote him repeatedly on national affairs. Lincoln exchanged confidential views with Frank P. Blair, Jr., who thought his Columbus speech the best answer yet made to Douglas. Thurlow Weed, for some obscure purpose of his own, had telegraphed Norman B. Judd on October 20, 1859: "Send Abraham Lincoln to Albany immediately." Of course Lincoln did not go. Horace Rublee, half-owner of the *Wisconsin State Journal* and head of the Wisconsin State Committee, sent messages indicating that he had become a warm admirer. From James Speed, a distinguished Louisville lawyer who would later become Attorney-General, came assurances that he would have been glad to see Lincoln in the Senate: "I feel that our rights and institutions would not have been in jeopardy in your hands." The prominent Ohio politician, Samuel Galloway, who felt that Chase would never do, urged the Illinoisan to be unobtrusive but receptive. "Your visit to Ohio has excited an extensive interest in your favor," he wrote on October 13, 1859. Long before the year 1860 began, State Chairman Judd and Editor Ray of the Chicago *Tribune* had concluded that Lincoln would probably be on the next Presidential ticket either in first or second place. And mixed with communications from all the men named we find in the long-sealed papers of Robert Todd Lincoln numerous complimentary letters from obscure people all over the map.

"If I have any chance," wrote Lincoln on March 15, 1860, "it consists mainly in the fact that the whole opposition (*to the Democrats*) would vote for me if nominated." This was in response to Samuel Galloway, who agreed with other Ohio leaders that Lincoln would best satisfy sentiment in their State. During March and April the correspondence of the Springfield attorney was filled with encouraging letters. James F. Babcock of New Haven wrote of the great impression he had made in Connecticut. "Since the [State] election I have heard your name mentioned more freely than ever in connection with the Chicago nominations, and by some who have had other views. . . ." Lyman Trumbull, remarking that Seward seemed very confident but that the situation was uncertain, added that Lincoln had made many friends by his eastern trip, and that nobody had spoken of his speeches but in the highest terms. In a subsequent letter of April 24, Trumbull reported that the Congressional delegations from Rhode Island, Connecticut, New Jersey, Pennsylvania (except Cameron), and Indiana all declared that Seward could never carry their States. David Davis described his conferences in Chicago with "Long John" Wentworth, both eager to see Lincoln named. And J. M. Lucas related that a gathering of fifteen men in a corner of the House of Representatives had taken a straw poll, with the result that seven proved to be for Lincoln, the rest for various aspirants.

It was now easier for the Chicago *Tribune* to declare that no man had ever risen so rapidly to political eminence as Lincoln; easier for scattered eastern sheets to speak of his nomination as a possibility. His principal strength remained in the Northwest, however, and the main result of the New York and New England successes was a reflex effect among more enthusiastic and hopeful Westerners.

As great a turning point in Lincoln's career as the Cooper Union address was the unexpectedly fervent and even riotous State convention in Decatur on May 8, an event which imparted to his cause all the political revivalism of Jackson's and Harrison's day. Thus far nothing had dramatized to the nation the heroic character of Lincoln's rise from backwoods poverty. His years of struggle, while taken as a matter of course in the West where such stories were common, were almost unknown in the East. A versatile Decatur politician named Richard J. Oglesby, a veteran of the Mexican War and a forty-niner, realized that some touch was needed to give their candidate the picturesque and stirring appeal of "Old Hickory" and "Old Tippecanoe." He talked with patriarchal John Hanks, with whom Lincoln had toiled in early days to clear land. When Hanks spoke of rail splitting, Oglesby had an inspiration. The two men plucked from an old fence, twelve miles east of Decatur, two rails which Hanks identified as his and Lincoln's handiwork; Oglesby took some friends into his confidence; and when the convention met he was ready for a spectacular *coup*. Three thousand men, including six hundred delegates, crowded into the improvised convention hall. Amid a tremendous demonstration, Lincoln was lifted over the heads of the mass to a seat on the platform. Then, at the moment when emotion ran highest, down the central aisle marched bearded old

Land Dept Ogle County Illinois

June 14/60

Dear Sir

Above is the Photograph of the next President of the U.S.

We remain very respty yours

Blackman & Packer

Lincoln Becomes the Railsplitter Candidate.

John Hanks and a fellow pioneer bearing two weather-beaten rails, flag-bedecked, with a great banner inscribed:

"Abraham Lincoln. The Rail Candidate For President in 1860. Two Rails From a Lot of 3,000 Made in 1830 by John Hanks and Abe Lincoln—Whose Father Was the First Pioneer of Macon County."

The storm of cheering, with hats, canes, and papers tossed aloft as the crowd surged and shouted, literally brought down part of the canvas roof of the structure. The uproar, continuing for fifteen minutes, was heard by all the wondering citizens of Decatur. Lincoln, yielding to the demand for a speech, explained how, when he first entered Illinois, he helped fell timber, make fences, and erect a cabin on the banks of the Sangamon. These might or might not be his own rails; at any rate, he had made many better ones! As a matter of fact, John Hanks's brother Charles presently wrote the Decatur *Magnet* that the original Lincoln fence had been burned up and replaced by new material. "I think, and am almost certain, that the rails that are now worshipped all over the North as Lincoln rails, were made by poor Bill Strickland, who is now old, blind, and helpless in the Macon County poorhouse." [36]

It had been anticipated that Norman B. Judd, the railroad official and attorney who had written the first city charter of Chicago and who had angrily abandoned the Democratic Party when the Nebraska bill was introduced, would be nominated for governor. Two other candidates, Leonard Swett and Richard Yates, however, obtained respectable support on the first three ballots, and on the fourth Swett released his delegates to Yates, giving the nomination to the eloquent Jacksonville lawyer. Taking the stand, Yates in a brilliant speech declared that he strongly favored the nomination of Lincoln for President. A committee on delegates to the Chicago convention being appointed, it repaired to a neighboring grove to make out its list. This was submitted to Lincoln, who revised it.[37] Thus closed the first day.

The next morning, John M. Palmer leaped to his feet with a resolution instructing the delegates in the Chicago convention to vote as a unit for Lincoln. When a spokesman for Seward's followers in northern Illinois objected, Palmer crushed him in an able speech. The Lincoln instructions were carried unanimously; four notable delegates at large were appointed—Judd, Gustave Koerner, David Davis, and Orville H. Browning; and after adopting a platform, the convention adjourned. It had greatly advanced Lincoln's chances. For one reason, the genuine enthusiasm at Decatur attracted attention all over the Middle West. For another, the carefully selected body of twenty-two delegates would make a hard sustained fight for Lincoln instead of voting briefly for him and then going over to another man. But above all, Oglesby's little drama which brought Lincoln before the country as the Rail Splitter, and thus identified him with all the pioneer virtues and the rousing cause of Free Labor, had a great and fast-widening psychological impact.[38]

The two rails that went down that Decatur aisle proved to be mighty levers. Democracy must be reborn in every generation; and who was so fit to bring about a rebirth in 1860 as this son of the West, who had advanced so rapidly from the axe and maul to leadership in expounding the best principles of the

36 Decatur *Magnet*, quoted in Havana, Illinois, *Squatter Sovereign*, July 21, 1860. See R. P. Morgan, "Birth of the Rail-Splitter Legend," in R. R. Wilson, ed., *Intimate Memories of Lincoln*, 260–267.
37 Arnold, *Lincoln*, 163.
38 Baringer, *Lincoln's Rise to Power*, 180–186.

new party? All over the country, already, men were reading a short biographical article on Lincoln which a Pennsylvania editor had based upon the autobiographical paper sent to Jesse Fell—a paper full of humanly appealing matter:

My paternal grandfather . . . was killed by the Indians. . . . My father . . . removed from Kentucky to what is now Spencer County, Indiana, in my eighth year. We reached our new home about the time the State came into the Union. It was a wild region, with many bears and other wild animals still in the woods. There I grew up. . . . Of course, when I came of age I did not know much. Still, somehow, I could read, write, and cipher to the rule of three, but that was all. I have not been to school since. The little advance I now have upon this store of education, I have picked up from time to time under the pressure of necessity. . . .

At twenty-one I came to Illinois, Macon County. Then I got to New Salem, at that time in Sangamon, now in Menard County, where I remained a year as a sort of clerk in a store. Then came the Black Hawk War; and I was elected a captain of volunteers, a success which gave me more pleasure than any I have had since. I went the campaign, was elated, ran for the legislature the same year (1832), and was beaten—the only time I ever have been beaten by the people.[39]

[III]

If the choice of Charleston as meeting place had been the most unfortunate in Democratic annals, that of Chicago can always be regarded as one of the happiest in Republican history. It was a recognition of the fast-growing strength of the prairies and their increasing attachment to Republican principles. The city was easily accessible by rail or lake, still charming in its semi-rural aspect, with wide dooryards and gardens, and fascinating in the bustling evidences of incessant activity and rapid growth. It now boasted of fourteen miles of dock frontage. From the cupola of the courthouse the visitor could see wide, flat vistas of wooden shops, lawns, and houses (even the magnate William B. Ogden lived in a large white frame dwelling, surrounded by fine trees); long rows of lumber yards on each side of the north and south branches of the Y-shaped Chicago River; out in the blue lake the new lighthouse, and long piers that sheltered steamers and sailboats; the new customhouse and post office; the roomy North Side Market, with drays discharging vegetables, meat, and fish; warehouses, breweries, the city water-works, and imposing hotels; and line after line of glistening tracks leading south, west, and east, all alive with smoking trains. Some delegates visited the shops lining Lake Street, where Potter Palmer's jewelry store was already famous; some dropped into the rooms of the Library Association which Walter L. Newberry had been chiefly instrumental in estab-

39 Lincoln, *Works*, I, 596, 597.

lishing, or the newly founded Historical Society; some went to the Board of Trade rooms to see samples of wheat, corn, sorghum, lumber, coal, and other Illinois products. Many inspected the modish North and South Side residential districts, where not a few families had grounds covering an entire block each.

Chicagoans had a go-ahead spirit. They had raised five thousand dollars, put a little army of carpenters at work on an empty lot at Market and Lake Streets, and thrown up what they called the largest auditorium in the country. The "Wigwam" was useful in itself and valuable as a symbol. Republican leaders hoped to fill the country with big and little wigwams housing party headquarters. The Chicago building, a hundred and eighty by a hundred feet, enclosed a broad wooden platform, a huge rectangular floor facing it, and a spacious gallery running around three sides—the whole seating about ten thousand people. Women of the city, called upon to decorate the building, had festooned the upright beams with bunting, rosettes, and evergreens. A great gilt eagle, a dozen portraits of American statesmen, and six busts adorned the platform. Raw and ugly as the hall was, its abundant windows gave plenty of air and light, its large exits permitted free movement, and it had well-nigh perfect acoustics. Gas lights were ready to furnish a brilliant evening illumination.[40]

Though Wednesday, May 16, was the date fixed for Governor Morgan to call the convention to order, by the previous Sunday the city was bursting with delegates, political friends, and sight-seers. Party leaders and city newspapers had persuaded the railroads to offer cheap excursion rates, while hotels had kept their charges reasonable. A sense that the hour of destiny had struck for the Party and that national history was to be made, together with the eager rivalry of Seward men, Chase men, Bates men, and all the others, brought hosts of onlookers from all quarters of the country and filled them with excitement.[41] All the chief buildings of the city rippled with flags and bunting in the bright May sunshine. Bands had blared on Saturday as the Wigwam was dedicated, and at dawn on Monday drum and bugle again filled the air. Hotel lobbies hummed like hives. Up and down the planked streets, greeted by sporadic bursts of cheering, tramped campaign clubs with banners, transparencies, and emblems. Everywhere, notabilities were being pointed out. Thurlow Weed, flanked by veterans like Moses H. Grinnell and James Watson Webb, with two brilliant young lieutenants, William M. Evarts and George William Curtis, opened headquarters for Seward at the Richmond House. David Davis rolled his portly

40 Caroline Kirkland, ed., *Chicago Yesterdays*, passim; for a Southern impression of Chicago, see N. O. *Picayune*, August 10, 1860; for Isaac H. Bromley's memories, *Scribner's Monthly*, November, 1893.
41 Charles Leib, a man peculiarly gifted in making enemies, had attached himself to Cameron. A. H. Reeder, March 10, 1860; Cameron Papers.

frame about the Lincoln headquarters in the Tremont, grunting placidly or snorting angrily as good or bad news came in; while Judd danced around talking with delegates, and Oglesby, Stephen T. Logan, Leonard Swett, and Joseph Medill conferred on strategy.[42]

It was soon evident, amid this bedlamite confusion, that a critical role would be played by what Party leaders called outside influences; that is, by rival cohorts of shouting, arguing, buttonholing men. The New York managers had brought from their home State thirteen cars of boisterous merrymakers who, with the pugilistic Tom Hyer at their head (men jested about Seward's Hyer-law platform), raised a thunderous racket. The Cameron managers had fetched in an almost equal number of Pennsylvanians, with two bands.[43] Michigan and Wisconsin had large contingents on hand, shouting, pleading, and threatening for Seward. St. Louis trains disgorged a wild body of Bates enthusiasts. It was obvious, however, that in cheering-power the Lincoln hosts held the advantage. Word had been circulated throughout the State that if friends of Old Abe wished to see him nominated, they should be on hand to create the requisite atmosphere of enthusiasm for his name. By thousands they had poured in from Danville, from Bloomington, from Springfield, from Peoria, from Quincy, from Rock Island. Many thousands more had mustered from Chicago and the belt of surrounding towns—Elgin, Aurora, Kankakee, Waukegan. The plan of David Davis's group was to give Lincoln a hundred votes on the first ballot, increase his roster steadily, and meanwhile release an irresistible mass enthusiasm in the hall.[44]

Long before the convention opened, the leaders of the rival groups were exerting themselves frenziedly to convert the wavering, to intimidate the fearful, to bargain with the purchasable, and to outmaneuver, outbluff, and outswap their opponents. Long before it began, delegates were being detached here and corralled there. It was plainly Seward against the field—and the Seward managers, encouraged by the Charleston debacle, were redoubling their efforts. Yet among the arrivals in Chicago were a surprising number of men who believed that it would be fatal to nominate the New Yorker. Given a seat by proxy from Oregon, Horace Greeley was early on the ground to spread doubt and objection. Gideon Welles of Connecticut arrived, armed in hostility to Seward by letters from Senator James Dixon, who stated two emphatic reasons for another candidate. First, Seward could not be elected; and second, if by some miracle he was, his elevation to the Presidency would be a disaster, for

---

42 Clark E. Carr, *The Illini*, 276.
43 Thomas A. Scott of the Pennsylvania Railroad secretly provided free transportation to Chicago for the entire Pennsylvania delegation and its attached persons, three hundred and seventy-six in all. Cameron Papers, April–May, 1860.
44 O. H. Oldroyd, *Lincoln's Campaign*, 71.

he was surrounded by corrupt rascals demanding free access to the treasury.[45] George Opdyke came from New York convinced that party interest demanded the naming of anybody but Seward.[46] Hannibal Hamlin of Maine, while esteeming the New York Senator personally, believed that it would be unwise to nominate him; he had been impressed by Lincoln's power in the debates with Douglas, and after reading the Cooper Union speech began persuading other Maine delegates that Lincoln would be a happy choice.[47]

Amos Tuck of New Hampshire, who had named Lincoln for Vice-President at the convention in 1856, was in Chicago, actively laboring among the New England delegates. He wrote Lincoln on Monday that he was sanguine. David Davis and Jesse Dubois were full of confidence. "We are quiet but moving heaven and earth," they telegraphed Lincoln the day before the opening. "Nothing will beat us but old fogy politicians. The hearts of the delegates are with us."

Nevertheless, as the eve of the convention found Chicago bursting at the seams with its crowds (fifteen hundred people slept in the Tremont House that Tuesday night), Seward maintained his lead. He was sure of more than one hundred and fifty votes on the first ballot out of the whole four hundred and sixty-six, while no other aspirant could count on more than fifty. Samuel Bowles summed up the situation with fair accuracy. Seward was absolutely certain of New York, Michigan, Wisconsin, and Minnesota; fairly certain of Iowa, California, and the greater part of New England. Against him in solid column stood Illinois, Indiana, Pennsylvania, and New Jersey, the leaders stoutly insisting that he could carry none of these States, and that, if he were nominated, the Bell-Everett ticket would make heavy inroads among the Republicans, defeating the party's State and Congressional tickets as well as its Presidential nominee.[48] The States of Ohio, Connecticut, Oregon, and Rhode Island inclined

45 Dixon to Gideon Welles, April 26, 1860; Welles Papers, LC. Dixon liked Seward personally, but wrote: "My apprehension is his administration would be the most corrupt the country has ever witnessed."
46 Opdyke to F. P. Blair, Jr., May 10, 1860; Blair-Lee Papers.
47 C. E. Hamlin, *Hannibal Hamlin*, 339–344. Young James G. Blaine, sent to Chicago as a Maine delegate, agreed with Welles, and did his utmost to convert Lot M. Morrill on the journey westward. What Morrill saw and heard in Chicago quickly brought him over to the Lincoln side. As a result of the labor of Hamlin and Blaine, on the first three ballots Maine gave Lincoln six votes against ten for Seward. Louis G. Hatch, *Maine, A History*, II, 421, 422; David Muzzey, *James G. Blaine*, 31.
48 Weed had made every effort to reach an agreement with the Cameron men. He had written Cameron on April 27 asking for a personal conference in Philadelphia, New York, or Washington; Simon Cameron Papers. Six Pennsylvania delegates were in Chicago as early as May 10, making preparations for the contest to carry Cameron through. They wrote Cameron that they had resolved that when Curtin came, they would put the issue squarely to him; he must stand for Cameron or for Seward. C. Casey to Simon Cameron, May 10, 1860; Cameron Papers. A. K. McClure and A. H. Reeder had been working hard for Cameron, but their willingness to make a prolonged fight was questionable.

toward the opponents of Seward.⁴⁹ The votes of the border States, Delaware, Maryland, and Missouri, were confidently claimed for Bates, while Virginia's delegates would be divided between him and Seward. Bowles indicated that the day might be swayed by a group of doubtful States which, standing in the position of compromisers between the earnest supporters and stubborn opponents of Seward, did not wish to force an unacceptable candidate upon either.⁵⁰

The border, it will be seen, was represented. The arriving delegations included groups from Kentucky, Maryland, and Virginia, where the existence of true Republican organizations was denied, along with a flagrantly bogus group pretending to be from Texas. All these questionable bodies were admitted, even "Texas" being allowed six votes. Meanwhile, much discussion dealt with the question whether the ticket should be nominated by a majority of all delegates seated, or merely of all the delegates present. In the end the majority-present rule won. Leaders of the party, anxious to preserve harmony, yielded to determined pressure in both these matters.

At noon on Wednesday, Morgan brought down his gavel before the largest, most brilliant, and most enthusiastic party gathering yet seen in the country. A galaxy of celebrities was present. The venerable Joshua Giddings, the battle-scarred David Wilmot, the dashing Frank P. Blair, Jr., the brilliant Carl Schurz, the crusading Eli Thayer—these were but a few of the well-known figures. Every corner of the building was jammed. The open doors showed crowds choking the streets. When Morgan moved that Wilmot, the first great battler for freedom in the Territories, be made temporary chairman, a tempest of applause swept the hall.

[IV]

For decades to come, participants were to retell the story of the convention until it became a part of the legendary lore of the republic. At the very outset, as Morgan, Wilmot, and the permanent chairman, George Ashmun, delivered brief speeches, a rapport was established between the thousand delegates and ten thousand spectators which seemed, as by an electric current, to fuse them into a single body in feeling and action. The stirring spectacle presented by the crowd, and its animated response to every appeal, created an irresistible temptation to oratory. While many delegates betrayed their uncertainty as to a

49 Ohio held a peculiar position. Ostensibly for Chase, it was really not with him. "The reason that Chase was so soon dropped," declared Giddings later, "was that his leading friends appointed by his request wanted to substitute Wade for him, and gave out notice as soon as we reached Chicago that we were to give Chase only a complimentary vote, and then go for Wade." See J. L. Sellers, "The Makeup of the Early Republican Party," *Trans. Ill. State Hist. Soc.*, 1930.
50 Springfield *Republican*, May 16, 1860.

nominee, the concourse inevitably began to express its preference; with the result that, in midafternoon of the opening day, correspondents were writing distant newspapers that although half the members seemed in doubt, and though the Blairs were still predicting Bates's nomination, with a Ben Wade movement in formation, Lincoln was rapidly assuming prominence as the head of the opposition to Seward.

Indeed, the New York *Tribune* told Easterners on Thursday morning that according to its regular correspondent, Lincoln seemed likely to be nominated. The Chicago *Tribune* had been striving amain to make converts. On Tuesday, it had carried a column editorial—"Abraham Lincoln, the Winning Man"— giving eight reasons why he should be named. Next day it reprinted the editorial. Its news stories on Wednesday and Thursday conspicuously favored Lincoln, and on Friday the seventeenth another editorial—"A Last Entreaty"— summarized the arguments for the Rail Splitter.[51] The marked antagonism arising between the New Yorkers and Westerners played into the hands of Lincoln's managers. While some of the best men of the Empire State were in Chicago, many rowdies, braggarts, and quarrelsome partisans were also present. As Greeley wrote, they used bad tactics. "Noisy barroom denunciations of anti-Seward men from this State as ingrates and traitors; claims for Gov. Seward not only of the exclusive leadership but even of the authorship of the Republican party; public boasts that ever so much money could be raised to carry Seward's election, and none at all for anybody else, with triumphant queries, 'If you don't nominate Seward, where will you get your money?'— these were the weapons only of the lowest stratum of New York politicians, yet they had a most damaging effect." Westerners replied that *they* had been the first to form a Republican organization, that they did not believe in carrying elections by money, and that they could earn what was needed by splitting rails at fifty cents a day. What was more effective, the Lincoln managers tried to make friends in all delegations, enemies in none.[52]

The principal event of the second day, the adoption of a platform, was lifted to high interest by the economic realism of the document and by a dramatic clash over the incorporation of Jeffersonian doctrine.[53] As an observant young Springfield lawyer, Shelby M. Cullom, later wrote, the platform of 1860 was in sharp contrast with that of 1856. While more conservative in phrasing, it was far more boldly constructive in content. Already, Republican action in Congress and State conventions had dictated a number of the planks;

51 Kinsley, *Chicago Tribune*, I, 115.
52 N. Y. *Weekly Tribune*, May 26, 1860.
53 The platform declared that the Constitution, the rights of the States, and the Union must be preserved. It asserted that every State had the right to determine and control its own domestic institutions, and denounced lawless invasions as the greatest of crimes.

free homesteads, tariff revision, internal improvements, a Pacific railroad, a daily overland mail, the immediate entry of Kansas. The subcommittee which put these doctrines into form included Austin Blair, Carl Schurz, Greeley, and John A. Kasson. Greeley, especially concerned over the homestead resolution, later boasted that he had written it exactly to his liking.[54] A plank assailing any abridgment of rights of citizenship which had heretofore been accorded to the alien-born, vigorous in tone, was the work of Schurz and Gustave Koerner.[55] The tariff plank was put in, one delegate wrote, to satisfy Pennsylvania, and was accepted with some hesitation outside the industrial States.[56] One by one, after midnight, most of the tired committee members retired, until at dawn Greeley and Kasson were left alone to finish. As the editor had to send a dispatch to his paper, Kasson put the last touches to the draft.[57]

The Pennsylvania delegation, traveling to Chicago determined to insist on a strong tariff plank, had been imperious in their demands. They took the attitude already expressed by the Philadelphia *North American*: The convention must understand that it could not carry Pennsylvania and New Jersey unless it stood squarely on protectionist ground. The largest gathering of iron men ever seen in Pennsylvania, representing nearly all ironworks in the eastern part of the State, had met in Philadelphia in March and appointed a committee which drew up stiff protectionist resolutions. Of this committee, three men were delegates to the Chicago convention. When they had found various leaders convinced that party harmony demanded caution, they were depressed. Western members of the platform committee were averse to any mention of the tariff at all, and had some support, apparently, from New England. A New Jersey delegate, Thomas H. Dudley, then made a determined battle in committee to obtain some action; and the result was a compromise plank, calling for a revenue tariff together with "such an adjustment of those imposts as to encourage the development of the industrial interests of the whole country." When the tariff plank was presented in Chicago, the Pennsylvania delegates indulged in a striking demonstration of joy. Privately, however, they were disappointed by the cooing-dove character of the resolution.

Lincoln, it may be noted, would have preferred no tariff plank at all. Just before the convention opened he wrote one Edward Wallace that he was and always had been a Henry Clay tariff man. "I now think," he went on, "the tariff question ought not to be agitated in the Chicago convention; but that all should be satisfied on that point with a presidential candidate, whose ante-

54 Greeley-Colfax Corr., June 20, 1860.
55 Gustave Koerner, *Memoirs*, II, 87.
56 W. C. Noyes foresaw no "serious mischief"; Lieber Papers, HL, no date.
57 A. B. Burk, ed., *Golden Jubilee of the Republican Party*.

cedents give assurance that he would neither seek to force a tariff law by Executive influence; nor yet to avert a reasonable one, by a veto, or otherwise."

The platform as a whole was generally regarded as admirable. It has been said that its mingled idealism and materialism represented the union of Jefferson and Hamilton—or Jefferson and Clay. Everyone liked its negative features—its denunciation of Lecomptonism, popular sovereignty, the movement to revive the slave trade, and disunion. Nearly everyone approved an innovation for which Eli Thayer later claimed credit, replacing the stereotyped Wilmot Proviso doctrine, out of date since the successful battle in Kansas, with a declaration that the normal condition of all Territories was freedom, and that legislation to maintain it was to be passed only when necessary.[58] Even Greeley agreed that Congress need not positively prohibit slavery in a Territory where it could not possibly exist. This was a conservative feature; and the conservatives also dropped the insulting and inaccurate phrase of 1856 about "twin relics of barbarism" from the platform. But Joshua Giddings discerned one fault. The resolutions failed to reaffirm those truths of the Declaration of Independence which had been quoted four years earlier. When he moved to add Jefferson's words upon life, liberty, and the pursuit of happiness to the preamble, conservative members objected that they were inappropriate, and the convention voted Giddings down. In humiliation, the venerable freesoiler rose to leave the hall. As friends clustered about to dissuade him, George William Curtis rose in the midst of the New York delegation. His tall form caught every eye and his rich, musical voice held every ear as he moved to amend the *second* resolution by the words of the Declaration. Chairman Ashmun, irritated, tried to pass on to other business. But Frank Blair supported the young editor and insisted upon a vote.

Will the convention, asked Curtis, go before the nation as rejecting the Declaration of Independence? "I rise simply to ask gentlemen to think well before, upon the free prairies of the West, in the summer of 1860, they dare to wince and quail before the assertions of the men of Philadelphia in 1776." A crash of cheers shook the rafters; the motion was unanimously carried; and ten thousand voices loosed a deafening salvo as Giddings, his snowy head radiantly erect, came back to his seat.[59]

[V]

The third day, Friday, brought the crisis of the struggle over nominations. At dawn, Seward's victory still seemed inevitable to most friends and many foes. Greeley, whose antagonism had become increasingly bitter as the excitement in

58 F. P. Rise, MS Life of Eli Thayer, Harvard Library.
59 Julian, *Giddings*, 372-375; *Harper's Weekly*, August 7, 1875.

Chicago mounted, had telegraphed the *Tribune* during the night that the failure of the opposing delegations to agree on any one man had made it almost certain. The Seward delegates, believing any concentration of the hostile forces impossible, breakfasted with triumphant faces. They made inquiries, in perfect good faith, as to the wishes of the supporters of Bates, Chase, Cameron, and Lincoln respecting a Vice-Presidential candidate. The convention was to open at ten. By eight o'clock the streets were full of people hastening to the Wigwam; by nine that structure was tightly packed, with a great concourse outside. Most of the delegates formed in procession, with bands playing lively airs, and as they trooped into the central area applause greeted every prominent figure. Several politicians were making speeches outside, and while the opening prayer was being offered the roars of their audiences came in recurrent gusts. An electric excitement seemed almost to make the air crackle as the chairman announced that the pending business was a nomination for the Presidency of the United States.

In reality, more had been done to achieve a last-minute union of forces against Seward than Greeley or other observers guessed. The astute leaders of the Illinois delegation, grasping the situation, had been busy all night, laying plans and moving from caucus room to caucus room. Such men as David Davis, Joseph Medill, John M. Palmer, and Dick Yates were a fair match, in energy, resourcefulness, and indomitable determination, for Thurlow Weed, Edwin H. Morgan, and Moses H. Grinnell of the New York delegation.[60] They were being aided by the Republican candidates for the governorship in Pennsylvania and Indiana, Andrew Curtin and Henry Lane, who were convinced that the nomination of Seward would be death to their hopes, while that of Lincoln would mean victory. At one in the morning, Murat Halstead, historian of the convention, saw the pale, haggard Lane racing from room to room in the Tremont House to rally the doubtful. The Illinoisans knew that Evarts, Schurz, and Austin Blair, floor leaders of the New York, Wisconsin, and Michigan delegations, hoped to plunge through to victory in the first two or three ballots. With two hundred and thirty-three votes necessary to nominate, Seward would come within seventy of that total on the first roll call. Could he then be stopped?

Lincoln's supporters believed he could. If to Illinois could be added Pennsylvania, Indiana, and New Jersey (these four States making what Greeley called

60 Arrangements for seating the delegates were in the hands of Judd and Medill. They saw to it that the New York delegation was at one end of the hall, with no State for neighbor that was not already for Seward; and that the doubtful Pennsylvania delegation was at the other end, with the Illinois men flanking it. Medill believed that this device weakened the power of Seward's lieutenants to apply pressure on wavering men. T. E. Strevey in Paul M. Angle, ed., *Papers in Illinois History*, 59, 60. See Leonard Swett's story in R. R. Wilson, ed., *Intimate Memories of Lincoln*, 292–298.

the Malakoff redoubt of the anti-Seward forces), and if enough scattered delegates could be recruited from New England and other areas, Lincoln might be made powerful enough to win. Let him make a strong showing on the first two ballots, and other States would respond.

During their sleepless night, the Lincoln enthusiasts left no measure neglected. They knew the importance of overwhelming the Seward gallery. Davis saw to the preparation of a thousand counterfeit tickets, which were issued to as many men drilled to cheer for Lincoln; and a Boanerges reputed to be able to shout clear across Lake Michigan, with a Stentor hurriedly brought in from Ottawa, were put in charge of this force. Lincoln had sent a paper to headquarters reading, "Make no contracts that will bind me." But as one lieutenant swore and others protested, Davis swept it aside with a curt: "Lincoln ain't here and don't know what we have to meet!" [61]

The Illinois leaders that night addressed two main pleas to the men of Indiana, Pennsylvania, and New Jersey. One was based on party expediency; the ultra-radical Seward could never carry these four crucial States. Curtin, David Wilmot—for some time favorable to Lincoln—and Henry Lane were ready to support this thesis. The other plea embraced an offer of post-election rewards. Necessarily, these offers were made orally and under circumstances of partial secrecy. The evidence is overwhelming, however, that David Davis virtually promised a Cabinet position to Caleb B. Smith, reputedly the most influential Indiana delegate. Smith was more than receptive; indeed, he seems to have laid a little trap to obtain the pledge, for, according to another Indianian, he made Davis believe that unless he got the promise of the Cabinet place, the delegation would plump for Seward—"when the truth was that none of us cared for Smith and after we got to Chicago and looked over the ground all were for Lincoln." [62] The precise moment when a majority of Indiana delegates (many of whom had at first leaned toward Bates) decided to vote for Lincoln cannot be determined. If we may judge from the statements of Carl Schurz, sensitive men immediately on arrival in Chicago found themselves attracted to Lincoln by the popular enthusiasm for him, and repelled from Seward by the low politicians, the champagne and cigars, the free money-spending, and the hole-and-corner whispering which characterized the New York headquarters as dominated by the stealthy-footed Weed. [63]

New Jersey was half won over that Thursday night by sheer force of argument—W. L. Dayton could not be nominated, Seward could not be elected. Pennsylvania presented a harder problem. Forcible Thad Stevens displayed a

61 So says Whitney in *Lincoln the Citizen*, 289. Weed, as spokesman for Seward, had obviously been making promises of future "recognition."
62 Gresham, *Walter Q. Gresham*, I, 110, 111.
63 Schurz, *Reminiscences*, II, 173 ff.

curious preference for the colorless McLean, while others liked Bates as a representative of old-fashioned high-tariff Whiggism. Launching themselves on this uncertain sea, Davis, Koerner, and other Illinoisans used every available plea. It was Koerner's task, aided by Germans in Chicago, to make it plain that Teutonic voters could never stomach Bates, and Davis's part to deal in more substantial considerations.

The Keystone delegates sat late discussing their duty. A special factor perhaps helped to bring the Pennsylvanians over to Lincoln's side. The Rock Island bridge had been constructed by two Pennsylvanians, William L. Scott and his brother-in-law John F. Tracy, men associated in railway building, shipping, and coal mining. Tracy, in fact, had gone to Chicago in 1854, and taken over the extension of the Rock Island Railroad, then a few miles west of Chicago, across the Mississippi and into Iowa. Tracy employed as attorney for the railroad Norman B. Judd, and it was through Judd that Lincoln was made special counsel in the famous bridge case. As it happened, the Chicago convention found a partner of Scott's and Tracy's named Morrow B. Lowry (who had charge of some of their Great Lakes shipping) a delegate from Pennsylvania. Lowry and Judd were good friends. Moreover, Lowry knew Lincoln, and had consulted with him in the bridge case. In after years, Lowry frequently boasted that he had been the active agent in bringing the Pennsylvania vote over to Lincoln.[64] At any rate, about midnight, Davis came down the stairs of the Tremont House from the Cameron rooms, and exultantly told Medill: "Damned if we haven't got them!" [65] As they had apparently been bought and sold once or twice before, this was saying a good deal. He had promised Cameron a Cabinet position. According to A. K. McClure, this pledge also was unnecessary; the delegation had already decided to support Lincoln when the Senator's friends maneuvered Davis into giving the inducement! What is certain is that the promise was made. It was given without authority, and to a man quite unfit for Cabinet position; but in time it was duly honored.

The decision of the Indiana, New Jersey, and Pennsylvania men to support Lincoln destroyed Bates's chances, and laid the foundation for Seward's defeat. At a later date, the various factors entering into this decision were subjected to diverse interpretations. Greeley believed that Indiana, the first to take the plunge, did much to bring Pennsylvania with her. A. K. McClure held that Pennsylvania could never have acted until assured of Lincoln's soundness on tariff revision.[66]

64 John C. Blackford, son of an intimate friend of Lowry's, to author, Seattle, July 25, 1939.
65 T. E. Strevey in Angle, ed., *Papers in Illinois History*, 58, 59.
66 See Greeley's long signed letter, N. Y. *Tribune*, May 26, 1860. Cf. T. M. Pitkin, "The Tariff and the Early Republican Party," MS Dissertation, Western Reserve Univ.

One other witness asserts that the critical moment came when committees from the Illinois, Indiana, New Jersey, and Pennsylvania delegations, meeting in David Wilmot's rooms on the fateful night, took a poll to decide which man, Lincoln, Cameron, or Dayton, had the most support. This is the story told by Charles Perrin Smith, in personal reminiscences deposited in the New Jersey State Library. Early in the week, he relates, a body of New England delegates, headed by John A. Andrew, had called upon the New Jersey delegation. They said that if Seward could not be elected, they would support anyone who could; but, pointing out that the opposition strength was divided among Cameron, Dayton, and Lincoln, declared that unless Illinois, Pennsylvania, New Jersey, and Indiana agreed on a single man, the New Englanders would go into the convention to vote for Seward. Smith states that on Thursday at noon the four doubtful States assembled at the Cameron rooms in an attempt to unite. Reeder presided. It was soon evident that nothing could be done by so large a body. The matter was therefore referred to a committee of three from each of the four States, which sat in David Wilmot's rooms from six until ten without reaching a decision. As a last recourse, one delegate proposed that it should be ascertained which of the three candidates had the greatest actual strength, and could carry the largest number of delegates from the four States, if the other two were dropped. This showed that Lincoln stood in the strongest position; and Pennsylvania and New Jersey then decided to turn to him after the first ballots.[67]

Many stories of these hectic hours are conflicting; many details confused. But the essential facts are clear: That Lincoln's managers fastened upon Indiana, Pennsylvania, and New Jersey as vital; that they established their Malakoff by a judicious combination of alarmist reports and promised rewards; and that they had perfected their position when the sun rose on May 18. It then remained for another factor to make itself felt—the great excited crowd, now an integral part of the convention machinery.

[VI]

The crowd was there; it had flooded into every nook of the Wigwam; it had invaded the stage, reserved for delegates and newspapermen; it milled

67 Some partially corroborative evidence is furnished by a dispatch to the Springfield *Republican* dated Chicago, May 16, afternoon session (Wednesday or first day). This recites that the Massachusetts delegation had organized under John A. Andrew as president. It was formally visited by the Pennsylvania, Illinois, and New Jersey delegations, which informed it that under no circumstances could they accept the nomination of Seward; for by that they would lose the State, Congressional, and local elections. E. H. Kellogg of Pittsfield then proposed that each of the three should submit the names of three men who could carry the State. Illinois presented the name of Lincoln alone; New Jersey those of Dayton, Lincoln, and Banks; and Pennsylvania those of Cameron, McLean, and Lincoln. Springfield *Republican*, May 17, 1860.

in a tumultuous throng about the building, communicating with its members inside by men posted on the roof. What pen, asks one who was present, could adequately describe this alert audience of ten thousand freemen; the low, wavelike roar of its ordinary conversation; the rolling cheers that greeted a popular favorite? There was something irresistibly stirring in its united voice.[68]

A thrill pervaded the concourse as it saw ballots being distributed, and as William M. Evarts rose to make his first nomination—then a process of unadorned simplicity. "In the order of business before the convention, sir," he said, "I take the liberty to name as a candidate to be nominated by this convention for the office of President of the United States, William H. Seward." Long-continued applause followed. Then Norman B. Judd was on his feet. "I desire, on behalf of the delegation from Illinois," he shouted, "to put in nomination, as a candidate for President of the United States, Abraham Lincoln of Illinois." [69] Instantly, the assemblage rose in a deafening response, wild with excitement; men shouting, women waving their handkerchiefs, and a tremendous roar echoing from the masses outside. This continued for several minutes. Then Dayton, Cameron, McLean, and Chase were nominated, each with much milder cheering, and various nominations were seconded. Smith of Indiana offered the second for Lincoln, and Schurz that for Seward.

The competition in applause was evident. "Abe Lincoln has it by the sound now," shouted one man. "Let us ballot!" And Judge Stephen T. Logan of Illinois vociferated: "Mr. President, in order or out of order, I propose this convention and audience give three cheers for the man who is evidently their nominee."

It was high noon as the balloting began. Nobody expected the first poll to do more than indicate the general trends. All the favorite sons received their due tribute—Collamer, Dayton, and others. Bates's following was lamentably small, for he trailed just behind Cameron and Chase, fifth in the whole roster. The two highest votes showed where the battle was to center: Seward, 173½, Lincoln, 102. As yet, the Seward managers did not lose their confidence. Some protesting delegate furnished a brief interruption. Eager for a full trial of strength, the audience growled its impatience, and "Call the roll! the roll!" came from a multitude of throats.

This time, the swing of the tide was unmistakable. The complimentary votes faded away, and the Lincoln column grew longer. Most of Cameron's delegates came to him; so did Collamer's ten; so did six from Chase and McLean. Seward's followers grew sick at heart as they saw their leader held at a practical standstill while Lincoln drew fairly abreast. The racing pencils quickly footed up the

68 Nicolay and Hay, *Lincoln*, II, 270, 271.
69 MS Proceedings, NYHS, 153-155.

totals: Seward, 184½; Lincoln, 181; Bates, 35; scattering, 42. If Lincoln could be kept immovable, there was still a chance that Seward's men might swing over to the other leader reputed to be radical, Chase. But the crowd, wilder than ever in its enthusiasm over Lincoln's gains, was shouting jubilantly. Then, without a pause, the third ballot began.

It had proceeded only to the fourth State, when Massachusetts suddenly changed four votes from Seward to Lincoln; and this heralded the avalanche. Rhode Island gave Lincoln two new votes; New Jersey for the first time gave him eight. Instead of forty-eight from Pennsylvania, he now received fifty-two. Instead of none from Maryland, he had nine—a token that the Blairs had given up Bates and were on Lincoln's side. Seward, losing one vote in Maryland and another in Kentucky, was actually dropping back. Once more the swift pencils of the spectators had the result before it was officially tabulated: Lincoln, 231½, Seward, 180. Some of the New Yorkers were in tears. If two delegates changed their votes, Lincoln was nominated.

"A profound stillness," writes one spectator, "fell upon the Wigwam; the men ceased to talk and the ladies to flutter their fans; one could distinctly hear the scratching of pencils and the ticking of telegraph instruments on the reporters' tables." An Ohio delegate jumped to his chair and announced four new Lincoln votes taken from the Chase column. A pause of one moment ensued; a teller waved his tally-sheet toward the skylight, and shouted a single word; the deep boom of the cannon on the roof threw echoes flying across the city; and from the crowd in the streets came a wild pandemonium of cheers, a wave of sound that mingled with the happy uproar inside the building.[70]

70 When the final total was announced, giving Lincoln 364 votes out of 466, Evarts rose and with a neat speech moved that the vote be made unanimous. The whole scene is described in the MS Proceedings, NYHS, 164–169.

The Four-Party Campaign

THE DISCORDS of Charleston and the enthusiasms of Chicago were both tokens that the country had been carried far along the course that led to sectional conflict. Midway between the two major gatherings, on May 9, the Constitutional Union Party met in Baltimore to try to turn time back; to demand that distracting sectional issues be banished from the national councils. Here Clay's despairing ghost was invoked for almost the last time.

The delegates cherished a momentary hope of playing a decisive role. As the candidacy of Douglas had provoked a Democratic schism, so they believed that Seward's candidacy might cause a Republican split; large sections of both parties then turning to their conservative organization. Nearly all the leaders of the promising Opposition movement of 1858-59 had joined in raising the Constitutional Union banner. Most of them came from the borderland: Crittenden of Kentucky, Rives and Goggin of Virginia, John P. Kennedy of Maryland, and Kenneth Rayner of North Carolina. In New York, a devoted group of adherents was led by Washington Hunt, D. D. Barnard, and James and Erastus Brooks; while in Massachusetts Edward Everett, Amos A. Lawrence, and Robert C. Winthrop lent their assistance. Winfield Scott sympathized with the cause. Clearly, the main strength of the party was among old-time Whigs. In still other respects it smacked of the past, many members being so venerable that opponents derided it as the Old Gentlemen's Party.

For a party of union, it at first showed a somewhat contentious spirit. While a Southern wing, largely survivors of the Know-Nothing organization, wished to nominate Sam Houston, most Northern and border men preferred a veteran Whig. On the second ballot the latter element swept through to victory, naming John Bell by a vote twice that of Houston. The strongest possible candidate, Crittenden, who had worked hard in Washington to organize the party, writing numberless letters and holding many conferences, emphatically insisted that he must not be considered. As he was well past seventy, this was reasonable. Bell, now in his sixty-fourth year, was universally acknowledged to be a man of character, ability, and patriotism, whose long public career had shown great integrity if some vacillation. When Edward Everett was unanimously named for Vice-President, not a few critics declared that he should have been placed first; but actually the convention made no mistake in preferring Bell. Everett, three years older, was a retiring, self-distrustful man, easily intimidated, and lacking in popular appeal. The ticket, which had intellectual distinction, inspired general respect—but no enthusiasm.

Everywhere conservative people, especially merchants, manufacturers, and professional men of old Whig antecedents, expressed high satisfaction with the Constitutional Union nominations, and almost everywhere they added that the party was of no use. Most conservative men were by definition averse to active labor in politics. The fervent unity of the Republicans in Chicago was a body blow to the Bell-Everett group. "All New England is warmly in favor of Old Abe and split rails," Amos A. Lawrence frankly wrote Crittenden.[1] Nor did the Constitutional Union platform satisfy realistic men. Declaring merely for the maintenance of the Constitution, the Union, and the laws, its evasion of the real issues gave it a fossil look; it would have done better for 1824 than for 1860. Nevertheless, the party, with at least some semblance of organization in most of the North and all of the South except South Carolina, set earnestly to work. Representative Boteler of Virginia was chairman of the national executive committee, which numbered John A. Gilmer of North Carolina, Marshall P. Wilder of Massachusetts, and other able men. A scanty newspaper guard, made up of surviving Whig or Know-Nothing sheets, rallied about Bell; the *National Intelligencer*, Louisville *Journal*, Nashville *Republican and Banner*, and the St. Louis *Intelligencer* in the border area being prominent.[2]

[I]

Meanwhile, as the Charleston convention delegates returned home, all responsible Democrats attached to the Union were filled with consternation. "What do you think of matters now?" Richard Malcolm Johnston asked Alexander H. Stephens. "Why," rejoined Stephens, "that men will be cutting one another's throats in a little while. In less than twelve months we shall be in a war, and that the bloodiest in history."

He and many other Southerners would have been glad to see the party unite behind Douglas and the Cincinnati platform.[3] To an apprehensive group at Macon, he sent a long public letter urging that the slave-code demand be dropped and that delegates be sent to the regular convention when it met again

---

1   May 25, 1860; Crittenden Papers, Duke Univ.
2   See pamphlet, "Bell and Everett," Washington, 1860.
3   Johnston and Browne, *Stephens*, 355, 356.

in Baltimore. Two other leading Georgians, Herschel V. Johnson and Governor Joseph E. Brown, took the same stand. From Democrats of all the border States, from the Soulé men in Louisiana, from the Forsyth forces in Alabama, from followers of Thomas B. Flournoy in Arkansas, and from numerous Texans, rose a demand for party reunion even if it meant accepting the Little Giant. In Washington, many of the fire-eaters were so visibly abashed by the disruption that Senator Hammond concluded that their big talk had been bosh.

Yet a swift-running tide was carrying the dissevered halves of the party further apart. The breach was essentially irreparable. The popular sovereignty Democrats of the North were vibrant with anger over what they termed party treason; the radicals of the South were equally savage over what they considered a threat to their sectional safety. While Dean Richmond, his blood up, declared he would stand or fall with the Northwest, the Dubuque *Herald* and other Douglas sheets of that section called the Yancey-Davis-Slidell crew a disunionist faction who should get out and stay out. Meanwhile, Robert Toombs heartily endorsed the bolt, and advised against any concession. Rhett's Charleston *Mercury* and Yancey's Montgomery *Advertiser* were declaring that the South would never accept a popular sovereignty candidate or platform. The Administration, with the *Constitution* chuckling over Douglas's failure, and Howell Cobb asserting that Southerners must never yield to the man, took the same ground. Both sides wanted to bring delegates from all the States together again in Baltimore. But while Douglas's managers wished to gain enough votes to nominate him, the Administration forces wished to nominate some other man on a platform embodying the Davis resolutions.

As soon as the convention ended, Washington boiled with political activity. A number of Southern extremists hoped that nothing whatever would be done to heal the schism; that the bolting delegates would meet in Richmond as practically a Southern convention; that they would present a united front for the slave-code demand; and that they would nominate Jefferson Davis and Joseph Lane, or two men like them.[4] A much larger body, backed (so far as we can determine) by dominant Southern sentiment, desired a general return of delegates to the Baltimore convention, where they might place such a man as Hunter on a platform acceptable to the South. Nine Southern Senators and ten Representatives signed an address advising the bolters to defer or abandon their Richmond gathering, go to Baltimore, and unite with other Southerners in procuring a satisfactory platform; and the *Constitution* applauded this plan.[5] They hoped that New York would assist in nominating a conservative man. Douglas's friends meanwhile strove to hold their old delegates and maneuvered to

4 Rhett, May 10, 1860; Porcher Miles Papers, Univ. of N. C.
5 "Tiber" in N. O. *Picayune*, May 16, 1860.

win new ones. Amid this jockeying, an acrimonious debate sprang up in the Senate.

It was begun by Jefferson Davis, who—ailing and haggard—spoke on May 8 for his long-pending resolutions. Containing no new ideas, his address was resolutely defiant. He would not surrender a comma of the radical platform. He asked for no immediate legislation, he said. (He knew well that he could not get it if he did ask, for the Democratic Senate no less than the Republican House would have refused to pass it. A. G. Brown, striving for several months to push forward a slave-code bill, had been unable to get a second for it, and Clingman of North Carolina avowed his belief that not a single Senator was willing to vote for it.) But Davis did ask that territorial legislatures be made to understand that Congress would not let them interfere with rights of persons or property guaranteed by the Constitution, and would apply a remedy if they did interfere. "We claim protection, first, because it is our right; secondly, because it is the duty of the general government." His arrogance grew more pronounced when he said that if safeguards, once demanded, were denied, Mississippi would secede. As for the Republican Party, its advent to power would be the signal for a break-up of the Union. They were asked, he scornfully remarked, to stand still and wait for an overt act. "Overt act! Is not a declaration of war an overt act?" We make no threat, he said; we only give the North warning.[6]

Douglas was waiting for him. He sought no quarrel, but when men urged him to "give the infernal scoundrels the devil," he said he would reply to Davis and Davis alone. Speaking again on May 17, the Mississippian declared that he would sooner have an honest man on a rickety platform than an untrustworthy candidate on the best platform possible. This was a thrust at the Little Giant. Douglas instantly saw the opening it presented. Indeed! he snorted. "Why break up the party on the platform, if you do not think that is of any consequence? . . . Why did you not tell us in the beginning of this debate that the whole fight was against the man, and not upon the platform?"[7]

Douglas's principal speech, delivered May 16–17, upheld his old thesis that non-intervention in the Territories was the historic Democratic doctrine, cherished until recently by all the chief party leaders. He too was ill and tired; during his recent disappointments he had begun drinking again; and, unsupported by any Senator except Pugh, he felt terribly alone. Going over familiar ground, he began less vigorously than usual. But he always gained new life from battle; and, as he went on, his ringing voice, his lucid argument, his energy

6 *Cong. Globe*, 36th Cong., 1st Sess., 1937–194:.

7 *Cong. Globe*, 36th Cong., 1st Sess., 2155, 2156. J. Hanly Smith sent Stephens his impression of Douglas's speech. "He has utterly demolished Jeff Davis—putting him under his heel and grinding him to powder. . . . As far as debate is concerned it is the grandest triumph of his life." May 19, Stephens Papers, LC.

fierce as a lion rending its prey, gave the address tremendous polemic force. He had arranged a dramatic effect. At intervals, he paused for a citation proving the adherence of some Democratic champion to non-intervention doctrine, and Pugh's crisp voice was heard reciting an apposite quotation from Daniel S. Dickinson, Franklin Pierce, Governor Winston of Alabama, the Florida legislature, a Georgia Democratic convention, President Buchanan, and even Yancey. This antiphonal chorus was impressive. Douglas made room for a frank revelation of personal feeling. He had been removed from his committee chairmanship in 1858, he said, because he had uttered statements identical with the public utterances of Buchanan and Breckinridge in 1856. A senatorial caucus had read him out of the party because he had espoused the Democratic platform of that year. He had fought that proscription until he had won a victory. "The Charleston convention affirmed the same platform. I am no longer a heretic. I am no longer an outlaw from the Democratic Party." [8]

In a rattling exchange of bitter personalities with Davis, Judah P. Benjamin, and others, the Illinoisan argued that he had been the choice of a majority in Charleston, declared the slave-code plank a novel invention brought forth for selfish purposes of the cotton kingdom leaders, and arraigned Yancey's avowed scheme "to precipitate the cotton States into revolution." Benjamin retorted that Douglas would not have had a majority but for the coercion of the unit rule in the New York, Indiana, and other delegations. In view of the Administration's use of patronage to capture delegates, this was not very impressive. When Davis declared that the seventeen certainly Democratic States were for the slave-code platform at Charleston, and that the sixteen States offering the Douglas platform did not include one that was surely Democratic, Douglas checked him resentfully. Maryland had opposed the Douglas platform at Charleston; was she surely Democratic? She had voted against Buchanan in 1856. Tennessee had opposed the Douglas platform; was she always Democratic? She had voted against Pierce in 1852, and of her ten Congressmen, only three were now Democrats. Kentucky was on Davis's list; yet Kentucky too had voted against Pierce in 1852. Illinois had never once failed the Democratic Party in a Presidential campaign. Could Davis say as much for Mississippi? He could not, for the Whigs had once carried the State. [9]

By these acrid defiances the gulf between the two factions was deepened and the failure of the impending convention at Baltimore rendered more probable. Various Southerners, including Benjamin, announced that the cotton kingdom delegates would arrive with unaltered instructions and a firm determination to wear the Northern Democrats into compliance. Mr. Benjamin is mistaken, re-

8 *Cong. Globe.*, 36th Cong., 1st Sess., App., 301–316.
9 *Cong. Globe.*, 36th Cong., 1st Sess., 1937; 1966; 2120–2122; 2143–2146.

torted Pugh, "if he supposes that the men who stood there at Charleston for two weeks in that atmosphere voting down your resolutions again and again, and voting for Stephen A. Douglas, are going to be tired when it comes to Baltimore, which is a much more agreeable atmosphere for them." [10]

[II]

The course of events inside the Southern States had meanwhile been highly interesting. Would the people support the bolters? Would they, even while supporting them, send them back to the new regular convention in Baltimore? Thus far the slave States stood divided. Delegates of eight of them had withdrawn at Charleston; delegates of seven, counting Delaware, had remained. It seemed evident that majority sentiment in the seven States and at least a strong minority sentiment in the others hoped for party reunion on a compromise basis; the Cincinnati platform, say, with a Southern nominee. Important Democratic journals of the upper South—the Richmond *Enquirer* and *Examiner*, Louisville *Courier*, and others—called for such a solution. The Nashville *Union and American* asked for the rejection both of the slave-code plank and the candidacy of Douglas.[11] Deep in the Lower South, such newspapers as the Montgomery *Confederation*, which declared that the issue of union or disunion was now drawn, implored all the Southern States to send delegations to Baltimore.[12] Stephens favored such action. To this course, Yancey, Rhett, and other extremists were strongly opposed. They declared the Cincinnati platform unacceptable because it was open to two interpretations; and they believed that the Douglas men would never yield but would try to force the Southerners in Baltimore to come to Canossa.

In the end, all of the bolting States but one decided to send delegates to the Baltimore gathering. South Carolina alone, swayed by Rhett, Porcher Miles, and

10 *Ibid.,* 2247.
11 The Wilmington *Weekly Journal* (May 3, 10, 17) was emphatic in condemning the bolters and in declaring its willingness to accept Douglas as candidate if justice were done the South. "Shall we leave the gallant barque to seek for safety in a cockboat? Are fifty-two seceders the 'Constitutional Democracy,' simply because they choose to assume that name? Not at all! Not at all!" It appealed to the Douglas men to withdraw the Illinoisan, and work for complete harmony at Baltimore. The New Orleans *Picayune* declared that Louisiana sentiment was overwhelmingly against a separate convention in Richmond, and for a return to Baltimore. Few were prepared to meet the issue presented by Yancey. "Louisiana will not sustain disunionism. However strongly she may feel the aggressions of a hostile Northern majority, she is true to the Constitution and the Union, and will continue so as long as she can maintain that position with honor. She will never secede, or cooperate with friends of secession, in view simply of threatened wrong, but will wait for overt acts." May 15, 1860.
12 Weekly *Confederation*, May 12, 1860; Phillips, *Toombs*, 191.

Gist, stood out, refusing to send representatives anywhere but to Richmond.[13] In Texas, the State committee reaccredited the former delegation to both Baltimore and Richmond. Similar action was taken by State conventions in Georgia and Florida, though about one-tenth of the Georgia convention withdrew and elected a separate, contesting, delegation for Baltimore alone. In Louisiana and Alabama spectacular fights developed. The opposition elements in these States, led by Pierre Soulé and John Forsyth, were outraged by what had happened in Charleston. When the Slidell forces reconvened the Louisiana State convention, commended the delegates, and sent them to Baltimore, Soulé flew to arms. Not intimidated by an enthusiastic Southern Rights mass meeting in New Orleans, he called an equally vociferous mass meeting of popular sovereignty men. This body convoked an opposition convention, which sent its own delegation to Baltimore.[14] Events followed much the same course in Alabama. The Yancey forces, dominating the State convention, approved the acts of the delegates in Charleston, and appointed a largely identical body to go to Baltimore and Richmond. On the same day, and in the same city of Montgomery, an opposing convention led by Forsyth and ex-Governor John A. Winston chose a contesting delegation for Baltimore.[15]

Most Douglas men, meanwhile, were adamant. They would yield nothing to seceders. The Charleston convention had declared the seats of the bolters vacant and called on the cotton States to elect new delegates. W. A. Richardson, who would be Douglas's floor manager again in Baltimore, said that if any seceders got into the convention without a reelection, his own self-respect would compel him to leave it. He had flatly told an agent of Secretary Cobb that the issue had been drawn between union or disunion, and that he was on the union side. Senator Pugh took the same attitude. These Southern dissidents have no business in Baltimore, he told the Senate, for they have left the party. "I will sit and vote until the fourth day of March, 1861, against allowing one man of them to come back again, unless he is newly elected as a delegate."[16] As most of the

13 The second Columbia convention in South Carolina was full of men of strong secessionist proclivities. The irreconcilables elected Rhett to Richmond, and the three other delegates at large. They were left in full control. But this was only after a vicious fight. Bitter feeling was aroused, and the State was left deeply divided.
14 Dumond, *Secession*, 65 ff.
15 Forsyth and Winston in Alabama were supported by J. J. Seibels of Montgomery, who was now certain that Yancey, Rhett & Co. aimed at breaking down the Union and creating a Southern Confederacy. He was much pleased by the opposition convention—"one of the most numerously attended, talented, and respectable bodies of men ever convened in Alabama." Our friends, he reported to Douglas on June 5, are in glorious spirits. Douglas Papers.
16 *Cong. Globe*, 36th Cong., 1st Sess., 2247. H. B. Payne wrote Douglas that the Northwestern delegates would stand firm to the last; "aut Caesar aut nihil." Regarding Virginia as of critical importance, he was anxious for Richardson to bargain with Hunter. "He can safely promise him anything from the Northwest in the future if he will now play the man." May 16; Douglas Papers.

cotton States were returning their original delegations, this question of readmission generated intense feeling.

[III]

It was a hot Monday morning, June 18, when the convention opened in the Front Street Theatre in Baltimore. Caleb Cushing, hearty, smiling, quick-witted, once more served as chairman. Howard of Tennessee no sooner offered a resolution that the sergeant-at-arms be instructed to admit all delegates of the convention as originally constituted at Charleston than a storm of mingled hisses and cheers arose. While Southerners applauded, the Douglas men manifested unalterable opposition. An angry quarrel seemed about to break forth. Sanford E. Church of New York proposed that the title of seceders be submitted to the committee on credentials, and that all delegates who were admitted be bound in honor to abide by the action of the convention and support its nominees.[17] This time, Douglas's followers loosed a burst of applause, while the cotton State men —who would submit to no conditions of loyalty—hissed. Clearly, the factions were at swords' point, and while Cushing rebuked the demonstrations, fierce words and gestures expressed the sectional bitterness. After a wrangle of three hours, the convention adjourned until five o'clock so that, as one member said, it might harmonize—a word which provoked an ironic laugh.

It was generally understood that the readopted Cincinnati platform could not be changed at Baltimore. The North could not yield on that point without dishonor; and the platform was fair to all sections. The real issue was the candidate. Ben Butler and other New England politicians hoped to have Horatio Seymour nominated for President, with Alexander H. Stephens for Vice-President. Some New York delegates shared this wish. But William S. Holman wrote his friend Allen Hamilton from Washington on May 15 that no Democrat could be elected except Douglas. "His friends and he himself count with absolute confidence on his receiving the nomination at Baltimore, and that the platform will remain unchanged."

From its bad beginning the convention went on to worse, as the committee on credentials fought and hesitated. In its first three days it did little except make the party ludicrous. Republican newspapers teemed with jeering articles. The people of Baltimore, who had hoped for a love feast followed by general jubilee, grew more and more disgusted. Twice or thrice a day, the convention would solemnly assemble; ladies in crinoline, newspapermen, prominent citizens, and idlers would fill the gallery; and then the delegates would adjourn. At noisy evening meetings rival groups listened to inflammatory speeches. Douglas men

17 *Proceedings, Charleston and Baltimore,* 160.

assailed the "disunionists" while Southerners attacked the "nigger lovers." Yancey, at hand to stir up trouble, declared that his opponents were ostriches, hiding their heads in the sand of popular sovereignty, all unaware that their great, ugly, ragged, abolition body was exposed.

By the third day, the shrewdest observers had divined the probable course of events. Greeley, or somebody equally perspicacious, inserted in the New York *Tribune* a remarkable forecast. New York delegates, he wrote, had been in a difficult situation; for if they voted to reject the seceders at Charleston they broke with the South, while if they voted to reject the new claimants under Soulé, Forsyth, and others, they broke with the Northwest. But a great light had just dawned upon them with the discovery that if they killed Douglas, his devoted friends were resolved to kill Horatio Seymour, so that they would lose the fruit of their meditated treachery. They were now resolved to go straight for Douglas, voting out the seceders and voting in the new Douglas delegates from the Lower South. Thereupon Cotton would bolt and make a ticket of its own, while Douglas would be nominated by the remainder of the convention.[18]

This was almost precisely what happened. On Thursday morning the credentials committee presented two reports. The Douglasite majority proposed to exclude the Louisiana and Alabama bolters, divide the Georgia seats evenly between seceders and new contestants, and admit a number of newcomers from Arkansas and other States; they were ready to let in all the original delegates from Texas and Mississippi, and most of those from Arkansas. The minority report, a document of great ability, provided for the admission of the original delegates from the Lower South. It argued that the convention had no right to declare seats vacant when a delegation withdrew, for bolting was not resignation; a valid resignation must be addressed to the appointing power. This statement produced a strong effect on a number of wavering delegates, and the New York delegation took time to confer. In the end, however, Dean Richmond and most others resolved to stand by Douglas, so that under the unit rule all thirty-five New York votes were cast for the majority report.

Friday, the twenty-second, after all the interminable waiting, witnessed a spectacular explosion. Amid intense excitement, the minority report was rejected by 150 to 100½.[19] The majority report was then taken up, part by part. The vote for replacing the Louisiana seceders by Pierre Soulé's contingent was emphatic—158 to 98. The vote to replace the Alabama bolters by Forsyth's group was 148 to 101½. Only in dealing with Georgia was the report altered, for here New York united with the Southern men in approving the admission of the

18 N. Y. *Tribune*, June 21, 1860.
19 Dumond, *Secession*, 86.

entire regular delegation. The convention then adjourned until evening. Since the New York delegates were perturbed and might vote for reconsideration, some hope for a reconciliation persisted. Dean Richmond had in his pocket a letter which Douglas, doubtless in anguish of spirit, had written at eleven o'clock on Wednesday night. The unity of the party and the maintenance of its principles, declared Douglas, were more important than the nomination of any man; and if his enemies were determined to destroy the Democracy and perhaps the nation rather than see him elected, he would withdraw in favor of some other reliable Union-loving Democrat of non-interventionist views. W. A. Richardson had a similar letter. The story had gone around Washington that after Douglas withdrew, Alexander H. Stephens would be brought forward and nominated.[20] But it was too late; resentments had again risen too high. Neither letter was made public. When the convention resumed work, it was in an atmosphere of doom.

The rattle of Cushing's gavel; the putting of the question; the steady march of the vote against the Southerners—and then the tall, spare form of Russell of Virginia, monotonously chanting "Mr. President!" caught every eye. Shouts of "Order!" and the frowns of the chair could not stop him. He announced in measured words that a large majority of the Virginia delegation had instructed him to say that they would no longer participate in the convention, and directed him to bid it a respectful adieu. This was the fateful turning point which all had feared, and the gathering listened in awe-struck silence. Then another voice broke the stillness, as Anderson of North Carolina gave notice that sixteen of his State's twenty delegates were withdrawing. Ewing of Tennessee succeeded him, announcing that his delegation was retiring to confer, and probably would not return. California and Oregon also departed. The Kentucky and Missouri delegations asked time to consult; some Marylanders declared they would share the fate of the South; and sixteen of the twenty-six Massachusetts men left to determine their course.

The disruption of the party was now complete. Other voices were heard— voices of confession, of explanation, of denunciation, of lamentation.[21] The members, wearied with excitement, adjourned at eleven. Thus ended all hope of Democratic victory, and, as many believed, of averting disunion.

The last day, Saturday, June 23, witnessed the resignation of Caleb Cushing,

20 J. Hanly Smith, July 6, 1860; Stephens Papers, LC.
21 Among those who spoke was W. B. Gaulden of Georgia, who said that he would remain in the convention. He added that he was a "nigger man," and gloried in the term. He had boasted at Charleston of the newly-imported Africans whom he owned. Now he praised Virginia as a nigger-breeding State, and when a Virginia delegate called him to order, he said that he meant no offence; he was a "nigger-breeder," Georgia was a "nigger-breeding" State, and he was proud of the business. N. Y. Tribune, Baltimore correspondence dated June 23.

whose agile departure by a side door was hailed with cries of "Good!" and "Now we shall have a fair chairman!" It witnessed much speechmaking, including Pierre Soulé's brilliant denunciation of the Slidell-Yancey men as an unscrupulous combination of politicians and traitors. This speech was the climax of Soulé's career, his last public service; for before him lay nought but disaster and final insanity. Above all, the last day witnessed the nomination of Douglas. On the first ballot, with 212½ votes cast, he received 173½; and on the second, 180½.[22] A deafening roar saluted the result. As the news was telegraphed over the country, followers organized celebrations in cities from Boston to Chicago and St. Louis. That evening in Washington, a procession marched to Douglas's house and elicited a brief speech. "Can the seceders," asked the Senator, "fail to perceive that their efforts to divide and defeat the Democratic party, if successful, must lead directly to the secession of the Southern States? I trust that they . . . will return to the organization and platform of the party before it is too late to save the country." Benjamin Fitzpatrick had been nominated for Vice-President, and when he declined, Herschel V. Johnson was chosen by the National Committee in his place.[23]

Meanwhile the bolters in Baltimore, with other Southern delegates who had not applied for admission or had been excluded, had gathered at noon Saturday in the Maryland Institute, and elected Caleb Cushing chairman of a new convention. Here Yancey was the ruling spirit. He had previously met in Richmond with something less than a hundred delegates to the Constitutional Democratic convention, a body which had accomplished virtually nothing. He had then pursued his way to Washington, where George Sanders made the preposterous suggestion that he accept the Vice-Presidential nomination on the Douglas ticket, reinforcing it with an intimation that Douglas's health was so bad that Yancey would soon succeed to the Presidency. He had been busy in the background at Baltimore. Now he was in his element as two hundred and thirty-one delegates from nineteen States (New York and Missouri represented by only two each) gathered for a briskly efficient session. A slave-code platform was unani-

22 The number of regularly elected and accredited delegates after the withdrawals was but 166½ votes, representing eleven States. Counting the irregular delegates seated from Louisiana and Alabama, the Soulé and Forsyth men who really had a certain title, thirteen States were represented with 182½ votes. Other irregulars and withdrawn delegates present as spectators were counted to bring the total up to 212½ votes. See Dumond, *Secession*, 89–91.

23 J. Hanly Smith states that Robert Toombs brought about Fitzpatrick's declination. "He got Mrs. Gwin and others to see Mrs. Fitzpatrick, who told her the Governor would be eternally ruined if he accepted—got her to crying until he promised to decline. I was at Brown's when the telegraph announced Fitz's nomination. I was beside Pugh of Alabama who went up to Fitz's room to find out what he was going to do. He came down and told me that Fitz accepted—he had just seen him and had it from his own mouth." August 18, 1860; Alex Stephens Papers, LC.

mously adopted, and on the first ballot the reluctant John C. Breckinridge and Joseph Lane were nominated for the Presidency and Vice-Presidency.[24]

Then on Sunday the tumult in Baltimore died away. During the turmoil and excitement, neither faction had been able to estimate the long-term effect of its own actions. As they caught the trains home, the delegates could quietly reflect upon their deeds and try sadly to calculate the result.

[IV]

Thus the campaign of 1860 began. It was a campaign full of color as "Wide Awakes" paraded and orators thundered; a campaign packed with emotion, especially in proud communities of the Deep South, but lacking all the ordinary excitements of close rivalry. The country had the sensation of watching one of the old double dramas of the Elizabethan stage, a play within a play; the outer drama determining whether Lincoln, Breckinridge, or Douglas should gain national leadership, while the far more fateful inner drama decided whether the republic should be torn in twain. The New York *World* remarked that the party battle was the tamest since Monroe had been sent to the White House. In one sense this was true; but in another sense men who watched the banners sway, the fireworks soar, and the fife-and-drum corps march, divined a crisis working yeastily beneath all this gaiety, a cataclysm almost ready to break. These observers could but watch, for events were getting out of control.

The campaign was quieter than the Frémont-Buchanan struggle for a variety of reasons: because the existence of four parties, with a constant effort to make alliances in various States, rendered it confusing; because no clear-cut practical issue (the fate of slavery in the Territories being certain anyhow) separated any two parties; because the Republicans had lost their first picturesque *élan;* and above all, because the result of the election was fairly certain from the outset—Lincoln would win. Nevertheless, Fate brooded over the scene.

Of the four candidates, three were familiar public figures. Douglas for ten years had been in the very center of the national stage. Bell, who had entered Congress while J. Q. Adams sat in the White House and had defeated Polk for the speakership in 1834, was a veteran scarred by many an engagement. As a Whig, he had held the secretaryship of war under Harrison, and had thereafter been in the Senate for a decade. As for Breckinridge, the fact that he was not yet forty did not mean that he was little known. He sprang from a noted family; his grandfather had been Attorney-General under Jefferson, his father a leader

24 Again J. Hanly Smith: "Mr. Toombs induced Breck to accept—asserted that he would carry the whole South like a storm, and that in less than forty days he would have the field clear for himself—Douglas being withdrawn." *Ibid.*

of rare promise whose career had been ended by death at thirty-four. He had made his political debut in dramatic fashion, reaching Congress in 1851 from Henry Clay's district by defeating a strong Whig opponent. A capable record in the House had prefaced his election as Vice-President in 1856.

Of this trio, Douglas alone, iron-willed, sleeplessly active, and holding a constructive vision of the nation's future, possessed great intellectual power and force of character. Bell was popularly assumed to be less impressive than his associate Everett, and, as Greeley suggested, Everett was respectable without being commanding. What most distinguished Bell was the judicial balance of his temper. Every American interested in public affairs knew that, though he and his wife were large slaveholders, he had always taken a conservative and nationalist position. He had supported Taylor's policy in 1850, had opposed the Kansas-Nebraska bill, and, in calm disobedience to the instructions of his home legislature, had voted against Lecompton. He had been reviled in the Lower South and applauded in the Northwest. But, while a man of principle, he was a lesser Clay in a time when not even a greater Clay could have succeeded. Breckinridge possessed far more fire and energy. More than six feet tall, straight as an oak, with a youthful dash that made him seem more a Highland chieftain than a serious legislator, he brought to the Senate debates a high-bred impressiveness of speech and manner. But he lacked originality, and, as a colleague later wrote, was to be grouped not with the constructors of institutions, but with those who fashion and polish what others design.[25]

The relatively unknown candidate was Abraham Lincoln. Although most literate Americans had read at least some fragments from his speeches, of the man himself the vast majority of Easterners and Southerners knew nothing. The initial tendency in hostile quarters was naturally to depreciate him, the Washington *Union* declaring that so insignificant a nominee could never carry New York and Pennsylvania, and the Albany *Atlas and Argus* saying that the first news of the choice in Chicago had been regarded as a hoax. But a fairer view quickly supervened. The great Know-Nothing organ, the New York *Express*, pronounced him a much better nominee than Frémont and a wiser selection than Seward. The New York *Sun*, Democratic but close to the masses, hailed him as a strong candidate, certain to make a good President. Although James Russell Lowell expressed regret in the October *Atlantic* that the more advanced New Yorker had not been named, Douglas was emphatic in telling a group of Washington Republicans that they had made no mistake: "Gentlemen, you have nominated a very able and a very honest man."

Curiosity regarding his personality and views was intense, and journalists and party leaders hastened to supply all the information they could find. That

25 H. L. Dawes, "Two Vice-Presidents," *Century Magazine*, July, 1895.

his self-made career, homely virtues, and original vein of thought had a broad potential appeal to the masses was evident to all. The Republican editors, led by Medill, Bryant, Greeley, and Bowles, at once emphasized the log cabin, flatboat, and country store background; they all described the scanty schooling, the eager pursuit of knowledge, and the development of a tough, sinewy, intensely logical mind. On the morrow of the nomination, the New York *Tribune* struck the general keynote by hailing him as "a Man of the People, raised by his own genius and integrity from the humblest to the highest position, having made for himself an honored name as a lawyer, an advocate, a popular orator, a statesman, and a Man." [26]

"If Lincoln should be elected," said a highly respected Democrat, "he will be a mere nullity in the Administration." (So went a newspaper paragraph the week of the nomination.)

"It strikes me," answered a Republican who heard the observation, "that a man who by his own genius and force of character has raised himself from being a penniless and uneducated flatboatman on the Illinois river to the position which Mr. Lincoln now occupies, is not likely to be a nullity anywhere."

Springfield was forthwith invaded by reporters and political visitors who labored amain to diffuse a correct understanding of the country lawyer on whom fate had so suddenly laid her finger. George Opdyke, soon to be mayor of New York, published in Bryant's *Evening Post* a significant vignette. He found Lincoln living in a house that was handsome but not pretentious, its rooms neatly but quietly furnished, and its library holding long rows of books. The candidate received callers with an urbanity which Opdyke found surprising; for if awkward abroad, at home he appeared easy if not graceful, and his conversation was fluent, agreeable, and polite. What was of more importance, his talk reflected an acute, decided, and original mind; he had views of his own, founded in the main on sound common sense, though now and then a striking phrase revealed some original insight. [27]

Very similar was the letter which the New York *Herald* published from a Springfield correspondent. He, too, found Lincoln in a dignified, comfortable residence suitable to a gentleman of means. He thought the candidate far from ugly, for when engaged in earnest conversation his features lightened into a highly engaging expression. Learning that the townsfolk all admired him, he quoted a typical citizen. "He is honest, talks sense, and is not too proud to sit down upon his doorstep in his shirt sleeves and chat with his neighbors." [28] The correspondent of the Baltimore *Patriot* dwelt upon Lincoln's patient

26 N. Y. *Weekly Tribune*, May 26, 1860.
27 Nevins, *Evening Post*, 263, 264.
28 N. Y. *Herald* correspondence, dated August 8, 1860.

shrewdness in dealing with crowds of callers and floods of mail. His intimate friends, aware that he had a deep insight into human nature and a sound judgment of men and motives, remarked that he had astonished them by his dexterity in meeting these new burdens.[29] He concealed an impatience which "Billy" Herndon noted:

"Lincoln is well and is doing well—has hundreds of letters daily—many visitors every hour from all sections. He is bored—bored badly. Good gracious, I would not have his place and be bored as he is. I could not endure it." [30]

The honest newspaper material effectively counteracted malicious Democratic talk of Lincoln's Hoosier style of living, gauche manners, and essential ignorance. It destroyed such slurs as the New York *Herald's* editorial quip that the Republicans had passed over Seward, Chase, and other statesmen to take up a fourth-rate lecturer who delivered his hackneyed compositions at $200 apiece. A generous testimonial to Lincoln's talents came from Bates, who in a widely published letter to Orville H. Browning wrote that he had known the man for more than twenty years, and that his truth, courage, and candor, his powers and will to use them, abundantly qualified him for the Presidency.[31] Another came from John Bell, who generously mentioned in a speech the high impression which Lincoln had made in Congress upon himself and others.

Something was accomplished, too, by the campaign biographies of Lincoln. Party leaders called for a million copies of some cheap life to be put in the hands of indifferent, ill-informed, and secluded voters. William Dean Howells, then an editorial writer on the *Ohio State Journal*, was commissioned by Follett, Foster & Co. of Cincinnati, to write one, which appeared in abbreviated form in June and in full text in July. It enjoyed a wide sale. It would have been a better book had Howells not missed one of the opportunities of his career by failing to go to Springfield to interview Lincoln. Nearly half the text was devoted to the period preceding Lincoln's Congressional term. John L. Scripps, Chicago newspaperman, undertook a very hasty and very brief biography (he was required to compress it within thirty-two printed pages) on joint commission by the New York *Tribune* and Chicago *Tribune;* selling in large lots for two cents a copy, it had a wide circulation.[32] Lincoln, after protesting that his early life could be condensed into Gray's sentence on the short and simple annals of the poor, prepared some biographical material for it. Horace White wrote its account of the Douglas-Lincoln debates. Other biographies appeared—one by James Q. Howard, one anonymously issued by Thayer & Eldridge of Boston,

29 Quoted by N. Y. *Weekly Tribune*, September 22, 1860.
30 June 19, 1860; Trumbull Papers.
31 N. Y. *Weekly Tribune*, June 30, 1860.
32 Horace White, June 27, 1860, Robert Todd Lincoln Papers. See E. J. Wessen's essay on campaign biographies in Angle, ed., *Papers in Illinois History*.

Press & Tribune.

SATURDAY, MAY 19, 1860.

"HONEST OLD ABE."

The People's Candidate for President.

"RAILS AND FLAT-BOATS."

Log Cabins and Hard Cider Come Again?

Biographical Sketch of Abraham Lincoln.

ABRAHAM LINCOLN is a native of Hardin county, Kentucky. He was born on the 12th day of February, 1809. His parents were both from Virginia, and were certainly not of the first families. His paternal grandfather, Abraham Lincoln, emigrated from Rockingham county, Virginia, to Kentucky, about 1781 or '2, where a year or two later he was killed by Indians, not in battle, but by stealth, while he was laboring to open a farm in the forest. His ancestors, who were respectable members of the Society of Friends, went to Virginia from Berks county, Pennsylvania. Descendants of the same stock still reside in the eastern part of that State.

Mr. Lincoln's father, at the death of his father, was but six years of age, and he grew up literally without education. He removed from Kentucky to what is now Spencer county, Indiana, in 1816. The family reached their new home about the time the State was admitted into the Union. The region in which they settled was rude and wild, and they endured, for some years, the hard experience of a frontier life, in which the struggle with nature for existence and security is to be maintained only by constant vigilance. Bears, wolves and other wild animals still infested the woods, and young Lincoln acquired more skill in the use of the rifle than knowledge of books. There were institutions here and there known by the flattering denomination of "schools," but no qualification was required of a teacher beyond "readin', writin' and cypherin'," as the vernacular phrase ran, as far as the rule of three. If a straggler supposed to understand Latin happened to sojourn in the neighborhood, he was looked upon as a wizard, and regarded with an

of the prominence now given to the chief actor in that exciting event, it cannot fail to be interesting to all.

The affair came off on the fourth day of October, 1854. The State Fair had been in progress two days, and the capital was full of all manner of men. The Nebraska bill had been passed on the previous twenty-second of May. Mr. Douglas had returned to Illinois to meet an outraged constituency. He had made a fragmentary speech in Chicago, the people filling up each hiatus in a peculiar and good humored way. He called the people a mob—they called him a rowdy. The "mob" had the best of it, both then and at the election which succeeded. The notoriety of all these events had stirred up the politics of the State from bottom to top. Hundreds of politicians had met at Springfield expecting a tournament of an unusual character—Douglas, Breese, Kœrner, Lincoln, Trumbull, Matteson, Yates, Codding, John Calhoun, (of the order of the Candle Box,) John M. Palmer, the whole house of the McConnells, Singleton, (known to fame in the Mormon War,) Thos. L. Harris, and a host of others. Several speeches were made before and several after, the passage between LINCOLN and DOUGLAS, but that was justly held to be the event of the season.

We do not remember whether a challenge to debate passed between the friends of the speaker or not, but there was a perfectly amicable understanding between Lincoln and Douglas, that the former should speak two or three hours and the latter reply in just as little or as much time as he chose. Mr. Lincoln took the stand at two o'clock—a large crowd in attendance, and Mr. Douglas seated on a small platform in front of the desk. The first half-hour of Mr. Lincoln's speech was taken up with compliments to his distinguished friend Judge Douglas, and dry allusions to the political events of the past few years. His distinguished friend Judge Douglas had taken his seat, as solemn as the Cock-Lane ghost, evidently with the design of not moving a muscle till it came his turn to speak. The laughter provoked by Lincoln's exordium, however, soon began to make him uneasy; and when Mr. L. arrived at his (Douglas') speech pronouncing the Missouri Compromise "a sacred thing which no ruthless hand would ever be reckless enough to disturb," he opened his lips far enough to remark, "A first-rate speech!" This was the beginning of an amusing colloquy.

"Yes," continued Lincoln, "so affectionate was my friend's regard for this compromise line, that when Texas was admitted into the Union

The Chicago *Tribune* Offers a Brief Biography of Lincoln.

and so on. Much the best of them was D. W. Bartlett's *Life and Public Services of the Hon. Abraham Lincoln*, a three-hundred-and-fifty-four-page book, with steel portrait carefully wrought. The previous year, Bartlett had brought out a volume on twenty-one men regarded as possible Presidential candidates, including such minor figures as Orr and Dickinson but omitting Lincoln.[33] Howard's book possessed some fresh qualities, for it was largely the product of a visit he had paid to Springfield in order to collect material for Howells.

Lincoln alone of the major candidates made no speech during the campaign. As he confidentially explained to friends, his conservative opinions had been so often expressed that honest seekers of his views could easily find them, while any new expression would be misrepresented by bad men North and South. This was true; but it was also true that his silence permitted continuous attacks on him as an enemy of the South.[34] In that section, countless voters had no access to his past views. In the North, an edition of his debates with Douglas was in its fourth printing even before his nomination, and sold widely thereafter. His Cooper Union address had been circulated far and wide. The *Political Textbook* for 1860, which the New York *Tribune* scattered over the North in six editions before the end of August, contained his house-divided speech, part of the Freeport debate, the Cooper Union address, and three lesser utterances. These sufficed not only to present his views but to illustrate his intellectual qualities. Judicious Northerners doubtless agreed with the London *Critic*: "We collect from the speeches of Mr. Lincoln that he has a mind of the straightforward rather than the subtle order; that he rather seizes upon great and prominent facts and argues them to plain conclusions than builds up elegant but fragile theories . . . ; that he is earnest more than passionate, and persuasive more than commanding. Indeed, every one of his speeches which we have read bears upon it evidence that he is 'Honest Old Abe.' "

The caution that characterized Lincoln's part in the campaign was illustrated by an incident of the notification ceremonies in Springfield. For the eminent committee which arrived on a special train from Chicago, Mrs. Lincoln had provided champagne and sandwiches. Two Illinois politicians exclaimed that the champagne would never do—it would offend temperance people; and though

33 Lincoln refused to look at the proofsheets of Howells's life. "When," he wrote, "by the lessons of the past, and the united voice of all discreet friends, I am neither [to] write or speak a word for the public, how dare I to send forth, by my authority, a volume of hundreds of pages, for adversaries to make points upon without end? Were I to do so, the Convention would have a right to reassemble, and substitute another name for mine." To Samuel Galloway, June 19, 1860; Lincoln Collection, Ill. State Hist. Lib. But he did later make detailed private corrections in a copy.

34 When Zach Chandler made an effort to bring Lincoln to Detroit for a speech, Lyman Trumbull reported that the candidate thought that this would be departing from a fixed line of conduct which his friends had approved. Trumbull, September 3, 1860; Chandler Papers.

Mrs. Lincoln spiritedly defended her arrangements, Lincoln substituted ice water. His acceptance speech was a mere expression of thanks and of his high sense of responsibility. Caution was recommended not only by party leaders but by William Cullen Bryant, who as "an old campaigner" urged Lincoln to avoid making promises, expressing opinions, or forming any arrangements for the future. "The people have nominated you without any pledges or engagements of any sort; they are satisfied with you as you are, and they want you to do nothing at present but allow yourself to be elected." The vast majority of your friends, Bryant continued, "want you to make no speeches, write no letters as a candidate, enter into no pledges, make no promises, nor even give any of those kind words which men are apt to interpret into promises." [35] Lincoln declined to answer letters from strangers upon political topics, most correspondents getting nothing but an acknowledgment. But caution was not alone responsible for his refusal to make explanations which might reassure the South. He was sincerely convinced that Southern threats of secession were mere political gestures. Like nearly all Northerners, he failed to grasp the passionate fears and resentments of the Southern people.

While Herndon took sole charge of the law practice, Lincoln spent the summer in the governor's room at the State House. Assisted only by his secretary, John G. Nicolay, he took pains to see callers great and small, his mingled dignity and bonhomie making a happy impression on all. Some of his most interesting interviews were with Southerners who came full of prejudice, but left satisfied with his loyalty to the full constitutional rights of the South. He held no political conferences, and though he talked casually with visiting Republican leaders, he left the direction of the campaign to E. D. Morgan's national committee with scarcely a private hint of his wishes. As Southern alarm was increasingly fanned that summer by press and oratory, the demand for a counteracting pronouncement by Lincoln grew. But he continued to resist it, maintaining that in view of his repeated statements that the Republican Party would never molest slavery within the States, a new enunciation would but give an impression of weakness and cowardice.

"Why do not uneasy men *read* what I have already said? and what our platform says?" he asked. "If they will not read, or heed these, would they read or heed a repetition of them?" But his statement did not cover the whole ground. Had he realized the mental and emotional state of the South since Harper's Ferry, he would possibly have taken a different view. At the same time, his papers contain much evidence that he comprehended the rabid growth of Yanceyism in the cotton kingdom and pondered the means of meeting it. He saw no hope of arresting it by aught he could say; a conciliatory statement would not

35 June 16, 1860; Robert Todd Lincoln Papers, LC.

affect the South but would affect the North, creating division in his party and giving Douglas a powerful lever for prying away votes.

[V]

All four parties maintained busy headquarters. The Breckinridge campaign was managed by Governor Isaac Stevens of Washington Territory, with offices in the capital. Douglas fought his own battle with modest aid from an organization headed by Miles Taylor, a Representative of Louisiana, and the two Wickliffes, father and son. August Belmont as treasurer was never able to supply adequate funds. In managing the Bell-Everett campaign, Boteler had desultory help from some former Whigs and Know-Nothings. The most efficient organization by far was that of the Republicans. Their machine, strong in half the North in 1856, stronger still in every subsequent election, was now given a tremendous reinforcement by politicians eager to find room on a victorious ship. Village politicians, crossroads squires, country editors, and ward-workers from Maine to Missouri, the backbone of the party, were turning toward the holders of future power; while the tough-fibred managers at the top—E. D. Morgan, Norman B. Judd, Caleb Smith, Gideon Welles, Austin Blair, Simon Cameron, and the like —left no opportunity unused. Two Illinois leaders, David Davis and Leonard Swett, took immediate steps to conciliate the crestfallen Thurlow Weed, while Orville Browning hastened to St. Louis to enlist Judge Bates. As the Seward-Weed men began laboring heartily for the cause, Bates published a long letter in the St. Louis *Democrat* arguing for Lincoln's election. Republican unity was perfect.[36]

While the eagle of victory rode on Republican standards, croaking ravens of imminent defeat perched on all the opposition flags. The Constitutional Unionists and the Breckinridge forces, with some initial hope of victory, soon lost heart; and if Douglas waged a magnificent battle, it was not for the Presidency but for a larger object.

For the Constitutional Unionists, D. D. Barnard penned the ablest argument in a hard-hitting pamphlet, "Truths for the Times," directed primarily against Lincoln. The real object of the Republican Party, he wrote, was to effect the destruction of slavery; some wishing to do this at once, some in an indefinite future. He quoted Sumner's recent statement that the proslavery power must die, once the Republicans triumphed, as a poisoned rat dies of rage in its hole; and his declaration that the free communities must become a belt of fire about the South, within which slavery would perish. He quoted Seward's assertion in March, 1858, that the interests of the white race demanded the ultimate emanci-

36 Bates, *Diary*, 132 (May 31, 1860).

pation of all men. He quoted Lincoln's phrase about putting slavery in the course of ultimate extinction. Some men tried to pretend that the sole object of the party was the exclusion of slavery from the Territories. This was hypocrisy; there was no more chance of slavery going into any existing Territory than of its going into the land of the Eskimos. With the feeling over slavery what it was, and value of slaves so high, wrote Barnard, the migration of masters with their bondsmen to regions where soil, climate, and productions absolutely forbade the profitable employment of black labor was utterly preposterous. No, the real aim of the Republican Administration would be to hasten the extinction of slavery; and as soon as the Administration took power it could and would do a great deal to give effect to its hostility to the institution. It would be an Administration of Northern antislavery men; it would fill the Federal offices with antislavery appointees; and it would carry out Seward's pledge to reform the Supreme Court.[37]

The gravamen of Barnard's argument was that the triumph of such a party must inevitably give the signal for secession. Southern disunionists were always watching for an opportunity to be driven from the Union by Northern aggression. Nor did he doubt for a moment that Southern conspirators had planned the disruption of the Charleston convention and the organization of a separate party on extreme Southern ground as steps toward an independent republic. The one way, therefore, to defer the crisis, checkmate the conspirators, and save the Union, was to defeat Lincoln. Unquestionably Barnard was right about the real intent of the Republican leaders. Their aim was not primarily to keep slavery out of the Territories, for it could not go there, but to put it in the way of ultimate extinction everywhere. His pamphlet was a contribution to realism. But the Republican reply to his argument was simple. Lincoln had candidly avowed his desire to see slavery put in the way of ultimate extinction—and what of it? He had promised not to touch it in the States; no sudden, arbitrary, or unjust step was intended; none could or would be taken.

Though both Bell and Everett maintained for some time a belief that they might win, their cause was hopeless from the outset. As late as July 30, Bell was convinced that his ticket would carry all but two or three of the slaveholding States, and that if it could win in Pennsylvania, or New York, or Ohio, it would obtain a majority in the electoral college.[38] He was anxious for a coalition in the North with the Douglas Democrats on some terms of equality. The electors chosen on a combined ticket should have freedom to vote for whichever man they could elect to the Presidency—and as Douglas could gain no Southern electors, this would obviously be Bell. Since the prime object of both parties

37 Pamphlet, dated Albany, August 15, 1860.
38 Bell to A. R. Boteler, July 2, 30, 1860; Boteler Papers.

was to save the Union, the Tennesseean saw no violation of principle in such an arrangement. Everett, who had accepted his empty honor reluctantly, was more moderate in his hopes. For some years he had been wholly withdrawn from politics; feeling himself Bell's superior, he disliked taking second place on the ticket; and he feared that his fund for saving Mount Vernon would suffer heavily.[39] As the campaign progressed, to be sure, even his slow blood moved faster. With a little show of real strength in the North, he believed the ticket could sweep the entire South.[40] But the show never appeared, and realists like Amos Lawrence admitted the hopelessness of the cause.

The fact was that the Constitutional Union Party could not breast the tremendous tide of enthusiasm for Lincoln in the North, the deep surge of loyalty to Breckinridge and State Rights Democracy in the South. The conservative businessmen and planters who ought to have toiled amain for Bell were just the men most prone to indifference and apathy. They would vote, but they would not take off their coats and go to work.[41] Only a fervent crusade for the Union could have succeeded, and the whole Bell-Everett enterprise was too balanced, Laodicean, and timid. The platform pronouncement for the Constitution, the Union, and the laws meant nothing. Whose Constitution—Clay's? Calhoun's? Seward's? What laws? Bell refused to answer, referring inquirers to his past course on slavery issues. On examination, these proved highly equivocal; and while it was possible to quote his proslavery utterances in the South and his antislavery statements in the North, it was also possible to reverse the process. Everett, too, declined to interpret the party's doctrines. The Constitution is platform enough, he fatuously remarked, and the public character of the candidates sufficient guaranty of their fidelity to it. Their characters might be well enough, but what of their backbones? Before long it was shown that some of Bell's utterances on behalf of slavery were more extreme than any of Breckinridge's, while some of Everett's early excoriations of slavery were severe enough for an abolitionist. The party was thus left looking as two-faced as Janus; a party that appealed to principle while clinging to unprincipled equivocations.[42]

It was clear that despite all its noble intentions and intense "respectability," the Bell-Everett movement would do no more than poll a sizable protest vote against disunion. Its feebleness made the temptation to vote-trading and expedient alliances irresistible. Half the Northern States soon reported Bell-Everett men engaged in dickers and trades. In New Jersey, they were willing to fuse with the Breckinridge forces; in Georgia, with the Douglas men; and in New

39 To Kennedy, May 17, 1860; Kennedy Papers.
40 He believed so even after election; MS Journal, November 8, 11.
41 G. S. Hilliard, September 21, 1860; Boteler Papers.
42 Bell, July 30, Boteler Papers; Everett, May 7, June 2, Crittenden Papers.

York with almost anybody—so the reports ran. It was only in the border areas that the Constitutional Unionists mustered a dominating power.

[VI]

Not even Breckinridge could give much grace or dignity to the thrust of the Southern Democracy. The nominee, far from being identified with the slave-code extremists, had so recently as 1856 made a distinctly non-interventionist speech. Far from adopting the principles of Slidell, Toombs, and Cobb, he had shrunk during the Lecompton contest from throwing his weight into one scale or the other, and had been charged with absenting himself from the Senate chamber lest he might have to break a tie vote. His generous letter to Douglas during the senatorial contest of 1858 was well remembered, as was the fact that he had cordially taken Douglas's hand when the Illinoisan, amid Southern scowls, reentered the Senate chamber in January, 1859.

Breckinridge played his part in the canvass with gentlemanly decorum. But it was impossible to give moderation and perfume to a political effort so largely vengeful in character; for the Breckinridge-Lane ticket had been devised by Slidell, Buchanan, Cobb, and others to kill Douglas and other party rebels. It was impossible, too, to divest the Breckinridge party of a disunionist aroma which hung about it even while the candidate was protesting his devotion to national integrity. It was all too patent that Yancey, Rhett, Iverson, A. G. Brown, and others looked to the organization to make secession unescapable.

The essentially sectional character of the party could not be mistaken. To be sure, many prominent Northerners clung to it. Yancey boasted that three previous candidates of the Democracy, Cass, Pierce, and Buchanan, were upholding Breckinridge, while only Martin Van Buren stood with Douglas—and he very quietly. Eight of the ten Democratic Senators from the North, Bright, Fitch, Bigler, Gwin, and others, were for Breckinridge, as were four-fifths of the Representatives. So were such men as Caleb Cushing and Daniel S. Dickinson.[43] Against these men, Douglas's best champions in the South, Soulé, Forsyth, Foote, and Jere Clemens, were a feeble detachment. Yet somehow the Northern names were not really impressive. They meant simply that party regularity and the power of the Administration, joined in some instances with an inveterate sympathy for the slave States and in others with a timid desire to placate the men who threatened secession, had brought a large number of old party wheelhorses into harness. Everybody comprehended that Breckinridge could not carry a single free State. Everybody knew also that (as Douglas correctly said) while not all of Breckinridge's followers were secessionists, every secessionist was a

43 W. L. Yancey, speech at Memphis, August 14, 1860 (pamphlet).

CIRCULAR.

National Democratic Committee Rooms,
No. 28 Four-and-a-Half street, Washington, D. C.

WASHINGTON CITY, *June* 30, 1860.

The undersigned, Committee of Finance appointed by the Executive Committee, address you in relation to the collecting of funds for the expenses of the campaign. We need not urge the importance of the promptest action, with the view of efficient organization throughout the country. The preparation and circulation of documents which will place our cause before the great body of the American people on its just ground of nationality, devotion to the equal rights of all, and which will exhibit the pre-eminent qualifications of our candidates, BRECKINRIDGE and LANE, is of the first consequence. We feel, also, that all our friends will appreciate the necessity of untiring correspondence to perfect and consolidate the organization of our party throughout the country.

The Executive Committee is now prepared at once to enter upon the duties which have been devolved upon them; and they now appeal for efficient pecuniary aid. We have bold and desperate opponents to meet, and we need for the purposes mentioned a large amount of funds. We hope that no delay whatever will occur in answering this circular. Contributions should be forwarded to the Chairman of the Committee. It will be our purpose to see that the utmost economy be practiced in the use of funds.

With this determination on our part, we appeal again to the liberality of our friends to furnish us with the necessary means, to the end that our documents may go to every town and hamlet in the country.

Believing that an appeal for prompt action will be at once responded to by you and all our friends, we subscribe ourselves your friends in the cause of the great Democratic party of the country,

ISAAC I. STEVENS, *Oregon, Chairman.*
AUGUSTUS SCHELL, *New York.*
ISAAC H. WRIGHT, *Massachusetts.*
JOHN R. THOMPSON, *New Jersey.*
ROBERT W. JOHNSON, *Arkansas.*
JOHN W. STEVENSON, *Kentucky.*
JESSE D. BRIGHT, *Indiana.*
JOHN SLIDELL, *Louisiana.*
WILLIAM FLINN, *Washington City.*

Address—
HON. ISAAC I. STEVENS, M. C.,
Chairman of the National Democratic Executive Committee,
Washington City, D. C.

The Breckinridge Democrats Appeal for Funds.

283

Breckinridge follower. "Parson" Brownlow named twenty-six Southern leaders, all members of Congress, governors, or ex-governors, who in supporting Breckinridge were openly preaching disunion in the event of Lincoln's election.[44]

The unofficial headquarters of the Breckinridge forces, naturally, were in the White House. There Slidell, Bright, Bigler, Lane, and other managers conferred with the President and laid plans; thence patronage was manipulated, and a subtle venom sent coursing through all the veins of the party. The animosity which many Administration men expressed for Douglas recalled the bitterest warfare between Jeffersonians and Burrites, or Hamilton and Adams men. The *Ohio State Journal* remarked that the rival Democratic factions of that State displayed a violence, a vindictiveness, and a passion of hate to which it knew no parallel. In no Southern State would the Breckinridge faction consent to any compromise or coalition—not even in Virginia, where Governor John Letcher among others deplored the schism.[45] It held rigidly aloof even in those border States where an alliance with popular sovereignty Democrats offered the only hope of defeating Bell. "They do well to call us bolters," vociferated Daniel S. Dickinson at the "Hard" convention in Syracuse on August 7; "for we intend to bolt the door fast against all hucksters, auctioneers, and jobbers."[46] The nominee of the Breckinridge men for governor in New York, James T. Brady, had opposed Buchanan's Lecompton policy, but for a much longer period he had evinced his hearty distrust and dislike of Douglas.

Almost from the outset, and largely because of the stiff aversion to compromise, the Breckinridge Democrats anticipated defeat. There being three hundred and three electoral votes, they needed one hundred and fifty-two to win. If they could gain one hundred and twenty electors in the South, with the seven of California and Oregon (where Federal officeholders were mobilized in a powerful phalanx for Breckinridge), they would require only twenty-five more votes in the North. But this would mean carrying New York, or Pennsylvania, or Ohio plus either Indiana or Illinois—and most Southerners soon realized that the task was almost impossible. Only a complete fusion of the Douglas-Breckinridge-Bell elements would have offered a chance of clean-cut victory over Lincoln.

The obvious strategy for the National Democrats, any broad fusion being impossible, was to give the Douglas forces a free field in the Northwest and the Bell-Everett Party a full opportunity in the border area in the hope of throwing the election into the House. Then some compromise Democrat might well be chosen President. But strategy was precisely what the Breckinridge men

44 Fite, *op. cit.*, 186, 187.
45 Crenshaw, *Slave States in 1860*, 141.
46 N. Y. *Weekly Tribune*, August 11, 1860.

neglected. No evidence whatever appears that the candidate, the national committee, or the advisers who tramped in and out of Buchanan's office, ever formed a serious plan. Some leaders believed that the contest would, in the end, shake down to a close race between Breckinridge and Lincoln, the two other candidates falling into the background; and that national conservatism would elect the Democrat. Other leaders, including Buchanan, believed that the grand goal was the destruction of Douglas. Still others, the extremists like Rhett, Yancey, and A. G. Brown, whom Senator Hammond cursed as odious wreckers of the national temple, looked forward to party defeat as opening the door to a Southern republic.[47] Let the slave States have done with the whole wretched system; let the South, instead of scrambling to win a President in the House, turn to manly resistance! Still other Breckinridge men, the great majority, confused, helpless, and despondent, were content merely to drift. As the campaign wore on, less and less talk of a possible House contest was heard, and more and more pessimism was expressed. As Sam Houston remarked, the American people liked to have their Presidential elections settled at the polls and dreaded a remission of the question to the House. Even in the Lower South a feeling existed that, calamitous as the election of Lincoln would be, a ferocious contest in Congress, all the factions and sections clashing in embittered antagonism, might well prove more disastrous.[48]

One Southern Democratic leader alone, Jefferson Davis, attempted a stroke of bold leadership to defeat Lincoln. Seeing certain defeat ahead, as he wrote years later in his memoirs, he undertook to bring together all the opposition groups. His hope appears to have been that some such man as Horatio Seymour, devoted to the Union and standing outside old factional quarrels, might be named in the stead of Breckinridge, Bell, and Douglas. He made approaches to all three candidates.

Bell and Breckinridge, he tells us, promised him that they would withdraw if Douglas would do so.[49] This is plausible; for both knew that they had little if any chance, and Bell in particular had been eager for fusion arrangements by his party. Most of Bell's party, reconciled to defeat, would have been ready to fall in behind any moderate and able man who showed firm attachment to the Union. The plan was wrecked, however, on the rock of Douglas's refusal. He wanted no bargain with Southern radicals. He had denounced all schemes for carrying the election into Congress. "By God, sir," he told Representative Edward McPherson of Pennsylvania, "the election shall never go into the House; before it shall go into the House, I will throw it to Lincoln." [50] He informed

47 To M. C. M. Hammond, July 4, 1860; Hammond Papers, LC.
48 Cf. Crenshaw, *Slave States in 1860*, 70–73.
49 Davis, *Rise and Fall*, I, 52.
50 N. Y. *Weekly Tribune*, October 20, 1860.

Davis that the proposed plan was impracticable, because, if he withdrew, his Northern Democratic supporters would turn to Lincoln rather than to any substituted Democrat. "I am in the hands of my friends," he stated in effect, "and my friends will not accept such a scheme." [51] His own plan for the party was simple. If he dropped out, no other Democrat could be elected, for none could carry vital Northern States. But if Breckinridge resigned in his favor, then he would be confident of party and personal success.

By late summer, the question was no longer of Lincoln's election but of the results of his impending victory; and, in the play within the play, it was the inner drama—the radicals of the South fervently whipping up secessionist sentiment and one candidate alone, Douglas, dealing courageously with the issue—which held the gaze of shrewd observers.

51 Milton, *Eve*, 487; Wilson, *Slave Power*, II, 52; N. Y. *Weekly Tribune*, September 15.

10

The Election of Lincoln

HOT AS the summer of 1860 became, the breath of sectional passion grew hotter still. Early in August, the veteran Mississippi unionist Henry S. Foote, who had once exchanged blows with Jefferson Davis and had always opposed the Southern extremists, undertook to warn the country of imminent catastrophe. He was in New York at the time; he had been irritated by complacent Northern statements that the recent elections in Missouri, Kentucky, and North Carolina indicated the South would submit to Lincoln's election; and he wrote the *Herald* in contradiction. All prominent Southerners visiting the North, he declared, agreed with him that secession was certain if Lincoln won. Even moderates thought so—and he quoted a letter from a unionist who, while deprecating rash action, believed that on the morrow of Lincoln's victory the Southern States would indignantly strike for revolution. Foote might have pointed to the Southern newspapers. The Richmond *Enquirer* spoke for dozens of them when it appealed to the spirit of '76: "Resistance to wrong and injury—to tyranny, whether of one man or eighteen millions—is the cherished birthright of every citizen of the Federal Union." [1]

In parts of the South, as men heard such orators as Reuben Davis assert that war was inevitable, mob feeling boiled near the surface. George W. Cable describes an incident illustrating the excitement that sometimes flashed up in New Orleans. A crowd suddenly roared down Royal Street, fierce in pursuit of a pallid fugitive. "Hang him, hang him!" the mob thundered. Before rescue came he was almost lynched. He was a vendor of campaign medals (for half the population, men, women, and children, wore ribanded Breckinridge emblems) who in opening his stock had failed to notice that a Lincoln and Hamlin badge had crept in among his wares. As the mob dispersed an onlooker spoke up: "Didn't I tell you? Bound to have war. It's already begun."

The storm-cloud background of the Breckinridge campaign in the Lower South lay in a concerted if rather unsystematic effort to create emotions which would give that section a monolithic unity in facing the North. Many politicians

1 N. Y. *Herald*, August 13, *Enquirer*, July 10, 1860; Foote was now a Tennesseean.

like Keitt, Porcher Miles, and Yancey, many editors like the Rhetts, were eager for the early destruction of the Union. Many more, like Slidell, who had stood for secession in 1856 if Frémont were elected and had threatened it again in 1858, were not eager—but were ready. A large number, while wishing that the Union could be preserved, made defiant utterances and urged extreme measures in order to frighten the free States into concessions; they hoped that the crisis would end in writing guarantees for the South into the Constitution. Jefferson Davis and R. M. T. Hunter well represented this group. Still others indulged in harsh denunciations of cowardice and submission simply in order to shame voters out of the Constitutional Union Party. Raucous warnings of Northern plots, of new John Brown invasions, of servile revolts, and of a Lincolnian program of race equality filled the air. Since Harper's Ferry, the Lower South was in a mood to respond. Men who traveled through the cotton States with eyes and ears open found great numbers of men deeply, terribly aroused. As the political pot seethed at barbecues and rallies, many communities became gripped by a rising excitement. Garibaldi's triumphs in Italy, the civil war in Mexico, and the visit of the Prince of Wales seemed in comparison with the crisis only trivial events.[2]

A thousand Southern voices were raised to inform the North that Lincoln's election would be the signal for disunion. Such fire-eaters as Wigfall of Texas and Durant Da Ponte of New Orleans, speaking for Breckinridge, declared secession the only possible alternative. They drew lurid pictures of abolitionist armies invading the South, firing homes, and murdering women and children. Lincoln's Presidency would mean emancipation, declared the Charleston *Mercury*, and emancipation would mean a loss not merely of political ascendency, but of every vital interest. "It is the loss of liberty, property, home, country—everything that makes life worth having." The terrors of submission would be tenfold worse than the terrors of disunion. It is idle to deny, exclaimed Keitt, that the North is to the South a hostile community. "Shall we permit a party stained with treason, hideous with insurrection, and dripping with blood, to occupy the government?"[3] One Mississippian in a campaign speech described the Union as "fettered antipathies." Incendiary pamphlets were being scattered broadcast throughout the section. One, penned by William D. Porter of Charleston, was typical in its denunciation of present tyrannies and its evocation of a vision of still greater evils in the future. While we are now submitting to Northern rapacity, cruelty, and hatred, wrote the author, the worst is yet to come. "When new States are admitted; when Abolition becomes stronger and stronger;

2 White, *Rhett*, 163; Crenshaw, 295, 296; Reuben Davis, *Recollections*, 390.
3 Charleston *Mercury*, October 11; N. Y. *Weekly Tribune*, July 28, 1860.

when the power to amend develops the power to destroy—how are we to stem the torrent or avoid the cataract?" [4]

But it was significant that abler, saner men than these hotheads also predicted disunion. Former Speaker Orr, writing on July 23 to his constituents, declared that, since the election of Lincoln was a certainty, they would have to decide whether they would submit to the rule of a party whose fundamental principle was open, undisguised, and declared war on their social institutions. He believed that honor and safety would require prompt secession and that, if the North did not concede new and firmer guarantees of Southern rights, the slave States should form a new government. Henry W. Hilliard of Alabama, speaking in Cooper Union, predicted that Lincoln's success would be followed by a convulsion which would shake the institutions of the country to their deepest foundations. Alexander H. Stephens, who opposed secession, predicted that South Carolina would secede, that the Gulf States would follow, and that after some hesitation by the border region, war would begin. Later, talking with a correspondent of the New York *Herald*, he repeated that Lincoln's election, now certain, would usher in an attempt at secession and revolution. Robert Toombs, while less sober and responsible than these men, was never a wild radical. Yet he was quoted as writing privately from Washington that he would come home to raise ten thousand troops; and when he crossed the Potomac again it would be with drawn sword. He added that thirty members of Congress were pledged to that unflinching position. [5]

Not a few men in the cotton kingdom knew that the governors were exchanging letters on possible ways and means of secession. Gist of South Carolina, on October 5, sent a confidential missive to his colleagues, declaring that concert of action was essential, that South Carolina desired some other State to take the lead or at least move simultaneously in seceding, and that if none did so, she would in his opinion secede alone. The governors of North Carolina and Louisiana replied that, with public opinion much divided, their States would probably not regard Lincoln's election as justifying secession; and even Joseph E. Brown declared that Georgia, if acting alone, would probably wait for an overt act. But the governors of Mississippi and Florida believed that their States would join any other in secession; while Governor Moore thought that Alabama would cooperate with any two or more. [6]

It was the obvious duty of the Administration to rebuke these counsels of

4 "State Sovereignty and the Doctrine of Coercion," pamphlet.
5 N. Y. *Weekly Tribune*, August 11, September 22, 1860; Johnston and Browne, *Stephens*, 356; N. Y. *Herald* September 29, 1860; Sumter, Ga., *Republican*, quoted N. Y. *Weekly Tribune* November 3, 1860.
6 Nicolay and Hay, *Lincoln*, II, 306–314.

disruption with a stern voice. Buchanan should have combined his support of Breckinridge with a Jacksonian admonition to all secessionists. Being what he was, he kept silent. The Administration organ, the *Constitution*, enjoying a temporary boom as a campaign sheet and loosing all its broadsides against Douglas, actually encouraged disunion measures. It declared that if Lincoln were elected, his antislavery Administration would have antislavery officeholders quietly at work in every community, introducing the abolition virus as adroitly as possible, and gradually sowing disaffection among the slaves; while the post office would be converted into a machine for scattering Helper and Garrison publications broadcast, and the Federal marshals would menace, not protect, the public peace. Could the South be expected to wait until it had thus been undermined? "We think not. . . . Let Lincoln be President, and how many months' purchase would the Union be worth?" [7] While the Directory encouraged Editor Browne to write in this vein, Southern Cabinet members were talking intransigently. Secretary Cobb, according to Washington correspondents, went about freely threatening a revolutionary break-up of the Union.[8]

[I]

If Buchanan was supine, Douglas was not. Beginning his campaign as a battle for the Presidency, he shortly converted it into one for the Union. Only for the first two months was the Douglas branch of the Democratc Party able to cherish any hopes. Then it became clear that the ticket would run second to Lincoln in most Northern States, to Breckinridge in most Southern, and to Bell in the borderland—that the party was fated to a crushing defeat in the electoral college. But Douglas, indomitable, indefatigable, never so formidable as when meeting hopeless odds, turned to a far greater object than popular sovereignty— to the cause of national unity. This, even more than the Lecompton struggle, was his finest hour.

He alone of the candidates traveled widely and spoke industriously. When after his nomination a friend told him that the attacks of vindictive enemies and the momentous nature of the issues involved in the contest would compel him to take the stump, he showed reluctance.[9] But the pressure of friends, his wife, and above all of events, soon brought him to the front. One admirer was reminded of Napoleon at Lodi. His temper sternly aroused, he spoke during the summer and fall in nearly every free State; he invaded Virginia, North Carolina, and the Deep South; everywhere he held large crowds, and everywhere he

7 Washington *Constitution*, September 21, 1860.
8 N. Y. *Weekly Tribune*, November 3, 1860.
9 S. J. Anderson, September 2, 1860; Stephens Papers, LC.

took the offensive. Fiery, ready, and able as ever, he imparted his combative spirit to followers. At Concord, New Hampshire, and in Milwaukee, he denounced the Administration with passionate vigor, giving the country revealing glimpses of his personal encounters with the President and eliciting from Buchanan a public letter in denial of some of his assertions. Everywhere he spurned appeasement.

In Boston, the veteran machine politician B. F. Hallett called at the Revere House with oleaginous words, saying that the party would soon be reunited. "Never!" rejoined Douglas. "If you voted against me at Charleston on principle, being for intervention, we cannot act together. If you voted against me out of personal hatred, I know very well how to act toward you!" His denunciation of treasonable schemes was scorching.[10]

The Little Giant had quickly seen that all the omens were unfavorable to his election. Apart from his running mate Herschel Johnson, and Soulé, Forsyth, Dixon of Kentucky, and Alexander H. Stephens, he had no prominent Southern adherents; even his old friend Clingman of North Carolina deserted him. Nor was the list of his Northern friends impressive. In New York, he commanded the aid of Horatio Seymour and Dean Richmond, while August Belmont was chairman of the National Committee, and ex-Governor Washington Hunt eventually joined his column. Forney of Pennsylvania, Reverdy Johnson of Maryland, Pugh and Henry B. Payne of Ohio, W. W. Wick of Indiana, William A. Richardson of Illinois, and H. H. Sibley of Minnesota, were loyal and hardworking as ever. These names, however, nearly exhausted the roster.

His newspapers were a scattered and generally ineffective band. In New York City, the influential Oswald Ottendorfer brought the *Staats-Zeitung* to his side, but he had only the *Herald* among English-language dailies to give him its capricious and sometimes damaging aid—for Bennett's sword wounded friend and foe alike.[11] The Philadelphia *Press* was a wavering and unhappy adherent. In Chicago, he suffered a blow when, late in July, Cyrus H. McCormick paid about ten thousand dollars for the struggling *Times* and combined it with the *Herald*—the faithful James Sheahan losing his editorship. McCormick had en-

---

10 N. Y. *Weekly Tribune*, August 4, September 15, 1860.
11 Bennett, always with an eye to the main chance, was half for Breckinridge, half for Douglas, and ready to leap to the Republican chariot. Joseph Medill had a friend sound him out early in the campaign. This agent found Bennett not unwilling to bargain with the Republicans, and urged Medill and Norman B. Judd to go see him. As Medill started east, he wrote Lincoln: "We deem it highly important to spike that gun; his affirmative help is not of great consequence, but he is powerful for mischief. He can do us much harm if hostile. If neutralized a *point* is gained. We think his terms will not be immoderate. He is too rich to want money. Social position we suspect is what he wants. He wants to be in a position to be invited with his wife and son to dinner or tea at the White House occasionally, and to be 'made of' by the big men of the party. I think we can afford to agree to that much."

dorsed Buchanan's political policies, while he remembered that Douglas had opposed the extension of his patents; and the *Daily Times* henceforth gave the Senator only lukewarm espousal, trying at the same time to conciliate the Breckinridge Democrats. Its editor was anxious to heal the breach in the party. It may be surmised that if Douglas had not felt certain of his defeat, he would have taken steps to prevent this transfer.[12] The *Missouri Republican*, the most influential Douglas paper in the border area, was the only sheet regarded as at all likely to carry its own State for him. The Albany *Atlas*, Buffalo *Courier*, and a few others did what they could. The weight of the Northern press was for Lincoln, however, as that of the South was for Breckinridge.

Of unmistakable significance were the difficulties which the Douglas organization encountered in raising funds. Belmont, impaneling a weighty committee and making an initial gift of a thousand dollars himself, hoped for a generous response in New York. Yet despite urgent entreaty, the steamship magnate George Law flatly declined to contribute, and the New York Central men who in Belmont's opinion could well afford to pay $100,000 to help gain the State were almost equally indifferent. Important merchants were fearful lest they offend Southern customers by supporting Douglas. In midsummer, Miles Taylor, the energetic Louisiana Congressman toiling in New York for the cause, found the coffers so bare that it seemed hopeless to continue the battle unless fresh sums could be raised. He set up a financial committee of his own under Horace F. Clarke, but it too failed. Frantic appeals from the Northwest for financial assistance had to be given a stony answer, Belmont informing Sibley that his group could not raise for the whole country as much money as Minnesota alone demanded. A little money was scraped together for Maine, whose September election would be taken by many voters as a straw in the wind; but a call upon each Congressional district for a hundred dollars brought nothing into the treasury. To the very end, poverty laid a palsying hand on the Douglasite effort. Wealthy interests of the North saw no reason for aiding a party certain of defeat and a candidate hated by half of the South.[13]

But the obvious imminence of defeat did not daunt Douglas. His protracted tours were undertaken not for votes, but to vindicate his recent course, ensure the downfall of his enemies, and above all to rally men to the Union. His first speeches were at his birthplace in Brandon, Vermont, and in Concord, Boston,

---

12 Hutchinson, *McCormick*, II, 43 ff. Poor Sheahan, forced to sell, with the sheriff at the door, not a dollar in his pocket, and debts of perhaps four thousand, felt maltreated. He wrote a friend that Douglas had treated him cruelly—"in the matter of the book of which I had hopes, he wantonly interfered to my injury." This was perhaps the life of Douglas, perhaps a projected history of the Kansas struggle. Sheahan probably did not realize the gravity of Douglas's financial embarrassments. See his letters July 28, August 3, Lanphier Papers, Ill. State Hist. Lib.

13 Milton, *Eve*, 488–490.

Portland, Providence, and other New England cities. Meeting Henry Wilson in Boston, he predicted Lincoln's election and said he would go South to urge the people to submit to the result and sustain the national fabric. Making good his word, in Virginia and North Carolina he spoke more courageously upon secession than any other man in the land.

Behind this Southern tour of Douglas's, indeed, lay his conviction that a widespread and intricate conspiracy had been formed to bring about a *coup d'etat* as early as November or December, and that only hard campaigning in the border States could prevent it. He forcibly expressed his fears to Charles Francis Adams, who recorded them in his unpublished diary. According to Douglas, radical leaders of the cotton kingdom wished to form a powerful new slaveholding republic around the Gulf of Mexico, embracing Cuba and the Mexican and Central American states. The Illinoisan learned that when the dissolution of the Baltimore convention made it evident that the Democratic Party would lose the government, certain Southern fire-eaters had laid a plot. They helped to nominate Breckinridge with the idea that they would concentrate upon him the votes of every slaveholding State. They would make special efforts to carry Virginia and Maryland. Then, whether the Republicans won the election or no candidate emerged with a majority, they would declare Breckinridge the rightful President, use their control of the Cabinet to take possession of the Washington departments, and call upon the Southern States to recognize their *de facto* government. The slaveholding area could thus be used as a unit to overthrow the existing regime. It is certain that Douglas believed this conspiracy a grim reality; certain that he thought various high figures in Washington involved in it; and certain that he felt that it could be defeated only by carrying Virginia (and if possible her neighbors) against Breckinridge.

Hence the Little Giant's dramatic invasion of Maryland, Virginia, and North Carolina, denouncing disunion on every hand. He had no idea of carrying these States himself. But as he later told Adams, he did wish to help secure the borderland against the radicals, to break the Yancey-Rhett-Ruffin line, and to make impossible the plan for precipitating the entire South into rash action. In due time he was able to assert that he had succeeded. The Bell-Everett ticket carried Virginia and Douglas himself carried Missouri, while Breckinridge won in Maryland by only seven hundred votes. If the Southern conspirators, with Secretaries Cobb, Thompson, and Floyd, had planned to seize the capital, Douglas thwarted their scheme.

At Norfolk on August 25, standing on the City Hall steps to address seven thousand people, he announced that he wanted no vote except from men who desired the Union preserved by the faithful execution of every line of the Constitution. Two questions were handed him on slips of paper. One asked whether, if Lincoln were elected, the Southern States would be justified in seceding. He gave an emphatic no. The other inquired whether, if the South did secede, he would advise resistance by force to their withdrawal. "I answer emphatically," returned Douglas, "that it is the duty of the President of the United States and all others in authority under him to enforce the laws of the United States as passed by Congress and as the courts expound them. And I, as in duty bound by my oath of fidelity to the Constitution, am to do all in my power to aid the government of the United States in maintaining the supremacy of the laws against all resistance to them, come from what quarter it would. In other words, I think the President of the United States, whoever he may be, should treat all attempts to break up the Union by resistance to its laws as Old Hickory treated the Nullifiers in 1832." [14]

Though this forthright utterance provoked a Southern storm, Douglas stuck to his position. At Raleigh, on August 30, he used even stronger language. "I would hang every man higher than Haman who would attempt to resist by force the execution of any provision of the Constitution which our fathers made and bequeathed to us." He told North Carolinians that no Illinoisan would ever consent to pay duty on corn shipped down the Mississippi. "Never on earth! We shall say to the custom house keeper that we furnish the water that makes the great river, and that we will follow it throughout its whole course to the ocean, no matter who or what may stand before us." At Baltimore, he warned the country again, as he had done in the Senate, that the Yanceys and Rhetts had laid a plot to sunder the nation and that America stood in dire peril. Every disunionist, he said, was a Breckinridge man, and he would countenance no fusion of his party with secessionists. "I am for burying Southern disunionism and Northern abolitionism in the same grave." Speaking to an immense picnic concourse at Jones's Wood in New York City, he asserted that he would consent to no alliance with the Breckinridge Democracy until its leaders promised an enforcement of the laws against seceders. "I wish to God," he vociferated, "that we had an Old Hickory now alive in order that he might hang Northern and Southern traitors on the same gallows." [15]

And carrying the campaign to the Northwest, he repeated his warning to an enthusiastic multitude who welcomed him to Chicago at the beginning of October. A deadly peril hung over the Union, he said, and all lovers of the Consti-

14 N. Y. *Weekly Tribune,* September 8, 1860.
15 N. Y. *Herald, Tribune, Times,* September 17, 1860; Milton, *Eve,* 493; N. O. *Picayune,* September 16, 1860. Edmund Ruffin talked with Governor Magoffin of Kentucky about Douglas's threats of coercion. The governor declared that if Lincoln's election were followed by secession, and the United States sent an army which tried to march through Kentucky, "every night's encampment will be made a graveyard." Ruffin, MS diary, September 13, 1860.

tution should awake from their sleep. The head of the Breckinridge electoral ticket in Virginia had asked if he would fight secession. He had answered unequivocally, and had demanded that the elector propound the same question to Breckinridge. "We cannot get an answer from him, and the Republicans justify Mr. Breckinridge in concealing his opinions on that subject. . . . I believe the Union is in peril, and all good men, all true men . . . should rally to put down these sectional parties." [16]

Never did Douglas's claims to statesmanship stand higher than when he thus pointed to a danger which most Republicans were denying or minimizing, and defied the Southerners and border men who were attacking him on the ground that he was a brutal coercionist. He gloried, like Jackson, in upholding coercion. He was not so happy when, assailing the Republicans as advocates of Negro equality, he appealed to race prejudice. His Chicago speech indicted Seward, who had spoken there a few days earlier, for doctrines more extreme than the New Yorker really held. When he declared that Seward wished to make the Negro in Illinois and other States the equal of the white man—something that Sumner intended, but not Seward—the crowd raised an angry shout of "Never! Never!" The Northwest responded as of old to Douglas's unconquerable energy. Mass meetings were held all over the section and delegations of Douglas men streamed in from neighboring towns. Hickory poles were raised, and the Democrats called their local organizations "Hickory Clubs," "Little Giants," and "Invincibles." These were in fact militant Union organizations.

When at Cedar Rapids, Iowa, Douglas heard that the Republicans had swept the October elections in Pennsylvania (as they simultaneously swept Indiana), he immediately turned to his secretary. "Mr. Lincoln is the next President," he said. "We must try to save the Union. I will go South."

It was the Deep South this time that he invaded. Passing through Springfield, Alton, and St. Louis, where large crowds, five thousand people even in Lincoln's home city, cheered him, and speaking at Memphis, Chattanooga, and Nashville, he was soon in Georgia and Alabama. Never had he made a more heroic effort. He was worn out by constant travels and speeches, often two or three in a day. His devoted wife and the hard-working secretary, James B. Sheridan, who accompanied him, knew that his health had deteriorated. Southern radicals denounced his journey savagely; ruffians threatened his life, and several incidents convinced him that efforts were being made to wreck the trains on which he rode.[17] But he was encouraged by ovations in Memphis and Jackson, Tennessee, while in Nashville the enthusiasm of the greatest crowd collected there in twenty years contrasted with the chilly reception given

16 Havana, Ill., *Squatter Sovereign*, October 20, 1860.
17 Milton, *Eve*, 498, 499.

Yancey the same night. One planter who heard Douglas at Jackson returned exclaiming that the occasion was the most notable event of his life, and that Douglas was the greatest statesman of the age. This auditor, who pronounced his effort masterly, asserted that the Little Giant had utterly demolished both the Southern secessionists and Northern Republicans, and concluded by saying that Douglas could create more enthusiasm among the masses than any other man living. The impression in Chattanooga was equally great.[18]

Even in Georgia and Alabama Douglas found many friends. His visit was encouraged by Alexander H. Stephens, who clung to a faint hope that civil war might yet be averted if public sentiment could be aroused against the extremists. In a speech at Crawfordsville, Stephens had said that while Douglas was not his first choice for President, he admired the man. He declared that the Senator had shown greater moral courage in defending his convictions of right against prejudice and fanaticism at home than any other statesman living; that he had stood by the South in her perils, and was indeed the most powerful friend the South ever had; and that the war now waged against him by office-holders and office-hunters, by malicious and envious pettifoggers, reminded him of wolves hounding to death a lordly buffalo.[19] Many Georgians and Alabamians were as determined as Stephens to keep the flag afloat so long as the government survived.[20] In Atlanta, where Stephens introduced Douglas with warm praise, a great crowd cheered the Senator's speech. At Macon, Herschel V. Johnson and Douglas spoke together. In Montgomery, where the *Mail* had said that Douglas's political garments were dyed with Southern blood,[21] he was greeted by a torchlight procession; and, though ruffians tried to pelt him with fruit and eggs, he made an eloquent plea against secession from the steps of the capitol.[22]

Unhappily, not all Douglas's followers attained his elevated level. Reverdy Johnson warned that the break-up of the Union and the ruin of all its hopes for mankind were imminent, but, unlike his leader, he rather justified than denounced a Southern revolt. Republican ascendancy, he said in Faneuil Hall, would be followed by the barring of slavery from all Territories, the abolition of the domestic slave trade, and the reversal of the Dred Scott decision; and with all security for slavery torn away, disunion would be inevitable. And Herschel Johnson explicitly said at Atlanta that if the South did secede, he would follow her fortunes for weal or woe.[23]

18 Diary of Harrod C. Anderson, October 24, 1860; Univ. of La. Archives.
19 Augusta *Constitutionalist*, quoted in Washington *Constitution*, September 6, 1860.
20 See letter quoted in Wash. corr. N. Y. *Tribune* dated October 26, 1860.
21 Quoted in Washington *Constitution*, September 20, 1860.
22 Washington *Constitution*, September 6, 20, etc., 1860; N. Y. Weekly *Tribune*, October 26, 1860.
23 Reverdy Johnson, "Speech of June 7, 1860" (pamphlet); Dumond, *Secession*, 111.

The principal attempt of the Douglas Democrats to effect a profitable alliance with another party was made in New York. Horatio Seymour, Dean Richmond, and other leaders, holding their Soft convention in Syracuse in mid-August, nominated a palpably weak ticket. Their candidate for governor, a respectable merchant-farmer of Hudson named William Kelly, was markedly inferior in parts and popularity to the candidate of the Breckinridge men, the brilliant James T. Brady. But the Douglasites, after welcoming Fernando Wood and his followers into their fold, did accomplish one brilliant stroke. They made a compact on much their own terms with the Bell-Everett party. An electoral ticket was drawn up which allotted twenty-three of the thirty-three places to Douglas men, and the other ten to the Constitutional Union Party. The understanding of at least some Constitutional Union leaders was that if these ten votes were needed to make Douglas President, they would be cast for him. Of course the Republicans raised a jeer at the expense of the alliance. Washington Hunt and James Brooks, they sneered, had sold out to the highest bidder. "The Syracuse auction," Greeley called it. Since on matters of principle the Douglas and Bell-Everett parties were far apart, the transaction did have an immoral look, and it is certain that Douglas disliked it.[24]

This and other efforts at fusion had, in general, two main objects. One was to try to cut down Lincoln's vote sufficiently to throw the election into the House. The second, and more hopeful, was to promote the chances of State and Congressional nominees. All over the North, by September, knots of politicians were sitting up late in offices and taverns intent on some bargain that would save a governorship from the Republicans, and send three or four men to Congress. But these cabals, though resulting in a few alliances among Douglas, Bell, and Breckinridge forces, for two reasons accomplished little. While the national leaders, and particularly Douglas, frowned upon them, the people were for the most part equally hostile; for the plain voter wished to support the candidate and platform of his choice, and not a hybrid ticket. Even in New York, therefore, where fusion temporarily looked most promising, astute judges prophesied that the alliance would run from fifty to a hundred thousand votes behind Lincoln. A full history of these movements would be tiresomely complex.

In the end, fusion of at least a partial nature was achieved by the Douglas and Bell forces in New York, by the Douglas and Breckinridge factions in Pennsylvania and Rhode Island, and by Breckinridge, Bell and Douglas men in New Jersey. Various Senators in Washington were particularly active on the Democratic side, for they calculated that if the election went into the House and that body became deadlocked, the Senate choice for Vice-President, Joseph Lane, would become Chief Executive. A long shot that! However, little real harmony was

24 N. Y. *Weekly Tribune*, September 15, 1860.

achieved anywhere. In Pennsylvania, for example, Forney and the diehard wing of the Douglasites refused pointblank to vote for any but Douglas electors. In New York, all the efforts of such businessmen as August Belmont, William B. Astor, and A. T. Stewart to bring about a union of the two Democratic factions met the stony opposition of Administration adherents. Oil and water would not mix.[25]

[II]

Alas that Douglas's vigilance was not matched by Republican leaders! Confident of victory from the beginning, the young Party grew more exultant as the canvass advanced, exhibiting a blind optimism which took all too little account of the peril hanging over the nation. Lincoln himself was deplorably complacent. On August 15, he wrote John B. Fry that he had received from the South many assurances that "in no probable event will there be any very formidable effort to break up the Union."

The Republicans divided their appeal to the voters into four main segments. First, as a matter of course they gave emphasis to their immovable stand against any extension of slavery into any Territory at any time, coupling with this position appropriate attacks upon the appetite of many Southerners for Caribbean acquisitions. We have seen that it was now accepted Republican doctrine that the normal condition of the Territories was freedom, and that neither Congress nor a territorial legislature could give legal existence to slavery in them. Second, using the Covode Report (of which a hundred thousand copies had been printed for franking) and other evidence, they asserted that the Democratic Party which had governed the country for eight years was a corrupt, bickering organization with a record barren of aught but quarrels, bargains, and blunders, and that the hour had struck for a vigorous new Administration, animated by constructive ideals. In the third place, they laid their greatest stress upon their economic planks; and, varying their tune to suit local and regional desires, they argued persuasively for a protective tariff, agricultural colleges, the homestead law, internal improvements, and the Pacific Railroad. Finally, they held out to the alien-born assurances that they would permit no unfriendly legislation.

These bread-and-butter appeals were indispensable, for the party, only half a dozen years old, badly needed cohesive organization. "There is very little of Republican principle in Pennsylvania and New Jersey," O. L. Ferry had written Gideon Welles on March 1, "while the great foreign element of the Northwest is ultra in all its views and unable to understand the propriety of any conces-

25 Greeley, *Amer. Conflict*, I, 326–328; Dumond, *Secession*, 110; Nichols, *Disruption*, 340–344.

sion." That is, the Middle Atlantic States were conservative; many Germans of the Middle West were radical. But organization was supplied with great vigor. Thurlow Weed raised what were then considered large sums of money. The Congressional Committee under Preston King, with Covode as treasurer, did as good work as the National Committee. W. H. Herndon wrote that in Sangamon County "we are organizing as we have never organized before"; and the same might have been said of numberless other counties all over the North. The party did its utmost, especially in the Northwest, to appeal to the foreign-born and to mobilize what Carl Schurz called a solid column of German and Scandinavian freesoilers. While the urban Irish and some settlements of German Catholics were doubtless Democratic, the Republicans by enlisting Schurz, Gustave Koerner, Friedrich Kapp, and other prominent German-Americans, and employing a phalanx of nearly a hundred German, Swedish, and Norwegian journals, made sure of a vote in the upper Mississippi Valley that was probably decisive in several States. Lincoln's letter to the *Staats Anzeiger* upon the Massachusetts proposal to withhold the ballot from fully naturalized citizens for two years was publicized to millions. He wrote:

I am against its adoption, not only in Illinois, but in every other place in which I have the right to oppose it. . . . It is well known that I deplore the oppressed condition of the blacks, and it would, therefore, be very inconsistent for me to look with approval upon any measure that infringes upon the inalienable rights of white men, whether or not they are born in another land or speak a different language from our own.

Flushed with hope, full of the energy of youth and inspired by reformative ardor, the Party indeed offered every attraction to progressive-minded Northerners. Nearly all the great editors, the distinguished men of letters, the leaders in law, theology, medicine, and learning, had been drawn into its ranks. In State after State it named gubernatorial candidates of shining ability and integrity: John A. Andrew in Massachusetts, Edwin D. Morgan in New York, Andrew G. Curtin in Pennsylvania, Richard Yates in Illinois, Oliver P. Morton in Indiana. To a great degree, the State campaigns carried the national ticket, and the combined effort of the future governors made Lincoln President. Meanwhile, in bright contrast with the stained, jaded veterans of the Buchanan-Breckinridge Democracy rode the champions who had swung to the saddle for Lincoln—Seward, making an admirable series of speeches in the Northwest; Charles Francis Adams, no stump orator, but so deeply aroused that he accompanied and aided Seward; Chase, redoubtable in Ohio and useful elsewhere; William M. Evarts, George William Curtis, John Sherman, Lyman Trumbull, Carl Schurz, and Francis P. Blair, Jr. The star of destiny seemed to sit visibly on the forehead of the organization.

When in August Missouri reelected the junior Blair, as the first Republican Representative from a slave State, a thrill of exultation ran through the ranks. This seemed one of the most important events of the campaign. Lyman Trumbull had gone to St. Louis to speak for Blair; so had Carl Schurz. The proslavery forces had denounced Blair as an abolitionist, using the foulest epithets. Such bitter feeling had been engendered that his life was in danger from ruffians, his public meetings provoked riots, and a heavy armed guard of Wide Awakes was needed to protect him. Carrying his district by nearly fifteen hundred votes, he proclaimed that his victory sealed the position of St. Louis as a Republican city. His Northern friends now felt that theirs was a Party not merely of defense but of invasion, which would yet win the whole borderland.

Pains were taken to disavow radical purposes and reassure the Southern people. Most Republican leaders deplored the course of Charles Sumner. That Senator, lately returned from Europe, broke his long silence on June 4 by delivering a four-hour harangue on "The Barbarism of Slavery," a stilted, schematic piece of invective, not lacking in literary polish or pedantic learning but abominable in taste. After listing five elements of barbarism in the slave system, he expatiated upon its practical results by the familiar method of comparing Northern and Southern manufactures, commerce, railroads, schools, and presses.[26] The speech was precisely what a Western editor called it, able, exasperating, and useless. Since Sumner denominated himself a Republican, it helped convince Southerners that the Party had a malevolent hatred of slavery as an institution, and of slaveholders as evildoers. Republican members of Congress generally agreed that it was vindictive and even brutal, that it pointed to no remedy for the evils it assailed, and that it simply impaired Sumner's influence, angered Southern leaders, and hurt the party.[27] Greeley's *Tribune* was obviously dismayed. A few other Republicans, such as Carl Schurz, went to unwise lengths in attacking slavery as a national evil. The general tone of speakers and press, however, was moderate and conciliatory.

It fell to Seward to make the most important effort to prove that the Party would be circumspect and rigidly constitutional in dealing with slavery, a task which brought out all his natural conservatism. In his western speeches he cooed as gently as any mourning dove of Auburn. The "irrepressible conflict" became, in his new interpretation, simply a phrase to signify a certain rivalry between slavery and free labor. The nation needed quiet, he said in Madison, Wisconsin, and the conflict between the slave and free States must end. "The time has come to repress it. The people will have it repressed. They are not to be forever disputing upon old issues and controversies. New subjects for national action will come up." The Republican Party would be the agent in this happy consumma-

26 But the speech had a strong appeal to antislavery radicals; Pierce, *Sumner*, III, 610–614.
27 William Salter, *Grimes*, 127.

tion, for once it was decided that slavery should never enter any Territory, "that will end the irrepressible conflict." [28] Thus manfully—and wisely—did Seward eat his rash words of two years earlier.

Pursuing the same theme, Republican editors and speakers labored to dissociate their party from the abolitionists, who, upon a budget of fifty dollars, had nominated Gerrit Smith for the Presidency. The noisier abolitionists like Wendell Phillips, who attacked Lincoln as a "knave" and "the slave-hound of Illinois," helped mightily in this dissociation. While the motives of antislavery extremists commanded respect, declared the New York *Tribune*, their methods had always been absurd and impractical. With such men the Republicans had no connection. The Party proposed to circumscribe slavery by prohibiting it in the Territories, but they did not propose to meddle with it in the States; for there they would use only moral implements. If slavery was ever to be overthrown in the South, it would have to be by the Southerners themselves—the other States could have no share in the work.[29] Greeley, too, it will be seen, had to eat a good many words.

Unfortunately, the prominence in the Party of a few such radicals as John A. Andrew (who at heart was an abolitionist, fierce in condemnation of the peculiar Southern institution) counteracted the bland terms of Seward and Trumbull, the *Tribune* and the *Evening Post*. Carl Schurz uttered words of folly, insulting the South and deriding the idea of secession. Many suspicious Democrats agreed with the New Orleans *Picayune* that as the Jacobin Clubs had triumphed over the Montagnards, so the Sumners, Andrews, Wades, and Zach Chandlers would triumph over the cautious Thurlow Weeds and Fessendens.[30] The fact was that the Republican Party already showed that sharp division between its moderate and radical wings which was to plague President Lincoln in years to come. The gulf between zealots like Giddings, Chase, Sumner, Julian, and Greeley, and such moderates as Weed, Cameron, Bates, Blair, and Corwin, was already wide and deep.

The main driving force of the Republican campaign was thrown behind the homestead issue in the Northwest, the tariff issue in Pennsylvania, New Jersey, and New England, the Pacific Railroad in the Mississippi Valley, and internal improvements everywhere.[31] A call went up for a campaign of education. Be-

28 *Works*, IV, 366.
29 N. Y. *Weekly Tribune*, September 8, 1860.
30 N. O. *Picayune*, September 11, 1860.
31 The fifth tract issued by the Republican Association of Washington (a series of great effectiveness) dealt with Administration policy upon the overland mail routes and Butterfield contract. It accused the Administration of illegal and improper acts to bring the overland mail down from St. Louis to the 32d parallel, thus traversing arid desert country merely to further the construction of a Pacific railroad along Southern lines. The argument had influence in the Middle West, including Missouri. St. Louis *Missouri Democrat*, August 16, 1859.

fore the end, it was estimated that not less than ten thousand set speeches had been made for the Party in New York alone, and fifty thousand in the Union.[32] Of books and pamphlets an abundance was provided. The *Campaign Textbook* prepared by Greeley and John F. Cleveland, a large volume in double columns of fine print, crammed with speeches, documents, and tables, and selling at sixty-six cents a copy in quantity lots, reached its fourteenth edition by the beginning of October. A pamphlet on the homestead bill, available in German as well as English, and a summary of the Covode findings were distributed by hundreds of thousands. In a typical rural county of Illinois—Madison—some six thousand campaign documents were distributed by the middle of June. Nor did the Republican managers confine themselves to their own party publications. Mid-Western communities reported a keen demand for disunion and proslavery speeches by Southern Democrats, which were used to win over shaky voters. Good use was made, too, of Cobb's report at the end of 1858 on the sad condition of the Treasury. The Republican press from Maine to Nebraska volleyed and thundered on those promises which seemed likeliest to capture votes.[33]

"This Homestead measure," a Minnesota delegate in Chicago had written Simon Cameron, "overshadows everything with us, and throughout the West." Everywhere from Ohio to Kansas the cry of free land had grown immensely popular.[34] People believed that it meant opportunity for the poor man and his children, rapid development of the country, and a growth in the wealth of the whole central valley. The sad situation of many settlers in Kansas and Nebraska, utterly destitute this summer and fall after a season of drought, was used to drive home the argument. Journalists pointed out that countless preemptors, unable to pay the government $200 in gold for a farm of one hundred and sixty acres, had obtained it by borrowing money to purchase a land warrant. A warrant for one hundred and sixty acres might be had as low as $150. But to get the $150, the borrower must pay interest at four and even five percent a month

32 N. Y. *Weekly Tribune*, November 10, 1860.
33 See scores of entries in Trumbull Papers, May-October, 1860.
34 Stephen Miller, April 2, 1860; Cameron Papers. This popularity is proved by the fact that Republican conventions in every Northern State and in Missouri and Kentucky this year adopted homestead planks; while Democratic conventions in every Northwestern State, four New England States, and New York and New Jersey, did the same. Files of N. Y. *Herald*, January-July, 1860. A change of one vote in twenty-seven would have given Douglas Iowa and Illinois; a change of one in twenty the whole Northwest. Without the homestead issue, or the vigorous appeal to the foreign-born, the Republicans would doubtless have lost important States. W. E. Dodd, "The Fight for the Northwest," *Am. Hist. Rev.*, XVI, 774-788; Donnal V. Smith, "Influence of the Foreign-Born of the Northwest in the Election of 1860," *Miss. Valley Hist. Rev.*, XIX, 192-204. Joseph Schafer in "Who Elected Lincoln?" in the *Am. Hist. Rev.*, XLVI, 51-63, reaches the conclusion that more Wisconsin Germans voted for Douglas in 1860 than for Lincoln, and that it was an upsurge of enthusiasm among old American groups which gave Lincoln the palm. But in Illinois and Iowa the Germans seem to have turned mainly to the Republican ticket. See Jay Monaghan's article, *Journal Ill. State Hist. Soc.*, XXV, 133-139.

REPUBLICAN
MASS MEETING.

A Grand Mass Meeting will be held at

ITHACA, ON FRIDAY, AUGUST 31, 1860,

AT NOON,

For the purpose of RATIFYING the Nomination of

LINCOLN AND HAMLIN
—AND THE—
STATE TICKET.

HORACE GREELEY,
OF NEW YORK.
GEN. B. F. BRUCE,
OF MADISON CO., AND

HON. C. L. BEALE

MEMBER OF CONGRESS FROM COLUMBIA CO..
Have been POSITIVELY ENGAGED, and will address the meeting.

HON. DAVID WILMOT,
OF PENNSYLVANIA,

Has been written to and is expected to be present.

Republican Orators at Ithaca, New York.

—and attorney's fees in addition. If a settler met a crop failure the first year, he had the hard alternative of making a forced sale of his land and improvements or submitting to foreclosure. Kansas editors·furnished many poignant instances. One Burgett Thomas was notified early in 1860 that he must pay $200 with four percent a month interest from August 28, 1860, and fees of $40, or lose his farm. A settler named Gannon was called upon to pay $282 with interest at forty-eight percent a year from September 3, 1859, and $50 fees, or be sold out. One earnest pamphleteer got out a series of letters with such captions as: "Land Sales! Land Sharks! Forty-eight per cent for money! How Democracy Protects Workingmen, Starving Women, and Helpless Babes! Need of a Homestead Law." [35]

The record established by Republican Congressmen in support of the Morrill tariff bill was effective in parts of the East, and particularly so in Pennsylvania, where the conservatism of Philadelphia had to be combatted. Half the iron of the country was made in the Keystone State. The protectionists pointed out that only two Republicans in both houses had been against Morrill's measures, and one of these was an Ohioan who believed the wool schedule too low. Arguments were specially addressed to the workingmen—for ironmasters and manufacturers needed none. The laboring masses of Pennsylvania had been deluded in 1846 and 1857, declared Republican campaigners; would they cheat themselves once more by voting the Democratic ticket? Irish, German, and other immigrants, wrote a pamphleteer, "begin to see that a judicious tariff policy, on manufactured goods, sustains them at work in our factories; and therefore I have witnessed meetings of laborious Germans, Irish workmen, and of Frenchmen, and all of them meeting as Republicans, to sustain Mr. Lincoln for President." [36] As William D. ("Pig-Iron") Kelley, destined to become the staunchest pillar of protectionism, made a successful run for Congress in Pennsylvania, Representatives Morrill and John Sherman delivered stirring tariff speeches in the State. The trend of sentiment there was unmistakable.

Nor was the tariff plank without some support in the Northwest. In view of the oft-stated thesis that this section naturally stood with the South for low tariffs, the support which Medill of the Chicago *Tribune* gave the demand is significant. He sent Chase repeated pleas to make it clear that he was not a free trader. "Nobody is in favor of a high protective tariff or prohibitive tariff," he wrote. "But the present one is ruinous. It is taxation without even incidental protection. There must be a change; the country will not receive, will not enjoy solid safe prosperity until we supply more of our own wants and import less from abroad of those staples which we can so well make at home." [37]

35 Thaddeus Hyatt Papers, 1860. KHS.
36 Hotaling, *The Questions in the Canvass,* pamphlet.
37 Chase Papers, LC, July-August, 1860; Cf. T. E. Strevey, *Joseph Medill and the Chicago Tribune during the Civil War Period,* MS Doctoral Dissertation, Univ. of Chicago.

For all their emphasis on economic questions, the Republicans did not neglect emotional appeals. Their rallies, picnics, and mass meetings were as numerous as in '56, while the Wide Awake and kindred organizations, embodying and drilling hundreds of thousands of young men, were a spectacular feature of the contest. Hartford Republicans laid claim to originating these solid columns of marching men, who, in glazed capes of varying colors and smart military caps, bearing oil-burning torches and bright transparencies, swung down countless streets to the crash of brass bands and the roar of cadenced cheering. Nothing like them had been seen in America before. Their disciplined forces, lending fervor and enthusiasm to the Northern canvass, played no small part in the final result. They took pride in the military precision of their evolutions, and in developing a set of songs, salutes, and emblematic displays which were tumultuously stirring.[88]

Particularly picturesque were the well-advertised Wide Awake parades in Lincoln's home city and in New York. To the Springfield display streamed delegations from all over the Northwest, enlivening the little Illinois capital as never in its history. In the metropolis, the grand rally of the banners of light, as Republicans called it, was said to have marshalled ninety thousand well-trained Lincolnites into line. Broadway was packed to view the spectacle, which moved even cynical reporters to flights of ecstasy. From roofs along the route poured up a steady gush of rockets, roman candles, volcanoes, and other fireworks. The street itself seemed a river of fire. The martial swell of the music, the resounding tramp of the men, the fountains of flame and many-colored lights which shot upward on each side, the cheering of the spectators, answered by the sharp "one, two, three" of the Wide Awakes, all combined to produce an unforgettable impression. When, to the music of the bands, the tens of thousands of marchers took up the chorus of the song, "Ain't You Glad You Joined the Republicans?" the effect was tremendous.

[III]

The cardinal error of the Republicans was their failure to treat the now imminent danger of secession with the candor and emphasis which it required. That failure had various roots. It seemed to the Party's interest to minimize a peril which, if nakedly exposed, might drive many to vote for a candidate acceptable to the South; optimism is always easier than pessimism; and many honestly believed that the cry of "wolf, wolf!" would prove as empty now as before. Yet, however explained, the attitude was part of that national levity which we have identified as one key to the disaster which was about to befall the nation.

38 For the origin of the Wide Awakes, see N. Y. *Herald*, September 19, 1860.

When Henry W. Hilliard of Alabama said in Cooper Union that Lincoln's election would be followed by a terrible civil convulsion, he was derided by the New York *Tribune*, which declared that the stale Southern threats would appall nobody but fools, and that the diabolical mask did not frighten men who knew at what toyshop it was bought.[39] Seward, in his Northwestern speeches, was all reassurance. He told his Minneapolis audience that the menaces to the Union were absurd—nobody was afraid. At La Crosse, he said that the homogeneity of the American people furnished assurances for the future which enabled men to trample underfoot every threat of disunion, every apprehension of national dismemberment.[40] Edward Bates, who knew the Southern people better than most Republicans, was equally ready to pooh-pooh the rising storm. He dismissed what he called the idle fears of nervous people with the assertion that only a few conceited egotists were talking of a Southern confederacy, and that the Southern people as a whole could never be guilty of such wicked folly as rending the country in half.[41] These men should have listened more carefully to Southern leaders and paid closer heed to other plain indices of opinion. Perhaps Schurz made the most fatuous statement of all. Telling his St. Louis audience that secession talk was absurd, for "the mere anticipation of a Negro insurrection will paralyze the whole South," he struck the most painful nerve of slaveholders while adding to the foolish sense of Northern security.

In great parts of the South it was a summer of unprecedented excitement, with subterranean upheavals and rumblings. The Knights of the Golden Circle, a filibustering society organized a half dozen years earlier to promote the conquest of a wide crescent around the Gulf, was shifting its front to become a secessionist society. At the same time it clung to its filibustering designs, as was shown by a letter of its founder, George Bickley, in the Richmond *Whig*. Bickley, exhorting the South to rescue Mexico from the brigands who were pillaging and destroying the country, summoned an army of fellow rescuers to meet him on the banks of the Nueces with arms, wagons, mules, provisions, and $20 apiece.[42] As Lincoln's election became certain, a wave of apprehension regarding Negro insurrections again swept the South. Reports of a plot in upper Georgia ended in the arrest at Dalton of thirty-six Negroes accused of planning to burn the town and kill all its people. In Talladega, Alabama, two whites and eight Negroes were arrested, and one white man was summarily hanged. Bowling Green, Virginia, was thrown into fever by the mere arrival of a stranger who somehow looked like an abolitionist. A Louisianan traveling from Dallas to Crockett, Texas, to buy a farm, was almost lynched when his appearance ex-

39 N. Y. *Weekly Tribune*, September 22, 1860.
40 Bancroft, *Seward*, I, 549, 550.
41 Letter, September 15, to Keokuk Republicans, N. Y. *Weekly Tribune*, October 6, 1860.
42 Gray, *Hidden Civil War*, 70; N. Y. *Weekly Tribune*, June 28, 1860.

cited distrust. And during July and August the alarm and frenzy in other parts of Texas became almost a mass hysteria.

Incendiary fires were reported in nearly a dozen Texas towns. One excited editor wrote that the flames were no sooner put out in one settlement than they were lighted in another—all, of course, "kindled by the torches of abolitionists." This was taken as evidence of a diabolical plot to devastate all northern Texas. The Cameron *Sentinel* announced that during the summer the town patrol had found four guns, a pistol, and a dirk in the hands of Negroes. From another town came a report that colored people had collected a hundred bottles of strychnine to poison the inhabitants. Of valid evidence of any conspiracy or plan of concerted outbreak on the part of the slaves there seems to have been none. Some Northern observers suspected that the real object of this artificial panic was to check antislavery feeling among the Methodists and Germans of the State. Many people preferred the discipline and ministry of the Methodist Episcopal Church to that of the Methodist Episcopal Church South, for it was not sectional but national and its discipline seemed in better accord with Christian doctrine. Its precepts included a strong statement on the evil of slavery, a request that members should emancipate their slaves, and a rule forbidding any slaveholder to be a traveling preacher. The feeling against the church and its more outspoken ministers had engendered mob violence in Missouri and other places. The wave of hysteria in Texas, the worst thus far known, resulted in the lynching of a moderate antislavery man named Bewley, mild of speech and peaceful in demeanor; and it prompted strong protests in the church press of the North.[43] Various Southern observers meanwhile believed that the Texas furor was concocted primarily to weaken the Bell-Everett ticket and to destroy the influence of Sam Houston and his Union-loving friends. Alex and Linton Stephens spoke scornfully of the "pretended insurrections" in the Lone Star State.

Even at the time, the New Orleans *Picayune* declared of the Texas furore that "much of the apprehension may be unreal and some of the facts imperfectly proved," while no modern Texas historian credits the wild rumors of the time. They were of a piece with the reports in northern Georgia and other places. Yet the important fact was that the stories of insurrection, arson, and murder, sweeping the South, aroused deep emotions of fear and resentment. A Mississippi brother of Joseph Holt, writing that within three weeks he had read of twenty-three abolitionist agents being lynched, attributed their "hellish" activities to Northern organizations. Even John H. Reagan believed the excited tales, for he shortly told Congress: [44]

43 Cf. letter by T. M. Eddy September 7, 1860, in *Northwestern Christian Advocate.*
44 N. Y. *Weekly Tribune,* September 8, 15; N. O. *Picayune,* August 19, 1860; *Cong. Globe,* January 15, 1861.

We found, for the last two or three years, the members of the Methodist Church North, and others, living in Texas, were propagating abolition doctrines there. We warned them not to carry on their scheme of producing disaffection among our Negroes; but they persisted, and did not cease until they had organized a society called the Mystic Red. Under its auspices, the night before the last August election the towns were to be burned down and the people murdered. There now lie in ashes near a dozen towns and villages in my district. . . . The poisonings were only arrested by information which came to light before the plan could be carried into execution. The citizens were forced to stand guard for months. . . . A portion paid the penalty of their crimes; others were driven out of the country. These things had their effect on the public mind. They were the result of abolition teachings; a part of the irrepressible conflict; a part of the legitimate fruits of Republicanism.

As election day approached, the sense of defensive solidarity in the South became intensified.[45] Organizations of minute men, military bodies well trained in the simpler evolutions, were formed in Alabama, South Carolina, and Georgia. Yancey, wearing a suit of Southern homespun, reviewed in New Orleans a parade of semi-military clubs, including the Yancey Rangers. Several States were systematically buying arms. In many communities such a spirit of terrorism was abroad that out-and-out Unionists dared not raise their voices. While a growing body of Southerners avowed that they actually wished Lincoln elected so as to precipitate the crisis, sober men who, like B. F. Perry of South Carolina and Goggin of Virginia, asserted their readiness to abide by Republican victory, were angrily hooted down. The New Orleans *Commercial Bulletin* declared that secession would cause the steamboats to rot at the levee, cotton to sink to ruinous levels, and real estate to become unsalable. Not so, retorted the Charleston *Mercury;* secession will usher in a new age of prosperity for the South.[46] When on the eve of election the opening of the one-hundred-and-three-

45 This is Crenshaw's phrase; *Slave States,* 234. The South, said the Washington *Constitution* on September 13, is "in a blaze." Southerners staying at White Sulphur Springs had passed indignant resolutions calling on their people to fight rather than submit to Northern tyranny. Stories were flying around the section of insults offered to slaveholders who travelled above the Potomac. The *Constitution* on September 28 quoted a letter of James L. Orr to Alexander H. Stephens, the former Speaker writing that it would be fatal to let the Black Republicans take possession of the army, navy, and treasury. "If the South should think upon this subject as I do, no Black Republican President should ever execute any law within her borders, unless at the point of the bayonet and over the dead bodies of her sons." Like the Boston *Post* and other Administration papers, the *Constitution* was asserting that the Union could never be preserved by force.

46 The New Orleans correspondent of the Charleston *Mercury* (November 6) described the military character of the Breckinridge clubs in Louisiana. W. Doubleday of New York sent Lincoln two letters from Captain Abner Doubleday, of the small garrison in Charleston Harbor; "the last of a large number, all, until recently, pointing to the purpose of the Charlestonians to seize the forts in their harbor." Robert Todd Lincoln Papers. Yancey, touring the country from Boston to Mobile, declared the right of every State which objected to Lincoln's inauguration to secede.

mile Charleston & Savannah Railroad was celebrated in Savannah with a large Carolina delegation present, the company refused to honor a toast to the President of the United States.[47]

Northern tempers rose in response to Southern taunts and defiances. By early fall, many Republicans and Douglas Democrats were thoroughly angry, feeling that the time had come to test whether the Union could survive a fair and legal election. When the thickening tokens of Republican victory produced alarm in mercantile circles and a fall in stock prices, Zach Chandler angrily charged certain interests with trying to bring on a financial crisis to defeat Lincoln. "The West have put up with this attempt to bully, coerce, or frighten them out of their political convictions long enough," he stormed. Seward, speaking at Auburn, dropped his easy optimism and uttered a ringing appeal for Northern unity irrespective of party. "It is time, high time," he said, "that we know whether this is a constitutional government under which we live. It is high time that we know, since the Union is threatened, who are its friends and who are its enemies." [48]

[IV]

Ironically, while the political struggle held the nation in a grip of passion and apprehension, scattered newspaper reports of the early census returns of 1860 appeared, reflecting the unbounded vigor and spectacular growth of the past decade. Still the country grew—still the youthful sinewy race tramped forward:

We debouch upon a newer mightier world, varied world,
Fresh and strong the world we seize, world of labor and the march.

It was not merely that the returns showed a growth of more than eight and a half million people in the decade, to a grand total of 31,443,500. The features of a new American society were appearing. Thus, the value of manufactures had risen from a little over a billion dollars in 1849 to $1,886,000,000 ten years later, and the railroad system had expanded from 8,500 miles to more than 30,000. Although the nation was still primarily rural, tokens of the coming urban age could be discerned. In 1850, one-eighth of the people had lived in centers of eight thousand or more; now nearly one-sixth dwelt in such cities. New York, with Brooklyn, counted well over a million inhabitants, and Philadelphia well over a half-million. Baltimore held third place with 212,000, and Boston, Cincinnati, and St. Louis could boast of between 160,000 and

47 Charleston *Mercury*, October 5, November 5, 1860.
48 Greeley, *Amer. Conflict*, I, 327.

180,000 each. The South was plainly falling behind in the race for population. Of the eight and a half million increase during the decade, the States of the future Confederacy could lay claim to only about two million.

Most arresting of all the new census figures were those which disclosed the tremendous growth of the Northwest. The eleven States and Territories

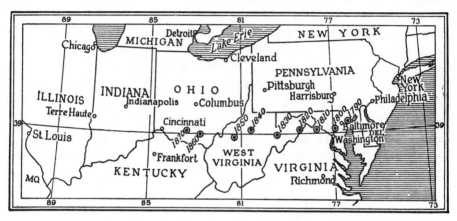

The Center of Population Swings into Freesoil Territory

which stretched from Ohio to Dakota inclusive had contained but 5,403,000 people when President Taylor died; now they counted 9,100,000. The popula-- tion of Illinois had almost doubled during the decade, that of Wisconsin had more than doubled, and that of Iowa had more than trebled. One striking fact could not escape even the casual analyst. Whereas in the North the old States grew vigorously alongside the new ones, in the South the old States were comparatively at a standstill. New York, for example, had enjoyed a popula- tion growth of nearly 900,000, and Pennsylvania of almost 600,000; but Vir- ginia's population had risen by only 175,000, and that of South Carolina by a mere 35,000. A Southern historian speaks of the exhaustion of Virginia and her coastal neighbors; and though the word is too strong, it is true that North Carolina's population increase of 77,000 compared but ill with Massachusetts' of 237,000.

Some of the most striking figures were not publicized at the time, although they bore directly upon the election. These were statistics pointing to the remarkable shift of Northwestern trade from the Gulf to the North Atlantic. In 1850 the North Central area had sent two-thirds as much corn to the South as it sent to the East; but in 1860 it sent only one-fourth as much. In 1850 it had shipped four times as much pork to the South (1,200,000 barrels) as it shipped to the East; in 1860 it sent the South only 570,000 barrels, and the

East 930,000 barrels. The swing in wheat movements from South to East was still more notable. In 1850 the Northwest had sent roughly half a million bushels southward, and five millions eastward; ten years later it still sent only a little more than half a million bushels to the South, but it shipped nearly 28,500,000 bushels eastward. The building of an efficient railroad system had enabled the East to capture trade that formerly went down the Mississippi, and to exchange its manufactures for Western foodstuffs. These commercial ties had their political consequences.

We have evidence in newspaper comment that the census of 1860 was being watched with interest; and attentive Southerners unquestionably saw in it new omens of the day when their section would be hopelessly outstripped in population, wealth, and political power.

[V]

The early State elections all pointed to the certain result. In September, Maine chose a Republican governor by more than eighteen thousand majority, and Vermont by more than twenty-two thousand. October brought the Pennsylvania and Indiana elections. In both States the Republicans decisively triumphed, electing their governor in Pennsylvania by thirty-two thousand and in Indiana by nearly ten thousand majority. Thereafter, the principal anxiety of the party managers was not over Lincoln, but their remaining State tickets. In Illinois, for example, Lyman Trumbull sent out a call for leaders in other States to come and help, for a desperate fight was being waged by the opposition to win the legislature. In the South, the Pennsylvania and Indiana result had a stunning effect. Voters stampeded from both the Bell and Douglas parties to the Breckinridge fold; for they saw that their only hope of defeating the Republicans (if they had any) lay in giving the Kentuckian a solid Southern vote. It seems probable that the early State elections also affected Douglas adversely in the North. The St. Paul *Pioneer and Democrat*, a Douglas organ, turned to Lincoln, declaring that the Little Giant was out of the race; while another Douglas paper, the Toledo *Herald and Times*, likewise advised its readers to vote the Republican ticket.[49]

49 Pennsylvania Democrats also forsook Douglas. A. K. McClure, Republican State Chairman, wrote Lincoln after the State election that the Democrats had utterly abandoned the national contest. "The Douglas straight ticket has now no force, and will not be pushed with any energy. Many of that camp will not vote at all—others will vote for you, and some will vote for the Douglas electors on the Reading ticket and scratch the balance. Our own men will, notwithstanding, vote, and poll more than they did for Curtin." October 15, 1860; Robert Todd Lincoln Papers. One Democratic observer had the courage to tell Buchanan the truth. "The fact is, and there is no use in assuming any other, the State is freesoiled and abolitionized. The tariff did something toward the result, but not all, as the terrible frontier majorities show." W. S. Hirst, October 12, 1860; Buchanan Papers.

It was evident by mid-September that Lincoln would carry all New England, all the Northwest, Ohio, and Pennsylvania. The last, infinitesimal chance of his opponents rested upon New York, where a huge city poll might just conceivably throw the contest into Congress.

Election day fell on November 6. No violence marred the polling. By an early hour next morning it was known that Lincoln had swept New York and at least fourteen other States, giving him a clear majority of electors. As returns from the border States, the South, and the Far West gradually came in, his total electoral vote rose to one hundred and eighty—a majority of fifty-seven. Some unexpected results presented themselves. The most astonishing disclosure was that Douglas, despite his lion-hearted fight, had won only twelve electors—nine in Missouri, three in New Jersey. The fact that the Breckinridge nomination had been made to kill was plainer than ever, for if the popular vote for Breckinridge had been added to Douglas's, the total would have exceeded that cast for Lincoln by three hundred and fifty thousand. As it was, Breckinridge obtained the seventy-two electoral votes of eleven slave States, and Bell the thirty-nine electors in Virginia, Kentucky, and Tennessee.

The followers of Douglas, if disheartened by his weak showing in the electoral college, could take comfort in his popular vote, which was 1,376,957 as against 1,866,452 cast for Lincoln. Breckinridge obtained only 849,781 votes, and Bell only 588,879. What the result would have been had the Democratic Party avoided its tragic schism none can undertake to say. If the whole Douglas, Bell, and Breckinridge vote, as finally cast, had been consolidated for any one of the three candidates, Lincoln would still have won with one hundred and sixty-nine electors, a majority of thirty-five. But if the Democratic Party had remained united, doubtless the danger of disunion would have seemed far slighter; the Constitutional Union Party would then probably have played a much smaller role; and far more spirited efforts would have been made in the North to rally all conservative voters against the Republican ticket. Had Douglas been nominated at Charleston, Lincoln might well—in view of the different trend which the campaign would have taken—have lost.

The results of the contest obviously illuminated certain faults in the nation's machinery for electing its Presidents. A good deal could be said in criticism of a system under which a candidate who polled only a large third of the popular vote could carry the electoral college so decisively. Lincoln had not received a single ballot in nearly one-third of the States, and had not gained a single elector in the entire South, yet he was now to be head of the entire country. The election was nevertheless constitutional, legally fair, and not more undemocratic in character than others before or since. Lincoln had an unimpeachable title. It could be pointed out that he had received substantial support in five slaveholding States: about 17,000 votes in Missouri, where he carried St. Louis, 3,800 in Delaware, 2,300 in Maryland, 1,900 in Virginia, and 1,300 in Kentucky. There were Northern States in which Breckinridge had likewise polled a meagre vote; he had less than a thousand followers in Wisconsin, only a thousand in Iowa, and only 2,400 in Illinois. One of the remarkable features of the election was the closeness of the race in half a dozen States. It was by margins of only a few hundred votes over the nearest oppo-

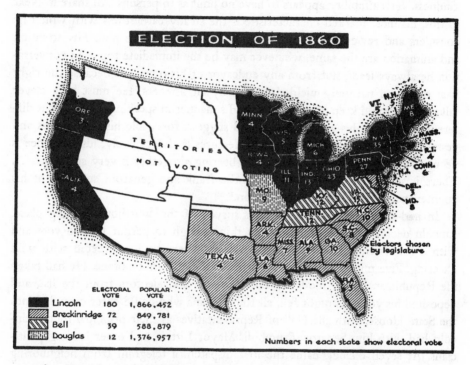

nent that Douglas carried Missouri, Bell carried Virginia, Breckinridge carried Maryland, and Lincoln carried Oregon and California. Altogether, it was a very curious, a very mixed, and except for its grand central result, a very inscrutable election.

[VI]

The most interesting scenes on election day naturally took place in Springfield. That pleasant prairie town, with its neat white-painted houses, its lines of maples, elms, box elders, and catalpas, their last leaves fluttering down in the chill winds, its central square surrounded by stores, hotels, and courthouse, and its dominating State Capitol, was tremulous with excitement as the polling began.

Strangers helped fill the streets—some of them "floaters," brought in as short-term residents to swell the normal vote of their party, more of them Republicans come to celebrate victory. Roving bands of music and occasional discharges of cannon enlivened the day. Lincoln, taking refuge in the governor's room of the State House, which commanded a full view of the courthouse opposite, settled himself in an armchair and chatted with numerous callers. The New York *Tribune* correspondent was struck by his winning manners and unaffected kindness. "His affability appears to have no limit as to persons. All share it. Next to this, his most marked characteristic is the steady earnestness with which he considers and reviews all subjects that are brought before him. His attention and animation are the same, whatever may be the immediate topic. In conversation he always leads, not from any endeavor of his own, but because the right is at once and naturally yielded to him by all listeners. He must be a clever talker who would keep even with him. His manner in speaking is somewhat different from what his appearance would suggest, for while his movements and gestures are quick, and the play of his features is always lively, his utterance is peculiarly measured and emphatic. His bearing altogether is very striking. . . . There is something beyond all art in the frank and generous sunshine of his countenance. It is full of fine expression." [50]

In mid-afternoon, after a cautious survey of the courthouse polling place, Lincoln decided that the crowd was thin enough to permit him to vote and with a few friends strolled across the way, where he was greeted with wild cheering. Five minutes later he was back in the governor's office. He had taken the Republican ballot, modestly cut his name and electors from the list, and deposited his vote. As night fell, all Republicans who could enter crowded into the State House, with the Hall of Representatives as their principal focus. Lincoln had with him Senator Trumbull, Mayor Litten, and other leading politicians. At seven o'clock came the first dispatch, a telegram from neighboring Decatur showing large Republican gains over 1856. [51]

The early news was overwhelmingly reassuring as to the Northwest, but left everyone uncertain of the East. Lincoln, anxious and elated by turns, decided about nine o'clock to walk to the telegraph office outside, where bulletins were coming in rapidly. Before ten, a telegram arrived from Simon Cameron: "Pennsylvania 70,000 for you. New York safe. Glory enough." But still there was no direct word from the crucial Empire State. The minutes ticked away until midnight. Lincoln proved the quietest of the watchers, manifesting quite as much interest in the local offices and the fate of fellow candidates as in his own fortunes. As the first Missouri news arrived, he straightened up, saying: "We shall

50 N. Y. *Weekly Tribune*, November 17, 1860.
51 Angle, *Here I Have Lived*, 251, 252; N. Y. *Tribune, Herald*, November 8, 1860.

now get some licks back"—but they were not severe licks. Then came a summons to his party to step over to a hall where Springfield women had prepared a supper. He walked through the door to see a gaily decorated room and a long table spread with food, while a hundred feminine voices chorussed: "How do you do, Mr. President?" The guests had hardly seated themselves when a messenger burst in waving a telegram from Simeon Draper which announced that New York was safe—that the fusion vote in the metropolis had been held to a mere twenty-seven thousand. This was almost too good to be true. A chorus of "You're elected now! It's all over!" shook the rafters, and the gathering burst into spontaneous song:

> Ain't you glad you joined the Republicans?
> Joined the Republicans—Joined the Republicans! [52]

Meanwhile, the same news had electrified the crowd at the State House. Men hugged each other, threw up their hats, hurrahed for Lincoln and New York, and even rolled on the floor in their delight. More dispatches poured in. Lincoln, back in the telegraph office, undoubtedly began to feel a sobering realization of his new burdens. When a late telegram—with which fat Jesse Dubois tore breathlessly into the State House—proclaimed that New York had gone Republican by fifty thousand, another scene of happy excitement took place. The old Capitol had never before heard such a roar. Then the President-elect, specially pleased by word of a party victory in Springfield, said good night and went home. The crowd began to break up, scattering over town the glad news: "New York fifty thousand for Lincoln!" All Springfield was agog; men shouting from housetops, from sidewalks, from buggies. Parties roamed the streets in the lightening dawn, chorussing: "Ain't I glad I joined the Republicans!" And as Lincoln closed the door of his house behind him, the boom of a cannon dragged into the square by young men of the town rolled forth to greet the morn.[53]

A very different scene took place that night in Mobile. Stephen A. Douglas had battled to the last; from Montgomery he had gone to Selma to speak, and then on election eve had told a great Mobile audience that their rights would be far safer in the Union than outside. He had spent election day quietly. After dinner he went with his secretary, Sheridan, to the office of John Forsyth's *Register* to await the news. The paper's telegraph service was good. Dispatches from the North and East soon made it plain that Douglas was overwhelmed and Lincoln victorious. This in itself was no shock to the Little Giant. Weeks before,

[52] See the description by the correspondent of the *Missouri Democrat,* quoted in the Havana, Illinois, *Popular Sovereign,* November 7, 1860.
[53] Springfield correspondence in N. Y. *Weekly Tribune,* November 16, 1860; Baringer, "Campaign Techniques in Illinois, 1860," *Trans. Ill. State Hist. Soc.,* 1932.

telling Anson Burlingame that Lincoln was sure of election, he had rejoiced in the weight that four Illinois men would soon have in Washington. "Won't it be a splendid sight, Burlingame," he had said, "to see McDougall returned Senator from California, Baker from Oregon, and Douglas and Old Abe all at Washington together?" [54]

But the news had to be accepted against the background of his recent observations. Completing his Southern tour, he had found new proofs that a conspiracy formed the previous spring to dissever the Union was nearing its climax. He had to interpret the news in the light of the intention of a hundred Southern leaders, from Slidell, Cobb, and Toombs down to Yancey and Rhett, to dissolve the Union once Lincoln won; in the light of the proclamation of even the friendly Atlanta *Confederacy:* "Let the consequences be what they may— whether the Potomac is crimsoned in human gore, and Pennsylvania Avenue is paved ten fathoms in depth with mangled bodies, or whether the last vestige of liberty is swept from the face of the American continent, the South will never submit to such humiliation and degradation as the inauguration of Abraham Lincoln." [55]

Forsyth asked his editorial associate to read Douglas an editorial for the *Register,* calling for a State convention to debate Alabama's course in the crisis. The best policy for Alabama Unionists, he explained to the Senator, would be to yield to the widespread demand for a convention, elect as many delegates as possible, and try to channel the proceedings into some safe outlet. Douglas dissented. If the Union men could not prevent a convention, he argued, they could not control it when it met. But Forsyth insisted on his view, and the editorial went to press. The Illinoisan, who saw more realistically than any leader except Stephens the disruption and bloodshed that lay ahead, left the office to return to the Battle House. As they walked through the desolate streets, his secretary observed that he was "more hopeless than I had ever before seen him." [56]

*   *   *   *   *

Men might, as always, dispute the meaning of the election. On the surface it seemed to offer no clean-cut national verdict for anything; certainly not for Lincoln and the Republican tenets. Yet its central import was actually plain: The nation had taken a mighty decision—the decision that slavery must be circumscribed and contained. Lincoln's 1,866,000 followers wished to contain the institution within existing limits by a flat Congressional refusal to recognize

54 N. Y. *Weekly Tribune,* September 8, 1860. James A. McDougall, who had been a Chicago lawyer and attorney-general of Illinois, was an intimate friend of Douglas.
55 Quoted in Dumond, *Secession Movement,* 104.
56 Wilson, *Slave Power,* II, 700; Milton, *Eve of Conflict,* 500.

it outside; the 1,375,000 adherents of Douglas wished to contain it by local-option type of popular sovereignty. But contained it would be, under either formula. No longer would a compact, determined Southern minority dictate national policy on the subject. The popular majority of the land had asserted itself, and a people's man, far stronger than the South supposed, stood ready to execute their will. Behind this decision that slavery had passed its flood tide and must henceforth stand still or recede, lay an implicit decision on the two rival assumptions that had divided South and North—one, the assumption that slavery was right and wholesome; the other, that it was wrong and deleterious. Slavery might persist indefinitely within the fifteen slave States, but as to its restriction, and as to the faith that it was in the path of ultimate extinction, the nation had come at last to an unavoidable determination.

From that decision there was but one appeal. Dreadfully clear now, to ears attuned to the future, sounded the drums and bugles.

11

The Lower South Secedes

THE MOMENT the election of Lincoln was certain, much of the Lower South gave way to a frenzy of excitement in which the clamor for secession of radical politicians and editors seemed to drown out the voices of conservative Unionists. Those who had been threatening the severance of the Union, and who had to make their threats good or confess impotence, united in a galvanic effort to revolutionize their States. Yancey, Iverson, Rhett, T. R. R. Cobb, Porcher Miles, and men of similar convictions had prepared to employ the first surge of resentment to carry a number of capitals into separate secession. In South Carolina, Alabama, and Mississippi the demand for action was so instant and aggressive that it took the North aback. Elsewhere, and especially in the broad border region, feeling was much calmer. While influential men called for separation, it was evident that the movement would be stubbornly resisted. As Northern opinion recovered from the first shock of dismay, it took heart from this division of sentiment and plucked up hope that even in the Lower South a national sentiment might, as in 1850–51, assert itself with effect. The swift events of the first month, however, proved that the new situation held grimmer perils than that of ten years earlier.

South Carolina was like a bed of charcoal suddenly leaping into flame. The legislature was sitting at Columbia to choose presidential electors. As the returns came in, Rhett, Milledge L. Bonham, Keitt, and Ruffin, all present in the city, delivered impassioned speeches. The State Rights flag, a red star on a white ground, was flung out over public buildings. In Charleston on Wednesday the seventh, crowds thronged the streets, the palmetto flag was hoisted over the *Mercury* office amid wild cheering, J. D. B. De Bow and others spoke, and the announcement that Federal Judge A. G. Magrath and Collector W. F. Colcock had resigned their offices inspired general enthusiasm. In the next few days a spate of news kept the people aroused. The legislature had authorized the governor to spend $100,000 for arms; Senator Chesnut had resigned his seat in Washington and Hammond had followed suit; telegrams from other States were tendering the support of volunteer corps. Everywhere the stars and stripes were coming down, and the red star or palmetto flags were going up. In Columbia,

Charleston, and other centers, militia units and minute men had redoubled their drilling. Bonfires, parades, and "resistance rallies" were the order of the day.[1]

The fever seemed to rage only less violently in Alabama and Mississippi, while in lowland Georgia it was intense. The night after the election, the largest mass meeting that Savannah had ever witnessed called for a State convention and rapid defensive measures. Another meeting, two nights later, amended the resolutions to demand immediate secession. In Augusta a similar assemblage cheered secessionist speeches. Toombs, T. R. R. Cobb (Howell's brother), and other radicals made bitter addresses; the colonial flag of Georgia was raised at various points; and citizens gathered at many county seats to organize minute men.[2] At Montgomery, where Yancey on the night of November 10 roused a crowd to wild emotion, people seemed almost unanimous for secession. Although dispatches from Mobile declared that commercial men opposed a separation, some observers reported that nine-tenths of the country districts in the lowlands were for disunion. Leaders of volunteers told the governor they would have eighty thousand men under arms by New Year's Day. All the prominent officers of Alabama—the governor, both Senators, all Representatives but one, the Supreme Court judges—were in favor of drastic action.

Meanwhile, in Mississippi an overwhelming demand had arisen for a special session of the legislature. The spirit animating much of the Lower South was voiced by the mother of E. Kirby Smith, writing from St. Augustine to that future Confederate general:

> I never expected to see a revolution, to see our long cherished stars and stripes hauled down—but so it is—you are so far removed from the scene of these acts that you can form no idea of the excitement which prevails among all classes—all ages—women as well as men. Our Cause is a just one, and I fully believe Providence will smile upon it—if we can pass through it without a baptism of blood and fire, shall we not have reason to thank God with our whole hearts?[3]

[I]

For several reasons, South Carolina was in the best position to give the secessionist forces vigorous leadership. Since in that State alone presidential electors were chosen by the legislature, the two houses had met November 5; they would

1 Ruffin, MS Diary, November 7, ff., 1860; Schirmer, MS Diary; Charleston *Courier*, November 8, 10, 1860; Mrs. Mary B. Chesnut, *A Diary from Dixie*. A caucus of South Carolina leaders was said to have met, October 25, at Senator Hammond's house to make plans; Nicolay and Hay, *Lincoln*, II, 328.

2 Stephens, writing from Crawfordsville on November 8, makes the astonishing statement: "The people here are taken greatly by surprise at the result. They did not anticipate it and thought I was only indulging in unnecessary apprehensions when I told them months ago how it would most probably be." *Toombs, Stephens, Cobb Corr.*, 502.

3 St. Augustine, January 7, 1861; Kirby Smith Papers, Univ. of N. C.

reconvene again on the twenty-sixth for the regular session and to elect a governor. No legislature in the country was less representative of the masses. Seats were apportioned according to a ratio compounded of the white population and the amount of taxes paid, so that the wealthy lowlands, with their heavy slave properties, held a marked advantage over the poorer up-country where the whites so strongly preponderated over the Negroes. Governor Gist, a wealthy planter and veteran State Rights man, had already prophesied the secession which he wished to make a reality. A month before the election, he had sent the before-noted letters to various Southern governors declaring that South Carolina would secede if she had any assurance of similar action by another or other States, and would desire their cooperation. As soon as his legislature met, he had informed it that in view of the probability of a Republican victory, which would give the South the prospect of becoming a mere province in a consolidated despotism, it should remain in session, and if Lincoln were chosen, should call a State convention to consider modes of redress.[4]

The legislature was ready to act. Differences arose as to the time schedule, one party demanding immediate and separate secession while another urged delay until joint action with other States could be arranged; but the issue was quickly resolved. On November 9, a bill passed calling a secession convention, to which the various districts should send as many delegates as their quotas in the legislature—thus preserving lowland domination. The election was to be held January 8, and the delegates were to meet a week later. This would give time for ascertaining the temper of other States. But when Charleston heard of the movement for delay, a great mass meeting entered a vehement protest; it was seconded by a body of influential Georgians who had come for the before-mentioned celebration of the opening of the Savannah-Charleston Railroad; and a committee of three was hurried to Columbia by special train. The legislature then reversed itself, fixing the election for December 6 and the convention for the seventeenth. The members, caustically wrote J. L. Petigru, were afraid to "trust the second thought of even their own people." It seems probable, however, that a decisive majority of South Carolinians wished to express themselves without delay, and to point the road for their sister States.[5]

The people have taken the helm, exultantly wrote Judge Longstreet to the Richmond *Enquirer*. They have carried the politicians before them. South Carolinians feel a universal resolution never to submit to Black Republican rule.

4 Nicolay and Hay, *Lincoln*, II, 306 ff., gives Gist's corr. with the governors. The S. C. *House Journal* and *Senate Journal* for 1860 mirror the rush of the radicals, though Speaker James Simons of Charleston was a moderate, and many members opposed precipitate action.

5 Carson, *James L. Petigru*, 361; Lillian A. Kibler, "Union Sentiment in S. C. in 1860," *Journal Southern Hist.*, IV, August, 1938.

"You might as well attempt to control a tornado as to attempt to stop them from secession." He praised the high spirits of the populace. "All is smiles, joy, and good fellowship." [6]

Mississippi was prepared, though with less precipitancy, to fall into line. Governor John J. Pettus had already written Gist that if any State acted, he believed his own would go with her. He hastened (November 13) to call the legislature into session on the twenty-sixth. Lincoln's election, he wrote, demonstrated that men eager to "destroy the peace, property, and prosperity of the Southern section" had gained control of the government, and that Mississippi must provide surer safeguards for life and liberty than could be hoped for "from Black Republican oaths." He also privately arranged a meeting in Jackson of part of the delegation in Congress to advise him. Here the usual disagreement arose between advocates of joint and disjoint secession; but when Reuben Davis offered a resolution calling on the governor to propose immediate and separate State action, it was adopted—the governor voting for it.[7] Gist had telegraphed Pettus asking whether the South Carolina convention should make secession effective at once or on March 4, and, again at the suggestion of Davis, a majority of the gathering decided that Gist should be advised in favor of immediate secession. The Jackson *Mississippian* was arguing that it would be wisest to secede while the national government still was in friendly hands.[8] To wait for joint secession might mean waiting forever.

"We are no longer one people," wrote a representative Alabama secessionist. "A paper parchment is all that holds us together, and the sooner that bond is severed the better it will be for both parties." As we have noted, the legislature early in the year had provided for calling a State convention if the Republicans won the Presidency. But when did Lincoln's election really take place—on November 6, or when the electoral college cast their ballots on December 5? Governor Moore, who had assured Gist that he believed Alabama would secede with any two or more cooperating States, decided that the true date fell in December. He made it known at once, however, that he would designate December 24 for the election of delegates, and January 7 as the day for the convention to meet; so that the canvass began forthwith in most counties. Here, again, the secessionist party divided into two main elements—one favoring immediate and if necessary separate action, the other demanding group secession. As the passing days made it obvious that other States would go out, however, the latter element gave way. It became evident that the opponents

6 Longstreet's letter, dated December 6, is copied in Charleston *Courier*, December 13.
7 N. Y. *Weekly Tribune*, November 21, 1860.
8 Reuben L. Davis, *Mississippi and Mississippians*, 391; Jackson *Mississippian*, November 13, 1860; Jefferson Davis, *Rise and Fall*, I, 57 ff.

of secession would meet certain defeat—that Alabama, like South Carolina and Mississippi, had sealed her determination.[9]

As for Georgia, keystone of the cotton kingdom arch, Governor Joseph E. Brown held aggressive disunionist views. He had urged his legislature, which met just before Lincoln's election, to adopt retaliatory measures against the North. He had also informed Gist that, in his opinion, Georgia would meet all the Southern States in convention, and might even take action without waiting for her sisters. The day after Lincoln's election, he sent the legislature a message recommending that it call a State Convention. Some delay took place, for opinion in Georgia was much more closely divided than in her neighbors. The hesitating legislators invited nearly a score of the strongest leaders of the State to address them. While Toombs spoke in fiery terms for immediate secession, Stephens argued for sober deliberation. In the end the legislature set January 2 for the election of a convention to meet a fortnight later.

Before November closed, the Mississippi and Florida legislatures had also called conventions, to be elected December 20 and 24. Thus, within three weeks of Lincoln's victory, five States had arranged for gatherings to pass upon secession—and nearly everyone assumed they would vote for leaving the Union. If nothing were done in Washington to halt the movement, South Carolina would assuredly withdraw before Christmas, and Mississippi, Alabama, Georgia, and Florida would probably do so before the end of January. Congress was to meet on Monday, December 3. The national government would have to act with celerity and wisdom in the next six weeks if it were to control the situation.

One hopeful factor was that all five States contained a Unionist party of no little strength and dignity. In the upper districts of South Carolina, many citizens—one observant minister thought them a majority—stood for maintenance of the Union. The able editor-politician, B. F. Perry, had published a strong attack upon secessionist scheme in the Charleston *Courier* of August 20, and he kept up his battle. Chief Justice John B. O'Neall, a nationalist since nullification times, believed that secession was madness and had the support of his associate, Judge Job Johnstone. Gabriel Cannon of Spartanburg was one of several State senators who counseled patience. "I am still for the Union," declared George S. Bryan of Charleston, "on the sole ground that the South has made Mr. Lincoln President." [10]

The respected jurist James L. Petigru, just entrusted with the codification of the State laws, protested to the last against the flowing tide. Charlestonians long remembered one dramatic moment of his career. Listening attentively to the

9 Denman, *Secession in Alabama*, 87 ff.
10 November 6, 1860; Kennedy Papers.

reading of Sunday prayers from the pulpit of his beloved St. Michael's, he started when he heard the usual invocation for the President of the United States omitted, and without hesitation walked up the aisle and out the door. It required all the varied excitements of the day, all the oratory of Keitt, Bonham, and Ruffin, all the urgings of Chesnut and Gist, and all the fiery editorials of the *Mercury* (whose normal paid circulation of five hundred and fifty compared badly with the three thousand circulation of the *Courier*) to convince Carolinians that the Unionist minority was too insignificant to be heeded.[11]

In Alabama, numerous merchants and professional men of Mobile, small farmers of the northern counties, and scattered lowland planters were insistent that the State should not secede without at least one final effort to secure redress of grievances within the Union. Yet national sentiment in Mobile, a city of thirty thousand with considerable trade connections with the North, found little effective expression. Such Unionists as John Forsyth of the *Register* and C. C. Langdon of the *Advertiser* (a journal established in 1833 to oppose nullification, and ever since then on the Union side) could accomplish nothing. Not until mid-December was a call issued for a meeting of men opposed to hasty action, and this gathering merely adopted a platform and nominated candidates favorable to cooperative secession. Alabama, ran its resolutions, should assert its independence only if the four neighboring cotton States did the same. In the ensuing election of convention delegates, advocates of separate secession swept Mobile County.

It was only in northern Alabama that the opposition made a formidable stand. This area, lying partly in the Tennessee Valley, sold much of its production across the Tennessee line, which it realized might soon become an international boundary. The last census had shown eight northern counties where the slaves were fewer than thirteen percent of the population. Cooperative secessionists here held a majority, while several counties were controlled by outright Unionists or men who at least wished secession delayed until it was proved that no other recourse existed. Before the national election, the Bell-Everett and Douglas men talked angrily of a conspiracy, pointing in proof to the legislature's provision for a convention in the event of a Republican victory, and to Yancey's successful efforts at Charleston to make that victory certain. The State, they had charged, was being railroaded into secession. Attacking the

---

11 The Charleston *Mercury*, while extensively copied outside the State, was not much read in it. It was supposed to cost the Rhett family $8,000 a year to maintain it. Charleston corr. N. Y. *Tribune*, dated November 7, 1860. See John B. O'Neall and John Chapman, *Annals of Newberry*, for the opposition. Petigru later was walking down Broad Street when a friend accosted him. "Have you heard the news, sir?" he asked. "Great news; Louisiana has seceded." "Good God, Williams," Petigru said in a tone of mild disgust, "I thought we had *bought* Louisiana." Undated sheet, Petigru Papers, S. C. Hist. Soc.

unfair ratio of representation in the legislature, they had accused the leaders of the conspiracy of being afraid to submit the issue of a convention to the whole people. A Huntsville friend of Governor Moore's wrote him:

> By vehement denunciations of this fancied conspiracy, and unmeasured eulogies upon the Federal Union, the leaders of these opposition parties have gradually led their followers into the adoption of doctrines touching the theory of our government, which in 1799 would have stamped them as rank federalists —insisting that their first and highest allegiance is to the Federal government— that there can be no lawful resistance to the pressures of the Federal government or of a violation of the compact by other States; that the only remedy is the right of revolution on the part, not of the State but the people of the State, and that *success* alone can exempt those participating in the revolution from traitor's doom; many of them insisting that the States occupy the same relation to the general government that our counties do to the State. . . . But a few days ago I heard the most influential leader of the Douglas party in this part of the State declare that if the people of South Alabama should succeed in putting the State out of the Union he would be in favor of putting this valley out of the State; contending at the same time that a separation of the State from the Federal government would operate as an utter annihilation of all government within the State. . . .[12]

Of the first five States to arrange conventions, Georgia was that where the separate secessionists had to fight their hardest battle and where Union feeling proved strongest. Alexander H. Stephens, Benjamin H. Hill, and Herschel V. Johnson all maintained a staunch conservatism. Nor were they without important followers. Less than a fortnight after Lincoln's victory, Judge Wayne of the Supreme Court arrived in Washington reporting that he thought four-fifths of the people of Savannah opposed immediate secession. Savannah, like Mobile, had important trade links with the North. A considerable minority of lowland planters, chiefly men who had clung to the Whig Party until its death, were steadfastly opposed to what they called premature action. The hilly country at the north of the State and the upper pine-barrens, where slaves were few, were strongholds of Union sentiment. Of the six diehard delegates who, in the end, were destined to vote against secession, four came from the hill region and two from the pinelands. In the middle black belt, feeling was almost evenly divided between radicals and conservatives.

When Governor Brown sent the legislature his message justifying the right of secession, asserting that "the time for bold and decided action has arrived," and proposing a tax of twenty-five percent on all merchandise manufactured in or imported from Massachusetts, New York, Michigan, and other States which had passed unfriendly legislation, he met rigorous opposition. It was because

---

12 S. D. Cabaniss, October 29, 1860; Governors' Papers, Ala. Dept. Arch and Hist.

public sentiment was so manifestly unclarified that the legislature asked the leading men of Georgia to debate the issues before it. Although the secessionists were, in Herschel V. Johnson's words, "impatient, overbearing, dictatorial, and intolerant," they did not dare to move precipitately.[13]

Toombs, in his rousing vindication of Southern rights delivered November 13 before the two houses, declared that the Republican Party patently intended to destroy the institution of slavery, and that guarantees from men already guilty of violating the Constitution would not be worth the paper on which they were inscribed. He was followed the next night by Stephens, whose appeal on behalf of Georgia's motto, "Wisdom, justice, and moderation," was one of the finest of his career. With haggard earnestness, Stephens argued that Lincoln, faced by hostile majorities in both House and Senate, could do nothing to jeopardize Southern security; that his bare election was no justification for destroying the institutions which generations of patriotic forebears had built up; and that, while the honor of Georgia must be maintained even if this meant eventual disunion, they should await an act of aggression before moving. He stood, he said, upon the Georgia platform of 1850 demanding equal rights in the Territories and enforcement of the Fugitive Slave Act. They should unite with the rest of the South in asking a repeal of unfriendly laws, and if the North refused a proper adjustment, "then let the consequences be with them." [14] Herschel V. Johnson, too, urged consultation with other slaveholding States and an appeal to the North for justice.

But despite all the evidence of scattered Union feeling, by December 6, the date of the South Carolina election, it was clear that the secessionists were overriding all opposition in four of the five foremost States—Georgia alone being doubtful. The course of events under the palmetto flag was eloquent of the situation. November found the State full of secession meetings, while Union men hardly dared assemble. Even B. F. Perry, who was defeated in his own county for the first time in twenty years, confessed himself paralyzed. "The election was hurried on without giving time for discussion," he writes in his autobiography. "I did not go out at all to electioneer, and the people of the district did not turn out to vote. The secessionists all went to the polls and did not cast more than a thousand votes, whilst the district could vote more than twenty-four hundred. The Union men thought that it was a foregone conclusion that the State would secede, and it was not worth their while to go to the polls." [15] Chief Justice O'Neall and Judge Johnstone, speaking from the steps of Newberry courthouse, were a target for eggs and turnips; and, according to

13 See U. B. Phillips, *Georgia and State Rights*; "From the Autobiography of Herschel V. Johnson, 1856–1867," *Am. Hist. Rev.*, XXX; Dumond, *Secession*, 142–144.
14 Extracts in Pendleton, *Stephens*, 159–163.
15 Perry, MS Autobiography.

O'Neall, "the majority of those entitled to suffrage" in that area did not vote. In the last week before the election, some observers discerned a strong conservative rally. One wrote the New York *Tribune* that if a true vote on the issue could be taken, a majority of South Carolinians would refuse to leave the Union. But on election day, the secessionists won from sea to mountains. And on the morrow Governor Gist issued another stirring message, urging immediate secession so that South Carolina might not exercise "a blighting and chilling influence upon the action of the other Southern States."

An explanation of the comparative impotence of Union men is not difficult to find. They were scattered, and, in such areas as northern Alabama and the Georgia hill country, isolated. They were handicapped, especially in South Carolina and Alabama, by apportionment laws and districting which penalized the small farmers. They had little organization, for neither the Bell-Everett nor Douglas forces had set up an efficient party machinery in the Lower South, and a good many Bell and Douglas leaders yielded to the secession impulse. The disunionists, on the other hand, availed themselves of the well-articulated Breckinridge organization. Most moderates and conservatives were by disposition inert, and stayed at home cautiously waiting while the radicals acted, spoke, and wrote with ebullient fervor. All the excitement of the time, too, favored the party of action—and an inflammatory spirit was sedulously maintained. "People are wild," wrote Senator Hammond on November 12. "The scenes of the French Revolution are being enacted already. . . . God knows the end." [16] Or as the British consul in Charleston put it, a few weeks later: "The public excitement is kept alive by the constant arrival of telegrams, many of the most absurd and mendacious character." [17] The brevity of the campaigns for electing the State conventions, moreover, gave no time for coolheaded reflection.

Then, too, as seeming majorities asserted themselves, many moderates thought it right to contribute to the moral unity of the State, and filled up the phalanx. This was the easy course to take. Greeley was unable to understand why the Bell-Everett party did so little outside the border region to make good their fidelity to the Constitution and the Union. He might have turned to the history of the American Revolution for illustrations of the power of an active minority to carry a population into revolt. He need only have consulted Burke's Speech on the Unitarian Petition for an analysis. "The greater number," wrote Burke, "is generally composed of men of sluggish tempers, slow to act and unwilling to attempt; and, by being in possession, are so disposed to peace, that they are unwilling to take early and vigorous measures for their defense, and they are almost always caught unprepared. . . . A smaller number, more expe-

16 Hammond to his brother; Hammond Papers, LC.
17 January 4, 1861; FO 5/780.

Washington D.C.
Nov. 30. 1850

Eli Whitney Esqr.

Sir, when the Adjt. Genl.
of Mississi. consulted me as to the best mode
of obtaining rifles for the volunteer companies of that state, I influenced him against
a preconceived plan of action, to propose to
you a contract for the manufacture of the
number required: My advice was based upon
the confidence reposed in you as a manufacturer and as a man. Recently it has been
reported to me that you had after much time
had been lost by depending upon you, in accordance with an agreement entered into, for said
manufacture, you have notified the authorities
of Mississi. that you declined to make the arms as
stipulated. The circumstances induce me to ask
of you an explanation, & will I hope lead you to
give me such a statement as will relieve me
of the impression created and justify me in
the advice given when I referred the Adjt. Genl.
to you as the best person with whom he could
make a contract. I have the honor to be yr obedt.

Jeffn Davis

Jefferson Davis Writes the Whitney Arms Works Concerning Rifles.

dite, awakened, active, vigorous, and courageous, who make amends for what they want in weight by their superabundance of velocity, will create an acting power of the greatest possible strength. When men are furiously and fanatically fond of an object, they will prefer it, as is well known, to their own peace, to their own property, and to their own lives. . . ." Toombs, Yancey, and Ruffin were furiously and fanatically devoted to their object.

Wherever opponents of secession attempted to use delay, the radicals resorted to social pressure, denunciation, and in sporadic instances to threats of violence. Volunteer companies, some old, some newly organized, all training lustily, tended to become centers of secessionist activity. The Knights of the Golden Circle, which under "General" George Bickley had held a convention at Raleigh in the spring of 1860, and which, as we have already seen, was actively recruiting an expeditionary force to take possession of Mexico and a home guard to serve Southern objects upon demand, uttered threatening growls. Bickley had boasted at the convention that his organization numbered nearly forty-eight thousand. According to F. A. P. Barnard, head of the University of Mississippi, Union men in his State had become targets for the harshest name-calling. When Governor Pettus took steps to have the convention called, the university professor of law, though a zealous secessionist, was aghast. Protesting that he knew the sentiment of people in all parts of the State, he declared the effort must fail. "I am perfectly satisfied," he said, "that it is impossible to take Mississipi out of the Union." Events quickly proved him wrong; and Barnard believed that it was largely because the opposition was cowed by taunting words like "poltroon," "submissionist," and "traitor" that it was quickly overcome.[18]

[II]

What hidden forces controlled this dramatic surge of Southern intransigence? Both at the time and later, many observers in the Northern and border States believed that an uprising so sudden and well-concerted could only be the fruit of a carefully matured plot. "The election of Lincoln is but a pretext," Douglas presently declared:

The present secession movement is the result of an enormous conspiracy which was matured a year ago. The conspiracy was formed by the leaders of the secession movement twelve months ago, and they have used every means to urge it on. They have caused a man to be elected by a sectional vote, to demonstrate that the Union was divided; and when the history of the country from the time of the Lecompton constitution to the date of Lincoln's election is written, it will appear that a scheme was maturing in the meantime which was for no end

18 See pamphlet, "Proceedings of the Convention of the Knights of the Golden Circle, Raleigh, May 7-11, 1860"; Fulton, *Barnard*, 272, 273.

except to break up the Union. They desired to break it up, and they used the slavery question as a means. They desired to create a purely sectional vote, to demonstrate that the two sections could not live together. The disunion card dictated that the South was to carry its own elections, and that the North was to elect Lincoln. Then a united South was to assail a divided North, and gain an easy victory. This scheme was defeated by the overthrow of the disunion candidates in Kentucky, Tennessee, and Virginia. Still the grand conspiracy existed, and the disunion movement was the result of it.[19]

This explanation was in time to be elaborated by Lincoln's secretary, John G. Nicolay, by John Minor Botts of Virginia, by the dashing commander of the Army of the Tennessee, John A. Logan, and other writers, all taking the view that secession was essentially the work of a small number of reckless, artful politicians whose plot carried six millions of reluctant or indifferent citizens into rebellion.[20] This conspiracy theory of secession furnishes no illumination of events. It is true that Rhett, Yancey, Wigfall, Porcher Miles, and others, bold, imperious, and in some respects unscrupulous men, had planned to make disruption of the Democratic Party a prelude to national disruption; and that numerous Southern extremists during 1859-60 were constantly corresponding and conferring, with disunion as their object. But it would have been impossible for even a far larger and better organized body of conspirators to have carried the South into this sweeping movement for independence had it not been that a large body of people in the cotton States had lost their old attachment to the Union, and had abandoned their old faith in the security it gave to their institutions and rights.

The central factor which made the secession movement possible, and which must be viewed as fundamental to the national schism, was a triple-fronted sentiment which, for a long generation, had been inculcated among the Southern people: A fervent belief in State Rights, including the right of secession, as the palladium of their liberties; an ever-deepening hatred for the freesoil movement in the North; and an increasing readiness to indulge the vision of a happy, opulent Southern republic. This sentiment had gradually sapped the once-powerful devotion of the Lower South to the Union. Alexander H. Stephens ranked preeminent as a Southern Unionist, yet he declared that if Georgia seceded he would bow to the will of the people. Such a declaration was worth little to the national bond.

Millions of Southerners felt much as Stephens did. They disliked secession for a number of reasons—because they revered the national concept established by the fathers, because they despised the fire-eaters (Rhett was never popular

19 Speech in Chicago May 1, 1861; Havana, Illinois, *Post*, June 13, 1861.
20 See Nicolay, *The Outbreak of Rebellion*; Botts, *The Great Rebellion*; Logan, *The Great Conspiracy*; Greeley, *American Conflict*, I, Chs. XXI-XXVI.

even in South Carolina), because they feared war and loss; but of militant, active Unionism, ready to give battle for the great ideal of Washington and Jackson, the majority of people in the Lower South had little. Their primary attachment was to their State or section. It was this lack of deep Union feeling, conjoined with the fear, irritation, and jealousy produced by Northern attitudes, and with a firm belief in the right of withdrawal, which made it possible for the extremists to bring about decisive action. The forces which had produced this psychology were all-important, and the so-called conspiracy, which was really a broad, groping, ill-coordinated impulse, was quite secondary.

The living social, economic, and intellectual interests of the Lower South, its sense of civic duty, its highest ambitions, had taken a turn divergent from the Union; and if Northerners had not learned what its state of mind was during the Congressional debate of 1859–60 and the Presidential compaign, a thousand men now informed them. Many voices, like that of Governor Gist, enunciated the right of peaceable secession. Many voices expressed a general prejudice. "I look upon the whole New England race," one Georgian had written, "as a troublesome, unquiet set of meddlers—their original stock a set of jailbirds, outlaws, and disturbers of the peace, who could not live among decent and civilized people in Europe; and this same intolerant and turbulent spirit has been transmitted to their posterity, and will cling to it to the latest generation." [21] Many voices expressed a resentment for past injuries, real and fancied. Northerners, declared Governor Pettus in his message of November 26 to the Mississippi legislature, have succeeded in educating a whole generation to hate the South. "They have attempted to degrade us in the estimation of other nations, by denouncing us as barbarians, pirates, and robbers, unfit associates for Christian or civilized men. They have excited our slaves to insurrection; advised them to burn our property and murder our people, and have furnished them with arms and ammunition to aid them in their bloody work." [22]

The secessionists also offered, however, reasoned and weighty if not cool-headed justifications of their cause. A belief that the outlook for the South would be hopeless in a Union no longer equal, just, and generous was stated with a thousand variations. Pettus wrote that the North had proclaimed that it would never rest satisfied until slavery was placed in a position ensuring its ultimate extinction; that these hard terms were offered fifteen States as if they were conquered and not coequal sisters; and that submission to such an ultimatum would establish a despotism under which the dearest rights of the South would be held at the sufferance of a hostile people. Governor Moore of Alabama similarly

21 J. Hanly Smith, Washington, April 3, 1860; Stephens Papers, LC.
22 Governor Brown of Georgia, harking back to Locke's ideas, wrote in his message of November 8 that the constitutional rights of Southerners had been violated by several free States to an extent justifying any measure necessary for their future protection.

insisted that safety demanded secession. The Black Republicans had elected a President; they would soon elect majorities in both houses; and then they would remake the Supreme Court. "Slavery will be abolished in the District of Columbia, in the dockyards and arsenals, and wherever the Federal Government has jurisdiction. It will be excluded from the Territories, and other free States will in hot haste be admitted to the Union, until they have a majority to alter the Constitution. Then slavery will be abolished by law in the States." Pamphleteers quoted leading Republicans in proof of their wish to end slavery. They pointed to Lincoln's words on ultimate emancipation, Sumner's statement that slavery must surely die, John Wentworth's assertion in the Chicago *Democrat* that the States must all be made free and the Republican Party would do it without bloodshed, the platform of 1856 which spoke of slavery and polygamy as relics of barbarism. Other writers warned the South that enemies like Sumner would rejoice in a revolution which made the slave the legal and social equal of the white man.

Even if the promise of Lincoln not to touch slavery within the States is taken at face value, declared some leaders, the South will be in dire danger. Senator Robert W. Johnson and Representative Thomas C. Hindman of Arkansas, addressing their constituents, foresaw disaster in the mere restriction of slavery. If the South submitted, the Republicans would limit slavery to its existing domain. This domain would be filled by the natural multiplication of colored people until the pressure of the blacks became intolerable. Finally, a conflict for racial supremacy would ensue; and either the Negroes would be exterminated, or the white man must abandon his Africanized country forever.[23] Meanwhile, asked other men, how much will slave property held under constant threat be worth? "The sole cause of the existing disunion excitement which is about to break up the government," wrote James A. Bayard to his son, "is the war which has been carried on for years past by all manner of devices by the antislavery fanatical sentiment upon more than $2,000,000,000 of property." [24]

It was in vain that Stephens reminded Southerners that they were no abject minority, and that for sixty out of seventy-two years they had controlled the government. In vain did men point out that the talk about a hurried admission of Nebraska, Washington, Dakota, Idaho, Nevada, and Arizona was nonsense, for these areas were far short of the population needed. In vain did moderates demonstrate that the Republicans could not possibly gain a majority in either house before March, 1863, and could not gain a sufficient majority to amend the Constitution under any circumstances.

23 January 8, 1861; E. L. Harvin, "Arkansas and the Crisis of 1860–61," MS, Univ. of Texas.
24 Washington, December 12, 1860; Bayard Papers, LC.

Apprehension for their future safety filled the minds of countless Southerners—and not without reason. Lincoln had said that a crisis must be reached and passed; that is, a critical decision be made *final*. This was the decision for the permanent containment of slavery, which meants its ultimate extinction. Southerners felt that if they assented to such a decision, they would have taken the first step on a road which could have but one ending. They could not guess how rapidly they might be hurried down the road, but they knew that much human history is a gloss on the text: "If ultimately, why not now?" They seemed safer against a premature revolution of their social and economic system outside the Union than in it. It probably did not occur to many Southerners, as it did to Buchanan, that the tide of world hostility to slavery was now so powerful that the South could better withstand it as part of the United States than as an isolated and exposed republic.

Then, too, many felt that it was not the old Union that they were leaving, for that was dead. "Equality and safety in the Union are at an end," Howell Cobb shortly informed his fellow Georgians. "The Union formed by our fathers was one of equality, justice, and fraternity. On the 4th of March it will be supplanted by a union of sectionalism and hatred." [25] So jangling had the national household become that not a few sincere lovers of concord believed that disunion would actually promote peace. The perpetual brawling over the slavery question was like some chronic dispute between husband and wife which only divorce could heal. The history of the Methodist Church seemed to illustrate the possibility of gaining harmony by a choice of separate ways. Before the church split, the General Conference was always a scene of disgraceful bickering; after the separation, Southern and Northern wings went forward peaceably and happily.

Next to the demands for safety and equality, the secessionist leaders emphasized familiar economic complaints. South Carolinians in particular were convinced of the general truth of Rhett's and Hammond's much publicized figures upon Southern tribute to Northern interests. Rhett had estimated that of the $927,000,000 collected in duties between 1791 and 1845, the South had paid $711,200,000, and the non-slaveholding States $216,000,000. Hammond had declared that the South paid about $50,000,000 and the North perhaps $20,-000,000 of the $70,000,000 raised annually by duties. In expenditure of the national revenues, the Senator thought the North got about $50,000,000 a year, and the South only $20,000,000. [26] These statistics were not the less persuasive because totally devoid of scientific quality. The theory that imports were paid

25 Address of December 6, 1860; *Toombs, Stephens, Cobb Corr.*, 505–516.
26 White, *Rhett*, 126–127; *Cong. Globe*, March 4, 1858. See Washington *Constitution*, November 13, N. Y. *Weekly Tribune*, November 17, 1860, for Southern economic complaints.

for out of exports was generally accepted in South Carolina. A widely distributed pamphlet published in Charleston, John Townsend's "The South Alone Should Govern the South," computed the total tribute of the section each year at $105,000,000, of which $20,000,000 was an exorbitant share of the tariff levies, $20,000,000 was profit on Northern manufactures, and $30,000,000 the profit of shipowners on the Southern export-import trade. What do we get in return for this? demanded Townsend. Nothing but insults and incitements to rebellion.[27]

Rhett, in his speech to the South Carolina legislature on November 10, touched the familiar chords anew. A generation earlier, according to his interpretation of history, the North had determined to live on the labors of the South. It had passed legislation to bring the whole carrying trade into American hands and lift the tariff to extortionate levels. When it had found its match in little South Carolina, it had changed its tactics. Northern leaders had resolved to increase the number of free States and unite them against the Southern people. They had forbidden the admission of any more slaveholding States, taken unfair measures to bring California into the Union, and bullied and shot the Southerners out of Kansas. How would he now meet the North? He would go to these plunderers, and tell them that the Union was dissolved. When the Yankees found their factories paralyzed and their shipping idle, they would come begging for the restoration of fraternal relations; but the Southern leaders should deal with the North as with any other foreign nation, and use their vast resources to enrich their own people. It is not likely that many readers accepted all of this statement. But it is certain that a great many Southerners believed at least part of it.

Other motives entered into the secessionist movement, some affecting one element and some another. Sheer pride counted for a great deal. The Lower South had been stung by derisive Northern comments upon its tendency toward gasconading threats and bombastic vaunts. The cotton kingdom could not let New York and Boston newspapers taunt it once more upon its windy resolutions and blustering manifestoes. Porcher Miles wrote that he was sick and disgusted with talk—he wanted action, and one State could "break up things generally." South Carolina newspapers and letters in the crisis repeated again and again the assertion that the State was too far committed, and must act or be disgraced. Allied with this pride was the feeling of many leaders that if they drew back once more, their last real opportunity would have vanished. Rhett said frankly that it would have been better to dissolve the Union in 1850, when the

---

27 Townsend, of St. John's Colleton, sums up a whole series of arguments for secession with great ability. The pamphlet, which quickly went into a third edition, must have had considerable influence. For a hostile response, see J. P. Kennedy's pamphlet of 1861, "The Border States: Their Power and Duty in the Present Disordered Condition of the Country."

States stood fifteen slaveholding, and fifteen free. What chance, he implied, would the South have in 1870 or 1880?

Many merchants of Charleston, Savannah, and Mobile, many railway pro-moters and other speculative men, hoped that with independence the cities, towns, and communications of their section might rise to larger opportunities. In Charleston, men pointed to maps showing what an immense region would soon export its produce and import its merchandise across their wharves. Inte-rior Tennessee, they declared, could ship its crops more cheaply to them than to New York. They talked of flourishing lines of steamers, nurtured by free trade, plying via the Azores to England, France, and Italy. Not a few planters, too, believed that their fortunes would be bettered if the South gained inde-pendence. A Cooper River magnate with two thousand slaves declared that he favored secession in order to make more money. "Most of us planters are deeply in debt; we should not be if out of the Union. We should have a direct trade with Europe. We should get a better price for our cotton, and our goods would cost us fifty per cent less than now. . . . We must do it now or never. If we don't secede now the political power of the South is broken." [28]

As another consideration, a revolutionary movement always serves aspiring men, and many a Southern politician who had never achieved high office under the Union dreamed of eminence under a new Confederacy. Fame might be won by merely helping build the foundations of the republic. When the election was held for delegates to the South Carolina convention, a Charleston diarist com-mented: "there were a large number of candidates anxious to hand their names down to Posterity as actors in the Southern Drama." [29] The future glories of the new nation inspired enthusiasts. Rhett invoked the historian of 2,000 A.D. who would write of the brave Southerners who had thrown off the chains of their oppressors. "And extending their empire across this continent to the Pacific, and down through Mexico to the other side of the great gulf, and over the isles of the sea, they established an empire and wrought out a civilization which has never been equalled or surpassed—a civilization teeming with orators, poets, philosophers, statesmen, and historians equal to those of Greece and Rome—and presented to the world the glorious spectacle of a free, prosperous, and illustrious people."

The widespread belief that secession might and probably would be bloodless contributed mightily to the radical sweep. Yancey, returning from his Northern tour in the campaign, declared he had good reason to believe that the with-drawal of any State would be peaceable. A. B. Longstreet had told a baccalaure-ate audience at South Carolina College that he would stake everything he was

28 Quoted in N. Y. *Weekly Tribune*, November 17, 1860.
29 Schirmer Diary, December 6, 1860.

worth upon Northern acceptance of a general Southern secession. Even if the Yankees did resist, the South stood the better chance of winning. "Away with this notion of whipping us into the Union, or whipping us at all!" [30] Some politicians went about declaring they would drink all the blood that was shed. "You may slap a Yankee in the face and he'll go off and sue you but he won't fight!" De Bow, who had traveled widely and whose work as editor and supervisor of the census gave him authority, scoffed at the idea of a conflict. If one occurred, he assured F. A. P. Barnard, it would take place between the Northern factions, and blood would flow in the streets of New York and Philadelphia before it did in the South. He may have seen Franklin Pierce's letter to Jefferson Davis predicting that, if war began, the Northern cities would witness fighting between the fanatical antislavery men and those good citizens who respected their obligations, and that the Northern radicals would find occupation enough at home. But it is more likely that De Bow was simply one of those self-deluded men whom W. J. Grayson describes in his autobiography:

In both sections of the Union were shortsighted men striving to avoid slight or imaginary evils by rushing into others of incalculable magnitude. In both, were heated shallow partisans scoffing at dangers because their limited faculties were unable to perceive them. The carnage, the desolation, the destruction of property, the enormous public debt, the insupportable taxes, the standing army, the fortified frontier, the ruin that awaits all parties, were beyond the reach of their feeble vision.[31]

[III]

Northern opinion in the anxious weeks just after the election was a maelstrom of conflicting currents, in which a few dominant tendencies rapidly became visible. At first, the characteristic national optimism held sway. Till after South Carolina's withdrawal, millions believed that the Southern "rant" and "bluster" need not be taken seriously, while others clung to hope of a speedy compromise. A great part of the North vehemently maintained that nothing must be done to hector or threaten the South. Some argued that the cotton

30 Wade, *Longstreet*, 323, 324; E. J. Arthur, February 16, 1861, to E. De Leon, De Leon Papers; Fulton, *Barnard*, 272–274. Hodgson in *Cradle of the Confederacy*, 469, 470, quotes Yancey on Northern acquiescence, and writes: "That secession might be, and doubtless would be, a peaceable measure, was almost universally believed by the secession party of the South."

31 Grayson's remarks are the more notable because they were penned in Charleston in the midst of the Civil War. He wrote that both sections were to blame for the conflict. "There are men, South as well as North, who used slavery as a trumpet to excite sedition, who desired dissolution of the Union and found slavery as the readiest means to bring it about, who sought a cement for party union and found the Negro the strongest within reach." MS Autobiography, R. D. Bass, editor, 290–292.

States could yet be coaxed back; some declared that if no violence took place the border States could all be held; and some asserted that, in any event, coercion was improper, impracticable, or both. Still another group took the view that the primary task was to attempt a compromise. If it failed, and only then, firmer policies might be formulated.

Business difficulties deepened the general consternation. The election was followed by all the premonitory symptoms of a sharp business panic. The stock market staggered uncertainly, the banks contracted their credit, and borrowers fell into distress. The South was just completing its cotton harvest, for the growing of which it had incurred the usual debts at the North. Now, in view of possible departure from the Union, it tended to hold on to the crop, meanwhile letting obligations to Northern merchants and jobbers stand over. It also moved to withdraw its specie balances from Northern banks. Its talk of direct trade with Europe worried Northern exporters, importers, merchants, and shippers. Money became tighter, and business circles, looking forward to a dark winter, grew anxious.

On November 13, the New York money market would not buy paper at all. Next day, borrowers of the highest quality were able to obtain funds at eight and ten percent, but very good names still sold at twelve percent, while the notes of jobbers connected with the South went at eighteen and twenty-four percent. The following week brought news of the suspension of various banks in the South and West, and failures continued throughout the fall. Material amounts of Southern railroad securities and State bonds were held in the North, and, as they declined, the paper currency of Western banks issued upon them depreciated. The Federal Treasury was in such weak condition, with expenditures steadily exceeding receipts, that when December opened it was unable to pay Congressional salaries and many other demands. As political uncertainty increased, so did the business dislocation.

Yet this business recession did not daunt most Northern freesoilers. Lincoln was frankly scornful of it. "I am not insensible to any commercial or financial depression that may exist," he assured Truman Smith on November 10; "but nothing is to be gained by fawning around the 'respectable scoundrels' who got it up. Let them go to work and repair the mischief of their own making; and then perhaps they will be less greedy to do the like again." And he curtly rejected the suggestions of Truman Smith and Henry J. Raymond that he offer some reassuring statement to the South. He could say nothing that he had not already said, he wrote; and to press fresh statements upon those who had refused to listen would not only show a want of self-respect—it "would have an appearance of sycophancy and timidity which would excite the contempt of good men, and encourage bad ones to clamor the more loudly."

Of the three thousand and more Northern newspapers, hardly half a hundred were at this time outright defenders of slavery. Conspicuous among this corporal's guard were three New York journals, the *Herald*, the *Day-Book*, and the *Daily News*, the first exhibiting James Gordon Bennett's cynicism and moral obtuseness, the second enjoying a considerable Southern circulation, and the third appealing to the Irish laborers of the city; one moribund sheet in Philadelphia, Buchanan's old organ the *Pennsylvanian*, and another in Washington, the *Constitution;* and Cyrus H. McCormick's Chicago *Times*. These journals declared that slavery was neither an evil nor a crime, that it was the status best fitting the inferior nature of the Negro, and that it could not be overthrown without destroying the fabric of Southern society. Some of them, notably the *Herald*, espoused Grayson's doctrine that the slave possessed greater economic security and social contentment than the hireling.

For various reasons, however, this proslavery element in the press exercised a diminishing influence. Bennett, for all his memorable work in improving the news-range and widening the democratic appeal of the press, was regarded as an erratic and unprincipled adventurer, while his *Herald* combined lurid sensationalism with a readiness to change its opinions with every veering wind. Men read it while despising it. The *Day-Book*, edited by the notorious Negrophobe, Dr. John Van Evrie, who published pseudo-scientific works on white supremacy and black subordination, was an eccentric, prejudiced racial organ. Both the *Pennsylvanian* and the *Constitution* were subsidized sheets, which died as soon as they lost the Administration advertising. As for the Chicago *Times*, which had gained real prestige when edited by Sheahan for Douglas, it was now suspect because conducted by one former Virginian, and owned by another.[32]

The great majority of Northern journals disliked slavery, believed in respecting the rights of the Southern States, and abhorred disunion. They took a position equally distant from the *Day-Book* and the *Liberator*. While they hoped for the eventual extirpation of slavery, they wished to see this accomplished in a way which would not ruin the Southern economy, bring the races to social and political equality, or fill the North with a mass of needy freedmen. Whether they inclined to the view of Breckinridge, Douglas, or Lincoln as to the position of slavery in the Territories, they condemned the fanaticism of both abolitionists and secessionists. But slavery was not the immediate issue. When the five cotton States which led the van arranged before the end of November for conventions, it became necessary for the Northern press to abandon generalities and take a stand on the question of secession.

Acquiescence or coercion? The fifty proslavery sheets, of course, chose the

32 See H. C. Perkins, "Defense of Slavery in the Northern Press on the Eve of Civil War," *Journal Southern Hist.*, IX, November, 1943.

former. Bennett's *Herald* sneered at Lincoln, remarking that as he had once split rails he was now splitting the Union. All thought of coercion was outrageous, it said. That would precipitate "a fratricidal conflict, which will destroy the industrial interests of all sections, and put us back at least a hundred years in the estimation of the civilized world." Scolding Lincoln for not begging the South to come back, the *Herald* in the end, half mockingly, half seriously, suggested that the seceding States should arrange a constitutional convention for their section, adopt whatever amendments for safeguarding slavery they thought proper, and submit them to the North for ratification. It would be a happy result if all the States came under the new roof except New England, to which the country could bid good-riddance. Already, the nation had suffered too much from "the provincial meanness, bigotry, self-conceit, love for isms, hypercritical opposition to anything and everything, universal faultfinding, hard bargaining, and systematic home lawlessness . . . which are covering their section of the country with odium." [33] Not only the New York *Day-Book* and *Daily News*, but the *Journal of Commerce* and the *Express* were nearly as complaisant. Ben Woods's *Daily News* declared that while no State had the right to withdraw, nothing could be done if withdrawal took place. The Brooks brothers' *Express*, denouncing personal liberty laws, the underground railroad, and abolitionist publications, implied that secession was an act of desperation.[34] And Gerard Hallock's *Journal of Commerce*, speaking for conservative businessmen, was for letting the seceders go.[35]

A median position was taken by the *Tribune*, which disappointed a multitude of readers by its indecisive tone. Immediately after the election, it declared that while the right to secede might be revolutionary, it nevertheless existed—if the secession really represented majority opinion. "Whenever a considerable section of our Union shall deliberately resolve to go out, we shall resist all coercive measures designed to keep it in. We hope never to live in a republic whereof one section is pinned to the residue by bayonets. But we must insist that the step be taken, if ever it shall be, with the deliberation and gravity befitting so momentous an issue. Let ample time be given for reflection; let the subject be fully canvassed before the people; and let a popular vote be taken in every case before secession is decreed." [36]

Very different, and very heartening to all believers in stern Union principles, was the stand taken by the *Evening Post* of Bryant and the *Times* of Raymond. The Jacksonian principles of the poet-editor prompted an immediate thunderpeal under the title "Peaceable Secession an Absurdity," which declared that no

33 Nevins, *Evening Post*, 273–274.
34 N. Y. *Express*, November 12, 13, 1860.
35 Perkins, *Northern Editorials on Secession*; files, November-December.
36 N. Y. *Weekly Tribune*, November 17, 1860.

government could have a day of assured existence if it tolerated views which deprived it of credit or future. "No, if a State secedes it is revolution, and the seceders are traitors. Those who are charged with the executive branch of the government are recreant to their oaths if they fail to use all lawful means to put down such rebellion." Bryant next day expressed his faith that Lincoln would restore American unity and make it perpetual. The *Times* meanwhile exhorted citizens to stand by the Union and the Constitution first, and talk of guarantees to the South only when their safety was assured. "We would yield nothing whatever to exactions pressed by threats of disunion." The *World*, a penny paper established by some religious-minded businessmen, warned the secessionists that they faced resistance. "It is of no use to mince matters," it remarked; "this rampant cotton rebellion will haul in its horns or we shall have civil war." [37]

This confusion of voices in the metropolis was echoed by a similar medley outside. The Dubuque *Herald*, a Douglas journal, defended the right of secession. So did the Bangor *Daily Union*, a Breckinridge paper, which remarked that while a sovereign State might be conquered and held as a subject province, no aggregation of power could ever force it to be a member of the Union. The Brooklyn *Eagle*, denying any State the right to secede, also denied the nation any right to prevent one from doing so. To coerce an unwilling member would be to convert the government into a sanguinary and odious despotism. The Cincinnati *Press* held that the revolt of the colonies offered a fair precedent for secession, and that the general voice of the North was for letting South Carolina go or stay, as she wished. Other journals simply urged the government to wait upon circumstances.

Yet a considerable and growing number of editors were for iron measures. Samuel Bowles's Springfield *Republican*, while willing to grant reasonable concessions, exclaimed on December 17: "Oh, for one hour of Jackson!" [38] Morton McMichael's Philadelphia *North American* pronounced the nation indissoluble. The Providence *Daily Post* insisted that the Union should be maintained with all the powers held by the government, and J. R. Hawley's Hartford *Courant* was equally emphatic. In the Middle West, the Chicago *Tribune*, accompanied by most Republican and many Douglasite newspapers, was ready for coercion. The Madison *State Journal* declared positively that the new President would not and could not be less prompt and decided than the President who had forced nullifiers to yield. We might as well face secession firmly, asserted the Washington *National Republican*, which was established just after the election to support the new Administration; for to talk about consenting to it is only to encourage with false hopes the traitors who will have to be quelled.

37 Nevins, *Evening Post;* Elmer Davis, *Times;* Perkins, *Northern Editorials.*
38 Merriam, *Bowles,* I, 277, 278. But Bowles blew cold as well as hot.

A clear majority of Northern newspapers, and certainly a heavy majority of Republican journals, denied the right of secession as explicitly as a majority of Southern sheets asserted it. For the two midwinter months in which some hope of compromise remained, however, only a minority of editors emphatically expressed the judgment that coercion was indispensable. While Bryant, Raymond, Forney, Medill, and others were militantly outspoken, Greeley and others hung back. It was only as the cotton kingdom plunged forward, as plans of adjustment proved futile, and as tempers grew hotter, that sentiment for coercion increased. Amid the crowd of events, the maelstrom of currents and counter-currents, hopes and fears alternated. So intelligent and decided an antislavery man as Charles Eliot Norton wrote to George William Curtis on December 17 that war was "most likely" and to Arthur Hugh Clough on February 10 that it was only "a remote possibility." [39] Such was the confusion, North and South, that conscientious men, torn between hope and despair, anger and conciliation, caution and impatience, changed in mood from day to day.

[IV]

That in this crisis the President was beset by the most awful anxieties, that he was racked between his long love for the South on one side and his attachment to the Union on the other, that in his deep aversion to violence he was tortured by the prospect of a fratricidal war, need not be said. No President ever faced a more difficult task. None, it may be added, ever faced a terrible crisis with feebler means of dealing with it effectively.

For what was the situation of the government? The nation had a President who within a few months would enter his seventieth year, tired, so infirm that at times he could not move outside his upstairs rooms, and utterly discredited. It had a Cabinet which was sharply divided over the permissibility of secession; Secretaries Cobb, Thompson, and Floyd standing defiantly for that right, and Cass, Holt, and Black denying it. It had a Congress which had been elected two years earlier, and which was dissevered as completely as the Cabinet; the Senate being Democratic, the House Republican, while both chambers broke into numerous factions on the questions of secession, compromise, and coercion. It had a public opinion which, largely because of the refusal of Republicans to face the certainty that Lincoln's election meant secession, and the failure of Southern extremists to face the certainty that secession meant war, was to the last degree ignorant and fluctuating. All these elements fell within a framework of government which kept a repudiated President in office four months after his party had been defeated, and the new Congress out of power for at least

39 Norton, *Letters*, I, 215–218.

that period. Had the nation possessed a ministerial form of government, a new leader would have taken over the reins immediately, with a united Cabinet behind him, and a close working relation with a new legislature. The stiffness of the American system, at times an advantage, now served it ill.

The main objective of Buchanan, the preservation of peace until compromise and sober second thought could bring the two sections together, was entirely sound. Most indices of public opinion suggest that the country desired caution, delay, and conciliation. A rough Jacksonian threat of force would have been repugnant to it. Buchanan believed that forbearance and moderation would keep the Upper South in the Union, that it would give time for placatory measures, and that the Lower South, finding itself alone and gradually softening under the offer of new guarantees, would return to its old allegiance. This was a reasonable policy. The President's use of appeasement had been unwise when it operated to bolster Southern unreason in the Lecompton dispute, in dealing with Douglas, and in pressing the slave-code demand; he should have checked and rebuked the radicals when that was still possible. But now that matters had come to an extremity, peaceable action was an imperative. Buchanan was unquestionably right in thinking that a military and naval demonstration against South Carolina in November of 1860 would have precipitated war. That angry State would have struck back. He was doubtless right in believing that most, if not all, of the South would have moved to defend the Carolinians. His resolve to explore every reasonable path toward reconciliation was sagacious statesmanship.

To be sure, it struck many Americans then and later as a supine course. Winfield Scott, a week before the election, had advised that six forts in the South be immediately garrisoned so strongly that their seizure would be impracticable. Some secessionist leaders, even, pronounced it a feeble policy. Ruffin jubilantly described it as such in his diary:

January 31, 1861. . . . I had not expected war between the old government and the seceded states, as a necessary or even probable result, provided all the southern states should secede at once, or even six or eight of the more southern states, with the early sympathy and early concurrence of the remaining and more northern slaveholding states. But I had certainly also expected, in the other contingency, of one only, or a few states seceding, that the first and immediate action of the federal government (denying the right of secession) would be to attempt the coercion and conquest of the seceded portion by a prompt and vigorous military attack. Instead of this no such attempt has yet been made, and nothing beyond the very partial and inefficient strengthening and reinforcing three of the many forts in the seceded and other southern states.

The imbecility of the executive department, added to the want of funds and means by the federal government, have prevented anything being done to coerce the seceded states. This impunity from federal attack must now continue until the 4th of March. . . . This has given four months of unforeseen and almost undisturbed time for action for the seceding states. Thus there has been avoided, what I certainly counted upon, the interregnum of lawful powers, or transition state of disorder, or illegal rule and perhaps revolutionary anarchy, expected to attend the change of government of every separately seceding state, and of all from the rule of the old to that of the new confederacy.

But Ruffin assumed that secession was fixed, irrevocable, and enduring, and that war must result from any attempt to disturb it. Buchanan's whole policy was to induce the Lower South to revoke its steps toward secession, and to guide the nation past war.

The correctness of this general policy, however, does not enable history to acquit Buchanan of weakness, vacillation, and timidity, his inseparable faults. His course passed through three fairly clear phases. The first was a period during which Cobb, Thompson, Slidell, and other Southern leaders still exerted almost their full influence, and he seemed ready to admit the main claims of the secessionists. The Directory, in fine, maintained its control over the Administration. The second was a brief interval during which he moved forward to a denial of the right of secession, but also denied that the government had any power to obstruct it. This acceptance of paralysis obviously could not last long. The impetuous action of the Lower South and the pressure of Northern sentiment forced the reluctant President to take a stand against Cobb, Thompson, and Slidell. Then the third period, following the reorganization of the Cabinet, found a strong Unionist group—Jeremiah Black, Joseph Holt, E. M. Stanton, and John A. Dix—maintaining the duty of the government to hold the forts and other Federal property in the South even if that course led to war. It is in the first two phases, falling in November and December, that we are immediately interested.

[V]

The initial Cabinet discussion held after Lincoln's election revealed that its members were violently divided in opinion, and that the President, anxious to learn the opinion of each, was as yet without sure conviction on the cardinal issues of secession and coercion. The date was November 9, and every member was present. Buchanan announced that they confronted the most momentous problem they had yet met, that of the course to be pursued in relation to Southern, and especially South Carolinian, threats of withdrawal. He raised for debate a specific proposal: That a convention of the States, as authorized in Article V of the Constitution, be called to devise some plan of adjustment. "He said," according to Floyd's diary, "that if this were done, and the North or non-slaveholding States should refuse it, the South would stand justified before the whole world for refusing longer to remain in a confederacy where her rights were so shamefully violated." [40] Cass, Black, Thompson, and Toucey favored calling a convention, and the two former spoke warmly in support of coercion if needed. Black, moreover, advocated immediate reinforcement of the Charleston forts. Cobb was saturnine and Floyd noncommittal on a convention, both feeling that nothing could be done to rescue the Union; while Holt opposed such a gathering on the ground that if it failed the secessionists would be more determined than ever.

Buchanan was working amain on a state paper which he thought of using either as a proclamation to expound his policy or as part of his annual message to Congress; and when he read the first draft to his Cabinet on November 10 a battle instantly opened between the two wings. His paper called upon the South to acquiesce in Lincoln's election, attacked the doctrine of secession, and hinted at the use of force to maintain the national authority. Cobb protested passionately. He had said the previous day that he thought disunion both inevitable and desirable. An implacable hater of the Republicans, he wished Georgia to secede in concert with the other Southern States; and he hoped that they would all take steps to leave on March 4, electing delegates to meet on that date to form a new Confederacy. Jacob Thompson held much the same views. He was anxious for Mississippi to secede; he believed that his political future lay with a Southern republic; he, too, thought that united action on March 4 would be the best course. When he heard Buchanan's paper he flared up angrily, denouncing its plea for acquiescence and its condemnation of secession. Floyd took the side of his fellow-Southerners. Like most Virginians, he was at this time opposed to secession or other rash steps and deplored the course of the Lower South. He even published over his own signature in a Richmond paper an essay rebuking secessionist attitudes. But he upheld the abstract right of withdrawal, and could not now abandon his stronger associates. He therefore attacked Buchanan's paper as false to the true State Rights doctrine and unjust to the temper of the Southern people.

On the other side, Cass, Black, Holt, and Toucey spiritedly espoused Buchanan's views. They gave the paper "extravagant commendation," records Floyd. Cass and Black were firm believers in Union principles. So was Holt, a man who had come into national politics as a staunch Jacksonian and adherent of Richard M. Johnson, and who represented the Union feeling in Kentucky. Toucey was simply a weak echo of the President. Like Buchanan, he was highly antagonistic to Northern "fanatics" and "agitators," but when his chief took a stand for national principles, he meekly followed. The Cabinet meeting broke

40 A thorough search has failed to reveal any more of Floyd's diary than is quoted in Pollard's *Lee*, 791 ff. Cf. P. G. Auchampaugh, "John B. Floyd and James Buchanan," *Tyler's Quarterly Hist. and Gen. Mag.*, XV, 71–90.

up without making any decision; but a deep cleavage had been revealed between its secessionist and antisecessionist wings.[41]

At this point, a President of spirit and acumen would have reorganized his Cabinet to make it a unit in harmony with his view, and would have pressed hard for the convention of States. The Cabinet schism sorely crippled the government. It was particularly inexcusable for Buchanan to retain Cobb and Thompson; to keep in the government two ministers who favored breaking that government down. As for the convention, if it were to be held, an immediate appeal to the country was essential. It could be called only by Congress on application of two-thirds of the State legislatures. The five States about to secede would probably spurn the idea and it would take time to get the others in motion. Bell-Everett men in the border region particularly favored a convention. Large numbers of conservative Democrats, and indeed numerous journals of all parties, were ready to support the plan. If Buchanan had given the movement energetic leadership, the convention might have served as a focus for national interest and Union sentiment; a body of men who inspired general respect could have been chosen; and their decisions might have saved the day. Unfortunately, Buchanan drifted. Doubtless fearing that the dismissal of Cobb and Thompson would raise a storm of anger in the cotton States, he kept his Cabinet intact. Actually, the expulsion of these two men would have yielded rewards as well as penalties, for it would have heartened Southern Unionists. Deciding to shift his responsibility to Congress, he dropped the convention plan.

It was a fatal error. Not a day should have been lost in calling for the grand national assize. An urgent request should have been sent the governors to convoke special legislative sessions. The mere spectacle of such executive energy in Washington would have encouraged the host of Southern unionists. A widespread demand that the country await the decision of the convention of States would have impeded the labors of the radical secessionists. Voices of moderation and statesmanship would have gained resonance as from a great amplifying apparatus. But neither vision nor boldness was part of Buchanan's nature, and he let the objections of the Directory deter him.

In this failure to unify his Administration and press for a bold national plan, Buchanan was influenced by the same Southern intimates who had surrounded him from the beginning. Horatio King, the First Assistant Postmaster-General and a close observer of events, wrote John A. Dix on November 10 that the President was "beset by secessionists who are almost exclusively occupying his

---

41 Curtis, *Buchanan*, II, *passim;* Nichols, *Disruption*, 382 ff.; Nicolay and Hay, *Lincoln*, II, Chs. XVIII–XXII; P. G. Auchampaugh, *James Buchanan and His Cabinet;* Frank W. Klingberg, "James Buchanan and the Crisis of the Union," *Journal Southern Hist.*, IX, November, 1943.

attention." He informs us that these men, Cobb and Thompson at their head, importuned and badgered Buchanan nightly until he was almost exhausted; until it was only with painful effort that he performed his duties, while some Cabinet sessions had to be held in his second-floor library because he was too unwell to go to his more distant office.[42] Soon after the election, Secretary Thompson was discussing with other Southerners ways and means of preventing Lincoln's inauguration. Within a month of the election, Secretary Cobb was addressing to Georgia a long exhortation to leave the Union. Yet these men were not merely kept in the government, but made the means by which Southerners of like views gained Buchanan's ear. Slidell, states King, was "among the most determined conspirators in seeking to destroy the Union." He remained intimate with Buchanan till the end of January, carrying his arrogance so far that when the President at that time dismissed Slidell's secessionist protégé, Beauregard, from the superintendency at West Point, the Senator sent the White House an insolent letter of rebuke.[43]

To the intense disgust of Cass, King, and others, the *Constitution*, still fed on Administration patronage, published articles day after day justifying secession. The morning after election, it asked whether the Southerner would submit to a Chief Executive chosen for his hostility to the South, or "make a struggle to defend his rights, his inheritance, and his honor." Greeley's Washington correspondent reported that when the first article appeared, Buchanan gave orders that the offenses should not be repeated and rebuked the Cabinet officer responsible. This may or may not have been true—but they continued. Finally, on December 14, King's disgust found vent in a letter to Attorney-General Black. "Is it not possible," he asked, "to relieve the Administration from the *infamy* which must attach to it for all time, so far as it is made responsible for the course of the *Constitution*, and for keeping men in responsible positions who are known and avowed disunionists? For God's sake, let us see the government placed squarely and unequivocally on the side of the Union!" Not until Christmas Day did Buchanan, "mortified" by an editorial declaring that the country must recognize secession or face civil war, notify W. M. Browne, the editor: "I am deeply sorry that I must in some authentic form declare the *Constitution* is not the organ of the Administration." At the end of January the disloyal sheet ceased publication.

While under this Southern pressure, Buchanan continued work on his state

42 King, *Turning On the Light*, 27 ff, 56, 57. King writes, p. 69 ff., that the conspirators had their headquarters in Washington, that many of them were in the pay of the United States, and that their object was first to embarrass and then break up or get control of the government. He earnestly defends Buchanan's patriotism and fidelity, but laments the influences surrounding him.

43 King, *op. cit.*, 33, 34, 113.

paper, turning to Attorney-General Black as his principal counsellor.[44] This strong-minded jurist, always positive in opinion and forcible in utterance, prepared some paragraphs asserting the indissoluble nature of the Union. "It can meet, repel, and subdue all those who rise against it," he wrote. He gave space to a severe castigation of the political course of both Southern and Northern extremists. When Cobb and Thompson saw these paragraphs, they violently rejected them as inflammatory. Buchanan thereupon told Black that he had gone too far, that his language was provocative, and that he should rewrite his sheets, confining himself to the strictly legal aspects of the situation. The Attorney-General did so. Thus Black's contribution to the President's document was watered down lest it ruffle Southern tempers; and at the same time it was decided, Cobb, Thompson, and Black all agreeing, that this document should take the form not of a proclamation but of part of the annual message to Congress.

When Black's legal paper was finally ready on November 20, its tenor proved sufficiently mild to suit the timid Buchanan. To be sure, it denied the right of secession. It offered a telling series of arguments for the perpetuity of the Union under the Constitution. Thompson had searched the debates of 1787 to find counter evidence, but he was no match for the Pennsylvanian. Apart from this stand on the abstract question, however, Black's contribution had lost all its initial fire; he temporarily turned his back on that advocacy of coercion which, if we accept Floyd's diary, he had twice previously affirmed. We can only guess at the psychological conflict which was raging in the breast of the tough-minded, courageous Scotch-Irishman, torn between prejudice and patriotism. He hated Republicanism and sympathized with the South; but he felt a devoted allegiance to the Union. His irresolution in these November weeks was pitiable. It almost matched the irresolution of the chief whom he loved but was now beginning to regard realistically. Black, however, was a man of iron qualities. The iron was being tempered by his inner fires, and he was soon to emerge as a resolute champion of the national authority and national idea.

His report contended that the national government had every power except *the* power which seemed needed in this crisis. In South Carolina, nearly all Federal officers—judges, marshal, district attorney—had resigned, while the

44 For Buchanan's dependence on Black, see Auchampaugh, *James Buchanan and His Cabinet,* 132, with citations. Buchanan remarked that he wished to stand between the quarreling parties in the country as a moderator, "with my hand on the head of each, counselling peace." The papers of W. H. Trescot in the South Caroliniana Library contain an undated "memorandum of views submitted to Cass and the President," which enforce the opinion that Congress alone could decide what policy was to be taken with reference to secession; that the President could only submit the situation to them and await their decision. This view, which played into the hands of the secessionists, Buchanan adopted.

collector seemed likely at any moment to be driven from his custom house. How could the laws be executed in these circumstances? Black concluded that no State, while in the Union, could absolve its people from obedience to the constitutional demands of the national government; that the collector could pursue his legal duties even if driven aboard a vessel in the port; that the President had a right to take such defensive measures as seemed necessary to protect forts, arsenals, navy yards, and other public property; and that he had a right to enforce the decrees of the courts on individuals. But Black also concluded that if antagonism to the United States forced the resignation of all national officers, the government was helpless. The laws in such an event could not be executed. Under these circumstances, the dispatch of military forces into a State with orders to act against the people would be an act of war against them. He advised Buchanan to transfer the decision for or against such acts of war to other hands:

Whether Congress has the constitutional right to make war against one or more States, and require the Executive of the Federal Government to carry it on by means of force to be drawn from the other States, is a question for Congress itself to consider. It must be admitted that no such power is expressly given; nor are there any words in the Constitution which imply it.[45]

This, obviously, was not the view which Jackson had taken in nullification days. Nor is it the view which some of the best constitutional authorities of later times have laid down.[46]

[VI]

The four weeks between the election and the opening of Congress meanwhile found the President desperately worried by the situation in Charleston harbor. Here stood three of the nine coastal forts in the South: Castle Pinckney, with eighteen heavy guns and four howitzers, commanding the city; the incomplete Fort Sumter, with seventy-eight guns on hand, some unmounted; and Fort Moultrie, with fifty-five guns. Some seventy-two thousand muskets were stored in the Charleston arsenal, and a quantity of powder in Castle Pinckney. At Pinckney on November 11 was housed only an ordnance sergeant, and at Sumter only a lieutenant and a few regulars to control the workmen. Moultrie was garrisoned, however, by two small companies of the First Artillery.[47]

Late in October, Winfield Scott, general-in-chief, had sent the President the before-mentioned recommendations which became known as his "views." He

45 Full text in Curtis, *Buchanan*, II, 319–324.
46 Corwin, *National Supremacy*, 242, 243.
47 *Official Records*, Series I, Vol. I, 70–72.

wrote that one or more of the Southern States would probably secede, that danger existed of a seizure of all of the nine forts, and that they should imme-- diately be garrisoned against surprise. While his interpolated political remarks were absurd, for he suggested an ultimate division of the nation into four con- federacies, his military opinions were to be treated with respect. Buchanan pon- dered his proposal. It was evident that spirited action by the government might give hotheaded Southerners a deterring sense of the gravity of their undertaking.

Charleston Harbor and the Forts

It was equally evident that to collect troops and throw them into the forts might exasperate other Southerners, intensify the excitement of the hour, and precipi- tate the very clash that the nation was anxious to avoid. Moreover, was the government justified in assuming that precautions were needed? With strong Union parties active in most Southern States, it seemed inadvisable to suggest that Washington anticipated their overthrow by men intent upon violent measures. Buchanan wisely put Scott's plan aside. But this left the question of strengthening the Charleston forts still acute.

The Charleston forts! Wearily pacing the library floor, dispiritedly cracking a few jokes at table for Miss Lane, lying awake hour after hour in the bedroom that looked out over the placid, moonlit Potomac, the aged President worried ceaselessly lest the hot South Carolinians make some lawless move against the three posts. The forts were so weak! Only a sergeant in Pinckney, with its guns dominating the city; only sixty-four men (of whom eleven were in arrest or confinement at last report) with a handful of officers, at Moultrie; only a tiny squad keeping order at unfinished Sumter! Daily, the fevered population uttered threats against them all. A storm might break at any moment. Every newspaper was discussing the question of reinforcements. Every time the Cabinet met, the quarrel on the subject broke out afresh—Cass and Black arguing for more troops, the Southern members vigorously protesting, and the President—with Toucey feebly seconding him—in the role of unhappy moderator.[48] It seemed certain that South Carolina would go out on December 20. What would happen to the forts then?

Buchanan's first instinct was to take the side of Cobb, Thompson, and Floyd in a scrupulous avoidance of any provocation whatever to the Carolinians. The day after Lincoln's election, Colonel John L. Gardner, commanding at Charleston, attempted a quiet transfer of ammunition from the city arsenal to Fort Moultrie, but was blocked by a hostile crowd. He was promptly transferred to Texas, and his place given to Major Robert Anderson.[49] This was a happy choice. Since Anderson was of Kentucky birth and Virginia ancestry, had married a Georgia girl, and displayed a friendly attitude toward slavery, he was fitted to play a conciliatory role in a Southern community. Yet he was thoroughly loyal to the Union, for which he had fought in the Black Hawk, Seminole, and Mexican wars. Hurrying to his post, he gave the three forts a close inspection. The result was dramatic. On November 24, again on November 28, and again on December 1, he called urgently for reinforcements.

It is not strange that the harassed President, never of decisive temper, presented a fluctuating front on this question of reinforcement. He had at first taken the Cobb-Floyd position, declining to send more troops. Anderson's first long dispatch, however, arriving November 27, put a new face on the matter. The South Carolinians evinced a settled determination, wrote the major, to leave the Union and seize Moultrie. They regarded Castle Pinckney as already practically in their possession. Nothing could be better calculated

48 Black later remarked in Cabinet that there had never been a time in English history when a minister who proposed to give up to an enemy a defensible military post would not have been brought to the block. King, *Turning On the Light*, 123.

49 *Official Records*, Series I, Vol. I, 69–73.

to prevent bloodshed than to put the forts in such a position "that it would be folly and madness to attack us." Anderson asked at least two companies for Sumter and Pinckney at once, and a reinforcement for his own Moultrie garrison, with ordnance stores and ordnance experts.[50] If he were thus strengthened, he believed South Carolina would not attempt to take the forts; if he were not, the secessionists would soon demand their surrender and launch an attack. Cass and Black now insisted more forcibly than ever that Buchanan should send aid to Anderson. Although Cobb, Thompson, and W. H. Trescot, Assistant Secretary of State, labored still to persuade the President that no reinforcements were needed, Buchanan gave way. He directed Floyd to send the required force to Anderson.

But Floyd took refuge in delay. He induced the President to consent to talk with General Scott before making his orders final—and Scott was too ill in New York to come to the capital. While the delay lasted, Cobb, Trescot, and Thompson hurriedly arranged a bargain between the Administration and South Carolina. The President agreed to revoke his decision to send troops to Charleston, while Governor Gist promised that national property there should not be seized. This was a precarious arrangement, subject to sudden disturbance. Floyd felt it necessary to send personal reassurances to South Carolina. A Charleston paper shortly published a letter of December 5 from an unnamed officer of distinction in Washington, quoting a conversation with the Secretary of War. "You may say to the people of South Carolina," Floyd remarked, "there will be no more troops sent to the forts at Charleston. I will resign before it shall be done." [51]

Meanwhile, as Cabinet differences over the two immediate issues, the doctrinal content of the message and the strengthening of the Charleston posts, continued unabated, the Southern group moved to improve their position. Floyd and one other Cabinet member, probably Cobb, invited Senators Jefferson Davis, Mason, and Slidell to hasten to Washington well in advance of the sitting of Congress. Davis, who responded with alacrity, tells us that he was especially wanted for his influence on the message. When he called at the White House, Buchanan informed him that the rough draft was completed but was still open to revision, and he would read it aloud. "He did so, and very kindly accepted all the modifications which I suggested. The message was, however, afterward somewhat changed, and, with great deference to the wisdom and statesmanship of the author, I must say that, in my judgment, the last

50 *Idem*, 75 ff.
51 Quoted in N. Y. *Weekly Tribune*, December 22, 1860. For Buchanan's vacillation, see Nichols, *Disruption*, 387. The articles on Black's acts by Col. Frank Burr in the Phila. *Press* of 1881 and 1883 are inaccurate in many points, but illuminating if used guardedly.

alterations were unfortunate—so much so that, when it was read in the Senate, I was reluctantly constrained to criticize it." [52] Davis's recollections may be inaccurate in detail, for his book was not published until 1881, and Buchanan may have accepted his suggestions for consideration, not outright incorporation. But the picture he gives of Presidential uncertainty is correct.

Until the day Congress opened, the wrangling within the Administration went on. Cass still maintained that the forts should be strengthened; he was curtly overruled. Major Anderson was ordered to take no step that would provoke an attack, and to wait patiently, though he must defend the forts to the last extremity if attacked. To emphasize these orders, Major Don Carlos Buell was sent southward to repeat them both orally and in writing. The embittered Cass was contemplating resignation. In discussions of the President's forthcoming message, Black maintained that while the President had no power to take *offensive* action against a State, he had the fullest power of *defensive* action in holding possession of the public property and in clearing away all obstruction to the execution of Federal law. He argued also that if a State seceded, Congress or a convention of States must take "necessary and proper measures" to deal with it. He, too, was overruled. [53]

The message was completed on December 2. The final Cabinet session on it saw Black contending vainly for his views on defensive action and necessary and proper measures. Buchanan refused to accept them. He declared that the Executive had no power to clear away obstructions in a State where no judicial authority existed to issue process, where there was no marshal to serve it, and where, even if a marshal could be found, the entire population would join in resisting him. He also declared that Congress, far from having any latitude to take "necessary and proper" measures against a State, had been expressly denied the power to coerce, and that such power was at variance with the spirit of the Constitution. Thompson, citing evidence that in 1787 the coercive power had been proposed at Philadelphia and rejected, had convinced Buchanan of *this* point. Black accepted his defeat with bad grace, and said that he did not see how he could submit to the President's decision. But he had to submit. The Southern members, reinforced by Davis, were in control on every issue except the abstract right of secession, which Buchanan denied. On the main practical matters—the forts, the rejection of coercion, the retention of the divided Cabinet—they could feel satisfied that they had made the controlling decisions; they could feel that they still dominated the Administration. [54]

52 Davis, *Rise and Fall*, I, 59.
53 Curtis, *Buchanan*, II, 323, 324.
54 Burr, in Phila. *Press*, March 4, 1883.

[VII]

Congress reconvened in an atmosphere of uncertainty, confusion, and frustration. All the members were present except Senators Chesnut and Hammond of South Carolina. The other States of the Lower South were fully represented, for they had much to gain and nothing to lose by keeping their seats in Washington. They could frustrate any Republican designs for taking control of the Senate; they could prevent the adoption of any threatening measures; they could encourage anti-war Democrats in the North; and, most important of all, they could urge members from the Upper South to join the new slaveholding republic. Most of the thirty Representatives and twelve Senators from the Lower South were not interested in restoring the Union, but they were intensely interested in peaceable separation. At the other extreme, the majority of Republicans were concerned with saving the Union only on the basis of their main plank, the containment of slavery. The prospects of any compromise were thus exceedingly slender.

Noon of December 4 brought the anxiously awaited message; and it is safe to say that no American state paper in time of crisis ever produced a more disappointing impression. The South was left dissatisfied and irritated—though some members agreed with Jesse D. Bright that Buchanan was more conservative than they had expected. Feeling in the North ranged from explosive indignation in radical Republican circles to a resigned sense of futility and helplessness among many Douglas Democrats and to partial satisfaction among some future Copperheads.

The essence of the message was that the Federal government held certain authorities and also certain disabilities which, taken together, resulted in complete paralysis. Secession, declared Buchanan, was unconstitutional, but there was no power in Congress or the Executive to compel a State to remain in the Union. It was the duty of the President to enforce the laws, but in the existing situation in South Carolina it was utterly impossible for him to do so. The government was "great and powerful," and its framers had not been "guilty of the absurdity of providing for its own dissolution"; but even if it possessed the right to make war against a State (which it did not), any exercise of that right would be unwise, for the resulting loss of blood and treasure would make a future reconciliation impossible. "The fact is," Buchanan wrote, "that our Union rests upon public opinion, and can never be cemented by the blood of its citizens shed in civil war. If it cannot live in the affections of the people, it must one day perish."

To this statement of national helplessness he prefixed an indictment of the Northern antislavery agitation as primarily responsible for the predicament of the nation. The incessant attack on Southern institutions, he said, had produced such alarm in the South that many a matron retired to bed at night uncertain whether she and her children would see the next dawn. Several of his assertions went far toward justifying and encouraging the secession which he elsewhere denounced as unconstitutional, unnecessary, and futile. Should the apprehension of Southern peril from servile revolt become intensified and pervade the masses, he remarked, "then disunion will become inevitable"—for self-preservation is man's first law. He assailed the personal liberty laws of various States, saying that Southerners had a right to ask their repeal. If this were denied them, the North would have willfully violated the Constitution. "In that event, the injured States, after having first used all peaceful and constitutional means to obtain redress, would be justified in revolutionary resistance to the government of the Union." Such utterances were far more likely to stimulate hesitant secessionists than to restrain them.

To meet the crisis, Buchanan suggested that an explanatory amendment respecting slavery be added to the Constitution. It should recognize the right of property in slaves in States where it already existed, or might thereafter exist; it should guarantee the protection of slave property in all Territories until they were admitted as States; and it should reaffirm the title of masters to the restoration of fugitive slaves, and declare all State laws impairing or defeating this title null and void.

The general Northern verdict on the message was that Buchanan stood by his views on the wrongfulness of secession theoretically, but ran away from them practically. The Philadelphia *North American* found the treatment highly characteristic of the President, in that "with much soundness of argument we have singular inadequacy of results." The Buffalo *Courier*, which had supported Douglas, was shocked by the way in which an excellent vindication of the constitutional authority of the government was coupled with "an ill-timed confession of weakness." The Cincinnati *Enquirer*, another Douglas paper, pronounced it silly to argue against secession without applying the corollary of coercion. "Seldom have we known so strong an argument come to so lame and impotent a conclusion." In general, Republican newspapers condemned the partisanship of the message, which scolded extremists on the Northern side while soothing them on the Southern; its historical errors; and its suggestion that they give up their interdiction of slavery in the Territories. They did not fail to comment scornfully upon the President's renewal of his proposal for buying Cuba, a step which, said the New York *Tribune*, would at once strengthen the slaveholding interest by ten or twelve additional members of Congress and as many Presidential electors—and which, commented the Des Moines *State Register*, would tax the nation several hundred million dollars to buy an island that might secede with the Gulf States before the ink used in drawing the bill of sale had dried on the paper.[55]

Repugnant to most Northerners, the message irritated most Southerners by its condemnation of secession. No sooner had it been read in the Senate than Clingman of North Carolina rose to denounce it, and to declare that its proposed concessions came too late. His State, he said, would not be satisfied with the repeal of all personal liberty laws. He favored immediate secession, spurning further parley with Northern men. A. G. Brown, Wigfall, and Iverson spoke in similar terms. "There will be no war," said Iverson. "In less than twelve months, a Southern Confederacy will be formed; and it will be the most successful government on earth." Even Jefferson Davis and Mason, who spoke in favor of waiting upon further efforts at an adjustment, were sharply critical of the message.

Yet Buchanan, before sending it to Congress, had been so confident that it might arrest the secession movement that he had asked Assistant Secretary Trescot to go at once to South Carolina with a copy for Governor Gist. He had plaintively told Trescot that he thought the South ought to find the message acceptable, for "all he had declared was that with regard to the laws of the United States and the property, he would discharge all the obligations of his official oath." The honest Trescot emphatically informed the President that the message would produce no effect. South Carolina was in headlong movement toward secession, he declared, and he proved it by describing the excitement and exaltation of the people, and by reading a letter from Gist which predicted withdrawal as soon as the convention should meet.[56]

Newspaper men, mingling with Southern members of Congress, found that many of them favored an early convention of the Southern States in order to lay down terms on which the section would remain in the Union; others favored a convention to organize a separate Confederacy whose members might rejoin the Union when proper concessions were made; still others were determined that the new Confederacy should assert and maintain its independence. Southern members of the House and Senate began to hold almost continuous conferences. No informed observer believed that any event could prevent the immediate secession of South Carolina, Mississippi, and Alabama, and few believed that the withdrawal of Georgia and Florida could be halted. Joseph Holt was hearing from his brother in Mississippi that that State would never turn back. He heard from a friend in New Orleans under date of December 14 that the cotton States were determined on secession: "I do not believe that these States would accept Union, if the North was to give every constitutional guarantee."

55 Editorials December 4, 5, 6 in papers named; *State Register*, December 10.
56 "Narrative of William Henry Trescot," *Am. Hist. Rev.*, XIII, 528–556.

[VIII]

Upon Buchanan's message, Lincoln uttered no recorded comment. As events soon showed, however, he differed radically from the President on two issues of paramount importance. Whereas Buchanan was for conceding to the South all its demands respecting the Territories, including a slave-protection code, Lincoln was bound by personal conviction and party pledge to insist that the national domain should be forever barred against the intrusion of slavery. The young new commonwealths of the West must, he had said, be given a clean bed, with no snakes in it. And whereas Buchanan wrote that it was his duty to enforce the laws and protect the national property, but that he could not, Lincoln held that it was *his* duty to do this, that he could, and he would. He had maintained his silence as the crisis developed. To a correspondent of the New York *Evening Post* who interviewed him in Springfield on November 14, he had made it clear that he would say nothing that might be construed as a token of weakness. "I know the justness of my intentions," remarked the President-elect, "and the utter groundlessness of the pretended fears of the men who are filling the country with their clamor. . . . My declarations have been made to the world without reservation. They have been repeated; and now, self-respect demands of me and the party that has elected me, that when threatened I should be silent." But he also made it clear to his interviewer that he was determined to yield no part of his own or his party's principles. He intended to adopt a policy for the whole country, reported the correspondent, and pursue it firmly and even obdurately to the end.[57]

Other evidences of his attitude reached the nation. Lincoln viewed the situation at first with an excessive optimism, believing (as did many other Illinois Republicans, including Lyman Trumbull and the editors of the Chicago *Tribune* and *Illinois State Journal*) that the secession clamor was largely bluff.[58] Nevertheless, the demand of the New York *Herald* and other papers that he redefine his position brought him to make one interesting experiment in reaching public opinion. Illinois Republicans arranged a grand jubilee for November 20. Trumbull was to speak, with Lincoln present. This meant that anything Trumbull said would be regarded as authorized; and to make this fact plain, Lincoln told the press that the speech would reflect his views—the New York *Herald* announcing the "Forthcoming Semi-Official Exposition" of the opinions of the President-elect. Moreover, Lincoln secretly wrote two paragraphs for the Senator to include in his address. The speech was highly moderate in

57 Nevins, *Evening Post*, 269, 270.
58 For an impression of Lincoln's optimism, see Donn Piatt, *Memories of Men Who Saved the Union*, 31–34. The *Illinois State Journal* said, December 12, of the action of the Lower South: "We do not apprehend any serious trouble from these incipient movements." Lincoln's secretary expected no secession; Helen Nicolay, *John G. Nicolay*, 57.

tone. Lincoln's paragraphs implied, with wishful blitheness, that the Union men of every State would themselves overthrow the disunionists. At the same time, the address made no concessions. Trumbull explicitly said that any interference by South Carolina with the collection of Federal revenues would be revolution, and that if any man assailed with force of arms the national authorities, the great mass of Americans would echo Jackson's stern words and deal hardly with these "traitors." [59]

The address, widely published and discussed, did not make the impression for which Lincoln had hoped. He expressed aggrieved disappointment in a letter to Raymond of the *Times*. Did a single newspaper previously in opposition to the Republicans use that speech to quiet public anxiety? "Not one, so far as I know. On the contrary, the Boston *Courier* and its class hold me responsible for that speech, and endeavor to inflame the North with the belief that it foreshadows an abandonment of Republican ground by the incoming administration; while the Washington *Constitution* and its class hold the same speech up to the South as an open declaration of war against them." Referring both to Northern zealots and Southern doctrinaries, he expressed disgust with the "political fiends" who were still possessed by "party malice, and not public good." [60] His resolution to make no public statements became fixed more firmly than ever.

Nevertheless, dispatches from Springfield made it known that he was studying Jackson's utterances in the nullification crisis. And the *Illinois State Journal*, whose editor was regarded as his personal spokesman, and whose columns at least once contained matter which on internal evidence might well be Lincoln's, was sufficiently militant in tone. On November 14, after remarking that the new President's policy would be peace, it added that if nullification raised its head he would have no discretionary power but to execute the laws. "Should it come to the worst, we feel satisfied from what we know of Mr. Lincoln that those who would destroy the law will be dealt with by the strong arm of the law." After Buchanan's message, the *State Journal* spoke still more sternly:

South Carolina . . . cannot get out of this Union until she conquers this government. The revenues must and will be collected at her ports, and any resistance on her part will lead to war. At the close of that war we can tell with certainty whether she is in or out of the Union. While this government endures there can be no disunion. . . . If the overt act on the part of South Carolina takes place on or after the 4th of March, 1861, then the duty of executing the laws will devolve upon Mr. Lincoln. The laws of the United States must be executed—the President has no discretionary power on the subject—his duty is emphatically pronounced in the Constitution. Mr. Lincoln

59　For Trumbull's speech see W. E. Baringer, *A House Dividing*, 32 ff.
60　Lincoln, November 28. 1860; *Works*, I, 656.

will perform that duty. Disunion by armed force is treason, and treason must and will be put down at all hazards. This Union is not, and will not, and cannot be dissolved until this government is overthrown by the traitors who have raised the disunion flag. Can they overthrow it? We think not.[61]

In private conversation with visitors and in reply to certain Southern letters, Lincoln did not hesitate to give assurances of fair treatment to the South. He was anxious that men understand that he would be a conservative President, acting in the interests of the whole country and not of one section. To a Kentucky judge who asked him to place one or more Southerners of non-Republican ties in the Cabinet, he explained that the party could not give up the fruits of victory, but promised to consider the plea. To two callers in mid-November, he spoke of his wish to maintain "a government of fraternity." [62] But on matters of well-understood principle he was adamant.

We can have no doubt as to what Lincoln would have thought of a curious episode which took place in Washington on December 9—the episode of Buchanan's so-called pledge to secession leaders. That day, four members of Congress from South Carolina held a conference with the President. They and one other followed it by sending Buchanan a letter. In this they expressed their conviction that the forts would not be molested until the State convention met, and until an offer had been made by an accredited representative to negotiate for an amicable settlement of all questions between the State and the Federal government; "provided that no reinforcements shall be sent into these forts, and their relative military status shall remain as at present." The President declared that he would never make any agreement not to reinforce the forts. But, he stated, he had no design at the moment to alter their status. Representatives Miles and Keitt later reported to the State convention that Buchanan had promised he would return their letter to them if for any reason he changed his policy. They declared that "the impression made upon the delegation was that the President was wavering, and had not wholly decided as to what course he would pursue." [63]

Thus the President made no pledge not to reinforce the forts. But he did promise (or so the South Carolina members understood) that he would not change their status without notifying the Congressmen.

[IX]

In the last half of December, a swift rush of events carried the nation past old landmarks and beacons, and into a tempestuous sea of uncertainty. On

61 December 20, 1860.
62 Baringer, *A House Dividing*, 52, 53.
63 King, *Turning On the Light*, 162; Buchanan, *Works*, XI, 56, 57; Crawford, *Genesis of the Civil War*, 38, 39.

December 13, Cass made his last effort to compel Buchanan to reinforce the Charleston posts. "These forts must be strengthened," he said. "I demand it." Buchanan replied that he was sorry to differ. "I have made up my mind. The interests of the country do not demand a reinforcement of the forces in Charleston. I cannot do it, and I take the responsibility on myself." Next day Cass resigned. Uncertain health and the pressure of his son-in-law, Henry Ledyard, contributed to this impulsive decision which he immediately tried to revoke—asking Black and Thompson to tell the President that he was willing to withdraw his letter.[64] Buchanan appointed Black to the Secretaryship of State, and named to Black's place a highly able, forceful, and erratic attorney of Pittsburgh, destined to a great and dubious place in American history— Edwin M. Stanton. The retirement of Cass further lowered the President's prestige, radical Northern newspapers interpreting it as the refusal of a patriotic statesman to remain longer in the family of a President who paltered with, if he did not abet, treason. At the same time, it did not really place the Secretary himself in an heroic light. Men of Harz-rock principles like Charles Francis Adams, recalling that Cass had for decades pursued a flabby, time-serving course on the slavery question, believed that he had created a false impression of a highly courageous stand against the Administration so that he could live with greater credit among his freesoil neighbors in Detroit.

At the age of fifty-seven, Stanton had achieved a position of high distinction at the American bar, and a reputation for fiercely positive opinions on public questions. Born in Steubenville, Ohio, the son of a Yankee Quaker of staunch abolitionist convictions, he had learned hatred of slavery at his father's knee and at that of a valued family friend—Benjamin Lundy, whose journal *The Genius of Universal Emancipation* the father assisted with money and labor. While a student at Kenyon College and under the influence of its head, Bishop Philander Chase, the lad had been converted to the Episcopal Church; and a fervent religious faith, almost morbid in some of its tendencies, had strengthened his aversion from human bondage. At Kenyon, too, he had aligned himself with strong feeling on the side of Andrew Jackson in combatting the Nullification movement. Later he had supported the Wilmot Proviso. No stauncher believer in the idea of national union could be found in the land, no sterner antagonist of disunion schemers and plotters—and, we may add, no more excitable, suspicious, and apprehensive prophet of coming dangers. To every task that he undertook Stanton gave a passionate determination, a fierce intensity, a power of instant action, and a terrible industry. He had shown in a long list of famous cases, including the patent action of McCormick vs. Manny, where he so brutally snubbed Lincoln, that he was one of the best

64 McLaughlin, *Cass*, 344.

lawyers of his day. Jeremiah Black believed that his successful work as special counsel for the government in resisting fraudulent land claims in California proved him the best living lawyer. He brought to public office an aggressive (and capricious) temper, tremendous driving force, and remarkable powers of organization. It was a stalwart fighter for the national principle who now entered the cabinet room; a pugnacious "little black terrier," as Montgomery Blair called him.

Both the promotion of Black and the appointment of Stanton constituted a telling gain for the Union cause in Washington. Equally important was the resignation of Cobb on December 8. He believed that secession was imperative. Between the Black Republicans and the people of the South, he wrote in a manifesto dated December 6, there was now no feeling but of bitter and intense hatred. Responding to what he called the paramount demands of his State, he hurried to Columbia and Macon to incite the people to create their own republic. Buchanan made an unfortunate choice in his stead. To deal with the desperate Treasury problems he selected a mediocre Maryland politician of Southern sympathies, Philip F. Thomas, so unfit that he was destined to a very brief tenure.

And on December 20 came the electrifying news of the secession of South Carolina. The convention met in Columbia on the seventeenth, adjourned to Charleston next day to escape a threatened smallpox epidemic, spent the nineteenth in talking about procedure, and at 1:30 on the afternoon of the twentieth unanimously adopted the ordinance of secession. Buchanan had sent Caleb Cushing to expostulate, but he was ignored. That evening, all the delegates having signed the engrossed copy of the ordinance, South Carolina was proclaimed an independent commonwealth.[65] Few farsighted men could have doubted the implications of this act. Ben Wade, on the day the convention met, delivered to the Senate a militant speech in which he proclaimed that the only way for a State to leave the Union was by making and winning a war, and that he would sacrifice everything to keep the flag flying over an intact nation. "Half a million Wide Awakes," tauntingly observed Senator Iverson at a committee meeting, "cannot inaugurate Lincoln." "Well, then," coolly replied a Republican Senator, "we will send a million." South Carolina at once appointed three commissioners (one of them Trescot, who resigned his place in the State Department) to negotiate with Buchanan for the cession of

---

65 Dumond, *Secession Movement*, 139–142. Bonfires, fireworks, bands, a military parade, and general illumination of the city celebrated the event. The *Mercury* sold six thousand copies of its extra. Crowds cheered the transparencies: "One voice and millions of strong arms to uphold the honor of South Carolina." *Mercury*, December 22, 1860. Commissioners from Alabama and Mississippi, Governor Perry of Florida, and other prominent Southerners were present at the convention.

national property to the commonwealth; and the new governor, Francis W. Pickens, wrote the President demanding that he be allowed to put a small guard of his own in Fort Sumter.

The nation was now in sore extremity. Inside and outside Washington, talk of war was increasing. The Mississippi and Florida elections, on December 20 and 24, resulted in the choice of conventions which would be strongly dominated by secessionists. One State was out, and four or five others certain to follow! Great elements in the border area were asserting that if the national government made war on the Lower South, they would stand by their brothers of the new, slaveholding Confederacy. The division of opinion in the North, some for outright coercion, some for generous concessions with coercion in reserve, and some for peace at any cost, seemed likely to paralyze that section. Justice Grier of the Supreme Court wrote from Washington on December 29 to his friend W. H. Smith in terms of despair. He feared that he was receiving his last salary check from the United States:

Everything is getting *worse and worse* here. Buchanan is *wholly unequal* to the occasion. He is surrounded by enemies of the Union. The Secretary of War wished to recall and censure the commander of Fort Moultrie—but was fortunately overruled by the Cabinet—Black Stanton and Holt the *honest* members of the Cabinet will probably withdraw unless Floyd is dismissed. Poor Toucey is *nobody*. Thompson is honest but a *secessionist*. I should not be astonished if the Cabinet should be wholly dissolved before ten days—and the country without a government.

We dined with the President yesterday. He is getting very *old*—very *faint*—poor fellow he has fallen on evil times. He put his confidence [in] and gave his power to his enemies and not to his friends and now he is enjoying the fruits of his mistakes. He *knows* Floyd to be a traitor and one who has conducted his office in a manner to disgrace the administration and plunder the country, and who is now plotting its destruction yet he hesitates to dismiss him. I should not be astonished from what I have heard privately, if Floyd was arrested and Buchanan impeached before 60 days. Everything is going to ruin unless the people rise in their majesty and rebuke the scoundrels north and south who are working together to divide the Union. This [division] would be certainly followed by civil war—*servile* war and ruin and misery to both parties. We are governed by fools and knaves we have not a *man* for the occasion. I expect to be at home on Thursday the 10th if nothing happens— and perhaps *sooner*—if the hero *Wise* should take the capital with his army.[66]

To what extent had Buchanan's management of the government in the crisis been censurable? A later generation was to condemn him in terms almost as severe as those of his Pennsylvania friend, Grier. In great part, this con- demnation was unjust. A clear distinction must be drawn, in reviewing his

66 Copy by courtesy of Carnegie Bookshop, New York.

acts, between his general policy, which was sound, and his mode of implementing it, which was weak, timid, and blundering.

The President was entirely right in determining upon a policy of peace, conciliation, and delay. This was the statesmanlike course, offering the one hope of preserving the Union without carnage, destruction, and hatred. But having chosen this policy, he showed all his characteristic feebleness, hesitation, and timidity in its execution.

At no fewer than four points did he fail to rise to the exigencies of the situation. (1) He should have lost no time after the election—not a day, not an hour—in preparing as eloquent and spirited an appeal to national sentiment, North and South, as he and his aides could pen. He should have rallied the patriotic feeling of the country as Jackson, Clay, and Webster had rallied it in the past. (2) He should have reorganized his Cabinet forthwith to give it unity and decision. It was something worse than a blunder to keep in the government two men, Cobb and Thompson, who were intent on the utter ruin of that government. No strong President would have hesitated to dismiss these marplots and give himself the support of a harmonious and truly Union-loving group of men.[67] (3) With a united Cabinet, he would certainly have reinforced Charleston as soon as Major Anderson set forth the facts demanding a stronger garrison. This would have angered many Southerners. But the government had every right to act; and action would have made it clear that secession meant war—dispelling an illusion which was giving secession sentiment one of its strongest supports. Either the government was going to fight to defend its forts, or it was not. Plainly it was, and the honest course was to show to all that disunion meant a fight. At this, many deluded men would have drawn back. (4) Most important of all, Buchanan should have pressed with instant vigor his plan for a national convention to formulate a scheme of adjustment. His weak decision to transfer responsibility to Congress was a choice of the easy path—but the wrong path. Congress was in the hands of the politicians, and mainly of small politicians at that. Two great groups of Congressmen, the radical secessionists and the radical Republicans, were committed to oppose any practicable scheme of accommodation. A national convention would have given the people an opportunity to choose their best statesmen and set aside small politicians; it would have been freer from party trammels than Congress; and

67 A New York friend of the President's niece, T. Bailey Myers, made bold to write her on December 8 urging a reconstruction of the Cabinet. If I were President, he stated, "I would resort to a change of ministers." He added that the chief difficulty of the country lay in "the want of a rallying point"; that "justly or not there is an utter want of confidence in the Cabinet on all hands"; that "New York will as a unit stand by the Union"; and that the actions of Cobb, Thompson, and Floyd "have shocked the public sense here and there is but one sentiment as to their course." Buchanan-Johnston Papers.

the memory of the great convention of 1787 could not but have given it an overwhelming sense of responsibility.

In the first six weeks after the election, great opportunities had been lost. The main responsibility for the future now lay with Congress. What would it do with its own opportunities?

12

The Administration Reorganized

CONFUSION NOW hath made its masterpiece, Americans might exclaim in Shakespeare's words as the old year gave way to the new. A clamor of discordant voices assailed the ear. Cave Johnson burst forth in a long Union letter to the Nashville *Banner*: Governor Thomas H. Hicks and Henry Winter Davis published appeals to the loyalty of Marylanders; and John Bell, while attacking Northern fanaticism, assured the South that the recent election gave no ground for secession. In New York, Mayor Fernando Wood was penning a sensational message to the aldermen, proposing that the city sever the bonds which placed it under up-State tyranny, declare its freedom, and levy a nominal duty on imports. At Norfolk, General John Tyler, son of the former President, fulminated: "Let the Union go to hell!" In New Orleans, the historian, Charles Gayarré, delivered a hot secession speech; in Missouri, the new governor, Claiborne F. Jackson, declared that all slaveholding States must stand united against oppression. While in Memphis a crowd burned in effigy Andrew Johnson, the Unionist Senator, in Philadelphia special police had to be used to protect Sumner in an intolerant speech. Ten thousand men all over the map, from Joseph Lane to Thurlow Weed, were presenting schemes of compromise.

As additional legislatures gathered, many State capitals became centers of fevered if rather aimless activity. Those of the North took up resolutions demanding strict enforcement of the laws, tendering support or swords to Major Anderson, and offering the government arms and recruits. Lawmakers of the South pealed defiance and authorized new purchases of weapons. In Massachusetts, Governor John A. Andrew ordered all the militia companies immediately filled up with trained and uniformed men. In Alabama, Governor Moore just after New Year's directed the occupation of Forts Morgan and Gaines. Coercionist resolutions were introduced in New England, and anti-coercionist resolutions in Virginia. While rumors of a servile revolt in southwestern Georgia worried Southerners, reports of Democratic disloyalty in New York City troubled Northerners. Everywhere, excited men were begging people to be cool. Everywhere outside of the Lower South, appeals were being made to

Union sentiment. *Harper's Weekly* published spirited pictures recalling the heroism of Nathan Hale and Sergeant Jasper. A hundred newspapers reprinted Longfellow's new poem, "Paul Revere's Ride."

But the drama of the hour was largely concentrated in three widely separated and curiously different cities, where political actors were simultaneously playing out three fateful scenes. One was Charleston, now filled with more excitement, effort, and hope than ever before in her eventful record. Her spires, domes, brightly painted houses, and massive warehouses seemed to rise with new pride over the sea and level, marshy land. The streets resounded with ruffling drum and calling bugle; darkies watched delightedly the drill of lads in gray jackets trimmed with black worsted braid; officers barked commands at working-parties building fortifications. A censor reigned at the telegraph office. The river fronts were carefully guarded, while at the Battery men prepared to obstruct the channels by sunken vessels. Here, looking out over the creaming waves, watchers found their eyes drawn to two points far down the seven-mile bay. One, just short of the throat leading to the open sea, was the square brick block of Fort Sumter rising gloomily from the breast of the waters. To the left of it, barely discernible on a low promontory of the mainland (Sullivan's Island), was Fort Moultrie. Great hopes and fears hung over these posts. Townspeople, startled at dawn by practice firing, thought of them with instant alarm.

Far to the north, under a darker sky and in a grimmer atmosphere, lay Washington, where action or inaction, wisdom or unwisdom, controlled the nation's destinies. An unusually inclement winter had set in. The white marble buildings were cold-looking, the ailanthus trees bare, the waters of the Potomac leaden-colored. As snow and rain smote the town, streets were alternately sheets of dazzling white, and stretches of viscid yellow mud. Social activities were at a low ebb; Northerners in particular, resenting the Southern inclination of the city, kept away from general gatherings. No one knew when some thunderbolt might fall. It was at a Congressional wedding that President Buchanan, hearing a disturbance in the entrance hall and sending to learn the reason, caught Mrs. Roger Pryor's whisper: "South Carolina has seceded. Mr. Keitt has a telegram." The police, fearing disorders—especially after the Richmond *Enquirer* recommended that Washington be occupied by force—were keenly alert. The hotels hummed with politicians and newspapermen; the public buildings blazed with light until after midnight; the committee rooms saw Democratic and Republican Congressmen in endless conferences; the Senate gallery filled up with curious crowds by ten or eleven in the morning. Yet despite this bustle the city lay in an aura of uncertainty and apprehension.

The third city was Springfield, that homely prairie agglomeration of ten thousand people, its checkerboard streets all unpaved, its wooden houses gauntly unattractive, its small business district affording but one decent hotel. The Illinois capital had grown busier and livelier. Flags and bunting were still in evidence. Every train discharged its deputations of advisers, office-hunters, and visitors, an average of perhaps one hundred and fifty a day. Men in frock coats and stovepipe hats hurried up the steps of the State House. Here, for two hours each morning and two each afternoon, the President-elect received all who came, from Senators in fine linen to farmhands in checked shirts. A ready "Come in" at every knock; a hearty handshake; an inquiry for names; a disposal of guests in the half-dozen armchairs that crowded the governor's small office; a running conversation—this was the regular order. As the days passed, Lincoln, burdened by callers, overwhelmed by mail, perplexed by questions of Cabinet and policy, grew more careworn. Yet he continued to impress newspapermen by the quaint originality and sagacity of his talk. "His phrases are not ceremoniously set," wrote Henry Villard, "but pervaded with a humorousness and, at times, with a grotesque joviality, that will always please. I think it would be hard to find one who tells better jokes, enjoys them better, or laughs oftener than Abraham Lincoln." [1]

Never in any public crisis, declared Greeley, had he seen such calmness, steadiness, and firmness as the masses now displayed. Was this true? On the contrary, every newspaper, every diary, every bundle of letters of the time, exhales bewilderment and anxiety. From the three million square miles of the country, from coastal plain, hill, and prairie, from the thirty million people, came an almost audible cry for rescue.

[I]

Inevitably, the secession of South Carolina on December 20 brought the situation in Charleston harbor to a new crisis. The position of Major Anderson seemed dangerous in the extreme. If Fort Moultrie had possessed the complement of some seven hundred men for which it had been designed, it could have been made almost impregnable, but its pitiful garrison of threescore were helpless. On the land side they were commanded by sand hills. If the South Carolinians took over Fort Sumter, a far stronger post, their seaward side would be equally exposed. The popular temper seemed ever more menacing. Governor Pickens wrote Buchanan on December 17 a confidential letter which he sent to Washington by hand, requesting that the President permit him to send a force not exceeding twenty-five men and an officer to take possession

1 Angle, *Here I Have Lived*, 253 ff.; Henry Villard, *Lincoln on the Eve of '61*, 13, 14.

of Sumter immediately.[2] He explained that this would give a feeling of safety to the highly excited community, and added the threat that if something of the kind were not done, he could not answer for the consequences. On the nights of the twentieth and twenty-first, steamers from Charleston kept guard around Sumter; and on the twenty-second, Anderson informed Washington that he felt no doubt the South Carolinians would seize the fort if and when they heard from Washington that it would not be turned over to the State.[3]

But would they hear this? Buchanan had removed Colonel Gardner from Fort Moultrie for trying to add to his ammunition supplies. He had stood out against the efforts of Cass, Black, and Holt to induce him to reinforce the forts. He had accepted the resignation of Cass, the ranking officer of his Cabinet, rather than send such reinforcements. He had just demonstrated anew in the "forty-musket affair" that he would go to great lengths to avoid offending the South Carolina authorities. On December 17, Captain J. G. Foster of Fort Moultrie, needing some muskets and being entitled to forty under an unfilled order of the Ordnance Department dated November 1, had drawn that number from the Federal arsenal in town. The city was instantly thrown into new commotion. The military authorities there, sending word to Foster that the governor had been promised that no arms should be removed from the arsenal, warned him that a violent demonstration was certain unless the muskets were returned. Angry dispatches were sent to Assistant Secretary Trescot. The President was informed that if the muskets did not come back, South Carolina might take them. On December 19, Secretary Floyd telegraphed Foster: "If you have removed any arms, return them instantly." He did so. Would so compliant an Administration deny Pickens his request for control over Fort Sumter?

Happily, it did. Pickens's emissary, carrying the letter to Washington, had Trescot obtain an interview at the White House on the twentieth. The two men were received in the library. Buchanan, after reading the message, promised a reply next day. As the South Carolinians were leaving, he called Trescot back and gave him the letter to read. The experienced diplomatist, whose brilliant talents, fine scholarship, and record of public service entitled him to this mark of confidence, easily detected that Buchanan was offended. Few men had quicker insight than Trescot, who had won the personal regard of Richard Rush, Edward Everett, and other superiors, had talked and walked with Macaulay, Hallam, and other eminent Britons, and, as Acting Secretary during Cass's illness in the past summer, had administered the State Department with skill. He at once saw that the governor's demand was egregious. If Pickens had

2 Full letter in Crawford, *Sumter*, 81–83.
3 *Official Records*, Series I, Vol. I, 105–107.

merely asked the President to instruct Anderson not to occupy Sumter, he might have obtained assurances to that effect. But what President could let the head of a seceding State, claiming separate and independent sovereignty, take over a national fort? Already, Republicans were muttering of impeachment, and such a capitulation would justify it.

Trescot, who knew that Black and Holt would never let Buchanan make such a surrender, went at once to Slidell and Jefferson Davis. They agreed that to press this demand would lead to a rebuff, and would release the President from his supposed pledge to the South Carolina Congressmen. A message flew to Charleston, and at once Pickens authorized Trescot to withdraw his ill-judged letter.[4] That same day Trescot talked with Secretary Floyd, who pledged him that the War Department would take no action which would injure South Carolina, or give any real ground for alarm. But the obliging Floyd spoke without knowledge of what his commander at Fort Moultrie was determining to do!

Major Anderson, meanwhile, was convinced that the South Carolinians were about to seize Fort Sumter.[5] He had abundant reason for so believing. The *Mercury* was insisting that it be taken. Resolutions had been introduced in the legislature for immediate possession of all the forts. While the secession convention sat, a party of Alabamians visited Sumter and gave it a careful inspection. On the twenty-sixth, the younger Rhett, warned from Washington that Anderson might remove to the fort, called on Pickens to urge him to take instant action. The city was full of talk of the imminent capture of both Moultrie and Sumter. Anderson, a man of resolute energy, knew that he had full liberty to transfer his force, for the orders received through Buell authorized him, whenever he had "tangible evidence of a design to proceed to a hostile act," to put his command into whichever post he deemed most defensible. By Christmas Day, when officers and citizens mingled pleasantly at a party given by Captain Foster and his wife, he had made up his mind.[6]

With great address, Anderson effected the transfer to Sumter under cover of darkness on the night of December 26. A small rearguard remained to hew down the flagstaff at Moultrie, spike the guns, and burn the gun-carriages. Charlestonians next morning, seeing the smoke of the fires rise above the deserted post, were deeply incensed. Believing at first that Washington had ordered the movement, and that Moultrie had been totally destroyed, men flew to arms. The people swarming on the piers and Battery, wrote one correspondent, showed chagrin, disappointment, and rage.

4 Crawford, *Sumter*, 83–86, gives Trescot's statement.
5 See his letter to his wife, Nicolay and Hay, *Lincoln*, III, 47, 48.
6 Doubleday, *Forts Sumter and Moultrie*, 47, 48.

Pickens immediately sent Major Anderson a peremptory demand that he return to Moultrie. The commander replied that he had a right to dispose his troops as he thought best, that he had removed to Sumter as the best means of avoiding bloodshed, and that he would stay there. At once the governor called upon ten military units to hold themselves ready for service, put a guard in possession of the national arsenal with its half-million dollars' worth of munitions, raised the palmetto flag over the custom house, postoffice, and branch of the Federal Treasury, and dispatched a small force to take possession of the totally unguarded Castle Pinckney. Late in the day, another force was sent against Moultrie, which the last national troops had just left; and at eight in the evening watchers in Charleston saw three rockets, the signal of occupation, soar aloft.[7]

[II]

News of Anderson's unexpected move produced consternation in Washington. Secretary Floyd, hearing of it early on the twenty-seventh, was taken aback. "It is impossible," he exclaimed. "It would be not only without orders, but in the face of orders." [8] Telegraphing Anderson for an explanation, he received a firm reply: "I abandoned Fort Moultrie because I was certain that if attacked my men must have been sacrificed and the command of the harbor lost." A Southern trio, Jefferson Davis, R. M. T. Hunter, and Trescot, carried the intelligence before noon to the White House. Cass had told a friend a few days earlier that the President was "pale with fear, for his official household is full of traitors, and conspirators control the government." The scene which now took place confirms this statement as to the President's perturbation. Buchanan, we are told by Trescot, was found by the three Southerners in a state of intense nervousness.

"Have you received any intelligence from Charleston in the last three hours?" inquired Davis. "None," responded the President. "Then I have a great calamity to announce to you," the Senator stated. He furnished his news. "And now, Mr. President," he melodramatically concluded, "you are surrounded with blood and dishonor on all sides."

"My God," wailed Buchanan, who stood at the mantelpiece crushing a cigar in his hand, "are misfortunes never to come singly? I call God to witness, *you*, gentlemen, better than anybody, *know* that this is not only without, but against my orders. It is against my policy." [9]

7 Nicolay and Hay, *Lincoln*, III, 61.
8 Crawford, *Sumter*, 143.
9 See Trescot's "Narrative and Letter," edited by Gaillard Hunt, *Am. Hist. Rev.*, April, 1908.

The Southerners urged him to lose no time in restoring the former position in Charleston harbor. If he would promise to do so, they said, the almost certain reprisals of South Carolina might even yet be stayed. But Buchanan agitatedly protested that he could not condemn Anderson until he had the full facts. "I must call a Cabinet meeting," he pleaded. The trio assured him that they did not wish him to condemn Anderson unheard. All they asked was that he promise to restore the old position, if, on inquiry, he found that Anderson had moved without being attacked. Three commissioners, R. W. Barnwell, J. H. Adams, and James L. Orr, had been appointed by the South Carolina convention to negotiate on the forts, and had arranged an interview with the President for that very afternoon. If Buchanan would give his promise, said Trescot, this meeting could take place, and amicable negotiations proceed. The President, however, refused to be rushed into action, and adjourned his talk with the commissioners until next day, the twenty-eighth.

It was fortunate that he insisted upon consulting his Cabinet, for that body now contained three strong men capable of fortifying his determination upon matters of vital principle: Black, Holt, and Stanton. The first fruits of the reorganization of the Cabinet were now to be garnered, and Buchanan's policy entered upon its second phase; that in which Southern influences ebbed and Northern potencies took their place.

The turning-point in Administration policy was reached in a swift series of unprecedentedly important Cabinet meetings. Trescot, Davis, and Hunter had hardly ceased their effort to drive the President into a humiliating submission when the Cabinet began to assemble. As Floyd came into the White House, he saw Major Buell there. He rapped out that Anderson had made a most unfortunate move. "It has made war inevitable!" he exclaimed. Buell defended his fellow-officer, but without avail. "It has compromised the President," added Floyd. When the Cabinet began its discussion, Floyd denounced Anderson in the same strident terms. The major had disobeyed instructions, he said, had taken a wholly unnecessary step in violation of a clear agreement between the President and South Carolina, and had brought the country to the verge of war. Black warmly interposed. Denying that Anderson had breached his orders, he called attention to the instructions of December 11 sent down by Buell. A messenger was hurried to the War Department for this paper, which was read aloud to the Cabinet, and was found to bear Floyd's endorsement. Either the President had never been shown it, or had completely forgotten it.[10]

At once Floyd shifted his ground; he could not deny his orders, but he

10 Buchanan, *Administration on the Eve of the Rebellion*, 187 ff.; Crawford, *Sumter*, 146; Nichols, *Disruption*, 428, 429; Nicolay and Hay, *Lincoln*, III, 66, 67.

did deny that Anderson had possessed "tangible evidence of a design to proceed to a hostile act." Stanton and Holt came to Black's assistance in defending Anderson, while Thomas (whose sympathies were with the South and whose son was soon to enter the Confederate armies) and Jacob Thompson assailed the officer. Black and Stanton asserted that it was impossible that the President had given any pledge to South Carolina, and demanded a specification of the time and place; both Floyd and Thompson insisted—in Buchanan's presence—that it *had* been given. The quarrel grew violent; tempers rose and words became hot. For purposes of his own, soon to appear, Floyd presented an extreme ultimatum.[11] He sat down and wrote out a demand that he be permitted to order the garrison withdrawn entirely from Charleston harbor. At this point, the feeling of Black and Stanton appears to have broken all bounds. Black threw in Floyd's face the statement that no English minister who supinely surrendered a fortified place to an enemy would have failed to reach the block. Stanton went further; he said that to accede to Floyd's demands would be a crime like Arnold's, that all the participants ought to be hanged like André, and that a President issuing such an order would be guilty of treason. At this Buchanan raised his hands in deprecation: "Oh, no! Not so bad as that, my friend—not so bad as that!"[12]

Excitement over the situation had filled the opposite end of Pennsylvania Avenue. When the Cabinet broke up without a decision, a determined body of Southern Senators—Yulee, Slidell, Mallory, Toombs, and others—gathered at the White House. They besought the President to revoke Anderson's movement. An equally determined band of Administration Democrats from the North also gained admittance and urged Buchanan to take no backward step. That weary, vacillating, alarmed potentate, the center of a paralyzing storm, was unable to make up his mind.

Night came on. After dinner the Cabinet met again. Newspapermen were eagerly awaiting word of the result. Until a late hour the debate continued. Midnight dispatches carried word to the country that by a vote of four to three, the members had decided against ordering Anderson back; that Toucey, under heavy Northern pressure, had joined Black, Stanton, and Holt.[13] Even yet, however, Buchanan had not definitely fixed his policy. "In this state of suspense," he tells us, "the President determined to await official information from Major Anderson himself. After its receipt, should he be convinced upon full examination that the Major, on a false alarm, had violated his instructions,

11 Text in Moore's *Rebellion Record*, I, 10.
12 Gorham, *Stanton*, I, 151 ff.
13 The N. Y. *Tribune*, December 31, carried a dispatch dated December 30 giving the four-to-three vote; other papers had the same news.

he might then think seriously of restoring for the present the former status quo of the forts." [14]

Next day, the three commissioners from South Carolina duly called to press a demand that all national forces be ordered out of Charleston waters. Barnwell, a Harvard graduate who had been Representative, Senator, and president of the South Carolina College, was chairman; Adams, a Yale graduate, was the former governor, and Orr the former Speaker. They were men of parts, and Barnwell could have figured much more lustrously in history but for his modesty.[15] Only Adams, an oldtime nullifier and a recent proponent of the African slave trade, was highly radical. They had a natural sense of their dignity in representing a new republic, and came not to sue for terms but to treat as equals. Buchanan had just heard of the seizures of Fort Moultrie, the Charleston arsenal, and the postoffice and customhouse. Nevertheless, he received the men courteously, not as diplomatic agents but as private gentlemen. To negotiate, they must appeal to Congress alone, he told them, and he could but communicate to Congress their proposals.

The discussion lasted two hours. Again and again, the three men told Buchanan that his pledge was dishonored, that he must withdraw the troops completely, and that if he refused a bloody issue was probable. When he resisted, they redoubled their efforts. Finally the President agonized aloud.

"Mr. Barnwell, you are pressing me too importunely," he expostulated. "You don't give me time to consider. You don't give me time to say my prayers. I always say my prayers when required to act upon any great state affair." [16]

The demands of the commissioners, reduced to writing, came before another tense Cabinet meeting that evening, Friday, the twenty-eighth. Southern Senators had maintained their pressure on the President, Toombs writing him that day that the evacuation of Sumter was imperative to prevent drastic and perhaps irrevocable action by some Southern States. Once more the atmosphere quickly became electric. Thompson argued pertinaciously in favor of a total evacuation of troops from South Carolina. Floyd lay on a sofa between the windows of the Cabinet room. At last, driven from various positions, Thompson took refuge in a tricky plea to national magnanimity. Carolina, he argued, was a tiny State with a sparse white population; the United States was a powerful nation with a vigorous government. The country could afford to say to South Carolina: "See, we will withdraw our garrison as an evidence that we mean you no harm."

14 Buchanan, *Administration on the Eve of the Rebellion*, 181. Cf. Davis, *Rise and Fall*, I, 215.
15 Jefferson Davis wished to make him Confederate Secretary of State; see letters of T. R. R. Cobb, *Papers So. Hist. Soc.*, XXVIII, and *Proceedings So. Hist. Assn.*, XI.
16 Letter of J. L. Orr, September 21, 1871; Crawford, *Sumter*, 148, 149.

At this Stanton's blood boiled. He knew that a storm of anger would sweep the North if Buchanan took such a step. "In every hotel and every street in this city," the Washington correspondent of the New York *Herald* had written, "we hear hardly anything but denunciation of the President for his course in refusing to strengthen Major Anderson." The sober, cautious *National Intelligencer* had just published an editorial of unparalleled severity. It had declared its belief that no loyal citizen could look with complacency on the Administration's easy tolerance of members and subordinates who were "avowedly and ostentatiously laboring for the destruction of the government." It had castigated Buchanan for not displaying in the restraint of traitors one-tenth the zeal he had shown in immolating luckless Democrats who had been so unfortunate as to believe in popular sovereignty. It had declared that if the President had no solid facts to support his refusal to reinforce the forts, the country would hold him to "a fearful responsibility" for the policy he had pursued.[17]

"Mr. President," Stanton exploded, "the proposal to be generous implies that the government is strong, and that we, as the public servants, have the confidence of the people. I think that is a mistake. No Administration has ever suffered the loss of public confidence and support as this has done. Only the other day it was announced that a million of dollars had been stolen from Mr. Thompson's department. The bonds were found to have been taken from the vault where they should have been kept, and the notes of Mr. Floyd were substituted for them. Now it is proposed to give up Sumter. All I have to say is that no Administration, much less this one, can afford to lose a million of money and a fort in the same week." [18]

To this burning arraignment Floyd dared make no reply, for his negligence, blundering, and general misfeasance, which at least bordered on malfeasance, had finally found him out. Year after year, he had permitted laxity and scandal in his department. The Fort Snelling and Willet's Point exposures were yet fresh in the public mind, Greeley's *Tribune* insisting that these affairs had cost the country $550,000.[19] The fact that Floyd himself had never been shown guilty of taking an unclean dollar did not clear him from the charge that he had assisted certain favorites to make many. Now he was floundering in a veritable Okefenokee Swamp of embarrassments. A dark and terrible story was just becoming public.

17 See N. Y. *Weekly Tribune*, December 29, 1860, for summaries of press criticism of the Administration.
18 Nicolay obtained this statement from Stanton; Nicolay and Hay, *Lincoln*, III, 74, 75. Cf. Stanton's full account of the crisis written October 8, 1863, in Gorham, *Stanton*, I, 151-159.
19 See editorial, "The National 'Cracksmen,'" N. Y. *Tribune*, December 27, 1860.

During and after the Mormon War, the Western contractors, Russell, Majors & Waddell, had furnished large quantities of supplies and transportation to troops. Congress had been tardy in passing some of the appropriations to meet government contracts. To aid the firm, whose credit was impaired by rashly ambitious operations and faulty management, Floyd had accepted a large amount of their drafts, some of them conditionally, others absolutely. Banks then advanced funds on this endorsed paper. In fact, Floyd *asked* banks to do so. In 1859, the President instructed the War Department to desist from such financial practises, but the Secretary continued. The most careful students of the papers of Russell, Majors & Waddell have concluded that while no direct, conclusive evidence exists that Floyd received money from Russell, "there is much to arouse suspicion that he did." The amount of the Secretary's acceptances ultimately reached a dizzy figure. Although the figure later given by a select House investigating committee, $6,179,395 of unconditional acceptances, and $798,000 of acceptances conditioned and payable out of the earnings of the firm, has been pronounced exaggerated, the sum was at any rate enormous. By July, 1860, William H. Russell knew that large amounts of these drafts, endorsed by Floyd, were about to mature. Since the banks refused to make him any further advances and insisted that he pay his endorsed notes, he was in terrible distress. If the paper went to protest, he would be ruined and Secretary Floyd disgraced.

In desperation, Russell turned to Goddard Bailey, an attorney, a South Carolinian, and a distant kinsman of Floyd's, now a clerk in the Land Office. Explaining that a protest of the acceptances would place Floyd in a terrible predicament, he induced Bailey to lend him $150,000 in Missouri and Tennessee State bonds. It appears that not until later did Russell learn that they belonged to the Indian Trust Fund of the Interior Department, of which Bailey was custodian. After he gained this information, however, the desperate contractor guiltily connived with Bailey in the embezzlement of further bonds, raising the grand total abstracted to $870,000. It was the old story; he hoped to make quick restitution, but his affairs grew worse and he could repay nothing.

In the closing weeks of 1860, when interest on the bonds had to be sent to the Indian tribes, the whole set of transactions was dragged to light. Bailey, on December 22, confessed to his friend Senator Rice and his superior Secretary Thompson. Black, Stanton, and the President were informed. On December 23, a Cabinet meeting subjected Bailey to a painful inquisition, and on the twenty-fourth the public was startled by an explicit announcement of the loss. Russell that day was arrested in New York, to be carried to Washington and jailed. Everyone was horrified—not least Secretary Thompson, who acted promptly and diligently to learn the truth. Just how much or little Floyd had known about Bailey's embezzlement of the bonds is not clear, though evidence exists that he had known something. When the House committee delved into the affair, a cheap adventurer named Robert W. Latham, who had worked for Floyd until 1859 and had been intimate with Russell, was examined. Many suspected him of having been a go-between who helped the Secretary to profit from the large Russell, Majors contracts. He proved a most refractory witness, and his constant refusals to answer questions bearing on such a connection did nothing to diminish public suspicion of Floyd. Instead, they left the impression that a secret arrangement of some kind had existed.[20]

It was immediately plain that Floyd would have to be dismissed. No Administration could let such a man continue to disgrace it. The House committee shortly termed the acceptances unauthorized by law, deceptive, and fraudulent. Any other President would have summoned the Secretary to a private interview, given him a bad half hour, and directed him to write his resignation. Not so Buchanan; heartsick to lose two old friends (for Mrs. Floyd had been much at the White House), he disregarded a strong Christmas Day letter from Black urging him to take peremptory action next morning,[21] and requested Vice-President Breckinridge to obtain the resignation. But Floyd refused to resign, declaring he must vindicate himself first. He wanted more time for several reasons; to continue resisting the Northern wing in the Cabinet, to make sure of some Southern berth, and to manufacture out of the South Carolina imbroglio a plausible excuse for his exit. Hence his written demand that the President allow him to evacuate all troops from the Charleston area. Black and Stanton were outraged by his conduct, and unhappy over the President's willingness to palter with the man.

It need not be said that much Northern sentiment, already inflamed by the President's message, the failure to reinforce the forts, and Cass's resignation, was raised to boiling point by the exposure of Floyd. "Why in the devil don't you present articles of impeachment against Buchanan and Floyd?" burst out Greeley in a letter of December 30 to Elihu Washburne. "People here are becoming frantic—absolutely frantic with rage at the treason. If Old Buck would show his countenance in these parts he would be hung so quick that Satan would not know where to look for his traitorous soul." Although this was outrageously unjust to the harried, overwrought President, it is understandable.

---

20 Full evidence on this affair is in 36th Cong., 2d Sess., House Doc. 78. Russell, whose indictment was quashed on a technicality in January, 1861, published a long explanatory statement in the press April 4, 1861. Facts in the case are carefully analyzed by Mary Lund Settle and Raymond Settle, *Empire on Wheels*, 95–131.
21 The matter should be settled "definitely, finally, and forever," wrote Black; Buchanan Papers.

[III]

But at any rate Floyd's dishonor produced one signal benefit in giving Union men full control of the Union's Cabinet. On Saturday the twenty-ninth the Secretary went out. He grounded his resignation on the statement that he could not countenance the President's violation of solemn pledges respecting Sumter, an excuse which failed to cloak his incompetence and perfidy. The comments of the Northern press were scorching. After giving brief testimony before the House committee on his acceptances, Floyd returned to Virginia, was banqueted, and made gasconading speeches. On January 25, 1861, he was indicted by a grand jury of the District of Columbia for malversation in office. Denouncing the action as a gross violation of principles of law and justice, and protesting his innocence, he visited Washington, gave bail, and called for a trial. A week after Lincoln took office, the Federal Attorney asked that the case be dropped for lack of evidence.

This was not the only complaint of the North against Floyd. Five days before Christmas he had given oral orders, later confirmed in writing, for the shipment of forty-six cannon from Pittsburgh to Ship Island, Mississippi, and seventy-nine cannon to Galveston, Texas. Angry municipal leaders had instantly organized to block the transfer, and by vigorous appeals had spurred the President to issue a Christmas Day order countermanding Floyd. Throughout half the North, a conviction now reigned that he was a dangerous traitor. He always maintained that his distribution of arms had been fair and legal. "My course," he wrote Wigfall, "was a proper one dictated by the true interests of the country, and I . . . am ready any moment to die for it if that be necessary." Subsequent official investigation indicated that his transfer in the spring of 1860 of one hundred five thousand muskets and ten thousand rifles from Northern to Southern arsenals was a correct transaction, designed to make room for more modern weapons in the North. Actually the Southern States did not ask for or receive their due quota of arms in 1860. It was only after Lincoln's election that Floyd's course with respect to arms shipments became—particularly in the order for the Pittsburgh cannon—censurable. He was a dangerous man—but rather from ineptitude than anything worse.[22]

22 Floyd's letter to Wigfall, February 3, 1861 (Wigfall Papers, LC), is written with fierce intensity. After assailing "the mean and sneaking malignity of some of those about the executive," he declares that Bailey, Russell, and Luke Lea know all about the bond affair and must exonerate him. "These men are all bound to swear in the most unequivalent [sic] manner that I did not and could not know anything whatever about the transactions." He added: "There has not during the time of my administration of the War Dept. been lost to the Govt. *one dollar*, either from accident or fraud, or embezzlement or theft, every dollar appropriated has been accounted for according to law. . . ." Jeremiah Black finally

The still unsettled question of Buchanan's reply to the South Carolina com-missioners now provoked a final Cabinet crisis. On Saturday night the body met again. The President showed his six remaining ministers a draft answer. This paper has disappeared from his records. That it conceded much more than was proper is evident from the debate which it provoked. The flaccid Toucey approved it. Thompson and Thomas opposed it only because it did not yield South Carolina an instant removal of all bayonets. Black, Stanton, and Holt, however, condemned it as excessively complaisant, and Black and Stanton at least were wrought up to a high pitch of indignation.

"These gentlemen," exclaimed Stanton, "claim to be ambassadors. It is pre-posterous! They cannot be ambassadors; they are lawbreakers, traitors. They should be arrested. You cannot negotiate with them; and yet it seems by this paper that you have been led into doing that very thing. With all respect to you, Mr. President, I must say that the Attorney-General, under his oath of office, dares not be cognizant of the pending proceedings. Your reply to these so-called ambassadors must not be transmitted as the reply of the President. It is wholly unlawful and improper; its language is unguarded and to send it as an official document will bring the President to the verge of usurpation." [23] Once more, the heat of the exchanges produced much plain speaking. When the President reserved the subject for further consideration, Black went home to spend a sleep-less night. He knew to what a degree the President was still under the influence of Davis, Mason, and other Southern leaders. He was told by both Stanton and Ben Butler, two men as clearheaded as they were aggressive, that any President who negotiated with Southern conspirators upon the segregation of government property and the alienation of American territory would be open to impeach-ment. He held this view himself. Before dawn on the thirtieth he had reached a determination.

That dawn was Sunday; the church bells were soon calling Washington to worship; but the Secretary of State had urgent business to dispatch. He informed Stanton, Holt, and Toucey that if the President sent the commissioners such a letter as that laid before the Cabinet, he would resign. Stanton declared he would follow. The agitated Toucey hurried to the White House with the news. Such resignations, coming after that of Cass, would utterly prostrate the Administra-

---

concluded that Floyd had been guilty only of reckless imprudence; *Essays and Speeches*, 13. But the House investigating committee unanimously termed his issue of acceptances "unauthorized by law and deceptive and fraudulent in character"; while the Supreme Court in 1868 held such issues illegal (7 *Wallace*, 666). Floyd's disposition of arms was treated, without explicit judgment, by the House Military Committee in a report of February 18, 1861; 36th Cong., 2d Sess., House Report 85.

23 Flower, *Stanton*, 88. This quotation has the ring of truth even if not literally accurate.

tion. Immediately, Buchanan sent for Black and bade him explain his views. We do not know the spirit in which they spoke to each other, but it seems probable that Black, always tempestuous, had betrayed such anger and chagrin the previous evening that an indirect approach to the President by Toucey was necessary. It is certain that he now freed his mind. He declared that the letter must be rewritten; he called for stamina, defiance, and the immediate reinforcement of Anderson.

In this stand, Black was buttressing an emphatic plea by General Scott, who had hurried a messenger to the White House door that morning with an urgent request that Buchanan listen to his views. "Will the President permit General Scott," he inquired, "without reference to the War Department and otherwise as secretly as possible, to send two hundred and fifty recruits from New York harbor to reinforce Fort Sumter, together with some extra muskets or rifles, ammunition, and subsistence stores? It is hoped that a sloop of war and cutter may be ordered for the same purpose as early as tomorrow." [24] Black was seconding also the expressions of a great part of the Northern press, now filled with indictments of the Administration as feeble and cowardly. From Maine to Iowa, tenterhook anxiety was felt for the safety of Anderson's tiny force.

Buchanan's weak stubbornness was not long in conflict with Black's inflexible resolution. The President handed the Secretary his draft letter for revision, saying, according to Black's son, that he might strike out what he thought objectionable and insert what he deemed necessary, if he only did it immediately.[25] The event proved that he really gave something like this blanket authorization. Black at once repaired to Stanton's office, talked over every point with him, and discussed the means of extricating the Chief Executive from his perilous situation. The pair then drafted a memorandum, of which Stanton seems to have written six paragraphs and Black two. Seldom if ever have the advisers of a President administered, even by implication, so severe a rebuke.

At no fewer than seven points did Black and Stanton traverse Buchanan's letter. They objected to his implied acknowledgment of the right of South Carolina to send diplomatic officers to treat with the United States. They objected to his expression of regret that the commissioners were unwilling to go on with the negotiation; there could be no negotiation, willing or unwilling. They objected above all to his intimated readiness to make some arrangement regarding the national forts; they were not subject to any arrangement whatever. They objected to his statement of belief that the government had no right

24 *Official Records*, Series I, Vol. I, 114.
25 Black, *Essays and Speeches*, 14.

to coerce a State to stay in the Union; the government certainly had a right to coerce those who attacked national property. They objected to his implied assent to the commissioner's statement that he had made an agreement on the forts; instead, he should make a flat denial of any bargain, pledge, or agreement. They objected to phrases casting doubt upon the propriety of Major Anderson's behavior. They objected to Buchanan's tolerance of the idea that the removal from Moultrie to Sumter did possible wrong to South Carolina. If these radical amendments were adopted, wrote Black and Stanton, the whole paper would have to be recast.[26]

The two heads concluded with some positive words upon the need for forceful action at Charleston. The warships *Brooklyn* and *Macedonian* should be ordered thither without delay. A messenger should be hurried to Anderson with word that the government would not desert him. Troops from New York or Old Point Comfort should immediately follow. "If this be done at once all may yet . . . be comparatively safe. If not, I can see nothing before us but disaster and ruin to the country." And the memorandum contained a stinging sentence upon "the fatal error which the Administration have committed in not sending down troops enough to hold *all* the [Charleston] forts."

Thus was finis written to appeasement. With Cobb and Floyd gone, with Thompson helpless, and with Black, Stanton, and Holt enforcing their views on the irresolute President by their readiness to resign if he retreated, the revolution in the executive branch was completed. As for ten years past, the United States had no President in the full sense of the word. A directory stood in the place of a single clear-sighted, strong-willed Chief Magistrate. But that directory was now made up of granite-constant Union men, aware of what the crisis demanded. Henceforth, Buchanan largely adopted the ideas of his stern-fronted fellow Pennsylvanians, Black and Stanton.

This was manifest in his courteous but firm reply to the commissioners, delivered December 30, essentially following Black's suggestions. He restated his desire to have Congress deal with the situation in such fashion as to avoid war over the Charleston forts. He explained away his alleged pledge to preserve the status of the forts. When he had learned of Anderson's transfer, he stated, his impulse had been to order him back to Moultrie; but the South Carolinians had immediately seized Moultrie, Pinckney, and other national property, radically altering the state of affairs. Now he was asked, under penalty of a possible attack on Sumter, to remove all the country's forces from the harbor. "This I cannot do; this I will not do," he wrote, in language at last befitting a successor of

26 Text of the memorandum in Black, *Essays and Speeches*, 14–17; for the relative parts played by Black and Stanton in drafting the "Written Objections," see Flower, *Stanton*, 90–93. As Buchanan's legal adviser, Stanton was nominal author.

Washington and Jackson. Major Anderson would be left where he was; his act would not be disowned; and Sumter would be defended "against hostile attacks from whatever quarter they may come." [27]

The remodeled executive department quickly showed its spirit in other ways. When the commissioners sent an insolent response to the President's letter, accusing him of breaking his pledge and choosing the path to war, it was returned with a brief endorsement that he refused to receive it. Jefferson Davis printed the response in the *Congressional Globe* with a cutting attack of his own on Buchanan, which several fellow-Senators echoed.[28] The moment he saw the commissioners' insulting note, Buchanan's hesitations over the strengthening of Anderson vanished. He exclaimed: "It is all now over and reinforcements must be sent." On December 31, he instructed the War and Navy Departments to take steps, under which orders were issued that day to send the sloop-of-war *Brooklyn* to Charleston with troops, ammunition, and stores.[29]

[IV]

The New Year's Day reception at the White House found Southern and Northern guests displaying a glacial hostility to each other, some secessionists, wearing blue cockades, ostentatiously passing the President without greeting him, and the general atmosphere as gloomy as a funeral. Slidell was not there. His sharp protest against the cancellation of Beauregard's appointment to West Point ("this crack of the overseer's whip over our heads," Holt termed it in speaking to Buchanan) would soon receive a tart rejoinder. Jefferson Davis wrote an editorial friend that Southerners no longer had any confidence in or respect for the President. "His weakness has done as much as wickedness could achieve." [30] No longer could the President have heart for his daily walk. His aspect of sad anxiety and illness inspired the compassion of many a beholder.

Reinforcements, as it turned out, were not to reach Charleston. When it was learned that the South Carolinians had sunk vessels to block the channel, General Scott decided to substitute for the *Brooklyn* the light-draught steamer *Star of the West*. Aboard her went two hundred well-trained recruits from Fort Columbus in New York. On January 5 she quietly sailed. Telegrams apprising Charleston of the fact were hastily sent by Senator Wigfall and Secretary

27 Too late, the South Carolina commissioners realized that they had overplayed their hand. On Sunday they backed water lustily; sending Trescot and Hunter to the White House, they suggested as a compromise that South Carolina should evacuate Moultrie, that Anderson be ordered back to that post, and that the Carolinians then promise to respect the *status quo* so long as Buchanan was President. Nichols, *Disruption*, 432.
28 January 9; *Cong. Globe*, 36th Cong., 2d Sess., 288 ff.
29 *Official Records*, Series I, Vol. I, 130 ff.; Curtis, *Buchanan*, II, 445, 446.
30 To E. D. De Leon, January 8, 1861; De Leon Papers, So. Caroliniana Library.

Thompson. The Carolinians had continued active in erecting batteries and preparing for a conflict. When the ship arrived off the port on January 9, Fort Moultrie and Morris Island fired upon her and drove her away. Happily, Major Anderson was for the moment in a fairly safe position. Washington had received from him a dispatch of December 31, which, after justifying his recent movement, concluded:

Thank God, we are now where the Government may send us additional troops at its leisure. To be sure, the uncivil and uncourteous action of the governor in preventing us from purchasing anything in the city will annoy and inconvenience us somewhat; still, we are safe. I find . . . only a small supply of soap and candles, and also of coal. Still, we can cheerfully put up with the inconvenience of doing without them, for the satisfaction we feel in the knowledge that we can command this harbor as long as our Government wishes to keep it.[31]

A new page had been turned. The third phase in Buchanan's policy, the phase in which he asserted the right to maintain possession of the forts and other property of the government even if this meant open war, and in which he turned a severe face upon secessionists, had been entered upon; and it was to continue until Lincoln came into power with a policy essentially identical.

And the Administration was now immeasurably strengthened when the two remaining Cabinet sympathizers with the South, seeing the utter impossibility of their position, resigned, and were succeeded by loyal men.

As the *Star of the West* was approaching Charleston, on January 8, Secretary Jacob Thompson indignantly left the Cabinet. He declared that it had been distinctly understood that no further troops should be ordered south without prior Cabinet consultation, yet he had first learned of the projected reinforcement of Sumter from outside sources. On the eleventh, Secretary Thomas, after just a month in the Treasury Department, also made his exit, announcing that he could not approve of the policy adopted toward South Carolina, and probably could not support the President in an attempted enforcement of the collection of duties there. He had been a hopeless misfit, for eastern financial circles had no confidence in him. The President made no sustained effort to find a new Secretary of the Interior, but allowed Chief Clerk Moses Kelly, an excellent executive, to fill out the term as Acting-Secretary. In Thomas's place, however, he made one of the happiest of all his appointments—John A. Dix. This former member of the Albany Regency and Senator from New York, more recently a railway president and an attorney in the metropolis, was an admirable selection from every point of view. A man of great ability, courage, and grasp, Dix for

31 *Official Records*, Series I, Vol. I, 120. When this dispatch to Adjutant-General S. Cooper was shown to the President, he attempted to countermand the *Star of the West* expedition, but it was too late.

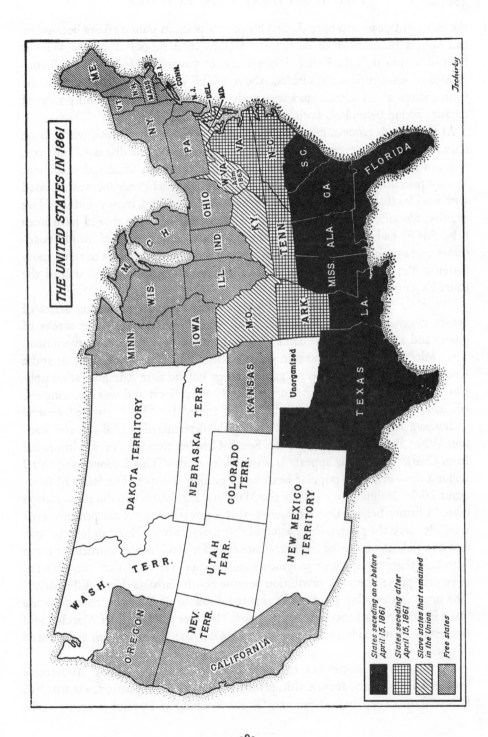

THE UNITED STATES IN 1861

Treburky

Legend:
- States seceding on or before April 15, 1861
- States seceding after April 15, 1861
- Slave states that remained in the Union
- Free states

the past eight years had been denied his proper place in public affairs because he had been a Barnburner or antislavery Democrat, a supporter of the Wilmot Proviso, and in 1848 the Free Soil candidate for governor. He held the full confidence of eastern financial circles. Above all, he was a staunch believer in the maintenance of the Union, and was ready to put all his courage and power of decisive action behind his faith.

At Buchanan's request, Dix took up quarters in the White House, where from ten to eleven nearly every night for the next seven weeks he discussed the great issues of the time with the President. He found Buchanan timid and credulous, an easy prey for artful men. It was obvious also that the President was obsessed with the idea that the North, in the war now about to begin, must avoid shedding the first blood; an idea which had made him yield when he should have been firm. But he had now awakened to the true character of some of his old coadjutors, and as conscientiousness was a cardinal trait, he was anxious to show more firmness. Beyond doubt Dix did his full share in strengthening the will of the Chief Executive.

Thus the year 1860 closed and 1861 opened with an inspiriting series of events which restored the courage of all loyal Northerners. After weeks of gloom and almost of despair came a radiant sunrise of faith in the government. The Unionist press grew warm in praise of Secretary Holt as a Democrat and a Kentuckian who had thrown his great prestige behind firm Administration policies. News that he was in close touch with General Scott and was restoring the efficiency of the War Department, almost ruined by Floyd, aroused general enthusiasm. Men told anecdotes illustrating the determination of Black and Stanton. When Buchanan's reply to the South Carolina demand for a withdrawal from Charleston harbor appeared, his defiant words—"This I cannot do; this I will not do"—lifted the popular heart like a pealing trumpet. The letter of Governor Hicks declining to convoke the Maryland legislature had the same clarion note. "I firmly believe that a disunion of this government would produce civil war," declared the governor; he asserted that practically all Marylanders thought that no valid reason existed for immediate secession; and he was scornful of those who held that, "against our judgments and solemn convictions of duty, we are to be precipitated into this revolution because South Carolina thinks differently." The press was quoting Buchanan's reputed dismissal of Southern threats to use force in preventing Lincoln's inauguration. "If I live till the 4th of March," said Buchanan, "I will ride to the Capitol with Old Abe whether I am assassinated or not."

As newspaper dispatches came from Charleston and Major Anderson's brother Larz returned from a visit, people learned of the dramatic scene that had followed the occupation of Sumter. On the morning of December 27, two officers dispatched by Governor Pickens had waited upon Major Anderson. The commander explained that while his sympathies lay with the South, he was determined to adhere firmly to his duty to the national government. "Well, sir," said Colonel Johnson Pettigrew of the First South Carolina Rifles, "however that may be, the governor directs me to say to you, courteously but peremptorily, to return to Fort Moultrie." "Make my compliments to the governor, and say to him that I decline to accede to his request; I cannot and will not go back," rejoined Anderson. "Then, sir," said Pettigrew, "my business is done," and he turned on his heel.

As noon approached that day, Anderson ordered his command to parade. The band took its station on the parapet, sixty feet above the waterline; the troops were drawn up on one side of a square, facing the flagstaff; the 150 workmen were formed on the other sides; and Major Anderson stood erect beside the bare staff. The chaplain moved to the center of the square, and as the battalion came to "parade rest," all uncovering, he raised his voice in prayer. Giving thanks for the safe arrival of the force in its new post, he asked that the flag might never be dishonored and might soon float again over a united, peaceful, and prosperous nation. Anderson, who had knelt, then arose; the battalion presented arms; the band broke into the national air; and amid the fervent cheers of the troops, the flag rose swiftly to the top of the staff and whipped out in the strong sea breeze.

Patriotic Northerners breathed more freely after these events and the reorganization of the Cabinet. They had feared that not merely the Charleston forts, but the government in Washington itself might be yielded by traitorous hands to the arrogant forces of secession—for arrogance seemed a striking quality of the cotton kingdom. Their spirits rose, and Jackson Day was celebrated with toasts, speeches, and cannonades which expressed undying devotion to the Union. Buchanan, reported his friends, now realized that he had been deceived and betrayed by the Southern leaders to whom he had given so much trust and made so many concessions. Disillusioned at last, he was convinced that Cobb, Jacob Thompson, Slidell, Jefferson Davis, and others had tried to use him as a tool; that while he had looked to them to help him maintain the Union, they had conspired to ruin him and the republic. He was ready to be guided by the strong men about him, Black, Holt, Stanton, and Dix; to some extent even by Seward, who was in touch with these men. The President, like his advisers, believed that by prompt action a sectional compromise might yet be achieved. The powerful border States, and especially Virginia, seemed to him in a strategic position to bring the two extremes together. But whatever happened, he was determined not to recognize secession nor to give up national property while he remained in the White House.

"You do the President great injustice," Dix shortly wrote the critical James

Watson Webb. "There is no warmer friend of the Union. I know no instance in history in which the head of a government was more grossly deceived by those in whom a generous confidence had been reposed." [32] Dix himself made a memorable contribution to Northern morale. One of his first acts was to order an officer of the Treasury Department to go to New Orleans, take over the revenue cutters there, and send them to New York. A Southern captain refused to surrender his vessel. On hearing this Dix (January 29) ordered the man arrested and the cutter seized, adding: "If anyone attempts to haul down the Union flag, shoot him on the spot."

The country at last had an Administration in which lovers of the Union could repose full confidence. The focus of public anxiety passed from the Cabinet room in the White House to other and more dangerous points.

32 Dix to Webb, February 1, 1861; Webb Papers.

13

The Failure of Compromise

MEANWHILE, what of the efforts of Congress to deal with the crisis? It had set to work in a blundering and legalistic fashion, but even if it had acted efficiently and sagaciously in the use of its mechanisms, it would have been doomed to failure. Three principal reasons, which by no means exhaust the list, may be assigned to explain the futility of its labors. In the first place, the heart of the great national scission lay in burning hatreds, gnawing distrusts, and inveterate prejudices which no new laws or statutory amendments could reach. In the second, two compact, determined wings of opinion and leadership, the radical Republicans and the secessionists, were committed to mutually incompatible positions. Finally, Congress, a body of politicians too close to party and sectional objects, too prone to posturing for effect, and too little inclined to think nationally, was ill adapted for the statesmanlike labor required. A new national convention would have been far more effective. If a fourth reason were to be named, it would lie in the belief of many Northerners and Southerners alike that their section would profit from temporary disunion followed by a peaceable reconstruction.

[I]

Nearly all informed leaders knew that the chances of successful action by Congress were exceedingly slender. After all, what was the situation? By the time Congress was well organized, in mid-December, five States had committed themselves to secession. On December 6, Senators Brown of Mississippi, Iverson of Georgia, and Wigfall of Texas had made speeches implying that the heroic South would depart no matter what delusive concessions were made to her. Iverson declared that Alabama would undoubtedly go out on January 7, and Georgia on January 16, and three if not five other States before March 4. Describing the enmity between the two sections as "deeper than hell," he said that in his opinion nothing under heaven could prevent such a consummation. Howell Cobb had included in his address to Georgians on December 6 a condemnation of compromise; every hour that Georgia stayed in the Union after Lincoln came into power would be "an hour of degradation, to be followed by certain and speedy ruin." Governor Gist on December 8 told the Alabama commissioner that two members of Congress had just written him "that Gen. Davis, Gov. Brown and others *have abandoned all idea of compromising the difficulty* and say that they desire South Carolina to get out of the Union without delay." [1] Much the same statement was made by a bustling politician, S. F. Butterworth, who wrote from Washington on December 2 to the active New York Democrat and lawyer S. L. M. Barlow. After giving much accurate information drawn from Southerners, Butterworth (who had advance knowledge of the President's message, and wanted a stock-exchange operation carried out on the basis of this knowledge) reported: "Jeff Davis says that no human power can save the Union, all the cotton states will go, no amendment short of protection of the institution by Congress in the territories will now satisfy the South, says that ninetynine-one hundreths of the people of Missi. are determined to secede."

As early as December 7, John H. Reagan wrote a friend from Washington that all idea of another Congressional compromise was vain and foolish.[2] Representative David Clopton of Alabama, less than a week later, informed Senator C. C. Clay that efforts to compromise differences and patch up the rotten concern would prove bootless. His frank description of secession commitments bulwarked this opinion:

The old man [Buchanan] is very anxious to avoid a collision, and wants secession postponed until the 4th March. His message was referred, in the House, to a committee of one from each State. Several of us, Pugh, Curry, Moore, and myself (Stallworth not here, but has since come) and others from other cotton States, declined to vote, believing that we ought to keep ourselves clear of all compromises. . . . The Republicans are quiet, say nothing, promise nothing, threaten nothing.

In my opinion, Alabama, Mississippi, Florida, and Texas will secede with South Carolina. Georgia will necessarily follow; but there has to be an iron wedge driven to split her off from the Union. Crawford, Jackson, Underwood, and Jones are firm, Love a grade lower, and Hill and Hardeman for the Union. Reagan is with the most advanced, Hamilton for the Union. Garnett, De Jarnette, Jenkins, Leake, Ryan, Edmundson, Stephenson, Ruffin and Craigie of North Carolina, and Anderson of Mississippi are doing nobly; and whilst from policy, they do not openly advocate the secession of the States, yet they say to us, Secede! and they can carry the border States with us. The general impression now, with all parties, is that a dissolution of the Union is inevitable. I cannot see how a collision of arms can be avoided. Be that as it may, far rather die a freeman than live like a slave to Black Republicanism. I would be an equal, or a

1 J. W. Garrett, Columbia, December 8, 1860, to Gov. Moore, Governors' Papers, Ala. Dept. Arch. and Hist.; my italics.
2 O. M. Roberts Papers, Univ. of Texas.

corpse. The argument is exhausted, further remonstrance is dishonorable, hesitation is dangerous, delay is submission. "To your tents, O Israel," and let the God of battles decide the issue.[3]

This letter found an echo in an open address which thirty Southern Senators and Representatives on December 13, only ten days after Congress opened, sent their constituents in Alabama, Georgia, Florida, Arkansas, Mississippi, North Carolina, and Louisiana. "The argument is exhausted," they declared. "All hope of relief in the Union, through the agency of committees, Congressional legislation, or constitutional amendments, is extinguished. . . . The Republicans are resolute in the purpose to grant nothing that will or ought to satisfy the South. We are satisfied the honor, safety, and independence of the Southern people are to be found in a Southern Confederacy. . . ."[4] One of the signers was Judah P. Benjamin. However hotheaded at times, the Louisiana Senator was a man who shrewdly gauged the moment. Already, on December 9, he had written S. L. M. Barlow of New York that compromise was hopeless:

It is a revolution; a revolution of the most intense character; in which belief in the justice, prudence, and wisdom of secession is blended with the keenest sense of wrong and outrage, and it can no more be checked by human effort for the time than a prairie fire by a gardener's watering pot. I see not how bloodshed is to be avoided, and at a meeting of Southern Senators yesterday, I implored them all to devote all their energies to devising means for rendering the separation peaceful if possible, rather than to vain discussions about the practicability of a settlement now totally out of our power to accomplish. On a comparison of views it was ascertained that Mississippi, Alabama, Louisiana, Florida, Arkansas, and Texas would secede separately as quickly as the forms of proceeding could be carried out, that Georgia would probably be led by the example, and many believe that Virginia and Maryland will join them before the 4th March, thus preventing the inauguration of Lincoln in the Federal capital. How all this is to occur without collision I cannot foresee; but some indulge the hope that the Middle States will join the South, and that New England will be left out of the Union to enjoy by herself her fanaticism and the blessings of such freedom as she prefers.[5]

And Benjamin illustrated the fervor of Southern feeling by his close. "I sicken," he wrote, "to contemplate the ruin and desolation thus gratuitously inflicted on my country by the blind and insane fury of a fanaticism which contemplated with calmness and even with complacency the reduction of fifteen States where civilization now flourishes into a new Haiti."

Meanwhile, Republican extremists were equally irreconcilable. Such leaders as Sumner, Wade, Zack Chandler, and Chase disliked the very idea of con-

3 December 13, 1860; Clay Papers, Duke Univ.
4 McPherson, *Political Hist. of the Rebellion*, 37.
5 S. L. M. Barlow Papers, Columbia Univ.

cession as implying timidity and apology. So did such editors as Bryant, Greeley, Bowles, and Medill. Two milder publicists, Henry J. Raymond of the New York *Times* and Thurlow Weed of the Albany *Evening Journal*, had just before the election suggested oblations to the spirit of union; Raymond proposing a Federal indemnity for rescued fugitives from slavery, and Weed going much further by asking why the North should not restore the Missouri Compromise line. Already unpopular in wide Republican circles, the Albany boss drew down upon his head a storm of wrath. Even his friend Preston King scolded him fiercely.[6] Immediately after the election, Senator Doolittle of Wisconsin, speaking for Northwestern Republicans, reasserted their determination that slavery should never be extended into any Territory by any means whatever. Many of the leaders had come to Washington in a stiffly unyielding temper. "The Republican Party today," Seward had written Weed after the first Senate caucus, "is as uncompromising as the Secessionists in South Carolina." He hoped that tempers on each side might moderate.[7]

And when the problem was reduced to its basic elements, how much room for compromise really existed? Associate Justice John A. Campbell of the Supreme Court was right when he wrote that the grievances of which the South complained were either not material or not remediable. The loss from fugitive slaves, for example, was not truly material; Campbell believed that not one Southerner in ten thousand ever knew a man who had lost a slave by Northern rescue. What the South really wanted was a cessation of the agitation against slavery. It could never be granted, because the slavery question agitated itself. Slavery was in conflict with the spirit of the age, and even if ten thousand Garrisons and Ben Wades were muzzled, the agitation would continue. What the North wanted (for the moment) was a cessation of the pressure for the expansion of slavery. But this pressure depended on economic and social forces independent of all such men as Wigfall, Iverson, and A. G. Brown. To name but one, slavery seemed usually to yield its best profits upon cheap lands, and this meant expansion. No, the basic question could not be compromised; one section must yield its fundamental position.

Each side in Congress naturally exhibited a deep suspicion of its opponents. Southern leaders believed that the Republicans meant to sing a Lorelei song of compromise to delay and cripple the secession movement until, their object of dividing and paralyzing the South attained, they would trample on all real concessions. Conversely, many Republican leaders believed that the secessionists, determined to go out even if they were offered apples of gold on platters of

6 "You and Seward," wrote King, "should be among the foremost to brandish the lance and shout for war." Weed, *Memoir*, 308, 309.
7 *Ibid.*

silver, were using talk of compromise as a screen. Behind fair words in Washington they were executing fell deeds in the South. Some of the playing for delay was sincerely based on patriotic motives. Union men in the South earnestly besought their Northern friends to delay the hotheads by irenic speeches and measures. "Their prayer is for time as strongly as that of Ajax is for light," wrote Senator Dixon of Connecticut.[8] It must be admitted, however, that the suspicions of both Northerners and Southerners had a substantial basis. Both sides harbored members who dissembled their real intent.

Charles Francis Adams, a member of the House committee appointed to deal with compromise, was a man of high probity. Yet his object in this committee is stated by his son to have been to maneuver for position and to gain time. We are told that he instinctively sought to demonstrate to Northern opinion that compromise was impossible by driving the Southern Representatives from one position to another, until their irreducible demands were shown to be impossible of concession. While he thus united the North, the peaceable attitude adopted might temporarily paralyze the South, and permanently hold the border States in the Union. Adams justified the duplicity inherent in this policy on the ground that he was but stripping the Southern radicals of their mask.[9]

On the other side, the Virginia historian Pollard informs us that radical Southern Senators had no real heart in the discussion of compromise. Determined to secede anyhow, they wished merely to affect public opinion; and while professing to desire a pacification of the nation, they secretly intrigued against it.[10] A Christmas Day letter of Douglas proves that he thought many leaders of both parties dissemblers and tricksters. Under these circumstances, tempers tended to harden. As December closed, Representative William S. Holman, an Indiana Democrat who earnestly prayed for adjustment, wrote home:

> We must expect to face all the consequences of a revolution that divides us into two nations on the slave line. I have not seen the slightest evidence of reaction since Congress met. Every *moment* and every *movement* tend to consolidate the Southern sentiment, and even the most conservative of the Southern men look to a united South as an inevitable result. In the midst of these contending elements there is no yielding on the part of the Republicans, not an inch to be given by the leaders, and in the main the Republican press sustain and back up their determination not to yield an inch. . . .[11]

Nevertheless, a few brave men, notable among them Crittenden and Douglas in the Senate and Tom Corwin and John Sherman in the House, were resolved

8 From Washington, December 22, 1860; Welles Papers, LC.
9 Charles Francis Adams, Jr., *Charles Francis Adams*, 128 ff. But there was more of a sincere desire for peace and settlement in the elder Adams than his son gives him credit for; his letters in the Dana Papers, Mass. Hist. Soc., show him working hard for agreement.
10 Pollard, *Jefferson Davis*, 68.
11 Allen Hamilton Papers, Ind. State Lib.

to struggle to the last for a fair settlement. Conspicuous among the battlers for compromise was the rudely eloquent Andrew Johnson, an anxious champion of peace and an impassioned defender of the Union. His speech of December 18, exhorting the Southerners to battle for their rights on the vantage-ground of the Constitution, and warning them that in the storm of civil war slavery would be cut down by the sword of destruction, was one of the memorable orations of the winter.

[II]

The action of the Senate, delayed by much ugly wrangling, did not begin until December 18, when it voted to form a Committee of Thirteen on the crisis. Two days later, Vice-President Breckinridge named a strong group who met for the first time that day. Two men of transcendent ability represented the Lower South, Jefferson Davis and Robert Toombs; three stood for the borderland, R. M. T. Hunter of Virginia, and Lazarus W. Powell and John J. Crittenden of Kentucky. The Northern Democrats were given spokesmen in Stephen A. Douglas, William M. Bigler of Pennsylvania, and Henry M. Rice of Minnesota. This left five places for Republicans. Breckinridge naturally named William H. Seward, and with him the quiet, moderate, industrious Jacob Collamer of Vermont, adding three Northwestern radicals—Ben Wade of Ohio, James R. Doolittle of Wisconsin, and James W. Grimes of Iowa. At first, Davis declined to serve because of the position he and his State were known to occupy, but under the advice of friends he changed his mind.[12]

It will be noted that the committee was named on the day that South Carolina seceded. Time was running out, and it would have to act rapidly. It is also to be noted that not one of the committee leaders was in close working relations with the President, especially after Davis broke with him, and that in this terrible convulsion all too little liaison existed between the executive and legislative branches. The astute and adroit Seward, curiously enough, became the principal intermediary between the Thirteen and the staunch Unionists of the Cabinet.

Leadership of the committee lay with Crittenden, who, though unhappily lacking the force, charm, and eloquence of Clay, had something of his breadth of vision. On the day the body was born, he made a speech presenting a well-rounded plan of adjustment quite in the Clay tradition. He proposed six amendments to the Constitution. The first would extend the line of 36° 30′ to California, prohibiting slavery in all Territories north of it, but recognizing and protecting the institution south of it; future States to be admitted with or with-

12 *Cong. Globe*, 36th Cong., 2d Sess., 158, 182.

out slavery as the people might decide. The second amendment would forbid Congress to abolish slavery in any place of national jurisdiction inside a slave State. The third would prohibit abolition in the District of Columbia so long as either Virginia or Maryland had slavery, or without the consent of the people of the District, or without compensation to those who asked it. The fourth amendment would protect from Federal interference the interstate transportation of slaves. The fifth would enable Congress to furnish compensation to owners of fugitive slaves rescued by force, this indemnity to be collected from the county responsible. The last amendment would forbid any future tampering with the Constitution as it applied to and shielded slavery. Annexed resolutions called for strict observance of the Fugitive Slave Law, repeal of the personal liberty laws, and efficient enforcement of the laws against the African slave trade.[13]

It need not be said that Crittenden had consulted with colleagues North and South before offering his broad scheme, and had received hopeful assurance of support.[14] Four Democratic members of the committee, Douglas, Powell, Bigler, and Rice, were ready to give general support to his plan. The vital question was whether Republicans, pledged to the exclusion of slavery from all new Territories, could consent to an amendment which, if the nation expanded southward, might permit great slaveholding accessions. Crittenden was aware of Republican sensitivity on this head. But he believed that the revival and extension of the Missouri Compromise line would prevent any expansion whatever; for while the North would stand adamant against all annexations southward, the South would forbid any acquisitions northward. Practically, therefore, the division on $36° \ 30'$ would settle the slavery issue in the Territories for all time. Of course many Republican leaders held the alternative view, that the plan would simply inaugurate a new contest for the balance of power: The free States would fix their covetous gaze on Canada and Alaska, the slaveholding States on Mexico and Cuba, and strife would be intensified rather than quieted.

The Committee of Thirteen commenced work on December 22. Davis shortly moved that no proposals should be reported to the Senate unless they had the support of a majority of both the Republican and the Democratic members of the body; that is, they must have four Democratic and three Republican votes. This seemed reasonable, for a one-sided recommendation would carry

13 Text in McPherson, *Pol. Hist. Rebellion*, 64, 65.
14 Crittenden wrote Larz Anderson March 20, 1861, of his resolutions: "They were the result of the joint labor of and consultation with friends, having the same object in view, and I believe that if those measures thus offered had been at a suitable time promptly adopted by the Congress of the United States, I would have checked the progress of the rebellion and revolution and saved the Union." Crittenden Papers, Duke Univ.

little weight. The rule was adopted. Thereupon the two leaders of the Lower South both submitted plans.[15]

Toombs, speaking for Southern extremists, asked for constitutional amendments granting recognition and protection to slave property in all Territories; providing for the surrender of fugitive slaves without writ of *habeas corpus* or jury trial; forbidding the passage of any law by Congress pertaining to slavery without the consent of a majority of slaveholding States; and stipulating that these and other constitutional provisions upon slavery (except that on the African slave trade) should not be altered without the consent of every slaveholding State. Davis made just one comprehensive suggestion. It was that the Constitution be amended to declare slave property on the same constitutional footing as any other species of property, and exempt from any impairment by the local law of any State, or by any enactment of the United States or of a Territory. This would establish slavery in all Territories and entitle it to full protection therein, while it would also estop the Northern States from passing any law limiting the recovery of fugitive slaves, or restricting the right of a slaveholder to bring his Negroes to free soil in transit or for a sojourn. Obviously, the Republicans could not accept either Toombs's or Davis's formula.

Douglas also had a plan, the chief features of which were that the status of each existing Territory should remain unchanged until, on attaining a population of fifty thousand, it should be admitted as a State with or without slavery; and that no further expansion of the nation should take place except with the consent of two-thirds of each house. He proposed to forbid any abolition of slavery in the District of Columbia except upon the same general conditions laid down by Crittenden; to prohibit any interference with the domestic slave trade, or any opening of the franchise or of office to the African race; and to furnish Federal compensation for rescued slaves. Very interestingly, he added a notation that land might be acquired at Federal expense for the colonization of colored people. His suggestions got little consideration, since his chief proposal, based on popular sovereignty principles, was repugnant to Republicans and Southern radicals alike. Indeed, the Crittenden plan alone out of seven offered in committee received really earnest attention.[16]

That Crittenden's scheme had wide and enthusiastic public support there could be no question. John A. Dix, Edward Everett, and Robert C. Winthrop no sooner saw it than they wrote strongly approbatory letters. Martin Van Buren declared that the amendments would certainly be ratified by three-

15 The Journal of the Committee is in the 36th Cong., 2d Sess., *Senate Committee Reports*, No. 288. For an analysis of its work, see Potter, *Lincoln and His Party in the Secession Crisis*, 171 ff.

16 A competent digest of all plans submitted is in Nicolay and Hay, *Lincoln*, III, 220–222.

fourths of the States. The Senator received hundreds of assurances from all over the North and the border States that his policy had reached the popular heart. It took time to hold meetings and get memorials signed, but before long resolutions and petitions were pouring in upon Congress. In New York City, sixty-three thousand people signed an endorsement of the plan; another document bore the names of fourteen thousand women, scattered from North Carolina to Vermont. From St. Louis came nearly a hundred foolscap pages of names, wrapped in the American flag. Greeley, who had as good opportunities for knowing public sentiment as any man in the country, later wrote that supporters of the Crittenden Compromise could claim with good reason that a large majority of people favored it.[17]

But the five Republicans in the committee were influenced not by general opinion but by personal conviction, party principle, and the voice of freesoil leaders and editors. The four minor Senators were to some extent inclined to wait for guidance on the preeminent Seward, who was expected by most people to be the controlling force in the next Administration. Seward, for his part, was disposed to be silent for the time, from a conviction noted in his journal that "concession, or solicitation, or solicitude would encourage, and demonstrations of firmness of purpose would exasperate." He preferred, also, to await a statement of policy from Lincoln. A week before the committee was appointed, he had learned that the President-elect desired him to be Secretary of State. He wrote at once to ask time for consideration, and left next day, December 14, with the intention of spending the holidays at home. Halting in Albany to talk with Thurlow Weed and others, he heard that on an invitation from Lincoln's friends, Weed was about to pay his second visit to Springfield. It seemed wise to see Weed on his return and find out what Lincoln had said on a variety of subjects.[18]

At this point a somewhat confusing incident occurred. Already, as we have seen, Weed had come out in favor of restoring the Missouri Compromise line. On Monday, the seventeenth, after talking with Seward, he renewed the proposal in his *Evening Journal*. His object, he tells us in his autobiography, was to do something to hold the border States in line, thus reducing the extent and strength of the "rebellion," and to keep the Northern people clearly in the right, so that if and when war came they would have greater unity. Of course he also hoped to do something for peace. Many people inaccurately leaped to the conclusion that his stand had been inspired or at least supported

17 Coleman, *Crittenden,* II, 237–258, presents detailed information on public support; see also Potter, *Lincoln and Secession Crisis,* 195 ff.

18 Weed, before visiting Springfield, suggested that a conference of governors be arranged and that Lincoln send it his views. Baringer, *House Dividing,* 204, 205; Weed, *Memoir,* 310; Nicolay and Hay, III, 252, 253.

by Seward. The fact was, however, that the Senator had a position all his own—a position which rendered him much more likely to follow Lincoln than to try to revive the old 36° 30′ line.

[III]

Lincoln had already made up his mind. Indeed, that central phalanx of the Republican Party which, comprehending not only all radicals but many moderates, believed that the doctrine of the exclusion of slavery from the Territories must be defended as their supreme citadel, was never for a moment moved by the Crittenden Compromise. Lincoln was less likely than anyone else to abandon a principle which he held vital.

On December 10 he had written Lyman Trumbull, who could tell the next Republican caucus: "Let there be no compromise on the question of extending slavery. If there be, all our labor is lost, and ere long, must be done again. . . . The tug has to come, and better now than at any time hereafter." Next day, in response to an inquiry from William Kellogg of the House committee on the crisis, he wrote again: "Entertain no proposition in regard to the extension of slavery. The instant you do they have us under again: all our labor is lost, and sooner or later must be done over." On the thirteenth he sent a similar letter to Elihu B. Washburne: "Prevent, as far as possible, any of our friends from demoralizing themselves and our cause by entertaining propositions for compromise of any sort on 'slavery extension.' There is no possible compromise upon it but which puts us under again, and leaves all our work to do over again. Whether it be a Missouri line or Eli Thayer's popular sovereignty, it is all the same. Let either be done, and immediately filibustering and extending slavery recommences. On that point hold firm, as with a chain of steel." [19]

This was one of the most fateful decisions of Lincoln's career. The reasons why he made it so quickly and emphatically, without consulting others, require a brief analysis.

"They will have us under again; all our work will have to be redone." By this Lincoln meant a good deal more than the naked words assert. It seems

19 The letter to Trumbull is in Tracy, *Uncollected Lincoln Letters*, 171; those to Washburne and Kellogg in the Thomas-Tandy edition of Nicolay and Hay, *Lincoln's Works*, VI, 77, 78. Lincoln's reply to Weed on December 17 was in the same vein. If the convocation of governors should meet, he wrote, Weed might tell them that "you judge from my speeches that I will be inflexible on the territorial question; that I probably think either the Missouri line extended, or Douglas's and Thayer's popular sovereignty would lose us everything we gain by the election; that filibustering for all south of us and making slave States would follow, in spite of us, in either case; also that I probably think all opposition, real and apparent, to the fugitive slave clause of the Constitution ought to be withdrawn." Weed, *Memoir*, 310, 311.

safe to say that he had two important ideas in mind. First, he meant that the whole work of his party in winning the election would have to be redone if the victorious candidate immediately surrendered the central tenet of the party. He could yield on peripheral points—not on the expansion of slavery. And Lincoln believed that the expansion of slavery was implicit in the Crittenden Compromise. He told Duff Green that the adoption of the line would still the controversy for the moment, but the quarrel would be renewed by the seizure and attempted annexation of Mexico.[20] Was this unlikely? The South had forced Pierce and Buchanan to take extreme attitudes on Cuba and Mexico. Not only the Knights of the Golden Circle, but a large clandestine organization in California had an eye on Sonora and other territory to the southward.[21] And what if Hawaii were annexed? The Republican Party had been born from a great principle—and now it was asked to sacrifice it under threat and menace. If it did so, how could it face honest Northern voters again?

More fundamentally, Lincoln had in mind his statement that "a crisis must be reached and passed," and the country brought to a completely new resolution respecting slavery. He had said explicitly that the nation as a whole must be persuaded to accept the containment of slavery within existing bounds as a prelude to the blest goal of ultimate extinction. His election on the principle of nonextension constituted the crisis; if the South accepted the election, realizing its import, the crisis *would* be passed; the nation could go on to consider slavery from a more constructive point of view. Its psychology on the great question would rapidly alter. But what if the nation backed away from a decision, and refused to accept the only principle on which a permanent solution, in keeping with nineteenth century progress, could be based? What if it turned back to the old policy of drift? Europe in 1848 had given the world the tragic spectacle of nations coming up to a healthy turning-point—and refusing to turn. Could the United States afford to do so? Could the one leader who had demanded that the country face the crisis now flinch and bid his party recede? To this question, Lincoln said *No.*

Talking with one of his Springfield friends, Lincoln partially summed up his view in a characteristically pungent sentence: "Well, we have got plenty of corn and pork and it wouldn't be exactly brave for us to leave this question to posterity." This was the report of his words sent to Washburne.

His letters to Kellogg, Trumbull, and Washburne were shown to leaders

20 Duff Green, December 28, 1860, to Buchanan; Buchanan Papers.
21 "We hope that Uncle Sam will soon own Sonora. . . . We have an organization here of about 4,000 men, and when they start I have a Captain's Commission, if it is not owned by the Government by 1862, we are going to take it from the cussed Mexicans. . . ." V. H. Claiborne, San Francisco, November 1, 1860, to "Dear Charles"; Brock Papers, HL.

and newspapermen. On December 22, his determination was revealed to the public in the New York *Tribune,* by an authorized statement in the editorial columns. Lincoln, announced the journal, "is utterly opposed to any concession or compromise that shall yield one iota of the position occupied by the Republican Party on the question of slavery in the territories, and. . . . he stands now, as he stood in May last, when he accepted the nomination for the presidency, square upon the Chicago platform."

Thurlow Weed, in his conference with Lincoln on December 20, discussed the question of compromise, though in his twelve-page record he confines himself almost entirely to the Cabinet slate.[22] He found Lincoln still possessed by an apparent cheerfulness, declaring that despite the threats of the cotton States, serious trouble might be averted by wisdom and forbearance. This, on the day South Carolina departed! Yet by this time Lincoln's optimism was probably more feigned than real. His strong, clear mind undoubtedly gauged the intentions of the cotton kingdom leaders accurately. But he could not talk of war without exposing himself to the accusation of exaggerating the crisis and fanning the flames. And whatever his fears, he did not intend to budge on the central issue.

When Weed showed him the new editorial in the *Evening Journal* advocating the Missouri Compromise line, he betrayed annoyance. Remarking that it was an attack on friend and foe alike, and would do "some good or much mischief," he inquired whether Weed thought Republican sentiment in New York would sustain it. The boss had to admit that it would not. Doubtless Lincoln spoke emphatically against opening the door to any extension of slavery. He had his own ideas as to how far concession might go in other matters, and embodied them in three resolutions which he asked Weed to show to Trumbull and Hannibal Hamlin, and to get Seward to introduce: [24]

Resolved: That the fugitive slave clause of the Constitution ought to be enforced by a law of Congress, with efficient provision for that object, not obliging private persons to assist in its execution, but punishing all who resist it, and with the usual safeguards to liberty, securing freemen against being surrendered as slaves—

That all state laws, if there be such, really or apparently, in conflict with such law of Congress, ought to be repealed; and no opposition to the execution of such law of Congress ought to be made—

That the Federal Union must be preserved.

22 Weed, *Autobiography,* 602–614.
23 Others also assumed an optimistic attitude. Henry J. Raymond had all the facilities of an editor for knowing the situation. He wrote from the *Times* office on January 21, 1861: "I think this crisis will work out gradually and leave things in much better condition than they were before—*provided* it is managed with firmness as well as forbearance." J. R. Hawley Papers.
24 Text in Bancroft, *Seward,* II, 10.

While this was all that Lincoln wrote at the time, he would not have objected to other assurances to the South. He had not the remotest thought of recommending that slavery be abolished in the District of Columbia, even under safeguards, or touched in Federal reservations within the slaveholding States. He had no idea of interfering with the domestic slave trade. He would not object to the confirmation of slavery in New Mexico, if further extension were prevented. He had said repeatedly that, far from harassing Southerners, he would give them a friendly Administration.[25] But on the containment of slavery he was adamant. Weed, returning east, met Seward on December 22 at Syracuse, for the Senator had been summoned back to Washington; and as the two rode together to Albany, they discussed all that Lincoln had said.

[IV]

The first committee vote on the Crittenden Compromise was taken that day in Seward's absence, and the proposal was defeated by the Republican majority. In a discussion of nearly seven hours, Douglas, Bigler, and Crittenden supported the plan. Hunter, Toombs, and Davis, speaking for Southern Democrats, declared they would accept it if the Republicans gave sincere assent, but not otherwise. On the vital point, the reestablishment of the Missouri Compromise line, Collamer, Doolittle, Grimes, and Wade all voted no. Thereupon Toombs and Davis cast negative votes, and the resolution failed, six to six. Returning to the sessions on December 24, Seward recorded a negative vote. Four days later, the committee reported to the Senate that it could reach no conclusion.[26]

This report, it must be kept in mind, almost coincided with the revolution in the Cabinet which placed Buchanan under staunch Union influence, and which made it certain that the demand for evacuating Sumter would be brusquely dismissed. It almost coincided with the action of Buchanan, under the stimulus of Horatio King and other Unionist advisers, in repudiating the Washington *Constitution* and its semi-treasonable utterances. Within a few days after the Thirteen reported their failure, Floyd was out and the Cabinet was fully revolutionized. In short, the Republican leadership was proving itself adamant on slavery extension at nearly the same time that the Administration became adamant on the issue of the Charleston forts.

It would be erroneous to say that these two events made continued secession certain; it was certain anyway. Ignoring compromise talk, Florida, Mississippi, and Alabama, on December 18, 20, and 24 respectively, had elected conven-

25 See Randall, *Lincoln the President*, I, 234–237, for a masterly statement on this head.
26 *Committee Journal*, 4, 8, *et seq.*

tions with decisive secessionist majorities. But the events did convince Southern radicals that they must push faster, further, and harder. Toombs, on December 23, telegraphed his State that the people of Georgia should thunder secession by unanimous voice in the election to be held on January 2. On January 5, a momentous caucus of Southern Senators was held. It is said that it took place in a room of the Capitol itself. Members from Alabama, Arkansas, Georgia, Louisiana, Florida, Mississippi, and Texas determined that immediate secession was imperative, that a convention should meet in Montgomery before February 15 to organize a Confederacy, and that they should temporarily hold their seats in an effort to protect their movement and impede hostile legislation. On January 8, Jefferson Davis wrote a friend:

We are advancing rapidly to the end of "the Union." The cotton States may now be regarded as having decided for secession. South Carolina is in a quasi war, and the probabilities are that events will hasten her and her associates into general conflict with the forces of the federal government. The black republicans exultant over their recent successes are not disposed to concede anything, and the stern necessity of resistance is forcing itself upon the judgment of all the slaveholding States. The Va. Legislature met yesterday and took promptly and boldly the Southern ground.[27]

In rejecting the Crittenden Compromise, the Republicans had taken what history later proved to have been a fearful responsibility, just as in thrusting secession steadily forward the Southern extremists were taking the same responsibility. Some Republicans, after war came, made an effort to divest themselves of the burden by contending that the true blame for the rejection fell upon Davis and Toombs, whose votes in the affirmative would have carried the compromise eight to four—or with Seward voting, eight to five. (Even then the measure would have died under the rule requiring a majority of both parties.) Edward Everett argued that the supposed willingness of Davis and Toombs to support the compromise was purely illusory, and that if the Republicans had come out for it, the two would have gone over to the opposition.[28] But we have unimpeachable evidence that the pair were sincere, and much additional evidence that, as Breckinridge told the Senate, "the leading statesmen of the lower Southern States were willing to accept the terms of settlement" proposed.[29] At any rate, Stephens, Toombs, Herschel Johnson, and Davis were ready to do so; though probably not Slidell, Howell Cobb, A. G. Brown, Iverson, Wigfall, or Benjamin.

Whether the secession of Florida, Alabama, Mississippi, and Georgia could

27 To E. De Leon; De Leon Papers.
28 "Address at Inauguration of Union League Club, Boston, April 9, 1863"; pamphlet.
29 See Potter, op. cit., 204–207; Rhodes, United States, III, 154, 155; Cong. Globe, 27th Cong., 1st Sess., 142.

under any circumstances have been arrested is another question, doubtless to be answered in the negative. Seward had written Lincoln just after Christmas that in his opinion the offer of the Missouri Compromise line would be utterly inutile in stopping them. Be it remembered that the address of various Southern Senators and Representatives declaring the argument exhausted and demanding a separate Southern Confederacy had been issued as early as December 14; that when Seward voted on the Crittenden proposal, four States were already committed to secession.

Since Lincoln and other leaders had said no, it was necessary for the Republicans to offer an alternative. The resolutions written by the President-elect were not presented, because Senators in Washington decided that the ground had been covered elsewhere and that the form of his proposal on the recovery of fugitives would excite party dissension. Seward now stepped to the front. On January 22, after Mississippi, Florida, and Alabama had all gone out, he rose in the Senate before an audience said to be unprecedented in size for one of his most telling efforts. The country rang with the shots just fired at the *Star of the West*. The Southern States were seizing one Federal post after another: The day before, Louisiana had taken over the arsenal at Baton Rouge and Forts St. Philip and Jackson, while, as he rose, Florida forces were occupying Fort Barrancas and the Pensacola navy yard. Yet his tone was bland as May.

He spoke of meeting prejudice with conciliation, exaction with concession, and violence with the right hand of peace. Never had he shown more literary felicity. Specially effective was the contrast he drew between a puissant warship of the United States, hailed with awe as she entered a foreign port flying her thirty-three stars, and a warship steaming in with a palmetto flag, to be greeted with the contemptuous words: "She comes from one of the obscure republics of North America. Let her pass on."

On the fundamental question of fresh extensions of slavery, Seward yielded nothing; but he went far in other respects, and his proposals were practical as well as patriotic. If Kansas were admitted under the Wyandotte constitution, he would consent to the consolidation of all remaining Territories into two States, to be organized under enabling acts similar to those of Oregon or Minnesota; the right to a future subdivision of each into several States being reserved. This would take the territorial question out of politics for all time. Presumably New Mexico-Arizona would come in as a slaveholding State, and certainly the region north of it would be a free State. Second, Seward proposed to satisfy the South on the sore point of efficient enforcement of the Fugitive Slave Law, while safeguarding the liberty of free blacks. In the third place, he was willing to write into the Constitution an amendment affirming the permanent exemption of slavery in the States from Congressional control. Fourth, he would support laws to prevent such invasions as that of John Brown. And finally, regarding physical bonds as the most powerful of all links, he wished to see both a northern and a southern railroad built to the Pacific with national help. His eloquent closing appeal for peace left more than one Senator in tears.[30]

In sober reality, Seward had little faith in Congressional schemes of compromise. He said so in his speech, frankly expressing his wish that, when the excitements of the hour had subsided, a new Constitutional convention could chisel out a settlement enduring as granite. By this time, his selection as Secretary of State had become public, and he expected to be one of the chief directors of the nation's destinies. "I will try to save freedom and my country," he had exuberantly written his wife on accepting. While he believed that secession could not be halted, he also believed that the Union might in time— perhaps in two years, he wrote Weed—be reconstructed. He trusted that he could be the chief architect of this reconstruction, this noble new edifice.

At about the time he wrote Lincoln that he would undertake the State Department, Seward approached Senator Gwin of California, who deplored secession, and said that he had a policy which he wished Gwin to understand he would pursue as head of the Cabinet. It was a plan for avoiding civil war and ultimately rebuilding the Union. Gwin writes:

His policy was, that if the separation of States could not be prevented, let the separation be a peaceful one; and to lead the public sentiment of the people of the North and South in the future, and especially of the South, in such a direction that they might see what a grand error that section had committed, and to reestablish the Union without the intervention of civil war. To carry out this policy, Mr. Seward's appointment as Secretary of State was an indispensable necessity, and to secure that appointment it was important that Mr. Lincoln should know that Mr. Seward's long services with the great leaders of the South in the Senate would inspire them with confidence that his appointment as Secretary of State would inaugurate a policy for the peaceable separation of the two sections, leaving it to be determined by the people in the future whether or not the two sections should be kept separate.[31]

This statement to Gwin ran parallel with the extempore speech which he had made to the New England Society in New York on December 22, when he laid heavy emphasis on the healing effects of time. The necessities which made the Union were enduring, he said, while the passions of men were short-lived and ephemeral; if the country kept calm, a discussion would ensue which, kindly in character, would soon show which side was in the wrong; and on

30 Bancroft, *Seward*, II, 16; Seward, *Seward at Washington*, II, 494.
31 MS Memoirs, Bancroft Library; cf. *Overland Monthly*, May–November, 1891.

the basis of concessions to correct this error, the discontented States would "come back into fraternal relations with us." That this was Seward's view is corroborated by the British minister, Lord Lyons, a warm friend, who wrote Lord John Russell on February 4, 1861:

> Mr. Seward's real view of the state of the country appears to be that if bloodshed can be avoided until the new government is installed, the seceding States will in no long time return to the Confederation. He seems to think that in a few months the evils and hardships produced by secession will become intolerably grievous to the Southern States, that they will be completely re-assured as to the intentions of the Administration, and that the Conservative element which is now kept under the surface by violent pressure of the Seces-sionists will emerge with irresistible force. From all these causes he confidently expects that when elections are held in the Southern States in November next, the Union party will have a clear majority and will bring the seceding States back into the Confederation. He then hopes to place himself at the head of a strong Union party, having extensive ramifications both in the North and in the South, and to make "Union" or "Disunion" not "Freedom" or "Slavery" the watchword of political parties.[32]

Making this unrealistic analysis of the situation, Seward was little worried by the rejection of the Crittenden Compromise or his own proposals. Why pay a heavy price for keeping the Lower South in the family when it would soon repent separation? He believed that any hostile external pressure, any foreign attack, would quickly restore a spirit of national solidarity; and in his speech to the New England Society he pictured the gallant South Carolinians, the moment they heard that New York was being attacked by the French, the Russians, or the British, rushing in a body to her defense. This was an idea which was to bear strange fruit early in Lincoln's Administration.

[V]

Early in January, Crittenden rose in the Senate to make the remarkable proposal that his compromise should be submitted to the people of the entire nation for their solemn judgment, as expressed by a popular vote. His reason for suggesting so novel a step, as he frankly confessed, was that he had come to fear he could never obtain a two-thirds vote for his plan in the Senate. The proposal inspired widespread enthusiasm. Douglas declared in the Senate on the same day it was made, January 3, that he ventured to prophesy that the Republicans themselves would approve the proposed amendments. Horatio Seymour wrote Crittenden that he was confident New York State would give the measure a majority of a hundred and fifty thousand. Horace Greeley later

32 *British Blue Book, United States*, 1862; pp. 62, 63.

declared that in a popular referendum, the compromise would have prevailed by "an overwhelming majority." But neither radical Northerners nor radical Southerners liked the plan. Because of Republican obstruction, interposing delay after delay, it never came to a vote in the Senate. The objection of men like Wade, Chandler, and Sumner, and of journals like the New York *Tribune*, was candidly stated. They said (1) that in the Lower South the secession elections had been unfair and fraudulent; (2) that the naked submission of the Crittenden Compromise alone was not enough—the entire controversy should be taken before the proper tribunal, which Greeley pronounced to be a Constitutional Convention; and (3) that some guarantees should be given in advance that the Southern States would accept the result of the election. Whether these were good or bad reasons, and whether it was for good or for ill that the American people were never given a chance of passing on this crucial compromise scheme, are questions on which no historian can pronounce a light judgment, and on which few would care to pronounce at all. But for Crittenden himself the repeated refusals of the Senate to vote on his referendum constituted a great tragedy.

The second critical decision on the Crittenden Compromise proper took place in open Senate on January 16. Crittenden had introduced his resolutions on the third, and had made a long argument in their behalf on the seventh—followed by a fierce disunion speech from Toombs. A motion to consider the resolution was now defeated by the adoption of a meaningless substitute, 25 to 23, with six Southern Democrats not voting. While the twenty-five adopting votes were all Republican, the six Democrats—Johnson of Arkansas, Iverson of Georgia, Benjamin and Slidell of Louisiana, and Hemphill and Wigfall of Texas—by their stubborn silence helped seal the fate of the measure. Crittenden, Andrew Johnson, and Douglas all severely censured the abstentionists.

While the vote was being taken Andrew Johnson, wrung with anxiety, hastened quietly to the side of Judah P. Benjamin, and whispered to him with tense earnestness: "Mr. Benjamin, vote! Let us save this proposition and see if we cannot bring the country to it. Vote, and show yourself an honest man." Making a scornful reply, Benjamin remained silent. More than a fortnight earlier he had delivered a speech announcing Louisiana's determination to secede, and threatening a bloody war. Obviously he wanted no compromise. As Johnson recrossed the Senate floor he saw Crittenden's venerable face pale with anguish and disappointment, the very image of gloom.

Had the six Southerners voted, the Crittenden resolutions would have had a majority of four. If the Senators from four seceding States had been in their seats, the majority would have been increased to twelve. Six of them were in Washington, but chose not to consider themselves competent to attend. According to Andrew Johnson, as soon as the vote was declared, Judah P. Benjamin sent a telegram to Louisiana, where the issue of secession was still undecided, notifying his State that the Crittenden scheme was lost, and the Black Republicans were carrying everything before them.[33] Provoking though the conduct of the six secessionists was, the fact remains that the chief responsibility for the defeat of the compromise falls upon the twenty-five Republicans who voted to slay it. A combination of Republicans and Northern Democrats could easily have carried the resolutions.

That responsibility the Republicans should squarely have accepted, and unquestionably Lincoln and his principal associates did so accept it. Once more, we must bear in mind that the central tenet of the Republican Party, ever since its foundation, had been the exclusion of slavery from all new Territories. We must also bear in mind that to Lincoln this doctrine of the containment of slavery represented much more than an objective, a goal. It represented rather a beginning, a new start. It represented, that is, the point at which one phase in the consideration of the great problems of slavery and race adjustment ended, and another phase began.

Once containment was tacitly accepted by the South, that section must also accept the corollary that slavery was a transitional and not a permanent institution; that the nation must look forward to a time, however distant, when it would be ended; that the country must take some initial step toward gradual abolition, perhaps combined with colonization abroad, and certainly combined with a fair plan of compensation. By arduous labor and heroic sacrifices, beginning in 1846 with the Wilmot Proviso and running through the spasmodic thrust of the Free Soil Party, the organization of the Republicans, their four Congressional campaigns, their two Presidential battles, and a tremendous mobilization of newspapers, orators, and pamphleteers, an Administration had been elected on a platform of containment. It had reached the end of the beginning. And now it was asked to begin all over again!

Such a surrender would have been endurable had it meant only a formal waiving of the interdiction of slavery in the West. After all, a mere handful of slaves could be found in all the Territories of the land. Nobody in his senses supposed that Negroes would ever be carried in any numbers into Nebraska, Dakota, Colorado, and Washington. In all New Mexico, despite favorable legislation, census-takers this year found only twenty-two slaves. On any practical basis, the issue of slavery in the Territories was empty. Nor was it likely, though it was certainly possible, that the Southern expansionists who had signally failed to gain any Cuban, Mexican, or Central American soil during the eight years of Pierce and Buchanan would be able to do so in the near

33 *Cong. Globe*, 37th Cong., 2d Sess., 587.

future. Northern opposition would be too dogged and powerful. So far as the actual diffusion of slavery went, the Republicans could have afforded to swallow the Crittenden Compromise—for the possibilities of slavery expansion were near their end.

The psychological and political effects of such an acceptance, however, would in Lincoln's eyes have been disastrous in the extreme. At one blow, all hope of lifting the slavery discussion, so long a futile debate between the positive-evil and positive-good schools and so totally out of key with the aspirations of civilization, to a new, enlightened, and constructive plane, would be ended. For what would be the moral result of accepting the Missouri Compromise extension? Forthwith, the hopes of the slavery extremists would rise anew. They would *toil* to make New Mexico a slave State; they would redouble their filibustering efforts; they would dream, however hopelessly, of Cuba, Lower California, Sonora, and Ceneral America. Instead of changing the climate of opinion, the recent Republican victory would leave it unaltered; instead of seeing a "crisis reached and passed," the country would see the perennial crisis lengthened.

No, the time had come to make a stand. The old American policy of drift, postponement, and politic evasion of fundamental issues would have to be stopped somehow, some day, in some fashion—and the Republican Party was pledged to stop it now. It was committed, in Lincoln's words, to placing the institution of slavery in a position where its ultimate extinction would be generally taken for granted.

To Lincoln, therefore, and all who shared his views, it seemed wise to stand on principle, hoping that it could be peaceably maintained. For great causes, great risks have to be taken. For some high causes, it is well that nations will fight and men gladly die. But Lincoln did not mean to make war in defense of his principle. He would coerce nobody to accept it. He would attack no slave-holding State, in the Union or out of it. Bound by oath to enforce the laws and protect the property of the government, he would not even do this in a needlessly offensive fashion, as, for example, by sending Federal officers where they would be resisted. To him the revival of the Missouri Compromise line did not mean assured peace; rather, it meant a temptation to war against Mexico and a certainty of continued bickering at home. He would not surrender the bright ideal he had so cogently stated in June, 1858, of a nation brought again to regard slavery as Washington, Madison, and Jefferson had regarded it. He meant to make good, if Providence permitted him, the great hope which some anonymous versifier in *Punch* had just forcibly expressed:

> Thus far shall Slavery go, no farther;
> That tide must ebb from this time forth. . . .

This is America's decision;
Awakening, she begins to see,
How justly she incurs derision
Of tyrants, while she shames us free;
Republican, yet more slaves owning
Than any under Empire groaning. . . .

Come, South, accept the situation;
The change will grow by safe degrees.
If any talk of separation,
Hang all such traitors if you please.
Break up the Union? Brothers, never!
No, the United States for ever,
Pure Freedom's home beyond the seas!

[VI]

While compromise was failing in the Senate, it was doing little better in the House, which was even worse adapted to the task of peacemaking; a body too large, too contentious, and too strongly Republican for mediatorial effort.

On motion of Boteler of Virginia, the House had agreed on December 4, by a vote of 145 to 38, to create a special committee of one from each State to consider the perilous condition of the country. The opposition was all Republican; but a number of Southern members refused to vote, Porcher Miles saying that South Carolina was already out of the Union in everything but form, and Pugh declaring that Alabama intended to follow South Carolina. Two days later, Speaker Pennington appointed the Committee of Thirty-three. His choices were maladroit. At a time when the fate of the nation hung in the balance, Pennington (a "dolt," an "old owl," wrote one observer) was showing a pitiful inability to control the chamber or drive public business ahead.[34] He could be credited with apportioning the Committee fairly among the parties, with sixteen Republicans, fourteen Democrats, and three Opposition members, while in Tom Corwin he chose an excellent chairman. But he failed to name a single Douglas man from the North; most of his Southerners were unrepresentative of public opinion in that section; and he chose too many radical Republicans. The body was far more likely to quarrel than agree.

On December 11 the Thirty-three held their first meeting. S. R. Curtis, an Iowa Republican, writes that they "seemed cordial conciliatory and deeply impressed with the importance of our position." [35] But on the twelfth, when Reuben Davis of Mississippi made a long speech on the causes of Southern

34 Charles Francis Adams, Jr., *Autobiography*, 44, 92.
35 MS Journal, Ill. State Hist. Lib.

disaffection, painting a most sinister picture of Republican objects, discord reared its head. Next day the situation grew worse.

The Committee passed a resolution written by Dunn of Indiana, expressing regret for Southern discontent, and declaring that whether this was without just cause or not, "more specific and effectual guarantees of their peculiar rights and interests" should be "promptly and cheerfully" granted. This was a handsome gesture, and went even further than a similar resolution which Rust of Arkansas had proposed. Yet at this very time it was announced that some of the Southern members had been collaborating with other Representatives and with Senators on the firebrand circular issued on December 14 with thirty signers—a manifesto declaring to the South that argument was exhausted and the Republicans would offer nothing that the section could accept. Reuben Davis declared that the Committee resolution was mere eyewash designed to mislead the South. While the resolution was telegraphed over the South with the design of restraining precipitate action, the manifesto was being just as assiduously telegraphed about with the object of promoting it.[36]

On the fourteenth Chairman Corwin made a long conciliatory speech (though he pronounced secession treason), proposing to take up issues *seriatim* and to seek, one by one, an adjustment. He suggested beginning with Henry Winter Davis's resolution calling upon the States to repeal all laws which conflicted with the Fugitive Slave Act. At once, unhappily, the wrangling recommenced. When Curtis introduced some coercionist resolutions, the Southern members protested in great indignation, and Reuben Davis declared that persistence in such a course would compel him to leave the Committee. From the beginning, two other Southerners, Hawkins of Florida and Boyce of South Carolina, had refused to serve. Curtis withdrew his motion. Thus the Committee pursued its stormy way. A weird variety of proposals was suggested to it, some reasonable, some hopeless, some fantastic. The Republicans were quite willing to give the South satisfaction on the question of fugitive slaves, and to urge the North to abandon its personal liberty laws. But the proposal to revive and extend the 36° 30' line was defeated by a solid Republican vote, with Henry Winter Davis, Opposition member from Maryland, assisting; a vote, that is, of 17 to 14.[37]

By Christmas, the once-hopeful Curtis had lost faith in the possibility of any effective result. "I see no way of uniting even Republicans on any terms of compromise," he wrote.

No member of the Thirty-three offered a plan which caught the national

36 The *Journal* of the Committee of Thirty-three is in 36th Cong. 2d Sess., *House Reports* No. 30. Reuben Davis's statement is in McPherson, *Pol. Hist. Rebellion*, 37.
37 *Committee Journal*.

attention like the Crittenden Compromise; but two distinguished Republicans did present schemes possessing great interest. One was John Sherman. This tall, spare, incisive Ohioan, now closing his third term in the House and about to open a great career in the Senate, had gained increased caution and moderation from his recent defeat as Speaker. He was eager to do anything to sustain the Union short of writing into the Constitution guarantees of the protection and extension of slavery. On December 12 he offered the House a resolution instructing the Committee of Thirty-three to divide all the Territories into States of convenient size with a view to their prompt admission. This would abolish the strife over slavery in the Territories by simply abolishing the Territories themselves. As they became States, the slavery issue would be settled by constitutional conventions and legislatures. Sherman's scheme quickly dropped into oblivion, but not before he had published a burning appeal to reason. The burden of his message was that the country could never huckster into fragments its nationality, its flag, its history.

"Disunion is war!" he wrote. He would not threaten it; he would indeed do almost anything to prevent it; but what honest man could deny that it would be inevitable? "If war results, what a war it will be! Contemplate the North and South in hostile array against each other. If these sections do not know each other *now*, they will *then*."

Still more striking was the role played by Charles Francis Adams. As a veteran observer of affairs, Adams was convinced that South Carolina and other cotton States were determined to erect a separate confederacy, and that nothing could stop them. The all-important object, he believed, was to hold Virginia, Maryland, Kentucky, and the other border States which stood shivering on the brink of secession. For this purpose, he would go to the outer verge of conciliation, standing firm only on principle. He felt certain that when a generous conciliatory offer was made to the cotton kingdom men, they would spurn it; for they meant to have a separate republic, and expand it around the Caribbean. Thus they would openly put themselves in the wrong. The border region, seeing them do so, would cling to the Union. If Virginia, Kentucky, Missouri and the rest could be held for even a year, their people would learn that Lincoln's Administration was fair and mild, and would realize once and for all the folly of secession.

In refusing to countenance the extension of slavery or to offer pledges of its territorial protection Adams, gratified to find Lincoln in full agreement with himself, stood firm as Monadnock. He would not affront the spirit of nineteenth century civilization by doing in 1860 what the nation's founders had refused to do in 1787. Delivering a trenchant speech to the Committee on December 20, he made it plain that he would prefer civil war to any such surrender. But he had a positive program to urge; a program which he shared with Henry Winter Davis, the handsome and eloquent Marylander. Both believed that everything depended on holding Virginia, Maryland, and other border States; both unhesitatingly opposed the Crittenden resolution; both saw that if they rejected the Crittenden proposals, they had to make an offer of their own.

The resulting Adams-Davis plan, hammered out—apparently with some aid from Seward—in protracted caucuses of Republican members of the Committee December 21-26, had for its central feature a bold proposal for the immediate admission of New Mexico (including present-day Arizona) as a State, letting her people decide for or against slavery. Adams waved aside all suggestions for giving statehood to the area north of 36° 30′; it was understood that Kansas must soon come in as a free State, but he believed that the rest of the region was unready. New Mexico, he argued, was the only area sufficiently populated to become a State, and the only area where slavery was an issue. At first most Republicans were shocked by the suggested admission of New Mexico, and Seward told Adams that party members on the Committee of Thirteen opposed it. Before long, however, they realized that the step was as adroit as it was bold.

In the caucus discussions of December 24-25 Adams and Davis explained that their plan had one advantage which was not visible at first glance. Whereas New Mexico, with her slave code, might enter the Union as a slave State, she must soon become free. Her terrain, climate, products, and traditions were hostile to slavery. Though peonage unhappily flourished there, slavery had never gained a real foothold. On the 25th John S. Watts of New Mexico, a former Federal judge of nine years' residence in the Territory, soon to become its Delegate in Congress, explained that slavery was impossible. His clear and decided testimony converted most of the Republicans. As Senator Crittenden privately said, the admission of New Mexico would simply give the Union another free State!

And Southerners perceived this too. When the proposal was introduced in the Committee, slave State members were as startled as if a bomb had exploded. They whispered nervously together, withdrew into an adjoining room to consult, and finally came back to announce that they could not entertain the plan. The Republicans were accepting the main part of Crittenden's proposal; they were offering the South a delusive possibility of one more slave State; but they were adamant against permitting slavery in "lands hereafter to be acquired" south of 36° 30′. The Adams-Davis plan thus cut through the nascent alliance between the border States and the cotton States as with a Saladin blade. It was acceptable to the former, repugnant to the latter. Miles Taylor of Louisiana and Warren Winslow of North Carolina, both extremists, announced that if the road was barred against slavery in lands thereafter acquired south of 36° 30′, they would no longer vote in Committee. When the Committee passed the New

Mexican proposal twelve to ten, only one slave State member, F. M. Bristow of Kentucky, voted alongside Adams and Davis for it.

These two adroit leaders could say they had compelled Southerners to admit that they did not want New Mexico as a new State. More than that, they had exposed some Southern members—in full view of the borderland—as willing to break up the Union because the Committee would not guarantee slavery in areas which the nation did not yet possess!

Early January found the Committee of Thirty-three so thin, because of Southern abstentions, that it could hardly keep a quorum. It found the rising excitement North and South powerfully affecting the body. Such Northern radicals as Sumner and Preston King had been painfully fearful that Adams might yield too much. Indeed, Sumner displayed a vindictive temper which made his associates feel that he looked forward to civil war almost with grim complacency. Meanwhile, Southern fire-eaters were equally fearful lest their Representatives concede too much. It is not strange that in the end the Committee wrote a record of too little, too lukewarm, and too late.

The Committee meeting on January 14 presented a remarkable spectacle. With twenty-nine members present (Houston of Alabama had seceded with his State), the body was unwilling to act either for or against the pending set of resolutions. No majority could be found to pass them; no majority could be found for adjournment without a report. Rust of Arkansas wished the Committee to break up without result, but was impotent to bring this about; other members wished to carry certain resolutions, and were equally impotent. Finally, Millson of Virginia offered a resolution directing Chairman Corwin to report the main proposals with his own opinions upon them. When this was carried 16 to 13, the Committee was left without responsibility, yet its chief suggestions were brought before the nation.[38]

In accordance with this resolution, Tom Corwin at once reported to the House, in addition to a series of declaratory resolutions, five specific "propositions." The first, which called for a repeal of personal liberty laws and a faithful execution of the Fugitive Slave Act, was passed by the House on February 27, 1861, by a vote of 137 to 53. The second, a constitutional amendment, providing that the Constitution should never be altered in such a way as to abolish or interfere with the domestic institutions of any State, including slavery, was carried in the House on February 28 by a vote of 133 to 65, and in the Senate on March 2 by 24 to 12. The third proposition, for the immediate

38 See John Sherman's letter in Rachel Sherman Thorndike, ed., *The Sherman Letters*, 92–104; McPherson, *Pol. Hist. Rebellion*, 52–62; *Committee Journal*; Henry Adams, "Secession Winter," Mass. Hist. Soc. Proc., XLIII, 674 ff.; W. C. Ford, ed., *Henry Adams Letters*, 1858–1891; Charles Francis Adams, Jr., *Autobiography*. For a fuller and kindlier view of Sumner, see Laura White's paper in the *W. E. Dodd Essays*.

admission of New Mexico, was defeated 115 to 71, though a number of Republicans, including Charles Francis Adams, Roscoe Conkling, and Eli Thayer, supported it. The fourth, granting to fugitive slaves a jury trial in the State from which they had fled, passed the House alone by the close vote of 92 to 83. Finally, the fifth proposition, to strengthen extradition procedure—an echo of Harper's Ferry—was decisively rejected.

It was the constitutional amendment which was most important; a self-denying amendment, which in theory would forever have chained the country in dealing with slavery inside the States. That it should have received sixty-six Republican and Opposition votes in the House, including those of Adams, Colfax, Corwin, Morrill, and John Sherman, and nine Republican or Opposition votes in the Senate, was a striking fact.

Nevertheless, when Corwin's report was submitted on January 14, Charles Francis Adams struck a pessimistic note. He stated in a separate document his melancholy conviction that no adjustment would suit the recusant States which did not fix in the Constitution an obligation to protect and extend slavery; that on this condition alone would they recognize the constitutional election of Lincoln. "He can never," he wrote, "give his consent to the terms demanded." [39] Six other minority reports were submitted. Inasmuch as, at the end, a considerable number of cotton kingdom members had systematically absented themselves from the Committee, the so-called majority report really emanated from a minority. Chairman Corwin was as bleakly discouraged as Adams. Ten days after the document went in, he wrote Lincoln that his month of toil had been a sad revelation.

"If the States are no more harmonious in their feelings and opinions than these thirty-three representative men," he wrote,[40] "then, appalling as the idea is, we must dissolve, and a long and bloody war must follow. I cannot comprehend the madness of the times. Southern men are theoretically crazy. Extreme Northern men are practical fools. The latter are really quite as mad as the former. Treason is in the air around us everywhere. . . . God alone, I fear, can help us."

But if these men were gloomily certain that the cotton kingdom could not be halted, they and Seward rejoiced that the borderland yet stood loyal, and hoped that with its aid the Union could yet be restored.

[VII]

It was the border States which, torn in sentiment and fearful of becoming a battleground, watched the drift toward disruption and war with the most

39 McPherson, *Pol. Hist. Rebellion*, 57.
40 Robert Todd Lincoln Papers.

harrowing anxiety. The Old Dominion, so long the leader in the American sisterhood and so prolific of great men, felt a commingled sorrow and fear of the liveliest character. Governor John Letcher ably expressed this emotion in his message of January 7 to the legislature. He declared it "monstrous to see a government like ours destroyed, merely because men cannot agree about a domestic institution, which existed at the formation of the government." Bitterly rebuking the governors of Mississippi and South Carolina for their disunionist proposals, and sternly indicting the North for its intolerant agitation, he proposed a national Peace Conference. The legislators, attached alike to the South and the Union, immediately took up the subject. On January 19, they invited all the States to send delegates to a convention which should meet in Washington on February 4, and whose members, with the Crittenden Compromise as a basis for discussion, should strive earnestly to adjust the unhappy controversy.

Thus was born the last sad effort to avert war. The gathering opened on the appointed date with a highly distinguished but somewhat superannuated roster of delegates.[41] John Tyler, who presided, David Wilmot, William C. Rives, Caleb B. Smith, Stephen T. Logan, and Thomas Ewing, with a number of others, belonged too plainly to the past. The New York *Herald* remarked that many of them were political fossils who would not have been disinterred but for the shock given the country by the crisis. They began by excluding reporters, which was wise, for the speechmaking was diffuse and aimless. The seven States of the Lower South, with Arkansas, boycotted the gathering; they were busy forming their Confederacy, and they thought compromise a game to hoodwink the border area. Michigan, Wisconsin, and Minnesota, with the two Pacific Coast States, were also unrepresented. This left twenty-one States with delegates. Republican radicals scoffed at the "venerable" conclave and predicted its total failure. According to John Bigelow, some of these radicals had a double object in their opposition: to prevent the adoption of anything like the Crittenden Compromise, and to keep Seward out of the Cabinet by discrediting the compromise idea.

A revealing incident illustrated the attitude of Northern extremists toward this gathering. The Michigan Senators were at first opposed to the participation of their State in the Conference; but both of them, on February 9, telegraphed the governor to send delegates. They did this on the ground that moderate members of the assemblage seemed likely to gain the day, and that more obstructionists were needed. "I hope you will send *stiff-backed* men or none," Zack Chandler wrote the governor on the eleventh, callously adding

41 For the Proceedings of the Peace Convention see L. E. Chittenden, ed., *Report of the Peace Convention.*

that he had no patience with those who were afraid of civil strife: "Without a little bloodletting, this Union will not, in my estimation, be worth a rush." This cynical letter Jefferson Davis was later to reprint in his memoirs—forgetting how many fiery Southerners were speaking in similar terms.

The dark prophecies of failure, although Rives, Reverdy Johnson, and former Secretary of the Treasury James Guthrie made strenuous exertions, were in the end fully realized. Such radicals as J. A. Seddon of Virginia, David Wilmot of Pennsylvania, and Lot M. Morrill of Maine did their utmost to obstruct the gathering. It was in vain that Rives made an eloquent appeal. "Virginia steps in to arrest the progress of the country on its road to ruin," he said. "I have seen the pavements of Paris covered . . . with fraternal blood! God forbid that I should see this horrid picture repeated in my own country. . . ." Ex-President Tyler told the delegates that they had a task as grand as that of the godlike fathers. "If you reach the height of this great occasion, your children's children will rise up and call you blessed." But it was all too late. The absence of thirteen States was too great a handicap; the fact that the convention possessed nothing but a thin moral authority was too evident; and the clash of radicals from each side was too savage. In the last days of the Buchanan Administration, the Conference agreed to resolutions resembling the abortive Crittenden plan. When they were laid before a Senate committee, that body rejected them 28 to 7,[42] while the House on March 1 refused to suspend its rules in order to consider them.

Virginia was the mother of the Peace Conference. Yet in the final House discussions five Virginia Congressmen opposed the plan it offered, and only three gave it support. It was an ironic fact that the failure of the gathering lent added strength to secession in Virginia.

All along the line, in the Senate, the House, and in Tyler's conclave of minor statesmen, efforts at compromise had proved futile. Had a Constitutional Convention, with the very ablest leaders of the nation in charge, been convoked at an early date, it is barely possible that the story might have been different. As matters stood, lovers of the Union could comfort themselves in February, 1861, with only one major consideration—the fact that although seven slaveholding States were leaving in anger, eight remained. In Virginia, Tennessee, Arkansas, Missouri, and North Carolina, the secessionist forces had thus far met repulse. The boasted Southern Confederacy was as yet but a fragment of the South. This fact gave encouragement to those who believed that the Union might yet be peaceably reconstructed on a sounder basis. Even in the cotton kingdom, this belief was still cherished by many. Jefferson Davis has recorded that a considerable number of men as late as February held the

42 The Senate action is in *Cong. Globe*, 36th Cong. 2d Sess., 1254, 1255.

hope, which he pronounced not unreasonable, that by the offer of suitable guarantees the North would make possible a reunited nation. Seward, a firm believer in voluntary reconstruction, looked at the matter a little differently. Young Henry Adams found him early in February in high spirits, chuckling himself hoarse with his stories. "He says it's all right. We shall keep the border States, and in three months or thereabouts, if we hold off, the Unionists and Disunionists will have their hands on each other's throats in the cotton States."

The realities, reflected in the drill of volunteer companies North and South, were far darker than these views indicated. Later generations find it hard to believe that many Southerners, like Judah P. Benjamin, thought that the North might actually agree to reconstruct the Union with the New England States thrust into outer darkness. They find it hard to believe that many Northerners, including Lincoln and Seward, indulged the fantasy that Southern Unionists might actually overpower by force of arms the Southern secessionists. It is depressing to recall with what continued levity many men spoke of civil war. The New York *Tribune*, on February 21, declared that if conflict came: "It would only be necessary for the Government of the North to concentrate at New York a small fleet of seagoing steamers and an army of 20,000 to 30,000 men to hold the entire South in perpetual check." Edmund Ruffin had written in the Richmond *Index* of January 13 that there was "not the slightest danger of war from the Northern States," for they could not win such a contest "without the sacrifice of fifty thousand lives of the Northern invaders, and one hundred million of dollars." From such fantastic misconceptions of the situation, self-deluded men in both great sections were to have a swift and harsh awakening.

14

The Rival Republic

WHILE COMPROMISE was grinding to a standstill, the dramatic process of creating a new Southern republic was attracting general attention. It might be viewed with all the eager hope of Yancey or Toombs, with the amused cynicism of W. H. Russell, the British correspondent who travelled to Montgomery to witness its birth, or the scornful hostility of Sumner, Wade, and countless other Northerners. But that it was an event of the first magnitude, none could doubt. It was necessarily built upon the completion of secession in the Lower South.

[I]

Mid-January found Milledgeville, on the Oconee River in central Georgia, filling up with delegates for the State convention. The eyes of most Southerners were fixed on the gathering, for the adherence of Georgia was essential to sectional unity. Jacob Thompson was writing Howell Cobb: "I have all along felt that as goes Georgia, so goes the whole South." The little town, with its capital, its cluster of four substantial churches, and its handsome residences, for it was much liked by wealthy Georgians, was soon crammed to bursting. One visitor, secretly a correspondent for the New York *Tribune*, found himself in such an incessant jostle that he dared take no written notes. On Tuesday the fifteenth, the two camps, the separate secessionists and cooperative secessionists, held caucuses and anxiously counted noses. During the next two days, crowded galleries watched the convention elect officers, give the South Carolina and Alabama commissioners a hearing, and do other preliminary work. Then a seal of secrecy was clapped on the session. Nothing could be picked up, grumbled newspapermen, but a few crumbs moistened by the prevailing whiskey.[1]

The tide of popular feeing in Georgia had been setting steadily toward an early abandonment of the Union. Alexander H. Stephens had written at the

1 N. Y. *Weekly Tribune*, February 2, 1861.

close of November that while large numbers would sustain his conservative position, the odds were against them. It was all too true, he thought, that most leading Georgians did not wish to remain on any terms. "They do not wish any redress of wrongs; they are disunionists *per se*, and avail themselves of present circumstances to press their objects; and my present conviction is that they will carry the State with them by a large majority." He kept reiterating these despondent statements.[2] Howell Cobb's long argument for secession issued simultaneously with his resignation had much effect; so did Toombs's public letter in the Savannah *Republican* of December 17, and his admonition to Georgians just before Christmas to thunder secession from the ballot box. The two men differed on one point, Cobb wishing secession immediately and Toombs preferring it on March 4; but on the need for a severance they stood together.

The election of delegates on January 2, held as a terrible storm smote Georgia, apparently resulted in a decisive victory for the separate secessionists. Only about two-thirds of the voters went to the polls and their verdict was roughly four to three for immediate action. Stephens, who struggled through the storm to vote and make a speech, believed that the weather had cost his side ten thousand ballots, for it favored the town dwellers and planters who had the best means of getting to the polls. "It really appears as if Providence was on the other side," he ejaculated.[3] As he prepared to leave for the convention, he wrote his brother that he had known for weeks that secession was certain, for the currents of the day were irresistible.

Yet the convention battle between the advocates of immediate and of postponed secession proved closer than had been anticipated. The gathering was one of remarkable ability. The radical leaders included Toombs, T. R. R. Cobb, and Francis S. Bartow, along with Governor Joseph E. Brown and Howell Cobb, who were invited to seats on the floor; the cooperationist leaders were Stephens, his brother Linton, Benjamin H. Hill, and Herschel V. Johnson. The latter group were handicapped by the lack of any preconcerted plan of action, by an old enmity between Stephens and Hill, and by the defeatist temper of Stephens. When the ordinance of secession was offered, Hill offered a substitute plan which Johnson had hurriedly drawn up. This series of resolutions declared the South in danger, proposed a convention of slaveholding

---

2 Cleveland, *Stephen*, 159, 160; Johnston and Browne, *Stephens*, 369 ff.

3 Johnston and Browne, *op. cit.*, 378, 379. Election figures vary; one set is 50,243 for immediate-action delegates and 37,123 for cooperationists. Pendleton, *Stephens*, 178. It should be noted that group attitudes were complex. The cooperationists included (1) those who wanted immediate secession but only by united State action; (2) those who wished to attempt compromise, and secede only when that failed; (3) those who desired to await an overt act of aggression by Lincoln before seceding; and (4) strict Unionists playing for delay. For a full elucidation see Dumond, *Secession Movement*, 113 ff.

States at Atlanta the next month, suggested some needed amendments to the Constitution, and deferred Georgia's decision until the North could be given an opportunity to reply. The substitute was lost 164 to 133. A change of but sixteen votes in the total of two hundred and ninety-seven would have reversed the result. Hill and others then joined in passing the secession ordinance 208 to 89, and all but half a dozen delegates signed it.[4]

Analysis of the vote showed that, like other Southern States, Georgia divided largely on economic and regional lines. The radical secessionists came from the Savannah River valley, the seacoast, and the tier of counties behind it, extending into southwest Georgia. Here dwelt most of the wealthy planters and large slaveholders. The townspeople, whether in Savannah, Augusta, Columbus, Macon, or Atlanta, were predominantly sympathetic with the planting interest. They included the merchants and factors who handled cotton and merchandise, the professional men who sprang largely from the planter class, and many retired or absentee landholders. It was noteworthy that all fifteen of the delegates from these five cities were immediate secessionists. On the conservative side, the great strongholds were, as we have noted, the pine barrens and the northern hill country. Here lived a population of small farmers, stockmen, and others with a pioneering tradition, whose immediate forebears had conquered the wilderness and fought the Indians. They liked the Union; their instinct was for the doctrines of Jackson, not Calhoun; they had little direct interest in slavery; and their concern for a peculiar Southern culture was slighter still. While exceptions to these generalizations were numerous, the convention decision was broadly a victory of plantation and town over the small farmer.[5]

When secession was announced, Milledgeville sprang into a spasm of illuminations, bonfires, Roman candles, cannon salutes, and speechmaking. Yet many were heavy-hearted. "I never felt so sad before," Herschel Johnson later wrote. "The clustering glories of the past thronged my memory, but they were darkened by the gathering gloom of the lowering future."[6] Georgia's action was widely regarded as decisive for the whole Lower South. With her great production of cotton, wheat, corn, and rice, her flourishing seaport of Savannah, her textile factories, her key railroad system, and her energetic population, the State was vital to a new republic. The step was described then

4 A. D. Candler, ed., *Confed. Records of Ga.*, I, 213 ff.; I. W. Avery, *Hist. Ga.*, 149 ff.; Hill, *Joseph E. Brown*, 44, 45; Pearce, *B. H. Hill*, 49–53.

5 A. J. Cole, "Sentiment in Ga. Toward Secession, 1850–61," MS, Univ. of Ill.

6 Flippin, *Johnson*, 192. Johnson always thought that "a fair and energetic canvass" would have shown a large majority of Georgians against secession; he always believed that ambitious Southern leaders wanted disunion as a means of establishing their personal power. *Idem.* 168–170.

and thereafter as one that electrified the cotton kingdom and determined the revolution; and while this is an overstatement, it is certain that it cleared up a great area of doubt and hesitation.

The Lower South was now swiftly completing its withdrawal from the Union. Already, on January 9, the Mississippi convention, sitting at Jackson, had passed its secession ordinance 84 to 15. On the tenth, Florida had followed, 62 to 7. On the eleventh the Alabama convention, its temper fired by Yancey, the Patrick Henry of the new cause, had decided upon withdrawal by a vote of 61 to 39. The Louisiana convention passed its secession ordinance on January 26 by a vote of 113 to 17, and on February 1 Texas took the same step, 166 to 8. Seven States were not as many as Ruffin and Yancey had hoped for, but they were regarded as sufficient for a viable new confederation.

[II]

On their face, the heavy convention majorities for secession seemed to point to an overwhelming disunionist strength. Actually, however, in every State the division of opinion ran deep, the forces opposing immediate secession were formidable, and, while the question defies settlement, perhaps a majority of citizens were Union men in the sense that they opposed secession altogether, or wished it deferred until other remedies had been exhausted, or hoped for a reconstruction of the nation on better terms within a few years. Certainly in the fifteen slave States taken as a whole, a heavy majority were against a permanent severance of ties. The apparently crushing victory of the immediate secessionists in the Lower South was accomplished by skillful use of the advantages before enumerated; their driving energy, superior organization, success in making action so rapid that the opposition could not mobilize, effective use of shibboleths and epithets, and capitalization on the demand for moral unity. They were aided in some States by favorable apportionment systems, and in nearly all by the excessive influence wielded by the planting class and its various allies.[7]

Public opinion in every such crisis necessarily moves like a great pendulum, gathering momentum. It was inevitable that the bright vision of a Southern republic should catch the imagination of multitudes of men and women. The spirit of nationalism, with its heady, volatile appeals—to traditionalism, to ancestral reverence, to folklore, to pieties of hearth and home, to the ideal of sacrifice—and its demand that the individual lose himself in a mass solidarity,

7 On this insoluble problem of the real sentiment of Southerners toward secession, see Potter, *Lincoln and Secession Crisis*, 208 ff.; Rhodes, *United States*, III, 273 ff.; Dumond, *Secession Movement*, Ch. X.

had already made impressive progress. As volunteer companies marched to the "Southern Marseillaise," as crowds began singing "The Bonnie Blue Flag," as slogans of freedom and justice ran through the press, a kindling sense of sectional patriotism swung even the dubious from their old allegiances. To join the new movement seemed (especially to youth) an affirmative, progressive, heroic act; to resist it seemed negative and timid. Every day, militancy grew. And as one step after another was taken, more doubters yielded to State loyalty, and to their feeling that the hard-pressed Southern people must at all hazards stand together.

All the standard agencies for moulding opinion were brought to bear upon conservatives. In Mississippi, for example, the Jackson *Mississippian*, Vicksburg *Sun*, and Natchez *Free Trader*, with other newspapers, spoke of moderation as a policy of imbecility, of delay as abject submission, and of Union men as enemies of the South. Many churches throughout the cotton kingdom preached resistance. The Thanksgiving sermons of the Rev. B. M. Palmer, head of the largest Presbyterian church in New Orleans, and the Rev. W. T. Leacock, his Episcopal colleague, two stirring exhortations to secession which were scattered broadcast in pamphlet form, were long remembered. "I warn my countrymen the historic moment once passed never returns," rumbled Palmer. "Sapped, circumvented, undermined, the institutions of your soil will be overthrown; and within five and twenty years the history of San Domingo will be the record of Louisiana." [8] The official journal of the powerful Baptist denomination in Mississippi urged citizens to insist upon their full rights within the old nation, or win them outside in a new.[9]

Plangent effects were produced by a steady reiteration of inflammatory news items from Washington and other centers. The Congressional leaders of secession had long been in close touch with the Washington correspondents of Southern newspapers, and many of the fire-eaters knew the art of manufacturing and coloring press intelligence. Many Southern editors, for their part, made a one-sided selection of the news. "Every morning for the past three or four weeks," complained A. H. Arthur of Vicksburg on January 10 to Joseph Holt,

8 The two sermons were printed together in "The Rights of the South Defended in the Pulpits," and were notable for their violent tone. Palmer declared that it was the South's duty under God "to conserve and perpetuate the institution of domestic slavery as now existing," and that "the abolition spirit is undeniably atheistic." Leacock was even fierier. Who could hesitate, he asked, "when we consider the treatment we have received from the hands of our enemies; our character they have defamed; our feelings they have lacerated; our rights they have invaded; our property they have stolen; our power they have defied; our existence they have threatened? Murderers and robbers have been let loose upon us, stimulated by weak or designing or infidel preachers, armed by fanatics, and sustaind by a band of assassins out of the very wealth which they have accumulated by their connection with us."

9 *Mississippi Baptist*, cited in Rainwater, *Mississippi*, 173, 174.

"we have been inundated with fresh dispatches from your region to keep up the courage of the leaders at home, and still further inflame the public mind." A week later another of Holt's correspondents, J. O. Harrison of New Orleans, wrote that the South was flooded with dispatches describing the unjust and coercive policy of the government. Censorship and intimidation meanwhile suppressed much news favorable to the cause of compromise and the Union. One Southerner after another, hearing indirectly of Andrew Johnson's great Union speech but unable to find any of it in the press, wrote him for copies, and spoke bitterly of the suppression of facts and opinion.

The companies of minute men, too, placing graybeards alongside striplings, were active propagandist agencies. State flags and badges helped win the wavering. When in Eufaula, Alabama, an enthusiastic lady flung from her window a banner of fifteen stars and fifteen stripes, the Eufaula Rifles promptly paraded and fired a fifteen-volley salute.[10] Such incidents were incessant and they had a cumulative effect.

In some areas, the secessionists frankly capitalized upon the illiteracy or apathy of the many voters who, as Helper and others had noted, knew all too little of public measures. In South Carolina, one radical exulted that ignorance played into the hands of his party. Secession had to be achieved by a select minority, he wrote. "I do not believe that the common people understand it; in fact I know that they do not understand it. . . . We must make the move and force them to follow."[11] The use of threats was not infrequent. Senator Iverson set a bad example when he suggested that the loyal Sam Houston was a Caesar who might yet find his Brutus. A Georgia secessionist, speaking of such men as the Stephens brothers, growled: "When the State goes out and we are on our own hook, those fellows will have to walk straight and keep quiet." The Savannah correspondent of the New York *Tribune* wrote in December that conservatives did not dare express their views with any force and warmth. A wealthy planter had confessed that he would be ejected from the State if he spoke his mind. "For," he said, "when a man once falls under the hand of the mob, though they only threaten him today, they will doubtless return tomorrow and burn his property, and the next day they will bring a rope with them."[12]

The extremists have taken our positions by storm, lamented one conservative of the Lower South. Nevertheless, Stephens was unjust in asserting that the people had run mad, and were "wild with passion and frenzy, doing they know not what."[13] The number who struggled to the last for delay, or yielded

10 Denman, *Secession in Alabama*, 89.
11 A. P. Aldrich, November 25, 1860; Hammond Papers.
12 *Weekly Tribune*, January 19, 1861.
13 Johnston and Browne, *Stephens*, 369, 370.

in the hope that the Union could yet be rebuilt, was formidable. Just how equivocal the character of the decision really was in some States will become evident from a brief examination of the secession struggle.

[III]

Although the Louisiana convention voted more than six to one for immediate departure, the true will of the people must always remain in doubt, for this result was attained by highly undemocratic means. The State had obvious reasons for exhibiting caution. It was closely linked with the Northwest by the commerce rolling up and down the Mississippi. Through the port of New Orleans passed every year a hundred million dollars' worth of cotton, and sixty-five millions in corn, wheat, pork, and other products; while importers distributed merchandise of all kinds through the upper valley. Enjoying an unprecedented prosperity, Louisiana feared that she would be separated from her rich Northern connections, and that a new nation built on slavery would foster the commerce of Norfolk, Charleston, and Savannah at her expense. Just after the election, Douglas, visiting New Orleans, spread a long letter in the press. Regrettable as Lincoln's election was, he wrote, it had been gained by constitutional means and offered no ground for secession; while the Democratic majority in both houses and the Democratic control of the Supreme Court rendered the new President powerless for evil, even if he had the disposition. This letter had attentive readers. A prominent citizen wrote that he believed that ninety-nine in a hundred people sincerely hoped for some adjustment to end the national dissension.[14]

The widespread notion that Louisiana was exclusively a land of opulent sugar and cotton plantations was a myth. More than two-thirds of the free population owned no slaves; three out of five agricultural holdings were farms; almost a third of all the cultivated land was tilled in units of less than a hundred acres.[15] Our best evidence is that the slavery system was economically injurious to a majority of the population. "Farmers were actually hurt by slavery and the plantation economy, which gradually deprived them of all opportunity to acquire Negroes and fertile land, or to participate on a large scale in the production of profitable staples."[16] The State had cast a much larger vote for the Bell and Douglas tickets combined than for Breckinridge.[17]

Yet the secessionists, directed by Slidell and his creature Governor Moore,

14 Quoted in *Ann. Cyc.*, 1861, p. 428.
15 *U. S. Census, 1860, Agriculture*, 202 ff.
16 Shugg, *Origins of Class Struggle in La.*, 78, 79; but F. L. Owsley and others dissent.
17 The figures were Breckenridge, 22,687; Bell 20,205; Douglas 7,625.

managed to carry everything before them. They did everything possible to stimulate disunionist sentiment. When South Carolina went out, they fired a hundred guns in New Orleans and displayed the pelican flag. Moore quickly summoned the legislature, dominated by the planter oligarchy and its allies of the New Orleans machine. Seats in this body were apportioned on the basis of total population, including slaves, so that the black belt of rich alluvial land and big plantations held a clear majority, while the white belt, with two-thirds of the free population, was in a minority. The system was one in which property, rather than white people, ruled the State.[18] On December 11, the legislators called for a State convention to be elected less than four weeks later, on January 7. Although the constitution stipulated that a referendum be held on the question of any such convention, this requirement was ignored; for the times, said the radicals, were too revolutionary.

Fraud was an old story in Louisiana elections, and this one seemed no better than others. To the last, the conservatives had hoped to carry the twenty-five delegates of New Orleans. Instead, it was announced that the city had gone for the immediate secessionists by a plurality of three hundred and eighty in a total vote of eight thousand three hundred and thirty-six—about half of the registration; while the whole State had elected eighty-three immediate secessionists against forty-seven cooperationists. Rumors sprang up that the cooperationists had really carried Louisiana by about three hundred votes. When the *Picayune*, which held that the separate secession of one State was a species of dictation to her Southern sisters, insistently demanded publication of the official returns, they were kept suppressed. Not until more than three months had passed and the whole subject had become academic, was the New Orleans *Delta* allowed to publish a tabulation of parish votes, and this was in a form which aroused suspicion of manipulation.[19]

The convention, meeting just after Governor Moore had seized the national forts and arsenals on his own authority, was as much under the sway of the planter oligarchy as the legislature; and it acted in what the historian Gayarré called a spirit of "sublime imprudence."[20] An effort to refer secession to a general Southern convention was defeated 73 to 47. An attempt to obtain a

18 For full treatment of representation, see Shugg, *Class Struggle*, 139 ff. The MS Diary of Alexander F. Pugh (Univ. of Texas Library) gives a good picture of the secessionist sentiment of one wealthy Louisiana planter. He thought that to ask cooperation was "humiliating;" January 9, 1861. The Liddell Papers, La. Univ. Library, contain letters showing how leaders of the planting interest worked for concert of action, and how confident they were that a few men could take control.

19 *Picayune*, January 8, et seq.; Shugg, *Class Struggle*, 162 ff. The city vote was given as 4,358 to 3,978; the State vote as 20,448 to 17,296. The N. O. *Picayune* had anticipated fraud. It stated on November 6 that the radical leaders were thoroughly ruthless, and frequently repeated this warning.

20 *Hist. La.*, IV, 692.

plebiscite on the secession ordinance was then voted down 84 to 43,[21] The majority displayed a joyous insouciance which depressed such of its own members as Richard Taylor.[22] A scrutiny of the convention vote and of the parish returns shows that, although no class voted as a unit, the wealthier slaveholding parishes were strongest for immediate action, while the small farmers elected most of the cooperationists. In Louisiana, as in South Carolina, the long-established domination of a planting and commercial aristocracy had made it easy to take the State out of the Union; not as part of a conspiracy, but by the use of powers always exercised when the economic, social, and political philosophy of the ruling group was imperilled.[23]

In Alabama we encounter a different pattern, and the victory of the immediate secessionists was more fairly won; yet the result was exceedingly close. North Alabama took a firm stand for delay, and won supporters in other areas. Had it not been for unexpected reverses in Mobile and Autauga Counties, the cooperationists would actually have gained control of the State convention. The outcome in Mobile was particularly remarkable. Although that county had given both Douglas and Bell much larger votes than Breckinridge, immediate secession gained the day nearly two to one. In this State, as in Louisiana, the vote for convention delegates was only seventy or seventy-five percent that given in the recent presidential election. A good deal of confusion enveloped the precise stand taken by some candidates, and the returns are not complete; but the radicals seem to have polled about 35,700 votes to the conservatives' 28,200, and the delegates stood fifty-four for immediate secession, forty-six for cooperative action. On the theory that conservative men were more likely to stay at home than the radicals, a full vote might have given them the victory.[24]

And the convention battle proved sternly exciting. Ex-Senator Jeremiah Clemens helped lead the cooperationist minority.[25] It showed such a stubborn

21 The *Picayune* had insistently asked for a referendum, but the *Delta* and *Crescent* replied that in such a crisis questions of form sank into insignificance.

22 Taylor, *Destruction and Reconstruction*, 13. Yet the *Picayune* had steadily warned of impending agony. It had said as early as November 4: "If the fires of civil war be kindled—and kindled they must be by any formidable movement in hostility to the Federal Government—they will burn until all is consumed that is perishable, and the land becomes a waste over which shall brood the silence of another and hopeless desolation."

23 Cf. Shugg, *Class Struggle*, 169.

24 It is roughly fair to say that of the fifty-two counties represented in the convention, twenty-nine were for immediate secession, twenty-three for some type of delay. The Montgomery *Weekly Post* of January 9, 1861, accused Governor Moore of taking high-handed steps, including seizure of the national forts, suspension of specie payments, and sending of commissioners to other States, in order to hurry Alabama into secession.

25 The cooperationists, discovering they were only eight fewer than the immediate secessionists, issued a public statement that Yancey could save the State for the Union by a wave of his hand; but of course Yancey's intention was just the opposite. On the first day, he and a longtime opponent, Thomas H. Watts, walked to the platform arm in arm, a token of unity against Northern "oppression." See G. M. Wrenn, "Ala. and the Formation of the Confederacy," Univ. of Texas Library.

spirit that Yancey, losing his temper, declared that any resistance to an ordinance of secession would be treason to the State. Nicholas J. Davis of Hunts-

VOTES FOR DELEGATES TO THE SECESSION CONVENTION

For separate state secessionists	For coöperationists
50-60%	50-60%
60-70%	60-70%
70-80%	70-80%
80-90%	80-90%
90-100%	90-100%

Cherokee County divided—three delegates for coöperation and one for separate state secession. No returns available for Lawrence County other than that a coöperationist delegate was elected.

Opinion in Alabama

ville, a Douglas man, instantly defied him. His constituents, he said, denied the sovereignty of the convention because of the way in which it had been called; they would sustain it only if it reflected the popular will, and the way to ascertain that was to hold a plebiscite on secession. He and his people were ready to meet Yancey at the foot of their mountains and settle this question of treason with the bayonet. In the end, the effort to refer secession to a general Southern convention to be held at Nashville on Washington's Birthday and the effort to gain a popular referendum on the subject were both voted down. But a change of a mere half dozen votes would have defeated the immediate secessionists in Yancey's own State.[26]

Moreover, the Alabama decision left great bitterness in its wake. No fewer than thirty-three delegates out of the hundred refused to sign the ordinance of secession on the ground that the State had not been allowed to consult her sisters before acting, and that the measure had not been submitted to the people for ratification. One county burned Yancey in effigy.[27] "In South Carolina the people have very little to do in politics but choose their own masters," angrily exploded Thomas M. Peters of Moulton, Alabama, in a letter of January 15 to Andrew Johnson. "And outside of South Carolina in the Cotton States politicians are trying the experiment of getting along without the people. Thus far they have succeeded. But in the end, unless we resort to a military government, there will be a revulsion, and as the Negro is the sole cause of our present troubles, the fury of the non-slaveholders will be turned on him and his masters; and we will have another tragedy of Actaeon and his dogs."

In Florida and Mississippi, by contrast, large secessionist majorities were obtained. The leading figures in Florida affairs were Senator Yulee, wealthy planter and railroad promoter, and Governor Perry, both warm secessionists. The State had been easily carried by Breckinridge. Immediately on Lincoln's election, nearly all the Democratic newspapers called for the disruption of the Union and the formation of a Southern Confederacy. When the legislature met, Perry appealed for separation from the faithless, perjured States of the North, and a convention bill passed both houses unanimously. One old Jacksonian, General Richard K. Call, opposed hasty action and distributed in pamphlet form a passionate address to the State, pleading with the people to await an overt act of wrong. The convention, however, sitting at Tallahassee, voted down a series of amendments which were designed merely to keep Florida waiting until the action of Georgia and Alabama was certain, and then formally seceded.

26 W. R. Smith, *Hist. and Debates of the Ala. Convention, passim.*
27 Hugh Lawson Clay of Huntsville had written C. C. Clay on January 11 that northern Alabama was ready to revolt. A meeting there had instructed the delegates to leave the convention if secession was not submitted to popular vote; one leader had made a violent speech, denouncing secession, assailing Governor Moore, and saying he "would have his neck stretched three feet and spend his money to the last dollar before he would consent to the dismemberment of the Union." Clay felt certain that "there will be a successful attempt made to excite the people of N. Alabama to rebellion vs. the State and that we will have civil war in our midst." Clay Papers, Duke Univ. Library. Cf. W. R. Smith, *Hist. and Debates,* 445–447; Denman, *Secession in Ala.,* 149.

According to the St. Augustine *Examiner*, which had recently been moderate, a large majority of the State held that "our grievances are not longer to be tolerated." [28]

In Mississippi also, most leaders were radical in outlook. "The Union is dead and in process of mortification," declared A. G. Brown, "and nothing now remains but to bury the rotten carcass." [29] Only three weeks were allowed in that State for the pre-convention campaign, and many voters learned so little of the issues that, feeling totally confused, they stayed away from the polls. The vote was only about sixty percent of that in the presidential election. About three-fourths of the delegates were immediate secessionists, motions for a special plebiscite and for cooperative action being defeated 74 to 25, and 70 to 29.[30] The gathering, which then voted secession by nearly six to one, was apparently a true reflection of the people: "Entirely representative of the social, economic, and political life of the State," concludes one student. At least three-fifths of the members belonged not to the class of rich planters, but to that of farmers, shopkeepers, and professional men, holding few slaves. In this State even more than in others, the cooperationists were not against secession if other means failed but hoped for an attempt to exhaust these means; they wanted time, as one member said, "for deliberation while we stood on the brink of the abyss."

Some Mississippians, nevertheless, realizing that disunion meant almost certain war, regarded any step on that road with dark foreboding. Two opposing members ventured into prophecy. The able planter-lawyer, James L. Alcorn, recalled many years later: "Judge J. S. Yerger was especially eloquent in picturing the workings of Conscription (which would of necessity be resorted to) upon the non-slaveholding classes of the South. I undertook to give a picture of the South when the Northern soldier would tread her cotton fields; when the slave would be free and the proud Southerner struck to the dust in his presence." [31]

In Texas, behind an outwardly overwhelming decision for immediate separation, we again meet factors which create grave doubt as to the real will of the people. Then, as later, the spirit of Texan life was more largely Western than

28 D. Dodd, "Secession Movt. in Fla., 1850–1861," Pt. II, in *Fla. Hist. Quarterly*, XII, October, 1933; C. M. Brevard, *Florida*, II. Call, who had been territorial governor, published an able letter in the Tallahassee *Sentinel* of December 22, 1860, and tried to hold public meetings.
29 Speech at Jackson in late November; Rainwater, *Mississippi*, 173.
30 *Journal of the State Conv.* (1861), pp. 9, 10.
31 Quoted by Rainwater, *Mississippi*, 213. This author's analysis of economic, geographic, and social factors is illuminating. He finds that many solid, conservative men of property, who had moved from the Whig into the Opposition Party, were against separate secession. The aggressive cutting edge of the secession movement was furnished by the petty planters, the lawyer-politicians, and the country editors, men still on the make. We shall later see a somewhat similar situation in another semi-frontier State, Arkansas.

Southern. The population comprehended a large German element, numerous traders and mechanics from the North, and a heavy sprinkling of stockmen, farmers, and planters of free-State origin. Everyone knew that Texas specially depended for her growth upon Northern capital, immigration from Europe and the North, and Northern mercantile credit. The six hundred and two thousand four hundred and thirty-two people registered by the census this year included the rather modest number of one hundred eighty thousand six hundred and eighty-two slaves. While Lincoln's election was at once followed by an outcry for dissolution of the Union, large moderate groups urged Texans to stand beside the border States in a conservative position. They pointed to the Federal moneys spent to win Texas, to the Federal troops guarding the Indian and Mexican frontiers, and to the millions which the Treasury annually paid Texas stockgrowers and farmers in maintaining defense and communications. The weekly *Alamo Express* of San Antonio predicted "untold evils" from secession, and it was abetted in its stand by the Dallas *Herald*, the Austin *Southern Intelligencer*, the San Antonio *Ledger* and *Herald*, the *Northern Standard*, and the German press.[32]

At the head of the opposition to immediate secession stood the rugged governor, Sam Houston, who for some stormy weeks withstood the demand for a special session of the legislature. When he yielded and called one to meet January 21, it was in terms indicating his desire to delay separate State action as long as possible. His utterances were outspoken. "You may," he said, "after the sacrifice of countless thousands of treasure and hundreds of thousands of precious lives, as a bare possibility, win Southern independence, if God be not against you; but I doubt it." [33] At the outset, the influential John H. Reagan was for cooperative secession, proposing that all the slaveholding States meet in convention, that they submit certain demands (including guarantees of equal Southern participation in the settlement of the common territory) to the free States, and that if these were denied (which he did not expect), they should then secede in a body. Just before Christmas, however, he wrote a public letter announcing that he had reached the conclusion that the North would never give adequate guarantees, and that his chief hope now was for a peaceable separation.[34] Not a few Texans thought of reestablishing a Lone Star republic; and certain of Houston's utterances squinted in that direction. Unlike some other States, he wrote the Alabama commissioner, Texas feels a spirit of imperial expansion, and expects to carry her institutions westward and southward.[35]

32 John H. Reagan also lists the Harrison *Flag*, Quitman *Clipper*, and McKinney *Messenger* among "submission sheets;" letter in *Texas Republican*, January 12, 1861. C. W. Ramsdell's brief treatment of secession in *Reconstruction in Texas* is excellent.
33 Marquis James, *Houston*, 409, 410.
34 December 23, 1860, to O. M. Roberts, et al., in Texas *Republican*.
35 January 7, 1861, to J. M. Calhoun; Smith, *Hist. and Debates*, 425 ff.

Ignoring Houston, many radical leaders had signed a call for a convention to meet in Austin on January 28. At once a violent campaign began. "The whole State was in a blaze of excitement," writes one Union observer. "Arbitrary arrests, broils, murder and hanging were the order of the day, and under the pressure large numbers of Union men were giving way, and the secessionists were receiving daily accessions to their strength. The people were either deceived into secession, led into it, or forced into it." [36] The Knights of the Golden Circle, whose active organizer Bickley was now a resident of Texas, played some small role, later much exaggerated, in the movement.[37] Moral intimidation was probably much more freely used than physical. One important citizen, William Pitt Ballinger, who feared that secession was a fatal step, found himself "excommunicated" from public affairs and shunned by old friends. "Thomas Harrison wrote me that the children of those not in the front of the present secessionists would be ashamed of their fathers," he records in his diary. "I am willing to bide the test of time on that subject." [38]

Because of the irregularity of the convention call, the vote for delegates was very light; in many well-settled counties only a third or fourth of the voters went to the polls. Nearly half of the one hundred twenty-two counties held no election and sent no delegates to the convention. The passage of the ordinance of secession, one hundred sixty-six to seven, was obviously no index of public sentiment whatever; and realizing this, the convention submitted the measure to the voters. The election was held February 23, when six other States were already out. Little over two weeks were allowed for the campaign. Pressure upon the conservatives was at once redoubled. Vigilance committees sprang up in various towns. In Waco, one such body proclaimed its intention to hang every "Lincolnite" who did not stop talking, and warned leading conservatives to shut up or leave town. Numerous Union men, we are told, left the State.[39]

On election day, eighty counties gave a vote of thirty-four thousand seven hundred and ninety-four for secession and eleven thousand two hundred and fifty-five against. Charges of fraud and unfair dealing at once came from all parts of the State. The machinery of election was in the hands of the secession-

36 James Pike, *Scout and Ranger*, 145.
37 James P. Newcomb, *Secession Times in Texas*, states that the perfect organization and secrecy of the K. G. C. made it a powerful instrument in the hands of the radicals. H. H. Bancroft in *Texas*, II, 435, takes the same view. But this is not the best judgment. See two essays in the Univ. of Texas Library: Julia L. Hering's "Secession Movement in Texas," and M. L. Arnold's "Later Phases of the Secession Movement in Texas."
38 December 31, 1860; MS Diary, Univ. of Texas Library.
39 Houston defiantly faced hostile audiences. At Waco his life was threatened, and at Galveston the crowd was so menacing that friends begged him not to appear. Here it was that, speaking the words on the cost of civil war quoted above, he warned Texans that the Northerners were determined to maintain the Union. They are not a fiery, impulsive people, he said, but "they move with the steady momentum and perseverance of a mighty avalanche, and what I fear is, they will overwhelm the South." Williams, *Houston*, 354.

ists, who were accused of refusing to receive opposition ballots or miscounting them; and for years afterward Union men declared that a true vote would have shown a majority against secession. Doubtless they were mistaken—but the whole course of events in Texas had certainly been such as to prevent a cool consideration of the issues and a fair popular verdict upon them.[40]

[IV]

All in all, we may wonder if the result in the Lower South would not have been different if South Carolina had not acted in such haste; if there and in Louisiana the governmental system had not been weighted heavily on the side of the wealthy planting interest; if in Georgia men like Stephens had exerted themselves more vigorously and the election had been held in sunny weather; if conservative Alabamians had been given more time to rally their forces in the northern counties and Mobile; and if a fair and calm election of delegates had been held in Texas. The amount of thick-and-thin Union sentiment in this section was not impressive. But the sentiment for delay and cooperative action might well have won the day; and a deliberative Southern convention, offering reasonable conditions to the North, might well then have furnished a solid foundation for compromise.

It will be seen that certain common features stamped the action of these seven States on secession. No really effective plebiscite on immediate as against cooperative action was held in any of them. In all except Georgia, the period allowed for discussing the issues and selecting delegates was deplorably short; usually but three or four weeks, and in Florida less than three. In all of them the vote for convention delegates fell surprisingly short of that just cast in the presidential election, being less by two-fifths, one-third, or one quarter. In a number of States (though not in Mississippi), the slaveholding aristocracy and its allies profited by advantages running even beyond those written into laws and constitutions. In Louisiana, for example, much of the slaveless population was too unstable in residence to qualify for voting, even if it cared to vote; in 1859, scarcely seven percent of the whites of New Orleans were registered

---

40 Analysis of the result in Texas shows a fairly close correlation between secession and slavery. In only three areas did this break down. A line of counties along the Red River boundary voted against secession apparently because they feared attack from the North (through Indian Territory) if Texas went out, and because the population was largely from the border States, Illinois, and Indiana; a group of slaveholding counties about Austin went against secession because of the influence of Houston and other leaders, of several able Union newspapers, and of German communities; and a group of six western counties (Hamilton, Brown, Young, and others) with almost no slaves voted for secession in apparent disgust over the failure of the government to give them adequate protection against the Indians. See Arnold, "Later Phases," 51 ff.; Ramsdell, Frontier and Secession, passim.

voters, and immigrants among them were subject to intimidation at the polls.[41] In all these States, too, observers agree on the emotional power and kinetic force of the spirit of Southern solidarity, speaking of it as a torrential current, an irresistible wind, carrying all before it.

It will also be noted that in their formal declaration of the reasons for secession, the seven States almost completely ignored any questions but those which pertained to slavery. Even South Carolina, in the clearheaded, dignified "Declaration of Immediate Causes" written by Memminger, made no mention of tariffs or other economic grievances. In Georgia, both the hot secessionist Toombs and the reluctant secessionist Stephens were old-time Whigs who had believed in the justice of moderate tariffs. The ablest statement of Alabama's reasons for secession, made by E. S. Dargan of Mobile, rested the action squarely on fear of emancipation. The South, he argued, had more than four million slaves; the removal of such a host was impossible; and if they were liberated without restraint, the result would be utter disaster. "They would either be destroyed by our own hands, the hands to which they look, and look with confidence, for protection, or we ourselves would become demoralized and degraded." [42]

All the seceding States held for a time an anomalous position. They were in their own eyes independent republics, yet they patently lacked the full governmental equipment of republics. Were the Federal laws dead within the States? Was the national coinage still valid? Should the national government continue to deliver mails? A. P. Calhoun told the South Carolina convention that having pulled down a temple which it had taken three-quarters of a century to erect, they must clear away the rubbish and erect another. "We are now houseless and homeless, and we must secure ourselves against storms." [43] The simple method of meeting the situation was to adopt the whole body of United States laws, and take over the whole corps of postmasters. In various States, as the conventions continued to sit and pass ordinances, a murmur arose against the doctrine that all powers were now lodged in a revolutionary group brought together under circumstances of intense excitement. Much fluttering of the pages of old histories for Revolutionary precedents took place in the weeks while men waited for a new Southern Confederacy to replace the United States with an indispensable central authority.

Meanwhile, the problem of relations with the Upper South and borderland raised anxious questions. Many hotheads of the cotton kingdom would have

41 Shugg, *Class Struggle*, 130.
42 Smith, *Hist. and Debates*, 93, 94.
43 N. Y. *Tribune*, December 20, 1860. Although Governor Pickens of South Carolina assumed charge of postal affairs and appointed a head of the postal department, Postmaster Alfred Huger of Charleston informed Joseph Holt that he would continue to account to Washington for the finances of his office; Holt Papers.

preferred to create a new nation without including the border States. The small number of men eager to reopen slave importations, and the much larger number intent upon establishing a free-trade republic, knew that Marylanders, Virginians, and Missourians would obstruct their aims. In Charleston, Savannah, and parts of Alabama and Mississippi in particular, a cotton republic thus seemed desirable. "We must beware lest the Border Slave States overslaugh us," William Gilmore Simms wrote Porcher Miles. "Their destiny involves more rapid changes than ours. . . . They will become manufacturing." [44] Moreover—and this is important—radical leaders were well aware that the Upper South and border would probably quit the Union (if at all) only with the expectation of reconstructing it. That seemed to be the dominant sentiment in North Carolina, Virginia, and Tennessee as well as in the slaveholding areas north of them. Hostile to any such policy, and taking "once out, always out," as their motto, many of the fire-eaters wanted nothing to do with States which hoped to reknit the old ligaments. Not a few of them denounced the border men as fainthearts, Laodiceans, and skulkers.

The more sober view, however, which all cooperationists strongly preached, was that the Lower South was bound both by duty and self-interest to gain the adherence of other slaveholding States. The erection of a mere cotton republic would do great wrong to the borderland, and irreparable injury to the institution of slavery. It was the Upper South which suffered most from Northern injuries and abolitionist propaganda; and could this region be left alone in resisting Yankee encroachment? Already, Northern writers were computing that for a little over ninety million dollars every slave in Maryland, Delaware, and Missouri could be purchased at the generous average price of five hundred dollars a head, and set free. For the Lower South to maintain its separate republic, many urged, would be a base and cowardly desertion of slaveholders in the sister States. Nor was this all. A cotton republic would not be strong enough to conquer Cuba or overrun Mexico in the teeth of European hostility. Slavery there, confined within narrow bounds, faced with world reprobation, and, as the blacks multiplied, operating to "Africanize" large districts, would in Seward's image eventually sting itself to death. [45]

In the chaotic situation which had developed by the beginning of February, many Gulf State men clearly perceived a terrible dilemma. They could probably not gain the accession of the Upper South, which they required, without striking a blow, and to strike a blow would precipitate all the horrors of a fratricidal war. Meanwhile, opinion in the great region from North Carolina and Virginia to Missouri was racked and torn by a thousand currents and counter-

44 February 26, 1861; Porcher Miles Papers, Univ. of N. C.
45 N. Y. *Weekly Tribune*, February 2, 1861; Rainwater, *Mississippi*, 182-185.

currents; and the idea that this populous area might soon be dragged into war by the impulsive cotton kingdom, while pleasing some, gave others the deepest anguish.

[V]

In Washington, the hope of compromise still existed. Charles Sumner saw Buchanan on February 2. "What, Mr. President," he inquired, "can Massachusetts do for the good of the country?" "Much," responded Buchanan, "no State more." "What is that?" "Adopt the Crittenden proposition," said the President.

"Is that necessary?" asked Sumner. "Yes." The Senator made an emphatic gesture. "Mr. President, Massachusetts has not yet spoken directly on these propositions. But I feel authorized to say—at least I give it as my opinion—that such are the unalterable convictions of the people, they would see their State sunk below the sea and become a sandbank before they would adopt these propositions."

Such an explosive statement was to be expected of Sumner, who, according to Edward Everett, was laboring under a morbid excitement which approached insanity. He had a magnificent project for acquiring Canada, and gladly accepting the secession of such slaveholding States as would not live in the Union under the tenets of the Republican platform.[46] But while the Crittenden Compromise was dead, other schemes of conciliation were not. Seward and Charles Francis Adams, whose opinions were fairly in unison, believed that by concessions on every point but territorial extension, they might yet save the Union. Both believed that the slavery issue had been substantially settled by the election. Both believed that to let this settlement be followed by a dissolution of the Union would be a terrible blunder as well as a catastrophe. Seward had written Lincoln on January 27 that a generous and hopeful attitude was indispensable; that the new Administration must collect the revenues and regain the forts; but that "every thought that we think ought to be conciliatory forbearing and patient, and so open the way for the rising of a Union Party in the seceding States which will bring them back into the Union." [47] Adams wrote to

46 Sumner stood at one extreme as Howell Cobb stood at another. On January 10, Cobb had written Porcher Miles that all the threat of coercion was attributable to the false position of Southern men talking of adjustment in Washington. "We ought to let it be distinctly understood, that we will accept no settlement—and if that position had been firmly taken at Washington from the beginning, the trouble would now be all over, and the country engaged in the discharge of the only remaining duty to be performed and that is, the terms of a *peaceable* and *perpetual* separation." Miles Papers, Univ. of N. C. Sumner narrates his talk with Buchanan in a letter of February 3, 1861, to John A. Andrew; Andrew Papers, MHS.

47 Robert Todd Lincoln Papers.

R. H. Dana in much the same terms. The first duty of the government, he thought, was to reestablish confidence by conciliatory language, to encourage the loyal Southerners, and to deprive the conspirators of the materials with which they had worked. Men in the Upper South were plucking up hope, the efforts to reject secession were growing more systematic, and if a fair understanding could only be reached in Congress or the question postponed until after Lincoln came in, "I think we shall have won the day." [48]

It was assuredly of good omen that neither the firing on the *Star of the West* nor the seizure of scattered forts and arsenals had enraged Northern opinion. While few Northerners were ready to admit that every outgoing State was entitled to all the national property within her limits, to be taken whenever a revolutionary agency chose, these "aggressive acts" had been accepted calmly. Even Horace Greeley spoke of them merely as highhanded.[49] The forbearance of Major Anderson in not returning the fire of the Charleston batteries on the Federal vessel was generally applauded, and Secretary Holt sent him the formal commendation of the President.[50]

Of calming psychological effect, too, in these last weeks of the Buchanan Administration, was the quasi-truce respecting Fort Sumter reached at Charleston between Major Anderson and Governor Pickens, and that respecting Fort Pickens at Pensacola arranged between various Southern Senators and President Buchanan. The attorney-general of South Carolina and one of Anderson's officers travelled jointly to Washington to initiate negotiations for determining the status of Sumter. The resulting parley came to nothing. South Carolina again demanded the surrender of the fort; the Administration again sharply refused it.[51] Secretary Holt delivered a grave warning to the State. "If with all the multiplied proofs which exist of the President's anxiety for peace and of the earnestness with which he has pursued it," he wrote, "the authorities of that State shall assault Fort Sumter, and peril the lives of the handful of brave and loyal men shut up within its walls, and thus plunge our common country into the horrors of civil war, then upon them, and those they represent, must rest the responsibility." This was a just anticipation of the verdict of history. An unwritten understanding continued, however, that the United States would not reinforce the fort without notice, and that South Carolina would meanwhile not yet attack it; an understanding the easier to respect because Anderson did not want reinforcements. Secretary Holt had told Anderson, nevertheless, that whenever

48 February 9, 1861; Dana Papers.
49 Signed article, N. Y. *Tribune*, January 8, 1861.
50 January 11; *Official Records*, Series I, Vol. I, 140.
51 Buchanan, *Administration*, 194 ff.; Curtis, *Buchanan*, II, 452; Crawford, *Sumter*, 222 ff.

he needed supplies or men, a prompt and vigorous effort to forward them would follow.[52]

The Fort Pickens truce was ampler and stronger. It was agreed that the government might provision the post but not disembark troops, and that in return the Florida authorities would make no attack. Buchanan gave firm orders through Holt to the provisioning force, which included a small body of troops: "The *Brooklyn* and other vessels of war on the station will remain and you will exercise the utmost vigilance and be prepared at a moment's warning to land the company at Fort Pickens and you and they will instantly repel any attack on the Fort." This was a display of proper vigor. He was anxious to maintain the truce while the Peace Convention under ex-President Tyler labored, and while other efforts at reconciliation were being made. But he was emphatic that the national forces should be ready to meet an attack on Pickens or preparations for an attack. "In either event, the *Brooklyn* and other vessels will act promptly." Had such a clear truce been made respecting Sumter, worry over the future would have been greatly lessened.

[VI]

Three days after the secession of Texas, and on the very day that the Peace Convention opened in Washington, February 4, delegates from six States met in Montgomery to launch their hopeful new Southern republic. South Carolina had proposed the gathering a month earlier. Delegates had in general been chosen by the various State conventions, in proportion to the number of electors each State possessed under the Constitution. They made up a distinguished body of men. Alexander H. Stephens asserts, indeed, that he was never associated with one of more ability; that nobody in it failed to rank above the average of the House in any of the sixteen Congresses in which he had served; and that several of the delegates might justly be placed among the first of the land.[53] Jefferson Davis, Yancey, Slidell, and Judah P. Benjamin were not present. But Toombs, the two Cobbs, Rhett, Memminger, Reagan, J. L. M. Curry, and Benjamin H. Hill were. The spirit in which they met was one of high enthusiasm and optimism. A patriotic harmony prevailed, and many of the wisest believed that their future was one of assured peace.

With Howell Cobb as presiding officer, and with each State given one vote, the convention moved with great celerity. Only four days after assembling, it adopted a Constitution for the provisional government of the Confederate

52 *Official Records*, I, I, 134–190.
53 Stephens, *War Between the States*, II, 325.

States of America; and on the fifth day it elected Jefferson Davis as provisional President. The choice necessarily had to be conservative in character, for while Rhett and Yancey were both highly receptive, their elevation to the leadership of the new nation would have frightened Virginia and the other hesitant States. At the outset, it was the general impression that the palm would be awarded to Toombs, who in the eyes of Stephens seemed far better equipped for the place than any rival. Davis would have preferred a high military post for himself. Unfortunately for Toombs, the Georgia delegation was divided, some members supporting him, some Howell Cobb; the veteran Democrats in the convention distrusted him as an old-time Whig; Yancey, when forced to withdraw, did so in favor of Davis; and after a good deal of complicated maneuvering, the Georgia Senator himself agreed to the austere Mississippian. Some small part may have been played in the rejection of Toombs by his well-known weakness for drink. By another unanimous vote, Stephens was selected for Vice President.[54]

No stronger pair of men could have been selected. Here were one representative of the older South, and one of the new frontier South; one of the old-time Whigs and one of the old-time Democrats; one of the Breckinridge men, and one of the Douglas men. Both were capable orators and parliamentarians. Davis had shown his skill and energy as an administrator in one of the most difficult of the government departments. Their election pleased cautious elements in the borderland; and the fact did not escape the North that, while the convention professed to be adamantine in spurning the old Union forever, both Davis and Stephens had followed a policy which made them seem not totally averse to its reconstruction.

The provisional Constitution had been drawn up by a committee of two from each State, with Memminger its chairman; and by general consent the Federal instrument was accepted as its basis. Within a few weeks a permanent Constitution was drafted. It differed from the old national model chiefly in its emphasis on State Rights, its careful guarantee of slavery (which it named without any cimcumlocution), and a number of interesting reform provisions. The general welfare clauses were omitted. Any Confederate official acting within the limits of a State might be impeached by the State legislature, though the Constitution, laws made under it, and treaties were declared "the supreme law of the land." The central government was forbidden to pass any law denying the right of property in slaves, and although the African slave trade was prohibited, the interstate rights of slaveholders were safeguard. Provision was made for a judicial system like that of the United States, including a Supreme Court. The restrictions upon the States followed in general the old pattern; they

54 See *So. Hist. Assn. Pubs.*, XI, 163 ff.; Johnston and Browne, *Stephens*, 389–391.

might not coin money, make alliances, form compacts with other States, or grant titles of nobility.

The most remarkable features of the new instrument sprang from the purifying and reforming zeal of the delegates, who hoped to create a more guarded and virtuous government than that of Washington.[55] The President was to hold office six years, and be ineligible for reelection. Expenditures were to be limited by a variety of careful provisions, and the President was given a budgetary control over appropriations which Congress could break only by a two-thirds vote. Subordinate employees were protected against the forays of the spoils system. No bounties were ever to be paid out of the Treasury, no protective tariff was to be passed, and no post office deficit was to be permitted. The electoral college system was retained, but as a far-reaching innovation, Cabinet members were given seats in Congress for the discussion of departmental affairs. Some of these changes were unmistakable improvements, and the spirit behind all of them was an earnest desire to make government more honest and efficient. The process of ratifying the new Constitution by the people of the respective States was destined to be slow; and the permanent government of the Confederacy was not to be inaugurated until Washington's birthday in 1862. Meanwhile, the provisional Administration served with all the authority that its leaders could give it.

On the evening of February 16, Jefferson Davis arrived in Montgomery, to be met with a storm of cheers as his erect figure was discerned emerging from the train. To the crowd at the station, he spoke a few sentences. "Our separation from the old Union is complete," he declared. "No compromise and no reconstruction can now be entertained." Two companies of Georgia militia, with a committee of the Confederate Congress and a deputation representing the city, escorted him to the Exchange Hotel, where a greater crowd awaited him. Their exultant shouts soon brought him out upon the balcony. Prominent among the distinguished men who surrounded him was William L. Yancey. He stepped forward, gesturing for silence that he might introduce Davis, and his voice rang out with clarion vibrance: "The hour and the man have met!"

55 We speak here of the permanent Constitution, adopted early in March. Texts of the Confederate and Federal Constitutions are given in parallel columns in Davis, *Rise and Fall*, I, 640–675.

15

Lincoln Takes the Helm

AS THE President-elect left Springfield for Washington on February 11, it was evident that the national crisis was gathering itself to some mighty climax; but no man could say what that climax would be. A complex web of intertwined and fateful questions would have to be decided within the next ten weeks.

Lincoln had as yet fully determined upon only two members of his Cabinet. Though compromise by the Missouri line was dead, lesser concessions to the South hung in balance in Washington; the House did not receive the report and proposals of the Committee of Thirty-three until three days after Lincoln's departure, while, for that matter, the Senate still had to take its final vote on the Crittenden scheme. Major Anderson had not determined when his garrison would need provisions and other stores, the South Carolina authorities marked time while the *Mercury* exhorted them to take the forts, and the new Confederate government remained without a policy as to Sumter and Pickens. The people of the border States still anxiously debated their future, and although Stephens told a Montgomery audience that the new nation might soon have more stars than the thirteen of the original Union, the battle of conservatives and radicals continued to rage in North Carolina and Virginia, in Kentucky and Tennessee. Seward believed the general excitement was abating, but Seward was always optimistic. To most people, the public bewilderment, apprehension, and irritability seemed as great as ever.

So great was the uncertainty that Lincoln was vastly relieved to learn at Columbus, Ohio, on the evening of the thirteenth, that the counting of the electoral votes had been safely completed in Washington that day. The country shared his feeling. Circumstantial stories of plans for a Virginia attack had been afloat. Joseph Medill had written Lincoln on New Year's Eve that the disunionists expected to have an army in the capital within five weeks.[1] Elihu B. Washburne had informed the President-elect on February 3 that a wide and powerful conspiracy to seize Washington undoubtedly existed. But Winfield Scott had

1 Robert Todd Lincoln Papers.

gathered troops and taken precautions. "I have said," he thundered to a New England visitor, "that any man who attempted by force or unparliamentary disorder to obstruct or interfere with the lawful count of the electoral vote should be lashed to the muzzle of a twelve-pounder and fired out of a window of the Capitol. I would manure the hills of Arlington with his body!" The New York attorney and civic leader, George Templeton Strong, noted in his diary that the metropolis was glad to have the critical day passed. "A foray of Virginia gents with Governor Wise at their head and Governor Floyd at their tail could have done infinite mischief by destroying the legal evidence of Lincoln's election (after they had killed and beaten General Scott and his Flying Artillery, that is)." [2]

[I]

The man who was journeying east to grapple with the crisis possessed more qualifications than men dreamed, but great public prestige he sadly lacked. Douglas had told a New Orleans audience, just after the election, that Lincoln, faced with hostile majorities in Congress, was entitled to commiseration rather than envy. While the adverse majorities were now melting away, the question of his power to push through such a thickening jungle of difficulties remained. Outside Illinois he was generally regarded as a secondary leader of commonplace gifts. A typical verdict of the hour characterized him as a fair Western lawyer, a good stump-speaker, and an adroit hand at electioneering, but a politician and not a statesman. C. H. Ray, who knew him well, wrote Governor Andrew that one reason for getting Chase into the Cabinet was that Chase's "great ability in affairs will give the force to Mr. Lincoln which nature has denied him." [3] The men who interviewed him during the winter—Weed, Chase, Cameron, Duff Green—had struck no note of pleased surprise over unexpected talents. His task was made harder by the general supposition that, like the four Presidents preceding him, he would be controlled by his intimate advisers.

But his Illinois intimates knew that he had plenty of backbone. C. H. Ray of the Chicago *Tribune*, stationed in Springfield, assured Elihu Washburne on January 7 that the Party leaders might trust Old Abe implicitly. "He is rising every day in the estimation of all who know him best. He is wiser and more sagacious than I thought he would prove to be. Our cause is dearer to him than anything else; and he will make no mistakes. Depend on that." And Horace White bore the same testimony: "There is no backdown in Old Abe, nor any toleration of that element in others."

2 L. E. Chittenden, *Recs. of President Lincoln*, 38; Strong MS Diary, Columbia Univ.
3 John Rutherfoord, December 19, 1860, Rutherfoord Papers, Duke Univ.; Ray, January 17, 1861, Andrew Papers, MHS.

Since election, he had been incessantly busy seeing politicians, answering letters, discussing Cabinet selections, paying a short visit to Chicago and conferring with Hannibal Hamlin there, tidying his personal affairs, and preparing his inaugural address. He had named John G. Nicolay, a Bavarian-born newspaperman of twenty-eight, frail-looking, wispy-bearded, and ceaselessly industrious, as secretary. Nicolay, overwhelmed with work, had presently suggested that John Hay—an active, brilliant young man from western Illinois, a Brown graduate of literary tastes—be retained as well, and Lincoln, after humorously demurring that he couldn't take the whole State to Washington, had consented.[4] Under the remorseless attack of job-hunters, Lincoln told Herndon that he was sick of his office before he got into it.

It is impossible to overemphasize the fact that his twin tasks of Cabinet-building and policy-making were inextricably entangled; that the stark battle being waged in Washington between the Seward-Adams moderates, who wished to show a conciliatory front toward the South in the hope of holding the border States and eventually rebuilding the Union, and the Sumner-Wade-Chandler implacables, who agreed with Greeley that the very word concession was hateful, was directly connected with efforts to manipulate the new President in the choice of his official family. The struggle on both these closely-linked fronts was to continue until the hour he entered the White House.

As Lincoln moved on toward Cleveland, Buffalo, and New York, Charles Francis Adams wrote Richard H. Dana that the negotiation between North and South was complicated by difficulties growing out of rival approaches to the new chief. "It is not to be disguised that two distinct lines of policy advocated by opposing parties within our ranks are developed. The index of one of them is Mr. Seward. That of the other [is] Mr. Chase. As yet there is no evidence before the public which will be adopted. Until it appears, there will be no firmness here. As yet I can form no opinion of the character of the chief. His speeches have fallen like a wet blanket here. They put to flight all notions of greatness. But he may yet prove true and honest and energetic, which will cover a multitude of minor difficulties." [5]

Antagonism between the moderate and the "iron-back" wings of the party, long jealous and suspicious, grew more bitter as each reached for power. Sumner was now ranting about Sewardism as a fatal policy of cowardice. To Congressional friends he orated, declaimed, and issued ukases after his wont, saying that the path of duty was plain as Washington Monument. Adams set him down as "crazy—actually frantic." He said he would give up nothing, not even the Personal Liberty law of Massachusetts. Characteristically, he denounced Seward

4 Thayer, *Hay*, I, 87; Helen Nicolay, *John G. Nicolay*, 1-65.
5 February 18, 1861; Dana Papers.

to his face. Just before the New Yorker made his great Senate speech on conciliation, Sumner went to his house, heard it read, and angrily protested. "I pleaded with him," he told friends, "for the sake of the cause, the country, and his own good name, to abandon all his propositions and simply declare that Mr. Lincoln would be inaugurated on the 4th March President of the United States, and to rally the country to his support." [6] Seward, laughing at Sumner as he seemed to laugh at everybody, was aware that he faced one of the most desperate battles of his life. For all his effervescent show of cheeriness, he looked thin, worn, and older than the previous summer. "The majority of those around me are determined to pull the house down," he said, "and I am determined not to let them." He was willing to risk his reputation in various ways to save the country. Not merely did he preach compromise where it was unpopular; he kept in close touch with Dix, Holt, and Stanton, encouraging and advising them as they managed the Administration.

Next to Weed, the ablest and most loyal of Seward's helpers was Charles Francis Adams, who possessed a weight of character that Weed lacked. The old family friendship of Seward and the Adamses had been reinforced the previous summer, when they stumped the Northwest together. The Senator hoped that Adams would be New England's representative in the Cabinet. Adams, for his part, believed that the destiny of the nation rested with the New Yorker. "All depends upon Lincoln *and the power of Seward in influencing his policy*," he wrote.[7] Like many others, Adams was annoyed by what he deemed the vacillating course of the President-elect, believing that he had begun well but failed to carry his policy through. Lincoln, thought Adams, should be like Seward—firm on the principle of non-extension of slavery, but conciliatory on other points, and suave in avoiding talk of coercion.

[II]

Lincoln's initial steps in forming his Cabinet had been taken before differences over policy could develop. The day after election, smitten with a crushing sense of the burden he was to take up, he made a tentative Cabinet slate. "It was almost the same that I finally appointed," he said later. But the problem was too difficult to be rapidly solved. His guiding principle, from which he never deviated, was to give places to the major leaders of the party, thus forming a ministry of all the talents—what Seward called "a compound Cabinet"—and reducing the danger of factional revolt against himself. If it could be kept in harmony, it would harmonize the party. Leaders and groups held such divergent

6 So he wrote Andrew, January 17, 1861; Andrew Papers.
7 February 28, 1861, Dana Papers; my italics.

views, however, that at times he despaired of realizing his object. An additional complication lay in the commitments his managers had made at the Chicago convention.

With the basic initial selection, that of Seward, we have already dealt. His position as the foremost leader of the party, his preeminent abilities, his long experience, and his genial personal qualities combined to make his appointment to the first position in the Cabinet almost imperative. With great friendliness toward the man, Lincoln could not be completely happy about the choice. He knew that Seward's undeserved reputation for radicalism made the South suspicious of him, that many Republicans disliked him for his real moderation, and that the Weed machine association was a handicap. Nevertheless, on the whole Seward's acceptance greatly strengthened his position. Another selection, that of Edward Bates as Attorney-General, was made without hesitation or difficulty. Not only was the Missourian fully equipped for this post by his legal erudition, fidelity to constitutional principles, and assuasive temper, but his appointment would gratify Union men in the border area. In December, Lincoln paid him the compliment of proposing to call on him in St. Louis. "I thought I saw an unfitness in *his coming to me*," writes Bates, "and that I *ought to go to him*." When they talked in Springfield on the fifteenth, Lincoln, discussing his whole Cabinet problem with candor, remarked that he thought Bates's participation in its work essential to his complete success. There was no refusing such an invitation.[8]

It was a weirdly unhappy comedy of errors which brought the wily Simon Cameron into a position where (though his appointment was still undecided when Lincoln left for the capital) a Cabinet assignment seemed almost a necessity. This drama, at times almost farce but in the end almost tragedy, began when David Davis and Swett promised Cameron's followers at the Chicago convention that he would be given a Cabinet seat. It was an unauthorized and disreputable bargain, but David Davis insisted that it be honored. So did Cameron's loyal Pennsylvania clansmen, and a number of old-time opponents, like David Wilmot, who had an eye on his senatorship. Seward was distinctly favorable to Cameron, and went so far as to urge Weed—unsuccessfully—to make a special trip to Springfield to press the nomination. Cameron himself, while protesting to various men that he did not want a post, left no wire unpulled and no stone unturned, until by extracting from Swett an invitation to visit Springfield, he was able late in December to push himself into Lincoln's presence. He faced a deeply troubled President-elect.[9]

Precisely what passed at this interview we do not know, and some have sur-

8 *Diary of Edward Bates*, 164–167; Nicolay and Hay, *Lincoln*, III, 351, 352.
9 Gideon Welles states that Swett's invitation was unauthorized; *Diary*, II, 390.

mised that the unwilling Lincoln let himself be browbeaten into offering an appointment. Cameron's own statement, now available in the papers of S. W. Crawford, would indicate that this is not true—that Lincoln had already yielded to Davis and others. Cameron writes:

At that interview a tender of the Secship of the Treasury was made by the President to Genl C. who replied that he was then in the Senate of the U. S. and satisfied with that position and that he was not seeking any other. But it was repeated by the President, who considered as arranged and then said "Now what am I to do with Chase." Why not offer him the War Dept. said Genl C. it is the most important department now as there is no doubt that a war is imminent. Will you take the War Dept. yourself, said Mr. Lincoln. I offer it to you. But I am not seeking for any position replied Genl C. and I would not decline of course what I had recommended to another. Genl C. returned at once to Harrisburg having remained but one day in Springfield. . . .[10]

It is unnecessary to accept this memorandum at face value. What is certain is that Cameron received from Lincoln a letter dated December 31, 1860, stating that "by your permission I shall at the proper time nominate you to the United States Senate for confirmation as Secretary of the Treasury or as Secretary of War—which of the two I have not yet definitely decided." Even if the President-elect did not believe that the unholy compact at Chicago had to be redeemed, he must have felt that to rebuff Cameron and the powerful Pennsylvania machine behind him would be politically dangerous.

The vituperative resources of the English language are large, but they were almost exhausted by the storm of condemnation which beat upon this selection as soon as it was suspected or known. William Cullen Bryant wrote Lincoln on January 3 that all observers of Cameron's career felt "an utter ancient and deep seated distrust of his integrity—whether financial or political." [11] Thaddeus Stevens went further; he pronounced Cameron "a man destitute of honor and honesty." [12] Matthew Carey informed the President-elect that Cameron stood charged in the courts of Pennsylvania with serious crime, that most good citizens "look upon him as the very incarnation of corruption," and that his appointment would be "a signal to all the vultures of the Union to flock around the Treasury." The fact that Cameron on January 21 made a conciliatory speech in the Senate, saying that Pennsylvania would do anything consistent with honor to save the Union, deepened the antagonism of the "iron-backs." [13] Governor Andrew G. Curtin and his faction expressed violent opposition, the State Chairman in Pennsylvania, A. K. McClure, telegraphing that the appointment

10 Undated memorandum in S. W. Crawford Papers, Ill. State Hist. Lib.
11 Robert Todd Lincoln Papers.
12 To E. B. Washburne, January 19, 1861; *Ibid.*
13 L. F. Crippen, *Cameron*, 229, 230.

would mean the destruction of the Party in that State. Lincoln, taken aback, summoned McClure to Springfield and listened to a circumstantial account of all Cameron's derelictions. The chairman bore letters from various men supporting his charge that, in view of "the notorious incompetency and public and private villainy" of the Pennsylvania boss, the selection would disgrace the republic.[14]

Lincoln now saw that he had acted prematurely. His proper course would doubtless have been to revoke his offer, drop Cameron completely, and keep him dropped. Instead, he followed a hesitant policy. First, he wrote the Senator on January 3 an abrupt letter, saying that "things have developed which make it impossible for me to take you into the Cabinet"; that this was partly because of McClure's interposition but more largely because of "a matter wholly outside Pennsylvania"; and that he wished Cameron to yield tacit assent by sending him a telegram reading, "All right." Unfortunately, McClure at the same time returned to Pennsylvania with loud and positive statements that no final decision had been reached on any Cabinet appointment for that State. This put Cameron, who had talked boastfully of Lincoln's offer, in an impossible predicament. If he sent the President-elect the desired telegram and kept quiet, the public would believe that he had lied about his selection, and that, after his lie, McClure had summarily put him in his place. He refused to budge.[15]

Not only that, but he employed all his varied political resources to bring fresh pressure upon Lincoln. Springfield was deluged with letters, telegrams, and signed memorials in Cameron's behalf. The Pennsylvania legislature passed resolutions of eulogy and endorsement. A stream of emissaries, including Senator-elect Edgar Cowan, was hurried to Springfield to expostulate. David Davis and Swett were rallied to return to the charge. Various Pennsylvania newspapers, led by the Philadelphia *Inquirer*, gave Cameron their support, some because they were allied with his machine, and some because they saw in him a pillar of protection. Under this bombardment, Lincoln wavered—for, after all, the allegations against the Senator were mainly vague, and McClure, when asked to document them, had declined to do so. The endorsements of Cameron soon outnumbered the protests three to one, and Lincoln was able to declare that "he is more amply recommended for a place in the Cabinet than any other man." [16]

In vain did various men, East and West, strive to resist this pressure. Horace White, declaring that Cameron's appointment would be positively

14 McClure, *Lincoln and Men of War-Times*, 41, 42, 141–143.
15 Burton J. Hendrick, *Lincoln's War Cabinet*, 108 ff.; Carman and Luthin, *Lincoln and the Patronage*, 39, 40.
16 To Lyman Trumbull; Tracy, *Uncollected Letters of Lincoln*, 173, 174.

awful, did so. So did C. H. Ray. So did Elihu Washburne. From New York came a deputation of three, George Opdyke, Hiram Barney, and Judge Hogeboom, supported by Greeley's *Tribune* and Byrant's *Post*, who in a three-hour interview told Lincoln what they thought were plain home truths. "If this goes on, and Thurlow Weed and Cameron get the reins," they declared, "no course will be left but a disgraceful compromise with the South. After that, the Administration will forfeit the confidence of the country, and the Democratic Party will regain its strength in all the free States." Some Springfield men hoped that the trio had given Lincoln an eye-opener; but Old Abe had a way of making up his own mind.

The upshot was that Lincoln sent Cameron a gentler letter, contritely disclaiming any intention of giving offense, or any doubt as to the Senator's ability and fidelity in a Cabinet post. He stuck to the withdrawal of his offer. At the same time, he made it clear that he was still considering Cameron's name. "If I should make a Cabinet appointment for Pennsylvania before I reach Washington," he wrote, "I will not do so without consulting you, and giving all the weight to your views and wishes which I consistently can." David Davis remained certain that Cameron would get a place, and assured him of the fact. Moreover, strong economic interests entered the contest in the Senator's behalf. The iron and coal men of Pennsylvania, hungry for tariffs, set to work and persuaded Curtin and McClure to withdraw their opposition. As Lincoln passed through Philadelphia, they had a spokesman there, the ironmaster James Milliken, to tell the President-elect that practically all elements wished Cameron appointed to the Treasury. The astute and tireless boss had succeeded! The New York *Times* on February 25 declared that although one of the bitterest political fights in all American history had been waged against him, he had won a complete victory, and it was a settled fact that he was to represent Pennsylvania in the Administration.[17]

One other promissory note of the Chicago convention was presented for payment, and in the end was met. Davis and Swett had pledged a Cabinet position to Caleb Blood Smith in return for Indiana delegates that Smith did not really control. This lawyer, politician, newspaper owner, and promoter of railways and canals, a commonplace contriver of Whig antecedents, had seconded Lincoln's nomination and spoken industriously during the campaign. It seemed important that Indiana receive some reward; Smith's interest in internal improvements suggested that he might do for the Interior Department; and Lincoln, after hesitating between him and Colfax, took the older man. You "are sure of a bright future in any event," he wrote Colfax; "with Smith it is now or

17 Crippen, *Cameron*, 239–242; Baringer, *op. cit.*, 288–291. He was to get the War post.

never." Corwin praised Smith as industrious, well-informed, and firm—but he was to prove firm in some wrong directions.[18]

[III]

As Adams remarked, the two opposed poles in the Party leadership were represented by Seward and Chase. Each man had followers in Lincoln's immediate entourage. While such moderate Illinoisans as David Davis heartily liked Seward and his policies, radicals like Norman B. Judd and the editors of the Chicago *Tribune* espoused Chase. Lincoln's choice of Seward for the State Department had no sooner been disclosed than the milk-of-the-word Republicans, the true-blue implacables, rallied for their own champion. "We," wrote C. H. Ray of the *Tribune* (meaning radical Chicagoans), "are doing what we can to get Mr. Chase into the Cabinet as a counterbalance to the schemers who hang upon the skirts of Mr. Seward." [19] To men like Sumner, Preston King, Wilmot, and Zack Chandler, the idea that Seward would dominate the Administration was horrible; just as to Weed, Charles Francis Adams, and Cameron, the idea of domination by Chase was ghastly.[20]

The drive to make certain that Chase would be offered one of the best Cabinet positions and would accept it (for as a newly-elected Senator he might prove coy) was entirely successful. By invitation, he visited Springfield on January 3. As in other interviews of the sort, Lincoln was candor itself. He first inquired if Chase would accept the Treasury if it proved possible for him to offer it; and then, as his visitor hesitated, explained that Seward was to be Secretary of State (for Chase could hardly stand second to any less important man), and that if Seward had declined, Chase would have been his second choice. This statement largely disarmed the touchy Ohioan of any pique. He felt a little offended that Lincoln did not approach him with the same prompt definiteness as Seward, but he could not deny that the New Yorker had superior claims to first place. The two separated with a quasi-understanding. While Lincoln, his fingers just badly burnt in the Cameron fire, did not quite commit himself to an

18 Corwin to Lincoln, January 18, 1861, Robert Todd Lincoln Papers. One aspirant for the Interior Department, Norman B. Judd, was pushed aside. Mrs. Lincoln, who was in Washington in mid-January, wrote David Davis on the 17th asking him to warn Lincoln against that appointment. She had heard people at a neighboring table that morning laughing at the idea of Judd for the place. "Judd would cause trouble and dissatisfaction, and if Wall Street testifies correctly, his business transactions have not always borne inspection." David Davis Papers, Ill. State Hist. Lib. The letter is interesting as evidence of Mrs. Lincoln's participation in political affairs.
19 January 17, 1861; Andrew Papers, MHS.
20 For Lincoln's own early ideas of Cabinet-making, see Welles, *Diary*, I, 82.

offer, he almost did so; and while Chase said he must consult friends, he almost promised to accept.[21]

At once, Chase and his friends bestirred themselves to give firmer outline to this understanding. It is impossible to detect an iota of hesitation in Chase's attitude. He wanted the Treasury because it was more important than a senatorship, because it would put him as a low-tariff man in a place that might otherwise go to the high-tariff Cameron, and above all, because it would enable him to checkmate Seward. He wrote a number of friends, hinting to George Opdyke of New York that he would like a deputation to visit Lincoln and press his nomination, and plainly telling J. S. Pike that the support of Greeley and Dana would be much appreciated. He probably wrote to Bryant, for that editor shortly sent a highly significant letter to the President-elect. It was important to nominate Chase to the Treasury Department, he stated, as a man of wisdom, rigid integrity, and force of character—"not to speak of the need of his presence as a counterpoise to another member who, to commanding talents, joins a flexible and indulgent temper, and unsafe associations." It was also important to hurry his nomination, for it was nearly certain that he would not take the place "unless it were offered him early." [22] Sumner was hot to see Chase safe in the Cabinet; "it is our only chance," he exclaimed.

As Congress labored throughout February, Seward and Adams still cherished the idea of conciliation, while Chase and Sumner steadily opposed all compromise. One of Chase's phrases gained wide currency: "Inauguration first, adjustment afterward"—by which he meant that unconditional submission by the South must precede any concessions. Seward, who believed it imperative to hold Virginia and the borderland and to build a groundwork of fraternal feeling for ultimate reconstruction, regarded such an attitude as calamitous. He had been intensely worried lest a secessionist victory in Virginia, which held elections for her convention on February 4, might precipitate an attack by Governor Wise upon Washington and open a war. The victory of the Union men heartened him enormously, for it seemed to indicate that his policy might well succeed. When the middle of February came without disturbance, he was still more relieved. Every day, he believed, was bringing the people nearer the tone, temper, and ideas that he hoped would prevail. Knowing that Lincoln was at work on his inaugural, he had written him a long letter in the hope of influencing its tenor:

21 R. B. Warden, *Chase*, 365 ff.; Schuckers, *Chase*, 201–203. Chase wrote Elihu Washburne on January 14: "Should he conclude it is desirable that I take the position, he will let me know; and then I shall decide with just as little reference to personal considerations as possible." Washburne Papers.
22 January 22, 1861; Robert Todd Lincoln Papers.

The appeals from the Union men in the Border states for something of concession or compromise are very painful since they say that without it those states must go with the tide. . . . In any case, you are to meet a hostile armed Confederacy when you commence. You must reduce it by force or conciliation. The resort to force would very soon be denounced by the North, although so many are anxious for the fray. The North will not consent to a long civil war. . . . For my own part I think that we must collect the revenues, regain the ports in the gulf, and if need be maintain ourselves here. But that every thought that we think ought to be conciliatory, forbearing, and patient, and so open the way for the rising of a Union Party in the seceding states which will bring them back into the Union.

It will be very important that your Inaugural Address be wise and winning.[23]

With every passing week the antagonism of the two factions became more acidulous, and more threatening to the harmony of the new Administration. Early in February, Greeley opened all the *Tribune* batteries upon Seward. He had reserved his fire for a time, merely because a severe struggle was raging at Albany for the senatorial seat soon to be vacated. The Seward-Weed forces had united behind the brilliant young William M. Evarts; the opposition, rallying against Weed with the cry, "Down with the dictator!", had divided its votes between Greeley and Ira Harris. The outcome left Greeley half-elated, half-frustrated. When Weed, sitting in the executive chamber nervously smoking, learned that Greeley was leading and Evarts was about to be overwhelmed, he suddenly transferred his votes to Harris, thus robbing the editor of the prize. Nothing was now too harsh for Greeley to say about the humiliating surrender of Seward to the compromise spirit. "Mr. Seward Renounces the Republican Party," ran one of the *Tribune* headlines. Bryant's *Evening Post* was equally virulent, for neither man could reconcile himself to the prospect of four years of government by what Samuel Bowles called "the New Yorker with his Illinois attachment." [24]

[IV]

The policies of the new President were as yet but adumbrations projected against two jutting principles, as rising mist might cling to two mountain crags. One principle was inflexibility on the territorial question. "I am for no compromise," Lincoln had written Seward, "which *asserts* or *permits* the extension of the institution on soil owned by the nation. And any trick, by which the nation is to acquire territory, and then allow some local authority to spread slavery over it, is as noxious as any other." The other principle was an anxious desire

23	January 27, 1861; Robert Todd Lincoln Papers. Punctuation slightly altered.
24	N. Y. *Weekly Tribune*, February 9, 1861; Merriam, *Bowles*, I, 318.

to maintain peace, first by taking no aggressive step, and second by making concessions on all points but that of new slaveholding territory. "As to fugitive slaves, District of Columbia, slave trade among the slave States, and whatever springs of necessity, from the fact that the institution is among us, I care but little; so that whatever is done be comely, and not altogether outrageous. Nor do I care much about New Mexico, if further extension be hedged against." [25]

One evidence of his desire to woo the South lay in his effort to find a Southern leader who could and would enter his Cabinet. Various men suggested that he retain, as head of the War Department, the capable Joseph Holt, who was not merely a native of Kentucky but a former resident of Mississippi. The Lower South, however, now hated Holt. Seward sat down on Christmas Day to propose Randall Hunt of Louisiana, and John A. Gilmer and Kenneth Raynor of North Carolina, while he later added Robert E. Scott of Virginia to the list.[26] Of these, Gilmer, a strong antagonist of secession and advocate of compromise, seemed the most promising. On Lincoln's authorization, the Senator wrote Gilmer (they were warm friends), inquiring as to his willingness to serve, but received only a hesitant, evasive answer. Lincoln himself had meanwhile invited him to come to Springfield; and he could not have been pleased when Gilmer not merely declined the visit, but called upon the President-elect to restate his policy toward the South in more satisfactory terms. When Seward talked with Scott of Virginia late in January, it appeared that he too would not do; he was too exacting in his demands on behalf of the slave States.

The fact was that, as even Seward was compelled to admit, such men as Gilmer, Scott, and W. C. Rives were now halfway secessionists, holding that their States could and should depart unless the government executed sweeping guarantees—guarantees that the North would find abhorrent. Lincoln's early belief that no really able and influential Southerner could be found except on terms that would mean hopeless future friction thus appeared justified, and the quest was abandoned.

In one respect the pathway ahead of the incoming President seemed to grow clearer. The departure of many Southern members from Congress gave a coalition of Republicans and Northern Democrats an opportunity to carry through some long-thwarted measures. On January 21, in a scene which thoughtful men found affecting, Senators Yulee and Mallory of Florida, Clay and Fitzpatrick of Alabama, and Davis of Mississippi had formally withdrawn from the Senate. All of them reproached the North, Clay's speech being a bitter indictment; all, and particularly Yulee, defended secession as springing from a profound sense

---

25 Seward, *Seward*, II, 504.
26 Senator Doolittle suggested Major Anderson, a Kentuckian, for the War Department; January 10, 1861, Robert Todd Lincoln Papers.

of duty to the Southern people and to posterity; and all voiced their regret at leaving old friends. Mallory spoke with horror of civil war—"imbrue your hands in our blood, and the rains of a century will not wash from them the stain"; but Davis expressed a magnanimous good will toward the North—"I wish you well; and such, I am sure, is the feeling of the people I represent towards those whom you represent." [27] Other members from seceding States, at appropriate times, uttered their farewells.

On the very day the five Senators departed, the bill to admit Kansas passed the Senate 36 to 16, with nine Northern Democrats joining the Republicans in its support. Much the same alliance carried legislation organizing the Territories of Dakota, Colorado, and Nevada. In accordance with the Republican platform statement that the normal condition of all Territories was that of freedom, it was assumed that no explicit exclusion of slavery was necessary. Since Lincoln would appoint the territorial officers, and since no sane Southerner would carry a slave into such regions, the assumption was quite sound. Nevertheless, Douglas did not miss his opportunity to point out that the organizing acts left slavery in the three Territories, so far as Congressional interference was concerned, precisely where his law of 1854 had left slavery in Kansas; that the Wilmot Proviso was relegated to oblivion. [28] His taunt did not disturb his opponents, who knew that the three Territories in 1861 stood in a very different position from that in which Kansas had stood when Pierce was in the Executive Mansion, and when Missouri was full of men eager to carry slavery into the valley of the Kaw.

The mild tariff bill of the preceding session, amended after a fashion which we shall discuss later, was carried through Congress with the aid of Democratic votes from Pennsylvania, New Jersey, and New York, and President Buchanan signed it as one of his last official acts. [29] Once more, the Pacific Railroad died amid unhappy wrangling over routes—but in the certainty of an early resurrection. Impressed by the popular interest in reform, Congress stopped the subsidy for the carriage of mails to the Pacific by steamship, revised the patent laws, and created a Government Printing Office to do the work heretofore farmed out on the scandalous terms exposed in the Covode Report.

27 *Cong. Globe.*, 36th Cong., 2d Sess., 484–487.
28 *Ibid.*, p. 1391. The fact was that Republicans did not need or want positive prohibition in these Territories; and sensible Southerners did not want positive protection of slavery, which would have been useless.
29 Lincoln dealt briefly with the tariff in his speech at Pittsburgh on February 14. Saying that "it is a question of national housekeeping," and that "it is to the government what replenishing the meal-tub is to the family," which was then true, he pledged himself to support the Chicago plank on the tariff; but he admitted that it was subject to varying interpretations, and said frankly that "I have by no means a thoroughly matured judgment upon this subject, especially as to details." N. Y. *Herald, Tribune*, February 15.

Although the cry of sectional legislation might be hurled against some of these enactments, they actually contained little of which the South could legitimately complain. The population in the three Territories obviously needed a governmental machinery near at hand. A higher tariff revenue had become exigent, and the new duties were moderate by any standard. In one field, too, sober Congressional leaders conspicuously avoided any provocative action. Buchanan having asked Congress for increased power to deal with disorders, the House spent days in discussing various proposals to enable the President to use the militia and accept volunteer forces to maintain the peace in Washington and to protect or recover Federal property elsewhere.[30] Among other steps, it set up a committee of five to investigate certain alleged plots, backed by subversive organizations, to prevent Lincoln from taking power. All this pother came to nothing, however, when the Democrats and the cooler Republicans in the House, fearful of offending Virginia and of closing the door to reconciliation elsewhere, refused to help carry any new measure looking to the employment of armed forces. Various leaders, including Charles Francis Adams, were anxious for the Northern States to arm and drill troops, without fuss or undue publicity, for the protection of the national government, and they wrote urgent letters to the State capitals.[31] But no force bill was allowed to pass. Lincoln, after reaching Washington, used his influence against any such measure.

Fort Sumter, where Major Anderson and Captain Abner Doubleday were energetically bossing laborers and soldiers who sweated to strengthen the post, was still the danger point. A host of South Carolinians burned to seize it. Governor Pickens was eager to attack as soon as he felt strong enough. Reports that he was about to strike had led Robert Toombs and ex-President Tyler to beseech him to stay his hand; and as he continued to breathe threats the Confederate Congress, much alarmed, passed a resolution on February 12 taking control of the question of the forts. At once Pickens sent a vehement protest to the president of Congress, Howell Cobb. It was vital, he wrote, to seize Sumter before Buchanan left office, so that the incoming Lincoln Administration would face the

---

30 There were in fact three principal measures. One, reported from the select committee on the President's message of January 8, empowered the President to accept the services of volunteers in protecting or recovering the forts and other national property. A second, from the same committee, gave the President such additional powers in collecting imports as he seemed to need in the port of Charleston. The third, reported from the House Military Affairs Committee, gave the President power to call out the militia in dealing with insurrections against the Federal authority; the existing laws covering only the use of militia against foreign invasions, or when the State governments asked for aid in quelling revolts against their peace and order. *Cong. Globe*, 36th Cong., 2d Sess., January 30–March 1, *passim*.

31 See Adams's letters, Andrew Papers; Medill's letters, Robert Todd Lincoln Papers. The steps which Northern and Southern State governments had been taking will subsequently be covered in detail, as will the situation in Virginia and the border States.

question of a declaration of war separated from any hostile act occurring since it held power! Radicals in Montgomery also wanted bold action. The Confederate Congress therefore made an aggressive move on February 22. It passed a resolution declaring that steps should be taken to obtain Forts Sumter and Pickens, by negotiation or force, as early as possible, and authorizing President Davis to make all necessary military preparations. Davis for his part wrote Pickens on March 1 that he wished to see Sumter in Confederate hands as quickly as possible, but that they must make sure of victory at the first blow; and the same day he ordered Brigadier-General Beauregard to take command at Charleston. In Washington, meanwhile, Acting-Secretary Holt warned Southern leaders again and again that the government could not give up Sumter, that it had as much right to reinforce it as to occupy it, that if Anderson required reinforcements they would be sent, and that any attack on Sumter would mean war. The stage had been set for a grand battle tableau—but still men waited.

[V]

"Lincoln is making little speeches as he wends his way toward Washington," wrote George Templeton Strong in his diary of February 18, "and has said some things that are sound and creditable and raise him in my esteem." It was true that he had said some good things. Standing on the balcony of the Bates House in Indianapolis, with the mayor and Governor Oliver P. Morton beside him, while a crowd of twenty thousand waited in the cold February twilight, he had said that maintenance of the Union depended upon the people. He had said that the word coercion needed definition: "If the United States should merely hold and retake its own forts and other property, and collect the duties on foreign importations," would that be coercion? He had said that the secessionists had a queer idea of the country: "In their view the Union, as a family relation, would seem to be no regular marriage, but rather a sort of free-love arrangement, to be maintained on passional attraction."

In Cincinnati, where he was greeted by an imposing procession and an enthusiastic crowd, he flung a pledge across the river to the Kentuckians: "We mean to treat you, as near as we possibly can, as Washington, Jefferson, and Madison treated you. We mean to leave you alone, and in no way to interfere with your institutions." In Pittsburgh and again in Albany, he had explained that he did not wish to speak prematurely on the issues: first, "I should see everything, hear everything, and have every light that can possibly be brought within my reach." Some of his extempore utterances were less felicitous. His repeated assertions that the crisis was all artificial, and that if tempers were restrained the trouble would soon come to an end, jarred on anxious citizens.

His rather clumsy attempts at wit were inappropriate to the tension of the hour. When at Westfield, New York, he asked for Grace Bedell, the little girl who had written him suggesting a beard, and said, "You see I let these whiskers grow for you, Grace," most people thought the episode undignified; as undignified as his invitation to a coal-heaver at Freedom, Pennsylvania, to clamber up on the train platform and measure heights. He did find private opportunity, however, to tell governors and local leaders that they must all stand firm in defense of the Union. On the nineteenth, he reached New York, where Strong had a glimpse of him:

Lincoln arrived here yesterday afternoon by Hudson River Railroad from Albany. I walked uptown at 3:30. Broadway crowded, though not quite so densely as on the Prince of Wales's Avatar last October. The trottoir well filled by pedestrians (vehicles turned off into side streets) and sidewalks by patient and stationary sightseers. Above Canal Street they were nearly impassable. At St. Thomas's Church I met the illustrious cortege moving slowly down to the Astor House with its escort of mounted policemen and a torrent of ragtag and bobtail rushing and hooraying behind. The great rail-splitter's face was visible to me for an instant and seemed a keen, clear, honest face, not so ugly as his portraits.

Four days later, on Saturday, newsboys at noon were crying extras in all the eastern cities. They told how a plot for Lincoln's assassination had been revealed to him at Harrisburg the previous evening; how he was to have been attacked as he rode from one station to another in Baltimore the next day; and how he thereupon left privily, disguised "in a Scotch cap and long military cloak," and by traveling all night reached Washington early in the morning. Though the alleged conspiracy sounded like a sensational piece of romancing, much evidence upon its reality has been preserved; and Lincoln's reluctant secret journey, made under the pressure of worried advisers, was wise. It was unfortunate that it detracted from the effect of his impressive short address at Independence Hall the previous morning.[32]

The eastward trip had taken eleven days; nine more were to be spent in Washington before the inauguration. Lincoln, housed in the best suite of Willard's Hotel (vacated for the time being by the wealthy William E. Dodge),

32 The Scotch cap and military cloak were fictions, and despite newspaper gibes, Lincoln's journey was entirely dignified. One element in the situation was distrust of George P. Kane, head of the Baltimore police, later arrested by General Banks and in time a Confederate officer. See Norma B. Cuthbert, *Lincoln and the Baltimore Plot, 1861,* which furnishes evidence from the Pinkerton files; R. W. Rowan, *The Pinkertons,* 82–118; Seward, *Seward,* II, 508–511. The story of the plot was temporarily discredited by W. H. Lamon in his *Life of Lincoln* because Lamon had a spiteful quarrel with Pinkerton; but it may now be regarded as valid. Nevertheless, the midnight journey did not add to Lincoln's prestige. Strong wrote in his diary for February 23: "It's to be hoped that the conspiracy can be proved beyond cavil. If it cannot be made manifest and indisputable, this surreptitious nocturnal dodging or sneaking of the President-elect into his capital city . . . will be used to damage his moral position and throw ridicule on his Administration."

was under the special guidance of Seward, who entertained him at breakfast and dinner the first day, took him to church the second, and escorted him on his visit of courtesy to President Buchanan. But Chase had taken quarters on the same floor of Willard's as Lincoln, and saw as much of him as possible. The President-elect had to receive everyone: the Illinois delegation in Congress headed by Douglas; the chief of the army, Winfield Scott; the Blair family, both father and sons, and an endless round of political callers. On his first Sunday in Washington he gave Seward a copy of his inaugural address, and that very evening the New York Senator indited a list of suggested emendations. Every observer was struck by the worn, haggard, troubled aspect of Lincoln's sensitive face.

About the incoming President, whose primary task was the completion of his Cabinet, swirled deep and murky currents of intrigue. To Seward, a perfect Cabinet would be one which included Charles Francis Adams for New England, Cameron for Pennsylvania, and Henry Winter Davis for Maryland—and which did not include Chase. Weed was in Washington, ably abetting his chieftain. To leaders of the radical wing, an ideal Cabinet would be one which included Gideon Welles for New England, someone like Wilmot for Pennsylvania, and Montgomery Blair for Maryland [33]—and which did not include Seward. Every motion that Lincoln made was watched by the rival forces with hope, dread, and suspicion. Greeley, who had come to the capital to do what he could, was almost frantic with anxiety. He wailed, on February 28, that Seward kept the incoming President perpetually surrounded, and that the compromisers would have full swing. "Old Abe is honest as the sun, and means to be true and faithful; but he is in the web of very cunning spiders and cannot work out if he would. Mrs. Abe is a Kentuckian and enjoys flattery—I mean deference. And God is above us, and all things will be well in the end. Life is not very long, and we shall rest by and by." [34]

But Lincoln intended, come what would, to be master in his own house. He meant to rule by a balance of factions and forces, in which he would hold pivotal authority. From the outset he had been determined, if possible, to have

33 Montgomery Blair, and indeed the whole Blair family, were at this moment radical with a fine Jacksonian fervor. They believed that if Buchanan had shown the nerve of Jackson, the Southern movement might have been checked at once. Montgomery wrote Governor Andrew on January 23 that he would not much care to serve in the same Cabinet with Seward and Cameron. "Neither of these gentlemen seem to me to appreciate the crisis or to comprehend what action it demands from the government. Violence is not in my judgment to be met with peace. Men intent on crime are not to be stopped from committing it by the promise of impunity, and it is my deliberate opinion that if such a policy is acted on we shall have a long and bloody war and permanent disunion. The truth is my dear friend that these gentlemen are wholly unfitted by mental and moral qualities for bearing sway in times of difficulty." Andrew Papers, MHS.
34 Greeley Papers, LC.

both Seward and Chase in his Cabinet and to give the direction to neither. He had no intention of yielding on the one side to Seward's objections to a "compound" Cabinet, nor on the other side to the last-minute battle of Chase, Greeley, and other radicals to close the door against Seward's ally in a policy of moderation, Cameron. As his biographers tell us, he listened patiently for a week to the voices of contending leaders, and found his original judgment as to the need for a balanced combination of talents unshaken.[35] He would not let Seward carry out the alleged agreements of a conference at Saratoga with David Davis the previous summer; he would not let the Chase-Sumner group be equally proscriptive on the other side. In the end, he decided to appoint Cameron to a place—which gave deep offence to the radicals or "iron-backs"; but also to appoint Welles and Montgomery Blair—which gave deep offence to Seward and his backers.[36]

By March 2, the heat generated by this battle had become so intense that informed Washingtonians looked for an explosion. Seward, the previous day, had presented an ultimatum: If Blair, Welles, and Chase all went in—and he particularly objected to Chase—he would go out. "There are differences between myself and Chase which make it impossible for us to act in harmony," he said. "The Cabinet ought, as General Jackson said, to be a unit." Lincoln expressed astonishment that at so late a day, after all the pains he had taken, and after all the negotiations that had taken place, he—facing so terrible a national upheaval—should be met with such a demand. He calmly asked Seward to reconsider the matter. Before he would yield, he was ready to part with the temperamental New Yorker. His friend Judd, hearing the gossip that was flying about, burst late one night into Lincoln's suite and asked whether he intended to put Henry Winter Davis in Blair's place as Postmaster-General. "Judd," replied Lincoln, "when that slate breaks again, it will break at the top."[37]

35 Nicolay and Hay, Lincoln, III, 368; Welles, Diary, II, 391.
36 Young Charles Francis Adams accepted the shelving of his father philosophically. Seward, he wrote R. H. Dana on February 28, had to drop the elder Adams and concentrate his energies on getting Cameron into the Cabinet; otherwise Lincoln would have fallen under the influence of the "iron-backs." To checkmate Chase, so violently pressed by the "ramwells," and to maintain his own peace-seeking policy, "Seward was obliged to abandon his wish to have my father in the Cabinet, and to throw his influence in favor of Cameron as a counterbalancing conservative force." But this was only one facet of the truth. Dana Papers, MHS.
37 Much light purports to be thrown on this Cabinet crisis by the mysterious Diary of a Public Man, attributed by Dr. Frank M. Anderson to Samuel Ward; and while its authenticity cannot be completely accepted, it bears some inner marks of veracity. See the editions by F. Lauriston Bullard and Dr. Anderson, with their introductions. Full treatment of all the complexities of the crisis would require much greater space than is here available. See Sandburg, Lincoln, I, 140-160; Randall, Lincoln the President, I, 256 ff; Nicolay and Hay, III, Ch. XXII; Hendrick, Lincoln's War Cabinet, 113-123; Carman and Luthin, Lincoln and the Patronage, 11-52; T. Harry Williams, Lincoln and the Radicals, 19-23, and the many biographies of Cabinet members.

Lincoln was actually ready to break his slate at the top—or to use the threat of such action to bring Seward to terms. Meeting George G. Fogg, who as secretary of the campaign committee had won his confidence, the morning after Seward's ultimatum, he described the situation. With a humorous twinkle, he remarked: "We must give up both Seward and Chase, I reckon; and I have drawn up here a list of the Cabinet leaving them both out." He showed Fogg a new slate which assigned the State Department to William L. Dayton of New Jersey and the Treasury to a New Yorker hostile to Seward. "I am sending this to Mr. Weed," dryly announced Lincoln.

That same day, Saturday, March 2, a New York deputation headed by Seward's friend Simeon Draper called to protest against Chase. They argued that Seward could never work with him. Lincoln, after listening patiently, remarked that the prime need of the nation was a hearty cooperation of all good men and all sections. At this the delegation pricked up hopeful ears, thinking he might say he would drop Chase. The President-elect drew a paper from a drawer. This, he explained, contained both his careful choice of Cabinet members, and an alternative list—the second list being in his opinion the poorer. As his hearers still radiated hope, he paused dramatically. Then he exploded his stick of dynamite! Mere mortals cannot have everything they like, he moralized. "This being the case, gentlemen, how would it do for us to agree on a change like this? How would it do for Mr. Chase to take the Treasury, and to offer the State Department to Mr. William L. Dayton?" He added that he could make Seward minister to Great Britain. And he bowed the stupefied delegation from the room.

In short, Lincoln made it plain that if Chase went, Seward must go too. And Seward had no mind to let the Administration be dominated by his rivals and enemies. He still hoped that time would justify the editorial prophecy just made by the New York *Herald*: "The destinies of the country are in Mr. Seward's hands. He will be the master spirit of the incoming Administration." He had embodied his oral ultimatum of Friday in a letter of March 2, informing Lincoln that circumstances seemed to make it his duty to withdraw his acceptance of the State Department; perhaps Draper's deputation had carried this with them. But when he heard from both Weed and Draper that if he persisted in his stand he would be shut out in the cold, he prepared to recede. On Sunday, Lincoln told Gideon Welles that although some difficulty still existed, he was satisfied that he could arrange the matter. He knew that his counter-ultimatum, "No Chase, no Seward," would be effective. "I can't afford to let Seward take the first trick," he told Nicolay.

On the morning of Monday, March 4, while the notes of the bands in the assembling procession drifted into the windows at Willard's, Lincoln penned a note, kindly but firm in tone, asking the Senator to countermand his withdrawal. "Please consider and answer by 9 o'clock tomorrow," he wrote. And that afternoon Seward, after a talk with Lincoln, came to terms. The New Yorker admitted to his wife that he had yielded. "The President is determined that he will have a compound Cabinet," he wrote; "and that it shall be peaceful, and even permanent." But even yet Seward did not begin to comprehend Lincoln's strength. After telling of his withdrawal and subsequent consent, he added: "At all events I did not dare to go home, or to England, and to leave the country to chance." Any Cabinet without himself was abandonment of the nation to chance! [38]

On the morning of the 5th Lincoln sent the Senate the names of his department heads. They were Seward as Secretary of State; Chase as Secretary of the Treasury; Cameron as Secretary of War; Gideon Welles as Secretary of the Navy; Caleb B. Smith as Secretary of the Interior; Edward Bates as Attorney-General; and Montgomery Blair as Postmaster-General. Four of the seven had been identified with the Whig Party before becoming Republicans; the other three had once been Democrats. Bates at sixty-seven was the oldest, and Montgomery Blair at forty-seven the youngest. Four members had a large national reputation, and Blair and Welles were quickly to earn one. Radical Republicans rejoiced that Chase had gained a place at Lincoln's right hand.

"Yes," exulted Greeley, "we *did*, by desperate fighting, succeed in getting five honest and noble men into the Cabinet—by a fight that you never saw equalled in intensity and duration. Gov. Chase, the ablest Republican living, who (as Gen. Dix said) was almost indispensable to the Treasury, got it at last, by the determined courage and clearheaded sagacity of Old Abe himself, powerfully backed by Hamlin, who is a jewel." Moderates also rejoiced, for their leader was head of the Cabinet. In reality neither of the two great factions of the party had won; the victory lay with the courage and wisdom of Abraham Lincoln.[39]

Meanwhile, a lesser struggle had been taking place over the contents and tone of the inaugural address. This paper had been written and set in type in Springfield, where David Davis and other intimates had read it. On the way east Lincoln showed it in Indianapolis to Orville H. Browning, who, while thinking it admirable, suggested one change. Lincoln had declared that he intended to *reclaim* the public property and national places lost to the South; Browning

---

38 For this Cabinet struggle, see Seward, *Seward*, II, 518; W. H. Lamon, *Recollections of Lincoln*, 49–51; Baringer, *A House Dividing*, 328, 329; Frank B. Sanborn, *Recollections of Seventy Years*, I, 26, 27; Welles, *Diary*, II, 391, 392; Nicolay and Hay, *Lincoln*, III, 370 ff.; N. Y. *Herald, Tribune, Times*, March 1–5, 1861.

39 March 12, 1861, Greeley Papers, LC. For criticism of the Cabinet, see Parker, *Morrill*, 124.

thought this too much of a threat; and Lincoln struck out the word. The most sensitive question remaining was whether, in addition to condemning secession as unconstitutional and unallowable, he should announce his purpose of protecting the property of the United States, South as well as North, executing all laws, and collecting the revenues. Any such statements will have a coercive look, said many; they will make it impossible for the Union men to hold Virginia, Maryland, Kentucky, North Carolina, and Tennessee; they will throw the border into revolution.

On this main point Lincoln stood his ground. Seward thought that instead of saying flatly that he would hold the forts and other public property, he should take refuge in an ambiguous statement that he would employ "the power confided to me" with efficiency but also with discretion. But Lincoln was adamant. He kept in his message a determined assertion: "The power confided to me will be used to hold, occupy, and possess the property and places belonging to the government, and to collect the duties and imposts." The one important change in content Lincoln made primarily on his own deeper reflection. In his original document he had spoken slightingly of any amendment of the Constitution, writing that he was not much impressed with the belief that it could be improved. Seward proposed a noncommittal statement. But Lincoln rewrote the passage, reversing his position. Stating that he would himself propose no amendments, he recognized the authority of the people over the question of constitutional change, concluding: "and I should, under existing circumstances, favor rather than oppose a fair opportunity being afforded the people to act upon it."

In lesser matters of style and tone, Seward was responsible for some marked improvements. When he objected to references to the Republican Party and Chicago platform, Lincoln, recognizing that they were improperly partisan, left them out. Lincoln elsewhere had written, "The Government will not assail you, unless you first assail it"; on Seward's advice, he omitted the last clause. Particularly did Seward improve the close of the document. Lincoln had ended with a prosaic statement that his oath required him to preserve, protect, and defend the government, and that it was for the secessionists and not himself to answer the question of peace or a sword. Seward, feeling the importance of sounding a higher note, and of concluding with words of affection and confidence, penned two paragraphs, and suggested that the President-elect take his choice. The second was truly inspired. Lincoln seized on it and gave it a perfection which has placed it among the nation's treasures of speech.[40]

40 On the inaugural address, see Browning, Diary, I, 455; Nicolay and Hay, Lincoln, III, 318 ff., 327–343; Randall, Lincoln, I, 297–310; and the well-informed Washington correspondence of the N. Y. Herald, March 2–5, 1861. David M. Potter in Lincoln and the Secession

[VI]

As a solemn public pageant, the inauguration ceremonies left nothing to be desired. The early morning was chill and cloudy, with a sharp northwest wind which swirled clouds of dust through the streets; but noon brought calm and a bright, cheerful sun. The usual host of visitors had surged into the capital, but with one sharp difference from previous years—few Southerners had come. Both Buchanan and Lincoln were busy at an early hour: the President signing bills at the Capitol, for the Senate had sat all night, and the President-elect giving a final touch to his address and receiving Bates, Welles, Cameron, Trumbull, David Davis, and other visitors. By nine o'clock crowds were filling the downtown streets, gazing at the volunteer soldiery who had begun to march and counter-march, and listening to the bands play patriotic music. Gradually the throng thickened; gradually the mounted marshals under B. B. French, with blue scarves, white rosettes, and blue-and-gold batons, got the procession into line. By noon double columns of troops flanked Willard's Hotel, and at 12:30 rolling cheers announced Buchanan's arrival in his open carriage.

General Scott had taken full precautions. As the procession to Capitol Hill got under way, riflemen were concealed on the roofs of scattered houses along Pennsylvania Avenue; platoons were stationed every hundred yards; cavalry guarded the side streets; and a guard of honor from the regular army and marines surrounded the presidential carriage so closely that it was often hard to see the occupants. Sharpshooters in the windows of the Capitol bent hawk-like eyes upon the crowd, and a battery of flying artillery was posted just north of that building. But the public saw little of all this. Its gaze was fixed on the fluttering flags and bunting, the gaily-dressed military corps, the pounding bands, and the float of thirty-four pretty girls representing as many States. Lincoln, entering the Capitol through a heavy plank passage-way, found Congress, the Supreme Court, and the diplomatic corps assembled in the Senate chamber. As attendants beat the dust of the avenue from his clothes, a reporter noted that he looked pale, fatigued, and anxious. Well he might, after the incessant conferences, interviews, dinners, receptions, and toils of the past ten days! He shook hands with friends. Then the march to the platform at the east portico began; and he was soon taking his place on that flag-dressed structure, the

---

Crisis holds that in declaring that he would not force unwelcome Federal officers upon any reluctant interior community, that he would exercise his authority "according to circumstances actually existing," and that he looked toward "a peaceful solution of the national troubles and the restoration of fraternal sympathies and affections," Lincoln was laying down both a formula and a plan; 327 ff. The mails would be delivered "unless repelled"; the duties would be collected, if at all, at sea. In short, Lincoln did not contemplate coercion, though he did insist that the Union "will constitutionally defend and maintain itself."

army and navy officers and uniformed diplomats splashing the black-coated groups about him with color.

Observant members of the great crowd (estimated at twenty-five thousand or more) facing the platform and the unfinished dome enjoyed some moments of drama. If we may believe Carl Schurz, Henry Watterson, and the author of *The Diary of a Public Man* (whose recollections, however, are not substantiated by any contemporaneous evidence) they saw Douglas, when Lincoln awkwardly sought a place for his tall hat, seize it and hold it on his knees as a symbolic act. They saw Lincoln's well-loved friend, the English-born Senator from Oregon, E. D. Baker, step forward and introduce the President-elect. They saw Lincoln lay down his manuscript, clap his hands in his pockets, and pull out a pair of steel-bowed spectacles—a surprise to those who knew him only through his pictures. As he read in his clear, shrill voice, which carried well to the outskirts of the assemblage, all listened in a solemn silence, as if moved by a conviction that the hour was big with their own fate and that of the nation. The sun shone down brightly on the gay dresses of the ladies, the uniforms and glittering weapons of the volunteer companies standing at rest on the outskirts, and the waving flags. Lincoln closed amid an intent hush. Then the crowd saw the bent, shrunken Chief Justice Taney, tottering with age and emotion, administer the oath to an incoming President whose views he deeply distrusted.[41]

The inaugural address had been awaited with feverish anxiety throughout the North, where nearly everyone felt that the nation was on the verge of its final decision for peace or war. Bulletins appeared in New York at noon: "Great excitement in Washington. The new President up all night. Great efforts to make him alter his inaugural. The President firm." This was a canard. Extras appeared there and in other cities at two o'clock, announcing that the ceremonies were safely under way; and multitudes of citizens, reading them, fervently exclaimed, "Thank God!" Evening editions carried first half and then all of the address. The comment of George Templeton Strong doubtless represents the first response of countless intelligent men. "I think there's a clank of metal in it," he wrote of the speech. "It's unlike any message or state paper of any class that has appeared in my time, to my knowledge. It is characterized by strong individuality and the absence of conventionalism of

41 The hat episode is also mentioned in J. G. Holland, *Lincoln*, 278 (1866). For a discussion of the authenticity of *The Diary of a Public Man* see James G. Randall in *Amer. Hist. Rev.*, XLI, 277-279. For the organization of volunteer companies in the District of Columbia to ensure the protection of the national capital and an orderly inauguration, see the interesting essay by Colonel Charles P. Stone in *Battles and Leaders of the Civil War*, I, 22, 23. Stone accuses Floyd of treasonable intentions. The *N. Y. Herald, Tribune,* and *Times* give full accounts of the inaugural ceremonies.

thought or diction. It doesn't run in the ruts of Public Documents number one to number ten million and one, but seems to introduce one to a *man*, and to dispose one to like him."

There was indeed a clank of metal in the address. Reciting the constitutional and historical arguments for deeming the Union perpetual, Lincoln declared: "It follows from these views that no State, upon its own mere motion, can lawfully get out of the Union; that laws and ordinances to that effect are legally void; and that acts of violence within any State or States against the authority of the United States are insurrectionary or revolutionary, according to circumstances." He proceeded:

I therefore consider that, in view of the Constitution and the laws, the Union is unbroken, and, to the extent of my ability, I shall take care, as the Constitution itself expressly enjoins upon me, that the laws of the Union be faithfully executed in all the States. . . . In doing this there needs to be no bloodshed or violence; and there shall be none, unless it be forced upon the national authority. The power confided to me will be used to hold, occupy, and possess the property and places belonging to the government, and to collect the duties and imposts; but beyond what may be necessary for these objects, there will be no invasion—no using of force against or among the people anywhere.

But the address was also full of expressions of a conciliatory spirit. Lincoln once more, and emphatically, declared that he had no purpose to interfere with slavery in the States where it existed. He asserted that in the matter of reclaiming fugitive slaves, Congress must make good the unanimous oath of its members to support the Constitution. He promised that where hostility to the United States in any interior community should be so great as to prevent resident citizens from holding Federal office, "there will be no attempt to force obnoxious strangers among the people for that object." Asking the nation to take time and think calmly, he appealed directly to the people of the South. "In your hands, my dissatisfied fellow-countrymen, and not in mine, is the momentous issue of civil war. The government will not assail you. You can have no conflict without being yourselves the aggressors. *You* have no oath registered in heaven to destroy the government, while *I* shall have the most solemn one to 'preserve, protect, and defend' it." And he ended, in poetic phrases for which Seward had supplied the framework of ideas:

I am loth to close. We are not enemies, but friends. We must not be enemies. Though passion may have strained, it must not break our bonds of affection. The mystic chords of memory, stretching from every battlefield, and patriot grave, to every living heart and hearthstone, all over this broad land, will yet swell the chorus of the Union, when again touched, as surely they will be, by the better angels of our nature.

[handwritten draft, struck-through words shown in best reading]

I close., We are not we must not vist be aliens
or enemies but countrymen fellow countrymen
and brethren. Although passion has strained
our bonds of affection too hardly they must
not be broken they will not. I am
sure they will not be broken. The
mystic chords which proceeding from every
so many battle fields and so many
many patriot graves pass through
all the hearts and hearths all the
hearths in this broad continent of ours
will yet. reason again harmonize in
their ancient music when touched in they
gently breathed upon again by the better
angel guardian angel of the nation

Seward wrote the paragraph above and submitted it for the close of the inaugural address, to read: "I close. We are not we must not be aliens or enemies but fellow countrymen and brethren. Although passion has strained our bonds of affection too hardly they must not, I am sure they will not be broken. The mystic chords which proceeding from so many battle fields and so many patriot graves pass through all the hearts and all the hearths in this broad continent of ours will yet again harmonize in their ancient music when breathed upon by the guardian angel of the nation." Lincoln revised this, shortened, transmuted it into slightly different meaning and a distinctly changed verbal music, adding it to the printer's proof text brought on from Springfield, as below:

[printed proof fragment, partly struck-through]

You can have no conflict, without being yourselves the aggressors. You have no oath registered in Heaven to destroy the government, while I shall have the most solemn one to "preserve, protect and defend" it.

[handwritten Lincoln revision]

I am loth to close. We are not enemies,
but friends— We must not be enemies. Though passion may
have strained, it must not break our bonds of affection.
The mystic chords of memory, stretching from every battlefield, and patriot grave, to every living heart and hearthstone, all over this broad land, will yet swell the chorus of the Union, when again touched, as surely they will
be, by the better angels of our nature.

460

It was natural that public response to the inaugural should be governed largely by party lines. The Chicago *Tribune*, the St. Louis *Democrat*, the New York *Evening Post* and *Tribune*, the Springfield *Republican*, all praised it warmly. So did such Republican leaders as Greeley, Sumner, Preston King, Hale, and Trumbull. On the other side, the Philadelphia *Pennsylvanian* called it a weak declaration of war on the South, a tiger's claw concealed under the fur of Sewardism; the Albany *Atlas and Argus* predicted that the attempt to collect revenues must lead to collision and war; and the New York *Herald* condemned it as bearing "marks of indecision, and yet of strong coercion proclivities." In the now all-important border States the secessionists regarded it as warlike, while many Union men seized on its mild phraseology as ground for hope. Thus in Virginia the fire-eating Richmond *Enquirer* declared that peace was now impossible—"Virginia must fight"; yet Governor John Letcher thought that it strengthened the hands of the conservatives. Many North Carolinians attacked it as a war message; but John A. Gilmer held that it offered cheering assurances which justified the South in waiting for the sober second thought of the North. Douglas said in the Senate on March 5 that after a careful analysis he had come to the conclusion that it was a peace and not a war speech; and John Bell declared that the South should accept it as a peace offering until by some act the North proved it otherwise.[42]

In the Lower South, however, it was generally treated as a justification of armed secession. The Charleston *Mercury* denounced Lincoln's "insolence" and "brutality"; Mobile and New Orleans journals grew inflammatory; and dispatches from Montgomery on the 5th universally construed the address as meaning that war was inevitable.

Far more important than the outward pageantry of the day were certain events of which the public knew nothing. On that historic March 4, the outgoing Secretary of War received from Major Anderson a disturbing dispatch, stating that the supplies of Fort Sumter were running low; intimating that he could not hold out much longer without help; and declaring that in his and his officers' opinion it would take at least twenty thousand troops to force their relief.[43] The South Carolinians had so strengthened the surrounding batteries, he wrote, that the fort might easily be reduced at any time. On that March 4, Martin J. Crawford of Georgia, Commissioner of the Confederate States, who had arrived in Washington only the previous day, held eager conferences with

42 Strong's comment on the inaugural is his MS Diary of March 5, 1861. The N. Y. *Herald* of March 5 and 6 contained an excellent resume of editorial opinion; the N. Y. *Times* of March 6 a number of excerpts. Jubal A. Early told the Virginia Convention that Lincoln's words showed he would perform his duty in moderate spirit; Munford, *Virginia's Attitude Toward Slavery and Secession*, 266. For a general survey see Randall, *Lincoln*, I, 303–308.

43 *Official Records*, Series I. Vol. I, 188 ff.

such Southern leaders as remained in the capital; and he mailed to Robert Toombs, Secretary of State in the Confederate Government, a long letter describing the situation. He wrote that Chase and Blair would compose the element in the Cabinet standing for coercion; that John Bell was in Washington, and was urgent in his entreaties to Lincoln not to disturb the Confederate States, but that he would not be heeded if the new Administration believed that it could act vigorously without losing the border States; and that "whatsoever the Republican Party can do without driving out Virginia it will do, and such coercive measures as the new Administration may *with safety* adopt it will most certainly." [43a] Ex-Senator Wigfall telegraphed from Washington that night to Charleston: "Inaugural means war. There is strong ground for belief that reenforcements will be speedily sent. Be vigilant."

Lincoln, as a matter of fact, wished to do everything within the limits of his duty to avoid a collision. When Scott, after studying Anderson's dispatch, reported to him that "evacuation seems inevitable . . . if indeed the wornout garrison be not assaulted and carried in the present week," he calmly instructed the general to give the subject further study. Nevertheless, the situation had become highly inflammable. Edward Everett, reading Lincoln's inaugural address, believed that its conciliatory tone was more than offset by the pledge to hold the forts and to collect the customs. "Either measure," he wrote in his diary, "will result in civil war, which I am compelled to look upon as almost certain." [44] Had he known what Major Anderson was reporting to Washington and what Commissioner Crawford was reporting to Montgomery, his forebodings would have been darker still.

* * * * * * *

Great and complex events have great and complex causes. Burke, in his *Reflections on the Revolution in France,* wrote that "a state without the means

43a Robert Toombs Letter-Book, Trescot Papers, South Caroliniana Library. Crawford's letter was dated March 3. His fellow Commissioners, John Forsyth and A. B. Roman, had not yet arrived. Bell, wrote Crawford, had assured Lincoln "that any attempt to reinforce the Forts, collect the revenue, or in any way whatever to interfere with your Government would be the signal for every border State to secede from the Union and join the Southern Confederacy. He advises an *indefinite* truce; the withdrawal of the troops from the Forts (except a sergeant with a nominal force); the flag of the U. S. to be kept floating on the fortifications to satisfy the war party North; in the meantime the Confederate States are to be left alone, to do as they may choose, prepare for war, strengthen defences, in short to do whatever may seem good to them. The advantages to the U. S. being, that the more we may do, looking to independence and safety, the greater will be the amount of taxation upon the people and the sooner will a current of dissatisfaction and discontent set in, resulting at last in a reconstruction upon the most permanent and durable basis." Crawford thought that part of the Administration was receptive to these ideas—but they would not prevail.

44 MS Diary, March 4, 1861.

of some change is without the means of its conservation," and that a constant reconciliation of "the two principles of conservation and correction" is indispensable to healthy national growth. It is safe to say that every such revolutionary era as that on which the United States entered in 1860 finds its genesis in an inadequate adjustment of these two forces. It is also safe to say that when a tragic national failure occurs, it is largely a failure of leadership. "Brains are of three orders," wrote Machiavelli, "those that understand of themselves, those that understand when another shows them, and those that understand neither by themselves nor by the showing of others." Ferment and change must steadily be controlled; the real must, as Bryce said, be kept resting on the ideal; and if disaster is to be avoided, wise leaders must help thoughtless men to understand, and direct the action of invincibly ignorant men. Necessary reforms may be obstructed in various ways; by sheer inertia, by tyranny and class selfishness, or by the application of compromise to basic principles—this last being in Lowell's view the main cause of the Civil War. Ordinarily the obstruction arises from a combination of all these elements. To explain the failure of American leadership in 1846–1861, and the revolution that ensued, is a bafflingly complicated problem.

Looking backward from the verge of war in March, 1861, Americans could survey a series of ill-fated decisions by their chosen agents. One unfortunate decision was embodied in Douglas's Kansas-Nebraska Act of 1854. Had an overwhelming majority of Americans been ready to accept the squatter sovereignty principle, this law might have proved a statesmanlike stroke; but it was so certain that powerful elements North and South would resist it to the last that it accentuated the strife and confusion. Another disastrous decision was made by Taney and his associates in the Dred Scott pronouncement of 1857. Still another was made by Buchanan when he weakly accepted the Lecompton Constitution and tried to force that fraudulent document through Congress. The Northern legislatures which passed Personal Liberty Acts made an unhappy decision. Most irresponsible, wanton, and disastrous of all was the decision of those Southern leaders who in 1858–60 turned to the provocative demand for Congressional protection of slavery in all the Territories of the republic.[45] Still other errors might be named. Obviously, however, it is the forces behind these decisions which demand our study; the waters pouring down the gorge, not the rocks which threw their spray into the air.

At this point we meet a confused clamor of voices as various students

45 We stated in an earlier chapter that Southern leaders in 1857 had time for a few more decisions, but they had to think fast and think straight. This slave-code demand represented their most flagrant error. It has been said that Jefferson Davis adopted it because his blatherskite rival A. G. Brown took it up. But a true statesman does not let an irresponsible rival force him into courses he recognizes as unwise.

attempt an explanation of the tragic denouement of 1861. Some writers are as content with a simple explanation as Lord Clarendon was when he attributed the English Civil War to the desire of Parliament for an egregious domination of the government. The bloody conflict, declared James Ford Rhodes, had "a single cause, slavery." He was but echoing what Henry Wilson and other early historians had written, that the aggressions of the Slave Power offered the central explanation. That opinion had been challenged as early as 1861 by the London *Saturday Review*, which remarked that "slavery is but a surface question in American politics," and by such Southern propagandists as Yancey, who tried to popularize a commercial theory of the war, emphasizing a supposed Southern revolt against the tariff and other Yankee exactions. A later school of writers was to find the key to the tragedy in an inexorable conflict between the business-minded North and the agrarian-minded South, a thrusting industrialism colliding with a rather static agricultural society. Still another group of writers has accepted the theory that the war resulted from psychological causes. They declare that agitators, propagandists, and alarmists on both sides, exaggerating the real differences of interest, created a state of mind, a hysterical excitement, which made armed conflict inevitable.

At the very outset of the war Senator Mason of Virginia, writing to his daughter, asserted that two systems of society were in conflict; systems, he implied, as different as those of Carthage and Rome, Protestant Holland and Catholic Spain. That view, too, was later to be elaborated by a considerable school of writers. Two separate nations, they declared, had arisen within the United States in 1861, much as two separate nations had emerged within the first British Empire by 1776. Contrasting ways of life, rival group consciousness, divergent hopes and fears made a movement for separation logical; and the minority people, believing its peculiar civilization in danger of suppression, began a war for independence. We are told, indeed, that two types of nationalism came into conflict: a Northern nationalism which wished to preserve the unity of the whole republic, and a Southern nationalism intent on creating an entirely new republic.

It is evident that some of these explanations deal with merely superficial phenomena, and that others, when taken separately, represent but subsidiary elements in the play of forces. Slavery was a great fact; the demands of Northern industrialism constituted a great fact; sectional hysteria was a great fact. But do they not perhaps relate themselves to some profounder underlying cause? This question has inspired one student to suggest that "the confusion of a growing state" may offer the fundamental explanation of the drift to war; an unsatisfactory hypothesis, for westward growth, railroad growth, business growth, and cultural growth, however much attended with "confusion," were unifying factors, and it was not the new-made West but old-settled South Carolina which led in the schism.

One fact needs emphatic statement: of all the monistic explanations for the drift to war, that posited upon supposed economic causes is the flimsiest. This theory was sharply rejected at the time by so astute an observer as Alexander H. Stephens. South Carolina, he wrote his brother on New Year's Day, 1861, was seceding from a tariff "which is just what her own Senators and members in Congress made it." As for the charges of consolidation and despotism made by some Carolinians, he thought they arose from peevishness rather than a calm analysis of facts. "The truth is, the South, almost in mass, has voted, I think, for every measure of general legislation that has passed both houses and become law for the last ten years." The South, far from groaning under tyranny, had controlled the government almost from its beginning, and Stephens believed that its only real grievance lay in the Northern refusal to return fugitive slaves and to stop the antislavery agitation. "All other complaints are founded on threatened dangers which may never come, and which I feel very sure would be averted if the South would pursue a judicious and wise course." Stephens was right. It was true that the whole tendency of Federal legislation 1842–1860 was toward free trade; true that the tariff in force when secession began was largely Southern-made; true that it was the lowest tariff the country had known since 1816; true that it cost a nation of thirty million people but sixty million dollars in indirect revenue; true that without secession no new tariff law, obnoxious to the Democratic Party, could have passed before 1863—if then.

In the official explanations which one Southern State after another published for its secession, economic grievances are either omitted entirely or given minor position. There were few such supposed grievances which the agricultural States of Illinois, Iowa, Indiana, Wisconsin, and Minnesota did not share with the South—and they never threatened to secede. Charles A. Beard finds the tap-root of the war in the resistance of the planter interest to Northern demands enlarging the old Hamilton-Webster policy. The South was adamant in standing for "no high protective tariffs, no ship subsidies, no national banking and currency system; in short, none of the measures which business enterprise deemed essential to its progress." But the Republican platform in 1856 was silent on the tariff; in 1860 it carried a milk-and-water statement on the subject which Western Republicans took, mild as it was, with a wry face; the incoming President was little interested in the tariff; and any harsh legislation was impossible. Ship subsidies were not an issue in the campaign of 1860. Neither were a national banking system and a national currency system. They were not mentioned in the Republican platform nor discussed by party debaters. The Pacific Railroad was advocated both by the Douglas Democrats and the Republicans; and it is noteworthy that Seward and Douglas were for building both a Northern and a Southern line. In short, the divisive economic issues are easily exaggerated. At the same time, the unifying economic factors were both numerous and powerful. North and South had economies which were largely complementary. It was no misfortune to the South that Massachusetts cotton mills wanted its staple, and that New York ironmasters like Hewitt were eager to sell rails dirt-cheap to Southern railway builders; and sober businessmen on both sides, merchants, bankers, and manufacturers, were the men most anxious to keep the peace and hold the Union together.[46]

We must seek further for an explanation; and in so doing, we must give special weight to the observations of penetrating leaders of the time, who knew at firsthand the spirit of the people. Henry J. Raymond, moderate editor of the New York *Times*, a sagacious man who disliked Northern abolitionists and Southern radicals, wrote in January, 1860, an analysis of the impending conflict which attributed it to a competition for power:

In every country there must be a just and equal balance of powers in the government, an equal distribution of the national forces. Each section and each interest must exercise its due share of influence and control. It is always more or less difficult to preserve their just equipoise, and the larger the country, and the more varied its great interests, the more difficult does the task become, and the greater the shock and disturbance caused by an attempt to adjust it when once disturbed. I believe I state only what is generally conceded to be a fact, when I say that the growth of the Northern States in population, in wealth, in all the elements of political influence and control, has been out of proportion to their political influence in the Federal Councils. While the Southern States have less than a third of the aggregate population of the Union, their interests have influenced the policy of the government far more than the interests of the Northern States. . . . Now the North has made rapid advances within the last five years, and it naturally claims a proportionate share of influence and power in the affairs of the Confederacy.

It is inevitable that this claim should be put forward, and it is also inevitable that it should be conceded. No party can long resist it; it overrides all parties, and makes them the mere instruments of its will. It is quite as strong today in the heart of the Democratic party of the North as in the Republican ranks; and any party which ignores it will lose its hold on the public mind.

Why does the South resist this claim? Not because it is unjust in itself,

46 South Carolina's Declaration of immediate causes of secession ignored economic issues, and concentrated upon slavery. Rhett's Address to the other slaveholding States did charge the North with gross injustice in tariff legislation; but the whole body of South Carolina's Representatives and Senators had voted for the existing tariff of 1857, and Rhett in defending his Address declared that to win the sympathy of Britain and France, a protest against protective tariffs would be more useful than a protest grounded on the slavery question. McPherson, *Political History*, 12–20.

but because it has become involved with the question of slavery, and has drawn so much of its vigor and vitality from that quarter, that it is almost merged in that issue. The North bases its demand for increased power, in a very great degree, on the action of the government in regard to slavery—and the just and rightful ascendency of the North in the Federal councils comes thus to be regarded as an element of danger to the institutions of the Southern States.

In brief, Raymond, who held that slavery was a moral wrong, that its economic and social tendencies were vicious, and that the time had come to halt its growth with a view to its final eradication, believed that the contest was primarily one for power, and for the application of that power to the slave system. With this opinion Alexander H. Stephens agreed. The Georgian said he believed slavery both morally and politically right. In his letter to Lincoln on December 30, 1860, he declared that the South did not fear that the new Republican Administration would interfere directly and immediately with slavery in the States. What Southerners did fear was the ultimate result of the shift of power which had just occurred—in its application to slavery:

Now this subject, which is confessedly on all sides outside of the constitutional action of the Government, so far as the States are concerned, is made the 'central idea' in the platform of principles announced by the triumphant party. The leading object seems to be simply, and wantonly, if you please, to put the institutions of nearly half the States under the ban of public opinion and national condemnation. This, upon general principles, is quite enough of itself to arouse a spirit not only of general indignation, but of revolt on the part of the proscribed. Let me illustrate. It is generally conceded by the Republicans even, that Congress cannot interfere with slavery in the States. It is equally conceded that Congress cannot establish any form of religious worship. Now suppose that any one of the present Christian churches or sects prevailed in all the Southern States, but had no existence in any one of the Northern States,—under such circumstances suppose the people of the Northern States should organize a political party, not upon a foreign or domestic policy, but with one leading idea of condemnation of the doctrines and tenets of that particular church, and with an avowed object of preventing its extension into the common Territories, even after the highest judicial tribunal of the land had decided they had no such constitutional power. And suppose that a party so organized should carry a Presidential election. Is it not apparent that a general feeling of resistance to the success, aims, and objects of such a party would necessarily and rightfully ensue?

Raymond and Stephens agreed that the two sections were competing for power; that a momentous transfer of power had just occurred; and that it held fateful consequences because it was involved with the issue of slavery, taking authority from a section which believed slavery moral and healthy, and giving it to a section which held slavery immoral and pernicious. To Stephens this transfer was ground for resuming the ultimate sovereignty of the States. Here we find a somewhat more complex statement of James Ford Rhodes's thesis that the central cause of the Civil War lay in slavery. Here, too, we revert to the assertions of Yancey and Lincoln that the vital conflict was between those who thought slavery right and those who thought it wrong. But this definition we can accept only if we probe a little deeper for a concept which both modifies and enlarges the basic source of perplexity and quarrel.

The main root of the conflict (and there were minor roots) was the problem of slavery *with its complementary problem of race-adjustment;* the main source of the tragedy was the refusal of either section to face these conjoined problems squarely and pay the heavy costs of a peaceful settlement. Had it not been for the difference in race, the slavery issue would have presented no great difficulties. But as the racial gulf existed, the South inarticulately but clearly perceived that elimination of this issue would still leave it the terrible problem of the Negro. Those historians who write that if slavery had simply been left alone it would soon have withered overlook this heavy impediment. The South as a whole in 1846–61 was not moving toward emancipation, but away from it. It was not relaxing the laws which guarded the system, but reinforcing them. It was not ameliorating slavery, but making it harsher and more implacable. The South was further from a just solution of the slavery problem in 1830 than it had been in 1789. It was further from a tenable solution in 1860 than it had been in 1830. Why was it going from bad to worse? Because Southern leaders refused to nerve their people to pay the heavy price of race-adjustment. These leaders never made up their mind to deal with the problem as the progressive temper of civilization demanded. They would not adopt the new outlook which the upward march of mankind required because they saw that the gradual abolition of slavery would bring a measure of political privilege; that political privilege would usher in a measure of economic equality; that on the heels of economic equality would come a rising social status for the Negro. Southern leadership dared not ask the people to pay this price.

A heavy responsibility for the failure of America in this period rests with this Southern leadership, which lacked imagination, ability, and courage. But the North was by no means without its full share, for the North equally refused to give a constructive examination to the central question of slavery as linked with race adjustment. This was because of two principal reasons. Most abolitionists and many other sentimental-minded Northerners simply denied that the problem existed. Regarding all Negroes as white men with dark skins, whom a few years of schooling would bring abreast of the dominant race, they thought that no difficult adjustment was required. A much more numerous body of Northerners would have granted that a great and terrible task of race adjustment existed—but they were reluctant to help shoulder any part of it. Take a million or two million Negroes into the Northern States? Indiana, Illinois, and even Kansas were unwilling to take a single additional person of color. Pay tens of millions to help educate and elevate the colored population? Take even a first step by offering to pay the Southern slaveholders some recompense for a gradual liberation of their human property? No Northern politician dared ask his constituents to make so unpopular a sacrifice. The North, like the South, found it easier to drift blindly toward disaster.

The hope of solving the slavery problem without a civil war rested upon several interrelated factors, of which one merits special emphasis. We have said that the South as a whole was laboring to bolster and stiffen slavery—which was much to its discredit. But it is nevertheless true that slavery was dying all around the edges of its domain; it was steadily decaying in Delaware, Maryland, western Virginia, parts of Kentucky, and Missouri. Much of the harshness of Southern legislation in the period sprang from a sense that slavery was in danger from *internal* weaknesses. In no great time Delaware, Maryland, and Missouri were likely to enter the column of free States; and if they did, reducing the roster to twelve, the doom of the institution would be clearly written. Allied with this factor was the rapid comparative increase of Northern strength, and the steady knitting of economic, social, and moral ties between the North and West, leaving the South in a position of manifest inferiority. A Southern Confederacy had a fair fighting chance in 1861; by 1880 it would have had very little. If secession could have been postponed by two decades, natural forces might well have placed a solution full in sight. Then, too, the growing pressure of world sentiment must in time have produced its effect. But to point out these considerations is not to suggest that in 1861 a policy of procrastination and appeasement would have done anything but harm. All hope of bringing Southern majority sentiment to a better attitude would have been lost if Lincoln and his party had flinched on the basic issue of the restriction of slavery; for by the seventh decade of nineteenth century history, the time had come when that demand had to be maintained.

While in indicting leadership we obviously indict the public behind the leaders, we must also lay some blame upon a political environment which gave leadership a poor chance. American parties, under the pressure of sectional feeling, worked badly. The government suffered greatly, moreover, from the lack of any adequate planning agency. Congress was not a truly deliberative body, and its committees had not yet learned to do long-range planning. The President might have formulated plans, but he never did. For one reason, no President between Polk and Lincoln had either the ability or the prestige required; for another reason, Fillmore, Pierce, and Buchanan all held that their duty was merely to execute the laws, not to initiate legislation. Had the country possessed a ministerial form of government, the Cabinet in leading the legislature would have been compelled to lay down a program of real scope concerning slavery. As it was, leadership in Washington was supplied only spasmodically by men like Clay, Douglas, and Crittenden.

And as we have noted, the rigidity of the American system was at this time a grave handicap. Twice, in the fall of 1854 and of 1858, the elections gave a stunning rebuke to the Administration. Under a ministerial system, the old government would probably have gone out and a new one have come in. In 1854, however, Pierce continued to carry on the old policies, and in 1858 Buchanan remained the drearily inept helmsman of the republic. Never in our history were bold, quick planning and a flexible administration of policy more needed; never was the failure to supply them more complete.

Still another element in the tragic chronicle of the time must be mentioned. Much that happens in human affairs is accidental. When a country is guided by true statesmen the role of accident is minimized; when it is not, unforeseen occurrences are numerous and dangerous. In the summer and fall of 1858, as we have seen, the revival of a conservative opposition party in the upper South, devoted to the Union, furnished a real gleam of hope. If this opposition had been given unity and determined leadership, if moderate Southerners had stood firm against the plot of Yancey and others to disrupt the Democratic Party, if Floyd had been vigilant enough to read the warning letter about John Brown and act on it, the situation might even then have been saved. Instead, John Brown's mad raid fell on public opinion like a thunderstroke, exasperating men everywhere and dividing North and South more tragically than ever. The last chance of persuading the South to submit to an essential step, the containment of slavery, was gone.

The war, when it came, was not primarily a conflict over State Rights, although that issue had become involved in it. It was not primarily a war born of economic grievances, although many Southerners had been led to think that they were suffering, or would soon suffer, economic wrongs. It was not a war created by politicians and publicists who fomented hysteric excitement; for while hysteria was important, we have always to ask what basic reasons made possible the propaganda which aroused it. It was not primarily a war about slavery alone, although that institution seemed to many the grand cause. It was a war over slavery *and* the future position of the Negro race in North America. Was the Negro to be allowed, as a result of the shift of power signalized by Lincoln's election, to take the first step toward an ultimate position of general economic, political, and social equality with the white man? Or was he to be held immobile in a degraded, servile position, unchanging for the next hundred years as it had remained essentially unchanged for the hundred years past? These questions were implicit in Lincoln's demand that slavery be placed in a position where the public mind could rest assured of its ultimate extinction.

Evasion by the South, evasion by the North, were no longer possible. The alternatives faced were an unpopular but curative adjustment of the situation by the opposed parties, or a war that would force an adjustment upon the loser. For Americans in 1861, as for many other peoples throughout history, war was easier than wisdom and courage.

RESPONSIBILITY OF McLEAN AND CURTIS FOR THE
DRED SCOTT DECISION

The evidence available does not warrant dogmatic statements on the prime responsibility for the annulment of the Missouri Compromise restriction; but there are reasons why we may entertain doubts as to the sole burden of McLean and Curtis. The truth seems rather to be that the responsibility falls upon a number of the judges, and that Wayne must be included among those whose share in bringing about a broad decision was greatest.

To begin with, we have the knowledge that, from the outset, Southern leaders like Stephens and Democratic journals like the *Union* were urging the slave State judges to write a broad decision. We have Catron's statement as early as February 6 that Daniel was prepared to deliver his opinion "at length." We have Judge Campbell's testimony that Wayne, at a conference February 14, prior to the reading of Nelson's judgment, moved that his limited decision be put aside and that Chief Justice Taney write another of sweeping character— a motion which carried. Campbell not only made this statement to Taney's biographer Tyler, but repeated it in a letter of October 30, 1879, to George Ticknor Curtis. After accurately reciting many details, Campbell wrote: "Judge Wayne made the motion. . . . He stated that the case had been twice argued with thoroughness; that public expectation had been awakened and a decision of the important question looked for; that the Court would be condemned as failing in a performance of its duty, and that his own opinion was decided that the Chief Justice should prepare the opinion of the Court, and discuss all of the questions in the cause. There was no debate about this. It seemed to be acquiesced in, though some did not approve it." [1] Wayne, according to G. T. Curtis, made public boast of his achievement the day it was won.

Senator Yulee of Florida also asserts that Wayne had accepted primary responsibility for the broad verdict. From two sources we have proof that Judge Benjamin R. Curtis identified Wayne as the prime mover in substituting a broad for a narrow judgment; for Judge Curtis told his brother this, and he also told Clement H. Hill, one-time Assistant Attorney-General of the United States, that Wayne not only persuaded the Chief Justice to recall the case from Judge Nel-

[1] Campbell to George T. Curtis, October 30, 1879; Campbell Papers, courtesy of Charles Warren.

son, but busied himself to induce the other judges to concur in Taney's decision.[2] For that matter, Wayne states in the first sentence of his own brief concurrence with Taney that *before* the Chief Justice wrote his opinion he had prepared one which he subsequently laid aside as superfluous.[3]

In the second place, the question of motive enters. What possible reason had Curtis and McLean for provoking a judgment that Congress possessed no power over slavery in the Territories? They knew that all freesoilers dreaded such a pronouncement, which would be hailed as a resounding triumph for slavery. To be sure, McLean has been accused of a political motive in wishing to strengthen himself with the Republican Party. But this accusation is unconvincing in view of the facts that since the convention of 1856 he was politically dead; that in 1860 he would be seventy-five and within a year of his grave; and that the first weeks of 1857, with the Democrats assuming power for another four years, were no time to think of political chances. Moreover, to take a step seemingly certain to strengthen the new Administration would be perverse political tactics. On the other hand, Southern members of the Court knew that a decision annulling the Missouri Compromise restriction would be hailed with joy in all slavery areas. Press, politicians—and President-elect—were telling them that it would unify their party and give it enduring advantages. They had a motive for acting, while the two freesoil members had none. It was with reference to this Southern and Democratic attitude that Montgomery Blair, accurately writing Martin Van Buren on February 5, 1857, that the Missouri Compromise would be invalidated, stated his belief that the decision would be influenced by *outside pressure* on the judges (Van Buren Papers).

The majority of the Court, moreover, had special reasons for deeming this an opportunity not to be lost. The Dred Scott case, the first which had permitted a clear-cut decision on the Compromise, might also be the last to occur in many years. Chief Justice Taney was now old and ailing. Kindly Judge Curtis wrote his brother in February: "Our aged Chief Justice, who will be eighty years old in a few days, and who grows more feeble in body, but retains his alacrity and force of mind wonderfully, is not able to write much." The outcry against the partisan and sectional character of the Court was making a sharp impression. Before a similar case occurred, the character of the panel might be altered completely. Taney, his patriotism alloyed by sectionalism, indubitably wished to use the Court to bulwark his own people and their institutions. His most acute biographer writes: "First and foremost it is necessary to remember his devotion to the South, of which he was a product, and his belief that, if the trend of events continued, the South was doomed. . . . His deepest fear seems

2 Curtis, *Const. Hist. U. S.*, 266–278; Curtis, *Benjamin R. Curtis*, I, 234–236.
3 19 *Howard*, 454.

to have been that when a northern political party assumed the reins of government the South would not act with sufficient unanimity to make rebellion effective." [4] Now was the moment, if ever, to strike a judicial blow for Southern rights in the Territories.

Still another consideration may be noted. While the statement of Grier and Catron as to the provocative stand of the two dissentients might seem credible with respect to McLean (whose opinion took up the issues in a curious inverse order, dealing with Congressional power before he considered in detail the action of the courts below), it is quite incredible as regards Judge Curtis. That conservative Whig of the Daniel Webster school, who had protested against Sumner's election, who had endorsed the Seventh of March speech, who had long represented the views of State Street business circles, was one of the last men in the country to act a radical part. The abolitionists attacked him as a "doughface." [5] His son's biography expressly states that every word of both his and McLean's opinions was written only *after* they had heard Taney's judgment read in conference.[6] Moreover, his judgment protested against the Court's sweeping action. He declares in it that after the Court had decided that Dred was a slave under Missouri law, it could not properly proceed to larger issues. "I dissent . . . from . . . the opinion . . . that a person of African descent cannot be a citizen of the United States; and I regret I must go further and dissent . . . from what I deem their assumption of authority to examine the constitutionality of the act of Congress commonly called the Missouri Compromise. . . . I feel obliged to say that, in my opinion, such an exertion of judicial power transcends the limits of the authority of the Court."

How could a justice who denied the Court's right to examine the issue of Congressional power, and rebuked it for doing so, have insisted upon discussing that issue when the Court first proposed to avoid it? To be sure, Judge Curtis argued that his own position was different; that since he held that the Federal courts possessed jurisdiction, he was bound to consider the merits of the case to ascertain if the judgment of the lower court were correct; and that he must declare the Supreme Court of Missouri wrong in its judgment, which conflicted with the weight of judicial opinion in the slave States and with its own

4 Swisher. *Taney*, 503–504. Curtis has been accused of taking the broad ground to curry favor with Boston, where he would later practice law. But (1) it is not clear that at this time he had determined to resign from the Court; (2) his legal eminence would have given him a lucrative practice no matter what his political views; (3) conservative Boston businessmen would have warmly approved if he had refused to rouse new sectional issues; and (4) his lifelong integrity makes such a charge absurd. As for McLean, he would certainly have been glad to pen a ringing dissent at the time of the first argument, in the December term of 1855, when it would have helped his chances in the Republican Convention of 1856. But that time was now past, and the situation was completely altered.

5 October 22, 1854, et seq.; Quincy Papers.
6 Curtis, *Benjamin R. Curtis*, I, 238.

previous decisions. His argument up to this point rested upon the validity of the eighth section of the Missouri Compromise Act. But the whole tenor of his opinion bears out the statement of his son and biographer that "every word" was written as a dissent from an opinion of the Chief Justice which he "had heard read in conference," and which had "elaborately maintained" the unconstitutionality of the Compromise.

It is not necessary, in setting aside the statements of Grier and Catron, to question the veracity of these men; we may merely question their accuracy. While we must not be dogmatic in passing upon this murky question of responsibility, it would seem that they give a partial and partisan view of a complex transaction.

Admittedly, when the judges began considering the case in conference a series of angry discussions ensued. Tradition states that one session grew so violent that Taney had to use his authority to restore order. As the debate became heated, judges on both sides doubtless manifested a desire to set down certain views on paper. Justice McLean would tell Wayne that if he expressed his erroneous ideas publicly, McLean would voice contrary opinions; Wayne and Daniel would retort in kind. Emerging from such a debate, when Catron and Grier wrote to Buchanan they would naturally describe the dissentients as the provocative members, just as McLean would naturally place the blame at a Southern door. We can go further; we can imagine several Southern judges discussing the case after a heated conference, agreeing that the views of Curtis and McLean were pernicious, and coming to regard the pair as trouble-makers, even if they wished to voice their conclusions only in private. In short, the letters of Catron and Grier can be explained simply as a distortion of the painful controversy then raging.

It is an indisputable fact that during the consultations of the court in the spring of 1856, on the first argument of the case before it, radical opinion both South and North had hoped for a decision on the Missouri Compromise question. The Washington correspondent of the New York *Tribune*, James Harvey, expressed the hope that with "aid from the Southern members of the court" a broad decision would be rendered. When Nelson at that time moved a reargument of the issues, it was (as Father Vincent C. Hopkins, S.J., shows in his monograph *The Dred Scott Decision*) both because he was uncertain of the proper scope of the decision, and because he doubted the wisdom of bringing the court "in collision with a popular election." After the victory of Buchanan, the desire of Republicans for a broad decision naturally abated, while that of Democrats outside the popular sovereignty school remained keen. It is significant that the critical motion on February 14, 1857, was made by Judge Wayne. He made it abruptly. As we have seen, he pointed to the public interest and expectation that the case had aroused. He declared that the court would fail in meeting the anticipations of the country if it did not render a broad decision. These are not the words of a man reluctantly spurred to action by two opponents; they are the words of a man speaking his own wishes and keenly conscious of outside pressures. A majority of other judges (Nelson being absent) readily assented; and thus the die was cast. From all the evidence, it seems clear that responsibility must be widely distributed, and that while McLean may have been a prime mover, Wayne—and probably Daniel—did not lag behind him.

It remains to say a few words about President-elect Buchanan's intervention. While no "conspiracy" was concocted between him and Taney, he did let key members of the Court know just what kind of decision he wanted, and just why he wanted it; so that the Court would save him from the peril of independent action on the disputed interpretation of popular sovereignty, quiet that disruptive question, restore unity to the party, and strike a crushing blow at the basic doctrine of the Republicans.[7] He moved the hesitant Grier to act. If Grier had not done so, Congressional power over slavery in the Territories might not have been adjudged null. Buchanan assumed a heavy partial responsibility for the Dred Scott decision. He had always taken a realistic view of the bench. He had long thought that politics should govern it. Six years earlier, he had written that the Democrats must control the Pennsylvania Supreme Court:

The mind that is strongly imbued with Democratic principles will naturally and necessarily take a different view of great constitutional and other highly important questions involving the rights and liberties of the people from that taken by a mind which has all its life delighted in high-toned federal doctrines. I agree that upon questions of mere *meum* and *tuum*, the politics of the judge could make no difference, but upon important questions involving the first principles of our government the difference might be very great. No Whig President has ever appointed a Democratic Judge of the Supreme Court of the United States, nor has a Democratic President appointed a Whig.[8]

It may be added that the Dred Scott decision was interestingly reviewed in one of the Insular Cases, *De Lima vs. Bidwell* (1901); and that the able argument of Frederic R. Coudert in this case contains much illuminating matter (182 U.S. 1).

7 See Grier's revealing phrase, "The cause of our anxiety to produce this result." Philip Auchampaugh considers Buchanan's note at length in "James Buchanan, the Court, and the Dred Scott Case," *Tenn. Hist. Mag.*, IX, January, 1926.
8 Buchanan to Mr. Hemphill, July 18, 1851; Buchanan Papers.

Appendix II

THE MORMON WAR

Almost no secondary account of the collision in Utah does justice to the Mormon position. This is presented with some fullness in H. H. Bancroft's *History of Utah* (1890) and B. H. Roberts's six-volume *History of the Church of Jesus Christ of Latter Day Saints* (1902–12), as well as in the writings of Brigham Young and the files of the *Deseret News*.

The conflict is incomprehensible without some grasp of a number of facts. (1) The Mormons at no time expected to establish an independent republic in Utah. They manifested their eagerness to become a member of the Union when early in 1849 they petitioned Congress to give them a government with the least possible delay; and they were pleased by Millard Fillmore's appointment of Young as governor of the Territory, September 28, 1850. (2) From an early date Gentiles had some valid complaints against the Mormons. When Young and other leaders found the overland trail pouring many emigrants through their community they were disturbed; and the result was non-intercourse regulations which greatly restricted trade with non-Mormons. Moreover, Mormons tended to regard the territorial government as applying primarily to Gentiles, for the church government controlled their own people. A dual system grew up, one civil and one religious, with two sets of courts. When litigation arose over chance affrays, trespass by emigrant cattle, marriages outside the church, and other matters, non-Mormons often felt treated with injustice. (3) From an early date the Mormons had valid complaints against the United States. Their land-titles were not secure; their memorials asking for statehood were treated with contempt; Congress gave Utah stingier appropriations than other Territories. (4) While all Territories suffered from the bad character of some Federal appointments, Utah had special reason to complain. Chief Justice George P. Stiles and Associate Justice W. W. Drummond were inefficient, tactless, and guilty of personal misconduct; and both deliberately fomented trouble by baseless accusations. (5) The turmoil over slavery in the East contributed to the discord; for especially after the Republican platform of 1856 denounced polygamy, attacks on the Mormons became politically popular.

In the end, provocative conduct by Federal officeholders was matched by provocative conduct on the part of Mormon leaders. Both sides, as Levi E. Young writes in *The Founding of Utah* (1923), were frequently rash and hotheaded. Buchanan did not sufficiently comprehend the special character of the Mormon community, which is vividly portrayed in Richard F. Burton's *The City of the Saints* (1861). They had an exceptional body of skilled artisans from the East and England; they were specially careful of education; they were a highly disciplined community. Brigham Young, for his part, did not sufficiently comprehend the American detestation of polygamy, the fear that Western travel routes would be blocked, or the eastern suspicion that he was trying to keep Utah an unassimilated enclave. Both men learned a lesson.

B. H. Roberts in the fourth volume of his comprehensive work on the Latter Day Saints attributes the Utah expedition to the mistaken impression of the national government that the Territory was in rebellion; to the influence of contractors who expected fat pickings from Secretary Floyd; and to the rivalry of the Democrats and Republicans in using the anti-Mormon issue to gain votes. He emphasizes the prejudice of the troops employed, quoting Captain J. R. Murdock: "All the way from the States to Laramie it was G—d d—n the Mormons." It is clear from his narrative that both the leadership in Washington and that in Salt Lake City altered its policy as events developed. Buchanan was at first determined upon rigorous measures; later, under pressure of American and European opinion, he became more forbearing. As for the Mormons, they were originally bent on armed resistance; then, after a council on March 18, 1858, they resolved on flight; and finally they made terms. Roberts's history is dry and one-sided, but accurate and extremely detailed. Naturally he pays warm tribute to Kane and Cumming. H. H. Bancroft's *Utah* is equally partisan, and bears evidence of having been compiled under Mormon aspices (see the *Nation*, February 27, 1890). For a corrective of the bias displayed in these books, general readers may consult William Alexander Linn's *The Story of the Mormons* (1902), which is strongly critical in tone. In this careful volume, based largely on the Helen Gould collection of Mormon materials, the sixth chapter deals with "Brigham Young's Despotism"; the eighth with "Some Church-Inspired Murders"; the eleventh with "Mormon Treatment of Federal Officers," Linn speaking of "the practical nullification of federal law"; and chapters 12–15 inclusive with "The Mormon War." Another work hostile to the Mormons, but more valuable than Linn's, is F. J. Cannon and G. L. Knapp, *Brigham Young and his Mormon Empire* (1913). Bernard De Voto includes in *Forays and Rebuttals* (1936) an admirable essay on Young and his achievement.

Official sources on the conflict fortunately provide a great mass of material. The annual report of the Secretary of War for 1858 contains documents on the Utah expedition by A. S. Johnston and other officers; that for 1858 gives more than two hundred pages to correspondence and reports on Utah affairs; and that for 1859 again includes a large body of official data on developments in the Department of Utah.. As noted in the text, House Exec. Doc. 71, 35th Cong., 1st Sess., treats of the expedition, its 215 pages being invaluable to students. Senate Exec. Doc. 2, 35th Cong., 2d Sess., covers the Mountain Meadow massacre and related matters. The National Archives contain much unpublished matter on the Utah expedition and Mormon affairs. Among the holdings may be mentioned a bound volume of general orders from New York headquarters relating to Utah; a volume of copies of headquarters letters 1857–59; a volume docketing the letters received by the Army of Utah 1857–59; and volumes containing copies of all letters written from headquarters of the Utah Forces or Department of Utah 1858–60. The Archives also have a package of letters and reports on the Mountain Meadow massacre, with a valuable map of the area.

For a general illumination of the Utah scene, no book compares with Richard F. Burton's *The City of the Saints*. Its tone is highly favorable. While the despotic tendencies of the theocracy and the crudities of Utah society did not escape the acute Englishman, he was impressed by Brigham Young's robust strength of mind and will, and still more by the miracle which Mormon industry had wrought within a dozen years in a wilderness waste. Burton had the insight to see that the conflict between the Mormon church-state and the nation grew out of an underlying social and economic conflict.

$$\boxed{\textit{Appendix} \\ \textit{III}}$$

PRESIDENT BUCHANAN AND FOREIGN AFFAIRS

In most important diplomatic matters, President Buchanan was inclined to disregard Secretary Cass, who was infirm of health, timid, and deficient in vigor. "He brought many questions to me which he ought to have decided for himself," later wrote Buchanan, adding that Cass also relied heavily on Cobb and Black.[1] The President prided himself upon his own success in the foreign field. Particularly did he gain much for the United States in dealing with Great Britain, as the British themselves acknowledged. "We have yielded to the Americans in some of our recent disputes," remarked the London *Times* in 1859, "but it is because they were right and we were wrong." The newspaper was doubtless referring to the controversy over the Mosquito Coast and Bay Islands in Central America, and to the dispute over the right of maritime visitation and search. On these issues Great Britain gave way completely and in good temper. But Buchanan's achievements were not as completely creditable as most American diplomatic histories, excessively nationalistic in tone, have implied.

Anglo-American relations when he entered office were a good deal better than men might have expected in view of recent events. President Pierce in 1856 had dismissed the British Minister, J. F. T. C. Crampton, and three British consuls, for their activity in enlisting Americans for Crimean War service. This was done after the British Government had disavowed any intention of violating American neutrality laws, and had expressed sincere regret if any violation had taken place. Many Americans thought the action excessively harsh. Senators Toombs and Butler deplored it; so did a number of newspapers, led by the Washington *National Intelligencer* and New York *Journal of Commerce*. Britons took credit for patient endurance of the American rebuke. The government, stated Delane's *Times*, on July 31, 1856, had done well to show meekness. "A few more strokes of the pen, a few more blustering speeches on the one side and a little dogged obstinacy on the other, and at this moment 28,000,000 of British subjects would have been equipping the materials for carrying destruction among 27,000,000 of kindred people on the other side of the Atlantic."

The British government and people were aware that in the Crimean War the United States had not shown a marked sympathy for the Allies. W. H.

1 *Works*, XI, 59.

Trescot, for example, who was to become Assistant Secretary of State in June, 1860, wrote a pro-Russian pamphlet on the subject. London knew how violently anti-British were the speeches constantly uttered by many leading American politicians. Douglas, at the Washington dinner to Kossuth, had gone out of his way to denounce "proud, haughty England," and to say that if American institutions triumphed she must "give up her monarchy, her nobility, her Establishment, the whole system of machinery by which she has been able to oppress her own people." Even Seward was addicted to twisting the lion's tail. Speaking in the Senate on January 31, 1856, he had threatened war, talked of overwhelming Britain, and painted a vision of Canada joining the United States in the struggle. British consuls kept their government informed of the anti-British activities of Irish clubs, and of the constant drilling of Irish organizations calling themselves Emmet Guards, Phoenix Rifles, and like names.

Happily, the British also knew that the Anglophobe utterances of the New York *Herald* and Stephen A. Douglas were not representative of dominant American feeling. Buchanan expressed the view of nearly all sensible men when he said of British and America: "No two countries have ever existed on the face of the earth which could do each other so much good or so much harm." Emerson's *English Traits* (1856), full of praise both for the English people and English civilization, was one of his most successful books. "After all," wrote Richard Rush to Trescot, "What a glorious old country it [Britain] is. . . . In some things it shoots ahead faster than even we do. In others of course it cannot. Next to our own country, why should we not love our mother country better than any other?" [2] When Consul Bunch in 1857 addressed a gathering of Southerners in Charleston to celebrate the opening of the Memphis & Charleston Railroad, the reception of his speech electrified him. The mayor of Memphis rose excitedly to shout: "Three cheers for old England!" The Charleston *Mercury* printed an extra edition to meet the demand for Bunch's speech, while he had more invitations to visit Southern communities than he could fill in a year. The greeting given the Prince of Wales in 1860 was largely a tribute to Britain. The New York *Times* declared that Americans, well aware that they drew their language, literature, laws, and political spirit from England, found in her "the type of everything cherished and endeared." [3] Just after Buchanan's Administration closed the New York *Evening Post* paid the general policy of the British Government a warm tribute:

Whatever the English people may have said or thought of us, nothing is plainer than that our people have looked with growing admiration at the brave stand of England, in Europe, for liberty. Foreign writers have assured us again

---

2   July 30, 1853; Trescot Papers, South Caroliniana Library.
3   May 21, 1861.

and again that the liberal policy of England in continental Europe was only a measure of annoyance to her rival powers, and that when she encouraged Garibaldi in Italy, or defended Turkey against Russia, she was moved simply by considerations of interest, and not principle. But we have denied the imputation, and our people have been firm in the belief that Great Britain was strong because she was right. . . . It is not too much to say that a great part of England's strength has lain in this conviction, that she was a great moral power.[4]

Buchanan had a valuable asset in handling Anglo-American affairs in his personal familiarity with British leaders. Lord Clarendon was an old friend to whom he wrote with candor on many subjects: the importance of keeping a strong British minister in Washington, the desirability of a British acceptance of the American construction of the Clayton-Bulwer Treaty, and the weakness of the dull Sir William Gore Ouseley as a special envoy to arrange matters with Nicaragua and Honduras. When Richard Cobden visited Washington in April, 1859, Buchanan frankly declared his preferences as to British leadership. "In the course of conversation in the evening," writes Cobden, "he expressed the hope that Lord Palmerston would not again become Prime Minister, as it would be unfavorable to the maintenance of friendly relations between England and America; that although personally partial to Lord Palmerston he (the President) regarded him as hostile to the United States and of belligerent character; that he (Lord Palmerston) was unpopular with the people of America, who considered him dictatorial; and that he (the President) could in any negotiations make concessions to Lord Aberdeen which he would not dare to make to Lord Palmerston."[5]

The Buchanan Administration gained much that was highly creditable; had it not been for the complicating factor of slavery, these gains would have been offset with less that was discreditable. Slavery entered strongly into Central American affairs.

The British Government had made pretensions in Central America which the United States declined to recognize, its claims to a protectorate over the Indians of the Mosquito Coast of Nicaragua and Honduras, and to ownership of the Bay Islands off the Honduran shore, being quite unacceptable to Washington. The United States held that the Clayton-Bulwer Treaty was retroactive in debarring Britain from these areas; London at first held that the treaty was merely prospective and hence recognized Britain's earlier acquisitions. However, yielding to the American argument, Great Britain agreed to give up all claim to the disputed areas. In 1859 she negotiated treaties with Nicaragua and Honduras granting them full sovereignty over the territory, and late in 1860 Buchanan announced to Congress that the United States was satisfied with the

4 May 28, 1861.
5 MS Diary, April 28, 1859, Midhurst, Sussex.

arrangement. Before ceding the Bay Islands to Honduras, however, Great Britain attempted to incorporate in the treaty a provision excluding slavery from them. This offended Southern Senators, and the clause was dropped.

In Central American affairs, moreover, sauce for the goose was by no means sauce for the gander. While Washington was warning Britain from the Mosquito Coast, a citizen of the United States, William Walker, was possessing himself of the government of Nicaragua, becoming president in July, 1856. In several Southern States his agents collected supplies and arms and enlisted recruits with a boldness which furnished an interesting commentary upon the American dismissal of Crampton. They kept recruiting offices open in New Orleans, Mobile, and other seaports, with offers posted of free land grants to every volunteer.

A Central American coalition, by a tremendous effort which the republics still count among their glories, overthrew Walker, who on May 1, 1857, took refuge with the United States Navy. Organizing a new expedition and easily evading the Federal authorities, he was soon back in Nicaragua again. His agent W. R. Henry meanwhile took open steps to organize a regiment of Texas Rangers and concentrate it at Galveston. The New Orleans *True Delta* made merry over the "vigilance" of Federal officers who did not notice the wonderful pile of coal on one of Walker's ships, with articles of strange character under it, and the curious presence of artillery and medical staffs among the crew. Walker's second invasion was cut short when late in 1857 Commodore Hiram Paulding arrested him and sent him back to the United States. Southern members of Congress fierily denounced the commodore; Buchanan in a special message of January 7, 1858, accused him of a grave error. When the President also seized the occasion to condemn lawless military expeditions which had aroused the suspicion and dread of Latin America, his words offended many Southerners.

Walker, always and increasingly an opportunist, utilized his final residence on American soil to pen a book, *The War in Nicaragua*, which was published early in 1860, and which combined a remarkably interesting and accurate record of his campaigns with an appeal to the South to reestablish slavery in Central America. The section, he wrote, must break through all barriers and "get her institution to tropical America" before restrictive treaties were made. He had planned a new descent upon Central America. But only a handful of men rallied to his standard; and, falling into the hands of the Honduran forces soon after he began his summer invasion of the little republic, he was shot on September 12, 1860. A blow to filibustering, his death was also a blow to schemes for the forcible expansion of slavery southward.

Slavery affected Anglo-American relations still more importantly when in 1859 a bitter dispute arose over the issue of maritime visit and search. Mr. Lewis

Einstein writes that Great Britain was trying to revive an offensive claim of the power of search "in the name of virtue," and that "to a great extent the slave trade was only the excuse." [6] How far this statement diverges from the facts will be plain to anyone who studies the published records of the Foreign Office, the best newspapers of the day, and William Law Mathieson's engrossing book *Great Britain and the Slave Trade, 1839–1865.*

It is a fact that the illegal carriage of slaves from Africa to Cuba was largely conducted under the American flag, by vessels sailing from American ports, and with capital from American sources. It is also a fact that while Britain and America kept squadrons off the African coast, the vigilance of the British warships had contrasted strikingly with the inefficiency of the American vessels —especially those under Southern officers. It is a further fact that in most instances no mode of detecting a suspected slaver existed except boarding her. Some of the slave-trading was done by foreigners in America, like the New York firm of Cunha, Reis & Co.; much of it was managed by Americans. The New York *Leader* of May 26, 1860, declared that an average of two vessels a week cleared the port bound for Africa and a slave cargo, and the New York *World* endorsed the figure. This was doubtless an exaggeration. Nevertheless, an informed writer in the New York *Evening Post*, under date of July 25, 1860, listed thirty-nine American ships known to have been in the slave trade during the Buchanan Administration, and the same paper a few days later gave a further list of eighty-five slave-trade ships fitted out from New York between February, 1859, and July, 1860. The British consul in New York, Archibald, had corroborative information from a secret informer. The inhumanity of the business defied description. The British naval commander on the West African station wrote in 1859: [7]

This expensive, cruel system is accompanied by the most terrible, most heart-rending loss of life that can well be conceived. In chained gangs the unfortunate slaves are driven by the lash from the interior to the barracoons on the beach; there the sea-air, insufficient diet, and dread of their approaching fate produce the most fatal diseases; dysentery and fever release them from their sufferings; the neighboring soil grows rich in the decaying remains of so many fellow-creatures, and the tracks are thick-strewn with their bones. On a short march of six hundred slaves, a few weeks back, intended for the *Emma Lincoln*, one hundred and twenty-five expired on the road. The mortality on these rapid marches is seldom less than twenty percent. Such, sir, is the slave trade under the American flag.

Soon after Buchanan became President, British warships seized several American vessels, suspected of being in the slave trade, off the African coast.

6 See his monograph on Cass in Bemis, *Amer. Secs. of State*, VI.
7 Quoted in Mathieson, *Great Britain and the Slave Trade*, 164.

The *Panchita* was arrested and sent in to New York. Inasmuch as the Anglo-American treaty of 1842 provided that the two nations should maintain naval units to enforce "separately and respectively" the laws prohibiting the slave trade, Secretary Cass made repeated protests. Soon afterward, in the spring of 1858, instances were reported of the British detention and search of American vessels in the Gulf of Mexico. A storm sprang up in Congress. Much of it represented a sincere desire to vindicate the old and fundamental American devotion to the principle of the freedom of the seas. But not a little of it was fomented by men who, like Keitt of South Carolina and Israel T. Hatch of New York, wished to use the incidents to destroy the Clayton-Bulwer Treaty and embark on Carribbean conquests. This bad treaty, declared Keitt, has bound "our feet while standing in the very porch of tropical power and wealth." "Cuba will be ours," declaimed Hatch; "England must surrender Roatan [British Honduras]." Reuben Davis of Mississippi said he abhorred the word negotiation—he would negotiate at the cannon's mouth.[8] A few men, like Garnett of Virginia, condemned the agitation for war as food for demagogues and stockjobbers. On June 15, 1858, the Senate unanimously voted a resolution pledging the United States to maintain the immunity of its merchantmen on the high seas.

President Buchanan ordered every naval vessel within reach to the Gulf with instructions to protect American ships from detention or search. A collision there might have had disastrous consequences. Happily, Lord Malmesbury, the Foreign Minister, quickly assented to the American position. At the same time he suggested that Cass might propose some method of meeting the fraudulent use of the American flag by slavers. Cass in return declared himself ready to receive any suggestion that Great Britain might be ready to make. At this point Mr. Einstein halts his narrative, and most histories of our foreign relations say little more on the subject.

The discreditable sequel is actually worth careful attention. It was now possible for any slaver to hoist the American flag, and no non-American warship might touch it. The profits of a successful voyage might be enormous. One trader named Mitchell boasted in New York in 1860 that by landing 1300 Africans in Cuba at $1,000 a head he had cleared a million dollars. The British Government proposed that American and British cruisers patrol the African coast in pairs so that one could deal with ships using the American flag, the other with ships flying no flag at all. Washington withheld its assent to the plan, though as previously noted, the American squadron was increased and given a more effective base. The importation of slaves into Cuba in 1859, still largely under American auspices, was estimated by the British authorities at about 30,000; in 1860, thanks to better naval dispositions and to a new Captain-General

8 *Cong. Globe*, 36th Cong., 1st sess., 2860 ff.

in Cuba, Serrano, the number was reduced to 18,000. Lord John Russell, in a debate in the Commons on February 26, 1861, summarized his fruitless expostulations with Secretary Cass:

I said, "If your national pride will not allow an English officer to search vessels belonging to the United States, employ cruisers of your own. If you will not allow British cruisers to put down the slave trade, put it down yourself, and take all the credit and glory which will attach to the successful extinction of the slave trade. Do it effectually—do it for the sake of your own character, for the sake of that great republic which I hope may still remain the United States of America." The President of the United States directed the Secretary of State to tell me that the American Government had already heard enough of these remonstrances on the part of the British Government, and hoped that they would not be continued.

Southern pressure largely accounted for the uncooperative attitude of the Buchanan Administration; pressure like that of Jefferson Davis, who told the Senate that he favored abrogating the article of the treaty which required maintenance of a squadron on the African coast, and the concentration of national attention on an armed force to protect the American flag.

Mexican policy was handled in the main by Buchanan, not Cass, and it too showed distinct marks of Southern pressure. The treatment in James Morton Callahan's *American Foreign Policy in Mexican Relations* offers an excellent summary. That the turmoil and disorder in Mexico were almost intolerable, and that American rights were flagrantly violated, there can be no question. The President's proposal in December, 1859, to enter Mexico with military force to obtain indemnity for the past and security for the future had some resemblances to President Theodore Roosevelt's subsequent proposals respecting Santo Domingo. Buchanan was correct in pointing to the danger of European intervention if the Mexican chaos continued: "It would not be surprising should some other nation undertake the task [of pacification], and thus force us to interfere at last, under circumstances of increased difficulty for the maintenance of our established policy." This was prophetic of French action. But American policy was suspect in that Buchanan's concept of indemnity for the past, like that of many Southerners, embraced the cession of Lower California, and if possible part or all of Sonora and Chihuahua. The complete failure of the two able ministers, John Forsyth and Louis McLane, to gain Buchanan's objects, makes a story which contrasts strikingly with his successes in dealing with Great Britain.

APPENDIX IV

POPULATION RETURNS AS AMERICANS READ THEM IN 1860–61

(From *Appleton's Annual Cyclopaedia*, 1861)

STATES	CENSUS OF 1860			
	White	Free Colored	Slave	Total
Alabama	526,534	2,630	435,132	964,296
Arkansas	324,186	137	111,104	435,427
California	376,200	3,816	.....	380,016
Connecticut	451,609	8,452	.....	460,151
Delaware	90,697	19,723	1,798	112,218
Florida	77,778	908	61,753	140,439
Georgia	591,638	3,459	462,232	1,057,329
Illinois	1,704,684	7,069	.....	1,711,753
Indiana	1,340,072	10,869	.....	1,350,941
Iowa	673,925	1,023	.....	674,948
Kansas	106,487	623	.....	107,110
Kentucky	920,077	10,146	225,490	1,155,713
Louisiana	357,642	18,638	333,010	709,290
Maine	627,081	1,195	.....	628,276
Maryland	516,128	83,718	87,188	687,034
Massachusetts	1,221,611	9,454	.....	1,231,065
Michigan	742,289	6,823	.....	749,112
Minnesota	171,793	229	.....	172,022
Mississippi	353,969	731	436,696	791,396
Missouri	1,064,369	2,983	114,965	1,182,317
New Hampshire	325,622	450	.....	326,072
New Jersey	647,084	24,947	.....	672,031
New York	3,831,730	49,005	.....	3,880,735
North Carolina	631,489	30,097	331,081	992,667
Ohio	2,303,374	36,225	.....	2,339,599
Oregon	52,343	121	.....	52,464
Pennsylvania	2,849,997	56,373	.....	2,906,370
Rhode Island	170,703	3,918	.....	174,621
South Carolina	291,623	9,648	402,541	703,812
Tennessee	826,828	7,235	275,784	1,109,847
Texas	421,411	339	180,682	602,432
Vermont	314,534	582	.....	315,116
Virginia	1,047,613	57,579	490,887	1,596,079
Wisconsin	774,392	1,481	.....	775,873
	26,727,512	470,716	3,950,343	31,148,571
TERRITORIES				
Colorado	34,153	44	.....	34,197
Dakotah	4,839	.....	.....	4,839
Nebraska	28,755	71	10	28,836
Nevada	6,803	54	.....	6,857
New Mexico	93,447	70	24	93,451
Utah	40,236	30	29	40,295
Washington	11,548	30	.....	11,578
Dist. of Columbia	60,788	11,107	3,181	75,076
	27,008,081	482,122	3,953,587	31,443,790

THE NUMBER OF FUGITIVE SLAVES

According to the Seventh Census, the number of fugitive slaves in the year ending June 1, 1850, was 1,011; according to the Eighth Census, the fugitives for the year ending June 1, 1860, totalled 803. These were out of a slave population of 3,200,000 in 1850 and 3,950,500 in 1860. Both tables of fugitives include all absconding and hiding slaves—those, for example, who took refuge in swamps or mountain areas near home. Indeed, the Eighth Census explicitly declares: "it is not pretended that all missing in the border states, much less any considerable number escaping from their owners in the more Southern regions, escaped into the free States." The census returns showed that the borderland (which complained little) had the most fugitives; the Lower South (which complained bitterly) had the least. Delaware suffered the highest proportionate losses in both 1849–50 and 1859–60; South Carolina and Georgia suffered little. In total numbers of missing slaves, Maryland and Kentucky stood at the head of the list.

No other statistics on the number of fugitive slaves possess any factual basis whatever. It is impossible to determine their number by examining the increase of Negro population in the North, or in Canada. Estimates by politicians and editors of the period are contradictory and unconvincing. Senator James M. Mason of Virginia put the annual loss of his State at about $30,000 in a speech of January, 1850, and above $100,000 in a speech the next August! He was obviously guessing. When J. F. H. Claiborne declared in 1860 that the South had lost 100,000 fugitive slaves in the past fifty years, and the New Orleans *Commercial Bulletin* of December 19, 1860, asserted it had lost 75,000, they were obviously guessing. Most Northern estimates of the fugitives ran below the census totals, and most Southern estimates well above. Senator Walker Brooke of Mississippi supported the census totals for his State when he assured the Senate in 1852 that slaves there seldom if ever escaped to the North.

The whole subject has been carefully studied by Mr. Claude Bragdon in a monograph deposited in the Columbia University Library. His conclusion is that the monetary loss in fugitive slaves, which according to the census may have reached $800,000 in 1860, but which really cannot be calculated with any accuracy, provoked the South much less than the bad faith attributed to the North in refusing to execute the Fugitive Slave Act. Mason told the Senate on December 11, 1860: "The loss of property is felt, the loss of honor is felt still more."

Bibliography

I: MANUSCRIPT COLLECTIONS

(MHS denotes Massachusetts Historical Society; HL denotes Huntington Library; LC denotes Library of Congress. In all its sections, this Bibliography is but partial and suggestive. A full list of sources would far transcend the space here available.)

Anderson Papers, La. State Univ. Archives; Diary of Harrod C. Anderson, La. State U. Archives; John A. Andrew Papers, MHS; Appleton-Sumner Correspondence, Boston PL; Bagby Papers, Univ. of N. C.; Bayard Papers, LC; "Bill of Sale Book 1853" (actually 1848–57), S. C. State Archives; Jeremiah S. Black Papers, LC, Pa. Hist. Soc.; Blair-Lee Papers, Princeton Univ.; Borden Papers, Univ. of Texas; Boteler Papers, Duke Univ.; L. O. Branch Papers, Duke Univ.; Briggs, Samuel, MS Journal; Brodhead Papers, Mo. Hist. Soc.; John Brown Papers, Chicago Hist. Soc., LC, Ohio Arch. and Hist. Soc., Boston PL., etc.; Bryant Papers, NYPL; Buchanan Papers, Pa. Hist. Soc., N. Y. Hist. Soc., LC; Buchanan-Johnston Papers, LC; A. Burt Papers, Duke Univ.; Cameron Papers, LC; Chamberlain Papers, Boston PL; Zachariah Chandler Papers, LC; Chase Papers, LC, NYPL, Ohio Arch. and Hist. Soc., etc.; Claiborne Papers, Miss. Dept. Archives and Hist.; Claiborne Papers, Univ. of N. C.; C. C. Clay Papers, Duke Univ.; Clay, Mrs. C. C., MS Recollections, Duke Univ.; Clayton Papers, LC; Colfax Papers, Indiana State Lib.; S. W. Crawford Papers, Ill. State Hist. Lib.; Francis P. Corbin Papers, NYPL; Thomas Corwin Papers, LC; John J. Crittenden Papers, LC; S. R. Curtis, MS Journal, Ill. State Hist. Lib.; Cushing Papers, LC, MHS; Dana, R. H., Jr,. Papers, MHS; Davis Papers, Duke Univ.; De Leon, Daniel, Scrapbook, South Caroliniana Lib.; De Leon Papers, South Caroliniana Lib.; Stephen A. Douglas Papers, Univ. of Chicago, Ill. State Hist. Soc., LC; Du Bose Family Papers, Ala. State Dept. Arch. and Hist.; Duff Green Papers, LC; Duyckinck, Evert, MS Diary, NYPL; W. H. English Papers, Indiana State Lib.; Everett Papers, MHS; Ewing Papers, LC; Fish Papers, LC, Columbia Univ.; H. F. French Papers, LC; Gaillard, S. Porcher, Journal, 1856–1858, South Caroliniana Lib.; Garrison Papers, Boston PL; Giddings Papers, Western Reserve Hist. Soc.; Gould, W. P., MS Diary, Ala. State Dept. of Arch. and Hist.; Governors' Papers, Ala. State Dept. of Arch. and Hist.; Governors' Letter Books, Va. State Lib.; William A. Graham Papers, Univ. of N. C.; Gratz, Henry H., MS Reminiscences, Mo. Hist. Soc.; Greeley-Colfax Papers, NYPL; Greeley Papers, LC; Gregg Account Book, 1854–1855, South Caroliniana Lib.; Allen Hamilton Papers, Indiana State Lib.; Hammond, Edward S., MS Plans . . . Views of Agriculture, South Caroliniana Lib.; Hammond, James H., MS Journal, South Caroliniana Lib.; James H. Hammond Papers, LC; Hoge, Dr. J. D., MS Journal, HL; Hopkins, Kate, and Carolina, MS Poems, 1850, South Caroliniana Lib.; Houston Papers, Texas State Hist. Lib.; Richard J. Hinton Papers, Kan. State Hist. Lib.; R. M. T. Hunter Papers, Va. State Lib.; Thaddeus Hyatt Papers, Kan. State Hist. Lib.; G. W. Julian Papers, Indiana State Lib.; Keitt Papers, Duke Univ.; Kennedy Papers, Peabody Institute; Charles Lanman Papers, LC; Lanphier Papers, Ill. State Hist. Lib.; Liddell Family Papers, La. State Univ. Archives; Lieber Papers, HL; Lincoln Papers, LC; Robert Todd Lincoln Papers, LC; Lincoln Collection, Ill. State Hist. Lib.; Bulwer Lytton Papers, Duke Univ.; Robert McClelland Letter Book, LC; McClernand Papers, Ill. State Hist. Lib.; Maury Papers, Univ. of N. C.; Charles S. May Papers, Detroit Public Lib.; Memminger Papers, Univ. of N. C.; Minor Family Papers, La. State Univ. Archives; Moore Papers, La. State Univ. Archives; Moran, B., MS Diary, LC; E. D. Morgan

BIBLIOGRAPHY

Papers, N. Y. State Hist. Lib.; Franklin Pierce Papers, LC; New Hampshire State Hist. Soc.; Pierpont Papers, Brock Collection, HL; J. S. Pike Papers, Calais (Me.) PL; Porcher Miles Papers, Univ. of N. C.; Pruyn, John V. L., MS Diary, New York State Hist. Lib.; Pugh Collection, Univ. of Texas Archives; Edmund Quincy Papers, MHS; Rives Papers, LC; Charles Robinson Papers, Univ. of Kansas, Kan. State Hist. Lib.; Edmund Ruffin Diary, LC; Rusk Papers, Univ. of Texas; Schirmer MS Diary, Charleston Hist. Soc.; George R. Smith Papers, Mo. Hist. Soc.; Gerrit Smith Papers, Syracuse Univ.; Kirby Smith Papers, Univ. of N. C.; Alexander H. Stephens Papers, LC; George Templeton Strong Diary, Columbia Univ.; Stuart Collection, HL; Charles Sumner Papers, Harvard Univ. Lib.; Swain Papers, N. C. Hist. Commission Lib.; Thayer, William W., MS Autobiography, LC; Judge Samuel Treat Papers, Mo. Hist. Soc.; William Trescot Papers, South Caroliniana Lib.; Lyman Trumbull Papers, LC; Wade Papers, LC; Thurlow Weed Papers, Univ. of Rochester; Weehaw Plantation Book, Charleston Hist. Soc.; Welles, Edward E., MS Diary, Miss. Dept. Arch. and Hist.; Gideon Welles Papers, LC, NYPL; Winthrop Papers, MHS; Daniel Woodson Papers, Kan. State Hist. Lib.; Yancey, W. L., MS Address to the Erosophic and Philomathic Societies, Ala. State Lib.; Yancey Papers, Ala. State Lib.

II: CONTROVERSIAL BOOKS, PAMPHLETS, AND REPORTS

Anon., "Five Years' Progress of the Slave Power" (pamphlet); Anon., "Letters for the People on the Present Crisis" (pamphlet, dated October 1, 1853); *The Abolition of Slavery in Cuba and Puerto Rico* (pamphlet, 1865); American Anti-Slavery Society, *Reports*, 1850–1861; Baines, Rev. Albert, *The Church and Slavery;* Barnes, Gilbert H. and Dumond, Dwight L., *Letters of Theodore Dwight Weld, Angelina Grimké Weld and Sarah Grimké, 1822–1844,* 1934; Barnard, F. A. P., Tuscaloosa Oration, July 4, 1851 (pamphlet); Birney, James G., *The American Churches the Bulwarks of American Slavery;* Bowen, Francis, *The Principles of Political Economy Applied to the Condition . . . of the American People,* 1856; Brown, G. G., Speech on Gradual Emancipation in Missouri (pamphlet, 1857); Cairnes, John E., *The Slave Power,* 1862; Christy, David, *Cotton is King,* 1855; Cobb, T. R. R., *An Inquiry into the Law of Negro Slavery,* 1858; De Bow, James D. B., *Industrial Resources of the Southern and Western States,* Three Vols., 1852–53; Dewees, Jacob, *The Great Future of Africa and America,* 1854; Donnan, Elizabeth, ed., *Documents, Illustrative of the History of the Slave Trade to America,* 1930–1932; Fisher, Ellwood, "The North and The South" (pamphlet, 1849); Fitzhugh, George, *Sociology for the South,* 1854; Fitzhugh, George, *Cannibals All! or, Slaves Without Masters,* 1857; Grayson, W. J., *Letters of Curtius,* 1851; Grayson, W. J., *The Hireling and the Slave,* 1854; Helper, Hinton R., *The Impending Crisis of the South: How to Meet It,* 1857; Hildreth, Richard, *The Slave: or, Memories of Archie Moore,* 1840; Hopkins, John H., *The American Citizen, His Rights and Duties,* 1857; Humphrey, Rev. Heman, *The Missouri Compromise* (pamphlet); Kettell, T. P., *Southern Wealth and Northern Profits,* 1860; Lowell, James Russell, *Anti-Slavery Papers,* Two Vols., 1902; May, Samuel J., *Some Recollections of Our Anti-Slavery Conflict,* 1868; Martineau, H., *Society in America,* 1837; Noyes, John H., *History of American Socialisms,* 1870; Parsons, D. D., *Inside View of Slavery;* Proceedings of the Convention of the Knights of the Golden Circle, Raleigh, May 7–11, 1860 (pamphlet); *The Pro-Slavery Argument, as Maintained by the Most Distinguished Writers of the Southern States,* 1853; A St. Louisian, "Letters for the People on the Present Crisis" (pamphlet); Stevens, C. E., *Anthony Burns, A History,* 1856; Townsend, John, *The South Should Govern the South* (pamphlet, 1860); Trenholm, W. L., *The South: An Address,* April 7, 1869 (pamphlet); Turner, Lorenzo D., *Anti-Slavery Sentiment in American Literature Prior to 1865,* 1929; Wolfe, S. M., *Helper's Impending Crisis Dissected.*

III: TRAVEL

Ampère, J. J., *Promenade on Amérique*, Two Vols., 1855; Ashworth, Henry, *A Tour in the United States, Cuba, and Canada*, 1859; Audubon, Marian W., and Hodder, Frank H., *Audubon's Western Journal, 1849–50;* Baxter, W. E., *America and the Americans*, 1855; Bishop, Mrs. I. L., *Aspects of Religion in the United States*, 1859; Bremer, Fredrika, *Homes of the New World*, Two Vols., 1853; Buckingham, James S., *America: Historical, Statistical, and Descriptive*, Three Vols., 1841; Buckingham, James S., *The Slave States of America*, 1842; Burns, Rev. Jabez, *Tour of the United States and Canada*, 1848; Caird, James, *Prairie Farming in America*, 1859; Chambers, William, *Things As They Are in America*, 1854; Cunynghame, Arthur, *A Glimpse at the Great Western Republic;* Dana, Richard A, *To Cuba and Back: A Vacation Ramble*, 1859; Dicey, Edward, *Six Months in the Federal States*, 1863; Gladstone, T. H., *Englishman in Kansas*, 1856; Grattan, T. C., *Civilized America*, Two Vols., 1859; Greeley, Horace, *An Overland Journey from New York to San Francisco in the Summer of 1859*, 1859; Ingraham, Joseph H., *The Southwest, by a Yankee*, 1835; Lyell, Sir Charles, *Travels in North America in the Years 1841–42*, 1845; Lyell, Sir Charles, *A Second Visit to the United States*, Two Vols., 1849; Mackay, Alexander, *The Western World*, Three Vols., 1849; Mackay, Charles, *Life and Liberty in America*, 1859; Martineau, Harriet, *Retrospect of Western Travel*, 1838; Monaghan, Frank, *French Travellers in the United States, 1765–1932: A Bibliography*, 1933; Nevins, Allan, *American Social History Recorded by British Travellers*, rev. ed., 1931; Olmsted, Frederick L., *A Journey in the Back Country in the Winter of 1853–54*, 1860; Olmsted, Frederick L., *A Journey in the Seaboard Slave States*, 1856; Olmsted, Frederick L., *A Journey Through Texas*, 1857; Pierson, George W., *Tocqueville and Beaumont in America*, 1938; Raumer, Ludwig von, *America and Her People*, 1846; Reid, H., *Sketches in North America, with some Account of Congress and the Slavery Question*, 1855; Russell, Robert, *North America: Its Agriculture and Climate*, 1857; Schaff, Philip, *Sketch of the Political, Social, and Religious Character of the United States of North America*, 1855; Sullivan, Sir E. R., *Rambles and Scrambles in North and South America*, 1853; Torrielli, Andrew J., *Italian Opinion of America as Revealed by Italian Travellers, 1850–1900*, 1941; Tremenheere, Hugh S., *Notes on Public Subjects in the United States and Canada*, 1856; Tuckerman, Henry T., *America and Her Commentators*, 1864; Wilson, James Grant, *Thackeray in the United States*, Two Vols., 1904.

IV: BIOGRAPHIES, DIARIES, REMINISCENCES; A SELECTED LIST

(Arranged alphabetically by *subject*. The *Dictionary of American Biography*, edited by Allen Johnson and Dumas Malone, furnishes a comprehensive guide to biographical data and sources.)

Charles Francis Adams, Jr., *Charles Francis Adams* (American Statesmen Series), 1900; *Charles Francis Adams, 1835–1915, An Autobiography, With a Memorial Address by Henry Cabot Lodge*, 1916; *The Education of Henry Adams: An Autobiography*, 1918; Worthington C. Ford, ed., *A Cycle of Adams Letters, 1861–1865*, two volumes, 1920; Worthington C. Ford, ed., *Letters of Henry Adams 1858–1891*, 1930; Harold Dean Cater, *Henry Adams and His Friends*, 1947. The first of these volumes is tantalizingly brief, and its chapter on the secession winter is by no means satisfactory. We need a full publication of the diary and principal letters of the elder Charles Francis Adams for the years 1850–1861. The auto-biography of the younger Charles Francis Adams has an enlightening chapter entitled "Washington, 1861," which in the famous autobiography of Henry Adams is matched by a chapter called "Treason (1860–1861)." The letters of the two sons show well what they did and thought, but leave the course of the elder Adams only partially elucidated. That he labored valiantly to preserve peace there can be no doubt.

Henry Greenleaf Pearson, *The Life of John A. Andrew, Governor of Massachusetts 1861–1865*, two volumes, 1904. A pedestrian compilation, in which the chapter "First Months as Governor" contains useful letters and documents on Andrew's prompt preparations for war.

M. A. De Wolfe Howe, *Life and Letters of George Bancroft*, two volumes, 1908; Russel B. Nye, *The Biography of George Bancroft*, 1944. These lives of the eminent historian, of which Mr. Howe's offers the fuller quotations from letters and Mr. Nye's the greater detail, show how a Jacksonian Democrat reacted against the policies of the proslavery men.

Howard K. Beale, ed., *The Diary of Edward Bates, 1859–1866*, 1933; Floyd E. McNeil, *Lincoln's Attorney-General, Edward Bates*, MS doctoral diss., University of Iowa. The diary is invaluable for the borderland opposition to Buchanan, the Republican campaign of 1860, and the making of Lincoln's cabinet.

Thomas Hart Benton, *Thirty Years' View*, 1854–1856; Theodore Roosevelt, *Thomas Hart Benton* (American Statesmen Series), 1886; William M. Meigs, *Life of Thomas Hart Benton*, 1905. The *View* is an elaborate survey of American politics from 1820 to 1850. Roosevelt's life, though a hasty piece of work, shows grasp of character; Meigs's biography is detailed, careful, and dull.

John Bigelow, *Retrospections of an Active Life*, five volumes, 1909–1913; Margaret Clapp, *Forgotten First Citizen: John Bigelow*, 1947. The first volume of the *Retrospections* covers Bigelow's career from youth to the spring of 1863, and offers interesting letters and comments on public affairs. Miss Clapp's fine biography covers the Frémont campaign, the panic of 1857, and the crisis of 1860–1861.

William Birney, *James G. Birney and His Times*, 1890; Dwight L. Dumond, *Letters of James G. Birney, 1831–1857*, two volumes, 1938. These works, besides throwing general light on the antislavery movement, contain a corrective of much writing by and about the Garrisonian school.

W. N. Brigance, *Jeremiah S. Black*, 1934; Chauncey F. Black, ed., *Essays and Speeches of Jeremiah S. Black, With a Biographical Sketch*, 1885. The essays include Black's replies to Douglas on territorial sovereignty, and a very hostile examination of the character and career of Seward. The biography furnishes a discriminating estimate of Black as Attorney-General. On his career as Secretary of State see the essay by Roy F. Nichols in S. F. Bemis, ed., *American Secretaries of State and Their Diplomacy*, VI, 387–406 (1928).

R. J. Hinton, *John Brown and His Men*, 1894; Franklin B. Sanborn, *The Life and Letters of John Brown*, 1885; Oswald Garrison Villard, *John Brown 1800–1859: A Biography Fifty Years After*, 1910; Robert Penn Warren, *John Brown, The Making of a Martyr*, 1929; Hill Peebles Wilson, *John Brown, Soldier of Fortune: A Critique*, 1913. Of these books Villard's massive biography is the ablest and most thorough. Its final chapter on Brown's influence, "Yet Shall He Live," is worth special attention. Wilson goes over the evidence with the object of showing that "the story reveals little which is creditable to Brown or worthy of emulation and much that is abhorrent"; Warren attempts a balanced view. Most other books on John Brown should be avoided as inaccurate and confusing. Among magazine articles Alexander R. Boteler's "Recollections of the John Brown Raid" in the *Century*, July, 1883, is specially interesting. Brown's life to the age of fifty deserves a careful book.

Parke Godwin, *A Biography of William Cullen Bryant, With Extracts From His Private Correspondence*, two volumes, 1883; Parke Godwin, ed., *Complete Prose Writings of William Cullen Bryant*, two volumes, 1884; John Bigelow, *William Cullen Bryant* (American Men of Letters Series), 1880. Bryant was a greater editor than is commonly realized, and has been more fortunate in his biographers than Greeley. The four volumes given us by Parke Godwin throw much light on the history of the times.

George Ticknor Curtis, *The Life of James Buchanan*, two volumes, 1883; John Bassett Moore, ed., *The Works of James Buchanan*, twelve volumes, 1908–1911; Philip G. Auchampaugh, *James Buchanan and His Cabinet on the Eve of Secession*, 1926. Curtis's work is stiff, unrevealing, and full of gaps; Auchampaugh's, though showing careful scholarly research, is ill-organized and partisan. A good modern biography of Buchanan based on the extensive collections of his papers remained in 1950 to be written.

Gaillard Hunt, *John C. Calhoun*, 1908; W. M. Meigs, *Life of John Caldwell Calhoun*, two volumes, 1917; Hermann Von Holst, *John C. Calhoun* (American Statesmen Series), 1882; R. K. Crallé, *Works of John C. Calhoun*, six volumes, 1851–1855; J. Franklin Jameson, ed., *Correspondence of John C. Calhoun*, 1900. All previous biographies of Calhoun are now being supplanted by the large work of Charles M. Wiltse, of which the second volume was published in 1949. The three older biographies all possess merit, though Von Holst was too unsympathetic to understand the man.

Salmon P. Chase, *Diary and Correspondence* (Ann. Report Am. Hist. Ass., 1902, II); Albert B. Hart, *Salmon Portland Chase* (American Statesmen Series), 1899; J. W. Schuckers, *Life and Public Services of Salmon Portland Chase*, 1874; Robert B. Warden, *Private Life and Public Services of Salmon P. Chase*, 1874. The life by Warden was undertaken at Chase's own request; that by Hart is the most scholarly and readable.

Carl Schurz, *Henry Clay*, two volumes, 1887; George R. Poage, *Henry Clay and the Whig Party*, 1936; Glyndon G. Van Deusen, *Life of Henry Clay*, 1937; C. Colton, *Life and Times of Henry Clay*, revised edition, six volumes, 1864. A full biography of Henry Clay by Bernard Mayo has been begun. The volumes by Schurz in the American Statesmen Series constitute a masterly work, interpreting the man and his times with insight. New facts and ideas are added by Van Deusen's biography. The work by Colton contains speeches and correspondence.

Rowland Dunbar, ed., *Jefferson Davis, Constitutionalist: His Letters, Papers and Speeches*, ten volumes, 1923; Jefferson Davis, *The Rise and Fall of the Confederate Government*, two volumes, 1881; Mrs. Jefferson Davis, *Jefferson Davis, A Memoir*, two volumes, 1890; Edward A. Pollard, *Life of Jefferson Davis, With a Secret History of the Confederacy*, 1869; William E. Dodd, *Jefferson Davis*, 1907; Hamilton J. Eckenrode, *Jefferson Davis, President of the South*, 1923; Allen Tate, *Jefferson Davis, His Rise and Fall: A Biographical Narrative*, 1929. Other biographies of Davis, including the two volumes by Robert M. McElroy, might be added. It is perhaps the fault of the subject that none seems satisfactory. The chapters on this period by Varina Howell Davis in the first volume of her life of her husband are more interesting and more genuinely informative than the *Rise and Fall* by Davis himself.

George Fort Milton, *The Eve of Conflict: Stephen A. Douglas and the Needless War*, 1934; Allen Johnson, *Stephen A. Douglas*, 1908; William Garrott Brown, *Stephen Arnold Douglas*, 1902; Clark E. Carr, *Stephen A. Douglas, His Life, Public Services, Speeches and Patriotism*, 1909. Based on the voluminous Douglas Papers, Milton's biography is one of the indispensable works on the period. But the volume by Brown is a keen-minded study of personality, and that by Allen Johnson offers an accurate and fair survey. A collection of Douglas's own letters would be highly useful. No student should neglect Frank E. Stevens's monograph on Douglas in Volume 16 of the *Journal of the Ill. State Hist. Soc.*, 1924, with its many facts not available elsewhere.

James E. Cabot, *A Memoir of Ralph Waldo Emerson*, two volumes, 1887; Van Wyck Brooks, *Emerson and Others*, 1927; Ralph L. Rusk, *Ralph Waldo Emerson*, 1949; Edward Waldo Emerson, ed., *Complete Works of Ralph Waldo Emerson* (Centenary Edition), *With a Biographical Introduction and Notes*, twelve volumes, 1903-1904. The literature on Emerson is vast; see the bibliography in the *Cambridge History of American Literature*, I, 551–566, complete to 1917. The Centenary Edition is the best collection of the works, but should be supplemented by the ten volumes of the Journals. Rusk's biography, built in part on his complete edition of Emerson's letters, is the best life.

W. P. and Francis J. Garrison, *Life of William Lloyd Garrison, 1805-1879*, four volumes, 1885–1889; John Jay Chapman, *William Lloyd Garrison*, 1913. The great four-volume biography is indispensable to all students of the antislavery movement, while Chapman's admiring memoir is a penetrating estimate of a remarkable personality.

L. D. Ingersoll, *Life of Horace Greeley*, 1873; W. A. Linn, *Horace Greeley, Founder and Editor of the New York Tribune*, 1903; James Parton, *Life of Horace Greeley, Editor of the New York Tribune*, 1868, 1872, etc.; F. N. Zabriskie, *Horace Greeley, the Editor*, 1890; Horace Greeley, *Recollections of a Busy Life*, 1868. None of the more recent biographies has quite the value of the books by Linn and Parton, themselves journalists of distinction. Greeley's *Recollections* has the frank graphic qualities of Franklin's autobiography, and should be widely known.

Thomas W. Higginson, *Cheerful Yesterdays*, 1898; *Letters and Journals of T. W. Higginson, 1846-1926*, 1921. These volumes give a good view of a radical antislavery leader who had the courage of his convictions.

William Dean Howells, *Years of My Youth*, 1916; *Literary Friends and Acquaintance*, 1900; Mildred Howells, *Life in Letters of William Dean Howells*, two volumes, 1928. These books, invaluable for the social and literary life of the time, also throw some illumination on political affairs.

C. H. Ambler, ed., *Correspondence of Robert M. T. Hunter, 1826-1876*, Ann. Report Am. Hist. Assn., 1916, II. Very useful for one school of Virginia thought.

George Fort Milton, *The Age of Hate: Andrew Johnson and the Radicals*, 1930; Robert W. Winston, *Life of Andrew Johnson, Plebeian and Patriot*, 1928; Lloyd P. Stryker, *Andrew Johnson: A Study in Courage*, 1929. Three excellent books on the self-made popular leader of Tennessee. That of Milton is fullest on the period before 1861.

Percy S. Flippin, *Herschel V. Johnson of Georgia, State Rights Unionist*, 1931; Percy S. Flippin, ed., "From the Autobiography of Herschel V. Johnson, 1856-1867," *Am. Hist. Review*, XXX, 1925.

Horatio King, *Turning on the Light*, 1895. One of the indispensable books for the secession winter of 1860-1861.

John G. Nicolay and John Hay., eds., *Abraham Lincoln, Complete Works*, two volumes, 1894; Nicolay and Hay, *Complete Works* (sometimes called Tandy or Tandy-Thomas edition), twelve volumes, 1905; Gilbert A. Tracy, *Uncollected Letters of Abraham Lincoln*, 1917; Paul M. Angle, ed., *New Letters and Papers of Abraham Lincoln*, 1930; Rufus Rockwell Wilson, *Uncollected Works of Abraham Lincoln*, 1947; Nicolay and Hay, *Abraham Lincoln: A History*, ten volumes, 1890; Albert J. Beveridge, *Abraham Lincoln, 1809-1858*, two volumes, 1928; Carl Sandburg, *Abraham Lincoln: The Prairie Years*, two volumes, 1926; Sandburg, *Abraham Lincoln: The War Years*, four volumes, 1939; William H. Herndon and Jesse W. Weik, *Abraham Lincoln, The True Story of a Great Life*, 1892 (reissue from the rare original three-volume work of 1889 called *Herndon's Lincoln: The True Story of a Great Life*); Ida M. Tarbell, *The Life of Abraham Lincoln*, two volumes, 1909, etc.; William E. Barton, *The Life of Abraham Lincoln*, two volumes, 1925; Lord Charnwood, *Abraham Lincoln*, 1916; James G. Randall, *Lincoln the President, Springfield to Gettysburg*, two volumes (American Political Leaders Series), 1946. These are among the most important works on Lincoln. For the huge library which has grown up about him and his career, see Jay Monaghan's *Lincoln Bibliography, 1839-1939*, two volumes, 1945, which is supplemented by the valuable bibliography in Randall's second volume. The ten volumes by Nicolay and Hay, an official life, are rather a history of the time than a strict biography. Beveridge's work is notable for its fairness and even sympathy in treating Douglas; Sandburg's for its fine poetic spirit and mass of detail; and Randall's for its analytical quality and profound scholarship. The best edition of the Herndon-Weik life is the one-volume edition with introduction and notes issued by Paul M. Angle in 1930, since reprinted. Those interested in appraising the biographical work done on Lincoln should not fail to read David Donald, *Lincoln's Herndon*, 1948, which has much valuable material on the history of the time; Benjamin P. Thomas, *Portrait for Posterity: Lincoln and His Biographers,* and Paul M. Angle, *A Shelf of Lincoln Books: A Critical Selective Bibliography of Lincolniana.*

Samuel Longfellow, *Life of Henry Wadsworth Longfellow,* three volumes, 1891; Charles Eliot Norton, *Letters of James Russell Lowell,* two volumes, 1893; H. E. Scudder, *James Russell Lowell: A Biography,* two volumes, 1901; Ferris Greenslet, *James Russell Lowell. His Life and Work,* 1905; Sara Norton and M. A. DeWolfe Howe, *Letters of Charles Eliot Norton,* two volumes, 1913. These books throw much light on American life, letters, and public affairs as seen from the area of Boston. They are also delightful to read. The Riverside edition of Lowell's works, ten volumes, 1890, is useful.

Theodore Parker, *Collected Works,* fifteen volumes, 1907–1913; John Weiss, *Life and Correspondence of Theodore Parker,* two volumes, 1864; Octavius B. Frothingham, *Theodore Parker,* 1874; Henry Steele Commager, *Theodore Parker: Yankee Crusader,* 1936. These are the more important materials for understanding a leader who summed up much of the reform spirit and crusading ideology of the time.

Roy F. Nichols, *Franklin Pierce: Young Hickory of the Granite Hills,* 1931; P. Orman Ray, ed., "Some Papers of Franklin Pierce, 1852–1862," *Am. Hist. Review,* X. The biography by Nichols embodies an excellent history of the Pierce Administration.

Laura A. White, *Robert Barnwell Rhett, Father of Secession,* 1931; Avery O. Craven, *Edmund Ruffin, Southerner: A Study in Secession,* 1932. Two admirable biographies, both compact, of leaders in the movement for Southern independence.

William H. Russell, *My Diary North and South,* two volumes, 1863. Reprinted in various editions. A graphic and honest piece of reporting by one of the great journalists of the century. Its sketches of Washington and the South in the secession winter and spring are excellent.

Carl Schurz, *Reminiscences,* three volumes, 1907–1908; Frederic Bancroft, ed., *Speeches, Correspondence and Political Papers of Carl Schurz,* six volumes, 1913; Joseph Schafer, *Intimate Letters of Carl Schurz, 1841–1869,* 1928. A keen observer and a delightful writer, Schurz shows great accuracy—despite his strong freesoil bias. Claude M. Fuess, *Carl Schurz, Reformer* (American Political Leaders Series), 1932, has good chapters on the fifties and the campaign of 1860.

Frederic Bancroft, *The Life of William H. Seward,* two volumes, 1900; Frederick W. Seward, *Seward at Washington as Senator and Secretary of State,* three volumes, 1890, 1891. These, with Seward's works published in five volumes by order of Congress, cover the political career of the New Yorker with great detail; but room remains for the full critical life now being written by Harry Carman and R. H. Luthin (Amer. Political Leaders Series).

John Sherman, *Recollections of Forty Years in the House, Senate, and Cabinet. An Autobiography,* two volumes, 1895; William Tecumseh Sherman, *Memoirs of General William T. Sherman,* two volumes, 1875; Rachel S. Thorndike, *The Sherman Letters,* 1910; M. A. DeWolfe Howe, ed., *Home Letters of General Sherman,* 1909; Theodore E. Burton, *John Sherman* (American Statesmen Series). John Sherman's *Forty Years,* though dull in style, has useful chapters on the birth of the Republican Party, the panic of 1857, the Congressional conflicts during the Buchanan Administration, and the beginning of Lincoln's Administration. William Tecumseh Sherman's *Memoirs* is much more entertaining, but often wildly inaccurate. Its impressions of the South just before the war are particularly good. A really adequate biography of John Sherman is being prepared by Jeanette Paddock Nichols and Roy F. Nichols.

Louis M. Sears, *John Slidell,* 1925. A useful biography of a man who seems doomed to remain little known because of the destruction of his papers.

George C. Gorham, *Edwin M. Stanton,* two volumes, 1899; Frank A. Flower, *Edwin McMasters Stanton,* 1905. Neither of these works approaches a satisfactory standard. They are supplemented by A. H. Meneely's *The War Department, 1861,* 1928. But an adequate study of Stanton and his work remains one of the great desiderata in the field of American history.

R. M. Johnston and W. H. Browne, *Life of Alexander H. Stephens,* 1878; Louis Pendleton, *Alexander H. Stephens,* 1908; Rudolph Von Abele, *Alexander H. Stephens,* 1946; J. Z. Rabun, *Alexander H. Stephens, 1812–1861,* MS diss., University of Chicago; M. L. Avary, ed., *The Recollections of Alexander H. Stephens,* 1910; Alexander H. Stephens, *A Constitutional View of the Late War Between the States,* two volumes, 1868–1870; James D. Waddell, *Biographical Sketch of Linton Stephens,* 1877. The best of these works are the old book by Johnston and Browne, rich in letters, and the new study by Rabun, based on a full examination of various collections of Stephens papers. *The Constitutional View* is to the historian a most disappointing work.

Charles Sumner, ed., *The Works of Charles Sumner,* fifteen volumes, 1870–1883; Edward L. Pierce, *Memoir and Letters of Charles Sumner,* four volumes, 1877–1893; Moorfield Storey, *Charles Sumner,* 1900; George H. Haynes, *Charles Sumner,* 1909. The compendious memoir by Pierce, though eulogistic and formal, is full of useful matter. It exhibits Sumner as an admirable letter-writer. A full and scholarly new biography is being prepared by David Donald.

Carl B. Swisher, *Roger B. Taney,* 1935; B. C. Steiner, *Life of Roger Brooke Taney,* 1922; Samuel Tyler, *Memoir of Roger B. Taney,* 1872. Tyler's volume includes an autobiographical fragment. Each of these books has materials of value, but Swisher's is the fullest and most scholarly.

Holman Hamilton, *Zachary Taylor, Soldier of the Republic,* 1945. This first half of a projected two-volume work brings Taylor to the eve of his Administration.

Ulrich B. Phillips, ed., *The Correspondence of Robert Toombs, Alexander H. Stephens, and Howell Cobb, Ann. Report. Am. Hist. Ass.,* 1911, Vol. II; Ulrich B. Phillips *The Life of Robert Toombs,* 1913; Pleasants A. Stovall, *Robert Toombs,* 1892; W. W. Brewton, *The Son of Thunder: Robert Toombs,* 1936. The correspondence of the three Southern leaders covers the years 1844–1882, and contains a frank and able presentation of the Southern standpoint. Phillips's life of Toombs is careful, critical, and thorough. W. P. Trent's *Southern Statesmen of the Old Regime,* 1897, contains an acute estimate of Toombs; and John C. Reed, *The Brothers' War,* 1905, is built mainly about the man.

John D. Wade, *Augustus B. Longstreet: A Study of the Development of Culture in the South,* 1924. A work as valuable in its field as W. P. Trent's *William Gilmore Simms* (American Men of Letters Series), 1892.

Edward Everett, ed., *Works of Daniel Webster,* six volumes, 1851; J. W. McIntyre, ed., *Writings and Speeches of Daniel Webster,* eighteen volumes (National Edition), 1903; George Ticknor Curtis, *Life of Daniel Webster,* two volumes, 1870; Claude M. Fuess, *Daniel Webster,* two volumes, 1930; C. H. Van Tyne, ed., *Letters of Daniel Webster,* 1902.

Harriet A. Weed, ed., *Life of Thurlow Weed (Autobiography),* 1883–1884; Thurlow Weed Barnes, *Memoir of Thurlow Weed,* 1883–1884. These form the two volumes of a set. The autobiography is particularly valuable. The best biography is Glyndon G. Van Deusen, *Thurlow Weed, Wizard of the Lobby,* 1947.

John T. Morse, ed., *Diary of Gideon Welles,* three volumes, 1911. This contains a useful introduction. It is beyond price in the light it throws on American history 1860–1869. But it should be read in the light of Howard K. Beale's article in the *Am. Hist. Review,* XXX, 547 ff., 1925, "Is the Printed Diary of Gideon Welles Reliable?"

Barton H. Wise, *The Life of Henry A. Wise of Virginia, 1806–1876;* Henry A. Wise, *Seven Decades of the Union,* 1871; John S. Wise, *The End of an Era,* 1899. *The Seven Decades* contains interesting matter on the Peace Convention and Virginia's secession; and the book by Governor Wise's son gives a really vivid impression of an old era ended and a new one begun.

V: GENERAL LITERATURE: A SELECTED LIST

The principal comprehensive works on the period 1846–1861 are the following:

Adams, James Truslow, *America's Tragedy*, 1934. A thoughtful sketch of the conflict of North and South from the seventeenth century to the end of Reconstruction. The author finds the chief root of the Civil War in slavery; but he adds that "the South was not fighting from 1820 onward merely against the North but against the time spirit, the course of modern life and thought."

Burgess, John W., *The Civil War and the Constitution, 1859–1865*, two volumes, 1901. An outline history, now considerably outdated, by a native of Tennessee who fought on the Union side and later became one of the moulders of Columbia University.

Chadwick, French E., *Causes of the Civil War, 1859–1861* (American Nation Series), 1906. In the main an excellent book, though its research is not deep, and it has more than its share of errors.

Channing, Edward, *A History of the United States*, Vol. V, *The Period of Transition*, 1921, Vol. VI, *The War for Southern Independence*, 1925. Taken together, these cover the period 1815–1865. Full treatment is impossible in such limited compass, and Channing lacks literary quality. But as a series of monographic investigations of select topics, with excellent footnote bibliographical references, the volumes are useful and stimulating.

Cole, Arthur C., *The Irrepressible Conflict, 1850–1865* (History of American Life), 1934. Excellent treatment of social and cultural forces.

Craven, Avery, *The Coming of the Civil War*, 1942. In his account of slavery ("a very ancient labor system, drastically adjusted to local American conditions") and the anti-slavery movement, and in his handling of specific issues like Lecompton and Sumter, the author leans to the Southern side. More than half of the book deals with the period before 1849. The treatment of sectional self-consciousness and sectional antagonisms, and of the frequent triumph of emotion over reason, is especially able. At the end Craven condemns Lincoln for "double-talk," failure to see clearly, and refusal to adopt a clear-cut program. An unconventional, opinionated, stimulating, and exasperating volume.

Dodd, William E., *The Cotton Kingdom: A Chronicle of the Old South*, 1919. A brilliant sketch of the planter civilization of the cotton States; best read in conjunction with William Garrett Brown's *The Lower South in American History*, 1902, and the books of Ulrich B. Phillips and Frederic Law Olmsted.

Hart, Albert Bushnell, *Slavery and Abolition* (American Nation Series), 1906. Still the best single volume on the subject.

Holst, Hermann Von, *Constitutional History of the United States*, eight volumes, 1885–1892. More detailed on some subjects than any other treatment; valuable for its full use of official documents, pamphlets, and Northern periodicals; greatly impaired by Von Holst's abolitionist leanings, ignorance of Southern conditions, and unsympathetic attitude toward many American ways and institutions.

Hosmer, James K., *The Appeal to Arms, 1861–1863* (American Nation Series), 1907. A useful outline history.

Macy, Jesse, *The Anti-Slavery Crusade: A Chronicle of the Rising Storm* (Chronicles of America Series), 1919. A good brief account of the abolitionist movement, underground railroad, Kansas struggle, and John Brown.

McMaster, John Bach, *History of the People of the United States*, eight volumes, 1883–1913. The seventh and eighth volumes are particularly useful for this period; good on public opinion, especially as reflected in the press, and on many aspects of social change.

Nichols, Roy Franklin. *The Disruption of American Democracy*, 1848. An exhaustive, scholarly, and interesting book on the Democratic Party and its disruption, 1857–1861, and on the Buchanan Administration.

Randall, James G., *The Civil War and Reconstruction*, 1937. Impartial, thorough, and able; based on a comprehensive knowledge of source materials and monographs, yet admirably digested. Indispensable to all students of the time. The full bibliography is the best general guide to the literature of the period 1850–1877.

Rhodes, James Ford, *History of the United States From the Compromise of 1850*, seven volumes (to 1877), 1893–1906. One of the great road-breaking works of American historiography, and a narrative history of broad swinging interest. Many separate sections have been left outdated by the progress of research; but taken as a whole the first three volumes, which cover the period 1850–1862, deserve careful reading.

Schouler, James, *History of the United States Under the Constitution*, seven volumes, 1894–1913. The fifth volume covers the Mexican War and the years down to Lincoln's inauguration. Good as an outline guide, though badly organized, inadequately documented, and full of Northern freesoil bias.

Smith, Theodore Clarke, *Parties and Slavery, 1850–1859* (American Nation Series), 1906. Shows in brief compass how sectional antagonism "came to permeate law and politics, literature and social intercourse."

Stephenson, Nathaniel W., *Abraham Lincoln and the Union: A Chronicle of The Embattled North* (Chronicles of America Series), 1918. Mainly on the Civil War.

Wilson, Henry, *History of the Rise and Fall of the Slave Power in America*, three volumes, 1872–1877. The last work of the rugged Massachusetts Senator and Vice-President, left incomplete at his death, this shows less prejudice than its title would indicate. Its superficiality and lack of perspective are obvious, but it embodies the special knowledge which Wilson gained from his long official career.

Most of the general and monographic works used by the author of the present volumes are in the list below, arranged alphabetically under authors; dates are not invariably given.

Abbott, Edith, *Historical Aspects of the Immigration Problem: Select Documents*, 1924; Adams, Grace & Hutter, Edward, *The Mad Forties*, 1946; Adams, James Truslow, *America's Tragedy*, 1934; Affleck, Thomas, *The Cotton (or Sugar) Plantation Record & Account Book;* Albion, Robert G., *Rise of New York Port, 1815–1860*, 1939; Alexander, DeAlva S., *Political History of the State of New York*, Vols. 1 and 2, 1906; Allen, James Lane, *Blue Grass Region of Kentucky*, 1892; Ambler, Charles H., *Sectionalism in Virginia from 1776 to 1861*, 1910; *The American Textbook for the Campaign of 1856*, 1856; Anderson, Galusha, *A Border City During the Civil War*, 1908; Anderson, Godfrey T., "The Slavery Issue as a Factor in Mass. Politics from the Compromise of 1850 to the Civil War," unpublished Univ. of Chicago doctoral diss.; Andrews, E. H., *Slavery & The Domestic Slave Trade*, 1836; Anon., *The Attaché in Madrid*, or, *Sketches of the Court of Isabella II*, 1856; Anon., *The Five Cotton States and New York*, 1861; *Appleton's Cyclopedia of American Biography; Appleton's Railway Guide, 1855–1861;* Aptheker, Herbert, *American Negro Slave Revolts;* Ardrey, R. L., *American Agricultural Implements;* Auchampaugh, P. G., *James Buchanan and His Cabinet on the Eve of Secession*, 1926; Bailey, T. A., *Diplomatic History of the American People*, revised ed., 1950; Bancroft, Frederic, *Slave Trading in the Old South*, 1931; Ballagh, J. C., *A History of Slavery in Virginia*, 1902; Barnes, Gilbert H., *The Anti-Slavery Impulse, 1830–1844*, 1933; Baringer, William E., *A House Dividing: Lincoln as President Elect*, 1945; Baringer, William E., *Lincoln's Rise to Power*, 1937; Bassett, John S., *Slavery in the State of North Carolina;* Becker, Jeronimo, *Relaciones Exteriores de España;* Beecher, Henry Ward, *New Star Papers, or Views & Experiences on Religious Subjects;* Belcher, Wyatt, *Economic Rivalry of Chicago & St. Louis, 1850–1880*, 1947; Bemis, S. F., ed., *The American Secretaries of State and Their Diplomacy;* Benjamin, J. G., *The Germans in Texas;* Benton, Thomas H., *Historical and Legal Examination of the Dred Scott Case*, 1857; Bettersworth, John K., *Confederate Mississippi*, 1943; Bidwell, P. W. and Falconer, J. I., *Agriculture in Northern United States, 1620–1860*, 1925; Biesele, R. L., *History of the*

German Set..ements in Texas, 1831–1861, 1930; Bigelow, John, *Jamaica in 1850,* 1851; Billington, Ray A., *The Protestant Crusade, 1800–1860,* 1938; Billington, Ray A., *Westward Expansion: A History of the American Frontier,* 1949; Bogen, Jules, *The Anthracite Railroads,* 1927; Botts, John M., *The Great Rebellion,* 1866; Boucher, Chauncey S., *The Secession & Cooperation Movements in South Carolina, 1848–52,* Washington U. Studies, pt. 2, no. 2, 1918; Boudin, Louis B., *Government by Judiciary,* Two Vols., 1932; Bowen, Francis, *Principles of Political Economy,* 2nd ed., 1859; Boyd, M. C., *Alabama in the Fifties,* 1931; Brearly, H. C., *Time-Telling Through the Ages,* 1924; Brisbane, Albert, *Association; or a Concise Exposition of the Practical Part of Fourier's Social Science,* 1843; Brooks, N. C., *History of the Mexican War,* 1849; Brooks, Van Wyck, *America's Coming-of-Age,* 1915; Brooks, Van Wyck, *The Flowering of New England, 1815–1865,* rev. ed., 1941; Brown, George W., *False Claims of Kansas Historians;* Brown, Herbert R., *The Sentimental Novel in America, 1789–1860;* Bruce, P. A., *The Economic History of Virginia in the Seventeenth Century,* Two Vols., 1896; Bruce, P. A., *The Plantation Negro as a Freeman;* Buckham, John W., *Progressive Religious Thought in America,* 1919; Burgess, John W., *Civil War and Constitution;* Burlingame, Roger, *March of the Iron Men,* 1938; Caffin, Charles H., *The Story of American Painting,* 1907; Cairnes, J. E., *The Slave Power,* 1863; Caldwell, R. G., *The Lopez Expedition to Cuba, 1848–1851,* 1915; Calkins, Ernest E., *They Broke the Prairie;* Capers, Gerald M., *The Biography of a River Town;* Carr, Lucien, *Missouri; A Bone of Contention,* 1894; Cash, W. J., *The Mind of the South,* 1941; Catterall, Helen T., *Judicial Cases Concerning American Slavery & the Negro;* Channing, Edward, *A History of the United States,* Vol. VI, 1925; Clark, T. D., *A Pioneer Southern Railroad;* Clark, Victor S., *History of Manufactures in the United States, 1607–1860,* 1916; Cleland, Robert S., *From Wilderness to Empire: California 1542–1900,* 1944; Cochran, T. C. & Miller, William, *The Age of Enterprise,* 1942, etc.; Cole, A. J., "Changes in Sentiment in Georgia toward Secession 1850–1860," Univ. of Ill. M.A. thesis; Cole, Arthur C., *Era of the Civil War, 1848–1870* (Centennial History of Illinois), 1919; Cole, Arthur C., *The Irrepressible Conflict 1850–1865,* 1934; Cole, Arthur C., *The Whig Party in the South,* 1913; Coleman, J. W., Jr., *Slavery Times in Kentucky,* 1940; Cooke, George W., *Unitarianism in America: A History of its Origin & Development,* 1902; Commons, John R. & Associates, *History of Labor in the United States,* Three Vols., 1921; Cooley, T. M. et al., *Constitutional History of the United States,* 1889; Corwin, Edward S., *National Supremacy,* 1913; Corwin, Edward S., *Twilight of the Supreme Court,* 1934; Cotterill, R. S., *The Old South,* 1936; Coupland, Reginald, *The British Anti-Slavery Movement;* Cox, Samuel S., *Three Decades of Federal Legislation 1855–85,* 1885; Crallé, R. K., ed., *Works of J. C. Calhoun,* 1851–1855; Craven, Avery, *The Coming of the Civil War,* 1942; Crawford, Col. Samuel W., *Genesis of the Civil War,* 1887; Crenshaw, Ollinger, *Slave States in the Presidential Election of 1860,* 1945; Cubberley, E. P., *Public Education in the United States,* 1919; Curtis, George T., *Constitutional History of the United States,* 1896; Dana, E. S. and others, *A Century of Science in America,* 1918; Dana, R. H., Jr., *Two Years Before the Mast,* 1840; Davenport, F. G., *Cultural Life of Nashville, 1825–60,* 1941; Davis, Elmer, *History of the New York Times,* 1921; Davis, Charles S., *The Cotton Kingdom in Alabama,* 1939; Davis, Edwin Adams, *Plantation Life in the Florida Parishes of Louisiana, 1836–1846;* Davis, Jefferson, *The Rise & Fall of the Confederate Government,* Two Vols., 1881; Davis, Reuben, *Recollections of Mississippi & Mississippians,* 1889; Denman, Clarence P., *Secession Movement in Alabama,* 1933; Dixon, Mrs. Archibald, *True History of the Missouri Compromise and Its Repeal;* Dodd, William E., *The Cotton Kingdom,* 1919; Dodd, William E., *Statesmen of the Old South, or From Radicalism to Conservative Revolt,* 1911; Dollard, John, *Caste and Class in a Southern Town;* Dorfman, Joseph, *The Economic Mind in American Civilization,* Three Vols., 1942–1949; Dorman, Lewey, *Party Politics in Alabama from 1850 through 1860,* 1935; Dumond, D. L., *Anti-Slavery Origins of the Civil War,* 1939; Dumond, D. L., *The Secession Movement 1860–1861,* 1931; Easterby, J. H., *The South Carolina Rice Plantation as Revealed in the Papers* of Robert F. W. Allston, 1945; Eaton, Clement, *Freedom of Thought in the Old South;* Eskew, Garnett L., *The Pageant of the Packets;* Ettinger, Amos A., *The Mission to Spain of Pierre Soulé, 1853–1855,* 1932; Fairchild, Henry P., *Immigration,* 1913; Faust, Albert B., *The German Element in the United States,* 1909; Fish, C. R., *Rise of the Common Man 1830–50,* 1927; Fite, Emerson D., *Presidential Campaign of 1860,* 1911; Flanders, Ralph B., *Plantation Slavery in Georgia,* 1933; Follett, M. P., *The Speaker of the House of Representatives,* 1896; Foner, Philip S., *Business and Slavery,* 1941; Foote, Henry S., *War of the Rebellion,* 1866; Franklin, John Hope, *The Free Negro in North Carolina, 1790–1860;* Garber, P. N., *The Gadsden Treaty,* 1923; Gates, P. W., *The Illinois Central Railroad & Its Colonization Work;* Gihon, Dr. John H., *Geary and Kansas,* 1857; Gilbert, E. W., *Exploration of Western America, 1800–1850,* 1933; Gildersleeve, Basil, *The Creed of the Old South, 1865–1915,* 1915; Gohdes, Clarence, *American Literature in Nineteenth Century England,* 1944; Gray, Lewis C., *History of Agriculture in the Southern States to 1860,* Two Vols., 1933; Gray, Wood, *Hidden Civil War: The Story of the Copperheads,* 1942; Greeley, Horace, *The American Conflict,* Two Vols., 1865; Grund, Francis J., *The Americans in Their Moral, Social, and Political Relations,* 1837; Guillet, Edwin C., *The Great Migration,* 1929; Halstead, Murat, *Caucuses of 1860,* 1860; Hamer, P. M., *The Secession Movement in South Carolina, 1847–52;* Hazard, Lucy L., *The Frontier in American Literature,* 1927; Hansen, Marcus Lee, *The Atlantic Migration, 1607–1860,* 1940; Harper, James H., *The House of Harper,* 1912; Harris, N. D., *History of Negro Servitude in Illinois;* Havighurst, Walter, *Long Ships Passing;* Harvin, E. L., "Arkansas and The Crisis of 1860–1861," MS, Univ. of Texas; Hendrick, Burton J., *Lincoln's War Cabinet,* 1946; Hendrick, Burton J., *Statesmen of the Lost Cause,* 1939; Hesseltine, William B., *Lincoln and the War Governors,* 1948; Hesseltine, William B., *A History of the South, 1607–1936,* 1936; Heyward, Duncan C., *Rice From Madagascar,* 1937; Hilliard, H. W., *Politics and Pen-Pictures,* 1892; Hodgson, Joseph, *Cradle of the Confederacy;* Homer, William, *The Higher Law in its Relations to Civil Government: with Particular Reference to Slavery & the Fugitive Slave Law,* 1852; Howard, Robert W., *Two Billion Acre Farm;* Howe, M. A. De Wolfe, *The Atlantic Monthly and Its Makers,* 1919; Hume, John, *The Abolitionists;* Hundley, D. R., *Social Relations in our Southern States,* 1860; Hungerford, Edward, *The Story of the Baltimore & Ohio Railroad,* Two Vols., 1928; Hungerford, James W., *The Old Plantation;* Ingle, Edward, *Southern Sidelights: A Picture of Social and Economic Life in the South a Generation Before the War,* 1896; Jackson, Luther P., *Free Negro Labor and Property Holding in Virginia, 1830–1860,* 1937; Jenkins, William S., *Pro-Slavery Thought in the Old South,* 1935; Johnson, Guion G., *Ante Bellum North Carolina, A Social History,* 1937; Johnston, J. H., "Race Relations in Virginia and Miscegenation in the South, 1776–1860," MS dissertation, Univ. of Chicago; Kahn, Morton E., *Djuka, The Bush Negroes of Dutch Guiana,* 1931; King, Horatio, *Turning on the Light: A Dispassionate Survey of President Buchanan's Administration,* 1895; Kinsley, Philip, *The Chicago Tribune: Its First Hundred Years,* Vol. I, 1847–1865, 1943; Kirkland, Caroline, *Chicago Yesterdays,* 1913; Klingberg, Frank J., *The Anti-Slavery Movement in England: A Study of English Humanitarianism,* 1926; *Know-Nothing Almanac, or True Americans' Manual,* 1850; Krout, John A., *The Origins of Prohibition,* 1925; Langston, B. H., "The South and the Kansas-Nebraska Bill," MS, Univ. of Texas; *Letters Relating to a Collection of Pictures Made by Mr. James Jackson Jarves* (privately printed 1859); Lewis, Lloyd, and Smith, Henry J., *Chicago;* Lewis, Oscar, *The Big Four,* 1938; Lunt, George, *Origin of the Late War,* 1866; Luthin, Reinhard H., *First Lincoln Campaign,* 1944; MacGill, Caroline E. & others, *Transportation in the United States Before 1860,* 1917; McGregor, J. C., *The Disruption of Virginia;* Macy, Jesse, *The Anti-Slavery Crusade,* 1919; Malin, James C., *John Brown and the Legend of '56,* 1942; Mansfield, E. D., *History of the Mexican War,* 1849; Martin, Edgar W., *The Standard of Living in 1860,* 1942; Mathieson, W. L., *Great Britain and The Slave Trade, 1839–1865;* A Mechanic, *Elements of Social Disorder: A Plea for the Laboring Classes in the U. S.,* 1844;

Mott, E. H., *Between the Ocean & the Lakes: the Story of Erie*, 1902; Mott, Frank L., *A History of American Magazines*, Three Vols., 1930–1938; Mott, Frank Luther, *American Journalism: 1690–1940*, 1941; Munford, Beverly B., *Virginia's Attitude toward Slavery and Secession*, 1910; Neuhaus, Eugen, *The History and Ideals of American Art*, 1931; Nevins, Allan, *The Evening Post: A Century of Journalism*, 1922; Nevins, Allan, *America Through British Eyes* (revised ed.), 1948; Nicholas, Roy F., *The Democratic Machine, 1850–54*, 1923; Nichols, Roy F., *The Disruption of American Democracy*, 1948; Nichols, Thomas Low, *Forty Years of American Life*, Two Vols., 1864; Nicolay, Helen, *Our Capitol on the Potomac*, 1924; Nicolay, John G., *The Outbreak of the Rebellion*; Nordhoff, Charles, *Communistic Societies in the U. S.*, 1875; O'Brien, Frank M., *The Story of the Sun*, 1918; Oldroyd, O. H., *Lincoln's Campaign, or the Political Revolution of 1860*; Osterweis, R. G., *Romanticism and Nationalism in the Old South*, 1949; Overdyke, Darrell, "The American Party in the Old South," MS doctoral dissertation, Duke Univ.; Overton, Grant, *Portrait of a Publisher and the First Hundred Years of the House of Appleton*, 1925; Owsley, Frank L., *King Cotton Diplomacy*, 1931; Page, Thomas N., *The Old Dominion: Her Making and Her Manners*, 1908; Parrington, Vernon L., *Main Currents in American Thought*, Three Vols., 1927–1930; Parson, G. C., *Inside View of Slavery*; Pattee, Fred Lewis, *The First Century of American Literature, 1770–1870*, 1935; Paxson, F. L., *History of the American Frontier, 1763–1893*, 1924; Perkins, Howard, ed., *Northern Editorials on Secession*, Two Vols., 1942; Petersen, William J., *Steamboating on the Upper Mississippi . . . Commerce & Navigation*, 1847; Peto, Sir S. Morton, *The Resources & Prospects of America*, 1865; Phillips, U. B., *The Course of the South to Secession*, 1939; Phillips, U. B., *Georgia and States Rights*, 1902; Phillips, U. B., *History of Transportation in the Eastern Cotton Belt, 1860*, 1908; Phillips, U. B., *Life and Labor in the Old South*, 1929; Phillips, U. B., *American Negro Slavery*, 1918; Phillips, William, *The Conquest of Kansas*; Pike, James S., *First Blows of the Civil War*, 1870; Pitkin, T. M., "The Tariff and the Early Republican Party," MS diss., Western Reserve Univ.; Pollard, Edward A., *The Lost Cause: A New Southern History of the War*, 1866; Quinn, Arthur H., *A History of the American Drama From the Beginning to the Civil War*, 1923; Randall, J. G., *The Civil War and Reconstruction*, 1937; Rainwater, Percy L., *Mississippi: Storm Center of Secession 1856–61*, 1938; Rantoul, Robert, *Letter to Robert Schuyler on the Value of the Public Lands of Illinois*, 1851; Ray, P. O., *Repeal of the Missouri Compromise*, 1909; Reed, John C., *The Brothers' War*, 1905; Rennick, S. G., *Report on Cattle Transportation*, 1856; Rhodes, James Ford, *History of the U. S. from the Compromise of 1850*, Vols. 1–3, 1892–1895; Richardson, James D., ed., *A Compilation of the Messages & Papers of the Presidents, 1789–1897*, 1896–1899; Richardson, R. N., *Texas, The Lone Star State*; Riegel, O. W., *Crown of Glory: The Life of J. J. Strang*; Rice., M. H., *American Catholic Opinion in the Slavery Controversy*, 1944; Rives, G. L., *The United States and Mexico 1821–1848*, Two Vols., 1913; Robbins, Roy M., *Our Landed Heritage*, 1942; Robinson, Charles, *The Kansas Conflict*, 1892; Robinson, Harriet H., *Early Factory Labor in New England*; Rodriques, J. I., *Estudio . . . sobre . . . la idea de la Anexion de la isla de Cuba a los Estados Unidos de America*; Russell, Robert R., *Economic Aspects of Southern Sectionalism, 1840–61*; Savage, William S., *The Controversy Over the Distribution of Abolition Literature*, 1938; Sawyer, W. E., "Evolution of the Morrill Act of 1862," MS doctoral diss., Boston Univ., 1948; Schafer, Joseph, *Social History of American Agriculture*; Schlegel, Marvin, *Franklin B. Gowen*, 1948; Schlesinger, Arthur M., Jr., *The Age of Jackson*, 1947; Schultz, Harold, "South Carolina & National Politics, 1852–1860," MS diss., Duke Univ.; Schweitzer, Albert, *On the Edge of the Primeval Forest*; Scroggs, W. O., *A Century of the Banking Progress*, 1924; Scrugham, Mary, *The Peaceable Americans of 1860–1861*; Shanks, Henry T., *The Secession Movement in Virginia 1847–1861*, 1934; Shippee, Lester Burrell, *Hist. Canadian-American Relations, 1849–1879*, 1939; Shugg, Roger W., *Origins of the Class Struggle in Louisiana*, 1939; Siebert, Wilbur H., *The Underground Railroad from Slavery to Freedom*, 1898; Simms, Henry H.,

A Decade of Sectional Controversy, 1942; Smith, J. H., *The War with Mexico*, Two Vols., 1919; Smith, Theodore C., *Liberty and Freesoil Parties in the Northwest*, 1902; Smith, William E., *The Francis Preston Blair Family in Politics*, Two Vols., 1938; Somers, Robert, *The Southern States Since the War*, 1871; Spring, Leverett W., *Kansas: The Prelude to the War for the Union*, 1907; Stanwood, Edward, *History of the Presidency from 1788 to 1920*, rev. ed., Two Vols., 1924; Stanwood, Edward, *Tariff Controversies in the Nineteenth Century*, Two Vols., 1903; Starr, John W., Jr., *One Hundred Years of American Railroading;* Stephens, Alexander H., *A Constitutional View of the Late War between the States . . .* , Two Vols., 1868–1870; Stephenson, N. W., *Lectures on Typical Americans and Their Problems;* Strevey, T. E., "Joseph Medill and the Chicago Tribune During the Civil War Period," MS doctoral diss., Univ. of Chicago; Stroupe, Henry S., "The Religious Press in the South Atlantic States 1802–1865," MS doctoral diss., Duke Univ., 1942; Sweet, W. W., *Religion on the Frontier; Vol. 1, The Baptists, 1783–1830*, 1938; Sweet, William W., *The Story of Religions in America*, 1930; Sydnor, Charles, *Slavery in Mississippi*, 1933; Tannenbaum, Frank, *Slave and Citizen: The Negro in the Americas;* Taylor, Richard, *Destruction and Reconstruction;* Thayer, Eli, *A History of the Kansas Crusade, Its Friends and Its Foes*, 1889; Thompson, Edgar T., ed., *Race Relations and the Race Problem*, 1939; Tilby, A. Wyatt, *Britain in the Tropics, 1527–1910;* Trexler, Harrison A., *Slavery in Missouri, 1804–1865*, 1914; Trollope, Anthony, *The West Indies and the Spanish Main;* Turner, A. J. *Genesis of the Republican Party;* Tyler, Alice F., *Freedom's Ferment;* Vance, Rupert B., *Human Geography of the South*, 1935; Van Oss, S. F., *American Railroads As Investments;* Vilá, Herminio Portell, *Historia de Cuba;* Walker, William, *The War in Nicaragua*, 1860; Wallas, Graham, *Human Nature in Politics* (third ed.), 1921; Warren, Charles, *The Supreme Court in United States History*, Two Vols., 1926; Weeks, S. B., *Anti-Slavery Sentiment in the South;* Whitfield, Theodore M., *Slavery Agitation in Virginia, 1829–32*, 1930; Wender, Herbert, *Southern Comercial Conventions 1837–1859*, 1930; Wertenbaker, T. J., *Patrician and Plebeian in Virginia*, 1910; Williams, T. Harry, *Lincoln and the Radicals*, 1941; Williams, M. W., *Anglo-American Isthmian Diplomacy, 1815–1915*, 1916; Wilson, Henry, *History of the Rise and Fall of the Slave Power in America*, Three Vols., 1872–77; Wilson, W. B., *History of the Pennsylvania Railroad Company;* Winsor, Justin, ed., *Memorial History of Boston*, Four Vols., 1881; Wise, John S., *End of an Era*, 1899; Woodson, Carter G., *Education of the Negro Prior to 1861*, 1915; Woodson, Carter G., *A Century of Negro Migration*, 1918; Woodson, Carter G., *The Negro in our History*, 1922; Zahler, Helene, *Eastern Workingmen and National Land Policy, 1829–1862*, 1941.

VI: ARTICLES IN PERIODICALS AND PAMPHLETS

Anon., "Prospect and Policy of the South, as seen by a Southern Planter," *Southern Quarterly Review*, Oct., 1854; Anon., *The New 'Reign of Terror' in the Slaveholding States, 1859–60* (pamphlet); Auchampaugh, P. G., "The Buchanan-Douglas Feud," *Journal Ill. State Hist. Soc.*, XXV, 5–48; Baltimore and Ohio R. R., *Annual Reports*, 1855–1861; Barnard, F. A. P., *Improvements Practicable in American Colleges* (pamphlet); Bauer, R. A. and A. H., "Day to Day Resistance to Slavery," *Journal Negro Hist.*, 27:388–419; Bean, W. G., "Anti-Jeffersonianism in the Ante-Bellum South," *North Carolina Hist. Rev.*, 12:103; Binckley, W. C., "The Question of Texan Jurisdiction in New Mexico under the U. S., 1848–50," *Southwestern History Quarterly*, 24:1–38; Bining, Arthur, "The Glass Industry of Western Pennsylvania," *Pa. Mag. Hist. and Biog.*, Dec., 1936; Botts, J. M., *A Letter to the Opposition Members . . .* (pamphlet); Letters of L. O. Branch, *N. C. Hist. Rev.*, 10:47; Cady, E. H., "William Dean Howells and the Ashtabula Sentinal," *Ohio Arch. and Hist. Quarterly*, 53:40–41; Cade, John B., "Out of the Mouths of Slaves," *Journal Negro Hist.*, 20:294–337; Calhoun, A. H., MS, "Vindication of John Calhoun," *Kan. State Hist. Lib.; Presidential Campaign of 1856, The Election and the Candidates* (pamphlet); Carman, Harry J., "Eng lish Views of Middle Western Agriculture, 1850–1879," *Agr. Hist.*, Jan., 1934; Carman, Harry J., and Luthin, R. H., "The Seward-Fillmore Feud and the Crisis of 1850," *New York Hist.*, 24:163–184; Carnathan, W. J., "The Proposal to Reopen the Slave Trade," *South Atlantic Quarterly*, 25:410–430; *Speech of Cass on Religious Freedom Abroad; Letter of the Most Rev. Archbishop Hughes on the Madai; Letter of Hughes in Reply to Lewis Cass* (pamphlet); *Case of Dred Scott in the Supreme Court of the United States* (pamphlet); Catterall, Helen T., "Some Antecedents of the Dred Scott Case," *Am. Hist. Rev.*, XXX, 56–71; Cotterill, R. S., "James Guthrie, Kentuckian," *Ky. State Hist. Soc. Reg.*, Sept., 1922; Cole, A. H., "Wholesale Commodity Prices in the United States, 1843–1862," *Rev. of Econ. Stats.*, Feb., 1929; Corwin, Edward S., "The Dred Scott Decision in the Light of Contemporary Legal Doctrines," *Am. Hist. Rev.*, XVII, 1911; Craik, E. L., "Southern Interest in Territorial Kansas," *Kan. Hist. Colls.*, 25:348; Craven, Avery, "Agricultural Reformers of the Ante-Bellum South," *Am. Hist. Rev.*, 33:302–314; *Speech of John W. Crisfield, 1856* (pamphlet); Dodd, W. E., "The Fight for the Northwest," *Am. Hist. Rev.*, XLV, 774–788; Donelson Papers, *Tenn. Hist. Mag.*, 3:259–291; Eaton, Clement, "The Resistance of the South to Northern Radicalism," *New England Quarterly*, VIII, 215; *Facts for the People of the South, or Know-Nothingism Exposed*, 1856 (pamphlet); Flanders, R. B., "Free Negro in Ante-Bellum Georgia," *North Carolina Hist. Rev.*, 9:1932; Fleming, W. L., "The Buford Expedition to Kansas," *Am. Hist. Rev.*, 6:38–48; Fleming, W. L., "Jefferson Davis, the Negroes and the Negro Problem," *Sewanee Rev.*, 16:407–427; "The Free School System of South Carolina," *Southern Quarterly Review*, Nov., 1856; Fraser, Jesse M., "Louisa C. McCord," *Bulletin No. 91*, Univ. S. C.; Galpin, W. F., "The Jerry Rescue," *New York Hist.*, Jan., 1945; "Letters of Governor John W. Geary to President Pierce," *Am. Hist. Rev.*, 10:124 ff., 350 ff.; Govan, Thomas P., "Was Plantation Slavery Profitable?" *Journal Southern Hist.*, 8:513–535; Haar, C. M., "Legislative Regulation of New York Industrial Corporations, 1800–1850," *New York Hist.*, April, 1941; Harmon, G. D., "Douglas and the Compromise of 1850," *Journal Ill. State Hist. Soc.*, 21:453–499; Harrington, Fred H., "The First Northern Victory," *Journal Southern Hist.*, 5:186–205; Hesseltine, William B., "Some New Aspects of the Pro-Slavery Argument," *Journal Negro Hist.*, 21:5; Hitchcock, Henry, "Modern Legislation Touching Marital Property Rights," *Journal of Social Science*, March, 1881; Hodder, F. H., "The Authorship of the Compromise of 1850," *Miss. Valley Hist. Rev.*, 22:525–536; Hodder, F. H., "The Genesis of the Kansas-Nebraska Act," *Wis. State Hist. Soc., Bull., No. 60*, 1912; Hodder, F. H., "Some Phases of the Dred Scott Decision," *Miss. Vall. Hist. Rev.*, XI (1929), 3–22; Hodder, F. H., "The Railroad Background of the Kansas-Nebraska Act," *Miss. Valley Hist. Rev.*, XII; Johnson, H. B., "German Forty-eighters in Davenport," *Iowa Journal Hist. and Politics*, XLIV, 3–53; Johnson, Hadley D., "How the Kansas-Nebraska Line Was Established," *Trans. Neb. State Hist. Soc.*, 2:85; Jordan, H. D., "A Politician of Expansion: Robert J. Walker," *Miss. Vall. Hist. Rev.* (1918); Julian, George W., "The First Republican National Convention," *Am. Hist. Rev.*, 4:313; Kennedy, John P., *The Border States: Their Power and Duty in the Present Disordered Condition of the Country* (pamphlet, 1861); Kibler, Lillian A., "Union Sentiment in South Carolina in 1860," *Journal Southern Hist.*, IV, Aug., 1938; Klem, Mary J., "Missouri in the Kansas Struggle," *Miss. Valley Hist. Assn. Proc.*, 9:393–413; Klingberg, Frank J., "James Buchanan and the Crisis of the Union," *Journal Southern Hist.*, IX, Nov., 1943; Landon, F., "Negro Migration to Canada," *Journal Negro Hist.*, 5:30; Learned, H. B., "Relation of Philip Phillips to the Repeal of the Missouri Compromise," *Miss. Vall. Hist. Rev.*, 8:303–317; Levermore, C. H., "Henry C. Carey and His Social System," *Pol. Sci. Quart.*, 5:555; Linthicum, Gordon, "Autobiography," *Miss. Hist. Soc. Pubs.*, IX; Lippincott, I., "History of River Improvement," *Jour. Pol. Economy*, XXII, 644; Loomis, N. H., "Asa Whitney, Father of Pacific Railroads," *Miss. Valley Hist. Assn. Proc.*, VI; "Literary Prospects of the South," *Russell's Magazine*, June, 1858; Luthin, R. H., "Lincoln Becomes a Republican," *Pol. Sci. Quart.*, LIX, No. 3; McCormac, E. I., "Justice Campbell and the Dred Scott Decision," *Miss. Vall. Hist. Rev.*,

XIX (1933), 565–571; McCulloch, M. C., "Founding the North Carolina Asylum for the Insane," *N. C. Hist. Rev.*, 13:185:July, 1936; Malin, J. C., "Beginnings of Winter Wheat Production," *Kan. Hist. Quart.*, X, No. 3; Moore, J. B., "A Great Secretary of State: Wm. L. Marcy," *Pol. Sci. Quart.*, Sept., 1915; Myers, C. M., "Rise of the Republican Party in Pa.," MS diss., Univ. of Pittsburgh; Nichols, Roy F., "Some Problems of the First Republican Presidential Campaign," *Am. Hist. Rev.*, 28:492; *North and South: Impressions of Northern Society Upon a Southerner* (pamphlet, 1853); Ordway, S. F., "John Bell," *Gulf States Hist. Mag.*, II, No. 1, 41, 42; Owsley, Frank L. and Harriet C., "The Economic Basis of Society in the Late Ante-Bellum South," *Journal Southern Hist.*, 6:21–45; Owsley, Frank L. and Harriet C., "The Economic Structure of Rural Tennessee," *Journal Southern Hist.*, 8:161–182; "The Peculiarities of the South," *North Amer. Rev.*, Oct., 1890; Perkins, Howard C., "A Neglected Phase of the Movement for Southern Unity, 1847–1852," *Journal Southern Hist.*, 12:153–203; Perkins, H. C., "Defense of Slavery in the Northern Press on the Eve of the Civil War," *Journal Southern Hist.*, IX, Nov., 1943; Persinger, C. E., "Bargain of 1844," *Oregon Hist. Quart.*, 24:137–146; Pierce, E. L., *Important Statistics in Regard to the Foreign Vote in the Presidential Election*, 1857 (pamphlet); Porter, William D., *State Sovereignty and the Doctrine of Coercion* (pamphlet); Phillips, Ulrich B., "The Central Theme of Southern History," *Am. Hist. Rev.*, 24:30; Ramsdell, C. W., "The Natural Limits of Slavery Expansion," *Miss. Valley Hist. Rev.*, 16:151–171; Ray, P. O., "Genesis of the Kansas-Nebraska Act," *Am. Hist. Assn. Report*, 1914, 1:259–280; Reagan, J. H., *Address to the Voters of the First Congressional District* (pamphlet); Rice, William G., "The Appointment of Governor Marcy as Secretary of State," *Mag. of Hist.*, Feb.-March, 1912; Sanger, D. B., "The Chicago *Times* and the Civil War," *Miss. Vall. Hist. Rev.*, 17:557–580; Savage, W. S., "Abolitionist Letters in the Mails," *Journal Negro Hist.*, 13; Schafer, Joseph, "Some Facts Bearing on the Safety Valve Theory," *Wis. Mag. Hist.*, Dec., 1936; Schafer, Joseph, "Who Elected Lincoln?" *Am. Hist. Rev.*, XLVI, 51–63; Sellers, E. M., "The Pittsburgh and Cincinnati Packet Line Minute Book, 1851–53," *Western Pa. Hist. Mag.*, Dec., 1936; Shannon, Fred A., "The Homestead Act and Labor Surplus," *Am. Hist. Rev.*, July, 1936; "A Slave Trader's Note Book," *North Amer. Rev.*, Nov., 1886; Smith, D. V., "Influence of the Foreign-Born of the Northwest in the Election of 1860," *Miss. Vall. Hist. Rev.*, XIX, 192–204; *Speeches in the Assembly of the State of New York in Exposition of the Know-Nothings* (pamphlet, 1855); Spring, L. W., "The Career of a Kansas Politician," *Am. Hist. Rev.*, Oct., 1898; Stenberg, Richard R., "The Motivation of the Wilmot Proviso," *Miss. Vall. Hist. Rev.*, 28:535–541; Stephenson, W. H., "Political Career of General J. H. Love," *Kan. State Hist. Pubs.*, III, 1930; Stone, Alfred H., "The Cotton Factorage System of the Southern States," *Am. Hist. Rev.*, 20:557; Sydnor, C. S., "The Free Negro in Mississippi," *Am. Hist. Rev.*, 32:769; "Narrative of William Henry Trescot," *Am. Hist. Rev.*, XIII, 528–556; Van Alstyne, R. W., "British Diplomacy and the Clayton-Bulwer Treaty, 1850–1860," *Journal Mod. Hist.*, 9; Wesley, C. H., "Lincoln's Plan for Colonizing the Emancipated Negroes," *Journal Negro Hist.*, 4:7; "Bunyan in Broadcloth, the House of Weyerhaeuser," *Fortune*, April, 1934; White, Laura A., "The South in the 1850's as seen by British Consuls," *Journal Southern Hist.*, 1:29–48; Wilkey, H. L., "Infant Industries in Illinois," *Journal Ill. State Hist. Soc.*, 32, No. 4; Woodson, Carter G., "History Made to Order," *Journal Negro Hist.*, 12:330–348; Yancey, W. L., *Speech at Memphis, August 14, 1860* (pamphlet).

Index

INDEX

A

Abolitionists, support of John Brown, 21–23; reaction to Brown's death, 98; nominate Gerrit Smith, 301; and Republican party, 301

Adams, Charles Francis, member of House, 114; and Douglas' fears, 293; aids Seward in Republican campaign, 299; role in Committee of Thirty-Three, 389, 406–410; views on compromise, 431, 432; as Seward's side, 439; labors for reconciliation, 444–446; urges Northern arming, 449; and struggle over Lincoln's cabinet, 452–455

Adams, J. H., and Charleston forts, 369; calls on Buchanan, 370; and Buchanan's policy, 380

African Labor Supply Association, 33

Alabama, and secession, 111, 128, 129; forbids manumission of slaves, 133; State Democratic convention, 177, 225; withdraws from Charleston Convention, 220, 221; and Baltimore Convention, 267; division on secession, 319, 323; occupies Forts Morgan and Gaines, 363; secession, 421–424

Albany *Atlas and Argus*, and Lincoln, 273; backs Douglas, 292

Alcorn, James L., opposes Mississippi secession, 425

Alcott, Bronson, impressed by Brown, 73

Allen, Henry W., resolutions for dissolving Union, 110, 111

Allstadt, John H., seized by Brown, 79

Anderson, Major Robert, in command at Charleston, 349; fears concerning Sumter, 366, 367; transfer from Moultrie to Sumter, 368; dispute in Washington, 369–372; position at Sumter, 381; calmness praised, 432, 433; strengthens Sumter, 449, 450; warns Sumter needs reinforcements, 461, 462

Andrew, John A., and Chicago Convention, 258; candidate for governor of Mass., 299; damages party by abolitionism, 301

Anthony, Henry B., as new Senator, 113

Anti-Slavery movement, in Europe, 133

Argentina, emancipation of slaves, 140

Arkansas, slave legislation, 153; withdraws from Charleston Convention, 221

Ashmun, George, chairman Chicago Convention, 251

Astor, John Jacob, and fund raising for Douglas, 47

Avery, W. W., presents report on platform at Charleston Convention, 214, 215

B

Babcock, James F., describes Lincoln's reception in Conn., 244

Bailey, Dr. Gamaliel, urges Chase to withdraw, 236

Bailey, Goddard, dealings with Russell and Floyd, 373, 374

Baker, Senator E. D., 458

Ballinger, William Pitt, opposes Texas secession, 427

Baltimore & Ohio Railroad, 71

Baltimore plot, Lincoln and, 451

Bangor *Daily Union*, and Southern secession, 339

Banks, A. D., opens Douglas headquarters in New York, 47

Banks, N. P., and Republican Convention, 234–260

Barksdale brothers, and Charleston Convention, 206–223

Barnard, D. D., urges formation of opposition party, 60; writes for Constitutional Unionists, 279, 280

Barnard, F. A. P., on failure of Southern unionists, 328

Barney, Hiram, praises Lincoln, 187

Barnwell, R. W., and Charleston forts, 369, 370, 380

Barnwell, W. H., urges help for slaves, 162

Bartlett, D. W., campaign biography of Lincoln, 277

Bates, Edward, as aspirant for presidency, 53, 234–260; praises Lincoln, 275; supports Lincoln, 279; minimizes possibility of civil war, 306; and Cabinet position, 440; and final Cabinet crisis, 453–455

Bayard, James A., at Charleston Convention,

About the Author

Allan Nevins was born at Camp Point, Illinois, on May 20, 1890. An editorial writer for the New York *Evening Post* during the period 1913–23, Nevins also wrote for *The Nation*, the New York *Sun*, and other newspapers and magazines. While enjoying a distinguished career in journalism, Nevins was also intrigued with history. A leading American historian, he taught at Columbia University (1928–58), becoming the DeWitt Clinton Professor of American History in 1931. In 1948 Nevins established Columbia's "Oral History Program," a cause he was much devoted to for the rest of his life. The prolific Nevins's most famous works included *Grover Cleveland* (1932) and *Hamilton Fish* (1936), both of which won Pulitzer prizes, as well as *The Emergence of Modern America* (1927), *John D. Rockefeller*, 2 Volumes. (1940), and his famous trilogy on Ford with Frank Hill: *Ford: The Lines, the Man, the Company* (1954); *Ford: Expansion and Challenge* (1957); and *Ford: Decline and Rebirth* (1963). President of the American Historical Association and President of the American Academy of Arts and Letters, Nevins also went on to help found *American Heritage* magazine. He died on March 5, 1971, and was posthumously awarded the National Book Award for his last installments of *Ordeal of the Union*. Lamented C. Vann Woodward, in his elegiac review of the posthumous volumes, "We are not likely to see more history of this character and scope for some time to come."

Other Titles in Our Civil War Library

R. E. Lee
Four Volumes
by Douglas Southall Freeman

R. E. Lee
An Abridgment
by Douglas Southall Freeman

Lee's Lieutenants
A Study in Command
by Douglas Southall Freeman

Grant and Lee
The Virginia Campaigns
by William A. Frassanito

Antietam
The Photographic Legacy of America's Bloodiest Day
by William A. Frassanito

Gettysburg
A Journey in Time
by William A. Frassanito

The Gettysburg Campaign
A Study in Command
by Edwin B. Coddington

The Greatest Battles of the Civil War
by John Macdonald

Why the North Won the Civil War
by David Donald

Company Aytch
by Sam Watkins